March 9–11, 2016
New Orleans, LA, USA

Advancing Computing as a Science & Profession

CODASPY'16

Proceedings of the Sixth ACM

Conference on Data and Application Security and Privacy

Sponsored by:

ACM SIGSAC

Advancing Computing as a Science & Profession

The Association for Computing Machinery
2 Penn Plaza, Suite 701
New York, New York 10121-0701

Notice to Past Authors of ACM-Published Articles
ACM intends to create a complete electronic archive of all articles and/or other material previously published by ACM. If you have written a work that has been previously published by ACM in any journal or conference proceedings prior to 1978, or any SIG Newsletter at any time, and you do NOT want this work to appear in the ACM Digital Library, please inform permissions@acm.org, stating the title of the work, the author(s), and where and when published.

ISBN: 978-1-4503-3935-3 (Digital)

ISBN: 978-1-4503-4470-8 (Print)

Additional copies may be ordered prepaid from:

ACM Order Department
PO Box 30777
New York, NY 10087-0777, USA

Phone: 1-800-342-6626 (USA and Canada)
+1-212-626-0500 (Global)
Fax: +1-212-944-1318
E-mail: acmhelp@acm.org
Hours of Operation: 8:30 am – 4:30 pm ET

Printed in the USA

Foreword

It is our great pleasure to welcome you to the sixth edition of the *ACM Conference on Data and Application Security and Privacy (CODASPY 2016)*, which follows the successful five editions held in February/March 2011-2015. This conference series has been founded to foster novel and exciting research in this arena and to help generate new directions for further research and development. The initial concept was established by the two co-founders, Elisa Bertino and Ravi Sandhu, and sharpened by subsequent discussions with a number of fellow cyber security researchers. Their enthusiastic encouragement persuaded the co-founders to move ahead with the always daunting task of creating a high-quality conference.

Data and applications that manipulate data are crucial assets in today's information age. With the increasing drive towards availability of data and services anytime and anywhere, security and privacy risks have increased. Vast amounts of privacy-sensitive data are being collected today by organizations for a variety of reasons. Unauthorized disclosure, modification, usage or denial of access to these data and corresponding services may result in high human and financial costs. New applications such as social networking and social computing provide value by aggregating input from numerous individual users and the mobile devices they carry and computing new information of benefit to society and individuals. To achieve efficiency and effectiveness in traditional domains such as healthcare there is a drive to make these records electronic and highly available. The need for organizations to share information effectively is underscored by rapid innovations in the business world that require close collaboration across traditional boundaries. Security and privacy in these and other arenas can be meaningfully achieved only in context of the application domain. Data and applications security and privacy has rapidly expanded as a research field with many important challenges to be addressed.

In response to the call for papers of CODASPY 2016 a total of 115 papers were submitted from Africa, Asia, Australia, Europe, North America, and South America. The program committee selected 22 full-length research papers (19% acceptance rate). These papers cover a variety of topics, including privacy of outsourced data, novel privacy techniques, forensics, applications, and access control and security of smart appliances and mobile devices. The program committee also selected 5 short papers for presentation. The program includes a poster paper session presenting exciting work in progress, as well as a panel session led by Murat Kantarcioglu on "Data Security in the Cloud: Post-Snowden Era." The program is complemented by keynote speeches by John Knight, Anita Nikolich, and Jeffrey Voas. This year's edition also features three workshops: the International Workshop on Security and Privacy Analytics, the International Workshop on Security in Software Defined Networks&Network Function Virtualization, and the ACM workshop on Attribute-Based Access Control.

The organization of a conference like CODASPY requires the collaboration of many individuals. First of all, we would like to thank the authors for submitting to the conference and the keynote speakers for graciously accepting our invitation. We express our gratitude to the program committee members and external reviewers for their efforts in reviewing the papers, engaging in active online discussion during the selection process and providing valuable feedback to authors. We also would like to thank Gail-Joon Ahn (the workshop chair), Adam Lee (the poster chair) and the committee of the poster track, Martín Ochoa (proceedings and publicity co-chair), Jaehong Park (proceedings co-chair), Enrico Lovat (web co-chair), Ram Krishnan (web and publicity co-chair), and Vassil Roussev, the local organization chair. Our special thanks go to our organizing chair Suzanne Tanaka. Finally, we would like to thank our sponsor, ACM SIGSAC, for their support of this conference.

We hope that you will find this program interesting and that the conference will provide you with a valuable opportunity to interact with other researchers and practitioners from institutions around the world. Enjoy!

Elisa Bertino
CODASPY'16 General Co-Chair
Purdue University

Ravi Sandhu
CODASPY'16 General Co-Chair
The University of Texas at San Antonio

Alexander Pretschner
CODASPY'16 Program Chair
Technische Universität München

Foreword

Table of Contents

Session: Reception and Poster Session

Keynote Address

Session: Android Security and Malware Detection

Session: Cloud Management and Access Control I

Session: Access Control II

Keynote Address

Session: Behavior/Data Flow Anomolies and Containment

Session: Data Flows in Web Applications and Query Paths

CODASPY 2016 Conference Organization

General Chairs: Elisa Bertino, *Purdue University, USA*
Ravi Sandhu, *University of Texas at San Antonio, USA*

Program Chair: Alexander Pretschner, *Technische Universität München, Germany*

Poster Chair: Adam J. Lee, *University of Pittsburgh, USA*

Workshop Chair: Gail-Joon Ahn, *Arizona State University, USA*

Organizing Chair: Suzanne Tanaka, *University of Texas at San Antonio, USA*

Panel Chair: Murat Kantarcioglu, *University of Texas at Dallas, USA*

Web Chairs: Enrico Lovat, *Technische Universität München, Germany*
Ram Krishnan, *University of Texas at San Antonio, USA*

Local Chair: Vassil Roussev, *University of New Orleans, USA*

Proceedings Chairs: Martín Ochoa, *Singapore University of Technology and Design, Singapore*
Jae Park, *The University of Alabama in Huntsville, USA*

Publicity Chairs: Ram Krishnan, *University of Texas at San Antonio, USA*
Martín Ochoa, *Singapore University of Technology and Design, Singapore*

Program Committee: Gail-Joon Ahn *(Arizona State University)*
Eliso Bertino *(Purdue University)*
Eric Bodden *(Fraunhofer IPT and Paderborn University)*
Barbara Carminati *(University of Insubria)*
Naranker Dulay *(Imperial College)*
Manuel Egele *(Boston University)*
William Enck *(North Carolina State University)*
Elena Ferrari *(University of Insubria)*
Philip W. L. Fong *(University of Calgary)*
Debin Gao *(Singapore Management University)*
Gabriel Ghinita *(University of Massachusetts, Boston)*
Hannes Hartenstein *(Karlsruhe Institute of Technology)*
Martin Johns *(SAP Research)*
James Joshi *(University of Pittsburgh)*
Murat Kantarcioglu *(University of Texas at Dallas)*
Günter Karjoth *(Lucerne University of Applied Sciences & Arts)*
Florian Kelbert *(Technische Universität München)*
Ram Krishnan *(University of Texas at San Antonio)*
Yves Le Traon *(University of Luxembourg)*
Adam J. Lee *(University of Pittsburgh)*

Program Committee (continued):

Qi Li *(Tsinghua University)*
Peng Liu *(The Pennsylvania State University)*
Fabio Martinelli *(IIT-CNR)*
Fabio Massacci *(University of Trento)*
Nick Nikiforakis *(Stony Brook University)*
Martín Ochoa *(Singapore University of Technology and Design)*
Balaji Palanisamy *(University of Pittsburgh)*
Jaehong Park *(University of Alabama in Huntsville)*
Alexander Pretschner *(Technische Universität München)*
Indrajit Ray *(Colorado State University)*
Vassil Roussev *(University of New Orleans)*
Ravi Sandhu *(University of Texas at San Antonio)*
Anna Squicciarini *(The Pennsylvania State University)*
Thorsten Strufe *(TU Dresden)*
Hassan Takabi *(University of North Texas)*
Mahesh Tripunitara *(University of Waterloo)*
Danfeng Yao *(Virginia Tech)*
Chuan Yue *(University of Colorado, Colorado Springs)*
Su Zhang *(Symantec Corporation)*

Poster Committee:

Adam J. Lee *(University of Pittsburgh (chair))*
Omar Chowdhury *(Carnegie Mellon University)*
Nicholas Farnan *(University of Pittsburgh)*
Roberto Hoyle *(Indiana University)*
Ram Krishnan *(University of Texas at San Antonio)*
Silvio Ranise *(FBK-CIT, Trento)*
Nicola Zannone *(Eindhoven University of Technology)*

Additional reviewers:

Adwait Nadkarni
Aisha Ali-Gombe
Alexandre Bartel
Andrea Saracino
Andrea Saracino
Arsen Hayrapetyan
Artsiom Yautsiukhin
Avinash Sudhodanan
Awad Younis
Ben Stock
Benjamin Andow
Bo Chen
Bo Tang
Carlos Rubio
Chao Li
Chen Zhong
Christopher Hénard
Cong Liao
Daniel Bernau
Daniel Ricardo Dos Santos
Daniel Wang
Giada Sciarretta
Gianpiero Costantino
Golden Richard
Harichandan Roy
Huseyin Ulusoy
Imrul Chowdhury Anindya
Irfan Ahmed
Jacques Klein
Jens Köhler
Jialin Liu
Jun Shao
Kevin Allix
Lannan Luo
Leila Bahri
Leila Karimi
Li Li
Luke Deshotels
Mahdi Alizadeh
Mariia Astrakhantceva
Martin Beck
Martin Härterich
Pietro Colombo
Purui Su
Qingji Zheng
Rui Zhao
Runhua Xu
Sathya Chandran Sundaramurthy
Shiva Houshmand
Siegfried Rasthofer
Sokratis Vavilis
Sowmya Myneni
Stefan Köpsell
Stefanie Roos
Steven Arzt
Subhojeet Mukherjee
Tahmina Ahmed
Tarik Moataz
Thomas Paul
Tonglin Li
Wenhui Hu
Wonkyu Han
Xiaobing Zhou

Additional reviewers (continued) :

Daoyuan Li
Davide D'Arenzo
Dieudonne Mulamba
Dongfang Zhao
Fahad Shaon
Fengguo Wei
Fengjun Li
Francois Fouquet
Matthieu Jimenez
Médéric Hurier
Michael Mabey
Mikhail Strizhov
Mingyi Zhao
Nico Schlitter
Panagiotis Ilia
Pavol Svaba
Peng Zhang
Xiaoyan Sun
Xin Jin
Yiming Jing
Yuan Cheng
Yuping Li
Zhi Wang
Zhongwen Zhang
Ziming Zhao

Sponsor:

Decoding the Mystery of the Internet of Things

Jeffrey Voas
NIST
100 Bureau Drive, MS 8930
Gaithersburg, MD 2089
1-301-975-6622
jeff.voas@nist.gov

ABSTRACT

System primitives allow formalisms, reasoning, simulations, and reliability and security risk-tradeoffs to be formulated and argued. In this work, six core primitives belonging to most distributed systems are presented. These primitives apply well to systems with large amounts of data, scalability concerns, heterogeneity concerns, temporal concerns, and elements of unknown pedigree with possible nefarious intent. These primitives form the basic building blocks for a Network of 'Things' (NoT), including the Internet of Things (IoT). This keynote offers an underlying and foundational science to IoT. To my knowledge, the ideas and the manner in which the science underlying IoT is presented here is unique. Further, this talk reflects my personal viewpoints and not those of NIST.

General Terms

Reliability, Security

Keywords

Distributed system; Internet of Things (IoT); Network of Things (NoT); Trustworthiness, Reliability, Security, Composability

1. INTRODUCTION

The current IoT landscape presents itself as a confusing mix of jargon, consumer products, and unrealistic predictions. There is no formal, analytic, or even descriptive set of the building blocks that govern the operation, trustworthiness, and lifecycle of IoT. This vacuum between the hype and the science, if a science exists, is evident. Therefore, a composability model and vocabulary that defines principles common to most, if not all networks of things, is needed to address the question: "what is the science, if any, underlying IoT?"

My research uses two acronyms, IoT and NoT, interchangeably —the relationship between NoT and IoT is subtle. IoT is an instantiation of a NoT, more specifically, IoT has it's 'things' tethered to the Internet. A different type of NoT could be a Local Area Network (LAN), with none of its' 'things' connected to the Internet. Social media networks, sensor networks, and the Industrial Internet are all variants of NoTs. This differentiation in terminology provides ease in separating out use cases from varying vertical and quality domains (e.g., transportation, medical, financial, agricultural, safety-critical, security-critical, performance-critical, high assurance, to name a few). That is useful since there is no one, static IoT.

Primitives are building blocks that offer the possibility of an answer to the aforementioned question by allowing comparisons between NoTs. They offer a unifying vocabulary that allows for composition and information exchange among differently purposed networks. They offer clarity regarding more subtle concerns, including interoperability, composability, and continuously-binding assets that come and go on-the-fly. Because no simple, actionable, and universally-accepted definition for IoT exists, the model and vocabulary proposed here reveals underlying foundations of the IoT, i.e., they expose the ingredients that can express how the IoT behaves, without defining IoT. This offers insights into issues specific to trust.

2. THE PRIMITIVES

The *primitives* I propose are: 1) Sensor, 2) Snapshot, 3) Aggregator, 4) Communication channel, 5) *e*Utility, and 6) Decision trigger:

1. A **sensor** is an electronic utility that digitally measures physical properties (e.g. temperature, acceleration, weight, sound, etc.) and outputs raw data.
2. A **snapshot** is an instant in *time*, utilized for synchronization of events fired by sensor, aggregator, communication channel, decision trigger, or *e*Utility.
3. An **aggregator** is a software implementation based on mathematical function(s) that transforms/consolidates groups of raw data into *intermediate* data.
4. A **communication channel** is a medium by which the data is transmitted (e.g., physical via USB, wireless, wired, verbal, etc.) between sensor, aggregator, communication channel, decision trigger, or *e*Utility.
5. A ***e*Utility** (external utility) is a software or hardware product or service, providing computing power that aggregators will likely not have.
6. A **decision trigger** creates the final result(s) needed to satisfy the purpose, specification, and requirements of a specific NoT.

3. THE ELEMENTS

To complete my model, I propose five elements: *environment, cost*, *geographic location*, *owner*, and *Device_ID*. Although not primitives, these elements play a major role in fostering the degree of trustworthiness that a specific NoT can provide.

CODASPY'16, March 9-11, 2016, New Orleans, LA, USA.
ACM 978-1-4503-3935-3/16/03.
http://dx.doi.org/10.1145/2857705.2857729

1. **Environment** – The universe that all primitives in a specific NoT operate in; this is essentially the *operational profile* of a NoT. Analogies are the various weather profiles in which an aircraft operates or a particular factory setting in which a NoT operates. Environment will likely be very difficult to define correctly.
2. **Cost** – The expenses (time and money) that a specific NoT incurs in terms of non-mitigated reliability and security risks; additionally, the costs associated with each of the primitive components needed to build a NoT. Cost is an estimation or prediction. Cost drives the design decisions in building a NoT.
3. **Geographic location** – Physical place where a sensor or *e*Utility operates or was manufactured. Manufacturing location is a supply chain trust issue. Note that the operating location may change over time. Note that a sensor's or *e*Utility's geographic location along with communication channel reliability may affect the timeliness of dataflow throughout the workflow. Geographic location determination may sometimes not be possible.
4. **Owner** - Person or Organization that owns a particular sensor, communication channel, aggregator, decision trigger, or *e*Utility. There can be multiple owners for any of these five primitives. Note that owners may have nefarious intentions that affect overall trust. Note further that owners may remain anonymous.
5. **Device_ID** – A unique identifier for a particular sensor, communication channel, aggregator, decision trigger, or *e*Utility. This will typically be created by the originator of the entity, but it could be modified or forged.

4. SUMMARY

To understand the inescapable *trust* issues associated with IoT, consider the attributes of the primitives and elements shown in Table 1. The three rightmost columns are my best guess as to whether the pedigree, reliability, or security of an element or primitive creates a trustworthiness risk.

The table poses questions such as: *What does trust mean for IoT when its abstractions are in continual flux due to natural phenomenon that are in continuous change and while its virtual and physical entities are unknown, partially unknown, or faulty?* Or: *If we have insecure physical systems employing faulty snapshots composed with incorrect assumed environments, where is the trust?*

Table 1: Primitive and Element Trust Questions

Primitive or Element	Attribute	Pedigree Risk?	Reliability Risk?	Security Risk?
Sensor	Physical	Y	Y	Y
Snapshot	Natural phenomenon	N/A	Y	?
Aggregator	Virtual	Y	Y	Y
Communication channel	Virtual and/or Physical	Y	Y	Y
***e*Utility**	Virtual or Physical	Y	Y	Y
Decision trigger	Virtual	Y	Y	Y
Geographic location	Physical (possibly unknown)	N/A	?	?
Owner	Physical (possibly unknown)	?	N/A	?
Environment	Virtual or Physical (possibly unknown)	N/A	Y	Y
Cost	Partially known	N/A	?	?
Device_ID	Virtual	Y	?	Y

Such questions demonstrate the difficulty of understanding IoT trustworthiness. A fuller explanation of these ideas can be found at https://dslsrv.gmu.edu/DecodingIoTv1.0.pdf.

Building Privacy-Preserving Cryptographic Credentials from Federated Online Identities

John Maheswaran
Yale University
john.maheswaran@yale.edu

Daniel Jackowitz
Yale University
daniel.jackowitz@yale.edu

Ennan Zhai
Yale University
ennan.zhai@yale.edu

David Isaac Wolinsky
Yale University
david.wolinsky@yale.edu

Bryan Ford
Swiss Federal Institute of Technology (EPFL)
bryan.ford@epfl.ch

ABSTRACT

Federated identity providers, *e.g.*, Facebook and PayPal, offer a convenient means for authenticating users to third-party applications. Unfortunately such cross-site authentications carry privacy and tracking risks. For example, federated identity providers can learn what applications users are accessing; meanwhile, the applications can know the users' identities in reality.

This paper presents Crypto-Book, an anonymizing layer enabling federated identity authentications while preventing these risks. Crypto-Book uses a set of independently managed servers that employ a (t, n)-threshold cryptosystem to collectively assign credentials to each federated identity (in the form of either a public/private keypair or blinded signed messages). With the credentials in hand, clients can then leverage anonymous authentication techniques such as linkable ring signatures or partially blind signatures to log into third-party applications in an anonymous yet accountable way.

We have implemented a prototype of Crypto-Book and demonstrated its use with three applications: a Wiki system, an anonymous group communication system, and a whistleblower submission system. Crypto-Book is practical and has low overhead: in a deployment within our research group, Crypto-Book group authentication took 1.607s end-to-end, an overhead of 1.2s compared to traditional non-privacy-preserving federated authentication.

Categories and Subject Descriptors

C.2.0 [**Computer-Communication Networks**]: General | Security and protection

1. INTRODUCTION

Federated identity services have gained widespread popularity among users as a simplifying means for managing their online identities. In particular, federated identity providers (*e.g.*, Facebook and PayPal) employ authentication protocols such as OAuth [20, 21] and OpenID [34] to offer their users the convenience of using single identity – and thus a single credential – to log into and access various third-party applications (*e.g.*, Wiki and StackOverflow). This convenience, however, comes at the privacy cost of enabling not only the federated identity providers themselves, but also the third-party application providers and advertising partners, to link a user's account and track her activities across applications.

In order to tackle the above privacy problem, this paper presents Crypto-Book, an architecture that enables users to log into third-party applications anonymously or pseudonymously using their existing federated identities. At a high level, Crypto-Book could be looked as an anonymizing layer between the user's federated identity providers and third-party applications consuming the identities. This anonymizing layer generates cryptographic pseudonyms for users based on their federated identities, thus enabling users to anonymously log into third-party applications with the pseudonyms. Such pseudonyms not only prevent the application providers from learning the user's actual identity/profile information, but also blocks the federated identity providers from linking a user's identity across different applications. Furthermore, Crypto-Book is capable of generating cryptographic pseudonyms from a combination of multiple federated identities (*e.g.*, both Facebook and PayPal identities) to remain secure in the event that one of user's federated identity provider accounts is compromised.

While there have been many cryptographic schemes for anonymous authentication [1–3, 5, 22, 23], these efforts typically assume that users have public keys that are known or validated through PKI – an assumption that has proven a major roadblock to widespread use [40]. On the contrary, Crypto-Book aims at providing a systematic effort that can incorporate different privacy-preserving cryptographic authentication methods without requiring any conventional PKI or PGP-style key management.

Crypto-Book's architecture contains three logical components: 1) a given *client* that represents the user; 2) a group of *credential producers* that interact with the client to manufacture cryptographic credentials for the client; and 3) *credential consumers* that validate these credentials and use them to create application-specific pseudonymous accounts for the client. The credential producers, each maintained or run individually, verify the user's claimed identity via the federated identity providers, then jointly manufacture privacy-preserving credentials, so that the user does not need to trust any one (or few) of these credential producers. While credential production itself uses standard threshold cryptography, a key systems challenge Crypto-Book addresses is ensuring that *all* of the credential producers can securely and independently authenticate the user's federated identity via the unmodified OAuth protocol, without demanding that the human user perform multiple tedious and seemingly-redundant OAuth logins in succession.

Users' privacy expectations, in practice, often depend on the third-party applications the user is visiting. The Crypto-Book ar-

CODASPY'16, March 9–11, 2016, New Orleans, LA, USA.

 ISBN 978-1-4503-3935-3/16/03...$15.00

DOI: http://dx.doi.org/10.1145/2857705.2857736

chitecture is therefore designed to support different forms of privacy protection through multiple "pluggable" cryptographic credential schemes. As examples of such designs, this paper presents and implements two distinct credential schemes within the Crypto-Book architecture.

- Crypto-Book can use partially blind signatures [1, 9] to create "at-large" anonymous access tokens enabling users to log into third-party applications, optionally revealing only *user-selected* information about the user to those applications, while protecting the user's identity from disclosure or linking. For example, a partially-blind credential could indicate that the user is over 21 years of age and has had a PayPal account in good standing for at least a year (detailed in §4).
- Using group credentials built on linkable ring signatures [26,35], Crypto-Book enables users to prove to be one of a set of federated identities (*e.g.* defined by a list of Facebook identities) without disclosing which member of the set they are, and **without requiring the *other* listed members to be Crypto-Book users or have cryptographic keypairs (detailed in §5)**.

These two pluggable credential schemes are intended only as a useful starting point and are not intended to be definitive: they could be improved in many ways utilizing more advanced cryptographic authentication techniques [38].

Our prototype implements these two credential schemes and supports both PayPal and Facebook as federated identity providers. We also prototyped three applications to evaluate Crypto-Book: 1) a Wiki system exploring the use-case of supporting anonymous but accountable editing on sites like Wiki; 2) an accountable anonymous chatting system, Dissent [41], offering scalable and traffic analysis resistant communication service; and 3) a SecureDrop [36] like application enabling a whistleblower to convince a journalist that she is a member of some authoritative group – such as a government official or company employee of a certain rank – without revealing her precise identity. We have deployed Crypto-Book login for a web site used within our research group and evaluated the overall login time, as well as various performance microbenchmarks for each stage of the credential pickup and login processes.

To summary, this paper makes the following contributions: 1) a practical architecture offering privacy-protected and accountable usage of existing federated identities; 2) multiple pluggable credential schemes supporting different degrees of privacy and anonymity; 3) credentials derived from multiple federated identities, increasing protection against identity compromise; and 4) comprehensive experiments demonstrating the practicality of the system.

2. BACKGROUND AND MOTIVATION

This section first describes privacy issues of federated identity services (§2.1), and then presents three motivating use-cases for Crypto-Book (§2.2).

2.1 Privacy Concerns with Federated Identity

Through federated identity based authentication, a user can log into third-party applications without having to maintain separate accounts for each of the applications. Well-known federated identity providers in practice include Facebook, Google+ and PayPal; representative third-party applications supporting federated identity authentication include Quora and StackOverflow. While federated authentication offers great convenience from the perspective of the user, it also introduces or exacerbates several privacy risks, of which Crypto-Book focuses on the following.

- The federated identity providers can learn every application or site the user logs into using her federated identity, and *every time* that they do so.
- Third-party applications can learn the user's true identity and often many profile details such as friends lists and location.
- Third-party applications can link users, and their corresponding profile details, across applications, sharing or selling the information to advertisers.
- If one of a user's federated identity accounts is compromised, the attacker is then able to access third-party applications using this account.

Furthermore, whenever a user visits any page containing federated identity providers' "Like" or "Share" buttons, the identity providers may again learn that the user visited that page, enabling even more detailed tracking and sale of personal information. Additionally, third-party applications often demand access to profile information, contacts lists, and even write access (permission to post on user's behalf) and it is sometimes unclear to users what these permissions will be used for, and not obvious after-the-fact how they were actually used.

2.2 Motivating Use-Cases for Crypto-Book

We now present three motivating use-cases for Crypto-Book. For each use-case, we have built and evaluated a representative application using the Crypto-Book framework.

Privacy-preserving "Login with Crypto-Book". Crypto-Book can be used to provide general, privacy-preserving login functionality to third-party applications. An application may choose to include a "Login with Crypto-Book" button which allows users to be authenticated via Crypto-Book. The difference between Crypto-Book privacy preserving login and existing federated authentication, *e.g.*"Login with Facebook", is that Crypto-Book login preserves the user's privacy and anonymity, while also protecting the third-party applications from abuse. The application learns that the user has been authenticated by Crypto-Book, and learns a pseudonym for the user, but does not know the user's actual identity, nor can the application map back from the pseudonym to the user's identity. For example, while Wiki allows anonymous editing, such privileges are often abused for vandalism. We built a system, CB-Wiki, that allows users to edit pages without revealing their identities but at the same time allows the Wiki site administrators to sanction site abusers. CB-Wiki leverages Crypto-Book to provide anonymous yet linkable editing in a Wiki system environment.

Abuse-resistant anonymous communications. Crypto-Book is additionally useful for authenticating users within anonymous chat applications. Organizations may wish to allow members to discuss sensitive issues without revealing their individual identities but at the same time limit access to their discussions to only members of the organization in an effort to prevent repressive authorities or other undesirable outsiders from viewing the communications. The Crypto-Book architecture could be used to give such applications a reason not to block Tor [16], by authenticating users anonymously in an abuse resistant manner. This would allow applications to counter anonymous abuse without compromising anonymity. The Tor Project issued a "call to arms" seeking solutions to this issue[1]. We built CB-Dissent on Dissent [12,41], an anonymous group communication application. CB-Dissent shows how the integration of anonymous authentication with anonymous communication systems can better protect the identities of the users.

[1]https://blog.torproject.org/blog/call-arms-helping-internet-services-accept-anonymous-users

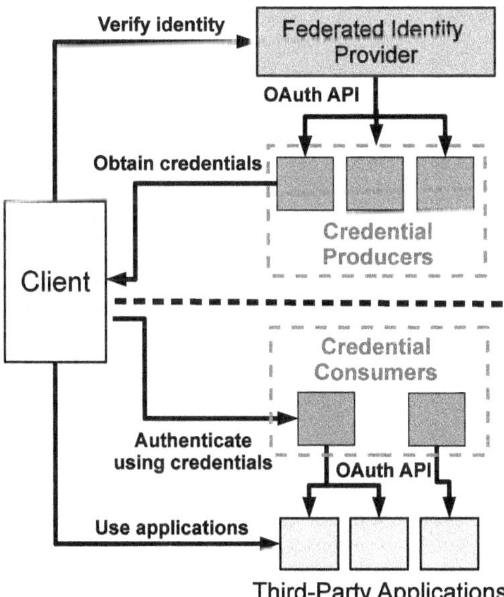

Figure 1: The Crypto-Book architecture overview. Crypto-Book consists of credential producers and credential consumers. Conventional federated authentication process only contains client, federated identity provider and third-party applications.

Group authenticated whistleblowing. Crypto-Book authentication supports verifiable whistleblowing by allowing a journalist taking possession of sensitive documents to authenticate the documents without compromising the anonymity of the source. To illustrate this usage model, we built CB-Drop by extending the SecureDrop [36] open-source whistleblowing platform. CB-Drop is able to provide anonymous document signing using Crypto-Book identities, allowing for verifiable leaks without compromising privacy. A whistleblower authenticates as a member of a group, so that a journalist, for example, can verify that the leak comes from one of the members of the ring, yet does not know which specific member leaked the document.

3. OVERVIEW

This section first presents a high-level overview of the Crypto-Book architecture (§3.1). We then present Crypto-Book's privacy goals (§3.2) and define our assumptions (§3.3). Finally, we detail two key components of Crypto-Book: credential producers (§3.4) and credential consumers (§3.5).

The purpose of this section is to show a basic working process of the Crypto-Book architecture. To highlight Crypto-Book as a "pluggable" architecture, the following two sections (§4 and §5) each detail a specific credential scheme that has been plugged into the Crypto-Book architecture, respectively.

3.1 Crypto-Book Architecture Overview

Figure 1 shows the overall Crypto-Book architecture. In the conventional scenario (*i.e.*, without Crypto-Book), a federated identity provider exposes an authentication API to third-party applications (*e.g.*, via OAuth [21]), which enables users to log into these applications with their federated identities. Such protocols, however, may expose users' identities or profile information to the third-party applications and permit linkage across applications (as mentioned in §2.1).

Crypto-Book addresses this concern by interposing two additional, disjoint layers – *credential producers* and *credential consumers* – between the federated identity providers and the third-party applications. In particular, *credential producers* interact with the federated identity providers to collectively map clients' federated identities to privacy-preserving cryptographic credentials. Clients then submit these credentials to *credential consumers*, which create cryptographic pseudonyms/accounts for the clients, allowing the clients to authenticate with cooperating third-party applications using these pseudonyms rather than their true federated identities.

3.2 Privacy Goals

Crypto-Book targets the following privacy goals: *anonymity*, *unlinkability*, and *accountability*.

- Anonymity means that no party can associate any operation within a third-party application with a specific client's federated identity; additionally, federated identity providers cannot learn what third-party applications a specific client has accessed.
- Unlinkability means that no party can link or track any client's pseudonymous identities across multiple third-party application providers.
- Accountability means pseudonymous identities who abuse applications can be identified and held accountable (*e.g.*banned) without revealing the corresponding federated identity.

Non-goals. Because Crypto-Book aims to preserve the anonymity of clients, defending against sybil attack [17] and network-level Denial-of-Service (DoS) attack have been out of our scope. These attacks are important in practice, but not specific to Crypto-Book. Well-known defenses for these two attacks could be applied.

3.3 Threat Model and Assumptions

Clients are potentially malicious in that they may abuse third-party applications, *e.g.*, posting low-quality content on Wiki. We do not consider network level attacks and assume that clients are able to connect to system components through an anonymous network such as Tor [16].

Both *federated identity providers* and *third-party application providers* are potentially malicious in that they try to break the privacy properties described in §3.2 – for example, de-anonymizing clients' data and linking some client to a specific federated identity. In addition, multiple application providers are allowed to collude with each other. Collusive application providers may try to track a client's identity across their applications. Federated identity providers can collude with application providers, and they may try to learn what applications a specific client is accessing or has accessed.

We assume that fewer than t of n ($t \leq n - 1$) credential producers are dishonest, and may collude with each other to attempt to forge user credentials. The remaining producers are honest-but-curious. In particular, these producers faithfully follow their protocols, but may try to exploit additional information that can be learned in doing so.

We assume that all the cryptographic primitives are operated correctly and work securely. We assume anonymous network communication (*e.g.*, Tor), linkable ring signatures and blind signatures cannot be compromised.

3.4 Credential Producers

Crypto-Book credential producers are a set of independently managed servers responsible for producing cryptographic credentials from verified federated identities. We assume each server is run by a respected, technically competent, and administratively independent anonymity service provider. We envision several commercial

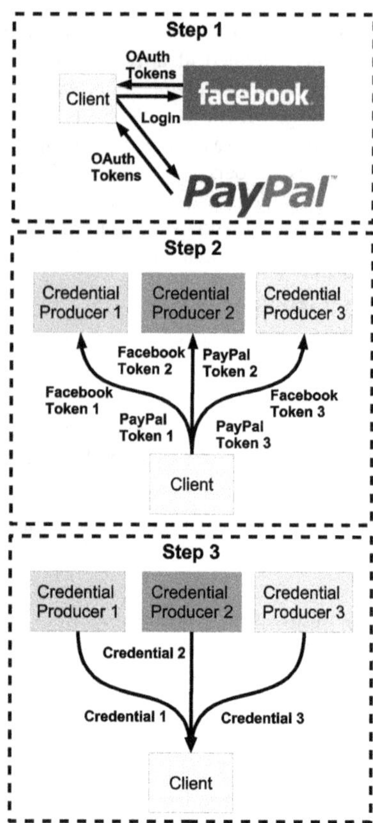

Figure 2: Client collects credentials from multiple credential producers.

or non-profit organizations each deploying a cluster of the credential producer servers, as either a for-profit or donation-funded community service.This assumption on servers has been demonstrated to be reasonable in practice [16, 41]. These servers can support various credential schemes (shown in §4 and §5), enabling Crypto-Book to satisfy different users' privacy expectations in practice.

To obtain cryptographic credentials, a Crypto-Book client contacts a threshold t of the n credential producers, each of which independently authenticates the user with respect to one or more federated identity providers. This process is outlined in Figure 2, and proceeds as the following three steps. **We note that credential production is performed only once for each third-party application that a client wishes to access, not on every authentication.**

Step 1. Each credential producer prompts the user to perform a non-anonymous OAuth federated authentication with each of the federated identity providers (*e.g.*, Facebook and PayPal). Each credential producer then redirects the client to the federated identity provider's login page for authentication. Upon successful authentication, the client receives a unique OAuth token corresponding to the specific federated identity provider and identity.

Step 2. The client sends these tokens to the producer who initiated that authentication. With these tokens, the corresponding credential producers can access and validate the user's profile information. Credential producers request only the minimum access necessary to verify that the identity is valid. Each credential producer verifies via federated identity provider's profile-access API (*e.g.*, the Facebook API) that the federated identity for which the OAuth token was obtained corresponds to the federated identity (*e.g.*, Facebook ID) that the user claimed to have. For multiple federated identity providers (*e.g.*, Facebook and PayPal), each credential producer also verifies that the user attributes (*i.e.*, date of birth and email address) are the same for both the Facebook and PayPal accounts. In order to obtain a verified PayPal account, a user needs to connect her real-world bank account or credit card, which requires showing her real-world identity (*e.g.*, driver license) in person at a bank. **This provides a higher barrier to entry and makes it much more difficult for someone to assume a fake identity.**

Step 3. After each producer verifies all identities with their respective providers, assuming all verify successfully, the producer returns a share of the cryptographic credential to the client. The client then combines the shares from all contacted producers and stores the resulting cryptographic credential for use in future privacy-protected logins.

3.4.1 Design Intuitions

It is crucial that each producer performs its own OAuth authentication and receives its own OAuth token. A strawman design uses only one OAuth workflow with a single OAuth token and forwards this token to each of the credential producers. The problem with this is that each credential producer can forward the token to other producers to impersonate the user. Having separate OAuth workflows for each producer protects against this.

While security requires each of multiple credential producers to verify one or more of the user's federated identities, we do not wish to subject the *human* user to a tedious process of typing passwords into many federated identity provider login dialogs in succession. The Crypto-Book client hides the multiple-independent-authentications from the human user, on the client side using a Chrome plugin.

Crypto-Book credential producers support multiple cryptographic credentials, requiring only that the credential be adaptable to a (t, n)-threshold cryptosystem; any set of at least t honest producers must be able to produce a valid credential which will be accepted by any honest credential consumer, while any set of fewer than t producers must not be able to produce such a credential.

3.5 Credential Consumers

Credential consumers map cryptographic credentials to cryptographic pseudonyms that can then be used to authenticate with third-party applications. The cryptographic pseudonyms produced by credential consumers are unlinkable to the actual federated identities from which they are derived. Credential consumers typically take one of two forms: OAuth provider or application-embedded consumer.

OAuth provider consumer. OAuth provider consumers operate externally to third-party applications. They map cryptographic credentials to anonymous identities and then expose those identities to third-party applications via the OAuth protocol. Applications interact with OAuth provider consumers just as they would directly with conventional federated identity providers. Third-party applications already using federated authentication require little modification to support OAuth provider credential consumers; such integration, however, requires that the application trust the OAuth provider. There is nothing, however, preventing a third-party application from running its own OAuth provider consumer, independent of the application but still under the same administrative domain.

Application-embedded consumer. An application-embedded credential consumer exists directly within a third-party application, either via an imported library or a custom implementation of the consumer. Using this approach the application need not trust an external provider, but at the cost of ease of integration with existing authentication mechanisms.

4. AT-LARGE CREDENTIAL SCHEME

This section presents the first of two concrete credential schemes we have built on top of Crypto-Book. The *at-large credential scheme* does not explicitly constrain the anonymity set of a user, but instead represents that the user has been verified as the owner of *some* federated identity. The anonymity set for each at-large credential is then implicitly all users who have ever collected a credential in the time period before the credential was used. Credential producers enforce the accountability of at-large credentials by restricting the number of credentials they produce for a given federated identity within a period of time (*i.e.* rate-limiting). We then extend at-large credentials to optionally include *credential attributes*, such as "age over 18" or "identity active for at least one year", which are also verified with the identity provider at the time of credential production.

4.1 Building Block: Blind Signatures

The blind signature [1,9,37] is a cryptographic primitive, where a *requester* can request a *signer* to sign one or more messages, while the signer cannot learn the signed message's content. Given the message-signature pair, a public *verifier* is able to verify the legitimacy of the signature. In our architecture, the client is the requester, each credential producer is a signer and the credential consumer is a verifier (of multiple signatures). In our work we use the blind signature scheme proposed by Shen *et al.* [37] which we outline below in the context of our system. The process involves the following five phases.

Initialization phase: The credential producer chooses a large prime p and α as a primitive root modulo p. In addition, the producer randomly chooses a number x $(2 < x < (p-2))$ and then computes $y = \alpha^x \mod p$. The producer publishes (y, α, p) as the public key, keeps x as the private key, and chooses a one-way hash function $h(g)$ such as SHA-1.

Blinding phase (client and credential producer): The client has a message m and wants to have it signed by the producer. First, the client sends a request to the producer for signing the message m. The producer then randomly chooses a number $\tilde{k}$, such that $\gcd(\tilde{k}, \phi(p)) = 1$. The producer computes $\tilde{r} = \alpha^{\tilde{k}} \mod p$. After computing $\tilde{r}$, the producer sends $\tilde{r}$ to the client. When the client receives $\tilde{r}$ from the producer, the client randomly chooses the set of values (a, b, c), so that parameters (a, b, c) are relatively prime to the value $\phi(p)$. The client then computes $r = \tilde{r}^a y^b \alpha^c \mod p$ and the hash value $h(m)$ generated by the hash function $h(g)$. The client then blinds m with the equation $\tilde{m} = a^{-1}(c + m + r) - \tilde{r} \mod \phi(p)$. After that, the client sends $\tilde{m}$ to the signer.

Signing phase (producer): When receiving the value $\tilde{m}$, the producer computes $\tilde{s} = (\tilde{k} + (\tilde{m} + \tilde{r}))x^{-1} \mod \phi(p)$. The producer then sends the value $\tilde{s}$ to the client.

Unblinding phase (client): After receiving $\tilde{s}$ from the producer, the client computes $s = a\tilde{s} + b \mod \phi(p)$ and obtains the message-signature (m, r, s). The client can then send the message-signature pair (m, r, s) to the credential consumer.

Verifying phase (credential consumer): When the consumer receives the message-signature pair (m, r, s), the verifier can use the one-way hash function $h(g)$ and the public key (y, α, p) to verify the legitimacy of the signature by checking $V_1 = V_2$ so that, $V_1 = y^s \mod p$ and $V_2 = r\alpha^{r+h(m)} \mod p$. If $V_1 = V_2$, then the verification passes; else the verification fails.

4.2 Producing At-Large Credentials

To produce an at-large credential, clients and credential producers play the requester and signer roles, respectively, in the blind signatures signing process (§4.1).

In practice, we assume that each credential consumer has a unique, publicly known identity, analogous to the application identity in the OAuth protocol. For a given consumer, we refer to this identity as id_c. In order to prevent replay attacks in which one credential consumer can use a client's successful login to impersonate the client at another consumer, at-large credentials are bound to a specfic consumer.

Initialization & blinding phases. To produce an at-large credential, a client first chooses a value r to serve as the credential's unique identifier. The value r must be kept secret and should be uniquely chosen for each at-large credential a client obtains. The client binds the identifier to a specific consumer to obtain the message $m = H(r, id_c)$ and requests a blind signature on m from at least t of the n credential producers, uniquely blinding the message m for each of the requests. In this way, the producers learn neither the credential identifier nor the identity of the consumer the credential is for.

Signing & unblinding phases. Upon receiving a signature request, a credential producer must first verify the requesting client's federated identity with the appropriate provider(s) (*e.g.* Facebook and PayPal). If verification succeeds, the producer then checks any rate-limit restrictions for the federated identity. If the limit has not been exceeded, the producer reponds with a blinded signature s_i' on (blinded) message m. The client waits for successful responses from at least t of the n credential producers and unblinds the signatures to obtain vector $s_1, s_2, \ldots, s_t$. This vector serves an at-large credential with identifier r, valid for the credential consumer with identity id_c.

4.3 Consuming At-Large Credentials

Credential consumers can specify which at-large credentials they accept based on the threshold of the credential, dictating the number of signatures required. To authenticate with a credential consumer with identity id_c and requiring a threshold t at-large credential, a client must provide the credential consumer with a credential identifier r along with a vector $s_1, s_2, \ldots, s_t$ of signatures from at least t *unique* credential producers. The consumer first hashes the provided credential identifier with its own identity to reproduce message $m = H(r, id_c)$ and then uses the public keys of the credential producers to verify that each of the provided signatures is, in fact, a valid signature on message m. If at least t signatures verify, the consumer authenticates the client using an anonymous identity derived (using a deterministic, one-way function) from credential identifier r.

4.4 Credential Attributes

Credential attributes allow credential consumers to enforce general restrictions on the at-large credentials they accept. For example, some credential consumers may require that all users be at least 18 years of age. Credential attributes can also be used to provide a higher barrier to entry by requiring, for example, that a Facebook identity has been active for at least one year.

The at-large credential scheme supports credential attributes by using partially blind signatures. *Partially blind signatures* [1] are a modification to blind signatures in which part of the message, the *info* tag, remains visible to the signer. This allows the signer and verifiers to share additional information about the context of the blind signature.

Clients bind attributes to at-large credentials by including each desired attribute in the info tag of their signing requests. Each credential producer then additionally verifies all of the attributes with the federated identity provider and produces a signature only if all check out. Credential consumers enforce credential attributes by ensuring that each signature presented by the client contains all required attributes in the info tag. An inherent restriction on credential attributes is that they must be verifiable with the federated identity provider.

4.5 Rate-Limits via Attributes

Credential attributes additionally allow for finer control over the rate-limits imposed on at-large credential production. Rather than relying on producers to choose a proper default rate for all applications (*e.g.* x credentials per identity per week), clients can instead specify a time interval (*e.g.* 3 days) with each credential request; only if the producer has not already issued the federated identity an at-large credential during the preceding interval does production succeed. As credential attributes are accessible by credential consumers, a consumer can inspect the interval associated with each credential and in turn elect to accept only those credentials satisfying criteria the consumer itself defines. Some consumers may accept 1-hour credentials while other, more abuse-conscious consumers may require 1-month credentials, allowing consumers themselves to determine the degree of accountability they wish to enforce.

4.6 Security/Privacy Properties

The at-large credential scheme is designed to provide the following properties, which correspond to our privacy goals:

- **Anonymity** During credential production, the producers learn the user's federated identity, but not the anonymous identity derived from the credential. During credential consumption, the third-party applications only learn the credential, but not the user's federated identity. Only the user herself knows both pieces needed to complete the mapping between identities.
- **Unlinkability** For any two at-large credentials, neither credential producers nor consumers can determine whether they correspond to the same federated identity.
- **Accountability** Each at-large credential is bound to a unique identifier. If a user misbehaves, the credential with which the user authenticated can be blacklisted by the consumer, effectively banning the user just as with any non-anonymous identity. Producers provide abuse resistance by limiting the rate at which new credentials are assigned to each federated identity.
- **Unforgability** Each at-large credential requires a signature from t of the n credential producers; no colluding group including fewer than t dishonest producers can produce a forged credential that will be accepted by an honest consumer.

We provide a security analysis of how Crypto-Book provides these properties and which attacks it does and does not protect against in our technical report [8].

4.7 Discussions

Crypto-Book's current at-large credential scheme requires the client to obtain a separate blind signature for each third-party application or site the user wishes to visit for the first time, to protect the user from being linked across applications. This limitation may be an inconvenience, especially if Crypto-Book's rate-limits interfere with a user's legitimate attempts to explore several third-party sites in a short time period. Adopting a more sophisticated cryptographic credential scheme such as BLAC [4,38] might allow the client to pick up a single credential and then "re-blind" it for use across multiple sites while maintaining cryptographic unlinkability and abuse-resistance. Since Crypto-Book's immediate goal is not to find the "ultimate" cryptographic credential scheme but to fit cryptographic credentials (of any kind) into a usable OAuth-compatible architecture, we leave more advanced at-large credential schemes to future work.

5. GROUP CREDENTIAL SCHEME

In this section, we plug another credential scheme, *group credential scheme*, into our Crypto-Book architecture.

As an alternative to at-large credentials, in which anonymity sets form implicitly, group credentials allow an individual to authenticate explicitly as some member of a larger, well-defined set of users. We describe a group credential scheme construction based on linkable ring signatures in this section.

5.1 Building Block: Ring Signatures

Ring signatures [35] rely on group signatures [10] and allow third-parties to verify that a message was signed by one of a well-defined set of private keys, but do not reveal which specific key. Ring signatures are particularly useful for associating properties of a group as a whole, such as credibility in our CB-Drop example, with the signed message. Liu *et al.* propose *linkable ring signatures* (LRS) [26]. LRS is an extended version of ring signatures with the additional property of *linkability* – for any two linkable ring signatures, a third party can determine whether or not the two signatures were produced using the same private key by comparing the *linkage tag* properties of the signatures. We use the linkability property to add accountability to anonymous credentials. The LRS process consists of four phases.

Initialization phase (credential producer and client): Let $G = \langle g \rangle$ be a group of large prime order q. Let $H_1 : \{0,1\}^* \to \mathbb{Z}_q$ and $H_2 : \{0,1\}^* \to G$ be independent hash functions. Each member (e.g. Facebook profile) i ($i = 1, ..., n$) has a distinct public key y_i, and private key x_i (assigned by the credential producers) so that $y_i = g^{x_i}$. Let $L = \{y_1, ..., y_n\}$ be the list of n public keys (assigned to federated identities by producers).

Signature generation phase (client): Given the list of public keys L, which the client collects from the producers, the client first uses her private key x_π, which corresponds to her public y_π ($1 \leq \pi \leq n$), to compute $h = H_2(L)$ and $\tilde{y} = h^{x_\pi}$. Then, she picks $u \in \mathbb{Z}_q$ and computes $c_{\pi+1} = H_1(L, \tilde{y}, m, g^u, h^u)$, where m is the message the client wants to sign with an LRS. Next, for $i = \pi+1, ..., n, 1, ..., \pi-1$, the client picks $s_i \in \mathbb{Z}_q$ and computes $c_{i+1} = H_1(L, \tilde{y}, m, g^{s_i} y_i^{c_i}, h^{s_i} \tilde{y}^{c_i})$. Finally, the client computes $s_\pi = u - x_\pi c_\pi \mod q$. The LRS for the message m is $\sigma_L(m) = (c_1, s_1, ..., s_n, \tilde{y})$.

Verification phase (credential consumer): Suppose a credential consumer receives a message m signed by $\sigma_L(m) = (c_1, s_1, ..., s_n, \tilde{y})$ and the consumer knows the public key list L (obtained from the producers), the consumer first computes $h = H_2(L)$. For $i = 1, ..., n$, the consumer computes $z_i' = g^{s_i} y_i^{c_i}$ and $z_i'' = h^{s_i} \tilde{y}^{c_i}$ and then $c_{i+1} = H_1(L, \tilde{y}, m, z_i', z_i'')$ if $i \neq n$. Finally, the consumer checks if $c_1 = H_1(L, \tilde{y}, m, z_n', z_n'')$. If so, the consumer accepts the signature and the client is authenticated; otherwise authentication fails.

Linkability checking (credential consumer): Given two signatures $\sigma_L'(m') = (c_1', s_1', ..., s_n', \tilde{y}')$ and $\sigma_L''(m'') = (c_1'', s_1'', ..., s_n'', \tilde{y}'')$ corresponding to messages m' and m'', the consumer can check whether the two signatures are from the same signer by checking if $\tilde{y'} = \tilde{y}''$. This allows the consumer to maintain a consistent pseudonym for each client.

5.2 Producing Group Credentials

A group credential consists of two components - the user's individual private key and the set of public keys of all other members of the desired anonymity set.

Credential production process begins with an initialization phase. Suppose a user Alice wants to collect her private key. She first connects to a credential producer through an anonymity network (such as Tor) and supplies a list of federated identities, including her own, as her desired anonymity set. The credential producers then work together to generate public/private key pairs for each federated identity using Pederson's PKG [35], in which all credential producers contribute to the overall value of the credential but each learns only a single share. Finally, for each identity in the anonymity set, each of the n credential producers holds a single share of the corresponding key, t of which are necessary to reconstruct the key.

After all keys have been generated, each credential producer sends an invitation to each of the federated identities (via Facebook message, for example) inviting them to join the Crypto-Book service and collect their private key. This indirection is necessary as if a user directly requested their private key a credential producer colluding with a credential consumer could potentially de-anonymize a user via a timing analysis attack by correlating the private key request with subsequent authentications.

Alice (and, independently, the other identities who have received invitations) then follows the invitations to collect a share of her private key from each of the credential producers. Before releasing the share, each producer first requires Alice to authenticate with her federated identity provider via OAuth, proving that she in fact owns the identity corresponding to the private key. After collecting shares from at least t of the n credential producers, Alice combines the shares to recover her private key.

Obtaining the set of public keys requires no interaction between client and federated identity provider. Instead, Alice directly contacts each credential producer and requests a share of the public key for each identity in her anonymity set. After receiving at least t shares of each key, Alice recovers the set of public keys. In practice, clients bundle all key requests for a given anonymity set and producers return all shares in a single response, to minimize transmission overhead and latency.

5.3 Consuming Group Credentials

Credential consumers authenticate group credentials by requiring users to supply a valid linkable ring signature over a message of the consumer's choosing; typically, a fresh, random value. Such a challenge prevents replay attacks and ensures that the user knows a valid private key for the ring.

The user first contacts the credential consumer with an authentication request. The consumer then replies with a challenge, which the user signs using their group credential and returns to the consumer. In some instances, the user also supplies the anonymity set to which the group credential corresponds; in others, this set is implicitly determined by the consumer itself. In either case, the consumer first asserts that the anonymity set contains valid Crypto-Book identities for the given consumer.

The consumer then collects public key shares for all members of the anonymity set from at least t credential producers and verifies the ring signature against the resulting public keys. If the signature verifies, authentication succeeds and the consumer maps the user to an anonymous account based on the linkage tag of the signature, creating a new account if this was the first authentication for the given tag.

5.4 Security/Privacy Properties

The group credential scheme is designed to provide the following properties:

- **Anonymity** During credential production, each credential producer learns only a single share of a user's private key. No colluding group of fewer than t dishonest produces can recover the private key needed to de-anonymize the user.
- **Accountability** Linkability of the signatures produced by group credentials ensures that a given credential always maps to the same anonymous identity. Thus group credential identities can be banned just as any non-anonymous identity.
- **Unforgability** Any valid group credential must include a private key for a valid Crypto-Book identity. Shares for such a key must be obtained from at least t credential producers. Thus no colluding group including fewer than t dishonest producers can produce a forged credential that will be accepted by an honest consumer.

We provide a security analysis of how Crypto-Book provides these properties and which attacks it does and does not protect against in our technical report [8].

5.5 Discussions

Crypto-Book's current group credential scheme uses linkable ring signatures whose size is linear in the anonymity set size; their efficiency on large anonymity sets could be improved using accumulator-based schemes [6, 7] at the cost of more complex computations.

Another disadvantage is that using any form of signatures for authentication leaves a non-repudiable trail, which might expose a user whose private signing key is later compromised. This limitation might be addressed by adopting techniques from deniable authentication protocols [15, 31].

Finally, in practice it may be hard for users to pick "good" anonymity sets. If all the other users a whistleblower conscripts into his "anonymity set" turn out to be implausible for some reason to an investigating adversary, *e.g.*, because none of the other members could have had access to the leaked document, then the chosen anonymity set may prove ineffective. We make no suggestion that group credentials are straightforward to use safely: only that, if the user's only other alternative is to disclose his identity completely (*e.g.*, to persuade the journalist of his credibility), then group anonymity may be better (and perhaps at least more "plausibly deniable") than no anonymity.

6. IMPLEMENTATION

We have implemented a Crypto-Book prototype. The prototype interfaces with Facebook, PayPal, or a combination of the two, as federated identity providers. We implemented credential producers, consumers, and clients for both at-large and group credentials and deployed the system on a distributed set of servers. Users can collect credentials from these producers using their existing federated identities.

We implemented at-large credentials based on blind [37] and partially blind signatures [1] and developed standalone credential producers and consumers for both schemes. For group credentials we implemented RSA-based ring signatures [35] and DSA-based linkable ring signatures [26]. We implemented (t, n)-threshold DSA key pair generation for group credentials using Pederson's distributed PKG [35].

In order to maintain the convenience users have come to expect of federated authentication, we have implemented a web-based Crypto-Book client, named CB-Login. CB-Login combines an application-embedded consumer with a Google Chrome extension to offer a one-click login experience akin to a privacy-preserving "Login with Facebook". The Chrome extension retrieves and manages group credentials and generates linkable signatures in the web browser, uploading the signatures to the CB-Login consumer. The consumer verifies the signatures and produces anonymous identities based on the linkage tags of the signatures. CB-Login requires no more user interaction than a traditional federated authentication.

6.1 Applications

We have implemented three applications on top of the Crypto-Book architecture: CB-Wiki, CB-Dissent and CB-Drop, concretizing the motivating use-cases outlined in §2.2. In addition, we also implemented OAuth provider functionality in our client CB-Login to allow other applications to more easily incorporate Crypto-Book as a federated identity provider.

CB-Wiki is a Wiki system based on MediaWiki [30] that allows users to log in as *anonymous* yet *accountable* pseudonymous identities rather than *personally identifiable* users. This design benefits both users, who can edit Wiki pages without disclosing their identity, and administrators, as if a user repeatedly vandalizes a page or conducts other forms of system abuses an administrator can issue warnings or other sanctions (*i.e.* banning) just as for any traditional, non-anonymous user.

CB-Dissent is a system that combines the Crypto-Book anonymous authentication architecture with the Dissent [12, 41] scalable anonymous messaging system. CB-Dissent is an anonymous authentication system that allows users to anonymously request a Dissent session (a set of Dissent servers) to be started and then to anonymously authenticate themselves and connect to that Dissent group. Unlike in traditional Dissent, in CB-Dissent servers do not learn the actual identities of the clients connected to them, but only that the client is a valid Crypto-Book identity.

CB-Drop builds on SecureDrop [36], an open-source whistleblower submission system developed by the Freedom of the Press Foundation. SecureDrop allows journalists to accept sensitive documents from anonymous sources via a web interface running as a Tor hidden service. CB-Drop adds credibility to leaks by allowing a source to anonymously sign a document using a relevant set of Crypto-Book identities before submitting it via SecureDrop. Upon retrieving the document, a journalist can then verify the signature, increasing confidence in the authenticity of the leak without compromising the source's anonymity.

7. EVALUATION

To evaluate the practicality of Crypto-Book we consider both end-to-end measurements in expected deployment scenarios and microbenchmarks focusing on scalability of specific components. We first describe the experimental setup and then evaluate credential production and consumption in both proposed credential schemes. We conclude by evaluating Crypto-Book in the context of our example applications. Evaluations of CB-Drop, as well as code modification metrics for CB-Wiki, CB-Dissent and CB-Drop are available in our technical report [8].

7.1 Experimental Setup

The experimental setup for the following evaluations include three classes of machines, based on role in the system:

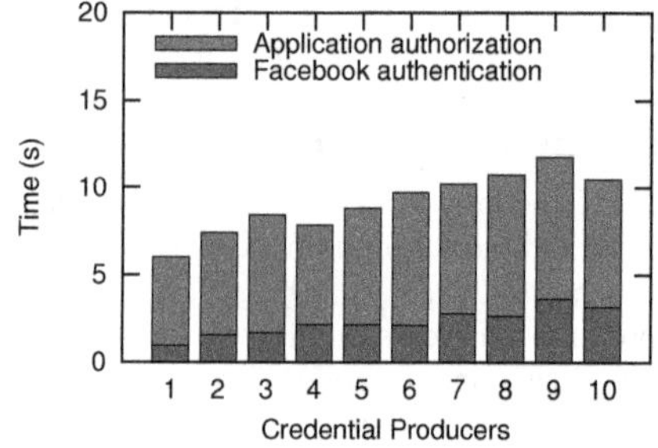

Figure 3: Facebook application authorization

Key Parameters	Signature Size (Bytes)
(1024,160)	210
(2048,224)	287
(2048,256)	325
(3072,256)	326

Table 1: Partially blind signature size

- **Clients** are consumer laptops with 2.4GHz Intel Core i5 processors and 8GB of RAM.
- **Credential producers** are nodes on the geographically distributed PlanetLab [11] network. A typical PlanetLab node has a 2.4GHz Intel Xeon processor and 4GB of RAM.
- **Credential consumers** are commercial shared hosting providers also with 2.4GHz Intel Xeon processors and 16GB of RAM.

In selecting experimental key pairs we followed NIST recommendations [33] for DSA keys where the tuple (L, N) specifies the bit-length of the p and q parameters, respectively. If a parameter tuple is not specified, it is assumed to be $(1024, 160)$.

7.2 Producing Credentials

In this section we evaluate the production of credentials in both the at-large and group credential schemes.

7.2.1 Facebook Application Authorization

In both the at-large and group credential schemes a first-time user must authorize a credential producer's application with a supported federated identity provider before retrieving any credentials from that producer. We evaluated the time taken to complete this step for a varying number of credential producers, with Facebook as the federated indentity provider. We used our Chrome extension to automate the authorization process and performed all authorizations in parallel. Results are presented in Figure 3, drawing distinction between time spent authenticating with Facebook and time spent authorizing the Crypto-Book application. The times shown are those of the last credential producer to return. **A client only ever needs to perform this setup step once, the first time they ever use Crypto-Book.**

7.2.2 At-Large Credentials

An at-large credential consists of partially blind signatures from t credential producers. As each signature is obtained independently from all others, we focus on time taken to obtain a single signature. As discussed in Section 4, a signature is generated collaborately by the client and a producer. Network overhead consists of two round trips between producer and client where the second trip is dependent on the size (and hence strength) of the signature. Signature sizes for varying signing key sizes are shown in Table 1.

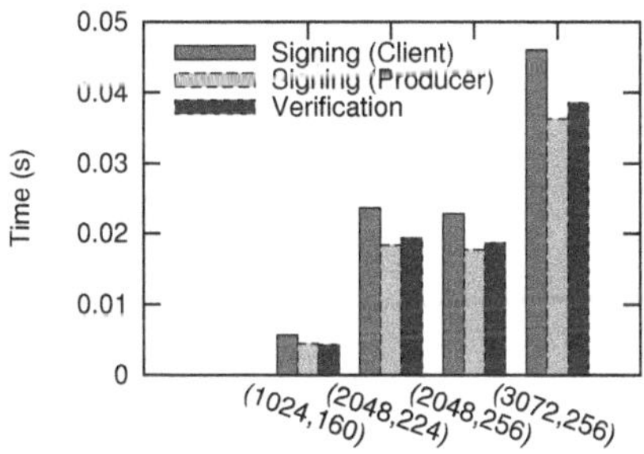

Figure 4: Partially blind signature operations

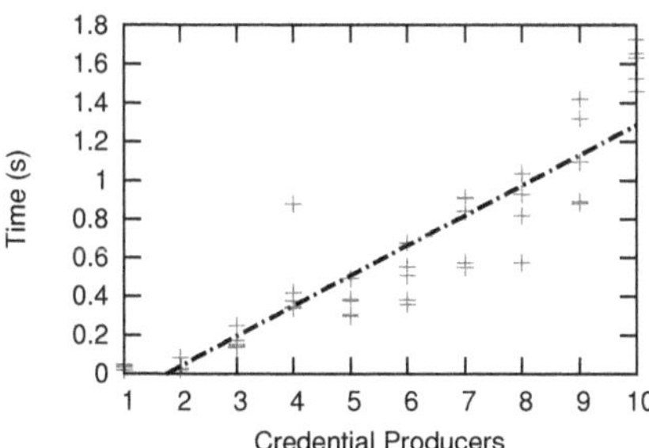

Figure 5: Distributed keypair generation

The computation costs for partially blind signature operations are shown in Figure 4. Credential production consists only of the signing operation, which, for a 2048-bit signing key, takes approximately 50ms of computation time, with effort divided fairly evenly between client and producer.

7.2.3 *Group Credentials*

Keypair Generation In our group credential scheme, the first time a key pair is requested it must be collectively generated by the credential producers. We evaluated the time required to generate a single key pair for a varying number of credential producers and present the results in Figure 5. Times shown include only operations involving producers; returning the keys to the client is evaluated separately. For a reasonable number of producers, we find that the results scale approximately linearly.

Key Retrieval We next evaluate the time taken for a client to retrieve a single key, either private or public, from the set of credential producers. Requests to all producers are performed in parallel. We present the results in Figure 6. For public keys, we find near constant response. Times shown for private keys include Facebook authentication, which accounts for the difference when compared to public key requests. **Private key requests will be rare, as after retrieval users retain their private keys locally, stored in the Chrome extension.**

7.3 Consuming Credentials

In this section we evaluate the consumption of credentials in both the at-large and group credential schemes.

7.3.1 *At-Large Credentials*

In evaluating the consumption of at-large credentials we assume that all credential producers' signing keys are well-known to all credential consumers. As a result, authentication via at-large credentials consists only of the transmission and verification of partially blind signatures. As shown previously in Figure 1, a threshold t at-large credential is approximately $300t$ bytes in size; at these sizes credential upload times are heavily dependant on network properties.

To evaluate the costs of verification we considered $t = 1$ at-large credentials for varying key size. Results are shown in Figure 4; for a 2048-bit key verification takes less than 20ms. As each signature verification is completely independent of all others, for expected values of t (≤ 10), signature verification can be performed largely in parallel.

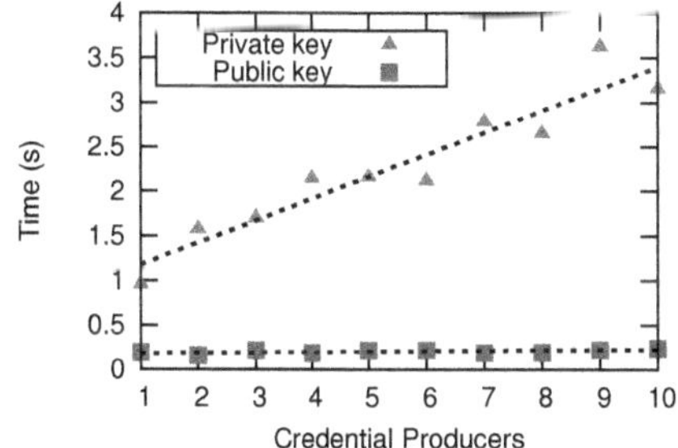

Figure 6: Retrieval of previously generated keys

Entity	Operation	Time (s)
Client	Produce LRS	0.257
Credential Consumer	Fetch Public Keys	1.011
	Verify LRS	0.035
Client-Consumer Network Latencies		0.304
	Total User-Observable	**1.607**

Table 2: End-to-end Group Authentication

7.3.2 *Group Credentials*

In order to perform an **end-to-end evaluation** of authentication using group credentials, we first created a group credential including ten Facebook identities belonging to members of the authors' research group. Users then each collected their group credential and used our Chrome extension to authenticate to an internal website with their Crypto-Book identity. We used an application-embedded consumer and three credential producers on networks different from the consumer's. We recorded timings for each phase of 117 authentications and present the averages in Table 2. On average, the total user-observable authentication time was 1.6 seconds; this is approximately a 1.2 second overhead compared to non-anonymous federated authentication with Facebook.

To investigate how group credential authentication scales with group size, we considered each operation from Table 2 separately. We found that by bundling public key requests we were able to fetch up to 1000 public keys in near-constant time, identifying the ring signature operations as the limiting factor for larger groups. We then measured the computation time for each ring signature operation, varying the ring size between 1 and 1000. Results for signing and verification are shown in Figures 7 and 8, respectively. Both operations scale linearly with ring size and, for ring sizes near 100 and 2048-bit keys, both operations complete in one second.

We additionally measured the size of the linkable ring signature produced for varying ring sizes. This signature is what the client sends to the credential consumer with each authentication, thus overall client-consumer network latency depends on signature size. Results are shown in Figure 9. We found that signature size scales linearly with ring size and that, for ring sizes near 100 and 2048-bit keys, signatures are less than 10kB.

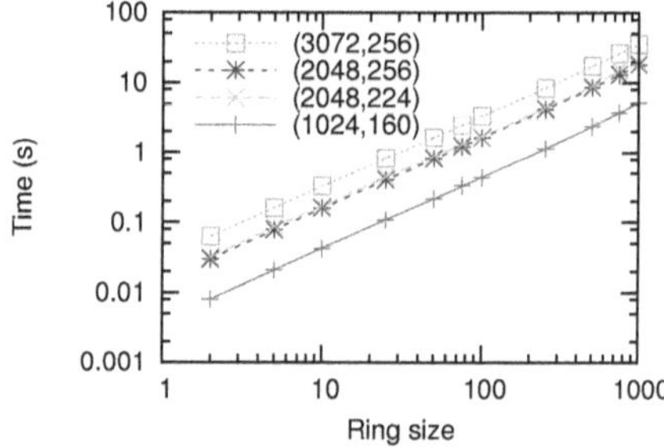

Figure 7: Linkable ring signature generation

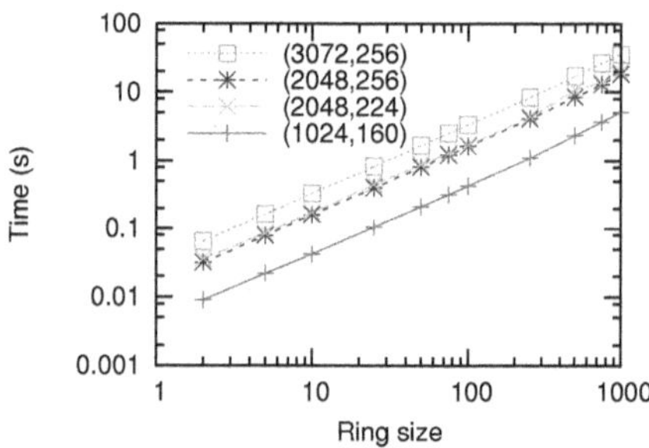

Figure 8: Linkable ring signature verification

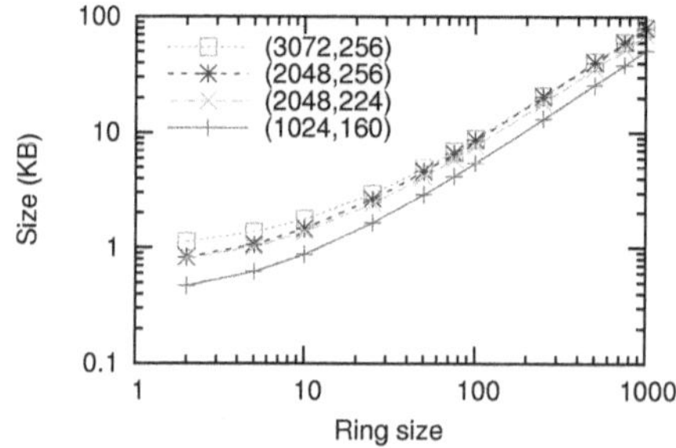

Figure 9: Linkable ring signature size

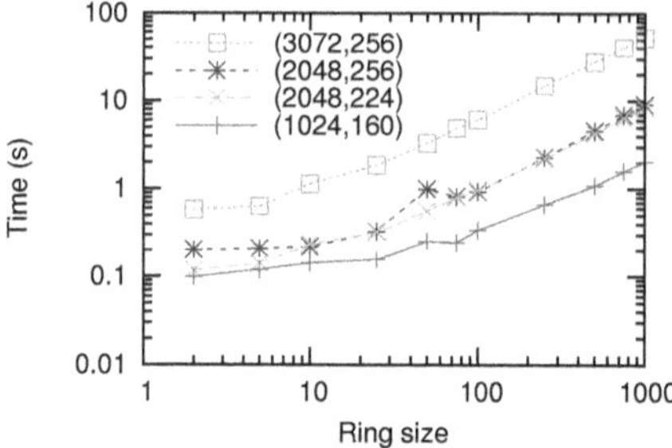

Figure 10: CB-Dissent authentication time

7.4 CB-Dissent Authentication

Finally, we evaluated group authentication in our CB-Dissent implementation. This experiment measures the time required for a client to authenticate with a single Dissent server acting as an application-embedded consumer. We again varied the group size between 1 and 1000, presenting the results in Figure 10. For a group size of 100 and 2048-bit keys, authentication again takes under 1 second. While this is a significant overhead compared to traditional pre-exchanged key authentication, it remains well within practical limits.

8. RELATED WORK

Existing work on anonymous credential systems include BLAC [4, 38] which supports blacklisting of anonymous credentials in certain situations. There have been a wide variety of other approaches to anonymous credential systems including those based on group signatures [2, 3, 5, 10], dynamic accumulators [6, 7] and Nymble systems [22, 23].

Felt and Evans [18] examine privacy protection in social networking APIs. The deployment of public key cryptography over social networks was considered by Narayanan *et al.* [32] where they considered key exchange over social networks. They considered using social networks as a public key infrastructure (PKI), they did not implement any applications that use the public keys.

Various schemes have been proposed to protect user data *within* an online social network [13, 19, 27, 28], by encrypting the content stored within the social network. However these schemes did not consider the privacy risks involved when a user uses their online social networking identity to identify themselves with third parties such as logging into other websites using their Facebook credentials. Dey and Weis [14] proposed PseudoID, a similar system based on blind signatures for privacy protected federated login, however their scheme does not handle key assignment as our work does. A similar blind signature based system was proposed by Khattak *et al.* [24]. Watanabe and Miyake [39] made initial efforts towards account checking however still did not consider key assignment. Opaak [29] is a system that attempts to provide some Sybil resistance through relying on a cellphone as a scare resource. SudoWeb [25] looked at limiting the amount of Facebook information disclosed to third party sites but did not consider fully anonymous online IDs.

9. CONCLUSIONS

We have demonstrated Crypto-Book, a practical and pluggable architecture for providing privacy preserving online identities based on federated identity providers. As two examples, this paper deploys two different credential schemes into Crypto-Book through adapting two cryptographic primitives, blind signature and linkable ring signature, respectively. The two deployments are capable of supporting different needs of privacy protection.

We have implemented three major applications, CB-Wiki, CB-Dissent, and CB-Drop, on top of Crypto-Book and shown them to have good scalability properties. We believe that Crypto-Book is a practical way to provide federated identity users with accountable pseudonyms and many applications could be developed on top of Crypto-Book.

There remain a large number of areas for future research based on our architecture as well as many applications that could be developed on top of Crypto-Book leaving open a wide range of areas for investigation building on our results in future work.

Acknowledgments

We wish to thank the anonymous CODASPY reviewers as well as Joan Feigenbaum, Ramki Gummadi and Anil Somayaji for their valuable feedback. This work is supported in part by NSF grants CNS-1407454 and CNS-1409599.

10. REFERENCES

[1] Masayuki Abe and Tatsuaki Okamoto. Provably secure partially blind signatures. In *20th CRYPTO*, 2000.

[2] Giuseppe Ateniese, Jan Camenisch, Marc Joye, and Gene Tsudik. A practical and provably secure coalition-resistant group signature scheme. In *20th CRYPTO*, 2000.

[3] Giuseppe Ateniese, Dawn Song, and Gene Tsudik. Quasi-efficient revocation of group signatures. In *7th FC*, January 2003.

[4] Man H Au, Apu Kapadia, and Willy Susilo. BLACR: TTP-free blacklistable anonymous credentials with reputation. In *19th NDSS*, February 2012.

[5] Dan Boneh, Xavier Boyen, and Hovav Shacham. Short group signatures. In *24th CRYPTO*, 2004.

[6] Jan Camenisch and Anna Lysyanskaya. Dynamic accumulators and application to efficient revocation of anonymous credentials. In *22nd CRYPTO*, August 2001.

[7] Jan Camenisch and Anna Lysyanskaya. An efficient system for non-transferable anonymous credentials with optional anonymity revocation. In *EUROCRYPT*, May 2001.

[8] Technical Report: Providing Abuse Resistant Pseudonyms for Federated Online Identities with Cobra. https://www.dropbox.com/s/c90jn2om7ahlth4/anon-tech-report.pdf?dl=0.

[9] David Chaum. Blind signatures for untraceable payments. In *CRYPTO*, 1982.

[10] David Chaum and Eugène Van Heyst. Group signatures. In *EUROCRYPT*, April 1991.

[11] Brent Chun, David Culler, Timothy Roscoe, Andy Bavier, Larry Peterson, Mike Wawrzoniak, and Mic Bowman. Planetlab: an overlay testbed for broad-coverage services. *ACM SIGCOMM Computer Communication Review*, 33(3):3–12, 2003.

[12] Henry Corrigan-Gibbs and Bryan Ford. Dissent: accountable anonymous group messaging. In *17th CCS*, October 2010.

[13] Leucio Antonio Cutillo, Refik Molva, and Thorsten Strufe. Safebook: A privacy-preserving online social network leveraging on real-life trust. *Communications Magazine, IEEE*, 47(12):94–101, 2009.

[14] Arkajit Dey and Stephen Weis. Pseudoid: Enhancing privacy in federated login. *Hot topics in privacy enhancing technologies*, pages 95–107, 2010.

[15] Mario Di Raimondo, Rosario Gennaro, and Hugo Krawczyk. Deniable authentication and key exchange. In *CCS*, 2006.

[16] Roger Dingledine, Nick Mathewson, and Paul Syverson. Tor: the second-generation onion router. In *13th USENIX Security Symposium*, August 2004.

[17] John R. Douceur. The Sybil attack. In *1st IPTPS*, March 2002.

[18] Adrienne Felt and David Evans. Privacy protection for social networking APIs. *W2SP*, 2008.

[19] Saikat Guha, Kevin Tang, and Paul Francis. Noyb: Privacy in online social networks. In *WOSN*, 2008.

[20] E. Hammer-Lahav. The OAuth 1.0 protocol, April 2010. RFC 5849.

[21] Ed Hardt. The OAuth 2.0 authorization framework, October 2012. RFC 6749.

[22] Ryan Henry, Kevin Henry, and Ian Goldberg. Making a nymbler nymble using verbs. In *PETS*, 2010.

[23] Peter C Johnson, Apu Kapadia, Patrick P Tsang, and Sean W Smith. Nymble: Anonymous IP-address blocking. In *PETS*, 2007.

[24] Zubair Ahmad Khattak, Jamalul-lail Ab Manan, Suziah Sulaiman, et al. Analysis of open environment sign-in schemes-privacy enhanced & trustworthy approach. *Journal of Advances in Information Technology*, 2(2):109–121, 2011.

[25] Georgios Kontaxis, Michalis Polychronakis, and Evangelos P Markatos. SudoWeb: Minimizing information disclosure to third parties in single sign-on platforms. In *Information Security*, pages 197–212. Springer, 2011.

[26] Joseph K Liu and Duncan S Wong. Linkable ring signatures: Security models and new schemes. In *ICCSA*, May 2005.

[27] Matthew M Lucas and Nikita Borisov. Flybynight: mitigating the privacy risks of social networking. In *Proceedings of the 7th ACM workshop on Privacy in the electronic society*, pages 1–8. ACM, 2008.

[28] Wanying Luo, Qi Xie, and Urs Hengartner. Facecloak: An architecture for user privacy on social networking sites. In *Computational Science and Engineering, 2009. CSE'09. International Conference on*, volume 3, pages 26–33. IEEE, 2009.

[29] Gabriel Maganis, Elaine Shi, Hao Chen, and Dawn Song. Opaak: using mobile phones to limit anonymous identities online. In *Proceedings of the 10th international conference on Mobile systems, applications, and services*, pages 295–308. ACM, 2012.

[30] MediaWiki. http://www.mediawiki.org.

[31] Moni Naor. Deniable ring authentication. In *22nd CRYPTO*, August 2002.

[32] Arvind Narayanan, Narendran Thiagarajan, Mugdha Lakhani, Michael Hamburg, and Dan Boneh. Location privacy via private proximity testing. In *Proc. of NDSS*, volume 2011, 2011.

[33] The FIPS 186-4 Digital Signature Algorithm Validation System. http://csrc.nist.gov/groups/STM/cavp/documents/dss2/dsa2vs.pdf.

[34] David Recordon and Drummond Reed. OpenID 2.0: A platform for user-centric identity management. In *Proceedings of the second ACM workshop on Digital identity management*. ACM, 2006.

[35] Ronald L. Rivest, Adi Shamir, and Yael Tauman. How to leak a secret. In *7th ASIACRYPT*, December 2001.

[36] SecureDrop. https://pressfreedomfoundation.org/securedrop/.

[37] Victor R. L. Shen, Yu fang Chung, Tzer Shyong Chen, and Yu An Lin. A blind signature based on discrete logarithm problem. *ICIC*, 7(9), September 2011.

[38] Patrick P Tsang, Man Ho Au, Apu Kapadia, and Sean W Smith. Blacklistable anonymous credentials: Blocking misbehaving users without TTPs. In *14th CCS*, October 2007.

[39] Ryu Watanabe and Yutaka Miyake. Account management method with blind signature scheme. *Engineering and Technology, World of Science*, (59):2069–2073, 2011.

[40] Alma Whitten and J. Doug Tygar. Why johnny can't encrypt: A usability evaluation of PGP 5.0. In *Proceedings of the 8th USENIX Security Symposium*, August 1999.

[41] David Isaac Wolinsky, Henry Corrigan-Gibbs, Aaron Johnson, and Bryan Ford. Dissent in numbers: Making strong anonymity scale. In *10th OSDI*, October 2012.

Neuralyzer: Flexible Expiration Times for the Revocation of Online Data

Apostolis Zarras
Technical University of Munich
zarras@sec.in.tum.de

Katharina Kohls
Ruhr-University Bochum
katharina.kohls@rub.de

Markus Dürmuth
Ruhr-University Bochum
markus.duermuth@rub.de

Christina Pöpper
Ruhr-University Bochum & NYU Abu Dhabi
christina.poepper@rub.de

ABSTRACT

Once data is released to the Internet, there is little hope to successfully delete it, as it may have been duplicated, reposted, and archived in multiple places. This poses a significant threat to users' privacy and their right to permanently erase their very own data. One approach to control the implications on privacy is to assign a lifetime value to the published data and ensure that the data is no longer accessible after this point in time. However, such an approach suffers from the inability to successfully predict the right time when the data should vanish. Consequently, the author of the data can only *estimate* the correct time, which unfortunately can cause the premature or belated deletion of data.

This paper tackles the problem of prefixed lifetimes in data deletion from a different angle and argues that alternative approaches are a desideratum for research. In our approach, we consider different criteria when data should be deleted, such as keeping data available as long as there is sufficient interest for it or untimely delete it in cases of excessive accesses. To assist the self-destruction of data, we propose a protocol and develop a prototype, called *Neuralyzer*, which leverages the caching mechanisms of the Domain Name System (DNS) to ensure the successful deletion of data. Our experimental results demonstrate that our approach can completely delete published data while at the same time achieving flexible expiration times varying from few days to several months depending on the users' interest.

1. INTRODUCTION

Social media and cloud storage services have changed the information culture of our society. In the era of Web 2.0 people willingly leave lasting digital traces of their lives while decisions on uploading such information are short-termed. In contrast to analog information, these traces remain available as long as the providers of these services decide to. As a consequence, data such as uploaded documents, communication contents, personal profiles, and posts can be accessed even years after their initial relevance ceased [5, 15, 21, 31]. While the decision to upload personal information to the Internet can be made by each user individually, the control of published data is passed to the service provider. Users depend on a responsible privacy policy while the transparency of the storage and provision process is lost in most cases. In addition, the confidence in the corresponding services has been damaged by a number of data scandals and insights into their archiving practices [16, 19, 22, 23, 32]. Unfortunately, these tendencies conflict with the users' right to be forgotten [8, 12].

As there is no solution on retroactively regaining control over externally stored data, a possible remedy to this problem is a proactive user-driven access control. For instance, the timed revocation of data equips users with control over personal information by revoking the access to data at a specific time after its publication, even if files are maintained by external service providers. Solutions such as Ephemerizer [28], Vanish [14], and EphPub [7] allow users to define a prefixed time when the data will be deleted. All these solutions rely on the very same concept: they encrypt the data and prevent access after the predetermined expiration date by destroying the decryption key. In these solutions, the decryption key is often spread within an existing infrastructure, for example, on distributed hash tables. As long as the key bits can be accessed, the published data remains available. The security goal of all timed revocation schemes is *retrospective privacy*, i. e., the schemes guarantee the revocation of access rights after the expiration time.

However, all the previously-mentioned schemes suffer from the same limitation: users should have *prior knowledge of the correct time* when to delete their shared data. Unfortunately, this is not always feasible and users' privacy preferences are also likely to change over time [1]. For instance, if a user uploads a picture from a party, she may want this picture to be accessible only for a certain period of time. In reality, knowing beforehand when the picture should be deleted is a complicated task that can cause additional overhead to individuals, while it remains most of the times without the desired results; the picture may be destroyed before all of her friends have seen it or it remains available for so long that it may have negative impact.

We address this problem by introducing the concept of *flexible expiration times*. In essence, this concept builds upon the security features of retrospective privacy. Although at first glance it is based on the same infrastructures as the above mentioned systems, at the same time it does not require to predefine an expiration date and therefore removes the respective load from users. Instead, deletion will be based on a suitable revocation model, for example, expiration after interest in the data drops or untimely revocation following excessive access. No matter which revocation model a user selects, the shared data will disappear after a period of time without the user's requirement of selecting this time.

CODASPY'16, March 09-11, 2016, New Orleans, LA, USA
© 2016 ACM. ISBN 978-1-4503-3935-3/16/03...$15.00
DOI: http://dx.doi.org/10.1145/2857705.2857714

Although the concept of flexible expiration times sounds simple enough, its actual design and implementation is not straightforward. The main reason is that we cannot directly modify the architecture of the distributed infrastructures we use. In essence, we require a widely accessible distributed infrastructure where we can design a solution that allows us to react on external systems' behavior without the necessity to modify or revise its architecture. Thus, it is crucial that the ephemeral storage we select provides mechanisms for extending the lifetime of the information we store based on different events (e. g., the receivers' accesses) or at least allow us to perform a roundabout solution to this direction. This constitutes a key difference to the previously mentioned proposals in this space.

In this paper, we investigate this problem space and propose *Neuralyzer*, a timed revocation scheme that allows dynamic access control of users' publicly available data. *Neuralyzer* extends existing approaches by applying flexible expiration times while providing retrospective privacy. More specifically, our prototype is based on the caching mechanisms of the Domain Name System (DNS), similar to the EphPub system [7]. To this end, it uses encryption to protect the data and then splits and distributes the parts of the decryption key over various DNS entries. The key is accessible to anyone who knows which entries has been used for the encoding of the key bits. At the same time, data access leads to the automatic extension of the lifetime of the key bits in the cache of the DNS servers. In essence, the key is valid as long as it is stored in the cache and vanishes once the cache entries are empty. To assess our results, we evaluate the performance of the designed framework regarding data lifetime for different access scenarios (i. e., drop of interest, excessive access, and manual revocation). Based on the results of a simulation study as well as a prototype implementation we show that our approach provides dynamic access revocation to published data. Overall, we believe that *Neuralyzer* can be an important building block to protect users from the long-term exposure of their online data.

In summary, we make the following main contributions:

- We identify the limitations of current schemes for the timed revocation of data and introduce the concept of *flexible expiration times* for online data.
- We propose a protocol to revoke the public access to data that should be forgotten based on three different access heuristics: (i) drop of interest, (ii) excessive access, and (iii) manual revocation.
- We assess the feasibility of our approach by implementing and evaluating a working prototype. Our experimental results demonstrate that our prototype is able to successfully destroy data with flexible expiration times.

2. DESIGN GOALS

In this section, we first state the problem we are addressing and introduce the term of retrospective privacy. Furthermore, we describe three different access heuristics as motivation for the concept of flexible expiration times. Finally, we present the threat model used throughout this paper.

2.1 Problem Statement

The security goal of our approach is to prevent access to shared data after its expiration time, summarized with the term of *retrospective privacy*. This is achieved under the application of different access heuristics which time the revocation of an object.

Retrospective Privacy. With the publication of information in the Internet, all physical control of data is passed to the respective service provider. Timed revocation schemes encrypt valuable information and revoke the access to a respective encryption key once an object should become inaccessible. If access to an expired object is successfully prevented, then *retrospective privacy* is fulfilled.

Access Heuristics. The data should be accessible only for a limited period of time. Hence, the proposed protocol must revoke access rights after that time. Predefined expiration times are the only revocation technique that have so far found attention with respect to the proposal of technical solutions [7, 14, 28]. These approaches are, however, independent of the access heuristic. We argue that predefined expiration times have drawbacks in terms of appropriateness and user friendliness (the users may not know the expiration time nor may want to decide on it beforehand) and thus more dynamic revocations schemes are desirable. Dynamic revocation can be achieved for instance based on the following types of heuristics that take into account the number of accesses over time:
Drop of interest: With reducing audience also the relevance of information can be assumed to disappear. Therefore, the system should detect drops in interest and revoke the accessibility of information to protect its future privacy. In essence, uploads of personal information may be of short-term interest, as such posts are frequently updated and often relate to recent events: A user uploads a picture from an event recently attended, however, does not want to be accessible forever, but only for a period where interest in the event is still present. Through applying the above heuristic, the picture will remain alive by enduring requests, though once the interest drops it will become inaccessible.
Excessive access: Users should be able to revoke the access to publicly available data in case of excessive access. Therefore, a protocol should have the capacity to automatically revoke the access in case of high demand. For instance, an advertising campaign provides free vouchers that should be limited in number. By applying the excessive access heuristic a maximum number of accesses to shared data can be constrained after which the data ceases to exist.
Manual revocation: Manual revocation of objects is an essential fallback method if an applied heuristic does not cover proper deletion. With the capability of manually revoking data any applied fixed or dynamic lifetime of an object can be expired on demand.

We claim that the described, possibly incomplete, list of access heuristics contains instances of desirable behavior. While technical approaches for all heuristics and evaluations of their applicability are desirable, in this paper we chose to focus on the first one (drop of interest) and its technical realization. We later also extend our investigations to the other access heuristics where applicable in the description of our solution and evaluation. We note that providing technical means to address all desirable access heuristics in parallel may not always be possible.

2.2 Threat Model

The security goal of our approach is to provide retrospective privacy, where the adversary is prevented from accessing content after its expiration. We assume that the attacker has no interest in accessing the published data *prior* to its expiration. In other words, the attacker learns the importance of the previously-published data only after that data has expired. This is due to the fact that data is publicly available in the Internet throughout its lifetime and thus is not assumed to be private. The privacy of data is protected only *after* its expiration. We also assume that the attacker can access meta information prior to their destruction, i. e., she can retrieve information about expired or soon to expire data from messages occurring

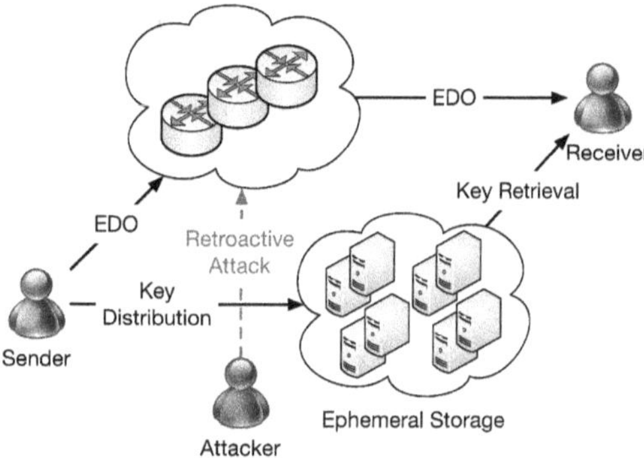

Figure 1: System model.

in the used protocol. Yet, she is not proactively trying to collect information to use it in the future for recovering expired data—if many people utilize the proposed scheme, the sheer amount of information to be collected for later use would simply be excessive.

Within these restrictions, the attacker is able to add custom messages to system (e. g., by injecting new messages, altering existing or replaying previous messages), however, she does not constantly monitor the communication channel of the sender and the receiver. Thus, she is capable of manipulating messages throughout the lifetime of an object, but does not do this in a targeted manner due to a lack of knowledge which objects may be of interest in the future. In addition to the discontinuous monitoring and altering of system-related communication, the attacker may have access to the internal memory of sender and receiver *after* the lifetime of an object.

3. HIGH-LEVEL IDEA

In our proposed model, we define three crucial parts that are involved in the definition of our approach: (i) the ephemeral storage, (ii) the sender, and (iii) the receiver (see Figure 1).

Ephemeral Storage. The lifeblood of our system is the mechanism to store the decryption key. The key should remain accessible only for a valid period of time and then disappear without leaving traces that can be backtracked to its successful recovery. To this end, we define *ephemeral storage* as a mechanism which assures that data is accessible only for a valid period and then disappears permanently. In essence, the ephemeral storage contains the critical information for the successful decryption of data and therefore should always be available and reachable during the data lifetime. This means that it must not suffer from severe down-times and be accessible by the majority of the online population. Therefore, we believe that only a popular infrastructure can serve as ephemeral storage.

Sender. The sender must be aware that, as long the ephemeral key exists, everyone with access to it can decrypt the data. The uploaded data to a server that the user does not own (e. g., Google Drive, Dropbox, etc.), allows to any receiver as well as the server itself to retrieve, decode, and store it permanently. Previous works made it harder for the server to accurately use the collected data [10, 26], but these approaches are outside the scope of this paper. Following our threat model, we assume that the server does not proactively collect this data.[1] With that in mind, the sender compiles the data to a data structure called Ephemeral Data Object (EDO) which contains the encrypted data and a link to the ephemeral storage that includes information for the construction of the decryption key, and then uploads it to a server from where it can be retrieved.

[1] If this assumption is not fulfilled, out-of-band channels can be set up and used to distribute the information required for key recovery.

Table 1: Summary of notation.

Notation	Explanation
S	: Sender
R	: Receiver
N	: Length of DNS portrayal
I	: Length of decryption key
$\|K\|_I : k_i \in K$	: Key of length I
$\|K'\|_I : k_i \in K'$	: Recovered key of length I
$\|C\|_{I \times N} : c_{i,n} \in C$	: Cache entries for key
$\|D\|_{I \times N} : d_{i,n} \in D$	: Domains of cache entries
$\|TTL\|_{I \times N} : ttl_{i,n} \in TTL$	: TTL values of cache entries
x	: Key threshold
t_1, t_2	: TTL thresholds

Receiver. A receiver who retrieves an EDO is able to decode it and decrypt its data before the key expires. To do so, the key must first be recovered from the ephemeral storage and then be reconstructed locally. Additionally, in our proposed model and following the *drop of interest* access heuristic, the receiver contributes to the viability of the EDO. Thus, it is crucial that the ephemeral storage provides mechanisms for extending the lifetime of the stored key based on the receivers' access. This way, the data will be accessible as long as there is sufficient interest for it and disappear afterward.

4. SCHEME DESCRIPTION

In this section, we provide the design details of our approach. We propose the utilization of the DNS resolvers' caching mechanisms as an instantiation for the ephemeral storage. In the following text, we first introduce the concept of *ephemeral bits* and then describe the details of the protocol design.

4.1 Ephemeral Bits

As in any other encryption system, data is encrypted to protect it from unauthorized access. Given that the encryption algorithm remains the same, the size of the key defines its resistance to brute force attacks. For instance, breaking a symmetric 256-bit key, which is used to encrypt data with the AES algorithm [9], by brute force requires 2^{128} times more computational power than a 128-bit key. In our approach, we use the same principle of defining the size of a key by dividing it into its key bits. However, and given the fact that we require the bits to be available only for a certain period of time and then automatically being destroyed, we refer to these key bits as *ephemeral bits*.

In our proposed scheme, we use the caching mechanisms of DNS resolvers to encode the ephemeral bits and enhance them with the property of self destruction. The utilization of DNS resolvers is well-suited for our approach because of their automatic mechanism to clear their caches within a predefined *Time to Live* (TTL) period [24]. Consequently, after a scheduled timeout, the key will disappear from DNS caches and the data can no longer be decrypted.

4.2 Protocol Description

Our approach allows data to be vanished once the interest for it drops. This way, if a retroactive attacker attempts to access the data after that point, she cannot recover it anymore. To do so, we introduce the data structure EDO that protects the publicly accessible data by encrypting it, encapsulating the encrypted content, and ensuring its disappearance when the expiration time is reached. The data contained in EDO becomes useless after a period of time, even if an attacker retroactively obtains a valid copy of the EDO. Overall, the lifetime of an EDO is divided into three phases: (i) construction, (ii) access, and (iii) revocation. For convenience Table 1 summarizes the notation we use throughout this section.

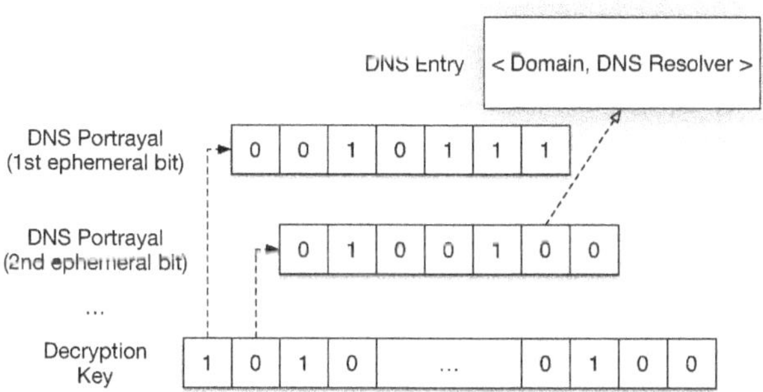

Figure 2: An example of key distribution in DNS servers. We note that initially, all entries in the DNS portrayal of a key bit 0 are in fact 0 (some of them may get set over time, as shown in the figure).

4.2.1 Construction Phase

In this phase, a sender S uploads to a third-party server data that will cease to exist after the interest for it drops. For each new EDO, our algorithm executes the following steps:

Step C1. First, it generates a random key. The size of the key defines the security of the encrypted data and therefore we recommend at least a 128-bit key. Then, it utilizes this key to encrypt the data using the AES algorithm.

Step C2. Next, it converts the key bits into ephemeral bits. Specifically, each ephemeral bit is encoded to a list of DNS entries, which we call *DNS portrayal*. Each DNS entry is represented by a pair of a domain name and a DNS resolver, illustrated in Figure 2. For this purpose, we use a list of DNS resolvers and a list of precompiled domains. The latter can be generated either by crawling the web or by selecting random IP addresses and performing reverse DNS lookups (details on how this can be achieved practically are provided in Section 4.3.1). Note that the selected domains must not be preloaded in the cache of the associated DNS resolvers. With that in mind, our algorithm can assign the value 1 in a DNS entry by performing a *recursive* DNS request which will set the cache entry.

For all bits k_i of the key, we proceed as follows: We do not take any action if $k_i = 0$ (apart of a non-recursive DNS query verifying that the respective DNS entry is indeed not set). For every $k_i = 1$, we execute recursive DNS queries for the respective domain names (defined in the EDO). As a result, values of the DNS portrayal for each key bit 1 are set to active (loaded in the cache), while the DNS portrayal for each key bit 0 remains unset (respective domain names are not in the cache).

Note that we do not initially assign the value 1 to *all* entries in the DNS portrayal if $k_i = 1$, but only to a certain number of them. Actually, we want to avoid that all DNS resolvers happen to clear their caches at the same time, which would prevent key updates during the access phase (detailed further below). The length of the DNS portrayal (N) and the number of entries required for a successful representation of an ephemeral bit (x) are defined by thresholds. We discuss the threshold values in Sections 4.3 and 5.

Step C3. In this final step, our algorithm compiles the EDO. An EDO contains the encrypted content and the list of domains D for each key bit k_i, represented by N cache entries $c_{i,n}$. As we will present in the access phase, this information is sufficient for successfully decrypting the EDO during its lifetime.

4.2.2 Access Phase

Once the EDO has been compiled, it can be distributed to third-party servers. A receiver R can retrieve the EDO and access its content as follows:

Step A1. First, it retrieves the encrypted content and extracts the list of domains D for each k_i from the EDO.

Step A2. In order to assign the correct values to each ephemeral key bit, our algorithm performs *non-recursive* queries to the DNS resolvers for their corresponding domain names. If the resolver contains the domain in its cache, our algorithm assigns the value 1 to this DNS entry otherwise the value 0. To minimize the errors that may occur from externally modified entries, we use an empirically calculated threshold x. If the sum of the returned values exceed this threshold, the algorithm sets the corresponding ephemeral key bit:

$$\texttt{recover}\begin{cases}\sum_{n=0}^{N-1} c_{i,n} \geq x : 1\\ \sum_{n=0}^{N-1} c_{i,n} < x : 0\end{cases}, \quad (1)$$

where x is the threshold value that enables for recovering errors in the cache entries. Such errors may be induced by random recursive DNS requests leading to $0 \rightarrow 1$ switches (due to DNS queries from users external to our scheme during the execution of the protocol), or failures at the DNS cache resulting in $1 \rightarrow 0$ switches (the DNS server has emptied its cache, for example, due to a reboot).

Step A3. In this step our algorithm extends the lifetime of EDO. To do so, it updates a random DNS entry of each DNS portrayal that represents an ephemeral key with the value 1 by executing a recursive request. However, we want to have variation in the remaining TTL values on the entries of each portrayal. This minimizes the danger of having resolvers that simultaneously empty their caches or at similar times. We achieve this by performing a recursive DNS request when the median or minimum TTL per DNS-portrayal is less than a preselected threshold. For instance, we can update the DNS entries if we see that the median TTL is less than $\text{TTL}_{max}/2$, or if the DNS entry with the minimum remaining time to empty its cache is less than $\text{TTL}_{max}/10$, where TTL_{max} is the maximum value assigned to the TTL by the DNS servers. It is worth to mention here that both conditions work in parallel and we update a DNS entry whenever one of these conditions, or both of them, is satisfied. In essence, without refreshing the cache entries, an object would expire as soon as a significant amount of 1-bit representations has switched from 1 to 0. Overall, to prolong the initial lifetime limit, each receiver performs a cache refreshment after a successful reconstruction of the EDO for all key bits $k_i = 1$:

$$\texttt{refresh}\begin{cases}(\texttt{median}(ttl_{i,n}) < t_1) \vee (\exists n : ttl_{i,n} < t_2) : 1\\ (\texttt{median}(ttl_{i,n}) \geq t_1) \wedge (\forall n : ttl_{i,n} \geq t_2) : 0\end{cases}, \quad (2)$$

where the `refresh` operation is only executed in case the median TTL $\texttt{median}(ttl_{i,n})$ or the TTL of a single value $ttl_{i,n}$ for a key bit k_i fall below thresholds t_1 or t_2. In this case, a random $c_{i,n}$ currently 0 is set to 1 by a recursive DNS request to the respective domain $d_{i,n}$. Note that the threshold values as well as the metrics (median/minimum TTL) can be adapted to a specific deployment scenario and are not necessarily bound to the above definition.

Step A4. In the final step of this phase, the ephemeral key has been successfully reconstructed. Then, the receiver uses this key to decrypt and access the encrypted data.

4.2.3 Revocation Phase

This is the last phase in the lifetime of an EDO. We expect that after some time there will be a drop of interest for a published EDO. Consequently, the number of accesses will decrease as well, which will cause *Step A3* of the access phase to be executed less and less frequently. This results in cleared caches of the DNS entries, such that, the ephemeral key cannot be reconstructed successfully. Therefore, the data will vanish, i. e., the encrypted data will be present but will be useless without a retrievable decryption key.

4.2.4 *Different Access Heuristics*

In this section, we discussed how our model operates in the case of *"drop of interest"*. We now describe how our scheme could handle different access heuristics with only small modifications.
Excessive Access. In this case, we want to revoke the access of an EDO in case the interest for it exceeds a certain upper bound of allowed accesses. For this reason we need to count the number of accesses to the EDO. As the DNS resolvers do not have an access counter that would be visible or accessible to normal users, we can enrich the EDO with a probabilistic self-destruction mechanism. More precisely, for every single access of EDO, we generate a random number. The decision to destroy the decryption key is based on whether the generated random number is larger than a specific bound defined by the highest number of acceptable accesses (e. g., for a allowed accesses, the bound would be $1 - 1/a$ if the random numbers are selected from $[0, 1]$). If the result leads to not allowing more accesses, the ephemeral key gets destroyed by performing recursive DNS requests for all key bits. This causes all the ephemeral bits to take the value `1`. In essence, this approach is like a dice with N sides and if we throw the proper side the ephemeral key is destroyed. This requires the sender to include the maximum number of accesses in the EDO and is based on the assumption that receivers of the EDO before the expiration time are not malicious (in accordance to our threat model).
Manual Revocation. Additionally, our approach supports the revocation of an EDO at a time its creator decides to. This can be done by performing recursive DNS requests to all DNS entries (similar to what we previously discussed). After that, the data will not be accessible any more, which is similar for a user to own the server in which the data was initially uploaded to and then decides to remove the data from the server. That said, we are aware that manual revocation entails the danger of a receiver or an attacker prematurely destroying the key. However, as we described in our threat model we try to protect the data only against a retroactive attacker, thus a proactive attacker is outside the scope of this paper.

4.3 Instantiation of the Scheme

Central to the application of the proposed scheme are the list of domain names used in the construction of the EDO and the length and threshold of the DNS portrayal. We detail both in the following. We then also reason about the error correction capabilities and scalability issues of the proposed scheme.

4.3.1 *List of Precompiled Domains*

The domain names which are used in our prototype are collected automatically by utilizing reverse DNS lookup. This method is based on the DNS infrastructure and allows the resolution of an IP address to its designated domain name (also known as forward DNS resolution). To generate a list of domains, we perform reverse DNS lookups to a range of IP addresses. In this procedure, we exclude addresses that have been reserved for special purposes by the Internet Engineering Task Force (IETF) and the Internet Assigned Numbers Authority (IANA). Before employing the domains we ensure using non-recursive DNS lookups that the domains are not currently cached in the DNS resolvers.

An alternative way to generate such a list is by crawling the Internet [30], using heuristics to reach less likely used websites. In both cases, our list of domain names should contain rarely used websites in order to reduce the chance of interference from legitimate DNS lookups. However, the randomized reverse DNS lookup approach above has the advantage that different users are more likely to select different domains so that their key storages do not interfere with each other.

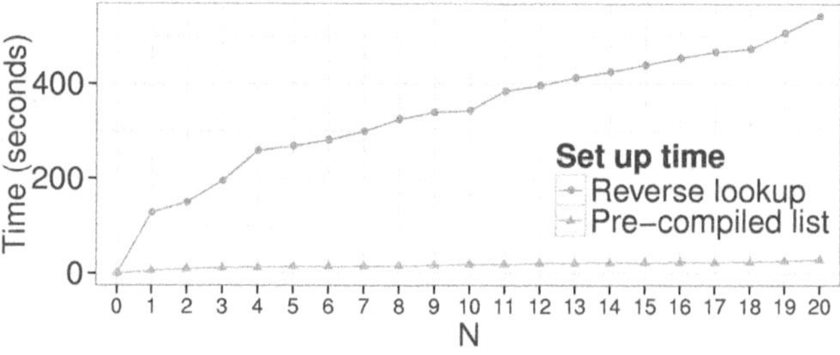

Figure 3: Time to construct an EDO for various lengths of the DNS portrayal.

Figure 3 illustrates an example of EDO generation with and without a precompiled list of domains for different numbers of DNS servers used for each key bit (size N of the DNS portrayal). The time consumption increases with a higher number of lookups. Measurements of 1024 random lookups (as would, e. g., be needed for $N = 8$) indicate an average duration of 0.31 seconds per successful operation. In this setup, no collisions of domains were encountered. We note that the domain lists can be compiled by the sender in advance to creating and publishing an EDO such that this does not create a bottleneck in the execution of the system.

4.3.2 *Size of DNS Portrayal*

The length N and the threshold x of the DNS portrayal determine the number of errors that our scheme can handle and influence how long the lifetime of the data can be extended. We consider as error any unexpected modification of the cache of a DNS resolver. That is, (i) a DNS resolver that empties its cache before the prescheduled TTL or (ii) an "accidental" recursive DNS request to our selected domain. To find representative error numbers, we monitored how the DNS entries behave in the real world. Our measurements of error frequencies are based on a set of 1853 DNS resolvers that had shown reliable service over a period of several months. We monitored the cached and uncached entries of 1000 randomly selected domains. For each resolver we collected all errors that occurred during the entire lifetime of entries. Results show that (i) with an error probability of $e_{1\to0} = 0.7\%$ a resolver empties its cache before the scheduled TTL expires and (ii) $e_{0\to1} = 0.1\%$ of accidental recursive requests were performed on the observed set of domains during out measurements. Although the exact error rates may vary over time, these numbers provide reasonable estimates for our derivations and simulation.

Both types of errors, that is bit flips $e_{1\to0}$ and $e_{0\to1}$, should be handled by our scheme. Based on this insight we can derive a minimal parameter setup $N = 3$ and $x = 2$ that enables correcting errors of type (i) and (ii) while providing the capability of refreshing cache entries. During initialization, i. e., when the key bits are first stored in the portrayal, the number of bits set to 1 must be larger than x; in later investigations, we use $\lceil \frac{N}{2} \rceil$ 1s for the initialization.

Beyond the minimal setup, an increase of the portrayal length N allows for increasing the scheme's correction capability whereas an increasing x threshold leads to a higher overhead in the presentation of bits (see Equation 5 for reference).

The initial lifetime (before lifetime extensions due to new accesses to the object) are given by the TTLs. Typical TTL values we observed for 1000 random lookups are characterized as follows: median of 86,400 s = 24 h, min. 72 s, max. 604,800 s = 14 days, standard deviation 110,704 s $\approx$ 30 h. Due to variations in the TTLs as well as due to errors, we initially do not set only one but multiple entries in each portrayal to 1.

4.3.3 Error Correction

Errors can cause the destruction of an encryption key before the heuristic would have triggered the revocation of an object. The application of a correction scheme should compensate such errors as long as the heuristics consider an object accessible. We consider the regular expiration of an entry as type-*(iii)* error for this purpose: as long as the applied heuristics did not trigger the destruction of the key, all changes in the key representation should not lead to the expiration of an object.

As the expiration of an entry is a necessary event, the error probabilities for $e_{1\to 0}$ and $e_{0\to 1}$ errors are highly distinct. Previous revocation systems utilized different correction schemes with individual characteristics: EphPub [7] uses Reed-Solomon (RS) error correcting codes (ECC) and Vanish [14] uses Shamir's Secret Sharing (SSS). The following paragraphs compare the performance of RS and SSS with the portrayal scheme applied in our scheme.

Error Correcting Codes. The RS code is an optimal BCH code (in non-binary mode) designed for correcting burst errors and it therefore performs best for errors that occur in row in an encoded word. In context of our scheme, the majority of type-*(iii)* errors occur randomly in 50 % of the cache entries and—since DNS servers and domain names are picked and distributed using a random selection—are uniformly distributed rather than bursty. An alternate to burst-optimal RS codes are Golay codes. The extended binary Golay code $[24, 12, 8]$ can correct uniformly distributed errors and would be more suitable for the occurrences of errors in our scheme. Different to standard ECC schemes, the parameters of our portrayal can be adapted to the type of errors occurring, that is the asymmetric distribution of 0- and 1-errors. Given this characteristic it is possible to achieve high correction rates while applying a smaller overhead to the key representation. With respect to the applied overhead and correction capabilities, the portrayal outperforms standard ECC schemes; we provide a detailed derivation in Appendix A. Thus, the portrayal is selected for providing robust lifetimes and the possibility of refreshing the key representation of an object.

Shamir's Secret Sharing. Secret sharing schemes distribute portions of a secret message over several users where a threshold t defines the number of shares required for reconstructing the original secret. When applied to an encryption key, the key can only be recovered when at least t shares are available at access time. Threshold values close to the number of shares lead to fast revocation and high security while smaller t values lead to a more robust system that can survive a higher number of errors. Overall, secret-sharing can provide theoretical security for revocation schemes that *do not* rely on the refreshing of entries: as soon as a bit error occurs in one share it becomes invalid and cannot be used for reconstructing the key. As our scheme requires the refreshing of bits, it must be robust to bit errors occurring through the expiration of cached entries.

4.3.4 Scalability

Without any centralized component in our proposed scheme it is not possible to store the domains that are already used for existing objects. Therefore it is not transparent whether an uncached entry for a domain is currently unused or represents a 0-entry or erroneous 1-entry in another portrayal. The probability of overlapping with an existing portrayal depends on the number of active domains: for instance for 510 million domain names [18] and a minimal portrayal with $N = 3$ and $x = 2$ overall 1,328,125 parallel users can share data via our model. The probability of overlapping entries at the initialization is approximately 1 % for 28,000 parallel users, as 50 % of bits in a portrayal are 0-bits that are prone to overlap with entries that are already used.

Table 2: Parameter space of simulation study.

Parameter	Variable space
I	: 128
N	: [4, 5, ..., 10]
x	: $\{1, 2\}$
t	: 43, 200
$e_{1\to 0}$	: $[0, 0.007]$
$e_{0\to 1}$	: $[0, 0.001]$
TTL_{min}	: 1, 200
TTL_{max}	: 604, 800

We note that high numbers of parallel users can increase the original probability for $e_{0\to 1}$ errors in addition to the error rate induced by accidentally performed recursive requests. In order to increase the robustness of our scheme for scenarios of massive parallel use, an additional encoding can be applied. For instance, in the portrayal of the encryption key, each bit can be encoded by a mixed tuple. A possible implementation could use a Manchester encoding, where 0-bits are encoded by 01 while 1-bits are encoded by 10. This allows to detect all 0 key bits that are already in use under the expense of doubled overhead.

5. SIMULATION STUDY

We conduct a simulation study to explore the parameter space, with respect to three performance parameters for the access heuristics of dropping interest and excessive access.

5.1 Simulation Setup

The parameters we investigate are shown in Table 2. They include the range of possible portrayal lengths N and the threshold values x and t for key recovery and TTL refreshing for a fixed key length $I = 128$ bit. We simulate the caching of entries and their TTL values, possible errors induced to the key shares, and different types of access patterns representing fluctuating numbers of receiver requests. The possibility of errors in the cache entries $e_{0\to 1}$ and $e_{1\to 0}$ each define the probability of a cache entry being flipped and are derived from measurements on the set of resolvers. The assignment of TTL values follows the measurements of EphPub [7].

Within a simulation run the lifetime of an object is monitored starting with its initialization until the destruction of the encryption key. It is executed step-wise with each step representing one second of object lifetime. The number of requests to an object at a time is simulated through different probability distribution functions (PDF): we applied an exponential and shifted normal distribution for the scenarios of dropping interest and an inverse exponential PDF for the scenario of excessive accesses. At each simulation step the cumulative number users performs an access on the object.

5.2 Performance Parameters

We consider the following performance parameters:

- *Sensitivity of expiration*: The sensitivity of expiration refers to the point of time when the access to an object gets revoked. While systems with high sensitivity react to the underlying metrics at an early point in time, more robust parameter setups extend the lifetime of an object.

- *Reliability of results*: For identical parameter setups, the lifetime of an object may vary in multiple simulation runs, as the system dynamics lead to a probabilistic model. Nevertheless, the reliable revocation of an object should still be ensured. We analyze the continuity of object lifetimes for highly sensitive as well as robust parameter setups.

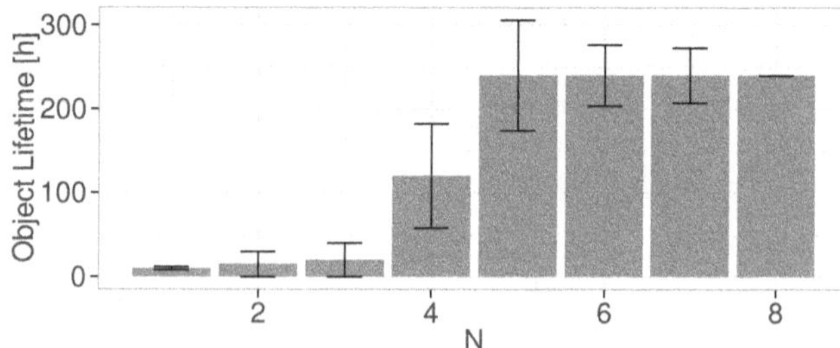

Figure 4: Error correction capabilities for $x = 2$ and increasing N. The error bars summarize the standard deviation of object lifetimes for 50 repetitions.

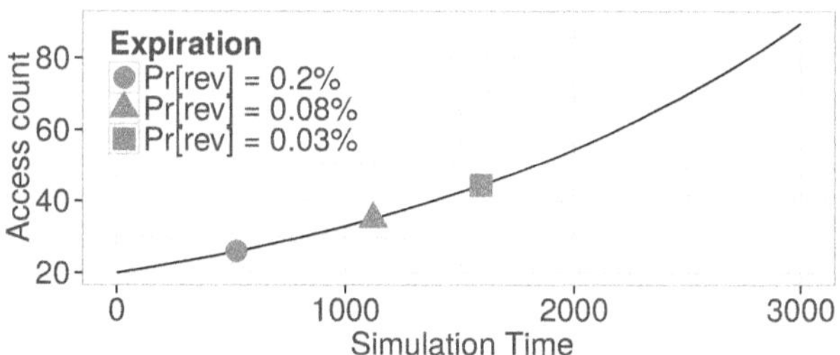

Figure 5: Lifetimes for $x = 2$, $N = 10$ and access heuristic for excessive access at an inverse exponential distribution of accesses.

- *Error correction capabilities*: Based on the optimal threshold $x = 2$, the correction capabilities can be increased by adapting the portrayal size N. Therefore a variation of the portrayal length leads to different object lifetimes.

5.3 Sensitivity of Expiration

Figure 4 summarizes the object lifetime for an increasing portrayal length N at the optimal threshold $x = 2$. With an increasing ratio $\frac{N}{x}$ the correction capabilities increase and lead to a prolonged object lifetime. This characteristic can be applied for defining the sensitivity of metrics in our scheme: to provide a robust revocation mechanism we need a ratio of at least 2.5 while smaller ratios lead to a system sensitive to a lack of refresh operations.

We measured the expiration time of an object with respect to exponentially (Figure 6a) and normally (Figure 6b) distributed access patterns. To provide an object with low sensitivity to dropping access rates, we simulated the object lifetime with $N = 10$, $x = 2$ and therefore a high ratio $\frac{N}{x} = 5$. For a scenario with access rates similar to a normal distribution the object expires as soon as the number of users is close to zero. In a parameter setup with increased sensitivity and $N = 4$, $x = 2$, $\frac{N}{x} = 2$ the expiration is triggered earlier, as a reduced number of expirations in cache entries can be covered. For a scenario with exponentially distributed access rates a highly sensitive parameter setup would require a more restrictive parameter setup.

Other than the Drop of interest heuristic, in case of Excessive access the key information should be destroyed if the number of accesses increases dramatically. Based on a probabilistic approach the expiration of an object can be reduced or prolonged by adapting the probability of destruction. As shown in Figure 5 higher probabilities lead to an early destruction of key information while reduced probabilities prolong the object lifetime. Nevertheless the revocation of an object cannot be determined as reliable as with the Drop of interest heuristic, as the moment of expiration is random.

5.4 Reliability of Results

Given the above parameter setups for a sensitive or robust revocation we analyzed the reliability of results for multiple repetitions. As shown in Figure 6, the dynamic characteristics of the simulation model lead to variations in the object lifetime: for 50 repetitions with TTL values distributed according to the measurements of common lifetimes, the results show slight deviations in the expiration time. Nevertheless the overall range is limited leading to a reliable destruction of key information for a given parameter set. Based on these characteristics it is possible to initialize an object with a target sensibility of the Drop of interest heuristic.

5.5 Error Correction Capabilities

Given the probability of naturally occurring errors in the cache representation of key bits, the x threshold is capable of correcting a limited amount of errors. We tested different x-thresholds based on a cache dimension of $N = 20$, which represents an acceptable creation duration. We applied the best performing setup to a simulation scenario with increasing error rates and accumulated the results for 100 random repetitions. As summarized in Figure 7, an average error probability of 10^{-4} already leads to a major decrease in the object lifetime when no correction threshold is applied (Figure 7a). However, $x = 2$ provides a constant lifetime up to an error rate of 10^{-3} and still allows for a performing system at 10^{-2} (see highlighted area), which is beyond the realistic error rates measured in the prototype implementation.

Overall, the simulation results lead to the conclusion that an application of the Drop of interest heuristic is possible with our scheme. Furthermore, a variation of system parameters such as the x-threshold enable for adjusting the sensitivity of the applied heuristic leading to a shift in the expiration time.

6. PROTOTYPE EVALUATION

To demonstrate the viability of our approach, we have implemented our proposed scheme as an autonomous framework called *Neuralyzer*. Our prototype is capable of dynamically encrypting data with a randomly generated key and then distribute the key bits across multiple real world DNS resolvers. To this end, we utilized the Python programming language and more specifically the PyDNS module, which allowed us to send both recursive and non-recursive DNS queries to our chosen DNS resolvers. Additionally, we used the AES algorithm (with a standard key size of 128 bits) of PyCrypto module to encrypt the data. Finally, each compiled EDO is encoded in a base64 format which is ideal for "shipping" the data across the Internet.

6.1 Expiration Time

We first consider the expiration of the publicly available data once the interest for it ceases to exist. In other words, the decryption keys of EDO should be available only as long as there is sufficient interest and disappear afterward.

To examine whether our protocol design is accurate we created two sets of EDO documents. Each set contained 100 documents compiled with our prototype. On the first set we did not apply any accesses at all, whereas on the second set we applied sufficient accesses (2 to 10 accesses per hour, random selection of their number and point in time) for a day, which is a typical lifespan for a normal tweet [33]. To assess the viability of the generated key bits in the DNS resolvers we performed non-recursive DNS queries to the corresponding servers. This way we did not affect the caches of the resolvers while we were able to monitor the TTL values on their caches, which means that we could monitor the existence of the decryption key without interfering with our experiment.

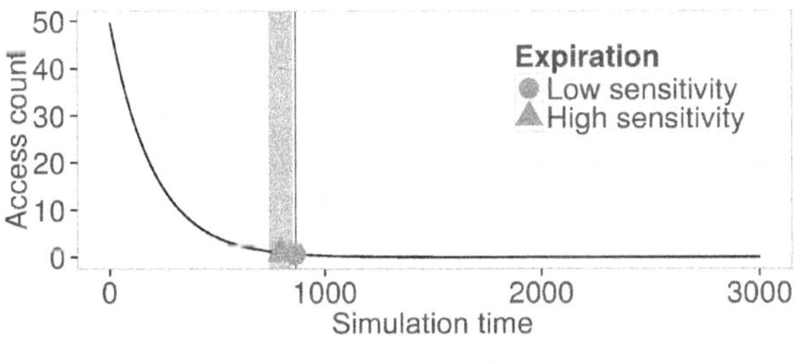

(a) Exponential Distribution.

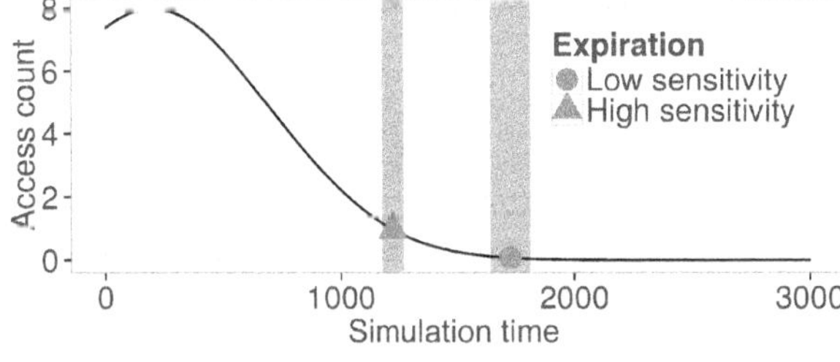

(b) Shifted Normal Distribution.

Figure 6: Expiration time for 50 repetitions of sensitive and robust parameter setup. The highlighted boxes represent the positive and negative standard deviation of measured lifetimes.

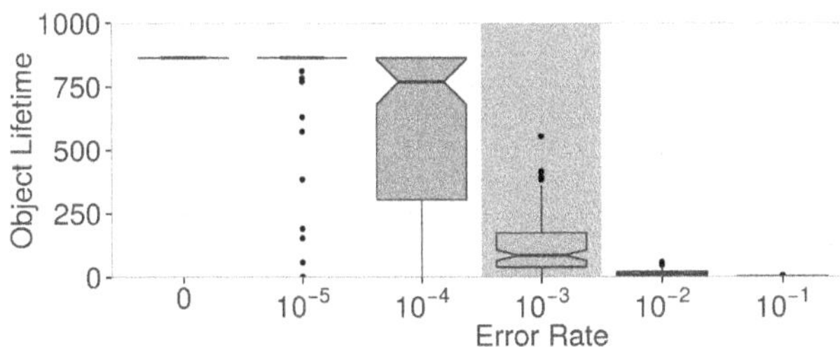

(a) Accumulated lifetime of EDO for $x = 0$ (no error correction).

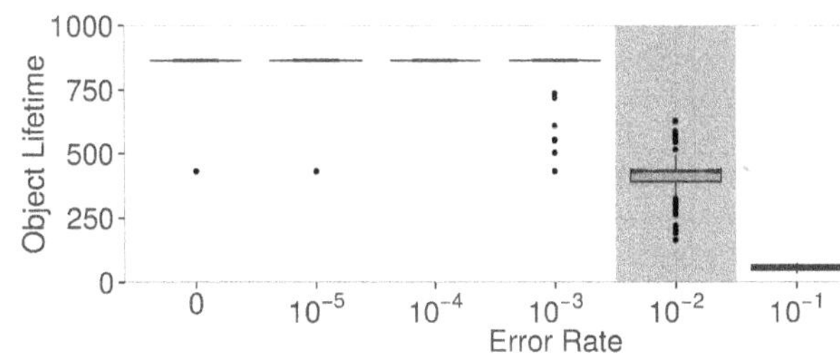

(b) Accumulated lifetime of EDO for $x = 2$ (minimal correction threshold).

Figure 7: EDO lifetime measured for different error rates at $N = 20$.

The outcomes revealed that in both scenarios the keys were destroyed during the expected time (same behavior for all documents). More precisely, the keys were vanished once the cache of the corresponding DNS resolvers emptied. Keep in mind that the TTL of the DNS resolvers cache define for how long the data will be available after their last access. In the first scenario, we noticed that after the first hour we could not decrypt the EDO documents any more. This happened due to the fact that the majority of the resolvers provided us with a TTL of 3600 seconds. In the second scenario, the keys remained available for the time that there existed sufficient interest for the documents. The major take away message from this experiment is the permanent deletion of the key once the interest drops. One anecdotal experience of this experiment is that we noticed during the day few resolvers to prematurely empty their caches or recursive DNS requests. However, none of these incidents were sufficient to destroy the decryption key.

6.2 Long Lasting Data

In contrast to certain types of data such as status updates on social media, comments on news websites, or publicly available pictures in cloud services in which the expected interest will be very limited and ranging from some hours to few days, there exist others such as posts on popular blogs or project documents that their creators expect to last longer, e. g., weeks or even months. The design of our model is meant to maintain the data as long as there is sufficient interest for it. We thus wanted to see if our approach operates in the real world as it is designed to, or an increased number of random recursive queries and errors in the caches of DNS resolvers over time will prematurely destroy the access to the compiled data.

To examine how *Neuralyzer* behaves in such long lasting data we created EDO documents, which we then accessed for a period of 33 days. In essence, we wanted to measure how a drop of interest scenario will behave in long lasting objects (in our case for a period of one month). Thus, the number of accesses dropped from over 400 accesses per day, which was at the beginning, to only a few accesses per day at the end. The outcomes of our experiments demonstrated that the number of random recursive queries and errors in the caches of DNS resolvers were not sufficient to revoke the access to the compiled EDO. More precisely, we were able to successfully reconstruct the decryption keys for a period of 30 days, as long as there was sufficient interest for the published data, and after that point in time the data were not accessible any more as Figure 8 illustrates. After the 33rd day there was no more accesses and this is the reason for the linear drop of accesses after this point in time. Consequently, this experiment along with the previous one demonstrates that *Neuralyzer* can achieve expiration times varying from hours to several weeks or months, depending on users' interest.

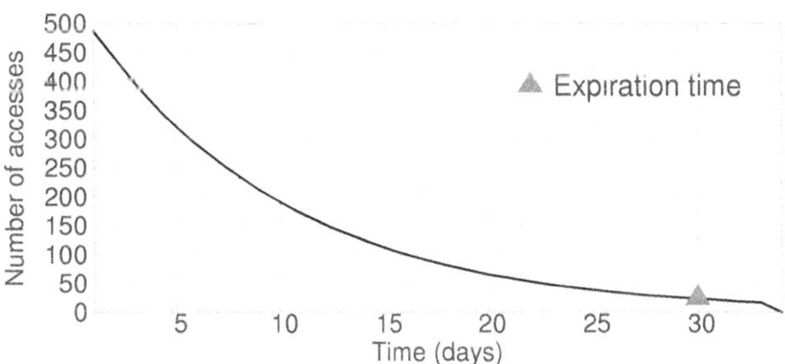

Figure 8: Number of accesses for a period of one month.

6.3 Accuracy of Excessive Accesses

Most of the times users do not really care about the publicity of their exposed information, e. g., status updates or tweets. However, there exist cases that the number of accesses play an important role, e. g., a blog post which the author does not desire to get viral.

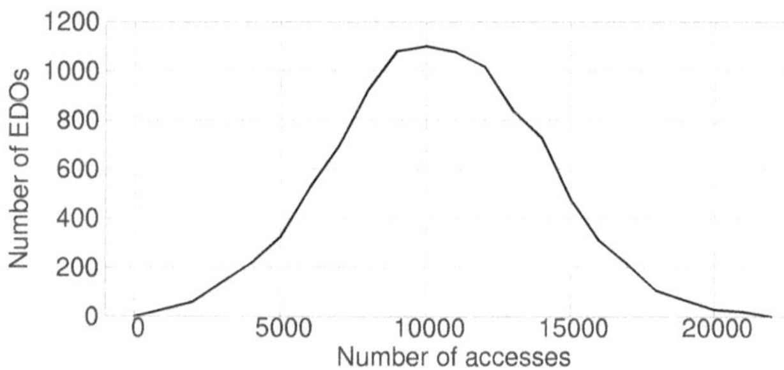

Figure 9: Standard deviation for the self destruction of EDOs.

The DNS infrastructure does not allow us to utilize or introduce a counter for the number of accesses to our publicly available EDOs. Therefore, we devised a probabilistic solution that could allow us to address this problem (Section 4.2.4). We next wanted to examine the accuracy of our approach. For this reason we created 10,000 EDOs and then we selected 10,000 to be a desired number of accesses. We then calculated the average number of accesses along with its standard deviation. Figure 9 depicts the number of accesses before an EDO is finally destroyed. More precisely, we found that each EDO was destroyed on average after 9928 accesses. The standard deviation value of our solution in terms of 3598 accesses (36% off from our assigned value) indicates that this approach can be selected as long as the number of accesses is acceptable as a rough estimate for the self-destruction of an object.

6.4 Manual Revocation Evaluation

Although our basic model is to revoke the access of publicly available data once the interest for it drops, there may exist cases where there is a pressing need for the immediate revocation of data. Although the concept behind of manual revocation is really simple, we nevertheless evaluated its effectiveness. To do so, we created 200 EDO documents and we divided them into two sets of 100 documents per set. In the first set we performed a manual revocation immediately after the creation of the encrypted documents while in the next set we performed the same action after they already had been accessed. This way we took into consideration (i) the case that an author of an EDO document wants to recall the access to the document right after it is been uploaded to a remote server, and (ii) the case that the document already have been accessed but the author does not desire any more publicity. As expected, in both cases we were able to completely destroy the decryption key in all 200 documents.

7. SECURITY ANALYSIS

We now analyze the presented scheme with respect to the security goal of retrospective privacy. Furthermore, additional attacks on the proposed system are discussed.

7.1 Retrospective Privacy

Retrospective privacy is fulfilled if an attacker is unable to access the contents of an EDO after its expiration. Under the assumption of a secure encryption system, this is possible in case the attacker manages to recover the decryption key of an object. Furthermore, we must take security issues of the DNS infrastructure into account.

7.1.1 Key recovery

Following the assumptions of Section 2.2, the attacker gains access to an encrypted EDO as well as the respective list of all destinations to where the key share was distributed after the object expired. Based on the DNS implementation, this results in a set of cache entries that previously represented the encryption key.

In an attack the expired and therefore still encrypted objects along with the list of key share domains are accessible to the adversary. At this point the information embedded in the acquired EDO can only be accessed if the attacker manages to recover the required amount of key bits from the list of queried domains for reconstructing the encryption key. The chance of successfully guessing the encryption key after expiration decreases over time.

Targeted guessing. Short after the expiration, a high number of cached 1-entries is still valid allowing the separation of 0- and 1-key bits based on an assumed threshold value: In the standard portrayal a threshold of $x = 2$ is optimal for the given error characteristics. Even though the correction capabilities for $e_{1\to 0}$ errors can be increased by using larger portrayal lengths N, the x threshold must be at least 2 for providing the correction of $e_{0\to 1}$ errors. An attacker therefore can assume $x = 2$. The number of valid 1 entries decreases over time, which increases the indistinguishability of key bits. Even though the threshold cannot be fulfilled correctly after some time, the existence of a 1-entry is more likely to be the remaining cache entry of a 1-bit of the key rather than a $e_{0\to 1}$ flip error. Therefore targeted guessing may lead to success if a sufficient number of 1-caches still exist. Both, the possible assumption of the optimal x threshold as well as targeted guessing of entries highly increases the chance of an attacker to successfully recovering the encryption key. Nevertheless, the overall success highly depends on the amount of time that passed between the revocation of an object and the actual attack on the key information.

Time. Over time the number of remaining 1-entries in the cache decreases, which also reduces the probability for an attacker to successfully recover the encryption key from remaining entries. The period of time in which a successful attack is likely can be analyzed based on the frequency of common TTL values.

As soon as the expiration of one entry $TTL(c_{exp})$ leads to the destruction of the key bit, a set of remaining 1-entries $c_{rem} \in C_{rem}$ must have had the same or higher TTL values at the initialization of c_{exp}:

$$\exists c_{rem} \in C_{rem} : TTL(c_{rem}) \geq TTL(c_{exp}) \tag{3}$$

That is, when c_{exp} was initially set and later triggered the destruction of the encryption key, all remaining entries that are also cached cannot have a TTL that is lower than that of c_{exp}. Due to this restriction two cases can be distinguished: In case (a) the majority of remaining entries has a TTL identical to c_{exp} and therefore expires at the same time. In this case the amount of information left for the attacker is insufficient for efficiently guessing the encryption key. In the second case (b) a majority of elements in C_{rem} has a TTL greater than the expired one. Based on the measurements on common TTL values, a lifetime of $86,400$ seconds (1 day) can be assumed for 58% of cache entries, the next greater TTL is $86,400 * 2$ and therefore provides another day to guess the remaining entries of the key. After that, the data is irrecoverably gone.

7.1.2 Security issues of the DNS infrastructure

Even though *Neuralyzer* utilizes the distributed and decentralized infrastructure provided by public DNS resolvers, several characteristics of this infrastructure can lead to security issues. Kührer et al. [20] found that in 2015 a significant amount (that is 20% of overall 6,753,748 resolvers in that specific measurement) of public resolvers run with BIND version 9.8.2, which can be manipulated through a remote code execution vulnerability. They also showed that a majority of public DNS resolvers are hosted by the top 25 networks wherein at least 20 offer telecommunication and broadband Internet services. Even though these results do not necessarily imply malicious behavior of service providers or the monitoring of traffic through a BIND vulnerability, the above can still lead to security issues for *Neuralyzer*. To overcome the threat of remote code execution, a fingerprinting of resolvers and the according software should be performed. When detecting a software version that can enable an attacker to perform monitoring of traffic on the public resolver, it should be excluded from the list of nodes that are considered in the portrayal of key bits.

In a scenario where the attacker is able to make use of the above issues, it must be assumed that the traffic of a fraction of resolvers of a portrayal can be monitored. This monitoring enables the attacker to save a history of cached/uncached entries during the lifetime of an object. In a retroactive attack this knowledge can help to reconstruct the encryption key from the remaining cache entries. As summarized in Section 7.1.1, even limited knowledge about the content of a portrayal can increase the probability of successfully guessing the related key bit dramatically. A simulation study on the amount of monitors required for learning about the encryption key shows that also smaller amounts of malicious resolvers are sufficient for reconstructing a significant portion of the key (see Appendix B for details). When extending the current filtering of resolvers to a selection of maximum distributed hosts of public resolvers, the threat of centrally controlled nodes can be reduced.

7.2 Further Attacks

Brute Force attack. A Brute Force attack on all possible DNS cache resolvers requires guessing of all potential destinations for bits of the key share. As summarized in EphPub [7] the number of possible entries exceeded 126 million in 2011 making a successful Brute Force key recovery unlikely for a DNS-based implementation. Moreover, the recovery of single key bits still requires the reconstruction of the full encryption key and a matching of this key to the explicit object it was applied to.

Sybil and infiltration attack. The Sybil attack, such as used by Zeng et al. [35] for showing vulnerabilities in the Vanish [14] system, is realized by controlling multiple virtual identities within the target infrastructure. Based on that the attacker is enabled to receive a large portion of the traffic occurring in a network allowing her to analyze the traversing packets. In context of a DNS-based implementation a Sybil cannot be realized through virtual nodes as there is no such thing as virtual identities for DNS resolvers. The required overhead for controlling the required amount of physical nodes in the DNS system makes a successful Sybil or infiltration attack therefore unlikely.

8. RELATED WORK

The automated deletion of data is not a new idea and researchers worked on this concept for quite a while. The first set of works involves trusted parties. Perlman proposed Ephemerizer, a trusted service that ensures timely expiration of emails [27, 28]. Nair et al. [25] extend the original idea of the Ephemerizer system through an identity-based cryptosystem. Systems such as X-Pire! [2] or the revocable backup system [6] also rely on a trusted key management server. Pöpper et al. [29] presented an approach utilizing porter devices for a secure storage of long term keys including explicit key deletion and forward-secret protocols, even under device compromise. Reimann et al. [30] proposed a revocation system that allows for long-term expiration dates of several months after publication. However, providing *flexible* expiration times of data using a *decentralized* infrastructure has not been proposed or investigated.

Vanish [14] was the first system not relying on a centralized, trusted system for the later revocation of data. Instead, it utilizes a decentralized architecture based on P2P distributed hash tables (DHT). Unfortunately, Vanish is susceptible to Sybil attacks [34] that can compromise the system by continuously crawling the DHT and saving each stored value before it expires. To overcome the vulnerabilities of Vanish, Zeng et al. [35] presented SafeVanish, which extends the length range of Vanish's key shares to substantially increase the attack cost, while it does also some improvement on the Shamir's Secret Sharing implemented in Vanish. In a survey about the vulnerabilities of self-destructing data systems, Geambasu et al. [13] implemented a framework for testing key-storage mechanisms based on different infrastructures and presented countermeasures to data-harvesting attacks. Casteluccia et al. [7] presented EphPub, a system that utilizes the DNS infrastructure and is capable of providing longer lifetimes for objects. Our major differences to EphPub is that we (i) designed a way for refreshing cache entries to prolong the lifetime of an object and (ii) applied access heuristics that manage the revocation of objects depending on the access behavior.

Another group of approaches is the cipher-text-policy attribute-based encryption (CP-ABE) schemes first introduced by Bethencourt [4]. With CP-ABE, access control policies can be enforced with attribute-based encryption where defined sets of credentials are required for encrypting sensitive data. These credentials are related to group or location attributes, e. g., specific enterprise departments, and included in a policy definition. Different to previous attribute-based encryption systems such as [11], attributes are used for a description of user credentials while access policies are defined by the encrypting party instead of storing this information in user keys. Hur et al. [17] presented a system providing the enforcement of access control policies even with revocation of attributes and thus access privileges. Balani and Ruj [3] took this concept to the cloud, outsourcing the decryption to a proxy server unable to retrieve information from the computations. Even though these approaches provide encryption-based handling of access policies they still cannot provide the dynamic revocation of files. That is the underlying crypto-infrastructure may be ported to a system such as the *Neuralyzer* while handling the key information must be performed in a decentralized manner.

9. CONCLUSION

In this paper, we proposed a novel approach for flexible revocation of online data. Other than recent work in this field, the central goal is to provide a metric-driven revocation mechanism that can be adapted to, e. g., the progression of user accesses over time instead of a predefined lifetime. To this end, the publicly accessible data is protected by encrypting it, encapsulating the encrypted content, and ensuring the destruction of the encryption key when the expiration time is reached. To assess our approach we created *Neuralyzer*, a proof-of-concept system based on the caching mechanism of public DNS resolvers that is able to refresh key information over time and expire its lifetime based on access novel heuristics. Results of a simulation study and experiments with a prototype implementation reveal that we can achieve flexible and reliable expiration times for the revocation of online data based on users' interest.

Acknowledgments

The research presented in this paper was supported by grant An-2014-0024 from MERCUR (Mercator Research Center Ruhr) and by the DFG Research Training Group GRK 1817/1.

10. REFERENCES

[1] O. Ayalon and E. Toch. Retrospective Privacy: Managing Longitudinal Privacy in Online Social Networks. In *Symposium on Usable Privacy and Security (SOUPS)*, 2013.

[2] J. Backes, M. Backes, M. Dürmuth, S. Gerling, and S. Lorenz. X-Pire!-A Digital Expiration Date for Images in Social Networks. *arXiv preprint arXiv:1112.2649*, 2011.

[3] N. Balani and S. Ruj. Temporal Access Control With User Revocation for Cloud Data. In *International Conference on Trust, Security and Privacy in Computing and Communications (TrustCom)*, 2014.

[4] J. Bethencourt, A. Sahai, and B. Waters. Ciphertext-Policy Attribute-Based Encryption. In *IEEE Symposium on Security and Privacy*, 2007.

[5] M. Bishop, E. R. Butler, K. Butler, C. Gates, and S. Greenspan. Forgive and Forget: Return to Obscurity. In *New Security Paradigms Workshop*, 2013.

[6] D. Boneh and R. Lipton. A Revocable Backup System. In *USENIX Security Symposium*, 1996.

[7] C. Castelluccia, E. De Cristofaro, A. Francillon, and M.-A. Kaafar. EphPub: Toward Robust Ephemeral Publishing. In *IEEE International Conference on Network Protocols (ICNP)*, 2011.

[8] C. Conley. The Right to Delete. In *AAAI Spring Symposium: Intelligent Information Privacy Management*, 2010.

[9] J. Daemen and V. Rijmen. *The Design of Rijndael: AES – the Advanced Encryption Standard*. Springer Science & Business Media, 2002.

[10] E. De Cristofaro, C. Soriente, G. Tsudik, and A. Williams. Hummingbird: Privacy at the Time of Twitter. In *IEEE Symposium on Security and Privacy*, 2012.

[11] T. Eissa and G.-H. Cho. A Fine Grained Access Control and Flexible Revocation Scheme for Data Security on Public Cloud Storage Services. In *International Conference on Cloud Computing Technologies, Applications and Management (ICCCTAM)*, 2012.

[12] European Commission. Factsheet on the "Right to Be Forgotten" Ruling, C-131/12. http://ec.europa.eu/justice/data-protection/files/factsheets/factsheet_data_protection_en.pdf, 2014.

[13] R. Geambasu, T. Kohno, A. Krishnamurthy, A. Levy, H. Levy, P. Gardner, and V. Moscaritolo. New Directions for Self-Destructing Data Systems. Technical report, University of Washington, 2011.

[14] R. Geambasu, T. Kohno, A. A. Levy, and H. M. Levy. Vanish: Increasing Data Privacy with Self-Destructing Data. In *USENIX Security Symposium*, 2009.

[15] R. Gross and A. Acquisti. Information Revelation and Privacy in Online Social Networks. In *ACM Workshop on Privacy in the Electronic Society (WPES)*, 2005.

[16] Huffington Post. Experts Say Facebook Leak of 6 Million Users' Data Might Be Bigger Than We Thought. http://www.huffingtonpost.com/2013/06/27/facebook-leak-data_n_3510100.html, Jun 2013.

[17] J. Hur and D. K. Noh. Attribute-Based Access Control With Efficient Revocation in Data Outsourcing Systems. *IEEE Transactions on Parallel and Distributed Systems*, 22(7):1214–1221, 2011.

[18] Internet Live Stats. Total Mumber of Websites. http://www.internetlivestats.com/total-number-of-websites/, Aug 2015.

[19] B. Krebs. Online Cheating Site AshleyMadison Hacked. http://krebsonsecurity.com/2015/07/online-cheating-site-ashleymadison-hacked/, Jul 2015.

[20] M. Kührer, T. Hupperich, J. Bushart, C. Rossow, and T. Holz. Going Wild: Large-Scale Classification of Public DNS Resolvers. In *ACM SIGCOMM Internet Measurement Conference (IMC)*, 2015.

[21] M. Madejski, M. L. Johnson, and S. M. Bellovin. The Failure of Online Social Network Privacy Settings. Technical report, Columbia University, 2011.

[22] C. D. Marsan. 15 Worst Internet Privacy Scandals of All Time. http://www.networkworld.com/article/2185187/security/15-worst-internet-privacy-scandals-of-all-time.html, Jan 2012.

[23] Mashable. 98,000 Hacked Snapchat Photos and Videos Posted Online. http://mashable.com/2014/10/13/the-snappening-photos-videos-posted, Oct 2014.

[24] P. V. Mockapetris. RFC 883, Domain Names – Implementation and Specification. 1983.

[25] S. K. Nair, M. T. Dashti, B. Crispo, and A. S. Tanenbaum. A Hybrid PKI-IBC Based Ephemerizer System. In *New Approaches for Security, Privacy and Trust in Complex Environments*, 2007.

[26] P. Papadopoulos, A. Papadogiannakis, M. Polychronakis, A. Zarras, T. Holz, and E. P. Markatos. K-Subscription: Privacy-Preserving Microblogging Browsing Through Obfuscation. In *Annual Computer Security Applications Conference (ACSAC)*, 2013.

[27] R. Perlman. File System Design With Assured Delete. In *IEEE International Security in Storage Workshop (SISW)*, 2005.

[28] R. Perlman. The Ephemerizer: Making Data Disappear. *Journal of Information System Security (JISSec)*, 1:51–68, 2005.

[29] C. Pöpper, D. Basin, S. Čapkun, and C. Cremers. Keeping Data Secret Under Full Compromise Using Porter Devices. In *Annual Computer Security Applications Conference (ACSAC)*, 2010.

[30] S. Reimann and M. Dürmuth. Timed Revocation of User Data: Long Expiration Times From Existing Infrastructure. In *ACM Workshop on Privacy in the Electronic Society (WPES)*, 2012.

[31] D. Rosenblum. What Anyone Can Know: The Privacy Risks of Social Networking Sites. *IEEE Security & Privacy*, (3):40–49, 2007.

[32] The Register. iCloud Fiasco: 100 Famous Women Exposed Nude Online. http://www.theregister.co.uk/2014/08/31/jlaw_upton_caught_in_celeb_nude_pics_hack, Aug 2014.

[33] Wisemetrics. Your Tweet Half-Life Is 1 Billion Times Shorter Than Carbon 14's. http://blog.wisemetrics.com/tweet-isbillion-time-shorter-than-carbon14/, Mar 2014.

[34] S. Wolchok, O. S. Hofmann, N. Heninger, E. W. Felten, J. A. Halderman, C. J. Rossbach, B. Waters, and E. Witchel. Defeating Vanish With Low-Cost Sybil Attacks Against Large DHTs. In *ISOC Network and Distributed System Security Symposium (NDSS)*, 2010.

[35] L. Zeng, Z. Shi, S. Xu, and D. Feng. SafeVanish: An Improved Data Self-Destruction for Protecting Data Privacy. In *International Conference on Cloud Computing Technology and Science (CloudCom)*, 2010.

APPENDIX

A. COMPARISON OF CORRECTION CAPABILITIES

In the following our portrayal **(P)** is compared to the Reed-Solomon **(RS)** and Golay **(G)** error correcting code with respect to each scheme's individual overhead. To do so, a fixed number of errors $T = 1000$ and key length $z = 128$ are defined that should be corrected by a scheme with minimum possible overhead.[2] For a binary input of length z the above schemes can correct the following number of errors in general:

$$\textbf{RS}\begin{cases}\frac{n-k}{2}\cdot\lceil\frac{z}{k\cdot m}\rceil & : n-k \text{ even}\\ \frac{n-k-1}{2}\cdot\lceil\frac{z}{k\cdot m}\rceil & : n-k \text{ odd}\end{cases}, \quad (4)$$

where $n = 2^m - 1$ with $7 \leq n \leq 2^{16} - 1$ is the codeword length, $3 \leq m \leq 16$ is the input word length, and $k < n$ is the number of words to be encoded in one code word.

$$\mathbf{P} : z(N - x - 1), \quad (5)$$

where N is the length of a portrayal, and x is the correction threshold. To be robust against flipping of bits in both directions, the total correction capability for $e_{0\rightarrow 1}$ must be at least 1. This requirement is fulfilled for $x \geq 1$ and $N \geq 3$.

The parameters for **G** are fixed and allow up to 3 corrections for the extended binary $G[24, 12, 8]$.

A **RS** code is optimal only for non-binary input and can be adapted to encoding the binary encryption key by setting $m = 8$ for representing 1 byte per word. Under this assumption the overhead and correction capability of **RS** (assumed $n - k$ even) is as follows for $T = 1000$:

$$\begin{aligned} T &\leq \frac{n-k}{2}\cdot\lceil\frac{z}{k\cdot m}\rceil && (6)\\ \Rightarrow 1000 &\leq \frac{255-k}{2}\cdot\lceil\frac{128}{k\cdot 8}\rceil|\cdot 2 && (7)\\ \Leftrightarrow 2000 &\leq 255-k\cdot\lceil\frac{128}{k\cdot 8}\rceil|k=1 && (8)\\ \Rightarrow 2000 &\leq 2032 && (9)\end{aligned}$$

To correct at least $T = 1000$ errors, **RS** must be applied with $m = 8, n = 255, k = 1$ leading to a total overhead of factor 16.

For any T and an input length $z = 128$ the overhead of **RS** is as follows:

$$2T \leq (n^m - 1 - k)\cdot\lceil\frac{128}{m\cdot k}\rceil \quad (10)$$

[2]In context of a scheme's correction capabilities the overhead defines the amount of additional bits required for a code that is capable of correcting the fixed error rate.

For a minimum threshold of $x = 2$, **P** provides the following overhead for $T = 1000$:

$$\begin{aligned} T &\leq z(N-x-1) && (11)\\ \Rightarrow 1000 &\leq 128(N-2-1) && (12)\\ \Leftrightarrow 1000 &\leq 128N|N=8 && (13)\\ \Rightarrow 1000 &\leq 1024 && (14)\end{aligned}$$

This leads to a parameter set of $N > 8, x = 2$ and a total overhead of factor 9 for the portrayal scheme. The correction capability for any error rate T for an input of length $z = 128$ is as follows:

$$\frac{T}{128} \leq N \quad (15)$$

For providing the same minimum correction rate with **G**, the input length must be extended: to correct at least $T = 1000$ errors, an input length of 334 is required leading to a total overhead of factor 63.

B. CONTROL OF M PUBLIC RESOLVERS

Under the assumption of an attacker who is able to utilize either a remote code execution vulnerability in the software of a resolver or a malicious service provider hosting a fraction of resolver, a relative amount of m entries, that is M entries in total, in the key representation is known by the attacker. To analyze the effects of such an attack on the security of *Neuralyzer*, two cases must be distinguished (for the following we assume a maximum number of resolvers used in the portrayal: each domain in the key portrayal is organized by exactly 1 resolver):

In the best case (bc) scenario (from a user's perspective) the number of different key bits affected by the attack is minimal. That is for the portrayal C_{IxN} the number of rows I is minimal while the number of columns N is maximal. For a key length I and portrayal size N the probability of being attacked in a best case distribution of M controlled domains is as follows:

$$Pr(bc) = \binom{I\cdot N}{M} \quad (16)$$

Opposed to the best case scenario the attacker has the maximum possible knowledge about the encryption key in case the controlled resolvers are distributed over a maximum number of rows I in the portrayal. We simulated this attack for different fractions m of controlled resolvers and varying key lengths I and portrayal sizes N. Results show that even for small m the attacker can gather a significant amount of information about the encryption key. For $m = 0.05$ an attacker can control from 14% (at $I = 128$, $N = 3$) up to 40% (at $I = 128$, $N = 10$) of rows in the key portrayal.

Differentially Private K-Means Clustering

Dong Su
Purdue University
su17@cs.purdue.edu

Jianneng Cao
Institute for Infocomm Research
caojn@i2r.a-star.edu.sg

Ninghui Li
Purdue University
ninghui@cs.purdue.edu

Elisa Bertino
Purdue University
bertino@cs.purdue.edu

Hongxia Jin
Samsung Research America
hongxia.jin@samsung.com

ABSTRACT

There are two broad approaches for differentially private data analysis. The *interactive* approach aims at developing customized differentially private algorithms for various data mining tasks. The *non-interactive approach* aims at developing differentially private algorithms that can output a synopsis of the input dataset, which can then be used to support various data mining tasks. In this paper we study the effectiveness of the two approaches on differentially private k-means clustering. We develop techniques to analyze the empirical error behaviors of the existing interactive and non-interactive approaches. Based on the analysis, we propose an improvement of DPLloyd which is a differentially private version of the Lloyd algorithm. We also propose a non-interactive approach EUGkM which publishes a differentially private synopsis for k-means clustering. Results from extensive and systematic experiments support our analysis and demonstrate the effectiveness of our improvement on DPLloyd and the proposed EUGkM algorithm.

Keywords

Differential privacy; k-means clustering; Private data publishing

1. INTRODUCTION

In recent years, differential privacy [10] has been increasingly adopted as the privacy notion of choice of data analysis while preserving individual privacy. Several broad classes of approaches exist for developing differentially private techniques for data analysis. In this paper we study differentially private k-means clustering. Clustering analysis plays an essential role in data management tasks. Clustering under differential privacy has also been studied in [3, 9, 19, 22, 24, 25, 34].

Our study has two goals. The first is to improve the techniques for performing k-means clustering differentially privately. The second is to use k-means clustering as a case study to compare several classes of methods for private data analysis, and to identify the strengths and weaknesses of these methods.

There are three state-of-the-art differentially private algorithms on k-means clustering. All of them are interactive approaches. The first method, which we call DPLloyd, makes the iterative Lloyd algorithm [3, 22] differentially private by adding noises to each step. The second method, which we call PGkM, uses PrivGene [34], a framework for differentially private model fitting based on genetic algorithms. We call them *iterative interactive* algorithms. The third algorithm uses the sample and aggregation framework [25] and is implemented in the GUPT system [24], which we call GkM.

An alternative to the interactive setting is the *non-interactive* setting, in which the data curator releases the data in one shot, while still preserving privacy. To the best of our knowledge, performing k-means clustering using the non-interactive approach has not been explicitly proposed in the literature. In this paper, we propose to combine the following non-interactive differentially private synopsis algorithms with k-means clustering. The dataset is viewed as a set of points over a d-dimensional domain, which is divided into M equal-size cells, and a noisy count is obtained from each cell. A key decision is to choose the parameter M. A larger M value means lower average counts for each cell, and therefore noisy counts are more likely to be dominated by noises. A smaller M value means larger cells, and therefore one has less accurate information of where the points are. We propose a method that sets $M = \left(\frac{N\epsilon}{10}\right)^{\frac{2d}{2+d}}$, which is derived based on extending the analysis in [27], which aims to minimize errors when answering rectangular range queries for 2-dimensional data, to higher dimensional case. We call the resulting k-means algorithm EUGkM, where EUG is for Extended Uniform Grid.

We conducted extensive experimental evaluations for these algorithms on 6 external datasets and 81 datasets that we synthesized by varying the dimension d from 2 to 10 and the number of clusters from 2 to 10. Experimental results are quite interesting. GkM was introduced after DPLloyd and was claimed to have accuracy advantage over DPLloyd, and PGkM was introduced after and compared GkM. However, we found that DPLloyd is the best method among these three interactive methods. In the comparison of DPLloyd and GkM in [24], DPLloyd was run using much larger number of iterations than necessary, and thus perform poorly. In [34], PGkM was compared only with GkM, and not with DPLloyd. More specifically, we found that GkM is by far the worst among all methods. However, DPLloyd, the earliest method is clearly the best performing algorithm among the three interactive algorithms. Through analysis, we found that why DPLloyd outperforms PGkM. The genetic programming style PGkM needs more iterations to converge. When making these algorithms differentially private, the privacy budget is divided among all iterations, thus having more iterations means more noise is added to each iteration. Therefore, the more direct DPLloyd outperforms PGkM.

CODASPY'16, March 09-11, 2016, New Orleans, LA, USA

DOI: http://dx.doi.org/10.1145/2857705.2857708

The most intriguing results are those comparing DPLloyd with EUGkM. For most datasets, EUGkM performs much better than DPLloyd. For a few, they perform similarly, and for the rest datasets DPLloyd outperforms EUGkM. Through further theoretical and empirical analysis, we found that while the performance of both algorithms are greatly affected by the two key parameters, the number of dimensions d and the number of clusters k, both of them are affected differently by these two parameters. DPLloyd scales worse when k increases, while EUGkM scales worse when d increases. Again we use analysis to demonstrate why this is the case.

In this paper we advance the state-of-the-art on differentially private data mining in several ways. First, we have introduced a new non-interactive method, EUGkM, for differentially private k-means clustering, which are highly effective and often outperform the state-of-the-art interactive methods and non-interactive methods. Second, we have developed techniques to analyze the error resulted from DPLloyd. Such kind of error analysis is missed in most differentially private data analysis papers. Third, based on the error analysis of DPLloyd, we proposed an improved version of DPLloyd which significantly reduces the clustering error. Fourth, we have extensively evaluated three interactive methods, and three non-interactive methods, and analyzed their strengths and weaknesses.

The rest of the paper is organized as follows. In Section 2, we give preliminary information about differential privacy and k-means clustering. In Section 3, we describe the existing three interactive approaches, DPLloyd, GkM, PGkM, two non-interactive approaches UGkM and MkM, improve DPLloyd and derive a new non-interactive approach EUGkM. In Section 4, we first show the experimental results on the performance comparison among the interactive and non-interactive approaches, and analyze their strengths and weaknesses. In Section 5, we discuss related works. We conclude in Section 6.

2. BACKGROUND

2.1 Differential Privacy

Informally, differential privacy requires that the output of a data analysis mechanism should be approximately the same, even if any single tuple in the input database is arbitrarily added or removed.

Definition 1 (ϵ-Differential Privacy [8, 10]). *A randomized mechanism $\mathcal{A}$ gives ϵ-differential privacy if for any pair of neighboring datasets D and D', and any $S \subseteq Range(\mathcal{A})$,*

$$\Pr\left[\mathcal{A}(D) \in S\right] \leq e^{\epsilon} \cdot \Pr\left[\mathcal{A}(D') \in S\right].$$

In this paper we consider two datasets D and D' to be neighbors if and only if either $D = D' + t$ or $D' = D + t$, where $D + t$ denotes the dataset resulted from adding the tuple t to the dataset D. We use $D \simeq D'$ to denote this. This protects the privacy of any single tuple, because adding or removing any single tuple results in e^{ϵ}-multiplicative-bounded changes in the probability distribution of the output.

Differential privacy is composable in the sense that combining multiple mechanisms that satisfy differential privacy for $\epsilon_1, \cdots, \epsilon_m$ results in a mechanism that satisfies ϵ-differential privacy for $\epsilon = \sum_i \epsilon_i$. Because of this, we refer to ϵ as the *privacy budget* of a privacy-preserving data analysis task. When a task involves multiple steps, each step uses a portion of ϵ so that the sum of these portions is no more than ϵ.

There are several approaches for designing mechanisms that satisfy ϵ-differential privacy, including Laplace mechanism [10] and Exponential mechanism [21]. The Laplace mechanism computes a function g on the dataset D by adding to $g(D)$ a random noise, the magnitude of which depends on GS_g, the *global sensitivity* or the L_1 sensitivity of g. Such a mechanism $\mathcal{A}_g$ is given below:

$$\begin{array}{lrl} & \mathcal{A}_g(D) & = g(D) + \mathsf{Lap}\left(\frac{\mathsf{GS}_g}{\epsilon}\right) \\ \text{where} & \mathsf{GS}_g & = \max\limits_{(D,D'):D\simeq D'} |g(D) - g(D')|, \\ \text{and} & \Pr\left[\mathsf{Lap}\left(\beta\right) = x\right] & = \frac{1}{2\beta} e^{-|x|/\beta}. \end{array}$$

In the above, $\mathsf{Lap}\left(\beta\right)$ denotes a random variable sampled from the Laplace distribution with scale parameter β.

2.2 k-means Clustering Algorithms

The k-means clustering problem is as follows: given a d-dimensional dataset $D = \{x^1, x^2, \ldots, x^N\}$, partition data points in D into k sets $\mathbf{O} = \{O^1, O^2, \cdots, O^k\}$ so that the Normalized Intra-Cluster Variance (NICV) is minimized

$$\frac{1}{N}\sum_{j=1}^{k} \sum_{x^\ell \in O^j} ||x^\ell - o^j||^2. \tag{1}$$

The standard k-means algorithm is the Lloyd's algorithm [18]. The algorithm starts by selecting k points as the initial choices for the centroid. The algorithm then tries to improve these centroid choices iteratively until no improvement can be made. In each iteration, one first partitions the data points into k clusters, with each point assigned to be in the same cluster as the nearest centroid. Then, one updates each centroid to be the center of the data points in the cluster.

$$\forall i \in [1..d]\ o_i^j \leftarrow \frac{\sum_{x^\ell \in O^j} x_i^\ell}{|O^j|}, \tag{2}$$

where $j = 1, 2, \ldots, k$, x_i^ℓ and o_i^j are the i-th dimensions of x^ℓ and o^j, respectively. The algorithm continues by alternating between data partition and centroid update, until it converges.

3. THE INTERACTIVE AND NON-INTERACTIVE APPROACHES

In this section, we describe and analyze three interactive approaches and three non-interactive approaches to differentially private k-means clustering.

3.1 DPLloyd and Proposed Improvements

3.1.1 DPLloyd

A differentially private version of the Lloyd's algorithm was first proposed by Blum et al. [3] and was later implemented in the PINQ system [22], a platform for interactive privacy preserving data analysis. We call this the DPLloyd approach. DPLloyd differs from the standard Lloyd algorithm in the following ways. First, Laplacian noise is added to the iterative update step in the Lloyd algorithm. Second, the number of iterations needs to be fixed in order to decide how much noise needs to be added in each iteration.

Each iteration requires computing the total number of points in a cluster and, for each dimension, the sum of the coordinates of the data points in a cluster. Let t be the number of iterations, and d be the number of dimensions. Then, each tuple is involved in answering dt sum queries and t count queries. To bound the sensitivity of the sum query to a small number r, each dimension is normalized to $[-r, r]$. Therefore, the global sensitivity of DPLloyd is $(dr + 1)t$, and each query is answered by adding Laplacian noise $\mathsf{Lap}\left(\frac{(dr+1)t}{\epsilon}\right)$.

3.1.2 Optimization Issues

The overall structure of DPLloyd is to first select initial values, and then iteratively improve them. This same algorithmic structure also applies to many other data analysis tasks, such as linear regression, SVM, etc. When making such an interactive and iterative algorithm differentially private, there are two important decisions one has to make.

The first decision is how to select the initial values? In the standard, non-private setting, a purely random choice may suffice, since one could repeat the algorithm multiple times and choose the best result among them. With privacy constraints, however, running the interactive algorithm multiple times results in each run can use only a fraction of the total privacy budget, and make the results being even less accurate.

The second decision is how many iterations one runs. A large number of iterations causes too much noises being added. A small number of iterations may be insufficient for the algorithm to converge. Existing approaches fix a number. However, intuitively the number of rounds would depend on the available privacy budget ϵ. With a smaller privacy budget, one should run fewer number of rounds, to avoid the results being overwhelmed by too much noise.

How to choose these parameters has not been carefully considered in the literature. In the implementation of DPLloyd in PINQ [19], it is proposed to run 5 iterations, with equal privacy budget allocation for each round. In [24], comparison of GkM with DPLloyd was done by running DPLloyd with 20, 80, and 200 iterations, resulting in incorrect claim that GkM outperforms DPLloyd. Dwork [9] considered the possibility of running k-means clustering without knowing the number of rounds in advance, and proposed to use exponentially decreasing allocation of privacy budgets, i.e., $\frac{\epsilon}{2}$ in the first round, $\frac{\epsilon}{4}$ in the second round, and so on. This mostly likely results in deteriorating performance when the number of rounds increases. The main reason is that in later rounds, when one gets closer to the optimal value, it is desirable to have a larger privacy budget.

Below, we propose an approach to improve the selection of initial centroids for k-means clustering, design a general framework for deciding the number of iterations and apply it to improve DPLloyd. The improved version of DPLloyd is called DPLloyd-Impr.

3.1.3 Selecting Initial Centroids

The quality of initial centroids greatly affects the accuracy of DPLloyd. A poor choice of initial centroids can result in converging to a local optimum that is far from global optimum, or not converging after the given number of iterations. While many methods for choosing the initial points have been developed [26], these methods were developed without the privacy concern and need access to the dataset. In [22], k points at uniform random from the domain are chosen as the initial centroids. We have observed empirically that this can perform poorly in some settings, since some randomly chosen initial centroids are close together. We thus introduce an improved method for choosing initial centroids that is similar to the concept of sphere packing. Given a radius a, we randomly generate k centroids one by one such that each new centroid is of distance at least a away from every corner of the domain $[-r,r]^d$ and each new centroid is of distance at least $2a$ away from any existing centroid. When a randomly chosen point does not satisfy this condition, we generate another point. When we have failed repeatedly, we conclude that the radius a is too large, and try a smaller radius. We use a binary search to find the maximal value for a such that it is the process of choosing k centroids succeed. This process depends only on the shape of the overall domain and not where the data points are, and thus does not affect privacy.

3.1.4 Optimizing Rounds and Budget Allocation

We introduce the following general approach of determining the number of rounds and privacy budget allocation. Our approach depends on the ability to analyze the amount of noise introduced in each round, manifested as the mean squared error (MSE). Given this, one also specifies a threshold for the maximum MSE. The basic idea is to choose the number of iterations so that we try to ensure that each iteration's MSE is no larger than the threshold, and use smaller number of rounds if necessary. Below we show how to apply this idea to DPLloyd.

3.1.5 Error Study of DPLloyd

DPLloyd adds noises to each iteration of updating centroids. We now analyze the mean squared error (MSE) between noisy centroids and true centroids in one iteration.

Consider one centroid and its update in one iteration. The true centroid's i'th dimension should be $o_i = \frac{S_i}{C}$, where C is the number of data points in the cluster and S_i is the sum of i'th dimension coordinates of data points in the cluster. Consider the noisy centroid $\widehat{o}$; its i'th dimension is $\widehat{o_i} = \frac{S_i+\Delta S_i}{C+\Delta C}$, where ΔC is the noise added to the count and ΔS_i is the noise added to the S_i. The MSE is thus:

$$\mathsf{MSE}(\widehat{o}) = \mathsf{E}\left[\sum_{i=1}^{d}\left(\frac{S_i+\Delta S_i}{C+\Delta C} - \frac{S_i}{C}\right)^2\right] \tag{3}$$

Derivation based on the above formula gives the following proposition.

Proposition 1. *In one round of DPLloyd, the MSE is*

$$\Theta\left(\frac{(kt)^2 d^3}{(N\epsilon)^2}\right).$$

Proof. Let us first consider the MSE on the i-th dimension.

$$\begin{aligned}
\mathsf{MSE}(\widehat{o_i}) &= \mathsf{E}\left[\left(\tfrac{S_i+\Delta S_i}{C+\Delta C} - \tfrac{S_i}{C}\right)^2\right] \\
&\approx \mathsf{E}\left[\left(\tfrac{C\Delta S_i - S_i\Delta C}{C^2}\right)^2\right] \\
&= \tfrac{\mathsf{E}[(\Delta S_i)^2]}{C^2} + \tfrac{\mathsf{E}[S_i^2(\Delta C)^2]}{C^4} + \tfrac{2CS_i\mathsf{E}[\Delta S_i\Delta C]}{C^4} \\
&= \tfrac{\mathsf{Var}(\Delta S_i)}{C^2} + \tfrac{S_i^2\mathsf{Var}(\Delta C)}{C^4}
\end{aligned}$$

The last step holds, because ΔS_i and ΔC are independent zero-mean Laplacian noises and the following formulas hold:

$$\begin{cases}
\mathsf{E}[\Delta S_i\Delta C] = 0 \\
\mathsf{E}[(\Delta S_i)^2] = \mathsf{E}[(\Delta S_i)^2] - (\mathsf{E}[\Delta S_i])^2 = \mathsf{Var}(\Delta S_i) \\
\mathsf{E}[(\Delta C)^2] = \mathsf{E}[(\Delta C)^2] - (\mathsf{E}[\Delta C])^2 = \mathsf{Var}(\Delta C),
\end{cases}$$

where $\mathsf{Var}(\Delta S_i)$ and $\mathsf{Var}(\Delta C)$ are the variances of ΔS_i and ΔC, respectively.

Suppose that on average $\frac{|S_i|}{2r\cdot C} = \rho$, where $[-r,r]$ is the range of the i'th dimension. That is, ρ is the normalized coordinate of i-th dimension of the cluster's centroid. Furthermore, suppose that each cluster is about the same size, i.e., $C \approx \frac{N}{k}$. Then, $\mathsf{MSE}(\widehat{o_i})$ can be approximated as follows:

$$\mathsf{MSE}(\widehat{o_i}) \approx \frac{k^2}{N^2}\left(\mathsf{Var}(\Delta S_i) + (2\rho r)^2 \cdot \mathsf{Var}(\Delta C)\right) \tag{4}$$

DPLloyd adds to each sum/count function Laplace noise $\mathsf{Lap}\left(\frac{(dr+1)t}{\epsilon}\right)$. Therefore, both $\mathsf{Var}(\Delta S_i)$ and $\mathsf{Var}(\Delta C)$ are equal to $\frac{2((dr+1)t)^2}{\epsilon^2}$.

From Equation (4) we obtain

$$\mathsf{MSE}(\widehat{o_i}) \approx \frac{k^2}{N^2}\left(\mathsf{Var}(\Delta S_i) + (2\rho r)^2 \cdot \mathsf{Var}(\Delta C)\right) \quad (5)$$

$$= 2(1+(2\rho r)^2)\left(\frac{kt(dr+1)}{N\epsilon}\right)^2. \quad (6)$$

As the noise added to each dimension is independent, from Equation 3 we know that the MSE is

$$\mathsf{MSE}(\widehat{o}) = \sum_{i=1}^{d} \mathsf{MSE}(\widehat{o_i}) \approx 2d(1+(2\rho r)^2)\left(\frac{kt(dr+1)}{N\epsilon}\right)^2 \quad (7)$$

When r is a small constant, this becomes $\Theta\left(\frac{(kt)^2 d^3}{(N\epsilon)^2}\right)$. □

Proposition 1 shows that the distortion to the centroid proportional to $t^2k^2d^3$, while inversely proportional to $(N\epsilon)^2$.

3.1.6 *Optimizing Privacy Budget Allocation Within Each Round*

An issue specific to DPLloyd and may not be shared by all iterative algorithms is that within each round of DPLloyd, the privacy budget needs to be divided among the count and the d sum queries. Suppose ϵ_0 is allocated to the count query, and ϵ_i is allocated to the sum query for the i-th dimension, for each $i = 1, 2, \ldots, d$. While all dimensions should be treated equally, i.e., $\epsilon_1 = \epsilon_2 = \ldots = \epsilon_d$, an interesting question is what should be the right value of $\frac{\epsilon_i}{\epsilon_0}$? The DPLloyd approach allocates the privacy budget according to the sensitivities of different queries; thus $\frac{\epsilon_i}{\epsilon_0} = r$, assuming that each dimension is normalized to $[-r, r]$. Different r values will result in different allocations of privacy budget.

We observe that the analysis in Section 3.1.5 calls for a fixed allocation of $\frac{\epsilon_i}{\epsilon_0}$, independent from how the data ranges are normalized. Plugging $\mathsf{Var}(\Delta S_i) = \frac{2r^2}{\epsilon_i^2}$ and $\mathsf{Var}(\Delta C) = \frac{2}{\epsilon_0^2}$ into Equation (5), one obtains

$$\sum_{i=1}^{d} \mathsf{MSE}(\widehat{o_i}) \approx \frac{k^2}{N^2}\sum_{i=1}^{d}\left(\mathsf{Var}(\Delta S_i) + (2\rho r)^2 \cdot \mathsf{Var}(\Delta C)\right)$$

$$= \frac{2r^2k^2}{N^2}\left(\sum_{i=1}^{d}\frac{1}{\epsilon_i^2} + \frac{4d\rho^2}{\epsilon_0^2}\right) \quad (8)$$

Minimization of the above subject to $\sum_{i=1}^{d} \epsilon_i + \epsilon_0 = z$ can be solved using the method of *Lagrange multipliers*, where z is the privacy budget allocated to the current round. The optimal proportion is

$$\epsilon_1 : \epsilon_2 : \cdots : \epsilon_d : \epsilon_0 = 1 : 1 : \cdots : 1 : \sqrt[3]{4d\rho^2} \quad (9)$$

To compute $\sqrt[3]{4d\rho^2}$, we need an estimation of ρ, the normalized coordinate of i-th dimension of the cluster's centroid. We note that $0 \le \rho \le 0.5$. If a cluster includes points perfectly balanced between the negative side and the positive side, then $\rho = 0$. If all points have r $(-r)$ as its i-th coordinate, then $\rho = 0.5$. We empirically compute ρ from 81 synthetic datasets that are not used for purpose of evaluation. We use $\rho = 0.225$ in this paper, and conjecture that it provides a good enough approximation for most scenarios.

We note that in the DPLloyd approach, if one chooses $r = 1$, i.e., normalizes each dimension to the range of $[-1, 1]$, one would allocate the privacy budget with a ratio of $\epsilon_i : \epsilon_0 = 1 : 1$, which is suboptimal in most cases.

3.1.7 *Determining the Number of Rounds*

Based on our analysis in Section 3.1.5, we make several observations. First, it makes no sense to run DPLloyd with a large number of rounds. From Proposition 1, the distortion on the centroid is on the order of $\Theta\left(\frac{t^2}{(N\epsilon)^2}\right)$. Thus, all one gets from running DPLloyd with too many rounds results large distortion on the cluster centroids. Second, one should dynamically determine the number of rounds based on parameters such as N and ϵ, since the distortion on the centroid is inversely proportional to $(N\epsilon)^2$.

By exploiting these observations, we propose a way to determine the number of iterations. We first determine a minimum privacy budget ϵ^m that needs to be allocated to each iteration (see below). Then, the privacy budget allocation across the iterations is decided by the following two cases. *Case 1:* $\epsilon \le 2\epsilon^m$. In this case, the total privacy budget is inadequate. If we distribute it to more than 2 iterations, then as stated before the added noise in each round would easily dominate the centroid improvement. Therefore, we decide that DPLloyd runs for two iterations only, each with privacy budget of $\frac{\epsilon}{2}$. *Case 2:* $\epsilon > 2\epsilon^m$. In this case, the total privacy budget is able to meet the requirement of assigning minimum budget to each iteration. We require that the total number of iterations is at most 7. Thus, the total number of iterations $t^- = \min\{\frac{\epsilon}{\epsilon^m}, 7\}$, and the privacy budget allocated to each of them is $\frac{\epsilon}{t^-}$.

We now come to the calculation of ϵ^m. The intuition is that if the centroid improvement of one iteration is effective, then the MSE value should not be too big. We use the heuristic that the MSE of all the centroids improvement should be no more than $0.004 \cdot r^d$. It follows from Equation 8 that

$$\frac{2r^2k^3}{N^2}\left(\sum_{i=1}^{d}\frac{1}{\epsilon_i^2} + \frac{4d\rho^2}{\epsilon_0^2}\right) \le 0.004 r^d, \quad (10)$$

where $\sum_{i=0}^{d} \epsilon_i = \epsilon^m$. According to the optimized ratio in Equation 9, the privacy budget ϵ^m is distributed between ϵ_i's as follows:

$$\begin{cases} \epsilon_0 = \frac{\sqrt[3]{4d\rho^2}}{d+\sqrt[3]{4d\rho^2}}\epsilon^m \\ \epsilon_i = \frac{1}{d+\sqrt[3]{4d\rho^2}}\epsilon^m, \text{for } i = 1, 2, \ldots, d. \end{cases}$$

Plugging the above into Inequality 10 we can find the minimal ϵ^m value,

$$\epsilon^m = \left(\frac{500k^3}{N^2}\left(d + \sqrt[3]{4d\rho^2}\right)^3\right)^{1/2}. \quad (11)$$

For the Gowalla dataset, $\epsilon^m \approx 0.011$; for the Adult-num dataset, it is approximately equal to 0.096.

3.2 PGkM

PrivGene [34] is a general-purpose differentially private model fitting framework based on genetic algorithms. Given a dataset D and a fitting-score function $f(D, \theta)$ that measures how well the parameter θ fits the dataset D, the PrivGene algorithm initializes a candidate set of possible parameters θ and iteratively refines them by mimicking the process of natural evolution. Specifically, in each iteration, PrivGene uses the exponential mechanism [21] to privately select from the candidate set m' parameters that have the best fitting scores, and generates a new candidate set from the m' selected parameters by crossover and mutation. Crossover regards each parameter as an h-dimensional vector. Given two parameter vectors, it randomly selects a number $\bar{h}$ such that $0 < \bar{h} < h$ and splits each vector into the first $\bar{h}$ dimensions in the vector and the remaining $h - \bar{h}$ dimensions (the lower half). Then, it swaps the lower halves of the two vectors to generate two child vectors. These vectors are then mutated by adding a random noise to one randomly chosen dimension.

In [34], PrivGene is applied to logistic regression, SVM, and k-means clustering. In the case of k-means clustering, the NICV formula in Equation 1, more precisely its non-normalized version, is used as the fitting function f, and the set of k cluster centroids is defined as parameter θ. Each parameter is a vector of $h = k \cdot d$ dimensions. Initially, the candidate set is populated with 200 sets of cluster centroids randomly sampled from the data space, each set containing exactly k centroids. Then, the algorithm runs iteratively for $\max\{8, (xN\epsilon)/m'\}$ rounds, where x and m' are empirically set to 1.25×10^{-3} and 10, respectively, and N is the dataset size.

We call the approach of applying PrivGene to k-means clustering PGkM, which is similarly to DPLloyd in that it tries to iteratively improve the centroids. However, rather than maintaining and improving a single set of k centroids, PGkM maintains a pool of candidates, uses selection to improve their quality, and crossover and mutation to broaden the pool.

By selecting multiple sets of centroids in each round and applying mutation, PGkM reduces the chance that the iterative process is stuck in a suboptimal solution. At the same time, doing this invariably slows down the converging process. At the same time, if one increases the number of iterations, each iteration becomes highly inaccurate. Thus whether PGkM is a suitable approach for a problem depends on whether the benefit of PGkM can compensate for the slow converging speed. Our experimental results in Section 4 show that for k-means clustering, this is not the case and PGkM performs poorly.

3.3 GkM

The k-means clustering problem was also used to motivate the *sample and aggregate* framework (SAF) for satisfying differential privacy, which was developed in [25, 31], and implemented in the GUPT system [24].

Given a dataset D and a function f, SAF first partitions D into ℓ blocks, then it evaluates f on each of the block, and finally it privately aggregates results from all blocks into a single one. Since any single tuple in D falls in one and only one block, adding one tuple can affect at most one block's result, limiting the sensitivity of the aggregation step. Thus one can add less noise in the final step to satisfy differential privacy.

As far as we know, GUPT [24] is the only implementation of SAF. Authors of [24] implemented k-means clustering and used it to illustrate the effectiveness of GUPT. We call this algorithm GkM. Given a dataset D, it first partitions D into ℓ blocks $D_1, D_2, \ldots, D_\ell$. Then, for each block D_b ($1 \leq b \leq \ell$), it calculates its k centroids $o^{b,1}, o^{b,2}, \ldots, o^{b,k}$. Finally, it averages the centroids calculated from all blocks and adds noise. Specifically, the i'th dimension of the j'th aggregated centroid is

$$o_i^j = \frac{1}{\ell}\sum_{b=1}^{\ell} o_i^{b,j} + \mathsf{Lap}\left(\frac{2(max_i - min_i)\cdot k \cdot d}{\ell \cdot \epsilon}\right), \quad (12)$$

where $o_i^{b,j}$ is the i'th dimension of $o^{b,j}$, $[min_i, max_i]$ is the estimated output range of i'th dimension. One half of the total privacy budget is used to estimate this output range, and the other half is used for adding Laplace noise.

We have found that the implementation downloaded from [23], which uses Equation (12), performed poorly. Analyzing the data closely, we found that min_i and max_i often fall outside of the data range, especially for small ϵ. We slightly modified the code to bound min_i and max_i to be within the data domain. This does not affect the privacy, was able to greatly improve the accuracy. In this paper we use this fixed version.

Here a key parameter is the choice of ℓ. Intuitively, a larger ℓ will result in each block being very small and unable to preserve the cluster information in the blocks, and a smaller ℓ, on the other hand, results in large noise added. (Note the inverse dependency on ℓ in Equation (12). Analysis in [24] suggests to set $\ell = N^{0.4}$. Our experimental results, however, show that the performance is quite poor. We can analytically show why that is the case.

There are two sources of errors in GkM. The first is that the aggregation from the cluster centers obtained from different subsamples may not be accurate. The second is due to the added noise. The MSE due to the added noise is on the order of $\frac{k^2 d^2}{\ell^2 \epsilon^2}$. Compared with the MSE analysis of DPLloyd, they are comparable when $\ell \approx \frac{N}{t\sqrt{d}}$, that is, when each block contains only a small number of data points. It is unlikely that one could learn k centroids from such small subsamples. At the same time, if one chooses $\ell = N^{0.4}$, then MSE will be linear in $\frac{k^2 d^2}{N^{0.8} \epsilon^2}$, which is much larger than that of the DPLloyd method.

3.4 Non-interactive Approaches

Interactive approaches such as DPLloyd and GkM suffer from two limitations. First, often times the purpose of conducting k-means clustering is to visualize how the data points are partitioned into clusters. The interactive approaches, however, output only the centroids. In the case of DPLloyd, one could also obtain the number of data points in each cluster; however, it cannot provide more detailed information on what shapes data points in the clusters take. The value of interactive private k-means clustering is thus limited. Second, as the privacy budget is consumed by the interactive method, one cannot perform any other analysis on the dataset; doing so will violate differential privacy.

Non-interactive approaches, which first generate a synopsis of a dataset using a differentially private algorithm, and then apply k-means clustering algorithm on the synopsis, avoid these two limitations. In this paper, we consider the following synopsis method. Given a d-dimensional dataset, one partitions the domain into M equal-width grid cells, and then releases the noisy count in each cell, by adding Laplacian noise to each cell count.

The synopsis released is a set of cells, each of which has a rectangular bounding box and a (noisy) count of how many data points are in the bounding box. The synopsis tells only how many points are in a cell, but not the exact locations of these points. For the purpose of clustering, We treat all points as if they are at the center of the bounding box. In addition, these noisy counts might be negative, non-integer, or both. A straightforward solution is to round the noisy count of a cell to be a non-negative nearest integer and replicate the cell center as many as the rounded count. This approach, however, may introduce a significant systematic bias in the clustering result, when many cells in the UG synopsis are empty or close to empty and these cells are not distributed uniformly. In this case, simply turning negative counts to zero can produce a large number of points in those empty areas, which can pull the centroid away from its true position. We take the approach of keeping the noisy count unchanged and adapting the centroid update procedure in k-means to use the cell as a whole. Specifically, given a cell with center c and noisy count $\tilde{n}$, its contribution to the centroid is $c \times \tilde{n}$. Using this approach, in one cluster, cells who have negative noisy count can "cancel out" the effect of other cells with positive noise. Therefore, we can have better clustering performance.

For this method, the key parameter is M, the number of cells. When M is large, the average count per cell is low, and the noise will have more impact. When M is small, each cell covers a large area, and treating all points as at the center may be inaccurate when the points are not uniformly distributed. We now describe two existing methods of choosing M and extend one of them.

3.4.1 MkM

Lei [16] proposed a scheme to release differentially private synopses tailored for the M-estimator. Given a d-dimensional dataset with N tuples, statistical analysis in [16] suggests that

$$M = \left(\frac{N}{\sqrt{\log(N)}}\right)^{\frac{2d}{2+d}} \quad (13)$$

We name the approach of applying the k-means clustering on this synopsis MkM.

3.4.2 UGkM

UG is a simple algorithm proposed in [27] for producing synopsis of 2-dimensional datasets that can be used to answer rectangular range queries (i.e., how many data points there are in a rectangular range) with high accuracy. The algorithm partitions the space into $M = m \times m$ equal-width grid cells, and then releases the noisy count in each cell. It is observed that for counting queries, a larger M value results in higher errors because more noises are added, and a smaller M value results in higher errors due to the fact that points within cells may be distributed nonuniformly, and queries including a portion of these cells may be answered inaccurately. To balance these two kinds of errors, it is suggested to set

$$m = \sqrt{\frac{N\epsilon}{10}}, \text{ or equivalently, } M = \frac{N\epsilon}{10} \quad (14)$$

It has been shown that UG performs quite well for answering rectangular range queries [27]. UG can be easily extended to d-dimensional dataset by setting $m = \sqrt[d]{M}$. We use UGkM to represent the UG-based k-means clustering scheme.

3.4.3 EUGkM

We now analyze the choice of M for higher-dimensional case. We use *mean squared error* (MSE) to measure the accuracy of est with respect to act. That is,

$$\mathsf{MSE}(est) = \mathsf{E}\left[(est - act)^2\right] = \mathsf{Var}(est) + (\mathsf{Bias}(est))^2,$$

where $\mathsf{Var}(est)$ is the variance of est and $\mathsf{Bias}(est)$ is its bias.

There are two error sources when computing est. First, Laplace noises are added to cell counts to satisfy differential privacy. This results in the variance of est. Since counting a cell size has the sensitivity of 1, Laplace noise $\mathsf{Lap}\left(\frac{1}{\epsilon}\right)$ is added. Thus, the noisy count has the variance of $\frac{2}{\epsilon^2}$. Suppose that the given counting query covers α portion of the total M cells in the data space. Then, $\mathsf{Var}(est) = \alpha\frac{2M}{\epsilon^2}$. Second, the given counting query may not fully contain the cells that fall on the border of the query rectangle. To estimate the number of points in the intersection between the query rectangle and the border cells, it assumes that data are uniformly distributed. This results in the bias of est, which depends on the number of tuples in the border cells. The border of the given query consists of $2d$ hyper rectangles, each being $(d-1)$-dimensional. The number of cells falling on a hyper rectangle is in the order of $M^{\frac{d-1}{d}}$. On average the number of tuples in these cells is in the order of $M^{\frac{d-1}{d}} \cdot \frac{N}{M} = \frac{N}{M^{\frac{1}{d}}}$. Therefore, we estimate the bias of est with respect to one hyper rectangle to be $\beta\frac{N}{M^{\frac{1}{d}}}$, where $\beta \geq 0$ is a parameter. We thus estimate $(\mathsf{Bias}(est))^2$ to be $2d\left(\beta\frac{N}{M^{\frac{1}{d}}}\right)^2$.

Summing the variance and the squared bias, it follows that

$$\mathsf{MSE}(est) = \alpha\frac{2M}{\epsilon^2} + \beta^2\frac{2dN^2}{M^{\frac{2}{d}}}.$$

To minimize the MSE, we set the derivative of the above equation with respect to M to 0. This gives

$$M = \left(\frac{N\epsilon}{\theta}\right)^{\frac{2d}{2+d}}, \quad (15)$$

where $\theta = \sqrt{\frac{\alpha}{2\beta^2}}$. We name the above extended approach as EUG (extended uniform griding approach). We use EUGkM to represent the EUG-based k-means clustering scheme.

4. PERFORMANCE AND ANALYSIS

Table 1: Descriptions of the Datasets.

Dataset	# tuples	# dims	# clusters
S1	5,000	2	15
Gowalla	107,091	2	5
TIGER	16,281	2	2
Image	34,112	3	3
Adult-num	48,841	6	5
Lifesci	26,733	10	3
Synthe	10,000 + O	[2, 10]	[2, 10]
Synthe-PT	10,000	[2, 10]	[2, 10]

O is # outliers and is uniformly sampled from [0, 100].

In this section, we compare and analyze the performance of the six methods described in Section 3.

4.1 Evaluation Methodology

We experimented with six external datasets and two sets of syntheticly generated datasets. The first external dataset is a 2D synthetic dataset S1 [12], which is a benchmark to study the performance of clustering schemes. S1 contains 5,000 tuples and 15 Gaussian clusters. The Gowalla dataset contains the user checkin locations from the Gowalla location-based social network whose users share their checking-in time and locations (longitude and latitude). We sample one locaiton of each user ID and obtain a 2D dataset of 107,091 tuples. We set $k = 5$ for this dataset. The third dataset is a 1-percentage sample of road dataset which was drawn from the 2006 TIGER (Topologically Integrated Geographic Encoding and Referencing) dataset [4]. It contains the GPS coordinates of road intersections in the states of Washington and New Mexico. The fourth is Image [12], a 3D dataset with 34,112 RGB vectors. We set $k = 3$ for it. We also use the well known Adult dataset [1]. We use its six numerical attributes, and set $k = 5$. The last dataset is Lifesci. It contains 26,733 records and each of them consists of the top 10 principal components for a chemistry or biology experiment. As previous approaches [24, 34], we set $k = 3$. Table 1 summarizes the datasets. For all the datasets, we normalize the domain of each attribute to [-1.0, 1.0].

We generate two sets of synthetic datasets. The first set of synthetic datasets, which we call Synthe, is generated by using the clusterGeneration [28] R package. It is designed for generating cluster datasets with specified degree of separation which is a quantitative measure of closeness between any cluster and its nearest neighboring cluster. Besides, the clusterGeneration package can generate clusters with arbitrary diameters, shapes and orientations.

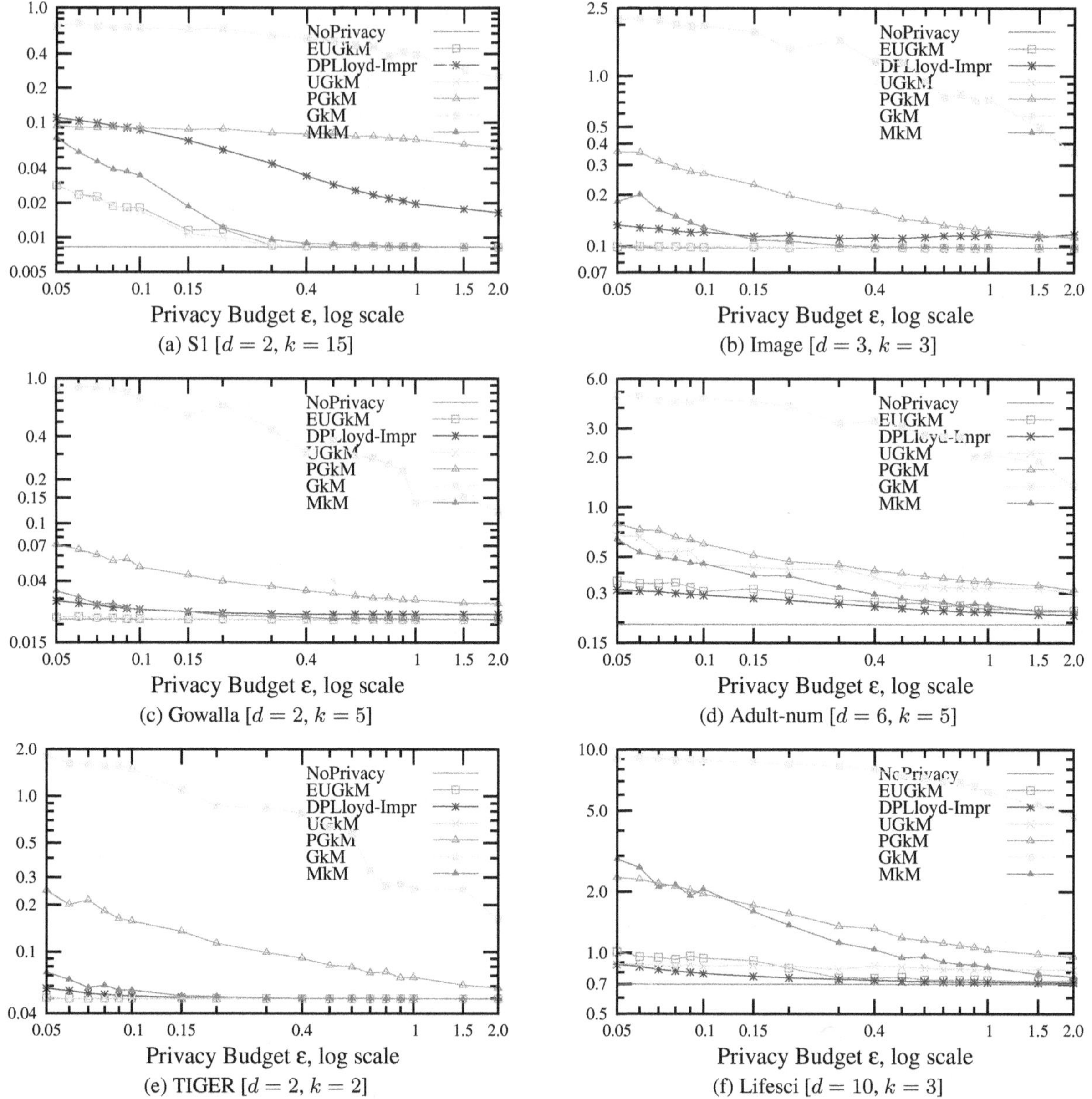

(a) S1 [$d = 2$, $k = 15$]

(b) Image [$d = 3$, $k = 3$]

(c) Gowalla [$d = 2$, $k = 5$]

(d) Adult-num [$d = 6$, $k = 5$]

(e) TIGER [$d = 2$, $k = 2$]

(f) Lifesci [$d = 10$, $k = 3$]

Figure 1: The comparison of DPLloyd-Impr, PGkM, GkM, EUGkM, UGkM and MkM by varying the privacy budget ϵ. x-axis: privacy budget ϵ in log-scale. y-axis: NICV in log-scale.

In this paper, we generate 81 dataset by varying k and d from 2 to 10. We fix the dataset size to 10,000 and distribute them into k clusters with size proportional to the ratio $1 : 2 : \ldots : k$. We also inject few outliers whose number is uniformly sampled from $[0, 100]$. For each dataset, we randomly sample its degree of separation from $[0.16, 0.26]$, which means from clusters with small overlapping to separated-but-close clusters.

The second set is mainly for tuning parameters of the EUGkM algorithm. We fix the dataset size to be 10,000, and vary k and d from 2 to 10 respectively. For each dataset, k well separated Gaussian clusters with equal size are generated. We call the second set of synthetic dataset as the Synthe-PT set, where PT stands for parameter tuning.

Implementations for DPLloyd and GkM were downloaded from [19] and [23], respectively. The source code of PGkM [34] was shared by the authors. We implemented EUGkM, UGkM and MkM.

Configuration. Each algorithm outputs k centroids $\mathbf{o} = \{o^1, o^2, \cdots, o^k\}$. The quality of the centroids $\mathbf{o}$ is evaluated by the Normalized Intra-Cluster Variance (NICV) (Eq.1).

We note that since both DPLloyd, EUGkM, UGkM and MkM use Lloyd-style iteration, they are affected by the choice of initial centroids. In addition, all algorithms have random noises added somewhere to satisfy differential privacy. To conduct a fair comparison, we need to carefully average out such randomness effects. GkM and PGkM do not take a set of initial centroids as input. GkM divides the input dataset into multiple blocks, and for each block invokes the standard k-means implementation from the Scipy pack-

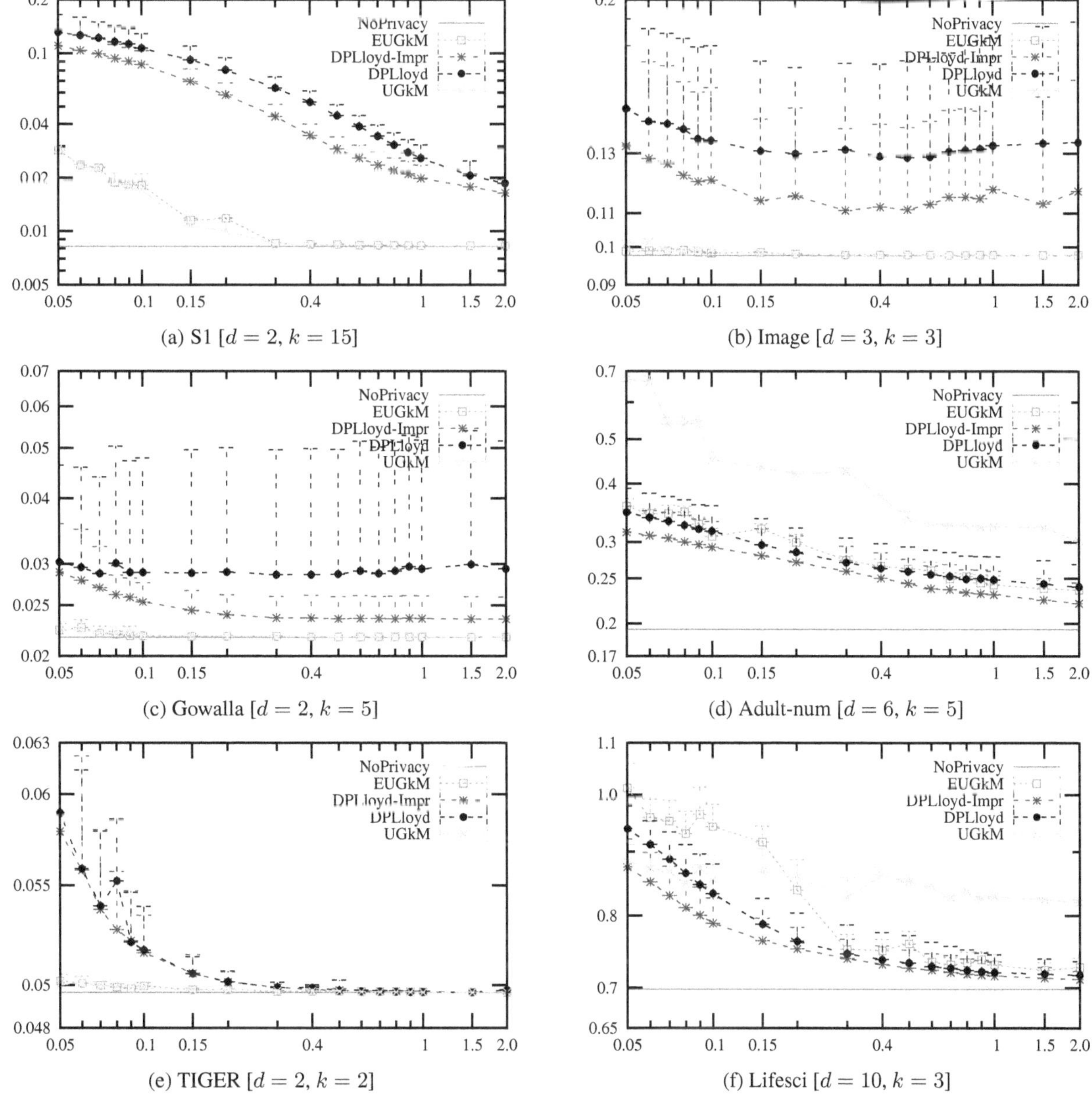

Figure 2: The close-up view of the comparison of DPLloyd-Impr, DPLloyd, EUGkM, and UGkM by varying the privacy budget ϵ. x-axis: privacy budget ϵ in log-scale. y-axis: NICV in log-scale.

age [30] with a different set of initial centroids to get the result, and finally aggregates the outputs for all the blocks. We run GkM and PGkM 100 times and report the average result.

DPLloyd-Impr generates 30 sets of initial centroids by using the proposed sphere packing method in Section 3.1.3. We run DPLloyd-Impr 100 times on each set of initial centroids, and report the average of the 3000 NICV values as the final evaluation of DPLloyd-Impr. For DPLloyd, we randomly generate 30 sets of initial centroids and use the same way to compute the averaged NICV values.

The non-interactive approach (EUGkM) has the advantage that once a synopsis is published, one can run k-means clustering with as many sets of initial centroids as one wants and choose the result that has the best performance relative to the synopsis. In our experiments, given a synopsis, we use the same 30 sets of initial centroids as those generated for the DPLloyd-Impr method. For each set, we run clustering and output a set of k centroids. Among all the 30 sets of output centroids, we select the one that has the lowest NICV relative to the synopsis rather than to the original dataset. This process ensures selecting the set of output centroids satisfies differential privacy. We then compute the NICV of this selected set relative to the original dataset, and take it as the resulting NICV with respect to the synopsis. To deal with the randomness introduced by the process of generating synopsis, we generate 10 different synopses and take the average of the resulting NICV values.

For EUGkM, we set the the parameter $\theta = 10$. We experimentally compare the EUGkM's performance on different θ choices and find that $\theta = 10$ for EUGkM works well in most cases. This parameter tuning for EUGkM is performed on the Synthe-PT dataset. Therefore, the following evaluation of EUGkM on the Synthe dataset

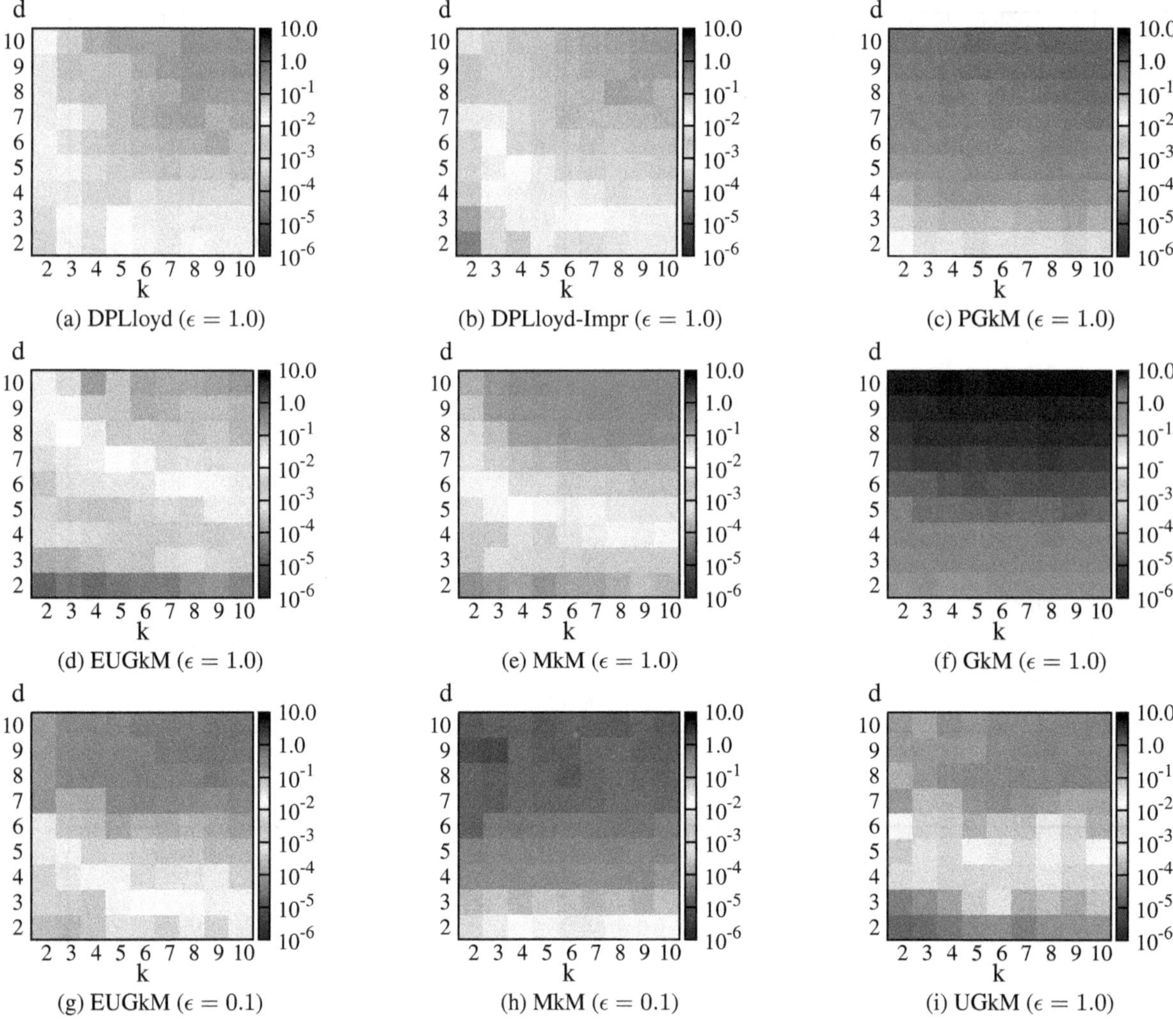

Figure 3: The heatmap by varying k and d on the Synthe datasets with $\epsilon = 1.0$ and $\epsilon = 0.1$

strictly satisfies differential privacy, since the parameter is determined on an independent set of datasets.

As the baseline, we run standard k-means algorithm [18] over the same 30 sets of initial centroids generated in DPLloyd-Impr and take the minimum NICV among all the 30 runs.

Experimental Results. Figure 1 and Figure 2 report the results for the 6 external datasets. For these, we vary ϵ from 0.05 to 2.0 and plot the NICV curve for the methods mentioned in Section 3. This enables us to see how these algorithms perform under different privacy budgets.

Figure 3 reports the results on the Synthe datasets. For these, we fix $\epsilon = 1.0$ and $\epsilon = 0.1$ and report the difference of NICV between each approach and the baseline. This enables us to see the scalability of these algorithms when k and d increase.

Among interactive approaches, DPLloyd-Impr has the best performance in most cases. It also outperforms DPLloyd in most cases. For non-interactive approaches, both EUGkM and UGkM clearly outperform MkM, especially for small ϵ values. EUGkM and UGkM has close performance on the low dimensional datasets. As the dimensionality increases, the advantage of EUGkM to UGkM becomes obvious. Comparing DPLloyd-Impr and EUGkM (Figure 2), we observe that in the four low dimensional external datasets (S1, Gowalla, TIGER and Image), EUGkM clearly outperforms DPLloyd-Impr at small ϵ value and their gap becomes smaller as ϵ increases. However, in the two high dimensional datasets (Adult-num and Lifesci), DPLloyd-Impr outperforms EUGkM almost in all given privacy budgets. The similar observations can also be found in Figure 3.

Figure 3 also exhibits the effects of the number of clusters and the number of dimensions. The EUGkM's performance is more sensitive to the increase of dimension, while DPLloyd-Impr gets worse quickly as the number of clusters increases.

4.2 The Analysis of the GkM Approach

From Figures 1 and 3, it is clear that GkM is always much worse than others. There are two sources of errors for GkM. One is that GkM is aggregating centroids computed from the subsets of data, and this aggregation may be inaccurate even without adding noise. The other is that the noise added according to Equation (12) may be too large. We find that setting $\ell = N^{0.4}$ in GkM, which corresponds to block size of $N^{0.6}$, is far from optimal, as the error GkM is dominated by that from the noise, and is much higher than the error due to sample and aggregation. Detailed explanations are deferred to Appendix 8.1.

4.3 The Analysis of the PGkM Approach

PGkM is a stochastic k-means method based on genetic algorithms. A stochastic method converges to global optimum [15]. On the contrary, DPLloyd is a gradient descent method derived from the standard Lloyd's algorithm [18], which may reach local optimum. However, PGkM is still inferior to DPLloyd in Figure 1.

There are two possible reasons. First, a stochastic approach typically takes a 'larger' number of iterations to converge [15]. Detailed explanations are deferred to Appendix 8.2. The second reason is that the low privacy budget allocated to select a parameter (i.e., a set of k cluster centroids) from the candidate set. In each iteration PGkM selects 10 parameters, and the total number of iterations is at least 8. Thus, the privacy budget allocated to select a single parameter is at most $\epsilon/80$. Therefore, PGkM has reasonable performance only for big ϵ value.

4.4 The Analysis of the EUGkM, UGkM and MkM Approaches

The difference between of the three non-interactive methods, EUGkM, UGkM and MkM is the choice of grid size M. The EUGkM method sets it to $\left(\frac{N\epsilon}{10}\right)^{\frac{2d}{2+d}}$, the UGkM method sets it to $\left(\frac{N\epsilon}{10}\right)$ and the MkM method sets it to $\left(\frac{N}{\sqrt{\log(N)}}\right)^{\frac{2d}{2+d}}$. Figure 1 and Figure 3 show that the performance of UGkM and EUGkM are superior to that of MkM. An important reason is that MkM does not take ϵ as a factor in M. Thus, it is nonadaptive to the variation of ϵ. This explains why EUGkM and UGkM perform much better than MkM for small ϵ values. On the other hand, although UGkM considers the impact of the privacy budget ϵ, it does not produce large enough grids for the high dimensional data. This explains why EUGkM performs better on high dimensional data than UGkM.

4.5 Estimating the Number of Clusters.

In cluster analysis, an important problem is to estimate the number of clusters, which has a deterministic effect on the clustering results. Such problem becomes more prominent in the differential privacy setting, since the data analyst cannot access the private database as many times as she/he wants.

Our EUGkM approach can address this problem. Several heuristics and statistics [29, 32] have been proposed to determine the number of clusters k automatically. Suppose we have a list of candidate values of k and one statistics ϕ for determining the best k. Once an EUGkM synopsis is published, we evaluate ϕ for each candidate k value on this noisy synopsis. The k value with the best ϕ score will be selected for the following k-means clustering. All the operations are performed on the released EUGkM synopsis. So the estimation process satisfies the differential privacy. This is another advantage of the non-interactive approaches over the interactive approaches on the k-means clustering.

We also experimentally evaluate the above method on the six external datasets and on six privacy budget values. This method gives very accurate estimations on the k values under most of the privacy budget settings. We omit the experimental results for space reasons.

5. RELATED WORK

The notion of differential privacy was developed in a series of papers [7, 11, 3, 10, 8]. Several primitives for answering a single query differentially privately have been proposed. Dwork et al. [10] introduced the method of adding Laplacian noise scaled with the sensitivity. McSherry and Talwar [21] introduced a more general exponential mechanism.

Blum et al. [3] proposed a sublinear query (SuLQ) database model for interactively answering a sublinear number (in the size of the underlying database) of count queries differential privately. The users (e.g. machine learning algorithms) issue queries and get responses which are added laplace noises. They applied the SuLQ framework to the k-means clustering and some other machine learning algorithms. McSherry [22] built the PINQ (Privacy INtegrated Queries) system, a programming platform which provides several differentially-private primitives to enable data analysts to write privacy-preserving applications. These private primitives include noisy count, noisy sum, noisy average, and exponential mechanism. The DPLloyd algorithm, which we compare against in this paper, has been implemented using these primitives.

Nissim et al. [25, 31] propose the sample and aggregate framework (SAF), and use k-means clustering as a motivating application for SAF. This SAF framework has been implemented in the GUPT system [24] and is evaluated by k-means clustering. This is the GkM algorithm that we compared with in the paper. Dwork [9] suggested applying a geometric decreasing privacy budget allocation strategy among the iterations of k-means, whereas we use an increasing sequence. Geometric decreasing sequence will cause later rounds using increasingly less privacy budget, resulting in higher and higher distortion with each new iteration. Zhang et al. [34] proposed a general private model fitting framework based on genetic algorithms. The PGkM approach in this paper is an instantiation of the framework to k-means clustering.

Interactive methods for other data mining tasks have been proposed. McSherry and Mironov [20] adapted algorithms producing recommendations from collective user behavior to satisfy differential privacy. Friedman and Schuster [13] made the ID3 decision tree construction algorithm differentially private. Chaudhuri and Monteleoni [5] proposed a differentially private logistic regression algorithm. Zhang et al. [35] introduced the functional mechanism, which perturbs an optimization objective to satisfy differential privacy, and applied it to linear regression and logistic regression. Differentially private frequent itemset mining has been studied in [2, 17]. The tradeoffs of interactive and non-interactive approaches in these domains are interesting future research topics.

Most non-interactive approaches aim at developing solutions to answer histogram or range queries accurately [10, 33, 14, 6]. Dwork et al. [10] calculate the frequency of values and release their distribution differentially privately. Such method makes the variance of query result increase linearly with the query size. To address this issue, Xiao et al. [33] propose a wavelet-based method, by which the variance is polylogarithmic to the query size. Hay et al. [14] organize the count queries in a hierarchy, and improve the accuracy by enforcing the consistency between the noisy count value of a parent node and those of its children. Cormode et al. [6] adapted standard spatial indexing techniques, such as quadtree and kd-tree, to decompose data space differential-privately. Qardaji et al. [27] proposed the UG and AG method for publishing 2-dimensional datasets.

6. CONCLUSION AND DISCUSSIONS

We have improved the state-of-the-art on differentially private k-means clustering in several ways. We have introduced a non-interactive methods for differentially private k-means clustering and improved one interactive methods based on a systemized error analysis. Concerning the question of non-interactive versus interactive, the insights obtained from k-means clustering are as follows. The non-interactive EUGkM has clear advantage, especially when the privacy budget ϵ is small. Considering the further advantage that non-interactive methods enable other analysis on the dataset, we would tentatively conclude that non-interactive is the winner in this comparison. We conjecture that this tradeoff will hold for many other data analysis tasks. We plan to investigate whether this holds in other analysis tasks.

7. ACKNOWLEDGMENTS

This paper is based upon work supported by the United States National Science Foundation under Grant CNS-1116991.

8. APPENDIX

8.1 Detailed Explanations for the Analysis of the GkM Approach

This section gives detailed explanations for the two sources of errors in the GkM approach as mentioned in the Section 4.2. We use the Figure 4 to show the effect of varying block size from around $N^{0.1}$ to N on the two sources of errors. In Figure 4, we show error from GkM, error from using the aggregation without noise (SAG), and error from adding noise computed by Equation 12) to the best known centroids (Noise). From the figure, it is clear that setting $\ell = N^{0.4}$, which corresponds to block size of $N^{0.6}$ is far from optimal, as the error GkM is dominated by that from the noise, and is much higher than the error due to sample and aggregation. Indeed, we observed that as the block size decreases the error of GkM keeps decreasing, until when the block size gets close to k. It seems that even though many individual blocks result in poor centroids, aggregating these relatively poor centroids can result in highly accurate centroids. This effect is most pronounced in the Tiger dataset, which consists of two large clusters. The two centroids computed from each small block can be approximately viewed as choosing one random point from each cluster. When averaging these centroids, one gets very close to the true centroids.

8.2 Detailed Explanations for the Analysis of the PGkM Approach

This section gives detailed explanations for the first reason why PGkM is still inferior to DPLloyd as mentioned in the Section 4.3. Generally, a stochastic approach typically takes a 'larger' number of iterations to converge [15]. Figure 5 compares the Lloyd's algorithm with Gene (i.e., the non-private version of PGkM without considering differential privacy). For Lloyd, we reuse the initial centroids generated in Section 4.1. Given a dataset, we run Lloyd on the 30 sets of initial centroids generated for the dataset, and report the average NICV. Generally, Gene overtakes Lloyd as the number of iterations increases and finally converges to the global optimum. However, Lloyd improves its performance much faster than Gene in the first few iterations, and converges to the global optimal (or local optimum) more quickly. For example, in the Image dataset, Lloyd reaches the best baseline after three iterations, while the Gene needs more than 10 iterations to achieve the same.

9. REFERENCES

[1] A. Asuncion and D. Newman. UCI machine learning repository, 2010.

[2] R. Bhaskar, S. Laxman, A. Smith, and A. Thakurta. Discovering frequent patterns in sensitive data. In *KDD*, pages 503–512, 2010.

[3] A. Blum, C. Dwork, F. McSherry, and K. Nissim. Practical privacy: The sulq framework. In *PODS*, pages 128–138, 2005.

[4] U. S. Census. Topologically integrated geographic encoding and referencing. http://www.census.gov/geo/maps-data/data/tiger.html.

[5] K. Chaudhuri and C. Monteleoni. Privacy-preserving logistic regression. In *NIPS*, pages 289–296, 2008.

[6] G. Cormode, C. M. Procopiuc, D. Srivastava, E. Shen, and T. Yu. Differentially private spatial decompositions. In *ICDE*, pages 20–31, 2012.

[7] I. Dinur and K. Nissim. Revealing information while preserving privacy. In *PODS*, pages 202–210, 2003.

[8] C. Dwork. Differential privacy. In *ICALP*, pages 1–12, 2006.

[9] C. Dwork. A firm foundation for private data analysis. *Commun. ACM*, 54(1):86–95, Jan. 2011.

[10] C. Dwork, F. McSherry, K. Nissim, and A. Smith. Calibrating noise to sensitivity in private data analysis. In *TCC*, pages 265–284, 2006.

[11] C. Dwork and K. Nissim. Privacy-preserving data mining on vertically partitioned databases. In *CRYPTO*, pages 528–544, 2004.

[12] P. Fränti. Clustering datasets. http://cs.joensuu.fi/sipu/datasets/.

[13] A. Friedman and A. Schuster. Data mining with differential privacy. In *KDD*, pages 493–502, 2010.

[14] M. Hay, V. Rastogi, G. Miklau, and D. Suciu. Boosting the accuracy of differentially private histograms through consistency. *Proc. VLDB Endow.*, 3(1-2):1021–1032, Sept. 2010.

[15] K. Kummamuru and M. N. Murty. Genetic k-means algorithm. *IEEE Transactions on Systems, Man, and Cybernetics, Part B*, 29(3):433–439, 1999.

[16] J. Lei. Differentially private m-estimators. In *NIPS*, pages 361–369, 2011.

[17] N. Li, W. Qardaji, D. Su, and J. Cao. Privbasis: Frequent itemset mining with differential privacy. *Proc. VLDB Endow.*, 5(11):1340–1351, July 2012.

[18] S. P. Lloyd. Least squares quantization in pcm. *IEEE Transactions on Information Theory*, 28(2):129–136, 1982.

[19] F. McSherry. Privacy integrated queries (pinq) infrastructure. http://research.microsoft.com/en-us/downloads/73099525-fd8d-4966-9b93-574e6023147f/.

[20] F. McSherry and I. Mironov. Differentially private recommender systems: Building privacy into the netflix prize contenders. In *KDD*, pages 627–636, 2009.

[21] F. McSherry and K. Talwar. Mechanism design via differential privacy. In *FOCS*, pages 94–103, 2007.

[22] F. D. McSherry. Privacy integrated queries: An extensible platform for privacy-preserving data analysis. In *SIGMOD*, pages 19–30, 2009.

[23] P. Mohan. Gupt: a platform for privacy-preserving data mining. https://github.com/prashmohan/GUPT.

[24] P. Mohan, A. Thakurta, E. Shi, D. Song, and D. Culler. Gupt: Privacy preserving data analysis made easy. In *SIGMOD*, pages 349–360, 2012.

[25] K. Nissim, S. Raskhodnikova, and A. Smith. Smooth sensitivity and sampling in private data analysis. In *STOC*, pages 75–84, 2007.

[26] J. M. Peña, J. A. Lozano, and P. Larrañaga. An empirical comparison of four initialization methods for the k-means algorithm. *Pattern Recogn. Lett.*, 20(10):1027–1040, 1999.

[27] W. H. Qardaji, W. Yang, and N. Li. Differentially private grids for geospatial data. In *ICDE*, pages 757–768, 2013.

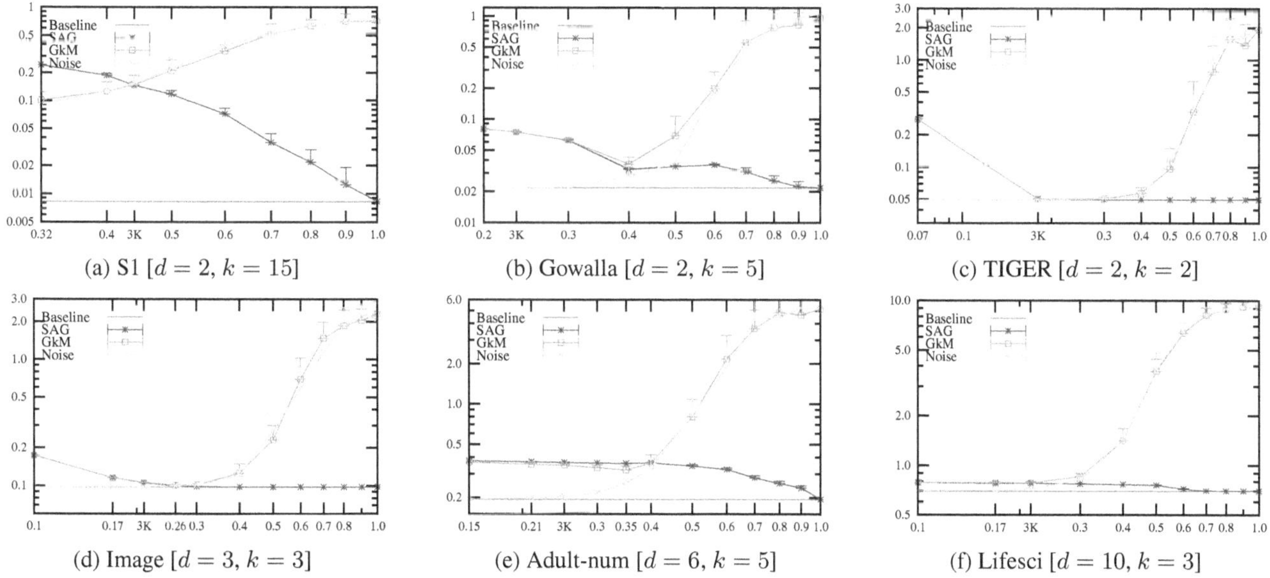

(a) S1 $[d = 2, k = 15]$ (b) Gowalla $[d = 2, k = 5]$ (c) TIGER $[d = 2, k = 2]$

(d) Image $[d = 3, k = 3]$ (e) Adult-num $[d = 6, k = 5]$ (f) Lifesci $[d = 10, k = 3]$

Figure 4: The analysis of the GkM Approach. x-axis: block size exponent in log-scale, y-axis: NICV in log-scale.

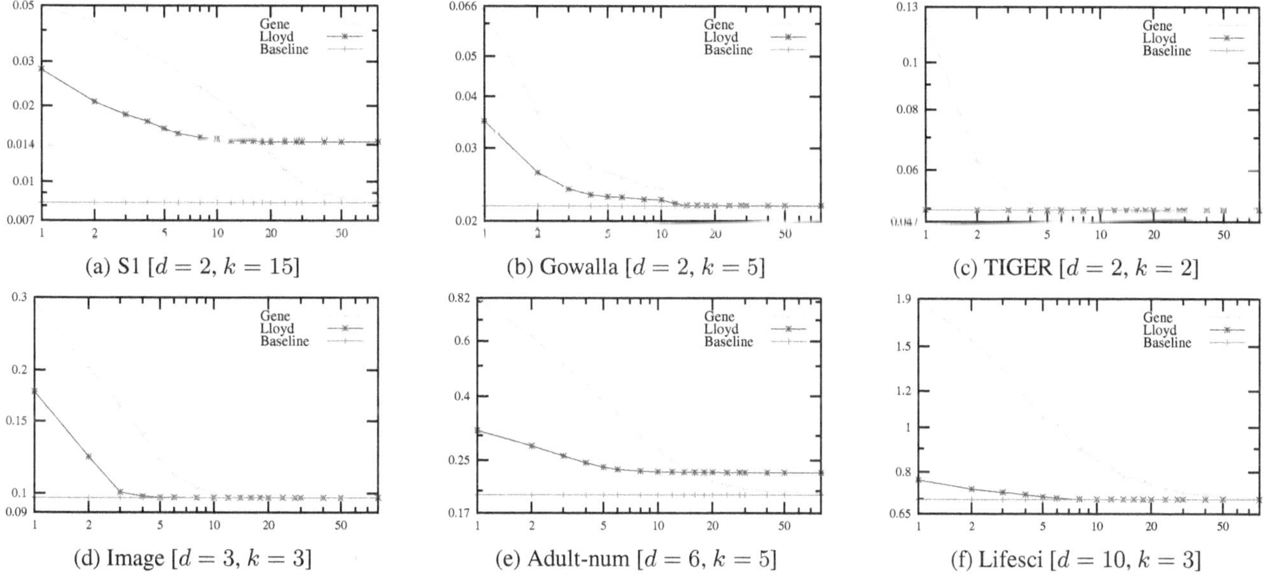

(a) S1 $[d = 2, k = 15]$ (b) Gowalla $[d = 2, k = 5]$ (c) TIGER $[d = 2, k = 2]$

(d) Image $[d = 3, k = 3]$ (e) Adult-num $[d = 6, k = 5]$ (f) Lifesci $[d = 10, k = 3]$

Figure 5: The comparison of the convergence rate of the genetic algorithm based k-means and Lloyd algorithm. x-axis: number of iterations in log-scale, y-axis: NICV in log-scale.

[28] W. Qiu. clustergeneration: Random cluster generation (with specified degree of separation). http://cran.r-project.org/web/packages/clusterGeneration/index.html.

[29] S. Ray and R. H. Turi. Determination of number of clusters in k-means clustering and application in colour image segmentation. In *ICAPRDT'99*, pages 137–143, 1999.

[30] Scipy.org. Scientific computing tools for python. http://scipy.org/.

[31] A. Smith. Privacy-preserving statistical estimation with optimal convergence rates. In *STOC*, pages 813–822, 2011.

[32] R. Tibshirani, G. Walther, and T. Hastie. Estimating the number of clusters in a data set via the gap statistic. *Journal of the Royal Statistical Society: Series B (Statistical Methodology)*, 63(2):411–423, 2001.

[33] X. Xiao, G. Wang, and J. Gehrke. Differential privacy via wavelet transforms. *IEEE Trans. Knowl. Data Eng.*, 23(8):1200–1214, 2011.

[34] J. Zhang, X. Xiao, Y. Yang, Z. Zhang, and M. Winslett. Privgene: Differentially private model fitting using genetic algorithms. In *SIGMOD*, pages 665–676, 2013.

[35] J. Zhang, Z. Zhang, X. Xiao, Y. Yang, and M. Winslett. Functional mechanism: Regression analysis under differential privacy. *Proc. VLDB Endow.*, 5(11):1364–1375, July 2012.

HCFI: Hardware-enforced Control-Flow Integrity

Nick Christoulakis
FORTH
christoulak@ics.forth.gr

George Christou
FORTH
gchri@ics.forth.gr

Elias Athanasopoulos
VU University, Amsterdam
i.a.athanasopoulos@vu.nl

Sotiris Ioannidis
FORTH
sotiris@ics.forth.gr

ABSTRACT

Control-flow hijacking is the principal method for code-reuse techniques like Return-oriented Programming (ROP) and Jump-oriented Programming (JOP). For defending against such attacks, the community has proposed Control-flow Integrity (CFI), a technique capable of preventing exploitation by verifying that every (indirect) control-flow transfer points to a legitimate address. Enabling CFI in real systems is not straightforward, since in many cases the actual Control-flow Graph (CFG) of a program can be only approximated. Even in the case that there is perfect knowledge of the CFG, ensuring that all return instructions will return to their actual call sites, without employing a shadow stack, is questionable. On the other hand, the community has expressed concerns related to significant overheads stemming from enabling a shadow stack.

In this paper, we acknowledge the importance of a shadow stack for supporting and strengthening any CFI policy. In addition, we project that implementing a full-featured CFI-enabled Instruction Set Architecture (ISA) in actual hardware with an in-chip secure memory can be efficiently carried out and the prototype experiences negligible overheads. For supporting our case, we implement HCFI by modifying a SPARC SoC and evaluate the prototype on an FPGA board by running all SPECInt benchmarks instrumented with a fine-grained CFI policy. The evaluation shows that HCFI can effectively protect applications from code-reuse attacks, while adding less than 1% runtime overhead.

1. INTRODUCTION

Exploitation of modern software is undoubtedly still possible, despite many mitigation techniques that have been enabled in production systems. Although a simple stack smashing [26] is unlikely to be sufficient for compromising a program due to non-executable data protection (DEP) [4], advanced exploitation techniques, based on code reuse, commonly known as Return-Oriented Programming (ROP) [31] and Jump-Oriented Programming (JOP) [7], are so powerful that can potentially take advantage of any vulnerability and transform it to a functional exploit. Code randomization techniques [23,28,30,37] attempt to make code reuse harder by shuffling the location of the code to be reused, but it has been demonstrated that even a simple information leak can reveal all of the process' layout and essentially bypass any randomization scheme [34].

Therefore, for fighting software exploitation, the community seeks protection schemes that are based on core principles. One promising direction is based on the observation that modern exploits introduce control flows that are not part of the program's Control-flow Graph (CFG). Control-flow Integrity (CFI) [3] suggests that a running program should exhibit only the control flows that are part of the program's original CFG as expressed by its source code. Essentially, CFI mandates that any indirect branch should not be possible to target the address of *any* instruction in the program, but rather be constrained in an allowable set of addresses that have been a priori determined. For example, consider that in principle a return instruction should be *only* able to transfer control to the call site responsible for the associated function call.

CFI, although a strong principle, has still two open issues related to the technique's *accuracy* and *performance*. As far as accuracy is concerned, it is not always trivial to compute the program's CFG. This is mainly because the source code might not be always available, dynamic code might be introduced at run-time [6], and heavy use of function pointers can lead to inconclusive target resolution. This problem has led researchers to develop CFI techniques that are based on a relaxed approximation of the CFG [41,42], also known as coarse-grained CFI. Unfortunately, coarse-grained CFI has been demonstrated to exhibit weak security guarantees and it is today well established that it can be bypassed [20].

Since approximation of the ideal CFG through code analysis does not have sound protection, at least for protecting backward edges, the community has suggested the use of a *shadow stack* [14]. A shadow stack is secure memory where, during a function call, the call site is saved. Once the function is to return, the information stored in the shadow stack is checked with the return address stored in the actual stack; in case there is a mismatch, a violation is recorded and the running process is halted. There is much criticism about the use of a shadow stack due to performance implications. However, it was recently demonstrated that even an *ideal* CFI implementation, without the use of a shadow stack, *is* vulnerable [10]. This is mainly because any CFG contains functions (e.g., `memcmp`) which are called by many different

CODASPY'16 March 9-11, 2016, New Orleans, LA, USA

DOI: http://dx.doi.org/10.1145/2857705.2857735

locations of the program and essentially allow the attacker to be flexible in creating call-preceded chains of gadgets for finally exploiting the program. It is thus vital for *any* CFI implementation to employ a shadow stack.

In this paper, we acknowledge that the use of a shadow stack is mandatory for any practical CFI deployment. We further attempt to quantify the performance of CFI and demonstrate that the technique can be applied to real systems with practically negligible overhead. For proving our case, we present HCFI, a full-featured hardware implementation of CFI. We extend an existing Instruction Set Architecture (ISA), with instructions dedicated for CFI and we deploy shadow memory inside the core. We modify a SPARC SoC and evaluate the prototype on an FPGA board by running all SPECInt benchmarks instrumented with the additional CFI-related instructions. The evaluation shows that HCFI can effectively protect applications from code-reuse attacks, while adding less than 1% runtime overhead.

Compared to similar hardware implementations, such as HAFIX [15], HCFI is (i) *complete*, since it protects both forward and backward edges, (ii) *faster*, since the experienced overhead is on average less than 1%, and (iii) *more accurate*, since it employs a full-functional shadow stack implemented inside the core. Especially, as far as shadow memory is concerned, HCFI uses a novel system for supporting multiple recursive calls. Each time a return address is to be saved in the secure memory it is checked with the top of the shadow stack and if the address is matched, indicating there is a recursive call, no additional memory is wasted. This dramatically simplifies the design and reduces the space requirements, but implies that a recursive call can return to its call site immediately from any depth, thus violating a perfect CFI policy. However, we anticipate that this policy relaxation has not severe security implications, since system calls and sensitive functions are not recursive and they do not call recursive functions (i.e., hijacking a recursive function called by a sensitive system call for jumping to the sensitive call site is not possible). Furthermore, in terms of completeness, we argue that HCFI is the most rich hardware implementation of CFI so far, supporting many problematic cases (such as `setjmp/longjmp`), which we discuss thoroughly in Section 3.

1.1 Contributions

This paper contributes the following.

1. We design, implement, and evaluate HCFI, a full-featured ISA for supporting processes hardened with CFI. The prototype is based on extending a SPARC SoC and it includes a hardware implementation of a shadow stack.

2. HCFI is complete and accurate. It protects both forward and backward edges, and the shadow stack implementation can handle recursion of arbitrary depth.

3. HCFI has practically negligible overhead. We evaluate HCFI with all SPECInt benchmarks and we record a runtime overhead of less than 1% on average, which, to the best of our knowledge, stands for the first hardware implementation for full CFI support with low cost.

4. HCFI is policy agnostic and can deal with all idioms that usually interfere with hardening indirect jumps, such as the use of `longjmp` and `setjmp`. For the purpose of presenting HCFI in this paper we enable a fine-grained CFI policy with shadow-stack support.

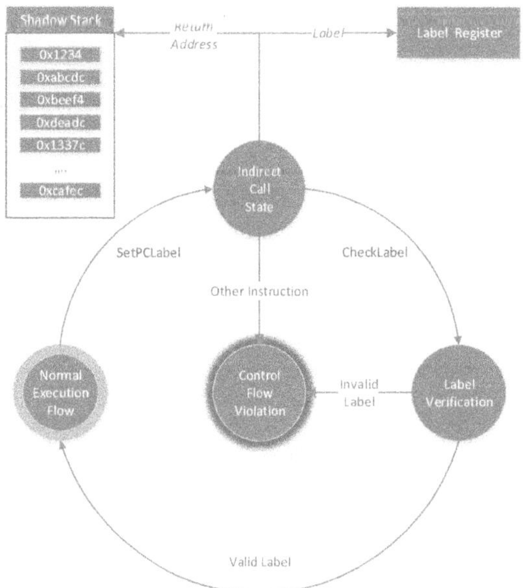

Figure 1: Indirect Call States. A SetPCLabel instruction is received, the appropriate memory modules are set, and the core enters a state where only CheckLabel instructions are accepted. Once a CheckLabel instruction is received, the labels are compared and execution returns to its normal flow.

1.2 Organization

This paper is organized as follows. In Section 2 we discuss the generic architecture of HCFI and in Section 3 we thoroughly present the technical details for implementing the prototype. We evaluate HCFI in terms of security in Section 4 and in terms of performance in Section 5. We discuss various aspects of our current and future work in Section 6. We review related work in Section 7 and, finally, we conclude in Section 8.

2. HCFI ARCHITECTURE

2.1 Control-Flow Integrity enforcement

Control-flow Integrity (CFI) aims at guaranteeing that the execution flow adheres to the path determined by the control-flow graph of the program. The control flow of a program can be manipulated either on the forward-edge, when the target of an indirect jump is altered, or on the backward-edge, when a saved return address has been changed. For forward-edges we ensure that an indirect jump can target only a function entry with the appropriate label that is generated during the CFG extraction. For backward-edges we validate that the function's return instruction targets the address of the original call site(Call-Ret pair). A more detailed discussion follows.

2.1.1 *Forward-edge*

The forward-edge is handled as discussed in the original CFI proposal [3]. Every indirectly called function is hardcoded with a label on its entry point. Before the indirect function call, the function's label is compared to a label assigned to the call site. Our approach differs in that we set the label before the indirect call executes, while the valida-

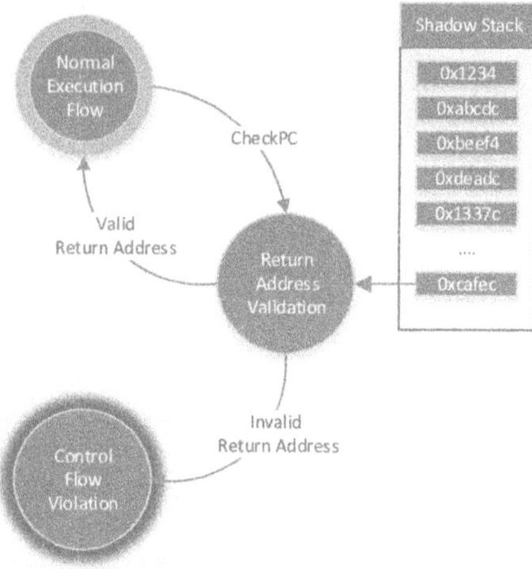

Figure 2: Return States. A CheckPC instruction is received, the Program Counter is compared with the top value of the stack and the execution continues normally.

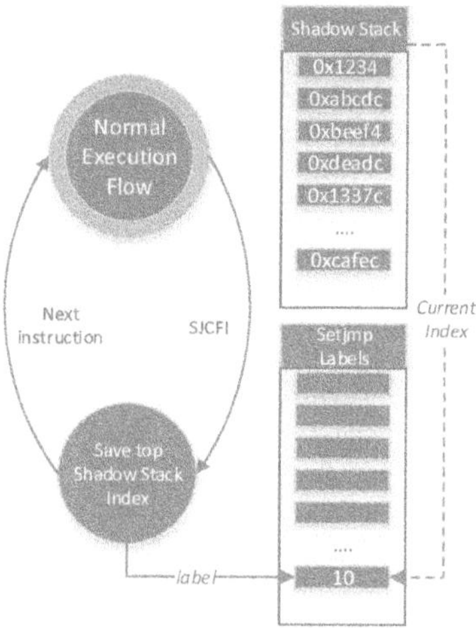

Figure 3: Setjmp Finite State Machine. An SJCFI instruction stores the current state of the Shadow Stack.

tion takes place immediately after function entry. Before the indirect control transfer, a SetPCLabel instruction, placed on the delay slot(described in subsection 3.2), stores a label in a non memory-mapped latch that resides inside the core. On the function entry, a CheckLabel instruction verifies that the label equals the one stored in the latch. If the comparison fails, a control-flow violation is detected, an exception is raised, and the system handles it appropriately.

2.1.2 Backward-edge

For the backward edges, a non memory-mapped stack, which also resides within the core, is deployed. The concept of a shadow stack is thoroughly studied in the literature [3, 10, 14]. The general concept is based on the notion that a function's return address points to the instruction lying directly below the call site. This is not always the case as it is common that a function does not return to the original call site.

The shadow stack of HCFI is implemented as follows. Before a call instruction executes, a copy of the return address is pushed to the shadow stack. When the callee function returns, the return address is compared with the one on the top of the shadow stack. If they are not equal, a control-flow violation is detected and handled appropriately by the system.

Notice that every direct call instruction is paired with a SetPC instruction placed on its delay slot. The SetPC instruction pushes the current Program Counter to the shadow stack module. After the callee function returns, a CheckPC instruction, placed in the delay slot of the return instruction, checks that the computed return address is equal with the address stored in the shadow stack incremented by four (one instruction below the SetPC). If the check fails, a hardware exception is raised, which is handled by the supervising firmware. An alternative way to process a mismatch between the shadow stack and the main stack, is to *silently* force the address obtained from the shadow stack as the return address. Aforesaid proposition can potentially enhance our architecture with fault tolerance capabilities, since any tampering of the return address would be rectified by the hardware.

2.2 Architecture Overview

HCFI is based on a series of modifications of Leon3 [18] core's pipeline. The architecture consists of unmapped *shadow* memory elements, more specifically a shadow stack, a shadow memory array, a shadow register, and six dedicated instructions which function upon the shadow memory elements. The shadow stack is utilized in enforcing backward-edge CFI through the detection of control-flow changes caused by arbitrary return address modifications, e.g. buffer overflows. Likewise, a single shadow register is used for enforcing forward-edge CFI, effectively protecting the execution flow from vulnerable function pointers. The shadow memory array is used for assisting setjmp/longjmp support. To access and utilize the shadow memory blocks, we extended the SparcV8 [1] instruction set with six instructions.

2.3 ISA Extension

We extended the SparcV8 ISA with six instructions designed to provide CFI functionality to the core.

SetPC: Paired with direct call instructions. The SetPC instruction is placed in the delay slot of the call instruction it is paired with. It pushes the currently executing Program Counter (PC) to the shadow stack. Also, if the next instruction is a CheckLabel, the SetPC instruction suppresses the CFI violation that would occur, since the Label Register's value has not been initialized, yet. This functionality is useful in cases where an indirectly called function is also called directly.

SetPCLabel: Paired with indirect call instructions. This instruction is placed in the delay slot of the indirect call it is paired with. Its 18 Least Significant(LS) bits carry the label used to validate the indirect call target. As with the SetPC instruction, the current Program Counter is pushed to the shadow stack. At the same time, the 18 LS bits are stored in the Label Register to be used later for validation. If the next instruction executed is not a CheckLabel, a CFI violation occurs.

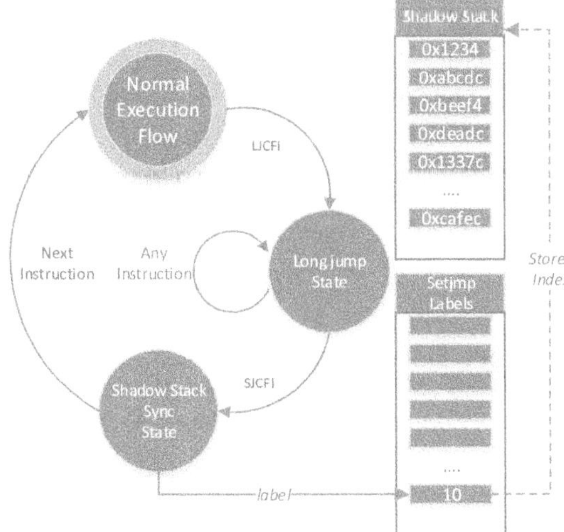

Figure 4: Longjmp Finite State Machine. An LJCFI instruction puts the core in a state waiting for an SJCFI instruction. The next SJCFI will not store the environment but restore it to the state that it was the last time an SJCFi instruction was executed on its own.

CheckLabel: Placed on the entry point of a function that is found during instrumentation to be called indirectly. It is the only instruction that can be legally executed after a SetPCLabel. Its 18 LS bits carry the label used to validate the indirect call target. It compares the label carried on its 18 LS bits with the value stored in the Label Register. If the labels match, the register is reset and the execution continues normally, otherwise a CFI violation is detected. Since the Label Register is zeroed out after every CheckLabel, and no function is assigned zero as a label, the Label Register cannot be reused without being set again.

CheckPC: Paired with return instructions. This instruction is placed in the delay slot of the return instruction it is paired with. It compares the program counter of the next instruction executed (after the branch takes place) with the top of the shadow stack. If PC equality is confirmed, the shadow stack is popped and the execution continues. Otherwise, a CFI violation occurs.

2.4 Shadow Stack Incompatibilities

Backward-edge control-flow integrity relies on the Call-Ret pair model of programs. That means that each time a return instruction jumps to an address different than the one it was called from, the Call-Ret pair model is violated which leads to a CFI violation. Unfortunately, there are cases that Call-Ret pairs are violated in a legitimate way.

2.4.1 Setjmp/Longjmp

The most common violation is setjmp/longjmp. When a longjmp occurs, the original stack may *unwind* by several frames. Standard solutions suggest unwinding the shadow stack till it is empty or a match is found. Such an approach would impose a greater performance overhead in our design. In the proposal by Davi et al. [15], a longjmp would not cause a control-flow violation but the intermediate labels would remain active, significantly relaxing CFI. We overcome these problems by using dedicated instructions for setjmp/longjmp support, without sacrificing any security or performance.

Additionally, some designs [27] propose popping the shadow stack till a valid return address is found or it is empty, causing additional delay cycles. Furthermore, unwinding the shadow stack can lead to inconsistencies. The address required could exist more than once in the shadow stack, and since the hardware could not blindly know which of the addresses is the correct call site, it could settle on the wrong one, causing a violation later in the execution. Other proposals do not support setjmp/longjmp functionality and any such jump would be perceived as a control-flow violation.

In order to achieve *on cycle* synchronization between the shadow stack and the normal stack, we decided on the addition of two dedicated instructions and a shadow memory array. Those new instructions are paired with the call instructions to the setjmp and longjmp functions themselves.

SJCFI: The first one, SJCFI, is paired with the setjmp function. It is placed two instructions below the call to setjmp - the instruction to which a call to setjmp would return to. It carries a unique label on it 8LS bits - different from the label used for forward edge enforcement. Much like setjmp, it serves two purposes, (i) it sets the environment to support a longjmp, and (ii) acts as a landing point for the jump itself.

In the first case, once a setjmp returns, the first instruction executed would be SJCFI. The label is used as an index to the new memory element. During SJCFI's execution, the index of the top element of the shadow stack is stored in the new memory component using the label as an index. This allows pairing this particular landing point to the current state of the shadow stack. Even though the addresses remain in the shadow stack, they cannot be exploited by an attacker as the only way to use them would be to raise the index, which cannot happen without overwriting the addresses with correct ones.

SJCFI also acts as a landing point for a longjmp. Since it is placed two instructions below the call to setjmp, and a longjump will return to its equivalent setjmp call site, it will be the first instruction executed after such a jump.

For SJCFI to support long jumps, an LJCFI instruction is assumed to have been already executed. In this case, SJCFI, instead of reading the index of the stack and writing it to the new memory element, reads the index from the memory element (once again using its label) and sets the stack to it. Since the index of the shadow stack corresponds with the stack frame once again, execution and CFI enforcement can continue normally. The next SJCFI instruction executed will use the first functionality unless another LJCFI was executed before that.

LJCFI: LJCFI instruction is only used to signify that a longjmp is underway. It is placed in the delay slot of a longjmp call and flags that a longjmp is executed. After the longjmp function is executed, the program counter should point to an SJCFI instruction, which will use the second of its functionalities, synchronizing the shadow stack and clearing the longjmp state flag.

The functionality of those two instructions is graphically represented in figures 3 and 4.

2.4.2 Tail-Call Elimination

Another case of Call-Ret pair violation is *tail call elimination*. As shown in figure 7, before calling *bar*, *foo's* return

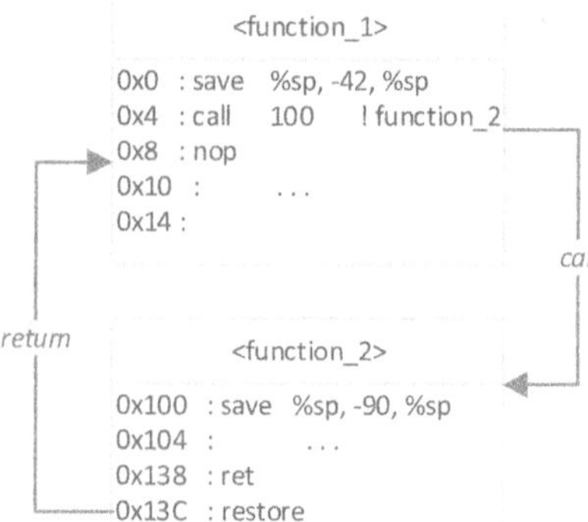
<function_1>
0x0 : save %sp, -42, %sp
0x4 : call 100 ! function_2
0x8 : nop
0x10 : ...
0x14 :
call
return
<function_2>
0x100 : save %sp, -90, %sp
0x104 : ...
0x138 : ret
0x13C : restore

Figure 5: SparcV8 assembly - direct function call without CFI instrumentation.

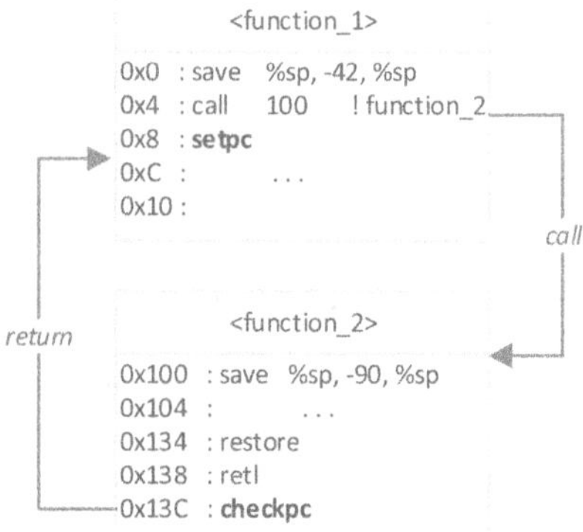
<function_1>
0x0 : save %sp, -42, %sp
0x4 : call 100 ! function_2
0x8 : setpc
0xC : ...
0x10 :
call
return
<function_2>
0x100 : save %sp, -90, %sp
0x104 : ...
0x134 : restore
0x138 : retl
0x13C : checkpc

Figure 6: SparcV8 assembly - direct function call with CFI instrumentation. A SetPC instruction is placed on the delay slot of the call instruction, and a CheckPC on the delay slot below the return. The restore instruction is pushed above the return and the return instruction changes to account for it.

address (stored inside the o7 register) is *moved* to global register g1. When the call instruction is executed, register o7 will be overwritten with the current program counter (0x20) which serves as *bar* function's return address. Finally, in the delay slot of the call instruction, the return address of *foo* is restored in register o7. The effect of the above code snippet is that *bar* function will return to *foo* function's call site. In our design, this optimization renders the shadow-stack inconsistent with the main stack. Thus, this particular optimization has to be disabled in order to run the benchmarks. Adding support for this optimization is possible, by simply not instrumenting the eliminated call site, though that might pose a great security concern.

2.5 Recursion Support

The memory available to the shadow stack is finite and implemented statically inside the core, where there is no dynamic memory allocation. Therefore, for supporting recursion, additional features should be implemented.

Before the SetPC and SetPCLabel instructions push the current PC to the shadow stack, the stack is topped and the two addresses are compared. If the addresses are different, the new address is pushed. Otherwise, the address is not

```
<foo>
0x0  :        ...
0x10 : mov    %o7, %g1
0x14 : call   bar
0x18 : mov    %g1, %o7
0x1C :        ...
```

Figure 7: SPARC V8 tail call elimination example. The calling function (foo) replaces the return address of the callee function (bar) with its own. Bar will return to the function that called foo, skipping it.

pushed, but the current index of the shadow stack is marked as *recursive* on a separate 128*1 bitmap.

During the CheckPC execution, if the address currently being compared has the recursion bit activated, it is not popped from the stack. If the address comparison results in a mismatch and the top address is recursive, the top address is popped and the PC is compared with the next one. If the addresses match, execution continues normally and, if the (now) top address is not marked as recursive, it is popped. Otherwise, should the comparison again result in a mismatch, the corresponding violation is raised.

2.6 Instrumentation

Instrumentation takes place at the assembly-level of C programs using a Python script (about 200 LoCs). We assume that input programs are products of standard C compilers (such as, GCC and Clang), and they do not include custom assembly idioms. Instrumentation by no means is limited to C-compiler generated assembly. In fact, any assembly code is instrumentable as long as a Call-Ret-like model is sustained.

In figures 5 and 6 we show the instrumentation of a direct call in the SparcV8 assembly language. The logic behind the instrumentation is fairly simple as it consists of pairing every call and return with a CFI instruction. For calls, a SetPC instruction is added below them, and for returns, a CheckPC.

The new instructions were designed to take advantage of the delay slot below branches in the SparcV8 architecture. With that in mind, any instructions residing in the delay slot must be moved out of the slot, before the branch. The most usual case of instructions that need to be moved are *restore* instructions as they almost always reside in the delay slot of their respective return instructions.

Since the *restore* instruction changes the focus of the register window, we must compensate for it moving before the return instruction. The *ret* instruction expects to find the return address in register i7, but because the register windows have shifted, the appropriate value is now stored in register o7. Thankfully, the Sparc assembler provides another instruction with this case in mind, *retl*.

In Figures 8 and 9 we show the instrumentation of an indirect function call in the SparcV8 assembly language. The backward-edge components remain essentially the same, with the only modification being that the SetPC instruction is switched with a SetPCLabel instruction. But now, the

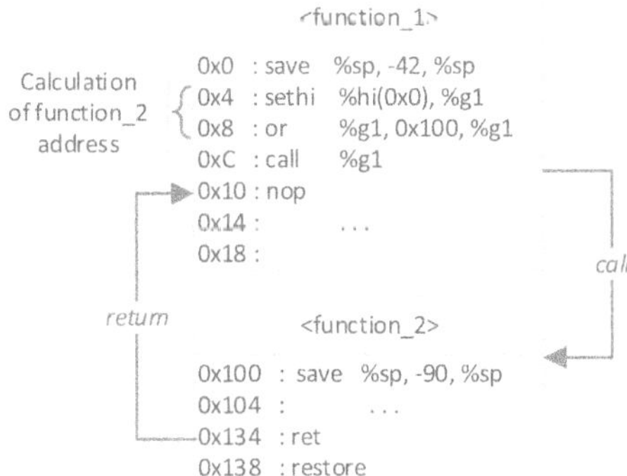
<function_1>
Calculation of function_2 address
0x0 : save %sp, -42, %sp
0x4 : sethi %hi(0x0), %g1
0x8 : or %g1, 0x100, %g1
0xC : call %g1
0x10 : nop
0x14 : ...
0x18 :
call
return
<function_2>
0x100 : save %sp, -90, %sp
0x104 : ...
0x134 : ret
0x138 : restore

Figure 8: SparcV8 indirect function call without CFI instrumentation. The address in loaded in a register which is used to perform the indirect call. Otherwise, the call performs similarly to the direct call.

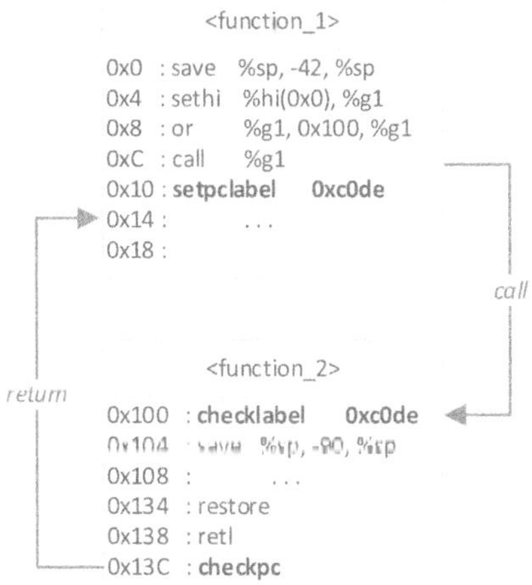
<function_1>
0x0 : save %sp, -42, %sp
0x4 : sethi %hi(0x0), %g1
0x8 : or %g1, 0x100, %g1
0xC : call %g1
0x10 : setpclabel 0xc0de
0x14 : ...
0x18 :
call
return
<function_2>
0x100 : checklabel 0xc0de
0x104 : save %sp, -90, %sp
0x108 : ...
0x134 : restore
0x138 : retl
0x13C : checkpc

Figure 9: SparcV8 indirect function call with CFI instrumentation. A SetPCLabel instruction is placed on the delay slot below the indirect call. A CheckLabel instruction is placed on the entry point of the indirectly called function. Finally, a CheckPC instruction is placed in the delay slot of the return instruction.

forward-edge components are also in use. Specifically, SetPCLabel, storing the hard-coded label for later comparison, and the CheckLabel instruction, placed on the function entry point, performing said comparison.

3. HCFI PROTOTYPE IMPLEMENTATION

In this section we describe the HCFI prototype implementation, we present the results of the hardware synthesis using an Virtex 6 [40] FPGA board, in terms of additional hardware needed compared to the unmodified processor, and finally we discuss how the proposed system can be easily ported to other architectures and systems.

3.1 Introduction to the Leon3 Softcore

We modified the Leon3 SPARC V8 processor [18], a 32-bit open-source synthesizable processor, to implement the security features required for a hardware-based CFI support. All hardware modifications require less than 500 lines of VHDL code. Leon3 uses a single-issue, 7-stage pipeline. Our implementation has 8 register windows, an 16 KB 2-way set associative instruction cache, and a 16 KB 4-way set associative data cache.

3.2 Delay Slot

In the SparcV8 architecture, as with many other RISC ISAs, exists the concept of a delay slot. In those architectures, any instruction directly below a branch is always executed as if before it, regardless of the result. Subsequently, the instruction slot below a branch is called a delay slot. HCFI was built with that mechanism in mind, though it is by no means a prerequisite.

3.3 Memory Element Additions

The implementation of the prototype presented in this paper requires several memory elements. Specifically, a dedicated 32 bit register, a dedicated 128*32 bit stack, a bitmap of 128 bits, and a dedicated 128*8 bit memory module. All memory elements are only accessible using the new CFI instructions of the prototype.

The register (Label Register) is used in storing the label used for indirect jump verification - forward edge. The stack (Shadow Stack) is used in storing the return addresses of the functions currently executing, so as to add a measure of redundancy and validate return instructions - backward edge. The bitmap holds the recursion bit for the return addresses of the Shadow Stack. The third memory module is used to provide setjmp/longjmp support.

All four memory elements are are not *memory-mapped*, and thus are only accessible through the use of the CFI instructions, while there is no interference with additional peripherals or supervising software. Since the memory elements do not rely on the data cache, or use any existing buses, they do not encumber the core's memory bandwidth. Also, since the elements do not reside in RAM, they can be accesed with just one cycle of delay for both reads and writes.

3.4 Leon3 Pipeline Modifications

The modifications required for supporting the new instructions, discussed in Section 2, to the core are exclusive to the pipeline. The design relies on a new `process`, the hardware equivalent of a software thread, for avoiding heavy modifications to the critical path of the pipeline. The process contains all the CFI functionality, while the Leon3 pipeline is only modified to handle the input and output for the process; such as the current and next Program Counter, signals indicating annulled instructions, exceptions, and the instructions themselves. We discuss here how each instruction is implemented.

SetPC: The basic function of the SetPC instruction is to push the current PC to the Shadow Stack during the memory stage of the execution. Additionally, during the execution stage of the pipeline, it sets a flag that is used to suppress the `Invalid Label` violation (discussed in subsection 3.5) that occurs if the next instruction executed is a CheckLabel. If the next instruction is not in fact a CheckLabel, the flag is reset. This implementation allows a function called directly to be called indirectly, as well. To avoid an exception, the violation must be suppressed, as the Label Register is not currently set.

For supporting recursion, the instruction first tops the stack during the register access stage of the execution. If the address is the same as the current PC, it does not push it to the stack but instead marks the current index as recursive. Otherwise, it performs as previously described.

SetPCLabel: This instruction also pushes the current PC to the Shadow Stack during the memory stage and supports recursive calls as SetPC does. Additionally, SetPCLabel sets the Label Register to the value carried in its 18 LS bits. The value is extracted from the instruction during the decode stage and is set to the Label Register during the memory stage of the execution. Finally, it forces a check that ensures that the next instruction executed is in fact a CheckLabel. If the next instruction is not a CheckLabel, then a violation is raised that will lead to an exception during the violating instruction's exception stage.

CheckPC: The CheckPC instruction serves a simple purpose. During the register access stage, it *tops* the Shadow Stack, increments the value by 4 (one instruction below the SetPC), and compares the result with the next Program Counter (nPC). If equality is confirmed, then the stack is *popped*. If the result is not the expected value, a violation is raised leading to an exception during the exception stage.

Much like the SetPC and SetPCLabel instructions, if recursion optimization is in place, the functionality shifts. If the top address in the stack is marked as recursive, it is not popped, so that it can be used again later. If the address comparison results in a mismatch and the top address is marked as recursive, the stack is popped and another comparison is performed two cycles later, during the memory access stage. If the new comparison holds, execution continues normally and, if the top address is not recursive, it is popped. If the comparison fails again, a mismatch violation is raised during the exception stage.

CheckLabel: This instruction, much like the SetPCLabel instruction, carries a label on its 18 LS bits. This label is extracted during the decode stage of the execution, and compared to the label stored in the Label Register during the execution stage. If label equality is not confirmed, then a violation is raised leading to an exception. The Label Register is reset during the memory stage.

The CheckLabel instruction requires that a SetPC or SetPCLabel instruction was the last instruction to execute. Otherwise the Label Register is not set and its contents are zeroed. This leads to a violation, as no function is assigned zero as a label, unless a SetPC is the last instruction executed, which suppresses the violation.

LJCFI: LJCFI raises a flag to signify that a longjmp is underway. It does not carry any labels or uses any memory beyond the signal used for the flag.

SJCFI: SJCFI carries a label in its 8LS bits that is extracted at the decode stage. During the execution stage, depending on whether the flag is set by LJCFI, it either reads the top value's index from the Shadow Stack or retrieves the new index from the new memory element, using the label as a pointer to it. Finally, during the memory stage, again depending on the flag, it either stores the Shadow Stack's index to the memory element with the label as a pointer, or it sets the index retrieved from the new memory element to the Shadow Stack.

3.5 Violations

The various problems and errors detected during execution are summed in the following violations:

Label Mismatch: Raised when the label stored in the Label Register is not equal to the label carried by the CheckLabel instruction. It can also mean that the Label Register has not been set at all. This is a forward-edge CFI violation.

PC Mismatch: Raised when a CheckPC instruction detects tampering on the return address. The address stored in the Shadow Stack is not the address to which the return instruction jumped. This is a backward-edge CFI violation.

Flow: Raised when the instruction executed after a SetPCLabel is not a CheckLabel. The indirect call targeted a function that has not been found to be a valid indirect target during instrumentation. This is a forward-edge CFI violation.

Empty: Raised when a CheckPC instruction tries to validate a return address while the stack is empty. More return addresses have been popped than have been pushed. This is a backward-edge CFI violation.

Full: Raised when a SetPC or a SetPCLabel instruction pushes a return address while the stack is full. This is not a CFI violation, but an error that is raised when the stack fills. For the implementation presented in this paper, a 128 word Shadow Stack is used and is capable to run all benchmarks. Nevertheless, a larger Shadow Stack can be easily placed in the core if needed.

In the prototype implemented on the Leon3 softcore, all violations are designed to lead to an illegal instruction exception that puts the Integer Unit in Error Mode thus halting the execution. Alternatively, a custom exception can be easily created and handled by either the hardware or the supervising software.

3.6 Portability to Other Architectures

The design of our implementation does not actively change the core's architecture, but simply adds a few components and checks. The design only touches on very basic concepts of computer architecture, like the Program Counter, interrupts and exceptions, that are present in any modern core. All modifications for supporting HCFI are only additive to the processor, and rely on components present in any architecture. Therefore, the design presented in this paper can be ported to any architecture with minimal effort, and, as shown in section 5.5, with a small area overhead footprint.

4. SECURITY EVALUATION

In this section we discuss the security guarantees provided by HCFI. In our threat model we assume that the attacker can exploit a vulnerability, either a stack or heap overflow, or use-after-free, present in the application's source code. This vulnerability can be further used to overwrite key components of the running process like return addresses, function pointers, or VTable pointers. We also consider that the attacker has successfully bypassed ASLR or fine-grained randomization [34], and has full knowledge of the process' memory layout. Nevertheless, the system enforces that (i) the `.text` segment is non-writable preventing the application's code from being overwritten, and (ii) the `.data` segment is non-executable [4] blocking the attacker from executing directly data with proper CFI annotation. Both of those principles are commonplace in today's systems preventing software exploitation.

4.1 Defence with CFI ISA extensions

By forcing every return instruction to adhere to the address stored at the top of the Shadow Stack, ROP attacks are effectively foiled. In all our tests, every change in the control flow of the application, provoked by a return instruction that was not consistent with the Shadow Stack's top value, led to a CFI violation being raised, leading to a trap in the core and the eventual termination of the execution.

Similarly, an indirect call not leading to a pre-approved function entry point would always raise a CFI violation and halt the execution. Thus, foiling again most JOP attacks by limiting the possible positions in the program that such a jump would be allowed to target. The granularity of the forward-edge protection is directly proportional to the depth of the analysis performed on compile time.

4.2 Efficacy

We run a multitude of small programs designed to violate the CFI principles in different ways, e.g. indirectly jumping with invalid labels, or no labels at all, modifying return addresses on runtime, stressing the Shadow Stack, and various others. Using behavioural simulation with Xilinx's [39] Isim tool, we had total transparency of every signal in the Leon3 softcore, and therefore the shadow memory elements themselves. We could observe every microbenchmark's effect on the Shadow Stack and the core in general. The observations were consistent with our expectations. Every control-flow violation expected was raised and detected, halting the execution. Finally, we further confirmed our observations by additonally running the microbenchmarks on the programmed FPGA board, again finding the expected results.

5. PERFORMANCE EVALUATION

5.1 Testing Environment

We synthesized and programmed the modified Leon3 softcore on a Xilinx ml605-rev.e FPGA board. The FPGA has 1024 MB DDR3 SO-DIMM memory and the design operates at 120 MHz clock frequency. It has also several peripherals including an 100Mb Ethernet interface. Since we are targeting embedded systems, we ran all tests without an operating system present. The benchmarks are SpecInt2000 [35] and a few microprocessor-based, namely Coremark [17], Dhrystone [38], and matmul [9].

5.2 BareFS

Since the Spec suite is not designed for use in embedded systems, and running on bare-metal has the drawback of not offering the functionality of either files or command line arguments, we had to modify the code of each benchmark in order for it to be able to read its input files and arguments. The modifications included hard-coding all input files and required command line arguments to buffers, as well as changing any instructions related to I/O so that all input comes from memory, and any possible output is either discarded, written to a new buffer, or sent to stdout/stderr.

We automated the modification process by creating a library, which overloads a large part of the standard library and a python script that, given the input files, creates a C file containing buffers initialised to the contents of the files. The library redefines all standard function calls (such as open, fopen, fscanf, fgets, etc) with custom ones.

5.3 NOP Equivalence & Profiler Verification

Due to the architecture of the Leon3 core, our CFI instructions have the same execution time as a NOP instruction. This allows us to perform various sanity checks during our testing phase, with regards to expected overhead. One such test consists of running all benchmarks, on an unmodified (vanilla) Leon3 core, with NOP instructions in place of our CFI instructions. All checks performed during the testing phase verified our results. Finally all results are also verified by using a profiler to count all calls, both direct and indirect, and returns executed during the benchmarks' runtimes. Again, all results are consistent.

5.4 Runtime Overhead

To measure the overall runtime overhead we run for multiple times each benchmark, instrumented with CFI instructions, on the modified core, which is programmed on the ml605-rev.e FPGA. Before each run, both the instruction and data cache are flushed. The results are depicted in Figure 10 and the runtime overhead is under 1%.

We have omitted gcc and eon from SpecInt2000. In the case of gcc, CFI violations occur during normal execution, since several return addresses change after being pushed to the shadow stack. This has been confirmed by Dang et al. [14]. For evaluating gcc we count NOP instructions, since they are equivalent to CFI instructions (see Section 5.3). While the overhead reported is without the full CFI instrumentation, counting NOP instructions is really close to measuring the actual CFI instrumentation.

We are also unable to sufficiently instrument eon (written in C++). The main problems are that we could not detect VTables and that some return addresses changed during runtime. An analysis of the code, on the assembly level, revealed that the program loaded return addresses from memory, a few stack frames below the current one.

Interestingly, the gap benchmark came very close to reaching the maximum theoretical overhead of 6.60%; measured by running the worst case scenario - a loop executing only indirect calls to a function, which, in turn, immediately executes a return instruction.

5.5 Hardware Overhead

We implemented our design firstly without setjmp/longjmp support or the recursion optimization. The resulting area overhead of our implementation, as detailed by the reports of the Xilinx tools used to synthesize the design, was very low, using an additional 0.65% registers and 0.81% LUTs (look-up tables). With setjmp/longjmp support and the recursion optimization in place, the area overhead increased significantly to 2.52% registers and 2.55% LUTs. The additions to the design do not seem to add to the critical path of the processor and thus do not lower the maximum frequency that the core can achieve on the board.

6. DISCUSSION & FUTURE WORK

HCFI's design does not offer support for multi-threaded environments. A single shadow stack located in the core is not sufficient to store the return addresses for all the processes that share the processor. Implementing an array

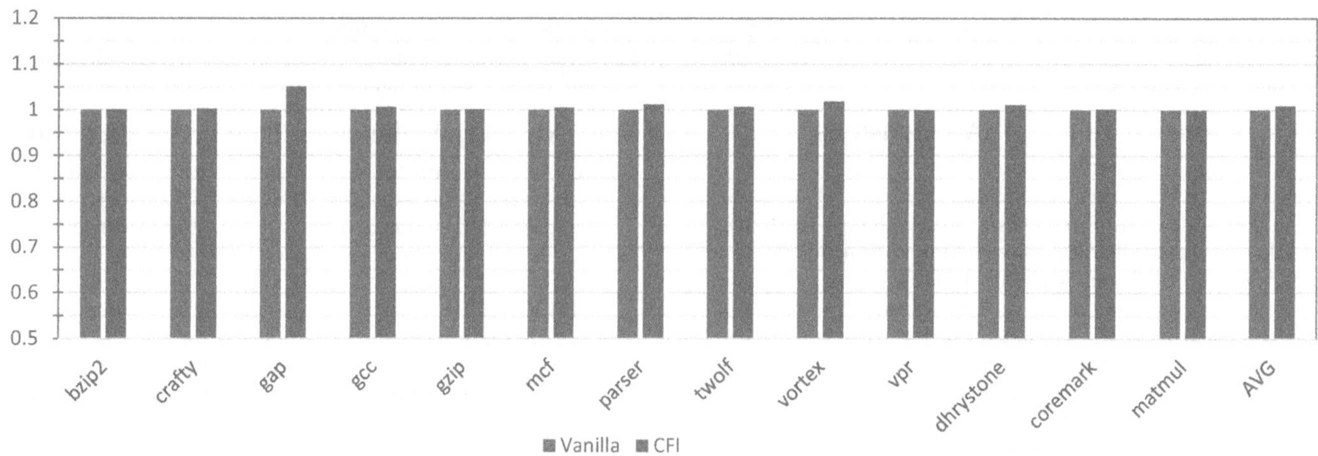

Figure 10: Presentation of the runtime overhead measured with our implementation compared to the runtime on a vanilla Leon3 core.

of shadow stacks inside the core would be a step towards achieving this functionality. Unfortunately, such a hardware implementation is not feasible, due to the substantial area overhead it would introduce; the array would have to be large enough to store the shadow stack for every active process.

This approach can be easily implemented by having a small array of shadow stacks indexed by the processes' IDs. When a context switch occurs, the operating system has to store the new running process' ID to a memory-mapped register that is visible to the control-flow integrity pipeline. The pipeline would, in turn, use it to select the appropriate shadow stack for the running process. When the process is terminated, a *cfiexit* instruction will be issued in order to invalidate the process' slot in the shadow stack array. Additionally, several software stacks could be integrated in one hardware stack. Instead of using an array of shadow stacks, the operating system could use one shadow stack for storing return addresses along with their respective process ID. Once a process terminates, all stale records contained at the shadow stack should be cleaned up by the operating system. Enabling multiple shadow stacks is part of our future work.

The most novel approach, that handles multi-threaded environments, is proposed by IAD [2]. They conclude that the optimal design for a shadow memory assisted architecture has to derive a large subset of the logic from the existing MMU subsystem. In essence, the core is augmented with a second MMU(Shadow MMU), that reserves a small part of the system's memory, and denies access to it for everything but itself and the the set of CFI instructions from the core's extended ISA.

Compared to our design, the above approach could provide the same level of security, but would trade-off performance for multi-threading support. The performance degradation is owed to the fact that the CFI instructions would now operate on the *slow* system memory, and not the dedicated memory located inside the processor's core. An obvious optimization, is to include enough memory for one process inside the core, much like in our current design, and utilize the shadow MMU in order to swap the CFI values of the executing thread at every context switch. With this optimization, the shadow MMU architecture would add minor performance overhead over our initial design, considering the overhead imposed by the context switch itself, and therefore it could be essentially used on top of HCFI. We plan to explore this integration in our future work.

7. RELATED WORK

Many mitigation techniques for protecting software are based on CFI. Most of them are software-based, although there are some attempts for delivering CFI-aware processors. In this section, we discuss a representative selection of CFI solutions and their limitations.

BinCFI [42] and CCFIR [41] are the first CFI implementations that can transparently work with binaries, where the source code is absent. Both techniques are based on relaxing the CFG a process should adhere to, by delivering coarser-grained CFI polices compared to the original CFI proposal [3]. Although coarse-grained CFI, as implemented in both BinCFI and CCFIR, is practical and aims at protecting directly binaries with really low overhead, the security implications cannot be overlooked, since it has been demonstrated that both techniques can be bypassed [20]. In a similar fashion, coarse-grained CFI techniques have been enabled using particular hardware features, such as the Last-branch Record (LBR) [13,29], however, again, it was quickly demonstrated that these policies are vulnerable as well [11,16,21,33].

Since coarse-grained CFI provides limited security, the community has further focused on (a) more fine-grained policies that can be applied at the compiler level and on (b) securing just the frequently exploited elements of a running process, and not all indirect branches, as for example are VTable pointers. For example, researchers have proposed techniques for securing VTables in binaries [5,12,19], however, since recovering the semantics of all C++ objects from binaries is not always possible, these systems are all subject to more sophisticated attacks [32]. In another direction, VTV [36], ShrinkWrap [22], and SafeDispatch [24] apply fine-grained CFI policies at the compiler level for protecting VTables. However, even fine-grained policies have been also demonstrated vulnerable, unless they include a shadow-stack implementation [10].

In this paper, we do not attempt to promote a new CFI

flavor, but, rather, to argue that a full-featured system that supports fine-grained CFI policies *and* an in-chip shadow stack can be implemented and offer strong security guarantees at a low cost (less than 1% overhead on average). Similar processors have been proposed in the literature, however none is as complete and as fast as ours. In Branch Regulation [25], neither forward or backward edge control-flow changes are secured adequately. Forward edges are augmented by coarse-grained CFI, which allows for branching to any function entry point or any point within the currently executing function. While backward edges are protected by a shadow stack that keeps track of the program's return addresses, the stack itself is not secured against tampering as it resides in mapped memory. HCFI implements a shadow stack that is *never* mapped on the host's memory.

Davi et al. [15] propose HAFIX, a system for backward edge CFI and, unlike Branch Regulation, HAFIX does use dedicated, hidden memory elements for storing critical information. Their implementation utilizes labels to mark functions as active call sites. However, this has the disadvantage of allowing the attacker to jump to any active function. This is important, since their method also allows for an attacker, using stack unwinding, to avoid the execution of CFIDEL instructions and eventually mark every function as an active one, thus effectively permitting jumps anywhere in the program, and therefore being possibly vulnerable.

Budiu et al. [8] propose the usage of hard-coded labels for both forward edge and backward edge control-flow integrity enforcement. The usage of labels for backward-edge protection certainly limits the attacker, but still allows him to take advantage of functions that are called by many call sites, such as `memcpy`. Essentially, this implementation is vulnerable, since it lacks of a shadow-stack implementation.

Finally, NSA's proposal on hardware CFI [2] facilitates a shadow stack to protect return addresses and landing point instructions to augment indirect-call transfers. In order to improve the flexibility of the shadow stack, they propose the use of a shadow MMU that will handle the management of the shadow memory. However, their proposal lacks granularity on forward-edge flow integrity, thus an attacker can point an indirect branch on any landing point instruction.

8. CONCLUSION

Many CFI policies have been proposed in current literature, however all of them have been demonstrated to be vulnerable. Recently, it was argued that even fine-grained CFI policies can be exploited, unless the policy is supported by a shadow stack. In this paper, we acknowledge that the use of a shadow stack is mandatory for any practical CFI deployment. We further attempted to quantify the performance of CFI and demonstrated that the technique can be applied to real systems with practically negligible overhead. For supporting our case, we presented HCFI, a full-featured hardware implementation of CFI. We extended an existing ISA by adding CFI assisting instructions and we deployed shadow memory inside the core. We modified a SPARC SoC and evaluated the prototype on an FPGA board by running all SPECInt benchmarks instrumented with the additional CFI-related instructions. The evaluation showed that HCFI can effectively protect applications from code-reuse attacks, while adding less than 1% runtime overhead. Compared to similar hardware implementations, HCFI is (i) *complete*, since it protects both forward and backward edges, (ii) *faster*, since the experienced overhead is on average less than 1%, and (iii) *more accurate*, since it employs a full-functional shadow stack implemented inside the core.

Acknowledgments This work was supported by the European Commission through the project SHARCS under Grant Agreement No. 644571.

9. REFERENCES

[1] The SPARC Architecture Manual, Version 8. www.sparc.com/standards/V8.pdf.

[2] Hardware Control Flow Integrity for an IT Ecosystem. https://github.com/iadgov/Control-Flow-Integrity/tree/master/paper, 2015.

[3] Abadi, M., Budiu, M., Erlingsson, U., and Ligatti, J. Control-flow integrity. In *Proceedings of the 12th ACM conference on Computer and communications security* (2005), ACM, pp. 340–353.

[4] Andersen, S., and Abella, V. Changes to functionality in microsoft windows xp service pack 2, part 3: Memory protection technologies, Data Execution Prevention. Microsoft TechNet Library, September 2004. http://technet.microsoft.com/en-us/library/bb457155.aspx.

[5] Aravind Prakash, Xunchao Hu, and Heng Yin. vfguard: Strict protection for virtual function calls in cots c++ binaries. In *Symposium on Network and Distributed System Security (NDSS)* (2015).

[6] Athanasakis, M., Athanasopoulos, E., Polychronakis, M., Portokalidis, G., and Ioannidis, S. The devil is in the constants: Bypassing defenses in browser jit engines. In *NDSS* (2015), The Internet Society.

[7] Bletsch, T., Jiang, X., Freeh, V. W., and Liang, Z. Jump-oriented programming: a new class of code-reuse attack. In *Proceedings of the 6th ACM Symposium on Information, Computer and Communications Security* (2011), ACM, pp. 30–40.

[8] Budiu, M., Erlingsson, U., and Abadi, M. Architectural support for software-based protection. In *Proceedings of the 1st workshop on Architectural and system support for improving software dependability* (2006), ACM, pp. 42–51.

[9] Burkardt, J., Puglielli, P., and Center, P. S. Matmul: An interactive matrix multiplication benchmark. *degrees from BITS, Pilani. He is a Fellow of the Institution of Engineers (India), Fellow of National Academy of Engineering (FNAE), Fellow of National Academy of Sciences (FNASc), Life Member ISTE(LMISTE). Professor Kothari has published/presented 640* (1995).

[10] Carlini, N., Barresi, A., Payer, M., Wagner, D., and Gross, T. R. Control-flow bending: On the effectiveness of control-flow integrity. In *24th USENIX Security Symposium (USENIX Security 15)* (Washington, D.C., Aug. 2015), USENIX Association, pp. 161–176.

[11] Carlini, N., and Wagner, D. Rop is still dangerous: Breaking modern defenses. In *23rd USENIX Security Symposium (USENIX Security 14)* (San Diego, CA, Aug. 2014), USENIX Association, pp. 385–399.

[12] Chao Zhang, Chengyu Songz, Kevin Zhijie Chen, Zhaofeng Cheny, and Dawn Song. Vtint: Protecting virtual function tables' integrity. In *Symposium on Network and Distributed System Security (NDSS)* (2015).

[13] Cheng, Y., Zhou, Z., Yu, M., Ding, X., and Deng, R. H. Ropecker: A generic and practical approach for defending against ROP attacks. In *21st Annual Network and Distributed System Security Symposium, NDSS 2014, San Diego, California, USA, February 23-26, 2013* (2014).

[14] Dang, T. H., Maniatis, P., and Wagner, D. The performance cost of shadow stacks and stack canaries. In *ACM Symposium on Information, Computer and Communications Security, ASIACCS* (2015), vol. 15.

[15] Davi, L., Hanreich, M., Paul, D., Sadeghi, A.-R., Koeberl, P., Sullivan, D., Arias, O., and Jin, Y. Hafix: hardware-assisted flow integrity extension. In *Proceedings of the 52nd Annual Design Automation Conference* (2015), ACM, p. 74.

[16] Davi, L., Sadeghi, A.-R., Lehmann, D., and Monrose, F. Stitching the gadgets: On the ineffectiveness of coarse-grained control-flow integrity protection. In *23rd USENIX Security Symposium (USENIX Security 14)* (San Diego, CA, Aug. 2014), USENIX Association, pp. 401–416.

[17] EEMBC. Coremark Benchmark. https://www.eembc.org/coremark/.

[18] Gaisler Research. Leon3 synthesizable processor. http://www.gaisler.com.

[19] Gawlik, R., and Holz, T. Towards automated integrity protection of c++ virtual function tables in binary programs. In *Proceedings of the 30th Annual Computer Security Applications Conference* (New York, NY, USA, 2014), ACSAC '14, ACM, pp. 396–405.

[20] Göktaş, E., Athanasopoulos, E., Bos, H., and Portokalidis, G. Out of control: Overcoming control-flow integrity. In *Security and Privacy (SP), 2014 IEEE Symposium on* (2014), IEEE, pp. 575–589.

[21] Göktaş, E., Athanasopoulos, E., Polychronakis, M., Bos, H., and Portokalidis, G. Size does matter: Why using gadget-chain length to prevent code-reuse attacks is hard. In *23rd USENIX Security Symposium (USENIX Security 14)* (San Diego, CA, Aug. 2014), USENIX Association, pp. 417–432.

[22] Haller, I., Göktaş, E., Athanasopoulos, E., Portokalidis, G., and Bos, H. Shrinkwrap: Vtable protection without loose ends. In *ACSAC* (2015), ACM, pp. 341–350.

[23] Hiser, J., Nguyen-Tuong, A., Co, M., Hall, M., and Davidson, J. W. Ilr: Where'd my gadgets go? In *Proceedings of the 2012 IEEE Symposium on Security and Privacy* (Washington, DC, USA, 2012), SP '12, IEEE Computer Society, pp. 571–585.

[24] Jang, D., Tatlock, Z., and Lerner, S. Safedispatch: Securing c++ virtual calls from memory corruption attacks. In *Symposium on Network and Distributed System Security (NDSS)* (2014).

[25] Kayaalp, M., Ozsoy, M., Abu-Ghazaleh, N., and Ponomarev, D. Branch regulation: Low-overhead protection from code reuse attacks. In *Computer Architecture (ISCA), 2012 39th Annual International Symposium on* (2012), IEEE, pp. 94–105.

[26] One, A. Smashing the stack for fun and profit. *Phrack magazine 7*, 49 (1996), 365.

[27] Özdoganoglu, H., Vijaykumar, T., Brodley, C. E., Kuperman, B., Jalote, A., et al. Smashguard: A hardware solution to prevent security attacks on the function return address. *Computers, IEEE Transactions on 55*, 10 (2006), 1271–1285.

[28] Pappas, V., Polychronakis, M., and Keromytis, A. D. Smashing the gadgets: Hindering return-oriented programming using in-place code randomization. In *Proceedings of the 2012 IEEE Symposium on Security and Privacy* (Washington, DC, USA, 2012), SP '12, IEEE Computer Society, pp. 601–615.

[29] Pappas, V., Polychronakis, M., and Keromytis, A. D. Transparent rop exploit mitigation using indirect branch tracing. In *Presented as part of the 22nd USENIX Security Symposium (USENIX Security 13)* (Washington, D.C., 2013), USENIX, pp. 447–462.

[30] PaX Team. Address Space Layout Randomization (ASLR), 2003. http://pax.grsecurity.net/docs/aslr.txt.

[31] Roemer, R., Buchanan, E., Shacham, H., and Savage, S. Return-oriented programming: Systems, languages, and applications. *ACM Transactions on Information and System Security (TISSEC) 15*, 1 (2012), 2.

[32] Schuster, F., Tendyck, T., Liebchen, C., Davi, L., Sadeghi, A.-R., and Holz, T. Counterfeit object-oriented programming: On the difficulty of preventing code reuse attacks in c++ applications. In *36th IEEE Symposium on Security and Privacy (Oakland)* (May 2015).

[33] Schuster, F., Tendyck, T., Pewny, J., Maass, A., Steegmanns, M., Contag, M., and Holz, T. Evaluating the effectiveness of current anti-rop defenses. In *Research in Attacks, Intrusions and Defenses - 17th International Symposium, RAID 2014, Gothenburg, Sweden, September 17-19, 2014. Proceedings* (2014), pp. 88–108.

[34] Snow, K. Z., Davi, L., Dmitrienko, A., Liebchen, C., Monrose, F., and Sadeghi, A.-R. Just-in-time code reuse: On the effectiveness of fine-grained address space layout randomization. In *Proceedings of the 34th IEEE Symposium on Security and Privacy* (May 2013).

[35] Standard Performance Evaluation Corporation (SPEC). SPEC CINT2000 Benchmarks. http://www.spec.org/cpu2000/CINT2000.

[36] Tice, C., Roeder, T., Collingbourne, P., Checkoway, S., Erlingsson, U., Lozano, L., and Pike, G. Enforcing forward-edge control-flow integrity in gcc and llvm. In *Proceedings of the 23rd USENIX Conference on Security Symposium* (Berkeley, CA, USA, 2014), SEC'14, USENIX Association, pp. 941–955.

[37] Wartell, R., Mohan, V., Hamlen, K. W., and Lin, Z. Binary stirring: Self-randomizing instruction addresses of legacy x86 binary code. In *Proceedings of the 2012 ACM Conference on Computer and*

Communications Security (New York, NY, USA, 2012), CCS '12, ACM, pp. 157–168.

[38] WEICKER, R. P. Dhrystone: a synthetic systems programming benchmark. *Communications of the ACM 27*, 10 (1984), 1013–1030.

[39] XILINX. ISE Simulator (ISim). http://www.xilinx.com/tools/isim.htm.

[40] XILINX. Xilinx Virtex 6 ml605 rev-e Evaluation Board. http://www.xilinx.com/support/documentation/boards_and_kits/ug534.pdf, 2012.

[41] ZHANG, C., WEI, T., CHEN, Z., DUAN, L., SZEKERES, L., MCCAMANT, S., SONG, D., AND ZOU, W. Practical control flow integrity and randomization for binary executables. In *Security and Privacy (SP), 2013 IEEE Symposium on* (2013), IEEE, pp. 559–573.

[42] ZHANG, M., AND SEKAR, R. Control flow integrity for COTS binaries. In *Usenix Security* (2013), pp. 337–352.

Remix: On-demand Live Randomization

Yue Chen, Zhi Wang, David Whalley
Florida State University
{ychen,zwang,whalley}@cs.fsu.edu

Long Lu
Stony Brook University
long@cs.stonybrook.edu

ABSTRACT

Code randomization is an effective defense against code reuse attacks. It scrambles program code to prevent attackers from locating useful functions or gadgets. The key to secure code randomization is achieving high entropy. A practical approach to boost entropy is on-demand live randomization that works on running processes. However, enabling live randomization is challenging in that it often requires manual efforts to solve ambiguity in identifying function pointers.

In this paper, we propose Remix, an efficient and practical live randomization system for both user processes and kernel modules. Remix randomly shuffles basic blocks within their respective functions. By doing so, it avoids the complexity of migrating stale function pointers, and allows mixing randomized and non-randomized code to strike a balance between performance and security. Remix randomizes a running process in two steps: it first randomly reorders its basic blocks, and then comprehensively migrates live pointers to basic blocks. Our experiments show that Remix can significantly increase randomness with low performance overhead on both CPU and I/O intensive benchmarks and kernel modules, even at very short randomization intervals.

CCS Concepts

•Security and privacy → Software and application security;

Keywords

ASLR; Code Reuse Attack Defense; Live Randomization

1. INTRODUCTION

With the ubiquitous deployment of data execution prevention (DEP) that can foil direct code injection [20, 21, 24], code reuse attacks have become a popular attack method. Instead of injecting foreign code, they reuse existing code to bypass DEP. These attacks could reuse either whole functions (e.g., return-to-libc or return-to-plt) or short code fragments called gadgets (e.g., return-oriented programming [12, 15, 45] or jump-oriented programming [11]). In a typical scenario, the attacker first launches a code-reuse attack to disable DEP by calling functions like `mprotect`, and then injects the malicious code into the victim process for more complex tasks. Control flow integrity (CFI) is an effective defense against code reuse attacks [1]. CFI guarantees that the runtime control flow follows the static control flow graph (CFG). Consequently, the attacker cannot arbitrarily manipulate the control flow to reuse the existing code. However, CFI has not been widely adopted. Early CFI systems have high performance overhead because CFI requires to instrument every indirect branch instruction. Recent implementations improve the performance by sacrificing preciseness [55, 54] and, in some cases, security [23, 28].

Code randomization is another effective defense against code reuse attacks. Unlike CFI, code randomization scrambles the reusable code by randomizing the code location, the code layout, or the instruction encoding [7, 22, 30, 33, 42, 49]. Many code reuse attacks rely on the exact locations or contents of the victim process. Code randomization causes these attacks to behave unpredictably. Most popular operating systems support a simpler form of code randomization called address space layout randomization (ASLR), in which (position-independent) executables are loaded at random base addresses [3, 5, 37]. ASLR offers limited randomness, especially on the 32-bit architectures [46]. Moreover, ASLR is particularly vulnerable to information leak attacks – a single leaked code or data pointer can de-randomize the whole process since every code section has a fixed offset to the base. To address this problem, fine-grained code randomization techniques have been proposed, for example, to rearrange functions [33], basic blocks [49], or instructions [30, 42]. A high entropy is the key to the security of code randomization.

One effective boost to randomness is on-demand live randomization. Live randomization works on a live, running process. It can be applied many times at undetermined periods of time, making the process a moving target for the attacker. Live randomization can eliminate the predictability associated with the compile-time or load-time randomization schemes. It can significantly improve the randomness for 32-bit architectures, which many computers and embedded devices still use. However, live randomization is challenging to implement correctly: when the code is changed, it is necessary to update all the code and the data that depend on the changed code to guarantee correctness. For example, if a `call` instruction is moved to a different address, we

CODASPY'16, March 09 - 11, 2016, New Orleans, LA, USA

ISBN 978-1-4503-3935-3/16/03...$15.00

DOI: http://dx.doi.org/10.1145/2857705.2857726

have to update every branch instruction that targets this instruction (or its preceding instructions), and search the stack for the corresponding return address and update it to the new one. Run-time changes to function entry points are even harder to fix – it is non-trivial to locate all the affected function pointers in the whole address space, including the code, the data, the stacks, and the heap. In particular, a linear search of the function address has false positives and could take a prohibitively long time to complete. Function addresses could also be stored by and in the OS kernel. For example, a process can register a handler for each signal of interest. The kernel saves this data in the kernel memory, unreachable by the process. If the handler is moved, the kernel must be notified with the updated address. To achieve that, one has to intercept the system calls that register signal handlers and re-register the handlers when necessary. Therefore, live randomization is challenging to implement. An existing live-randomization system customizes the compiler to generate enough meta-data to facilitate its job [27]. However, it still has yet to overcome the aforementioned challenges. For example, there is unsolvable ambiguity (e.g., pointers in unions or pointers stored as integers) in pointer migration that requires developers' manual effort.

In this paper, we propose Remix, an efficient, practical live randomization system for both user processes and kernel modules. Remix randomly shuffles the process' basic blocks *within* their respective functions to change the run-time code layout (a basic block is a linear sequence of instructions that has only one entry point and one exit point [50]. An exit point is often a branch instruction, such as `jmp` or `ret`. It could also be a non-branch instruction that falls through to the next basic block.) That is, functions remain at their original, expected locations, while basic blocks are moved around but never cross the function boundaries. This design can significantly reduce the complexity of live randomization: *first*, there is no need to fix function pointers because function entry points are not moved. This avoids the complicated pointer migration that may involve unresolvable ambiguity [27] (function addresses are still randomized once at the load time by ASLR). Basic block addresses may still appear in both the code and data sections (e.g., jump tables). But these appearances are mostly limited to the local scopes and thus are relatively easy to fix. *Second*, it is straightforward to support partial randomization since each change is confined to a local scope. For example, Remix can be used to randomize selected kernel modules. Randomized and non-randomized kernel modules can co-exist in a single kernel in harmony. *Third*, compared to systems that globally rearrange basic blocks [49], Remix maintains better locality. Compilers make an effort to optimally lay out the code for better performance. Global rearrangement of basic blocks could potentially lead to poor locality and substantial performance loss. Remix instead shuffles basic blocks locally. It can also bundle closely-related basic blocks together (e.g., tight loops) to further reduce the performance overhead. Simplicity and efficiency are two major advantages of Remix. They make Remix an ideal technique to compose with other defenses. For example, Remix should be used with ASLR so that functions are randomized at least once (during program startup). Other examples of compatible techniques include defenses against JIT-ROP [47] or Blind-ROP [10] attacks [6, 19, 26] and function-level re-randomization [27]. Remix can significantly increase the unpredictability of those systems with on-demand, live randomization of basic blocks.

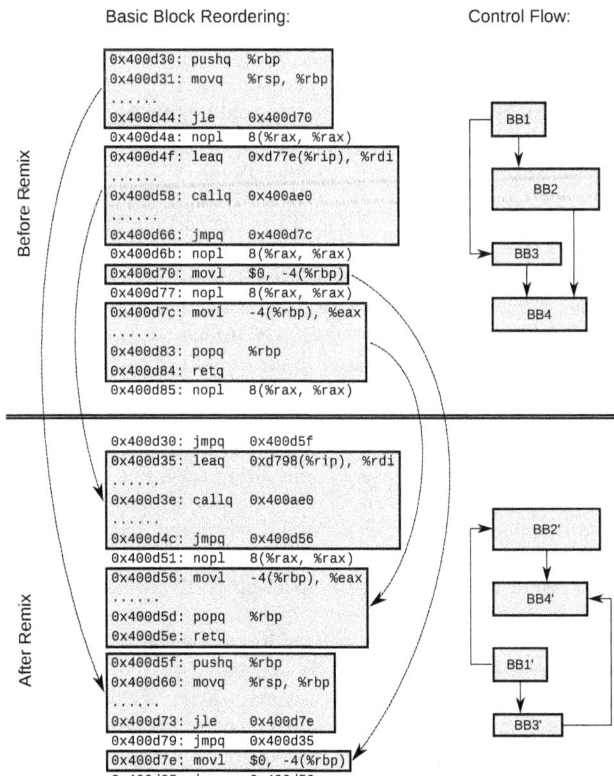

Figure 1: An Example of Remix on x86-64

We have implemented a prototype of Remix for Linux applications and FreeBSD kernel modules. Our prototype uses a slightly modified LLVM compiler to reserve spaces needed for basic block reordering (it can also support binary-only programs by leveraging existing `NOP` instructions used to align instructions, albeit with less gain in randomness.) Our experiments with standard benchmarks and applications show that Remix can substantially improve the randomness with a minor overhead (e.g., 2.8% average performance overhead and 14.8% average increase in binary size for SPEC CPU2006).

The rest of the paper is organized as the following. We first present the design and implementation of Remix in Section 2 and Section 3, respectively. The evaluation results are given in Section 4, followed by a discussion of potential improvements to Remix in Section 5. Finally, we compare Remix to the state-of-the-art in Section 6 and conclude the paper in Section 7.

2. DESIGN

2.1 Overview

Remix aims at increasing randomness for protected processes through live randomization of basic blocks while keeping function entry points unmoved. Figure 1 shows an example of applying Remix to a simple 64-bit x86 (x86-64) function. After Remix, the basic blocks have been reordered. Any gadgets discovered before Remix immediately become obsolete, and their execution likely will cause exceptions like illegal opcode or general protection error. Even though it is conceptually straightforward, reordering basic blocks faces a number of challenges:

First, the function might not have enough space to accommodate the reordered basic blocks. For example, some basic blocks end with a short jump instruction that takes a single byte of offset. Their targets could be moved by Remix beyond the reach of one byte. It is thus necessary to substitute the short jump with a long jump, which takes four bytes for the offset. In addition, some basic blocks do not end with a branch instruction. They instead fall through to the next basic block. The `movl $0, -4(%rbp)` instruction in Figure 1 (at address `0x400d70`, before Remix) is such an example. The instruction at `0x400d7c` starts a new basic block because the instruction at `0x400d66` jumps to it, making it an entry point. Remix has to add a new jump instruction to connect the fall-through basic blocks. To accommodate reordered basic blocks, we modify the compiler to emit a five-byte NOP instruction after each basic block. This provides enough space to insert a long jump (also five bytes) for each basic block. This errs on the safe side – there is always enough space to accommodate the reordered basic blocks. Remix can also support binary-only programs without recompilation by leveraging the existing NOP instructions in functions.

Second, when a basic block or its succeeding blocks are moved to other positions, it is necessary to fix their exit points to maintain the correct control flow: if the exit instruction is a direct branch, we only need to update its offset to the new address of its successors (a basic block has two successors if it is a conditional branch.) For example, the `jle` instruction (Figure 1) has two branches. When it is moved, Remix adds a direct `jmp` instruction (at `0x400d79` after Remix) because the original branch falls through to the `movl` instruction at `0x400d70`. If the exit instruction is an indirect branch, Remix analyzes its structure and handles it accordingly. For example, indirect calls can be left alone because function entry points are not moved by Remix. Indirect jumps are more complicated with several possibilities (Section 2.3.2). They are in fact related to the third challenge, how to migrate basic block pointers.

Third, there exist pointers to basic blocks in the process' code and data sections. For example, the stack consists of local variables and return addresses. A return address points to the instruction after the originating call instruction (the return site). If a call instruction is moved by Remix, we have to substitute the original return address on the stack with the new one. In addition, the compiler generates jump tables to speed up `switch`/`case`-like structures. A jump table contains basic block pointers to handle its cases. It has to be patched when basic blocks are moved. Jump tables have several possible structures. Remix must handle all those different cases. The kernel has its own set of basic block pointers that have to be converted to maintain the correct control flow. In the rest of this section, we present in detail how Remix solves these problems.

2.2 Basic Block Reordering

Remix shuffles basic blocks within their respective functions to increase run-time randomness. Algorithm 1 gives a high-level overview of this process. Specifically, Remix first parses the code into basic blocks, and generates a random ordering of these basic blocks to guide the process. Remix then lays out the basic blocks according to that ordering, and saves the mapping between their old and new positions in a table (m). This table is used to convert basic block

Algorithm 1 Basic Block Reordering

```
1:  for each function f do
2:      s = GenerateRandomOrder(f);
3:      m = LayoutBasicBlocks(s);
4:      for each instruction i do
5:          if i ∈ DirectCall then
6:              FixDispS(i, m);
7:          else if i ∈ DirectJump then
8:              FixDispS(i, m);
9:              addr = CalcPrevTarget(i);
10:             FixDispD(i, m, addr);
11:         else if i ∈ IndirectJump then
12:             if IsJumpTable(i) then
13:                 AddToJumpTableList(jt, i);
14:             end if
15:         end if
16:         if i ∈ PC-RelativeInsn then
17:             FixDispS(i, m);
18:         end if
19:     end for
20:     ConvertBasicBlockPointers (m, jt);
21: end for
```

pointers. Note that the first instruction of a function (i.e., the function entry point) is replaced by a direct jump to the first basic block. As shown in Figure 1, Remix does not terminate a basic block with a call instruction. We choose this design for two reasons: first, Remix keeps functions at their original locations. Call instructions thus do not require complicated handling. Second, by design, a call instruction falls through to the next instruction. An extra jump must be inserted after the call instruction if the fall-through instruction is moved by Remix. Many applications use a large number of call instructions. This would substantially increase the binary size and reduce the performance.

Reordering basic blocks changes their positions. Some instructions need to be updated to maintain the original control flow. They consist of instructions that have a program-counter (PC) relative operand (e.g., the various branch instructions). Most of them have a constant displacement that can be adjusted to offset the position changes made by Remix. We need to consider two types of position changes – the instruction itself and the destination of the instruction. We use two functions, `FixDispS` and `FixDispD`, in Algorithm 1 to handle these two cases, respectively. The majority of the instructions to be patched are branch instructions, i.e., indirect/direct calls and jumps (line 5-15 in Algorithm 1):

- **Indirect Call:** an indirect call invokes a function indirectly through a function pointer. Function pointers remain valid because Remix does not move function entry points. As such, indirect calls can be left unchanged.
- **Direct Call:** a direct call targets the function at a certain displacement to itself. Even though the function stays at its position in the memory, the call instruction could have been moved to a different place. Accordingly, direct calls should be fixed with the `FixDispS` function.
- **Direct Jump:** a direct jump often targets another basic block. Both the source and the destination instructions

might change the positions. To fix a direct jump, Remix first adjusts the instruction's displacement to offset the source instruction movement with `FixDispS`. It then calculates the original target and adjusts the displacement to offset the target instruction movement. In addition, a conditional jump has two branches, one for the true condition and the other for the false condition. One of the branches is a fall-through to the next instruction. Remix handles this case by treating the fall-through as an implicit jump to the next basic block. The same approach is applied if a basic block falls through to the next one without a branch instruction (e.g., BB3 in Figure 1).

- **Indirect Jump:** indirect jumps are more complicated to handle than the other branch instructions. They can target both functions and basic blocks. The former does not need any changes, but the latter can involve several different cases that must be handled by Remix. We elaborate these cases in Section 2.3.2.
- **PC-relative Addressing Mode:** in addition to branch instructions, we also need to patch instructions with the PC-relative addressing mode, which are often used by the compiler to generate position-independent code. A program must be compiled as a position-independent executable (PIE) to benefit from ASLR (on Linux). A PIE program can run at any location in the address space. To achieve that, it calculates the run-time addresses of its code and data relative to the current program counter. The newer x86-64 architecture natively supports the PC-relative addressing mode. For example, instruction `lea 0x200000(%rip),%rbp` adds `0x20,0000` to the current program counter and saves it to the `rbp` register. The older x86-32 architecture has no native support for this addressing mode. Instead, the compiler uses a simple built-in function to retrieve the return address from the stack, which has been pushed to the stack earlier by the caller. Accordingly, this function returns the address of the return site (i.e., PC+5). To ensure correctness, Remix needs to update these instructions and functions. Fortunately, the compiler uses this mode (almost) exclusively to calculate the run-time function and data addresses, both of which are not changed by Remix. Only the PC-relative instructions and functions (on the x86-32 architecture) may have been moved. This can be easily compensated with `FixDispS`.

When updating instructions, the new displacement might grow larger than what can fit in the original instruction. For example, x86-64 has two formats of relative jumps – short jumps with a one-byte displacement and long jumps with a four-byte displacement (x86-32 also supports short jumps with a two-byte displacement.) It is rather easy to overflow short jumps especially in large functions. One feasible solution is to restrict the moving distances of short jumps within the one-byte limit. However, this could quickly become over-complicated if several short jumps are close to each other. We might end up with several basic blocks unchanged or only moved by a short distance. Remix instead configures the compiler to always generate the equivalent long jumps with four-byte displacements. This is also the case for call instructions which have either a two-byte or a four-byte displacement.

Figure 1 gives an example of applying Remix to a short x86-64 function. After Remix, four basic blocks are moved to new positions. Branch and PC-relative instructions, including `jle`, `callq`, `jmpq` and `leaq`, are updated to maintain the control flow. Moreover, two `jmpq` instructions (`0x400d79` and `0x400d85`, after Remix) are inserted for the fall-through of basic blocks. Another `jmpq` instruction (`0x400d30`) is placed at the function entry point targeting the first basic block.

2.3 Basic Block Pointer Conversion

User-space programs built by compilers often do not need or have direct access to basic blocks. Accordingly, most programs have no explicit pointers to basic blocks. However, the compiler might spontaneously create such pointers when compiling the source code. For example, a return address on the stack points to the instruction following the corresponding `call` instruction. Besides, the compiler often uses jump tables to speed up the `switch/case` statements. After Remix reorders basic blocks, these pointers become invalid and thus have to be updated. In the rest of this section, we discuss these cases in detail.

2.3.1 Return Address Conversion

A call instruction automatically pushes its return address to the stack so that the callee can continue the execution from there upon return. The return address points to the instruction following the call instruction, i.e., the return site. When Remix performs live randomization of the process, the stack has already contained return addresses. If these addresses are not subsequently updated, the process will return to wrong locations, eventually causing exceptions such as illegal opcode or segmentation fault.

To convert return addresses, we traverse the whole stack (starting at the top of the stack in register `rsp`), and search for and update every address that points to a valid return site. With this condition, the chance of a stack variable being accidentally treated as a return address is very slim. In addition, return address conversion is straightforward and deterministic if the program maintains stack frame pointers. A stack frame is a continuous block of memory on the stack that keeps data for an active function. If frame pointers are maintained, each frame contains a pointer to the previous frame, and the return address is stored at a known location in the frame. Therefore, we can traverse stack frames and update all and only return addresses. By default, modern compilers like `gcc` do not generate code to maintain frame pointers in an optimized compilation.

2.3.2 Indirect Jump Related Conversion

Indirect jumps are used by the compiler and standard libraries for a number of purposes. They can target either functions or basic blocks. No change is needed for the former, but the latter requires us to update the associated basic block pointers.

Function Pointers: the compiler uses indirect jumps (to functions) mostly to support shared libraries, C++ vtable, and tail/sibling calls. For example, the compiler generates the PLT and GOT tables for calls to external functions in a shared library [35]. The library is loaded at a random address unknown until the program runs. At the run-time, the linker resolves the address of each called external function and saves it in a GOT entry. A PLT entry is an executable trampoline that represents the actual function. It essentially is an indirect jump to the function address saved in its associated GOT entry. The PLT table is placed in a special

```
(A) jmpq     *0x480000(,%rax,8)

(B) jmpq     *0x8(%rax,%rcx,8)

(C) movslq  (%r9,%rbp,4),%rcx
    add      %r9,%rcx
    jmpq     *%rcx
```

Figure 2: Jump Table Examples

section. Remix leaves this section unchanged. Tail/sibling call optimization is also interesting. The compiler normally allocates a new stack frame for each function call. However, there are cases where the callee can safely share the caller's stack frame. Such a call is dubbed the tail call or the sibling call, depending on the location of the call instruction. A typical example of the tail call is tail-recursive functions [52], but compilers like gcc support the broader definition of tail/sibling call. They can identify these cases and reuse the callers' stack frames. If the callee is a function pointer, the compiler generates an indirect jump (instead of an indirect call) in order to reuse the stack frame. Remix does not need to change indirect jumps introduced by tail/sibling call optimization.

Saved Context: indirect jump is also used by the standard C library to restore saved context. For example, the `setjmp` and `sigsetjmp` functions save their calling context to a jump buffer, while the `longjmp` and `siglongjmp` functions restore the context saved by `setjmp` and `sigsetjmp`, respectively. Both functions use an indirect jump to continue the execution at the saved instruction pointer. After reordering basic blocks, Remix needs to update all the jump buffers. The most efficient solution is hooking the functions that save the context and record the locations of the jump buffers. Note that the saved registers in the jump buffer are encoded by glibc in a special format (PTR_MANGLE). The alternative approach to search the whole address space for jump buffers incurs unnecessary performance overhead as these functions are seldom used.

Jump Tables: jump tables are often generated by the compiler to speed up `switch/case` statements. If some cases are continuous, the compiler stores their handlers in a table, and uses the switch variable as an index to quickly locate the corresponding handler. On x86-64, various patterns of jump tables can be used [17] as shown in Figure 2. They all have a base address, an index register, and a scale. An entry in the jump table can be addressed by $(base + index * scale)$. For example, the bases of case A, B, and C are constant `0x480000`, register `rax`, and register `r9`, respectively, and the indexes are in the `rax`, `rcx`, and `rbp` respectively (in case C, `rbp` is used as a general-purpose register, not the stack frame base pointer.) Interestingly, while case A and B store the actual handler addresses in the table since they directly jump to the selected entry, case C stores the offsets between the table base and the handlers. Each offset is only four bytes (a pointer is 8 bytes on the x86-64 architecture.) To calculate the handler address, the code reads the offset into register `rcx` and adds it to the table base in register `r9`.

Handlers for a `switch/case` statement are some basic blocks of the enclosing function. Remix thus has to update them after reordering basic blocks. The first two cases are rather straightforward to handle: jump tables are typically placed in the `.rodata` section. We search this section looking for at least 3 consecutive addresses pointing to the code section. If these addresses are close enough to each other (e.g., no more than 1MB apart) and all point to a valid instruction, Remix updates them accordingly. Even though false positives are possible, we did not find it to be a problem during our experiments. This approach does not work on the third case whose jump table consists of offsets, not instruction addresses. A simple solution is to export some meta data (e.g., the table base and length) from the compiler for Remix to patch the table at the run-time. Remix then can locate each handler and adjust its offset by the displacement between the old handler address and the new one. Our prototype uses this approach. Another viable solution is to use pattern matching to locate the code similar to case C (registers might be different) and use an intra-procedural, backward program slicing [2, 56] to locate the table base and length. For example, the index (register `rbp` in case C) is often compared to the table's upper and lower limits to make sure that it is within the table's boundary. This gives us the valid range of the index and hence the table length. As for the table base, the compiler generates case C mostly for position-independent code (e.g, shared libraries). The table base is calculated at the run-time using the PC-relative addressing mode, which has its own patterns (Section 2.2). As such, the table base can be calculated using the program counter and an offset. This approach is more complicated but it is the only choice if the source code is not available.

Exception tables can be similarly patched. Each exception table entry consists of a code range and a handler. If an exception happens in that range, it should be handled by the associated handler. However, Remix might move a faulting instruction out of the range and cause no handler or a wrong handler to be called. To address that, we can either revert the faulting instruction to its original location or avoid moving basic blocks into and out of the range. Our prototype has yet to implement this feature. Nevertheless, we can complete our experiments (including the Apache server and a kernel file system) without any problem. Even though exception handling is exploited by malware or DRM software to *obfuscate* control flows, regular applications do not use it that way (i.e., they use it for exceptions, not regular control flows.) since exception handling is relatively slow.

2.4 Live Randomization of Kernel Modules

Live randomization of the kernel code faces many of the same challenges as that of user applications. For example, the kernel can be compiled to use jump tables for tight `switch/case` statements. The kernel may also use exception tables – the kernel often needs to access the user memory. To protect itself from untrusted applications, the kernel must verify every user address it accesses, an expensive operation that requires traversing the process' paging structures. Moreover, the vast majority of user addresses are benign and safe to access. To avoid unnecessary verification, the kernel accesses the user memory without a prior verification. Instead, it registers a page fault handler that will be called by the kernel if the memory access fails. These cases can be similarly handled as in the user-space.

Nevertheless, there are some differences between the kernel and user applications. For example, the kernel often embeds manual assembly code, which may not follow the paradigms of the compiled code. That code has to be handled case-by-case (for once). The return address conversion is more complicated than the user space because the changed return addresses could exist in any of the active kernel stacks (if a process is running in the user-space, its kernel stack is empty.) All these stacks need to be updated at once. In addition, a hardware interrupt can interrupt any instruction in the kernel or the user space. The interrupted address is saved on the kernel stack. If the interrupted instruction is in the kernel and has been moved, we can directly update the saved interrupt context. However, if the interrupted instruction is in the user space, Remix cannot update the kernel interrupt context, which is protected from the user space. Consequently, in the user space, Remix should not move an instruction that may be interrupted, i.e., the instruction that is currently executing. In our prototype, we stop the whole process (to guarantee consistency) and use a small agent to reorder basic blocks. The agent does not randomize itself. Even though it is possible to randomize the whole kernel, our prototype currently supports live randomization of kernel modules (e.g., the ReiserFS file system).

2.5 Performance Optimization

In this section, we present our strategies to improve the run-time performance of protected processes and to reduce the randomization latency.

2.5.1 *Probabilistic Loop Bundling*

Compilers make an effort to optimize the layout of the generated code for better performance. For example, gcc has an option to align loops to a power-of-two boundary (`-falign-loops`). If enabled, gcc inserts a number of NOPs before the loops to properly align them in the cache. If the loops are executed many times, the performance gain from the alignment outweighs the time wasted in executing NOPs. Remix, as well as other basic block randomization systems, disrupts this careful layout of the code. Because Remix randomly rearranges basic blocks, its final performance impact is somewhat unpredictable due to the complex interactions between the program and the cache hierarchy. For example, our early experiments find that Remix incurs low overhead for most SPEC CPU2006 benchmarks, but there are a couple of outliers with more than 15% overhead. To address that, we propose probabilistic loop bundling.

Loops are critical to the overall performance. A process often spends most of its execution time in loops. Changing the layout of loops might incur the largest impact to the performance. Accordingly, Remix focuses its optimization on the loops. It can probabilistically bundle the basic blocks of loops. A bundled loop has the same internal layout of basic blocks as the original, non-randomized loop. Within the boundary of a function, we consider the destination of a backward jump as the beginning of a loop and the jump as its end (even though this loop detection is quite rough, it is sufficient for our purpose.) We also control the size of a bundled loop by limiting the number of the jump and return instructions it contains. This avoids bundling large loops – for some functions, their bodies consist of a single large loop. Before the first randomization, Remix detects loops in the original code and records the layout of their basic blocks. During the live randomization, Remix flips a coin with certain probability to decide whether or not to bundle a loop. If a loop is bundled, its basic blocks are restored to the original, compiler-generated layout. The whole bundle is then treated as a single basic block and takes part in the randomization. In other words, a bundled loop is still moved around but its internal basic blocks remain relatively static. If possible, we make bundled loops to be 16-byte aligned. Our prototype bundles loops with a probability of $\frac{1}{3}$. i.e., about $\frac{2}{3}$ of the loops are randomized. Finally, we want to emphasize that each live randomization individually selects which loops to bundle. No loops will always be bundled.

Software	glibc	httpd	nginx	lighttpd	OpenSSL
NOP Space	42.9	19.3	26.2	22.1	19.9

Table 1: Average NOP Space per Function

2.5.2 *Meta-data Maintenance*

Remix reorders basic blocks from time to time to make the code layout unpredictable. This is a time consuming process especially for large programs. In addition, Remix has to stop the whole process during randomization to ensure consistency. Otherwise, a multi-threaded process might have unsuspecting threads executing partially randomized functions. To this end, Remix maintains some meta-data to facilitate live randomization. For example, it builds an index for basic blocks and some important instructions (e.g., `call` instructions and jump tables). The meta-data is built from the ground up in the first run and kept updated afterwards. With the meta-data, Remix can significantly reduce the randomization latency. To protect the meta-data from being leaked, we allocate its memory at a random location. Even though the meta-data is stored in the process' address space, it is isolated from the process itself because no pointers to the meta-data exist in the process (our prototype stores the base address for the meta-data out of the process. See Section 3.) Information leak vulnerabilities in the process cannot disclose the meta-data location or its content. To be more cautious, we could move the meta-data to random locations at undetermined intervals.

2.6 Binary-only Program Support

If the source code is available, Remix uses a (slightly) customized compiler to reserve enough space for extra jumps necessary to connect reordered basic blocks (Section 2.1). However, the source code is not always available, especially for commercial or legacy programs. Remix has a compatibility mode to support binary-only programs by leveraging the existing NOP padding in the code. As previously mentioned, compilers often insert NOP instructions to align functions and loops to a power-of-two boundary. As such, there are NOPs between and inside functions. Table 1 shows the average NOP space per function (in bytes) for several popular software packages. Remix can use the NOP space for its purpose. We treat small and large functions differently: small functions naturally contain less NOP instructions, but short jumps (2 bytes each, one byte for the opcode and the other byte for the displacement) are often enough to chain basic blocks; Large functions have more NOP space available, but basic blocks might be moved far apart from each other. To chain two basic blocks, we use short jumps whenever possible and long jumps otherwise. If the space runs short, we bundle some basic blocks together to reduce the extra jumps needed (similar to the loop bundling). During each live randomization, Remix picks different sets of basic blocks to bundle together. This ensures that a different code layout is generated each time.

3. IMPLEMENTATION

We have implemented a prototype of Remix for the Linux applications and the FreeBSD kernel modules on the x86-64 architecture. The FreeBSD kernel is chosen because it has better support for the LLVM/Clang compiler. In this section, we describe our prototype in detail.

We slightly modify the LLVM/Clang compiler to insert a 5-byte NOP instruction (`nopl 8(%rax, %rax)`) after each basic block. To achieve that, we add one line to the `EmitBasicBlockEnd` function in LLVM. These 5-byte NOPs also serve as delimiters for basic blocks because LLVM itself does not use this type of NOP (it does use other formats of NOPs, such as `xchg %ax,%ax`.) This makes basic block identification straightforward for Remix. To ensure that LLVM only generates long jumps (Section 2.2), we pass `-mc-relax-all` to the LLVM backend. However, it unnecessarily relaxes other instructions, such as `add` and `sub`, to full displacements as well. With more invasive changes to LLVM (likely in the `fixupNeedsRelaxation` function), we could make LLVM relax only branch instructions. We use Capstone, a cross-platform multi-architecture disassembly framework, to disassemble instructions in the memory. Linux enforces $w \oplus x$ for user applications, in which a block of memory is either writable or executable, but not both simultaneously. As such, we use the `mprotect()` system call to temporarily make the `.text` and `.rodata` sections writable. After live randomization, we set their permissions back.

A major implementation challenge is to guarantee the consistency of the process, especially for a multi-threaded process. All the threads should enter a consistent state before live randomization, and have their data updated before the execution is resumed. A viable solution is to use a kernel module and pause all the threads at the system call boundary. In our prototype, we use the `ptrace` interface to stop the whole process (for single-threaded processes, a timer signal can also serve this purpose.) Similarly, we need to put the kernel in a quiescent state and update all the affected kernel stacks consistently.

Ptrace is an interface for process tracing and debugging. It allows one process to inspect and control the execution of another process. We start the target program under the control of a small utility program, which is responsible for initiating live randomization at random intervals (for brevity, we call it the initiator.) When it is time for live randomization, the initiator sends a `SIGSTOP` signal to the target process and waits for it to stop. For each stopped thread, the initiator has full access to its execution context, including the registers and the program counter. Even though we could randomize the code with ptrace, the ptrace interface is too slow for this task – each access to the target process' memory must be conducted through an expensive system call. Instead, we pre-load a small agent in the target process and use ptrace to activate the agent. The agent performs the live randomization and returns the control back to the initiator when it finishes. The initiator can subsequently restores the process' state and resumes its execution at the interrupted instructions. However, these instructions might have been moved to different positions. To fix that, the initiator requests the agent to translate the interrupted program counters to their new values. To avoid interfering with the target process' heap and stacks, the agent uses the `mmap` system call to allocate new memory for its own heap and stack. The agent makes system calls directly instead of using the equivalent libc functions because it might be libc that Remix is currently randomizing (if so, libc is in an inconsistent state.) To prevent the agent from being exploited by code reuse attacks, the initiator relocates the agent from time to time. Moving the agent is much simpler than the live randomization of regular processes because the agent is small, position-independent, and self-contained (i.e., it does not rely on other libraries.)

In the FreeBSD kernel, live randomization is triggered by a timer. When the timer expires, we call the `smp_rendezvous` function to put all the CPUs in a consistent, quiescent state. `Smp_rendezvous` sends inter-processor interrupts to signal all the CPU cores. They rendezvous and execute the same set of functions. In our prototype, one core performs live randomization while others wait for it to finish. That core reorders the basic blocks of the target kernel module and searches the kernel stacks and other data structures for the affected basic block pointers. After randomization, all the cores are resumed and continue the interrupted execution.

Software	Apache	nginx	lighttpd
Average Basic Block #	15.3	18.8	14.4
Average NOP Space	19.3	26.2	22.1

Table 2: Statistics of Three Web Servers

4. EVALUATION

In this section, we first analyze the security guarantee of Remix and then measure its performance overhead with standard benchmarks.

4.1 Security

Remix randomly reorders basic blocks within their respective functions to increase entropy. It complements the existing ASLR support in commodity operating systems. ASLR randomly places the executable in the address space. It only provides a coarse-grained protection against code reuse attacks. The leak of a single code pointer, such as a function pointer or a return address, is often sufficient to de-randomize the whole executable. The attacker often leverages an information leak vulnerability to de-randomize the victim process before full-on attacks [51]. Remix can significantly improve ASLR's resilience to this type of information leak. It reorders the basic blocks of each function at random intervals. The actual code layout is unpredictable and keeps changing from time to time. Even if two systems run the exactly same programs, their run-time code layouts are different. Table 2 shows the average number of basic blocks per function for three popular web servers, Apache, nginx, and lighttpd. They all have about 16 basic blocks per function on average. Therefore, Remix adds about four bits of entropy to each instruction of these programs. This leads to about 20% to 25% boost in the entropy for 32-bit systems [46]. More importantly, Remix introduces the time as a variable to address space layout, making it a moving target. The compiler often spontaneously inserts NOP instructions to the generated programs to align functions or loops. Table 2 also shows the average NOP space per function (in bytes) for those programs. The NOP space can be leveraged to further increase the entropy by randomly placing NOPs between basic blocks. For short functions with less than 4 basic blocks, we also insert some additional NOP space to improve the entropy.

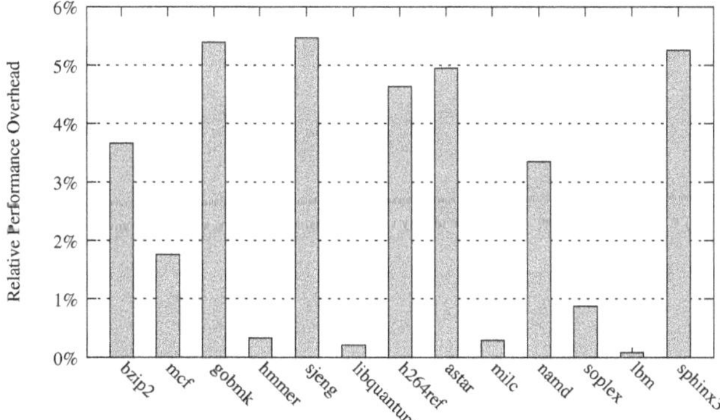

Figure 3: SPEC CPU2006 Performance Overhead

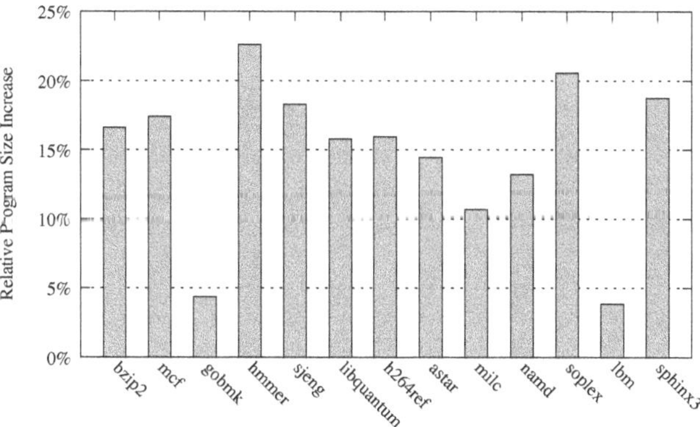

Figure 4: SPEC CPU2006 Size Increase

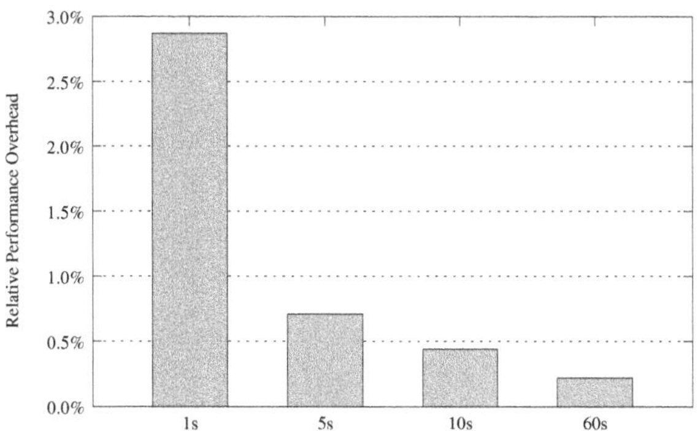

Figure 5: Apache Web Server Performance Overhead

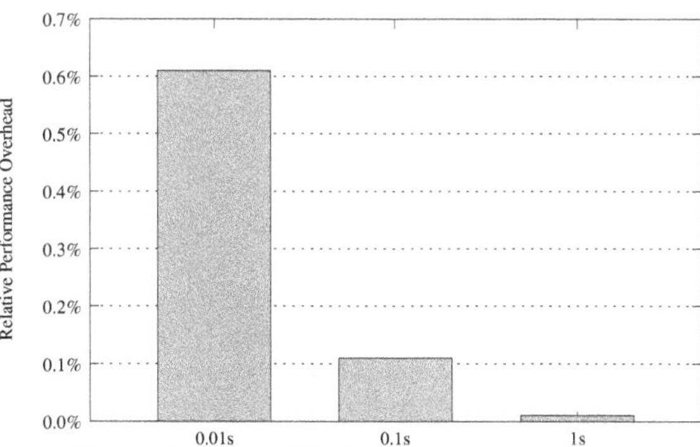

Figure 6: ReiserFS Performance Overhead

Recently, researchers have proposed a few novel attacks against fine-grained code randomization. For example, JIT-ROP (Just-in-time ROP [47]) repeatedly exploits a memory leak vulnerability to recursively map out the victim process' address space, and synthesizes code reuse attacks on demand. JIT-ROP is particularly detrimental to code randomization techniques that randomize the process only once at the compile or load time [49]. Remix's live randomization could potentially disrupt the JIT-ROP attack (if the code happens to be randomized by Remix during the attack), but it is not always effective. A sure defense against JIT-ROP is execute-only memory, in which the code can only be executed but not read. Fortunately, execute-only memory is being adopted by major CPU architectures [4, 19, 31] and can be emulated in the software [6, 26]. Remix should incorporate the execute-only memory as a defense-in-depth solution. For performance reasons, our prototype implants an agent and its meta-data into the target process. However, it is unlikely that JIT-ROP could find these artifacts. Even though they exist in the process' address space, they are isolated from the process itself because the process has no pointers to them. In addition, we could move them to random locations from time to time. JIT-ROP carefully maps the victim process' address space to avoid accessing invalid memory. Blindly probing the Remix memory most certainly will trigger a general protection exception and be foiled. BROP [10] is another attack against fine-grained code randomization, which exploits a victim process many times to essentially brute-force it in order to locate useful gadgets (it assumes the process would be restarted upon crash.) During this long process, Remix likely has randomized the process a few times, making the probed gadgets useless.

4.2 Performance

The performance impact of Remix mostly comes from the following two aspects: first, live randomization has to stop the whole process or the kernel to ensure consistency. This introduces some latency to the whole process. Second, Remix rearranges the code layout. Modern computer architectures rely heavily on the cache for performance. Changing the process' code layout can affect its cache profile and by extension the performance. We measure both aspects with standard benchmarks (SPEC CPU2006) and a number of popular applications. All the experiments are performed on a third-generation Intel Core i7 machine with 16 GB of memory. The operating system is the 64-bit Ubuntu 14.04.2 LTS. LLVM version 3.6 is used as the base compiler.

To measure the execution overhead, we randomize the SPEC CPU2006 benchmarks once (with a probability of $\frac{1}{3}$ for loop bundling) and compare their performance to the baseline built with the unmodified LLVM compiler. All the experiments are repeated 20 times. The standard deviation of the experiments is negligible. Figure 3 shows the performance overhead caused by Remix (C++ benchmarks with exceptions currently are not supported yet.) The overhead for most benchmarks are less than 5% with an average of 2.8%. To reserve space for reordering basic blocks, Remix inserts a 5-byte NOP instruction after every basic block. It also relaxes various instructions to use larger constants (e.g., `jmp` and `call`). This could substantially increase the program binary size. Figure 4 shows the size increase of SPEC CPU2006. The average increase in size is 14.8%. We use ApacheBench to measure the performance impact of live randomization intervals. We run the Apache server and ApacheBench on two directly connected machines. We use ApacheBench to send $5 * 10^6$ requests to the server with a concurrency of 10. We set Remix to periodically randomize the server with an interval of 1, 5, 10, and 60 seconds, respectively. As expected, one-second interval incurs the highest overhead (2.9%). The overhead gradually decreases as the time interval increases. At the ten-second interval, the overhead is only 0.44%.

Remix not only supports user-space applications but also kernel modules. Our experiments are based on the FreeBSD kernel as it has better support for the LLVM/Clang compiler. We use Remix to live randomize the ReiserFS kernel driver [44]. IOZone, a user-space file system benchmark [40], is used to measure the performance of ReiserFS under different randomization intervals. We test the stride read of a large file in the automatic mode with a record size from 4KB to 512MB. The performance overhead of Remix is negligible even with a randomization interval of 0.01 seconds (Figure 6). This is expected as the performance bottleneck is in the disk I/O. We also test the read/re-read operations and get very similar results.

5. DISCUSSION

In this section, we discuss some possible improvements to Remix. *First*, Remix reorders basic blocks within their respective functions. The entropy increase by Remix is thus limited by the number of basic blocks in the function. Smaller functions have fewer basic blocks and thus benefit less from Remix. In our prototype, we insert extra NOP space in small functions to increase the entropy. Furthermore, we could incorporate fine-grained code randomization [30] specifically for these small functions. One of the key benefit of reordering basic blocks within functions is that function entry points remain at their intended location. Consequently, there is no need to migrate stale function pointers, which in general is an unsolvable problem. However, this does not necessarily require that basic blocks remain within function boundaries. We could randomly place basic blocks in the whole address space, and use a long jump at each function entry point to jump to its first basic block. This system has the benefits of binary stirring's higher entropy gain and Remix's simpler live randomization. However, its spatial locality of the randomized code is even more fragmented than our current design. It is necessary to carefully study the optimal basic block layout for better performance and security. Meanwhile, Remix does not *lively* move functions to avoid the complex runtime fixing of stale function pointers. Functions are nevertheless randomized at least once during the program startup by ASLR. Remix is a highly composable technique. It can be naturally integrated with systems that lively randomize functions [27] or with other techniques.

Second, some programs contain code that cannot be automatically randomized by Remix, such as inline assembly code, which sometimes does not follow the (relatively) clean paradigm as the compiled code. For example, kernels often use inline assembly in trampolines for interrupt handlers. A trampoline prepares the kernel stack to handle pending interrupts. The addresses of these trampolines are stored in the interrupt vector table. When an interrupt is triggered, the CPU indexes into this table and dispatches the corresponding handler. If these trampolines are reordered, we need to update the interrupt vector table. In addition, some programs have code that cannot be cleanly disassembled (e.g., the obfuscated code), and programs like just-in-time compiler can dynamically generate binary code. There does not seem to have a universal solution to these diverse problems. We instead have to handle them case-by-case. For example, we could incorporate the design of Remix into the JIT compiler so that dynamically generated code can also be randomized.

Third, Remix performs live randomization of the target process at an undetermined interval. The choice of this interval is a trade-off between randomization latency and security. As mentioned earlier, Remix provides probabilistic protection against information-leak based attacks such as JIT-ROP [47] (Section 4.1). That is, the protection is in effect if Remix happens to randomize the target process during the attack. As such, an interesting criterion to decide the live randomization interval is how likely Remix can disrupt these attacks. Our prototype uses an interval of ten seconds as a trade-off between randomization latency and security. Like other code randomization systems, Remix is, after all, a probabilistic defense. A more complete, defense-in-depth system should combine Remix with specific defenses against those attacks (e.g., execute-only memory to prevent JIT-ROP).

Lastly, Remix inserts an extra NOP instruction after each basic block to reserve space for reordering basic blocks. A program built by Remix is still a valid one that can be executed standalone. It is just larger (14.8% average size increase for SPEC CPU2006) and probably runs slower. Our tests show that Remix-built programs run mostly as fast as or only slightly slower than the original programs. This result is expected as modern processors have an efficient and intelligent instruction prefetching system. However, there are a few outliers that execute even faster than the baseline. This is probably caused by the complex interaction between the instruction alignment and the cache hierarchy. Native client (NaCl) shows similar results [53]. NaCl is a software fault isolation system that can safely execute native code in the web browser. In NaCl, the untrusted code is divided into equal-sized fragments, and no instructions can cross the fragment boundary. NOP instructions are used to pad the fragments if necessary.

6. RELATED WORK

In this section, we present the state-of-the-art in the research of code reuse attacks and defenses.

ROP Defenses: the first category of related work is various defenses against return-oriented programming (ROP). ROP exploits short snippets of the existing code, called gadgets, for malicious purposes [12, 45]. Gadgets of ROP end with a return instruction. This allows the attacker to chain a number of gadgets together using a crafted stack. ROP has been demonstrated to be Turing-complete when given a reasonably sized code base. Variations of ROP that do not rely on return instructions have also been proposed [11, 15]. Code randomization and control-flow integrity are two systematic defenses against ROP (we will discuss them in this section later.) Besides, there are a wide variety of diverse ROP defenses. For example, G-free eliminates usable gadgets at compile time by removing unaligned free-branch instructions [41]. Return-less also leverages a customized compiler to remove intended and unintended return instructions [36]. KBouncer [43] and ROPecker [16] detects ROP attacks by checking whether the path to a sensitive system call contains too many indirect branches to "short" gadgets.

Recent work shows that this approach might not be effective [13]. In particular, the threshold is very difficult to determine [29].

Software Diversity: the second category of closely related work is software diversity, in which the program code or data are diversified to foil attacks that depend on knowing particular program attributes [34]. For example, ROP chains the gadgets together by arranging their addresses on the stack. Each gadget ends with a return instruction, which pops the next gadget address from the stack and executes it. As such, ROP needs to know the gadget addresses. To defeat ROP, code randomization aims at making gadget addresses unpredictable. Code randomization systems differ in the randomization granularity. Address space layout randomization (ASLR) is a popular coarse-grained code randomization system. It places the program binary as a whole at a random base address [48]. Consequently, ASLR has limited entropy on the 32-bit architectures [46]. Because the program internal layout is not changed, ASLR is especially vulnerable to information leak attacks. A single leaked code pointer can de-randomize the whole process. ASLP works at a finer granularity than ASLR [33]. It permutes functions and static data objects in addition to randomizing the section bases. In comparison, Remix works on the basic blocks and also supports live randomization of running processes. Binary stirring is one of the fine-grained code randomization systems. It also works at the basic block level. However, it stirs basic block globally for once at the load time. Remix instead reorders basic blocks within their respective functions. This localizes the changes required to compensate the moved basic blocks. It allows a relatively simple implementation of live randomization. Giuffrida et al. proposes a live randomization system that relies on heavy compiler customization to output meta-data for the pointer conversion [27]. In particular, it needs to migrate function pointers which may involve unsolvable ambiguity and require manual efforts. Remix confines the changes (mostly) to functions, and thus are easier to implement. At an even finer granularity, some systems randomize the instruction set through encoding or encryption to defeat code injection and code reuse attacks [8, 32]. ILR randomizes the location of every instruction [30]. It uses a process virtual machine (Strata) to execute the scattered code. IPR rewrites instruction sequences with equivalent same-length instructions [42]. It can eliminate about 10% useful gadgets and probabilistically break 80% of them. It supports various concrete transformations, such as atomic instruction substitution, instruction reordering, and register reassignment. Data randomization has also been proposed to prevent data-based attacks [9, 18].

Code randomization systems are often vulnerable to information leak attacks. For example, the coarse-grained ASLR could be de-randomized by even one leaked code pointer. Fine-grained code randomization systems like binary stirring are more resilient to leaked code pointers, but are still vulnerable to the leak of memory contents. For example, JIT-ROP repeatedly exploits a memory leak vulnerability to map the victim process' code in order to launch an on-demand ROP attack [47]. A few systems have been proposed to enhance fine-grained code randomization to withstand JIT-ROP attacks [6, 19, 26]. They all utilize the execute-only memory in which the code can only be executed but not read. Remix only provides probabilistic defense against JIT-ROP attacks (Section 4.1). Remix should integrate execute-only memory when it is available in the commodity hardware. Such a combination would significantly raise the bar of code reuse attacks.

Control-Flow Integrity: Control-flow integrity is another effective defense against code reuse attacks [1]. It inserts in-line monitors to confine the run-time control flow to the program's (static) control-flow graph. CFI systems vary in the protection granularity. Fine-grained CFI provides a strong protection against most control-flow hijacking attacks, but often has high performance overhead. It also requires a precise control-flow graph that still is not readily available in the commodity compilers. Recent research effort focuses on reducing CFI performance overhead for commodity programs [54, 55]. They trade the protection granularity for performance, leading to potential vulnerabilities [23, 28]. Opaque CFI uses coarse-grained control-flow integrity to strengthen fine-grained code randomization against certain types of information leak attacks [38]. Instead of validating the exact target address, OCFI ensures that the target is within a certain randomized bound. RockJIT leverages modular CFI to protect the JIT compiler and the dynamically generated code [39]. It builds a fine-grained CFG from the source code of the JIT compiler, and keeps the control-flow policy updated with the new generated code. Even though most CFI systems are implemented in the software, hardware architectural support for CFI has been proposed that can substantially simplify and speed up CFI systems [25].

In addition to control-flow integrity, researchers have proposed other security properties that can prevent code reuse attacks. For example, data-flow integrity (DFI) enforces that run-time data flow must follow the data-flow graph [14]. DFI can prevent many memory vulnerabilities from being exploited. Code-pointer integrity (CPI) separates sensitive data, such as code pointers and pointers leading to code pointers, from regular data to protect them from unauthorized modification.

7. SUMMARY

We have presented the design and implementation of Remix, a live randomization system for user-space applications and kernel modules. Remix randomly reorders basic blocks within their respective functions at undetermined time intervals. it can substantially increase the entropy of ASLR, one of our most important defenses against code reuse attacks. By randomizing the code layout, Remix can significantly enhance ASLR's defense against certain types of information leak vulnerabilities. Remix is a flexible and composable defense technique due to its unique design and efficiency. It brings to the composed systems extra entropy that changes with the time. Our experiments with both standard and application benchmarks show that Remix only incurs a small performance overhead.

8. ACKNOWLEDGMENTS

We would like to thank the anonymous reviewers for their insightful comments that greatly helped improve the presentation of this paper. This work was supported in part by the US National Science Foundation (NSF) under Grant 1453020. Any opinions, findings, and conclusions or recommendations expressed in this material are those of the authors and do not necessarily reflect the views of the NSF.

9. REFERENCES

[1] M. Abadi, M. Budiu, U. Erlingsson, and J. Ligatti. Control-Flow Integrity: Principles, Implementations, and Applications. In *Proceedings of the 12th ACM Conference on Computer and Communications Security*, 2005.

[2] H. Agrawal and J. R. Horgan. Dynamic Program Slicing. In *ACM SIGPLAN Notices*, volume 25, pages 246–256. ACM, 1990.

[3] Apple. OS X MountainLion Core Technologies Overview. http://movies.apple.com/media/us/osx/2012/docs/OSX_MountainLion_Core_Technologies_Overview.pdf.

[4] ARM: the Architecture for the Digital World. http://www.arm.com/.

[5] Linux Kernel Address Space Layout Randomization. http://lwn.net/Articles/569635/.

[6] M. Backes, T. Holz, B. Kollenda, P. Koppe, S. Nürnberger, and J. Pewny. You Can Run but You Can't Read: Preventing Disclosure Exploits in Executable Code. In *Proceedings of the 21st ACM Conference on Computer and Communications Security*, 2014.

[7] M. Backes and S. Nürnberger. Oxymoron: Making fine-grained memory randomization practical by allowing code sharing. In *Proceedings of the 23rd USENIX Security Symposium*, 2014.

[8] E. G. Barrantes, D. H. Ackley, S. Forrest, and D. Stefanović. Randomized Instruction Set Emulation. *ACM Transactions on Information and System Security*, 8(1):3–40, 2005.

[9] S. Bhatkar and R. Sekar. Data Space Randomization. In *Proceedings of the 5th Conference on Detection of Intrusions and Malware, and Vulnerability Assessment*, 2008.

[10] A. Bittau, A. Belay, A. Mashtizadeh, D. Mazieres, and D. Boneh. Hacking Blind. In *Proceedings of the 35th IEEE Symposium on Security and Privacy*, 2014.

[11] T. Bletsch, X. Jiang, V. W. Freeh, and Z. Liang. Jump-oriented Programming: A New Class of Code-reuse Attack. In *Proceedings of the 6th ACM Symposium on Information, Computer and Communications Security*, 2011.

[12] E. Buchanan, R. Roemer, H. Shacham, and S. Savage. When Good Instructions Go Bad: Generalizing Return-Oriented Programming to RISC. In *Proceedings of the 15th ACM Conference on Computer and Communications Security*, 2008.

[13] N. Carlini and D. Wagner. Rop is Still Dangerous: Breaking Modern Defenses. In *Proceedings of the 23rd USENIX Security Symposium*, 2014.

[14] M. Castro, M. Costa, and T. Harris. Securing Software by Enforcing Data-flow Integrity. In *Proceedings of the 7th Symposium on Operating Systems Design and Implementation*, 2006.

[15] S. Checkoway, L. Davi, A. Dmitrienko, A.-R. Sadeghi, H. Shacham, and M. Winandy. Return-oriented Programming without Returns. In *Proceedings of the 17th ACM Conference on Computer and Communications Security*, 2010.

[16] Y. Cheng, Z. Zhou, M. Yu, X. Ding, and R. H. Deng. ROPecker: A Generic and Practical Approach for Defending against ROP Attacks. In *Proceedings of the 21st Network and Distributed Systems Security Symposium*, 2014.

[17] C. Cifuentes and M. Van Emmerik. Recovery of Jump Table Case Statements from Binary Code. In *Proceedings of 7th International Workshop on Program Comprehension*, 1999.

[18] C. Cowan, S. Beattie, J. Johansen, and P. Wagle. Pointguard TM: protecting pointers from buffer overflow vulnerabilities. In *Proceedings of the 12th conference on USENIX Security Symposium*, 2003.

[19] S. Crane, C. Liebchen, A. Homescu, L. Davi, P. Larsen, A.-R. Sadeghi, S. Brunthaler, and M. Franz. Readactor: Practical Code Randomization Resilient to Memory Disclosure. In *Proceedings of the 36th IEEE Symposium on Security and Privacy*, 2015.

[20] Memory Protection Technologies. http://technet.microsoft.com/en-us/library/bb457155.aspx.

[21] x86 NX support. http://lwn.net/Articles/87814/.

[22] L. Davi, C. Liebchen, A.-R. Sadeghi, K. Z. Snow, and F. Monrose. Isomeron: Code randomization resilient to (just-in-time) return-oriented programming. In *Proceedings of the 22nd Network and Distributed Systems Security Symposium*, 2015.

[23] L. Davi, A.-R. Sadeghi, D. Lehmann, and F. Monrose. Stitching the Gadgets: On the Ineffectiveness of Coarse-Grained Control-Flow Integrity Protection. In *Proceedings of the 23rd USENIX Security Symposium*, 2014.

[24] Data Execution Prevention. http://en.wikipedia.org/wiki/Data_Execution_Prevention.

[25] U. Erlingsson, M. Abadi, and M.-D. Budiu. Architectural Support for Software-based Protection, Mar. 13 2012. US Patent 8,136,091.

[26] J. Gionta, W. Enck, and P. Ning. HideM: Protecting the Contents of Userspace Memory in the Face of Disclosure Vulnerabilities. In *Proceedings of the 5th ACM conference on Data and application security and privacy*, 2015.

[27] C. Giuffrida, A. Kuijsten, and A. S. Tanenbaum. Enhanced Operating System Security Through Efficient and Fine-grained Address Space Randomization. In *Proceedings of the 21st USENIX Conference on Security Symposium*, 2012.

[28] E. Göktas, E. Athanasopoulos, H. Bos, and G. Portokalidis. Out of Control: Overcoming Control-Flow Integrity. In *Proceedings of the 35th IEEE Symposium on Security and Privacy*, 2014.

[29] E. Göktaş, E. Athanasopoulos, M. Polychronakis, H. Bos, and G. Portokalidis. Size Does Matter: Why Using Gadget-chain Length to Prevent Code-reuse Attacks is Hard. In *Proceedings of the 23rd USENIX Security Symposium*, 2014.

[30] J. Hiser, A. Nguyen-Tuong, M. Co, M. Hall, and J. W. Davidson. ILR: Where'd My Gadgets Go? In *Proceedings of the 33rd IEEE Symposium on Security and Privacy*, 2012.

[31] Intel. *Intel 64 and IA-32 Architectures Software Developer's Manual*, 2014.

[32] G. S. Kc, A. D. Keromytis, and V. Prevelakis. Countering Code-injection Attacks with

Instruction-set Randomization. In *Proceedings of the 10th ACM Conference on Computer and Communications Security*, 2003.

[33] C. Kil, J. Jun, C. Bookholt, J. Xu, and P. Ning. Address Space Layout Permutation (ASLP): Towards Fine-Grained Randomization of Commodity Software. In *Proceedings of the 22nd Annual Computer Security Applications Conference*, 2006.

[34] P. Larsen, A. Homescu, S. Brunthaler, and M. Franz. Sok: Automated Software Diversity. In *Proceedings of the 35th IEEE Symposium on Security and Privacy*, 2014.

[35] J. R. Levine. *Linkers and Loaders*. Morgan Kaufmann, 1999.

[36] J. Li, Z. Wang, X. Jiang, M. Grace, and S. Bahram. Defeating Return-Oriented Rootkits with "Return-less" Kernels. In *Proceedings of the 5th ACM SIGOPS EuroSys Conference*, 2010.

[37] A. I. Mark Russinovich, David Solomon. *Windows Internals, 6th Edition*. Microsoft Press, 2012.

[38] V. Mohan, P. Larsen, S. Brunthaler, K. Hamlen, and M. Franz. Opaque Control-Flow Integrity. In *Proceedings of the 22nd Network and Distributed Systems Security Symposium*, 2015.

[39] B. Niu and G. Tan. RockJIT: Securing Just-in-time Compilation Using Modular Control-flow Integrity. In *Proceedings of the 21st ACM Conference on Computer and Communications Security*, 2014.

[40] W. D. Norcott and D. Capps. Iozone Filesystem Benchmark. *URL: www.iozone.org*, 2003.

[41] K. Onarlioglu, L. Bilge, A. Lanzi, D. Balzarotti, and E. Kirda. G-Free: Defeating Return-oriented Programming Through Gadget-less Binaries. In *Proceedings of the 26th Annual Computer Security Applications Conference*, 2010.

[42] V. Pappas, M. Polychronakis, and A. D. Keromytis. Smashing the Gadgets: Hindering Return-Oriented Programming Using In-place Code Randomization. In *Proceedings of the 33rd IEEE Symposium on Security and Privacy*, 2012.

[43] V. Pappas, M. Polychronakis, and A. D. Keromytis. Transparent ROP Exploit Mitigation Using Indirect Branch Tracing. In *Proceedings of the 22nd USENIX Conference on Security*, 2013.

[44] H. Reiser. ReiserFS, 2004.

[45] H. Shacham. The Geometry of Innocent Flesh on the Bone: Return-Into-Libc without Function Calls (on the x86). In *Proceedings of the 14th ACM Conference on Computer and Communications Security*, October 2007.

[46] H. Shacham, M. Page, B. Pfaff, E.-J. Goh, N. Modadugu, and D. Boneh. On the Effectiveness of Address-space Randomization. In *Proceedings of the 11th ACM Conference on Computer and Communications Security*, 2004.

[47] K. Z. Snow, F. Monrose, L. Davi, A. Dmitrienko, C. Liebchen, and A.-R. Sadeghi. Just-in-time Code Reuse: On the Effectiveness of Fine-grained Address Space Layout Randomization. In *Proceedings of the 34th IEEE Symposium on Security and Privacy*, 2013.

[48] P. Team. PaX Address Space Layout Randomization (ASLR), 2003.

[49] R. Wartell, V. Mohan, K. W. Hamlen, and Z. Lin. Binary Stirring: Self-randomizing Instruction Addresses of Legacy x86 Binary Code. In *Proceedings of the 19th ACM Conference on Computer and Communications Security*, 2012.

[50] Wikipedia. Basic Block. http://en.wikipedia.org/wiki/Basic_block.

[51] Wikipedia. Pwn2Own. http://en.wikipedia.org/wiki/Pwn2Own.

[52] Wikipedia. Tail Call. http://en.wikipedia.org/wiki/Tail_call.

[53] B. Yee, D. Sehr, G. Dardyk, J. B. Chen, R. Muth, T. Orm, S. Okasaka, N. Narula, N. Fullagar, and G. Inc. Native Client: A Sandbox for Portable, Untrusted x86 Native Code. In *Proceedings of the 30th IEEE Symposium on Security and Privacy*, 2009.

[54] C. Zhang, T. Wei, Z. Chen, L. Duan, L. Szekeres, S. McCamant, D. Song, and W. Zou. Practical Control Flow Integrity and Randomization for Binary Executables. In *Proceedings of the 34th IEEE Symposium on Security and Privacy*, 2013.

[55] M. Zhang and R. Sekar. Control Flow Integrity for COTS Binaries. In *Proceedings of the 22nd USENIX Security Symposium*, 2013.

[56] X. Zhang, R. Gupta, and Y. Zhang. Precise Dynamic Slicing Algorithms. In *Proceedings of the 25th International Conference on Software Engineering*, 2003.

Derandomizing Kernel Address Space Layout for Memory Introspection and Forensics

Yufei Gu
The University of Texas at Dallas
800 W. Campbell RD
Richardson, TX 75080
yufei.gu@utdallas.edu

Zhiqiang Lin
The University of Texas at Dallas
800 W. Campbell RD
Richardson, TX 75080
zhiqiang.lin@utdallas.edu

ABSTRACT

Modern OS kernels including Windows, Linux, and Mac OS all have adopted kernel Address Space Layout Randomization (ASLR), which shifts the base address of kernel code and data into different locations in different runs. Consequently, when performing introspection or forensic analysis of kernel memory, we cannot use any pre-determined addresses to interpret the kernel events. Instead, we must derandomize the address space layout and use the new addresses. However, few efforts have been made to derandomize the kernel address space and yet there are many questions left such as which approach is more efficient and robust. Therefore, we present the first systematic study of how to derandomize a kernel when given a memory snapshot of a running kernel instance. Unlike the derandomization approaches used in traditional memory exploits in which only remote access is available, with introspection and forensics applications, we can use all the information available in kernel memory to generate signatures and derandomize the ASLR. In other words, there exists a large volume of solutions for this problem. As such, in this paper we examine a number of typical approaches to generate strong signatures from both kernel code and data based on the insight of how kernel code and data is updated, and compare them from efficiency (in terms of simplicity, speed etc.) and robustness (e.g., whether the approach is hard to be evaded or forged) perspective. In particular, we have designed four approaches including brute-force code scanning, patched code signature generation, unpatched code signature generation, and read-only pointer based approach, according to the intrinsic behavior of kernel code and data with respect to kernel ASLR. We have gained encouraging results for each of these approaches and the corresponding experimental results are reported in this paper.

CCS Concepts

•Security and privacy → Operating systems security; Operating systems security; Virtualization and security; •Applied computing → System forensics;

CODASPY'16, March 09 - 11, 2016, New Orleans, LA, USA

ISBN 978-1-4503-3935-3/16/03. . . $15.00

DOI: http://dx.doi.org/10.1145/2857705.2857707

Keywords

Kernel Address Space Layout Randomization; Virtual Machine Introspection; Memory Forensics

1. INTRODUCTION

Address space layout randomization (ASLR) [27] has become a prominent defense against the attacks that use a hard-coded address to compromise vulnerable systems. Examples of such attacks include Internet worms that use the same virtual address to compromise the control flow of the same vulnerable program, or some kernel rootkits that overwrite the same virtual address to hide or redirect the kernel control flow. At a high level, ASLR randomizes the base address of program code and data including both heap and stack. Consequently, traditional memory exploits through return-into-libc [10, 19] or return oriented programming (ROP) [24, 9] can be mitigated because of the memory address diversity enabled by ASLR. ASLR has also been pushed to the kernel space due to the existence of the exploitable vulnerabilities in OS kernels as well as the threats from kernel rootkits. Modern OS kernels such as Windows, Linux, and Mac OS all have adopted ASLR to randomize both the kernel code and the kernel data including those in kernel global, heap and stack regions. As such, the address of kernel code and data (e.g., system call dispatcher table) will be relocated to different memory locations in different runs.

The implication of kernel ASLR has twofold: on one hand it significantly decreases the success rate of kernel memory exploits as well as some kernel rootkit attacks; on the other hand it also hinders the application of online kernel introspection [14] and offline kernel memory forensics, both of which need to interpret (or reconstruct) kernel events outside of the (guest) OS. Specifically, for an introspection and forensic tool to be effective, it often requires a pre-knowledge of the OS kernel such as where kernel code and important kernel data structure is located. For instance, to interpret a system call event, it requires to know the address of the system call tables (e.g., [13]); to intercept the kernel object allocation and deallocation, it requires to know the addresses of the functions that manages the kernel heaps (e.g., [30]); to traverse certain dynamically allocated kernel objects, it needs to know their rooted global addresses (e.g., [12]). Unfortunately, kernel ASLR will randomize these addresses, and we must derandomize them for introspection and forensics.

From the offense perspective, there are already several attempts to derandomize the user space ASLR. In particular, Shacham et al. [25] demonstrated the first brute-force linear search approach, which only requires 2^{16} probes at worst (2^{15} on average) to derandomize the address space of a vulnerable program for a 32-bit ASLR implementation. Such a brute-force approach was also used in recent BROP [8] attack to bypass the ASLR protection. Additionally, another way to derandomize ASLR is through information leakage. Roglia et al. [21] demonstrated a surgical approach to return to randomized libc by exploiting information about the base address of libc in victim process memory and also combing the code fragments available at fixed locations and use them to discover the address of other libc functions. Meanwhile, unlike this single memory disclosure, recent JIT-ROP [26] attack leverages multiple memory disclosures to bypass fine-grained ASLR through repeatedly abusing a memory disclosure to map an application's memory layout on-the-fly and dynamically discover the attack gadgets.

Interestingly, while we can use these offensive techniques, which have only the *remote access* to derandomize the user space ASLR, we have the *local access* of the entire memory for introspection or forensics applications and we can leverage such an advantage to derandomize the kernel ASLR. For instance, memory forensics tools such as Volatility [29] uses a KDBG signature (a sequence of bytes) to derandomize Windows kernel address space. In other words, there are too many options (e.g., too many signatures) to perform the derandomization when having the physical access of the kernel memory. Given such a large volume of solution space, there is however no study that has searched for the optimal solutions in terms of both robustness (i.e., hard to evade) and efficiency (i.e., having a fast performance).

Therefore, in this paper, we conduct the first systematic study to search for the optimal solutions for introspection and forensics to derandomize the kernel ASLR. In particular, since the key challenge lies in deriving the strong and robust signatures inside kernel memory, we systematically examine both kernel read-only code and data that can be used to derandomize the ASLR. For read-only kernel data, we examine the strings and entries of code pointers (e.g., jump tables) and we propose to use the entries of the code pointers as the signatures. For kernel code, we examine how kernel code is updated, from which to derive the robust signatures. We also perform a comparison study among these approaches by using robustness and efficiency metrics.

In summary, this paper makes the following contributions:

- We make the first systematic study in searching for the optimal solutions of derandomizing kernel ASLR for virtual machine introspection and memory forensics.
- We revisit, examine, and devise four different approaches from kernel code and data perspective. Among them, three are novel approaches that have not been reported, and they explore the intrinsic properties of kernel code and also the way of how kernel code and data is updated.
- We have implemented these approaches and compared them using the metrics of robustness and efficiency. We have tested 20 recent Linux kernels, and the detailed experimental results are reported in this paper.

2. BACKGROUND AND RELATED WORK

Software is so complicated today especially for an OS kernel, and it contains inevitable vulnerabilities. As discussed earlier, due to the existence of exploitable vulnerabilities inside OS kernels and those rootkit attacks, modern OSes all have pushed ASLR into kernel space, for instance:

- **Microsoft Windows**. Starting from Windows Vista (released in January 2007) [2], Microsoft has enabled ASLR inside the kernel space.
- **Linux**. Starting from the kernel version 3.14 (released in March 2014) [5], Linux supports the kernel ASLR. While currently it is disabled by default, users can turn it on by configuring the kernel compilation options and then rebuilding the kernel.
- **Mac OS**. Starting from OS X Mountain Lion 10.8 (released in July 2012) [4], the entire system (include the kernel) supports ASLR.

Therefore, kernel ASLR has become a de facto standard for modern OS. At a high level, it relocates both kernel code and data into different locations in different runs of the kernel. Consequently, we must derandomize the kernel address space layout before performing the introspection or forensics analysis.

State-of-the-art. A straightforward approach to derandomize the kernel ASLR would be devising strong signatures from OS kernel code or data, and then searching for them to derandomize the address. Volatility [29], a memory forensic analysis tool, uses such an approach to derandomize the Windows kernel (currently it does not support Linux kernel yet). Specifically, Volatility uses the Windows KdDebuggerDataBlock (KDBG), a data structure maintained by the Windows kernel for debugging purposes. KDBG contains a list of the running processes and loaded kernel modules. It also contains some version information. Identifying this data structure in memory can reveal many useful information including certain code addresses of the kernel. Meanwhile, the header of this data structure also contains some unique binary for different Windows versions, which can serve as signatures.

Therefore, Volatility contains a kdbgscan plugin, which is particularly designed to scan the KDBG, from which to derandomize the ASLR. A list of the signatures used by kdbgscan is presented in Table 1. We can notice that these signatures are very short (at most 14 bytes in length), and more importantly, these data are located in writable kernel data sections, which means a non-collaborative guest OS can easily cheat the introspection or the forensics tool. We have verified that the signatures used by kdbgscan can be easily modified without crashing the kernel. Therefore, we need robust signatures to derandomize the kernel ASLR. Our paper focuses on how to derive such robust signatures.

Other related works. There are also efforts focusing on fingerprinting guest OS kernel version. While derandomzing kernel ASLR and kernel version fingerprinting are different problems, they share certain similarity in that they both have to derive and search for strong signatures from an OS kernel. Meanwhile, kernel version fingerprinting can be used as a first step for derandomizing the ASLR for a specific kernel, though it might also be possible to use the strong and unique signatures to directly derandomize the kernel ASLR without the fingerprinting step. Therefore, kernel fingerprinting technique can help derandomize the kernel ASLR. The signatures used in the kernel ASLR derandomization can also complement the kernel fingerprinting depending on whether they are unique or not.

In the past a few years, there are a number of efforts focusing on how to fingerprint the guest OS version when having the physical access of the computer (e.g., in the cloud environment for cloud providers). UFO [20] is one such a system that explores the discrepancies in the CPU state for different OSes. By profiling, extracting, and differing the values in CPU registers such as GDT, IDT, CS, CR, and TR, UFO can generate unique signatures for a family of Windows kernels.

OS-Sommelier [15] is another system that explores robust signatures from kernel code to fingerprint the guest OS. More specifically,

Kernel Version	Signature (Byte Sequence)	Size (Bytes)
VistaSP0x86	00 00 00 00 00 00 00 00 4b 44 42 47 28 03	14
VistaSP1x86	00 00 00 00 00 00 00 00 4b 44 42 47 30 03	14
VistaSP2x86	00 00 00 00 00 00 00 00 4b 44 42 47 30 03	14
VistaSP0x64	00 f8 ff ff 4b 44 42 47 28 03	10
VistaSP1x64	00 f8 ff ff 4b 44 42 47 30 03	10
VistaSP2x64	00 f8 ff ff 4b 44 42 47 30 03	10
Win7SP1x64	00 f8 ff ff 4b 44 42 47 40 03	10
Win7SP1x86	00 00 00 00 00 00 00 00 4b 44 42 47 40 03	14
Win7SP0x86	00 00 00 00 00 00 00 00 4b 44 42 47 40 03	14
Win7SP0x64	00 f8 ff ff 4b 44 42 47 40 03	10
Win2008SP1x86	00 00 00 00 00 00 00 00 4b 44 42 47 30 03	14
Win2008SP2x86	00 00 00 00 00 00 00 00 4b 44 42 47 30 03	14
Win2008SP1x64	00 f8 ff ff 4b 44 42 47 30 03	10
Win2008SP2x64	00 f8 ff ff 4b 44 42 47 30 03	10
Win2008R2SP0x64	00 f8 ff ff 4b 44 42 47 40 03	10
Win2008R2SP1x64	00 f8 ff ff 4b 44 42 47 40 03	10
Win8SP0x86	00 00 00 00 00 00 00 00 4b 44 42 47 60 03	14
Win8SP1x86	00 00 00 00 00 00 00 00 4b 44 42 47 60 03	14
Win8SP0x64	03 f8 ff ff 4b 44 42 47 60 03	10
Win8SP1x64	03 f8 ff ff 4b 44 42 47 60 03	10
Win2012x64	03 f8 ff ff 4b 44 42 47 60 03	10
Win2012R2x64	03 f8 ff ff 4b 44 42 47 60 03	10

Table 1: KDBG Signatures used by Volatility to Derandomize the Kernel.

it computes the core kernel code hash to precisely fingerprint an OS, and these core kernel code is identified by correlative disassembling, code and signature normalization, and resilient signature matching techniques. OS-Sommelier$^+$ [16] further combines kernel data structure for the fingerprinting. Instead of precisely identifying the core kernel code from the memory snapshot and computing the hash, Sdkernel [23] utilizes an approximate matching tool Sdhash [22] to extract kernel fingerprints from the content of the disk images. Sdkernel would work well for disk forensics but not on memory since kernel code can be significantly changed due to the dynamic patching issues discussed in §3.2.

Most recently, Ahmed et al. [6] proposed the use of relocation tables in the program binary code to compute their fingerprints. Their key idea is that relocation tables tend to be distinct, and the relative addresses among the relocation entries can hence be used to build unique signatures. Their experimental results show that this approach can achieve very high accuracy but not 100% for Windows binaries (they have not tested any Linux binaries yet).

3. OVERVIEW

In this section, we give an overview of what we aim to achieve in this paper. We first define our research problem in §3.1, then enumerate the challenges faced to derandomize the kernel ASLR in §3.2, and finally present an outline of the approaches we will study in §3.3.

3.1 Problem Statement

The goal of our work is to investigate the optimal solutions for derandomizing the kernel address space for introspection and forensics. Under such application scenarios, we have the physical access of the target computers, and consequently there exist a large number of solutions for this problem. Therefore, we would like to also answer the questions of what the solution space is and which solution is more optimal. To this end, we define two metrics to evaluation the possible solutions.

- **Robustness:** Since there could exist non-cooperative guest OS running in a cloud (e.g., criminals who want to defeat the memory forensics, or kernel rootkits that have tampered with the kernel memory), the signatures generated for the derandomization should be robust; namely, it should be quite challenging for an adversary to modify the signatures, or generate fake ones to mislead the derandomization process.

- **Efficiency:** Given the fact that the size of the kernel memory is usually very large and there could also be millions of VMs running in a cloud, we would prefer faster approaches — the faster the derandomization takes (or the simpler the approach is), the better.

Threat Model, Scope, and Assumptions. We focus on derandomizing the kernel ASLR for cloud providers or forensic investigators where they have the physical access of the OS memory. We assume there are non-cooperative cloud users (e.g., cyber criminals), or there exists kernel malware which can manipulate or forge the signatures. Also, we focus on x86 platform, and the OS we aim to derandomize are the recent Linux kernels since version 3.14. Meanwhile, we do not attempt to compare all the possible approaches, and instead we would like to design and compare the approaches that tend to be simple, robust, and efficient.

3.2 Challenges

Intuitively, while we can use those sophisticated offensive techniques such as the brute-force probing [25] or memory disclosure attack [21, 26] to derandomize the kernel ASLR, a more efficient approach would be to derive robust signatures from both kernel code and data, and use them for the derandomization. Therefore, the central problem we aim to solve is how to derive such signatures. In the following, we discuss the challenges faced during this step.

3.2.1 Kernel Code is Non Static

The most straightforward approach is to directly use the entire kernel code as the signatures, and search for the memory to locate them. However, such an approach cannot have 100% accuracy because kernel code is actually non static [17], and there exists various complicated kernel patching techniques during the kernel loading and even during the kernel run-time. More specifically, modern Linux kernel, the target of our work, often involves the following dynamic kernel code patching:

- **Relocation**. Relocation is typically needed by a linker when linking object code to produce the final executable for user space program. Relocation is also needed when loading kernel modules or loading ASLR-enabled kernel. Specifically, as the current ASLR basically shifts the base address of kernel code and kernel global data, there is a need to dynamically patch the static hard coded addresses in both kernel code (e.g., certain memory address operand) and kernel data (e.g., jump table entries in read-only global data sections). The location of these static addresses are described in the relocation entries in relocation table sections of the binary code (e.g., `.rel.text`, `.rel.data` and `.rel.rodata` sections). Two examples of the relocation patching are illustrated in Fig. 1. We can see from the first example that when this `mov` instruction gets loaded into different memory locations, its target memory address operand has been accordingly patched (e.g., from `0xa7b000` to `0xcb7b000`).

- **Alternative Instructions**. One optimization strategy used by modern Linux kernel is to dynamically replace some (old) instructions with more efficient alternatives. The benefits of this mechanism is to allow distributors to ship generic kernels which can then be self-optimized according to the

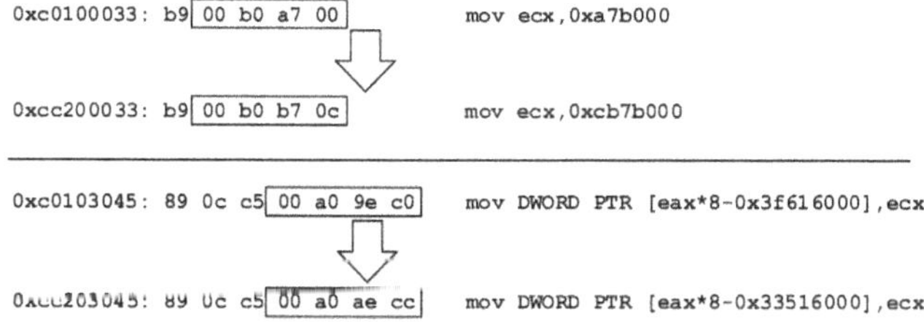
0xc0100033: b9 00 b0 a7 00
mov ecx,0xa7b000
0xcc200033: b9 00 b0 b7 0c
mov ecx,0xcb7b000
0xc0103045: 89 0c c5 00 a0 9e c0
mov DWORD PTR [eax*8-0x3f616000],ecx
mov DWORD PTR [eax*8-0x33516000],ecx

Figure 1: Relocation patching.

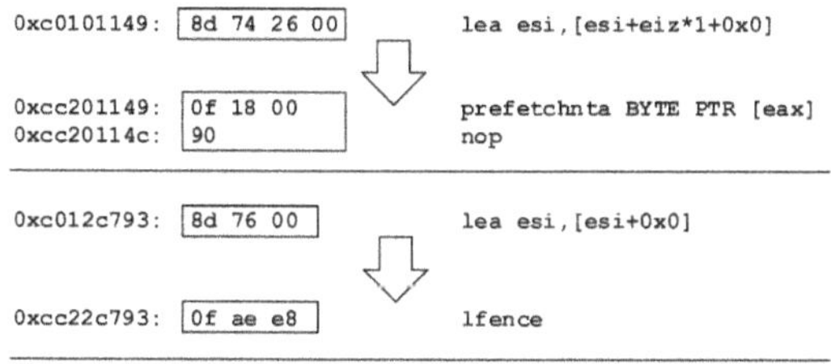
0xc0101149: 8d 74 26 00
lea esi,[esi+eiz*1+0x0]
0xcc201149: 0f 18 00
0xcc20114c: 90
prefetchnta BYTE PTR [eax]
nop
0xc012c793: 8d 76 00
lea esi,[esi+0x0]
0xcc22c793: 0f ae e8
lfence

Figure 2: Alternative instruction patching.

CPU configuration at load time. For instance, the code built for older CPUs can take advantage of the alternative instructions added later in the newer CPUs. To use such patching, kernel developers have to explicitly declare the instruction substitution through macro definition statement in the kernel source code. For example, the following code snippet shows how an old `lock` and `addl` instruction sequence is replaced by `mfence` instruction if the CPU has XMM2 enabled:

```
#define mb() alternative("lock; addl $0,0(%%esp)",
"mfence", X86_FEATURE_XMM2)
```

These alternative patching definitions will be translated by compilers and then stored in special data sections such as `.altinstructions` and `.altinstr_replace` section in the kernel binary code. The kernel will apply alternative instructions by invoking `apply_alternative` function at load time. Fig. 2 also shows two examples of this alternative instruction patching.

- **Symmetric Multiprocessing**. In addition to the relocation and alternative instruction patching, kernel also has some other special patching. One example is the critical section locking and unlocking of the execution of Symmetric Multi-Processing (SMP) CPUs [3]. Note that SMP is an architecture that allows multiple CPUs to share the same memory. It is widely used in modern computers.

  Since in SMP mode, multiple CPUs can simultaneously access the same piece of memory, there are some regions of the kernel code that would become critical sections. In this situation, the critical section must be locked. However, kernel only activates these locks if it is operating in a multiple CPU environment. The SMP patching can occur at both load time and run time. During the loading phase, if kernel detects it runs in SMP mode, it will apply the SMP unlock and lock patching, as illustrated in Fig. 3.

  Additionally, the Linux kernel also supports enabling and disabling SMP CPUs at run time. This makes such patching

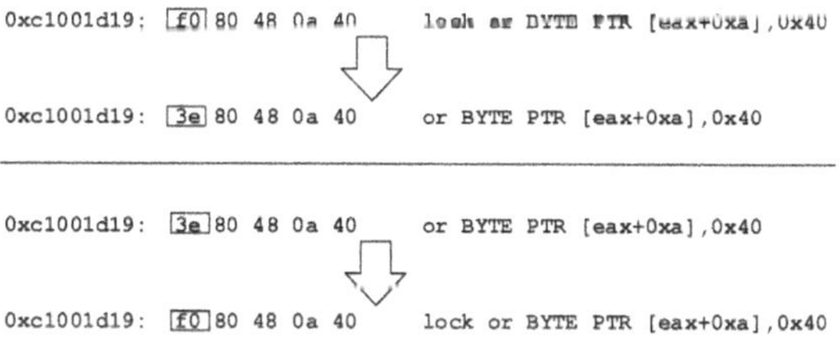
0xc1001d19: f0 80 48 0a 40
lock or BYTE PTR [eax+0xa],0x40
0xc1001d19: 3e 80 48 0a 40
or BYTE PTR [eax+0xa],0x40
0xc1001d19: 3e 80 48 0a 40
or BYTE PTR [eax+0xa],0x40
0xc1001d19: f0 80 48 0a 40
lock or BYTE PTR [eax+0xa],0x40

Figure 3: SMP unlock and lock patching.

  occur at run time. In particular, Linux kernel uses the functions `alternatives_smp_lock` and `alternatives_smp_unlock` to a live kernel in memory to add or remove locks.

- **Function Tracing**: Function tracing is a mechanism which requires runtime code patching. The tracer is usually used to debug the kernel or measure performance. It is commonly called at the beginning of each function within the kernel. For performance reasons, each tracer call is replaced by a NOP slide when the tracing feature is currently disabled. For example, instruction `call mcount` is patched by a NOP instruction, e.g., `xchg %ax, %ax`. As such, the system will run with virtually no overhead when function tracing is disabled.

  Similar to relocation patching, function tracing patching is also informed by special data sections (e.g., `__mcount_loc`) that tracks where these tracing functions are located in the `.text` section. This special data section is generated during the compile time. Then during the kernel booting phase, before SMP is initialized, kernel will scan this special data section and update all the function tracing call site into NOPs. When tracing is enabled, the NOPs are patched back to calls.

In addition to those outlined above, there also exists other sophisticated kernel code patching such as jump label optimization and load-time hypercall patching [17]. They all show strong evidence that kernel code is non static and we have to deal with this challenge while deriving code signatures.

3.2.2 *Kernel Data is Huge*

Unlike kernel code (which tends to be small), there is a huge volume of kernel data located in different data sections (e.g., global, heap, and stack) in the memory. Apparently, writable data such as those in kernel heap and stack cannot be used as signatures, though their shape might be able to serve as the signatures [18, 28]. Therefore, the most intuitive approach would be to use the read-only data (such as the strings) as the signatures. However, string may be manipulated by adversaries [11, 7], and we must use the immutable ones. As a result, the key challenge lies in how to search for the unique and immutable kernel data and use them as the signatures.

3.3 Study Overview

Again, the goal of this work is to explore the possible optimal approaches to derandomizing kernel ASLR for introspection and forensics applications, and compare them in terms of robustness and efficiency. Since a program including OS kernel is composed of code and data, we divide the possible approaches into code-based and data-based, as illustrated in Fig. 4.

- **Kernel Code-based Approaches**. Modern Linux kernel contains several mega-bytes of code. Thus, too much information

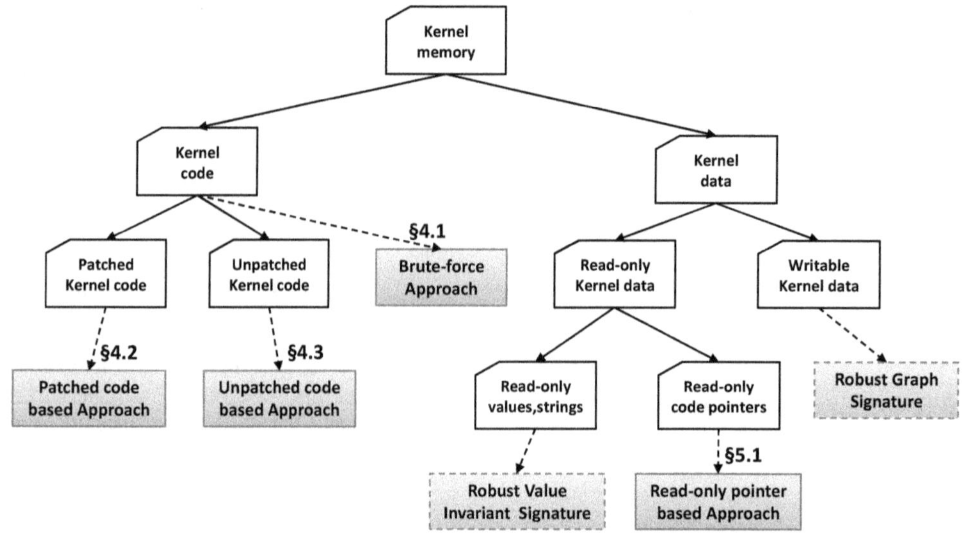

Figure 4: An Overview of the Investigated Approaches in Our Study.

can be used as the signatures. At a high level, the longer the signature is, the more robustness it is (because adversaries need to spend more efforts forging it for instance). On the other hand, we would prefer less sophisticated approaches because we also aim for efficiency. Similar to the brute-force approach used to break the ASLR [25], one of the simplest approach would be to directly scan the entire kernel memory and locate the base address of the kernel code, and we call this brute-force-approach (§4.1). However, this approach is not ideal because kernel code is not static and it would not achieve a 100% byte-by-byte matching. Therefore, more natural approaches would be to generate the derandomization signatures based on the patched code and unpatched code:

  - **Signatures from Patched Code**. While kernel patching is so complicated, there could be approaches that leverage the rules in the patching and derive the signatures. We can hence explore the intrinsic properties enforced by the patching and generate the signatures, and we will demonstrate one such an approach in §4.2.

  - **Signatures from Unpatched Code**. If we can distill the patched code, the rest will be the unpatched one, from which we can generate the signatures. Certainly the challenge will be how to identify those unpatched code, we will discuss a novel approach we devised in §4.3.

- **Kernel Data-based Approaches**. Kernel data can be divided into writable kernel data, and read-only data. Correspondingly, there exist different approaches based on this:

  - **Writable kernel data**. For writable data such as those located in kernel heap, we cannot directly use their values as the signatures, and instead we may use their shapes of the data structure as signatures, as demonstrated by earlier approach SigGraph [18]. In this study, we will not evaluate the feasibility of such an approach as it is too sophisticated, though it is possible to be used.

  - **Read-only kernel data**. Then we can look at the kernel read-only data. Constant strings are one of such candidates. However, strings can be manipulated by strong adversaries without crashing the kernel. While it is possible to systematically identify these non-manipulable strings (e.g., through fuzzing as in robust value invariant signatures [11]), we believe again this is too sophisticated, and instead we would like to focus on other non-manipulable data. We will discuss another novel approach we designed in §5.1.

4. DERIVING SIGNATURES FROM KERNEL CODE

4.1 Brute-force Code Matching Approach

The first and simplest approach is to directly scan the kernel code in memory using the entire code image from the disk. For a 32-bits Linux kernel, there are a maximum of 16 bits used in the randomization according to the default kernel configuration. Therefore, assume the kernel code has K bytes, the worst case complexity of this byte-by-byte brute-force scanning would take $2^{16}K$ number of comparisons. While there could be some optimizations, such as only using a subset of pages instead of all disk code for the scanning.

However, a caveat is that there will be no 100% byte-by-byte matching of the in-memory code and the in-disk code because of the dynamic patching of the kernel code (as discussed in §3.2). Fortunately, there will be only one peak match ratio, since it is very unlikely that there are two copies of the same kernel code in the memory. Therefore, we present a rigorous algorithm in Algorithm 1 for this peak-value based brute-force approach we used in our evaluation. Basically, it uses a byte-by-byte matching for each page (by calling `PageMatching`, which returns how many bytes get matched) and if more than half page of the data gets matched (line 8), then it compares with the next page. If all the code in disk has been checked, and the final match ratio has the highest peak value, then we output the based address of the kernel code (line 15).

The advantage of this brute-force approach is that it is the simplest (no sophisticated analysis required), and has very strong robustness since it uses the entire kernel code as the signatures. The disadvan-

Algorithm 1: A Brute-Force Based Code Matching Approach

Data: Kernel Page Size 4096;
Input: Kernel memory snapshot: M with M_p pages; Kernel code in disk D with D_p pages;
Result: The base address of the randomized kernel code

```
begin
    peak ← 0;
    R ← 0;
    for i ∈ {0..M_p} do
        matched ← 0;
        j ← 0;
        while j < D_p do
            M[i] ← GetVirtualPageContent (M, i);
            if (k ← PageMatching (M[i], D[j]) and k > 2048) then
                j ← j + 1; matched ← matched + k ;
            else
                j← 0; break;
        if ((j == D_p) and (matched/D > peak)) then
            peak ← matched/D; R ← GetVirtualAddr (M, i − j);
    return R;
```

Algorithm 2: Relocation Entry Based, Patched Code Signature Matching Approach.

Data: V_b: the base address of the kernel in the disk; n: the number of the randomization bits; $PhyKernAlign$: the kernel address alignment for the randomized kernel, which is usually at page level granularity.
Input: Kernel memory snapshot: M; Kernel code in disk D;
Result: The base address of the randomized kernel code

```
begin
    for i ∈ {0..2^n} do
        ProbBaseAddr← 0xc0000000 + i * PhyKernAlign;
        matched ← false;
        for each relocation offset O_j ∈ {rel.text} and with type R_386_32 do
            if (M[ProbBaseAddr+ O_j - V_b] - D[O_j - V_b]) != M[ProbBaseAddr+ O_{j+1} - V_b] - D[O_{j+1} - V_b])
            then
                matched ← false;
                break;
            else
                matched ← true;
        if (matched) then
            return ProbBaseAddr;
    return 0;
```

tage is it is very slow as shown in our experiment in §6 and also it may have false negatives as discussed in §7 when facing strong adversaries.

4.2 Patched Code Based Approach

While there are too many instructions that can be patched, we notice that there are still certain rules we can leverage. One is that kernel must know where to patch and how to patch. In particular, for relocation-based patching, kernel needs to use the information stored in relocation entries such as `.rel.text`, which means we can also leverage them to locate where to patch; for alternative instructions, kernel binary code also stores what those alternative instructions are and how to patch them (by invoking the internal kernel function `apply_alternative`). While we can re-execute the logic implemented in `apply_alternative` to locate the alternative instruction patched code, it is less complicated to locate the relocation-based patched code. For function tracing patching, we also need to parse the offset stored in the corresponding special data sections, which tends to be complicated. Therefore, we eventually decide to only look into how to use the relocation entries that can be directly acquired by tools such as `readelf` for our derandomization.

According to the standard ELF format specification [1], a relocation entry in a 32-bit ELF file is defined as a record consisting of two fields: the `offset` field and the `info` field, where the `offset` field gives the location at which the patching needs to be applied. Therefore, one insight we have is we can use the `offset` information stored in `.rel.text` for each relocation entry to probe and locate them in the kernel memory. The other insight is the data that needs to be patched are static memory address. Compared with static memory address that are in the disk file, all the patched memory address should be shifted by a constant value, which is the randomized offset we aim to get.

In fact, relocation entry had recently been used by CodeIndentifier [6] to fingerprint the Windows binary code. An example that illustrates this approach is presented in Fig. 5. Basically, it iterates each relocation entry defined in the `.rel.text` in Windows PE files, acquires its in-disk value V_d at offset o_i, then computes a signature value S using the difference between V_d and the base address of the code V_b in disk, namely V_d - V_b. This signature value shall remain a constant for this particular relocation entry. Then it searches the memory to locate the code by probing the value V_m and checking whether its distance to the randomized kernel base address V_x (we aim to find) is S. For instance, as shown in Fig. 5, the S value of $V_m - V_x$ for the first relocation entry is 0x7015d8, and the forth relocation entry is 0x7ca780. Only when all the relocation entries match the S values, does it mean successfully identifying the fingerprints of the code.

With respect to ELF binary, we can notice that not all the relocation entry can be used by CodeIdentifier. Specifically, for the 2nd and 3rd relocation entry, it has the type of `R_386_PC32`, which means the loader/linker shall places the PC-relative 32-bit address of the symbol into the specified memory location. However, when loading them into memory, they have already been updated with the relative addresses and there is no need to patch them. Also, interesting, the code snippet shown in Fig. 5 contains a function tracing disabling patching where instruction "`call c0683c80`" gets patched to NOP "`xchg %ax, %ax`".

Therefore, if we can remove the 2nd and 3rd relocation entry and use the first and forth ones (with type `R_386_32`, which means linker/loader will place an absolute 32-bit address of the symbol into the specified memory location) to compute the signature, we should be able to locate the corresponding kernel code. As such, we use a different approach to compute the signature compared to CodeIdentifier. In particular, instead of computing different signature value for each relocation entry, we compute it using the difference of the value in the memory snapshot V_m and the value in the disk V_d (i.e., $V_m - V_d$). In this way, we will always get a constant value for all the relocation entries, which is the in fact the randomized offset.

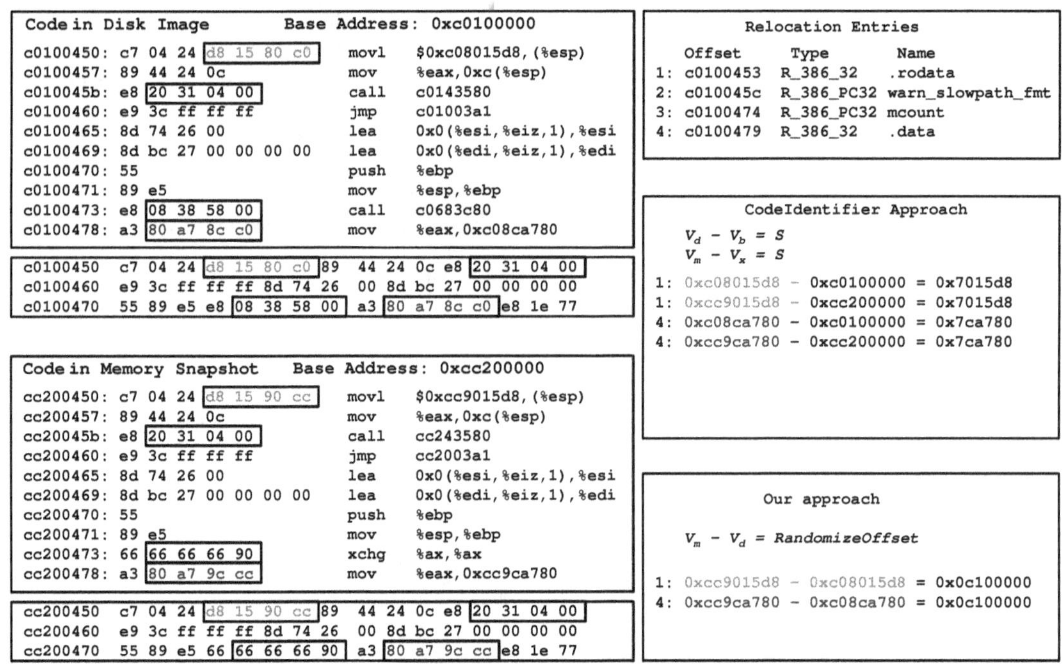

Code in Disk Image Base Address: 0xc0100000
c0100450: c7 04 24 d8 15 80 c0 movl $0xc08015d8,(%esp)
c0100457: 89 44 24 0c mov %eax,0xc(%esp)
c010045b: e8 20 31 04 00 call c0143580
c0100460: e9 3c ff ff ff jmp c01003a1
c0100465: 8d 74 26 00 lea 0x0(%esi,%eiz,1),%esi
c0100469: 8d bc 27 00 00 00 00 lea 0x0(%edi,%eiz,1),%edi
c0100470: 55 push %ebp
c0100471: 89 e5 mov %esp,%ebp
c0100473: e8 08 38 58 00 call c0683c80
c0100478: a3 80 a7 8c c0 mov %eax,0xc08ca780
c0100450 c7 04 24 d8 15 80 c0 89 44 24 0c e8 20 31 04 00
c0100460 e9 3c ff ff ff 8d 74 26 00 8d bc 27 00 00 00 00
c0100470 55 89 e5 e8 08 38 58 00 a3 80 a7 8c c0 e8 1e 77
Code in Memory Snapshot Base Address: 0xcc200000
cc200450: c7 04 24 d8 15 90 cc movl $0xcc9015d8,(%esp)
cc200457: 89 44 24 0c mov %eax,0xc(%esp)
cc20045b: e8 20 31 04 00 call cc243580
cc200460: e9 3c ff ff ff jmp cc2003a1
cc200465: 8d 74 26 00 lea 0x0(%esi,%eiz,1),%esi
cc200469: 8d bc 27 00 00 00 00 lea 0x0(%edi,%eiz,1),%edi
cc200470: 55 push %ebp
cc200471: 89 e5 mov %esp,%ebp
cc200473: 66 66 66 66 90 xchg %ax,%ax
cc200478: a3 80 a7 9c cc mov %eax,0xcc9ca780
cc200450 c7 04 24 d8 15 90 cc 89 44 24 0c e8 20 31 04 00
cc200460 e9 3c ff ff ff 8d 74 26 00 8d bc 27 00 00 00 00
cc200470 55 89 e5 66 66 66 66 90 a3 80 a7 9c cc e8 1e 77
Relocation Entries
Offset Type Name
1: c0100453 R_386_32 .rodata
2: c010045c R_386_PC32 warn_slowpath_fmt
3: c0100474 R_386_PC32 mcount
4: c0100479 R_386_32 .data
CodeIdentifier Approach
V_d - V_b = S
V_m - V_x = S
1: 0xc08015d8 - 0xc0100000 = 0x7015d8
1: 0xcc9015d8 - 0xcc200000 = 0x7015d8
4: 0xc08ca780 - 0xc0100000 = 0x7ca780
4: 0xcc9ca780 - 0xcc200000 = 0x7ca780
Our approach
V_m - V_d = RandomizeOffset
1: 0xcc9015d8 - 0xc08015d8 = 0x0c100000
4: 0xcc9ca780 - 0xc08ca780 = 0x0c100000

Figure 5: Using Relocation Entry to Generate Code Signatures

For instance, as illustrated in Fig. 5, for the first and forth relocation entries, we will get the same value of 0xc100000.

We also present a rigorous algorithm in Algorithm 2 to illustrate the detailed matching process. Specifically, we probe each possible base address (the maximum is controlled by the n bits entropy used in the randomization) starting from the kernel base address (line 3), if the distance of all the relocation entry point between the randomized kernel and the static disk image (namely $V_m - V_d$) remains a constant value (line 5 - line 10), then we identify and return the randomized base address V_x which is the probed base address (line 12); otherwise, we keep iterating and probing other possible base addresses.

4.3 Unpatched Code Based Approach

Having generated the signatures from patched code for the de-randomization, next we would like to investigate the approaches to generate the signatures from unpatched code. As discussed in §3.2, there are many cases that certain pieces of kernel code can be patched. It is quite challenging to identify the instructions that will not be patched. Meanwhile, we can also notice that we actually do not have to identify all the unpatched code, as long as we can identify the ones that will not be patched and use them as the signatures. That is, we can aim for soundness instead of completeness for unpatched code identification.

Though kernel has complicated cases for load time or run time patching, we realize that all the patching currently only operates individually and there is no dependence between two patched points. For instance, kernel only patches one point at a time based on the information stored in the binary code (e.g., the relocation entry). Therefore, an insight we have is that the instructions that (implicitly or explicitly) increase or decrease stack pointers will not be patched; otherwise, the kernel must patch them simultaneously. For instance, if there is a `push` instructions, there must be a `pop` or equivalent instructions. Otherwise, the stack cannot be kept balanced. This property of stack related instructions keeps themselves from being patched. As a result, they can be served as the candidates for our unpatched code signatures.

Algorithm 3: Unpatched Code Signature Generation

Input: Kernel code C in disk;
Result: A set S which contains all $tuples$({offset, instruction}) of each unpatched code

1 **begin**
2 $S \leftarrow \emptyset$;
3 **for** *each instruction* $i \in C$ **do**
4 **if** `ChangeStackPointer` (i) **then**
5 $O_i \leftarrow$ `GetOffset` (i);
6 $C_i \leftarrow$ `GetInstrCode` (i);
7 $S \leftarrow S \cup \{<O_i, C_i>\}$
8 **return** S;

An algorithm of how we generate the unpatched code signature based on the stack operations is presented in Algorithm 3. Basically, we first disassemble the kernel code. Then we collect the instructions that will modify the stack pointers (line 4 - line 7). We consider two categories of instructions in `ChangeStackPointer` function (line 4): one is those implicit stack pointer changing instructions including `push`, `pop` and `leave` that will change the stack size without explicitly modifying the `esp` value; the other ways is the explicit instructions that directly changes the value of `esp`, e.g. "`sub %esp, 0x68`". Our signatures consist of these identified instructions as well as their offsets (line 7, 8).

Then to match the signatures with the memory snapshot, we just probe whether all the instruction at offset $O_i + R$ in memory contains the same instruction C_i as the one in disk O_i. If so, we output R as the randomized offset. The detailed matching algorithms is elided since this is quite simple.

Approach	Total	Signature Generation	Signature Matching	C++	Python
Brute Force	669	0	32	649	20
Patched Code	807	0	110	759	48
Unpatched Code	817	41	107	756	61
Readonly Pointer	822	0	124	773	49

Table 2: Implementation Complexity (Units: LOC).

5. DERIVING SIGNATURES FROM READ-ONLY KERNEL DATA

Data in general can be classified into writable data and read-only data. As discussed earlier, for writable data, when there are pointers involved, the shape of the points-to graph might be able to serve as a signature [18] to derandomize the kernel. We consider this approach is too complicated and instead we focus on read-only kernel data. Meanwhile, for read-only data, strings should be one intuitive candidate for the signatures. However, strings can often be mutated without crashing the kernel. As discussed earlier, while similar to robust signatures approach proposed by Dolan-Gravitt et al. [11], we could use fuzzing to identify those non crashable strings as the signature. Again, we believe this approach is also too sophisticated and leave it for future work. In the following, we discuss a new approach we developed based on the read-only pointers in the `.rodata` section.

5.1 Read-only Pointer Based Approach

Program including OS kernel contains static code pointers, for instance, the system call tables, the indirect jump tables, etc. These static code pointers when compiled are actually stored in the `.rodata` section. Changing the value of these static code pointers will change the semantics of the program code, and it might also lead to the kernel crashes.

Similar to the relocation entries in `.rel.text` that contains those to be patched memory address inside kernel code, there are also relocation entries in `.rel.rodata` that contains the offset in the `.rodata` to inform loader to patch the memory addresses (basically they are pointers) stored in this `.rodata` section. Therefore, we can use them to build read-only data signatures.

The approach is also surprisingly simple. Similar to Algorithm 2, we iterative each relocation entry in `.rel.rodata` (instead of `.rel.text`), and then compare the values between disk version and the memory version. If all entry has the same shifted offset, we return this randomized offset. Detailed algorithm is also elided for simplicity.

6. EVALUATION

We have implemented the four approaches presented in §4 and §5, and these implementation code can be found at github.com/utds3lab/derandomization/. Basically, we implemented each approach with a mixture of C++ and Python. The python code is called by C++ and is used to parse the output from `objdump` and `readelf`. The implementation complexity in terms of lines of code (LOC) for each of approach is presented in Table 2. In particular, we use python to parse the address and offset from the `rel.text` and `rel.rodata` sections produced by `readelf` of the kernel binary code. Meanwhile, we use Python to parse the disassembled code produced by `objdump` and get the offset and instruction of the stack pointer change related instructions as the signatures.

OS Kernels	Brute Force	Patched Code	Unpatched Data	Readonly Pointer
Linux-3.14.8	95.45%	100.00%	100.00%	100.00%
Linux-3.14.11	95.45%	100.00%	100.00%	100.00%
Linux-3.14.30	95.46%	100.00%	100.00%	100.00%
Linux-3.15	95.39%	100.00%	100.00%	100.00%
Linux-3.15.2	95.39%	100.00%	100.00%	100.00%
Linux-3.15.4	95.39%	100.00%	100.00%	100.00%
Linux-3.16	95.40%	100.00%	100.00%	100.00%
Linux-3.16.2	95.40%	100.00%	100.00%	100.00%
Linux-3.16.6	95.40%	100.00%	100.00%	100.00%
Linux-3.17	95.39%	100.00%	100.00%	100.00%
Linux-3.17.2	95.39%	100.00%	100.00%	100.00%
Linux-3.17.6	95.39%	100.00%	100.00%	100.00%
Linux-3.18	95.40%	100.00%	100.00%	100.00%
Linux-3.18.2	95.40%	100.00%	100.00%	100.00%
Linux-3.18.4	95.40%	100.00%	100.00%	100.00%
Linux-3.18.6	95.40%	100.00%	100.00%	100.00%
Linux-3.19	95.40%	100.00%	100.00%	100.00%
Linux-3.19.2	95.41%	100.00%	100.00%	100.00%
Linux-3.19.4	95.41%	100.00%	100.00%	100.00%
Linux-4.0	95.41%	100.00%	100.00%	100.00%
mean	95.41%	100.00%	100.00%	100.00%

Table 4: Match Ratio.

In this section, we present our experimental result. We took 20 Linux kernels from version 3.14 to 4.0 for the evaluation. We first tested the effectiveness of each approach with respect to the testing Linux kernels in §6.1, and then we report the performance overhead of each approach in §6.2.

To obtain the physical memory dumps, we run each of the tested Linux kernels in a VMware Workstation configured with 512M bytes RAM (131,072 pages with 4K bytes each) for the guest OS. After the guest OS has booted up, we took a memory snapshot and used it for the testing. Our host machine has an Intel Xeon CPU with 48G memory, installing a Red Hat Enterprise Linux Workstation 6.5 with Linux kernel 2.6.32.

6.1 Effectiveness

Robustness. To evaluate the robustness of each approach, we use the size of the signatures as the metric, though there could be other metrics to measure the robustness of the signature. Again, the intuition is the longer the signature, the more robust the approach is, because an adversary needs to spend more efforts to cheat the system with longer signatures. The "Total Bytes" column in Table 3 shows the signature size of each approach.

We can notice that brute-force approach has the strongest robustness. On average it contains close to 5.88 Mega-bytes data. It will be extremely difficult to forge such signatures except that an adversary could load multiple copies of the code into kernel memory and cheat this approach. The next strongest signature is the read only pointer based approach. On average it contains 342 Kilo-bytes data. If an adversary wants to cheat this approach, it has to simultaneously patch more than 80 Kilo-bytes pointers. For patched code approach, its signature size is 283 Kilo-bytes. Regarding the unpatched code approach, its signature has only 230 Kilo bytes on average, and eventually it only keeps on average 3.91% of kernel code in the signatures.

We also reported how many signature bytes per page for each approach in Bytes/Page column in Table 3. Note that these data can provide the statistics with respect to the performance of each approach. Basically, more bytes comparison in a page, the slower the approach will be as we show in Fig. 7. We can notice unpatched code has the least data to compare in a page, whereas brute force approach has an entire page to compare.

OS-kernels	Brute Force		Patched code		Unpatched code		Readonly pointer	
	Total Bytes	Bytes/Page	Total Bytes	Bytes/Page	Total Bytes	Bytes/Page	Total Bytes	Bytes/Page
Linux-3.14.8	5,787,280	4,096	278,156	196	225,632	159	331,956	656
Linux-3.14.11	5,788,560	4,096	278,192	196	225,647	159	332,084	656
Linux-3.14.30	5,802,328	4,096	278,900	196	225,933	159	332,416	656
Linux-3.15	5,793,980	4,096	280,476	198	227,514	160	336,204	659
Linux-3.15.2	5,794,108	4,096	280,480	198	227,514	160	336,208	659
Linux-3.15.4	5,794,940	4,096	280,504	198	227,518	160	336,212	659
Linux-3.16	5,844,284	4,096	281,812	197	229,065	160	340,964	658
Linux-3.16.2	5,846,844	4,096	281,840	197	229,084	160	340,956	658
Linux-3.16.6	5,850,044	4,096	281,916	197	229,213	160	341,068	658
Linux-3.17	5,889,452	4,096	284,832	198	230,785	160	344,240	660
Linux-3.17.2	5,889,324	4,096	284,880	198	230,794	160	344,252	660
Linux-3.17.6	5,894,696	4,096	285,416	198	230,886	160	344,396	661
Linux-3.18	5,929,000	4,096	286,508	198	232,155	160	346,384	662
Linux-3.18.2	5,929,704	4,096	286,516	198	232,159	160	346,448	662
Linux-3.18.4	5,930,280	4,096	286,608	198	232,167	160	346,448	662
Linux-3.18.6	5,931,816	4,096	286,612	197	232,242	160	346,480	662
Linux-3.19	5,977,424	4,096	288,156	197	233,339	159	348,064	662
Linux-3.19.2	5,980,280	4,096	288,216	197	233,466	159	348,104	663
Linux-3.19.4	5,982,136	4,096	288,268	197	233,503	159	348,172	663
Linux-4.0	6,015,102	4,096	289,532	197	235,018	160	351,676	656
mean	5,882,580	4,096	283,891	198	230,182	160	342,137	660

Table 3: Signature Size.

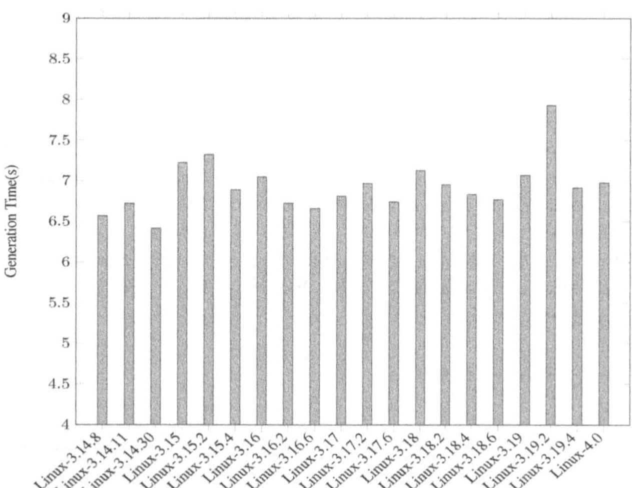

Figure 6: Signature Generation Performance.

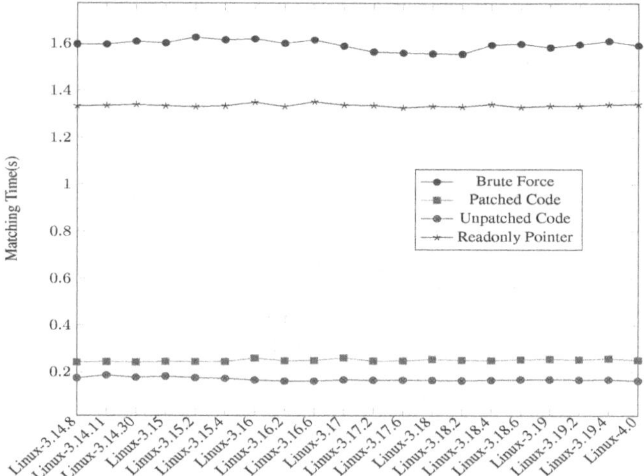

Figure 7: Signature Matching Performance.

Precision. Next, we tested the precision of each approach with benign kernels. Regarding the non-cooperative kernels, it is discussed in §7. The match ratio for each approach is presented in Table 4. We can see that the peak match ratio for brute-force approach is 95.41% (which means usually 4.59% of code has been patched) on average for all these kernels. For all other approaches, it has a perfect 100% match ratio.

6.2 Performance

We also measured the performance of each approach. The faster the performance, the more likely to be used in practice. As mentioned above, we tested 20 latest Linux kernels. The size of the memory snapshot is set to 512M bytes.To load the memory snapshot as well as the kernel code, it took on average 0.677 seconds. For a fair comparison among all these approaches, we exclude the snapshot loading time. Also, only the unpatched code approach requires the preprocessing of the kernel code to generate the signatures, and this performance is presented in Fig. 6 for all these kernels. We can see that on average it took 6.9 seconds for the signature generation. Note that this pre-processing runs with pure python environment, which explains why it took such a larger amount of time than even brute-force matching.

Regarding using the signature for the matching and derandomization, this performance is presented in Fig. 7. We can see that brute-force approach has the worst performance. It took on average 1.6 seconds to derandomize a Linux kernel. The next worst one is the read only pointer based approach, since it needs to check over 85 thousands of pointers and perform the distance subtraction computation for each pointer. The unpatched code is the fastest, and it only requires about 0.2 seconds on average to derandomize a kernel.

7. DISCUSSIONS AND FUTURE WORK

In this study, we aim to systematically examine the possible optimal approaches from both kernel code and kernel data to derandomize kernel ASLR. We have presented four approaches from the perspective of basic brute-force code, to patched code, unpatched code, and read only pointers. However, we have not compared with a few other possible approaches such as from writable-data, or other read only data to generate the signatures. We leave these to future works.

In our evaluation, we tested our approaches with only benign Linux kernels, and we did not evaluate the memory snapshot running by adversaries such as uncooperative cloud users. The fundamental reason is due to the fact that there is a large attack surface, and it is hard to enumerate all of them. Fortunately, what an adversary they can only play with in the attack is to generate bogus data to mislead the signature matching, because the signatures we used are either code or pointer related, changing them will change the semantics or even crashing the kernel. Therefore, we can analyze the consequences of these non-cooperative attacks.

Specifically, for brute-force code scanning approach, it could fail to derandomize a kernel when directly using the Algorithm 1. For instance, when an adversary simply loads a copy of the kernel code into the kernel memory (by writing a simple kernel module to do so), this approach can get a 100% peak match ratio for this code copy instead of the 95% we tested with the benign kernel. Therefore, even though it has the strongest robustness in terms of signature size, it will have false positive (not providing the correct address) and false negative (missing the correct address) when facing bogus data cheating attack. One possible mitigation would be to relax the peak value to make it more conservative. For instance, through empirical evaluation we can acquire a threshold of the peak value for the benign kernel, and then use it to derandomize the kernel. In this way, it will not have false negatives but it will have false positives since the bogus data will be included.

For all other approaches, while an adversary can also create bogus data, we will not have false negatives since the match ratio is 100%. In other words, the only consequence is that we will not be able to quickly pinpoint the derandomization address but the candidates are among the final results. With additional pruning or a combination with other approaches, it is very likely to produce the correct result. In fact, without too many efforts, we have designed four simple approaches (with just about three thousands lines of code in total), and we believe these four approaches can be combined to prune the false positives (i.e., the bogus data generated by attackers). We leave the investigation for more robust signatures under the presence of strong adversary in another avenue of our future work.

8. CONCLUSION

Many modern OS kernels today have started to randomize their kernel address space. Consequently, when performing introspection or forensic analysis of the kernel memory, we must derandomize and use the correct addresses. In this paper, we present the first systematic study of how to derandomize a kernel when given a memory snapshot of a running kernel instance. Unlike the derandomization approaches used in developing memory exploits in which only remote access is available, with introspection and forensics applications, we can use all of the information available in kernel memory to generate signatures and derandomize the kernel address space layout. We have explored a number of typical approaches to generate strong signatures from both kernel code and data based on the insight of how kernel code and data is updated, and compare them from efficiency and robustness perspective. In particular, we have designed four approaches from brute-force code scanning, to robust signature generation from patched code and unpatched code, as well as from read-only kernel data, respectively. We show that brute-force approach is simple, but it is slow and may have false positives and false negatives to bogus data misleading attack. For all other approaches, they run faster and they will not have false negatives, but there might be false positives when facing strong adversaries. However, these false positives could be pruned when combining with multiple strong signatures for instance.

Acknowledgement

We would like to thank the anonymous reviewers for their helpful comments. This research was partially supported by AFOSR Award FA9550-14-1-0119, NSA Award H98230-15-1-0271, and NSF Award 1453011. Any opinions, findings, conclusions, or recommendations expressed do not necessarily reflect the views of the sponsors.

9. REFERENCES

[1] Elf file format. *http://www.skyfree.org/linux/references/ELF_Format.pdf.*

[2] Microsoft security intelligence report. *http://www.microsoft.com/security/sir/strategy/default.aspx#!section_3_3.*

[3] Smp alternatives. *http://lwn.net/Articles/164121/.*

[4] Os x mountain lion core technologies overview. *http://movies.apple.com/media/us/osx/2012/docs/OSX_MountainLion_Core_Technologies_Overview.pdf*, June 2012.

[5] Linux 3.14. *http://kernelnewbies.org/Linux_3.14*, Mar 2014.

[6] I. Ahmed, V. Roussev, and A. A. Gombe. Robust fingerprinting for relocatable code. In *Proceedings of the 5th ACM Conference on Data and Application Security and Privacy, CODASPY 2015, San Antonio, TX, USA, March 2-4, 2015*, pages 219–229, 2015.

[7] H. Y. Aravind Prakash, Eknath Venkataramani and Z. Lin. Manipulating semantic values in kernel data structures: Attack assessments and implications. In *Proceedings of the 43rd Annual IEEE/IFIP International Conference on Dependable Systems and Networks(DSN-PDS 2013)*, Budapest, Hungary, June 2013.

[8] A. Bittau, A. Belay, A. Mashtizadeh, D. Mazières, and D. Boneh. Hacking blind. In *Proceedings of the 2014 IEEE Symposium on Security and Privacy*, SP '14, pages 227–242. IEEE Computer Society, 2014.

[9] E. Buchanan, R. Roemer, H. Shacham, and S. Savage. When good instructions go bad: generalizing return-oriented programming to risc. In *Proc. 15th ACM Conf. Computer and communications security (CCS'08)*, pages 27–38, Alexandria, Virginia, USA, 2008. ACM.

[10] S. Designer. "return-to-libc" attack. *Bugtraq*, August 1997.

[11] B. Dolan-Gavitt, A. Srivastava, P. Traynor, and J. Giffin. Robust signatures for kernel data structures. In *Proceedings of the ACM Conference on Computer and Communications Security (CCS)*, November 2009.

[12] Y. Fu, Z. Lin, and D. Brumley. Automatically deriving pointer reference expressions from executions for memory dump analysis. In *Proceedings of the 2015 ACM SIGSOFT International Symposium on Foundations of Software Engineering (FSE'15)*, Bergamo, Italy, September 2015.

[13] Y. Fu, Z. Lin, and K. Hamlen. Subverting systems authentication with context-aware, reactive virtual machine introspection. In *Proceedings of the 29th Annual Computer Security Applications Conference (ACSAC'13)*, New Orleans, Louisiana, December 2013.

[14] T. Garfinkel and M. Rosenblum. A virtual machine introspection based architecture for intrusion detection. In

Proc. Network and Distributed Systems Security Sym. (NDSS'03), February 2003.

[15] Y. Gu, Y. Fu, A. Prakash, Z. Lin, and H. Yin. Os-sommelier: Memory-only operating system fingerprinting in the cloud. In *Proceedings of the 3rd ACM Symposium on Cloud Computing (SOCC'12)*, San Jose, CA, October 2012.

[16] Y. Gu, Y. Fu, A. Prakash, Z. Lin, and H. Yin. Multi-aspect, robust, and memory exclusive guest os fingerprinting. *IEEE Transactions on Cloud Computing*, 2014.

[17] T. Kittel, S. Vogl, T. K. Lengyel, J. Pfoh, and C. Eckert. Code validation for modern os kernels. In *Malware Memory Forensics Workshop (MMF)*, December 2014.

[18] Z. Lin, J. Rhee, X. Zhang, D. Xu, and X. Jiang. Siggraph: Brute force scanning of kernel data structure instances using graph-based signatures. In *Proc. 18th Annual Network and Distributed System Security Sym. (NDSS'11)*, San Diego, CA, February 2011.

[19] Nergal. The advanced return-into-lib(c) exploits: Pax case study. *Phrack*, 10(58), 2001.

[20] N. A. Quynh. Operating system fingerprinting for virtual machines, 2010. In DEFCON 18.

[21] G. F. Roglia, L. Martignoni, R. Paleari, and D. Bruschi. Surgically returning to randomized lib(c). In *Proceedings of the 25th Annual Computer Security Applications Conference (ACSAC)*, pages 60–69. IEEE Computer Society, Dec. 2009. Honolulu, Hawaii, USA.

[22] V. Roussev. Data fingerprinting with similarity digests. In *Advances in digital forensics vi*, pages 207–226. Springer, 2010.

[23] V. Roussev, I. Ahmed, and T. Sires. Image-based kernel fingerprinting. *Digit. Investig.*, 11:S13–S21, Aug. 2014.

[24] H. Shacham. The geometry of innocent flesh on the bone: return-into-libc without function calls (on the x86). In *Proc. 14th ACM Conf. Computer and communications security (CCS'07)*, pages 552–561, Alexandria, Virginia, USA, 2007. ACM.

[25] H. Shacham, M. Page, B. Pfaff, E.-J. Goh, N. Modadugu, and D. Boneh. On the effectiveness of address-space randomization. In *Proceedings of the 11th ACM Conference on Computer and Communications Security*, CCS '04, pages 298–307, New York, NY, USA, 2004. ACM.

[26] K. Z. Snow, F. Monrose, L. Davi, A. Dmitrienko, C. Liebchen, and A.-R. Sadeghi. Just-in-time code reuse: On the effectiveness of fine-grained address space layout randomization. In *Security and Privacy (SP), 2013 IEEE Symposium on*, pages 574–588. IEEE, 2013.

[27] P. Team. Pax address space layout randomization (aslr). *http://pax.grsecurity.net/docs/aslr.txt*.

[28] D. Urbina, Y. Gu, J. Caballero, and Z. Lin. SigPath: A Memory Graph Based Approach for Program Data Introspection and Modification. In *Proceedings of the 19th European Symposium on Research in Computer Security*, Wroclaw, Poland, September 2014.

[29] A. Walters. The volatility framework: Volatile memory artifact extraction utility framework. https://www.volatilesystems.com/default/volatility.

[30] J. Zeng and Z. Lin. Towards automatic inference of kernel object semantics from binary code. In *Proceedings of the 18th International Symposium on Research in Attacks, Intrusions and Defenses (RAID'15)*, Kyoto, Japan, November 2015.

Patching Logic Vulnerabilities for Web Applications using LogicPatcher

Maliheh Monshizadeh
Department of Computer Science
University of Illinois at Chicago
Chicago, IL
mmonsh2@uic.edu

Prasad Naldurg
IBM Research India
Bangalore, India
pnaldurg@in.ibm.com

V. N. Venkatakrishnan
Department of Computer Science
University of Illinois at Chicago
Chicago, IL
venkat@uic.edu

ABSTRACT

Logic vulnerabilities are an important class of programming flaws in web applications. These vulnerabilities occur when a desired property pertaining to an application's logic does not hold along certain paths in the application's code. Many analysis tools have been developed to find logic vulnerabilities in web applications. Given a web application with logic vulnerabilities, the question is whether one can design methods to patch application code and prevent these vulnerabilities from being exploited. We answer this question by developing an approach and tool called LogicPatcher for patching of logic vulnerabilities. We focus on correct *patch placement*, i.e. identifying the precise location in code where the patch code can be introduced, based on path profiling. As we show in this paper, finding the appropriate location as well as generating the right patch can get complicated and require deep code analysis. We demonstrate the utility of LogicPatcher by automatically fixing several critical parameter tampering and authorization vulnerabilities in large web applications.

1. Introduction

Logic vulnerabilities cause a program to operate incorrectly or exhibit unexpected behavior. The ability to fix security-sensitive logic vulnerabilities in web applications, caused by incorrect control checks or improper data computation, is an important requirement in the SANS Critical Security Control (CSC) [1] for effective cyber-defenses. When such errors are exploited, they can affect the security of millions of users.

The main research issues in this context are vulnerability analysis, prevention, and correction of logic errors. While the focus of most prior research [9, 18, 15, 22] is on vulnerability analysis, and some on prevention [11], we study the problem that has received less attention, that of correcting these errors in source code. Manual inspection of the source code in order to develop security patches for reported vulnerabilities does not scale as some of these applications can be very large. As shown in this paper, however, the problem of fixing these errors automatically is far from straightforward, and requires a thorough analysis of large amount of source code. In the case of legacy web applications, if the vendor or the developer of a web application is no longer in business, or simply failed to fix the problem, the burden is on the customers of the application to either change their application or patch the vulnerabilities themselves. Patching an application requires a thorough understanding of the application and the error, something that deployment professionals do not have time for.

1.1 Logic Vulnerabilities

In the web applications context, logic vulnerabilities may manifest in one of two categories: 1) as a logic error in a computation (data dependent) or 2) as a logic error in program control, i.e., a vulnerability caused by a missing or an incorrect control check in the program. Web applications often do not come with correctness specifications – properties that attest behavior at various program points. The lack of such program specifications makes it very difficult to identify original functional requirements and validate their correctness. Therefore, fixing the first category, i.e., computation errors is challenging, as the true intention of the computation is unknown to the analysis tools. However, the second category of logic vulnerabilities is relatively easier to generate patches for, given that this subset of logic vulnerabilities are detectable through inconsistency analyses on applications. We term this set of vulnerabilities as application inconsistency vulnerabilities (AIVs), the type of logic vulnerability that arises from inconsistent design and implementation of security checks in an application. Existing tools for AIVs [18, 15] can not only detect that *something* is missing or is incorrect, but also infer *what exactly* is missing and suggest ways to correct it.

In addition to generating correct conditions for these checks, the correct placement of these is also a difficult problem. Detected vulnerabilities may be embedded deeply in the code, beyond such easily analyzable or stand-alone constructs such as user interfaces or end-user communication modules. Manually locating these errors may require rigorous analysis of the source-code, with many interdependencies. Modifying or adding code snippets to fix these errors will now imply we take extra care not to change the logic and the functionality of the interdependent code, and only fix the vulnerable path(s). To address this, we have designed and implemented LogicPatcher, a static analysis tool that takes a patch condition, i.e., a reported vulnerability and a path descriptor as input, and suggests optimal or near-optimal candidate path placement locations. Using our automated tool, application customers or system administrators can confirm and test the candidate patches instead of going through the arduous work of manual code inspection.

Due to fundamental and practical issues in verification of code correctness, the candidate patches need to be verified by a separate approach, either manually or automatically through formal verification. For reasons of scope, we discuss the issues of patch generation and patch placement for AIVs in this paper, and leave the formal verification step for future work. Additionally, we have employed several static code analysis techniques which increase our confidence in the correctness of the candidate patches. We evalu-

CODASPY'16, March 09 - 11, 2016, New Orleans, LA, USA

ISBN 978-1-4503-3935-3/16/03...$15.00

DOI: http://dx.doi.org/10.1145/2857705.2857727

ated 9 open-source web applications and out of 29 vulnerable files we have generated patches for 27 of them correctly.

1.2 Main issues

At a high level, we need to identify the candidate patch locations for the application while preserving the logic of the program. This goal becomes challenging as we do not know much about the functionality of the program in the first place. The only information we have aside from the source code of the application, is the reported vulnerabilities and their locations in the code.

Patch Generation: In order for the generated patch to work, it should first have the necessary instructions which will prevent the exploits. While the generated patch should work, it should not interfere with the main functionality of the program.

Patch Placement: We need to find the proper location for the patch, which assures that the patch will not change the logic or the functionality of the application along other execution paths. For patch generation, we rely on outputs from AIV detection tools such as Rolecast and MACE [18, 15]. Our work in patch placement is related to FixMeUp [19], a static analysis tool that suggests patches for access control vulnerabilities. Our research finds a wider scope for solving this problem. We believe that we can generate security patches for any type of logic vulnerability caused by missing or inconsistent checks, with minimal guidelines about the vulnerability, and find optimal or near optimal placement of the suggested changes directly. We summarize the contributions of our research: 1) Precise formulation of logic vulnerabilities in order to patch the applications, 2) Design and implementation of an analysis tool called LogicPatcher, 3) Finding candidate placements of the generated patches along the vulnerable path(s), and 4) Generation of security patches for reported logic vulnerabilities for 9 open-source applications.

This paper is organized as follows: Section 2 presents a running example used in the rest of this paper. Section 3 explains the high-level overview of our approach. Section 4 describes the architecture of LogicPatcher and the implementation details. Section 5 presents the evaluation of our approach. Section 6 presents related work. In Section 7 we conclude.

2. Background and Challenges

Application Inconsistency Vulnerabilities (AIVs) are cause by lack of consistency in the design / implementation of security checks. Some of them include:

- *E-commerce logic inconsistencies* These vulnerabilities result from inconsistent checking of business validation logic in the application code. Prior work on detecting these vulnerabilities include using model checking [9], modeling correct payment logics combined with static analysis [20], and invariant generation and blackbox testing [16]. In all these cases, the vulnerability analysis tools report inconsistencies in checks, and these inconsistencies are subsequently verified for the presence of vulnerabilities.
- *Client-server inconsistencies* The validation performed by client-side JavaScript can be used as a specification to check the server-side for vulnerabilities. [6, 7, 3] take this approach towards vulnerability detection. In this case, the vulnerability is a client-side check that must have been performed by the server.
- *Access control inconsistencies* Inconsistency in application authorization logic along different execution paths result in application vulnerabilities. [18, 15, 22, 10] look for these types of inconsistencies, which are subsequently confirmed for the presence of actual vulnerabilities.

2.1 Vulnerabilities to Be Patched

AIVs seen in Table 1 often have one characteristic in common: they lack conditions (if-statements) in one or more execution paths.

Table 1: Inconsistency Checking Analysis Tools

Tool	Description
Waler [9]	Detection of program invariable violations through model checking
JIGSAW [23]	Detection of resource access inconsistencies
MACE [15]	Detection of authorization & authentication inconsistencies
RoleCast [18]	Detection of authorization & other logic inconsistencies within authorization roles
WAPTEC [7]	Detection of client and server input validation inconsistencies

That is, some conditions are not met along some paths. This problem makes these paths and eventually the whole application vulnerable to various exploits.

To patch this type of vulnerability, the developer needs to have some basic knowledge about the vulnerability to be able to patch it effectively. In particular three different items affect the patching process: $< C, P, E >$ in which C is the missing condition which needs to be added to vulnerable paths, P is the particular vulnerable path, and E is the exception handling policy the developer considers if the condition failed at execution time.

The Conditions Set The set of missing conditions C is expressed in terms of variables, values and conditional operators. For example, {`strlen($password)`,`8`,>=} defines a condition on the length of the variable `$password`. The variables used in C can be functions of input variables (e.g. `strlen($password)`) or they can be internal variables related to server-state (e.g. `$_SESSION['username']`). The values also can be constants or derived from some server-state (e.g. the result of a DB query).

The Vulnerable Path(s) P is the path from the source to the sensitive operation (*sink*). Security analysis tools can usually generate execution traces which shows the possibility of the exploiting the vulnerability.

The Exception Handling Policy Set The set E defines the set of actions which are allowed to be executed if the conditions C do not hold. For example, the developer may choose to use `exit()` or `die("message")` or she may choose to log the failed operation in the system. The semantics of the actions specified in E depends on the application, the usage and developer's choice.

2.2 Goals & High-level Challenges

Our high-level goal is: given a inconsistency logic vulnerability, we want to generate a candidate patch to retrofit the vulnerable sink. To generate such security patch analyses must be performed to 1) generate a proper patch and 2) place the patch in a proper location.

There are some high-level challenges involved in the process of generating security patches for vulnerable web applications. Given that most web applications lack program specifications, our approach should be able to work on the source code with minimal input from the developers/application admins. That is, the patch generation and placement modules should rely on the extracted logic of program and inferred security policies.

Missing Check Dependencies A security patch is basically a generated code snippet which is going to be placed somewhere along the vulnerable path(s). The code snippet may contain variables which should have semantical and syntactic values at the location they are going to be placed. Therefore, the data dependencies for these variables should be kept intact and meaningful. Forward and backward data dependencies of the variables used in the code snippet will assure that the dependencies are correct and consistent along different paths and throughout the application.

The following example, derived from a real-world vulnerable application, shows a sink (the DELETE query) in which the variables used in the query are dependent on some previous instructions. Although the value used in the sink depends on the user input (e.g. `$_POST['username']`), it also depends on some server state (e.g. the data stored in `users` table which determines if the username is valid in the application). If the sink missed the authentication, along with the check in Line 2, other instructions (on validation of the username and password) should accompany the check in the patch. Therefore, we need analysis to determine the instructions with dependencies on the input values and the server-state.

```
1  session_start();
2  if(isset($_POST['username']) &&
       isset($_POST['password'])){
3      $result = mysql_query("SELECT userid FROM users
4              WHERE username = " + $_POST['username'] +
                   " AND password = " +
                   $_POST['password']);
5      if ($result) {
6          $_SESSION['username'] = $_POST['username'];
7          if($action == 'delete'){
8              $res = mysql_query("DELETE FROM posts
                   WHERE author=" +
                   $_SESSION['username'] + "AND
                   post_ID=" + $_POST['post_id']);
9              if($res) echo("Deleted post
                   successfully");}}}
```

Listing 1: Sink Control and Data Dependency

Overprotecting The patching process includes adding some code snippets (patches) to the source code which will retrofit certain vulnerable sinks. Therefore, we need to make sure that the changes made to the application source code do not in any way affect the functionality and logic of the program in the execution paths which were not vulnerable. In particular, we need to assure that the logic of the program in other non-vulnerable paths is not changed due to the insertion of the patch. The *path-sensitivity* of the patching problem requires us to know which path it is going to retrofit. Our analysis can gain this information about the vulnerable path from the vulnerable location (sink) and can use this information to distinguish execution paths.

Optimization Although the main goal of automatic retrofitting of the web application against logic vulnerabilities is to make sure that the vulnerabilities are correctly patched, but we also prefer that the resulting web application source remains optimized in terms of both time and space. That is, we prefer to add one patch at a location where it prevents several vulnerable locations than adding multiple patches into multiple locations in the code. To place the patches to optimal locations in an application, our approach considers various scenarios with different candidate places, it then identifies which candidate place is optimal for an application with one or multiple vulnerable sinks. More detailed discussion about optimization of the patching process is in Subsection 3.4.

3. Approach

Figure 1 shows the overview of our approach. There are two two main steps: 1) generate the appropriate patch, 2) place the patch in an appropriate location in the original code.

Input Our approach uses general information about the vulnerability to start its analysis. This information includes: 1) the missing condition, C, 2) the path to the vulnerable sensitive operation (*sink*), P, and 3) the exception policy E.

Error Handling Policy LOGICPATCHER requires an (optional) exception handling logic E as input. If no inputs are provided, the default exception handling strategy is to terminate of the program. This way if the placed security condition C is not met by the program state, the program terminates without entering in a non-secure state. Though termination is one option, the developers may want to take other actions if a malicious input is given to the program. Logging and sending alerts to system administrators are among popular actions that one may take after a malicious attack. To better help users of the tool in deciding the exception handling methods, LOGICPATCHER provides an option to analyze exception handling options in the source code (see Appendix A).

3.1 Patch Generation

The Missing Conditions Automatic detection tools usually report AIVs in terms of the missing conditions as well as the details about the location of the vulnerability. They express these conditions in terms of conditions on 1) user inputs or 2) conditions on the internal server state. A condition is a tuple of $< Var, Val, Rel >$ in which Var is the variable, Val is the value for the variable which may be a constant value or a dynamic one, and Rel is the relational operator. Our approach can use the missing conditions C and the vulnerable execution trace (path) P to compute the program slice for these constraints. This program slice is called the *patch*.

The security conditions to be added to the patch include variables which specify the available information *context*. This information context defines the type of the patch as well as the instructions which need to be added to patch.

Program Slicing A missing condition, when inserted in code, may need to be accompanied by some other data- and control-dependent instructions if necessary. To preserve the data dependencies, we may add other instructions to the patch. That is, given a condition $< Var, Val, Rel >$, we perform backward program slicing so that the variables Var and values Val involved in the condition set C will be meaningful and valid at the patch location.

3.2 Patch Placement

The problem of patch placement may seem to be trivial at first glance. However, the location of the vulnerability is not necessarily the location where the security patch should be placed. A logic vulnerability patch is basically a constraint written as an conditional statement. To insert an conditional statement we need to find the starting point and the ending point for the conditional statement block.

An important challenge in patching an execution paths is to ensure that the patch does not affect other execution paths, an occurrence we call *overprotection*, since adding a security condition to a path which was not vulnerable may make that execution path unavailable, and prevent it from being executed under legitimate circumstances. To place the generated patch, the approach should find candidate places in the code where it can insert the beginning and ending of the conditional statement block without interfering with other execution paths and other sinks.

Multiple Paths to one Vulnerable Sink When only some of the execution paths to a sink are vulnerable, we need to make sure that we are fixing those vulnerable paths only and are not changing other paths. When there are multiple execution paths to a vulnerable sink, our approach must assure that the vulnerable(s) path is patched, as well as ensure other non-vulnerable paths remain intact. Based on this goal, we categorize different scenarios when placing the patch.

To show these scenarios, we provide an example of a sink (a DELETE query). The code example deletes some records from the table `$table`. This example derived from a real-world example in `phpNS` application (simplified for more clarity). The main command to delete is executed in `function.php`.

```
function delete_item($table,$where) {
  $res = mysql_query("DELETE FROM ".$table ."
       ".$where);
  log_this('delete','User
       <i>'.$_SESSION['username'].'</i> has
       <strong>deleted</strong> a tables contents.
       Table: '.$table.' '.$where);}
```

Listing 2: Delete Query phpNS, function.php

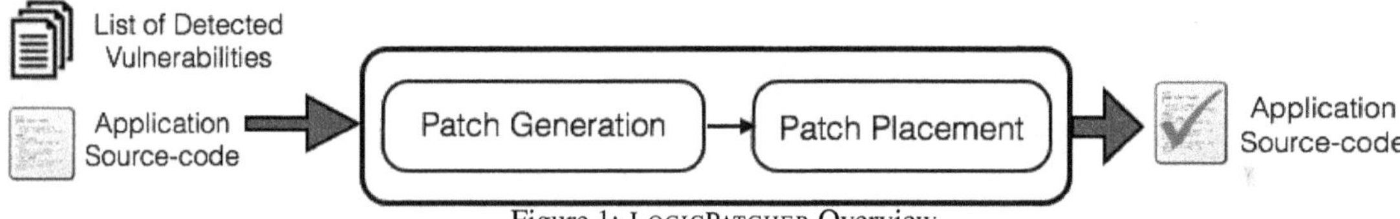

Figure 1: LOGICPATCHER Overview

Analysis shows that this query is vulnerable to authorization bypass in some of the paths, for instance it lets the authenticated normal users to delete *any* comment in the system if they can guess the comment ID (which is an incremental integer value and not hard to guess). The missing condition is to check whether the current user is the owner (the author) of the comments and if so, she can delete the comments. Now let us consider different scenarios where the other execution paths in the application affect our decision about patch placement. For code in Listing 3, all of the paths leading to the sink are vulnerable since both paths allow authenticated users to delete any comments.

```
if ($do == "comments") {
  if ($_GET['action'] == 'delete') {
    $where = "WHERE id =".$_POST['id'];
    delete_item('comments',$where);
    log_this('delete_comments','User
        <i>'.$_SESSION['username'].'</i> has
        <strong>deleted</strong> the comments:
        "'.$where"');}}
else if($do == "all") {
  if ($_GET['action'] == 'delete') {
    delete_item('comments',"");
    log_this('delete all comments','User
        <i>'.$_SESSION['username'].'</i> has
        <strong>deleted</strong> all comments');}}
```

Listing 3: Deleting a comment, article.php

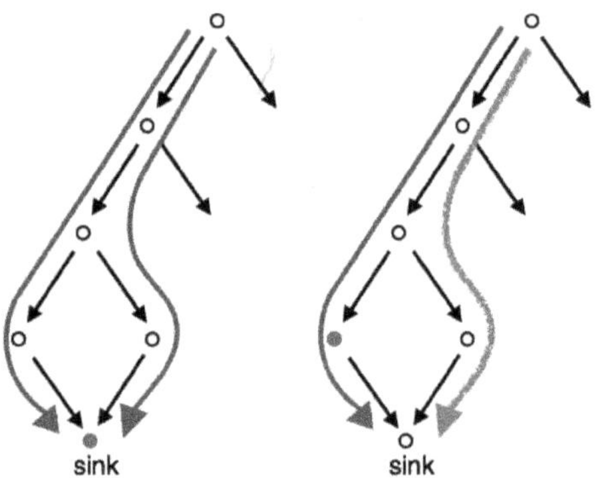

Figure 2: a) Execution paths for Listing 3, b) Execution paths for Listing 5

An abstract control flow graph of this example is depicted in Figure 2 (a) where both paths to the sink are vulnerable and therefore we can simply place the patch at the sink location. Since all of the paths to a sink are vulnerable, then patching the query or patching the path to the query is straightforward: it can insert the patch just before sink location. We can place the patch, which is a check for the author of the comment (users should be able to delete their own comments), in the `delete_item` function if this function is used only for deleting comments. Listing 4 shows the candidate place for the patch.

```
function delete_item($table,$items) {
  XXXX: placing the Patch here : XXXX
  $res = general_query("DELETE FROM ".$table." WHERE
      id IN (".$items.")");
  log_this('delete','User
      <i>'.$_SESSION['username'].'</i> has
      <strong>deleted</strong> a tables contents.
      Table: '.$table.'. Items: '.$items);}
```

Listing 4: Patching scenario 1, phpNS, function.php

Another scenario is shown in Listing 5 in which only some of the paths to the query are vulnerable. The path to deleting a comment is the vulnerable one but the other path to delete an article is not since it restricts the query to the author of the article.

Figure 2 (b) shows the control flow representation of Listing 5. If we place the patch inside `delete_item` function, then we are adding code to non-vulnerable paths, in which we will check for the author of comments, and so we are injecting an irrelevant check to the code which makes the query unavailable for those non-vulnerable paths.

```
if ($do == "comments") {
  if ($_GET['action'] == 'delete') {
    $where = "WHERE id =".$_POST['id'];
    delete_item('comments',$where);}}
else if($do == "articles") {
  if ($_GET['action'] == 'delete') {
    $where = "WHERE id =".$_POST['id'] "AND
        author=".$_SESSION['userID'];
    delete_item('articles',$where}}
```

Listing 5: Non-vulnerable Paths to the Sink, article.php, phpNs application

Unlike the earlier scenario, in these case, we certainly cannot patch the path at query location. To patch the vulnerable path, we must ensure that the patch is only accessible along the vulnerable path. Our approach finds the nearest location from the sink where the patch would not interfere with other paths. The candidate location for this example is shown in Listing 6.

```
if ($do == "comments") {
  if ($_GET['action'] == 'delete') {
    $where = "WHERE id =".$_POST['id'];
    XXXX: placing the patch here XXXX
    delete_item('comments',$where);}}
else if($do == "articles") {
  if ($_GET['action'] == 'delete') {
    $where = "WHERE article_ID = " .$_POST['id']."
        AND author=".$_SESSION['userID'];
    delete_item('articles',$where);}}
```

Listing 6: Patching scenario 2, phpNS, article.php

Other Paths to Other Sinks Now consider a scenario in which some paths to the sink are vulnerable, but the vulnerable paths are not entirely disjoint from other non-vulnerable paths to other sinks. Listing 7 shows the example where the code is shared with other users in the system (in this case `admin` user(s)). Based on the previous solution, we may place the patch before calling function `delete_item`, however, we are restricting the admin users from deleting comments of other users, where there is no such policy in the application demanding that.

```
if($_SESSION['group'] == "admin"){
  $admin = true;}
if ($do == "comments") {
  if ($_GET['action'] == 'delete') {
    $where = "WHERE id =".$_POST['id'];
    delete_item('comments',$where);}}
else if($do == "articles") {
  if ($_GET['action'] == 'delete') {
```

```
        delete_item('articles',"WHERE article_ID = "
        .$_POST['id']." AND
        author=".$_SESSION['userID']);}}
```

Listing 7: Other Execution Paths in article.php

Figure 3 (a) shows this scenario. Although the nearest node to `sink1` is node `x`, we cannot place the the patch right after this node, because it will interfere with the non-vulnerable path.

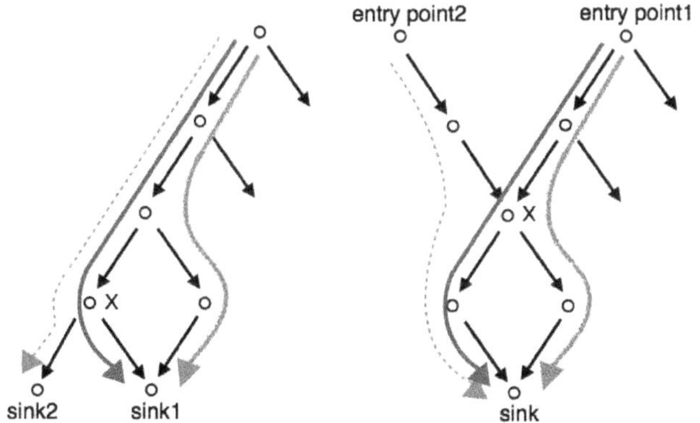

Figure 3: a) Interference with Other Execution Paths: CFG representation of Listing 7, b) Interfering Execution Paths: Non-disjoint Paths

The above example, or even the one shown in Figure 3 (b)), where two or more non-vulnerable paths are not entirely disjoint from the vulnerable path, show that in some cases the overlap between the paths make it impossible to place the patch along the vulnerable path without interfering with non-vulnerable ones.

In order to uniquely patch the vulnerable path, we need to be able to uniquely identify it. Therefore, our approach uses *Path Profiling* techniques [5] to uniquely identify the execution paths in the instrumented application. Path Profiling algorithm assigns a unique state to each execution path and instruments the program with state transitions on each path. The changes in the transition state should be in a way that by reaching the end of each path, we reach the same state which was assigned to the path. Path Profiling algorithm introduced in [5] computes the state transitions efficiently.

After identifying the path, and checking for interfering paths, if inserting the condition *C* alone results in interference between vulnerable and non-vulnerable paths, then the path id (hash ids generated in path profiling) will be merged with condition *C*, to make it non-interfering, as shown in Listing 8.

```
if(C && PATH == <hash_path_x>){
   /*vulnerable sink and its dependent instructions*/}
```

Listing 8: Merging Path Profiling info

3.3 Algorithm

A high-level overview of our algorithm is shown in Algorithm 1. We start our analysis by parsing and generating the control-flow graph (CFG) of the source code. After creating the CFG, we should identify the CFGNodes which are data- or control-dependent on the sink. This is a crucial step since we are going to wrap the sink inside an introduced security condition *C*; therefore we need to also include these dependent instructions inside the condition block so that the program executes consistently during run-time. Sets `instructions_before_sink` and `instructions_after_sink` are used to gather these dependent instructions.

Finding the right Scope The previous scenarios show that it is important to reason about the patch and the placement of the patch

Algorithm 1: Overview of the Patching Algorithm on a Single File

```
input : C: Missing Check
input : P: Vulnerable Path to the Vulnerable Sink
input : E: Security Exception Handling Policy
// Step 1:  Generating the Patch
CFG := getCFG(sourceFile);
foreach Condition cond ∈ C do
    instructions_before_sink,Vars, Vals := ∅;
    Vars.add(getVar(cond));
    Vars.add(getVal(cond));
    // non-constant values
    // Step 1.1:  Backward Program Slicing
    for cfgNode ∈ CFG do
        // Starting from sink backward
        foreach Variable newVar ∈ cfgNode do
            if newVar is data-control dependent on Vars then
                Vars.add(newVar);
        if cfgNode.include(Vars) then
            instructions_before_sink.add(cfgNode);
// Step 2:  Finding the Patch Scope:  Algorithm 2
// Step 3:  Patch Placement
// Step 3.1:  Forward Live Variable Analysis
instructions_after_sink := ∅;
for cfgNode ∈ CFG do
    // Starting from sink forward
    foreach Variable v ∈ cfgNode do
        if v is data-control dependent on sink operation then
            instructions_after_sink.add(cfgNode);
            break;
return instructions_before_sink, instructions_after_sink, functionScope;
```

with respect to other execution paths in the application.Our approach uses static analysis techniques to generate and place the patch in a proper location and it also reasons about the possibility of multiple vulnerabilities and how LogicPatcher should generate and place the patches so that they would also not interfere with each other.

Recall that the input to LogicPatcher is a vulnerable sink location *P*, the missing (authorization) condition *C*, and the security exception handling policy *E*. LogicPatcher generate 1) the patch *S* which is a set of instructions; 2) the candidate location *L* for the patch to be inserted in. *L* consists of the patch context (i.e. filename where the patch introduced), and two candidate locations to insert the start and ending of the missing condition.

First our approach needs to identify the function context where we should inject the missing condition. Since the execution paths are intra- and inter-procedural according to where in path we inject the missing condition, LogicPatcher may work with different function contexts.

Consider this sequence of function calls `f() −> g() −> h()` where function `f`calls function `g` and also function `g` can call function `h` and function `h` includes the vulnerable sink. The first challenge is identify the proper function context; that is, whether LogicPatcher should add the missing condition to function `h()`, `g()` or `f()`.

To answer this question we should think about our second goal: not to overprotect the application, which means that we should not add the condition to the execution paths which were not vulnerable in the first place. So we first examine the number of function calls to each of this functions – starting from the innermost function `h()` and going backward to `f()` – and if the sequence of such function calls includes paths which are not vulnerable we go one step backward.

After this step, the location of the function is found and the scope of the variables involved in the patch is identified. Now LogicPatcher needs to find the start and end block for the condition itself. The start point for the condition can come just before the vulnerable sink inside the candidate function f.

Algorithm 2: Finding the candidate file and scope

```
input : CFGNode vuln_sink, List vulnerablePaths, missingAuthzCheck
input : Candidate file name, Candidate start point, candidate end point
Function (findFunction(h)) currentFunction := h;
callerFunctions := all callGraphNodes who call currentFunction;
if callerFunctions.size == 1 then
    // only one path
    candidate patch function := currentFunction;
else if callerFunctions are all in vulnerable paths then
    // all paths leading to the currentFunction are
       vulnerable
    // so we can patch the current function
    candidate patch function := currentFunction;
else
    // traverse backward
    // and put the check before calling the
       currentFunction
    foreach function f ∈ callerFunctions do
        findCandidatePatchFunction(f);
```

For the end point of the check, we first need to analyze the data dependencies after the sink. To address this problem, we do an inter-procedural Live Variable Analysis (LVA) on the output of the sink operation to find the scope of the code where the output is still live. This analysis may add other variables to the set due to data dependencies.

Live Variable Analysis A patch puts the vulnerable sink inside an conditional statement block with the condition C. If we simply put only the sink inside a conditional statement, we may change the original semantics of the application. Merely including the sink instruction to the conditional statement block may make other instructions after the sink invalid. Listing 9 shows an example where the result of the query is used to other operations.

```
result = execute_query(...);
if(result){ echo("successful transaction.");}
else{ handle_exception();}
```

Listing 9: Result of sink is used for another operation

Now one only puts the sink (the query) inside the condition block, then the result value would not be accessible for paths which do not execute the true branch of condition C. Therefore, our approach needs to reason about a candidate location for ending the condition block.

```
if(missing_condition \mytt{C}){
  result = execute_query(...);}
if(result){
  do_something();}
```

Listing 10: Wrongly patched version of 9

The correct patch for Listing 9 is shown in Listing 11.

```
if(missing_condition \mytt{C}){
  result = execute_query(...);
  if(result){
    do_something();}}
```

Listing 11: The correct patch for 9

What is changed in Listing 11 is that every instruction which is control- or data-dependent on the value of the sink operation is now also contained by the condition block. To find all of the instructions which are dependent on the sink value, we should first find the variables which are dependent on the value of the sink. Each instruction which includes such variables, will be added to the instruction list which is going to be added to the condition block.

To find the *sink-dependent* variables LOGICPATCHER performs forward data-control dependency analysis starting from the sink location and put the ending of the block where the result of the sink is no longer used. LOGICPATCHER uses similar ideas for *Live Variable Analysis* to find which variables are dependent on the sink. The implementation details of this algorithm is shown in the implementation Section.

3.4 Discussion

Patching the Sink Based on the type of vulnerability and the information context available in the execution paths, there may be two options to patch the application at the source level: 1) patching the execution paths leading to the sensitive operations (*sinks*), and 2) patching the sink itself by changing the access parameters of the sensitive operation.

For example, when the sink type is a DB query, to patch the vulnerability we may be able to augment the query where clause if the columns in the DB table hold the condition variables. This way the query becomes more restrictive. However, it is not always the case that the values are available for access parameters. For example, when the missing authorization information is not available in the query or in any of the columns of the table, we need to add the missing conditions to the execution paths leading to the vulnerable sink.

As an example, consider the following query. This query is accessible for all logged-in users of a blog application. The following query is detected as vulnerable because it lets the authenticated user to delete *any* blog post if she can provide a valid post ID.

```
$sql = "DELETE FROM blogdata WHERE post_id=$post_id";
```

Listing 12: Query to be Patched

To patch the vulnerability, we may have the option to place the condition `authorID == $_SESSION['userID']` in the `WHERE` clause in the query as shown in Listing 13 if the `blogdata` table contains the column `author_ID` . Alternatively, we can place the condition in the path leading to the query as shown in Listing 14.

```
$sql = "DELETE FROM blogdata WHERE post_id=$post_id AND
    author_ID=$author_id";
```

Listing 13: Patched Query

```
if(getAuthor($post_id) == $author_id ||
    $author_id=="admin"){
  $sql = "DELETE FROM blogdata WHERE post_id=$post_id";}
```

Listing 14: Patched Path

Patching Multiple Vulnerabilities In real world, it is often the case that an application may have more than one logic vulnerability. It is because some logic vulnerabilities go together i.e. they may have the same or similar root cause(s). In patching logic vulnerabilities therefore we should examine how we can patch the application in a way that is both 1) correct and 2) efficient. Reasoning about patching multiple vulnerabilities is crucial because we do not want to repeat the patch(es) firstly because it may change the logic of the program and secondly because repeating the patch at multiple locations is not time- and space-efficient. In finding the optimal location for patching multiple vulnerabilities in an application several scenarios may occur:

1) Vulnerabilities of the same type: A patch consists some security checks which would control values on some variables or some server-side state. Vulnerabilities of the same type may share these checks entirely or partially. In this scenario, we should place the checks if they are being added previously.

2) Vulnerabilities with various types, but the same root cause: In another scenario, the vulnerabilities may be of various type and therefore they do not share the security checks in the patch, however, they share a common prefix in the code. i.e., they share paths.

In this case, even though the checks themselves are not shared, but the patch may change data-dependencies for the variables used in the patch or they may change the server-side state. Hence, we must watch out for the instructions included in each patch to make sure they do not interfere with each other.

3) Independent Vulnerabilities: Vulnerabilities are independent when they do not share a common prefix in the code or they do not have the same cause. These vulnerabilities can be patch independently. Our approach takes each vulnerability one by one and generated the candidate patch for it.

3.5 Limitations

LogicPatcher is a 'best effort' tool which suggest security patches to developers/system administrators. A separate formal verification or manual effort must be made to verify the correctness of the generated patches and the resulting source code. This is because of some high-level limitations which are involved in using automated tools to patch security vulnerabilities which we discuss in the rest of this subsection.

Lack of Program Specification The main reason that our approach cannot assure the correctness of the patches is that our approach does not require specifications on the functionality of the program, functions and program statements in the source code. For instance, during the patch generation, our tool must decide which instructions should be wrapped by the security condition C. This would be much easier if the tool had more knowledge about the sensitive instructions rather than performing static data- and control-dependency analyses.

Although we do not verify the correctness of the patches automatically, we believe that the proposed approach *by design* minimizes undesirable side-effects on the functionality of the applications. For instance, in the presence of interfering execution paths, as discussed in Section 3, we use path profiling to prevent the introduction of new control instructions in non-vulnerable paths.

The generated patch consists of the missing condition, and its control and data dependencies. Thus, the correctness of the generated patch depends on the correctness of the data and control dependency analysis. We use backward program slicing and live variable analysis techniques to create the patch. These data and control dependency techniques are performed statically and therefore they may be imprecise. However, we use a very conservative approach to analyzing the dependencies along the execution paths and so we do not miss any dependent instructions. For instance, in backward program slicing, even though the dependencies of DB query instructions are not available statically, our tool adds those instructions in the patch if condition C is dependent on the result of the query and also it adds the query string variables to the set of variables of interest. This may seem to cause overprotection problems, however, the path profiling procedures ensure that the instructions protected by C are going to be used only in the vulnerable path.

Cascading Sinks There are some complications involved with patching applications in which the developers use cascading sinks. Assume that the developers perform two sensitive operations (reading and writing to db tables, or files) in the same execution path, and one of these sensitive operations is vulnerable. The decision to whether include both sinks in the missing condition statement block or just include the vulnerable sink depends on whether the data- and control-dependency analyses detect the two operations as related or not. The problem may cause some side effects (as we will see in Section 5 under correctness discussion) on the generated patch and correctness of the code.

4. Implementation

We have designed and implemented a tool which, given a list of application vulnerabilities in a web application, it will generate security patches for the vulnerabilities and will place them in the source-code of the application so that each sink is no longer vulnerable to that particular vulnerability. Figure 4 shows the architecture of LogicPatcher in two major steps: 1) patch generation and 2) patch placement. As shown in this figure, each phase has various analysis components. In this section we go over the implementation of each of these components.

4.1 Inputs to LogicPatcher

LogicPatcher starts the analysis with two sets of inputs:(1) source files and (2) list of detected vulnerabilities which is expressed as the tuple $< C,P,E >$ (ref Sec 2.1) . In our experience, providing such input does not need any additional effort. Security tools usually report the vulnerabilities with these details.

4.2 Patch Generation

To generate the security patch, LogicPatcher uses static data- and control-flow analysis to preserve the original semantics of the program in the presence of a new security condition C. A security condition has a set of variables and values which should be have the same semantics as other consistent paths while used in the security condition. Therefore LogicPatcher uses static analysis to identify the instructions which include these variables and values. These instruction then are then added to the patch.

LogicPatcher starts with using a PHP parser and Control Flow Graph (CFG) generator to get the CFG of the application. It then traverses the CFG of one of the consistent paths backward from the sink location to find the related instructions to condition C's variables and values. This analysis is intra- and inter-procedural which enables LogicPatcher to reason about consistency of the patch throughout the entire application. After adding all the related instructions to the patch, LogicPatcher compares these instructions to the instructions which are in the vulnerable path P. The reason for this comparison is that our approach avoids the insertion of instructions to a path twice as it may cause side-effects.

4.3 Patch Placement

As discussed in Section 3, along the execution path leading to the vulnerable query, there are several candidate locations to put the patch. If we put the patch at the beginning of the entry point, we may cause so many side-effects because other instructions are going to be affected by the patch. So the best choice is to put it as close as possible to the query itself to minimize the side-effects.

To find a correct place for the patch to be inserted in the code, LogicPatcher uses several code analysis techniques. These techniques assure that LogicPatcher inserts a patch into the vulnerable path and it does not affect other execution paths.

Path Enumeration To enumerate all of the execution paths, LogicPatcher uses Pixy [13] to parse all of the PHP files in the source code and build the Control Flow Graph (CFG) of the application. LogicPatcher then traverses the CFG nodes in the graph and lists all of the paths for each entry point. It finally gathers all of the execution paths for all of the entry points in the application. Our path enumeration is intra- and inter-procedural.

LogicPatcher starts uses one entry point at a time to enumerate all of the paths starting from that entry point. For non-control instructions LogicPatcher adds the CFG node for the instruction to the current path to be constructed. Each time LogicPatcher visits a control instruction (i.e. if-statement, function call, function return) it changes the list which holds the paths.

For if-statements it clones a path into two different paths and puts the paths back into the list of paths. For a function call instruction, LogicPatcher first saves the return address (the next instruction to be executed after the function return) in a hash structure and then traverses the CFG for the function. By visiting a function return, LogicPatcher searches the hash and adds the CFG node for the return address to the current path.

Path Profiling As discussed in Listing 5, there may be cases where

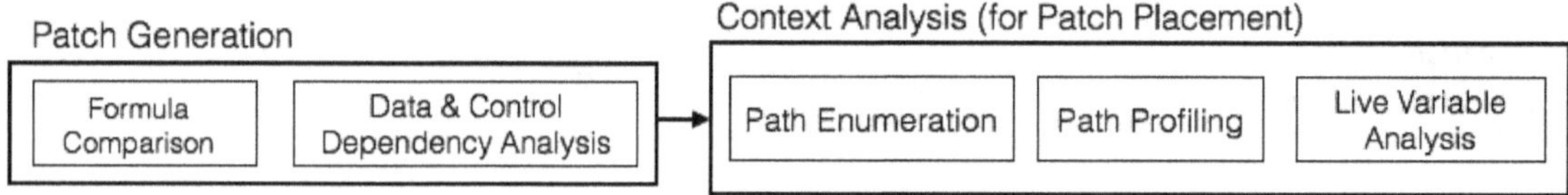

Figure 4: Patch Generation and Patch Placement in LOGICPATCHER

placement of the patch in a vulnerable path interferes with other execution paths since it is not disjoint from the other paths and therefor we may need to introduce extra control flags to assure that the patch is going to be added to the vulnerable path only. In order to patch the vulnerable path and only the vulnerable path, LOGICPATCHER needs to keep track of the vulnerable path and uses some criteria to uniquely identify it.

Path profiling techniques [5] enable LOGICPATCHER to achieve this goal. The path profiling concept first enumerates all of the paths and assigns a unique number to paths to each sink or exit location. It then computes the transition numbers and instruments the application. At execution time, by each transition, the computed value for the transition is going be added to the state of application. Eventually when it reaches the sink or exit location it arrives to the same assigned number to the path. LOGICPATCHER uses the same ideas to keep track of the vulnerable path and for efficiency it uses an abstracted version of the path which only includes control-instructions: conditions, loops, exit, return, and function calls.

Live Variable Analysis As discussed in Section 3, there are instructions after the sink which need to be included in the condition block during the patching. Since we need to know the last location where the dependent variables are used (the result value of the sink operation is still *alive*), we need to perform a backward dependency analysis, which is going to show the last location where the variables are used. LOGICPATCHER uses *Live Variable Analysis* (LVA) [2] ideas to keep track of the variables which are data- or control-dependent on the result of the sink operation.

To perform the analysis, LVA algorithm takes the current context (i.e. the current file which the patch is going to be inserted in) as input and performs a backward analysis to compute the `In`, `Out`, `Def` and `Used` sets. The last instruction where all sink-dependent variables are still alive is going to be marked. The end of the condition block will be just after the marked instruction. Since the value of the sink operation may be used in return statements and be variables in other file contexts may be dependent on the sink, LOGICPATCHER performs intra- and inter-procedural LVA. Note that the end block will be inserted to the file context where the condition is going to be added, therefore the block syntax is preserved by LOGICPATCHER.

Output LOGICPATCHER generates a candidate security patch which includes the missing condition C. It also gives out the candidate location to place the patch which is somewhere along path P. In cases where path profiling is needed, LOGICPATCHER produces an instrumented version of the code along with new control conditions, which assure that the patch is only executable along the vulnerable path.

4.4 Discussion

There are some technical limitations associated with static analysis of programs for patching PHP applications with current open-source tools. These problems however are not derived from the design of LOGICPATCHER, and they do not limit the applicability of our approach for patching applications.

Object-Oriented PHP features LOGICPATCHER uses Pixy [13] for parsing and creating the control flow graph of the application. Some complex features in PHP such as object-oriented features are not handled by Pixy.

Table 2: PHP Applications

Application	SLOC	# php Files	# of Sink Locs	# of Resources	Vulnerability Type
phpns 2.1.1alpha	4224	30	40	13	Authz/Authc
DCPPortal 5.1.44	89074	362	308	34	param tampering Authc/Authz
myBloggie 2.1.3	6261	59	24	5	param tampering Authc/Authz
miniBloggie 1.1	1283	11	5	2	Authc/Authz
SCARF 1.0	978	19	13	7	Authc/Authz
SnipeGallery	9.1k	37	25	3	param tampering
SPHPBlog	26.5k	125	122	11	param tampering
PHPNews	6.4k	20	57	6	param tampering
Landshop	15.4k	88	541	9	param tampering

Path enumeration in the presence of loops Path enumeration is the most crucial component of our approach. It is used by both for patch placement and path profiling algorithms. Therefore the precision of path enumerates affects the precision of our tool. However, with static analysis of PHP code and limitations in the libraries we use, there are some cases where enumerating the paths statically is a challenge. Currently our path enumeration approach treats loops similar to if-statements and therefore each loop is treated in two different branches: 1) it is not going to be executed and 2) it is going to be executed once.

5. Evaluation

LOGICPATCHER, designed for patching PHP web applications, is implemented in Java in about 1.5K lines of code. We use open-source tools and libraries (TAPS [8] and Pixy [13]) to get the control flow graphs for PHP applications. The experiments described in this section were performed on a MacBook Pro (2.4 GHz Intel, 4.0 GB RAM).

We examine 9 open-source PHP applications which are summarized in Table 2. The test suite was picked from reported logic vulnerabilities [15, 18, 19] in PHP web applications from previous research studies, which also gave missing conditions and path locations. The results of our evaluation are categorized into three subsections: (1) the generated patches by LOGICPATCHER and sample patch and patch locations suggested by our tool, (2) the precision of LOGICPATCHER on generation and placement of the patches, and (3) scalability of our approach.

5.1 Candidate Patch Locations

myBloggie is a simple blogging application which lets users add, delete and update blog posts to/from a database. The application has two types of security issues: access control and parameter tampering vulnerabilities. There are six privilege escalation problems in `myBloggie`, which allow an unauthenticated user to delete and update blog posts. LOGICPATCHER generated a patch which checks the validity of the session variables and the level of the user `$userid['level']`. The patch includes termination instructions if the security check is not met.

miniBloggie is a blogging software with standard features such as adding, deleting, and updating blog posts and comments. This application has one vertical privilege escalation(i.e., access to privileges in higher role) vulnerability. LogicPatcher fixed miniBloggie by adding the following constraint:

```
if (isset($_SESSION['user']) && isset($_SESSION['pwd'])){
  $sql = "DELETE FROM blogdata WHERE post_id=$post_id";
  $query = mysql_query($sql) or die("Cannot query the
      database.<br>" . mysql_error());}
else{ header( "Location: ./login.php" );}
```

Listing 15: Patch generated for del.php, miniBloggie

SCARF is an open-source conference management software. This application is vulnerable to both vertical and horizontal privilege escalation(same role different user). The vertical escalation vulnerability is caused by lack of authorization checks in certain files. For example, in generaloptions.php the check for administrative role is omitted which lets other users to gain access to operations in this file. Our tool generated the following patch for the file, and placed the patch before the first sensitive operation (DB query) in the file.

```
if ($_SESSION['privilege'] == 'admin'){...}
else{ exit();}
```

Listing 16: Patch generated for generaloptions.php, SCARF

Several horizontal escalation vulnerabilities found in SCARF are caused by use of `$_GET['session_id']` instead of `$_SESSION['user_id']`. This vulnerability happens at the query location in the access parameters used in the WHERE clause. Therefore, for the database columns which were identified to hold the `$_SESSION['user_id']`, LogicPatcher augmented the WHERE clause in the vulnerable queries with the necessary constraints on the column values. For the WHERE clauses in which the column was present but the value was set to `$_GET['session_id']`, LogicPatcher replaced the value with `$_SESSION['user_id']`.

DCPPortal is an open-source content management system which is vulnerable to both vertical and horizontal privilege escalation. The reason for vertical privilege escalation vulnerabilities is the use of cookies from untrusted sources. LogicPatcher suggested using session variables instead of cookies, preserving a one-to-one correspondence between the cookie and the session variables (username, role, permissions, etc). We also generated the program slices with necessary computations for each of the new session variables. For example, for checking the admin role we added:

```
session_start();
if($_SESSION"dcp5_member_id"] == 5){...}
```

Listing 17: Patch generated for DCPPortal

SnipeGallery a photo album application, allows users to arrange albums hierarchically by selecting a parent category for each new album from a drop down list. By selecting a value not in that list, the new album becomes invisible. LogicPatcher generated the patch to check for the availability of the values in the list, before performing any sensitive operations, preventing the vulnerability.

SPHPBlog is a blog system. It uses files to store blog posts, comments, rating, etc. This application is vulnerable to parameter tampering as it does not check if the user selects values from the drop-down list, or if it is an arbitrary value. Entered values are stored in various files, which is a security threat to the server LogicPatcher generated the patch to check the values for the drop-down lists.

PHPNews is a news management software and is vulnerable to parameter tampering attacks. In admin.php, the application allows administrators to modify certain files through a form which contains name of the file as a hidden field. The server-side code fails to validate that the file name is not tampered and as a result attackers can update existing files, create arbitrary files and / or corrupt files of other applications deployed on the same web server.

Landshop is a real estate application which is vulnerable to both parameter tampering and horizontal privilege escalation attacks. This application includes a form with a hidden field not relevant to that form. When the value of this field is set to the ID of an existing listing (which are displayed prominently on the site), that listing is deleted from the application whether the user is the owner or not. LogicPatcher patched this application by 1) augmenting the WHERE clause query to include the ownership constraints and 2) generate the program slice to create the ownership value.

phpns, In `phpns`, application, we have a case of non-disjoint paths because of the existence of a generic function `delete_item`. This function is used to delete rows from any table in the DB and the table (the resource) name depends on the path leading to this function. That is, in `manage.php` and `article.php` we have:

```
delete_item('articles',$items_f);
```

Listing 18: manage.php, `phpns`

```
delete_item('comments',$items_f);
```

Listing 19: article.php before the patch, `phpns`,

However, only one of these execution paths is vulnerable to vertical privilege escalation, and therefore only one of these function calls should be patched by an authorization check. In this case, we use path profiling to restrict the path which deletes comments (Listing 19) to authenticated users. The generated candidate patch is shown in Listing 20:

```
if($_SESSION['username']){//added security check, checks
    if the a valid username exists in the session
  delete_item('comments',$items_f);}
```

Listing 20: article.php after the patch, `phpns`,

5.2 Effectiveness

We evaluated the effectiveness of our tool by manually inspecting the generated patches. We also compare the newer versions of applications in our test suite (if available) with our the patches. There are two aspects to the effectiveness of LogicPatcher: correctness of the patches and optimizing patch placement.

Correctness The correctness of the patching depends on: 1) the correctness of the generated patch, and 2) the correctness of the scope and location of the patch. We have confirmed that LogicPatcher could correctly patch 27 of 29 vulnerable files in 9 web applications in our test suite. As discussed in the Limitations subsection in Section 3, cascading sinks are one of the reasons LogicPatcher might generate incorrect or inconsistent patches. The following example in `Scarf` application shows the code before and after the patch:

```
if (isset($_POST['paper_id'])) {
  query("UPDATE papers SET title='$title',
      abstract='$abstract', $pdfSetString
      session_id='$session' WHERE paper_id='$id'");
  query("DELETE FROM authors WHERE paper_id='$id'");}
```

Listing 21: editpaper.php, Scarf Application before the patch

```
if (isset($_POST['paper_id'])) {
  if($_POST['authors'] == $_SESSION['user'] && PATH ==
      <hash-path1>){
    query("UPDATE papers SET title='$title',
        abstract='$abstract', $pdfSetString
        session_id='$session' WHERE paper_id='$id'");}
  if($_POST['authors'] == $_SESSION['user'] && PATH ==
      <hash-path2>){
    query("DELETE FROM authors WHERE paper_id='$id'");}}
```

Listing 22: editpaper.php, Scarf Application after applying the candidate patch

Table 3: Application Complexity

Application	# of paths	vulnerable file(s)	Entry Point Locs	Analysis time (s)
phpns 2.1.1alpha	709	1	21	3759
DCPPortal 5.1.44	588	12	210	2452
myBloggie 2.1.3	98	7	45	1620
miniBloggie 1.1	14	1	6	732
SCARF 1.0	86	3	16	250
SnipeGallery	530	1	32	2415
SPHPBlog	251	1	76	5613
PHPNews	36	2	10	179
Landshop	362	1	44	1205

As it is shown in Listing 22, because two different sinks exist in the same path and they are not disjoint, the path profiling procedure will create two different hash values for the functions, and each sink is wrapped in a different set of conditions. However, these two queries should come together to preserve the consistency of the DB data.

Optimization The second aspect of the effectiveness of our tool is to check whether the patch placement was optimal. For the same missing condition *C*, our tool should be able to find the best location to inject *C* so that multiple vulnerabilities are prevented. Currently, the path enumeration and path profiling procedures use the information about vulnerable paths and missing conditions one at a time. If the same missing condition causes multiple vulnerabilities and paths are disjoint from correct paths, optimal patches are generated. However, if any interference exists in the code, then the path profiling procedure may suggest several patch locations for multiple vulnerabilities for the same cause. We plan to address optimizing of multiple patch placement in future work.

5.3 Scalability

We evaluate LOGICPATCHER on variety of web applications with sizes ranging from 1K to 90K. as shown in Columns 2-3 in Table 2 show the size and number of PHP files in the applications, and column 4 gives an estimation of the number of sink locations (query locations, file operations, etc) in the source-code of the applications. Column 5 in Table 2 shows number of resources to be analyzed. By resources, we mean the number of DB queries in case the vulnerabilities are related to DB operations and number of different files when the sink type is file operation.

Table 3 shows statistics about the complexity of each application. In particular, it shows the total number of paths (column 2), the number of files which are vulnerable and need to be patched (column 3). Column 4 shows the number of program entry points, which together with the number of paths affect the patch placement process. That is, if the number of paths increase while the number of entry points remain the same, the number of disjoint paths would decrease. This in turn will increase the analysis times which are shown in column 5 of Table 3. About 90% of the analysis time is spent on path enumeration which is used by the patch placement module. This analysis is only needed once and it does not add any overhead to the application execution at run-time.

6. Related Work

The problem of finding logic errors in software has been studied originally in the context of e-commerce business validation logic. Prior work towards detecting computational logic errors include model checking [9], modeling correct payment logics combined with static analysis [20], and invariant generation and blackbox testing [16]. Other works in this context look at finding inconsistencies using server and client side validation, by comparing the checks performed by client-side JavaScript as an implied specification to check for server-side vulnerabilities [6, 7, 3].

In terms of finding security logic errors, RoleCast [18] is one of first works for web applications, using patterns to model authorization requirements and check if any sensitive operations are performed after authorization. Relatedly, MACE and AutoISES [15, 22] look at conditions along program paths to detect inconsistencies. MACE [15] employs a precise and fine-grained authorization model that is supported by user annotations, comparing the consistency of checking conditions across different requests to the same resources along different code paths, giving it the ability to detect a larger class of vulnerabilities. AutoISES [22] can detect bugs in standard C libraries through mining for common security-related patterns and identifying deviations from these as vulnerabilities. Srivastava et al. [21] detect security vulnerabilities through comparing different implementations of the same API using security policies as inputs. Any inconsistency between the security policy and any of the implementations or between different implementations are reported as errors.

The problem of fixing security errors has received less attention. Ganapathy et al. [11] study correct enforcement of authorization rules in legacy applications, such as X SERVER using a reference monitor for authorization policies. Also, static analysis tools have been used to generate patches in vulnerable software automatically, including repair by generating invariants from correct executions statically [12], placement of sanitization functions by taint analysis [14], and searching for violations in pre-defined patterns [17], requiring to a few lines of edits in the source code, or restricted to specific code transformations within a single procedure [4].

The work closest in spirit to LOGICPATCHER is FixMeUp[19], for fixing access control bugs in web applications due to incorrect conditions. At a high level, LOGICPATCHER is tackling a problem of broader scope, that of fixing logic vulnerabilities caused by missing or inconsistent checks, with minimal guidelines about the vulnerability. FixMeUp requires an explicit and correct high-level specification of access control checks to generate a low level policy specification and a program transformation template, computed using interprocedural backward slicing similar to LOGICPATCHER. In our work, the focus is on correct patch placement in existing code, different from their statement matching and replacement semantics. Also we do not require explicit roles or a specification of correct access control check in advance. LOGICPATCHER works using only correct conditions and path identifiers as input, and optimizes patch placement directly.

7. Conclusions

We present LOGICPATCHER, a tool for automatically patching application inconsistency vulnerabilities in web applications. Though LOGICPATCHER is best effort, and works without explicit functional or policy specifications, we showed that we were able to generate near-optimal patches and fix important vulnerabilities on 9 open source PHP web applications that were previously studied in literature from the point of view of vulnerability detection, inspite of inherent limitations such as cascading sinks. Verifying the correctness of these patches by hand demonstrates that LOGICPATCHER works well in identifying the correct scope and placing the patch in optimal code locations.

8. Acknowledgement

The authors would like to thank the anonymous reviewers for their constructive comments. This material is based upon work supported in part by the National Science Foundation under Grant Nos. NSF-CNS 1065537, NSF-CNS 1514142, NSF-DGE 1069311, DARPA FA8750-12-C-0166 and DARPA FAFA8650-15-C-7561. Any opinions, findings, and conclusions or recommendations expressed in this material are those of the author(s) and do not necessarily reflect the views of the National Science Foundation or the U.S. government.

9. References

[1] Sans critical security controls for effective cyber defense, 2015.

[2] AHO, A. V., SETHI, R., AND ULLMAN, J. D. *Compilers: Principles, Techniques, and Tools*. Addison-Wesley Longman Publishing Co., Inc., Boston, MA, USA, 1986.

[3] ALKHALAF, M., CHOUDHARY, S. R., FAZZINI, M., BULTAN, T., ORSO, A., AND KRUEGEL, C. Viewpoints: Differential string analysis for discovering client- and server-side input validation inconsistencies. In *Proceedings of the 2012 International Symposium on Software Testing and Analysis* (New York, NY, USA, 2012), ISSTA 2012, ACM, pp. 56–66.

[4] ANDERSEN, J., AND LAWALL, J. L. Generic patch inference. In *23rd IEEE/ACM International Conference on Automated Software Engineering ASE 08* (2008).

[5] BALL, T., AND LARUS, J. R. Efficient path profiling. In *Proceedings of the 29th Annual ACM/IEEE International Symposium on Microarchitecture* (Washington, DC, USA, 1996), MICRO 29, IEEE Computer Society, pp. 46–57.

[6] BISHT, P., HINRICHS, T., SKRUPSKY, N., BOBROWICZ, R., AND VENKATAKRISHNAN, V. N. Notamper: Automatic blackbox detection of parameter tampering opportunities in web applications. In *Proceedings of the 17th ACM Conference on Computer and Communications Security* (New York, NY, USA, 2010), CCS '10, ACM, pp. 607–618.

[7] BISHT, P., HINRICHS, T., SKRUPSKY, N., AND VENKATAKRISHNAN, V. N. Waptec: Whitebox analysis of web applications for parameter tampering exploit construction. In *Proceedings of the 18th ACM Conference on Computer and Communications Security* (New York, NY, USA, 2011), CCS '11, ACM, pp. 575–586.

[8] BISHT, P., SISTLA, A. P., AND VENKATAKRISHNAN, V. N. Taps: Automatically preparing safe sql queries. In *Proceedings of the 17th ACM Conference on Computer and Communications Security* (New York, NY, USA, 2010), CCS '10, ACM, pp. 645–647.

[9] FELMETSGER, V., CAVEDON, L., KRUEGEL, C., AND VIGNA, G. Toward automated detection of logic vulnerabilities in web applications. In *Proceedings of the 19th USENIX Conference on Security* (Berkeley, CA, USA, 2010), USENIX Security'10, USENIX Association, pp. 10–10.

[10] GANAPATHY, V., JAEGER, T., AND JHA, S. Automatic placement of authorization hooks in the Linux Security Modules framework. In *Proceedings of the 12th ACM Conference on Computer and Communications Security* (Nov. 2005), pp. 330–339.

[11] GANAPATHY, V., JAEGER, T., AND JHA, S. Retrofitting legacy code for authorization policy enforcement. *2012 IEEE Symposium on Security and Privacy 0* (2006), 214–229.

[12] JIN, G., SONG, L., ZHANG, W., LU, S., AND LIBLIT, B. Automated atomicity-violation fixing. In *Proceedings of the 32Nd ACM SIGPLAN Conference on Programming Language Design and Implementation* (2011).

[13] JOVANOVIC, N., KRUEGEL, C., AND KIRDA, E. Pixy: A static analysis tool for detecting web application vulnerabilities (short paper). In *Proceedings of the 2006 IEEE Symposium on Security and Privacy* (Washington, DC, USA, 2006), SP '06, IEEE Computer Society, pp. 258–263.

[14] LIVSHITS, B., AND CHONG, S. Towards fully automatic placement of security sanitizers and declassifiers. In *Proceedings of the 40th Annual ACM SIGPLAN-SIGACT Symposium on Principles of Programming Languages* (New York, NY, USA, 2013), POPL '13, ACM, pp. 385–398.

[15] MONSHIZADEH, M., NALDURG, P., AND VENKATAKRISHNAN, V. N. Macc: Detecting privilege escalation vulnerabilities in web applications. In *Proceedings of the 2014 ACM SIGSAC Conference on Computer and Communications Security* (New York, NY, USA, 2014), CCS '14, ACM, pp. 690–701.

[16] PELLEGRINO, G., AND BALZAROTTI, D. Toward black-box detection of logic flaws in web applications. In *NDSS 2014, Network and Distributed System Security Symposium, 23-26 February 2014, San Diego, USA* (2014).

[17] PERKINS, J. H., KIM, S., LARSEN, S., AMARASINGHE, S., BACHRACH, J., CARBIN, M., PACHECO, C., SHERWOOD, F., SIDIROGLOU, S., SULLIVAN, G., WONG, W.-F., ZIBIN, Y., ERNST, M. D., AND RINARD, M. Automatically patching errors in deployed software. In *Proceedings of the ACM SIGOPS 22Nd Symposium on Operating Systems Principles SOSP 09* (2009).

[18] SON, S., MCKINLEY, K. S., AND SHMATIKOV, V. Rolecast: finding missing security checks when you do not know what checks are. In *Proceedings of the 2011 ACM international conference on Object oriented programming systems languages and applications* (New York, NY, USA, 2011), OOPSLA '11, ACM, pp. 1069–1084.

[19] SON, S., MCKINLEY, K. S., AND SHMATIKOV, V. Fix me up: Repairing access-control bugs in web applications. In *In Network and Distributed System Security Symposium* (2013).

[20] SON, S., AND SHMATIKOV, V. Saferphp: Finding semantic vulnerabilities in php applications. In *ACM PLAS* (2011).

[21] SRIVASTAVA, V., BOND, M. D., MCKINLEY, K. S., AND SHMATIKOV, V. A security policy oracle: Detecting security holes using multiple api implementations. In *Proceedings of the 32Nd ACM SIGPLAN Conference on Programming Language Design and Implementation* (2011).

[22] TAN, L., ZHANG, X., MA, X., XIONG, W., AND ZHOU, Y. utoises: Automatically inferring security specifications and detecting violations. In *Proceedings of the 17th Usenix Security Symposium* (2008).

[23] VIJAYAKUMAR, H., GE, X., PAYER, M., AND JAEGER, T. Jigsaw: Protecting resource access by inferring programmer expectations. In *Proceedings of the 23rd USENIX Conference on Security Symposium* (Berkeley, CA, USA, 2014), SEC'14, USENIX Association, pp. 973–988.

APPENDIX

A. Error Handling

As described in Section 4 LOGICPATCHER mines the security exception handling information from source-code. This pre-processing step helps the user of LOGICPATCHER to consistently handle exceptions throughout the whole application. LOGICPATCHER users can decide which of the mined instructions should be included in E. Table 4 shows some sample handling methods used by different applications.

Table 4: Mined Security Exceptions by LOGICPATCHER

Application	Security Exception Handling Method
DCPPortal	no else branch Termination Redirect to Login page
SCARF	Termination Redirect to Login page
SPHPBlog	Redirect to Login page
SnipeGallery	Redirect to Login page
PHPNews	Termination Redirect to Login page
MiniBloggie	Termination Redirect to Login page
MyBloggie	Termination
PHPNS	Termination Redirect to Login page
Landshop	Termination

Toward Large-Scale Vulnerability Discovery using Machine Learning

Gustavo Grieco
CIFASIS-CONICET, Rosario
gg@cifasis-conicet.gov.ar

Guillermo Luis Grinblat
CIFASIS-CONICET, Rosario
grinblat@cifasis-conicet.gov.ar

Lucas Uzal
CIFASIS-CONICET, Rosario
uzal@cifasis-conicet.gov.ar

Sanjay Rawat*
System Security Group, Vrije Universiteit, Amsterdam
s.rawat@vu.nl

Josselin Feist
VERIMAG, Université Grenoble Alps
josselin.feist@imag.fr

Laurent Mounier
VERIMAG, Université Grenoble Alps
laurent.mounier@imag.fr

ABSTRACT

With sustained growth of software complexity, finding security vulnerabilities in operating systems has become an important necessity. Nowadays, OS are shipped with thousands of binary executables. Unfortunately, methodologies and tools for an OS scale program testing within a limited time budget are still missing.

In this paper we present an approach that uses lightweight static and dynamic features to predict if a test case is likely to contain a software vulnerability using machine learning techniques. To show the effectiveness of our approach, we set up a large experiment to detect easily exploitable memory corruptions using 1039 Debian programs obtained from its bug tracker, collected 138,308 unique execution traces and statically explored 76,083 different subsequences of function calls. We managed to predict with reasonable accuracy which programs contained dangerous memory corruptions.

We also developed and implemented VDiscover, a tool that uses state-of-the-art Machine Learning techniques to predict vulnerabilities in test cases. Such tool will be released as open-source to encourage the research of vulnerability discovery at a large scale, together with VDiscovery, a public dataset that collects raw analyzed data.

1. INTRODUCTION

In spite of the progress made in programming languages and software engineering techniques, most of the programs we routinely use (from operating system components to main office or web applications) still contain numerous bugs. However, some of these bugs are clearly more dangerous than the others: the ones which may affect the security of the whole system, hereafter referred to as software *vulnerabilities*. As a consequence, a serious issue for software editors is not only to find bugs, but also to identify which ones correspond to vulnerabilities and require in-depth analysis to estimate their dangerousness, and if necessary, rapidly distribute some adequate patch.

Nevertheless, vulnerability detection is not a simple operation. As has been pointed out in [1],

> *"The* ***defect*** *caused an* ***infection****, which caused a* ***failure*** *and when we saw the failure we tracked the infection, and finally found and fixed the defect."*

In the context of vulnerability discovery, a failure (i.e., an observable incorrect program behavior) could be a crash or an infinite loop. Tracking the infection is possible by *monitoring* the program execution until it finally reaches the defect, i.e. some code calling to an insecure library function. We can observe that all of the three points are related to each other in a way that the presence of one can be used to infer the presence of the other. In other words, a defect will manifest itself in the infection in a very *peculiar* way, which in turn, will lead to a failure.

Some static analysis techniques have been proved successful in finding classical programming flaws, like buffer overflows or null-pointer dereferences, but they suffer from a high percentage of *false positives*. More importantly, only a few tools are able to operate on the binary code. As a result, one of the most effective vulnerability detection techniques still relies on large fuzzing campaigns, feeding the target program with various inputs in order to produce *crashes* that need to be (manually) analyzed afterwards. This is a time-consuming activity.

For instance, an operating system like Debian contains more than 30,000 programs and 80,000 bug reports. Methodologies and tools for an OS scale program testing in a limited time budget are still missing. Microsoft Security Development Lifecycle (SDL) [2], for example, is a well known security assurance process, but it is intended for a more incremental approach for testing. It introduces various security enabling measures throughout all phases of development process. Testing an already developed large product seems to be out of scope of SDL. Therefore, there is a strong need for techniques to be used as fast predictors, to quickly

*author was associated with IIIT Hyderabad, India

CODASPY'16, March 9–11, 2016, New Orleans, LA, USA.

ISBN 978-1-4503-3935-3/16/03...$15.00
DOI: http://dx.doi.org/10.1145/2857705.2857720

identify which programs are more likely to contain a vulnerability, in order to direct the fuzzing process.

Given the complexity of modern software, the relationship between defect, infection and failure is not easy to notice, especially by a human analyst. Machine learning and data mining techniques [3] have been used to learn such subtle relationships in a wide range of applications [4, 5, 6], when the complexity involved is too high. In this work, we resort to the application of Machine Learning techniques to learn such dependencies in the case of a failure.

The objective of our work is to make a step in this direction by presenting a scalable machine learning approach that uses lightweight static and dynamic features to predict if a test case is *likely* to contain a software vulnerability. As far as we know, this is the first large scale study on vulnerability discovery for binary only programs.

1.1 Contributions

The main contribution of this paper is to demonstrate the feasibility of a large-scale study of binary programs in order to predict vulnerabilities according to some procedure to perform vulnerability discovery. In order to build a predictor, we started by defining and evaluating different sets of features that can be automatically extracted from binary programs. Such features are designed to be scalable: they are extracted using very lightweight static and dynamical analysis.

To show the effectiveness of our approach, we set up a very large experiment to detect easily exploitable memory corruptions using 1039 Debian programs obtained from its bug tracker. To perform a reasonable evaluation of our methodology, we collected 138,308 unique execution traces and statically explored 76,083 different subsequences of function calls. We managed to predict which programs contained dangerous memory corruptions with a 55% of accuracy and which programs resulted robust with a 83% of accuracy.

We also developed and implemented VDiscover, a tool that uses state-of-the-art Machine Learning to predict vulnerabilities in test cases. Our tool will be released with an open-source license to encourage the research of vulnerability discovery at large scale, together with VDiscovery, a public dataset that collects raw analyzed data.

The paper is organized as follows. We dedicate Sec. 2 to explain the background on vulnerability discovery. Later, we overview the proposed methodology in Sec. 3 and we explain it in detail in Sec. 4. Data generation and feature extraction is presented in Sec. 5. Then, Sec. 6 is devoted to introduce the Machine Learning techniques used in this paper. Experimental setup is detailed in Sec. 7 and results are presented and discussed in Sec. 8 followed by a survey of related work in Sec. 9. Finally we draw some conclusions and point possible future work directions in Sec. 10.

2. BACKGROUND

Many different vulnerability discovery procedures (VDP) has been proposed in the Computer Security literature to detect potentially vulnerable issues in software. As expected, every VDP has particular requirements and biases to identify (specific) vulnerabilities. In this section, we highlight the attributes of different VDP proposed by several authors.

2.1 Fuzzing and Smart Fuzzing

Currently, one of the most effective approaches to find vulnerabilities in large software is based on fuzzing techniques [7], i.e., feeding the target application with *unexpected inputs* and looking for abnormal program termination. The crucial step in fuzzing is clearly to choose relevant unexpected inputs, likely to reveal potential vulnerabilities. Several techniques can be used.

One of the simplest techniques is *random mutation* of known correct inputs. It requires only a basic knowledge of the target application. However, most of the mutated inputs are likely to be rejected in the early steps of the program execution either at parsing or because of checksum verification.

To overcome this problem, another input generation technique is to better control the mutations using some knowledge about the input format, like in grammar-based fuzzing [8]. However, this technique is effective only with a high level of expertise on the target application.

Such *black-box* fuzzing techniques are rather easy to implement and they are highly scalable since they do not involve complex computations nor heavy program monitoring techniques. Nevertheless, they suffer from two drawbacks: first, they do not allow to control the program execution and second, huge fuzzing campaigns are required to obtain valuable results. Furthermore, the crashes obtained should be processed *a posteriori*, first to filter redundant information (crashes resulting from the same bugs), and second to sort out between harmless bugs and more serious ones. This operation requires a high-level of expertise and is really time-consuming.

To overcome these limitations, some *white-box* fuzzing approaches have been proposed [9, 10]. The underlying idea is to generate the application inputs with the help of its code.

Clearly, the benefit of these "smart-fuzzing" techniques is to better control the program exploration according to a given objective (e.g., either maximizing code coverage, or focusing on specific parts, more likely to be vulnerable). Hence, many tools have been developed in this direction (Klee [11], TaintScope [12]) and their ability to find vulnerabilities has been illustrated on several case studies.

Moreover, some works make use of concolic execution for vulnerability detection [13, 14, 15]. The idea is to enforce the path predicate Π_{path} corresponding to a crashing execution sequence by adding "exploitability conditions" Π_{exp}, namely sufficient conditions on register and memory contents to be fulfilled in order to make the crash exploitable by an external user. Thus, if the solver can find program inputs satisfying $\Pi_{path} \wedge \Pi_{exp}$ then it automatically produces a concrete (proof-of-concept) exploit, saving the manual and tedious exploitability analysis. A typical example is the Mayhem tool presented in [13], close to our work as far as the objective is concerned, i.e., finding the bugs that are exploitable without using sourcecode. However, our work takes a different approach by learning the characteristics of exploitable bugs using very light-weight program analysis and Machine Learning and thereby avoiding the use of somewhat more complex techniques like heavy instrumentation and symbolic execution. This choice clearly makes our analysis very fast, and applicable to very large data-sets in order to rapidly extract suspicious programs.

2.2 Static Analysis

Historically, static analysis tools were used to prove the absence of bugs inside a program [16][17], and they proved

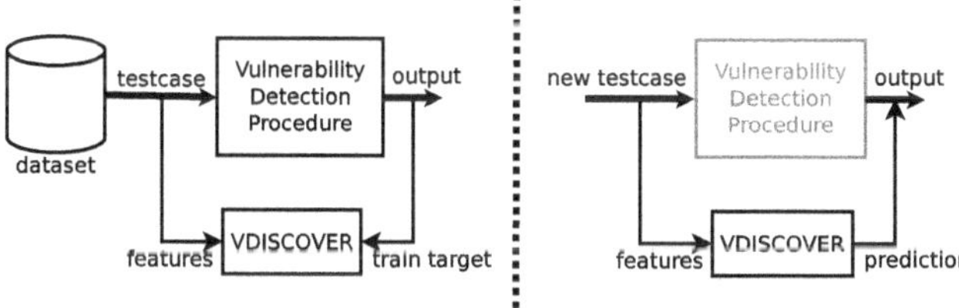

Figure 1: Summary of train and recall phases in VDiscover

to be particularly effective in specific application domains like embedded systems or aeronautic applications. Their main advantage is clearly to provide sound reports on the whole set of program executions. However, using these techniques on more general-purpose software is much harder and time consuming. This is essentially due to the over-approximations performed during the analysis to preserve soundness, since static analysis is undecidable [18]. Providing good approximation techniques for general program constructions (involving dynamical memory allocations and complex data structures) is hard, and therefore the number of false positives produced is usually huge.

However a few works have been proposed to apply static analysis techniques in the context of vulnerability detection. They offer lightweight static analysis [19, 20], either on source or binary code, and they generally focus in a specific kind of vulnerability [21]. Also, they sacrifice soundness in order to serve as "bug finders", allowing to better control the trade-off between precision and scalability.

Nevertheless, even if it appears that pure static analysis techniques are not precise enough to be used as standalone general vulnerability detection techniques, they offer highly valuable preprocessing information to combine with other approaches like concolic execution or Machine Learning.

3. OVERVIEW

Our study aims to define and evaluate some machine learning techniques that can be used to predict whether a binary code may contain certain vulnerabilities. We propose a methodology that works in two phases: training and recall.

In the training phase, a large amount of test cases are collected from the binary code in a *training dataset.* These test cases are characterized by static features extracted from the disassembled binaries and dynamical features extracted from its execution analysis. These features are based on the use patterns of the C standard library. Additionally, test cases are evaluated using a vulnerability detection procedure: such procedure flags as vulnerable or not every test case in the train dataset. The objective of this phase is to use the extracted features and the vulnerability discovery procedure to train a predictor using supervised machine learning techniques.

After that, in the recall phase, a *trained classifier* is used to predict if new test cases, extracted from new programs, will be flagged as vulnerable or not. Later, a flagged test case can be prioritized in further analysis. It is also important to note that our approach is not replacing the outcome of a vulnerability detection procedure. Figure 1 summarizes both phases of our approach.

3.1 Building a Predictor

Our tool aims to deal with a very large number of test cases to decide which ones should be further analyzed to look for security vulnerabilities. Needless to say, we want our predictor to distinguish between flagged and unflagged test cases as correct as possible. In this work, accuracy is measured in terms of the errors predicting flagged test cases (false negatives, also called type II error) and the errors predicting unflagged test cases (false positives, also called type I error). VDiscover aims to minimize both types of errors during the training phase. On the one hand, the reduction of false positives allows to discover more vulnerabilities in a shorter time. On the other hand, reducing false negatives decreases the number of misses vulnerabilities in this predictive analysis.

The extraction and processing of our features to predict also included some distinctive design principles. Such principles are:

1. **No source-code required**: Our features are extracted using static and dynamic analysis for binaries programs, allowing our technique to be used in proprietary operating systems.
2. **Automation**: Some Machine Learning applications rely on heavily engineered features to obtain a good performance. This typically requires a human expert to review candidate features before the training phase. In this work, we will focus only on feature sets that can be extracted and selected automatically, given a large enough dataset.
3. **Scalability**: Since we want to focus on scalable techniques, we only use lightweight static and dynamic analysis. Costly operations like instruction per instruction reasoning are avoided by design.

4. METHODOLOGY

In order to show experimental results on the performance of VDiscover to predict vulnerabilities in new test cases, we need a concrete vulnerability detection procedure (VDP) and a dataset to train our tool. In particular, we evaluated our technique using a simple fuzzer to detect easily exploitable memory corruptions on a large corpus of test cases. Despite the evaluation of our technique will be limited to the use of a simple fuzzer as VDP, it is important to note that detection of this kind of vulnerability is not a fixed component of VDiscover. In fact, the adaptive computation performed by machine learning techniques provides a convenient machinery to predict the presence of vulnerabilities using another VDP.

4.1 Detecting Memory Corruptions

Our vulnerability detection procedure comprises two components: a fuzzer to mutate the original test case and a dynamic detection module to identify easily exploitable memory corruptions.

We used a simple fuzzer to explore a large number of variations of a test case. It performs only two types of mutations: replacement of one byte by another and expansion of a random byte at some position in the original input. Using it, we defined a fuzzing campaign that mutates and executes each test case 10,000 times, large enough to catch some interesting memory corruptions.

We also need to define when a program is vulnerable to a potentially or easily exploitable memory corruption and how that can be detected automatically. Detecting this type of vulnerability is not as easy as it sounds, especially without source code or debugging information. We define two ways of detecting memory corruptions, through explicit and implicit evidence of them.

Explicit signs of stack and heap memory corruptions are:

1. Corruption of stack memory: Some of the Debian binaries are compiled with stack protections provided by the GNU C standard library, so in case of stack corruption such protections will abort the execution. Additionally, we can inspect the call stack when a program crashed, looking for return addresses of called functions. If we find at least one invalid return pointer, then we immediately conclude that the stack frames were corrupted.

2. Corruption of heap memory: We take advantage of the heap consistency check made by the GNU C standard library. If we find a call to abort related with this check, we conclude that a heap corruption happened.

Implicit hints of memory corruptions include:

1. Corrupted or unexpected arguments in some functions: A few key functions like `strcpy`, `memcpy`, `fread`, `fwrite`, among others have its arguments inspected during execution. For example, a call to memcpy indicates a potential memory corruption if it has a very large count parameter value (e.g., bigger than 2^{24}).

2. Corruption of a pointer to a function: If a crash is detected, we inspect if the instruction pointer is pointing to an invalid or a non-executable page.

4.2 Memory corruption for fun and profit

To illustrate how important it is to prevent memory corruption, we present a small example of this issue that can easily be exploited to hijack the control flow of a faulty program. The vulnerable condition in this example can be detected using the procedure detailed in 4.1 and the affected program is flagged as vulnerable in VDISCOVERY.

We will show in detail the analysis of a crash in xa, a small cross-assembler for the 65xx series of 8-bit processors (used in computers such as the Commodore 64). This command line utility is located in the Debian package xa65. The version 2.3.5 can be crashed using an unexpectedly large input in one of its arguments. The insecure code is shown in Figure 2a. This crash is the result of a buffer overflow caused by the improper use of sprintf at lines 9–10. It is worth mentioning that this memory corruption is *not* directly exploitable by overwriting the return address of a function call since the invocation of sprintf will write in global memory (at lines 2–3).

An alternative way to exploit this bug is available, since a pointer to a *FILE* structure is controllable by an attacker. A large input in the sprintf argument can be used to overflow the array, and rewrite the fperr *FILE* pointer. By abusing the fact that the *FILE* structure contains a virtual function table, we can craft a fake *FILE* structure with a pointer to our own payload. Once this layout is placed in memory, we should just wait for the program to execute a fprintf (line 19) with our malicious *FILE* structure (and to use our fake virtual function table), which happens just after, inside the logout function. This technique is not new at all, in fact, it was well known by Greek hackers more than 10 years ago [22]. Despite that, it still works today when it is tested on a fully updated installation of Debian Sid.

We will also illustrate how VDISCOVER extracts patterns to detect vulnerable programs using a small piece of x86 assembly code from the xa utility shown in Figure 2b, since this program contains many examples of vulnerable code. Such code reads data from the environment (line 1) and calls to strcpy (lines 5–7) without checking the size of the input variable.

5. DATASET

It is not possible to learn from a single test case using a Machine Learning approach. A large amount of them are needed during a training procedure. Also, additional example cases are required to evaluate a trained predictor. Unfortunately, at the time of writing, we found no suitable dataset to perform the evaluation of our technique.

The need for these cases were our main motivations to construct VDISCOVERY, our dataset. It was created by analyzing 1039 test cases taken from the Debian Bug Tracker. Every test case uses a different executable program and they are distributed over 496 packages. They were originally packed along their inputs by the Mayhem team using their symbolic execution tool and submitted to the Debian Bug Tracker [23]. The programs comprised in VDISCOVERY are quite diverse and included data processing tools from scientific packages, simple games, small desktop programs and even an OCR. Using VDISCOVER, we can unpack and parse the necessary input sources (command line, standard input, files, etc.) in order to instantly reproduce each test case.

5.1 Classes

After using the previously defined vulnerability discovery procedure described in Sec. 4.1, test cases are divided in two classes: *flagged as vulnerable* and *not flagged as vulnerable.* A program is said to be *flagged as vulnerable* if there is at least one trace that exhibits a vulnerable memory corruption pattern. As expected, our dataset suffers from a severe class imbalance [24]. Only 8% of the programs are flagged. This is an issue we have to tackle before the predictor starts learning from it, as explained in Sec. 7.

5.2 Features

In this work, two sets of features are defined and evaluated: dynamic features extracted from the execution of test cases and static features extracted from the binary programs. Both set of features try to abstract the use patterns of the C standard library and they are represented as variable-length sequences. Nevertheless, they aim to capture different aspects of it. On the one hand, static features are extracted by detecting potential subsequences of function calls. On the other hand, dynamic features are captured from execution traces containing concrete function calls augmented with its arguments.

Features are not necessarily correlated with the concrete vulnerability that we are trying to detect. In fact their objective is to provide a redundant and robust similarity measure that a Machine Learning model can employ to predict whether a test case will be flagged as vulnerable or not. Such

```c
/* global variables */
static char out[MAXLINE],
static FILE *fpout, *fperr, *fplab;
...

int main(int argc,char *argv[])
{
  ...
  sprintf(out, "Couldn't open source \
                file '%s'!\n", ifile);
  logout(out);
  ...
}

void logout(char *s)
{
  fprintf(stderr, "%s",s);
  if(fperr)
    fprintf(fperr,"%s",s);
}
```

(a)

```
1  call getenv
2  test %eax,%eax
3  je @15
4  lea -0x100c(%ebp),%ebx
5  mov %eax,0x4(%esp)
6  mov %ebx,(%esp)
7  call strcpy
8  movl $0x123,0x4(%esp)
9  mov %ebx,(%esp)
10 call strtok
11 ...
12 ...
13 ...
14 ...
15 ret
```

(b)

Figure 2: Different routines of /usr/bin/xa in C and x86 assembly

prediction will be based on previously seen examples during the training phase.

5.2.1 Static Features

Static features are supposed to capture information relevant to a whole program, and they should be obtained without running the code on particular inputs. Classical static analysis techniques use graph-based representations to express the code structure, like call graphs, control and data-flow graphs, etc. However, building such structures is costly and not always possible from a stripped binary code.

The approach we propose is to "approximate" a code structure as a set of finite sequence calls to the standard C library. Such a sequence set can be viewed as an abstraction of the program call graph where only some function calls are considered, and where the graph structure is flattened.

These static features can be extracted directly from the binaries using a very lightweight static analysis. First, the binary is disassembled using a linear sweep algorithm. The set I of direct calls to C standard library functions is extracted from the disassembled code. Elements of I will be used as starting points for a random exploration of the program control-flow graph. We build the set S of library function calls by repeatedly using the algorithm described informally below:

1. select an element c of I and insert it in an empty sequence σ;
2. follow the subsequent instructions of c in the disassembled code, and:
   - if a call or jump to a C standard library function is found, append it to σ and continue with the next instruction;
   - if an unconditional jump to the address x is found, continue at address x;
   - if a conditional jump is found, randomly select a branch and continue on this branch;
   - otherwise, skip the instruction and continue with the next one;
3. when a return statement or an indirect jump is reached, the sequence σ is terminated and added to the resulting set S.

As expected, this simple procedure extracts feasible and unfeasible subsequences of C standard library calls by a random walk on a part of the program control flow graph.

Example. In Figure 2b, if we start from the call to getenv at (1), two possible subsequences of C standard library calls can be extracted, according to the conditional jump at (3). The resulting set S is then:

$$\{[\text{getenv}; \text{strcpy}; \text{strtok}; \ldots], [\text{getenv}]\}$$

Computational Cost. The extraction of this kind of features requires to completely disassemble a program: the executable of the analyzed test case. After that, the lightweight static analysis performed is stateless and the random walking only needs to collect a sample of the potential C standard library calls.

5.2.2 Dynamic Features

Dynamic features are supposed to capture a sample of the behavior of a program in terms of its concrete sequential calls to the C standard library. Additionally the final state of the execution is included. Such features are extracted by executing for a limited time a test case and hooking program events, collecting them in a sequence. We define program events as either a call to the C standard library function (abstracted simply as fc_i) with its arguments or the final state of the process:

$$fc_i(arg_1, .., arg_n) \mid FinalState$$

The final state will be analyzed to determine which event will be the last one of a trace. In this work, a program can finish with an exit, an abnormal termination, an induced abnormal termination or, it can run out of time.

$$Exit \mid Crash \mid Abort \mid Timeout$$

An important difference with the static features is the amount of data that can be potentially extracted from a test case. Even for small programs, the collection of traces can create a very large dataset, since a simple loop can be unfolded into an arbitrarily long sequence of events.

Nevertheless, it is really difficult for a Machine Learning classifier to discover useful relations using these traces of raw events. The fact that the arguments of function calls are low level computational values, like pointers and integers, becomes an issue for learning patterns in traces. There are two important reasons for this.

In first place, it will induce an enormous range of different values (e.g., 2^{32} in 32-bit). If we want to train our classifier with discrete sequences of events, it is essential to drastically reduce the range of different events. In second place, these values convey very little information by themselves. So, it is necessary to augment them with relevant information in order to be able to learn from them.

To address these two issues, we decided to *tag* every argument value with a suitable sub-type. The sub-typing relation we defined is shown in Figure 3. It is loosely inspired by TIE [25] and PointerScope [26] sub-typing systems for reverse engineering.

In the case of the pointers (`Ptr32`), it is very useful to know the region where they are pointing to: for instance, `HPtr32` indicates heap, `SPtr32` stack and `GPtr32` global memory. Also it is relevant to know if they are dangling (`DPtr32`) or null (`NPtr32`).

In the case of integers (`Num32`), since they convey even less information than pointers, it is useful to know if they are zero, small, large or very large. To formalize this kind of imprecise knowledge, our approach is to divide them in logarithmic buckets so a sub-type of the generic integer type gives an idea of how large it is, e.g `Num32B`n indicates a 32-bit number between 2^n and $2^{(n+1)}$. In case of looking for suspiciously small or large arguments, for example, reading or writing bytes, it is useful to use such sub-types.

Example. After executing the vulnerable code in Figure 2b, VDiscover captures the following piece of trace presented here in comparison with the ltrace [27] output:

ltrace	VDiscover
getenv('XAINPUT')	getenv(GPtr32)
strcpy(0xbfffc0fc, 'input')	strcpy(SPtr32,HPtr32)
strtok('input', ',')	strtok(HPtr32,GPtr32)

Computational Cost. The extraction of this kind of features requires the execution of a test case. In order to do that, the analyzed binary and its dynamically linked libraries are instrumented to detect calls to C standard functions. White-listing is also performed, discarding internal function calls from the libraries contained in the C standard library package. Such restriction in our dataset aims not only to minimize the cost of instrumentation but also to reduce the complexity of the resulting features. It therefore allows different Machine Learning techniques to learn from this kind of features more easily.

It is also worth to mention that we designed VDiscover to require the collection of **a single trace** during the recall phase. In our experiments, such trace is collected using the fuzzer detailed in 4.1 to reduce the bias of the test cases (generated using a symbolic executor). Otherwise, the original test case should be used.

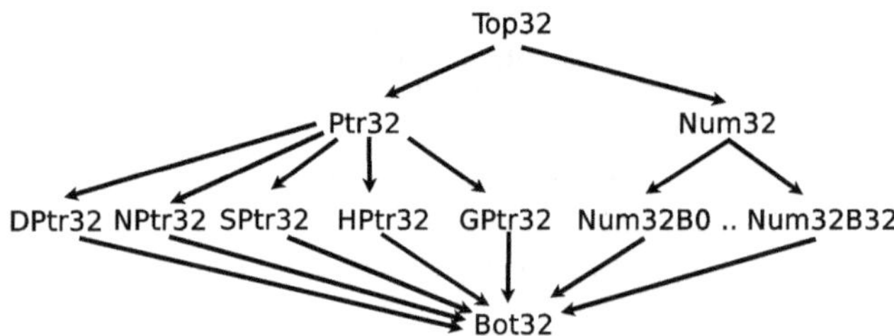

Figure 3: Sub-typing relation used to process the function arguments in the traces

6. A MACHINE LEARNING APPROACH

6.1 Models

A wide variety of Machine Learning and statistical models address the classification problem. We can sort these models ranging from those with few parameters, linear boundary surface and easy to train, to models with many parameters, nonlinear boundary surface and very hard to train. The *logistic regression* model [3] is between the former. It models the log conditional probability of category outputs (given the inputs) as an affine transform of the inputs. In our case these inputs are either the static or the dynamic features after being preprocessed.

The logistic regression model can be extended to a non-linear model by adding one or more intermediate nonlinear transforms –known as *hidden layers*– between the input and the affine transform. These layers also consist of an affine transform plus an element-wise nonlinearity. The resulting model is the most common version of a *multilayer perceptron* (MLP). Notice that when using an MLP model we must choose certain design parameters (*hyperparameters*) such as the number of layers and the dimension of each intermediate representation (number of *hidden units*).

The parameters (or *weights*) of each layer are obtained by maximizing the log-likelihood over the training data. This formulation casts the learning process as an optimization problem over the weights. The optimization is performed using the *stochastic gradient descent* (SGD) algorithm which is commonly used for training artificial neural networks [3]. The SGD algorithm is suitable for handling large datasets since training examples are seen in small batches. The optimization algorithm has its own hyperparameters that must be chosen beforehand together with model hyperparameters.

Additionally, we complete the list of Machine Learning models considered for comparison with the *random forest* method [28]. Random forest is an ensemble of decision trees trained on bootstrap data sets with a random selection of features. This model is a widely adopted method for classification due to its resistance to overfitting and the small number of hyperparameters that are required to optimize during the training phase.

6.2 Validation and regularization

All Machine Learning methods are susceptible to overfitting, i.e. explaining certain particular features present in a finite training set which damage the performance for new and unseen examples. This behavior implies that an error estimation over the training set is overly optimistic. Therefore a separated set of unseen samples is required for an unbiased error estimate. Furthermore if we want to use this

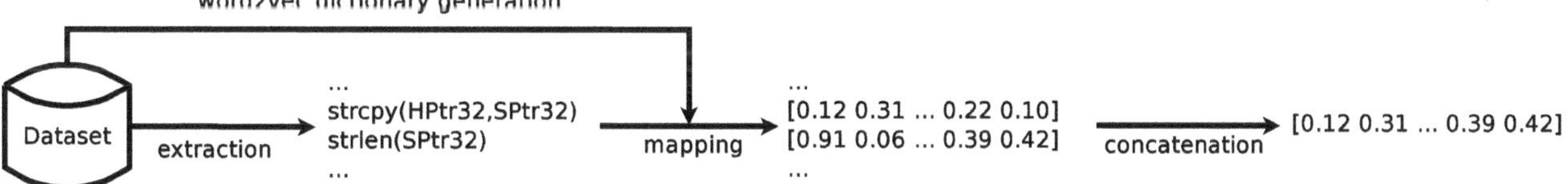

Figure 4: Preprocessing of dynamic features using word2vec

estimation for choosing the best set of hyperparameters we must use a *validation* set for this purpose and leave an unseen *test* set for the final unbiased error estimate [3]. This means that we must split the available data in three parts: the training, validation and test sets.

The validation set is used for monitoring the error over unseen samples during training. By stopping training when validation error reaches a minimum some degree of overfitting can be avoided. This *early stopping* technique [3] also biases the model to having small weights since they are initialized with small random values.

Another way for improving generalization is the recently proposed *dropout* training technique [29]. This technique has been widely adopted in recent years for improving generalization error over a large variety of neural networks [30, 31]. We applied it to both logistic regression and MLP.

7. EXPERIMENTAL SETUP

7.1 Data Preprocessing

Before starting to train the vulnerability predictor of VDISCOVER, the features of our dataset were preprocessed. Data preprocessing is essential to be able to train and test Machine Learning models out of the box. This procedure should also reduce the dimensionality of the sequential data in VDISCOVERY, since training Machine Learning models require to use fixed-length inputs.

In order to process the different sets of features, we used two procedures taken from the text processing and mining field. We started considering each trace as a text document. Such approach is very similar to the ones already used to deal with traces in other works [32, 33]. Also, for each preprocessing procedure, different parameters were used, since they can have a large impact in the accuracy of a trained classifier:

- bag-of-words: this widely used [34] preprocessing technique was applied. For each feature set, we used 1-grams, 2-grams and 3-grams to get suitable representations to train and test our vulnerability predictor.
- word2vec: this preprocessing technique was recently designed for learning continuous vector representations [35] of words in large text datasets. We selected it since it was successfully used in a variety of text mining applications [36, 37]. As shown in Figure 4, word2vec was used to generate a vectorial representation of all possible events. Then, for each trace, a vector was formed selecting events from the beginning and the end of each trace. We experimented with 20, 50, 100 or 200 vectorized events concatenated in order to characterize complete executions.

A critical issue in our dataset is the class imbalance. We addressed it using a well tested solution known as *random oversampling* [24] in order to facilitate the learning process of different classifiers.

7.2 Training Procedure and Models

In order to perform a valuable evaluation of the different features and classification methods, we processed several training datasets with only static or only dynamical features, so every set of features was evaluated independently.

For each feature set, a total of 40 predictive experiments were made splitting the dataset in three **completely disjoint program sets**: train, validation and test. As we explained in Sec. 6, such condition is essential to report honest results. We want our trained classifiers to generalize beyond the examples available in the training set of programs.

In our experiments, we trained several machine learning classifiers: logistic regression, MLP of single hidden layer and random forest. Mature and well tested software packages like scikit-learn [38] and pylearn2 [39] were employed to train and test different classifiers.

7.3 Error Evaluation

The use of a highly imbalanced dataset requires additional care when accuracy is computed after the prediction of a test set. Otherwise, a trivial classifier predicting every program as unflagged will report a misleading accuracy. In order to use a sensible test error measure, we account false positives and false negatives as percentages. To obtain a single error percentage, we can average false positives and false negatives into a *balanced test error.* Unless stated otherwise, we refer to this quantity as *test error.*

8. RESULTS AND DISCUSSION

8.1 Results

Tables 1a, 1b and 1c summarize the test errors on vulnerability detection. Our most accurate classifier was a **random forest trained using dynamical features.** To show the accuracy of such classifier, we present the corresponding confusion matrix in Table 3a in terms of the test cases that VDISCOVER detects as flagged or not. Using the most accurate classifier, we can estimate the reduction in the effort needed to discover new vulnerabilities. If we recall the percentage of programs found vulnerable (8%) and non-vulnerable (92%) in our dataset presented in 5, we can compute which is the percentage of all the programs VDISCOVER flags as potentially vulnerable using a weighted average:

$$8\% * \overbrace{0.55}^{\substack{\text{true}\\\text{positives}}} + 92\% * \overbrace{0.17}^{\substack{\text{false}\\\text{positives}}} = 4.4\% + 15.64\% = 20.04\%$$

Input	Logistic Regression	MLP
200 events	38% ± 1	35% ± 1
100 events	**34%** ± 1	37% ± 1
50 events	35% ± 1	36% ± 1
20 events	37% ± 1	35% ± 1

(a) Dynamic features (word2vec)

Input	Logistic Regression	Random Forest
1-grams	40% ± 1	32% ± 1
1-2-grams	40% ± 1	**31%** ± 1
1-3-grams	40% ± 1	**31%** ± 1

(b) Dynamic features (bag-of-words)

Input	Logistic Regression	Random Forest
1-grams	**37%** ± 1	43% ± 1
1-2-grams	**37%** ± 1	41% ± 1
1-3-grams	**37%** ± 1	40% ± 1

(c) Static features (bag-of-words)

Table 1: Average test error of vulnerability prediction using VDISCOVER

Variable	Importance
fflush:0=Ptr32	6%
StackCorruption	6%
MemoryCorruption	4%
malloc:0=Num32B24	4%
fread:1=Num32B8	3%
memset:0=GPtr32	3%
memset:1=Num32B0	2%
strcat:1=SPtr32	2%
strcat:1=GPtr32	2%
exit:0=Num32B32	2%
strncpy:0=SPtr32	2%
strrchr:0=SPtr32	2%

(a) With relevant features

Variable	Importance
strrchr:1=Num32B8	11%
printf:0=GPtr32	9%
_IO_getc:0=Ptr32	4%
malloc:0=Num32B32	3%
getenv:0=GPtr32	3%
strcasecmp:1=GPtr32	3%
open:1=Num32B8	3%
fprintf:0=Ptr32	3%
Timeout	2%
strcasecmp:0=SPtr32	2%
fopen:0=SPtr32	1%
malloc:0=Num32B16	1%

(b) Without relevant features

Table 2: A comparison of variable importance between trained vulnerability predictors with and without features relevant to memory corruptions

Consequently, by analyzing 20.04% of our test set pointed as potentially vulnerable by VDISCOVER we can detect 55% of vulnerable programs. As expected, without the help of our tool, a fuzzing campaign will randomly select test cases to mutate. It needs to analyze 55% of the programs to detect 55% of the vulnerable programs. Therefore, in terms of our experimental results, we can detect same amount of vulnerabilities 274% faster ($\approx$ 55%/20.04%).

8.2 Feature Analysis and Robustness

After performing the series of experiments detailed in this section, the results suggest that the proposed methodology was appropriate for the prediction task. Nevertheless, it is important to investigate further how the trained Machine Learning model is differentiating and characterizing test cases.

In order to evaluate the robustness of the best predictor, it is important to know which features are more important and how they are used to predict. Despite model interpretability is a very desirable property, there is no general approach to understand how and why trained models take decisions in the recall phase. Fortunately, we can easily extract an importance score for each variable in the feature set from a trained random forest [28].

To analyze the model robustness, first we want to define a special subset of dynamic features: the *features relevant to the specific VDP*. In our experiments, these features are defined according to the procedure to detect easily exploitable memory corruption as explained in 4.1. They include features associated with certain function calls (e.g. strcpy, memcpy, etc.) as well as the final state indicating if the there is a crash, abort or exit.

Without loss of generality, we decided to analyze one of the simplest models we trained: a random forest using bag of words (1-gram) of dynamic features that achieved a reasonable accuracy (32%). The most significant variables are shown in Table 2a where *relevant features* are in bold. *Relevant features* are widely used as the most important ones for prediction. Still, the resulting classifier is not completely dominated by only a few features. Nevertheless, at this point, it is critical to know if *relevant features* are responsible for all or most of the accuracy in the prediction task. If this is the case, the predicted model is just looking for trivial evidence to detect vulnerabilities in memory corruption.

A simple yet effective way to estimate the real importance of a set of features is to remove them from the original dataset and re-train the predictor. Such procedure will force the model to predict without them. We can estimate how important *relevant features* are in the prediction comparing the accuracy of the re-trained predictor. Interestingly enough, after re-training without the *relevant features*, the test error in prediction is only marginally higher (35%) than our best predictor. Most significant variables for the re-trained predictor are shown in Table 2b.

Using this simple procedure, we show that the resulting predictor is robust, in the sense that the removal of some features still allows to get a reasonable prediction for flagged test cases. We hypothesize that the model is taking advantage of the generality of the features to detect behaviorally similar test cases. Using such similarity allows it to predict correctly instead of looking for features relevant to the memory corruption itself.

8.3 Speed

VDISCOVER is implemented in Python using the python-ptrace binding [40] and GNU Binutils. It is designed to scale avoiding to use extremely slow operations like instruction per instruction execution. Nevertheless, in terms of code optimization there is very little work done.

The extraction of dynamic features is performed for every analyzed binary hooking its global offset table and detecting calls to C standard library functions. A very lightweight value analysis of the arguments of every call is also performed. The instrumented executions are on average only 7 times slower, a trade-off we considered acceptable given the obtained results.

As it was explained in Sec. 5, static feature extraction is defined as a stateless procedure, in which a part of control flow graph is random-walked to collect subsequences of function calls. Nevertheless, there is no need to explicitly reconstruct the control flow graph, so the feature extraction cost is dominated by the parsing and disassembly of the analyzed binary. Fortunately, we employ GNU Binutils which is highly optimized for this task, taking no more that a few seconds to extract static features in a modern desktop computer.

It is also worth to mention that VDISCOVER works with ELF x86 binaries on Linux. Despite the fact that the current implementation is limited to that platform, there is no reason to think that the same approach cannot work in other operating systems without ptrace (e.g. Windows) if there is support for breakpoints and peek/poke memory of a process.

8.4 Comparison

As far as we know, no other technique was designed to perform vulnerability discovery at a large scale without source code, so we have not found a fair approach to compare our work with others. Nevertheless, we found a suitable tool to give a fast evaluation of the bug severity in memory corruptions: !Exploitable. It also works performing a lightweight analysis of a test case. This tool was originally developed by Microsoft [41] and later adapted to run in Linux using GDB by the CERT [42].

Unlike our tool, !Exploitable *requires* a crash to analyze its final state and the failing assembly instruction. It outputs an *exploitable category* according to heuristics encoded in prefixed rules: *exploitable*, *probably exploitable*, *probably not exploitable* or *unknown*. After running all the test cases in VDISCOVERY, we collected the categories answered by *!Exploitable*. A summary of our experiments is shown in Table 3b.

In order to make a sensible comparison between !Exploitable and VDISCOVER, it is necessary to map such categories to binary answers about the exploitability of the programs in our dataset. A reasonable choice is to consider vulnerable programs if they are flagged as *exploitable* or *probably exploitable*. Computing the balanced error from Table 3b results in 44% of test error while VDISCOVER is at 31%.

On the one hand, our tool represents a substantial improvement in the prediction to discover new vulnerabilities. On the other hand, !Exploitable analyzes crash executing programs at native speed and requires no training at all. Unfortunately, in our experiments, the accuracy of !Exploitable is close to a random guess (e.g. a test error of 50%) and thus results in poor performance to predict vulnerability at

	Flagged	**Not Flagged**
Flagged	**55%**	17%
Not Flagged	45%	**83%**

(a) VDISCOVER

	Flagged	**Not Flagged**
Exploitable	14%	5%
Probably Exploitable	21%	18%
Probably Not Exploitable	43%	59%
Unknown	22%	18%

(b) !Exploitable

Table 3: Comparative between VDISCOVER and !Exploitable predictions of test cases

a large scale. It is important to note that this comparison is limited to the VDP selected for the experimental evaluation.

8.5 Data Limitations

As expected, lightweight extraction of features from binary programs has several limitations: a prediction error of 31% in the testing of VDISCOVER shows that there is room for improvement. The confusion matrix from Table 3a presents a visible unbalance between the accuracy of the detection of flagged and non-flagged test cases. We hypothesize that the relatively small number of flagged test cases available during the training phase is limiting the classifiers accuracy.

It seems natural to try to combine both features sets to improve prediction accuracy. Unfortunately, the results of this strategy are quite disappointing. The test prediction error were similar to the ones obtained using only static features. We found no effective way of combining different sets of features to improve prediction accuracy. We believe that the train phase is affected by the fact that static features are less diverse than dynamic ones because they are shared by all the traces of the same program. In other words, the number of independent training samples is reduced to the number of different programs as soon as we include the static features. Machine Learning algorithms assume independence of the training examples and, in the presence of this (artificial) persistence in the static feature values for a large set of flagged test cases, it tends to use this subset of features for discrimination. Therefore, the generalization capabilities are not better than using only static features.

The use of features also has its limitations. For instance, static features cannot be used to analyze different test cases of the same program, since the program is only statically analyzed without taking into consideration its actual input. This limitation did not affect our experiments, since our dataset only contains one test case per program but it is certainly an issue if VDISCOVER is used to evaluate a large set of test cases. Additionally, static features should be considered naturally more imprecise than dynamic features in general, since every non-trivial binary program contains many distinctive procedures.

The use of dynamic features has its own limitations: learning from traces is difficult because they have variable size and they can contain different amounts of useful information. For example, a complex program can use libraries. As expected, each library will have their own intrinsic patterns and a trace from such program will contain interleaved events from different libraries making pattern recognition a very challenging task.

9. RELATED WORKS

A very close work, albeit for a different problem of malware analysis, is reported in [43]. Similar to our approach, its authors have used static and dynamic features to form vectors of binary features of malware behavior. This vector is used in a supervised Machine Learning algorithm to produce rules for further classification. In spite of the reported similarities, there are differences in the way the vectors are generated. Unlike the reported work, our static and dynamic feature extraction is much lighter and hence introduces a very small overhead. It is important to note that extracting features from the actual malware process and code is a very challenging task, since most of these programs are packed or encrypted, and designed to avoid running normally under a virtualized environment. Therefore, we do not claim that our technique can be easily adapted to analyze malware.

Another close work is reported in [44], where the idea is to detect vulnerable code patterns from vulnerable source code. Similar to our approach, the main idea is to form a vector of characteristics that capture the semantic and syntactic structure of the function code and then use a machine learning approach to classify new functions. However, unlike ours, the proposed technique works with the source code of the program and has the different objective of finding vulnerable code patterns.

It is also worth to mention that there are plenty of approaches reported in the past wherein machine learning techniques are applied for attack detection (in the context of intrusion detection systems) [45, 46, 47]. However, we would like to point out that though the objective of finding *subtle and hidden* dependencies by using Machine Learning remains the same, our work involves a much fine-grained approach to extract feature vectors, which is more tuned towards the problem at hand i.e., classifying the bug on the basis of its severity.

10. CONCLUSIONS AND FUTURE WORK

As we have shown in previous sections, the large scale prediction of programs flagged and unflagged as vulnerable using static/dynamical features is feasible even without source code. The reached error rate of 31% suggests that there are patterns in the features that can be detected using a machine learning algorithm. Given such promising results, we are already working on the evaluation of different VDP as well as some directions that we plan to explore in the near future.

On the one hand, regarding static features, it could be a good idea to search for similarities between program slices, e.g. by creating a tree representing the possible sequences of C standard library calls. Using this tree could help to detect similar behavior during the training of the classifier.

On the other hand, regarding dynamical features, it is expected that interesting patterns could appear at different locations along the traces. Convolutional neural networks (CNN) [3] have been developed to model patterns in images with translation invariance along the image 2D array. This dramatically reduces the number of parameters to train with respect to a standard multilayer perceptron, improving generalization capabilities. We then expect that a 1D version of a CNN can improve the current performances over traces. There is a promising ongoing work in this direction.

In conclusion, this study shows that Machine Learning applications on a large scale binary-only vulnerability detection can have the potential to significantly increase the number of vulnerabilities found at operating system scale.

11. REFERENCES

[1] A. Zeller, *Why Programs Fail: A Guide to Systematic Debugging*. Morgan Kaufmann Publishers Inc., 2005.

[2] Microsoft Corporation, "Microsoft Security Development Lifecycle," MicrosoftSecurityDevelopmentLifecycle, 2012.

[3] C. M. Bishop *et al.*, *Pattern recognition and machine learning*. springer New York, 2006, vol. 1.

[4] H. Drucker, S. Wu, and V. N. Vapnik, "Support vector machines for spam categorization," *Neural Networks, IEEE Transactions on*, vol. 10, no. 5, 1999.

[5] G. E. Hinton and R. R. Salakhutdinov, "Reducing the dimensionality of data with neural networks," *Science*, vol. 313, no. 5786, 2006.

[6] A. Genkin, D. D. Lewis, and D. Madigan, "Large-scale bayesian logistic regression for text categorization," *Technometrics*, vol. 49, no. 3, 2007.

[7] M. Sutton, A. Greene, and P. Amini, *Fuzzing: Brute Force Vulnerability Discovery*. Addison-Wesley Professional, 2007.

[8] P. Godefroid, A. Kiezun, and M. Y. Levin, "Grammar-based whitebox fuzzing," *SIGPLAN Not.*, 2008.

[9] P. Godefroid, M. Y. Levin, and D. A. Molnar, "Sage: whitebox fuzzing for security testing." *Commun. ACM*, 2012.

[10] V. Ganesh, T. Leek, and M. Rinard, "Taint-based directed whitebox fuzzing," in *Proceedings of the 31st International Conference on Software Engineering*, ser. ICSE '09. IEEE Computer Society, 2009.

[11] C. Cadar, D. Dunbar, and D. R. Engler, "Klee: Unassisted and automatic generation of high-coverage tests for complex systems programs." in *OSDI*. USENIX Association, 2008.

[12] T. Wang, T. Wei, G. Gu, and W. Zou, "Checksum-aware fuzzing combined with dynamic taint analysis and symbolic execution." *ACM Trans. Inf. Syst. Secur.*, 2011.

[13] S. K. Cha, T. Avgerinos, A. Rebert, and D. Brumley, "Unleashing mayhem on binary code," in *Proceedings of the 2012 IEEE Symposium on Security and Privacy*, ser. SP '12. IEEE Computer Society, 2012.

[14] S.-K. Huang, M.-H. Huang, P.-Y. Huang, H.-L. Lu, and C.-W. Lai, "Software crash analysis for automatic exploit generation on binary programs," *Reliability, IEEE Transactions on*, March 2014.

[15] T. Avgerinos, S. K. Cha, A. Rebert, E. J. Schwartz, M. Woo, and D. Brumley, "Automatic exploit generation," *Commun. ACM*, 2014.

[16] P. Cousot, R. Cousot, J. Feret, L. Mauborgne *et al.*, "The astreÉ analyzer." ser. Lecture Notes in Computer Science. Springer, 2005.

[17] P. Cuoq, F. Kirchner, N. Kosmatov, V. Prevosto *et al.*, "Frama-c - a software analysis perspective." ser. Lecture Notes in Computer Science. Springer, 2012.

[18] W. Landi, "Undecidability of static analysis." *LOPLAS*, 1992.

[19] D. Evans and D. Larochelle, "Improving security using extensible lightweight static analysis." *IEEE Software*, 2002.

[20] F. Yamaguchi, N. Golde, D. Arp, and K. Rieck, "Modeling and discovering vulnerabilities with code property graphs," in *Proceedings of the 2014 IEEE Symposium on Security and Privacy*, ser. SP '14. IEEE Computer Society, 2014.

[21] S. Rawat and L. Mounier, "Finding buffer overflow inducing loops in binary executables," in *Proceedings of Sixth International Conference on Software Security and Reliability (SERE)*. IEEE, 2012.

[22] killah@hack.gr, "File Stream Pointer Overflows Paper," http://www.ouah.org/fsp-overflows.txt, 2003.

[23] M. Team, "Reporting 1.2K crashes," https://lists.debian.org/debian-devel/2013/06/msg00720.html, 2013.

[24] H. He and E. A. Garcia, "Learning from imbalanced data," *Knowledge and Data Engineering, IEEE Transactions on*, vol. 21, no. 9, 2009.

[25] J. Lee, T. Avgerinos, and D. Brumley, "Tie: Principled reverse engineering of types in binary programs."

[26] M. Zhang, A. Prakash, X. Li, Z. Liang, and H. Yin, "Identifying and analyzing pointer misuses for sophisticated memory-corruption exploit diagnosis," 2012.

[27] J. Céspedes, "ltrace," http://www.ltrace.org, 2014.

[28] L. Breiman, "Random forests," *Machine learning*, 2001.

[29] G. E. Hinton, N. Srivastava, A. Krizhevsky, I. Sutskever, and R. R. Salakhutdinov, "Improving neural networks by preventing co-adaptation of feature detectors," 2012.

[30] A. Krizhevsky, I. Sutskever, and G. E. Hinton, "Imagenet classification with deep convolutional neural networks," in *Advances in neural information processing systems*, 2012.

[31] Y. Taigman, M. Yang, M. Ranzato, and L. Wolf, "Deepface: Closing the gap to human-level performance in face verification," in *Computer Vision and Pattern Recognition (CVPR), 2014 IEEE Conference on*. IEEE, 2014.

[32] H. Pirzadeh, A. Hamou-Lhadj, and M. Shah, "Exploiting text mining techniques in the analysis of execution traces," in *Software Maintenance (ICSM), 2011 27th IEEE International Conference on*, Sept 2011.

[33] W. Xu, L. Huang, A. Fox, D. Patterson, and M. I. Jordan, "Detecting large-scale system problems by mining console logs," in *Proceedings of the ACM*

SIGOPS 22Nd Symposium on Operating Systems Principles, 2009.

[34] I. H. Witten and E. Frank, *Data Mining: Practical Machine Learning Tools and Techniques, Second Edition (Morgan Kaufmann Series in Data Management Systems)*. Morgan Kaufmann Publishers Inc., 2005.

[35] T. Mikolov, K. Chen, G. Corrado, and J. Dean, "Efficient estimation of word representations in vector space," 2013.

[36] L. Wolf, Y. Hanani, K. Bar, and N. Dershowitz, "Joint word2vec networks for bilingual semantic representations," *International Journal of Computational Linguistics and Applications*, vol. 5, no. 1, 2014.

[37] S. P. F. G. H. Moen and T. S. S. Ananiadou, "Distributional semantics resources for biomedical text processing."

[38] F. Pedregosa, G. Varoquaux, A. Gramfort, V. Michel, B. Thirion, O. Grisel *et al.*, "Scikit-learn: Machine learning in Python," *Journal of Machine Learning Research*, vol. 12, 2011.

[39] I. J. Goodfellow, D. Warde-Farley, P. Lamblin, V. Dumoulin *et al.*, "Pylearn2: a machine learning research library," 2013.

[40] V. Stinner, "python-ptrace," http://python-ptrace.readthedocs.org, 2014.

[41] Microsoft Security Engineering Center (MSEC) Security Science Team, "!Exploitable," http://msecdbg.codeplex.com, 2013.

[42] Jonathan Foote, "CERT Triage Tools," http://www.cert.org/vulnerability-analysis/tools/triage.cfm, 2013.

[43] I. Santos, J. Devesa, F. Brezo, J. Nieves, and P. Bringas, "Opem: A static-dynamic approach for machine-learning-based malware detection," in *International Joint Conference CISIS'12-ICEUTEt'12-SOCOt'12 Special Sessions*, ser. Advances in Intelligent Systems and Computing. Springer Berlin Heidelberg, 2013, vol. 189.

[44] F. Yamaguchi, F. Lindner, and K. Rieck, "Vulnerability extrapolation: Assisted discovery of vulnerabilities using machine learning," in *Proceedings of the 5th USENIX Conference on Offensive Technologies*, ser. WOOT'11. USENIX Association, 2011.

[45] S. Forrest, S. A. Hofmeyr, A. Somayaji, and T. A. Longstaff, "A sense of self for unix processes," in *Proceedings of the 1996 IEEE Symposium on Security and Privacy*, ser. SP '96. IEEE Computer Society, 1996.

[46] S. Rawat, V. P. Gulati, and A. K. Pujari, "Transactions on rough sets iv." Springer-Verlag, 2005, ch. A Fast Host-based Intrusion Detection System Using Rough Set Theory.

[47] T. G. and C. P., "Learning rules from system calls arguments and sequences for anomaly detection," in *Proc. ICDM Workshop on Data Mining for Computer Security (DMSEC)*. Springer, 2003.

To Fear or Not to Fear That is the Question: Code Characteristics of a Vulnerable Function with an Existing Exploit

[1]Awad Younis, [1]Yashwant K. Malaiya, [1]Charles Anderson, and [1]Indrajit Ray
[1]Computer Science Department, Colorado State University, Fort Collins, CO 80523, USA
{younis,malaiya,anderson,indrajit}@cs.colostate.edu

ABSTRACT
Not all vulnerabilities are equal. Some recent studies have shown that only a small fraction of vulnerabilities that have been reported has actually been exploited. Since finding and addressing potential vulnerabilities in a program can take considerable time and effort, recently effort has been made to identify code that is more likely to be vulnerable. This paper tries to identify the attributes of the code containing a vulnerability that makes the code more likely to be exploited. We examine 183 vulnerabilities from the National Vulnerability Database for Linux Kernel and Apache HTTP server. These include eighty-two vulnerabilities that have been found to have an exploit according to the Exploit Database. We characterize the vulnerable functions that have no exploit and the ones that have an exploit using eight metrics. The results show that the difference between a vulnerability that has no exploit and the one that has an exploit can potentially be characterized using the chosen software metrics. However, predicting exploitation of vulnerabilities is more complex than predicting just the presence of vulnerabilities and further research is needed using metrics that consider security domain knowledge for enhancing the predictability of vulnerability exploits.

Keywords
Vulnerabilities Severity; Exploitability; Software security; Exploits; Data mining and machine learning; Feature selection; Prediction; Software metrics.

1. INTRODUCTION
Identifying and addressing software vulnerabilities is important before software release because a single software vulnerability can lead to a breach with a high impact to an organization. However, identifying and addressing potential vulnerabilities can take considerable expertise and effort. Recently, researchers [1], [2], [3], [4] have started investigating ways to predict code areas which are more likely to be vulnerable so security testers can focus on them.

Software vulnerabilities, pose different levels of potential risk. A vulnerability with an exploit written for it presents more risk than the one without an exploit because the existence of an exploit allows an attacker to take advantage of a vulnerability and potentially compromise the affected systems. Allodi and Massacci in [5] have shown that out of the 49599 vulnerabilities reported by the National Vulnerability Database, only 2.10% are in fact exploited. Younis and Malaiya in [6] have also found that only 6.8% out of 486 vulnerabilities of Microsoft Internet Explorer have reported exploits. K. Nayak et al. [7] have reported that combining all of the products they have studied only 15% of disclosed vulnerabilities are ever exploited. Thus, identifying *what characterizes a vulnerability having an exploit* is needed; it can identify code that are more likely than others to have exploits and help security testers focus on areas of highest risk, thus saving limited resources and time. It should be noted that having a reported exploit does not necessarily mean some company or individuals have suffered a real attack. It means that a proof for exploiting a vulnerability exists. Obtaining data on real attacks is challenging because such data is generally kept confidential. Therefore, we will use the presence of an exploit as the ground truth for characterizing exploited vulnerabilities.

Discriminating between a vulnerability that has no exploit from the one that has an exploit is challenging because both of them have similar characteristics. Besides, the number of vulnerabilities with a reported exploit are few compared to the vulnerabilities without a reported exploit. Although vulnerability exploitability can be characterized by external factors such as attacker profile, software market share, etc., the focus of this study is on predicting vulnerability exploitability using internal attributes. This can help software developers predict vulnerabilities exploitability on the development side rather than the deployment side.

The objective of this research is to investigate what could characterize a code containing a vulnerability with an exploit. To address this objective, we have studied 183 vulnerabilities from the National Vulnerability Database [8] for the Linux Kernel and Apache HTTP server. The two software systems have been selected because of their rich history of publicly available vulnerabilities, availability of reported exploits, the existence of an integrated repository, availability of the source code, and their diversity in size, functionalities, and domain. For every selected vulnerability, we verify whether it has an exploit reported in the Exploit Database or not [9]. Eighty-two vulnerabilities have been found to have an exploit. Ten of them are for Apache HTTP server and 72 for Linux Kernel. We then mapped these vulnerabilities to their locations at the function granularity level.

After that, we characterize the vulnerable functions with and without an exploit using the selected eight software metrics: Source Line of Code, Cyclomatic complexity, CountPath, Nesting Degree, Information Flow, Calling functions, Called by functions, and Number of Invocations. The reasons why these metrics have been selected are discussed in section 3.1. Based on the metrics values of the vulnerable functions with and without an exploit, we first test the individual selected metrics discriminative power using Welch t-test [10]. Next, we select a combination of these metric using three feature selection methods: correlation-based, wrapper, and principal component analysis. Then, we test the predictive power of the selected subset of metrics using four classifiers: Logistic Regression, Naïve Base, Random Forest, and Support Vector machine.

CODASPY'16, March 09-11, 2016, New Orleans, LA, USA
 ISBN 978-1-4503-3935-3/16/03…$15.00
DOI: http://dx.doi.org/10.1145/2857705.2857750

Table 1. Software Metrics

Metrics	Description
Source Line of Code	**SLOC** measures the size of a code [13]. A higher value of SLOC indicates that an entity is to be difficult to test.
Cyclomatic complexity	**CYC** measures the number of independent paths through a program unit [14]. The higher this metric the more likely an entity is to be difficult
CountPath	**CountPath** measures the number of unique decision paths. A higher value of the CountPath metric represents a more complex code structure [13].
Nesting Degree	**ND** measures the maximum nesting level of control structures in a function. The higher this metric the more likely an entity is to be difficult to test [15].
Information Flow	**Fan-In** measures information flow, which represents the number of inputs a function uses. [16]. The more inputs from external sources the harder to trace where they came from.
Calling Functions	**In-Degree** measures the number of functions that call the function corresponding to the node [17]. The more dependent upon a peace of code, the higher the chance it has a defect.
Called by Functions	**Out-Degree** measures the number of functions that the function corresponding to the node calls [17]. The more depends upon other code, the higher the chance to have a defect.
Number of Invocations	It measures the number of functions that needed to be called before invoking the vulnerable function [18]. The higher this metric the more difficult to reach the vulnerable code.

The results demonstrate that vulnerabilities having an exploit can be characterized. The investigation also shows that predicting exploitation of vulnerabilities is more complex than predicting the presence of vulnerabilities and hence further research that considers metrics from security domain is needed to improve the predictability of vulnerability exploits.

This paper is organized as follows. In section 2, the background of the vulnerabilities, vulnerability databases, exploit database, software metrics, confusion matrix, and feature subset selection methods are discussed. In the next section, the hypotheses are examined and the methodology of testing them is presented. In sections 4, the case studies along with the results are introduced. Section 5 presents the discussion whereas section 6 presents the related work. Finally, concluding comments is given along with the issues that need further research.

2. BACKGROUND

2.1 Vulnerability and Exploit Databases

A software vulnerability is defined as "an instance of [a mistake] in the specification, development, or configuration of software such that the execution can violate the [explicit or implicit] security policy" [11]. Vulnerability' databases are maintained by several organizations such as National Vulnerability Database (NVD) [8] as well as the vendors of the software. An exploit is a method: piece of software, a chunk of data, or a sequence of commands, that identifies and takes advantage of vulnerability [20]. EDB is an exploit database that records exploits and vulnerable software [9].

2.2 Software Metrics

A software metric is a measure of some property of a piece of software. Table 1 summarizes the eight selected metrics. We have selected these metrics based on prior research on fault and vulnerability prediction.

2.4 Confusion Matrix

The confusion matrix table shows the actual vs. the predicted results. For the two class problem a vulnerability is either *has an exploit* or *has no exploit*. The following terms are defined based on Table 2.

Table 2. Confusion matrix

		Prediction	
		Has an Exploit	**Has no Exploit**
Actual	**Has an Exploit**	TP= True Positive	FN=False Negative
	Has no Exploit	FP= False Positive	TN= True Negative

True Positive (TP): the number of the vulnerabilities predicted as having an exploit, which do in fact have an exploit. False Negative (FN): the number of vulnerabilities predicted as not having an exploit, which turn out to have an exploit. False Positive (FP): the number of vulnerabilities predicted as having an exploit when they have no exploit. True Negative (TN): the number of vulnerabilities predicted as not having an exploit when there is no exploit.

2.5 Feature Subset Selection

Two commonly known types of feature subset selection methods are the filter and the wrapper approach. In the filter approach, the feature selection is performed independently of the learning algorithm and it selects a subset based only on the data characteristics. The wrapper approach, however, conducts a search for a good subset using the learning algorithm as part of the evaluation function [19].

2.5.1 Correlation-based feature selection

Correlation-based feature selection (CFS) evaluates subsets of attributes instead of individual attributes [20]. This technique uses a heuristic to evaluate subset of attributes. The heuristic balances how predictive a group of features are and how much redundancy is among them. In this study, CFS is used with the Greedy stepwise forward search through the space of attribute subsets.

2.5.2 Wrapper Subset Evaluation

The wrapper feature subset evaluation conducts a search for a good subset using a learning algorithm (classifier) as part of the evaluation function. In this study, repeated five-fold cross-validation is used as an estimate for the accuracy of the classifier while a greedy stepwise forward search is used to produce a list of attributes, which are ranked according to their overall contribution to the accuracy of the attribute set with respect to the target learning algorithm [21].

2.5.3 Principal Component Analysis

Principal Component Analysis (PCA) is a statistical technique that transforms a set of possibly correlated variables into a set of linearly uncorrelated variables [22]. These linearly uncorrelated variables are called principal components. The transformation is accomplished by first computing the covariance matrix of the original variables and after that finding its Eigen vectors, principal components. The principal components have the property that most of their information content is stored in the first few features so that the remainder can be discarded. It should be noted that in this paper, PCA is used with the ranker search method that ranks attributes by their individual evaluations.

3. HYPOTHESES AND METHODOLOGY

In this section, we provide our hypotheses that are needed to be researched and then provide the methods to test them.

3.1 Hypotheses

It should be noted that the metrics in section 2.3 have been classified into four classes: size (SLOC), structure (CYC, CountPath, ND), ease of access (Number of Invocations), and communication (Fan-In, In-Degree, Out-degree) so to ease the analysis and observation. The rationale behind using the selected metrics to derive our hypothesis is explained as follows.

In the software security field, experts argued that complexity is the enemy of security [1]. It is believed that complexity can be the cause of subtle vulnerabilities that are hard to test and analyze [23] and hence providing a chance to attackers to exploit them. However, we consider the fact that predicting a presence of a vulnerability is different from predicting its exploitation because the latter involves the attacker behavior. As the measures of the complexity vary, we consider the possibility that the potential exploit writers would prefer to exploit less complex code [24]. Besides, in [25], the researchers have observed that the complexity measures for Windows 7 and 8 were negative and they argued that the reason could be that attackers favor simpler vulnerable targets. Based on these reasons, we set up the following research hypotheses related to code complexity (size and structure metrics):

H1: *The values of the size metric for vulnerabilities with an exploit are lower than for vulnerabilities without an exploit.*

H2: *The values of the structure metrics for vulnerabilities with an exploit are lower than for vulnerabilities without an exploit.*

Sparks et al. [26] studied the penetration depth of reaching a node in a control flow graph. They found that the nodes at greater depths (>10 edges) become increasingly difficult to reach. If crafting an input that can reach a vulnerable statement for a single method is difficult, we believe that crafting an input to call a method containing a vulnerable statement from other methods could be even harder. If we further assume the target system is a closed system, it gets even harder for the attackers to figure out the sequences of calls and inputs that are needed to trigger them. Younis et al. [18] observed that the degree of a call depth of vulnerable functions varies among vulnerabilities. Some of the vulnerabilities have only one degree of depth, while others have 13. Thus, we set up the following research hypothesis for the ease of access (Number of Invocations metric):

H3: *The values of the ease of access metric for vulnerabilities with an exploit are lower than for vulnerabilities without an exploit.*

On the other hand, Younis et al. [18] argued that the more functions are called by the vulnerable function, the higher the effect if the vulnerable function is exploited. They have shown that some vulnerable functions call more than 10 functions while other functions call only one or two functions. Based on the attack surface concept [27], however, the more a function is exposed to the outside environment the larger attack surface. Thus, we argue that the higher the communication a function has, the larger its attack surface gets. From this reasoning, we set up the following research hypothesis for the communication (Fan-In, In-Degree, Out-degree metrics):

H4: *The values of communication metrics for vulnerabilities with an exploit are higher than for vulnerabilities without an exploit.*
As argued by Manadhata and Wing [28], no single metric can be an indicator of software quality for all types of software. Besides, according to [19], a feature (or two features) that is completely useless by itself (themselves) can be useful when taken with others (together). Therefore, determining the combination of multiple features (metrics) is important. Thus, we set up the following research hypothesis:

H5: *There is a combination of metrics that significantly predicts vulnerabilities with an exploit.*

3.2 Evaluation Strategy for the Hypotheses

We first investigate the discriminative power of the proposed individual metrics and then test their predictive capability when they are combined. A metric has a discriminative power if it can "discriminate between high-quality software components and low-quality software components" [29]. In this paper, a vulnerable function is classified as exploited if there exists a reported exploit for it and as not exploited if there exists no reported exploit for it at the time of our study. To evaluate the discriminative power of the proposed hypotheses, H1, H2, H3, and H4, we test their null hypotheses. Because our data has unequal sample size, unequal variances and is skewed, we used the Welch t-Test [10]. The Welch t-test is an adaptation of t-test to compare the means of two samples when the two samples have unequal variances and unequal sample sizes and it also is known to provide a good performance for skewed distributions. The difference between the means of the two group is considered discriminative when the result from the Welch t-test are statistically significant at the $p < 0.05$ level.

However, to evaluate the predictive power of the hypothesis H5 (combined metrics), on the other hand, two challenges have to be addressed. First, how can we select the subset metrics? Second, how can we evaluate the predictive power of the selected subset? To address the first challenge, we use feature subset selection methods. There are two commonly used feature subset selection methods: the filter and the wrapper approach. In this paper, we use correlation-based feature selection (CFS) and wrapper subset evaluation (WRP) methods. The first method has been selected because it selects the subset features based on only the characteristics of the data while the second method selects the features based on the learning algorithm and this can help us observe an advantage of one method over the other. However, according to [17], combining several metrics can be affected by the multicollinearity and that is due to the inter-correlation among metrics. To account for the multicollinearity problem, we use the Principal Component Analysis (PCA) and compare its result with two selected methods.

To address the second challenge, we evaluate the performance of a binary classification technique to assess the predictive power of the selected subset metrics. A binary classifier can make two possible types of errors: false positives and false negatives. These two types of errors are defined in section 2.4. To measure the performance of a classifier, we mainly use recall, precision and false positive ratio. In addition, we also report the harmonic mean of the precision and recall, using the F-measure, and the accuracy. It should be noted that a high recall value is required even at the cost of the precision and that is because of the significant impact of one exploited vulnerability. It is also desirable to have a low false positive rate because that helps avoiding a waste of an inspection effort. P. Morrison et al. in [25] suggested that the value 0.7 of the recall and precision measures are considered reasonable for the prediction models in the realm of software quality.

Recall is defined as the ratio of the number of vulnerabilities correctly predicted as having an exploit to the number of

Table 4. Apache HTTP Server Vulnerabilities' Measures									
Vulnerability	**In-Degree**	**Out-Degree**	**CountPath**	**ND**	**CYC**	**Fan-In**	**No of Invocation**	**SLOC**	**Exploit Existence**
CVE-2009-1891	1	9	9000	6	68	45	2	211	**NEE**
CVE-2010-0010	4	9	145	4	11	16	4	38	**EE**
CVE-2013-1896	26	5	8	1	5	37	3	29	**EE**

vulnerabilities that actually have an exploit as shown by the following: Recall = TP / TP+FN. Precision, on the other hand, is defined as the ratio of the number of vulnerabilities correctly predicted as having an exploit to the total number of vulnerabilities predicted as having an exploit as shown by the following: Precision = TP / TP+FP. False positive rate is defined as the ratio of the vulnerabilities incorrectly predicted as having an exploit to the total number of vulnerabilities that have no exploit: FP rate = FP / FP+TN.

We have considered four classifiers for this study and they are namely: Logistic Regression (LR), Naïve Bayes (NB), Random Forests (RF), and Support Vector Machine (SVM). LR has been selected because it is a standard statistical classification technique whereas NB has been selected because it is a simple classifier and it has often outperformed more sophisticated classifiers [4]. Besides, RF has been selected because it is more robust to noise such as inter-correlated features while SVM has been selected because it is less prone to overfitting.

4. EXPERIMENTATION

The purpose of the experiment is to investigate whether there is a difference in characteristics between a vulnerable function without exploits and a function with exploits. We have selected two software systems namely: Linux Kernel and Apache HTTP Server. The two software systems have been selected because of their rich history of publicly available vulnerabilities, availability of reported exploits, existence of an integrated repository (which enables us to map vulnerabilities to their location in the source code), availability of the source code (which enables us to collect the measures of the proposed metrics), and their diversity in size, functionalities, and domain.

4.1 Data Collection

In this study, the data about vulnerabilities and exploits of Linux kernel and Apache HTTP Server were collected from NVD [8] and the EDB [9] respectively from the period 2002 to 2014. Table 3 shows the number of the selected vulnerabilities and their exploits. It should be noted that we have considered all reported vulnerabilities that have an exploit for the two selected software system. We only considered some of the vulnerabilities that do not have an exploit. These vulnerabilities have been mainly selected based on their age and information about their locations. We tried to select the vulnerabilities that are at least 3 or 4 years old, so that their lack of exploit is not due to their recent discovery.

Table 3. Vulnerabilities and Exploits			
Software	**EE**	**NEE**	**Total Each**
Linux Kernel	72	81	**153**
Apache	10	20	**30**
Total All	**82**	**101**	**183**

4.2 Computing the Metrics

To collect the selected metrics, we use a function as a logical unit for analysis. Before we can take the measures of the selected metrics, the location of the vulnerable function is needed to be identified. The location can be found by looking at the report in the vulnerability database. The following steps have been followed to identify the location:

- From the vulnerability database, identify the vulnerability.
- From the Bug Repository (Bugzilla) and Version Archive:
  - Identify the vulnerable version (e.g., Apache 1.3.0)
  - Identify files by mapping CVE number to Bug ID
  - Identify the vulnerable function

Once the vulnerable version and the vulnerable function have been identified, we can now compute the metrics at the function level from the source code [30] and [31].There are different tools that can be used to compute these metrics. We have chosen the commercial tool Understand [32]. This tool has been chosen because it is user-friendly and it has a good set of APIs that allows interaction with programming languages such as Python, Perl, and C++. For the selected vulnerable version we have performed the following using our own python script:

- Search inside all folders in the *main* folder and find all .c files and store them in a list
- From the list, select the .c files that contain the vulnerabilities
- For every selected file, find the vulnerable function(s)
- Using the commercial tool Understand, compute the selected metrics.

Showing the whole measures for the selected software is limited by the number of pages, thus Table 4 shows the measures of the selected metrics for some of Apache HTTP Server vulnerabilities. As can be seen, the measures of the vulnerabilities are distinguished by the availability of exploit as either an exploit exist (EE) or no exploit exist (NEE).

4.3 Discriminative Power Test

4.3.1 Apache Dataset

Table 5 shows the results of testing the hypotheses H1, H2, H3, and H4 for the discriminative power of the individual metrics for the Apache HTTP Server dataset. It should be noted that we have performed an outliers test for all computed metrics to avoid their effect on the mean. Only one metric, calling functions, has been found to have outliers.

H1: As can be seen, the size metric has shown to have smaller values for vulnerabilities with exploits than those without an exploit and this difference is statistical significant at p-value 0.021. Therefore, the Welch t-test result suggests that the vulnerabilities with an exploit tend to have a smaller size than the vulnerabilities without an exploit.

H2: Looking at the structure metrics values, however, only the CountPath metric has shown statistical significant difference, the p-value is 0.011, for vulnerabilities with exploits compared to those without an exploit. Thus, the Welch t-test result implies that the vulnerabilities with an exploit tend to have smaller CountPath

Table 5. Result of Discriminative Power Test for Apache HTTP Server Dataset

Class of Metrics	Metrics		EE (Observations = 10) Mean	EE Variance	NEE (Observations = 20) Mean	NEE Variance	t-value	P-Value
Size	SLOC		54.2	134.4	698.4	18148.2	-2.49	**0.021**
Structure	Cyclomatic complexity		13.6	27.3	83.8	766.6	-1.95	0.063
	Nesting Degree		3.7	2.5	3.4	3.7	0.43	0.669
	CountPath		45.4	2462.3	3072	13840876.5	-2.83	**0.011**
Ease of Access	Number of Invocations		2.9	0.4	2.5	0.6	1.55	0.136
Communication	Information Flow		14.69	93.5	17.5	150.6	-0.73	0.472
	Calling functions	**Outliers**	5.7	70.3	1.4	0.7	1.53	0.163
		No outliers	5.2	64.6	1.2	0.3	1.6	0.151
	Called by functions		4.9	9.1	8.4	37.5	-2.01	**0.054**

than the vulnerabilities without an exploit. On the other hand, while the Cyclomatic complexity values are smaller for vulnerabilities with an exploit, though the difference is not significant, Nesting Degree values are higher for vulnerabilities with an exploit and this is a contrary to what we anticipated. However, according to [33], the recommended maximum for Nesting Degree is 5 and those two values are less than this number. This suggests that Nesting Degree is smaller for both vulnerabilities with an exploit and those without an exploit.

H3: The ease of access metric has shown slightly higher values for vulnerabilities with exploits which is not what we anticipated. The median for the vulnerabilities with and exploits and without an exploit is 3.0 and 2.5 respectively. Therefore, the Welch t-test result suggests that the vulnerabilities with an exploit tend to have a slightly more number of invocations than those without an exploit but this difference is not significant. However, Sparks et al. in [26] found that the nodes at greater depths (>10 edges) become increasingly difficult to reach. Therefore, we conclude that the degree of depth (around 3.0) for both groups is smaller.

H4: As can be seen from the communication metrics values, only calling functions metric has shown to have higher values for vulnerabilities with exploits than for the vulnerabilities without an exploit. However, this difference is not statistically significant. On the other hand, information flow and called by functions metrics have shown a smaller values for vulnerabilities with an exploit and that is not what we anticipated.

4.3.2 Linux Kernel Dataset

We also obtained the results of testing the hypotheses H1, H2, H3, and H4 for the discriminative power of the individual metrics for the Linux Kernel dataset. We have performed an outlier test for all computed metrics so that to avoid its effect on the mean. All metrics' values have been found to have outliers except for one metric, number of invocations. We have run the Welch t-test on both data with and without outliers.

H1: The size metric values for the data without outliers show that the size of the vulnerabilities with an exploit and without an exploit is almost the same and this is not what we anticipated. Therefore, based on the p-value, we accept that there is no difference between the vulnerabilities with an exploit and without an exploit.

H2: The values of the structure metrics without outliers are smaller for vulnerabilities with an exploit than for those without an exploit except for the CountPath metric where its values have been found to be higher, which is not what we anticipated. However, these differences are not statistically significant. Therefore, the Welch t-test result implies that none of these differences are statistically significant.

H3: The values of the ease of access metric show that the mean of the vulnerabilities with an exploit are almost the same compared to the vulnerabilities without an exploit and this is not what we anticipated. Therefore, the Welch t-test result suggests that there is no significant difference between the vulnerabilities with an exploit and those without an exploit. However, as it was discussed in section 4.3.1 under the H3 paragraph, the mean of the measures of these two groups are considered to be small.

H4: The communication metrics have shown to have smaller values. This is not what we anticipated. However, looking at the p-values, we can see that the differences are not statistically significant. Thus, we cannot reject the null hypothesis that there is no difference between the vulnerabilities with an exploit and those without an exploit.

4.4 Predictive Power Test

To test predictive power of the metrics, we need to select a subset of the proposed metrics. To do that, we implemented CFS, WRP, and PCA feature selections techniques using Waikato Environment for Knowledge Analysis (WEKA) [34]. WEKA is a popular open source toolkit implemented in Java for machine learning and data mining tasks. Once the metrics subsets have been selected, we implemented the four selected classifiers: LR, NB, RF, and SVM using WEKA. It should be noted that the parameters for the chosen feature selection techniques and classifiers are initialized with the default settings of the WEKA toolkit. It should be also noted that the results are obtained by performing 10-fold cross-validation so that the variability in prediction are reduced. Cross-validation is a technique for assessing how accurately a predictive model will perform in practice [35]. However, it is more important to identify exploited vulnerabilities even at the expense of incorrectly predicting some not exploited vulnerabilities as exploited vulnerabilities. This is because a single exploited vulnerability may lead to serious security failures. Thus, we use recall as our main performance measure to compare among the classifiers' performance. The results of testing metrics predictive power are shown in the following two subsections.

4.4.1 Apache Dataset

Table 6 shows predictive power results for the Apache dataset. Column one and two contain the classifiers and their performance measures respectively. We first start with testing every classifier using the whole selected metrics and collect the performance measures provided by WEKA, as shown in column three. For

Table 6. Result of Predictive Power Test for Apache HTTP Server Dataset

Model	Performance Measures	All metrics (%)	Correlation-Based (CFS) (%)	Wrapper Subset (WRP) (%)		PCA (%)
				BN	RF	
Logistic Regression	Recall	60	**73**	73	67	**74**
	Precision	60	**73**	72	64	**75**
	F-Measure	53	**73**	73	64	**74**
	Accuracy	60	**73.3**	73.3	66.6	**73.3**
	FPR	50	**33**	38	52	**28**
Naïve Bayes	Recall	70	70	**77**	80	63
	Precision	84	84	**79**	81	72
	F-Measure	70	70	**77**	80	64
	Accuracy	70	70	**76.7**	80	63.3
	FPR	15	15	**22**	20	28
Random Forest	Recall	**77**	70	73	**83**	73
	Precision	**76**	69	72	**84**	73
	F-Measure	**76**	70	73	**84**	73
	Accuracy	**76.6**	70	73.3	**83.3**	73.3
	FPR	**32**	40	38	**18**	33
Support Vector Machine	Recall	67	67	73	73	67
	Precision	44	44	81	81	44
	F-Measure	53	53	67	67	53
	Accuracy	66.7	66.7	73.3	73.3	66.7
	FPR	67	67	53	53	67

convenient interpretation, we express the performance measures in terms of percentage, where a 100 % is the best value and 0 %is the worst value. Then, we select a subset of those metrics using CFS, WRP, and PCA feature selection techniques and test the chosen classifier using the selected subsets and provide the performance measures as shown in column four, five, and six respectively.

Considering the value 0.7 (70%) of recall and precision measures as reasonable [25], we show for every metrics subset the highest recall for a classifier in bold. Now, we will compare the classifiers performance measures using different subset metrics. We will first start with using the whole metrics. As can be seen, only NB and RF report the best recall and precision value. Moreover their accuracy and precision performance measures are either 70 or more. Even though NB reports the best precision, the reported harmonic mean, F-measure, by RF is better. It should be also notated that FPR reported by NB is lower than the one reported by RF. However, when the subset metrics selected by the correlation-based feature selection, we see that not only LR has improved but it has done better than the other classifiers. Neither the BN nor the SVM has shown any improvement.

On the other hand, when the other subset of the metrics, selected by the wrapper subset selection method was used, RF has reported the best performance compared to the other classifiers and the best among any the other features selection technique the RF used. It should be noted that WRP conducts a search for a good subset using a classifier. We applied the four classifiers as a part of WRP in order to select the best combination of metrics. However, as the other classifiers, SVM and LR, did not show better results than NB and RF, we only reported the NB and RF results. When the subset selected by the PCA method was used, however, LR has reported the best performance.

We have observed that the feature selection technique has an impact on the classifiers performances. More precisely, the LR has its best performance when PCA technique has been used while the NB, RF, and SVM has their best performance when the WRP has been applied. In addition, we have observed that the RF recall's value did not score below 70%. Besides, even though the SVM recall value has improved when the metrics subset selected by the WRP was used, its FPR remains above 50. Moreover, when the PCA technique was used, only LR reports a good performance and the other three classifiers either remained the same (RF and SVM) or performed their worst (NB).

H5: It can be concluded that there is a combination of metrics that significantly predicts vulnerabilities that have an exploit using Apache dataset.

4.4.2 Linux Kernel Dataset

The metrics predictive power results for the Linux Kernel dataset show that none of the classifiers has a 70 % recall value. However, let us investigate if any of the classifiers has a recall score of at least 50%. When the whole metrics have been used, none of the classifiers has a recall score of 50%. However, when the CFS feature selection technique has been used, RF has a 50% recall score. It should be noted that while the NB and LR have improved when the CFS was used, compared when using the whole metrics, SVM performed worse than when it used the whole metrics. On the other hand, when the WRP has been used, only NB and RF has their recall score improved. When the PCA technique has been used, however, only NB and SVM have shown a recall score above 50%. Though using the feature selection techniques has slightly improve the performance of the chosen classifiers, their FPRs have a score close to or greater than 50%. This shows that the classifiers have difficulty to learn from this dataset and hence behaved almost randomly. It should be noted that the SVM, when the PCA was used, has performed the best compared to the other classifiers.

H5: We can conclude that there is a combination of metrics that significantly predicts vulnerabilities that have an exploit using Linux Kernel dataset but at low recall score.

4.5 Threats to Validity

In this paper we have considered the datasets for only two products, the Apache HTTP server and Linux Kernel. However, they are both very significant examples. The Apache HTTP server has more than 169 belonging to different categories. Besides, its line of code varies between 50,712 LOC to 358,633 LOC. We recognize that the number of vulnerabilities that have an exploit reported for them in Apache HTTP server is low. However, we are just scratching the surface based on what is available. On the other hand, Linux Kernel has larger number of vulnerabilities, more than 1200. Its size in line of code has ranged from 10,239 LOC to 15,803,499 LOC. It also has a greater variety of vulnerabilities. As there are other potential factors that can influence the probability of development of an exploit for a vulnerability that have not been examined in this study. Finally, exploits that have not yet been publically reported were not considered in our study.

5. DISCUSSION

One of our main observations is that some metrics have a good discriminative and predictive power for Apache dataset. However, they do not have significant discriminative and predictive power for the Linux Kernel dataset. Moreover, we also observed that, unlike in Apache dataset, some metrics such as CountPath, values have been found to be higher for vulnerabilities with exploit in Linux dataset. One possible reason could be the value of the target. *The exploits developers may be willing to exploit vulnerabilities in an operating system even if it requires more effort because having a root access could be worth the effort.* Besides, when compared to Apache, Linux Kernel has more exploits. This shows that this might be because Linux Kernel is a more valuable target for the attackers. To verify this, we looked into the initial release dates of the both products and we found that the difference in age is not very significant (Linux is 23 years old and Apache 20 years old), and also looked into the usage statistics and market share data and we found Apache market share is around 57% [36] whereas Linux Kernel is about 52.4 % [37].

Based on the Apache dataset, we have also observed that when a function is vulnerable and has an exploit, its SLOC, CYC, and CountPath values have been found to be lower than the vulnerable functions without an exploit. A similar result has been observed by [25] when they try to predict the existence of a vulnerability. *It seems that the attackers favoring simpler vulnerable targets,* especially when the goal is to deny a service, such as the one provided by Apache, using the least effort. Using the WRP as a method to select a combination of metrics has the best impact on the classifiers performance. However, in [25], security domain knowledge metrics have to be considered in order for the vulnerability prediction performance to be enhanced.

6. RELATED WORK

In this section, we summarize related works based on their approach: works that address vulnerabilities exploitability, the studies that use software metrics to predict vulnerability location and existence, and works that use the graph-based metrics.

***CVSS Metrics*:** CVSS metrics are the de facto standard for measuring the severity of vulnerabilities [38]. CVSS Base Score measures severity based on exploitability (the ease of exploiting vulnerability) and impact (the effect of exploitation). However, CVSS exploitability measures have some limitations. First, they assign static subjective numbers to the metrics based on expert knowledge. In contrast, we focus on reducing subjectivity in assessing vulnerability exploitation by basing our analysis on software attributes that can be objectively derived from the source code. Second, two of CVSS's factors (Access Vector and Authentication) have the same value for almost all vulnerabilities [5]. Third, there is no formal procedure for evaluating the third factor (Access Complexity) [38]. Consequently, it is unclear if CVSS considers the software structure and properties as a factor.

***Assessing vulnerability exploitability*:** Gegick et al. [39] argued that vulnerabilities that are located in low risk areas of the code should be prioritized differently from the ones that are located in high risk areas of the code. Their results show that the combined usage of the internal metrics has predicted the attack-prone components with a high accuracy and zero false negative rates. While the authors granularity analysis was at the component level ours is at the function level, which might reveal some more important information [40]. Moreover, we used different internal code-level metrics. In addition, they used reported security failures to identify a component as an attack prone and a non-attack-prone. In contrast, we used the availability of exploit to identify a vulnerable function as either exploited or not exploited function.

Bozorgi et al. [41] proposed a Machine Learning and Data mining technique that uses features mined from known vulnerability reports to predict the possibility of vulnerability exploitability. They compare their results with the CVSS Exploitability metrics and found that their approach can classify vulnerability exploitability better than the CVSS. We consider the relationship between some software internal metrics, which are extracted from the source code, and the availability of exploits. This is particularly important for newly released software where vulnerability reports are not available.

Allodi and Massacci in [42] and [43] have proposed the black market as an index of risk of vulnerability exploitation. Their approach assesses the risk of vulnerability exploitation based on the volumes of the attacks due to the vulnerability exploits sold in the black market. In contrast, in this paper we try to investigate the relationship between software metrics and the availability of exploits, as data about vulnerabilities attacked in the wild is not always available. This could help software developers predict vulnerabilities exploitation on the development side instead of the deployment side.

***Using software metrics*:** Several researchers have studied the possibility of using software metrics to predict vulnerable entities (components, classes, modules, files, and functions/methods) or the existence of vulnerabilities. Shin and Williams [1] and [2] investigated the possibility of using complexity metrics as predictors for the location of security problems. Chowdhury and Zulkernine [3] investigated the usability of complexity, coupling and cohesion metrics as predictors of vulnerabilities' location. However, in [4], Zimmermann et al. studied several software metrics including code complexity and dependency as predictors for the existence of vulnerabilities. Our work, on the other hand, focuses on predicting the exploitability of a vulnerability.

***Using Graph-based Metrics*:** Bhattacharya et al. [44] studied the possibility of applying graph-based approaches to software engineering tasks. Using the source code, they construct a graph model and use graph metrics to measure some properties. Their results show that graph metrics can detect significant structural changes, and can help estimate bug severity, prioritize debugging efforts, and predict defect-prone releases. In this paper, we use different graph metrics and investigate whether they are correlated with a vulnerability severity rather than a bug severity. Besides, we use the availability of an exploit to identify the severity of a vulnerability.

7. CONCLUSIONS AND FUTURE WORK

In this study, we investigated the possible relationship between the metrics and the existence of a vulnerability exploit. We studied 183 vulnerabilities and mapped them to their locations at the function level. We then characterized these functions using eight software metrics. The metrics have been evaluated for their discriminative and predictive power. The results show that the difference between a vulnerability that has no exploit and a vulnerability that has an exploit can be characterized to some extent using software metrics known for characterizing the presence of vulnerabilities for some of the products. However, the study shows that predicting exploitation of vulnerabilities is more complicated than predicting the presence of vulnerabilities and thus using metrics that consider security domain knowledge is important for enhancing the performance of a vulnerability exploitation prediction effort.

Even though the two selected applications have a rich history of reported vulnerabilities, considering software with a different domain, such as an open source browser like Firefox, increases the size of the dataset and that might reveal significant information. Improving the classifiers performance and capturing vulnerabilities exploitability may require further empirical investigations of software metrics specifically applicable to the security realm. Thus, further research is needed which considers the metrics related to attack surface [28], reachability and dangerous system calls metrics [18, 45], graph-based metrics [44], and static analysis tool warnings metrics [39]. Moreover, using an alternative approach such as a text mining technique [46] to predict vulnerability exploitability might lead to an interesting results.

Identification of previously unknown (i.e. zero-day) vulnerability take considerable expertise and effort using fuzzers, and many of the resulting vulnerabilities may pose little risk if no exploits are written for them. If the methods considered here can be extended for identifying code which is more likely to have an exploited vulnerability, the vulnerability testers can save considerable time.

8. REFERENCES

[1] Shin, Y. and Williams, L. "Is complexity really the enemy of software security?" *in Proc. ACM Workshop Quality Protection*, 2008, pp. 47–50.

[2] Shin, Y. and Williams, L. "An empirical model to predict security vulnerabilities using code complexity metrics," *in Proc. ACM-IEEE Int. Symp. Empirical Softw. Eng. Meas.*, 2008, pp. 315–317.

[3] I. Chowdhury and M. Zulkernine, "Using complexity, coupling, and cohesion metrics as early indicators of vulnerabilities," *J. Syst. Archit.*, vol. 57, no. 3, pp. 294–313, 2011.

[4] T. Zimmermann, N. Nagappan, and L. Williams, "Searching for a needle in a haystack: Predicting security vulnerabilities for windows vista," *in Proc. Int. Conf. Softw. Testing, Verification Validation*, 2010, pp. 421–428.

[5] L. Allodi and F. Massacci, "My Software has a Vulnerability, should I worry?," *arXiv preprint arXiv*:1301.1275, 2013.

[6] A. Younis and Y.K. Malaiya. "Comparing and Evaluating CVSS Base Metrics and Microsoft Rating System". *The 2015 IEEE International Conference on Software Quality, Reliability and Security*, 2015, pp. 252-261.

[7] K. Nayak, D. Marino, P. Efstathopoulos, T. Dumitra, "Some vulnerabilities are different than others". *In: Proceedings of the 17th International Symposium on Research in Attacks, Intrusions and Defenses*, 2014, pp. 426–446.

[8] "National Vulnerability Database Home.". Available: http://nvd.nist.gov/. [Accessed: 24-May-2015].

[9] EDB: Exploits Database by Offensive Security. Available: http://www.exploit-db.com/. [Accessed: 24-May-2015].

[10] M. Fagerland and L. Sandvik. "Performance of five two-sample location tests for skewed distributions with unequal variances." *Contemporary clinical trials*, vol. 30, pp.490-496, 2009.

[11] A. Ozment, "Improving vulnerability discovery models," *in Proceedings of the 2007 ACM workshop on Quality of protection*, New York, NY, USA, 2007, pp. 6–11.

[12] S. Frei, D. Schatzmann, B. Plattner, and B. Trammell, "Modeling the Security Ecosystem - The Dynamics of (In)Security," in Economics of Information Security and Privacy. Springer US, 2010, pp. 79–106.

[13] N.E. Fenton, S.L. Pfleeger, Software Metrics: A Rigorous and Practical Approach, PWS Publishing Co., Boston, MA, USA, 1997.

[14] T.J. McCabe, A complexity measure, *IEEE Transactions on Software Engineering* 2 (4) (1976) 308–320.

[15] W.A. Harrison, K.I. Magel, A complexity measure based on nesting level, *ACM Sigplan Notices* 16 (3) (1981) 63–74.

[16] S. Henry, D. Kafura, Software structure metrics based on information flow, *IEEE Transactions on Software Engineering* (1981) 510–518.

[17] N. Nagappan, T. Ball, A. Zeller, Mining metrics to predict component failures, *in Proceedings of the 28th International Conference on Software Engineering*, Shanghai, China, May 2006, pp. 452–461.

[18] A. Younis, Y.K. Malaiya and I. Ray, "Assessing Vulnerability Exploitability Risk Using Software Proprieties", *Software Quality Journal*: 1-44, Mar 2015.

[19] G. Forman, "An extensive empirical study of feature selection metrics for text classification." The Journal of machine learning research, 3, p.1289-1305, 2003.

[20] M. Hall and L. Smith. Practical feature subset selection for machine learning. *In Proceedings 21st Australasian Computer Science Conference*, University of Western Australia, Perth, Australia, February 1996.

[21] R. Kohavi, G.H. John, "Wrappers for feature subset selection" *Artificial Intelligence*, 97(1-2), p. 273-324, 1997.

[22] I. Jolliffe, Principal component analysis. John Wiley & Sons, Ltd, 2002.

[23] B. Schneier, Beyond Fear: Thinking Sensibly about Security in an Uncertain World. Springer-Verlag, 2003.

[24] E. Alatal, V. Nicomettel, M. Kaâniche1, M. Dacier, and M. Herrb, "Lessons Learned from the Deployment of a High-Interaction Honeypot", EDCC'06: *in Proc. 6th European Dependable Computing Conf. Coimbra*, Portugal, 2006, pp. 39–46.

[25] P. Morrison, K. Herzig, B. Murphy, and L. Williams, "Challenges with Applying Vulnerability Prediction Models", Proceedings of the 2015 Symposium and Bootcamp on the Science of Security, 2015. Microsoft Research: http://research.microsoft.com/apps/pubs/default.aspx?id=240601. [Accessed: 24-March-2015].

[26] S. Sparks, S. Embleton, R. Cunningham, and C. Zou, "Automated vulnerability analysis: Leveraging control flow for evolutionary input crafting," *in Computer Security Applications Conference*, 2007. ACSAC 2007. Twenty-Third Annual, 2007, pp. 477–486.

[27] M. Howard, J. Pincus, and J. Wing, "Measuring Relative Attack Surfaces," *in Computer Security in the 21st Century*, D. T. Lee, S. P. Shieh, and J. D. Tygar, Eds. Springer US, 2005, pp. 109–137.

[28] P. K. Manadhata and J. M. Wing, "An Attack Surface Metric," *Software Engineering, IEEE Transactions* on, vol. 37, no. 3, pp. 371 –386, Jun. 2011.

[29] IEEE, "IEEE Standard for a Software Quality Metrics Methodology," *IEEE Std* 1061-1998 (R2004), IEEE CS, 2005.

[30] Apache-SVN. The apache software foundation. Available: http://www.svn.apache.org/viewvc/. [Accessed: 24-May-2015].

[31] Linux Kernel Archive. Available: https://www.kernel.org/ [Accessed: 24-May-2015].

[32] Scientific Toolworks Understand. Available: http://www.scitools.com/. [Accessed: 24-May-2015].

[33] LocMetrics. Available: http://www.locmetrics.com/index.html. [Accessed: 24-May-2015].

[34] WEKA Toolkit. Available: http://www.cs.waikato.ac.nz/ml/weka. [Accessed: 24-May-2015].

[35] I.H. Witten, E. Frank, Data Mining: Practical Machine Learning Tools and Techniques (2nd ed.), Morgan Kaufmann, San Francisco, 2005.

[36] Usage Statistics and Market Share of Web Servers for Websites. Available: http://www.w3techs.com/technologies/overview/web_server/all. [Accessed: 24-May-2015].

[37] Usage Statistics and Market Share of Web Servers for Websites. Available: http://w3techs.com/technologies/details/os-unix/all/all. [Accessed: 24-May-2015].

[38] P. Mell, K. Scarfone, and S. Romanosky, "A complete guide to the common vulnerability scoring system version 2.0," in Published by FIRST-Forum of Incident Response and Security Teams, 2007, pp.1–23.

[39] M. Gegick, L. Williams, J. Osborne, and M. Vouk. "Prioritizing software security fortification through code-level metrics." *In Proceedings of the 4th ACM workshop on Quality of protection*, 2008, pp. 31-38.

[40] T. Zimmermann, R. Premraj, A. Zeller, "Predicting defects for eclipse". *In Proceedings of the Third International Workshop on Predictor Models in Software Engineering*, 2007, pp. 9–15.

[41] M. Bozorgi, L. K. Saul, S. Savage, and G. M. Voelker, "Beyond heuristics: learning to classify vulnerabilities and predict exploits," *in Proceedings of the 16th ACM SIGKDD international conference on Knowledge discovery and data mining*, New York, NY, USA, 2010, pp. 105–114.

[42] L. Allodi and F. Massacci, "A preliminary analysis of vulnerability scores for attacks in wild," *ACM Proc. of CCS BADGERS*, 2012, pp.17-24.

[43] L. Allodi and F. Massacci, "My Software has a Vulnerability, should I worry?,", 2013 , arXiv preprint arXiv:1301.1275.

[44] P. Bhattacharya, M. Iliofotou, I. Neamtiu, and M. Faloutsos, "Graph-based analysis and prediction for software evolution," *in Proc. Intl. Conf. on Softw. Eng. (ICSE). ACM*, 2012, pp. 419–429.

[45] A. Younis and Y.K. Malaiya," Using Software Structure to Predict Vulnerability Exploitation Potential," The 8th IEEE International Conference on Software Security and Reliability, 2014, pp. 13-18.

[46] R. Scandariato, J. Walden, A. Hovsepyan, W. Joosen. Predicting vulnerable software components via text mining. *IEEE Trans Softw Eng*, 40 (10) (2014), pp. 993–1006.

On the Effectiveness of Sensor-enhanced Keystroke Dynamics Against Statistical Attacks

Valeriu - Daniel Stanciu
VU University Amsterdam
The Netherlands
valeriu.stanciu@cti.pub.ro

Riccardo Spolaor
University of Padua
Italy
rspolaor@math.unipd.it

Mauro Conti
University of Padua
Italy
conti@math.unipd.it

Cristiano Giuffrida
VU University Amsterdam
The Netherlands
giuffrida@cs.vu.nl

ABSTRACT

In recent years, simple password-based authentication systems have increasingly proven ineffective for many classes of real-world devices. As a result, many researchers have concentrated their efforts on the design of new biometric authentication systems. This trend has been further accelerated by the advent of mobile devices, which offer numerous sensors and capabilities to implement a variety of mobile biometric authentication systems. Along with the advances in biometric authentication, however, attacks have also become much more sophisticated and many biometric techniques have ultimately proven inadequate in face of advanced attackers in practice.

In this paper, we investigate the effectiveness of sensor-enhanced keystroke dynamics, a recent mobile biometric authentication mechanism that combines a particularly rich set of features. In our analysis, we consider different types of attacks, with a focus on advanced attacks that draw from general population statistics. Such attacks have already been proven effective in drastically reducing the accuracy of many state-of-the-art biometric authentication systems. We implemented a statistical attack against sensor-enhanced keystroke dynamics and evaluated its impact on detection accuracy. On one hand, our results show that sensor-enhanced keystroke dynamics are generally robust against statistical attacks with a marginal equal-error rate impact (<0.14%). On the other hand, our results show that, surprisingly, keystroke timing features non-trivially weaken the security guarantees provided by sensor features alone. Our findings suggest that *sensor dynamics* may be a stronger biometric authentication mechanism against recently proposed practical attacks.

CODASPY'16, March 09-11, 2016, New Orleans, LA, USA

DOI: http://dx.doi.org/10.1145/2857705.2857748

1. INTRODUCTION

Password-based systems have been the most common form of authentication for many years. Albeit simple, password-based authentication is prone to several attacks such as guessing attacks, dictionary attacks, and shoulder surfing attacks. With the advent of mobile computing, such attacks have dramatically increased their effectiveness.

In a mobile context, password-based authentication is even more problematic due to the peculiar nature of the devices. Most of such problems relate to the users being unaware of privacy leakage or exhibiting incautious behavior. Indeed, users often choose passwords that are easy to type and thus easy to guess. They also tend to leave visible finger marks on the touchscreen (i.e., smudges), which can lead to password leaks [1]. Moreover, an unaware user could be victim of shoulder surfing attacks due to the exposure of mobile devices [30, 24]. In addition, new increasingly sophisticated attacks are rampant. For example, researchers have demonstrated the proneness of mobile password authentication to automated attacks based on videos captured by low-end cameras and motion analysis through repeated reflections [33]. As an another example, more advanced attacks that rely only on hands dynamics [28] can achieve even 50% penetration rate at the first attempt. Given the ever-growing amount of highly-sensitive information (e.g., credit card transactions, confidential emails, and personal photos) stored on mobile devices, there is an increasing demand for stronger mobile authentication techniques.

To address the emerging threats to password-based mobile authentication, many researchers have recently devised a number of biometric authentication systems [14] for mobile devices. Biometric authentication identifies users by relying on their behavioral or physiological characteristics, such as fingerprints, body geometry, voice, gestures or signature. Since modern mobile devices offer an increasingly complex and diverse set of user-driven features, they provide an ideal platform for capturing and analyzing biometric traits. Prior research efforts have explored a broad range of mobile authentication techniques, including authenticating users based on their walking patterns [17], phone call gestures [5], touch gestures [23, 6, 7, 18, 27] or keystroke dynamics [15, 4, 11, 31]. However, most existing biometric authentication mechanisms either yield insufficient accuracy for real-world deployment or have recently proven ineffective against advanced statistical attacks [26, 29, 25]. The recent sensor-enhanced keystroke dynamics [9], in turn, yields promising accuracy results against zero-effort attack conditions, but its real effectiveness in face of advanced statistical attacks remains unexplored.

Contributions

In this paper, we assess the effectiveness of sensor-enhanced keystroke dynamics against statistical attacks drawing input data from general population statistics. Sensor-enhanced keystroke dynamics relies on both mobile devices built-in sensors (e.g., accelerometer, gyroscope) and keystrokes timing (e.g., hold time) information for user authentication purposes. This rich set of features can be potentially generalized to different biometric authentication systems, thereby motivating our focus in this paper. In order to conduct our investigation, we implemented a state-of-the-art statistical attack that forges mobile user inputs based on real population statistics. Next, we ran the attack on a pool of 20 users using our forged input samples. We have assessed the effectiveness of our attack and its impact on the end-to-end accuracy of sensor-enhanced keystroke dynamics, also evaluating its effects on the individual features (i.e., sensor-based and timing-based). Our experimental results show that sensor-enhanced keystroke dynamics is resilient to both zero-effort and advanced statistical attacks in practice. Finally, our results suggest that timing features are generally detrimental to detection accuracy in statistical attack scenarios, but they still achieve a measurable accuracy improvement in face of zero-effort attacks.

Roadmap

The remainder of the paper is organized as follows. In Section 2, we survey related work, provide background information on sensor-enhanced keystroke dynamics, and present modern attacks against biometric authentication systems. In Section 3, we present the threat model, our attack methodology, and implementation. In Section 4, we present experimental results, and discuss our findings. In Section 5, finally, we draw conclusions and discuss directions for future work.

2. RELATED WORK

In the literature, there have been numerous attempts to attack biometric authentication systems. In the following, we first provide background information to adequately introduce the main concepts and then detail prior efforts related to our work.

2.1 Equal Error Rate

Measuring the accuracy of a biometric identification system is a well-studied problem [32]. Briefly, the performance of a system is characterized by two metrics:

- False Match Rate (FMR), which expresses the number of impostors accepted as legitimate users;
- False Nonmatch Rate (FNMR), which expresses the number of legitimate users rejected as impostors.

The parameters of an authentication system can be tuned according to its specific purpose, that is, facilitating authentication for the average user, but accepting more impostors (i.e., with a high FMR), or offering better security but constraining the user to a more strict authentication behavior (i.e., with a high FNMR).

In the literature, e.g., [7], [19], [12], the Equal Error Rate (EER) is a common accuracy metric. The EER reflects the accuracy of the authentication system when the False Match Rate and the False Nonmatch Rate are equal. It is expressed as a single value between 0 and 1, with lower values representing better accuracy. Following the common approach in the literature, we rely on the EER to measure accuracy and compare our results against prior work.

2.2 Sensor-enhanced Keystroke Dynamics

Keystroke dynamics have been widely used as biometrics for characterizing users' behavior. From hardware to software keyboards, from fixed- to free-text input, from traditional to mobile devices, keystroke dynamics has successfully exploited intrinsic typing characteristics for authenticating interactive users. In detail, keystroke dynamics relies on timing *key-press* and *key-release* events, associating them in different ways and deriving features such as the key hold time, inter-key-press time, etc.

With the advent of mobile devices, a fairly large number of sensors became available for biometric authentication purposes, such as accelerometer, gyroscope, temperature, air pressure, and many others. In this paper, we specifically focus on movement sensors, i.e., accelerometer and gyroscope, which have proven effective for authentication purposes in the context of *sensor-enhanced keystroke dynamics* [9].

Sensor-enhanced keystroke dynamics [9] augments keystroke timing features borrowed from traditional keystroke dynamics with sensor-based features derived from real-time data sampled from movement sensors. Building on this rich feature set, prior sensor-enhanced keystroke dynamics solutions implemented different detection algorithms, including the mean and k-nearest neighbors (kNN, with k=1) algorithms based on Euclidean (unweighted, weighted, normed, normed weighted) and Manhattan (unweighted, weighted, scaled, scaled weighted) distances. Such detection algorithms have been evaluated against zero-effort attacks, ultimately reporting a 0.08% EER [9].

2.3 Zero-effort Attacks

Zero-effort attacks [16, 14] are the common setting to evaluate the accuracy of biometric authentication systems and their resilience to attacks. In short, a zero-effort attack refers to an impostor generating inputs to bypass an authentication system without any knowledge of other users and their behavioral characteristics. For our evaluation, this translates to evaluating the accuracy of our authentication system for every user against any other user who participated in the experiment. This evaluation strategy has been widely used in prior work in the field [7, 12, 18].

As mentioned earlier, a zero-effort attack setting was also previously used to evaluate the accuracy of sensor-enhanced keystroke dynamics [9]. Nevertheless, accuracy measurements solely based on zero-effort attacks are not alone sufficient to thoroughly assess the robustness of biometric authentication systems against modern attacks [22]. In this paper, we thereby consider more sophisticated (statistical) attacks to thoroughly evaluate the accuracy of sensor-enhanced keystroke dynamics in practice.

2.4 Other Attacks

Many prior efforts have shown that zero-effort attacks achieve significantly lower EER than more sophisticated non-zero-effort attacks in practice [22, 2, 8, 13, 20, 21, 3, 26, 29, 25]. In what follows, we discuss the most relevant efforts for our work and draw appropriate comparison.

Rahman et al. [21] propose a snoop-forge-replay attack against a keystroke-based continuous verification system. Their technique is based on snooping keystroke samples from the user using a keylogger [10] and reuse the samples to evade detection. Their attack achieves extremely high EERs, between 43.0% and 96.5%, with average EER increases between 69.3% and 2,919.3%. Such high EER increases naturally stem from the attack setting, which relies on real keystrokes "stolen" from the victim to create the forged inputs. We assume that, in such an attack setting, the system has already been irremediably compromised and we construct our attack only based on external population statistics (i.e., without any prior knowledge about the victim).

Other researchers [26] have demonstrated practical statistical attacks against touch-based authentication systems. Such attacks rely on a "Lego" robot to physically issue forged inputs based on statistical analysis of the touch patterns of a population. The authors in [26] have reported EER increases between 339% and 1,004%, with mean EER values between 30% and 55%. Unlike such attacks, we consider an ideal (and thus pessimistic) setting with no physical constraints for the attacker, providing worst-case results for the accuracy of sensor-enhanced keystroke dynamics.

Other researchers have proposed statistical attacks to evaluate the accuracy of keystroke dynamics [29]. Such attacks, somewhat closer to our work, also rely on statistically drawn inputs issued by a physical robot. The attacks presented in [29], however, are more focused on raising concerns about synthetic forgery attacks rather than detailing the statistical attack design and impact in practice. Serwadda et al. [25] provide a step forward, with a detailed accuracy analysis of keystroke dynamics against statistical attacks based on timings drawn from general population statistics. The attack presented in [25] groups keystroke dynamics features in probability trees and relies on a binning procedure to extract statistically relevant features from a given population. Our attack draws from the methodology presented in [25], but focuses on sensor-enhanced keystroke dynamics and scales to a much higher number of features and inputs.

3. ATTACK METHODOLOGY

In this section, we present the methodology we followed to perform the attack. We first introduce the threat model (Section 3.1), then give details about feature selection (Section 3.2) and detection (Section 3.3) algorithms, and finally discuss how we implemented the attack (Section 3.4).

3.1 Threat Model

We consider an attacker seeking to bypass a sensor-enhanced keystroke dynamics authentication system based on password-based keystroke dynamics combined with accelerometer and gyroscope sensor information. If the attacker enters the correct password with the expected typing behavior, then authentication is successful. Otherwise, authentication fails, even if the typed password is correct.

We assume the password to be known to the attacker. This is a common assumption in biometric authentication, since the main purpose of the accuracy analysis is to assess the extra security added by biometric characteristics.

We also assume an ideal attacker able to perfectly forge a particular typing pattern. In other words, we assume the attacker to be a "perfect machine" able to learn and reproduce human typing patterns. In particular, in order to obtain worst-case accuracy results, we assume the attacker is not limited by any physical constraints. This model matches the assumptions made in prior sensor-enhanced keystroke dynamics efforts [9].

Finally, we assume the attacker can draw from general population statistics (except the victim) to generate impostor samples and try to bypass the authentication system. This is a common assumption in statistical attack scenarios [25], which normally impose no restrictions on the population data available to the attacker.

3.2 Feature Selection

Sensor-enhanced keystroke dynamics relies on features derived from keystroke timings and sensor data continuously sampled while typing. In particular, the features we select from the sensor distributions sampled over time are based on standard statistical metrics, that is root mean square, minimum and maximum value, number of local maxima and minima, mean delta, sum of positive values, sum of negative values, mean value, mean value during keystroke events, and standard deviation. We rely on these statistical metrics to identify features for both gyroscope and accelerometer samples. For keystroke dynamics, we rely on two main features: *KHT* (*Key Hold Time*) and *KIT* (*Key Interval Time*, or inter-key-press time), for each key and pair of keys typed, respectively. Each sample is represented as a vector of F feature values, where F is the total number of features according to the distance metrics considered.

3.3 Detection

To authenticate users and detect impostors, we rely on standard threshold-based binary classification. Similar to prior efforts [9], we experimented with two classes of detection algorithms, k-nearest neighbors (kNN, with k = 1), and the mean algorithm (comparing the test samples against the mean training sample rather than against all the training samples). We omitted the SVM and Naive Bayes algorithms from our analysis, after unsuccessful early attempts. Finally, we based our detection algorithms on a number of distance metrics commonly used in the literature [9]: Euclidean, Euclidean normed, Manhattan, Manhattan scaled, and their weighted versions (weights representing the importance of a given feature in the feature vectors).

3.4 Attack Design and Implementation

This section presents the design and implementation of our statistical attack and details the challenges involved. Figure 1 illustrates a general overview of our attack strategy.

Our statistical attack strategy consists of four main steps:

- Statistically analyze the samples of a given population to identify common characteristics, that is the most frequent combinations of feature values.
- Generate forged input samples based on the previously discovered characteristics.
- Feed the forged samples to the authentication system.
- Analyze the impact of the attack.

To analyze the impact of the attack, we rely on leave-one-out cross-validation and EER calculations under statistical attacks, as follows:

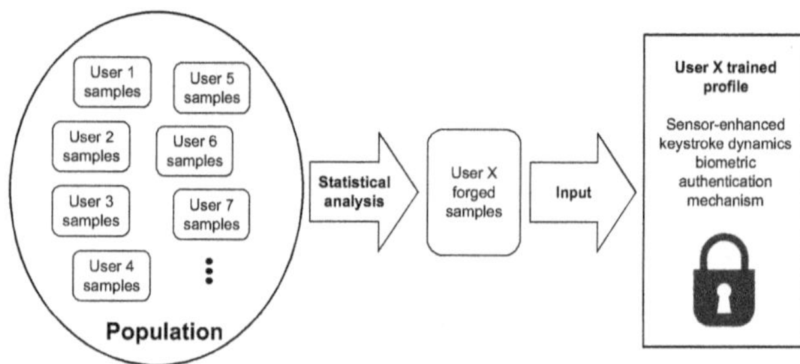

Figure 1: Statistical attack overview.

- For each user in the population, we iteratively "leave one sample out" and create a *training set* containing the remaining samples.
- Unlike zero-effort attacks, we create a *testing set* for each user with inputs statistically generated using the common characteristics from other users' samples.
- For each iteration, we calculate the corresponding EER and acceptance threshold for the given user (based on the reported False Match and False Nonmatch rates) and evaluate the effectiveness of our attack.

To identify common characteristics in the population and generate forged input samples based on statistical analysis, we have devised the procedure depicted in Algorithm 1. The algorithm receives the following parameters in input: an array of real-world input samples (*realInputs*), an array of weights (*weights*) for each feature (calculated across the population by an SVM classifier), the number of bins (*numberOfBins*) each [0; 1] feature value distribution should be partitioned into, and the number of most relevant bins (h) to consider to forge input samples.

```
Input: realInputs[ ]; //Real-world input samples
Input: weights[ ]; //Feature weights
Input: numberOfBins; //Number of bins for each feature
Input: h; //Number of bins for forged input generation
Output: forgedInputs[ ]; //Forged input samples

/* Generate bins sorted by feature weights and occurrences */
binnedInputs[ ] := binInputs(realInputs);
sortBinsByOccurrence(binnedInputs);
sortFeaturesByWeight(binnedInputs, weights);

/* Initialize bin indexes to 0 */
binIndexes[ ] := initBinIndexes();

foreach realInputs do
    forgedInput := generateInput(binnedInputs, binIndexes, h);
    addForgedInput(forgedInput, forgedInputs);
end

return forgedInputs;
```

Algorithm 1: Procedure to create forged input samples.

Given the input parameters, the algorithm runs a binning procedure that iterates over all the samples and feature values received in input and, for each feature value visited, increments the corresponding bin. The bins uniformly partition the original [0; 1] feature value intervals in *numberOfBins* smaller (and identical) value intervals. After running this procedure, the algorithm obtains, for each feature, an array of bins sorted by number of occurrences in descending order (see Figure 2). In other words, for each feature, the first N bins determine the N most common feature values across the population. In Algorithm 1, all the sorted per-feature bins are ultimately assembled and sorted by feature weights in descending order in the *binnedInputs* array. Next, the algorithm initializes the *binIndexes* array containing, for each feature, the bin to use to generate the next guess. Initially, all the indexes are set to 0.

Binned feature values sorted by number of occurrences →

Features sorted by discriminability ↓	V0	V1	V2	V3	V4	V5	V6	V7	V8	V9 ...
KHT 0	14x	13x	10x	10x	10x	8x	8x	7x	6x	6x
KIT 2	10x	8x	7x	7x	6x	6x	6x	5x	5x	4x
AvgAccY	16x	15x	15x	14x	14x	13x	12x	8x	8x	8x
AvgAccX	13x	13x	13x	13x	12x	11x	11x	10x	10x	10x
RMSAccX	18x	18x	17x	16x	15x	15x	12x	12x	8x	7x
RMSGyro	12x	12x	12x	12x	11x	10x	10x	8x	8x	8x
...										

Figure 2: Bin generation example.

The next step is to identify the relevant bins for each feature and generate forged input samples. To identify the relevant per-feature bins, we simply select the first h bins with most occurrences. To generate the forged input samples, we traverse all the features available and generate combinations of features values associated only to the first h per-feature bins. A naive strategy, which instead considers all the possible per-feature bins without discrimination, would face a prohibitively large guess space and have trouble scaling. In Algorithm 1, our generation strategy is implemented by the *generateInput* subprocedure, which runs *realInputs* times to generate as many forged input samples as real-world samples given in input.

The order in which the combinations are generated is dictated by the discriminability offered by the our feature weights (calculated by an SVM classifier). The features with higher discriminability are considered first, thanks to the sorting strategy adopted when generating the *binnedInputs* array. As an example, suppose we have only three features, KHT0 (key hold time for keystroke 0), KIT2 (time between keystroke 2 and keystroke 3), and AvgAccY (average acceleration on Y axis), as represented in Figure 2. Also suppose the value of h is set to 2, AvgAccY has the highest discriminability, and KHT0 has the lowest one. In this example, the first five combinations generated by the algorithm would be {V0, V0, V0}, {V0, V0, V1}, {V0, V1, V0}, {V0, V1, V1}, and {V1, V0, V0}.

Algorithm 2 presents the *generateInput* subprocedure, which receives our *binnedInputs*, *binnedIndexes*, and h parameters in input, and each time returns a forged input sample (*forgedInput*) in output. First, the subprocedure iterates through the features represented in the *binnedInputs* array. For each feature, the subprocedure relies on its bin index to locate the corresponding relevant feature value in the *binnedInputs* array and add it to the forged input sample. Next, the subprocedure updates the *binIndexes* array to select a new combination of feature values at the next subprocedure call. This is done by using a global counter (*guessCounter*), which, at each invocation of the subprocedure, is incremented and converted into base h to encode the next combination in the *binIndexes* array. This allows our search strategy to potentially explore all the possible $h^{\#features}$ combinations, while always prioritizing the most discriminative features thanks to the sorting strategy adopted when generating the *binnedInputs* array. Finally, the subprocedure returns the generated forged input sample including all the necessary feature values.

```
Input: binnedInputs[ ]; //Binned input samples
Input: binIndexes[ ]; //Current indexes
Input: h; //Maximum number of bins to use for each feature
Output: forgedInput; //Forged input sample

/* Initialize an empty forged input sample */
forgedInput[ ] := initForgedInput();

foreach binnedInputs as binnedInput do
    /* Retrieve current feature index */
    i = getFeatureIndex(binnedInput);

    /* Get corresponding relevant feature value */
    v = binIndexes[i];

    /* Add current feature value to forget input sample */
    addFeatureValue(v, forgedInput);

end

/* Update bin indexes */
guessCounter++; //Global variable
currentGuess = guessCounter;

foreach binIndexes as binIndex do
    binIndex = currentGuess % h;
    currentGuess = currentGuess / h;
end
return forgedInput;
```

Algorithm 2: Forged input generation subprocedure.

4. EVALUATION

We evaluated our statistical attack against all the detectors considered, that is, combinations of detection algorithms and distance metrics. Moreover, we experimented with all the combinations of features, namely keystrokes-only (i.e., keystroke dynamics), sensors-only (i.e., sensor dynamics), and keystrokes and sensors (i.e., sensor-enhanced keystroke dynamics).

To reproduce the experimental setting from prior work [9], we based our analysis on a dataset generated by 20 different test subjects (students in our department). The test subjects were asked to type 20 different samples of 2 passwords negotiated with our test subjects in advance, i.e., "internet" and "satellite" (easy to type in a mobile setting, yet sufficiently long to provide adequate protection). We gathered keystroke and sensor samples in a controlled environment, on a Samsung Nexus S with a soft keyboard in landscape mode. We sampled sensor value distributions at a frequency of 17 Hz. To obtain targeted results, we focused our attack and accuracy analysis on whole words rather than n-graphs.

For each detector, we ran the experiments while varying the number of bins between 25 and 300, with a step size of 25 (using less than 25 bins would have severely lowered accuracy in statistics, while using more than 300 bins would have generated overly specific results, given that we had about 350 samples to statistically group). To highlight the cases in which the attack was most damaging, we first report only the highest EERs across all the bin configurations. We also experimented with different values of h, but we ultimately resorted to $h = 3$ for all the configurations. Given the large feature space, increasing h (beyond 3) did not significantly affect the results. Table 1 summarizes our results.

We first mounted our attack against our keystroke dynamics configuration. As shown in Figure 4a, our experiment reported EER increases between 210.09% (using the "mean, euclidean normed weighted" combination) and 452.92% (using the "kNN (k=1), euclidean normed" combination)—i.e., mean EER values between 31.47% and 50.56% for the input combination with the highest impact. In contrast, Serwadda et al. [25] reported EER increases of between 28.6% and 84.4% for statistical attacks against keystroke dynamics.

Table 1: EER increases and ranges under our attack

	Min. EER increase	Max. EER increase	Min. EER	Max. EER
Keystroke Dynamics	210.09%	452.92%	31.47%	50.56%
Sensor Dynamics	28.29%	1368.14%	0.22%	3.89%
Sensor-Enhanced Keystroke Dynamics	148.1%	3143.36%	0.22%	14.91%

We believe the discrepancy with previous results [25] to be caused by the following reasons:

1. We relied only on the most probable combinations generated by our algorithms, while Serwadda et al. [25] also used forged inputs randomly sampled throughout the entire guess space.
2. For each user, we generated a much larger number of forged input samples (around 350, rather than 50 [25]).
3. We considered a different environment, focusing on mobile rather than traditional [25] devices.

Despite the discrepancies, our results confirm and even provide stronger evidence that keystroke dynamics is vulnerable to statistical attacks. Next, we mounted our attack against our sensor-based configurations. Our results show that both configurations, that is sensors dynamics and sensor-enhanced keystroke dynamics, provide strong resistance against statistical attacks. While we did observe EER increases due to statistical attacks in our experiments, such increases were small, resulting in fairly limited impact in practice as detailed below.

In the sensor-only configuration (see Figure 4b), we reported EER increases between 28.29% and 1368.14% and EER values between 0.22% and 3.89% ($numberOfBins = 200$, $h = 3$). Our best performer, the "kNN (k=1), euclidean weighted" combination, reported EERs of 0.22% under our statistical attack and 0.09% under zero-effort attacks, confirming the sensor-only configuration to be robust against statistical attacks and appropriate for adoption.

In the sensor-enhanced keystroke dynamics configuration (see Figure 4c), the smallest EER under our statistical attack was the same as in the previous sensors-only configuration (i.e., 0.22% for "kNN (k=1), euclidean weighted"). However, other detectors reported much higher EER increases than in the sensors-only configuration. As an example, for "kNN (k=1), euclidean", the EER increase reaches 14.92% from the original 0.46% under zero-effort attacks. This suggests that adding keystroke timing features to even robust sensor features can significantly degrade the performance of some (but not all) detectors under statistical attacks.

To validate our results, we tried several more combinations of values for h and $numberOfBins$. Significantly increasing h results in the most important features being consistently assigned the same feature values for all the forged input samples, potentially biasing the results. When gradu-

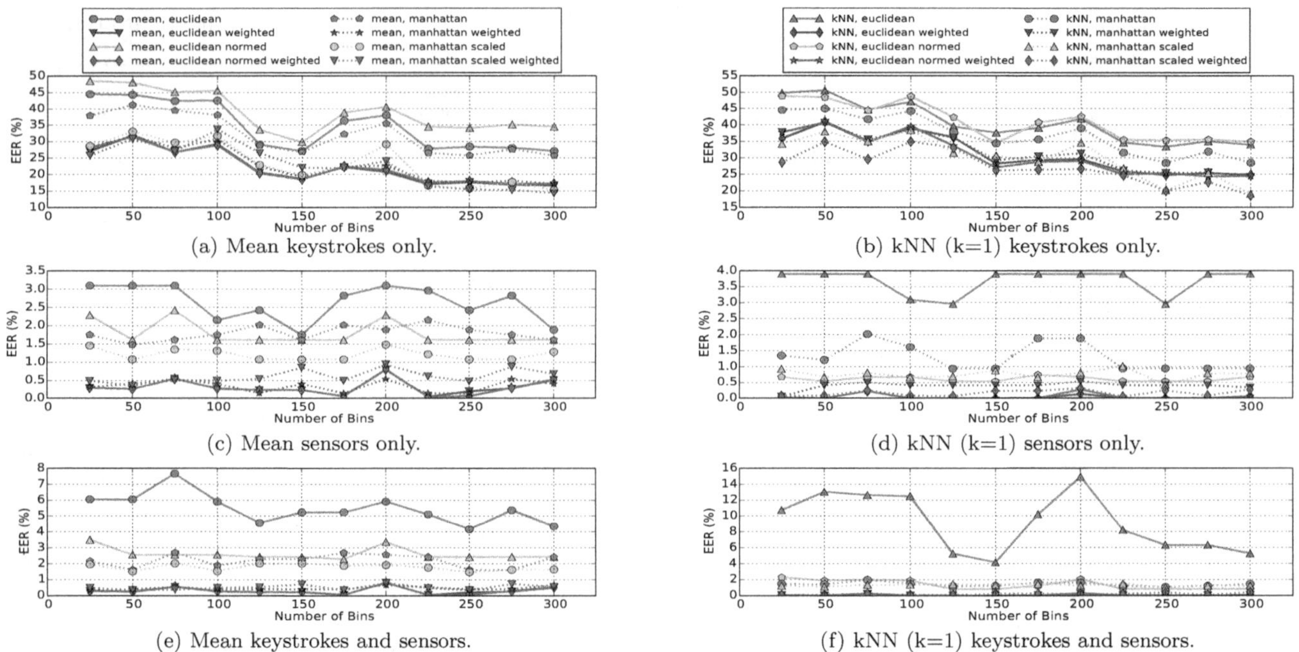

(a) Mean keystrokes only.

(b) kNN (k=1) keystrokes only.

(c) Mean sensors only.

(d) kNN (k=1) sensors only.

(e) Mean keystrokes and sensors.

(f) kNN (k=1) keystrokes and sensors.

Figure 3: EER rate vs. number of bins used in our statistical attack.

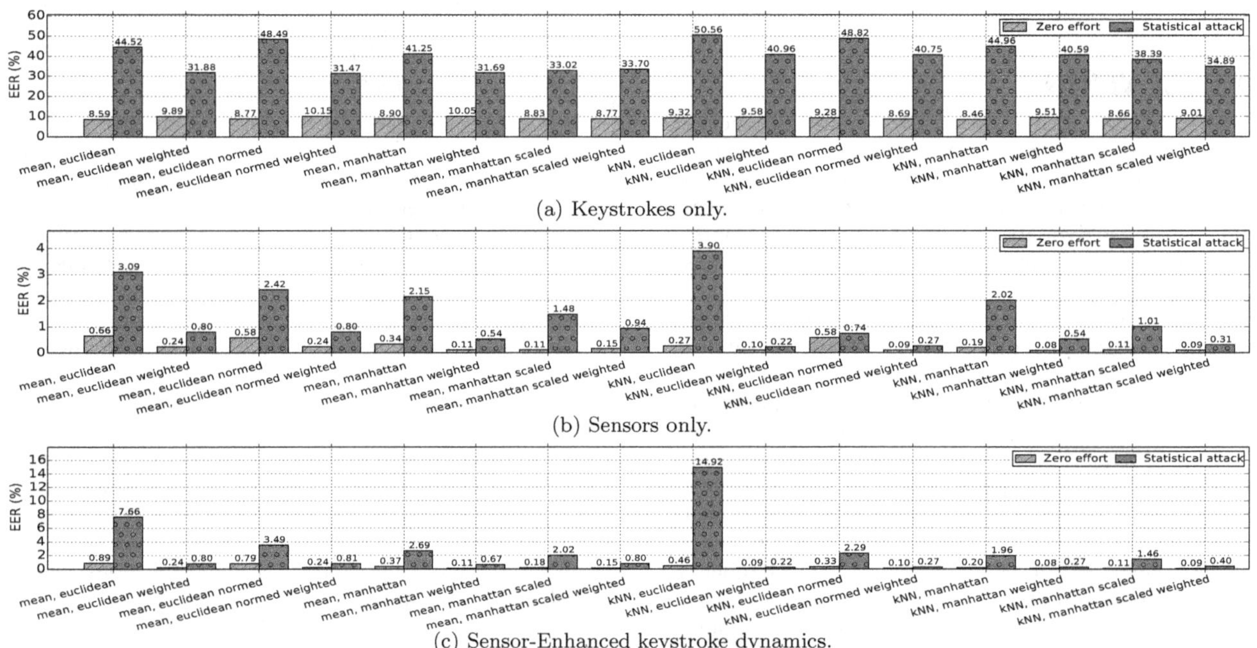

(a) Keystrokes only.

(b) Sensors only.

(c) Sensor-Enhanced keystroke dynamics.

Figure 4: Comparison between EERs obtained by zero-effort attacks and our statistical attack.

ally increasing h (up to 300), we observed EER variations of 5-10% (compared to our previous results) for our keystroke dynamics configuration. However, we observed no noticeable EER variations for our sensors-only or sensor-enhanced keystroke dynamics configurations.

When gradually increasing the $numberOfBins$ (between 25 and 300, with increments of 25), in turn, we observed that the optimal number of bins depends on the number of features and on the detector used. In particular, in our keystroke dynamics configuration, we obtained optimal results for a small number of bins (less than 100). In our sensor-based configurations, in contrast, we obtained optimal results for a much larger number of bins (higher than 200). We believe this behavior to stem from the different number and discrimination power of the features used. For example, keystroke dynamics has more limited features, so the calculated thresholds are generally wider. As a result, having wider bins (smaller number of bins) can provide better spread for the attack. With 25 bins (0.04 interval size per bin), traversing the features for $h = 3$ covers 12% of the most probable values. On the other hand, having 70-80 different unique features, with more discriminative power, provides tighter thresholds. Hence, it is more complicated for a forged input sample based on wide bins to fit into the thresholds (i.e., succesfully authenticate), translating to the need for more than 200 tighter bins.

Another finding that emerges from Figure 3 is that, on average, the attack is more effective against mean-based rather than kNN-based detectors. This means that, on average, kNN-based detectors are more resistant against statistical attacks. In addition, in most of the cases, weighted detectors offer better accuracy than unweighted detectors in face of statistical attacks. Weighted detectors also tend to provide better results for a large number of bins. We believe this is due to weighted detectors being able to achieve tighter thresholds and better raise the bar for the attacker, similar to the behavior observed earlier for sensor-based features.

5. CONCLUSION

In this paper, we analyzed the behavior of state-of-the-art biometric authentication systems based on sensor-enhanced keystroke dynamics under statistical attacks. Our goal was to establish whether the combination of keystroke timings and mobile sensor-based features offers a sufficiently robust authentication mechanism against sophisticated attacks.

For our purposes, we designed and implemented a statistical attack against sensor-enhanced keystroke dynamics. Our approach is to forge statistically relevant inputs by drawing from the characteristics of a given population and attempt to evade detection. We attacked sensor-enhanced keystroke dynamics for all the three combinations of features used in prior work [9]. Our results confirm that basic keystroke-dynamics authentication is very prone to statistical attacks, with the best classifier available yielding an EER of 28.83% and an EER increase of 184% compared to the zero-effort attack. When sensors are considered, in turn, we obtained much more promising results. The best classifier reported an EER of 0.22% for both sensors-only and sensor-enhanced keystroke dynamics, with EER increases of 123.28% and 148.09% (respectively). The effective percentage increase in these cases is 0.12-0.13%. Our results show that the effectiveness of statistical attacks against these two mechanisms is low, demonstrating their robustness in practice. Moreover, our results suggest that sensor dynamics alone is a stronger mobile biometric authentication mechanism against statistical attacks, since it proved robust for all the classifiers we considered (not only the weighted ones) while full sensor-enhanced keystroke dynamics performed poorly for unweighted classifiers.

To conclude, we have shown that, by using sensor-based biometric features, it is possible to build highly accurate mobile authentication systems, robust against both human and modern statistical attacks.

6. ACKNOWLEDGMENTS

Mauro Conti is supported by a Marie Curie Fellowship (PCIG11-GA-2012-321980). This work is also supported by the EU TagItSmart! project (H2020-ICT30-2015-688061), the EU-India REACH project (ICI+/2014/342-896), the Italian PRIN TENACE project (20103P34XC), the Univ. Padua PRAT-2013 project on malware detection, and by the ReCover project funded by NWO.

7. REFERENCES

[1] A. J. Aviv, K. Gibson, E. Mossop, M. Blaze, and J. M. Smith. Smudge attacks on smartphone touch screens. 2010.

[2] B. Biggio, Z. Akhtar, G. Fumera, G. L. Marcialis, and F. Roli. Security evaluation of biometric authentication systems under real spoofing attacks. *IET biometrics*, 1(1):11–24, 2012.

[3] I. Chingovska, A. Rabello dos Anjos, and S. Marcel. Biometrics evaluation under spoofing attacks. *IEEE TIFS*, 9(12):2264–2276, 2014.

[4] N. L. Clarke and S. Furnell. Authenticating mobile phone users using keystroke analysis. *International Journal of Information Security*, 6(1):1–14, 2007.

[5] M. Conti, I. Zachia-Zlatea, and B. Crispo. Mind how you answer me!: transparently authenticating the user of a smartphone when answering or placing a call. In *Proceedings of ACM ASIACCS*, 2011.

[6] A. De Luca, A. Hang, F. Brudy, C. Lindner, and H. Hussmann. Touch me once and i know it's you!: implicit authentication based on touch screen patterns. In *Proceedings of ACM CHI*, 2012.

[7] M. Frank, R. Biedert, E.-D. Ma, I. Martinovic, and D. Song. Touchalytics: On the applicability of touchscreen input as a behavioral biometric for continuous authentication. *IEEE TIFS*, 8(1):136, 2013.

[8] D. Gafurov, E. Snekkenes, and P. Bours. Spoof attacks on gait authentication system. *IEEE TIFS*, 2(3):491–502, 2007.

[9] C. Giuffrida, K. Majdanik, M. Conti, and H. Bos. I sensed it was you: authenticating mobile users with sensor-enhanced keystroke dynamics. In *Proceedings of DIMVA*, 2014.

[10] C. Giuffrida, S. Ortolani, and B. Crispo. Memoirs of a browser: A cross-browser detection model for privacy-breaching extensions. In *Proceedings of ACM ASIACCS*, 2012.

[11] X. Huang, G. Lund, and A. Sapeluk. Development of a typing behaviour recognition mechanism on android. In *Proceedings of IEEE TrustCom*, 2012.

[12] S.-s. Hwang, S. Cho, and S. Park. Keystroke dynamics-based authentication for mobile devices. *Computers & Security*, 28(1):85–93, 2009.

[13] A. K. Jain and K. Nandakumar. Biometric authentication: System security and user privacy. *IEEE Computer*, 45(11):87–92, 2012.

[14] A. K. Jain, A. Ross, and S. Pankanti. Biometrics: a tool for information security. *IEEE TIFS*, 1(2):125–143, 2006.

[15] E. Maiorana, P. Campisi, N. González-Carballo, and A. Neri. Keystroke dynamics authentication for mobile phones. In *Proceedings of ACM SAC*, 2011.

[16] A. J. Mansfield and J. L. Wayman. *Best practices in testing and reporting performance of biometric devices.* Centre for Mathematics and Scientific Computing, NPL, 2002.

[17] J. Mäntyjärvi, M. Lindholm, E. Vildjiounaite, S.-M. Mäkelä, and H. Ailisto. Identifying users of portable devices from gait pattern with accelerometers. In *Proceedings of IEEE ICASSP*, 2005.

[18] Y. Meng, D. S. Wong, R. Schlegel, et al. Touch gestures based biometric authentication scheme for touchscreen mobile phones. In *Information Security and Cryptology*, pages 331–350, 2013.

[19] F. Okumura, A. Kubota, Y. Hatori, K. Matsuo, M. Hashimoto, and A. Koike. A study on biometric authentication based on arm sweep action with acceleration sensor. In *Proceedings of IEEE ISPACS*, 2006.

[20] K. Rahman, K. S. Balagani, V. V. Phoha, et al. Making impostor pass rates meaningless: A case of snoop-forge-replay attack on continuous cyber-behavioral verification with keystrokes. In *Proceedings of IEEE CVPRW*, 2011.

[21] K. A. Rahman, K. S. Balagani, and V. V. Phoha. Snoop-forge-replay attacks on continuous verification with keystrokes. *IEEE TIFS*, 8(3):528–541, 2013.

[22] A. Rattani and N. Poh. Biometric system design under zero and non-zero effort attacks. In *Proceedings of IEEE ICB*, 2013.

[23] N. Sae-Bae, K. Ahmed, K. Isbister, and N. Memon. Biometric-rich gestures: a novel approach to authentication on multi-touch devices. In *Proceedings of ACM CHI*, 2012.

[24] F. Schaub, R. Deyhle, and M. Weber. Password entry usability and shoulder surfing susceptibility on different smartphone platforms. In *Proceedings of ACM MUM*, 2012.

[25] A. Serwadda and V. V. Phoha. Examining a large keystroke biometrics dataset for statistical-attack openings. *ACM TISSEC*, 16(2):8, 2013.

[26] A. Serwadda and V. V. Phoha. When kids' toys breach mobile phone security. In *Proceedings of ACM CCS*, 2013.

[27] M. Shahzad, A. X. Liu, and A. Samuel. Secure unlocking of mobile touch screen devices by simple gestures: You can see it but you can not do it. In *Proceedings of ACM MobiCom*, 2013.

[28] D. Shukla, R. Kumar, A. Serwadda, and V. V. Phoha. Beware, your hands reveal your secrets! In *Proceedings of ACM CCS*, 2014.

[29] D. Stefan, X. Shu, and D. D. Yao. Robustness of keystroke-dynamics based biometrics against synthetic forgeries. *Computers & Security*, 31(1):109–121, 2012.

[30] F. Tari, A. Ozok, and S. H. Holden. A comparison of perceived and real shoulder-surfing risks between alphanumeric and graphical passwords. In *Proceedings of ACM SOUPS*, 2006.

[31] C.-J. Tasia, T.-Y. Chang, P.-C. Cheng, and J.-H. Lin. Two novel biometric features in keystroke dynamics authentication systems for touch screen devices. *Security and Comm. Networks*, 7(4):750–758, 2014.

[32] J. L. Wayman. Error rate equations for the general biometric system. *Robotics & Automation Magazine*, 6(1):35–48, 1999.

[33] Y. Xu, J. Heinly, A. M. White, F. Monrose, and J.-M. Frahm. Seeing double: Reconstructing obscured typed input from repeated compromising reflections. In *Proceedings of ACM CCS*, 2013.

On the Feasibility of Cryptography for a Wireless Insulin Pump System

Eduard Marin, Dave Singelée, Bohan Yang, Ingrid Verbauwhede and Bart Preneel
KU Leuven, ESAT-COSIC and iMinds
Kasteelpark Arenberg 10, B-3001 Leuven-Heverlee, Belgium
firstname.lastname@esat.kuleuven.be

ABSTRACT

This paper analyses the security and privacy properties of a widely used insulin pump and its peripherals. We eavesdrop the wireless channel using Commercial Off-The-Shelf (COTS) software-based radios to intercept the messages sent between these devices; fully reverse-engineer the wireless communication protocol using a black-box approach; and document the message format and the protocol state-machine in use. The upshot is that no standard cryptographic mechanisms are applied and hence the system is shown to be completely vulnerable to replay and message injection attacks. Furthermore, sensitive patient health-related information is sent unencrypted over the wireless channel.

Motivated by the results of our attacks, we study the feasibility of applying cryptography to protect the data transmitted over the air and prevent unauthorized access to the insulin pump. We present a solution based on AES in combination with an updated message format optimized for energy consumption. We implement our solution on a 16-bit micro-controller and evaluate its security properties and energy requirements. Finally, we discuss potential strategies for further reducing the energy consumption.

Keywords

Cryptography; proprietary wireless communication protocol; software radio-based attacks

1. INTRODUCTION

Wearable and Implantable Medical Devices (IMDs) such as pacemakers, neurostimulators and insulin pumps are currently used to monitor and treat physiological conditions within the patient's body. For example, patients with diabetes require a precise daily dosage of insulin, combined with a strict schedule for diet, physical activity and insulin injections. The dosage can be automated via an insulin pump. Unlike self-injection, insulin pumps provide more flexibility, tighter control of the patient's diabetes and better predictability by delivering more precise insulin doses.

CODASPY'16, March 09-11, 2016, New Orleans, LA, USA

 ISBN 978-1-4503-3935-3/16/03. . . $15.00
DOI: http://dx.doi.org/10.1145/2857705.2857746

Nowadays, most insulin pumps have a radio that enables wireless communication with various peripherals (e.g. a glucose meter), a more powerful embedded processor and connectivity to a back-end computing infrastructure. While these advances bring substantial clinical benefits, new security and privacy threats emerge. More specifically, the wireless interface of these devices is of particular concern as it could be exploited by adversaries to perform remote attacks; adversaries might eavesdrop the wireless channel to compromise the patient's privacy, or even worse, send unauthorized commands to the insulin pump.

Contributions. Our first contribution is to show that (at least) two commercial insulin pump models use proprietary wireless communication protocols without any security protection. By fully reverse-engineering the wireless communication protocol, we are able to: (i) discover sensitive information on the patient sent in the clear over the air and (ii) send unauthorized commands to the insulin pump. Our second contribution is a practical case study on the feasibility of using cryptography to secure the wireless channel between these devices. We present a cryptographic AES-based solution with an updated message format optimized for energy consumption, an important requirement for these devices. We evaluate the security properties and energy requirements of our solution. Finally, we implement our solution on a 16-bit micro-controller, similar to the one used in the insulin pump system, and discuss possible ways to further reduce the energy consumption.

Disclosure of results. Our study examines a widely adopted insulin pump system that is being used by many diabetic patients worldwide. Given the sensitive nature of our results, we deliberately omit some details (e.g. model and manufacturer) as they would allow anyone to easily reproduce our attacks on insulin pump systems used by patients.

Paper outline. The remainder of this paper is organized as follows. Section 2 provides an overview of related work. Section 3 describes the devices that are part of the insulin pump system. Section 4 shows the laboratory setup used to eavesdrop the wireless channel and perform the remote attacks. The methodology of how to reverse-engineer the proprietary wireless communication protocol is explained in Section 5. Section 6 shows several software radio-based attacks that are carried out on the insulin pump, whereas a cryptographic solution to secure the wireless link is presented and evaluated in Section 7, particularly focusing on the energy consumption. Section 8 provides a final conclusion on the paper.

2. RELATED WORK

2.1 Attacks on medical devices

Recently, it has been shown that some medical devices are vulnerable to security attacks. Halperin et al. surveyed a wide range of security issues, and explained the need to balance the security and privacy of IMDs with safety and effectiveness [11]. Halperin et al. also performed a security and privacy analysis of a widely used Implantable Cardioverter Defibrillator (ICD). More specifically, they carried out several software radio-based attacks that could compromise both the safety and privacy of the patient [12]. Similar attacks were also executed on the wireless channel between an insulin pump and a remote control, as shown by Li et al. [8]. The main focus of their paper was to show different types of attacks that adversaries could perform after fully reverse-engineering the wireless communication protocol. In this paper, we validate and extend their attacks by fully reverse-engineering the wireless communication protocol between all the peripherals of the insulin pump system. This includes the wireless link between: (i) the remote control and the insulin pump, (ii) the glucose meter and the insulin pump, (iii) the glucose sensor and the insulin pump and (iv) the USB stick and the insulin pump. This paper also describes the methodology of how to reverse-engineer the proprietary wireless communication protocol.

2.2 Countermeasures

Researchers have proposed several countermeasures to solve or mitigate the vulnerabilities found on medical devices. Li et al. suggested using rolling codes, as used in garage doors, to protect against unauthorized entities [8]. However, some rolling codes do not offer strong authentication. Another weak point of their proposal is that it assumes that the remote control and the insulin pump share an encryption key, but it does not explain how this key is updated and revoked. The solution proposed by Gollakota et al. consists of introducing an external device, known as "shield", which acts as a relay between the IMD and the external device programmer [10]. The "shield" has been prototyped for a cardiac device to mitigate some of the security problems, but it has not been tested for wearable medical devices, such as insulin pumps. Anomalous detection is also a promising technique that could be used in combination with other security mechanisms to prevent unauthorized access, as shown by Hei et al. [13]. They proposed to use past glucose trends to detect anomalous behaviours. However, while strict policies can increase the detection rate, they may also result in false alarms. Undoubtedly, cryptography is the only strong approach for securing the data transmitted over the wireless communication and preventing unauthorized access. The use of cryptography, though, is challenging because IMDs are resource-constrained devices that require reduced size, low peak power and a low duty cycle. Key management also presents important challenges in terms of scalability, usability and the capacity to deal with emergency situations [14]. This makes it non-trivial to propose cryptographic solutions that increase the level of security and privacy of the system without jeopardizing the patient's safety. In this paper, we address this problem by proposing an AES-based solution optimized for the insulin pump system. Furthermore, we investigate how the energy cost of this security solution can be reduced without compromising the security.

3. INSULIN PUMP SYSTEM

This section describes the devices that are part of the insulin pump system (see also Figure. 1).

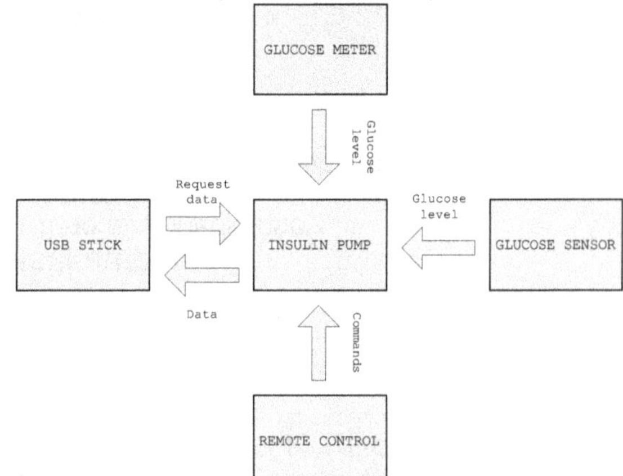

Figure 1: Insulin pump system.

The *insulin pump* can administer two types of insulin doses: a bolus dose, which is pumped quickly to the patient after meals, or a basal dose, which is continuously delivered at an adjustable rate. The *remote control* allows patients to send commands wirelessly to their insulin pump from a distance up to 1-2 meters. The *glucose meter* and the *glucose sensor* (attached to the body) measure the glucose's concentration in the patient's blood, and send this value wirelessly to the insulin pump. This is then used as an indicator for the patient to adjust the dose. The *USB stick (with software for therapy management)* is a remote monitoring tool that collects data from the patient's insulin pump, and then uploads these data to a website managed by the manufacturer.

Before any of these devices can communicate with the insulin pump, the patient needs to manually enter the device's serial number on the insulin pump (except for the USB stick). This serial number is typically printed on the back of the device. This pairing process only needs to be done once. From then onwards, these devices can interact with the insulin pump as long as the patient does not modify the list of valid serial numbers stored on the insulin pump. If any of these devices is lost, damaged or stolen, the patient can manually remove its serial number from the list of valid devices, and enter the serial number of the new device.

4. LABORATORY SETUP

In our laboratory we employed available Commercial Off-The-Shelf (COTS) hardware including a Universal Serial Radio Peripheral (USRP) [4], an oscilloscope, an insulin pump, a remote control, a glucose meter, a glucose sensor and a USB stick. Initially, we used the USRP, a commercial antenna and a receiver program to eavesdrop the wireless channel and intercept messages. Using this setup, the sending/receiving communication range is more than 5 meters. In practice, adversaries can extend this range to several orders of magnitude. At a later stage, we were able to transmit messages by means of the USRP, the antenna and a transmitter program. Our receiver and transmitter programs were built in LabVIEW [2], a software tool which allows to interact with the USRP.

5. METHODOLOGY

The first step in the security and privacy analysis of this insulin pump system is to understand which data are sent and how these data are exchanged between devices. This is a difficult task because the protocol specifications are kept secret, since IMDs manufacturers often rely on obscurity to provide security, also known as *security-through-obscurity*. However, experience has shown that these proprietary solutions can be broken via several reverse-engineering techniques. More specifically, we follow a black-box based approach, i.e. we only give some inputs to the devices and then look at their outputs. In other words, we conduct an operation on the device (e.g. we press any of the remote control buttons), and then we look at the produced message format.

Our black-box approach can be divided into four steps:

1. Find the wireless communication parameters: Several wireless communication parameters, including the transmission frequency, modulation and symbol rate, need to be first discovered. This step is crucial, as using slightly different values would result in an erroneous received message.

2. Reverse-engineering: Secondly, we eavesdrop the wireless channel to intercept messages sent from any of the peripherals to the insulin pump (and vice versa). We then analyse these messages to discover both the message format as well as the protocol state-machine. For example, the existence of the remote control's serial number within the message might be revealed by intercepting and comparing two messages sent by two different remote controls while performing the same action, i.e. pressing the same button.

3. Obtain the serial number: Most active attacks can only be mounted if the serial number of a valid device, i.e. in the list of patient's devices with which the insulin pump can communicate, is known. There are several means to obtain the serial number of any of the patient's devices: (i) we could either peek at the back of the device itself, (ii) get it through an insider working in the hospital, (iii) eavesdrop once the wireless channel or (iv) brute-force it.

4. Perform the attacks: Once the previous steps are completed, various attacks including replay, message injection and privacy attacks can be carried out on the insulin pump. In the next section, we will describe these attacks more in detail.

6. EXPERIMENTAL RESULTS

This section describes various types of active and passive software radio-based attacks that we can perform on the insulin pump.

6.1 Wireless communication parameters

The *transmission frequency* of any wireless device is publicly available on-line, and it can be easily obtained through its Federal Communications Commission (FCC) ID [1]. By checking the remote control's FCC ID, we discovered that this device transmits at 868.35 MHz. Fig. 2 shows the waveform of the signals transmitted by the remote control. By observing this waveform, we found that the *modulation scheme* uses the presence of a carrier wave to indicate a binary '1' and its absence to indicate a binary '0'. This type of modulation is known as On-Off Keying (OOK). To find the *symbol rate*, we opened our remote control and looked at the raw bits (i.e. bits before modulation) to be transmitted by tapping one pin of its micro controller. Using the oscilloscope, we measured the duration of a bit, which corresponds to the duration of a symbol. Following the same steps, we found that the other peripherals also use the same wireless communication parameters.

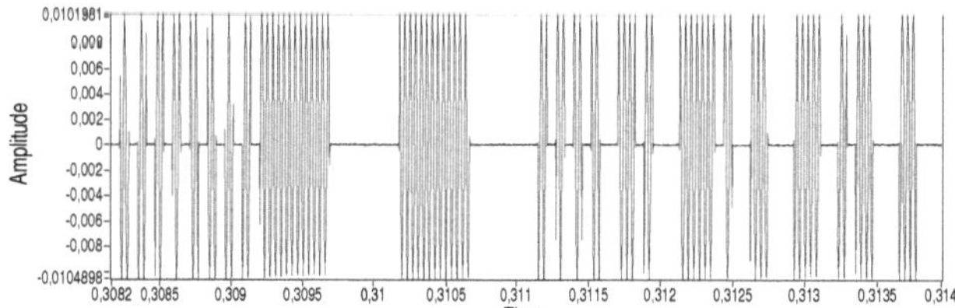

Figure 2: Waveform of the signal transmitted by the remote control.

6.2 Reverse-engineering the wireless communication protocol

In this section, we show how to reverse-engineer the wireless communication protocol between the insulin pump and its peripherals.

We found that the messages sent from any of the peripherals to the insulin pump (and vice versa) consist of common message fields and information bits that depend on the peripheral being used. In particular, all messages have a common start-of-frame and frame synchronization sequences. The former consists of a series of "1s" and "0s" sent consecutively to wake up the insulin pump from power saving mode, whereas the latter is used to indicate that the information bits are about to start. Next, there is a 6-bit sequence used to distinguish between the four types of devices that can communicate with the insulin pump. We will now explain how to discover the information bits sent by each peripheral more in detail.

6.2.1 Remote control - insulin pump

As explained in Section 2, in 2011, Li et al. reverse-engineered the wireless communication protocol between the remote control and the insulin pump [8]. In our experiments, presented below, we obtained similar results and hence validated their findings.

We started our tests by capturing the messages sent by the remote control while performing the same operation (i.e. pressing the same remote control's button) several times. The result of this test showed that the remote control produces messages that differ in 24 bits each time. On the one hand, by computing the entropy of these bits, we determined that 12 bits seemed to be uniformly distributed, which made us think that a Code Redundancy Check (CRC) could be used to detect bit errors in the transmissions. CRCs are easy to implement and very effective at detecting bit errors caused by noise in the communication channel. In order to find the CRC generator polynomial, rather than brute-forcing all possible polynomials, we took the GCD of two observed messages (in polynomial form). This allowed us to discover that a standard CRC commonly used in mobile networks, known as CRC-8-WCDMA, is being used. On the other hand, the remaining 12 bits are repeated after 256 messages and hence they are used as a message counter, which is increased every time the patient presses any of the remote control's buttons.

Afterwards, we ascertained whether pressing different buttons on the remote control or using different remote controls causes some part(s) of the message to change. These tests led us to conclude that a 12-bit sequence depends on the button being pressed, and a 36-bit sequence depends on the remote control being used. Furthermore, by looking at two 36-bit sequences and their corresponding 6-digit remote control's serial numbers, we found that each digit is represented by 6 bits. A mapping sequence is then used to convert each 6-bit sequence to a 4-bit hexadecimal number. Thus, due to this mapping sequence, the serial number only contains 24 unique bits. Note that for security reasons we do not disclose the table containing the mapping sequences in the paper. Fig. 3 shows the remote control's message format.

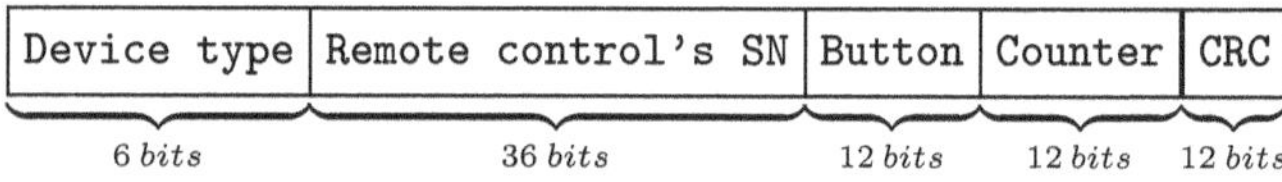

Figure 3: Remote control's message format.

6.2.2 *Glucose meter - insulin pump*

Several messages sent by two different glucose meters, wherein a wide range of glucose levels were measured, were first intercepted. Based on our previous results, we investigated whether using different glucose meters causes some part(s) of the message to change. We found that the glucose meter's serial number is represented by 36 bits (6-bit per digit) and that it uses the mapping sequence previously found. This is followed by the information field, which remains empty (i.e. all zeros) for all captured messages. Subsequently, we grouped messages with identical and different glucose level, separately, in several clusters. By comparing the messages in these clusters, we discovered that 12 bits are used to transmit the measured glucose level. Finally, there is a 12-bit CRC that is computed using the CRC-8-WCDMA. Fig. 4 shows the glucose meter's message format.

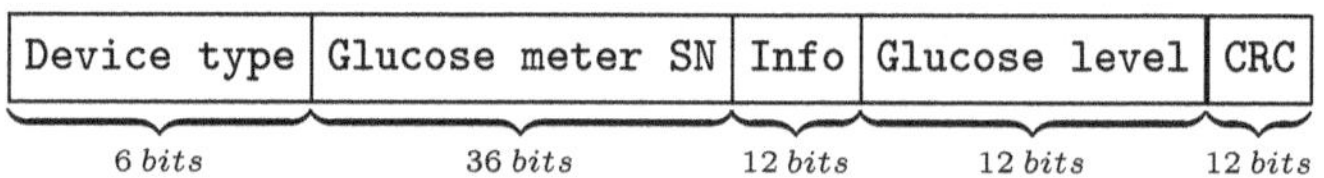

Figure 4: Glucose meter's message format.

6.2.3 *Glucose sensor - insulin pump*

Given the similarities between the previous message's formats, the first step was to determine whether the messages sent by the glucose sensor contain its serial number. This test showed that, unlike the previous cases in which we found a 36-bit serial number, the glucose sensor's serial number is represented by 84 bits. In order to discover the rest of the message, we then looked at several consecutive messages sent by the glucose sensor. This allowed us to find a 6-bit counter along with the current and past eight measured glucose levels. Because of the longer message's length in comparison with the messages sent by the previous peripherals, these messages use a 24-bit CRC (instead of a 12-bit CRC). We found that the CRC being used is the standard CRC-16-CCITT. Fig. 5 shows the glucose sensor's message format.

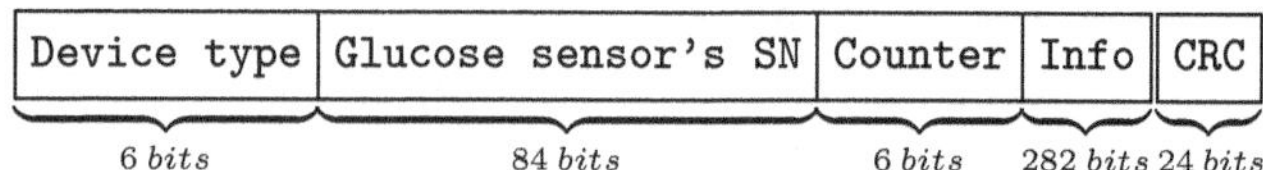

Figure 5: Glucose sensor's message format.

6.2.4 *USB stick - insulin pump*

Without looking at the bits being transmitted, we first studied the message exchange process between the USB stick and the insulin pump. For this, we placed the insulin pump close to our USRP while keeping the USB stick (connected to our laptop) further away, thus, getting more power from the insulin pump, as shown in Figure. 6. During a communication session, the USB stick and the insulin pump send to each other a fix number of messages. The USB stick always initiates the communication by sending a "wake up" message several times to the insulin pump. If the remote control and the insulin pump are within the same communication range, the latter replies to this message and the interrogation process starts, as shown in Figure. 6. From that point onwards, two different consecutive phases can be distinguished: in the first phase, the USB stick requests data such as the model, firmware or the current settings from the insulin pump, whereas in the second phase the insulin pump first sends a message to the USB stick and the latter responds with an ACKnowledgement message (ACK).

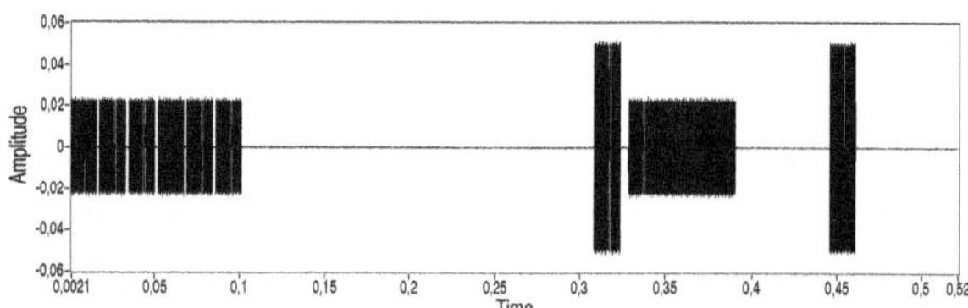

Figure 6: Communication between the USB stick (connected to the computer) and the insulin pump. From left to right, the message sent several times by the USB stick to wake up the insulin pump, the response sent by the insulin pump to the first USB stick's message, the second message sent by the USB stick to the insulin pump and the response sent by the insulin pump to the second USB stick's message.

Once we understood the message exchange process between these devices, we started to analyse the messages sent from the USB device to the insulin pump (and vice versa). A first test consisted on capturing several messages sent by the USB stick while interrogating two different insulin pumps. This test revealed that the insulin pump's serial number is transmitted in both messages; the ones sent by the USB stick and the ones sent by the insulin pump. We found that the mapping sequence previously discovered is also used. By comparing two consecutive messages sent by the USB stick and the insulin pump, respectively, we found a 12-bit message type (or message identifier) sequence which indicates the USB stick message the insulin pump replies to.

Subsequently, insulin pump's data such as the model, firmware or current settings are transmitted within the message. The length of this field (denoted by x in Figure. 7) depends on the information requested/provided by the devices. Finally, similarly to the cases above, there is a 12-bit CRC at the end of the messages that is computed using the CRC-8-WCDMA. Fig. 7 shows the message format being used by the USB stick and the insulin pump.

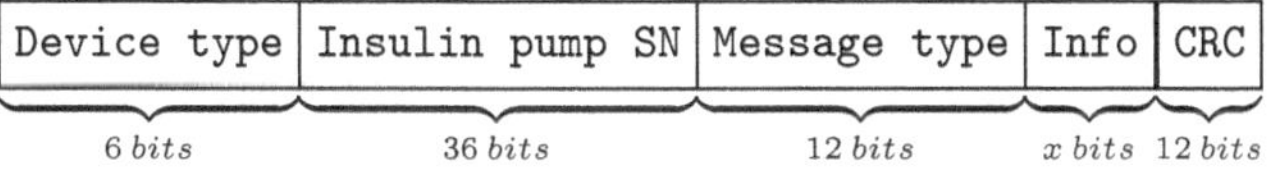

Figure 7: USB stick/insulin pump's message format.

6.3 Software radio-based attacks

In this section, we focus on the active and passive attacks that we can carry out on the insulin pump after having reverse-engineered the wireless communication protocol.

Replay attacks: We first investigated the feasibility of carrying out replay attacks, as these attacks can even be conducted without reverse-engineering the protocol; knowing the transmission frequency being used by the devices is sufficient. At first, we intercepted several messages sent by the remote control to the insulin pump and simply re-sent each message without demodulating the signal. Our experiments demonstrated that some sort of anti-replay mechanism is being used. This anti-replay mechanism does not allow to re-send the last message accepted by the insulin pump, but it does not impede us to send any other arbitrary message previously recorded. Thus, just by obtaining two different messages while performing an action (e.g. activate the insulin pump), we can alternatively re-send these messages as many times as needed in a protocol instance. Following the same approach, we also successfully performed this attack on the wireless link between: (i) the glucose meter and the insulin pump and (ii) the USB stick and the insulin pump. In both cases, messages were accepted the first time they were re-sent, meaning that no anti-replay mechanism is being used.

Message injection attacks: With the knowledge gained during the reverse-engineering process, we can create messages containing a valid serial number and successfully send them to the insulin pump. As a result, we can activate/suspend the insulin pump, deliver a high amount of insulin to the patient and send any arbitrary glucose value to the insulin pump. In addition to this, two different types of message injection attacks can be mounted on the wireless link between the USB stick and the insulin pump. On the one hand, we can emulate the insulin pump's behaviour by replying to USB stick transmissions. This attack, though, has several limitations. Since the USB stick initiates the communication, triggered when a doctor clicks a button in the website managed by the manufacturer, the attacker has to wait for such an event and hijack the session, potentially even having to block the communication from the genuine insulin pump. On the other hand, we can also impersonate the USB stick to trigger an interrogation process. This could compromise both the security and privacy of the patient, as it might be launched either to discover sensitive patient health-related information or to drain the insulin pump's battery.

Privacy attacks: Our analysis of the wireless communication protocol reveals that messages sent from any of the peripherals to the insulin pump (and vice versa) are not encrypted. Therefore, these messages disclose the type of device with which the insulin pump is communicating and its serial number, the current and past patient glucose levels, the insulin pump's model/software version, the current insulin pump's settings, the basal rate information or the total amount of insulin taken by the patient.

7. SECURITY DEFENCES

In the previous sections, we executed several active and passive attacks on the insulin pump that could compromise the safety and privacy of the patient. In this section, we present a cryptographic solution based on AES [9] that provides data confidentiality, authentication and freshness at a reasonable energy cost. Furthermore, we propose an optimized message format to reduce the energy cost. Without loss of generality, we will only focus on the wireless link between the remote control and the insulin pump. However, our solution can be applied as well to the wireless link between the insulin pump and any of the other peripherals.

7.1 Key management

The remote control and the insulin pump need to share two independent symmetric cryptographic keys: one for encryption and one for authentication. We will now briefly explain the process of generating, transporting, updating and revoking these keys.

Key generation: To reduce the software footprint and the redundant computation on the remote control, both keys are generated by the insulin pump. To guarantee an appropriate level of entropy, a true randomness source is required. This randomness could originate either from the Static Random-Access Memory (SRAM) [16] or a True Random Number Generator (TRNG) [6].

Key transport: After the key generation process, both keys have to be securely transported from the insulin pump to the remote control. For this, we suggest to make physical contact between both devices via a secure channel (e.g. we connect a cable between devices), similarly as the Resurrecting Duckling approach proposed by Stajano and Anderson [15].

Key update: The patient is required to update the cryptographic keys every time the battery is replaced, i.e. every three weeks. During this process, the anti-replay counter is re-initialised to zero.

Key revocation: If the patient's remote control is lost, stolen or damaged, both keys have to be revoked. If this occurs, the key generation procedure has to be executed with the new remote control. From that point onwards, the old keys are removed from the insulin pump.

7.2 Our approach

7.2.1 AES-based encryption and MAC

Our solution makes use of two cryptographic primitives: AES-128 in counter (CTR) mode to encrypt messages and AES-128 as a MAC. To find the energy requirements of our solution, we implemented both AES-128 in CTR mode and AES-128 MAC for openMSP430 [5] on a Spartan-6 FPGA. This is a representative mid-range micro-controller similar to the one used in the insulin pump. This software implementation can be easily converted to any other 16-bit micro-controller. Our implementation has been compiled with GNU Tools for Texas Instruments MSP430 micro-controllers optimized for code size with -Os gcc flags. In the rest of this section, we will investigate how to optimize this solution.

Table 2: Energy cost (per day) of each solution for the remote control (RC) and the insulin pump (IP).

Solution	Confidentiality	Authentication	Computation cost	Communication cost	Total cost	Cost increase
No security (original system)	✗	✗	RC: 0 mJ IP: 0 mJ	RC: 26.32 mJ IP: 8.77 mJ	RC: 26.32 mJ IP: 8.77 mJ	RC: - IP: -
No security (new message format[a])	✗	✗	RC: 0 mJ IP: 0 mJ	RC: 18.9 mJ IP: 6.30 mJ	RC: 18.9 mJ IP: 6.30 mJ	RC: -28.19% IP: -28.16%
MAC + opt SN encryption	✓	✓	RC: 0.64 mJ IP: 0.65 mJ	RC: 35.10 mJ IP: 11.86 mJ	RC: 35.74 mJ IP: 12.51 mJ	RC: +35.79% IP: +42.64%
Only encryption	✓	✗	RC: 0.32 mJ IP: 0.32 mJ	RC: 20.25 mJ IP: 6.75 mJ	RC: 20.57 mJ IP: 7.07 mJ	RC: -21.84% IP: -19.38%
Only MAC	✗	✓	RC: 0.32 mJ IP: 0.32 mJ	RC: 39.15 mJ IP: 13.05 mJ	RC: 39.47 mJ IP: 13.37 mJ	RC: +50% IP: +52.45%

[a]Original remote control's message format without the mapping sequence.

Table 1: Implementation on MSP430 @16 Mhz, 1.8V.

Operation	ROM (Byte)	Cycles	Time (μs)	Energy (μJ)
MAC generation	2684	9430	590	2.14
MAC verification	2760	9561	598	2.16
Encryption/Decryption	2664	9404	588	2.13
Encryption + MAC generation	2879	18865	1180	4.27
Decryption + MAC verification	2847	18964	1186	4.30

7.2.2 *Communication cost vs. computation cost*

Although our solution provides data confidentiality and authentication to prevent the remote attacks previously shown, the use of cryptography increases the energy consumption in both the remote control and the insulin pump. The energy consumption can be divided into two main components: the computation and the communication cost. The former indicates the cost of performing operations such as encrypting/decrypting messages, whereas the latter refers to the cost of transmitting/receiving bits to/from a device.

On the one hand, to calculate the *computation cost*, we measure the number of clock cycles needed to perform an operation. By looking at the power consumption (in the micro-controller specifications [3]) and knowing the number of clock cycles required, we can compute its energy cost, as shown in Table 1. (Note that all the operations described in this table consider a 128-bit block). On the other hand, to compute the *communication cost*, we looked at the datasheet specifications of the remote control's radio transmitter and the insulin pump's radio receiver [7]. As a result, we found that the cost of transmitting and receiving one bit at 868.35 MHz using an OOK modulation scheme is $2.25\mu J$ and $0.75\mu J$, respectively.

Assumptions: To demonstrate the practicality of our solution, we consider the following worst case scenario. We assume that there is a patient in a very crowded hospital full of patients who all use an insulin pump. We assume that each patient has 5 meals per day, during which any of the remote control's buttons are pressed 30 times, so 150 remote control's buttons are pressed per patient daily. Given the 2 meter communication range between the remote control and the insulin pump, we can estimate the interference, i.e. the number of messages received from other patients' remote control. Assuming a density of 4 people per square meter, the number of patients within a radius of two meters is 52. In other words, the insulin pump of the patient receives 7800 messages sent by other patients' remote control daily.

7.2.3 *New message format*

When observing the original message format (see Figure. 3), we note that several message fields can be optimized or removed when adding security countermeasures. In the new message format, the mapping sequence used to convert each 4-bit hexadecimal sequence to a 6-bit sequence can be removed, as it provides no extra security and it is costly to transmit extra bits. As a result, the length of several fields is reduced, resulting in an energy reduction (see Table 2). In the rest of this section, we will further optimize this new message format to reduce the communication cost without significantly increasing the computation cost.

7.2.4 *MAC + optimized SN + encryption*

Our solution consists of encrypting the messages sent by the remote control using AES-128 in CTR mode, and then append a AES-128 MAC tag to each message. Intuitively, authenticated encryption like Counter with CBC-MAC (CCM) could be used. However, from an energy point of view, there is no advantage on using CCM in comparison with our solution because of the small message length.

Message format: we notice that we can further optimize the message format proposed in section 7.2.3. For example, the CRC used in the original message format to verify the message's integrity can be removed, as the MAC by itself already provides integrity protection. To prevent replay attacks during the three weeks lifetime of the key, a counter needs to be increased every time the patient presses any of the remote control buttons. This counter needs to be large enough to avoid reuse of previous values. In contrast to the original design, the insulin pump will now only accept a message if and only if the counter of the message is higher than the value of the previously received message.

Remote control's serial number optimization: As the MAC by itself is used to authenticate the remote control, another possible optimization is to reduce the length of the remote control's serial number. However, there is an important trade-off between the communication cost and the computation cost. On the one hand, if there is no remote control's serial number in the messages, the insulin pump would have to verify the MAC of the messages sent by the patient's remote control as well as other patients' remote control within the communication range. This approach increases the computation cost while reducing the communication cost. On the other hand, if the entire remote control's serial number is sent, the insulin pump would only need to verify the MAC of the messages sent by the patient's remote control. However, although this approach requires less computations, more bits need to be sent/received.

Therefore, we investigate if it is possible to reduce the remote control's serial number length while keeping the cost of verifying some extra MACs at a reasonable level. The relation between the energy consumption and the remote control's serial number length for both the remote control and the insulin pump is shown in Figure. 8. When analysing this figure, we notice that the most optimal serial number's length in the remote control (i.e. when no serial number is used) is the option that introduces the largest energy cost in the insulin pump. In this context, though, we take the serial number's length where the total energy cost in the insulin pump is the lowest (i.e. 12-bit), as the patient can not receive the treatment if the insulin pump has no battery.

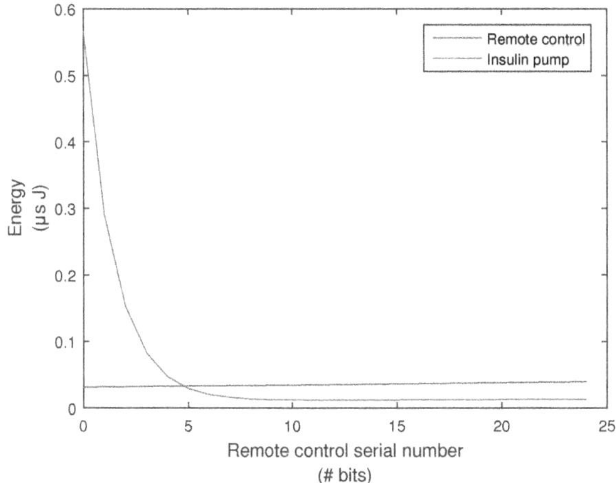

Figure 8: Relation between the energy consumption and the remote control serial number's length for both the remote control and the insulin pump.

As a result, because of using a 12-bit remote control serial number (instead of a 24-bit serial number), the insulin pump does not only receive messages sent by the patient's remote control, but also from other remote controls with the same optimized 12-bit serial number within the communication range. Given the assumptions explained in section 7.2.2 and assuming a uniformly distributed 12-bit serial number, the expected number of collisions per day is $7800 \cdot (2^{-12})$, namely, 2 collisions.

Optimized solution: Fig. 9 shows the encryption-then-MAC schematic. Initially, the message is encrypted using the encryption key and a fresh counter value. The message contains two fields: the device type and information bits. Subsequently, the 12-bit remote control's serial number (not encrypted), the ciphertext and the counter are used to generate a 64-bit tag, which is appended to the message.

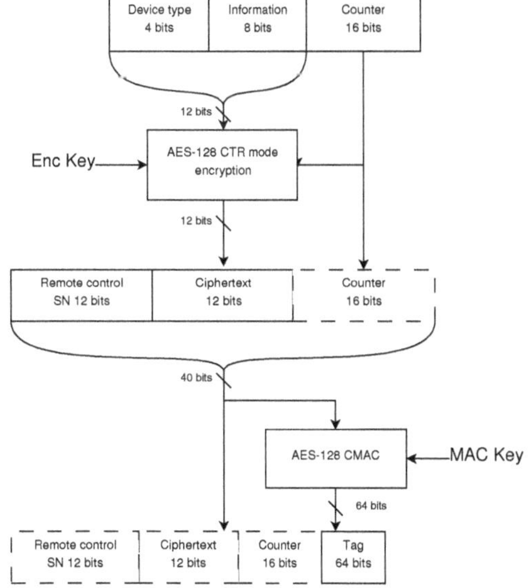

Figure 9: Encryption-then-MAC schematic.

When the insulin pump receives a message from a remote control (not necessarily from the patient's remote control), the former checks whether the 12-bit serial number equals the 12-bit serial number of the valid remote control. If this condition is satisfied, the authenticity and freshness of the message are verified. The insulin pump verifies the 64-bit tag, and if this is valid, it decrypts the message to check whether the counter is higher than the value of the previously received message. If both conditions are fulfilled, the message is accepted, otherwise it is discarded.

Total energy cost: Because of the message format introduced in section 7.2.3 and all the other optimizations, the message length, compared with the original remote control's message format, is increased from 78 to 104 bits. Given the solution that we propose and the assumptions above mentioned, the remote control sends 26 extra bits per message, 150 times per day, which results in an extra communication cost of 8.77mJ. Similarly, the insulin pump receives 26 extra bits per each of the 150 messages sent by the patient's remote control as well as 2 messages sent by other patients' remote control caused by collisions in the serial number. This corresponds to an extra communication cost of 2.92mJ and 0.16mJ, respectively. To encrypt-then-MAC each of these 150 messages, the remote control requires 0.64mJ. Likewise, the insulin pump needs to verify the MAC and then decrypt the 150 messages sent by the patient's remote control and the 2 additional messages sent by other patients' remote controls. To perform these operations, an extra computation cost of 0.65mJ is required.

7.3 Discussion

Table 2 shows the security properties of the different security solutions with their corresponding energy costs for both the remote control and the insulin pump.

Our results show that in all these solutions the computational cost is negligible compared to the cost of transmitting/receiving bits, which evidences the importance of optimizing the message format. On the one hand, we demonstrate that the data confidentiality requirement can be easily accomplished if these devices transmit/receive messages with an optimized format. We show that, by using a reduced message format to lower the communication cost, even adding encryption/decryption still requires a lower energy cost compared to the original design (without security and a non-optimized message format). On the other hand, we show that the authentication requirement is more difficult to accomplish, as this can only be achieved by appending a MAC to the message, which inevitably increases the message length and so the cost of transmitting/receiving bits.

How can the energy costs be further reduced? Our results show that the computation cost is about the 2% of the total energy cost of our final solution. So, even if the cost of computing cryptographic operations could be theoretically reduced to zero, the total energy cost would only be slightly decreased. Therefore, the problem does not solely lie in the design of lightweight cryptographic algorithms but particularly on finding ways to reduce the communication cost, e.g. further optimize the message format proposed in section 7.2.3. Another possibility would be to use a 32-bit tag rather than a 64-bit tag (as currently used in our solution). However, even though 32-bit MACs are considered to be secure against on-line attacks, attacks where an attacker can capture messages and then try all possible keys off-line could still be carried out. While not practical in this insulin pump system, another option could be to compute the MAC over several messages rather than doing it per every message. Our work clearly shows that there is a need for lightweight integrity solutions which do not significantly increase the message size.

8. CONCLUSIONS

In this work we have demonstrated, by reverse-engineering two models of a commonly used insulin pump system, that security through obscurity is a dangerous design approach. Our protocol analysis resulted in the identification of serious security and privacy vulnerabilities. We discovered that no defences against replay and message injection attacks were present, and sensitive patient health-related information was disclosed unencrypted in the wireless communication.

To prevent these active and passive software radio-based attacks, we showed how to secure the wireless link using a security solution based on AES in combination with an optimization of the message format. We evaluated and implemented this solution on a low-cost 16-bit micro-controller similar to the one used in the insulin pump, and compared its security properties and energy costs with alternative solutions that provide less security. We show that there is a need for future research on how to protect the message integrity without largely increasing its length.

In accordance with the principle of responsible disclosure, we have notified the manufacturer six months before disclosure.

9. ACKNOWLEDGMENTS

The authors would like to thank Pieter Gillard and Saskia Vanderwegen for their support and the anonymous reviewers for their helpful comments. This work was supported in part by the Research Council KU Leuven: C16/15/058.

10. REFERENCES

[1] Federal Communications Commission (FCC) ID. http://www.fcc.gov/encyclopedia/fcc-search-tools.

[2] LabVIEW. http://www.ni.com/labview.

[3] MSP430FRxx FRAM Ultra-low-power Microcontrollers. http://www.ti.com.

[4] NI USRP-2920. http://www.ni.com.

[5] OpenMSP430 Project. http://www.opencore.org/.

[6] Random Number Generation Using the MSP430. http://www.ti.com/lit/an/slaa338/slaa338.pdf.

[7] TX6001, RX6001 datasheets. http://www.rfm.com.

[8] L. Chunxiao, A. Raghunathan, and N. Jha. Hijacking an insulin pump: Security attacks and defenses for a diabetes therapy system. In *e-Health Networking Applications and Services (Healthcom), 2011 13th IEEE International Conference on*, pages 150–156, Jun 2011.

[9] J. Daemen and V. Rijmen. *The Design of Rijndael: AES - The Advanced Encryption Standard.* Information Security and Cryptography. Springer, 2002.

[10] S. Gollakota, H. Hassanieh, B. Ransford, D. Katabi, and K. Fu. They Can Hear Your Heartbeats: Non-invasive Security for Implantable Medical Devices. *SIGCOMM Comput. Commun. Rev.*, 41(4):2–13, Aug. 2011.

[11] D. Halperin, T. S. Heydt-Benjamin, K. Fu, T. Kohno, and W. H. Maisel. Security and Privacy for Implantable Medical Devices. *IEEE Pervasive Computing, Special Issue on Implantable Electronics*, 7(1):30–39, Jan. 2008.

[12] D. Halperin, T. S. Heydt-Benjamin, B. Ransford, S. S. Clark, B. Defend, W. Morgan, K. Fu, T. Kohno, and W. H. Maisel. Pacemakers and implantable cardiac defibrillators: Software radio attacks and zero-power defenses. In *Proceedings of the 29th Annual IEEE Symposium on Security and Privacy*, pages 129–142, May 2008.

[13] X. Hei, X. Du, S. Lin, and I. Lee. PIPAC: Patient infusion pattern based access control scheme for wireless insulin pump system. In *INFOCOM, 2013 Proceedings IEEE*, pages 3030–3038, Apr 2013.

[14] M. Rostami, A. Juels, and F. Koushanfar. Heart-to-heart (H2H): authentication for implanted medical devices. In *2013 ACM SIGSAC Conference on Computer and Communications Security, CCS'13, Berlin, Germany, November 4-8, 2013* [14], pages 1099–1112.

[15] F. Stajano and R. J. Anderson. The Resurrecting Duckling: Security Issues for Ad-hoc Wireless Networks. In *Proceedings of the 7th International Workshop on Security Protocols*, pages 172–194, London, UK, 2000. Springer-Verlag.

[16] A. Van Herrewege, V. van der Leest, A. Schaller, S. Katzenbeisser, and I. Verbauwhede. Secure PRNG Seeding on Commercial Off-the-shelf Microcontrollers. In *Proceedings of the 3rd International Workshop on Trustworthy Embedded Devices*, TrustED '13, pages 55–64, New York, NY, USA, 2013. ACM.

Multi Cloud IaaS with Domain Trust in OpenStack

Navid Pustchi
Institute for Cyber Security
Dept. of Computer Science
Univ of Texas at San Antonio
tam498@my.utsa.edu

Farhan Patwa
Institute for Cyber Security
Univ of Texas at San Antonio
farhan.patwa@utsa.edu

Ravi Sandhu
Institute for Cyber Security
Dept. of Computer Science
Univ of Texas at San Antonio
ravi.sandhu@utsa.edu

ABSTRACT

As cloud services have been firmly accepted by enterprises, the current challenge is how to share these resources among increasing number of cloud platforms. Currently, cloud platforms such as OpenStack, the *de facto* open-source platform for cloud Infrastructure-as-a-Service (IaaS), offer limited cross-cloud access capabilities in their federation APIs. In this paper, we present a fine-grained cross-cloud domain-trust model enabling resource sharing between domains across distinct homogeneous clouds. We further present a formalized description of core multi-cloud OpenStack access control (MC-OSAC) with proposed domain trust extension. We have implemented a proof of concept with extending OpenStack identity and federation services to support cross-cloud domain trust. Our approach does not introduce any authorization overhead within current OpenStack federation model.

CCS Concepts

•**Security and privacy** → **Access control;**

Keywords

Multi Cloud; Multi Domain; Federation; Access control; Trust Management

1. INTRODUCTION

Cloud federation is a promising mechanism to share resources across multiple public or private clouds in order to fulfill demanding IT portfolio of enterprises. Cloud service provider (CSP) lock-in as one main drawbacks of cloud adoption by industry can be avoided by federation strategy. Federation allows use of multiple cloud providers while data and applications reside in distinct clouds with different security or privacy measures. Cloud federation offers greater resource pooling, flexibility and dynamicity for organizations. In this scenario, single or multiple collaborating organizations aim to share resources dispersed across multiple CSPs. OpenStack [2] and Amazon Web Services (AWS) [1] as leading cloud platforms currently support coarse-grained federation mechanisms. However, federation administration in terms of relation establishment and federated-user assignments to resources across domains are not supported.

CODASPY'16 March 09-11, 2016, New Orleans, LA, USA

ACM ISBN 978-1-4503-3935-3/16/03.

DOI: http://dx.doi.org/10.1145/2857705.2857745

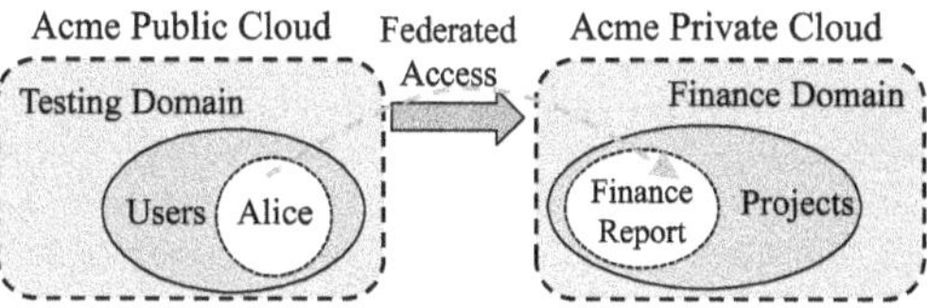

Figure 1: Cross-Cloud Domain Federation.

In this paper, we present a fine-grained mechanism to establish trust between domains across clouds and enable domain administrators to manage trust and user assignment. Our contribution is scoped within federation in homogenous cloud IaaS platforms. In contrast to other cloud federation [6] models, our scope of contribution is to extend OpenStack with domain-trust federation.

To motivate the problem, we use an enterprise such as Acme in figure 1 which stores it's financial data in Acme's private cloud and development applications in Acme's public cloud. Finance domain hosts finance projects in private cloud while Testing domain in public cloud hosts software developer users. Alice as a software developer is working on reports which finance data access is necessary. For security and privacy reasons financial data should not be transferred to other domains. Meanwhile, for administrative reasons it is impractical to provision or assign other domains' users permanently in Finance domain. The practical approach is for Testing domain administrator to establish a relation between two domains in which Finance domain administrator is authorized to assign Alice to Finance report projects. Upon task completion Finance domain administrator can remove user assignments. Testing domain administrator can remove federated relation with Finance domain at any time.

2. BACKGROUND

OpenStack is an open-source cloud IaaS platform consisting of RESTful API services such as Nova (Compute), Keystone (identity), Neutron (networking), and so on. Keystone is both the authentication and authorization service in OpenStack. OpenStack access control model consists of entities such as users, groups, projects, domains, and roles.

Users are individuals authenticated to Keystone while each group is a set of users. Projects define a container of cloud resources such as virtual machines, storage, and etc. Domain is an administrative boundary which owns users, groups, and projects. Each cloud consist of multiple domains representing an organization (in public clouds), a department of an organization, or an individual who uses cloud services. Roles are global within a cloud boundary. Users and groups are both assigned to roles within project or domain scope. Currently OpenStack supports cloud admin and domain admin roles whereas domain admin can only administer within it's residing domain.

As of Kilo release OpenStack federation API supports SAML assertions [5] (Keystone generates and consumes assertions). Specifically Keystone to Keystone federation is supported which it allows authenticated users (Keystone as identity provider) to swap their token for a SAML assertion. This assertion is redirected to another Keystone (Keystone as service provider) to get a token back from the second Keystone. Federated user is then mapped to a user or group from second Keystone and based on assigned roles, it can request a project scoped token. Such coarse-grained model does not allow domain administrators to manage user and resources shared within federated clouds.

3. MULTI-CLOUD OSAC MODEL

In multi-cloud model, cross-domain access is granted upon domain-trust between two domains across distinct clouds.[1] In addition to OSAC model [8], federation relation is represented by trustor clouds (identity provider) and trustee clouds (service provider) which is a many-to-one relation. Identity providers are set of clouds which trust to federate their users to the current cloud. Similarly service providers are set of clouds in which current cloud trust to federate its users to their resources. For example in figure 1 for Acme Private Cloud, Public Cloud is an identity provider and in Acme Public Cloud, Private Cloud is a service provider. In MC-OSAC, administrative model consists of two levels of administrative roles: *cloud-admin* and *domain admin*. *Cloud-admin* refers to cloud-level administrators managing all cloud identity service components. *Domain-admin* is administrator role at domain-level which manages components within its associated domain.

In MC-OSAC we enable domain-trust by remote assignment which is administered by *domain-admin*. Mapping rules define a set of accepted remote users or groups to local domain users and groups. Federated users are mapped to local users and groups by remote mapping in a many-to-one relation as it is depicted in figure 2. We define domain-trust in MC-OSAC as a many-to-many relation between domains in federated clouds.

Trust properties characterizes which *domain-admin* controls trust relation or cross-domain assignments. Our trust type is specifically motivated by previously defined type-β trust [7]. We define type-β domain-trust as:
If $domain_A \trianglelefteq_\beta domain_B$ *($\trianglelefteq$ is trust notion),* $domain_B -$ *admin is authorized to assign* $domain_A$ *users to its projects.* $Domain_A -$*admin controls trust relation.*[2] In trust relation,

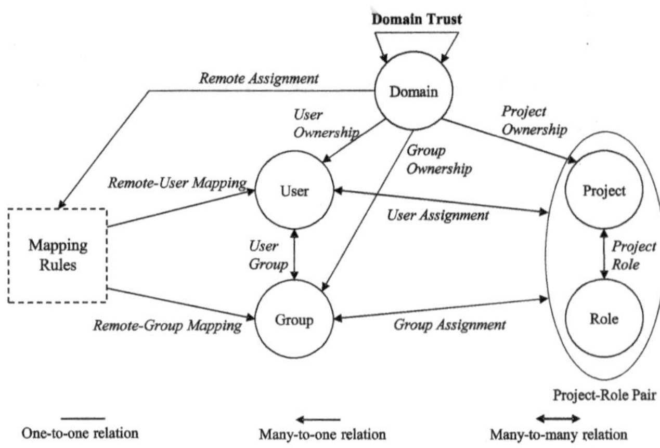

Figure 2: Multi Cloud OpenStack Access Control Model (MC-OSAC) with Domain-Trust.[4]

$domain_A$ is trustor domain and $domain_B$ is trustee domain.

Recall our Acme federation example in figure 1, Testing *domain-admin* establishes type-β domain-trust between Finance domain. Finance *domain-admin* can assign Alice to set of projects in its domain and upon collaboration completion Finance *domain-admin* removes assignments. Testing *domain-admin* can remove trust relation which results in removing all assignments of its users to projects in Finance domain. This approach enables collaborating domains to form collaboration relation dynamically while upon task completion, they can end collaboration with ease.

4. IMPLEMENTATION

In this section, implementation considerations are discussed. Keystone as authentication and authorization service is organized as a group of internal services exposed on one or many endpoints. Such internal services are identity, assignment, resource, token, policy, catalog, and federation. In order to deploy our model in OpenStack platform, we modified assignment, policy, and federation internal services in Keystone. We assumed each OpenStack Cloud belongs to a single organization while domains represent departments of each organization. In the case of collaboration, multiple domains from distinct OpenStack clouds share resources within specified domain-trust. In our model domain-trust relation is stored in the trustee cloud as *federation-domain-trust* table. Figure 3 depicts entries for such table. Trust relation is stored as remote-domain name, local-domain id, and trust-type.

We implemented the model with two OpenStack DevStack instances. To establish domain-trust and cross-domain user assignments, policy service and policy module was modified to enable *domain-admin* assignments. In assignment service, we added methods to restrict assignments to trusted domains. To enable remote assignments, in federation service we added methods to enable and restrict remote mapping (user and group) only within residing *domain-admin*'s domain.

In our model, cross-domain trust establishment steps are

[1]Since our contribution is at domain-level, we do not focus on cloud federation at cloud-level.

[2]We use type-β for simplicity, other types of trust as α, γ, and δ are also applicable to our model [6].

[4]It is slightly different from OSAC model where Tokens, PRMS, and Services are omitted due to our scope of contribution.

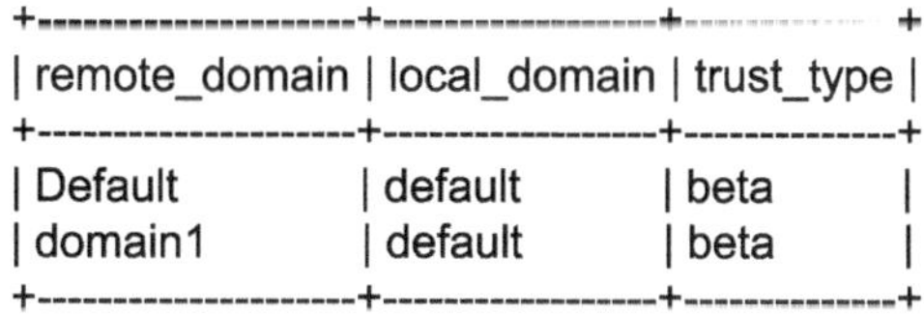

remote_domain	local_domain	trust_type
Default	default	beta
domain1	default	beta

Figure 3: Federation Domain-Trust Table.

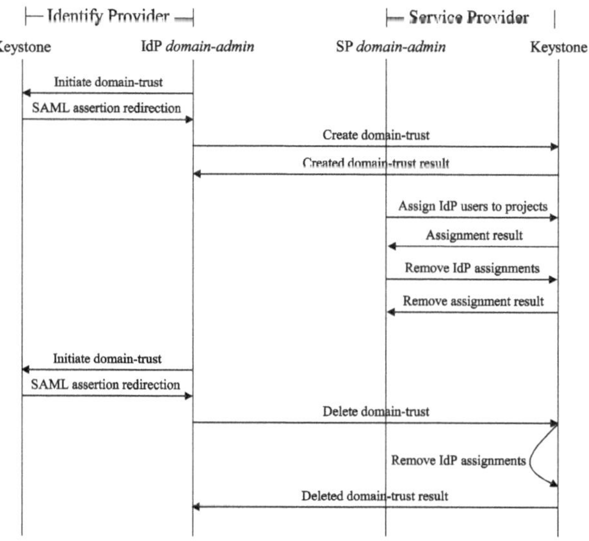

Figure 4: Cross-Domain Trust Establishment and Assignment Process.

as follows.
1. A *domain-admin* in trustor cloud initiates trust relation by selecting a trusted cloud from service provider list (note that prior to scoping a token with a project, federated users can list domains with an unscoped token in OpenStack federation).
2. *Domain-admin* token is swapped with SAML assertions and redirected to service provider.
3. *Domain-admin* is mapped to *remote-domain-admin* role which is enabled to modify *federated-domain-trust* table, then *domain-admin* creates the trust relation.

In case of trust relation deletion, Keystone removes all mappings matched with remote-domain name. The cross-domain remote assignment establishment steps are as follows.
1. A *domain-admin* in trustee cloud initiates remote assignment by selecting a trusted-cloud's domain from identity provider list and *federated-domain-trust* table.
2. *Domain-admin* creates remote assignment of trustor-cloud's domain to its user or groups.
3. *Federated-domain-trust* table is checked for proper trust relation as well as user or group domain, afterwards remote assignments are created.

In case of removing remote assignments, *domain-admin* can only remove mappings it has created. Figure 4 shows the flow to establish and delete a trust relation and remote assignments in MC-OSAC model. After remote assignments is created, incoming federated users from trustor-cloud's domain are mapped to specified roles dependent on users and groups assigned based on mapping rules. Within project-role pair permission in OpenStack, federated users can request project scoped token to access authorized resources.

5. RELATED WORK

We categorize previous research into collaboration with domain-trust and federation. In [7], authors describe a domain-trust within a single cloud and extensions to OpenStack is described in [8]. In federation, focus has been on authentication federation such as [3] and [4] which identity federation in OpenStack is presented. In authorization federation, recent work discussed use of domain trust within multi-cloud environment to enable collaboration, as authors stated in [6].

Presented model in this work is proposed with focus on cloud IaaS platforms and compatibility with current federation approaches. Our model is more similar to [6], from where we adapt domain-trust concept and realize it to extend OpenStack cloud IaaS platform.

6. CONCLUSIONS

We presented and implemented a multi-cloud model with domain-trust for resource sharing, where collaboration is enabled through cross-domain user-role assignments. Our approach considers applicability to other types of trust beyond presented trust. For future, we plan to investigate and implement other trust types. Finally as future research, we envision to develop multi-cloud models to incorporate attributes within current cloud platforms.

Acknowledgement

This research is supported by NSF Grant CNS-1111925 and CNS-1423481.

7. REFERENCES

[1] Amazon Web Services. http://aws.amazon.com/es/ec2.

[2] OpenStack. http://www.openstack.org/.

[3] D. W. Chadwick. Federated identity management. In *Foundations of security analysis and design V*, pages 96–120. Springer, 2009.

[4] D. W. Chadwick, K. Siu, C. Lee, Y. Fouillat, and D. Germonville. Adding federated identity management to OpenStack. *Journal of Grid Computing*, 12(1):3–27, 2014.

[5] J. Hughes and E. Maler. Security assertion markup language (saml) v2.0 technical overview. *OASIS SSTC Working Draft sstc-saml-tech-overview-2.0-draft-08*, pages 29–38, 2005.

[6] N. Pustchi, R. Krishnan, and R. Sandhu. Authorization federation in IaaS multi cloud. In *Proc. of Security in Cloud Computing*, pages 63–71. ACM, 2015.

[7] B. Tang and R. Sandhu. Cross-tenant trust models in cloud computing. In *Proc. of Int. Conf. IRI*, pages 129–136. IEEE, 2013.

[8] B. Tang and R. Sandhu. Extending OpenStack access control with domain trust. In *Network and System Security*, pages 54–69. Springer, 2014.

SPICE: A Software Tool for Bridging the Gap Between End-user's Insecure Cyber Behavior and Personality Traits

Anjila Tamrakar[1], Justin D. Russell[2], Irfan Ahmed[1], Golden G. Richard III[1], Carl F. Weems[2]
[1]University of New Orleans, 2000 Lakeshore Dr. New Orleans, LA - 70122
[2]Iowa State University, Ames, IA - 50011
atamraka@uno.edu, jrusse10@iastate.edu, {irfan, golden}@cs.uno.edu, cweems@iastate.edu

ABSTRACT

End users are prone to insecure cyber behavior that may lead them to compromise the integrity, availability or confidentiality of their computer systems. For instance, replying to a phishing email may compromise an end user's login credentials. Identifying tendency toward insecure cyber behavior is critically important to improve cyber security posture and thesis of this paper is that the susceptibility of end-users to be a victim of a cyber-attack may be predicted using personality traits such as trait anxiety and callousness.

This paper presents an easily configurable, script-based software tool to explore the relationships between the personality traits and insecure cyber behaviors of end users. The software utilizes well-established cognitive methods (such as dot probe) to identify a number of personality traits for a user and further allows researchers to design and conduct experiments through customizable scripting to study the end-users' insecure cyber behaviors. The software also collects fine-grained data on users for analysis.

Keywords

Software Psychology; Personality traits; computer security; Human factor; Test-bed

1. INTRODUCTION

Current efforts on improving the secure cyber behavior of end users are mostly limited to education, training, and awareness campaigns that do not tend to have long-lasting impacts on user behavior. Technical controls are also enforced to improve certain aspects of user behavior, such as maintaining strong passwords and the use of encryption, but these have no impact on other issues, such as effectively preventing users from responding to phishing emails, or downloading and running executable from anonymous sources.

A first step to an effective solution is to study end users who have greater tendencies toward insecure cyber behavior. In particular, exploring any reliable relationship among personality traits and cyber behavior of end users can help in developing user-centric mechanisms for maintaining their proper cyber security postures. For example, automatically generating variants of user interfaces and alerting systems that tap individual psychological traits might prevent users from engaging in insecure cyber behavior unintentionally.

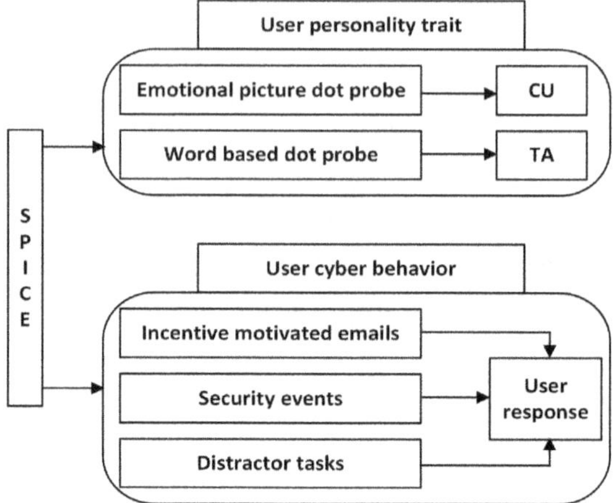

Figure 1: Overall architecture of *SPICE.*

In this paper, we propose SPICE (Software Package for Investigating Computer Experiences) - a script based, easily customizable research tool for acquiring data on an end-user's personality traits, and (in)secure cyber behavior. As shown in Figure 1, SPICE currently utilizes dot-probe tasks to identify two personality traits, trait anxiety (TA), and callousness unemotional trait (CU). It further creates a multistage simulated scenario (using configuration parameters, and customizable scripts) involving both distraction and routine tasks such as accounting, monitoring of stock rates, responding to an email, and updating software. Some tasks allow a user to opt into an insecure behavior such as providing a web link in an email to click. To the author's best knowledge, SPICE is the first tool designed to study the relationship between personality traits and cyber security behavior of end users.

2. PERSONALITY TRAITS

2.1 Anxiety and Callousness

Psychology researchers note that degree of attention and preferential biasness towards visually presented stimuli are associated with personality traits [4] such as TA and CU that may be important risk or protective factors in cyber

CODASPY'16 March 09-11, 2016, New Orleans, LA, USA

ACM ISBN 978-1-4503-3935-3/16/03.

DOI: http://dx.doi.org/10.1145/2857705.2857744

security. A consistent finding in psychology proposes that individuals who tend towards CU traits are more likely to commit cybercrimes as a result of lacking sympathy for victims or personal connections with an organization [2]. Similarly, TA may be a vulnerable factor in users succumbing to attacks such as social engineering, given links between anxiety and neuroticism. On the other hand, TA also may be a protective factor in improving rule-following and conscientiousness.

Personality traits have been widely studied with standardized sets of self-report and interview based questions. Predispositions for attending to, processing, and biasness towards stimuli can be identified with dot probe technology.

2.2 Dot Probe Task

This method [3] involves presentation of a fixation symbol ("X") at the center of the computer screen, then simultaneous presentation of stimuli (e.g. a pair of picture, words) on the computer screen (e.g. one on the top, one on bottom), immediately followed by removal of stimuli and presentation of a probe (e.g."*" or "<" / ">") in the location of one of the stimuli. The theory behind this assessment technique is that the faster the probe is detected, the more likely the participant was attending to the stimulus that was located in the same position as the probe. Therefore, shorter probe detection latencies for one category of stimuli over another indicate a selective attention bias towards the category with the shorter probe detection latency. Biases in the selection of attention cause individual differences in emotional vulnerability and are usually used in determining callous unemotional trait and trait anxiety. The main purpose of this task in our software architecture is to collect the independent variable attentional facilitation and threat bias index.

2.2.1 *Emotional Picture dot probe task*

The stimuli presented in this task are pictures representing distress, positive and neutral content with possible stimuli pairings: neutral-neutral, distress-neutral, positive-neutral. Callous-unemotional individuals have been shown to demonstrate shorter detection latencies for images of pain, distress and sufferings than non-callous individuals. The distress and positive facilitation index is calculated as follows:

Distress Attentional Facilitation Index

$$(Y) = 1/2[((N\uparrow) - (D\uparrow)) + ((N\downarrow) - (D\downarrow))] \quad (1)$$

Positive Attentional Facilitation Index

$$(Y) = 1/2[((N\uparrow) - (P\uparrow)) + ((N\downarrow) - (P\downarrow))] \quad (2)$$

Where, N $\uparrow$ = only neutral picture appear on the screen, with the dot probe behind the top picture (Probe top); D$\uparrow$= distressing picture on top, probe on top; N$\downarrow$ = only neutral picture appear on the screen, probe on bottom; D$\downarrow$= distressing picture on bottom, probe on bottom; P$\uparrow$= positive picture on top, probe on top; P$\downarrow$= positive picture on bottom, probe on bottom.

*All variables are mean response time

The distress/positive attentional biases are the mean latencies to detect probes that appear in the location of the neutral picture to the location of the distress/positive picture and indicate a bias to attend to distress/positive content respectively. The task consists of a block of practice stimuli (16 picture pairs) followed by 4 blocks of test stimuli (24 picture pairs each). The user is assisted to take a break between each block.

2.2.2 *Word based dot probe task*

The stimuli presented in this task are a pair of words of negative and neutral type, in a vertically aligned fashion succeeded by presentation of fixation ("+++") and followed by probe (">" or "<") at the location of one of the word pair. Individuals with anxiety have shorter probe detection latencies for mild threat stimuli (a word like 'fear'). The task consists of the practice block (10 pairs of words) followed by two blocks of 96 pairs of words each. The threat bias index (TBI) is calculated as follows:

Threat Bias Index

$$(Y) = ((NT) - (T)) \quad (3)$$

Where, T= median response time to probes presented in the position of the threat word; NT= median response time to probes presented in the position of the non-threat word.

3. INSECURE CYBER BEHAVIOR

Simulating a real world environment is crucial to capture user behaviors in a related, immersive scenario. However, simulating every aspect of a situation is obviously impossible. Instead of simulating everything, we designed our tool to capture a user's cyber behavior in the context of general but important security related activities that can capture user's intentions to harm others/take risks/be secure/be meticulous. We present users with the hypothetical situation that they are acting as a new employee in an accounting firm after having a similar experience in another company. We present a multi-tasking environment where user has to participate in various parallel tasks listed below:

1. Solve accounting problems (mathematics problems)
2. Monitor stock prices of competitors' companies and respond to market updates
3. Attend to emails and respond as quickly as possible
4. Attend to various system-related security events, such as software updates, antivirus scanning, etc.

These parallel tasks tend to keep the user busy and encourage their normal behaviors even in the testing scenario.

3.1 Mathematical problems

Mathematical problems are based on the established work by Hopko et al [1] and we present them as a distractor task to the user. As per our hypothetical situation, the more mathematical problems a user solves correctly, the more compensation is provided, which presents mathematical problems as a major task. Thus users are not aware of the intention to capture their secure/insecure cyber behavior. In the process of solving mathematical problems, other tasks (emails and security events) interrupt the user. The interrupting task may be related, such as emails that on responding may provide a hint to solve a subsequent mathematical problem, resulting in more incentive. Other unrelated task such as security events may also appear as interrupting tasks. Thus we provide an incentive-motivated environment but the user can opt to choose or not to participate in those cases.

3.2 Security events

SPICE present varying user interfaces related to security that tap users' knowledge and tenacity to victimize others/be victimized, maintain security postures like keeping their system updated and safe etc. These user interfaces are presented before, after or during solving mathematical problems. Followings are the security events presented to the user:

1. Software updates like Flash update, Java update
2. Anti-virus scan
3. Virus alert
4. Drive by download

3.3 Emails

Email represents a strong communication factor in any working environment. We present emails of various nature ranging from company welcome emails to incentive-motivated emails and random advertising emails. The user response towards these helps us gather knowledge about the users' propensity to participate in potentially unethical behavior. For example: email from colleagues offering a link to hack other company illegally; emails from adversaries asking employees to reset their username and passwords; emails from random persons sending a link to receive reward etc. These clearly demonstrate user's intentions based on their actions and responses.

In our tool, we present the option to force a user to at least open the email but we leave all other decisions to the user. This can be employed to illustrate that emails are important; otherwise the emails may not be attended to at all, especially given our scenario where incentives are related to the mathematical problems that are presented.

3.4 Stock market ticker

We show a ticker displaying information about the stock market. The user may need to keep track of the stock market while solving the mathematical problems. This is one of the other distractor tasks used in our tool.

4. SOFTWARE CUSTOMIZATION

Customizability is one of important feature in SPICE. It is easy to modify the contents and manage flow of occurrence of different events for the design of the experiment.

4.1 Scripting

SPICE employs a tag-based, customizable scripting for configuring the experimental environment. A tag-based script follows the basic rules and patterns as shown below.

1. *<dot-probe>*
2. *<block>0</block>*
3. *<up> neu_img_1.jpg,neg_img_2.jpg, ...</up>*
4. *<up-type> Neutral, Neutral, ...</up-type>*
5. *<down> neg_img_1.jpg,pos_img_1.jpg, ...</down>*
6. *<down-type> Neutral, Neutral, ...</down-type>*
7. *<probe-position>Down, Up, ...</probe-position>*
8. *</dot-probe>*

Line 1 and 8 represents the start and end tag of dot probe. Line 2 represents the block number. Lines 3/5 represent the list of images to be shown in the top/bottom positions on the screen during the task while lines 4/6 are the types of images in lines 3/5. The tags used are predefined tags and in between the tags are content that is customizable by the user. We use a similar tag-based script for word-based dot probe, emails, and mathematical problems.

4.2 Event sequencing

In a simulated scenario, the tool allows managing the order of occurrence of different events. Flow order is maintained as a simple list as shown below that describes the order in which the emails, security events and mathematical problems are presented to the user.

Flow-order=["Email-120000", "M", "software-update", "virus-alert", "M", "Email-120002-f"]
maths_sec_events=[["flash-update", "Java-update"], ["Email-120003-f", "Email-120004-f","anti-virus-scan"]]

Where, M = mathematical problem,
Email-XXXXXX = email with id XXXXXX from email script,
Email-XXXXXX-f = email with id XXXXXX from email script with force feature, and
"software-update", "virus-alert", "flash-update", "Java-update", "anti-virus-scan" are security events.

Security events and emails can occur before or after mathematical problems as depicted in *Flow-order*. Similarly, emails and security events can also occur within each mathematical problem, which is maintained in a separate variable as *"maths_sec_events"*. *maths_sec_events* is a double array that represents the event within each mathematical problem.

5. CONCLUSION

We have presented SPICE, an easily configurable, script-based software tool to explore the relationships between the personality traits and insecure cyber behaviors of end users. SPICE is designed to capture data detailing the personality traits and cyber behaviors of a large population of users, to create data sets that will be helpful in studying the variations of cyber behavior across different personality types.

6. ACKNOWLEDGMENTS

The authors would like to thank CNS-SaTC for the support by NSF-1358723

7. REFERENCES

[1] D. R. Hopko, D. W. McNeil, C. Lejuez, M. H. Ashcraft, G. H. Eifert, and J. Riel. The effects of anxious responding on mental arithmetic and lexical decision task performance. *Journal of Anxiety Disorders*, 17(6):647–665, 2003.

[2] E. R. Kimonis, P. J. Frick, J. L. Skeem, M. A. Marsee, K. Cruise, L. C. Munoz, K. J. Aucoin, and A. S. Morris. Assessing callous–unemotional traits in adolescent offenders: Validation of the inventory of callous–unemotional traits. *International journal of law and psychiatry*, 31(3):241–252, 2008.

[3] C. MacLeod, A. Mathews, and P. Tata. Attentional bias in emotional disorders. *Journal of abnormal psychology*, 95(1):15, 1986.

[4] S. P. Tipper and J. Driver. Negative priming between pictures and words in a selective attention task: Evidence for semantic processing of ignored stimuli. *Memory & Cognition*, 16(1):64–70, 1988.

Privacy-Preserving Mining of Sequential Association Rules from Provenance Workflows

Mihai Maruseac
UMass Boston
mmarusea@cs.umb.edu

Gabriel Ghinita
UMass Boston
gabriel.ghinita@umb.edu

ABSTRACT

Provenance workflows capture movement and transformation of data in complex environments, such as document management in large organizations, content generation and sharing in in social media, scientific computations, etc. Sharing and processing of provenance workflows brings numerous benefits, e.g., improving productivity in an organization, understanding social media interaction patterns, etc. However, directly sharing provenance may also disclose sensitive information such as confidential business practices, or private details about participants in a social network. We propose an algorithm that privately extracts sequential association rules from provenance workflow datasets. Finding such rules has numerous practical applications, such as capacity planning or identifying hot-spots in provenance graphs. Our approach provides good accuracy and strong privacy, by leveraging on the exponential mechanism of differential privacy. We propose an heuristic that identifies promising candidate rules and makes judicious use of the privacy budget. Experimental results show that the our approach is fast and accurate, and clearly outperforms the state-of-the-art. We also identify influential factors in improving accuracy, which helps in choosing promising directions for future improvement.

1. INTRODUCTION

Provenance workflows are increasingly important in characterizing industrial processes, scientific computations, social media interactions and content generation. Provenance is vital in understanding and optimizing processes involved with complex data management tasks. In recent years, numerous research efforts focused on capturing and analyzing the information provided by provenance workflows. A survey of existing techniques and important research directions in studying provenance can be found in [5]. Sharing provenance brings numerous benefits. For example, chemists can exchange process data for synthesizing new drugs. Corporations may better integrate operations with business partners.

Consider the example in Figure 1, which shows several document flows between departments in a company. Even though most documents would follow the path $Production$ to $Accounting$ and then $Sales$, some might flow through $Audit$, $Compliance$ and then CEO. The existence of such a document might reveal a high-risk event (e.g., a compliance oversight) which might impact the organization's future if publicly released. The objective of sanitizing provenance is to prevent an adversary from identifying such high-risk events, while at the same time allowing researchers to extract useful aggregate level information from the provenance.

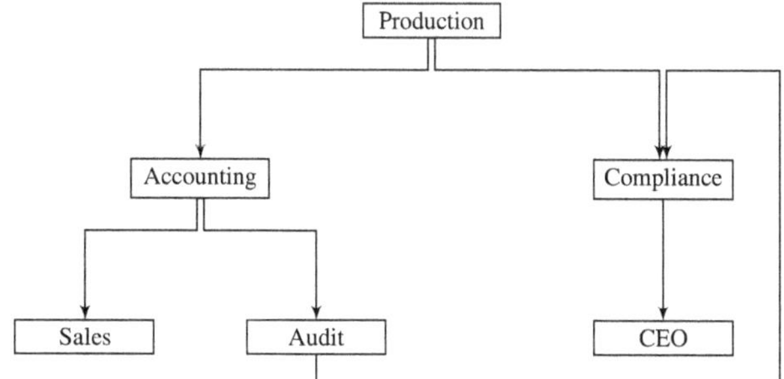

Figure 1: Document Workflows in an Organization

The differential privacy (DP) [1] framework is designed specifically for such aggregate-level release of information, and it is widely accepted as the de-facto standard for privacy-preserving data publication. DP preserves aggregate information, but it prevents an adversary from inferring whether any particular data item was present in the input dataset or not. For example, it would be impossible to detect if a certain secret chemical element was used in synthesizing a specific drug. Several techniques for rule mining with differential privacy have been proposed, culminating with the work in [3], which outperforms other existing techniques. However, such work focuses on itemset mining, and ignores sequence information, which is essential for provenance processing. None of the existing approaches we are aware of focus on provenance data, which is more challenging due to high sparsity.

In this paper, we focus on privately extracting sequential association rules from provenance data. We use the exponential mechanism of differential privacy, and introduce a powerful selection heuristic that identifies promising rules to sample. Experimental results show that our approach is fast, and it clearly outperforms existing techniques with respect to accuracy of extracting sequential association rules from provenance data.

2. PRELIMINARIES

Provenance workflows. Consider an undirected graph $G = (V, E)$, where each node $x_i \in V$ represents an entity which generates, receives or forwards data (e.g., department of an organization, user of a social network, etc.). The set E of edges captures the connections between these entities. Nodes are labeled with natural numbers, that is $V \subset \mathbb{N}$ and $E \subset \mathbb{N}^2$. A provenance workflow is a path in graph G, allowing a node to be visited multiple times to capture provenance loops. A path is a sequence $\pi_i = x_1^{(i)} \rightarrow x_2^{(i)} \rightarrow$

CODASPY'16 March 09-11, 2016, New Orleans, LA, USA

ACM ISBN 978-1-4503-3935-3/16/03.
DOI: http://dx.doi.org/10.1145/2857705.2857743

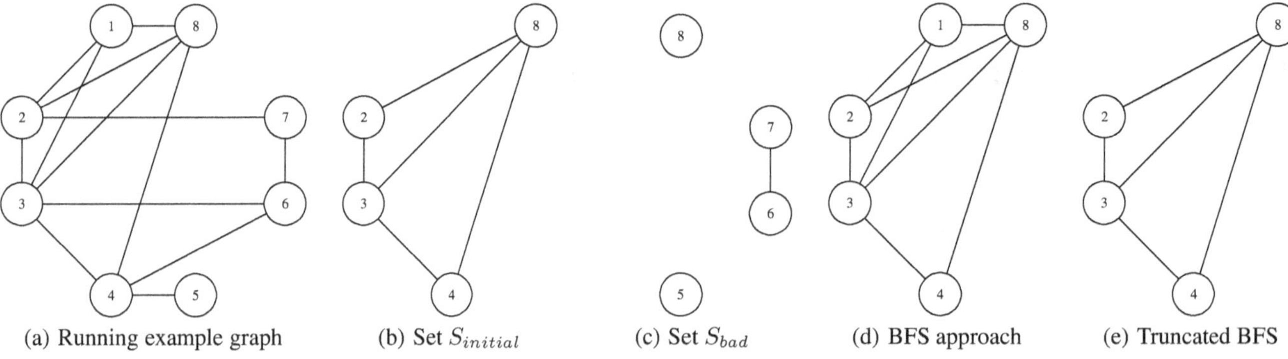

(a) Running example graph (b) Set $S_{initial}$ (c) Set S_{bad} (d) BFS approach (e) Truncated BFS

Figure 2: Running example graph (a); sets S_i generated with the algorithm in [3] (b,c) and with our approach (d, e)

Node	Real Count	Noisy Count
4	100	142
3	90	86
2	63	70
8	67	65
7	50	52
6	34	30
5	25	29
1	10	5

Table 1: Real and noisy node counts (sorted by noisy count)

$\dots x_{t_i}^{(i)}$ where each $x_i \in V$ is a node in G, t_i is the length of the path π_i and there is an edge between any two consecutive nodes in the path. In Figure 1, $\pi_1 = Production \rightarrow Accounting \rightarrow Sales$ and $\pi_2 = Production \rightarrow Accounting \rightarrow Audit \rightarrow Compliance \rightarrow CEO$ are workflows.

Differential privacy (DP) [1] guarantees that for any two *sibling* datasets $\mathcal{D}_1, \mathcal{D}_2$ that differ in a single workflow π, the probability of an adversary learning which of the two datasets was used to obtain a certain output $\mathcal{A}$ is bounded by $\left|\ln \frac{Pr[\mathcal{A}(\mathcal{D}_1)]}{Pr[\mathcal{A}(\mathcal{D}_2)]}\right| \leq \epsilon$, where parameter $\epsilon > 0$ represents the *privacy budget*. To achieve privacy for numerical queries, the Laplace mechanism adds to each query result noise randomly distributed according to a Laplace distribution with parameter $\lambda = S/\epsilon$ where S is the *sensitivity* of the query, i.e., the maximum change in the result of the query for any two sibling databases. On the other hand, the *exponential mechanism* [4] allows to privately sample data, by associating each possible output o a weight $q(o)$, where q is a *quality function*. Formally, each possible output o is selected with probability proportional to $\exp\left(\frac{\epsilon q(o)}{2S}\right)$ where S is the sensitivity of q.

3. PROPOSED APPROACH

A *sequential association rule* is an implication $X \Rightarrow Y$ where X and Y are fragments of a path in G. We define a *path fragment* as a sequence $X = x_1 \rightarrow x_2 \rightarrow \dots \rightarrow x_{l_X}$ of length l_X where nodes $x_1 \dots x_{l_X} \in V$ are linked by edges in E. For each path fragment X, we associate a metric called *support*, denoted by $\sigma(X)$, which is the number of workflows π_i in the database which contain the sequence X. The intuition of an association rule $X \Rightarrow Y$ is that a provenance workflow which contains X also contains Y and that the path fragment X is followed by the path fragment Y (in other words, the workflow also contains the path fragment $X \rightarrow Y$). The *confidence* of a rule is defined as $c(X \Rightarrow Y) = \frac{\sigma(X \rightarrow Y)}{\sigma(X)}$. Our objective is to privately extract high-confidence sequential association rules from the provenance database. One distinguishing characteristic of our work in comparison with existing techniques (e.g., [3]) is that we take into account sequence information, whereas other approaches are concerned with frequent itemsets, regardless of the order of appearance of items. Specifically, our algorithm must be able to analyze both the rule $1 \rightarrow 2 \Rightarrow 3$ and $2 \rightarrow 1 \Rightarrow 3$ whereas for existing approaches ([3]) these rules look identical.

```
ProvenanceSequenceMine
Input: Dataset D, graph G = (V, E), privacy budget ε
       requested number of rules k, maximum length of rules l_max
Output: Set of k rules
       /* — Step 1 — */
1.     items = ∅;
2.     for i ∈ V do
3.         σ'(i) = σ(i) + Laplace(ε_1^{-1});
4.         items = items ∪ {(i, σ'(i))};
5.     sort_decreasingly(items, σ');
       /* — Step 2 — */
6.     heap = ∅;
7.     for x_i ∈ V do
8.         S_i = BFS(G, x_i, l_max, items);
9.         for r ∈ generate_rules(G, S_i) do
10.            insert_rule_heap_EM(heap, r, ε − ε_1)
11.    return top_heap(heap, k);
```

Figure 3: Pseudocode of Two-Step Proposed Approach

The proposed algorithm has two steps, summarized by the pseudocode in Figure 3. The first step (lines 1-5) uses a small fraction of the privacy budget, $\epsilon_1 = \alpha \times \epsilon$, to compute basic statistics on the input database. For each node, we query the total number of times any document has passed through that node in order to obtain an estimation of the hotspots in the workflows. We protect these counts with the Laplace mechanism. For example, Figure 2(a) illustrates a provenance workflow graph, and Table 1 captures statistics for a set of workflows. For instance, node 4 has been visited by a total of 100 documents (i.e., real count of workflows) and after Laplace noise addition the sanitized count becomes 142.

The main contribution of the algorithm lies within the second step. From the list of noisy counts obtained in Step 1, we select sets S_i of cardinality l_{max} nodes from which we generate association rules of lengths up to l_{max}. Next, from all sets S_i, we use the exponential mechanism to select the k rules with the highest (noisy) confidence. Heap operations follow the framework of reservoir sampling [2] to allow for an efficient sampling of rules by trading some memory space to reduce time complexity.

Central to our approach is the choice of quality function q used within the exponential mechanism (EM), which must capture well the confidence of a rule, but at the same time must preserve privacy. In addition, it is important to devise an effective heuristic to prune the total number of candidate rules considered by EM, as the total number of candidates grows exponentially, but only relatively few candidates yield high-confidence rules. To illustrate the importance of these factors, we first show the limitations of the approach in [3] which does not account for provenance graph structure. In [3], a

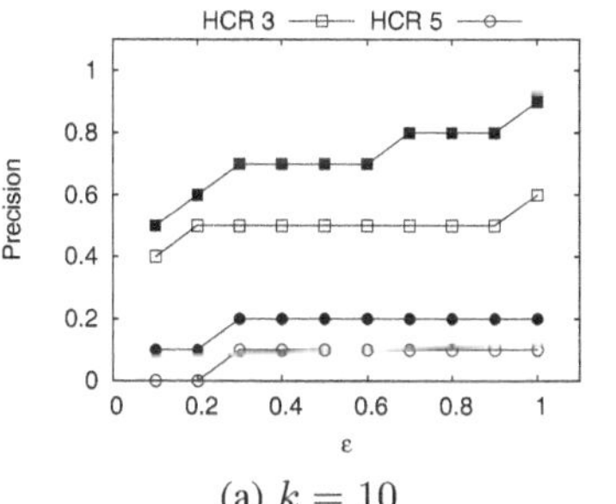

(a) $k = 10$

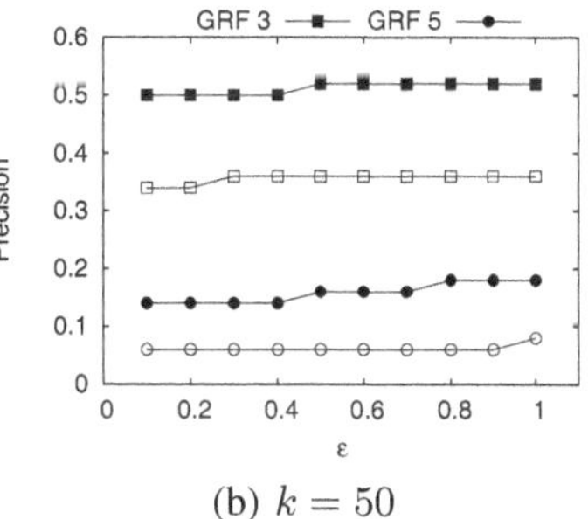

(b) $k = 50$

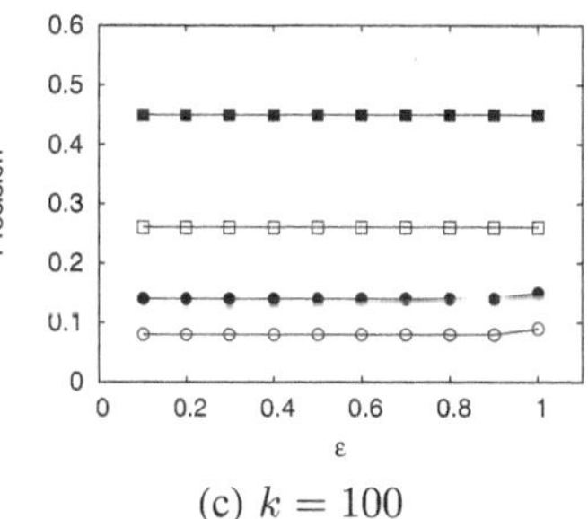

(c) $k = 100$

Figure 4: Accuracy of the proposed approach in comparison with benchmark [3]

sliding window of size l_{max} is constructed, with noisy counts from Step 1 in descending order. For example, in Figure 2(a), assume $l_{max} = 4$. The approach in [3] would generate rules with items from the set $S_{initial} = \{4, 3, 2, 8\}$ (the most 4 frequent elements in the workflows) making sure that there is always a path between the nodes in the rule. Hence, it can generate the rule $8 \rightarrow 2 \Rightarrow 3$ but it cannot generate rule $8 \rightarrow 2 \Rightarrow 4$ because there is no edge $(2, 4)$ in the subgraph spanned by the set $S_{initial}$, as seen in Figure 2(b).

However, as [3] does not account for graph structure, a future position of the sliding window will generate the set $S_{bad} = \{8, 7, 6, 5\}$ which generates the subgraph shown in Figure 2(c). This graph has only a single edge $(6, 7)$, hence it can only generate rules involving repetitions of the two nodes linked by it, for example $6 \Rightarrow 7$. It is likely that from set S_{bad} we can only generate rules with poor quality. If such sets are abundant, which is the case if we use the sliding window approach, the majority of rules inserted in the heap will have bad quality, increasing the chances of sampling bad rules and reducing the accuracy of the algorithm.

In contrast, we use the graph structure to select nodes from which to generate candidate rules. Any workflow which passes through a frequent node will also pass through at least one of its neighbors. It is more likely for a frequent node to occur in the middle of several intersecting workflows. Hence, we propose to generate the sets S_i by considering nodes $x_i \in V$ in descending order of the noisy counts from Step 1. For each x_i we add to the set S_i, we also add the nodes obtained in a breadth-first search (BFS) traversal of the graph starting at x_i. We truncate the search when at least l_{max} elements are found in S_i. In the running example, for node 8, we obtain set $S_8 = \{8, 1, 2, 3, 4\}$ with the corresponding subgraph shown in Figure 2(d), after the first level of the BFS traversal.

This example also shows another limitation: even though we are guaranteed to always generate connected subgraphs, their size can grow far larger than l_{max}. For any such set S_i we have that $|S_i| \geq l_{max}$ so we can generate rules of lengths up to l_{max}. However, there are $\binom{|S_i|}{l_{max}}$ ways to select the l_{max} items from S_i,leading to an exponential blow-up in the candidate generation phase of the algorithm. To address this issue, we devise a strategy that stops the BFS traversal as soon as l_{max} items have been inserted into the set S_i, thus transforming the search from a truncated BFS to an iterative deepening approach. Because this will most likely interrupt the traversal in the middle of a level, we need to prioritize the order in which the neighbors of a node are visited. Specifically, we visit the nodes in decreasing order of the noisy counts from Step 1.

The pseudocode of Step 2 is captured in lines 6-10 of Figure 3. Note that, Step 2 only makes use of the relative ordering of graph nodes, and not their associated noisy counts. Hence, the privacy budget allocated to the first step can be fairly small, dedicating most of ϵ to rule sampling in Step 2.

4. EXPERIMENTAL EVALUATION

We implemented a C prototype of the proposed technique, and we use as benchmark the method from [3]. We consider a workflow database modeled as a graph with 10 nodes and 50 edges on top of which we generate $10,000$ provenance documents with path lengths uniformly distributed between 5 and 7. The experiments were run on an Intel Core i7-3770 3.4 GHz CPU machine with 8 cores and 16 GB of RAM, running Linux OS. As evaluation metric, we consider the precision of returned rules, i.e., the fraction of rules with confidence above a threshold $c_0 = 0.4$ (we omit other thresholds due to space limitations). We extract between $k = 10$ and $k = 100$ sequences with lengths between $l_{max} = 3$ and $l_{max} = 5$. In all runs, the execution time was always below three seconds.

Figure 4 (a)-(c) shows that our graph-centric approach (label GRF) consistently outperforms the benchmark from [3] (label HCR). For the lowest number of extracted rules $k = 10$, our method reaches precision of 100% for larger ε values. As the length of the rules grows, the accuracy of both methods decreases due to the combinatorial increase in the number of candidate rules. However, our method is still able to outperform the benchmark, and is less adversely affected by the increase of l_{max}.

As expected, both methods are negatively impacted by the increase in k, as the privacy budget needs to be divided across more invocations of the exponential mechanism. Our method still outperforms the benchmark, but further research is necessary to identify ways to increase precision for larger k.

5. CONCLUSION

We proposed a novel method to mine sequence association rules from provenance workflows with differential privacy. Experimental results show that the approach is able to effectively make use of provenance graph information to improve mining accuracy, and clearly outperforms existing techniques. In future work, we will investigate methods to further enhance precision by using more information from the structure of the graph and by considering alternative privacy budget allocation strategies.

Acknowledgments. This work has been supported by NSF award CNS-1111512.

6. REFERENCES

[1] C. Dwork, F. McSherry, K. Nissim, and A. Smith. Calibrating noise to sensitivity in private data analysis. In *TCC*, pages 265–284, 2006.

[2] M. Kolonko and D. Wäsch. Sequential reservoir sampling with a nonuniform distribution. *ACM Trans. Math. Softw.*, 32(2):257–273, June 2006.

[3] M. Maruseac and G. Ghinita. Differentially-Private Mining of High-Confidence Association Rules. *Proc. of CODASPY*, 2015.

[4] F. McSherry and K. Talwar. Mechanism design via differential privacy. In *Proc. of IEEE Symp. on Foundations of Computer Science*, pages 94–103, 2007.

[5] Y. L. Simmhan, B. Plale, and D. Gannon. A survey of data provenance in e-science. *SIGMOD Rec.*, 34(3):31–36, Sept. 2005.

Risk-based Analysis of Business Process Executions

Mahdi Alizadeh
Eindhoven University of Technology
m.alizadeh@tue.nl

Nicola Zannone
Eindhoven University of Technology
n.zannone@tue.nl

ABSTRACT

Organizations need to monitor their business processes to ensure that what actually happens in the system is compliant with the prescribed behavior. Deviations from the prescribed behavior may correspond to violations of security requirements and expose organizations to severe risks. Thus, it is crucial for organizations to detect and address nonconforming behavior as early as possible. In this paper, we present an auditing framework that facilitates the analysis of process executions by detecting nonconforming behaviors and ranking them with respect to their criticality. Our framework employs conformance checking techniques to detect possible explanations of nonconformity. Based on such explanations, the framework assesses the criticality of nonconforming process executions based on historical logging data and context information.

CCS Concepts

•**Security and privacy** → **Security services;** *Information accountability and usage control;*

Keywords

Auditing, Risk Assessment, Alignments, Conformance Checking.

1. INTRODUCTION

Organizations are often exposed to a wide range of security incidents. These incidents might harm a company's reputation, adversely affect its clients and result in a significant financial loss. In response to a number of scandals like the Enron and HIH Insurance cases, a number of regulations and guidelines such as Sarbanes-Oxley Act, Basel III and COBIT, have been enacted. These regulations mandate organizations to have frameworks in place for auditing and managing operational risks.

Organizations often use process models to define activities and procedures to reach their business goals. However, in most organizations process models are not used to enforce a particular way of working. Thus, in practice, reality may deviate from the prescribed behavior. These deviations can correspond to infringements of security policies and have severe consequences for an organization. Therefore, organizations should be able to detect and analyze them as early as possible and take proper actions to mitigate their impact.

Auditing mechanisms currently in use are mostly human-driven and appear to be grossly ineffective. The main problem is that manual auditing of process executions is costly, error-prone and time consuming. In addition, it is not transparent (i.e., not replicable) as the decision whether a certain situation corresponds to an infringement depends on the judgment of the auditor. Moreover, organizations typically have limited resources and cannot deal with all the risks to which they are exposed. It is widely accepted that measuring the criticality of nonconforming behavior gives the opportunity to investigate the most critical infringements earlier. However, the analysis of process executions is not a trivial task because several process perspectives (e.g., control flow, data and users) should be taken into account.

In this work, we poses the basis for the definition of a risk-based auditing framework to assist security analysts in the detection of nonconformity in process executions and in assessing its criticality. To detect deviations in process executions, we rely on alignment-based conformance checking [1, 3]. Alignments provide explanations of nonconformity by pinpointing what went wrong in a process execution. However, alignments are often constructed using a predefined cost function, which can lead to incorrect diagnostics [1]. In particular, the underlying assumption is that the alignments with minimal cost (with respect to an arbitrary cost function) always provide the most probable explanations of nonconformity. We discard this assumption and compute the risks posed by nonconforming process executions by considering both the likelihood that an alignment reflects what actually happened in the system and the severity of the deviations identified by the alignment. Assessing the risk posed by nonconforming process executions makes it possible to rank such executions with respect their criticality, thus enabling security analysts to focus on the most severe incidents.

2. APPROACH

Process executions may deviate from the prescribed behavior. Organizations should be able to detect and analyze nonconforming behavior as earlier as possible to promptly react to security incidents and, thus, limit their impact. In particular, they should be able to prioritize security incidents with respect to their criticality. To assist analysts in the analysis of process executions, we propose a risk-based auditing framework. The framework allows the detection of nonconformity in process executions and the assessment of its criticality. Fig. 1 presents an overview of the framework.

The first step of the framework is to detect nonconforming behaviors (*Conformance Checking*). To this end, we rely on alignment-based conformance checking. Intuitively, an alignment relates events in an event log to activities in a process model and vice versa, thus

CODASPY'16, March 09-11, 2016, New Orleans, LA, USA.

ACM ISBN 978-1-4503-3935-3/16/03.

DOI: http://dx.doi.org/10.1145/2857705.2857742

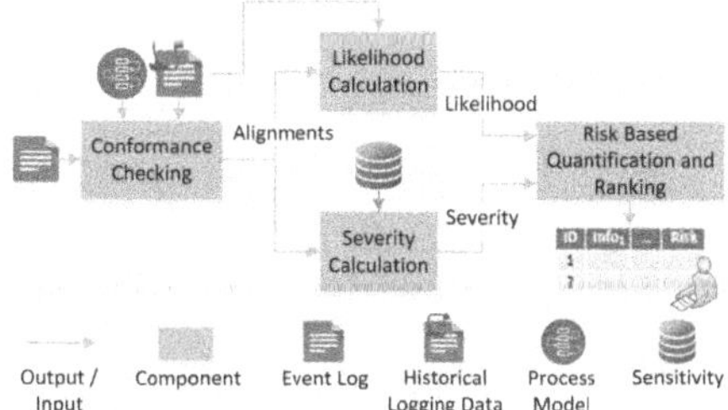

Figure 1: Risk-based Auditing Framework

pinpointing the nonconformity between a process execution and a process model.

The criticality of nonconforming process executions is assessed by computing the operational risks posed by such process executions. In particular, we compute the likelihood that an alignment provides the actual explanation of nonconformity and the severity of the deviations pinpointed in the alignment. The likelihood of an alignment is determined with respect to historical logging data, i.e. past process executions (*Likelihood Calculation*). The severity of an alignment is computed on the basis of the information available about the process execution, e.g. the executed activity, the user who executed it and data that were accessed (*Severity Calculation*).

The risk associated to an alignment is computed by combining its likelihood and severity (*Risk Based Quantification and Ranking*). It is worth noting that more than one explanation of nonconformity may exist for a given process execution. To this end, we compute the possible alignments for a process execution and aggregate the corresponding risks. The aggregated risk represents the operational risk posed by the process execution.

Nonconforming process executions are ranked and visualized with respect to their criticality (i.e., risk level). A security analyst, thus, can evaluate them focusing on the most severe incidents. Based on this analysis, organizations can take the appropriate actions to mitigate the losses. In the remainder of the section, we describe the main components of our framework.

2.1 Conformance Checking

We use alignment-based conformance checking [1, 3] to detect the possible explanations of nonconformity between process executions and the prescribed behavior. Alignment-based conformance checking compares the observed behavior (recorded in logs) with a process model (defining the intended system behavior). We consider process models in the form of classical Petri nets. Petri nets consist of transitions, places, and directed arcs between them. Transitions are labeled with the tasks they represent. The state of a Petri net is represented by a multi-set of tokens on the places of the net, called marking. A transition is enabled if all its input places contain at least a token. When an enabled transition is fired, a token is taken from each of its input places and a token is added to all its output places. A sequence of transitions is a complete firing sequence if firing transitions in the sequence leads from the initial marking to the final marking of the net.

Fig. 2 shows a process model for handling credit requests in form of a Petri net. A process execution starts by filing a loan request (c). Depending on the amount of the requested loan either simple (s) or advanced (a) assessment is performed. If the assessment is negative, the customer can renegotiate the loan amount (n). Otherwise, the loan application is either approved (p) or rejected (r). The process terminates by informing the customer of the decision (i).

A logged instance of a task is called *event*. The sequence of

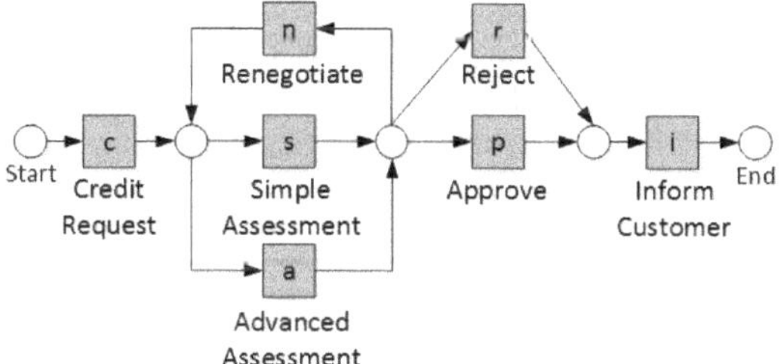

Figure 2: A process model for handling credit requests

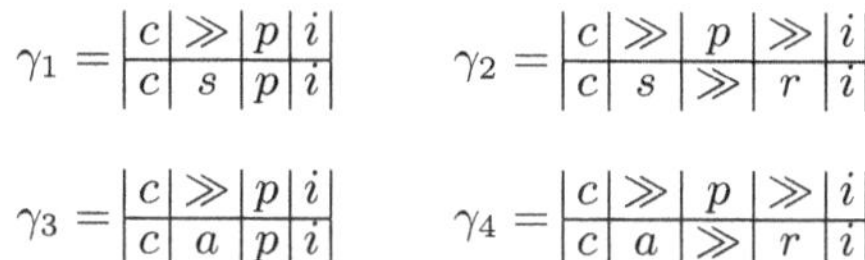

Figure 3: Alignments between the net in Fig. 2 and $\sigma_1 = \langle c, p, i \rangle$

events corresponding to a process instance is called *trace*. Given a trace and a Petri net, an *alignment* maps the trace to a complete firing sequence of the net (see [3] for a formal definition of alignment). Take, for example, a trace $\sigma_1 = \langle$credit request, approve, inform customer$\rangle$. Fig. 3 shows four possible alignments between σ_1 and the net in Fig. 2. The top row of alignments shows the sequence of events in the trace; the bottom row shows a complete firing sequence of the net. Deviations are explicitly shown by columns that contain $\gg$. For example, the third column in γ_2 shows that an event occurs in the trace although it is not allowed according to the net, i.e. *move on log*. The second column in γ_1 shows that a task must occur in σ_1 according to the net, but it is absent in the trace, i.e. *move on model*. Other columns for which events match the label of transitions represent *synchronous moves*.

As shown in Fig. 3, there can be more than one alignment between a trace and a Petri net. To determine the quality of alignments, a cost is assigned to each move in the alignment. The cost of an alignment is defined as the sum of the cost of the moves forming the alignment. For instance, consider a cost function that assigns 1 to moves on log/model and 0 to synchronous moves. According to this cost function, γ_1 and γ_3 have cost 1, and γ_2 and γ_4 have cost 3.

In this work, we use the approach to compute the cost function proposed in [1]. This approach uses historical logging data to determine the cost of moves based on the probability that an activity is executed in a certain state of the process instance. The cost of an alignment, thus, provides a measure of its reliability, i.e. to what extent it is close to what actually happened. We use this measure to compute the likelihood of alignments as shown in the next section.

2.2 Likelihood Calculation

An alignment provides an explanation about the possible deviations that could have occurred during the process execution. Several explanations of nonconformity can exist between a trace and a net. However, not all these explanations are equally probable. We account for the uncertainty in an explanation of nonconformity by computing the likelihood of the corresponding alignment. In particular, the likelihood of an alignment represents how likely an alignment reflects the reality, i.e. its reliability.

To measure the likelihood of an alignment, we use the cost of the alignment obtained using the approach in [1]. Intuitively, alignments that have a low cost are more likely to represent the correct relation between a trace and a model. Let π denote the function that computes the cost of an alignment according to the approach

Alignment	Cost	Likelihood	Severity	Risk
γ_1	2	0.5	0.5	0.25
γ_2	5	0.2	1.6	0.32
γ_3	5	0.2	1.0	0.20
γ_4	10	0.1	2.1	0.21

Table 1: Computation of the risk for the alignments in Fig. 3

proposed in [1]. Given an alignment γ and historical logging data $\mathcal{L}$, the likelihood of γ is:

$$\ell(\gamma) = \frac{1}{\pi(\gamma, \mathcal{L})} \tag{1}$$

Table 1 presents the cost and likelihood of the alignments in Fig. 3. The table shows that γ_1 is the alignment with minimal cost and, thus, it provides the most probable explanation of nonconformity for trace σ_1 and the net in Fig. 2. This is reflected in Table 1 by the fact that γ_1 has the greatest likelihood.

2.3 Severity Calculation

The criticality of a process execution is determined by its impact on organizational goals. We compute this impact based on the severity of the deviations that occurred in a process execution. The severity of deviations typically depends on the application domain and context information. In particular, various business process perspectives should be taken into account to determine the impact of a deviation. For instance, the impact of a deviation might depend on the tasks diverging from the prescribed behavior, the user causing the deviation and the data accessed [2].

To measure the severity of an alignment, we need a cost function ω that assigns a non-negative cost to each move based on the (negative) impact that the move has on organizational goals. Intuitively, a move with a higher severity cost has a higher impact. The severity of an alignment is computed as the sum of the moves forming the alignment. Given an alignment $\gamma = \langle m_1, ..., m_n \rangle$, where m_i ($i \in \{1, \ldots, n\}$) is an alignment move, and a severity cost function ω, the severity of γ is:

$$\lambda(\gamma) = \sum_{i=1}^{n} \omega(m_i) \tag{2}$$

The definition of a severity cost function that takes into account context information is part of our future work. Here, we use a simple cost function (Table 2) for illustrative purposes. This cost function defines the severity of skipping a given task (move on model) or executing a given task when it was not supposed to be executed (move on log). For instance, this cost function specifies that informing a client (*i*) multiple times is considered less severe than skipping the loan assessment (*s* or *a*). Moreover, the cost function assigns cost 0 to synchronous moves. The fourth column of Table 1 presents the severity of the alignments in Fig. 3 according to the severity cost function in Table 2.

2.4 Risk-based Quantification

To compute the risk level of an alignment we combine its likelihood and severity. Given an alignment γ between a trace and a net, the risk level of γ is:

$$\rho(\gamma) = \ell(\gamma) \times \lambda(\gamma) \tag{3}$$

In practice, there can be more than one alignment between a trace and a model [1, 3]. These alignments provide different explanations of nonconformity for the trace; each explanation can exhibit different operational risks. The calculation of the risk posed by the execution of a trace should take into account these risks. Thus, we

Activity	Model Move	Log Move
Credit Request (*c*)	0.1	0.1
Simple Assessment (*s*)	0.5	0.1
Advanced Assessment (*a*)	1	0.1
Inform Customer (*i*)	0.1	0.1
Renegotiate (*n*)	0.1	0.1
Approve (*p*)	0.1	1
Reject (*r*)	0.1	0.1

Table 2: Sample severity cost function

compute the risk posed by the execution of a trace by aggregating the risk level of its alignments. Let $\gamma_1, ..., \gamma_n$ the alignments constructed between a trace σ and a net, the risk posed by σ is:

$$\bar{\rho}(\sigma) = \sum_{i=1}^{n} \rho(\gamma_i) \tag{4}$$

Intuitively, the risk posed by the execution of a trace is a weighted average of the severity of the alignments constructed between the trace and a net, where the likelihood of an alignment is used as the weight for the alignment. In our example, the risk posed by the execution of trace σ_1 is equal to 0.98.

So far, we have focused on the risk assessment for a single trace. This risk assessment process can be repeated for every nonconforming process execution. This makes it possible to rank nonconforming process executions with respect to their risk level. This way, auditors can focus on the most critical incidents.

3. CONCLUSION

This work poses the basis for a novel risk-based framework for analyzing the criticality of process executions. The framework uses alignments to obtain diagnostics about process executions. The risk of nonconforming process executions is determined as the combination of the likelihood that an explanation of nonconformity corresponds to the reality and its severity. In particular, the framework computes likelihood based on historical logging data and severity based on context information. By ranking nonconforming process executions with respect to their criticality, the framework enables a security analyst to focus on the most severe incidents.

Acknowledgments This work has been funded by the NWO Cyber Security programme under the PriCE project and the Dutch national program COMMIT under the THeCS project.

4. REFERENCES

[1] M. Alizadeh, M. de Leoni, and N. Zannone. History-based construction of log-process alignments for conformance checking: Discovering what really went wrong. In *Proceedings of International Symposium on Data-driven Process Discovery and Analysis*, CEUR Workshop Proceedings 1293, pages 1–15. CEUR-WS.org, 2014.

[2] S. Banescu and N. Zannone. Measuring privacy compliance with process specifications. In *Proceedings of International Workshop on Security Measurements and Metrics*, pages 41–50. IEEE, 2011.

[3] W. M. P. van der Aalst, A. Adriansyah, and B. F. van Dongen. Replaying history on process models for conformance checking and performance analysis. *Wiley Interdisc. Rew.: Data Mining and Knowledge Discovery*, 2(2):182–192, 2012.

Automatic Summarization of Privacy Policies using Ensemble Learning

Noriko Tomuro
College of Computing and Digital Media (CDM)
DePaul University
Chicago, IL USA
tomuro@cs.depaul.edu

Steven Lytinen
College of Computing and Digital Media (CDM)
DePaul University
Chicago, IL USA
lytinen@cs.depaul.edu

Kurt Hornsburg
MobileEvolution
Vienna, Austria
kurt.hornburg@mobileevolution.eu

ABSTRACT
When customers purchase a product or sign up for service from a company, they often are required to agree to a Privacy Policy or Terms of Service agreement. Many of these policies are lengthy, and a typical customer agrees to them without reading them carefully if at all. To address this problem, we have developed a prototype automatic text summarization system which is specifically designed for privacy policies. Our system generates a summary of a policy statement by identifying important sentences from the statement, categorizing these sentences by which of 5 "statement categories" the sentence addresses, and displaying to a user a list of the sentences which match each category. Our system incorporates keywords identified by a human domain expert and rules that were obtained by machine learning, and they are combined in an ensemble architecture. We have tested our system on a sample corpus of privacy statements, and preliminary results are promising.

General Terms
Privacy, Languages, Algorithms, Experimentation

Keywords
Privacy Policy; Natural Language Processing; Machine Learning

1. INTRODUCTION
A wide variety of companies require their customers to agree to a Privacy Policy (or Terms of Service) when purchasing products and services. These policies are often quite intrusive, including conditions about how a customer's personal information will be gathered and retained, shared by subsidiaries or sold to other companies, and so on. The vast majority of customers agree to these policies without reading them carefully if at all [1]. This means that for many people, their personal data is stored, used, and/or shared without them being aware that this is the case.

One potential approach to helping a customer understand privacy policies is through text summarization. While automated approaches to text summarization are certainly not infallible, a customer would be more likely to read a short, computer-generated summary of a privacy policy than the full text. We have developed a prototype of an automatic text summarization system which is specific to privacy policies. The system generates a summary by identifying important sentences in a policy, and presenting those sentences to a user according to which of 5 "statement categories" is addressed by each sentence. Although there are only few previous works which attempted automatic privacy policy analysis (e.g. [2][3]), our system is unique in several ways. First, it incorporates both the knowledge of a human domain expert (provided as keywords), and the knowledge obtained automatically through machine learning. The two types of knowledge are combined in an ensemble architecture to exploit the synergy between them. Second, our system represents both types of knowledge in the form of if-then rules, which are human-readable and easy to understand. Also the system is implemented as a web application, and publicly accessible (http://slytinen-ntomuro.rhcloud.com/index.jsp). We conducted a preliminary evaluation of the system's performance. The results were promising – with the initial set of rules which are yet to be refined, the system showed relatively high recall and precision.

CODASPY'16, March 09-11, 2016, New Orleans, LA, USA.
ACM 978-1-4503-3935-3/16/03.
http://dx.doi.org/10.1145/2857705.2857741

2. PRIVACY SUMMARIZER SYSTEM
The main goal of the system is to summarize a privacy policy by extracting key sentences which address its major points, and displaying them in a concise manner. We identified 5 privacy categories as the most important, essential information to understand a privacy policy, and defined our own *Statement Categories* in the form of questions:

- Statement 1 (Clear Purpose): For what purposes does the company use personal information?
- Statement 2 (Third Parties): Does the company share my information with third parties?
- Statement 3 (Limited Collection): Does the company combine my information with data from other sources?
- Statement 4 (Limited Use): Will the company sell, re-package or commercialize my data?
- Statement 5 (Retention): Will the company retain my data? What is their retention policy?

We created our dataset of privacy policies by downloading the privacy policy page of many major companies from a wide range of business areas. So far there are a total of 76 policies in the dataset. A domain expert manually annotated the individual sentences in (randomly selected) 25 policies with the statement categories. This annotated subset corpus consisted of 335 sentences which are statement category 1-5, and 4424 sentences which didn't address any of the categories. We used this corpus to build our system, as described in detail in section 3.

Our system is implemented as a web application. Figure 1 shows its interface. The system incorporates all 76 policies, and they are shown in a dropdown menu; when the user selects a statement, the summary is displayed as shown in Figure 2.

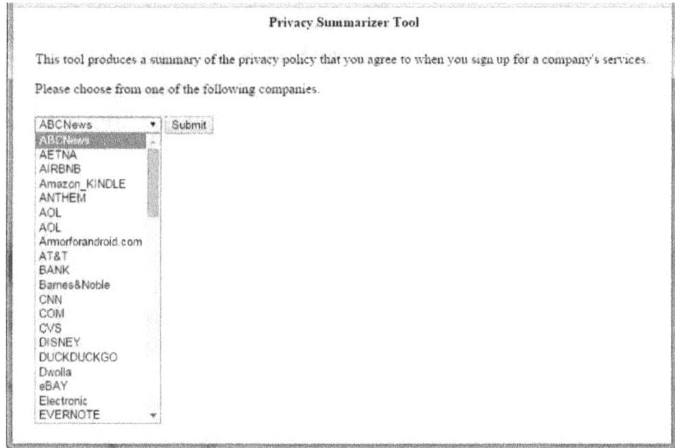

Figure 1. User Interface of the System.

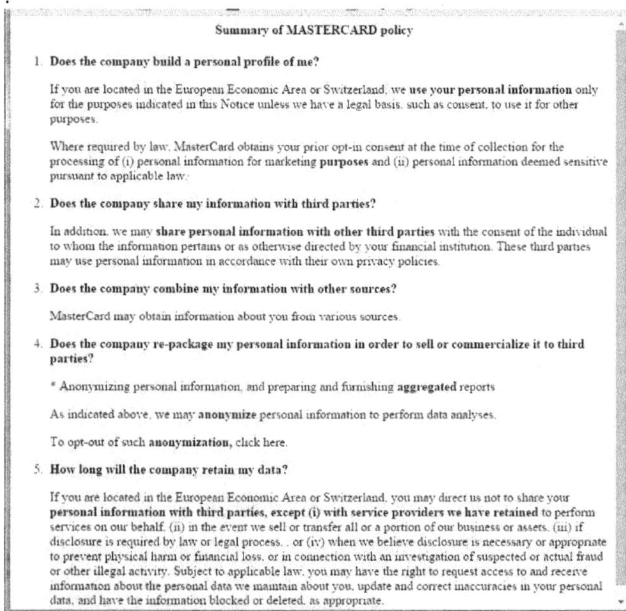

Summary of MASTERCARD policy

1. **Does the company build a personal profile of me?**

   If you are located in the European Economic Area or Switzerland, we **use your personal information** only for the purposes indicated in this Notice unless we have a legal basis, such as consent, to use it for other purposes.

   Where required by law, MasterCard obtains your prior opt-in consent at the time of collection for the processing of (i) personal information for marketing **purposes** and (ii) personal information deemed sensitive pursuant to applicable law.

2. **Does the company share my information with third parties?**

   In addition, we may **share personal information with other third parties** with the consent of the individual to whom the information pertains or as otherwise directed by your financial institution. These third parties may use personal information in accordance with their own privacy policies.

3. **Does the company combine my information with other sources?**

   MasterCard may obtain information about you from various sources.

4. **Does the company re-package my personal information in order to sell or commercialize it to third parties?**

   * Anonymizing personal information, and preparing and furnishing **aggregated** reports

   As indicated above, we may **anonymize** personal information to perform data analyses.

   To opt-out of such **anonymization,** click here.

5. **How long will the company retain my data?**

   If you are located in the European Economic Area or Switzerland, you may direct us not to share your **personal information with third parties, except (i) with service providers we have retained** to perform services on our behalf, (ii) in the event we sell or transfer all or a portion of our business or assets, (iii) if disclosure is required by law or legal process, , or (iv) when we believe disclosure is necessary or appropriate to prevent physical harm or financial loss, or in connection with an investigation of suspected or actual fraud or other illegal activity. Subject to applicable law, you may have the right to request access to and receive information about the personal data we maintain about you, update and correct inaccuracies in your personal data, and have the information blocked or deleted, as appropriate.

Figure 2. Summary of a policy extracted by the system.

Note that a summary is a list of sentences which the system extracted from the policy files, as is, with no modification (i.e., sentences themselves are not shortened). Also currently the development is at an early stage, and the interface is still rough. Furthermore, at this moment the system displays all sentences that matched each of the 5 statement categories. We plan to improve the interface, and display just one or two *best* sentences that matched the statement.

3. DETAILS OF THE SYSTEM

The system is composed of three components which are organized in a two-level ensemble hierarchy, as shown in Figure 3. The first level consists of two components – a pattern matcher based on manually crafted patterns (the "Keyword Matcher"), and another matcher based on patterns automatically derived by a Machine Learning algorithm (the "JRIP matcher"). Then the component on the second level (the "Combiner Classifier") receives the output of the two level-1 matchers and produces the final result, which is the statement category of the sentence fed in the system (category 1/2/3/4/5 or 0 for no-category).

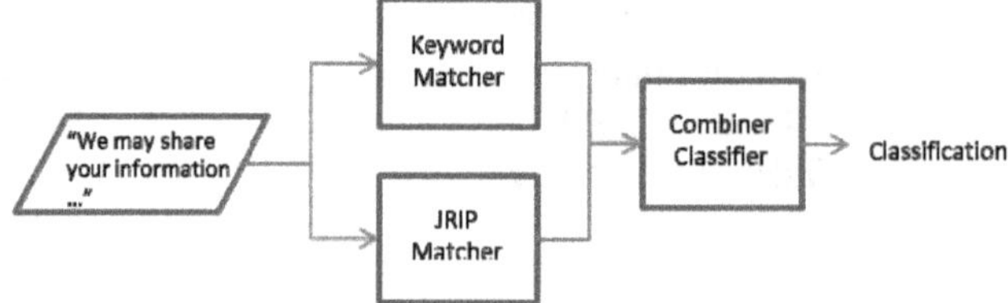

Figure 3. Schematic components of the system

3.1 Keyword Matcher

The Keyword matcher is based on the keywords provided by a human domain expert. The keywords are manually crafted into several 'patterns' (in the form of regular expressions) for each of the 5 statement categories.

As an example, the keywords provided by the human expert for statement 3 were as follows:

KEY WORDS:
Combine, supplement, associate, in conjunction, link
Personal information, your information, the information
Third-parties, partners, other companies, other sources

And the regular expressions written for this category included the following pattern:

```
(combin|supplemen|associa).{0,100}(third|other|informat|data)
```

Note that ".{0.100}" (occurrence of any character (.) between 0 and 100 times) is an example effort to specify the allowable distance between two keywords (where words in an enclosed parentheses in a pattern are essentially synonyms). We observed most keywords appear in a sentence at the subject or main verb or direct object position. So we wrote patterns to specify that two keywords should appear close to each other (in a local context) to avoid spurious false-positive matches.

For a given sentence the keyword matcher applies all patterns in the 5 sets of patterns (statement category 1-5) and produces 5 resulting values – one for each category. The value is a yes or no, indicating whether or not any of the patterns of the category matched the sentence. Note that, with this scheme, a sentence could match with more than one category.

3.2 JRIP Matcher

The JRIP matcher is based on the rules derived (automatically) by a Machine Learning (ML) algorithm called RIPPER [4]. We used a particular implementation of the algorithm in a ML tool called Weka [5] (in which the algorithm is named JRIPPER).

RIPPER is a classification algorithm, which classifies a given input instance into one of the predefined target categories. We first trained the algorithm using the subset corpus of 25 annotated policies, and obtained a set of 'rules' for each category. The derived rules are a model, in particular a decision rule expressed in the form of an if-then statement and keyed by the words in the sentence. Ordering of the selected words is unimportant for the JRIPPER-derived rules. For example, the rules for statement 3 included the following.

```
(combine >= 1) and (group <= 0) => category=3
(associate >= 1) and (account <= 0) and (access <= 0)
   and (device <= 0) => category=3
(combine >= 1) and (datum >= 1) => category=3
```

Note the values appearing with a word with a <= or a >= are a number of occurrences of the word in the given sentence, and an expression "category=X" after the symbol => is the decision of the rule – the statement category X. For example, the first rule above indicates that a sentence containing one or more occurrences of the word "combine" and not containing "group" should be categorized as statement category 3.

Note that we trained the JRIPPER algorithm using sentences of the categories 1 through 5 and excluded category-0 sentences. We did so because only 5% of the sentences were identified as relevant (category 1-5), and the vocabulary would have otherwise been dominated by terms from category-0 sentences.

Similar to the Keyword matcher, the JRIP matcher applies all 5 sets of rules (statement category 1-5) to each sentence and produces 5 yes/no resulting values. Also just like the Keyword matcher, a sentence could match with more than one category.

3.3 Combiner Classifier

The combiner classifier on the second level receives the output of the two matchers on the first level (totaling 10 yes/no values) and produces the final output – the statement category of the given sentence which the system predicts (1/2/3/4/5 or 0). To develop a model for this classifier, we used the RIPPER algorithm again because of the interpretability of the generated rules. But for the training data, we included some category-0 sentences so that the classifier would learn to identify irrelevant sentences as well as relevant (category 1-5) ones.

As an example, the generated rules included the following. Note that "regexpN" represents the Keyword matcher's result for the statement category N, while "jripN" represents the JRIP matcher's result for category N. Note also that the final classification is mutually exclusive – only one category for a sentence (and 'category 0' was one of the options).

```
(regexp5 = yes) => category=5
(jrip3 = yes) => category=3
(regexp3 = yes) and (jrip1 = no) and (jrip4 = no) => category=3
(regexp2 = yes) and (regexp1 = no) => category=2
```

4. EVALUATION

To evaluate the system, we used the same dataset used for the Combiner classifier, which included a 5% random sampling of the category-0 sentences in addition to the 335 category 1-5 sentences (thus the total number of sentences was (4424*.05) + 335 = 221 + 335 = 556). The table below shows the results for category 1-5. Note that these were obtained by a 10-fold cross-validation.

Meanings of the table's columns are as follows.

- # Actual – The number of sentences of the category, as labeled by the human domain expert.
- # TP (True-Positive) – The number of sentences which the system correctly classified as this category.
- # FP (False-Positive) -- The number of sentences which the system incorrectly classified as this category.
- Recall -- # TP / # Actual. The ratio of the true sentences recalled by the system.
- Precision -- # TP / (#TP + # FP). The ratio of the true sentences in all sentences classified as this category by the system.

Table 1. Results of cross-validation test

Statement	# Actual	# TP	# FP	Recall	Precision
1	81	49	16	0.605	0.754
2	87	30	9	0.345	0.769
3	57	42	13	0.737	0.764
4	59	38	14	0.644	0.731
5	51	41	13	0.804	0.759
Total	335	200	65	0.597	0.755

Based on the results, we can see that approximately 6 in 10 relevant sentences (as judged by the human expert) are correctly labeled by the system. Statement 2 seems very difficult to identify, with recall = 0.345. Overall, precision is somewhat higher than recall; about 3 in 4 sentences (on average) marked as relevant by the system are correctly classified.

5. CONCLUSIONS AND FUTURE WORK

We plan to continue working and improve the system in the future work. The most immediate issue is to reduce false-positives – when irrelevant/category-0 sentences are identified as relevant (category 1-5). The regular expressions which we have crafted are particularly overproductive, and we expect to be able to achieve higher precision with further refinement of these rules. We also plan to develop a component which utilizes non-lexical features (e.g. sentence length, position of a sentence relative to document headers) and to add this as a third module in the first level of our system, to be incorporated into the learning ensemble.

6. REFERENCES

[1] Jensen, C., and Potts, C. 2004. Privacy Policies as Decision-Making Tools: An Evaluation of Online Privacy Notices. In *Proceedings of the SIGCHI Conference on Human Factors in Computing Systems.*

[2] Constante, E., Sun, Y., Petkovic, M. and den Hartog, J. 2012. A Machine Learning Solution to Assess Privacy Policy Completeness. In *Proceedings of the ACM Workshop on Privacy in the Electronic Society*, 91-96.

[3] Zimmeck, S. and Bellovin, S. 2014. Privee: An Architecture for Automatically Analyzing Web Privacy Policies. In *Proceedings of the 23rd USENIX Security Symposium.*

[4] Cohen, W. 1995. Fast Effective Rule Induction. In *Proceedings of the Twelfth International Conference on Machine Learning*, 115-123.

[5] Witten, I., Frank, E. and Hall, M.. 2011. *Data Mining: Practical Machine Learning Tools and Techniques*, Third Edition. Morgan Kaufmann.

An Authorization Service for Collaborative Situation Awareness

Alexandru Ionut Egner, Duc Luu, Jerry den Hartog, Nicola Zannone
Eindhoven University of Technology
{a.i.egner, m.luu, j.d.hartog, n.zannone}@tue.nl

ABSTRACT

In international military coalitions, situation awareness is achieved by gathering critical intel from different authorities. Authorities want to retain control over their data, as they are sensitive by nature, and, thus, usually employ their own authorization solutions to regulate access to them. In this paper, we highlight that harmonizing authorization solutions at the coalition level raises many challenges. We demonstrate how we address authorization challenges in the context of a scenario defined by military experts using a prototype implementation of SAFAX, an XACML-based architectural framework tailored to the development of authorization services for distributed systems.

CCS Concepts

•Security and privacy → Access control; Authorization;

Keywords

Access control; XACML; Security-as-a-Service

1. INTRODUCTION

A Combined Joint Task Force (CJTF) is a complex military coalition created for a specific mission. It is typically composed of military branches (e.g., navy, air force) belonging to different authorities (e.g., several NATO members), which can cooperate with non-military bodies (e.g., civilian agencies, NGOs). With this type of highly collaborative missions, situation awareness is achieved from intel gathered from a large number of heterogeneous data sources (e.g., UAV, motion sensors) and analysis services (e.g., imagery analysis, HUMINT). Sharing information is thus essential for the success of a CJTF. However, due to the sensitive nature of data, each party within the coalition imposes stringent security constraints that govern sharing of information.

The operational model adopted by a CJTF enables each authority to retain control over their data. To this end, each authority employs its own authorization solution and defines its own policies to regulate who is allowed to access its resources. In particular, each authority can choose its own access control model, define policies according to its domain knowledge and best practices, augment policy evaluation with customized capabilities, etc. This, however, can have an impact on the exchange of information between parties within the coalition and can result in poor cooperation. Therefore, the success of a coalition requires harmonizing access rights across different authorities. In particular, the authorization systems employed by the authorities need to interoperate with each other and act like a global authorization system at the CJTF level.

Access control standards such as XACML [1] already provide a baseline for the development of authorization services suited for distributed systems. In particular, XACML has been proven to be suitable for the specification and enforcement of access control policies in open systems. One of XACML's strengths is that it supports augmenting policy evaluation through extensibility points such as User Defined Functions (UDF).

Existing implementations of XACML, however, are not flexible enough to face challenges characteristic to military coalitions. These implementations are usually monolithic and cannot be easily adapted to different deployment configurations, depending on the requirements of each authority. For instance, components for policy evaluation and management, which already exist as part of the access control systems of the authorities forming the coalition, cannot be reused for new missions. In addition, existing implementations do not support features fundamental to the military domain, such as delegation of authority [3, 7], concept alignment [8] and geolocation policies [2]. Although they can be extended to support additional capabilities, this is often done in an ad-hoc way. In particular, the logic of UDFs is typically implemented as part of the Policy Decision Point (PDP), which impacts both extensibility (PDP needs to be modified and redeployed) and separation of concerns (PDP should only be responsible for the evaluation of requests).

We have developed SAFAX [6], a novel XACML-based architectural framework. The driving idea underlying SAFAX is to provide authorization as a service. Each component of SAFAX is designed as a loosely-coupled service, thus allowing a variety of deployment configurations. In a major departure of existing XACML implementations, UDFs are realized as self-configuring clients that consume external services, making it possible to extend a PDP's capabilities without changing the PDP itself. In this paper we demonstrate the feasibility of creating secure collaborative situation awareness using SAFAX. To this end, we apply a prototype implementation of SAFAX to a scenario in the military domain within the context of the IN4STARS 2.0 project. It is worth noting that, although we demonstrate the framework in the context of a military scenario, it is domain independent and can be applied to different application domains (e.g., eHealth systems, cloud services).

CODASPY'16 March 09-11, 2016, New Orleans, LA, USA

ACM ISBN 978-1-4503-3935-3/16/03.

DOI: http://dx.doi.org/10.1145/2857705.2857740

2. AUTHORIZATION FRAMEWORK

SAFAX [6] is an XACML-based architectural framework tailored to the development of authorization services for open and distributed systems. An overview of the authorization framework is shown in Figure 1. The components forming the architecture are designed as loosely-coupled services and can be logically separated into three main blocks: *(i)* domain-specific components - Policy Enforcement Point (PEP), Context Handler (CH) and Policy Information Point (PIP), *(ii)* core components, which represent the baseline of the authorization service and *(iii)* external services, which can be used to evaluate custom constraints in the policies.

Domain-specific components depend on the application environment and are under the control of the coalition members. These components are responsible for handling the conversion between the attribute representation in the application environment and the attribute representation in the XACML format (CH), retrieving the information necessary for policy evaluation (PIP) and enforcing access decisions (PEP). The only implementation requirements are that they adhere to the XACML reference architecture [1] and that they are deployed as web services. External services provide additional capabilities for policy evaluation. For instance, they can be used to retrieve trust information from external sources (e.g., attributes certified by a trusted authority) or relocate the computation of complex functions relieving the burden on the PDP (e.g., geolocation function [2], concept alignment [8]).

The core components represent the baseline of the authorization service. Below, we briefly describe the core components of the authorization framework:

- **Policy Decision Point (PDP)** is responsible for evaluating access requests against policies and providing access decisions. SAFAX can support several PDP services for different versions of XACML or PDP implementations with additional functionalities (e.g., transparency [5], probabilistic decisions [4]). Each PDP service is identified by a unique URL (PDP-URL).
- **PDP Configuration (PDPC)** allows authorities to select the PDP service to be used for evaluation. Moreover, the PDPC allows the configuration of PDP services by setting a number of parameters including the root combining algorithm.
- **Router** is responsible for distributing access requests to the proper PDP service for evaluation based on the PDP-URL.
- **Policy Administration Point (PAP)** facilitates storage and management of access control policies, regardless of the location where resources are stored.
- **Service Repository** allows registered service to dynamically discover, bind and consume other services. Services can be components of the authorization framework (e.g., PDP, PIP) or external services registered as UDFs. In SAFAX, UDFs are decoupled from the PDP and implemented as external, pluggable services.

By designing SAFAX components as loosely-coupled services, the framework provides great flexibility in terms of deployment, configuration, and integration. In particular, the authorization service (i.e., core components) can be outside the control of an authority depending on the required deployment configuration. For instance, army branches such as infantry or armored brigades, can delegate part of the authorization decision making to a trusted authorization service (e.g., one provided by the army). This facilitates the integration of components that deploy different authorization solutions (e.g., based on different versions of XACML). Another strength of the framework comes from the implementation of the UDFs' logic as external services. This makes it possible to enrich the context of a request during evaluation and enable the computation of the complex functions, while keeping the system scalable.

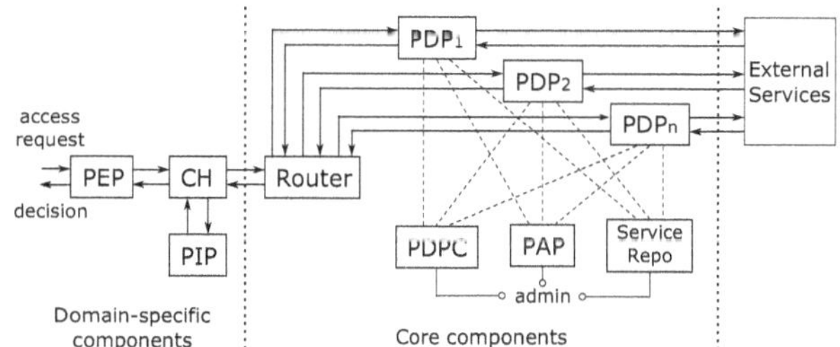

Figure 1: Overview of the Architectural Framework

3. DEMONSTRATION

The SAFAX framework has been realized as an authorization service[1], in which every component of the framework is implemented as a RESTful service. We demonstrate the feasibility of the authorization service in a collaborative situation awareness scenario elaborated by military experts in the context of the IN4STARS 2.0 project. In this case study, two instances of the service were deployed at authorities A_1 and A_2, under different deployment configurations. In both configurations, the core components of the authorization service were deployed within the boundaries of the authority. Each authority employs a credential-based trust management service based on GEM [7] to retrieve user credentials issued by the other authority. Moreover, A_2 deploys a geolocation service based on GeoXACML [2] for the evaluation of constraints on spatial information and a concept alignment service [8]; A_1 relies on these services for the evaluation of its policies.

Both authorities define policies to regulate access to their resources and deploy them in their own PAPs. A_1 contributes to the coalition with intel reports. To protect these resources, A_1 defines a policy that grants access to reports providing intel about the mission's area only to *mission members* having *role* intel officer.

Authorities can customize the PDP to be used for the evaluation of their policies through the PDPC (Figure 2a). This makes it possible to reuse components in the context of other missions, which on the other hand would not be possible using existing monolithic implementations. In our scenario, A_1 chooses a PDP service for policies expressed in XACML v2. As confidentiality of data is considered to be of utmost importance, A_1 chooses deny-overrides as the root combining algorithm. The PDPC also assigns a unique identifier to the PDP (PDP Code), which is part of the PDP-URL (shown at the bottom of Figure 2a).

Suppose that A_1 receives a request from a mission member belonging to A_2 to access an intel report. The request, however, does not contain all the attributes needed for policy evaluation. One the one hand, the requester may not know which attributes are used in the evaluation. On the other hand, A_1 does not trust the value that requesters provide for certain attributes (e.g., resource *type* and *classification*). These attributes can be retrieved from the PIP deployed at A_1 (through the CH). Figure 2b shows the interface of the PIP service along with the attributes assigned to the resources shared by A_1. However, not all attribute values may be locally available for the evaluation of a request. For instance, the requester is within A_2's trust domain and A_1 has no knowledge of his *role*. Thus, the PDP retrieves the value of this attribute from A_2 through an external service (the credential-based trust management service) during policy evaluation.

A_1 consumes the concept alignment service at A_2 for harmonizing the terminology used within the coalition (e.g., the *role* ex-

[1]The authorization service is available at http://security1.win.tue.nl/safax/.

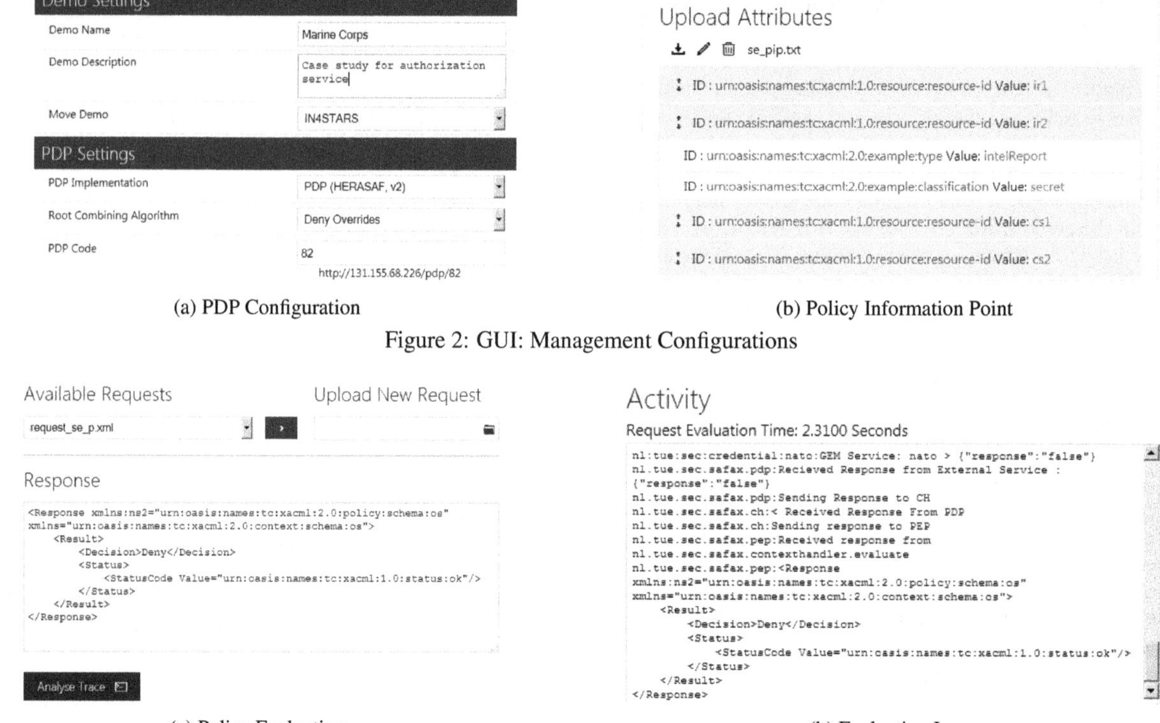

(a) PDP Configuration (b) Policy Information Point

Figure 2: GUI: Management Configurations

(a) Policy Evaluation (b) Evaluation Log

Figure 3: GUI: Evaluation

pected in the policy of A_1 is *intel officer*, while the same role provided with the request is defined as *intel analyst* by A_2). Moreover, A_1 consumes the geolocation service at A_2 to determine whether the requested intel report concerns the mission's area. The PDP's use of external services extends its capabilities in a flexible way, which is essential for enabling collaborations. This constitutes an advantage of SAFAX over other monolithic approaches, as it increases scalability by shifting part of the computational burden away from the PDP.

Upon receiving the request, the Router of the authorization service employed by A_1 forwards it to the PDP identified by the PDP Code contained in the PDP-URL. To manage multiple requests-responses, the Router augments each request sent to a PDP with a unique Transaction ID, internal to the SAFAX framework. In our example, the requester is not an intel officer. Thus, the request is denied as shown by the PDP response in Figure 3a. For debugging purposes SAFAX supports the visualization of the log messages generated during the evaluation of access requests. A snippet of the log can be found in Figure 3b.

4. CONCLUSION

In this paper we demonstrated the feasibility of secure collaborative situation awareness using an authorization service based on SAFAX. In particular, we have shown the deployment of the authorization service under two different configurations within the context of a military coalition. The demonstration highlights the importance of decoupling UDFs from the PDP and illustrates the benefits of relying on external services for attribute retrieval and relocation of computation for complex functions.

Acknowledgments This work has been funded by the EDA project IN4STARS2.0, ITEA2 projects FedSS and M2MGrid, EU FP7 project AU2EU and the Dutch program COMMIT under the THeCS project.

5. REFERENCES

[1] eXtensible Access Control Markup Language (XACML) Version 3.0. OASIS Standard, OASIS, 2013.

[2] OGC Geospatial eXensible Access Control Markup Language (GeoXACML) 3.0 Core. OGC Discussion Paper, Open Geospatial Consortium, 2013.

[3] XACML v3.0 Administration and Delegation Profile Version 1.0. OASIS Standard, OASIS, 2014.

[4] J. Crampton, C. Morisset, and N. Zannone. On missing attributes in access control: Non-deterministic and probabilistic attribute retrieval. In *Proc. of SACMAT*, pages 99–109. ACM, 2015.

[5] S. Damen, J. den Hartog, and N. Zannone. CollAC: Collaborative access control. In *Proc. of CTS*, pages 142–149. IEEE, 2014.

[6] S. P. Kaluvuri, A. I. Egner, J. den Hartog, and N. Zannone. SAFAX - An Extensible Authorization Service for Cloud Environments. *Frontiers in ICT*, 2(9), 2015.

[7] D. Trivellato, N. Zannone, and S. Etalle. GEM: A distributed goal evaluation algorithm for trust management. *TPLP*, 14(3):293–337, 2014.

[8] D. Trivellato, N. Zannone, M. Glaundrup, J. Skowronek, and S. Etalle. A semantic security framework for systems of systems. *Int. J. Cooperative Inf. Syst.*, 22(1), 2013.

Evaluating Analysis Tools for Android Apps: Status Quo and Robustness Against Obfuscation

Johannes Hoffmann[*]
Ruhr-University Bochum

Teemu Rytilahti[*]
Ruhr-University Bochum

Davide Maiorca[†]
University of Cagliari

Marcel Winandy[*]
Ruhr-University Bochum

Giorgio Giacinto[‡]
University of Cagliari

Thorsten Holz[*]
Ruhr-University Bochum

ABSTRACT

The recent past has shown that Android smartphones became the most popular target for malware authors. Malware families offer a variety of features that allow, among the others, to steal arbitrary data and to cause significant monetary losses. This circumstances led to the development of many different analysis methods that are aimed to assess the absence of potential harm or malicious behavior in mobile apps. In return, malware authors devised more sophisticated methods to write mobile malware that attempt to thwart such analyses. In this work, we briefly describe assumptions analysis tools rely on to detect malicious content and behavior. We then present results of a new obfuscation framework that aims to break such assumptions, thus modifying Android apps to avoid them being analyzed by the targeted systems. We use our framework to evaluate the robustness of static and dynamic analysis systems for Android apps against such transformations.

1. INTRODUCTION

Malicious software for mobile devices became prevalent in the last few years. While the first such samples were rather simple and unsophisticated, the complexity of today's malicious apps is steadily increasing. Especially malware for Android-based smartphones has significantly advanced in the recent past.

To counter this development, analysis tools must keep up with the constant evolution of malware. The typical arms race in computer security between attackers and defenders is especially distinctive in this area. Researchers from both academia and industry developed a large number of analysis methods for Android apps in recent years. These tools explored many different approaches and they took into account lessons learned from analyzing malware for desktop computers. However, existing analysis methods cannot simply be ported to Android due to many intricacies of the platform.

In this paper, we evaluate the robustness of state-of-the-art analysis tools for Android apps. Such an empirical evaluation is needed to assess how reliable existing tools are.

In summary, we make the following contributions in this short paper: (1) We briefly describe basic assumptions underlying existing analysis methods (*e. g.*, ability to reconstruct a CG) and explore how these assumptions can be thwarted (*e. g.*, flattening the CG). Our goal is to produce an obfuscated app with the same semantics as the original one, but which withstands existing analysis tools. (2) We develop a comprehensive framework that employs obfuscation techniques that aim to thwart the assumptions on which the aforementioned tools base their analysis. Our framework is available upon request. (3) We empirically evaluate our obfuscations by using our framework, and found that they severely hamper state-of-the-art tools, thus successfully evading both static and dynamic systems.

An accompanying technical report is available [10]. This technical report additionally includes a thorough survey of existing analysis tools, the assumptions they rely upon as well as more thorough evaluation results.

2. PROGRAM ANALYSIS ASSUMPTIONS

Analysis tools have several basic assumptions on which their analysis is based. For example, to perform an analysis a tool could rely on (1) having access to the call graph (CG) of the app, (2) being able to follow data flows, or (3) being able to find API function names in the code. We found that the number of underlying assumptions for all existing methods is rather small.

To produce an obfuscated app, a viable strategy is thus to systematically thwart these assumptions by means of obfuscation. For example, we can degenerate the CG such that it does not contain meaningful information, hide all literals and strings to conceal methods' semantics and invoked API methods. Additionally, types can be hidden such that bytecode only refers Java's most generic type `j.l.Object` where possible which further conceals the semantic. To this end, we systematically replace method calls, field and array accesses with indirect calls by leveraging the Reflection API.

[*]firstname.lastname@rub.de
[†]davide.maiorca@diee.unica.it
[‡]giacinto@diee.unica.it

CODASPY'16 March 09-11, 2016, New Orleans, LA, USA

ACM ISBN 978-1-4503-3935-3/16/03.
DOI: http://dx.doi.org/10.1145/2857705.2857737

The resulting app has the same semantics as the unobfuscated one, but it withstands tools which base their analysis on those basic assumptions as they are not fulfilled anymore.

3. EVALUATING THE ROBUSTNESS OF ANALYSIS TOOLS

We implemented a framework that is capable of obfuscating arbitrary Android apps with techniques briefly introduced in the previous section (for a more detailed description see our technical report [10]). Our system directly obfuscates DEX code without converting it into an intermediate format (such as JAR), and performs automatic obfuscations. In this section, we present results produced by static and dynamic analysis systems against apps obfuscated with our framework.

We have produced self-written samples that exhibit characteristics that should be detected and analyzed by the target systems. All our samples are based on a "Hello World" app but contain additional functions:

- *Direct*: creates three threads performing suspicious actions: 1) sends an SMS; 2) sends Browser's search terms over a socket; 3) like the second, but IMEI instead of searches.
- *Sleep*: calls `Thread.sleep()` to sleep 5 mins before sending an SMS.
- *Alarm*: same as *Sleep*, but uses *AlarmManager* for delaying the sending.
- *EmuDetect (ED)*: detects whether it runs in an emulator before sending an SMS and the IMEI.

We also tested whether anti-tainting techniques were able to thwart dynamic analyzers which make use of taint tracking. The aforementioned actions are often used by malware and should therefore be reported by analysis systems. Our emulator detection is rather straightforward and it is well-detectable. In general, all tests are implemented in a straightforward fashion by using standard APIs, and should thus be easily detectable.

3.1 Evaluation of Dynamic Analysis Systems

In these experiments, we tested the capabilities of dynamic systems to detect evasive behaviors under obfuscation. Because of samples' properties, such behaviors should easily be detectable.

To test such systems, we wrote the four above described applications that exhibit malicious and evasive behavior. Such applications sum up attacks that can be easily developed to thwart dynamic analysis. If a dynamic system fails at detecting such attacks, it would most likely also fail with more complex strategies. We analyzed our obfuscated samples with five well known dynamic analysis systems. We did not specifically evaluate *DroidBox* [2] as Mobile Sandbox is based on it.

We show a summary of the results of our tests in Table 1. Satisfying analysis results—meaning the analysis system was resistant to our modifications—are marked with an "✓". If provided results for that application do not contain hints for suspicious behavior (such as simply marking it as "unsuspicious"), we mark them in the table with a "↯". If the system does not support an analysis of a tested feature, we mark it as "*n. a.*".

The analyzed services base their taint tracking on *TaintDroid* [7], which should detect possible leaks and report them. If leaked information is being sent back to us and the service report does not provide information about it, but does so when the original and not obfuscated application is analyzed, we know that our obfuscation techniques are successfully evading taint analyses. Lost taints are marked with a "↯" in the "Taints" section of the table. If taint tracking is not supported we mark it as "*n. a.*".

Table 1: Results for dynamic analysis services.

Vendor	Direct	Sleep	Alarm	ED	Taints
Andrubis	✓	↯	✓	↯	↯
ForeSafe	↯	↯	↯	↯	*n. a.*
Mobile Sandbox	✓	✓	✓	↯	↯
NVISO	✓	↯	↯	↯	↯
Tracedroid	✓	↯	✓	↯	*n. a.*

The results obtained by the tested analysis systems presented in Table 1 demonstrate many shortcomings of existing analysis methods. Next, we provide details about them.

Andrubis [1] provides information about all network activity and rates tested apps with a maliciousness value, which were in our case always towards malicious. It failed to detect malicious actions for the *Sleep* and *EmuDetect* tests, and no emulator identifiers apart from the IMEI were changed.

Mobile-Sandbox [16] checks for malware, determines required permissions, and identifies possible entry points. It is the only analyzer that is able to correctly analyze both delaying samples, but fails the emulator detection and anti-taint test.

NVISO [13] only marked the *Direct* sample as malicious. In its provided report, all relevant information about the samples' intentions can be found, although some only in the provided PCAP file. All other samples were ranked as non-malicious and as the emulator is detectable, the ability to send an SMS goes undetected.

ForeSafe [8] provided a screenshot of apps, meaning that they weresuccessfully started, but the reports did not detect malicious activities. Our server was contacted thrice, indicating that the app was run multiple times. The IMEI and other identifiers were unchanged. ForeSafe was the only system to fail to detect maliciousness even from non-obfuscated samples, except for the SMS sending.

Tracedroid [17] reports contain a lot of information and provide a complete execution trace, including the calls (with parameters) done reflectively, completely revealing what has happened. It however fails at detecting activities performed by *Sleep* and *EmuDetect* samples.

3.2 Evaluation of Static Analysis Systems

We continue our evaluation with publicly available static analyzers. All these systems are from academia and are free to download. As our framework flattens the call graph almost completely, we expect that static tools cannot properly analyze the program's control and data flows. They additionally see almost no types, literals, nor strings.

Most public static analyzers focus on Inter-Component Communication vulnerabilities. All these tools search for corresponding sinks and sources, *i. e.*, Intents, Receivers and Content Providers. *Epicc* [14], *ComDroid* [5] and *FlowDroid* [9] were unable to properly analyze data being passed around after obfuscation. The same was true for, *Amandroid* [18], *DIDFAIL* [12] and presumably with other static flow analyzers. Because of the implicit control flows, we stop information leaks that might be detected by the precise control flow handling of *EdgeMiner* [3]. All tested tools generated no results on our obfuscated test samples. The only information available to these tools was the one defined in the Manifest file.

All the other tested public static analyzers failed at gathering information from our obfuscated test apps. For example, *SAAF* [11] was not able to retrieve meaningful information from generated program slices. The obfuscations also broke tools that rely on Java decompilation, such as *DroidChecker* [4]. We provide more details about this topic in our accompanying technical report [10]. *StaDynA* [19] was able to construct call-graphs for obfuscated applications as expected, but due to a bug in AndroGuard [6] it failed to do it for some samples. In general, their approach might be used to form proper call-graphs for further analysis, but we could not provide detailed results.

Our results show that automatically applied obfuscation to programs often completely defeats static analyzers. Most information accessible by them is only of generic value, and does not lead to informative analysis reports. The heavy use of reflections can be flagged suspicious, but it should not be used solely for tagging apps as malicious due to its wide-spread use.

4. CONCLUSION

In this short paper, we evaluated how current state-of-the-art analysis tools can cope with heavily obfuscated apps. We have developed a framework for automated obfuscation of Android apps. Our framework implements fine-grained obfuscation strategies that can be used as test benches for evaluating the robustness of analysis tools.

In our analysis, we targeted both static and dynamic analyzers, including also decompilers (which we present among other topics and much more details in our extended technical report [10]). Our test results let us conclude that many analysis tools are not capable of analyzing obfuscated apps in a satisfying manner.

The worrying aspect is that the code modifications as described in Section 2 can be automatically applied on arbitrary apps without needing access to source code. Malicious software can easily piggyback obfuscated apps, and clandestinely execute their payload while most detection systems remain blind. To this end, the recent work by Zhauniarovich *et al.* [19] and Rasthofer *et al.* [15] shows a great promise, helping to bring static analysis methods again usable even against heavily obfuscated apps.

5. REFERENCES

[1] Anubis – Malware Analysis for Unknown Binaries. https://anubis.iseclab.org/.

[2] DroidBox. http://code.google.com/p/droidbox/.

[3] Y. Cao, Y. Fratantonio, A. Bianchi, M. Egele, C. Kruegel, G. Vigna, and Y. Chen. EdgeMiner: Automatically Detecting Implicit Control Flow Transitions through the Android Framework. In *Symposium on Network and Distributed System Security (NDSS)*, 2015.

[4] P. P. Chan, L. C. Hui, and S. M. Yiu. DroidChecker: Analyzing Android applications for capability leak. In *ACM Conference on Security and Privacy in Wireless and Mobile Networks*, WISEC '12, 2012.

[5] E. Chin, A. P. Felt, K. Greenwood, and D. Wagner. Analyzing inter-application communication in Android. In *Intern. Conf. on Mobile Systems, Applications, and Services (MobiSys)*. ACM, 2011.

[6] A. Desnos and G. Gueguen. Android: From reversing to decompilation. *In Proc. of Black Hat Abu Dhabi*, 2011.

[7] W. Enck, P. Gilbert, B.-G. Chun, L. P. Cox, J. Jung, P. McDaniel, and A. Sheth. TaintDroid: An Information-Flow Tracking System for Realtime Privacy Monitoring on Smartphones. In *OSDI*. USENIX Association, 2010.

[8] ForeSafe. ForeSafe Online Scanner. http://www.foresafe.com/scan.

[9] C. Fritz, S. Arzt, S. Rasthofer, E. Bodden, A. Bartel, J. Klein, Y. le Traon, D. Octeau, and P. McDaniel. Highly precise taint analysis for Android applications. Technical Report TUD-CS-2013-0113, TU Darmstadt, 2013.

[10] J. Hoffmann, T. Rytilahti, D. Maiorca, M. Winandy, G. Giacinto, and T. Holz. Evaluating Analysis Tools for Android Apps: Status Quo and Robustness Against Obfuscation. Technical Report TR-HGI-2016-001, Horst Görtz Institute for IT-security, 2016.

[11] J. Hoffmann, M. Ussath, T. Holz, and M. Spreitzenbarth. Slicing Droids: Program Slicing for Smali Code. In *SAC*. ACM, 2013.

[12] W. Klieber, L. Flynn, A. Bhosale, L. Jia, and L. Bauer. Android taint flow analysis for app sets. In *Proceedings of the 3rd ACM SIGPLAN International Workshop on the State of the Art in Java Program Analysis*, SOAP '14. ACM, 2014.

[13] NVISO. NVISO ApkScan – Scan Android applications for malware. http://apkscan.nviso.be/.

[14] D. Octeau, P. McDaniel, S. Jha, A. Bartel, E. Bodden, J. Klein, and Y. Le Traon. Effective Inter-component Communication Mapping in Android with Epicc: An Essential Step Towards Holistic Security Analysis. In *USENIX Security Symposium*, 2013.

[15] S. Rasthofer, S. Arzt, M. Miltenberger, and E. Bodden. Harvesting runtime data in android applications for identifying malware and enhancing code analysis. Technical Report TUD-CS-2015-0031, TU Darmstadt, 2015.

[16] M. Spreitzenbarth, F. C. Freiling, F. Echtler, T. Schreck, and J. Hoffmann. Mobile-Sandbox: Having a Deeper Look into Android Applications. In *SAC*. ACM, 2013.

[17] V. van der Veen and C. Rossow. Tracedroid. http://tracedroid.few.vu.nl.

[18] F. Wei, S. Roy, X. Ou, and Robby. Amandroid: A precise and general inter-component data flow analysis framework for security vetting of android apps. In *Proceedings of the 2014 ACM SIGSAC Conference on Computer and Communications Security*. ACM, 2014.

[19] Y. Zhauniarovich, M. Ahmad, O. Gadyatskaya, B. Crispo, and F. Massacci. StaDynA: Addressing the Problem of Dynamic Code Updates in the Security Analysis of Android Applications. In *Proceedings of the 5th ACM Conference on Data and Application Security and Privacy*, CODASPY '15, 2015.

Scalable and Secure Logistic Regression via Homomorphic Encryption*

Yoshinori Aono
NICT, Japan
aono@nict.go.jp

Takuya Hayashi
NICT, Japan
takuya.hayashi@nict.go.jp

Le Trieu Phong†
NICT, Japan
phong@nict.go.jp

Lihua Wang
NICT, Japan
wlh@nict.go.jp

ABSTRACT

Logistic regression is a powerful machine learning tool to classify data. When dealing with sensitive data such as private or medical information, cares are necessary. In this paper, we propose a secure system for protecting the training data in logistic regression via homomorphic encryption. Perhaps surprisingly, despite the non-polynomial tasks of training in logistic regression, we show that only additively homomorphic encryption is needed to build our system. Our system is secure and scalable with the dataset size.

Keywords

Logistic regression, additively homomorphic encryption, outsourced computation

1. INTRODUCTION

1.1 Background

Logistic regression is a standard method in supervised machine learning to classify data. It is widely applied in various fields of science and engineering. Specifically, it has been successfully used in medical research to help deciding, for example, a patient has a disease or not.

In several tasks using logistic regression, data contributors (and the data analyst as well) are geographically distributed, raising the need of a central server to *receive*, *store*, *share*, and *process* the data. However, the large data collection at the central server may easily become a significant target for attacks. Even if the access to the server is properly controlled, the server itself cannot be completely trusted due to the sensitive nature of the data.

*A full version of this paper is available as [1].

†Corresponding author.

CODASPY'16 March 09-11, 2016, New Orleans, LA, USA

ACM ISBN 978-1-4503-3935-3/16/03.

DOI: http://dx.doi.org/10.1145/2857705.2857731

1.2 Our contributions

We build a system for secure logistic regression. Both training data and predicting data in our system are protected under encryption, so data secrecy is ensured. In addition, the output of our system can achieve differential privacy. Specifically, our secure system is constructed via following technical steps and contributions:

(1) We turn the original logistic regression into what we call homomorphism-aware logistic regression via function approximations.

(2) We show how to use additively homomorphic encryption with the homomorphism-aware logistic regression. We also point out how to add differential privacy into the system.

1.3 Related works

The works [2,3] consider private prediction in logistic regression, given that the regression coefficients (i.e. θ^* in Section 2.1) are publicly known. This work complements [2] by protecting the training data in producing the regression coefficients. Approximate versions of logistic regression have appeared in other contexts such as differential privacy [5]. This work complements [5] by showing the secrecy of training data can be gained via encryption. In addition, this work combines well with the functional mechanism for differential privacy in [5] to obtain both data secrecy and output privacy. See Section 3.4.

2. LOGISTIC REGRESSION AND ITS APPROXIMATION

2.1 Original logistic regression

Consider a (N_{data}, d)-dataset of N_{data} records and d dimension

$$\left\{x^{(i)}, y^{(i)}\right\}_{1 \le i \le N_{\text{data}}}$$

in which $x^{(i)} = \left(1, x_1^{(i)}, \dots, x_d^{(i)}\right) \in \mathbb{R}^{d+1}$, $y^{(i)} \in \{0,1\}$. Define the following cost function $J : \mathbb{R}^{d+1} \to \mathbb{R}$, with variable

$\theta = (\theta_0, \theta_1, \ldots, \theta_d) \in \mathbb{R}^{d+1}$,

$$J(\theta) = \frac{\lambda}{2N_{\text{data}}}\sum_{j=1}^{d}\theta_j^2 + \frac{1}{N_{\text{data}}}\sum_{i=1}^{N_{\text{data}}}\Big[-y^{(i)}\log(h_\theta(x^{(i)})) - (1-y^{(i)})\log(1-h_\theta(x^{(i)}))\Big] \quad (1)$$

in which $0 < h_\theta(x) < 1$ is the value of the sigmoid function $h_\theta : \mathbb{R}^{d+1} \to \mathbb{R}$ given by

$$h_\theta(x) = \frac{1}{1+\exp(-\theta^T x)} = \frac{1}{1+\exp(-\sum_{j=0}^{d}\theta_j x_j)}.$$

The training phase of logistic regression aims at finding the minimizer which optimizes the cost function, namely computing $\theta^* = \text{argmin}_\theta J(\theta)$. For the predicting phase of logistic regression, see [2].

2.2 Homomorphism-aware logistic regression via approximation

The cost function $J(\theta)$ in Section 2.1 includes logarithm functions, causing obstacles when all the data are in encrypted form. In this section, via approximation of the logarithm functions, we derive what we call homomorphism-aware logistic regression. First, note that,

$$\log(h_\theta(x)) = \log\left(\frac{1}{1+\exp(-\theta^T x)}\right)$$
$$\log(1-h_\theta(x)) = \log\left(\frac{1}{1+\exp(\theta^T x)}\right)$$

so if we approximate the following function of $u \in \mathbb{R}$ by a degree k (e.g., $k=2$) polynomial namely, if $\log\left(\frac{1}{1+\exp(u)}\right) \approx \sum_{j=0}^{k} a_j u^j$ then we obtain following approximations

$$\log(1-h_\theta(x)) \approx \sum_{j=0}^{k} a_j(\theta^T x)^j \quad (2)$$

$$\log(h_\theta(x)) \approx \sum_{j=0}^{k}(-1)^j a_j(\theta^T x)^j \quad (3)$$

in which we choose[1] $a_0 = -0.714761$, $a_1 = -0.5$, $a_2 = -0.0976419$. The approximate function of $J(\theta)$ is formed by using the polynomials at (2) and (3) to replace the corresponding logarithm functions in (1), as follows.

$$J_{\text{approx}}(\theta) = \frac{\lambda}{2N_{\text{data}}}\sum_{j=1}^{d}\theta_j^2 + J^*_{\text{approx}}(\theta) \quad (4)$$

in which,

$$J^*_{\text{approx}}(\theta) = \frac{1}{N_{\text{data}}}\sum_{i=1}^{N_{\text{data}}}\sum_{j=1}^{k}\left(y^{(i)} - y^{(i)}(-1)^j - 1\right)a_j(\theta^T x^{(i)})^j - a_0.$$

Denote

$$A_{j,r_1,\ldots,r_j} = \sum_{i=1}^{N_{\text{data}}}\left(y^{(i)} - y^{(i)}(-1)^j - 1\right)\left(x_{r_1}^{(i)}\cdots x_{r_j}^{(i)}\right) \quad (5)$$

[1]by using the function `fit` of `gnuplot`.

we can finally express

$$J^*_{\text{approx}}(\theta) = \frac{1}{N_{\text{data}}}\sum_{j=1}^{k}\sum_{r_1,\ldots,r_j=0}^{d} a_j(\theta_{r_1}\cdots\theta_{r_j})A_{j,r_1,\ldots,r_j} - a_0 \quad (6)$$

Since degree $k=2$ is mainly used in later sections, we give the explicit formulas of (5) as

$$A_{1,r_1} = \sum_{i=1}^{N_{\text{data}}}\underbrace{\left(2y^{(i)}-1\right)\left(x_{r_1}^{(i)}\right)}_{\text{owned by the } i^{\text{th}} \text{ data source}} \quad (7)$$

$$A_{2,r_1,r_2} = \sum_{i=1}^{N_{\text{data}}}\underbrace{(-1)\left(x_{r_1}^{(i)}x_{r_2}^{(i)}\right)}_{\text{owned by the } i^{\text{th}} \text{ data source}} \quad (8)$$

for later references.

3. OUR SYSTEM FOR SECURE LOGISTIC REGRESSION

3.1 Model 1 (Rivest et al., 1978)

In this subsection, we recap the model of [4].

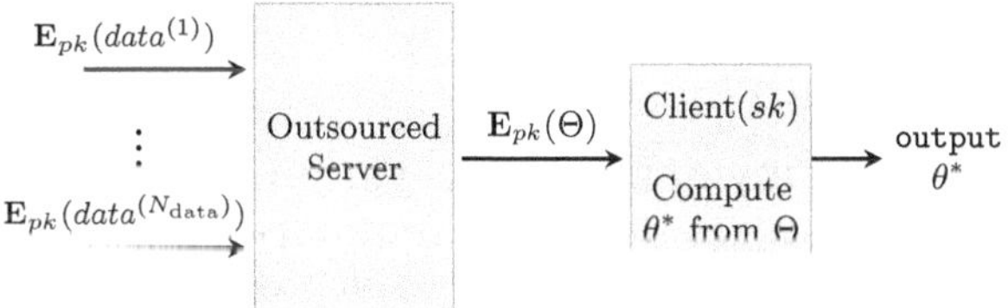

Figure 1: Outline of Model 1.

Model outline. The general picture of the protocol is in Figure 1. We use $\mathbf{E}_{pk}(data^{(1)}), \ldots, \mathbf{E}_{pk}(data^{(N_{\text{data}})})$ to represent the encryption of the data under a public key pk from various geographically distributed data contributors. After receiving the encrypted data, using homomorphic property of $\mathbf{E}_{pk}$, the computing server does necessary computations and sends the output $\mathbf{E}_{pk}(\Theta)$ to the data analyst, from which Θ is recovered by decryption, and the final result θ^* is obtained (from Θ).

Key generation. The client generates the public and secret key pair (pk, sk) and publicly distributes pk. The client is assumed to be honest.

Data encryption. Data from the client or many contributors is encrypted and sent to the outsourced server.

Protection goal. The outsourced server is assumed *honest-but-curious*: it is curious on any information from the data, and yet is honest in instructed computations. This curious nature of the server is considered a threat. The protection goal of our protocol in Figure 1 is to hide any information of the data from the server.

3.2 Model 2: encryption + differential privacy

Figure 2 extends Figure 1 by considering differential privacy, namely output privacy in the sense that the output θ^* reveals nothing meaningful from any specific input $data^{(i)}$. For that purpose, we view the server and the client and their interactions as an interactive mechanism $\mathcal{I} = (\text{Server}, \text{Client})$ with inputs $data^{(1)}, \ldots, data^{(N_{\text{data}})}$ and output θ^*.

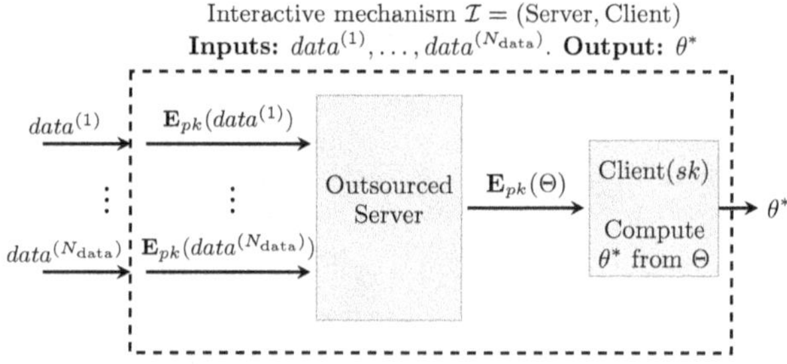

Figure 2: Outline of model 2.

Let D and D_* be two neighbor databases, namely $D = \{data^{(1)}, \ldots, data^{(N_{\text{data}})}\}$ and $D_* = \{data^{(1)}, \ldots, data_*^{(N_{\text{data}})}\}$, differing only at the final item, i.e., $data^{(N_{\text{data}})} \neq data_*^{(N_{\text{data}})}$. Denote $\mathcal{I}(D) \Rightarrow \theta^*$ as a shorthand for saying that the interactive mechanism $\mathcal{I}$ in Figure 2 outputs θ^* with input D, we have the following definition.

DEFINITION 1. *(Differential privacy) The interactive mechanism $\mathcal{I}$ = (Server, Client) in Figure 2 has ϵ-differential privacy, if and only if*

$$\Pr[\mathcal{I}(D) \Rightarrow \theta^*] \leq \exp(\epsilon) \cdot \Pr[\mathcal{I}(D_*) \Rightarrow \theta^*]$$

for any output θ^*.

3.3 Securing data via encryption

We present our secure system for logistic regression under the model outlined in Figure 1. Overall, in the following, the workload of the parties characterized by dataset size N_{data} and dimension d ($\ll N_{\text{data}}$ presumably) is in Table 1.

Table 1: Costs in dataset size N_{data} and dimension d.

	Storage	Computation
Server	$O(N_{\text{data}}d^2)$	$O(N_{\text{data}}d^2)$
Client	N/A	$O(d^2)$
Data sources	N/A	$O(d^2)$

	Communication
Each data source → server	$O(d^2)$
Server → client	$O(d^2)$

Encryption at data sources. Each data source i computes real numbers $a_{1,r_1}^{(i)} = \left(2y^{(i)} - 1\right) x_{r_1}^{(i)} \in \mathbb{R}$ and $a_{2,r_1,r_2}^{(i)} = (-1)\left(x_{r_1}^{(i)} x_{r_2}^{(i)}\right) \in \mathbb{R}$ for all $0 \leq r_1, r_2 \leq d$. Counting distinctly, these are $d+1$ and $(d+1)(d+2)/2$ numbers respectively, so that the data source needs to prepare totally

$$n_d = \frac{(d+1)(d+4)}{2} \tag{9}$$

real numbers using its d-dimensional data. In later sections, for the convenience of indexing, we denote these n_d numbers from data source i as $dat^{(i)} = (dat_1^{(i)}, \ldots, dat_{n_d}^{(i)}) \in \mathbb{R}^{n_d}$.

Next, the data source encrypts the above $O(d^2)$ real numbers, using some additively homomorphic encryption scheme, to produce the ciphertext

$$CT^{(i)} = \mathbf{E}_{pk}\left(\{a_{1,r_1}^{(i)}\}_{0 \leq r_1 \leq d}, \{a_{2,r_1,r_2}^{(i)}\}_{0 \leq r_1, r_2 \leq d}\right)$$

or equivalently $CT^{(i)} = \mathbf{E}_{pk}(dat^{(i)})$, in which concrete instantiations of the encryption $\mathbf{E}_{pk}$ together with real number encodings will be described in later section.

Cloud server computation. The server receives and stores $CT^{(i)}$ for $1 \leq i \leq N_{\text{data}}$ from all data sources. It then computes the following ciphertext additions

$$CT = \sum_{i=1}^{N_{\text{data}}} CT^{(i)} \tag{10}$$

and sends CT to the client.

Client decryption. The client decrypts CT using its secret key. Due to the additive homomorphism of $\mathbf{E}_{pk}$, what the client obtains is $\sum_{i=1}^{N_{\text{data}}} dat^{(i)} \in \mathbb{R}^{n_d}$ or equivalently,

$$\sum_{i=1}^{N_{\text{data}}} a_{1,r_1}^{(i)} \in \mathbb{R}, \sum_{i=1}^{N_{\text{data}}} a_{2,r_1,r_2}^{(i)} \in \mathbb{R}$$

for all indexes $0 \leq r_1, r_2 \leq d$. These are exactly the coefficients given in (7) and (8) of the cost function at (6). Using the coefficients, the client then finds the minimizer $\theta^* = \text{argmin}_\theta J_{\text{approx}}(\theta)$.

CLAIM 1. *The above system is secure against the semi-honest server in Figure 1 (and Section 3.1).*

3.4 Adding differential privacy

Recall that, a noise $x \in \mathbb{R}$ has Lap(σ) distribution if its probability density function is $\frac{1}{2\sigma}\exp(-|x|/\sigma)$. To combine with [5] to obtain ϵ-differential privacy, the only change we need is the computation of the server given at (10). Namely, the server generates Laplace noises $e = (e_1, \ldots, e_{n_d}) \in \mathbb{R}^{n_d}$ in which all components are from the Lap(Λ_d/ϵ) distribution where $\Lambda_d = 2n_d = (d+1)(d+4)$, and does the following computation in the replacement of (10)

$$CT = \mathbf{E}_{pk}(e) + \sum_{i=1}^{N_{\text{data}}} CT^{(i)}. \tag{11}$$

CLAIM 2. *The system in Section 3 with the change at (11) satisfies ϵ-differential privacy (Definition 1).*

4. CONCLUSION

We show that secure logistic regression is efficiently possible at scale. This is a step towards helping to protect sensitive data while being able to integrate them for analysis and sharing.

5. REFERENCES

[1] Y. Aono, T. Hayashi, L. T. Phong, L. Wang. Scalable and Secure Logistic Regression via Homomorphic Encryption. *IACR Cryptology ePrint Archive*, 2016.

[2] J. W. Bos, K. E. Lauter, and M. Naehrig. Private predictive analysis on encrypted medical data. *Journal of Biomedical Informatics*, 50:234–243, 2014.

[3] M. Naehrig, K. E. Lauter, and V. Vaikuntanathan. Can homomorphic encryption be practical? *CCSW 2011*, pages 113–124. ACM, 2011.

[4] R. L. Rivest, L. Adleman, and M. L. Dertouzos. On data banks and privacy homomorphisms. *Foundations of secure computation*, 4(11):169–180, 1978.

[5] J. Zhang, Z. Zhang, X. Xiao, Y. Yang, and M. Winslett. Functional mechanism: Regression analysis under differential privacy. *PVLDB*, 5(11):1364–1375, 2012.

AspectDroid: Android App Analysis System

Aisha Ali-Gombe
aaligomb@uno.edu

Irfan Ahmed
irfan@cs.uno.edu

Golden G. Richard III
golden@cs.uno.edu

Vassil Roussev
vassil@cs.uno.edu

Dept. of Computer Science
University of New Orleans
New Orleans LA 70148

ABSTRACT

The growing threat to user privacy related to Android applications (apps) has tremendously increased the need for more reliable and accessible app analysis systems. This paper presents AspectDroid, an application-level system designed to investigate Android applications for possible unwanted activities. AspectDroid is comprised of app instrumentation, automated testing and containment systems. By using static bytecode instrumentation, AspectDroid weaves monitoring code into an existing application and provides data flow and sensitive API usage as well as dynamic instrumentation capabilities. The newly repackaged app is then executed either manually or via an automated testing module. Finally, the flexible containment provided by AspectDroid adds a layer of protection so that malicious activities can be prevented from affecting other devices. The accuracy score of AspectDroid when tested on 105 DroidBench corpus shows it can detect tagged data with 95.29%. We further tested our system on 100 real malware families from the Drebin dataset [1]. The result of our analysis showed AspectDroid incurs approximately 1MB average total memory size overhead and 5.9% average increase in CPU-usage.

CCS Concepts

•**Security and privacy → Malware and its mitigation;**
•**Software and its engineering →** *Dynamic analysis;*

Keywords

Android, Instrumentation, AspectJ, Dynamic Analysis

1. INTRODUCTION

Many Android applications are well-known for privacy violations and data leakage [2]. For instance, they may transfer personal data outside the devices of end-users without their consent. Andrubis [3] performed an analysis on over a million malicious and benign apps, and found that 38.79% of the apps have various forms data leakage. The security and privacy concerns surrounding these revelations increases the need for reliable and accessible app analysis systems.

In this paper, we present `AspectDroid`, a dynamic analysis system for Android applications based on the AspectJ instrumentation framework. AspectDroid performs static bytecode instrumentation at the application level, and does not require any particular support from the operating system or Dalvik virtual machine. It is a fully automated system that weaves in monitoring code at compile time, using a set of predefined security concerns such as data/resource usage and possible abuse, new code execution, and other non traditional behaviors like reflective calls and native code execution.

AspectDroid has an automated testing engine that provides a means of executing the instrumented application while stimulating random user and system events without human interaction. Since apps can be monitored using real life scenarios, both with regards to the platform on which the application is executed as well as events involving real data, AspectDroid allows definition of a containment policy such allowing sink calls or and blocking or manipulating sink data content.

We use two well-known datasets of Android apps for thoroughly evaluating the effectiveness and efficiency of AspectDroid. The first dataset contains 105 Android apps from the DroidBench project and is used to detect data leaks (by apps), and effectiveness of containment policies. The results show that AspectDroid can accurately detect data leaks with 95.29% F-score accuracy, and can effectively allow, block or manipulate data at sinks without crashing applications. The second dataset contains 100 malware families from the Drebin dataset and is used to detect four important aspects of an Android application: data exfiltration, use of reflection and dynamic class loading, use of native code and SMS abuse. The results of our analysis show that Device ID, Subscriber ID and Sim serial number are the most widely exfiltrated phone data; five malware families use reflection for malicious purposes such as invoking the methods of a background service to spoof user accounts and passwords; eight families have some level of SMS abuse, such as sending SMS to all contacts on the user's phone posing as the user; and nine families invoke native processes.

We also used the second dataset to measure the instru-

CODASPY'16 March 09-11, 2016, New Orleans, LA, USA

ACM ISBN 978-1-4503-3935-3/16/03.

DOI: http://dx.doi.org/10.1145/2857705.2857739

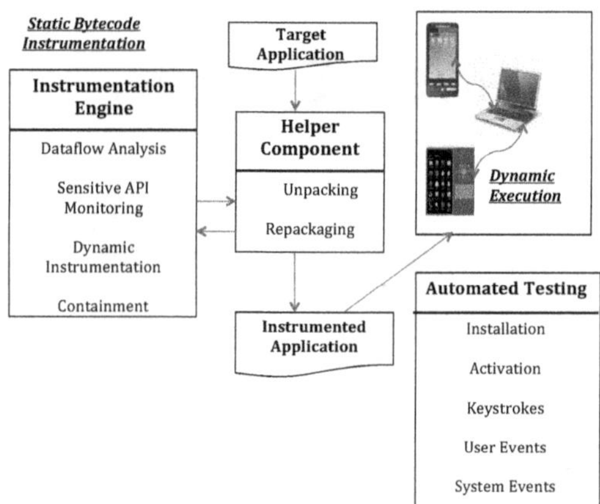

Figure 1: *AspectDroid* system architecture

mentation overhead on both static weaving and dynamic execution. The results show that AspectDroid has limited memory overhead of around 1MB, and a reasonable 5.9% CPU-Usage overhead.

2. SYSTEM DESIGN

AspectDroid is an Android app analysis system that consists of three modules: an *instrumentation engine*, an *automated tester*, and a *helper component* (see Figure 1).

The task of the *instrumentation engine* is to inject monitoring code into the target app statically based on some specific cross-cutting concerns. The injected code executes alongside the original code and performs custom logging and other analytical functions with the help of the *automated tester*. Finally, the *helper component* provides some utility/supporting functions needed before and after the instrumentation phase.

2.1 Instrumentation engine

The instrumentation engine (IE) forms the backbone of AspectDroid and is designed to address four objectives; *Dataflow analysis, Sensitive API monitoring Dynamic instrumentation Containment policy enforcement*

2.1.1 Dataflow analysis

AspectDroid performs application-level tainting of target data source(s). Our approach is built around the fact that standard Java and Android libraries use specific method naming conventions to express common types of operations. Thus, we utilize the consistent use of specific verbs, such as *read, open, write, put, connect,* and *execute*, to define broad signatures to capture actions such as file/stream/network access. More specific signatures, such as *getLongitude* are used to define narrower joinpoints. Based on all the signatures, we define pointcuts to select various *source, propagation and sink* joinpoints.

Taint sources represent the data of interest; in our case, we are interested in sources that are relevant to the privacy and security of the user and the data stored on the device. We define *vital* sources as phone-related data, component providers, file reads and user input APIs. Specialized pointcuts are created using signatures to intercept these API joinpoints. After execution, the return value is stored as a key in a *taint map* with a corresponding special tag for each unique source as the value

Taint sinks are defined as points where our application communicates with an external component, either within the device or the outside world. In our data flow analysis, we seek to monitor only those sinks that form a *possible* exfiltration point for the data sources defined above. The data sinks are broadly categorized as network, e.g., writing to a *Socket*, *URLConnection*, etc.; SMS sends; File writes (both ordinary files and shared preferences); and IPC. We use the same signature semantics to pick the sink joinpoints. We also leverage the *around advice* of such joinpoints to check if its arguments, or target, contain tainted data.

Taint Propagation. Knowing data sources and sinks alone cannot accurately determine data exfiltration; we also need to identify the data propagation process as represented by the sequence of variable assignments along the path from source to sink. The tainted data can be part of an object's field and the object can be manipulated in different ways. The following list illustrates our seven (7) point rules in picking a propagation's joinpoint:

1. Rule 1: Joinpoint that returns a low-level data type and contains a tainted argument.
2. Rule 2: Joinpoint that returns a low-level data type and contains a tainted target.
3. Rule 3: Joinpoints that convert a tainted array to other data types.
4. Rule 4: Joinpoints that create an array from other tainted data types.
5. Rule 5: Object Constructor joinpoint that contains a tainted argument.
6. Rule 6: All joinpoints with other object return type that contains tainted arguments.
7. Rule 7: All joinpoints with other object return type that contains tainted target.

In order to optimize the weaving process and reduce the complexity of the instrumentation, the propagation's joinpoints for every source are created on method calls that fall within the control flow path of the source call's enclosing method.

2.1.2 Sensitive API monitoring

Access to resources and sensitive data are requested through specialized API calls. Access to media, telephony (SMS and calls), reflection invocation and native code execution are important points of interest in performing in-depth analysis, therefore we define pointcuts that pick the joinpoints corresponding to such APIs. The advice at such joinpoints logs the corresponding target, arguments(s) and return value.

2.1.3 Dynamic instrumentation

AspectDroid implements *dynamic instrumentation*: at the joinpoint where `Dexclassloader` loads the new dex file, the weaved advice captures the absolute path to the file, sends it to the automated testing engine, and waits for notification to proceed. On receipt, the component will pull the referenced dex file with `adb` and instrument it as necessary. The resulting dex file is pushed back to its original directory and the normal program flow is resumed. This dynamic instrumentation feature considerably expands the coverage of the functionality of target applications.

2.1.4 Containment

AspectDroid targets the analysis of all kinds of applications, including malware. As such, we need a containment policy that will restrict malicious apps from going wild. Within the design of our instrumentation aspects, we built some flexible containment policies such that analyst can choose if sink calls are to be executed, blocked or manipulated. *Execution* containment policy allows the sink to proceed with its original target object and parameters. *Blocked* policy completely stops the joinpoint from executing by returning `null` to its around advice. This policy means if the program is on the verge of sending data over the network, that call will be skipped and program execution will continue. *Manipulated* policy modifies the parameters associated with the sink joinpoint if it contains tainted data. For example, if a `sendMessage` joinpoint is sending out location information, the data will be replaced with some random string, and the joinpoint will be allowed to continue.

2.2 Helper component

The helper component contains modules that automate key utility actions and ease the flow of *AspectDroid*. In particular, it implements unpacking, re-packaging and application signing.

2.3 Automated testing

For bulk testing, these events are designed to mirror real-life events on a regular Android device:

1. Installation of the repackaged app on a device/emulator.
2. Activation of the main activity as specified in the manifest.
3. Random keystrokes that simulate user touch and gesture on the app using *monkey*.
4. User input is simulated within the instrumentation framework using *EditText* user input types.
5. Incoming and outgoing SMS and calls are generated using *uiautomator*.
6. GPS coordinates are simulated and triggered on the emulator via telnet.
7. Device settings related to the network (wifi and cellular network), Bluetooth, and location access are set on and off on the emulator.
8. Information obtained from various joinpoints is logged in trace files.

3. TESTING AND EVALUATION

The objectives of the evaluation were to quantify the system's accuracy, ability to thwart malicious actions, and execution overhead. We tested the accuracy of our data flow algorithm and our containment policies on 105 applications from the DroidBench corpus. Our results indicate *AspectDroid* can detect data leak with F-score accuracy of 95.29%.

Table 1: Malware Analysis Result

	Malicious Apps
Data Exfiltration	*AckPosts, Aks, Ancsa, jSmsHider, Saiva, Vidro, Gonca, RootSmart, RATC, JSExploit-DynSrc, Xsider, Ssmsp, Mobsquz,FakeTimer, DroidKungFu, Spy.GoneSixty, Kmin, GGTrack, MobileTx Dougalek, FakeDoc, Loozfon, Placms*
Telephony Abuse	*MobileTx, Iconosys, UpdtKiller Pirater, Mania, FakeInstaller FakePlayer, Foncy*
Reflection and Dynamic Class Loading	*Mobsquz, FakeDoc FaceNiff, BaseBridge DroidDream*
Native Code	*Ancsa, Qicsom, RATC DroidKungFu, Xsider DroidSheep, Gmuse FakeDoc, FaceNiff*

Using 100 real malware families from the Drebin dataset, *AspectDroid* examines them for data exfiltration, reflective invocation and dynamic class loading, SMS abuse and native code as shown in Table 1. Finally, the dynamic execution overhead for *AspectDroid* has an average of 1MB memory overhead and 5.9% CPU usage overhead.

4. CONCLUSION AND FUTURE WORK

In this paper we've discussed *AspectDroid*, our hybrid system for Android application analysis, which provides a comprehensive, efficient and flexible alternative for analysis of Android applications to detect illicit activity. We have shown that *AspectDroid* can detect data leaks with acceptable accuracy while keeping its resource overhead minimal. As part of our future work, we intend to improve *AspectDroid*'s manipulation containment policy as well as provide a more generic automated testing module.

Acknowledgment

This work was partially funded by the NSF grant, CNS #1409534.

5. REFERENCES

[1] Arp, D., Spreitzenbarth, M., Hübner, M., Gascon, H., Rieck, K., and Siemens, C. Drebin: Effective and explainable detection of android malware in your pocket. In *Proceedings of the Annual Symposium on Network and Distributed System Security (NDSS)* (2014).

[2] Gibler, C., Crussell, J., Erickson, J., and Chen, H. Androidleaks: Automatically detecting potential privacy leaks in android applications on a large scale. In *Trust and Trustworthy Computing*, vol. 7344 of *Lecture Notes in Computer Science*. 2012, pp. 291–307.

[3] Weichselbaum, L., Neugschwandtner, M., Lindorfer, M., Fratantonio, Y., van der Veen, V., and Platzer, C. Andrubis: Android malware under the magnifying glass. *Vienna University of Technology, Tech. Rep. TRISECLAB-0414-001* (2014).

On Energy Security of Smartphones

Xing Gao[1,2], Dachuan Liu[1,2], Daiping Liu[1], Haining Wang[1]
[1]University of Delaware, Newark, DE, USA
[2]College of William and Mary, Williamsburg, VA, USA
{xgao, dachuan, dpliu, hnw}@udel.edu

ABSTRACT

The availability of smartphones is still severely restricted by the limited battery lifetime. To help users understand the energy consumption, major mobile platforms support fine-grained energy profiling for each app. In this paper, we present a new threat, called energy collateral attacks, which can abuse and mislead all existing energy modeling approaches. In particular, energy collateral attacks are able to divulge battery stealthily through interprocess communication, wakelock, and screen. To defend against those attacks, we propose E-Android to accurately profile the energy consumption in a comprehensive manner. E-Android monitors energy collateral related events and maintains energy consumption for relevant apps. We utilize E-Android to measure the energy consumption under the attack of six energy malware and two normal scenarios. While Android fails to disclose all these energy-malware-based attacks, E-Android can accurately profile energy consumption and reveal the existence of energy malware.

1. INTRODUCTION

Smartphones have brought great convenience to our daily life. However, the limited battery still seriously impacts the availability of smartphones. Previous works center on profiling energy consumption of each app. They breakdown the power consumption of a smartphone by every component and build energy models. A well designed battery interface is further developed to visualize energy consumption to smartphone users. As a result, existing energy malware is not hard to detect under the combination of energy accounting and battery interface.

In this paper, we reveal that a set of mechanisms could be exploited to cause biased energy profiling and user confusion. Based on those mechanisms, we propose new energy attack techniques that can neatly sidestep current energy accounting, resulting in stealthy energy consumption in Android smartphones. We term them as energy collateral attacks.

Android apps rely on inter-process communication (IPC) for communication. Current energy accounting approaches overlook IPC in Android. Our first attack vector is IPC-based, in which energy malware can trigger other innocent apps to waste energy through the IPC mechanism.

The second attack vector is wakelock- and screen-based. Existing methods to model the energy consumption of screen fall into two categories. The first takes screen as an independent module. The second allocates screen energy to foreground app. Both mechanisms give malicious apps the possibility to deceive energy accounting. Energy malware could simply enhances the brightness or uses the screen wakelock to keep screen on. Besides screen, wakelock could also be acquired to keep CPU awake. Failing to release the wakelock can drain tremendous amount of extra energy. Thus, by interrupting other apps to release wakelock, malicious app can force the system running in a high power state.

To defend against energy collateral attacks, we design E-Android to reveal collateral energy consumption. E-Android consists of three major components: (1) an extension of Android framework, (2) an enhanced energy accounting module, and (3) a revised battery interface. E-Android collects apps' user IDs and the type of operations. E-Android also carefully monitors the activities of task stacks to accurately identify an energy collateral attack. The collateral energy consumption will be appropriately charged to the initiated source. E-Android is able to handle sophisticated situations such as collateral attack chains. We modify two battery interfaces to work jointly with E-Android.

We conduct a series of experiments to evaluate energy collateral attacks as well as the functionality of E-Android. We build six types of energy malware running in a Nexus 4 mobile phone. Our results indicate that all energy collateral attacks can successfully waste energy without being noticed. They also prove that E-Android is able to detect and expose all energy malware.

2. ENERGY COLLATERAL ATTACK

2.1 Potential Attack Vectors

IPC-based Attack Vector. We first look into a simple scenario. Bob uses the Message app to film a half minute video and send it to Alice. A small camera window is embedded in the Message UI. All operations seem to occur in the Message app. Thus, it is reasonable to expect that the Message should be accounted for the corresponding energy consumption. We illustrate the energy consumption measured by Android official app in Figure 1. The result, however, indicates that the Message only consumes a quite small

CODASPY'16, March 9–11, 2016, New Orleans, LA, USA.

ACM ISBN 978-1-4503-3935-3/16/03..
DOI: http://dx.doi.org/10.1145/2857705.2857738

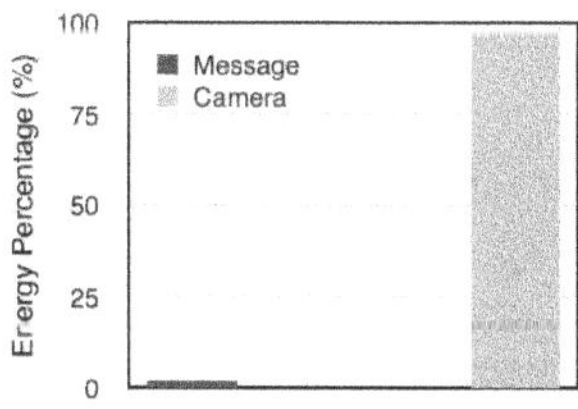

Figure 1: Energy consumption when filming in the Message.

portion of energy. The energy drained by video filming is assigned to the Camera.

The fact is that, when Bob clicks "Record Video" in the Message, the Message sends an *Intent* to request the Camera app. It is the Camera app that actually records the video. After the recording, the video is returned to the Message app. Interestingly, camera is reported as the most energy draining app [1]. However, we observe that energy consumption sometimes involves the communications between apps, and hence other apps should also be responsible for those indirect energy consumptions.

This scenario frequently occurs in Android since IPC serves as the only approach for the communication between apps. While the intent mechanism plays a critical role in Android, existing energy accounting modules overlook such factors.

Wakelock- & Screen-based Attack Vector. Android turns a device into deep sleep after some idle time to save energy. To override the aggressive power saving policy, Android introduces the wakelock, which is a special power management module to keep devices awake.

A wakelock must be released once acquired. Otherwise, battery will be drained up to 25% per hour [2]. Android does not release wakelock until the process has been killed. Pathak et al. [2] observed that a lot of developers fail to understand how to properly use wakelock. One improper usage is that, an app only releases wakelock when the process is destroyed. Normally, the app would be destroyed when the user quits the app, without causing any problem. However, a foreground activity could be easily interrupted by popup activities and then fails to properly release wakelock.

Mis-releasing wakelock also challenges the screen modeling policy. A wakelock could be acquired by a service. If the consumed energy is only allocated to the foreground app rather than the initiator, the energy modeling would confuse users on the internal energy consumptions.

2.2 Energy Malware

We define energy collateral attack as the misconducts that drain energy by exploiting specific attack vectors without being exposed via the battery interface. We assume that malware has been installed on the device with some necessary permissions. Also, several victims have been installed.

Attack #1. *Energy malware hijacks components belonging to other apps.* Existing energy modeling does not consider IPC communication. This mechanism enables malware to drain the target device's energy through a combination of legal operations, and hence bypass the energy monitoring.

Attack #2. *When malware is launched by user, malware open other apps concurrently and make them run in background.* It has been long reported that a background app definitely drains battery. Thus, triggering background apps is a very effective way to drain battery.

Attack #3. *Bind to services without unbinding.* Malware could further launch attacks on background services, where heavy computational workload normally runs as recommended by Android. A started service will not be terminated even the started component is destroyed and must be stopped by `stopService()` or `stopSelf()` to avoid running indefinitely. Similarly, a bound service must be unbound. Thus, an exported service bound by malware will keep alive infinitely and drain battery even after the victim attempts to stop service.

Attack #4. *Interrupt attacked apps to background.* Malware could also forcibly switch the victim to background through normal operations such as opening the launcher. Sophisticated malware could utilize other techniques to interrupt the foreground app without being noticed by users. For example, attackers can switch the app to background when the user attempts to quit the app.

The misinterpretation of wakelock could make the energy attack even more serious. Since the app enters background instead of being killed, it might fail to release wakelock. Since the wakelock is un-released by the victim, energy accounting will tax the energy into the victim, without disclosing malware behind curtain.

Attack #5. *Drain energy through changing screen configuration.* For both screen accounting policy, malware could easily bypass the battery interface. The brightness acts as the determining factor for screen energy consumption. Malware could change the brightness. Many apps enhance the brightness when they are running in foreground. Therefore, users probably would not perceive the malicious adjustment of brightness by malware. In particular, to avoid being noticed, malware could secretly escalate the brightness with a few levels. Such a slight enhancement might not affect users, but cut the battery lifetime. Advanced energy malware could camouflage as Android auto screen settings, by setting a higher value after obtaining current auto set brightness.

Attack #6. *Acquire screen wakelock without releasing.* Wakelock could also be utilized to conduct screen energy attack. Malware could easily keep screen on by intentionally acquiring but not releasing wakelock. The wakelock could even be acquired by service. The consumed part of screen energy will be allocated to the foreground app or Android launcher, rather than malware.

Multi- & Hybrid Attack. Sophisticated malware could combine the above attacks together for more effective attacks. Attackers could also conduct multiple attacks on the same attacked app. Also malware could conduct an attack on one victim, which unintentionally involves another, leading energy attack chains.

Attack Scenarios. Energy collateral attacks could be abused to launch denial of service attacks. Malware could reduce the battery's lifetime and degrade a user's experience. Furthermore, energy collateral attacks could mislead a user's attention to an innocent app and cause unfair competition.

Unlike traditional attacks targeting at leaking personal private information or controlling system resources, energy attacks aim to significantly reduce the battery's lifetime, as the battery is the most scarce resource of a mobile device. Also, energy attacks could be conducted accompanying with traditional attacks.

3. DEFENSE

We introduce E-Android to assist the battery interface to reveal collateral energy consumption. E-Android is com-

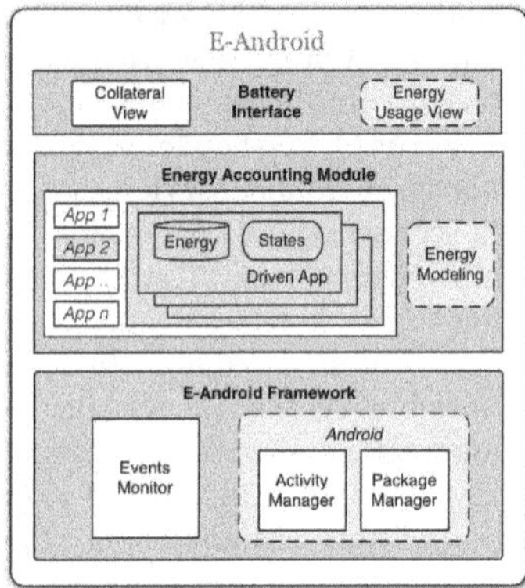

Figure 2: E-Android Architecture

posed of three major components: an extension of Android to log all potential energy operations, an enhanced energy accounting module to calculate energy consumption considering the collateral effects, and a revised battery interface to inform users of all related information.

We demonstrate the architecture of E-Android in Figure 2. Basically, E-Android monitors a series of events that potentially lead to energy collateral attack, e.g., starting an activity, changing screen settings. Each time an event is triggered, E-Android checks the user ID of both apps. If different, E-Android records the user ID of both apps as well as the type of the operation and notifies energy accounting module. The module then updates the relevant energy data.

The battery interface itemizes apps that consume a lot of energy. E-Android ranks apps by total energy consumptions with collateral energy combined. Moreover, for each app, E-Android provides a detailed inventory specifying contribution of all attack related apps. The breakdown assists users in better understanding the energy consumption.

We modified the framework of Android 5.0.1 to implement E-Android. We included the collateral attack modeling features to both Android official battery interface and powerTutor [3].

4. EXPERIMENTS

We demonstrated that energy collateral attacks could sidestep Android and deplete battery. To verify the functionality of E-Android, we compared the results of E-Android with those of Android.

We first conducted experiments simulating reality cases. We opened the Message app 30 seconds and then used it to take a 30s short video. Such case is similar to the malware attack #1. A more complicated scenario, which is similar to hybrid attack, is that we use the Contacts to open the Message, then films a 30s video.

Figures 3a and 3b illustrates the results for both reality cases. The '+' stands for the results of E-Android. In the original energy modeling, the Camera app expends much more energy than the Message app, regardless of the fact that the Camera is opened by the Message. In E-Android, the Message is also charged for the portion of energy consumed by the Camera.

We also implemented six types of energy malware as we mentioned before. Each experiment lasts 60 seconds. In the first two cases, malware either directly or simultaneously opens other activities. The results are similar. For malware

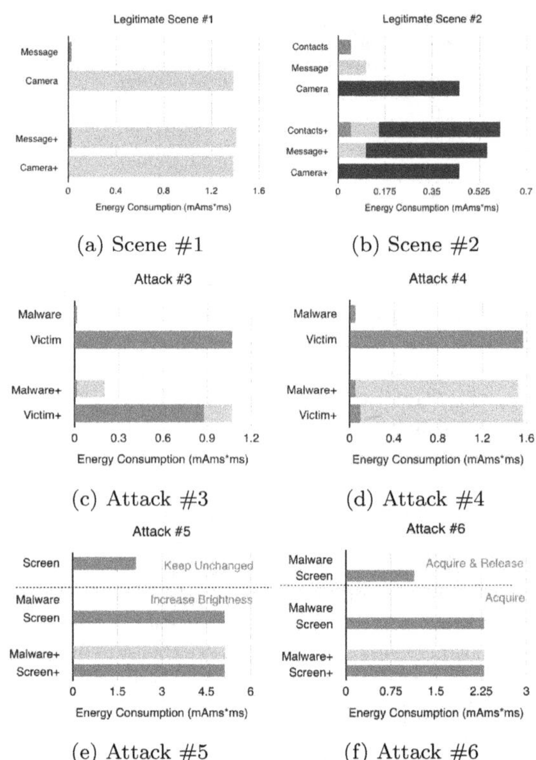

(a) Scene #1 (b) Scene #2

(c) Attack #3 (d) Attack #4

(e) Attack #5 (f) Attack #6

Figure 3: Functionality results

#3, our malware binds the victim's service once it detects the service is started. The connection bound by malware forces the service to run continuously after the attacked app stops the service. The malware #4 detects the quit dialog of the victim based on the shared virtual memory size of SurfaceLinger. It sends a transparent page to cover the dialog and start homepage once "OK" is clicked. In attack #5, we first measured regular screen energy consumption. Then, we measured the energy consumption after malware enhances brightness. While Android turns screen off after 30s, we measured the energy consumed by screen for 60 seconds under the conditions that malware #6 releases/not releases the wakelock.

The value is directly read from the Android battery interface. We displayed the results of attack #3 and attack #4 in Figures 3c and 3d, as well as the results of attack #5 and attack #6 in Figures 3e and 3f. As the figures show, all those attacks could successfully bypass the supervision of the battery interface. However, E-Android can detect all these attacks.

5. REFERENCES

[1] Top 10 android battery-sucking vampire apps. http://betanews.com/2014/02/27/top-10-android-battery-sucking-vampire-apps/.

[2] A. Pathak, A. Jindal, Y. C. Hu, and S. P. Midkiff. What is keeping my phone awake?: characterizing and detecting no-sleep energy bugs in smartphone apps. In *ACM MobiSys*, 2012.

[3] L. Zhang, B. Tiwana, Z. Qian, Z. Wang, R. P. Dick, Z. M. Mao, and L. Yang. Accurate online power estimation and automatic battery behavior based power model generation for smartphones. In *CODES+ISSS*, 2010.

DIVERSITY

John Knight
University of Virginia
Charlottesville, Virginia, USA

Abstract

Diversity works well in nature where it is the basis of natural selection, a phenomenon that helps biological populations survive as they are challenged by hazards in their environments. Diversity also has a long history in engineering where it is used to counter the effects of design faults. Engineered systems are subject to failure, and significant losses can result from the failure of safety- and security-critical applications. A system that includes identical replicates of one or more components can survive *degradation* faults, i.e., faults that arise during operation as components age. But identical replicates do not help a system to survive *design* faults, i.e., faults that are the result of defects in the basic design. Identical replicates will contain the same defect and so will fail together on the same inputs. All software faults are design faults, because software faults are not the result of software "wearing out" over time. Defects that arise in requirements, specification and coding of software are all design faults.

A variety of different types of diversity have been developed to deal with design faults. Design diversity couples together systems with identical functionality but with different designs. The different systems are referred to as *versions*, and the versions are executed in parallel with the results subject to a vote. If erroneous outputs are produced because of design defects in some of the versions, the correct outputs will be produced provided the erroneous outputs are in a minority. There is no guarantee that the different designs will not contain the same faults, and so voting could select an erroneous output. Data diversity couples together identical *copies* of a given system but executes them in parallel with transformed data. The inverse transformation is applied to the outputs. Artificial diversity applies an algorithmic transformation, such as relocating the address space by a random amount, to a system thereby producing *variants* that differ in a systematic way. Artificial diversity is an effective method of avoiding the "software monoculture".

All forms of diversity have been applied successfully in the field of cyber security. Artificial diversity is especially important because: (a) when applied carefully it transforms information useful to an attacker, such as the fixed and known locations of variables, into a high-entropy search problem, (b) it incurs little to no execution-time overhead, and (c) it is applied mechanically – no development effort is required. Artificial diversity has been shown to provide strong security protection to systems that contain certain classes of vulnerability whether the problem vulnerabilities are known or unknown.

A unique characteristic of artificial diversity is that artificially diverse variants can be constructed and combined into an operational system with a property known as secretless security. For certain classes of vulnerability, such a system is provably protected against attacks and no secrets need to be kept.

CCS Concepts

• Security and privacy→ Systems security; Software and application security; Software security engineering

Keywords

Design diversity; data diversity; artificial diversity; secretless security; software security

CODASPY'16, March 9–11, 2016, New Orleans, LA, USA.
ACM ISBN: 978-1-4503-3935-3/16/03.
DOI: http://dx.doi.org/10.1145/2857705.2857728

SMASheD: Sniffing and Manipulating Android Sensor Data

Manar Mohamed
University of Alabama at Birmingham
1300 University Boulevard
Birmingham, Alabama
manar@uab.edu

Babins Shrestha
University of Alabama at Birmingham
1300 University Boulevard
Birmingham, Alabama
babins@uab.edu

Nitesh Saxena
University of Alabama at Birmingham
1300 University Boulevard
Birmingham, Alabama
saxena@uab.edu

ABSTRACT

The current Android sensor security model either allows only restrictive *read access* to sensitive sensors (e.g., an app can only read its *own* touch data) or requires special install-time permissions (e.g., to read microphone, camera or GPS). Moreover, Android does not allow *write access* to *any* of the sensors. Sensing-based security applications therefore crucially rely upon the sanity of the Android sensor security model.

In this paper, we show that such a model can be effectively circumvented. Specifically, we build *SMASheD*, a legitimate framework under the current Android ecosystem that can be used to *stealthily* sniff as well as manipulate many of the Android's restricted sensors (*even touch input*). *SMASheD* exploits the Android Debug Bridge (ADB) functionality and enables a malicious app with only the INTERNET permission to read, and write to, multiple different sensor data files at will. *SMASheD* is the first framework, to our knowledge, that can sniff and manipulate protected sensors on unrooted Android devices, without user awareness, without constant device-PC connection and without the need to infect the PC.

The primary contributions of this work are two-fold. *First*, we design and develop the *SMASheD* framework. *Second*, as an offensive implication of the *SMASheD* framework, we introduce a wide array of potentially devastating attacks. Our attacks against the touchsensor range from accurately logging the touchscreen input (*TouchLogger*) to injecting touch events for accessing restricted sensors and resources, installing and granting special permissions to other malicious apps, accessing user accounts, and authenticating on behalf of the user — essentially almost doing whatever the device user can do (secretively). Our attacks against various physical sensors (motion, position and environmental) can subvert the functionality provided by numerous existing sensing-based security applications, including those used for *(continuous) authentication*, and *authorization*.

1. INTRODUCTION

Sensing-enabled computing is rapidly becoming ubiquitous. With mobile device manufacturers embedding multiple, low-cost hardware sensors onto the devices and mobile OS providers adding full software support for developing applications using these sensors, there is a transformational growth in the adoption of mobile devices.

The most common categories of sensors available on the current breed of mobile devices, smartphones, smartwatches and smartglasses, include: (1) *user input sensor* (touchscreen and hardware buttons), (2) *audio-visual sensors* (microphone and camera), (3) *navigational sensors* (e.g., GPS), (4) *motion sensors* (e.g., accelerometer and gyroscope), (5) *position sensors* (e.g., magnetometer and proximity), and (6) *environmental sensors* (e.g., pressure, and temperature). Mobile device sensors are a cornerstone of a wide range of security and privacy applications, including those geared for authentication and authorization (e.g., [6, 7, 15, 20]).

Since mobile sensors provide potentially sensitive information about the host device, the device's user or the device's surroundings, protecting sensor data from abuse by malicious applications becomes paramount. Consequently, most mobile platforms have established a sensor security access control model. Specifically, Android, one of the most popular mobile OSs and the subject of this paper, follows a model where *read access* to many sensitive sensors is very restrictive (e.g., an app can only read its *own* touch data) or requires special install-time permissions granted by the user (e.g., to access microphone, camera or GPS). The read access to most other sensors, including motion, position and environmental sensors, is not restricted within this model because Android may not consider these sensors as explicitly sensitive. Moreover, Android security model does not allow *write access* to *any* of the sensors. Clearly, the sensing-based applications therefore crucially rely upon the sanity of the Android sensor security model.

In this paper, we demonstrate that the current Android sensor security model can be effectively circumvented to a large extent. Specifically, we build *SMASheD*, a legitimate systems framework under the current Android ecosystem that can be used to *stealthily* sniff (read) as well as manipulate (write to) many of the Android's restricted sensors. To be precise, *SMASheD* can be used to: (1) directly sniff the touchsensor, (2) directly manipulate the touch, motion, position and environmental sensors, and (3) indirectly, using the touch inject capability, sniff the audio-visual and navigational sensors. *SMASheD does not* require the device to be rooted.

SMASheD exploits the Android Debug Bridge (ADB) functionality and enables a malicious app with only the INTERNET permission to read from, and write to, multiple sensor data files at will. ADB is a functionality designed to allow Android app developers with extended permissions to systems resources that are otherwise protected by the Android sensor security model. This workaround is legitimate and has been used by many apps in Google Play Store such as screenshot apps [9], sync and backup apps [3], and touch record/replay apps [22]. All of these apps ask the user to connect her device to a PC via USB, launch ADB and run a native service

CODASPY'16, March 09-11, 2016, New Orleans, LA, USA

DOI: http://dx.doi.org/10.1145/2857705.2857749

with ADB privilege. The app then communicates with this service to obtain access to the resources which Android deems as protected.

As part of *SMASheD*, we develop a service that provides read and write sensor events functionality. This functionality can be hidden inside any service that requires the ADB workaround, e.g., a screenshot service. When installing an app, the user is usually made aware of the permissions that she is granting to the app. However, while installing and executing the service through ADB, the user is completely oblivious as to what permissions the service might have. Also, *SMASheD* can be published for debugging or any other benign purposes but can contain malicious code that will utilize the functionality provided by the service for malicious purposes. Moreover, such services can be exploited by malicious apps in a similar way as presented in [11]. Our *SMASheD* platform encompasses a native service and an Android app.

Our Contributions: In this paper, we expose the vulnerability underlying the ADB workaround allowing us to read from and write to many Android sensors currently protected by the Android access control model. Equipped with this powerful capability, we then go on to present the offensive implications in many security contexts. The research contributions of our work are outlined below:

1. **A Framework to Sniff & Manipulate Android Sensors** (Section 3): We design and develop the *SMASheD* framework to sniff and manipulate many restricted Android sensors.
2. **Powerful Adversarial Applications** (Section 4): As a significant offensive implication of the *SMASheD* framework, we introduce a broad array of potentially devastating attacks. Our attacks include the following:
   (a) Logging the touchscreen input, leading to the first full-fledged, highly accurate *TouchLogger*.
   (b) Injecting touch events for accessing restricted sensors and resources (e.g., microphone, camera or GPS), installing and granting special permissions to other malicious apps (translating into many known malware schemes, such as [17, 23, 24], without the need for the user to grant special permissions), accessing user accounts and authenticating on behalf of the user – essentially *almost doing whatever the device user can do* (secretively).
   (c) Manipulating various physical sensors (motion, position and environmental) in order to subvert the functionality provided by many sensing-based security applications, including those used for *(continuous) authentication* (e.g., [6, 7]), and *authorization* (e.g., [10, 20]).

2. BACKGROUND: ANDROID SENSOR SECURITY MODEL

Android's core security principle is to protect user data, system resources and apps from malicious apps. Android utilizes the Linux approach of process isolation to enforce the isolation of apps and operating systems components. This isolation is achieved by assigning each app a unique User Identifier (UID) and Group Identifier (GID) at the app installation time. Therefore, each app is enforced to run in a separate Linux process, called *Application Sandbox*, and the Linux process isolation ensures that an app cannot interfere with other apps or access system resources unless permissions are explicitly granted. In order to allow apps to communicate with each other and access system resources, Android provides a secure Inter-Process Communication (IPC) protocol.

Discretionary Access Control (DAC) is the typical access control employed in Linux. In DAC, the owner/creator of the data sets the access permissions of the data to three types of users: the owner, the users in the same group and all other users. When an app is installed, Android creates a home directory for the app (i.e., /data/data/app-name) and allows only the owner to read from and write to this directory. The apps signed with the same certificate are able to share the data among each other.

File system permissions are also used to restrict the access of system functionality. For example, /dev/cam permission is set to allow only the owner and the users in the camera group to read and write to the camera sensor as shown in Listing 1. When an app requests the CAMERA permission, and if the permission is granted, the app is assigned the camera Linux GID, which would allow it to access /dev/cam. The mapping between the Linux groups and permission labels are set in platform.xml, and ueventd.rc is responsible for setting the owners and groups for various system files.

Some Android resources do not require any permission. In particular, reading motion, position and environmental sensors is globally permitted. Most of the other resources require read-write permissions, and these permissions have four levels:

1. *Normal*: The app needs to request the access, however, the system grants the permission automatically without notifying the user (e.g., vibrate).
2. *Dangerous (protection level 1)*: The system grants the permission to the app only if the user approves granting this permission (e.g., accessing camera, microphone, or GPS).
3. *Signature (protection level 2)*: The system grants the permission to the app only if the requesting app is signed with the same certificate as the app that declared the permission, without notifying the user (e.g., allowing two apps signed by the same developer to access each other components, inject event).
4. *SignatureOrSystem (protection level 3)*: The system grants the permission only to the apps that are in the Android system image or that are signed with the same certificate as the app that declared the permission (e.g., system reboot).

In any Linux system, an executable runs with same permission as the process that has started it. ADB shell is already assigned to several groups (graphics, input, log, adb, sdcard_rw, etc). Therefore, any executable that starts through the ADB shell is granted the same level of access to the resources which belong to any of these groups. As shown in Listing 1, since the directory "/dev/input/*" which contains the sensor files, belongs to "input" group, and the ADB shell has read-write access to all the resources associated with "input" group, any executable that is initiated by ADB shell can read from and write to the "/dev/input/*" resources. This is the key idea upon which our *SMASheD* framework is based, allowing us to sniff and manipulate many of the Android's sensors.

Listing 1: ueventd.rc file

```
...
/dev/input/*    0660    root    input
/dev/eac        0660    root    audio
/dev/cam        0660    root    camera
...
```

3. SMASHED DESIGN, IMPLEMENTATION AND THREAT MODEL

In this section, we explain the design, implementation and threat model of our proposed *SMASheD* framework.

3.1 Design Overview

As mentioned in Section 2, the current Android security model considers many resources as sensitive and thus limits the access of these resources only to the apps that are signed by the system (protection level 3 for the permissions declared by the system and protection level 4). These protected resources include: injecting user events into any window (INJECT_EVENTS), taking screen shots (READ_FRAME_BUFFER), and reading system log files (READ_LOGS). However, Android allows access to these resources through the ADB shell for development purposes, by assigning the ADB shell to the groups that can access these resources. For example, the ADB shell is assigned to the input group which allows any process with the ADB shell privilege to read from and write to any of the files in the /dev/input/ directory. This directory contains the files associated with user input, motion, position and environmental sensors.

Moreover, Android's current directory structure has the /data/local/tmp/ directory which is assigned to shell user and shell group, and gives read, write and execute permission to the shell user and any user in the shell group. This folder allows the user to run executable files on their Android devices through ADB shell.

Many developers have exploited these capabilities given to the ADB shell to grant permissions to their apps that are not otherwise allowed. This ADB workaround is performed by developing a native service, pushing it into the /data/local/tmp/ directory and running the service through the ADB shell. This way the native service grants all the permissions that are granted to the shell. Finally, to allow other apps to communicate with the service, both the app and the service open sockets and communicate through it. This approach has been utilized by many apps that are already published in Google Play Store such as apps that allow the users to take screenshots programmatically [9], sync and backup [3], USB tethering [2], and touch record/replay [22].

The above design allows any app with only the INTERNET permission to communicate with the service. Hence, the app with only the INTERNET permission will obtain access to the resources that the service provides *without the user's knowledge*. This vulnerability has been explored in [11], focusing mainly on screenshot apps published in Google Play Store. The authors developed an app, Screenmilker, which communicates with the native services of many screenshots apps. They showed that Screenmilker is able to collect user's sensitive data, such as user's credentials on many banking apps by sending requests to the screenshot's native service to take screenshots while the user is inputting her credentials. (A detailed comparison of our *SMASheD* framework with related prior work is later provided in Section 6).

In this paper, we are exploring and extending this vulnerability further, and with potentially much broader consequences. We focus on INJECT_EVENTS permission. There are already some apps in Google Play Store, such as *FRep* – Finger Replayer [22], which allow users to record their touch interactions with their devices and replay them later. *FRep* has already been installed by 100,000 to 500,000 users. These apps also utilize the ADB workaround, similar to the screenshot apps, in order to gain access to the read and inject touchscreen data. Also, as the communication between the touch repeater app and its native service is done through a socket, the native service becomes accessible to any app installed on the phone with only the INTERNET permission. Therefore, if the user installs any malicious apps with the INTERNET permission, these apps can also communicate with the service and read/inject touch events maliciously.

We implement the *SMASheD* framework which encompasses three components: *SMASheD* server: a native service that provides the sensor data reading and injection capabilities, scripts: two simple scripts used to copy the *SMASheD* server to the device and to start the server, and *SMASheD* app: an app that runs a status detection module in the background, and depending on the phone's status and the desired functionality, it sends requests to the *SMASheD* server to read or inject sensor events. Figure 1 depicts the overall *SMASheD* architecture.

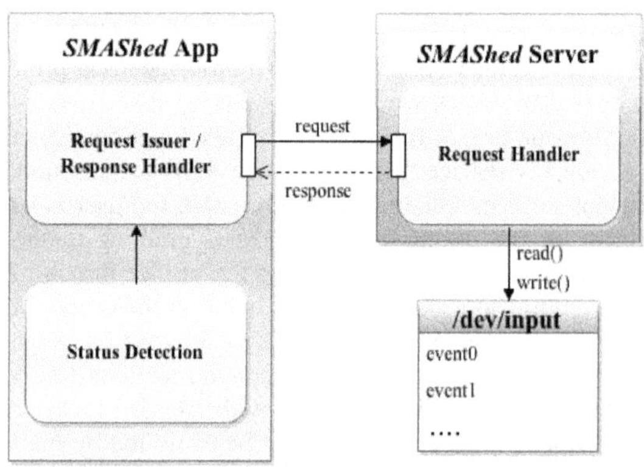

Figure 1: The architecture of *SMASheD*

3.2 SMASheD Server

Our system works with the sensors whose events are made available to apps through low-level event interface and have files under the directory /dev/input/, and not through system services (e.g., camera, microphone, and GPS). This includes user input, motion, position and environmental sensors. For each of these sensors, a corresponding file named event$x$ exists in the directory /dev/input/. Android allows reading and injecting sensor events through ADB commands $getevent$ and $sendevent$, respectively.

Each hardware event generates multiple input events. Each input event encompasses $time$, $type$, $code$ and $value$.

- $time$ represents the time at which the event occurred.
- $value$ represents the value of the event.
- $code$ is the event code and it precisely defines the type of the event. For example, REL_X, REL_Y, REL_Z represent relative changes in X, Y and Z axes, respectively.
- $type$ is the event type, which groups the event's codes under a logical input construct. Each event type has a set of applicable event codes. For example, EV_ABS represents the absolute axis value changes, EV_REL represents the relative axis value changes. A special event type, EV_SYN, is used to separate input events into packets of input data changes occurring at the same moment in time.

For a complete list of the applicable events' types and codes, we refer the reader to linux/input.h[1].

As an example, a simple touchscreen press-release event generates around 19 input events. Listing 2 in Appendix A displays a sample output of executing $getevent$ command, pressing on the screen at point (946,1543), and then releasing the touch. BTN_TOUCH DOWN and BTN_TOUCH UP indicate the beginning and the end of the touch, ABS_MT_POSITION_X and ABS_MT_POSITION_Y represent the touch's x and y positions.

We implemented a native service designed in C with code similar to Android's $getevent$ and $sendevent$ for reading and injecting the sensor events. First, the service scans /dev/input/ directory to find out what sensors are available in the device. Although the file names in the directory are event0, event1, etc, we use *EVIOCGVERSION ioctl* function to retrieve the name of the sensor that corresponds to each file. To read from and write to the sensors' files, we use *read()* and *write()* functions.

[1]https://github.com/torvalds/linux/blob/master/include/uapi/linux/input.h

To allow other apps to communicate with the service, the service creates a socket. The socket keeps on listening to the incoming requests. In the current implementation, the service accepts three kinds of requests: *read*, *stop* and *inject*.

- *read*: The service reads the input events from all the sensors. We can limit the read to a subset of sensors to improve the efficiency. The service continues reading until it receives a *stop* request.
- *stop*: The service stops reading the sensor events. Then, it either writes the events to a file, and sends the file name as a response to the request or sends all the read input events.
- *inject*: Inject needs to have a file name or a list of sensors events as an argument. The service injects the sensors events in the incoming list or in the file to their corresponding sensors files.

3.3 Scripts

We wrote two shell scripts to start the service. The first shell script is responsible for pushing the native service and the second script to /data/local/tmp/ folder on the device, and for starting the second script. The second script starts running the service. In this way, the service will run with the same privileges as the shell user. The service will then keep running until the phone is switched off or it gets killed by the user.

3.4 SMASheD App

We implemented an Android app, which only requires the INTERNET permission. The app connects to the *SMASheD* server through socket and sends requests to *read* and *inject* events. For example, it may send *read* touch events when a banking app is open to retrieve the password input by the user.

In order to determine whether a specific app that the attacker might be interested in is running, our app has a service that starts when the app is launched and keeps running in the background. The service runs *ps* command periodically, every 100 ms, until the app that the attacker is interested in is launched (status detector shown in Figure 1). Once the app under attack is running and on the foreground, *SMASheD* app connects to the *SMASheD* server through socket and sends *read* request with the list of sensors (e.g., touchscreen data only, all sensors, etc). Once the user exits the app or moves out of the app, *SMASheD* app sends *stop* request to the *SMASheD* server. In case the purpose of reading is to replay the sensor events later in the same device, to reduce the communication between the *SMASheD* server and app, the *SMASheD* server stores the read events in a file and only sends the file name to the *SMASheD* app. Otherwise, the *SMASheD* server sends all the sensor events.

Also, the *SMASheD* app can send *inject* request along with a list of sensor events to inject or a file name previously acquired from the service, whenever it wants to inject sensor events.

3.5 Threat Model

Our threat model is highly realistic, facilitated under three scenarios:

1. **Already Installed Benign ADB Services**: Apps that read and inject touch events (e.g., FRep [22]) are already available in Google Play Store and installed by many users. Given such an already installed benign app, our attacks that read/inject touch events work under the exact same threat model as [11] by using a malicious app that communicates with the service associated with the already installed app.
2. **Future Benign ADB Services**: Benign developers can publish an app/service that reads/injects sensors events for providing some benign functionality (e.g., debugging or testing). Once such an app is installed, attacker will launch our attacks similar to [11].
3. **Malicious ADB Services**: The attacker can create a benign-looking (malicious) screenshot app, adding read/inject sensor events functionality to its service. The attacker just needs to fool users into installing this app. Note that when user installs a service using ADB, he/she is not notified about the resources the service is accessing. Therefore, the user will not be able to differentiate between services that only take screenshots from services with added malicious functionality. Moreover, if the attacker can gain physical access to an unlocked Android device, the attacker can quickly install the malicious service on the device (e.g., in a lunch-time attack) [16].

The first and second threat model scenarios exploit the vulnerability of the services that expose their ADB functionalities to all the apps installed on the same device with INTERNET permission (same as [11]). The last scenario exploits Android's vulnerability of granting all the shell privileges to any service installed via ADB *without notifying the user.*

SMASheD works on unrooted devices, and does not require an infected PC (unlike [8]) or a constant connection between the device and a PC (e.g., unlike monkeyrunner [2]).

4. ATTACKS USING SMASHED

In this section, we present various attacks that can be performed based on the sensor data reading-writing capability provided by *SMASheD*. The entire spectrum of attacks that *SMASheD* can enable, especially those involving touch injection, is possibly very broad. As such, our exposition is not exhaustive. However, we introduce some of the most interesting and potentially devastating attacks targeting both real-world applications and research systems.

4.1 Sniffing Touchscreen Input (Touchlogger)

We will demonstrate how *SMASheD* can be used as a TouchLogger in order to sniff a user's sensitive information. According to Android security model, an app cannot read touch events performed by the user on other apps [6]. However, we will show how it is possible to infer the keys that the user has pressed, and therefore extract sensitive information efficiently and with 100% accuracy. We note that *SMASheD* is not only able to detect user key presses but it can also log any interaction of the user with the touchscreen.

The *SMASheD* app can send *read* request to the *SMASheD* server to obtain all the events the user performs on the touchscreen. However, getting only the raw touch events is not enough to hamper the user privacy. Moreover, the attacker will be interested only in a small subset of these events. For example, an attacker will be interested in learning the password of the user on banking apps but not the input corresponding to user's interaction with a game.

According to the information the attacker wants to learn about the user, the attacker can modify the service in the *SMASheD* app so it sends *read* request when the app corresponding to the data the attacker wants to collect is launched. Moreover, if the attacker wants only to learn the keys the user presses while the app is running, he can send the *read* request when both the app and the keyboard are on the phone's foreground.

To evaluate the ability of *SMASheD* to extract the username and password from various banking apps, we repurposed the original *SMASheD* app. When the *SMASheD* app is launched, it gets the list of installed apps on the device using *getPackageManager* API. Note that no permission is required to get the list of installed apps. Then, the *SMASheD* app looks for the apps that are already installed and are of interest to the attacker. The *SMASheD* app also finds the soft keyboards installed. The *SMASheD* app starts running its status

[2]http://developer.android.com/tools/help/monkeyrunner_concepts.html

detection service in the background, which regularly executes *ps* command to find out the list of running applications. Once any of the apps that the attacker wants to collect user data from appears in the output of the execution *ps* command, the service gets that app process ID, PID_{app}. The service also gets the process ID of the keyboard, PID_{kb} from the execution of the *ps* command. The service then executes $ps - tPID_{app}$ command, which returns the list of threads of that process; whenever an app is on the foreground, the list of threads of that app has a thread named "GL updater".

If the app is running the "GL updater" thread, the service also checks if the keyboard is running "GL updater" thread. If both the app and the keyboard app have "GL updater" thread running, *SMASheD* detects that both of them are in the foreground and sends *read* request to the *SMASheD* server. When user exits the app or the keyboard (which can be detected by checking if the app is no longer in the list returned by executing the *ps* command, or if "GL updater" is not in the list of the thread running for either the app or the keyboard), the *SMASheD* app sends *stop* request to the *SMASheD* server. As a response to the *stop* request, the *SMASheD* server sends all the touch events to the *SMASheD* app. The *SMASheD* app parses the events and extracts the events with event type ABS_MT_POSITION_X and ABS_MT_POSITION_Y (Listing 2 in Appendix A). Finally, it maps the x and y coordinates to keys (keyboard layout can be detected by determining which soft keyboard the user is using, the orientation of the device and the screen dimensions) and sends the text typed, for example, to the attacker's web service via HTML request, or via other methods as we will discuss in Section 4.2.3.

4.2 Manipulating Touchscreen Sensor

The ability of injecting touch events could be extremely dangerous. In essence, it will allow the malware to do whatever the user can do with her device. The primary challenge for the attacker is to be stealthy. To do so, the attacker should inject the touch events while the user might not be attending to the phone, such as when the user is asleep or the phone is left inside a pocket or a purse. Such contextual scenarios can be determined by monitoring various motion and environmental sensors on the phone, as shown by prior research [14]. For example, the attacker can monitor the proximity and light sensors to infer when the phone is inside a pocket or placed in dark [25]. Moreover, *SMASheD* can change the phone settings, e.g., decrease screen brightness, mute sound and erase logs/-traces to make the attacks "user-invisible."

Following subsections layout some of the attacks that *SMASheD* can perform given its capability to inject touch events.

4.2.1 Installing Apps Bypassing Permissions

SMASheD can install apps (benign or malicious) with extended permissions, available from Google Play Store, or any other website by injecting touch events on the infected device. To do so, *SMASheD* first sends an intent either to open the URL of the website where the malicious app resides, or to Google Play Store's app page. As the interface of the Google Play Store app is standard, *SMASheD* can inject touch events on the install button and then the accept button to grant the app with the requested permission. The position of the touch events can be calculated based on the screen dimensions. *SMASheD* can then close the Play Store app and clean-up any installation-related notifications. Similarly, *SMASheD* can open the malware-hosting website, download the APK, install the malware by clicking on the downloaded APK, grant the malware the desired permissions, and clean-up the traces. The installed malware apps can then do whatever they are designed to do against the phone or the user.

4.2.2 Permission Escalation

SMASheD can utilize already installed apps to compromise user's privacy. For example, *SMASheD* can open the camera app and collect images of the user's surroundings to learn sensitive information about the user, similar to PlaceRaider [23], but without asking the user to grant the CAMERA permission to the *SMASheD* app. Similarly, *SMASheD* can open an audio recording app and monitor the ambient audio. Also, *SMASheD* can open any installed app having the GPS permission, acquire the location of the user, and take a screenshot of the app displaying the location by pressing and holding down the Power and Volume Down buttons. *SMASheD* then can either send the snapshot to the attacker or perform simple image processing to extract the user location, given that *SMASheD* knows the app's layout and the screen dimensions.

Other possible attacks include: making phone call to premium rate numbers by opening the phone dialer and pressing the calling button, sending SMSs via a messaging app, sending the contact list of the user by opening the contact app, and sharing all the contacts via email or SMS with a remote attacker, changing the phone settings (such as toggling WiFi, GPS, etc) through the Settings app, muting the phone, and so on.

4.2.3 Data Exfiltration

Whenever *SMASheD* needs to send any data to a remote attacker (e.g., previously sniffed passwords, credit card numbers or pictures), it can stealthily transmit this data utilizing other apps, such as email or SMS. As some malware detection mechanisms detect malicious apps based on abnormal data usage, *SMASheD* can remain surreptitious and undetected by such systems. Moreover, *SMASheD* can delete the logs from the email and SMS apps so that users cannot trace back. This simple strategy will prevent *SMASheD* from being detected by either the device user or the anti-virus apps. Such an exfiltration will also avoid the need for doing any data processing on the infected device itself but rather allow the attacker to outsource all processing to a remote machine.

4.2.4 Phone Unlock

In order to allow *SMASheD* to access any of the device resources that require the device to be unlocked, *SMASheD* needs to unlock the device first. To do that, *SMASheD* first utilizes the TouchLogger presented in Section 4.1 to log the user's PIN or pattern unlock while the user unlocks his phone. Then, whenever *SMASheD* wants to unlock the phone, it will simply inject the recorded PIN or pattern unlock onto the touchscreen.

4.2.5 Accessing User Accounts

SMASheD can be used to open different apps that require authentication, and log into user's accounts. To do so, *SMASheD* will first extract the user's credentials for the target account by using the TouchLogger described in Section 4.1. *SMASheD* will then utilize this credential to log into the user account from her device. Accessing the user accounts from the *SMASheD* infected device is important for several reasons. Many web services and banks implement a second factor authentication approach which may only allow the user to login from a registered device. Similarly, many banks require the user to answer security questions when she logs in from a different device, and others send notification to the user specifying the devices that are used to access her account. After having logged into the user accounts, *SMASheD* can, for example, access the account and perform any kind of the allowed banking transactions, read user's emails, send fake emails, forward the emails to a remote attacker, or read user's private data from or post messages on social media sites — the possibilities are endless.

4.2.6 Attacking Biometric Authentication

Recently, a significant amount of research has been done to authenticate a user transparently using biometrics. The touch-based biometrics are applied either as a second factor authentication mechanism during the device unlock or as a continuous authentication mechanism when the user is performing some activity on the device. Among these, some systems analyze the keystrokes of the users to capture the biometrics while others analyze touch gestures provided by the users. We now analyze a variety of these biometrics systems proposed in the literature and provide a systematic methodology to attack them using *SMASheD*.

Keystroke Biometrics: *Maiorana et al.* [13] present an approach to authenticate users based on their typing habits on the smartphones. Their approach relies on the analysis of keystroke dynamics. The system acquires and processes the time stamps generated by the mobile phones related to key press and release. Using these, the system further calculates different features such as Manhattan distance, Euclidean distance and statistical features and generate a template for each user. During the authentication, the system computes the normalized distance and compares that with a threshold.

To authenticate against such system, *SMASheD* needs to learn how the user types. During the learning phase, *SMASheD* can record the user's keystroke behavior and compute the features in a similar way to the authentication system. After learning, it can create the keystrokes such that the time interval *SMASheD* presses and releases the keys closely correlates with that of the user. Note that *SMASheD* can simply record and replay the user's keystroke without computing the features and the system may still fail to detect such malicious input. However, creating new keystrokes after learning the features is more detrimental to the user as the attacker can recreate any events or activities he likes.

Touch Gesture Biometrics: *Frank et al.* [6] present "Touchalytics", a continuous touch-based authentication system which utilizes the strokes performed by the user while using her phone. Touchalytics focuses on single touch gestures such as sliding horizontally and vertically. To authenticate using touch, Touchalytics records the touch coordinates, finger pressures, the screen areas covered by each finger, and times. Touchalytics extracts 30 different features from these raw inputs. Touchalytics uses these features to build a profile of the user and utilizes it later to identify the user.

Since Touchalytics is monitoring and matching the touch with the trained data for horizontal and vertical slides only but not with other actions, *SMASheD* can perform tap/click and pinch without getting detected. However, to navigate up/down or right/left where *SMASheD* has to provide such horizontal/vertical slides, *SMASheD* needs to record the previous authentic slides from the user, and later inject them as desired. While outsider attacks using robots [18] have previously been reported against Touchalytics, the *SMASheD* attack represents the first known insider attack to our knowledge.

Shahzad et al. [19] present "GEAT" for screen unlocking based on simple gestures. Along with the user touch input, GEAT uses other features such as finger velocity, device acceleration, stroke time, inter-stroke time, stroke displacement magnitude, stroke displacement direction, and velocity direction. GEAT segments each stroke into sub-strokes of different time duration where, for each sub-stroke, the user has consistent and distinguishing behavior. GEAT utilizes these features to train and later identify the user.

Since GEAT is only authenticating when user wants to unlock the screen, *SMASheD* can record all the raw touch and device acceleration data during the legitimate authentication by the user. It can later just replay the touch providing the recorded data such that the features would fully match.

Luca et al. [5] present another transparent authentication approach that enhances password patterns with an additional security layer. They study the touch stroke gestures corresponding to the horizontal slide and the pattern unlock. Their approach uses dynamic time warping for the analysis of touch gestures using different features including XY-coordinates, pressure, size, time, and speed of the touch.

SMASheD cannot only thwart the password pattern to unlock the device but also foil the additional security layer provided by this system. As discussed in the Section 4.1, *SMASheD* first simply sniffs the password pattern. In addition, *SMASheD* records the pressure, size, time and speed of the touch when the legitimate user performs the pattern unlock gesture. Now, when the *SMASheD* app needs to unlock the device, it simply injects the previously recorded touch events to circumvent the authentication functionality.

4.2.7 Attacking Touch-based Authorization

Roesner et al. [15] propose the *user-driven access control* system where permission is granted using user actions rather than using manifests or system prompts. It introduces *access control gadgets* (ACGs). Each user-owned resource exposes UI elements, ACGs, which are embedded by the apps. The user's UI interaction with the ACG grants the app permission to access the corresponding resources. The system assumes that the kernel has complete control of the display and the apps cannot draw outside the screen space designated for them. Furthermore, it assumes that the kernel dispatches UI events only to the app with which the user is interacting.

The threat model of the system tries to restrict access such that only one app gets the permission from the user interaction, while other apps do not. It does not assume that the touch can be injected. No app will have permission to use the resource until the user explicitly interacts with the ACGs embedded by the app. To attack this system, *SMASheD* can provide the touch input to any app. For example, if *SMASheD* wants to make a phone call, it needs to interact with and provide touch to the phone calling ACG of the app. Since the system receives the touch, it will permit the app to make the phone call. In summary, *SMASheD* can fully bypass this system by injecting simple touch events.

Chaugule et al. [1] present a defense against unauthorized malicious behavior by utilizing the keypad or touchscreen interrupts. The system differentiates between malware and human activity by analyzing the presence of touch input which generates a hardware interrupt. Their approach especially focuses on preventing unauthorized messaging. The system assumes that the operating system is within the Trusted Computing Base and the hardware is not compromised. It assumes that the kernel memory interfaces are not exported to userspace so that userspace applications are not allowed to write into kernel memory and alter kernel control flow. They claim that there is no direct way in which the touchscreen interrupt handler will be called from userspace code unless the operating system is tampered with.

SMASheD can break this claim by providing the touchscreen interrupt without tampering with the operating system. *SMASheD* can provide touch screen input while sending the text message. When the touch event is injected, it will provide the necessary hardware interrupt that the system is looking for and hence any app will be authorized to send the messages.

4.3 Manipulating Other Sensors

In this section, we first describe the systems which provide different security or non-security functionality based on the motion, position and environmental sensors. Then, we provide an attack scheme against each system using the sensor event injection capability of *SMASheD*.

Attacking these systems may not be straightforward. The best scenario to manipulate the sensor readings is the one where the current sensor readings are not being altered by the natural events. For example, when the phone is in a pocket, the light sensor may not change or report constant values. Since the sensor file will not be altered by the natural environment in this case, the malware can manipulate the sensor data as it likes. Also if the system is implementing a statistical approach (such as based on mean, standard deviation, etc., of the sensor data), the malware may not even need to manipulate the sensors for the whole duration when the system is monitoring the sensors. *SMASheD* can insert some values that significantly changes these statistical features which causes the system to misjudge the sensing context, thereby failing to provide its intended security functionality. For the other systems, which implement specialized algorithms based on continuous sensor data, *SMASheD* needs to inject sensor readings at different timestamps that correlate to the sensor values during benign case.

4.3.1 Attacking Authentication Systems

Conti et al. [4] propose a system that transparently authenticates the user by analyzing her hand movement gesture while she is making or answering a phone call. It uses accelerometer and orientation sensor to detect the proposed gesture. The system uses the dynamic time warping distance (DTW-D) algorithm to verify if the authorized user is making or answering the phone call.

To attack this system, *SMASheD* can record the accelerometer and orientation sensor data when the user is making or receiving a valid call. Later, when *SMASheD* wants to make a call (e.g., to premium rate numbers or to user's contacts), it can replay the previously recorded sensor data.

Gascon et al. [7] present an approach to continuously authenticate users on smartphones by analyzing their typing motion behavior. Along with touch input, it also records the timestamps when the keys are pressed or released. The system uses different motion and position sensors such as accelerometer, gyroscope and orientation sensors to capture behavioral biometrics so as to authenticate the user. It extracts various features leading to a 2376-dimensional vector representing the typing motion behavior of a user in a given time frame. The system is trained with the linear SVM classifier.

To attack this system, *SMASheD* needs to learn how the user presses each character, and then reproduce it later. During the learning phase, *SMASheD* continuously records all the raw sensor data until it gets necessary information used by the system for all the keys during the legitimate key presses. Once the learning phase is complete, *SMASheD* can provide the touch injects with proper timings and the corresponding sensor readings. Since the motion and position sensors are continuously recording the data from the hardware, *SMASheD* may need to wait for a favorable time, e.g., when the phone is static, otherwise the natural readings may interfere with the injected sensor readings possibly leading to rejection by the system.

4.3.2 Attacking Authorization Systems

We now consider various systems that provide the authorization functionality to access mobile device resources/services. The main purpose of these systems is to differentiate a human user from a bot so as to authorize access to the requesting app. To authorize human-vs-bot actions, these systems capture different explicit and implicit gestures provided by the user measured using multiple sensors.

Li et al. [10] present "Tap-Wave-Rub". They propose multiple gestures that can be used for the purpose of authorization. An implicit gesture, such as tapping the phone with another device (*tap*), is used to provide NFC permission to the requesting app. The system uses accelerometer sensor to detect the *tap* gesture. An explicit gesture, such as waving a hand in front of the phone (*wave*) or rubbing a finger near the proximity sensor (*rub*), is used to grant permissions for the services where no implicit gesture can be used. To detect *wave* and *rub* gestures, the system uses proximity sensor. *Shrestha et al.* [21] also present "WaveToAccess", in which another mechanism for *wave* gesture detection is proposed. It utilizes the light sensors to infer the fluctuation in light due to hand waving and the accelerometer sensor to reduce the possibility of detecting other events as hand wave. Both Tap-Wave-Rub and WaveToAccess assume that the kernel is immune and the sensor data cannot be manipulated by the malware.

SMASheD attacks the assumption made by these systems. To generate the *tap*, *wave* or *rub* gesture, the attacker can record his own gesture and later inject the recorded values via *SMASheD*. Alternatively, *SMASheD* can record the gesture provided by the user during the benign case and replay it later. A simpler attack can be performed on *wave* and *rub* gestures in Tap-Wave-Rub, in which *SMASheD* fluctuates the proximity sensor in quick succession so that the system infers the corresponding gesture.

Shrestha et al. [20] later present a similar defense to mobile malware using *transparent human gestures*. The system uses the hand movement gesture to prevent unauthorized access of the services such as phone calling, picture snapping and NFC tapping. It looks for multiple, motion, position and environmental sensor data to detect the calling, snapping and tapping gestures. The assumption that the system makes is the device is already infected with malware. However, the device kernel is healthy and is immune to the malware infection, and also that the malware is not capable of manipulating the sensors.

SMASheD can attack the assumptions made by these systems. The attacker can record the sensor data that is being used by these systems to detect the gesture during call, snap or tap. Now, when malware is trying to make a call, snap photo or tap NFC tag, *SMASheD* can replay all these sensor data fooling the system to believe that the user is performing the activity.

5. SMASHED MITIGATION

To protect against the adversarial applications of *SMASheD* (Section 4), we suggest the following potential mitigation strategies. Although these strategies may not fully prevent the attacks, they may help reduce the impact of the underlying vulnerability.

First, we believe that it is important to raise people's awareness of the possible security risks associated with installing services through the ADB shell. Second, we suggest following the permission models of Android for native services that are executed through the ADB shell. In the current model, any native service that starts through the ADB shell is granted all the permissions that the shell has without notifying the user. These permissions include accessing logs, frame buffer, motion, position, environmental, and user input sensors. An attacker may not reveal all the resources that the service is accessing. For example, the attacker could publish a service as a snapshot service while injecting code that accesses sensor files as well. This may be prevented if the service is only granted permissions after informing the user. Third, we suggest enforcing security policies for the communication between processes running on the device through sockets. We recommend that Android monitors the open sockets on the device and the apps that are accessing those sockets. Whenever an unusual communication is detected, Android should at least inform the user. Whether or not users would pay attention to such notifications is an independent concern. However, we believe that the potential risks should be conveyed to the users.

6. RELATED WORK

Our paper is not the first to study the vulnerability underlying the ADB workaround. Recently, Lin et al. [11] developed Screenmilker, a malicious app that can glean sensitive information from the mobile device's screen (specifically passwords of banking apps) by communicating with a snapshot service installed through ADB. Screenmilker exploits the vulnerability of snapshot services of exposing their ADB capabilities to any app with only INTERNET permission installed on the same device.

Also, Hwang et al. [8] presented "Bittersweet ADB", a set of conceptual attacks using ADB ranging from private data leakage to usage monitoring and behavior interference. The threat model in [8] assumes that the user has enabled USB debugging on her phone and forgot to disable it and later her PC got infected with a malware such as the one explained in [12] which installs an ADB service on the connected device. Then, whenever the user connects her device to her infected PC, the malware on the PC installs a malicious service with ADB capabilities on the user phone. The authors also developed an app that can enable USB debugging without user knowledge. Although Android 4.2.2 and higher display a dialog asking the user to allow debugging via PC when the device is connected to a PC, the authors assume that the users would just accept. The authors proposed the use of static analyzer to detect the proposed attacks. The static analyzer checks if the private information resulted from executing ADB command is sent outside the Android device via socket API.

In our paper, we extensively expanded the scope and the impact of the ADB vulnerability to much more devastating, stealthy and accurate attacks than the one proposed in [11] and with a weaker (more realistic) threat model than [8]. We comprehensively and systematically exposed the vulnerability of sniffing and manipulating many protected Android sensors, and translated it into a wide spectrum of catastrophic attacks against real-world and research systems. Our proposed framework is the first, to our knowledge, that sniffs and manipulates protected sensors on unrooted Android devices, without user awareness, without constant device-PC USB connection (unlike the monkeyrunner tool) and without the need for an infected PC (unlike [8]).

7. CONCLUSION AND FUTURE WORK

In this paper, we called the Android's sensor security model into question. We exploited Android's ADB workaround to develop a framework that can effectively sniff and manipulate many sensors currently protected by Android's access control model. Our framework can be used to: (1) directly sniff the touchscreen sensor data, (2) directly manipulate the touchscreen, motion, position and environmental sensor data, and (3) indirectly, using the touch inject capability, sniff the audio-visual and navigational sensors. Based on this framework, we introduced a wide spectrum of potentially devastating attacks that can compromise user privacy and subvert many security applications that rely upon different sensors.

We believe that our framework can facilitate many other applications beyond the ones we presented, which we also plan to explore in our future work.

References

[1] A. Chaugule, Z. Xu, and S. Zhu. A specification based intrusion detection framework for mobile phones. In *Applied Cryptography and Network Security*, 2011.

[2] ClockworkMod. Clockworkmod tether (no root). https://goo.gl/qg2e80.

[3] ClockworkMod. Helium. https://goo.gl/ceW329, 2013.

[4] M. Conti, I. Zachia-Zlatea, and B. Crispo. Mind how you answer me!: transparently authenticating the user of a smartphone when answering or placing a call. In *ACM Symposium on Information, Computer and Communications Security*, 2011.

[5] A. De Luca, A. Hang, F. Brudy, C. Lindner, and H. Hussmann. Touch me once and i know it's you!: Implicit authentication based on touch screen patterns. In *SIGCHI Conference on Human Factors in Computing Systems*, 2012.

[6] M. Frank, R. Biedert, E. Ma, I. Martinovic, and D. Song. Touchalytics: On the applicability of touchscreen input as a behavioral biometric for continuous authentication. *IEEE Transactions on Information Forensics and Security*, 2013.

[7] H. Gascon, S. Uellenbeck, C. Wolf, and K. Rieck. Continuous authentication on mobile devices by analysis of typing motion behavior. In *Sicherheit*, 2014.

[8] S. Hwang, S. Lee, Y. Kim, and S. Ryu. Bittersweet adb: Attacks and defenses. In *ACM Symposium on Information, Computer and Communications Security*, 2015.

[9] E. Kim. No root screenshot it. https://goo.gl/hksbHY, 2013.

[10] H. Li, D. Ma, N. Saxena, B. Shrestha, and Y. Zhu. Tap-wave-rub: Lightweight malware prevention for smartphones using intuitive human gestures. In *ACM conference on Security and privacy in wireless and mobile networks*, 2013.

[11] C.-C. Lin, H. Li, X. Zhou, and X. Wang. Screenmilker: How to milk your android screen for secrets. In *Network and Distributed System Security Symposium*, 2014.

[12] F. Liu. Windows malware attempts to infect android devices. http://goo.gl/x2Dwc2. Accessed: 2015-08-08.

[13] E. Maiorana, P. Campisi, N. González-Carballo, and A. Neri. Keystroke dynamics authentication for mobile phones. In *ACM Symposium on Applied Computing*, 2011.

[14] J.-K. Min, A. Doryab, J. Wiese, S. Amini, J. Zimmerman, and J. I. Hong. Toss'n'turn: smartphone as sleep and sleep quality detector. In *ACM conference on Human factors in computing systems*, 2014.

[15] F. Roesner, T. Kohno, A. Moshchuk, B. Parno, H. J. Wang, and C. Cowan. User-driven access control: Rethinking permission granting in modern operating systems. In *IEEE Symposium on Security and Privacy (SP)*, 2012.

[16] D. Rogers. *Mobile Security: A Guide for Users*. lulu.com, 2013.

[17] R. Schlegel, K. Zhang, X.-y. Zhou, M. Intwala, A. Kapadia, and X. Wang. Soundcomber: A stealthy and context-aware sound trojan for smartphones. In *Network and Distributed System Security Symposium (NDSS)*, 2011.

[18] A. Serwadda and V. V. Phoha. When kids' toys breach mobile phone security. In *Conf. on Computer & Communications Security*, 2013.

[19] M. Shahzad, A. X. Liu, and A. Samuel. Secure unlocking of mobile touch screen devices by simple gestures: You can see it but you can not do it. In *Mobile Computing & Networking*, 2013.

[20] B. Shrestha, M. Mohamed, N. Saxena, and S. Tamrakar. Curbing mobile malware based on user-transparent hand movements. In *Pervasive Computing and Communications*, 2015.

[21] B. Shrestha, N. Saxena, and J. Harrison. Wave-to-access: Protecting sensitive mobile device services via a hand waving gesture. In *Cryptology and Network Security*. Springer, 2013.

[22] strAI. Frep - finger replayer. https://goo.gl/2F5k7J, 2015.

[23] R. Templeman, Z. Rahman, D. Crandall, and A. Kapadia. Placeraider: Virtual theft in physical spaces with smartphones. *Network and Distributed System Security Symposium (NDSS)*, 2013.

[24] N. Xu, F. Zhang, Y. Luo, W. Jia, D. Xuan, and J. Teng. Stealthy video capturer: a new video-based spyware in 3g smartphones. In *ACM conference on Wireless network security*, 2009.

[25] J. Yang, E. Munguia-Tapia, and S. Gibbs. Efficient in-pocket detection with mobile phones. In *ACM conference on Pervasive and ubiquitous computing adjunct publication*, 2013.

APPENDIX

A. SAMPLE OUTPUT FROM GETEVENT

Listing 2: Sample output from running *getevent* for a single press release

```
[69934.435503] EV_ABS ABS_MT_TRACKING_ID   0000038d
[69934.435533] EV_KEY BTN_TOUCH            DOWN
[69934.435564] EV_ABS ABS_MT_POSITION_X    000003b2
[69934.435564] EV_ABS ABS_MT_POSITION_Y    00000607
[69934.435595] EV_ABS ABS_MT_TOUCH_MAJOR   00000012
[69934.435595] EV_ABS ABS_MT_TOUCH_MINOR   00000009
[69934.435625] EV_ABS ABS_MT_WIDTH_MAJOR   00000002
[69934.435625] EV_ABS 003c                 ffffffa6
[69934.435778] EV_SYN SYN_REPORT           00000000
[69934.452105] EV_ABS ABS_MT_TOUCH_MAJOR   00000024
[69934.452105] EV_ABS ABS_MT_TO UCH_MINOR  0000001b
[69934.452135] EV_ABS ABS_MT_WIDTH_MAJOR   00000008
[69934.452135] EV_ABS 003c                 fffffffd
[69934.452166] EV_SYN SYN_REPORT           00000000
[69934.462847] EV_ABS 003c                 00000000
[69934.462877] EV_SYN SYN_REPORT           00000000
[69934.494371] EV_ABS ABS_MT_TRACKING_ID   ffffffff
[69934.494402] EV_KEY BTN_TOUCH            UP
[69934.494402] EV_SYN SYN_REPORT           00000000
```

On the Origin of Mobile Apps: Network Provenance for Android Applications

Ryan Stevens
UC Davis
rcstevens@ucdavis.edu

Jonathan Crussell
UC Davis
jcrussell@ucdavis.edu

Hao Chen
ShanghaiTech University
chenhao@shanghaitech.edu.cn

ABSTRACT

Many mobile services consist of two components: a server providing an API, and an application running on smartphones and communicating with the API. An unresolved problem in this design is that it is difficult for the server to authenticate which app is accessing the API. This causes many security problems. For example, the provider of a private network API has to embed secrets in its official app to ensure that only this app can access the API; however, attackers can uncover the secret by reverse-engineering. As another example, malicious apps may send automatic requests to ad servers to commit ad fraud.

In this work, we propose a system that allows network API to authenticate the mobile app that sends each request so that the API can make an informed access control decision. Our system, the Mobile Trusted-Origin Policy, consists of two parts: 1) an app provenance mechanism that annotates outgoing HTTP(S) requests with information about which app generated the network traffic, and 2) a code isolation mechanism that separates code within an app that should have different app provenance signatures into *mobile origin*. As motivation for our work, we present two previously-unknown families of apps that perform click fraud, and examine how the lack of mobile origin information enables the attacks. Based on our observations, we propose *Trusted Cross-Origin Requests* to handle point (1), which automatically includes mobile origin information in outgoing HTTP requests. Servers may then decide, based on the mobile origin data, whether to process the request or not. We implement a prototype of our system for Android and evaluate its performance, security, and deployability. We find that our system can achieve our security and utility goals with negligible overhead.

1. INTRODUCTION

Many mobile services consist of two components: a server providing an API, and an application running on smartphones and communicating with the API. An unresolved problem in this design is that it is difficult for the server to authenticate which app is accessing the API. For example, Snapchat[1] wishes to allow only its official app to access its API. However, attackers reverse-engineered the API and produced malicious third-party apps to steal Snapchat users' credentials and photos [11]. Unfortunately, there is no robust way to protect against such an attack on Android or iOS. For example, common iOS HTTP libraries automatically include the app's name in the HTTP header of outgoing requests, but attackers can easily forge the header either by setting the value manually or by using sockets directly. As long as apps can use sockets directly, relying on HTTP libraries to provide app provenance in HTTP requests would be insufficient. An alternative is to embed a secret key in the app to create an authentication token for accessing the API, but attackers can reverse-engineer the app to uncover the secret, as in the case of Snapchat. Clearly we need a better solution.

To solve this problem, we propose a system that inserts unforgeable *app provenance* in outgoing requests, which the servers can then use to identify the app making the request. To do so, we add a network proxy on the device that observes all outgoing HTTP(S) communications and injects an app identifier into the HTTP header (this approach could be extended to work with other application layer protocols, but as we will show in Section 8.3, the majority of apps communicate over HTTP). This unforgeable app identifier in the header allows the server to identify the app and enforces access control accordingly. The benefit of using a proxy is that the proxy is agnostic to how the network requests were generated, including using HTTP libraries, sockets, WebView, or native code (in Android). In Section 6, we build such a system for Android and evaluate it in Section 7. We call this approach Trusted Cross-Origin Requests (TCOR for short), as we trust the operating system to add the unforgeable header. If widely deployed, it would enable private network APIs for apps, and even enable API providers to "sell" their API to developers without fear of API keys being stolen.

However, the proxy alone can identify provenance only at the app granularity, which cannot detect all forgery attacks because of the way how mobile apps are developed. For example, on Android, many apps include ad libraries to display ads to generate revenue. These ad libraries are provided by a third party called an ad provider, but are included as part of the app's code. Thus, our proxy presented above would

[1]Snapchat is a smartphone messaging service that allows users to send ephemeral images that cannot be stored by the receiver.

CODASPY'16, March 09-11, 2016, New Orleans, LA, USA

DOI: http://dx.doi.org/10.1145/2857705.2857712

not be able to distinguish between ad requests generated by the ad library and those forged by the app. When apps automatically generate ad requests without user interaction, they are committing ad fraud, as no real user is viewing or clicking ads. To motivate the need to protect against such an attack, we present two previously-undisclosed families of Android click fraud malware in Section 3. To defend against this attack, we need a mechanism to divide an app's code into different *mobile origins* — e.g., app code and ad library — so that the proxy can distinguish network requests by mobile origin and tag the correct mobile origin in the HTTP header. Since inner-app code isolation has been studied in Android, we use an existing system called LayerCake [21] for implementing code isolation in our system.

We have discussed the need for two security mechanisms in smartphone operating systems: app provenance in network requests and inner-app code isolation. We will call the combination of these mechanisms the Mobile Trusted-Origin Policy (MTOP for short), loosely motivated by browsers' Same-Origin Policy. Our contributions are as follows:

- We propose the Mobile Trusted-Origin Policy and Trusted Cross-Origin Requests to provide both app provenance in network requests and inner-app code isolation to enable private network API and defend against ad fraud.
- We report two previously-unknown families of click fraud apps by leveraging existing methodology for detecting ad fraud behavior in apps and clustering apps based on code similarity. For each family, we classify their fraudulent behavior and identify what aspects of mobile systems they use to perform fraud.
- We implement Mobile Trusted-Origin Policy on Android and evaluate its performance, security, and deployability. We find that our system can achieve our security and utility goals with reasonable performance overhead.

2. BACKGROUND

2.1 Android Advertising

Figure 1 shows an overview of Android app advertising:

- The *publisher* is the app owner that is paid to show ads in her app. Publishers register with *ad providers*, who maintain relationships with publishers and *marketers*. Marketers pay ad providers to have their ads shown.
- An ad provider gives a registered publisher an *ad library* to embed in her app and a *publisher ID* to identify her. The ad library has an API to display ads.
- When instructed to show an ad, the ad library sends an *ad request* to the ad provider's *ad server*. The ad request contains the publisher ID and any ad *targeting* information (e.g. the user's age or gender).
- The ad server responds with ad metadata that includes a URL for the ad's content and a *click URL* where to redirect the user if the ad is clicked.
- Publishers are paid for *impressions*, where an ad is successfully requested and shown, and for *clicks*, when the user clicks the ad. Clicks are tracked by redirecting the user through the ad server before sending them to the marketer's webpage.

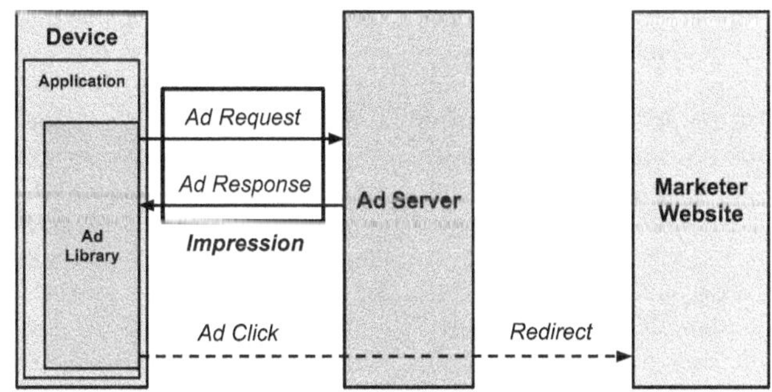

Figure 1: Overview of the Android in-app advertising model.

The primary difference between this ad serving model and the web ad serving model is how ad code is included with the publisher's content. Instead of code libraries, websites include external Javascript through `<iframe>` objects, called *ad tags*. This is necessary as the Javascript code must be hosted on the ad server to make network requests to the server due to the restrictions of the Same-Origin Policy. Once the ad request is made, the infrastructure to select and track ad views remains unchanged. In fact, many ad libraries choose to implement the requesting and display of ads by opening web ad tags in a `WebView` environment, which acts as an embedded browser in the app's UI.

3. MOTIVATION

In this section we motivate the need to mediate apps' network requests via MTOP. We first discuss private web APIs and then present two previously unpublished families of Android click fraud malware.

3.1 Private Web APIs

As previously mentioned, it is difficult for a network API provider to reliably ensure that only its mobile app can access its API. This difficulty contrasts with the case of such APIs for web apps, because web code is restricted by the Same-Origin Policy, preventing a web app on another website from completing a cross-domain network request. A recent study by Viennot, et. al. [26] found that thousands of apps embedded authentication tokens for web services, including API tokens for cloud computing services such as Amazon Web Services, as well as OAuth tokens for various social media sites. This is a high security risk because attackers can uncover these tokens by reverse-engineering, but developers have no other solutions for authenticating their apps with network APIs. Once an API token has been discovered, attackers can craft phishing apps or trojans that imitate the functionality of a legitimate one while secretly stealing user credentials or monitoring their behavior, as mentioned with Snapchat in the introduction. In addition, unscrupulous developers could use competitors APIs to bolster their own apps' functionality. All this can be done without exploiting the underlying operating system, motivating the need for a system-centric solution.

3.2 Case Study: Click Fraud

Ad fraud (or *click fraud*) is the practice of "viewing" and "interacting" with ads in an automated way to artificially inflate revenue. For example, an unscrupulous website publisher may inflate her ad revenue by having an automated script visit her website and click on ads. Ad fraud is a serious security issue as digital marketers who pay to have their ads shown will not receive any commercial benefit for ads shown to scripts.

In order to receive revenue, fraudsters must remain undetected while issuing large numbers of ad requests and clicks. To do so, fraudsters use botnets to instruct real devices to run code that periodically visits the fraudsters' webpages in the background and clicks on the ads located there, to generate revenue for the fraudsters. The use of bots allows fraudsters to use the characteristics of the compromised devices to generate varied ad traffic (for example, fraudulent requests from a botnet would use many different IP addresses). Unfortunately, Android apps distributed through a market can give fraudsters these same characteristics without the need to exploit users' machines.

3.2.1 Click Fraud Detection

To find apps that perform click fraud, we first run them through MAdFraud [3]. MAdFraud automatically identifies ad requests and clicks in mobile app traffic that is recorded from running the apps in an emulator. It uses simple rules to flag apps with suspicious ad behavior, which are candidates for further investigation. As a starting point, we use the initial MAdFraud dataset of 130,339 apps collected from 19 Android markets, which flagged 12,421 apps as potentially performing ad fraud. We then ran an additional 60,726 apps through MAdFraud, from the developers that uploaded these flagged apps. In total, MAdFraud identified 615 apps which send ad clicks without user interaction, which is too many to manually investigate. We chose to use AnDarwin [2] to cluster any detected click fraud apps into families based on code similarity. This significantly reduces the number of apps which need to be manually investigated.

Originally, AnDarwin excluded any feature appearing in at least N apps. This threshold-based approach is problematic for comparing our small set of apps that issue clicks as 1) we may set the threshold too low and exclude all click modules (code for committing click fraud that is shared across an app family), or, 2) we may set the threshold too high and fail to exclude libraries. Instead, we take an approach inspired by term-frequency inverse-document-frequency (TF-IDF). Rather than exclude features that are present in many apps, we instead give them a small weight based on the inverse of the number of apps they appear in. Now that features have weights, we cannot compare apps using the Jaccard similarity, as done in the original work. Instead, we compare apps using the Cosine similarity of their feature vectors which are weighted using the IDF weights. Ultimately, AnDarwin placed our 615 click fraud apps into 65 clusters. From our analysis of the app families, we found two clear examples of Android click fraud malware: Pixcel and AppsGeyser.

3.2.2 Pixcel

The first family of click fraud apps we present all contain a common package called `com.pixcel.core`, which contains code to perform fraud against a number of ad providers. The package implements an Android service which issues ad and click requests in the background when started. The ad fraud service first makes a request to `nucleardroid.com` to receive parameters used for issuing fraudulent ad traffic. An example response is shown in Figure 3 in the Appendix. The response contains instructions for the service, indicating which ad providers to perform fraud against (in this case Madvertise, Mobfox, and Tapjoy), which publisher IDs (sometimes called "siteid") to use, and how many fraudulent requests to make to each. A timing component uses parameters in the response (specifically, the **`countperday`** parameter) to start the service at regular intervals, or it defaults to running hourly if no parameters have been loaded. For each ad provider, the Pixcel package contains a custom module that is able to send ad requests to the ad provider's ad server, parse the response, and then issue click requests if instructed to do so. Interestingly, each custom module has very different code from the ad library of the associated ad provider. This implies that the authors of Pixcel spent the time to reverse engineer the ad server's API, instead of simply modifying an existing library. Figure 4 shows a code snippet (after decompilation) from the ad fraud service that issues fraudulent requests and clicks after receiving instructions. For each entry returned by **`nucleardroid.com`**, it dynamically instantiates the appropriate custom module to issue ad requests and clicks. The custom modules first issue **`countfake`** ad requests (from Figure 3), followed by **`counttry`** impressions and click requests.

The apps containing Pixcel are from various developer accounts and Android markets. Table 1 shows a breakdown of app packages which contain Pixcel and which markets these apps reside. Some markets have removed the Pixcel apps between the time we crawled the market and the time we discovered Pixcel. The markets may have discovered the fraud separately, or they may have removed them as many of the apps are "spam" apps that contain little content and are all essentially identical except for superficial cosmetic differences. To measure which ad providers Pixcel targets, we queried the Nucleardroid server hourly for three days and observed which ad providers and accounts are returned, using the package names in Table 1 as parameters. In total, Nucleardroid returned instructions to perform fraud using 43 publisher accounts from 5 different ad providers[2]. Since discovering Pixel, we have reported the fraud to each targeted ad provider and had the publisher accounts terminated.

The Pixcel module is an interesting case study. The practice of receiving instructions from a centralized server prior to performing fraud is reminiscent of botnets, where bots receive instructions from a command and control server. From looking at the responses, its clear the fraudsters wish to remain stealthy. Not only do they rotate which ad providers and publisher IDs they use, but they also balance the number of clicks with the number of impressions issued. In addition, because the publisher ID and behavior are chosen dynamically, the fraudsters can easily modify the app's behavior if one of their accounts is terminated. Given that Pixcel attempts to remain stealthy and can be easily reconfigured, it would be more effective to prevent ad fraud on the device than via detection of individual cases. By adopting the Mobile Trusted-Origin Policy presented in subsequent sections, such fraud techniques would not be possible.

3.2.3 AppsGeyser

Here we discuss a second family of apps which issue click requests when run. These apps are all made with the Apps-

[2]Tapjoy, Madvertise, Vserv, MobFox, and Mojiva

Package Name	Markets	Distinct Apps	Install Count
com.pixcel.DroidSaver	Play*, Opera, SlideME*	3	10,619
com.pixcel.FoxSaver	Play*, Opera, SlideME*	3	5,547
com.pixcel.OlympicWallpapers2012	Play*, Opera, SlideME*	2	2,077
com.pixcel.PRDroid	Play*, Opera, SlideME	3	4,963
com.pixcel.MorzeDroid	Play*, Opera, SlideME	2	3,874
com.pixcel.NuclearFlashlight	Opera, SlideME	2	4,072
com.wallpapersdroid.bestcarwallpapers	Opera, SlideME*	2	2,596
com.wallpapersdroid.housemdwallpapers	Opera, SlideME*	2	997
com.wallpapersdroid.offroadcarwallpapers	Opera, SlideME*	2	1,139
com.wallpapersdroid.porschewallpapers	Opera, SlideME*	2	2,936
com.wallpapersdroid.luxurycarwallpapers	Opera	1	238
com.wallpapersdroid.lamborghiniwallpapers	Opera	1	337
com.wallpapersdroid.bmwwallpapers	Opera	1	490
com.wallpapersdroid.peugeotwallpapers	Opera	1	148
com.wallpapersdroid.animalworldwallpapers	Opera	1	225
com.wallpapersdroid.supersedanswallpapers	Opera	1	84
com.wallpapersdroid.mobilewallpapers	Opera	1	335
com.wallpapersdroid.coolwallpapers	Opera	1	221

Table 1: Information about the apps containing the Pixcel click fraud module. An astericks next to a market denotes that the app is no longer available through the market. Distinct apps are counted based on the SHA-1 hash of the APK file. For markets that provide a range for install counts, we use the lower bound to ensure that our total install count is a lower bound on the actual number of installs.

Geyser framework[3], and perform fraud by loading malicious Javascript into a `WebView` that displays ads.

The AppsGeyser framework allows developers to develop web applications with HTML and Javascript and then wrap them in an Android app that can be distributed through Android Markets. We found 211 click fraud apps that were built using AppsGeyser, based on our clustering. Apps built through AppsGeyser will show advertisements when run. As part of the AppsGeyser business model, AppsGeyser receives a portion of revenue for ads shown in the apps in exchange for providing their app building service for free.

The AppsGeyser framework loads ads using a `WebView`. Upon starting the app or refreshing an ad, the framework makes a request to `ads.appsgeyser.com/`, which returns Javascript that bootstraps the `WebView` for showing ads. Under normal circumstances, benign Javascript is loaded and ads are displayed as usual. This Javascript sets up timers for refreshing the ad after some amount of time, configures the "close" button in the top right corner of the ad space, and sets up an `onClick` listener for handling when the user clicks an ad. Finally, a request is made to `postupdate.info/delivery/ajs. php` with some parameters, which returns an ad tag from another ad provider that eventually loads and displays the ad. In our experiments, we observed that these ad tags used a variety of ad providers, including InMobi, InnerActive, Jumptap, Madgic, MassiveImpact, Mocean, and Vserv. The practice of reselling ads from one ad provider to another is common practice, so fetching third party ad tags is not fraud.

However, rarely, we find apps making a request for additional Javascript content located at `postupdate.info/carousel/ad_track.js`. This additional Javascript contains obfuscated code that performs click fraud. The de-obfuscated Javascript content can be found in the Appendix. When run, it scrapes the HTML DOM for any anchor tags, as well as the DOM of any included `<iframe>` objects. For each URL, it creates a 1 pixel by 1 pixel invisible image, sets the `src` attribute of this image to be the click URL, and then inserts this image into the DOM. The result of this is that all click URLs in the populated ad tags of the third-party ad providers will be followed, which results in fraudulent click requests. There is a 1-to-1 mapping between requests to `postupdate.info/carousel/ad_track.js` and clicks detected by MAdFraud.

Normally, this kind of attack would not be feasible due to the Same-Origin Policy of browsers and `WebView`. However, we found that some ad requests to third-party ad providers contain the `Access-Control-Allow-Origin: *` header in the servers' response, which explicitly disables the Same-Origin Policy on delivered content [16]. Due to this vulnerability, the Javascript is able to extract click URLs and follow them by creating image objects which point to the click URLs. A properly configured Same-Origin Policy could have prevented these attacks, and the case study illustrates how trivially ad fraud can be performed without origin protections. This is especially disconcerting given that AppsGeyser app code runs in the same WebView as the ad code. If AppsGeyser were configured to have the app code and ad code run in separate mobile origins, then apps would be protected from misconfigurations in ad code. Additionally, with Trusted Cross-Origin Requests, WebViews with SOP misconfigurations or that have the SOP disabled (using the `setAllowUniversalAccessFromFileURLs()` API) would at least have app provenance information appended to outgoing requests in the case that malicious Javascript was loaded into the insecure WebView.

4. GOALS

Our goal is to provide app provenance for network requests so that servers can differentiate authorized and unauthorized app traffic. In order to do so, we must also isolate code within an app into separate protection domains, called *mobile origins*, when the code should have different app prove-

[3]`http://www.appsgeyser.com/`

nance signatures. Section 5.1 describes how our framework unambiguously identifies and reports mobile origins. The Mobile Trusted-Origin Policy provides the following security benefits:

- Code in one mobile origin should not be able to access or manipulate the code and/or data from other mobile origins. However, code from separate origins can communicate using message passing. On Android, this communication is done through Intents. (On the web, cross-origin communications can be done using *cross-document messaging.*)
- Code should be able to communicate with only authorized web domains, where the definition of "authorized" is left up to the receiver of the communication. This is because we wish to protect against network forgery attacks without restricting the rich functionality of legitimate apps. Many legitimate apps communicate with several different domains. If we were to require each app communicate with only one domain, as the web's Same-Origin Policy does, we would break many benign apps.

We discuss the first point in Section 5.2 and the second in Section 5.3. The former requirement isolates app code and third-party libraries. The latter requirement ensures that malicious apps cannot use the device as a network bot to send unwanted or fraudulent traffic to arbitrary websites, as well as restricts private API to only authorized apps.

4.1 Assumptions

We make the following assumptions in designing our system:

- The user, mobile operating system, and system apps are trusted, but user-installed apps are untrusted and potentially malicious.
- There exist mechanisms to split and sandbox app and library code on the user's device. In our implementation, we chose LayerCake.
- Malicious code cannot exploit the operating system or sandbox to escalate privilege.
- The user has not rooted the device (a rooted device has no restrictions regarding which apps can run code as the superuser).

4.2 Non-Goals

Our goal is to prevent malicious apps running on a benign user's device from attacking the other apps on the device or using the device as a bot to attack network sites. Thus, we do not consider the case where attackers run their code on their own devices or operating systems (just as the web's Same-Origin Policy does not consider the case where attackers launch attacks on their own machines or modified browsers), because such attacks would not have the properties that make the attacks presented in Section 1 useful, such as access to user data or a diverse range of IP addresses. Additionally, we do not aim at preventing other forms of attacks. For example, our framework does not defend against apps that exfiltrate sensitive user data to the attacker's server. Other systems have already been proposed to detect these kinds of attacks [8, 13]. Just as the SOP does not protect web apps against malicious code injected via cross-site scripting (XSS), the MTOP does not protect vulnerable apps that are tricked to run untrusted code.

5. DESIGN

Here we discuss the design of MTOP in order to achieve the goals presented in the previous section. In Section 6, we describe how we implemented the following design.

5.1 Identifying Mobile Origins

Our first challenge is how to determine the mobile origin of code and data contained in an app. To identify mobile code origins, we need a globally unique identifier for each app that an attacker cannot forge. For Android, one might consider an app's package name as its mobile origin, as the package name identifies the app uniquely on the device (e.g. *com.example.game*). Unfortunately, package names are not globally unique, as different apps on different markets may have the same package name. Instead, we take advantage of digital signatures. Code signing allows content to be unambiguously and unforgeably assigned an origin: libraries are signed by the library developer's key before being distributed, and apps are signed by the app developer's key before being uploaded to markets. The public key used to verify the app's signature is sufficient for identifying the app's mobile origin; given a large key size, app public keys should be globally unique.

This is analagous to how Android uses signatures to allow apps to share a UID: two apps which are signed by the same key may share a UID (effectively running both apps in the same mobile origin). This differs from how certificates are used for authentication on the web (i.e., in SSL/TLS). Authenticating a website requires that the certificate be signed by a certificate authority. This is because users need to make security decisions based on the identity information stored in the certificate, so they need the certificate authority to bind the identify to the certificate. By contrast, our system requires a trust relationship between the server and developer to be set up beforehand. Once established, the server is expected to remember the binding between its partners and their certificates, allowing the server to easily determine if a certificate is trusted (e.g., is the certificate its own or its partner's); it does not rely on the identity information in the certificate and therefore requires no certificate authority. Without reliance on a certificate authority, developers are free to self-sign their apps, which is already common practice in Android app publishing.

In the case of ad servers which receive ad requests from reselling, any resold ad requests (i.e., the publisher ID is from a trusted affiliate) would simply be trusted; the ad server would not check the TCOR header and assume their affiliate did the check. This is reasonable since affiliate ad networks require a certain amount of trust (often times the context of the original request is lost in resold ad requests, making ad fraud detection difficult on affiliate traffic [24]). Ad spammers would not have incentive to forge affiliate requests, as they would not receive revenue for the requests.

5.2 Origin Sandboxing

In the current version of Android, apps are sandboxed from each other, however, all code included within an app runs in the same sandbox. For example, a developer who wishes to monetize her apps may include ads, but this requires including an ad provider's library with her app's code. The library code runs with all the privileges that her app has been granted, which leads to privacy concerns; for example ad libraries automatically use these privileges to collect user data [23]. To reap the benefits of the Mobile Trusted-Origin Policy, app and library code should be split into separate origins and run in separate sandboxes.

There are several ways that app and library code can be split. Because of the aforementioned privacy infringements from ad libraries, recent research has primarily focused on splitting app and ad code. This previous work provides an excellent foundation upon which to enforce our policy. Some examples include:

- AdSplit [22]: Adds provenance to data and actions, such that the operating system can enforce policies dictating how data and actions can pass between app and ad code.
- AFrame [27]: Separates ad libraries into their own apps, leveraging Android's existing access control policies. Modifies the framework to allow app UIs to be embedded within each other.
- LayerCake [21]: Like AFrame, runs library code in a separate process. Unlike AFrame, generalizes to any scenario that requires UIs to be embedded within each other, ensuring the code that controls each UI will not run in the same sandbox.

Any of these approaches could be used to sandbox code and data from separate origins on Android. Leveraging AFrame and LayerCake requires libraries to be distributed as separate Android apps. On the other hand, AdSplit would allow an app to contain multiple origins and sandboxing could be achieved within a single app. We build our system on top of LayerCake and discuss our reasoning for doing so in Section 6.1.

5.3 Trusted Cross-Origin Requests

In Section 3.2, we saw an example of a family of apps that can issue fraudulent ad requests and clicks because there is no mechanism in Android to mediate apps' network communications. To mitigate this, our framework should be able to restrict which domains code can contact, so that untrusted code cannot silently forge arbitrary network requests from the user's device. On the web, code can only talk to the origin (i.e., domain) from which it was fetched. However, mobile apps are expected to be able to communicate with many domains (an email client app, for example), and thus a policy that only allows communication to one domain would be overly restrictive in the mobile space. To alleviate this, we propose *Trusted Cross-Origin Requests*, which shifts the decision of whether a mobile origin is authorized to contact a domain from the OS to the server the app is contacting. The mobile origin of the app is included in outgoing HTTP requests by the operating system, such that it cannot be forged by apps. If the server wishes to accept the origin, it responds with the requested content as usual. However, requests from unauthorized origins should receive a `Client Error 4xx` HTTP response status code, such as `403 Forbidden`, to indicate that the request was unauthorized.

An alternative to this design would be to let the app developer annotate each app with a list of authorized domains, e.g., by adding elements to the app's *Manifest* file, which is already used to grant permissions. This approach is problematic for two reasons. First, since we do not trust apps in our threat model, we cannot just let the app developer declare which domains her app can visit. Therefore, the market or the user must determine whether to authorize the app to visit those declared domains; however, neither party has enough information to make an informed decision. Second, this would break the existing advertising model as some content is hosted on the digital marketer's domain, which the developer cannot know ahead of time. For these reasons, we choose to let the server authorize.

Our approach has a similar effect to *cross-origin resource sharing* (CORS) on the web [16], where the server indicates in its response which origins in the web page may read the content in the response. CORS makes sense for browsers, as the browser always receives the content in the response; the CORS header only enables cross-origin reads for the specified domains. However, for the Mobile Trusted-Origin Policy, apps that make unauthorized network requests will not receive any content. Therefore, it is more economical for the server to refuse to deliver content to unauthorized apps up front.

To add Trusted Cross-Origin Requests to Android, we propose adding a custom HTTP header, `X-Mobile-Origin`, that contains information about the app that is making the request. This header will be added by the device and the server will be free to use it as needed. Some HTTP servers are designed to communicate with all clients and may ignore the header completely. On the other hand, servers that host a private API may restrict communications to only a few origins. Finally, some servers may wish to maintain a whitelist of authorized apps. Server whitelists are commonplace among services already — e.g., publisher IDs for ad providers, username/password credentials for web APIs, or symmetric keys as in Section 3.1. However, these credentials are all subject to replay attacks once the attacker has identified or reverse-engineered them from the apps. By contrast, the signatures used by Mobile Trusted-Origin Policy cannot be replayed as long as the developer's signing key has not been compromised.

To mitigate the privacy concern that a network eavesdropper may determine what apps a user is running by examining the `X-Mobile-Origin` header, we require apps that need this header to opt in by requesting a special permission, which our system uses when modifying the proxied traffic. Apps that do not opt in will have an empty value for `X-Mobile-Origin` in outbound requests (see Section 8.2).

6. IMPLEMENTATION

Using the design presented in the previous section, we develop an implementation of the Mobile Trusted-Origin Policy for Android.

6.1 Origin Sandboxing

As previously mentioned in Section 5.2, we use LayerCake to sandbox code and data from different mobile origins. We chose to build our framework on LayerCake because it is simpler than AdSplit, general enough to handle more than just ad libraries, and is implemented for a more recent version of Android than the alternatives. LayerCake adds the concept of *embedded activities* to Android, allowing for one app's UI to be embedded in another app without the parent or child UI being able to forge touch events on the other.

In this way, libraries can be separated into a different apps, and sandboxing is achieved through Android's current app isolation mechanisms. The decision to use LayerCake means that code from different origins will need to be distributed as separate apps. Regular apps and libraries may communicate using **Intents**, which allow apps to send messages between each other in Android. This may seem heavy-handed, but it is reasonable given that not all libraries will need to be run in a separate origin, only libraries which require a unique TCOR header. Additionally, various network-enabled libraries on Android already require another app to be installed to work such as the Facebook SDK [4] or Adobe Air [5].

6.2 Trusted Cross-Origin Requests

6.2.1 Failed Attempts

Our first idea was to use app rewriting [5] to modify apps so that all calls to make HTTP requests are wrapped in code that appends the origin header. This works in the simplest of cases but has many drawbacks. First, it requires rewriting every app to add the header logic. Second, and more severe, it also requires rewriting every app to remove existing logic that would forge the header. The second drawback would be very difficult to solve as it would require extensive program analysis. Third, it is prone to omission as existing rewriting tools require a list of method signatures to rewrite. Finally, this approach does not cover native code and would have difficulties when apps use non-library methods for making HTTP requests (such as writing to a TCP socket directly).

Next, we considered modifying the popular Android HTTP libraries to automatically append the origin header. However, this solution has many of the same limitations as the rewriting solution: it cannot handle apps that include their own HTTP libraries, native code, or apps that use TCP sockets directly.

6.2.2 Framework Modifications

Our solution solves all of the above issues by using a transparent HTTP proxy to capture and set the origin header for all HTTP requests made by apps installed on the device. We handle HTTPS traffic by installing a new certificate authority (CA) on the device and allowing our proxy to man-in-the-middle apps' HTTPS connections using the private key of the new CA. Figure 2 shows an overview of our implementation.

We implement the Mobile Trusted-Origin Policy for Android using a new system app. Our system app has two components: a Service that manages the proxies and a `BroadcastReceiver` that listens for apps being installed or removed. When an app is installed, the `BroadcastReceiver` instructs the Service to create a new proxy and then generates a user-ID-specific `iptables` rule that redirects all outbound HTTP and HTTPS traffic from the app to the newly created proxy. Since each app in Android is installed with a unqiue Linux user ID, UID granularity is sufficient[6] When an app is removed, the `BroadcastReceiver` removes the `iptables` rules and terminates the app's proxy.

[4]`https://developers.facebook.com/docs/android/`

[5]`https://play.google.com/store/apps/details?id=com.adobe.air`

[6]There is an exception to this rule: apps signed by the same key may share a UID. Given that we define mobile origin by signing key, this is not a problem.

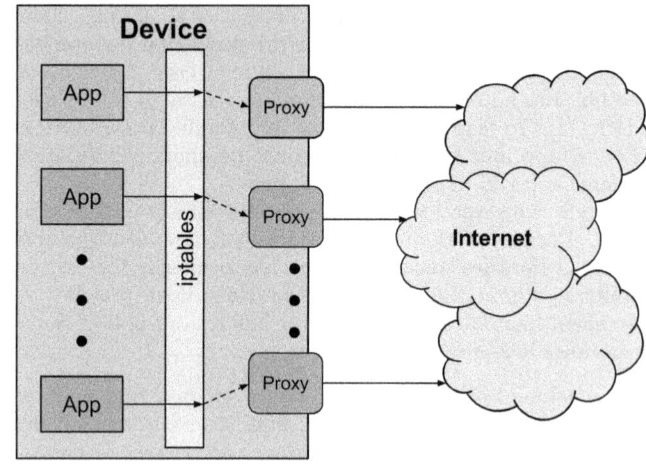

Figure 2: Overview of our implementation of the Mobile Trusted-Origin Policy for Android.

Once the `iptables` rule is in place and the proxy is running, the app can begin to make HTTP requests. These requested will be transparently redirected through our proxy which acts as forwarding proxy. For every request, the proxy modifies the HTTP request header to include the origin of the app that made the request before forwarding the request to the server. The origin header is populated with the SHA1 of the public key used to sign the app, which the proxy retrieves from Android's `PackageManager` when the app was installed. This signature will be unique to apps from the same developer, assuming that private keys are not disclosed. The proxy then forwards the response from the server back to the app which made the request.

For HTTPS traffic, there are a few additional steps. On first boot, the system app creates a new CA and installs it as a trusted authority on the device, keeping the new CA's private key (we should not do this at system compilation time as we do not want different devices to share the same CA, in case the private key becomes known). When an app makes an HTTPS connection, it will be redirected to the proxy. The proxy first fetches the destination server's certificate, extracts identity information from the sever certificate, creates a new certificate using the extracted server's identify information, and signs the new certificate using the new CA's private key. Then, the proxy returns the new certificate to the app during the SSL/TLS handshake. This allows the proxy to perform a man-in-the-middle modification on the HTTPS requests from the app to the server where it modifies the HTTP headers to include the app's origin. In the special case that the server's certificate is not signed by a trusted CA, our system proxy will sign the new certificate with an ephemeral key, so that we do not elevate the trust level of the destination server.

7. EVALUATION

Here we evaluate to what extent MTOP achieves the goals presented in Section 4. We evaluate our security goals and make a special case for deployment concerns, as any real-world adoption of our system would have to deal with partial deployment on devices, at least initially. Finally, we investigate the performance overhead of proxying HTTP traffic and adding the TCOR header.

7.1 Security

In Section 4, we defined two goals of our framework: 1) sandbox code and content from separate mobile origins, and 2) allow servers to detect unauthorized communications via mobile origins. We achieve the first goal by separating libraries and regular apps into separate Android apps and using LayerCake to allow them to share the screen. We achieve the second using the TCOR which allows servers to decide which mobile origins can communicate with it. Because our proxy determines mobile origin per UID, even HTTP requests generated by the app in a `WebView` (a UI object that acts as an embedded browser window), will have the correct mobile origin header. However, this means that any `<iframes>` in loaded websites will also be Trusted Cross-Origin Requests as they will also contain the app's origin header. For this reason, web APIs that allow for writes should contain *cross-site request forgery* tokens to protect from these "cross-mobile-origin request forgery" attacks.

Malicious code authors may attempt to circumvent TCOR by proxying their traffic through their own server to remove the header. As mentioned in Section 4, we do not consider the case where attackers run their code on their own devices or operating systems. In this case, proxying traffic would have the side effect of limiting all malicious traffic to a small set of IP addresses, which could be detected by private web APIs or ad networks.

7.2 Deployment

We consider the difficulty of deploying the Mobile Trusted-Origin Policy, and what security concerns arise if there is partial adoption from devices, servers, and apps.

7.2.1 Complete Deployment

When all mobile devices support MTOP, no app can fabricate its mobile origin, so receiving servers will be able to differentiate legitimate and unauthorized traffic from apps, effectively prohibiting unauthorized cross-domain communications. Note that just because cross-domain communications are forbidden doesn't mean that servers can rely on this property for client authentication. For example, a web server should not assume that all incoming XMLHttpRequests are generated by its pages, and neither should a mobile server assume that all incoming requests are generated by its apps, because an attacker can generate both these requests from his computer without using a web browser or mobile OS.

7.2.2 Partial Deployment

When Mobile Trusted Origin Policy is partially deployed on mobile devices, it has the following implications.

Servers not supporting Mobile Trusted-Origin Policy. If a server does not wish to support MTOP, meaning it accepts communications from all apps, it needs no modification to handle requests from devices supporting Mobile Trusted-Origin Policy. These servers can simply ignore the TCOR HTTP headers (provided that the HTTP header would not conflict with any headers added by the client itself).

Servers supporting Mobile Trusted-Origin Policy. When a server supports MTOP but not all mobile devices do, the server would encounter two problems when handling requests from these non-compliant devices:

1. The requests from the server's authorized apps would not have the required HTTP header.

2. A malicious app would be able to fabricate the required HTTP header.

To solve the first problem, the server's authorized apps could add the required HTTP header by itself as a temporary compatibility measure. The second case, on the other hand, essentially reduces non-compliant devices to the current security model. As discussed above, the mobile server should not rely on Mobile Trusted-Origin Policy for client authentication (just as a web server should not rely on the Same-Origin Policy for client authentication), instead our system allows the server to identify and reject unwanted requests from compliant devices. As more devices deploy Mobile Trusted-Origin Policy, such unwanted traffic will decrease.

When a server starts to support Mobile Trusted-Origin Policy, it adds the mobile origins of its authorized apps to its whitelist. However, a special case arises when the server provides third-party libraries for apps. When these apps embed the libraries, requests from the libraries would be rejected by the server because the mobile origin of these libraries would be those third-party apps rather than the library itself. To handle this case, the server should release its code in a standalone app instead.

Fortunately, even low levels of adoption can be useful for reducing attacks like click fraud. Fraudsters will have two choices when devices start to append the *X-Mobile-Origin* headers): 1) they can detect when this occurs and not perform their fraud, or 2) they can perform their fraud regardless. In the former case, fraudsters will lose out on the revenue they would have gained from installs on MTOP-enabled devices. In the latter case, MTOP would append the mobile origin to the fraudulent app's HTTP requests, which may help servers identify fraudulent traffic (and which apps are generating it). This hurts the fraudsters regardless of the choice that they make.

7.2.3 Legacy Apps

Apps which do not contain network-enabled libraries do not need to be modified to work with our framework. Apps which do contain network-enabled libraries, on the other hand, would likely be incompatible with our framework, as traffic generated from the libraries would have the mobile origin of the parent app. Library developers would be incentivized to modify their library to be a standalone app in order to protect against unauthorized access to their web APIs, and app developers would be incentivized to upgrade their apps in order to be able to use the functionality of these libraries.

7.3 Performance

We evaluate the additional delay to network requests introduced by our proxy implementation. As our implementation is built on LayerCake, we inherit its performance characteristics. Roesner and Kohno [20] determine that LayerCake introduces minor overhead when UI embedding is used, and negligible overhead to input event dispatch delay.

Webpage Size	Load time (ms)					
	HTTP			HTTPS		
	w/o Proxy	with Proxy	Overhead	w/o Proxy	with Proxy	Overhead
Small (431B)	7	17	10	27	85	58
Large (580KB)	238	250	12	308	521	213

Table 2: Comparison of the average time required for an app to load a small webpage (averaged over loading 10,000 times) and a large webpage (averaged over loading 1,000 times) while using our proxy vs. not using our proxy.

Our proxy-based approach introduces overhead on HTTP traffic from apps as the traffic must pass through our proxy. To determine whether the overhead is manageable, we perform two experiments: loading a small webpage (431 B) 10,000 times and loading a large webpage (580KB) 1,000 times. For both experiments, the website is hosted on a nearby server and the phone (a Nexus 4) is connected to the Internet via USB. Table 2 summarizes the results. It took 168 seconds and 68 seconds to load the small website 10,000 times with and without the proxy, respectively, so the proxy introduced only 10 millisecond overhead in each page load. For loading the large webpage 1,000 times, it took 250 seconds and 238 seconds with and without the proxy, respectively, so the proxy introduces only 12 milliseconds overhead in each page load. Such overhead caused by our proxy is negligible and therefore should be unnoticeable to users.

We perform the same benchmark for our HTTPS proxy. Our HTTPS proxy introduces a significant inital latency (about 1.5 seconds) the first time when it makes a request to a host, as the proxy must fetch the server's certificate, extract its identify information, and create a new one. (By comparison, without our proxy, the app still needs to fetch the server's certificate but need not create a new one.) However, subsequent requests to the same host are much faster since they reuse the newly created certificate. It took 854 seconds and 273 seconds to load the small website 10,000 times with and without the proxy, respectively, resulting in an overhead per page load of 58.1 milliseconds. The proxy must establish two SSL connections each time an app connects using HTTPS, meaning the cost of fetching a small webpage is dominated by the cost of the SSL handshakes. For the large webpage, it took 521 seconds and 308 seconds to make 1,000 requests with and without the proxy, respectively. Fetching the larger webpage amortizes the cost of the handshakes over a longer connection, meaning that the larger webpage had a significantly lower overhead per byte compared to the smaller one.

8. DISCUSSION

8.1 Other Operating Systems

Mobile Trusted-Origin Policy could apply to other smartphone operating systems besides Android. An interesting case is Firefox OS. Firefox OS is a mobile phone operating system which distributes apps as HTML and Javascript, and enforces the web's Same-Origin Policy to prevent externally loaded Javascript from accessing device functionality or reading app data. Additionally, app code is restricted from communicating with arbitrary websites according to the restrictions of the web's Same-Origin Policy. Despite this, Firefox mobile apps may request privileges to circumvent this restriction (the `network-http` permission or `systemXHR` permission). In fact, this permission is the most commonly requested among apps on the Firefox mobile app market [6]. Given this, Firefox OS could still benefit from using the Trusted Cross-Origin Requests HTTP header to prevent apps from making unauthorized network requests. Firefox OS would be free to implement the remainder of the Mobile Trusted-Origin Policy using the existing Same-Origin Policy built into the OS.

8.2 Privacy

Our framework may create privacy concerns as it enables a network snooper to determine which apps a user has installed by observing the `X-Mobile-Origin` values in outbound HTTP requests. We note there are a number of ways network eavesdroppers may already infer what apps a user is running, for example by network profiling [4], observing publisher IDs in ad requests [23], or by simply observing HTTP user-agent strings of apps in iOS. Regardless, our system relies on a partial mitigation to reduce the privacy impact of the TCOR headers. Apps which require a TCOR header must opt-in to having them added by requesting a special permission which our system uses when modifying the proxied traffic. Apps which opt-in will have the `X-Mobile-Origin` header added as usual. Apps which do not will have an empty value for `X-Mobile-Origin` in outbound requests. What is important to note is that all apps are subject to having their traffic proxied, regardless of whether they opt-in, meaning the origin headers cannot be forged by apps which choose to opt-out.

8.3 Limitations

We use the app's verification key to create its mobile-origin signature. However, in Android, developers may sign many of their apps with the same key, meaning our system defines mobile origin at the developer level. An alternative design would be to use a combination of the verification key and the app's package name, but since two apps on different markets may have the same package name (as discussed in 5.1), this only provides per-developer, per-market granularity. Finally, the code signature itself could be used, but since apps may be updated, this would be too granular, causing servers to have to update their signature each time an app updates.

Our implementation only adds origin information for HTTP traffic on port 80 and HTTPS traffic on port 443. Thus, servers which wish to enforce origin-based policies should listen on one of these ports. Apps which communicate via other protocols will not have their origin included with outbound requests. To estimate how many apps connect with a protocol other than HTTP(S), we ran a random sample of 1,000 Android apps through PyAndrazzi [15], a dynamic analysis tool which performs UI state exploration. From the resulting network logs, we found that of the 793 apps with network connections to known ports, 622 apps (78%) only connect over HTTP, while 786 apps (99%) only use HTTP or HTTPS (based on destination port number)[7].

A limitation of our proxy for HTTPS connections is certificate pinning, where the client app specifies the exact certificate it expects the server to respond with, instead of relying on certificate authorities. Apps which use certificate pinning will get certificate errors from our proxy, which resigns the remote server's certificate so it can perform its man-in-the-middle. According to [9], approximately 10% of the top apps on Google play use certificate pinning. Breaking certificate pinning is a limitation of the prototype implementation rather than of MTOP. This necessitates further research into how to send the provenance information. For example, it could be added at a lower level protocol (e.g., as an IP option).

9. RELATED WORK

One of the goals of the Mobile Trusted-Origin Policy is to prevent a user's device from being turned into a "bot" without exploiting the device's operating system, simply because a malicious app was downloaded. Botnets are collections of compromised user machines (called bots) which can be instructed to generate fraudulent network traffic. The damage caused by botnets is well documented in previous literature. For example, botnets can be used to perform ad fraud [24], send spam emails [25], and perform distributed denial-of-service attacks [10].

9.1 Mobile Ad Fraud

There is limited prior work investigating mobile app ad fraud. Liu, et al. [18] investigate *display fraud* on Windows Phone, which uses techniques that analyze the UI of apps to determine if developers are obfuscating ads or coercing users to click ads by placing them near buttons and other actionable UI elements. Our proposed framework prevents this attack as the app cannot interfere with the ad app's UI. Crussell et al. [3] built a system, MAdFraud, to automatically extract ad requests and clicks from network traces to investigate apps performing *ad fraud*: apps making ad requests when in the background and issuing clicks without user interaction. Our work performs a detailed investigation of two click fraud app families and proposes a framework that prevents the ad fraud found by MAdFraud. In addition, Symantec [1] and Lookout [12], two security companies, provide case studies of malware which issues fraudulent clicks to search engines. These include a type of click fraud called *search engine poisoning*, where search engine results can be influenced by clicking on search engine links to increase their page rank. We note that despite similar nomenclature, this type of click fraud is independent of ad click fraud.

9.2 Inner-App Code Isolation

Grace, et. al. [14] and Stevens, et. al. [23] investigate the practice of Android ad libraries leveraging permissions of the parent app to exfiltrate sensitive user data. As a result of these infringements, there have been proposals for different ways to separate ad libraries and apps into different security domains on Android. LayerCake [21] and AFrame [27] achieve this by separating the app and ad library into separate processes, relying on the built-in Linux process isolation mechanisms to put them into separate security domains. This requires distributing the app and library as separate Android apps which share a UI, while the systems ensure that touch events cannot be forged between security domains. Moshchuk, et. al. [19] develop a content-based isolation mechanism for Windows called ServiceOS, in which the operating system is able to sandbox code based on where the code came from, like the browser's SOP. This allows for isolation beyond application granularity (for smartphones) or user granularity (for desktops). These systems can isolate library and app code, but do not provide a way to mediate apps' network access to prevent the attacks in Section 3.

[7]PyAndrazzi cannot log in to services, and thus may not expose all the network functionality of an app. For apps that perform log in over HTTPS, however, PyAndrazzi will still attempt to submit the form with dummy values, and thus we expect to see the outgoing HTTPS connection regardless, even if the log in fails.

9.3 App Provenance for Network Requests

AdSplit [22], on the other hand, is built on Quire [7], which adds call stack provenance to IPC and RPC calls. Quire's RPC attestations, while able to to protect against the attacks in Section 3, rely on the presence of a manufacturer-embedded private key on the device to sign the RPC call stacks. Another work, AdAttester [17], provides impression and click attestations for ad requests by leveraging ARM's TrustZone hardware, preventing apps from sending forged impressions and clicks. Like AdSplit, it requires a private key stored on the device to sign its attestations. Not only would compromise of this key allow for forged attestations to be made, but it is unclear whether servers would be able to enumerate all the certificates associated with these deployed keys, as each device and manufacturer would need to have its own. Our MTOP, on the other hand, does not require a secret to be embedded on the device, and servers would need to enumerate only signatures for authorized apps, instead of for all devices which may contact the server. We note that it is already common for servers to whitelist apps, e.g., in the form of publisher IDs for ad providers and username/-password credentials for web APIs.

10. CONCLUSION

We proposed the Mobile Trusted-Origin Policy, which consists of two parts: 1) an app provenance mechanism which annotates outgoing HTTP(S) requests with information about which app generated the network traffic, and 2) a code isolation mechanism that separates code within an app which should have different provenance signatures into what we call a "mobile origin". To handle point (1), we propose Trusted Cross-Origin Requests, which allows servers to decide if an app's communication is authorized by including app provenance in outgoing HTTP requests. To motivate such a system, we investigated two families of click fraud malware in Section 3.2 and observe how the lack of origin protections enables the fraud to occur. Finally, we implement MTOP on Android, using a network proxy to add the TCOR header to outgoing HTTP requests and HTTPS requests, evaluating its deployability and performance.

Acknowledgements This paper is based upon work supported by the Intel Science and Technology Center for Secure Computing and UC Davis RISE award.

References

[1] Eric Chien. *Motivations of Recent Android Malware.* Tech. rep. Technical Report, Symantec Security, 2013.

[2] Jonathan Crussell, Clint Gibler, and Hao Chen. "An-Darwin: Scalable Detection of Semantically Similar Android Applications". In: *Computer Security–ESORICS 2013.* Springer, 2013, pp. 182–199.

[3] Jonathan Crussell, Ryan Stevens, and Hao Chen. "MAdFraud: Investigating Ad Fraud in Android Applications". In: *Proceedings of 12th International Conference on Mobile Systems, Applications and Services.* 2014.

[4] Shuaifu Dai, Alok Tongaonkar, Xiaoyin Wang, Antonio Nucci, and Dawn Song. "Networkprofiler: Towards automatic fingerprinting of android apps". In: *INFOCOM, 2013 Proceedings IEEE.* IEEE. 2013, pp. 809–817.

[5] Benjamin Davis and Hao Chen. "RetroSkeleton: Retrofitting Android Apps". In: *Proceeding of the 11th annual international conference on Mobile systems, applications, and services.* ACM. 2013, pp. 181–192.

[6] Daniel DeFreez, Bhargava Shastry, Hao Chen, and Jean-Pierre Seifert. "A First Look at Firefox OS Security". In: *Workshop on Mobile Security Technologies.* 2014.

[7] Michael Dietz, Shashi Shekhar, Yuliy Pisetsky, Anhei Shu, and Dan S Wallach. "QUIRE: Lightweight Provenance for Smart Phone Operating Systems." In: *USENIX Security Symposium.* 2011.

[8] William Enck et al. "TaintDroid: An Information-Flow Tracking System for Realtime Privacy Monitoring on Smartphones." In: *Proceedings of the 9th USENIX Symposium on Operating Systems Design and Implementation.* Vol. 10. 2010, pp. 1–6.

[9] Sascha Fahl et al. "Why Eve and Mallory love Android: An analysis of Android SSL (in) security". In: *Proceedings of the 2012 ACM conference on Computer and communications security.* ACM. 2012, pp. 50–61.

[10] Felix C. Freiling, Thorsten Holz, and Georg Wicherski. "Botnet Tracking: Exploring a Root-Cause Methodology to Prevent Distributed Denial-of-Service Attacks". In: *Computer Security–ESORICS 2005.* Vol. 3679. Lecture Notes in Computer Science. Springer Berlin Heidelberg, 2005, pp. 319–335.

[11] Sean Gallagher. "Snapchat images stolen from third-party Web app using hacked API". In: *Ars Technica* (Oct. 2014). URL: http://arstechnica.com/security/2014/10/snapchat-images-stolen-from-third-party-web-app-using-hacked-api/.

[12] John Gamble. *MaClickFraud: Counterfeit Clicks and Search Queries.* 2013. URL: https://blog.lookout.com/blog/2013/11/01/maclickfraud-counterfeit-clicks-and-search-queries/.

[13] Clint Gibler, Jonathan Crussell, Jeremy Erickson, and Hao Chen. "AndroidLeaks: Automatically detecting potential privacy leaks in Android applications on a large scale". In: *Trust and Trustworthy Computing.* Springer, 2012, pp. 291–307.

[14] Michael C Grace, Wu Zhou, Xuxian Jiang, and Ahmad-Reza Sadeghi. "Unsafe exposure analysis of mobile in-app advertisements". In: *Proceedings of the fifth ACM conference on Security and Privacy in Wireless and Mobile Networks.* ACM. 2012, pp. 101–112.

[15] Kristen Kennedy, Eric Gustafson, and Hao Chen. "Quantifying the Effects of Removing Permissions from Android Applications". In: *Workshop on Mobile Security Technologies.* 2013.

[16] Anne van Kesteren. "Cross-Origin Resoucrce Sharing". In: *World Wide Web Consortium W3C* (Jan. 2014). URL: http://www.w3.org/TR/cors/.

[17] Wenhao Li, Haibo Li, Haibo Chen, and Yubin Xia. "AdAttester: Secure Online Mobile Advertisement Attestation Using TrustZone". In: *Proceedings of the 13th Annual International Conference on Mobile Systems, Applications, and Services.* ACM. 2015, pp. 75–88.

[18] Bin Liu, Suman Nath, Ramesh Govindan, and Jie Liu. "DECAF: Detecting and Characterizing Ad Fraud in Mobile Apps". In: *Presented as part of the 11th USENIX Symposium on Networked Systems Design and Implementation (NSDI 14).* Seattle, WA: USENIX, 2014.

[19] Alexander Moshchuk, Helen J Wang, and Yunxin Liu. "Content-based isolation: rethinking isolation policy design on client systems". In: *Proceedings of the 2013 ACM SIGSAC conference on Computer & communications security.* ACM. 2013, pp. 1167–1180.

[20] Franziska Roesner, James Fogarty, and Tadayoshi Kohno. "User Interface Toolkit Mechanisms for Securing Interface Elements". In: *Symposium on User Interface Software and Technology* (2012).

[21] Franziska Roesner and Tadayoshi Kohno. "Securing Embedded User Interfaces: Android and Beyond". In: *Proceedings of the 22nd USENIX Security Symposium* (2013).

[22] Shashi Shekhar, Michael Dietz, and Dan S. Wallach. "AdSplit: Separating smartphone advertising from applications". In: *Proceedings of the 21st USENIX Security Symposium.* 2012.

[23] Ryan Stevens, Clint Gibler, Jonathan Crussell, Jeremy Erickson, and Hao Chen. "Investigating User Privacy in Android Ad Libraries". In: *Workshop on Mobile Security Technologies.* 2012.

[24] Brett Stone-Gross et al. "Understanding fraudulent activities in online ad exchanges". In: *Proceedings of the 2011 ACM SIGCOMM conference on Internet measurement conference.* ACM. 2011, pp. 279–294.

[25] Gianluca Stringhini, Oliver Hohlfeld, Christopher Kruegel, and Giovanni Vigna. "The Harvester, the Botmaster, and the Spammer: On the Relations Between the Different Actors in the Spam Landscape". In: *Proceedings of the 9th ACM Symposium on Information, Computer, and Communication Security.* ACM. 2014.

[26] Nicolas Viennot, Edward Garcia, and Jason Nieh. "A measurement study of Google Play". In: *The 2014 ACM international conference on Measurement and modeling of computer systems.* ACM. 2014, pp. 221–233.

[27] Xiao Zhang, Amit Ahlawat, and Wenliang Du. "AFrame: isolating advertisements from mobile applications in Android". In: *Proceedings of the 29th Annual Computer Security Applications Conference.* ACM. 2013, pp. 9–18.

APPENDIX

```
POST //NuclearCoreWeb//NuclearCoreServlet HTTP/1.1
Content-Type: text/plain; charset=ISO-8859-1
Host: core.nucleardroid.com:8080
User-Agent: Apache-HttpClient/UNAVAILABLE (java 1.4)

{"namespace":"com.pixcel.MorzeDroid","request":"getAd"}
HTTP/1.1 200 OK
Server: Apache-Coyote/1.1
X-Powered-By: Servlet/3.0; JBossAS-6
Date: Thu, 13 Feb 2014 23:04:34 GMT

{"countperday":5,"items":[{"countfake":5,"counttry":2,"name":"Madvertise-1","enable":true,"namespacelist":["com.
pixcel.MorzeDroid"],"siteid":"QCPWyzAF","publisherid":"","countsuccess":3,"adname":"Madvertise","namespace":"com
.pixcel.MorzeDroid"},{"countfake":5,"counttry":2,"name":"MobFox-1","enable":true,"namespacelist":["com.pixcel.Mo
rzeDroid"],"siteid":"84baac85e1f8a3092bd7cd4847dd0483","publisherid":"","countsuccess":1,"adname":"MobFox","name
space":"com.pixcel.MorzeDroid"},{"countfake":5,"counttry":2,"name":"Tapjoy-1","enable":true,"namespacelist":["co
m.pixcel.MorzeDroid"],"siteid":"c9e2a2f6-fb99-4131-bba0-944be954493d","publisherid":"IQAnj1JzUVHSFvRqja1R","coun
tsuccess":3,"adname":"Tapjoy","namespace":"com.pixcel.MorzeDroid"}],"enable":true,"namespace":"com.pixcel.MorzeD
roid"}
```

Figure 3: Example Nucleardroid query.

```
Iterator localIterator = localJSONAd.getAdItems().iterator();
while (localIterator.hasNext()) {
  JSONAdItem localJSONAdItem = (JSONAdItem)localIterator.next();
  if (localJSONAdItem.isEnable()) {
    LogHelper.log("processingAd: ad item: " + localJSONAdItem.getName() + " processing");
    BaseGenerator localBaseGenerator = GeneratorFactory.getGenerator(getApplicationContext(), localJSONAdItem);
    if (localBaseGenerator != null)
      try {
        localBaseGenerator.fakeRequest();
        waiteOne();
        localBaseGenerator.clickRequest();
    } catch (Exception localException2) { }
  } else {
    LogHelper.log("processingAd: ad item: " + localJSONAdItem.getName() + " disabled");
  }
}
```

Figure 4: De-compiled Java for Pixcel's ad fraud service.

```
setTimeout(function() {
  var i=1;
  var frames=document["body"]["getElementsByTagName"]("iframe");
  for(var j=0; j<frames["length"]; j++) {
    var content =
      frames[j]["contentWindow"] ? frames[j]["contentWindow"]["document"] : frames[j]["contentDocument"];
    if(content) {
      var atags= content["body"]["getElementsByTagName"]("a");
      if(atags["length"]) {
        _0x432cx7(atags[0]["href"], clickUrls[Math["min"](i, clickUrls["length"]-1)]);
        i++;
  } } }
  function _0x432cx7(href, clickUrl) {
    var div=document["createElement"]("div");
    div["innerHTML"]="<iframe src=\"javascript:'<!doctype html><html><head><meta charset=\'utf-8\'></head><body
        >' + decodeURIComponent('" + encodeURIComponent("<img src=\""+href+"\"/>")+"') + '</body></html>'\"></
        iframe>";
    div["style"]["width"]="1px"; div["style"]["height"]="1px";
    div["style"]["visibility"]="hidden";
    document["body"]["appendChild"](div["firstChild"]);
    if(clickUrl) {
      var img=document["createElement"]("img");
      img["setAttribute"]("src", clickUrl);
      img["style"]["width"]="1px"; img["style"]["height"]="1px";
      img["style"]["visibility"]="hidden";
      document["body"]["appendChild"](img)
} } }, 3000);
```

Figure 5: De-obfuscated Javascript from postupdate.info/carousel/ad_track.js.

Inferring the Detection Logic and Evaluating the Effectiveness of Android Anti-Virus Apps

Zhenquan Cai
Centre for Strategic Infocomm Technologies
30 Science Park Road, 117512, Singapore
cai.zhenquan.is@gmail.com

Roland H. C. Yap
School of Computing
National University of Singapore
13 Computing Drive, 117417, Singapore
ryap@comp.nus.edu.sg

ABSTRACT

Malware on Android has been reported to be on the rise. There are many anti-virus (AV) apps available on Android. However, most AVs are presented as black-boxes without details given about their workings. In this paper, we propose to determine the key elements used by the AVs, which we call inferring the AV detection logic, through a black-box testing methodology. We perform a large scale experiment on 57 Android AVs using 2000 malware variants to evaluate whether the detection logic can be found and whether the AVs can detect the malware. Our experiments show that a majority of AVs detect malware using simple static features. Such features can be easily obfuscated by renaming or encrypting strings and data, which can make it easy to evade some AVs. We also observe trends showing that AVs use common features to detect malware across all families.

1. INTRODUCTION

Google's Android is considered to be the dominant player for the mobile operating system market and is reported as having over 84% of the market share in 2014 [17]. Reports from anti-virus companies suggest that Android malware are on the rise. F-Secure reported that Android continues to be the most targeted platform by cybercriminals, accounting for 99% of global malware in 2014 [6].

Android apps are typically written in Java and compiled to bytecode for the Dalvik virtual machine (DVM). Like in the Java virtual machine (JVM), there is a close correspondence between the bytecode and source code. Hence, the task of analyzing Dalvik bytecode binaries may be easier than native code binaries. However, there are some challenges. Android enforces an app sandbox and every app runs within the sandbox. Like normal third-party apps, Android anti-virus apps (AV) also operate within the sandbox. In contrast, traditional AVs on desktops may operate with many special privileges, including the use of kernel drivers. Furthermore, mobile phones have limited processing power and battery life which limits the amount of analysis. Network bandwidth may be limited or the device may not be connected to the network, so using the cloud may not be feasible. Thus, the challenge is that an Android AV may be quite limited in what it can do. Furthermore, the AVs are usually presented as black-boxes so it is unclear as to: (i) their effectiveness; and (ii) the detection logic employed.

CODASPY'16, March 09 - 11, 2016, New Orleans, LA, USA

ISBN 978-1-4503-3935-3/16/03...$15.00

DOI: http://dx.doi.org/10.1145/2857705.2857719

In this paper, we present an approach which tries to determine what key elements of an Android app are used in Android AVs[1] to report it as being malware – we call this "infer the detection logic" of the AV. Our detection is based on obfuscation of the Android app package (APK) file and to do this, we propose 20 simple APK features.

We present, to the best of our knowledge, the first systematic large-scale characterization of Android AVs where we focus on determining their internal detection logic. We employ a corpus of 200 real-world malware samples (20 families with 10 instances per family). In order to determine the logic used by these black-box AVs, we propose a variety of obfuscation techniques to target particular features of the APK file. Our experiments evaluate 57 Android AVs on 2,000 malware variants (200 original malware and 2000 obfuscated variants across families). The experiments show that the detection logic for most (55/57) AVs can be found. We found that only a few AVs do consistently well to detect our malware variants across different families and many of the poorer performing AVs use only simple features. Although the performance of AVs have been found to vary, we believe that the poor average performance is still surprising. We believe our results also explain the difference between reports which claim good AV detection versus other research showing that AVs can be evaded using obfuscation.

The remainder of this paper is structured as follows. Section 2 surveys the related work and motivates our work. Section 3 gives background on Android and proposes app features and obsfucation techniques. Section 4 presents our system design for inferring AV detection logic. Section 5 presents our experiments and AV evaluation results. Section 6 concludes.

2. RELATED WORK

2.1 Mobile Malware Landscape

The proliferation of malware on smartphones has led to a number of studies into its characterization. Felt. et. al. [15] surveyed a dataset of 46 Android, iOS and Symbian malware samples collected between January 2009 and June

[1] In the rest of the paper, we will simply write AVs to mean Android AVs.

2011. They concluded that the two most common behaviors of malware are sending premium SMS and stealing information. Zhou et. al. [24] focused on Android and surveyed a much larger dataset of 1,260 Android malware samples in 49 malware families collected between August 2010 and October 2011. They observed that the most common malware are legitimate apps repackaged with malicious payloads.

2.2 Mobile Malware Detection

In response to the malware threat, several detection techniques have been proposed to detect malware. Using a dataset of 1,500 benign and 1,450 malicious samples, PMDS [22] applies machine learning methods on permissions extracted from the manifest. PMDS detects malware based on known malware signatures containing combinations of permissions and claims a 92+% detection rate. DREBIN [10] applies machine learning methods on eight features, including permissions, extracted from the manifest and bytecode. They use a larger dataset of 123,453 benign and 5,560 malicious samples and claim a 94% detection rate.

Kirin [12] extracts permissions defined in the manifest and matches them against security rules containing dangerous combinations of permissions. Kirin is different from PMDS in that it conservatively considers all kinds of potentially dangerous configurations. RiskRanker [16] focuses on detecting zero-day malware and performs a two-order risk analysis to uncover potentially malicious apps. RiskRanker first flags high-risk apps if they contain platform-level exploits and medium-risk apps if they leak information without requiring user interaction. Then, RiskRanker looks out for flagged apps that perform encrypted native code execution and dynamic loading of a secondary app.

It is unclear what detection techniques real-world Android AVs use. In a real-world AV, it may be necessary to have low false positives, otherwise users may complain. Anecdotal evidence suggests that AV companies study malware to learn signatures for detecting them – this is also consistent with our results that seeding VirusTotal with malware affects detection.

2.3 Evaluating Android AVs

There is a large number of AVs available on Google Play that claim to effectively detect malware. In a recent independent test conducted by AV-TEST [11], all 32 tested AVs achieved a detection rate of at least 90%, with 14 of them rated as having perfect detection. In another independent test by AV-Comparatives [9], 16 out 19 tested AVs were also rated as having close to perfect detection. However, Fedler et al. [14] showed that the detection rates of the 11 tested AVs dropped drastically against slightly modified malware. Recently Qihoo 360 [5] was reported as submitting an antivirus engine for independent testing which is different from the actual shipped engine. Resolving such potentially conflicting results is one of our motivations for evaluating the capabilities of AVs.

As far as we are aware, existing work on this area has been limited. Rastogi et. al. [21] evaluated 10 AVs using a dataset of 6 malware samples in 6 malware families. They applied 8 obfuscation techniques on the samples and testing the variants on the AVs and found all of them failed to detect the variants. Zheng et. al. [23] also evaluated 10 AVs using a dataset of 222 samples in 38 families. They applied 4 obfuscation techniques and observed that average detection rates dropped 25-50% for the variants.

While these studies have shown that the use of obfuscation techniques can decrease the detection rates of AVs, what is needed is a more comprehensive evaluation to more accurately assess the behavior of AVs. This requires investigating a sufficient number of AVs on a sufficiently large number of malware families with enough instances per family. Our results show that the detection rates of AVs vary considerably, so selecting a small number of AVs could lead either to a good or poor detection result depending on the chosen subset. For example, if the last 10 AVs in Table 4 are selected, overall detection rates will be poor. In a similar fashion, detection rates of malware instances also vary, e.g. the BASEBRIDGE family is better detected than the BOXERSMS in Table 4. Furthermore, our objective is not only to examine the robustness of these AVs with respect to evasion but also to determine the key features influencing their detection mechanisms.

3. FEATURES OF ANDROID APPS & OBFUSCATION

We first discuss constraints on the operation of Android AVs and how an Android app may be identified based on various static features. We then present obfuscation techniques which modify those features.

3.1 Android AVs Overview

Unlike traditional desktop AVs, Android AVs are no different from normal third-party apps, which means that they also operate within the Android sandbox. We hypothesize that a typical Android AV scanning process operates as follows: 1) the `PackageManager` service is used to get a list all user-installed apps on the device; and 2) the AV reads and scans this list of (`.apk`) files located in `/data/app/`. Since Android AVs are constrained by the sandbox, we believe that they are primarily based on detecting malware based on the static features of `.apk` files.[2] While in principle, one could get around the sandbox with techniques such as emulation or outsourcing the APK to the cloud for analysis, it may be impractical in actual usage on a mobile device – runtime overhead can be high, battery life reduced, and increased network costs.

3.2 APK File Format

An `.apk` file is a zip file with the following directories and files:

- **assets/**: This directory provides an alternative location for developers to save and query app resources like a normal file system.
- **lib/**: This directory contains compiled native code or private libraries.
- **META-INF/**: This directory stores the signed certificate of the app and a manifest file listing all files in the package and their hashes.[3]
- **res/**: This directory is the main location for developers to organize app resources using various subdi-

[2] `/proc` in Android also gives information about running processes but that may not help the APK scanning process since the app may not be running.

[3] This directory can be modified in place if the app is resigned with another certificate.

rectories. These resources are given resource IDs for developers to access through the R class or from XML resources.

- **AndroidManifest.xml**: This is the Android manifest file that describes the components of the app and the permissions required by the app.
- **classes.dex**: The `classes.dex` binary file contains all compiled (`.java`) files of the app, and hence the core logic of the app. The layout and contents of this binary are specified in the Android documentation [3]. This binary can also be decompiled using `apktool` [1] into (`.smali`) files.[4]
- **resources.arsc**: The `resources.arsc` binary file contains all resource names, identifiers and values. Resource values indicate whether a particular resource is precompiled in this binary or stored in a separate directory.

3.3 App Static Features

Let $S(m)$ denote the set of static features $\{S_0, ..., S_n\}$ of malware m. Based on the APK file format, we identified the following APK file components and their underlying static features that can be used as potential signatures by AVs:

3.3.1 Permissions

S_0: **Permission declarations**: Every app declares a set of permissions that is granted by the user during app installation. We do not consider S_0 for obfuscation as it is required for the app for its full functionality.[5]

3.3.2 File Metadata

S_1: **Hash and signature of (.apk) file**: The hash is the most trivial feature but can only identify the exact malware sample. Every app must be signed with a self-signed certificate before they can be installed on the device.

3.3.3 Known Strings

S_2: **Package name**: Every app has its own unique package name.

S_3: **Class names**: These refer to the names of the classes defined in the app, e.g. `Lpackage/name/ClassName;`

S_4: **Method names**: These refer to the names of the methods defined in the app, e.g. `Lpackage/name/ClassName;->MethodName(I)Z;`

S_5: **Field names**: These refer to the names of the fields defined in the app, e.g. `Lpackage/name/ClassName;->FieldName:Ljava/lang/String;`

S_6: **Parameter names**: These refer to the names of the parameters passed to a method, e.g. `.param p0, "ParamName" # Ljava/lang/String;`

S_7: **Local variable names**: These refer to the names of the local variables wihin a method body, e.g. `.local v0, LocalName:I`

S_8: **Strings values**: These refer to the constant strings defined in the app, e.g. `const-string v0, "string constant"`

S_9: **Field values**: These refer to the values of the fields defined in the app, e.g. `.field public FieldName:Lpackage/name/ClassName; = "field value"`

S_{10}: **Annotation values**: These refer to the string values contained in the annotation directives defined in the app.

3.3.4 Resources

S_{11}: **String resources**: These are saved in the `res/values` directory and provide string data values for the app.

S_{12}: **File resources**: These typically can be found in the `assets/`, `lib/`, `res/raw/` and `unknown/` directories. Malware could hide its payload here.

S_{13}: **Data payloads**: Malware payloads can be hidden in the `classes.dex` binary using the `fill-array-data` instruction that is used to embed variable-length bytes.

3.3.5 API Calls

S_{14}: **Android API calls**: These refer to the classes and methods in the Android framework referred to by the app.

3.3.6 Byte Sequences

S_{15}: **File size**: This is the size of the `classes.dex` binary.

S_{16}: **Methods**: These refer to the (number of) methods and byte sequences in each method body.

S_{17}: **goto instructions**: This is a simple feature to summarize control flow in a method based on the number of `goto` instructions.

S_{18}: **invoke instructions**: These refer to the (number of) `invoke` instructions in the app which are used to call a specified method.

S_{19}: **fill-array-data instructions**: These refer to the (number of) `fill-arraydata` instructions in the app. It can be used by malware to embed variable-length byte data in the app.

S_{20}: **aput-byte instructions**: These refer to the (number of) `aput-byte` instructions in the app. Such instructions may also be used by malware to embed a single byte per instruction in the app.

3.4 Obfuscation Techniques

We propose the use of obfuscation to modify the app so as to change app features but preserve app behavior. Let O denote the set of obfuscating functions $(O_1, ..., O_n)$. Each obfuscating function O_i obfuscates one static feature S_i of malware m where $1 \leq i \leq n$ and $S_i \in S(m)$. We distinguish a special repacking and resigning obfuscation, O_1, which only repacks and resigns the malware without any semantic change. The O_1 obfuscation is required by all other techniques. From the previous identified static features, we propose 20 obfuscation techniques to change a specific static feature in an app. We can coarsely classify these techniques under three broad categories: (i) C1: Change Identifier Names; (ii) C2: Encrypt Strings and Bytes; and (iii) C3: Expand DEX Binary. Based on these three categories, we propose the following obfuscation techniques:

O_1: **Repack and resign**: We change the hash of the `.apk` file. This is done using `apktool` to unpack and repack the file without making modifications. Then, we use `jarsigner` to resign the file.

3.4.1 C1: Change Identifier Names

O_2: **Change package name**: We rename the `<manifest>` element's `package` attribute in the `AndroidManifest.xml` file.

O_3: **Change class names**: We rename all classes defined in the app.

[4]Smali is an assembly language designed for Android app decompilation.

[5]As permissions should not be reduced to avoid app crashes, obfuscation would require adding new permissions.

O_4: **Change methods names**: We rename all methods defined in the app.
O_5: **Change fields names**: We rename all fields defined in the app.
O_6: **Change parameter names**: We rename all parameters passed to methods defined in the app.
O_7: **Change local variable names**: We rename all local variables in methods defined in the app.

3.4.2 C2: Encrypt Strings and Bytes

O_8: **Encrypt strings**: We encrypt all constant strings defined in the app.
O_9: **Encrypt field values**: We encrypt all field values defined in the app.
O_{10}: **Encrypt annotation values**: We encrypt all annotation values defined in the app.
O_{11}: **Encrypt string resources**: We encrypt all string values defined in the the `res/values/strings.xml` file.
O_{12}: **Encrypt file resources**: We encrypt all raw files in the `assets/`, `lib/`, `res/raw/`, `unknown/` directories.
O_{13}: **Encrypt data payloads from fill-array-data instructions**: We encrypt all bytes held by `fill-array-data` instructions.
O_{14}: **Encrypt Android API calls**: We encrypt API calls to the Android framework by using Java reflection to invoke an encrypted method name. An additional decryption method is inserted to decrypt at runtime. For each of the above obfuscations, an appropriate additional decryption method is inserted to decrypt at runtime.

3.4.3 C3: Expand DEX Binary

O_{15}: **Insert dummy bytes**: We change the size of the `classes.dex` binary. This is done by initializing a dummy array in the beginning of every method using a conditional but the array need not be used.
O_{16}: **Insert dummy methods**: We change the number of methods in the `classes.dex` binary. This is done by declaring a dummy method in every class which is called in the beginning of every method using a conditional but during execution, the method need not be called.
O_{17}: **Insert dummy gotos**: We use a simple heuristic to change the control flow of all methods in the app. This is done by inserting multiple goto statements in the beginning of every method which eventually flow to the beginning of the original code.
O_{18}: **Insert dummy invoke instructions**: We insert a dummy `invoke` instruction that is equivalent to a `nop` before every `invoke` instruction we encounter in the app.
O_{19}: **Insert dummy fill-array-data instructions**: We insert a dummy `fill-array-data` instruction that initializes a dummy array before every `fill-array-data` instruction we encounter in the app.
O_{20}: **Insert dummy aput-byte instructions**: We insert a dummy `aput-byte` instruction that inserts a dummy byte before every `aput-byte` instruction we encounter in the app. The dummy byte will be overwritten by the actual byte.

3.5 Our Objectives

Table 1 summarises our obfuscation techniques with those in the literature [21, 23]. In this paper, we employed variations of all techniques proposed in existing work and new ones.[6] Our experiments show that some of the new features we proposed are used by the higher-rated AVs.

Our Work	[21]	[23]
O_1: Repack and resign	✓	✓
O_2: Change package name	✓	-
O_3: Change class names	✓	-
O_4: Change methods names	✓	✓
O_5: Change fields names	✓	-
O_6: Change parameter names	-	-
O_7: Change local variable names	-	-
O_8: Encrypt strings	✓	✓
O_9: Encrypt field values	-	-
O_{10}: Encrypt annotation values	-	-
O_{11}: Encrypt string resources	-	-
O_{12}: Encrypt file resources	✓	-
O_{13}: Encrypt data payloads from fill-array-data instructions	-	-
O_{14}: Encrypt Android API calls	-	-
O_{15}: Insert dummy bytes	✓	-
O_{16}: Insert dummy methods	-	✓
O_{17}: Insert dummy gotos	✓	✓
O_{18}: Insert dummy invoke instructions	-	-
O_{19}: Insert dummy fill-array-data instructions	-	-
O_{20}: Insert dummy aput-byte instructions	-	-

Table 1: Comparison of obfuscation techniques
Key : (✓) is used by previous work, (-) our additional techniques

In this paper, we test whether an AV is effective against obfuscated malware and also analyse the features used by the AV for detecting particular malware instances. This allows us to identify the detection logic used by AVs which allows us to investigate: (a) similarities and differences of AVs on specific instances; (b) extending this to malware families.

4. SYSTEM DESIGN

Our system consists of the following three phases: Generation, Identification and Rating.

4.1 Generation

In the generation phase, we perform cumulative obfuscation, a chosen ordered sequence of obfuscation processes. The function of an obfucation process is to take an APK instance and transform it to a new APK instance which differs from the original according to the static feature(s) being transformed. An obfuscation process transforms a single static feature as follows:

An *obfuscation process* $O_i(m)$ where m is the original malware produces m_i, the obfuscated variant on feature S_i.

A cumulative obfuscation process is an ordered sequence of obfuscation processes composed together as follows:

$$O^i(m) = m^i = \begin{cases} m_i \text{ if } i = 0 \\ O_i(O^{i-1}(m)) \text{ if } i > 0 \end{cases}$$

where m is the original malware and m^i is the obfuscated variant on the set of features $\{S_0, S_1, \ldots, S_i\}$.

We modify our general cumulative obfuscation process in a small way. Due of the large number of obfuscation tech-

[6] We note that [21] did not provide implementation details.

niques, we choose to obfuscate sets of static features at a time. We classify the techniques into the following ten feature sets:

F1. Repack and resign: O_1
F2. Change package name: O_2
F3. Change class-level identifier names: O_3, O_4, O_5
F4. Change method-level identifier names: O_6, O_7
F5. Encrypt strings: O_8, O_9, O_{10}
F6. Encrypt resources: O_{11}, O_{12}
F7. Encrypt bytes: O_{13}
F8. Encrypt API calls: O_{14}
F9. Insert dummy bytes, methods, gotos: O_{15}, O_{16}, O_{17}
F10. Insert dummy instructions: O_{18}, O_{19}, O_{20}

We have chosen this sequence roughly in order of increasing implementation difficulty and change to the app/APK. Without loss of generality, other obfuscation processes can be obtained by re-ordering the obfuscation sequence.

4.2 Identification

In the identification phase, we pass the malware samples and their obfuscated variants to VirusTotal [7] collecting the detection results from the AVs in VirusTotal.[7] If an AV outputs the same detection results for at least $T\%$ of samples in the family, we say that the results are representative of the family with confidence threshold T. We choose a $T = 80$ to cover corner cases where the AV may output a different detection result(s) for one or two samples. In practice, we found that $T = 100$ is feasible in most cases.

We record the detection result of an AV on a malware family M as a vector

$$L(AV, M) = (L_1, L_2, ..., L_n)$$

where $L_i = +$ if obfuscated variants in M on feature sets $\{F1, F2, \ldots, Fi\}$ is detected by the AV and $L_i = -$ if it is not detected. We call $(L_1, L_2, ..., L_n))$ the *logic vector*.

For example, if the logic vector from our cumulative obfuscation process is all +'s, i.e. (+,+,+,+,+,+,+,+,+,+), this means that the malware obfuscated with all our techniques is still detected by the AV. We give another example using malware samples from the ADRD family. The logic vector of AVG on this family is represented as (+,+,+,+,+,+,+,+,−,−). This means that the samples obfuscated with the ordered sequences $\{F1, \ldots, F9\}$ and $\{F1, \ldots, F9, F10\}$ evades detection by AVG.

A logic vector $(L_1, L_2, \ldots, L_m, \ldots, L_n)$ is *cumulatively monotonic* if each $L_i = +$ for $i = 1, \ldots, m$ and $L_i = -$ for $i = m+1 \ldots, n$.

An AV is said to exhibit cumulative monotonicity if applying more obfuscation after evasion does not change the detection result. Intuitively, such a property would seem likely to apply and indeed we found it to be the case in our experiments.

4.3 Rating

In the rating phase, we propose a standard benchmark to rate the AVs for comparative evaluation. Our benchmark is intended to give a reasonably objective assessment as it is supported by tests which analyse a set of features relevant to Android apps. We feel this is fairer than simply relying on the ratings given by AV and security testing companies.

We suggest a scale using the size of the logic vector to rate the AVs – in our case, it is from 0 (weak) to 10 (strong). A lower rating suggests that the AV is more easily evaded. AVs that fail to detect original malware are rated 0 by default. AVs with the logic vector (−,−,−,−,−,−,−,−,−,−), i.e. the AV fails to detect repacked and resigned malware, are also rated 0. We call such AVs as *weak AVs*. Those with (+,+,+,+,+,−,−,−,−,−) will be rated 5 while those with (+,+,+,+,+,+,+,+,+,+) will be rated 10. The 10-rated AVs detect original and all obfuscated variants of malware, so we call them *strong AVs*. However, this does not suggest that these AVs are always among the best as there may be other aspects we did not consider. We have also manually investigated the strong AVs found with additional tests.

5. EVALUATION

We present our evaluation results based on a prototype implementation of our system and a public dataset of malware samples.

5.1 Prototype

We prototype our system in Python based on `apktool` to unpack and repack an app. The prototype decompiles the `(.dex)` bytecode into `(.smali)` code. Our obfuscation techniques are applied to `(.smali)` code that are recompiled back to `(.dex)` bytecode. The prototype then sends the obfuscated variants to VirusTotal and generates the AV detection logic based on the detection results.

5.2 Dataset

We used 5,560 malware samples from the Drebin [10] dataset. This dataset has been used extensively by many researchers. These samples were collected in the period of August 2010 to October 2012. We passed these samples to VirusTotal for re-analysis and obtained updated detection results from 57 AVs in November 2014.[8] We reduced the dataset to 1,285 samples that are detected by at least 40 out of 57 AVs. This is because we want to have a sufficient large number of families and samples per family that are detected by the majority of AVs. The samples must also be sufficiently old so that AV detection logic are well established. From the 1,285 samples, we derived a common family classification for the samples based on the detection results. We then selected 20 malware families shown in Table 2. Our final dataset consists of 200 randomly selected malware samples consisting of 10 samples each from 20 families.

We expand our dataset by generating obfuscated variants of the samples. Such variants are assumed to be unseen by the AVs (at the test time). We perform our cumulative obfuscation process to generate 10 malware variants, each obfuscated with a set of features (see Section 4.1). We generate a total of 200 original x 10 = 2,000 variants. In total, we analyse 57 Android AVs (see Figure 1) on 200 original malware and 2,000 obfuscated variants from 20 families.

5.3 VirusTotal Testing

VirusTotal has a disclaimer which discourages using their service for AV comparative analysis since they are using

[7]VirusTotal is used because it provides a scanning service using many AVs. An example of a VirusTotal report on an APK sample can be found at this URL [8] (the SHA256 hash of the file is in the URL).

[8]The VirusTotal public API accepts a maximum of 4 requests per minute.

Index	Family	Index	Family	Index	Family	Index	Family
1	ADRD	6	FAKETIMER	11	KUNGFU	16	PJAPPS
2	ANSERVER	7	GEIMINI	12	LEGANA	17	RUFRAUD
3	BASEBRIDGE	8	GINGERMASTER	13	LIGHTDD	18	SHASTROSMS
4	BOXERSMS	9	GOLDDREAM	14	LOTOOR	19	SMSHIDER
5	FAKENOTIFY	10	KMIN	15	OPFAKE	20	YZHC

Table 2. Malware families.

command-line versions of the AVs that that do not perform behavioural analysis. We believe that this argument does not hold for our work on Android AVs as they operate in a sandbox and monitoring behavior is difficult. Hence, the VirusTotal detection results still provide a good basis for our work.

Nevertheless, we have also manually investigated detection results of AVs directly on a device. We install a subset (24/57) of the AVs listed in VirusTotal (as not all AVs are readily available) and download a random sample from each of the 20 families onto a Samsung Galaxy Note II device. We found the sample results on the device AVs to be the same as VirusTotal. Thus, we believe our testing results to be representative on those AVs.

5.4 Results

We processed the detection results obtained during the identification phase and generated logic vectors for each AV across 20 malware families. Due to space constraints, we only present the logic vectors for all AVs across four (4 out of 20) malware families in Tables 3 and 4. However, our analysis is based on the complete results. The first column of each family denotes the detection results for the original malware sample. For columns Fi, a positive (+) symbol indicates that the AV detected more than the threshold (8 instances) obfuscated variants in the malware family on feature set $\{F1, F2, \ldots, Fi\}$. A negative (−) symbol indicates otherwise. We call Fj the *deciding feature* used for detection if there is a transition from (+) to (−) from columns $F(j-1)$ to Fj. From the transition, we infer that the AV uses the deciding feature Fj to detect malware. The final column of each family is our assigned rating.

Tables 3 and 4 clearly shows the transitions and hence the deciding features used by AVs across families. These transitions typically happen earlier for the lower-rated AVs and later for the higher-rated ones. We can see that there is considerable variance between AVs on the same family (column variance) and also variance for the same AV across different families (row variance). We highlight two observable trends. Based on the horizontal trends, we see some AVs (e.g. AVG, Cyren) using a common deciding feature for at least three families. Based on the vertical trends, we see families like ANSERVER and BASEBRIDGE being detected by AVs predominantly based on a common deciding feature. We next summarize our analysis on the complete results for AV ratings, AV detection logic and malware family detection logic.

5.4.1 Rating AVs

We compute the average ratings of each AV across 20 malware families and present them in Figure 1. We see some of the reputable brands in the AV industry, AVG (rating: 6.85) and F-Secure (rating: 4.6), ranked in the top 5 AVs. We were surprised to find that close to half (25/57) of the AVs have an average rating of below 2. This suggests that most of these AVs can be easily evaded by either repacking malware or changing the package name in malware. We found 8 AVs (rating: 0) do not detect our original malware or repacked variant at all. We leave out these 8 AVs for the rest of our analysis (note that they are listed in Table 3 and 4).

We manually investigate the top three AVs (AhnLab-V3, Alibaba, K7GW) with ratings of 10 and found the following peculiarities. AhnLab-V3 detected all 200 m^{20} variants[9] under the same classification, Android-Trojan/Malct.bb8a. On the other hand, K7GW detected all 200 m^{20} variants as Trojan (004b3add1). Since the original malware instances come from 20 families, this suggests that there is some other common feaure among these variants that is detected. We resigned these variants with a different self-signed certificate and managed to completely evade K7GW. The obfuscation process for the m^{20} variants then partially evaded AhnLab-V3 (139/200 detected) and Alibaba (70/200 detected). We also found that the detected variants were now given a different family-related classification. This suggests that the previous classification was solely used for our APK files signed with our original self-signed certificate. We note that the Alibaba result detected the variants but the classification was mixed between family related and signed certificate related categories. It may be the case that these AVs obtain their top ratings not only because they go beyond our list of static features but also because they reacted quickly to new seed malware, i.e. from the malware uploaded to VirusTotal.

5.4.2 Comparing AV Detection Logic

We want to look for high-level patterns of the AVs' detection logic across different malware families. Looking at Tables 3 and 4, we observe that the detection logic of the AVs across malware families vary extensively, likely this depends on the nature of the family or specific instances. There is no simple trend. However, many AVs seem to use deciding features that are more easily obfuscated. Naturally, the strong AVs use more features as scoring is proportional to the number of '+' symbols which means that evasion will probably need to apply many obfuscation processes. It is also interesting to note that all AVs exhibited the monotonic property across all malware families.

For each AV, we try to derive a common detection logic based on 20 malware families. Based on the complete obfuscation testing results, we aggregate (sum up the number of '+' symbols in each column) the row of 20 logic vectors for each AV. We call this result vector the *aggregated logic vector*. Based on the transitions in number of '+' symbols, we highlight the deciding features (transitions represented

[9]Each original malware instance has one m^{20} variant obsfucated under all features. Note that, it happens in our experiments that cummulative motonicity is preserved, so it also detects $m^1, \ldots, m^{19}$.

AVs	ADRD												ANSERVER											
	Original	F1	F2	F3	F4	F5	F6	F7	F8	F9	F10	Rating	Original	F1	F2	F3	F4	F5	F6	F7	F8	F9	F10	Rating
ALYac	-	-	-	-	-	-	-	-	-	-	-	0	-	-	-	-	-	-	-	-	-	-	-	0
AVG	+	+	+	+	+	+	+	+	+	-	-	8	+	+	+	+	+	+	+	+	+	-	-	8
AVware	+	+	+	-	-	-	-	-	-	-	-	2	+	+	+	+	+	+	-	-	-	-	-	5
Ad-Aware	+	+	+	-	-	-	-	-	-	-	-	2	+	+	+	+	+	+	-	-	-	-	-	5
AegisLab	+	+	+	+	+	-	-	-	-	-	-	4	+	+	+	+	+	+	-	-	-	-	-	5
Agnitum	-	-	-	-	-	-	-	-	-	-	-	0	-	-	-	-	-	-	-	-	-	-	-	0
AhnLab-V3	+	+	+	+	+	+	+	+	+	+	+	10	+	+	+	+	+	+	+	+	+	+	+	10
Alibaba	+	+	+	+	+	+	+	+	+	+	+	10	+	+	+	+	+	+	+	+	+	+	+	10
Antiy-AVL	+	-	-	-	-	-	-	-	-	-	-	0	+	+	+	+	+	+	-	-	-	-	-	5
Avast	+	+	+	+	+	-	-	-	-	-	-	4	+	+	+	+	+	+	-	-	-	-	-	5
Avira	+	+	+	-	-	-	-	-	-	-	-	2	+	+	+	+	+	+	-	-	-	-	-	5
Baidu-International	+	-	-	-	-	-	-	-	-	-	-	0	+	-	-	-	-	-	-	-	-	-	-	0
BitDefender	+	+	+	-	-	-	-	-	-	-	-	2	+	+	+	+	+	+	-	-	-	-	-	5
Bkav	-	-	-	-	-	-	-	-	-	-	-	0	-	-	-	-	-	-	-	-	-	-	-	0
ByteHero	-	-	-	-	-	-	-	-	-	-	-	0	-	-	-	-	-	-	-	-	-	-	-	0
CAT-QuickHeal	+	+	+	+	+	-	-	-	-	-	-	4	+	+	+	+	+	+	-	-	-	-	-	5
CMC	-	-	-	-	-	-	-	-	-	-	-	0	-	-	-	-	-	-	-	-	-	-	-	0
ClamAV	+	+	+	+	+	-	-	-	-	-	-	4	+	+	+	+	+	+	-	-	-	-	-	5
Comodo	+	-	-	-	-	-	-	-	-	-	-	0	+	+	+	+	+	+	-	-	-	-	-	5
Cyren	+	+	+	+	+	+	+	+	+	-	-	8	+	+	+	+	+	+	+	+	+	-	-	8
DrWeb	+	+	+	-	-	-	-	-	-	-	-	2	+	+	+	+	+	+	-	-	-	-	-	5
ESET-NOD32	+	+	+	-	-	-	-	-	-	-	-	2	+	+	+	+	+	+	-	-	-	-	-	5
Emsisoft	+	+	+	-	-	-	-	-	-	-	-	2	+	+	+	+	+	+	-	-	-	-	-	5
F-Prot	+	+	+	+	+	+	+	+	+	-	-	8	+	+	+	+	+	+	+	+	+	-	-	8
F-Secure	+	+	+	-	-	-	-	-	-	-	-	2	+	+	+	+	+	+	-	-	-	-	-	5
Fortinet	+	+	+	+	+	-	-	-	-	-	-	4	+	+	+	+	+	+	-	-	-	-	-	5
GData	+	+	+	-	-	-	-	-	-	-	-	2	+	+	+	+	+	+	-	-	-	-	-	5
Ikarus	+	+	+	+	+	-	-	-	-	-	-	4	+	+	+	+	+	+	+	+	+	+	-	9
Jiangmin	+	-	-	-	-	-	-	-	-	-	-	0	+	+	+	+	+	+	-	-	-	-	-	5

AVs	BASEBRIDGE												BOXERSMS											
	Original	F1	F2	F3	F4	F5	F6	F7	F8	F9	F10	Rating	Original	F1	F2	F3	F4	F5	F6	F7	F8	F9	F10	Rating
ALYac	-	-	-	-	-	-	-	-	-	-	-	0	-	-	-	-	-	-	-	-	-	-	-	0
AVG	+	+	+	+	+	+	+	+	+	-	-	8	+	+	+	+	+	+	+	+	+	-	-	8
AVware	+	+	+	+	+	+	-	-	-	-	-	5	+	+	+	-	-	-	-	-	-	-	-	2
Ad-Aware	+	+	+	+	+	+	-	-	-	-	-	5	+	+	+	-	-	-	-	-	-	-	-	2
AegisLab	+	+	+	+	+	+	-	-	-	-	-	5	+	+	-	-	-	-	-	-	-	-	-	1
Agnitum	-	-	-	-	-	-	-	-	-	-	-	0	-	-	-	-	-	-	-	-	-	-	-	0
AhnLab-V3	+	+	+	+	+	+	+	+	+	+	+	10	+	+	+	+	+	+	+	+	+	+	+	10
Alibaba	+	+	+	+	+	+	+	+	+	+	+	10	+	+	+	+	+	+	+	+	+	+	+	10
Antiy-AVL	+	+	+	+	+	+	-	-	-	-	-	5	+	-	-	-	-	-	-	-	-	-	-	0
Avast	+	+	+	+	+	+	-	-	-	-	-	5	+	+	+	-	-	-	-	-	-	-	-	2
Avira	+	+	+	+	+	+	-	-	-	-	-	5	-	+	+	-	-	-	-	-	-	-	-	2
Baidu-International	+	-	-	-	-	-	-	-	-	-	-	0	+	-	-	-	-	-	-	-	-	-	-	0
BitDefender	+	+	+	+	+	+	-	-	-	-	-	5	+	+	+	-	-	-	-	-	-	-	-	2
Bkav	-	-	-	-	-	-	-	-	-	-	-	0	-	-	-	-	-	-	-	-	-	-	-	0
ByteHero	-	-	-	-	-	-	-	-	-	-	-	0	-	-	-	-	-	-	-	-	-	-	-	0
CAT-QuickHeal	+	+	+	+	+	+	-	-	-	-	-	5	+	+	+	-	-	-	-	-	-	-	-	2
CMC	-	-	-	-	-	-	-	-	-	-	-	0	-	-	-	-	-	-	-	-	-	-	-	0
ClamAV	+	+	+	+	+	+	-	-	-	-	-	5	+	+	+	+	+	+	-	-	-	-	-	5
Comodo	+	+	+	+	+	+	-	-	-	-	-	5	+	+	+	+	+	+	-	-	-	-	-	5
Cyren	+	+	+	+	+	+	+	+	+	-	-	8	+	+	+	-	-	-	-	-	-	-	-	2
DrWeb	+	+	+	+	+	+	-	-	-	-	-	5	+	+	+	-	-	-	-	-	-	-	-	2
ESET-NOD32	+	+	+	+	+	+	-	-	-	-	-	5	+	+	+	+	+	+	-	-	-	-	-	5
Emsisoft	+	+	+	+	+	+	-	-	-	-	-	5	+	+	+	-	-	-	-	-	-	-	-	2
F-Prot	+	+	+	+	+	+	+	+	+	-	-	8	+	+	+	-	-	-	-	-	-	-	-	2
F-Secure	+	+	+	+	+	+	-	-	-	-	-	5	+	+	+	+	+	+	-	-	-	-	-	5
Fortinet	+	+	+	+	+	+	-	-	-	-	-	5	+	+	+	-	-	-	-	-	-	-	-	2
GData	+	+	+	+	+	+	-	-	-	-	-	5	+	+	+	-	-	-	-	-	-	-	-	2
Ikarus	+	+	+	+	+	+	-	-	-	-	-	5	+	+	+	+	+	+	+	+	+	+	-	9
Jiangmin	+	+	+	+	+	+	-	-	-	-	-	5	+	-	-	-	-	-	-	-	-	-	-	0

Table 3: Logic vectors.
Key: + = malware detected, - = malware not detected

ADRD

AVs	Original	F1	F2	F3	F4	F5	F6	F7	F8	F9	F10	Rating
K7AntiVirus	-	-	-	-	-	-	-	-	-	-	-	0
K7GW	+	+	+	+	+	+	+	+	+	+	+	10
Kaspersky	+	+	+	+	+	-	-	-	-	-	-	4
Kingsoft	+	-	-	-	-	-	-	-	-	-	-	0
Malwarebytes	-	-	-	-	-	-	-	-	-	-	-	0
McAfee	+	-	-	-	-	-	-	-	-	-	-	0
McAfee-GW-Edition	+	-	-	-	-	-	-	-	-	-	-	0
MicroWorld-eScan	+	+	+	-	-	-	-	-	-	-	-	2
Microsoft	+	+	+	+	+	-	-	-	-	-	-	4
NANO-Antivirus	+	+	+	-	-	-	-	-	-	-	-	2
Norman	+	-	-	-	-	-	-	-	-	-	-	0
Panda	-	-	-	-	-	-	-	-	-	-	-	0
Qihoo-360	+	-	-	-	-	-	-	-	-	-	-	0
Rising	-	-	-	-	-	-	-	-	-	-	-	0
SUPERAnti-Spyware	-	-	-	-	-	-	-	-	-	-	-	0
Sophos	+	+	+	-	-	-	-	-	-	-	-	2
Symantec	+	+	+	-	-	-	-	-	-	-	-	2
Tencent	+	-	-	-	-	-	-	-	-	-	-	0
TheHacker	-	-	-	-	-	-	-	-	-	-	-	0
TotalDefense	-	-	-	-	-	-	-	-	-	-	-	0
TrendMicro	+	-	-	-	-	-	-	-	-	-	-	0
TrendMicro-HouseCall	+	-	-	-	-	-	-	-	-	-	-	0
VBA32	+	-	-	-	-	-	-	-	-	-	-	0
VIPRE	+	+	+	-	-	-	-	-	-	-	-	2
ViRobot	-	-	-	-	-	-	-	-	-	-	-	0
Zillya	-	-	-	-	-	-	-	-	-	-	-	0
Zoner	-	-	-	-	-	-	-	-	-	-	-	0
nProtect	-	-	-	-	-	-	-	-	-	-	-	0

ANSERVER

AVs	Original	F1	F2	F3	F4	F5	F6	F7	F8	F9	F10	Rating
K7AntiVirus	-	-	-	-	-	-	-	-	-	-	-	0
K7GW	+	+	+	+	+	+	+	+	+	+	+	10
Kaspersky	+	+	+	+	+	+	-	-	-	-	-	5
Kingsoft	+	+	+	+	+	+	-	-	-	-	-	5
Malwarebytes	-	-	-	-	-	-	-	-	-	-	-	0
McAfee	+	+	+	+	+	+	-	-	-	-	-	5
McAfee-GW-Edition	+	-	-	-	-	-	-	-	-	-	-	0
MicroWorld-eScan	+	+	+	+	+	+	-	-	-	-	-	5
Microsoft	+	+	+	+	+	+	-	-	-	-	-	5
NANO-Antivirus	+	+	+	+	+	+	-	-	-	-	-	5
Norman	-	-	-	-	-	-	-	-	-	-	-	0
Panda	-	-	-	-	-	-	-	-	-	-	-	0
Qihoo-360	+	+	+	+	+	+	-	-	-	-	-	5
Rising	+	+	+	+	+	+	-	-	-	-	-	5
SUPERAnti-Spyware	-	-	-	-	-	-	-	-	-	-	-	0
Sophos	+	+	+	+	+	+	-	-	-	-	-	5
Symantec	+	+	+	+	+	+	-	-	-	-	-	5
Tencent	+	-	-	-	-	-	-	-	-	-	-	0
TheHacker	-	-	-	-	-	-	-	-	-	-	-	0
TotalDefense	-	-	-	-	-	-	-	-	-	-	-	0
TrendMicro	+	+	+	+	+	+	-	-	-	-	-	5
TrendMicro-HouseCall	+	+	+	+	+	+	-	-	-	-	-	5
VBA32	+	+	+	+	+	+	-	-	-	-	-	5
VIPRE	+	+	+	+	+	+	-	-	-	-	-	5
ViRobot	-	-	-	-	-	-	-	-	-	-	-	0
Zillya	-	-	-	-	-	-	-	-	-	-	-	0
Zoner	+	+	+	+	+	+	-	-	-	-	-	5
nProtect	-	-	-	-	-	-	-	-	-	-	-	0

BASEBRIDGE

AVs	Original	F1	F2	F3	F4	F5	F6	F7	F8	F9	F10	Rating
K7AntiVirus	-	-	-	-	-	-	-	-	-	-	-	0
K7GW	+	+	+	+	+	+	+	+	+	+	+	10
Kaspersky	+	+	+	+	+	+	-	-	-	-	-	5
Kingsoft	+	+	+	+	+	+	-	-	-	-	-	5
Malwarebytes	-	-	-	-	-	-	-	-	-	-	-	0
McAfee	+	+	+	+	+	+	-	-	-	-	-	5
McAfee-GW-Edition	+	-	-	-	-	-	-	-	-	-	-	0
MicroWorld-eScan	+	+	+	+	+	+	-	-	-	-	-	5
Microsoft	+	+	+	+	+	+	-	-	-	-	-	5
NANO-Antivirus	+	+	+	+	+	+	-	-	-	-	-	5
Norman	+	-	-	-	-	-	-	-	-	-	-	0
Panda	-	-	-	-	-	-	-	-	-	-	-	0
Qihoo-360	+	+	+	+	+	+	-	-	-	-	-	5
Rising	-	-	-	-	-	-	-	-	-	-	-	0
SUPERAnti-Spyware	-	-	-	-	-	-	-	-	-	-	-	0
Sophos	+	+	+	+	+	+	-	-	-	-	-	5
Symantec	+	+	+	+	+	+	-	-	-	-	-	5
Tencent	+	-	-	-	-	-	-	-	-	-	-	0
TheHacker	-	-	-	-	-	-	-	-	-	-	-	0
TotalDefense	+	+	-	-	-	-	-	-	-	-	-	1
TrendMicro	+	+	+	+	+	+	-	-	-	-	-	5
TrendMicro-HouseCall	+	+	+	+	+	+	-	-	-	-	-	5
VBA32	+	+	+	+	+	+	-	-	-	-	-	5
VIPRE	+	+	+	+	+	+	-	-	-	-	-	5
ViRobot	-	-	-	-	-	-	-	-	-	-	-	0
Zillya	-	-	-	-	-	-	-	-	-	-	-	0
Zoner	-	-	-	-	-	-	-	-	-	-	-	0
nProtect	-	-	-	-	-	-	-	-	-	-	-	0

BOXERSMS

AVs	Original	F1	F2	F3	F4	F5	F6	F7	F8	F9	F10	Rating
K7AntiVirus	-	-	-	-	-	-	-	-	-	-	-	0
K7GW	+	+	+	+	+	+	+	+	+	+	+	10
Kaspersky	+	+	+	-	-	-	-	-	-	-	-	2
Kingsoft	+	-	-	-	-	-	-	-	-	-	-	0
Malwarebytes	-	-	-	-	-	-	-	-	-	-	-	0
McAfee	+	-	-	-	-	-	-	-	-	-	-	0
McAfee-GW-Edition	+	-	-	-	-	-	-	-	-	-	-	0
MicroWorld-eScan	+	+	+	-	-	-	-	-	-	-	-	2
Microsoft	+	+	+	-	-	-	-	-	-	-	-	2
NANO-Antivirus	+	+	+	-	-	-	-	-	-	-	-	2
Norman	+	-	-	-	-	-	-	-	-	-	-	0
Panda	-	-	-	-	-	-	-	-	-	-	-	0
Qihoo-360	+	-	-	-	-	-	-	-	-	-	-	0
Rising	-	-	-	-	-	-	-	-	-	-	-	0
SUPERAnti-Spyware	-	-	-	-	-	-	-	-	-	-	-	0
Sophos	+	+	+	-	-	-	-	-	-	-	-	2
Symantec	+	-	-	-	-	-	-	-	-	-	-	0
Tencent	+	+	+	-	-	-	-	-	-	-	-	2
TheHacker	-	-	-	-	-	-	-	-	-	-	-	0
TotalDefense	-	-	-	-	-	-	-	-	-	-	-	0
TrendMicro	+	-	-	-	-	-	-	-	-	-	-	0
TrendMicro-HouseCall	+	-	-	-	-	-	-	-	-	-	-	0
VBA32	+	-	-	-	-	-	-	-	-	-	-	0
VIPRE	+	+	+	-	-	-	-	-	-	-	-	2
ViRobot	-	-	-	-	-	-	-	-	-	-	-	0
Zillya	-	-	-	-	-	-	-	-	-	-	-	0
Zoner	-	-	-	-	-	-	-	-	-	-	-	0
nProtect	-	-	-	-	-	-	-	-	-	-	-	0

Table 4: Logic vectors.
Key: + = malware detected, - = malware not detected

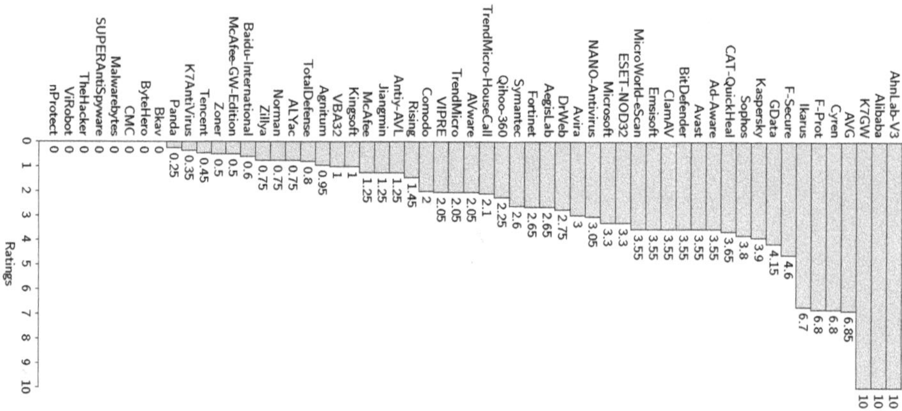

Figure 1: Average AV ratings.

as 1st: ■, 2nd: ▲, 3rd: •, 4th: ∘) that are used in detection. A blank row indicates that we do not detect the AV using our set of features. A decreasing number at column Fi suggests that the current feature Fi is used as a deciding feature for some families. We present the processed results on static features in Table 5. We illustrate with an example using BitDefender. We aggregate all 20 logic vectors of BitDefender and obtain the aggregated logic vector (20,20,7,7,7,2,2,2,2,2) which means the deciding features are $F3, F6$ in the same order. The first transition suggests that $F3$ is used as a deciding feature for detecting some families.

We highlight a few interesting findings on the AVs' detection logic. Based on coarse-grained classification, we observe that a majority of AVs detect some families using the more trivial deciding features in $C1$ that can be more easily obfuscated. Feature $F3$ (changing class, method, field names) is the most commonly used deciding feature in $C1$. This suggests that these AVs use class-level identifier names as a deciding feature for detecting some families. However, we note that most AVs are not limited to features in $C1$. Some lower-rated AVs may also use deciding features in $C2$ to detect other families. We also observe that a few higher-rated AVs use deciding features in $C3$ that will require more major modifications to malware. We see that close to half (26/57) of the AVs use $F1$ as a deciding feature. These are also the lower-rated AVs that can be evaded by simply repacking. We observe that $F6$ is the most used deciding feature among all features, suggesting that most AVs detect some families based on resources. We find that features $F7, F8$ appear not to be used by all AVs.

5.4.3 Malware Family Detection Logic

Similar to the previous comparison across AVs, we also want to look for high-level patterns of how a malware family is detected by different AVs. For each malware family, we also try to derive a common detection logic based on the 57 AVs. Based on the complete test results, we aggregate the row of 57 logic vectors for each family and highlight the deciding features (transitions represented as 1st: ■, 2nd: ▲, 3rd: •, 4th: ∘) used in detection. We present the processed results on static features in Table 6. For example, the aggregated logic vector of the PJAPPS family is (26,26,15,15,7,7,7,7,5,3) which suggests that the deciding features are $F1, F3, F5, F9$.

We highlight a few interesting findings on the logic to detect malware families. We observe a high number of transitions for all families, suggesting that different AVs probably use different deciding features to detect the same family. This is not surprising since different AVs can have differences in their AV signatures for different malware instances. We see that more than half (14/20) of the families can be detected using features across $C1, C2, C3$. We also observe that all families can at least evade some AVs by simply repacking. There appears to be a trend that features $F1, F3, F5, F6, F9$ are used in detecting all families.

5.4.4 Testing On More Recent Malware

Our test dataset contains malware collected between August 2010 to October 2012. It seems highly likely that AVs have already gathered large numbers of these samples and their variants to generate a comprehensive collection of signatures for detection. Towards the end of our evaluation, we tested with some recent malware collected from 2014 to 2015 to see if the resuls are any different from older malware. As the sample size is small, we do not detail the results but we find the overall pattern to be similar with results based on our current dataset. However, the results are more sparse since there are less samples. We observe that a majority of AVs detect these recent malware based on a single static feature. This suggests that AVs update their signatures and improve their detection logic as they see more related malware as is also shown in the next sub-section.

5.4.5 The Effect of Seeding Malware

We had initially tested two months earlier 200 m^{10} variants. We retested after another two months and found that the number of AVs that detected these variants sharply increased. This means that these AVs reacted within two months to our seed variants. We also find that a majority of these AVs are the better rated ones. This is consistent with anecdotal evidence that AV vendors continually analyse new malware so as to improve the detection rate of their AV over time.

6. DISCUSSION AND CONCLUSION

This paper shows that with sufficient testing, we are able to infer high-level patterns in the AV detection logic even-

	Static Features									
	C1				C2				C3	
AV	F1	F2	F3	F4	F5	F6	F7	F8	F9	F10
ALYac						■				
AVG					■	▲			●	○
AVware	■		▲		●	○				
Ad-Aware			■			▲				
AegisLab	■	▲			●	○				
Agnitum	■		▲			●				
AhnLab-V3										
Alibaba										
Antiy-AVL	■					▲				
Avast			■		▲	●				
Avira			■		▲	●				
Baidu-International	■		▲			●				
BitDefender			■			▲				
CAT-QuickHeal			■		▲	●				
ClamAV	■				▲	●				
Comodo	■					▲				
Cyren			■						▲	
DrWeb			■			▲				
ESET-NOD32			■		▲	●				
Emsisoft			■			▲				
F-Prot			■						▲	
F-Secure			■		▲	●				
Fortinet	■		▲		●	○				
GData			■			▲				
Ikarus					■	▲			●	○
Jiangmin	■					▲				
K7AntiVirus	■		▲			●				
K7GW										
Kaspersky			■	▲	●	○				
Kingsoft	■					▲				
McAfee	■		▲			●				
McAfee-GW-Edition	■					▲				
MicroWorld-eScan			■			▲				
Microsoft			■		▲	●				
NANO-Antivirus			■		▲	●				○
Norman	■					▲				
Panda	■					▲				
Qihoo-360	■		▲			●				
Rising	■				▲	●				
Sophos			■		▲	●				
Symantec	■		▲		●	○				
Tencent	■		▲			●				
TotalDefense	■	▲				●				
TrendMicro	■		▲		●	○				
TrendMicro-HouseCall	■		▲		●	○				
VBA32	■					▲				
VIPRE	■		▲		●	○				
Zillya	■					▲				
Zoner	■					▲				

Table 5: AV detection logic.
Key: ■= 1st, ▲= 2nd, ●= 3rd, 4th: ○

though the AVs are black boxes. Based on our dataset, we can conclude that most AVs do poorly on detecting obfuscated variants of previously detected malware. However, our seeding experiments show that the detection can improve over time and some AVs seem to react much faster than others. We find that AVs do not have a common detection logic that works across different families. However, we find that there are certain deciding features that are more commonly used in detection. We also apply our prototype on recent malware and observe similar patterns in AV detection logic. Our experimental results suggests that Android AVs are still very much limited in what they can do. For Android

	Static Features									
	C1				C2				C3	
Family	F1	F2	F3	F4	F5	F6	F7	F8	F9	F10
ADRD	■		▲		●				○	
ANSERVER	■					▲			●	○
BASEBRIDGE	■					▲			●	
BOXERSMS	■		▲			●				
FAKENOTIFY	■		▲		●	○				
FAKETIMER	■		▲		●					
GEIMINI	■		▲		●				○	
GINGERMASTER	■					▲			●	
GOLDDREAM	■		▲		●				○	
KMIN	■		▲		●				○	
KUNGFU	■		▲		●	○				
LEGANA	■		▲		●	○				
LIGHTDD	■		▲		●				○	
LOTOOR	■					▲			●	○
OPFAKE	■	▲	●		○					
PJAPPS	■		▲		●				○	
RUFRAUD	■		▲			●			○	
SHASTROSMS	■		▲		●				○	
SMSHIDER	■					▲			●	
YZHC	■		▲		●				○	

Table 6: Family detection logic.
Key: ■= 1st, ▲= 2nd, ●= 3rd, 4th: ○

AVs to be truly effective, they have to move beyond the app sandbox. Fedler et. al. [13] proposed an additional API for AVs to monitor file system modifications and scan arbitrary files. However, such a proposal will require a major overhaul of the Android app framework and require increased trust in the AV apps. Google runs Bouncer [2] to scan every app uploaded to Google Play. However, Bouncer [19, 20] has been shown to be easily fingerprinted and hence evaded. All Android devices are also pre-installed with Verify Apps [4] to regularly check that all installed apps are behaving in a safe manner. However, it has also shown that Verify Apps uses simple static features [18] like package names and its detection rate of 15.32% among 1260 malware samples was low, consistent with Tables 3 and 4.

7. ACKNOWLEDGEMENTS

This research is supported by the National Research Foundation, Prime Minister's Office, Singapore under its National Cybersecurity R&D Program (Award No. NRF2015-NCR-NCR002-001) and administered by the National Cybersecurity R&D Directorate.

8. REFERENCES

[1] https://code.google.com/p/android-apktool/

[2] http://googlemobile.blogspot.sg/2012/02/android-and-security.html

[3] http://source.android.com/devices/tech/dalvik/dex-format.html

[4] https://support.google.com/accounts/answer/2812853?hl=en

[5] https://www.av-test.org/fileadmin/pdf/VB-AVC-AVT-press-release.pdf

[6] https://www.f-secure.com/documents/996508/1030743/Threat_Report_H1_2014.pdf

[7] https://www.virustotal.com

[8] https://www.virustotal.com/en/file/fe8e99a5d0577691d3db5a6b1ed8d578bc21ee66d18164360c03-d0516926da7b/analysis

[9] Mobile Security Review September 2014, *AV-Comparatives*, 2014.

[10] D. Arp, M. Spreitzenbarth, M. Hubner, H. Gascon, and K. Rieck. DREBIN: Effective and Explainable Detection of Android Malware in Your Pocket. In *Network and Distributed System Security Symposium*, 2014.

[11] 32 Protection Apps for Android Put to the Test. *AV-TEST*, 2014.

[12] W. Enck, M. Ongtang, and P. McDaniel. On Lightweight Mobile Phone Application Certification. In *ACM SIGSAC Conference on Computer and Communications Security*, 2009.

[13] R. Fedler, M. Kulicke, and J. Schutte. An Antivirus API for Android Malware Recognition. In *International Conference on Malicious and Unwanted Software*, 2013.

[14] R. Fedler, J. Schtte, and M. Kulicke. On the Effectiveness of Malware Protection on Android. *Fraunhofer AISEC*, 2013.

[15] A.P. Felt, M. Finifter, E. Chin, S. Hanna, and D. Wagner. A Survey of Mobile Malware in the Wild, In *ACM CCS Workshop on Security and Privacy*, 2011.

[16] M. Grace, Y. Zhou, Q. Zhang, S. Zou, and X. Jiang. RiskRanker: Scalable and Accurate Zero-day Android Malware Detection. In *International Conference on Mobile Systems, Applications, and Services*, 2012.

[17] Smartphone OS Market Share, Q3 2014. *IDC*, 2014.

[18] X. Jiang. An Evaluation of the Application Verification Service in Android 4.2. 2012.

[19] J. Oberheide and C. Miller. Dissecting the Android Bouncer. In *SummerCon*, 2012.

[20] N. Percoco and S. Sean. Adventures in Bouncerland. In *BlackHat*, 2012.

[21] V. Rastogi, Y. Chen, and X. Jiang. DroidChameleon: Evaluating Android Anti-malware Against Transformation Attacks, In *ACM Symposium on Information, Computer and Communications Security*, 2013.

[22] P. Rovelli and Y. Vigfusson. PMDS: Permission-Based Malware Detection System. In *International Conference on Information Systems Security*, 2014.

[23] M. Zheng, P.P.C. Lee, and J.C.S. Lui. ADAM: An Automatic and Extensible Platform to Stress Test Android Anti-virus Systems. In *Conference on Detection of Intrusions and Malware & Vulnerability Assessment*, 2012.

[24] Y. Zhou and X. Jiang. Dissecting Android Malware: Characterization and Evolution. In *IEEE Symposium on Security and Privacy*, 2012.

Novel Feature Extraction, Selection and Fusion for Effective Malware Family Classification

Mansour Ahmadi
Department of Electrical and Electronic Engineering
University of Cagliari, Italy
mansour.ahmadi@diee.unica.it

Dmitry Ulyanov
Skolkovo Institute of Science and Technology, Russia
dmitry.ulyanov@skolkovotech.ru

Stanislav Semenov
National Research University Higher School of Economics, Russia
stasg7@gmail.com

Mikhail Trofimov
Moscow Institute of Physics and Technology, Russia
mikhail.trofimov@phystech.edu

Giorgio Giacinto
Department of Electrical and Electronic Engineering
University of Cagliari, Italy
giacinto@diee.unica.it

ABSTRACT

Modern malware is designed with mutation characteristics, namely polymorphism and metamorphism, which causes an enormous growth in the number of variants of malware samples. Categorization of malware samples on the basis of their behaviors is essential for the computer security community, because they receive huge number of malware everyday, and the signature extraction process is usually based on malicious parts characterizing malware families. Microsoft released a malware classification challenge in 2015 with a huge dataset of near 0.5 terabytes of data, containing more than 20K malware samples. The analysis of this dataset inspired the development of a novel paradigm that is effective in categorizing malware variants into their actual family groups. This paradigm is presented and discussed in the present paper, where emphasis has been given to the phases related to the extraction, and selection of a set of novel features for the effective representation of malware samples. Features can be grouped according to different characteristics of malware behavior, and their fusion is performed according to a per-class weighting paradigm. The proposed method achieved a very high accuracy ($\approx$ 0.998) on the Microsoft Malware Challenge dataset.

Keywords

Windows Malware, Machine learning, Malware family, Computer security, Classification, Microsoft Malware Classification Challenge

1. INTRODUCTION

CODASPY '16, March 09-11, 2016, New Orleans, LA, USA

DOI: http://dx.doi.org/10.1145/2857705.2857713.

In recent years, malware coders developed sophisticated techniques to elude traditional as well as modern malware protection mechanisms. On the other hand, developers of anti-malware solutions need to develop counter mechanisms for detecting and deactivating them, playing a cat-and-mouse game. The huge number of malware families, and malware variants inside the families, causes a major problem for anti-malware products. For example, McAfee Lab's antimalware solutions reported more than 350M total unique malware samples in Q4 of 2014, that represents a growth of 17% with respect to the analogous data in Q3 [5]. Symantec reported more than 44.5 million new pieces of malware created in May 2015 [6]. Analyzing the malicious intent in this vast amount of data requires a huge effort by anti malware companies. One of the main reasons for this high volume of malware samples is the extensive use of polymorphic and metamorphic techniques by malware developers, which means that malicious executable files belonging to the same malware `family` are constantly modified and/or obfuscated. In particular, polymorphic malware has a static mutation engine that encrypts and decrypts the code, while metamorphic malware automatically modify the code each time it is propagated.

Malware detection and classification techniques are two separate tasks, that are performed by anti-malware companies. Firstly, an executable needs to be analyzed to detect if it exhibits any malicious content: Then, in the case a malware is detected, it is assigned to the most appropriate malware family through a classification mechanism. There are various ways for detecting malware in the wild, and detecting a zero-day malware is still a challenging task. For example, Kaspersky recently discovered a new variant of Duqu, Duqu 2.0, in their own internal networks in July of 2015 [3]. The detection of this kind of advanced malware is usually carried out within a sandbox environment by leveraging on a powerful heuristic engine. After the malware detection step, malware need to be categorized into groups, corresponding to their families, for further analysis. As far as a very high number of malware variants is concerned, the need for the automation of this process is clear-cut.

The analysis of malicious programs is usually carried out by static techniques [39, 48, 34] and dynamic techniques [45, 37, 9, 46]. Analyzers extract various characteristics from the programs' syntax and semantic such as operation codes [40] and function call graph [23] from the disassembled code, or string signatures [22] and byte code n-grams [44, 2] from the hex code, or different structural characteristics from the PE header, such as dependencies between APIs [48] and DLLs [34]. Some other works [42] also explored the analysis of metadata such as the number of bitmaps, the size of import and export address tables besides the PE header's content. The aforementioned content-based detection systems, like those considering bytecode n-grams, APIs, and assembly instructions, are inherently susceptible to false detection due to the fact of polymorphism and metamorphism. In addition, these techniques are not appropriated in the case of malware samples such as the one with `0OyCuplj2VTc9ShXZDvnxz` hash name, that does not contain any APIs, and also contains a few assembly instructions because of packing.

In this paper, we propose a learning-based system which uses different malware characteristics to effectively assign malware samples to their corresponding families without doing any deobfuscation and unpacking process. Although unpacking may lead to the extraction of more valuable features if the packers are known, unpacking is a costly task, and dealing with customized packers is even more challenging. Hence, we aim to perform classification without the need to unpack the sample. In addition, the system doesn't need to be evaluated on any packed goodware, because the problem of malware classification already assumes all of the samples to be malware. Finally, as this paper focuses on malware classification, we didn't make any analysis of evasion mechanisms employed to evade detection.

For each malware sample, we compute not only a set of content-based features by relying on state-of-the-art mechanisms, but also we propose the extraction of powerful complementary statistical features that reflects the structure of portable executable (PE) files. The decision of not using more complex models like n-grams, sequences, bags or graphs, allowed us to devise a simple, yet effective, and efficient malware classification system. Moreover, we implemented an algorithm, inspired by the forward stepwise feature selection algorithm [25], to combine the most relevant feature categories to feed the classifier, and show the trade-off between the number of features and accuracy. To better exploit both the richness of the available information, in the number of the malware samples for training the classifier, and the number of features used to represent the samples, we resorted to ensemble techniques such as bagging [29].

We evaluated our system on the data provided by Microsoft for their malware Challenge hosted at Kaggle[1], and achieved 99.77% accuracy. The source code of our method is available online[2].

In summary, the original contributions of this paper are the following:

- The extraction and evaluation of different features based on the content and the structure of a malware that is performed directly on the packed executable file, and doesn't require the costly task of unpacking,
- A novel technique that extracts information on the structural characteristics of PEs, to accurately classify even obfuscated malware,
- The use of a limited number of features compared to other state-of-the-art systems, so that the method is apt to be used in large-scale malware categorization tasks,
- An algorithm for feature fusion that outputs the most effective concatenation of features categories, each category being related to different aspects of the malware, thus avoiding the combination of all the possible feature categories, and providing a trade-off between accuracy and the number of features,
- The assessment of the performances of the proposed malware classification on a dataset recently released by Microsoft, that can be considered one of the most updated and reliable testbeds for the task at hand.

The rest of the paper is organized as follows: a survey on the related work is presented in section 2; section 3 presents the details of the proposed method. Results of the experiments are discussed in section 4, and conclusions and future work will wrap up the paper.

[1] `https://www.kaggle.com/c/malware-classification`

[2] `https://github.com/ManSoSec/Microsoft-Malware-Challenge`

2. RELATED WORK

Prior to the development of signatures for anti-malware products, the two main tasks that have to be carried out within the scope of malware analysis are malware detection, and malware classification. While the goal of malware detection mechanisms is to catch the malware in the wild, malware classification systems assign each sample to the correct malware family. These systems can be roughly divided into two groups, based, respectively, on dynamic or static analysis.

Dynamic analysis. Researchers have put a lot of effort in proposing behaviour-based malware detection methods that capture the behavior of the program at runtime. One way to observe the behavior of a program is to monitor the interactions of the program with the operating system through the analysis of the API calls [45, 37]. In order to devise an effective and more robust system, some approaches considered additional semantic information like the sequence of the API calls [9], and the use of graph representations [27, 20, 26]. These approaches monitor the program's behaviour by analyzing the temporal order of the API calls, and the effect of API calls on registers [21], or by extracting a behavioural graph based on the dependency between API call parameters. Additionally, in contrast to the above program-centric detection approaches, some proposals address the issue by a global, system-wide approach. For example, Lanzi et al. [30] proposed an access activity model that captures the generalized interactions of benign applications with operating system resources, such as files and the registry, and then detects the malware with very a very low false positive rate. A recent survey on 36 research papers on dynamic analysis techniques [38] pointed out that the common shortcomings of dynamic analysis techniques are the problematic and somewhat obscure assumptions regarding the use of execution-driven datasets, and the lack of details and motivation on the security precautions that have been taken during the experimental phase. Moreover, recent malware is shipped with dynamic anti-analysis defenses that hide the malicious behaviour in the case a dynamic analysis environment is detected [36] and the lack of code coverage, as dynamic analysis is not designed to explore all or, at least, multiple execution paths of an executable [32].

Static analysis. On the other hand, static approaches perform the analysis without actually executing the program. The research literature exhibits a large variety of static analysis methods. SAFE [17] and SAVE [43] have been among the most influential approaches in heuristic static malware detection, as these works inspired many researchers in this area. The above two works proposed the use of different patterns to detect the presence of malicious content in executable files. Since that time, a large variety of techniques have been explored based on different malware attributes, such as the header of the PE, the body of the PE, or both of them. Analysis is further carried out either directly on the bytecode [44, 2], or by disassembling the code and extracting opcodes and other relevant detailed information on the content of the program [40]. The main issue in static analysis is coping with packing and obfuscation. Recently, some paper addressed this issue by proposing a generic approach for the automatic deobfuscation of obfuscated programs without making any assumption about the obfuscation technique [47]. Static techniques have been also employed to assess if a malware detected in the wild is similar to a previously-seen variant, without actually performing the costly task of unpacking [24, 34].

All of the malware detection and malware classification systems rely on the extraction of either static or dynamic features. So, basically, the same features used for malware detection are used for malware classification purposes. As this paper focuses on malware classification based on the extraction of static features, Table 1 summarize the prominent static techniques tailored to both the detection and the classification of PE malware designed for MS Windows systems. As far as the experiments reported in the literature have been performed on different datasets, we haven't reported the related performances, as a comparison of the attained accuracy would have not been fair. Table 1 shows, in the `type` column, if the paper is related to malware detection or classification. The column `feature` shows if the features are extracted from the PE header or from the PE body. Finally, the `structure` column reports on the extraction of any complex features, related, for example, to a relationship or a dependency among PE elements.

Table 1: Static analysis techniques on Windows malware.

Year	Authors	Type		Features		Structure
		Det	**Class**	**Header**	**Body**	
2008	Ye et al. [48]	✓		API	–	Itemset
2009	PE-Miner [42]	✓		STC	STC	–
2009	Tabish et al. [44]	✓		BYT	BYT	N-gram
2009	Griffin et al. [22]	✓		BYT	BYT	Sequence
2009	Hu et al. [23]	✓		–	FC	Graph
2010	Sami et al. [39]	✓		API	–	Itemset
2011	Nataraj et al. [35]		✓	BYT	BYT	–
2012	Jacob et al. [24]		✓	STC	BYT	N-gram
2013	Santos et al. [40]	✓		–	OP	Sequence
2014	Nissim et al. [2]	✓		BYT	BYT	N-gram
2015	DLLMiner [34]	✓	✓	DLL	–	Tree

`API`: Application Programming Interface
`BYT`: Byte code, `FC`: Function Call
`STC`: Structural features, `OP`: Operation code

3. SYSTEM ARCHITECTURE

As this paper focuses on malware classification, the most relevant issue is related to the choice of the features that will be used to represent each malware sample for the classification task. Our approach was guided by the rationale that to attain accurate and fast classification results, so we should integrate different types of features, such as content-based features as well as structural features.

3.1 Malware representation

Before entering into the details of the features that we extracted for the classification task, we will briefly review the different ways in which a malware sample can be represented. Two common representations of a malware sample are by the hex view, and the assembly view. The hex view represents the machine code as a sequence of hexadecimal digits, which is the accumulation of consecutive 16-bytes words, like in the following representation:

```
004010D0 8D 15 A8 80 63 00 BF 55 70 00 00 52 FF 72 7C 53
```

The first value represents the starting address of these machine codes in the memory, and each value (byte) bears a meaningful element for the PE, like instruction codes or data.

The task of disassembling a binary executable into its sequence of assembly instructions can be performed by two main techniques, namely by the linear sweep algorithm, and the recursive traversal algorithm [41]. Although neither approach is absolutely precise, the recursive approach is usually far less susceptible to mistakes than the linear sweep algorithm because the code is disassembled according to the jump and branch instructions. The Interactive Disassembler (IDA) [1] tool is one of the most popular recursive traversal disassembler, which performs automatic code analysis on binary files using cross-references between code sections, knowledge of parameters of API calls, and other information. For example, IDA interprets the aforementioned byte sequence as shown in Figure 1.

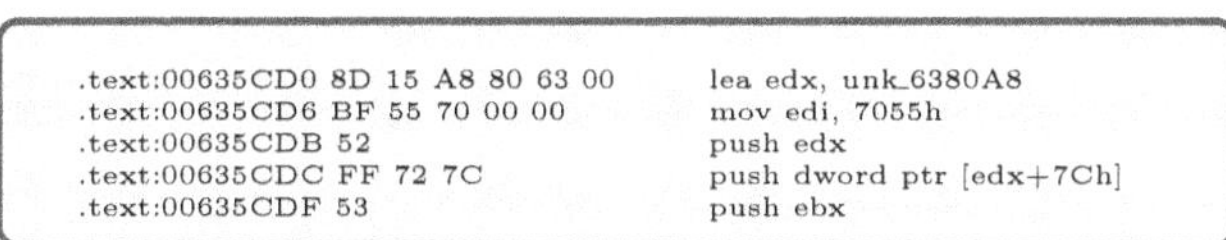

.text:00635CD0 8D 15 A8 80 63 00
.text:00635CD6 BF 55 70 00 00
.text:00635CDB 52
.text:00635CDC FF 72 7C
.text:00635CDF 53
lea edx, unk_6380A8
mov edi, 7055h
push edx
push dword ptr [edx+7Ch]
push ebx

Figure 1: Assembly view.

3.2 Features

For accurate and fast classification, we propose to extract features both from the hex view, and from the assembly view to exploit complementary information brought by these two representations. These complementary information are usually related to the essence of maliciousness, like obfuscation, and the experimental results will show how the combination of information from the two views can help improving the effectiveness of the whole system. In the following subsec-

tions we provide details on each feature that has been used and the reasoning of selecting them.
It is worth to point out the reason why we are not considering features extracted from the PE header. While it is well known that the PE header can be a rich source of information, the task at hand is more challenging as the PE header is not available, according to the rules of the Microsoft challenge that provided the dataset used in this paper.

3.2.1 Hex dump-based features

1. `N-gram`:
   A N-gram is a contiguous sequence of n items from a given sequence. N-gram is intensively used for characterizing sequences in different areas, e.g. computational linguistics, and DNA sequencing. The representation of a malware sample as a sequence of hex values can be effectively described through n-gram analysis to capture beneficial information about the type of malware. Each element in a byte sequence can take one out of 257 different values, i.e., the 256 byte range, plus the special ?? symbol. The "??" symbol indicates that the corresponding byte has no mapping in the executable file, namely the contents of those addresses are uninitialized within the file. This value can be discarded as, from an experimental point of view, it turned out that better results are achieved by taking into account just the 256 symbols. Examples of N-gram analysis include 1-gram (**1G**) features, which represent just the byte frequency, and thus are described with a 256-dimensional vector, and 2-gram features, which measure the frequency of all 2-byte combinations, thus having dimension of 256^2. As far as low computational complexity is concerned in our assumption, 1-gram is just considered in the experiments.

2. `Metadata`:
   We extract the following metadata features (**MD1**), namely, the size of the file, and the address of the first bytes sequence. The address is an hexadecimal number, and we converted it to the corresponding decimal value for homogeneity with the other features values.

3. `Entropy`:
   Entropy (**ENT**) is a measure of the amount of *disorder*, and can be used to detect the possible presence of obfuscation [31, 10]. Entropy is computed on the byte-level representation of each malware sample and the goal is to measure the *disorder* of the distribution of bytes in the bytecode as a value between 0 (Order) and 8 (Randomness). First, we apply the sliding window method to represent the malware as a series of entropy measures E $= e_i : i = 1, ..., N$, where e_i is the entropy measured in each window, and N is the number of windows, and then the entropy is calculated using the Shannon's formula:

   $$e_i = -\sum_{j=1}^{m} p(j) \log_2 p(j) \qquad (1)$$

   where p(j) is the frequency of byte j within window i, and m is a number of distinct bytes in the window. Then, we consider statistics of entropy sequences obtained using the sliding window method, that is, we calculate the entropy for each window of 10000 bytes and then we consider a number of statistical measures like quantiles, percentiles, mean, and variance of the obtained distribution. In addition, we compute the entropy of all the bytes in a malware.

4. `Image representation`:
   An original way to represent a malware sample is to visualize the byte code by interpreting each byte as the gray-level of one pixel in an image [35]. As shown in Figure 2, the resulting images have very fine texture patterns (e.g. see Figure 2a, and Figure 2b), that can be used as visual signatures for each malware family. Although matching visual patterns need a huge processing time, some features that describe the textures in an image [4] such as the Haralick features (**IMG1**), or the Local Binary Patterns features (**IMG2**) can be efficient and quite effective for the malware classification task. The representation of malware as images may sometimes cause problems, as in the case shown in Figure 2c, where the texture patterns of the two images are almost similar, even if the two malware samples that are represented belong to different classes. In addition, we have to take into account the case in which the resources (`.rsrc`) section of a PE file contains image files (e.g. see Figure 2d). As the same image files can be used as resources for different malware families, the extracted image patterns from these part of the malware may produce false positives. As far as the .rsrc section may not be always in the same position within a PE file, removing those parts from our analysis was not an easy task. Therefore, as these features are used in conjunction with other feature, we consider the texture patterns computed over the whole image.

5. `String length`:
   We extract possible ASCII strings from each PE using its hex dump. Since this method extracts a lot of garbage along with actual strings, the usage of string features directly is inappropriate. Consequently, to reduce noise and to avoid overfitting, only histograms related to the distribution of length of strings (**STR**) is used.

3.2.2 Features extracted from disassembled files

1. `Metadata`:
   After disassembling, we computed the size of the file, and the number of lines in the file, and included these features within the Metadata category (**MD2**).

2. `Symbol`:
   The frequencies of the following set of symbols (**SYM**), `-`, `+`, `*`, `]`, `[`, `?`, `@`, are taken into account as a high frequency of these characters is typical of code that has been designed to evade detection, for example by resorting to indirect calls, or dynamic library loading. In indirect calls, the address of the callee is taken from the memory/register. Although the implementation of calls depends both on the architecture, and on the optimal decision of compiler, indirect calls may reveal

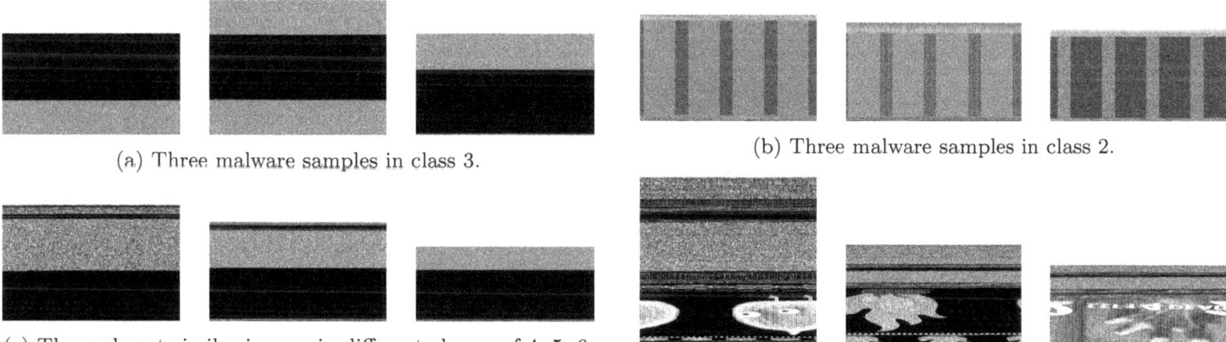

(a) Three malware samples in class 3.

(b) Three malware samples in class 2.

(c) Three almost similar images in different classes of 4, 5, 6.

(d) Some images embedded in malware.

Figure 2: Image representation of malware samples.

some information on data location obfuscation [33]. Dynamic library loading is another mechanism where an executable file loads a library into memory at runtime, and accesses its functions based on their address, so that static analyzers cannot capture the name of the imported functions.

3. `Operation Code`:
   Operation codes (**OPC**) are the mnemonic representation of machine code, which symbolize assembly instruction. The full list of x86 instruction set is large and complex, so we select a subset of 93 operation codes based either on their commonness, or on their frequent use in malicious applications [14], and measure the frequency of them in each malware sample. While instruction replacement techniques can be used to evade detection [18], their effects on malware classification tasks is limited, both for its rare use, and, consequently, for its negligible contribution to the computation of the statistics.

4. `Register`:
   Most of the processor registers in x86 architecture are used for dedicated tasks, but in some cases register renaming is used to make the analysis harder [18]. Consequently, the frequency of use of the registers (**REG**) can be a useful helper for assign a malware sample to one family, as the experiments will show.

5. `Application Programming Interface`:
   We also measure the frequency of use of Windows Application Programming Interfaces (**API**). As far as the total number of APIs is extremely large, considering them all would bring little or no meaningful information for malware classification. Consequently, we restricted our analysis to the top 794 frequent APIs used by malicious binaries based on an analysis on near 500K malware samples [7]. This feature category is discriminative for a subset of malware samples, because some samples might contain any API call because of packing, while some other samples might load some of its APIs by resorting to dynamic loading through the `LoadLibrary` API. For example, the sample with hash code `0OyCuplj2VTc9ShXZDvnxz` was packed with aspack[3], and it does not contain any API call, and most of the disassembled code just contains data define instructions like `db` (see Figure 3) and `dd` (see Figure 4).

```
DATA:0042F259 E1        db 0E1h ; á
DATA:0042F25A 36        db 36h ; 6
DATA:0042F25B 4E        db 4Eh ; N
DATA:0042F25C 12        db 12h
DATA:0042F25D 45        db 45h ; E
DATA:0042F25E 0B        db 0Bh
DATA:0042F25F 4A        db 4Ah ; J
DATA:0042F260 43        db 43h ; C
DATA:0042F261 6A        db 6Ah ; j
DATA:0042F262 18        db 18h
DATA:0042F263 DB        db 0DBh ; Û
DATA:0042F264 A7        db 0A7h ; §
```

Figure 3: A part of `0OyCuplj2VTc9ShXZDvnxz` (Packed, Changing section name); The sample contains no API call, and just few assembly instructions.

6. `Section`:
   A PE consists of some predefined sections like `.text`, `.data`, `.bss`, `.rdata`, `.edata`, `.idata`, `.rsrc`, `.tls`, and `.reloc`. Because of evasion techniques like packing, the default sections can be modified, reordered, and new sections can be created. We extract different characteristics from sections (**SEC**), which are listed in Table 2. In Section 4.2 we will point out that this category is the one with the higher influence in the classification performances.

7. `Data Define`:
   As shown in Figure 3 and Figure 4, some malware samples do not contain any API call, and just contain few operation codes, because of packing, In particular, they mostly contain `db`, `dw`, and `dd` instructions, which are used for setting byte, word, and double word respectively. Consequently, we propose to include this novel set of features (**DP**) for malware classification as it has a high discriminative power for a number of malware families. The full list of features in this category is presented in Table 3.

8. `Miscellaneous`: We extract the frequency of 95 manually chosen keywords (**MISC**) from the disassembled code. Some of these keywords are related to the interpretation of IDA from the code, like 75 adjacent dash-lines which show the border of blocks of PE, and counting them represent the number of blocks in PE. Others

[3]http://www.aspack.com/

```
.aspack:004BFA2C 20 20 20 00 34 34 34 00 56 56 56 00 0B 0B 0B 7B+    dd 202020h, 343434h, 565656h, 7B0B0B0Bh, 0FF292929h, 0FC282828h
.aspack:004BFA2C 29 29 29 FF 28 28 28 FC 2D 2D 2D FE 2C 2B 2A FF+    dd 0FE2D2D2Dh, 0FF2A2B2Ch, 0FF060504h, 0FF824B03h, 0FFE89325h
.aspack:004BFA2C 04 05 06 FF 03 4B 82 FF 25 93 E8 FF 40 A6 F5 FF+    dd 0FFF5A640h, 0FFFAA737h, 0FFFCAC37h, 0FFFBAD2Eh, 0FFFBAC23h
.aspack:004BFA2C 37 A7 FA FF 37 AC FC FF 2E AD FB FF 23 AC FB FF+ dd 0FFFBAE1Dh, 0FFFAAD16h, 0FFFBB014h, 0FFFAB71Eh, 0FFFFBE14h
.aspack:004BFA2C 1D AE FB FF 16 AD FA FF 14 B0 FB FF 1E B7 FA FF+ dd 0FF8B6A34h, 0FF282E3Ah, 0FF363634h, 0FF323134h, 0FFDE9C14h
.aspack:004BFA2C 14 BE FF FF 34 6A 8B FF 3A 2E 28 FF 34 36 36 FF+    dd 0FFFEBC16h, 0FFF7AA10h, 0FFF9AB13h, 0FFFCB221h, 0FFFBAC21h
.aspack:004BFA2C 34 31 32 FF 14 9C DE FF 16 BC FE FF 10 AA F7 FF+    dd 0FFFAAB2Bh, 0FFFCAE36h, 0FFFBA835h, 0FFF9A941h, 0FFF19E32h
.aspack:004BFA2C 13 AB F9 FF 21 B2 FC FF 21 AC FB FF 2B AB FA FF+ dd 0FFC2720Ah, 0FF321D02h, 0FE000004h, 0FE0A0909h, 0FC080808h
.aspack:004BFA2C 36 AE FC FF 35 A8 FB FF 41 A9 F9 FF 32 9E F1 FF+    dd 0FE060606h, 0E0101010h, 181B1B1Bh, 10101h, 202020h
```

Figure 4: A part of `00yCuplj2VTc9ShXZDvnxz` (Packed, Changing section name); The sample contains no API call, and just few assembly instructions.

Table 2: List of features in the SEC category.

Name	Description
section_names_.bss	The total number of lines in .bss section
section_names_.data	The total number of lines in .data section
section_names_.edata	The total number of lines in .edata section
section_names_.idata	The total number of lines in .idata section
section_names_.rdata	The total number of lines in .rdata section
section_names_.rsrc	The total number of lines in .rsrc section
section_names_.text	The total number of lines in .text section
section_names_.tls	The total number of lines in .tls section
section_names_.reloc	The total number of lines in .reloc section
Num_Sections	The total number of sections
Unknown_Sections	The total number of unknown sections
Unknown_Sections_lines	The total number of lines in unknown sections
known_Sections_por	The proportion of known sections to the all section
Unknown_Sections_por	The proportion of unknown sections to the all sections
Unknown_Sections_lines_por	The proportion of the amount of unknown sections to the whole file
.text_por	The proportion of .text section to the whole file
.data_por	The proportion of .data section to the whole file
.bss_por	The proportion of .bss section to the whole file
.rdata_por	The proportion of .rdata section to the whole file
.edata_por	The proportion of .edata section to the whole file
.idata_por	The proportion of .idata section to the whole file
.rsrc_por	The proportion of .rsrc section to the whole file
.tls_por	The proportion of .tls section to the whole file
.reloc_por	The proportion of .reloc section to the whole file

Table 3: List of features in the DP category.

Name	Description
db_por	The proportion of `db` instructions in the whole file
dd_por	The proportion of `dd` instruction in the whole file
dw_por	The proportion of `dw` instruction in the whole file
dc_por	The proportion of all `db`, `dd`, and `dw` instructions in the whole file
db0_por	The proportion of `db` instruction with 0 parameter in the whole file
dbN0_por	The proportion of `db` instruction with not 0 parameter in the whole file
dd_text	The proportion of `dd` instruction in the text section
db_text	The proportion of `db` instruction in the text section
dd_rdata	The proportion of `dd` instruction in the rdata section
db3_rdata	The proportion of `db` instruction with one non 0 parameter in the rdata section
db3_data	The proportion of `db` instruction with one non 0 parameter in the data section
db3_all	The proportion of `db` instruction with one non 0 parameter in the whole file
dd4	The proportion of `dd` instruction with four parameters
dd5	The proportion of `dd` instruction with five parameters
dd6	The proportion of `dd` instruction with six parameters
dd4_all	The proportion of `dd` instruction with four parameters in the whole file
dd5_all	The proportion of `dd` instruction with five parameters in the whole file
dd6_all	The proportion of `dd` instruction with six parameters in the whole file
db3_idata	The proportion of `db` instruction with one non 0 parameter in the idata section
db3_NdNt	The proportion of `db` instruction with one non 0 parameter in unknown sections
dd4_NdNt	The proportion of `dd` instruction with four parameters in unknown sections
dd5_NdNt	The proportion of `dd` instruction with five parameters in unknown sections
dd6_NdNt	The proportion of `dd` instruction with six parameters in unknown sections
db3_zero_all	The proportion of `db` instruction with 0 parameter to `db` instruction with non 0 parameter

are some strings like `hkey_local_machine` which represent the access to a specific path of the Windows registry, and the rest are related to the code like `dll` which shows the number of imported DLLs. Because of the limitation of the pages of the paper, the full list will be available in our online repository.

3.3 Feature fusion

The simplest way for combining feature categories is to stack all the feature categories in a single, long feature vector, and then run a classifier on them. However, it is often in the feature selection process that some of the features turn out to be irrelevant for class discrimination. Including such irrelevant features leads not only to unnecessary computational complexity, but also to the potential decrease of the accuracy of the resulting model. Within the vast literature on feature selection, we focused on two approaches. One approach is the *best subset* selection technique [25] that can be summarized as follows. Starting with subsets containing just one feature, a classifier is trained, and the subsets with the highest value of the objective function used to assess the performance (e.g., accuracy, loss functions, etc.) is retained. Then, the process is repeated for any subset containing f features, where f is increased by one at each step so that, for example, all the possible subsets of two features $\binom{f}{2} = \frac{f(f-1)}{2}$ are considered. The other technique that we considered is the *forward stepwise selection* technique which starts with a model containing no feature, and then gradually augments the feature set by adding more features to the model, one by one. This technique for feature selection is computationally more efficient than the *best subset selection* technique because the former just considers $\sum_{i=1}^{f}(f-k) = \frac{f(f+1)}{2}$ subsets, while the latter considers all 2^f possible models, using a greedy approach.

Based on the above considerations, we implemented an original version of the forward stepwise selection algorithm, where instead of considering one feature at a time, we considered all the subset of features belonging to a *feature category* at a time. At each step, the feature set that produces the minimum value of logloss (see section 3.5) will be added to the model. The process stops when adding more features does not decrease the value of logloss.

3.4 Classification

As for the feature selection task, over the years a large number of classification techniques have been proposed by the scientific community, and the choice of the most appropriate classifier for a given task is often guided by previous experience in different domains, as well as by trial&error procedures. However, recently some researchers evaluated the performances of about 180 classifiers arising from different families, using various datasets, and they concluded that random forests and SVM are the two classification mechanisms that have the highest likelihood to produce good performances [19]. On the other hand, most of the winners in the very recent Kaggle competitions used the XGBoost technique [8], which is a parallel implementation of the gradient boosting tree classifier, that in most of the cases produced better performances than those produced by random forests. The XGBoost technique is available as a library, implemented as a parallel algorithm that is fast and efficient, and whose parameters are completely tunable. The high performance and effectiveness of XGBoost is the main motivating reason for using this library for the task at hand. In addition, we also used bagging [15] to boost our single model, which is simple, classifier independent, and yet an efficient method to improve the classification quality. More details on the classification technique will be provided in the experimental section.

3.5 Evaluation measures

The performance in classification has been assessed by using two measures, namely, the accuracy, and the logarithmic loss. The accuracy has been measured as the fraction of correct predictions. As classification accuracy alone is usually not enough to assess the robustness of the prediction, we also measured the logarithmic loss (`logloss`), which is a `soft` measurement of accuracy that incorporates the concept of probabilistic confidence. It is the *Cross entropy* between the distribution of the true labels and the predicted probabilities. As shown in equation 2, it is the negative log likelihood of the model,

$$logloss = -\frac{1}{N}\sum_{i=1}^{N}\sum_{j=1}^{M} y_{ij} log(p_{ij}) \tag{2}$$

where N is the number of observations, M is the number of class labels, log is the natural logarithm, y_{ij} is 1 if observation i is in class j and 0 otherwise, and p_{ij} is the predicted probability that observation i is in class j.

4. EXPERIMENTS AND RESULTS

4.1 Data

Microsoft released almost half a terabyte of data related to 21741 malware samples, where 10868 samples are used for training, and the rest is for testing. The ID of each malware sample is a 20 characters hash value. The files are from nine different malware families, namely `Ramnit (R)`, `Lollipop (L)`, `Kelihos_ver3 (K3)`, `Vundo (V)`, `Simda (S)`, `Tracur (T)`, `Kelihos_ver1 (K1)`, `Obfuscator.ACY (O)`, `Gatak (G)`. The class label of each file is represented by an integer from 1 to 9, where '1' represented the first malware family in the above list, and '9' the last one. There are two files for each malware sample, one containing the hex code, and the other one containing the disassembled code (see Section 3.1). Microsoft removed the PE header to ensure file sterility. The distribution of data across the 9 families is shown in Figure 5.

4.2 Feature importance

Although there is no strict consensus about the meaning of importance, we refer to two common ways to measure

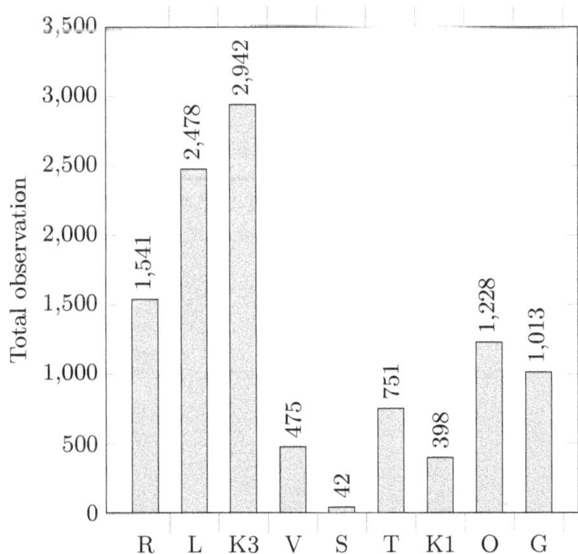

Figure 5: The distribution of data across malware families.

the importance of the features when decision tree classifiers are used, i.e., the *mean decrease accuracy*, and the *mean decrease impurity* [16]. These two metrics respectively measure the decrease in accuracy or the decrease in impurity[4] associated with each feature. In both cases, the importance of a given feature is proportional to the amount of decrease in accuracy or impurity related to that feature. While in Section 4.3 we will discuss the relationship between each feature category and the classification accuracy based on the feature fusion algorithm, in this section we report the importance of the features based on the *mean decrease impurity* to give a better insight on the relevance of each feature category for the attribution of the family to a given malware sample. For this purpose, we used the Random Forest algorithm, and the results are reported in Figure 6. It is worth to point out that Figure 6 shows that the two novel structural feature categories that we propose in this paper, namely `SEC` and `DP`, are among the top important features that most contribute to the decrease in the impurity of the classification tree.

4.3 Results

Table 4 and Table 5 respectively show the classification performances related to each individual feature category, and the performances related to the combination of feature categories. In particular, Table 5 provides useful information for data analysts to evaluate the trade-off between the number of features used, and the significance of the increase of the classification performances. We proceeded by leveraging on the feature fusion algorithm, by adding one by one the feature category that achieves the lowest logloss on training data. The attained results suggest that the combination of all the feature categories except the **IMG2** category lead to the lowest logloss on all training data, while the combination of all the feature categories leads to the lowest logloss on training data by employing cross validation. According to these results, we fine tuned the parameters of the XGBoost algorithm on these two feature configurations, as well as for the Bagging technique (see Table 6). In particular, by

[4]Gini impurity is a standard decision-tree splitting metric.

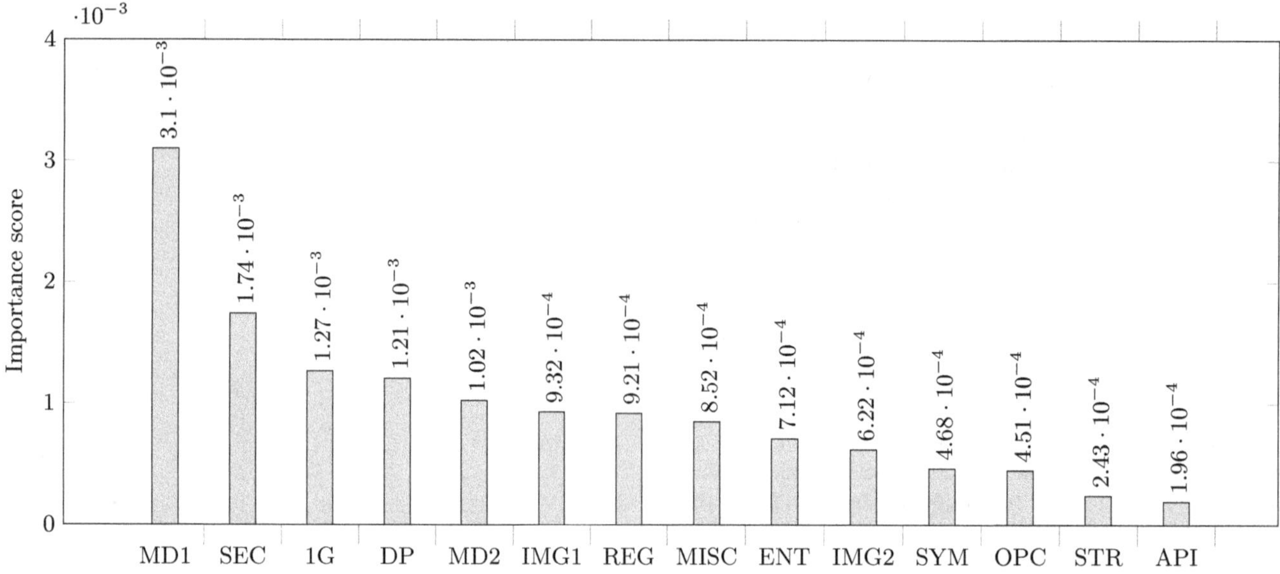

Figure 6: Importance of each feature category based on the *mean decrease impurity*.

adding the external bagging technique, we created a training set with eight times more samples instead of just using the plain training set. We considered all L train samples and sampled $Alpha \times L$ more samples with replacement, where the best value of $Alpha$ was found by grid search and set to one.

The proposed methodology for the classification of malware allowed achieving a very promising accuracy on the training set of 99.77%, as well as a very low logloss of 0.0096 on the combination of all categories, and 99.76% accuracy and 0.0094 logloss on the combination of the best feature categories, based on the outcome of the feature fusion algorithm. The log normalized confusion matrix of the final model is shown in Figure 7.

As far as the class labels of the test data were not provided by Microsoft, the only possible way to perform the evaluation on test data is through the submission of the predictions of our model to the competition website. Hence, we ran the experiments on test data and achieved a very low logloss, which is 0.0064 on combination of best categories and 0.0063 on combination of all categories.

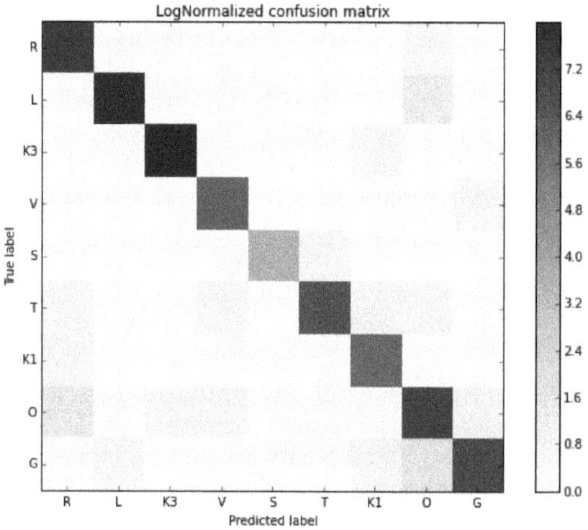

Figure 7: The normalized confusion matrix.

4.4 Feature extraction time

We run the experiments on a laptop with a quad-core processor (2 GHz), and 8GB RAM. Figure 8 and Figure 9 represents the required time for extracting different feature categories. The tasks of feature extraction and classifier training can be time consuming when the structure of the features is complex, and the size of datasets is large. For example, the 2-Gram category has more than 65K features, which requires a significant amount of time for their extraction (10213 seconds in total in our experiments), for training a model, and for selecting the most relevant ones. As 3-Gram and 4-Gram features are made up of a larger number of components, the time frame required to extract those features is excessively large.

4.5 Comparison and Discussion

To the best of our knowledge, this is the first paper based on the malware dataset that was recently released by Microsoft. Consequently, the effectiveness of the proposed approach can be assessed by comparing the reported results with the ones attained by the winner of the Microsoft malware challenge [5]. The winner of the competition attained 0.9983 accuracy, and 0.0031 logloss, on 4-fold cross validation, and 0.0028 logloss on test data, thus confirming the effectiveness of the proposed method, as the significance of this small difference is statistically negligible. While the performances are quite close, it is worth pointing out the differences between the method proposed in this paper and the one followed by the winning team. The proposed method is characterized by a limited computational complexity compared to the winning method, both in terms of the number and type of features, and in the classification technique em-

[5]http://blog.kaggle.com/2015/05/26/microsoft-malware-winners-interview-1st-place-no-to-overfitting/

Table 4: List of feature categories and their evaluation with XGBoost.

Feature Category	# Features	Train Accuracy	Train Logloss	5-CV Accuracy	5-CV Logloss
Hex dump file					
ENT	203	0.9987	0.0155	0.9862	0.0505
1G	256	0.9948	0.0307	0.9808	0.0764
STR	116	0.9877	0.0589	0.9735	0.0993
IMG1	52	0.9718	0.1098	0.9550	0.1645
IMG2	108	0.9736	0.1230	0.9510	0.1819
MD1	2	0.8547	0.4043	0.8525	0.4279
disassembled file					
MISC	95	0.9984	0.0095	0.9917	0.0306
OPC	93	0.9973	0.0146	0.9907	0.0405
SEC	25	0.9948	0.0217	0.9899	0.0420
REG	26	0.9932	0.0352	0.9833	0.0695
DP	24	0.9905	0.0391	0.9811	0.0740
API	796	0.9905	0.0400	0.9843	0.0610
SYM	8	0.9815	0.0947	0.9684	0.1372
MD2	2	0.7655	0.6290	0.75616	0.6621

Table 5: Gradual addition of feature categories based on feature fusion.

Feature Category	# Features	Train Accuracy	Train Logloss	5-CV Accuracy	5-CV Logloss
C1: MISC+ENT	298	1.0	0.0037	0.9907	0.0322
C2: C1+SEC	323	1.0	0.0019	0.9920	0.0278
C3: C2+API	1117	1.0	0.0016	0.9927	0.0251
C4: C3+1G	1373	1.0	0.0015	0.9930	0.0237
C5: C4+REG	1399	1.0	0.0014	0.9933	0.0226
C6: C5+OPC	1492	1.0	0.00137	0.9935	0.0220
C7: C6+MD1	1494	1.0	0.00132	0.9937	0.0214
C8: C7+DP	1518	1.0	0.00130	0.9938	0.0210
C9: C8+STR	1634	1.0	0.00128	0.9939	0.0206
C10: C9+IMG1	1686	1.0	0.00128	0.9940	0.0203
C11: C10+MD2	1688	1.0	0.00128	0.99411	0.0201
C12: C11+SYM	1696	1.0	0.00128	0.99418	0.0199
C13: C12+IMG2	1804	1.0	0.00130	0.9942	0.0197

Table 6: Employing bagging and parameter optimization for XGBoost.

Feature Category	# Features	5-CV Accuracy	5-CV Logloss	Test Logloss
Combination of all categories (C13)	1804	**0.9977**	**0.0096**	**0.0063**
Combination of best categories (C12)	1696	**0.9976**	**0.0094**	**0.0064**

ployed. Firstly, the winning team relied on a large set of well-known features, while we designed the proposed system not only by focusing on the features in the literature that proved to be effective, but also designing novel structural features that could provide a gain in performance with a limited computational cost. As an example, the winning team relied on the extraction of byte code N-gram and operation code N-gram, that require large computational resources both during the training phase, and the testing phase. The complexity of the classification step employed in the proposed method is lower than the ones of the winning team. Both methods rely on the ensemble paradigm, where the winning team resorted to an ensemble of different classifiers in a semi-supervised setting, while we resorted to a standard implementation of XGBoost with bagging. Thus, we can conclude that the proposed method exhibits a better trade-off between computational complexity and performances.

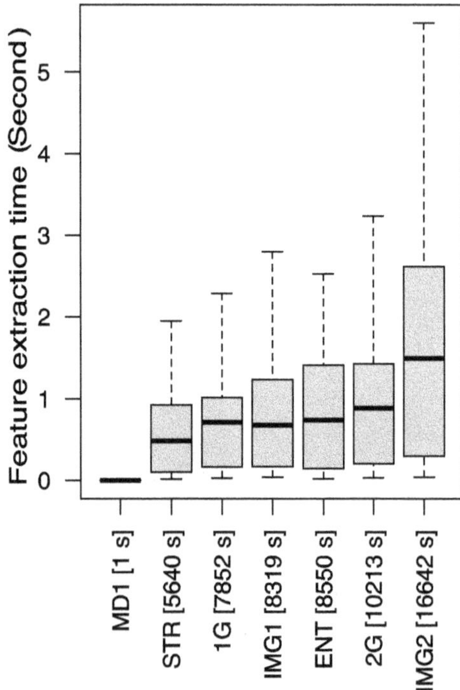

Figure 8: The required time of feature extraction from byte code for each app. The time in bracket shows the total time of extraction for all training samples.

The proposed method has not yet been tested for robustness against evasion attacks [11, 28] or poisoning attacks [13, 12] because these kinds of attacks are more frequent against malware detectors rather than against malware classifiers. Attacks against malware classifiers may be used to mislead automatic signature extractors, that analyze malware samples belonging to a family to design effective signatures. As the effectiveness of such attacks depends on a deep knowledge of the malware classifier, as well as of the signature extractor, and this knowledge cannot be reliably inferred from the outside of the system without insider support, we can conclude that these kind of attacks are highly rare. On the other hand, an analysis of the robustness of the system against evasion and poisoning attacks is worth to be carried out if the proposed system is modified to act as a malware detector.

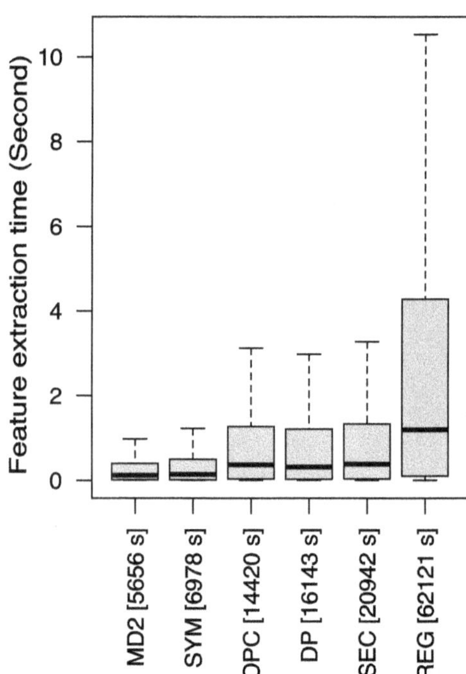

Figure 9: The required time of feature extraction from disassembled code for each app. The time in bracket shows the total time of extraction for all training samples.

5. CONCLUSION AND FUTURE WORK

We presented a malware classification system characterized by a limited complexity both in feature design and in the classification mechanism employed. To attain this goal, we proposed a number of novel features to represent in a compact way some discriminant characteristics between different families. In particular, we focused on the extraction of novel structural features, that, if compared to content-based features, are easier to compute, and allow the classification of obfuscated and packed malware without the need of deobfuscation and unpacking processes. Reported results allowed assessing the effectiveness of these features both with respect to classification accuracy, and to impurity.

The main motivation behind the choice of a *light* system is its suitability for an industrial use, where the trade-off between complexity and performances can be a key issue. Very often, the gain in performances of complex systems on validation data is negligible compared to the performances of less complex ones. In addition, the use of a reduced set of features may ease the task for an analyst to understand the classification results from the set of features related to a given sample, as compared to complex systems. While we haven't addressed this issue in this paper, we believe in its noteworthiness to gather information about the core common characteristics of malware samples within a family.

6. REFERENCES

[1] Ida : Disassembler and debugger. `https://www.hex-rays.com/products/ida/`, 2013.

[2] Novel active learning methods for enhanced {PC} malware detection in windows {OS}. *Expert Systems with Applications*, 41(13):5843 – 5857, 2014.

[3] Duqu is back. http://www.kaspersky.com/about/news/virus/2015/Duqu-is-back, 2015.

[4] Mahotas features. http://mahotas.readthedocs.org/en/latest/features.html, 2015.

[5] Mcafee labs threats report, february. http://www.mcafee.com/us/resources/reports/rp-quarterly-threat-q4-2014.pdf, 2015.

[6] Symantec intelligent report, may. https://www.symantec.com/content/en/us/enterprise/other_resources/intelligence_report_05-2015.en-us.pdf, 2015.

[7] Top maliciously used apis. https://www.bnxnet.com/top-maliciously-used-apis/, 2015.

[8] Xgboost. https://github.com/dmlc/xgboost, 2015.

[9] M. Ahmadi, A. Sami, H. Rahimi, and B. Yadegari. Malware detection by behavioural sequential patterns. *Computer Fraud & Security*, 2013(8):11 – 19, 2013.

[10] D. Baysa, R. Low, and M. Stamp. Structural entropy and metamorphic malware. *Journal of Computer Virology and Hacking Techniques*, 9(4):179–192, 2013.

[11] B. Biggio, I. Corona, D. Maiorca, B. Nelson, N. ÅărndiÄĞ, P. Laskov, G. Giacinto, and F. Roli. Evasion attacks against machine learning at test time. In H. Blockeel, K. Kersting, S. Nijssen, and F. Å¡eleznÃ¡, editors, *Machine Learning and Knowledge Discovery in Databases*, volume 8190 of *Lecture Notes in Computer Science*, pages 387–402. Springer Berlin Heidelberg, 2013.

[12] B. Biggio, B. Nelson, and P. Laskov. Poisoning attacks against support vector machines. In *29th Int'l Conf. on Machine Learning (ICML)*. Omnipress, Omnipress, 2012.

[13] B. Biggio, K. Rieck, D. Ariu, C. Wressnegger, I. Corona, G. Giacinto, and F. Roli. Poisoning behavioral malware clustering. In *Proceedings of the 2014 Workshop on Artificial Intelligent and Security Workshop*, AISec '14, pages 27–36, New York, NY, USA, 2014. ACM.

[14] D. Bilar. Statistical structures: Fingerprinting malware for classification and analysis. In *Blackhat*, 2006.

[15] L. Breiman. Bagging predictors. *Mach. Learn.*, 24(2):123–140, Aug. 1996.

[16] L. Breiman, J. Friedman, R. Olshen, and C. Stone. *Classification and Regression Trees.* Wadsworth and Brooks, Monterey, CA, 1984. new edition [?]?

[17] M. Christodorescu and S. Jha. Static analysis of executables to detect malicious patterns. In *Proceedings of the 12th Conference on USENIX Security Symposium - Volume 12*, SSYM'03, pages 12–12, Berkeley, CA, USA, 2003. USENIX Association.

[18] M. Christodorescu, S. Jha, S. Seshia, D. Song, and R. Bryant. Semantics-aware malware detection. In *Security and Privacy, 2005 IEEE Symposium on*, pages 32–46, May 2005.

[19] M. Fernández-Delgado, E. Cernadas, S. Barro, and D. Amorim. Do we need hundreds of classifiers to solve real world classification problems? *J. Mach. Learn. Res.*, 15(1):3133–3181, Jan. 2014.

[20] M. Fredrikson, S. Jha, M. Christodorescu, R. Sailer, and X. Yan. Synthesizing near-optimal malware specifications from suspicious behaviors. In *Proceedings of the 2010 IEEE Symposium on Security and Privacy*, SP '10, pages 45–60, Washington, DC, USA, 2010. IEEE Computer Society.

[21] M. Ghiasi, A. Sami, and Z. Salehi. Dynamic vsa: a framework for malware detection based on register contents. *Engineering Applications of Artificial Intelligence*, 44:111 – 122, 2015.

[22] K. Griffin, S. Schneider, X. Hu, and T.-C. Chiueh. Automatic generation of string signatures for malware detection. In *Proceedings of the 12th International Symposium on Recent Advances in Intrusion Detection*, RAID '09, pages 101–120, Berlin, Heidelberg, 2009. Springer-Verlag.

[23] X. Hu, T.-c. Chiueh, and K. G. Shin. Large-scale malware indexing using function-call graphs. In *Proceedings of the 16th ACM Conference on Computer and Communications Security*, CCS '09, pages 611–620, New York, NY, USA, 2009. ACM.

[24] G. Jacob, P. M. Comparetti, M. Neugschwandtner, C. Kruegel, and G. Vigna. A static, packer-agnostic filter to detect similar malware samples. In *Proceedings of the 9th International Conference on Detection of Intrusions and Malware, and Vulnerability Assessment*, DIMVA'12, pages 102–122, Berlin, Heidelberg, 2013. Springer-Verlag.

[25] G. James, D. Witten, T. Hastie, and R. Tibshirani. *An Introduction to Statistical Learning: With Applications in R.* Springer Publishing Company, Incorporated, 2014.

[26] F. Karbalaie, A. Sami, and M. Ahmadi. Semantic malware detection by deploying graph mining. *International Journal of Computer Science Issues*, 9(1), 2012.

[27] C. Kolbitsch, P. M. Comparetti, C. Kruegel, E. Kirda, X. Zhou, and X. Wang. Effective and efficient malware detection at the end host. In *Proceedings of the 18th Conference on USENIX Security Symposium*, SSYM'09, pages 351–366, Berkeley, CA, USA, 2009. USENIX Association.

[28] C. Kruegel, E. Kirda, D. Mutz, W. Robertson, and G. Vigna. Automating mimicry attacks using static binary analysis. In *Proceedings of the 14th Conference on USENIX Security Symposium - Volume 14*, SSYM'05, pages 11–11, Berkeley, CA, USA, 2005. USENIX Association.

[29] L. I. Kuncheva. *Ensemble Methods*, pages 186–229. John Wiley & Sons, Inc., 2014.

[30] A. Lanzi, D. Balzarotti, C. Kruegel, M. Christodorescu, and E. Kirda. Accessminer: Using system-centric models for malware protection. In *Proceedings of the 17th ACM Conference on Computer and Communications Security*, CCS '10, pages 399–412, New York, NY, USA, 2010. ACM.

[31] R. Lyda and J. Hamrock. Using entropy analysis to find encrypted and packed malware. *IEEE Security and Privacy*, 5(2):40–45, Mar. 2007.

[32] A. Moser, C. Kruegel, and E. Kirda. Exploring multiple execution paths for malware analysis. In *Proceedings of the 2007 IEEE Symposium on Security*

and Privacy, SP '07, pages 231–245, Washington, DC, USA, 2007. IEEE Computer Society.

[33] A. Moser, C. Kruegel, and E. Kirda. Limits of static analysis for malware detection. In *Computer Security Applications Conference, 2007. ACSAC 2007. Twenty-Third Annual*, pages 421–430, Dec 2007.

[34] M. Narouei, MansourAhmadi, G. Giacinto, H. Takabi, and A. Sami. Dllminer: Structural mining for malware detection. *Security and Communication Networks*, 2015.

[35] L. Nataraj, S. Karthikeyan, G. Jacob, and B. S. Manjunath. Malware images: Visualization and automatic classification. In *Proceedings of the 8th International Symposium on Visualization for Cyber Security*, VizSec '11, pages 4:1–4:7, New York, NY, USA, 2011. ACM.

[36] J. Qiu, B. Yadegari, B. Johannesmeyer, S. Debray, and X. Su. A framework for understanding dynamic anti-analysis defenses. In *Proceedings of the 4th Program Protection and Reverse Engineering Workshop*, PPREW-4, pages 2:1–2:9, New York, NY, USA, 2014. ACM.

[37] K. Rieck, T. Holz, C. Willems, P. Dussel, and P. Laskov. Learning and classification of malware behavior. In *Proceedings of the 5th International Conference on Detection of Intrusions and Malware, and Vulnerability Assessment*, DIMVA '08, pages 108–125, Berlin, Heidelberg, 2008. Springer-Verlag.

[38] C. Rossow, C. Dietrich, C. Grier, C. Kreibich, V. Paxson, N. Pohlmann, H. Bos, and M. van Steen. Prudent practices for designing malware experiments: Status quo and outlook. In *Security and Privacy (SP), 2012 IEEE Symposium on*, pages 65–79, May 2012.

[39] A. Sami, B. Yadegari, H. Rahimi, N. Peiravian, S. Hashemi, and A. Hamze. Malware detection based on mining api calls. In *Proceedings of the 2010 ACM Symposium on Applied Computing*, SAC '10, pages 1020–1025, New York, NY, USA, 2010. ACM.

[40] I. Santos, F. Brezo, X. Ugarte-Pedrero, and P. G. Bringas. Opcode sequences as representation of executables for data-mining-based unknown malware detection. *Information Sciences*, 231(0):64 – 82, 2013. Data Mining for Information Security.

[41] B. Schwarz, S. Debray, and G. Andrews. Disassembly of executable code revisited. In *Proceedings of the Ninth Working Conference on Reverse Engineering (WCRE'02)*, WCRE '02, pages 45–, Washington, DC, USA, 2002. IEEE Computer Society.

[42] M. Shafiq, S. Tabish, F. Mirza, and M. Farooq. Pe-miner: Mining structural information to detect malicious executables in realtime. In E. Kirda, S. Jha, and D. Balzarotti, editors, *Recent Advances in Intrusion Detection*, volume 5758 of *Lecture Notes in Computer Science*, pages 121–141. Springer Berlin Heidelberg, 2009.

[43] A. H. Sung, J. Xu, P. Chavez, and S. Mukkamala. Static analyzer of vicious executables (save). In *Proceedings of the 20th Annual Computer Security Applications Conference*, ACSAC '04, pages 326–334, Washington, DC, USA, 2004. IEEE Computer Society.

[44] S. M. Tabish, M. Z. Shafiq, and M. Farooq. Malware detection using statistical analysis of byte-level file content. In *Proceedings of the ACM SIGKDD Workshop on CyberSecurity and Intelligence Informatics*, CSI-KDD '09, pages 23–31, New York, NY, USA, 2009. ACM.

[45] C. Willems, T. Holz, and F. Freiling. Toward automated dynamic malware analysis using cwsandbox. *Security Privacy, IEEE*, 5(2):32–39, March 2007.

[46] T. Wüchner, M. Ochoa, and A. Pretschner. Malware detection with quantitative data flow graphs. In *Proceedings of the 9th ACM Symposium on Information, Computer and Communications Security*, ASIA CCS '14, pages 271–282, New York, NY, USA, 2014. ACM.

[47] B. Yadegari, B. Johannesmeyer, B. Whitely, and S. Debray. A generic approach to automatic deobfuscation of executable code. In *IEEE Security and Privacy*. IEEE, 2015.

[48] Y. Ye, D. Wang, T. Li, D. Ye, and Q. Jiang. An intelligent pe-malware detection system based on association mining. *Journal in Computer Virology*, 4(4):323–334, 2008.

Auditing Security Compliance of the Virtualized Infrastructure in the Cloud: Application to OpenStack

Taous Madi
CIISE
Concordia University
Montreal, QC, Canada
t_madi,su_majumencs.concordia.ca

Suryadipta Majumdar
CIISE
Concordia University
Montreal, QC, Canada
su_majum@encs.concordia.ca

Yushun Wang
CIISE
Concordia University
Montreal, QC, Canada
yus_wang@encs.concordia.ca

Yosr Jarraya
Ericsson Security Research
Ericsson Canada
Montreal, QC, Canada
yosr.jarraya@ericsson.com

Makan Pourzandi
Ericsson Security Research
Ericsson Canada
Montreal, QC, Canada
makan.pourzandi@ericsson.com

Lingyu Wang
CIISE
Concordia University
Montreal, QC, Canada
wang@encs.concordia.ca

ABSTRACT

Cloud service providers typically adopt the multi-tenancy model to optimize resources usage and achieve the promised cost-effectiveness. Sharing resources between different tenants and the underlying complex technology increase the necessity of transparency and accountability. In this regard, auditing security compliance of the provider's infrastructure against standards, regulations and customers' policies takes on an increasing importance in the cloud to boost the trust between the stakeholders. However, virtualization and scalability make compliance verification challenging. In this work, we propose an automated framework that allows auditing the cloud infrastructure from the structural point of view while focusing on virtualization-related security properties and consistency between multiple control layers. Furthermore, to show the feasibility of our approach, we integrate our auditing system into OpenStack, one of the most used cloud infrastructure management systems. To show the scalability and validity of our framework, we present our experimental results on assessing several properties related to auditing inter-layer consistency, virtual machines co-residence, and virtual resources isolation.

Keywords

Cloud, Virtualization, OpenStack, Security Auditing, Formal Verification, Co-residence, Isolation

1. INTRODUCTION

Several security challenges faced by the cloud, mainly the loss of control and the difficulty to assess security compliance of the cloud providers, leave potential customers reluctant towards its adoption. These challenges stem from cloud-enabling technologies and characteristics. For instance, virtualization introduces complexity, which may lead to new vulnerabilities (e.g., incoherence between multiple management layers of hardware and virtual components). At the same time, concurrent and frequent updates needed to meet various requirements (e.g., workload balancing) may create even more opportunities for misconfiguration, security failures, and compliance compromises. Cloud elasticity mechanisms may cause virtual machines (VMs) belonging to different corporations and trust levels to interact with the same set of resources, causing potential security breaches [30]. Therefore, cloud customers take great interest in auditing the security of their cloud setup.

Security compliance auditing provides proofs with regard to the compliance of implemented controls with respect to standards as well as business and regulatory requirements. However, auditing in the cloud constitutes a real challenge. First, the coexistence of a large number of virtual resources on one side and the high frequency with which they are created, deleted, or reconfigured on the other side, would require to audit, almost continuously, a sheer amount of information, growing continuously and exponentially [13]. Furthermore, a significant gap between the high-level description of compliance recommendations (e.g., Cloud Control Matrix (CCM) [14] and ISO 27017 [20]) and the low-level raw logging information hinders auditing automation. More precisely, identifying the right data to retrieve from an ever increasing number of data sources, and correctly correlating and filtering it constitute a real challenge in automating auditing in the cloud.

We propose in this paper to focus on auditing security compliance of the cloud virtualized environment. More precisely, we focus primarily on virtual resources isolation based on structural properties (e.g., assignment of instances to physical hosts and the proper configuration of virtualization mechanisms), and consistency of the configurations in different layers of the cloud (infrastructure management layer, software-defined networking (SDN) controller layer, virtual layer and physical layer). Although there already exist var-

CODASPY'16, March 09-11, 2016, New Orleans, LA, USA

DOI: http://dx.doi.org/10.1145/2857705.2857721

ious efforts on cloud auditing (a detailed review of related works will be given in Section 2), to the best of our knowledge, none has facilitated automated auditing of structural settings of the virtual resources while taking into account the multi-layer aspects.

Motivating example. The following illustrates the challenges to fill the gap between the high-level description of compliance requirements as stated in the standards and the actual low-level raw audit data. In CCM [14], the control on Infrastructure & Virtualization Security Segmentation recommends *"isolation of business critical assets and/or sensitive user data, and sessions"*. In ISO 27017 [20], the requirement on segregation in virtual computing environments mandates that *"cloud service customer's virtual environment should be protected from other customers and unauthorized users"*. Moreover, the segregation in networks requirements recommends *"separation of multi-tenant cloud service customer environments"*.

Clearly any overlap between different tenants' resources may breach the above requirements. However, in an SDN/-Cloud environment, verifying the compliance with the requirements requires gathering information from many sources at different layers of the cloud stack: the cloud infrastructure management system (e.g., OpenStack [27]), the SDN controller (e.g., OpenDaylight [24]), and the virtual components and verifying that effectively compliance holds in each layer. For instance, the logging information corresponding to the virtual network of tenant `0848cc1999-e542798` is available from at least these different sources:

- Neutron databases, e.g., records from table "Routers" associating tenants to their virtual routers and interfaces of the form `0848cc1999e542798 (tenants_id)` || `420fe1cd-db14-4780` (vRouter_id) || `6d1f6103-9b7a-4789-ab16 (vInterface_id)`.

- Nova databases, e.g., records from table "Instances" associating VMs to their owners and their MAC addresses as follows: `0721a9ac-7aa1-4fa9 (VM_ID)` || `0848cc1999e542798 (tenants_id)` and `fa:16:-3e:cd:b5:e1 (MAC)`|| `0721a9ac-7aa1-4fa9(VM_ID)`.

- Open vSwitch databases information, where ports and their associated tags can be fetched in this form `qvo4429c50c-9d (port_name)`||`1084(VLAN_ID)`.

As illustrated above, it is difficult to identify all the relevant data sources and to map information from those different sources at various layers to the standard's recommendations. Furthermore, potential inconsistencies in these layers make auditing tasks even more challenging. Additionally, as different sources may manipulate different identifiers for the same resource, correctly correlating all these data is critical to the success of the audit activity.

To facilitate automation, we present a complied list of security properties relevant to the cloud virtualized environment that maps into different recommendations described in several security compliance standards in the field of cloud computing. Our auditing approach encompasses extracting configuration and logged information from different layers, correlating the large set of data from different origins, and finally relying on formal methods to verify the security properties and provide audit evidence. We furthermore implement the verification of these properties and show how the data can be collected and processed in the cloud environment with an application to OpenStack. Our approach shows scalability as it allows auditing a dataset of 300,000 virtual ports, 24,000 subnets, and 100,000 VMs in less than 8 seconds.

The main contributions of our paper are as follows:

- To the best of our knowledge, this is the first effort on auditing cloud virtualized environment from the structural point of view taking into account consistency between multiple control layers in the cloud.

- We identify a list of security properties from the literature that may fill the gaps between security standards recommendations and actual compliance validation and allows audit automation.

- We report real-life experience and challenges faced when trying to integrate auditing and compliance validation into OpenStack.

- We conducted experiments whose results show scalability and efficiency of our approach.

The remainder of this paper is organized as follows. Section 2 reviews the related work. Section 3 describes our methodology. Section 4 provides an overview of our auditing framework. Section 5 describes the formalization of security properties. Section 6 details the integration of our auditing framework into OpenStack. Section 7 experimentally evaluates the performance of our approach. Finally, we conclude our paper discussing future directions in Section 8.

2. RELATED WORK

To the best of our knowledge, no work has been tackling auditing consistency views between different layers and structural configuration of virtualization in the cloud. Several works target the verification of forwarding and routing rules, particularly in OpenFlow networks (e.g., [34, 16]). For instance, Libra [34] uses a divide and conquer technique to verify forwarding tables in large networks. It encompasses a technique to capture stable and consistent snapshots of the network state and a verification approach based on graph search techniques that detects loops, black-holes and other reachability failures. Sphinx [16] enables incremental real-time network updates and constraints validation. It allows detecting both known and potentially unknown security attacks on network topology and data plane forwarding. These works are complementary to our work as they aim at verifying operational properties of networks including reachability, isolation and absence of network misconfiguration (e.g., loops, black-holes, etc.). However, they target mainly SDN environments and not necessarily the cloud.

In the context of cloud auditing, several works (e.g., [9, 29]) focus on firewalls and security groups. Probst et al. [29] present an approach for the verification of network access controls implemented by stateful firewalls in cloud computing infrastructures. Their approach combines static and dynamic verification with a discrepancy analysis of the obtained results against the clients' policies. However, the proposed approach does not address challenges related to the cloud such as virtualization and resources sharing. Bleikertz [9] analyzes Amazon EC2 cloud infrastructure using reachability graphs and vulnerability discovery and builds attack graphs to find the shortest paths, which represents the critical attack scenarios against the cloud. These works are complementary to our work as they only focus on layer 3 and layer 4 components, whereas layer 2 components can be at the origin of several problems, which is addressed in our work.

Other works focus on virtualization aspects. For instance, Bleikertz et al. [10] propose a general purpose security analysis of the virtualized cloud infrastructure based on formal verification techniques (e.g., model checking, theorem proving, etc.). Therein, the configuration of the infrastructure is captured using graph-based representations and security goals are expressed using VALID specifications [?]. The automated analysis mechanisms allow checking configuration states (against zone isolation and single point of failure problems) and configuration states changes against high-level security policies. In contrast to our work, their work is more oriented towards detecting attack states than auditing security controls compliance.

Bleikertz et al. [11] extend the previous work to tackle near-real time security analysis of the virtualized infrastructure in the cloud. Their objective is mainly the detection of configuration changes that impact the security. A differential analysis based on computing graph deltas (e.g, added/removed nodes and edges) is proposed based on change events. The graph model is maintained synchronized with the actual configuration changes through probes that are deployed over the infrastructure and intercept events that may have a security impact. In contrast to our work, they aim at the verification of operational properties such as reachability analysis. Furthermore, their analysis relies only on the information on the virtualized infrastructure configuration provided by the cloud infrastructure management system, namely VMware, and thus they do not verify consistency between the cloud infrastructure management system and the actual virtual implementation. In our case, we use direct querying of virtual resources to assess multi-layer configurations consistency.

In [17], an autonomous agent-based incident detection system is proposed. The system detects abnormal infrastructure changes based on the underlying business process model. The framework is able to detect cloud resource and account misuse, distributed denial of service attacks and VM breakout. This related work is more oriented towards monitoring changes in cloud instances and infrastructures and evaluating the security status with respect to security business flow-aware rules.

Xu et al. [33] investigate network inconsistencies between network states extracted from OpenStack and the configuration of network devices. They use Binary Decision Diagrams (BDDs) to represent and verify these states. Similarly to our work, they tackle inconsistency verification. However, this represents only one example of the problem we tackle. Furthermore, we are interested in auditing, thus our approach supports a wider view than simple verification, where log files are as important source of information as configuration.

Congress [2] is an open policy framework for cloud services. It enforces policies expressed by tenants and then monitors the state of the cloud to check its compliance. Furthermore, Congress attempts to correct policy violations when they occur. Our work shares the policy inspection aspect with Congress. Thus, the properties we are audit in the current paper can be integrated in Congress. The multi-domain cloud at the user level with OpenStack as an application is audited in Majumdar et al. [21], whereas this paper deals with different layers and structural configuration of virtualization.

3. METHODOLOGY

In this section, we present some preliminaries and describe our approach for auditing and compliance validation.

3.1 Threat Model

We assume that the cloud infrastructure management system has implementation flaws and vulnerabilities, which can be potentially exploited by malicious entities. For instance, a reported vulnerability in OpenStack Nova networking service, OSSN-0018/2014 [26], allows a malicious VM to reach the network services running on top of the hosting machine, which may lead to serious security issues. We trust cloud providers and administrators, but we assume that some cloud users and operators may be malicious [12]. We trust the cloud infrastructure management system for the integrity of the audit input data (e.g., logs, configurations, etc.) collected through API calls, events notifications, and database records (existing techniques on trusted auditing may be applied to establish a chain of trust from TPM chips embedded inside the cloud hardware to auditing components, e.g., [7]). We assume that not all tenants trust each other. They can either require not to share any physical resource with all the other tenants, or provide a white (or black) list of trusted (or untrusted) customers that they are (not) willing to share resources with. Although our auditing framework may catch violations of specified security properties due to either misconfiguration or exploits of vulnerabilities, our focus is not on detecting specific attacks or intrusions.

EXAMPLE 1. *For illustrating purposes in our running example, we consider two tenants. Tenant Alpha can be exposed to malicious outsiders and insiders. A malicious insider could be either an adversary (tenant Beta) sharing the same cloud resources with tenant Alpha or a malicious operator with a higher access privilege.*

3.2 Modeling the Virtualized Infrastructure

In a multi-tenant cloud Infrastructure as a Service (IaaS) model, the provider's physical and virtual resources are pooled to serve on demands from multiple customers. The IaaS cloud reference model [32] consists of two layers: The physical layer composed of networking, storage, and processing resources, and the virtualization layer that is running on top of the physical layer and enabling infrastructure resources sharing. Figure 1 refines the virtualization layer abstraction in [32] by considering tenant specific virtual resources such as virtual networks and VMs. Accordingly, a tenant can provision several VM instances and virtual networks. VMs may run on different hosts and be connected to many virtual networks through virtual ports. Virtualization techniques are used to ensure isolation among multiple tenants' boundaries. Host virtualization technologies enable running many virtual machines on top of the same host. Network virtualization mechanisms (e.g., VLAN and VXLAN) enable tenants' network traffic segregation, where virtual networking devices (e.g., Open vSwitches) play a vital role in connecting VM instances to their hosting machines and to virtual networks.

In addition to these virtual and physical resources illustrated as nodes, Figure 1 shows the relationships between tenants' specific resources and cloud provider's resources. These relations will be used in section 5 for the formalization of both the virtualized infrastructure model and the security properties. For instance, *IsAttachedOnPort* is a relationship with arity 3. It attaches a VM to a virtual subnet through a virtual port. This model can be refined with several levels of abstraction based on the properties to be checked.

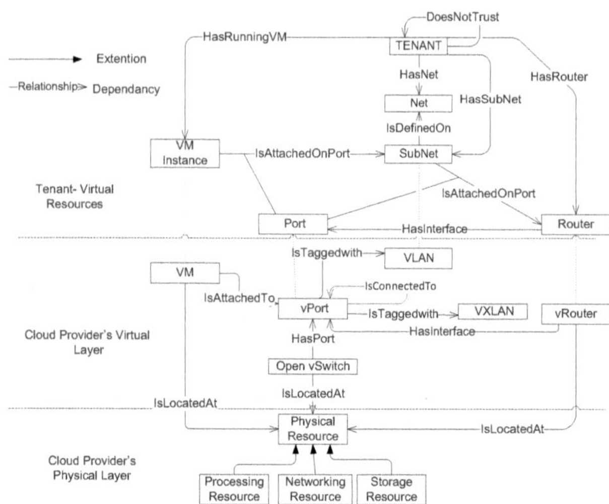

Figure 1: A generic model of the virtualized infrastructures in the cloud

3.3 Cloud Auditing Properties

We classify virtualization related-properties into two categories: Structural and operational properties. Structural properties are related to the static configuration of the virtualized infrastructure such as the assignment of instances to physical hosts, the assignment of virtual networking devices to tenants, and the proper configuration of isolation mechanisms such as VLAN configuration of each port. Operational properties are related to the forwarding network functionality. Those are mainly reachability-related properties such as loop-free forwarding and absence of black holes. Since the latter category has received significant attention in the literature (e.g. [34], [9], [16]), the former category constitutes the main focus of the current paper. As the major goal of this work is to establish a bridge between high-level guidelines in the security standards and low-level logs provided by current cloud systems, we start by extracting a list of concrete security properties from those standards and the literature in order to more clearly formulate the auditing problem. Table 1 presents an excerpt of the list of security properties we consider for auditing relevant standards (e.g., ISO 27002 [19], CCM [14]). Therein, we also classify properties based on their relevance to the stakeholders. In the following, we provide a brief description followed by an illustrating example for the sample properties, namely, absence of common ownership of resources, no co-residence, and topology consistency. More detailed properties' descriptions are provided in Appendix A.

Virtual resources isolation (no common ownership). The no common ownership property aims at verifying that no virtual resource is co-owned by multiple tenants.

EXAMPLE 2. *(No common ownership) Neutron OpenStack service allows tenant administrators to create virtual routers to connect their subnets. It also allows creating interfaces on those routers. OSSA-2014-008 [25] is a Neutron vulnerability that allows a tenant to create a virtual port on another tenant's router without checking his identity. Exploiting such vulnerability leads to the violation of no common ownership property, as virtual ports are tenant specific resources that should not be shared among tenants. As illustrated in Figure 2, Port_84 belongs to Beta as he is the initiator of the command for port creation. Since the port is connected to Router_A5 initially belonging to Alpha, the port would be considered as a common resource for both tenants.*

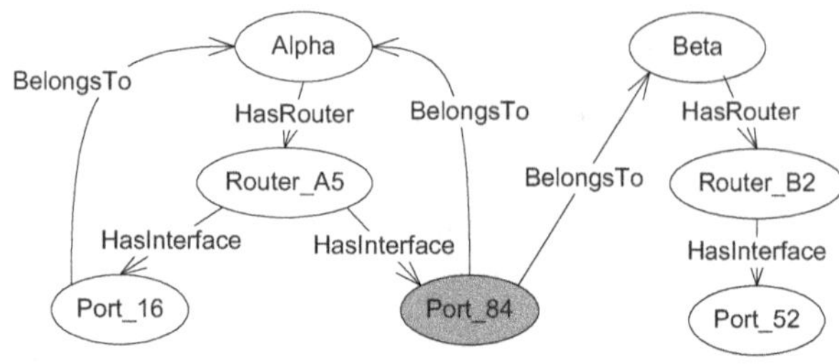

Figure 2: Model instance for *No common ownership*

No co-residence. This property consists of verifying the effective physical isolation of tenants' resources.

EXAMPLE 3. *(No co-residence) According to [36], it is possible to successfully identify the location of a target VM and to trigger the creation of malicious VMs to co-reside in the same host as the target VM. Once co-located with its target, a malicious VM can exploit vulnerabilities in the hypervisor[28] or use side channel techniques to violate other guests confidentiality and integrity and the hypervisor's availability. Suppose that VM_01 and VM_02 are two VMs belonging to tenant Alpha and running initially at Compute Node_85, and VM_03 is owned by tenant Beta and runs initially at Compute Node_96. Assume that tenant Alpha requires to physically isolate its VMs from those of tenant Beta, however, for load balancing reasons, VM_02 is migrated from Compute Node_85 to Compute Node_96. It is clear that this VM migration event will lead to a violation of the physical isolation property (See Figure 3).*

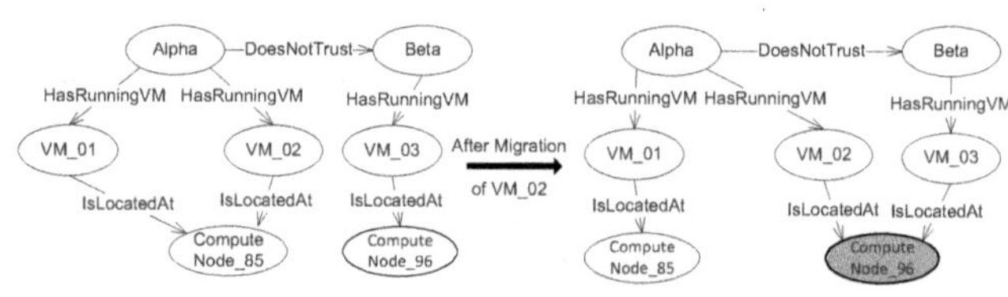

Figure 3: Model instance for *No co-residence*

Topology consistency. Topology consistency consists of checking whether the topology view in the cloud infrastructure management system, matches the actual implemented topology, while considering different mappings between the physical infrastructure, the virtual infrastructure, and the tenants' boundaries.

EXAMPLE 4. *(Port consistency) We suppose that a malicious insider managed to deliberately create a virtual port vPort_40 on Open_vSwitch_56 and label it with the VLAN identifier VLAN_100 that is already assigned to tenant Alpha. This would allow the malicious insider to sniff tenant's Alpha traffic by mirroring the VLAN_100 traffic to the created port vPort_40. This clearly would lead to the violation of the network isolation property.*

As illustrated in Figure 4, we build two views of the virtualized topology: The actual topology is built based on data collected directly from the networking devices running at the virtualization layer (Open vSwitches), and the perceived topology is obtained from the infrastructure management layer (Nova and Neutron OpenStack databases). The dashed lines map one to one the entities between the two topologies (not all the mappings are shown for more readability). We can observe that vPort_40 is attached to VLAN_100, which maps to Net_01 (tenant Alpha's network), but there is no entity at the infrastructure management layer that maps to the entity vPort_40 at the virtualization layer, which reveals a potential security breach.

4. AUDIT READY CLOUD FRAMEWORK

Figure 5 illustrates a high-level architecture of our auditing framework. It has five main components: data collection and processing engine, compliance validation engine, audit report engine, dashboard, and audit repository database. The framework interacts mainly with the cloud management system, the cloud infrastructure system (e.g., OpenStack), and elements in the data center infrastructure to collect various types of audit data. It also interacts with the cloud tenant to obtain the tenant requirements and to provide the tenant with the audit result. Tenant requirements encompass both general and tenant-specific security policies, applicable standards, as well as audit queries. For the lack of space, we will only focus on the following major components.

Our data collection and processing engine is composed of two sub-engines: the collection engine and the processing engine. The collection engine is responsible for collecting the required audit data in a batch mode, and it relies on the cloud management system to obtain the required data. The role of the processing engine is to filter, format, aggregate, and correlate this data. The required audit data may be distributed throughout the cloud and in different formats. The processing engine must pre-process the data in order to provide specific information needed to verify given properties. The last processing step is to generate the code for compliance validation and then store it in the audit repository database to be used by the compliance validation engine. The generated code depends on the selected back-end verification engine.

The compliance validation engine is responsible for performing the actual verification of the audited properties and the detection of violations, if any. Triggered by an audit request or updated inputs, the compliance validation engine invokes our back-end verification and validation algorithms. We use formal methods to capture formally the system model and the audit properties, which facilitates automated reasoning and is generally more practical and effective than manual inspection. If a security audit property fails, evidence can be obtained from the output of the verification back-end. Once the outcome of the compliance validation is ready, audit results and evidences are stored in the audit repository database and made accessible to the audit reporting engine. Several potential formal verification engines can serve our needs, and the actual choice may depend on the property being verified.

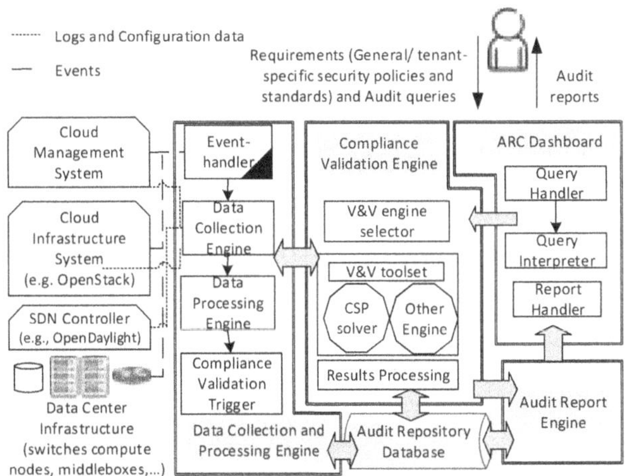

Figure 5: A high-level architecture of our cloud auditing framework

5. FORMAL VERIFICATION

As a back-end verification mechanism, we propose to formalize audit data and properties as Constraint Satisfaction Problems (CSP) and use a constraint solver, namely Sugar [31], to validate the compliance. CSP allows formulation of many complex problems in terms of variables defined over finite domains and constraints. Its generic goal is to find a vector of values (a.k.a. assignment) that satisfies all constraints expressed over the variables. If all constraints are satisfied, the solver returns SAT, otherwise, it returns UNSAT. In the case of a SAT result, a solution to the problem is provided. The key advantage of using CSP comes from the fact that it enables uniformly presenting the system's setup and specifying the properties in a clean formalism (e.g., First Order Logic (FOL) [8]), which allows to check a wide variety of properties [35]. Moreover using CSP avoids the state space traversal, which makes our approach more scalable for large data sets.

5.1 Model Formalization

Depending on the properties to be checked, we encode the involved instances of the virtualized infrastructure model as CSP variables with their domains definitions (over integer), where instances are values within the corresponding domain. For example, *Tenant* is defined as a finite domain ranging over integer such that *(domain TENANT* 0 *max_tenant)* is a declaration of a domain of tenants, where the values are between 0 and *max_tenant*. Relations between classes and their instances are encoded as relation constraints and their supports, respectively. For example, *HasRunningVM* is encoded as a relation, with a support as follows: (relation $HasRunningVM$ 2 $(supports(vm1, t1)(vm2, t2))$). The support of this relation will be fetched and pre-processed in the data processing step. The CSP code mainly consists of four parts:

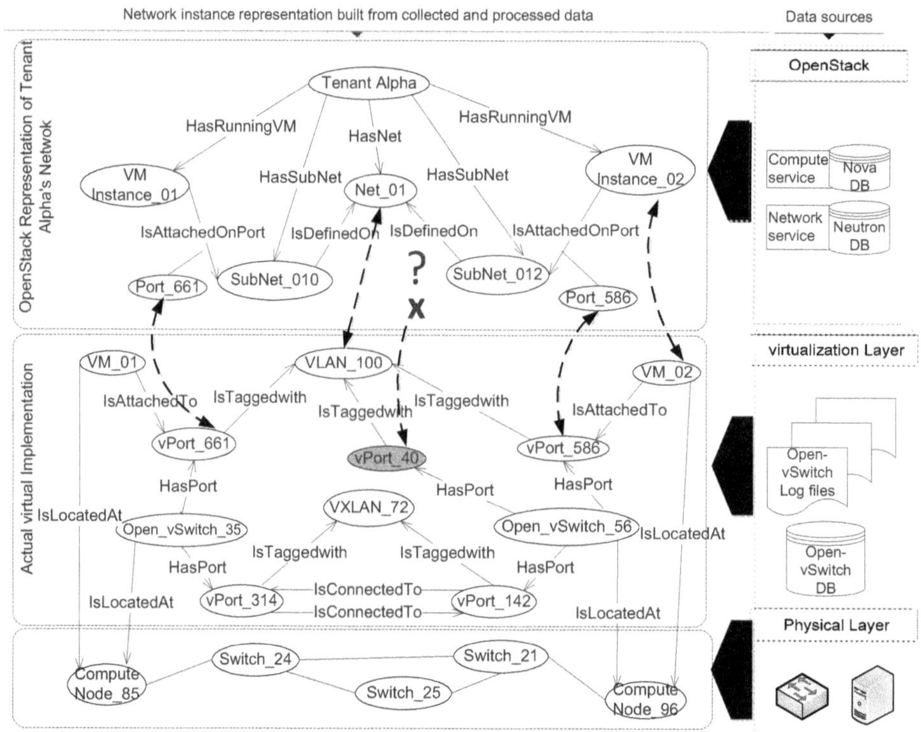

Figure 4: Virtualized infrastructure model instance showing an OpenStack representation and the corresponding actual virtual layer implementation. VXLAN_72 and its ports are part of the infrastructure implementation and do not correspond to any component in tenant Alpha's resources.

Subject	Properties and Sub-Properties		Standards			
			ISO27002 [19]	ISO27017 [20]	NIST800 [23]	CCM [14]
Tenant	Data and proc. location correctness		18.1.1	18.1.1	IR-6, SI-5	SEF-01, IVS-04
	Virt. resource isolation (e.g., No Common Ownership)		-	-	-	STA-5
	Physical isolation (e.g., No Co-residency)		-	13.1.3	SC-2	IVS-8, IVS-9
	Fault tolerance	Facility duplication	17.1, 17.2	12.1.3, 17.1, 17.2	PE-1, PE-13	BCR-03
		Storage service duplication				
		Redundant network connectivity				
Provider	No abuse of resources	Max number of VMs	-	-	-	IVS-11
		Max number of virtual networks				
	No resource exhaustion		-	-	-	IVS-05
Both	Topology consistency	inf. management view/virtual inf.	-	13.1.3	SC-2	IVS-8, IVS-9
		SDN controller view/ virtual inf.				

Table 1: An excerpt of security properties

- *Variable and domain declaration.* We define different entities and their respective domains. For example, t is a variable defined over the domain $TENANT$, which range over integers.
- *Relation declaration.* We define relations over variables and provide their support from the audit data.
- *Constraint declaration.* We define the negation of each property in terms of predicates over the involved relations to obtain a counter-example in case of a violation.
- *Body.* We combine different predicates based on the properties to verify using Boolean operators.

Relations in Properties	Evaluate to *True* if
$BelongsTo(r, t)$	The resource r is owned by tenant t
$HasRunningVM(vm, t)$	The tenant t has a running virtual machine vm
$DoesNotTrust(t1, t2)$	Tenant $t2$ is not trusted by tenant $t1$ which means that $t1$'resources should not share the same hardware with $t2$' instances
$IsLocatedAt(vm, cn)$	The instance vm is located at the compute node cn
$IsAssignedPortVLAN$ (p,v,t)	the port p is assigned to the VLAN v which is in turn assigned to tenant t
$HasPortVLAN(vs, p, v)$	The port p is created at the virtual switch vs and assigned to VLAN v

Table 2: First Order Logic predicates

5.2 Properties Formalization

Security properties would be expressed as predicates over relation constraints and other predicates. We express the sample properties in FOL. The corresponding CSP formalization is given in Appendix B. Table 2 summarizes the predicates required for expressing the properties. Those predicates correspond to CSP relation constraints used to describe the current configuration of the system. Note that predicates that do not appear as relationships in Figure 1 are inferred by correlating other available relations.

No common ownership. We check that a tenant specific virtual resource belongs to a unique tenant.

$$\forall \mathtt{r} \in \mathtt{Resource}, \forall \mathtt{t1}, \mathtt{t2} \in \mathtt{TENANT} \quad (1)$$
$$\mathtt{BelongsTo(r, t1)} \wedge \mathtt{BelongsTo(r, t2)} \quad \rightarrow (\mathtt{t1} = \mathtt{t2})$$

No co-residence. Based on the collected data, we check that the tenant's instances are not co-located in the same compute node with adversaries' instances.

$$\forall \mathtt{t1}, \mathtt{t2} \in \mathtt{TENANT}, \forall \mathtt{vm1}, \mathtt{vm2} \in \mathtt{INSTANCE}, \quad (2)$$
$$\forall \mathtt{cn1}, \mathtt{cn2} \in \mathtt{COMPUTEN} :$$
$$\mathtt{HasRunningVM(vm1, t1)} \wedge \mathtt{HasRunningVM(vm2, t2)} \wedge$$
$$\mathtt{DoesNotTrust(t1, t2)} \wedge \mathtt{IsLocatedAt(vm1, cn1)} \wedge$$
$$\mathtt{IsLocatedAt(vm2, cn2)} \rightarrow \mathtt{cn1} \neq \mathtt{cn2}$$

Topology consistency. We check that mappings between virtual resources over different layers are properly maintained and that the current view of the cloud infrastructure management system on the topology, matches the actual topology of the virtual layer. In the following, we consider port consistency as a specific case of topology consistency. We check that the set of virtual ports assigned to a given tenant's VLAN by the provider correspond exactly to the set of ports inferred from data collected from the actual infrastructure's configuration for the same tenant's VLAN.

$$\forall \mathtt{vs} \in \mathtt{vSWITCH}, \quad \forall \mathtt{p} \in \mathtt{Port} \quad \forall \mathtt{t} \in \mathtt{TENANT} \quad \forall \mathtt{v} \in \mathtt{VLAN} \quad (3)$$
$$\mathtt{HasPortVlan(vs, p, v)} \Leftrightarrow \mathtt{IsAssignedPortVLAN(p, v, t)}$$

EXAMPLE 5. *Listing 1 presented in Appendix B is the CSP code to verify the no common ownership, no co-residence and port consistency properties for our running example. Variables along with their respective domains are first declared (see Listing 1 lines 2-10). Based on the properties of interest, a set of relations are defined and populated with their supporting tuples, where the support is generated from actual data in the cloud (see Listing 1 lines 12-17). Then, the properties are declared as predicates over these relations (see Listing 1 lines 19-24). Finally, the disjunction of the predicates is instantiated for verification (see Listing 1 line 26). As we are formalizing the negation of the properties, we are expecting the UNSAT result, which means that none of the properties holds (i.e., no violation of the properties). We present the verification outputs in Section 6.*

6. APPLICATION TO THE OPENSTACK

This section describes how we integrate our audit and compliance framework into OpenStack. First, we briefly present the OpenStack networking service (Neutron), the compute service (Nova) and Open vSwitch [1], the most popular virtual switch implementation. We then detail our auditing framework implementation and its integration in OpenStack along with the challenges that we faced and overcame.

6.1 Background

OpenStack [27] is an open-source cloud infrastructure management platform that is being used almost in half of private clouds and significant portions of the public clouds (see [15] for detailed statistics). The major components of OpenStack to control large collections of computing, storage and networking resources are respectively Nova, Swift and Neutron along with Keystone. Following is the brief description of Nova and Neutron:

Nova [27] This is the OpenStack project designed to provide massively scalable, on demand, self service access to compute resources. It is considered as the main part of an Infrastructure as a Service model.

Neutron [27] This OpenStack system provides tenants with capabilities to build rich networking topologies through the exposed API, relying on three object abstractions, namely, networks, subnets and routers. When leveraged with the Modular Layer 2 plug-in (ML2), Neutron enables supporting various layer 2 networking technologies. For our testbed we consider Open vSwitch as a network access mechanism and we maintain two types of network segments, namely, VLAN for communication inside of the same compute node, and VXLAN for inter compute nodes communications.

Open vSwitch [1]. Open vSwitch is an open source software switch designed to be used as a vSwitch in virtualized server environments. It forwards traffic between different virtual machines (VMs) on the same physical host and also forwards traffic between VMs and the physical network.

6.2 Integration to OpenStack

We focus mainly on three components in our implementation: the data collection engine, the data processing engine, and the compliance validation engine. The data collection engine involves several components of OpenStack e.g., Nova and Neutron for collecting audit data from databases and log files, different policy files and configuration files from the OpenStack ecosystem, and log files from various virtual networking components such as Open vSwitch to fully capture the configuration. The data is then converted into a consistent format and missing correlation is reconstructed. The results are used to generate the code for the validation engine based on Sugar input language. The compliance validation engine performs the verification of the properties by feeding the generated code to Sugar. Finally, Sugar provides the results on whether the properties hold or not. Figure 6 illustrates the steps of our auditing process. In the following, we describe our implementation details along with the related challenges.

Data collection engine. We present hereafter different sources of data in OpenStack along with the current support for auditing offered by OpenStack and the virtual networking components. The main sources of audit data in OpenStack are logs, configuration files, and databases. Table 3 shows some sample data sources. The involved sources for auditing depend on the objective of the auditing task and the tackled properties. We use three different sources to audit configuration correctness of virtualized infrastructures:

- *OpenStack.* We rely on a collection of OpenStack databases, hosted in a MySQL server, that can be read using component-specific APIs such as Neutron APIs. For instance, in Nova database, table *Compute-node*

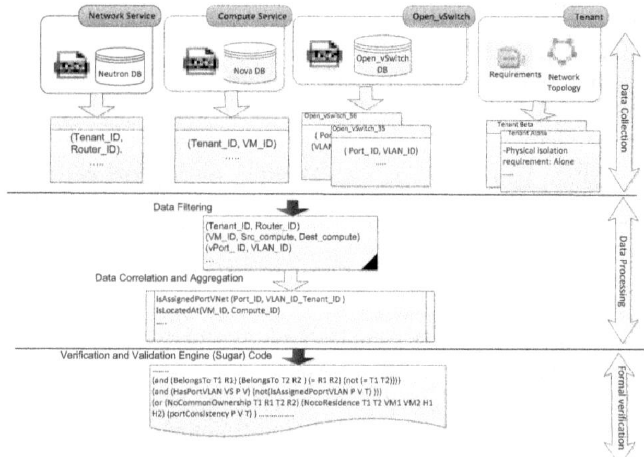

Figure 6: An instance of our OpenStack-based auditing solution with the example of data collection, formatting, correlation building and Sugar source generation

Relations	Sources of Data
BelongsTo	Table *Instances* in Nova database and *Routers, Subnets* and *Ports* in Neutron database, Neutron logs
DoesnotTrust	The tenant physical isolation requirement input
IsLocatedAt	Tables *Instances* in Nova database
IsAssignedPortVLAN	*Networks* in Nova database and *Ports* in Neutron database
HasPortVLAN	Open vSwitch instances located at various compute nodes
HasRunningVM	Table *Instances* in Nova database

Table 3: Sample Data Sources in OpenStack, Open vSwitch and Tenants' requirements

contains information about the hosting machines such as the hypervisor's type and version, table *Instance* contains information about the project (tenant) and the hosting machine, table *Migration* contains migration events' related information such as the source-compute and the destination-compute. The Neutron database includes various information such as security groups and port mappings for different virtualization mechanisms.

- *Open vSwitch.* Flow tables and databases of Open vSwitch instances located in different compute nodes and in the controller node constitute another important source of audit data for checking whether there exist any discrepancies between the actual configuration and the OpenStack view.

- *Tenant policies.* We consider security policies expressed by the customers, such as physical isolation requirements. As expressing tenants' policies is out of the scope of this paper, we assume that they are parsable XML files.

Data processing engine. Our data processing engine, which is implemented in Python, mainly retrieves necessary information from the collected data according to the targeted properties, recovers correlation from various sources, eliminates redundancies, converts it into appropriate formats, and finally generates the source code for Sugar.

- Firstly, for each property, our plug-in identifies the involved relations. The relations' support is either fetched directly from the collected data such as the support of the relation *BelongsTo*, or recovered after correlation, as in the case of the relation *IsAssignedPortVLAN*.

- Secondly, our processing plug-in formats each group of data as an n-tuple, i.e., *(resource, tenant),(port, vlan, tenant)*, etc.

- Finally, our plug-in uses the n-tuples to generate the portions of Sugar's source code, and append the code with the variable declarations, relationships and predicates for each security property (as discussed in Section 5). Different scripts are needed to generate Sugar source code for the verification of different properties.

Compliance Validation. The compliance validation engine is discussed in details in Section 5. In the following example, we discuss how our auditing framework can detect the violation of the no common ownership, no co-residence and port inconsistency security properties caused by the attack scenarios of our running example.

EXAMPLE 6. *In this example, we describe how a violation of no common ownership, no co-residence and port-consistency properties may be caught by auditing.*

Firstly, our program collects data from different tables in the Nova and Neutron databases, and logs from different Open vSwitch instances. Then, the processing engine correlates and converts the collected data and represents it as tuples; for an example: (18038 10) (6100 11000) (512 6020 18033) where Port_84: 18038, Alpha: 10, VM_01: 6100, Open_vSwitch_56: 512, vPort_40: 18033 and VLAN_100: 6020. Additionally, the processing engine interprets each property and generates the associated Sugar source code (see Listing 1 for an excerpt of the code) using processed data and translated properties. Finally, Sugar is used to verify the security properties.

We show for each property how the violation is detected:

a) *No common Ownership. The predicate CommonOwnership will evaluate to true if there exists a resource belonging to two different tenants. As Port_84 has been created by Beta, BelongsTo(Port_84, Beta) evaluates to true based on collected data from Neutron logs. Port_84 is defined on Alpha's router, hence, BelongsTo(Port_84, Alpha) evaluates to true based on collected data from Neutron database. Consequently, the predicate CommonOwnership evaluates to true. In this case, the output of sugar (SAT) is the solution of the problem, (r1 = 18038; r2 =18038; t1 =10; T2=11), which is actually the proof that Port_84 violates the no common ownership property.*

b) *No co-residence. In our example (see Figure 3), the supports HasRunningVM((VM_02, Alpha)(VM_03, Beta)), IsLocatedAt((VM_02, Compute_Node_96)(VM_03, Compute_Node_96) and DoesNotTrust(Alpha, Beta), where VM_02:6101, VM_03:6102, and Compute_Node_96:11100, make the predicate evaluate to true meaning that the no co-residence property has been violated.*

c) Port-consistency. *The predicate PortConsistency evaluates to true if there exists a discrepancy between the OpenStack view of the virtualized infrastructure and the actual configuration. The support HasPortVLAN(Open_vSwitch_56, vPort_40, VLAN_100) makes the predicate evaluate to true, as long as there is no tuple such that IsAssignedPortVLAN (Port, VLAN_100, Alpha) where Port maps to vPort_40:18033.*

Challenges. Checking the configuration correctness in virtualized environment requires considering logs generated by virtualization technologies at various levels, and checking that mappings are properly maintained over different layers. Unfortunately, OpenStack does not maintain such overlay details.

At the OpenStack level, ports are directly mapped to VXLAN IDs, whereas at the Open-vSwitch level, ports are mapped to VLAN tags and mappings between the VLAN tags and VXLAN IDs are maintained. To overcome this limit, we devised a script that generates logs from all the Open vSwitch instances. The script recovers mappings between VLAN tags and the VXLAN IDs from the flow tables using the *ovs-ofctl* command line tool. Then, it recovers mappings between ports and VLAN tags from the Open-vSwitch data base using the *ovs-vsctl* command line utility.

Checking the correct configuration of overlay networks requires correlating information collected both from Open vSwitch instances running on top of various compute nodes and the controller node, and data recovered from OpenStack data bases. To this end, we extended our data processing plug-in to deduce correlation between data. For example, we infer the relation *(portvlantenant)* from the available relations *(vlanvxlan)* recovered from Open vSwitch and *(portvxlantenant)* recovered from the Nova and Neutron databases. In our settings, we consider a ratio of 30 ports per tenant, which leads to 300,000 entries in the relation *(portvxlantenant)* for 10,000 tenants. The number of entries is considerably larger than the number of tenants, because a tenant may have several ports and virtual networks. As a consequence, with the increasing number of tenants, the size of this relation grows and complexity of the correlation step also increases proportionally. Note that, correlation is required for several of our listed properties.

An auditing solution becomes less effective if all needed audit evidences are not collected properly. Therefore, to be comprehensive in our data collection process, we firstly check fields of all varieties of log files available in OpenStack, all configuration files and all Nova and Neutron database tables. Through this process, we identify all possible types of data with their sources.

7. EXPERIMENTS

Here we discuss the performance of our work by measuring the execution time, memory, and CPU consumption.

7.1 Experimental setting

We deployed OpenStack with one controller node and three compute nodes, each having Intel i7 dual core CPU and 2GB memory running Ubuntu 14.04 server. Our OpenStack version is DevStack Juno (2014.2.2.dev3). We set up a real test bed environment constituted of 10 tenants, 150 VMs and 17 routers. To stress the verification engine and assess the scalability of our approach as a whole, we furthermore simulated an environment with 10,000 tenants, 100,000 VMs, 40,000 subnets, 20,000 routers and 300,000 ports with a ratio of 10 VMs, 4 subnets, 2 routers and 30 ports per tenant. To comply verification, we use the V&V tool, Sugar V2.2.1 [31]. We conduct the experiment for 20 different audit trail datasets in total.

All data processing and V&V experiments are conducted on a PC with 3.40 GHz Intel Core i7 Quad core CPU and 16 GB memory and we repeat each experiment 1,000 times.

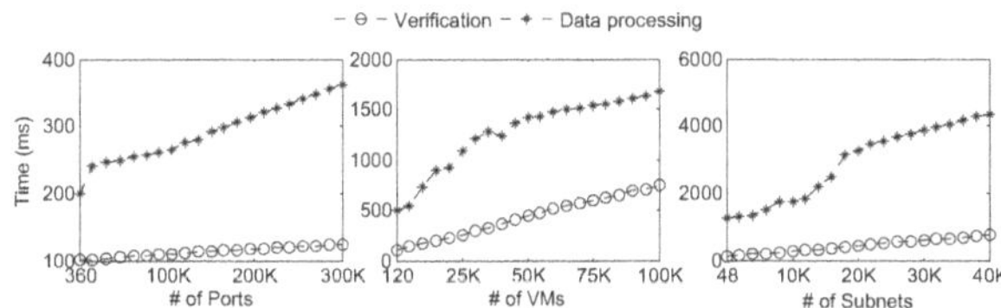

(a) Time required for data processing and verification for the port consistency (left), no co-residence (middle) and no common ownership (right) by varying number of ports, VMs and subnets respectively.

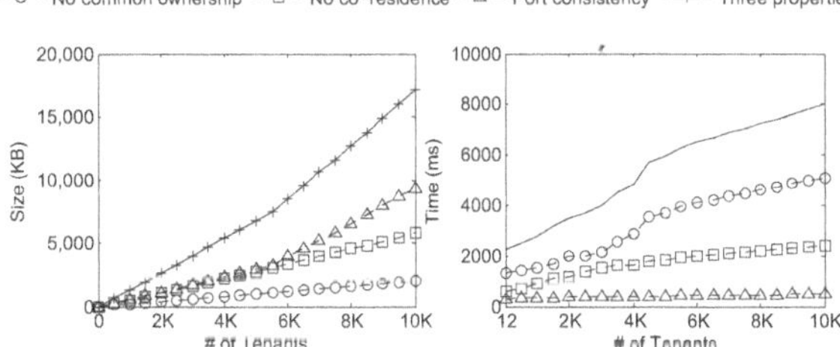

(b) Total size (left) of collected audit data and time required (right) for auditing the port consistency, no co-residence, no common ownership and sequentially auditing three properties (worst case) by varying number of tenants.

Figure 7: Execution time for each auditing step, total size of the collected audit data and total time for different properties using our framework

7.2 Results

The first set of our experiment (see Figure 7) demonstrates the time efficiency of our auditing solution. Figure 7(a) illustrates the time in milliseconds required for data processing and compliance verification steps for port consistency, no co-residence and no common-ownership properties. For each of the properties, we vary the most significant parameter (e.g., the number of ports, VMs and subnets for port consistency, no co-residence and no common ownership properties respectively) to assess the scalability of our auditing solution. Figure 7(b) (left) shows the size of the collected data in KB for auditing by varying the number of tenants. The collected data size reaches to around 17MB for our largest dataset. We also measure the time for collecting data as approximately 8 minutes for a fairly large cloud setup (10,000 tenants, 100,000 VMs, 300,000 ports, etc.). Note that data collection time heavily depends on deployment options and complexity of the setup. Moreover, the initial data collection step is performed only once for the auditing process (later on incremental collection will be performed at regular intervals), so the time may be considered reasonable. Figure 7(b) (right) shows the total execution time required for each property individually and in total. Auditing no common ownership property requires the longest time, because of the highest number of predicates used in the verification step; however, it finishes in less than 4 seconds. In total, the auditing of three properties completes within 8 seconds for the largest dataset, when properties are audited sequentially. However, since there is no interdependency between verifying different security properties, we can easily run parallel verification executions. The parallel execution of the verification step for different properties reduces the execution time to 4 seconds, the maximum verification time required among three security properties. Additionally, we can infer that the execution time is not a linear function of the number of security properties to be verified. Indeed, auditing more security properties would not lead to a significant increase in the execution time.

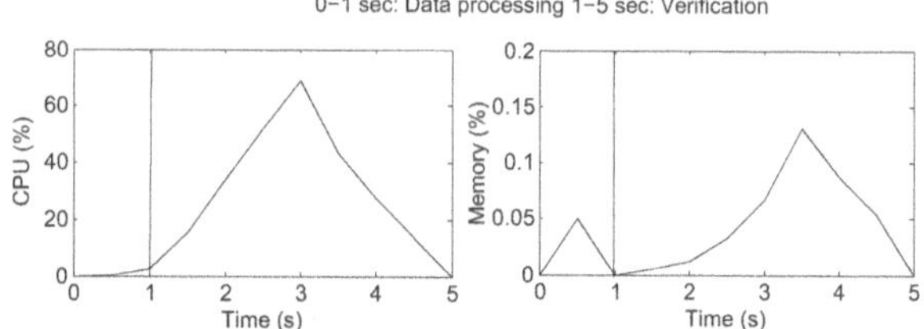

(a) Peak CPU and memory usage for each step of our auditing solution over time when there are 10,000 tenants, 40,000 subnets, 100,000 VMs and 300,000 ports.

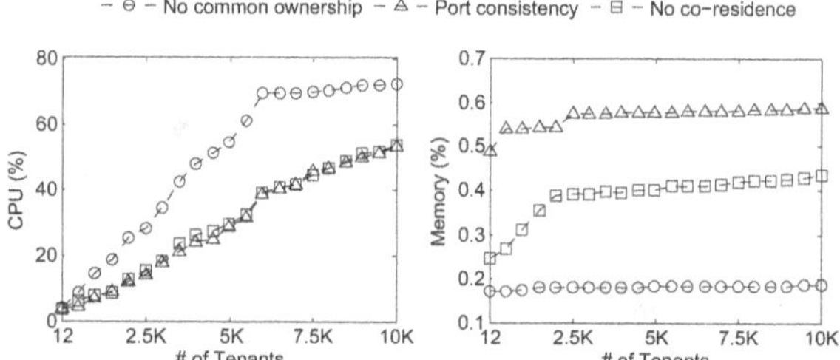

(b) CPU (left) and memory (right) usage for each step of our auditing solution over time when there are 6,000 tenants, 24,000 subnets, 60,000 VMs and 180,000 ports.

Figure 8: CPU and memory usage for each step and for different properties of our auditing solution over time

The objective of our second experiment (Figures 8(a)(left) and 8(b)(left)) is to measure the CPU usage (in %). In Figure 8(a)(left), we measure the peak CPU usage consumed by data processing and verification steps while auditing the no common ownership property. We notice that the average CPU usage is around 35% for the verification, whereas it is fairly negligible for the data processing step. According to Figure 8(b)(left), the CPU usage grows almost linearly with the number of tenants. However, the speed of increase varies depending on the property. It reaches a peak of over 70% for the no common ownership property for 10,000 tenants. This is due to the huge amount of tenant specific resources (e.g. for 10,000 tenants the number of the resources involved may reach 216, 000).

Note that, we conduct our experiments in a single PC; if the security properties can be verified through concurrent and independent Sugar executions, we can easily parallelize this task by running several instances of Sugar on different VMs in the cloud environment. Thus the parallelization in the cloud allows to reduce the overall verification time to the maximum time for any individual security property.

Our final experiment (Figures 8(a)(right) and 8(b)(right)) demonstrates the memory usage of our auditing solution. Figure 8(a)(right) shows that data processing step has a minor memory usage (with a peak of 0.05%), whereas the highest memory usage observed for the verification step for our largest setup is less than 0.19% of 16GB memory. The Figure 8(b) (right) shows that the port consistency property has the lowest memory usage with a percentage of 0.2% whereas no common ownership has the highest memory usage, which is less than 0.6% for 10,000 tenants. Our observation from this experiment is that memory usage is related to the number of relations, variables and constraints involved to verify each property.

Discussion. In our experiments, we audited several security properties e.g., no common ownership and port consistency, for up to 10, 000 tenants with a large set of various resources (300, 000 ports, 100, 000 VMs, 40, 000 subnets) in less than 8 seconds. The auditing activity occurs upon request from the auditor (or in regular intervals when the auditor sets regular audits). Therefore, we consider the costs of our approach to be reasonable even for large data centers. Although we report results for a limited set of security properties related to virtualized cloud infrastructure, promising results show the potentiality of the use of formal methods for auditing. Particularly, we show that the time required for our auditing solution grows very slowly with the number of security properties. As seen in Fig 7a, we anticipate that auditing a large list of security properties in practice would still be realistic. The cost generally increases almost linearly with the number of tenants.

8. CONCLUSION

In this paper, we elaborated a generic model for virtualized infrastructures in the cloud. We identified a set of relevant structural security properties to audit and mapped them to different standards. Then, we presented a formal approach for auditing cloud virtualized infrastructures from the structural point of view. Particularly, we showed that our approach is able to detect topology inconsistencies that may occur between multiple control layers in the cloud. Our evaluation results show that formal methods can be successfully applied for large data centers with a reasonable overhead. As future directions, we intend to leverage our auditing framework for continuous compliance checking. This will be achieved by monitoring various events, and triggering the verification process whenever a security property is affected by the changes. A second area of investigation is to extend the list of security properties with the operational properties. This would allow to check the compliance of the forwarding network functionality with the access control lists and routing policies.

9. ACKNOWLEDGMENTS

The authors thank the anonymous reviewers for their valuable comments. This work is partially supported by the Natural Sciences and Engineering Research Council of Canada and Ericsson Canada under CRD Grant N01566.

10. REFERENCES

[1] Open vswitch. Available at: http://openvswitch.org/.

[2] Policy as a service ("congress"). Available at: http://wiki.openstack.org/wiki/Congress.

[3] Federal data protection act. http://www.gesetze-im-internet.de/englisch_bdsg, August 2009.

[4] IBM Corporation. Ibm point of view: Security and cloud computing, 2009.

[5] C. S. Alliance. Security guidance for critical areas of focus in cloud computing v 3.0, 2011.

[6] C. S. Alliance. The notorious nine cloud computing top threats in 2013, February 2013.

[7] M. Bellare and B. Yee. Forward integrity for secure audit logs. Technical report, Citeseer, 1997.

[8] M. Ben-Ari. *Mathematical logic for computer science*. Springer Science & Business Media, 2012.

[9] S. Bleikertz. Automated security analysis of infrastructure clouds. Master's thesis, Technical University of Denmark and Norwegian University of Science and Technology, 2010.

[10] S. Bleikertz, T. Groß, and S. Mödersheim. Automated verification of virtualized infrastructures. In *Proceedings of CCSW*, pages 47–58. ACM, 2011.

[11] S. Bleikertz, C. Vogel, and T. Groß. Cloud radar: near real-time detection of security failures in dynamic virtualized infrastructures. In *Proceedings of the 30th Annual Computer Security Applications Conference*, pages 26–35. ACM, 2014.

[12] S. Butt, H. A. Lagar-Cavilla, A. Srivastava, and V. Ganapathy. Self-service cloud computing. CCS '12, pages 253–264, New York, NY, USA, 2012. ACM.

[13] Cloud Security Alliance. Top ten big data security and privacy challenges, 2012.

[14] Cloud Security Alliance. Cloud control matrix CCM v3.0.1, 2014. Available at: https://cloudsecurityalliance.org/research/ccm/.

[15] datacenterknowledge.com. Survey: One-third of cloud users' clouds are private, heavily OpenStack, 2015. Available at: http://www.datacenterknowledge.com.

[16] M. Dhawan, R. Poddar, K. Mahajan, and V. Mann. Sphinx: Detecting security attacks in software-defined networks. In *NDSS Symposium*, 2015.

[17] F. Doelitzscher, C. Reich, M. Knahl, A. Passfall, and N. Clarke. An agent based business aware incident detection system for cloud environments. *Journal of Cloud Computing*, 1(1), 2012.

[18] F. H.-U. Doelitzscher. *Security Audit Compliance For Cloud Computing*. PhD thesis, Plymouth University, February 2014.

[19] ISO Std IEC. ISO 27002:2005. *Information Technology-Security Techniques*, 2005.

[20] ISO Std IEC. ISO 27017. *Information technology-Security techniques (DRAFT)*, 2012.

[21] S. Majumdar, T. Madi, Y. Wang, Y. Jarraya, M. Pourzandi, L. Wang, and M. Debbabi. Security compliance auditing of identity and access management in the cloud: Application to openstack. In *IEEE CloudCom*, 2015.

[22] T. E. Network, , and I. S. Agency. Cloud computing benefits, risks and recommendations for information security, December 2012.

[23] NIST, SP. NIST SP 800-53. *Recommended Security Controls for Federal Information Systems*, pages 800–53, 2003.

[24] Opendaylight. The OpenDaylight platform, 2015. Available at: https://www.opendaylight.org/.

[25] OpenStack. Ossa-2014-008: Routers can be cross plugged by other tenants. Available at: https://security.openstack.org/ossa/OSSA-2014-008.html.

[26] OpenStack. Nova network configuration allows guest vms to connect to host services, 2015. Available at: https://wiki.openstack.org/wiki/OSSN/OSSN-0018.

[27] OpenStack. OpenStack open source cloud computing software, 2015. Available at: http://www.openstack.org.

[28] D. Perez-Botero, J. Szefer, and R. B. Lee. Characterizing hypervisor vulnerabilities in cloud computing servers. Cloud Computing '13, pages 3–10, New York, NY, USA, 2013. ACM.

[29] T. Probst, E. Alata, M. Kaâniche, and V. Nicomette. An approach for the automated analysis of network access controls in cloud computing infrastructures. In *Network and System Security*, pages 1–14. Springer, 2014.

[30] T. Ristenpart, E. Tromer, H. Shacham, and S. Savage. Hey, you, get off of my cloud: Exploring information leakage in third-party compute clouds. CCS '09, pages 199–212, New York, NY, USA, 2009. ACM.

[31] N. Tamura and M. Banbara. Sugar: A CSP to SAT translator based on order encoding. *Proceedings of the Second International CSP Solver Competition*, pages 65–69, 2008.

[32] TechNet. Nova network configuration allows guest vms to connect to host services cloud services foundation reference architecture - reference model, 2013.

[33] Y. Xu, Y. Liu, R. Singh, and S. Tao. Identifying sdn state inconsistency in openstack. SOSR '15, pages 11:1–11:7, New York, NY, USA, 2015. ACM.

[34] H. Zeng, S. Zhang, F. Ye, V. Jeyakumar, M. Ju, J. Liu, N. McKeown, and A. Vahdat. Libra: Divide and conquer to verify forwarding tables in huge networks. In *(NSDI 14). Seattle, WA: USENIX Association*, pages 87–99, 2014.

[35] S. Zhang and S. Malik. Sat based verification of network data planes. In D. Van Hung and M. Ogawa, editors, *Automated Technology for Verification and Analysis*, volume 8172 of *Lecture Notes in Computer Science*, pages 496–505. Springer International Publishing, 2013.

[36] Y. Zhang, A. Juels, A. Oprea, and M. K. Reiter. Homealone: Co-residency detection in the cloud via side-channel analysis. SP '11, pages 313–328, Washington, DC, USA, 2011. IEEE Computer Society.

APPENDIX

A. SECURITY PROPERTIES

In the following, we provide a brief description of the most pertinent properties presented in Table 1.

Data and processing location correctness. One of the main cloud specific security issues is the increased complexity of compliance with laws and regulations [18]. The cloud provider might have data centers spread over different continents and governed by various court jurisdictions. Data and processing can be moved between the cloud provider's data centers without tenants awareness, and fall under conflicting privacy protection laws. The Germany's data protection act [3] stipulates that personal data can only be transferred into countries with the same adequate level of privacy protection laws.

Virtual resources isolation (No common ownership). Resource sharing technology was not designed to offer strong isolation properties for a multi-tenant architecture and thus has been ranked by the CSA among the nine notorious threats related to the cloud [6]. The related risks include the failure of mechanisms separating virtual resources between different tenants of the shared infrastructure, which may lead to situations where one tenant has access to another tenant's resources or data.

No co-residency. Cloud providers consolidate virtual machines, possibly belonging to competing customers, to be run on the same physical machine, which may cause major security concerns as described in [36]. According to the CSA standard [5], customers should be able to express their willingness to share or not the physical hosts with other tenants, and they should be provided with the related evidences.

Redundancy and fault tolerance. Cloud providers have to apply several measures to achieve varying degrees of resiliency following the criticality of the customer's applications. Duplicating facilities in various locations, and replicating storage services are examples of the measures that could be undertaken. Considering additional redundancy of network connectivity and information processing facilities has been mentioned in ISO 27002:2013 [19] as one of best practices.

No abuse of resources. Cloud services can be used by legitimate anonymous customers as a basis to illegitimately lead criminal and suspicious activities. For example, cloud services can be used to stage DDoS attacks [6].

No resource exhaustion. The ease with which virtual resources can be provisioned in the cloud introduces the risk of resource exhaustion [22]. For example, creating a huge amount of VMs within a short time frame drastically increases the odds of misconfiguration which opens up several security breaches [5].

Topology consistency. As stated in [4], it is critical to maintain consistency among cloud layers. The architectural model of the cloud can be described as a stack of layered services: Physical layer, system resources layer, virtualized resources layer, support services layer, and at the top cloud-delivered services. The presence of inconsistencies between these layers may lead to security breaches, which in turn makes the security controls at higher layers inefficient.

B. CONSTRAINTS AND CODE

The CSP constraint to no common ownership property:

$$\begin{aligned}(\texttt{and}\ \ \texttt{BelongsTo}(\texttt{r1},\texttt{t1})\ \ \texttt{BelongsTo}(\texttt{r2},\texttt{t2})\\ (\texttt{r1}=\texttt{r2})(\texttt{not}(\texttt{t1}=\texttt{t2}))\end{aligned} \tag{4}$$

The CSP constraint for this no co-residence property:

$$\begin{aligned}(\texttt{and}\ \ \texttt{DoesNotTrust}(\texttt{t1},\texttt{t2})\ \ \texttt{HasRunningVM}(\texttt{vm1},\texttt{t1})\\ \texttt{HasRunning}(\texttt{vm2},\texttt{t2})\ \ \texttt{IsLocatedAt}(\texttt{vm1},\texttt{h1})\\ \texttt{IsLocatedAt}(\texttt{vm2},\texttt{h2})\ \ (\texttt{h1}=\texttt{h2}))\end{aligned} \tag{5}$$

The CSP constraint corresponding to topology consistency:

$$\begin{aligned}(\texttt{or}(\texttt{and}\ \ \texttt{HasPortVLAN}(\texttt{vs},\texttt{p},\texttt{v})\\ (\texttt{not}\ \ \texttt{IsAssignedPortVLAN}(\texttt{p},\texttt{v},\texttt{t}))\\ (\texttt{and}\ \ \texttt{IsAssignedPortVLAN}(\texttt{p},\texttt{v},\texttt{t})\\ (\texttt{not}\ \ \texttt{HasPortVLAN}(\texttt{vs},\texttt{p},\texttt{v})))\end{aligned} \tag{6}$$

Listing 1: Sugar source code for common ownership, co-residence and port consistency verification

```
//Declaration
(domain TENANT 0 60000) (domain RESOURCE 0 216000)
(domain INSTANCE 0 100000) (domain HOST 0 1000)
(domain PORT 0 300; 000) (domain VLAN 0 60000)
(domain VSWITCH 0 1000)
(int T1 TENANT) (int T2 TENANT)
(int R1 Resource) (int R2 Resource)
(int VM1 INSTANCE) (int VM2 INSTANCE)
(int H1 HOST) (int H2 HOST)(int V VLAN)
(int T TENANT) (int P PORT) (int vs VSWITCH)
//Relations Declarations and Audit data as their support
(relation BelongsTo 2 (supports (18037 10)(18038 10) (18039 10)(18040 10)(18038 11)(18042 11)(18043 11)(18044 11)(18045 11)(18046 12)(18047 12)))
(relation HasRunningVM 2 (supports (6100 10)(6101 10)(6102 11)(6103 11)(6104 11)(6105 11)))
(relation IsLocatedAt 2 (supports(((6089 11000)(6090 11000)(6093 11000)(6101 11100)(6102 11100))
(relation DoesNotTrust 2 (supports(9 11)(9 13)(9 14)))
(relation IsAssignedPortVLAN 3 (supports (18028 6017 9)(18029 6018 9)(18030 6019 10)(18031 6019 10)(18032 6020 10) ))
(relation HasPortVLAN 3 (supports(511 18030 6019)(511 18031 6019 10)(512 18032 6020)(512 18033 6021)))
//Security properties expressed in terms of predicates over relation constraints
(predicate (CommonOwnership T1 R1 T2 R2)
(and (BelongsTo T1 R1) (BelongsTo T2 R2 ) (= R1 R2) (not (= T1 T2))))
(predicate (coResidence T1 T2 VM1 VM2 H1 H2) (and (DoesNotTrust T1 T2) (HasRunningVM VM1 T1)
(HasRunningVM VM2 T2) (IsLocatedAt H1 VM1) (IsLocatedAt H2 VM2) (=H1 H2)))
(predicate (portConsistency P V T)(or (and (IsAssignedPoprtVLAN P V T)(not(HasPortVLAN VS P V)))
(and (HasPortVLAN VS P V) (not(IsAssignedPoprtVLAN P V T)))))
\\The Body
(or (CommonOwnership T1 R1 T2 R2) (coResidence T1 T2 VM1 VM2 H1 H2) (portConsistency P V T) )
```

Security Constraints in Temporal Role-Based Access-Controlled Workflows*

Carlo Combi
Dipartimento di Informatica,
Università di Verona, Italy
carlo.combi@univr.it

Luca Viganò
Department of Informatics,
King's College London, UK
luca.vigano@kcl.ac.uk

Matteo Zavatteri
Dipartimento di Informatica,
Università di Verona, Italy
matteo.zavatteri@univr.it

ABSTRACT

Workflows and role-based access control models need to be suitably merged, in order to allow users to perform processes in a correct way, according to the given data access policies and the temporal constraints. Given a mapping between workflow models and simple temporal networks with uncertainty, we discuss a mapping between role temporalities and simple temporal networks, and how to connect the two resulting networks to make explicit *who can do what, when*. If the connected network is still executable, we show how to compute the set of authorized users for each task. Finally, we define security constraints (to prevent users from doing unauthorized actions) and security constraint propagation rules (to propagate security constraints at runtime). We also provide an algorithm to check whether a set of propagation rules is safe, and we extend an existing execution algorithm to take into account these new security aspects.

Keywords

Access-controlled workflow, TRBAC, temporal separation of duties, security constraint propagation rules, STNU.

1. INTRODUCTION

Context and motivation. Workflow technology has emerged as a key technology to specify and manage business processes within complex organizations. Recent research has focused on the issues related to workflow temporalities, such as uncertain durations of tasks, temporal constraints between (even non consecutive) tasks, deadlines and so on [7]. As complex tasks need the suitable access to data and systems, *role-based access control (RBAC) models* play an important part as they both deal with the classical security analysis (concerning authorization inspection, administrative models, and hierarchies) and allow one to consider also temporal aspects [1, 3, 16, 23, 25].

Thus, in the business process context, RBAC models and workflow models need to be suitably merged, in order to allow users to perform processes in a correct way according to the given data access policies and the temporal constraints.

To properly manage temporal constraints of workflows, solutions have been proposed that are based on a mapping between workflow models and *simple temporal constraint networks with uncertainty (STNU)* [27] and that allow one to deal with *controllability* of workflow models. In a nutshell, an STNU, and its corresponding workflow, is *controllable* if it is always possible to execute the network without violating any constraint no matter what the uncertain durations (of tasks) turn out to be [27].

Even if both a temporal workflow model and a temporal access control model pass their security analyses successfully, in general we cannot be sure that their composition behaves as we expect. Hence, we need a way to analyze what happens when we put an access control model on top of a workflow model. As a temporal workflow can be translated into an equivalent STNU, if we were able to extend this network to take into consideration the security aspects, we could have some chances of reasoning on their interplay.

Contributions. In this direction, we have merged *temporal role-based access control (TRBAC)* and temporal workflow models to seamlessly manage temporal constraints when executing tasks together with possible temporal constraints related to the availability of agents able to execute tasks according to their roles. Thus, the first two contributions of this paper are: proposing a mapping of valid intervals of roles into an equivalent simple temporal network, and merging it with the STNU specifying the workflow model.

The enabling times of the roles in TRBAC models are usually specified according to periodic expressions using *calendars* [21]. We propose the concept of *configuration*, which corresponds to an STNU containing both the representation of a temporal workflow and the related role-based access model, considering periodic role-enabling intervals within a given, limited time window. A configuration allows us to check if the workflow is executable with respect to the access control model. That is, it allows us to understand if these two models are consistent with each other. If so, then we are able to compute which users belonging to which roles are authorized to execute the tasks.

Moreover, a further contribution is the definition of *security constraints (SCs)*, not directly expressible in role-based access models, along with their *security constraint*

*This work was partially supported by the PRIN 2010-2011 Project "Security Horizons". We thank the anonymous reviewers for their comments and suggestions.

CODASPY'16, March 09-11, 2016, New Orleans, LA, USA
© 2016 ACM. ISBN 978-1-4503-3935-3/16/03...$15.00
DOI: http://dx.doi.org/10.1145/2857705.2857716

propagation rules (SCPRs). The former are used to prevent users from doing unauthorized actions (e.g., starting/ending a task) if the current time satisfies the constraint itself, whereas the latter are used to propagate these security constraints depending on what is going on. If different users make different choices, then SCPRs will propagate different SCs. This *dynamic* approach reacts to observations of the occurring runtime events. As far as we know, this is the first attempt to use temporal networks to model (and enforce) security (policies).

Organization. Section 2 reviews essential background of simple temporal networks (STNs), STNUs, a mapping from workflow models to STNUs, and TRBAC. Section 3 provides a new mapping to translate the enabling intervals of roles of TRBAC into an STN and a connection mapping to connect the workflow STNU to the access control STN. It also shows how to derive the set of authorized users for each time point in these networks. Section 4 introduces a case study also specifying three security policies that are supposed to hold in that context. Section 5 defines SCs and SCPRs to enforce (temporal) security policies when executing a temporal workflow. It also discusses a safeness algorithm for a set of SCPRs. Section 6 discusses how to extend an already existing execution algorithm for STNUs so as to take into account these rules too. Section 7 discusses related work. Section 8 draws conclusions and discusses future work.

The proofs of our results are given, along with further details, in [8].

2. BACKGROUND

In this section, we briefly review the theoretical foundations of STNs [14] and STNUs [19], how to map a workflow into an STNU, and role based access models.

2.1 Simple Temporal Networks

Definition 1. A Simple Temporal Network (STN) *is a pair* $\langle \mathcal{T}, \mathcal{C} \rangle$*, where* $\mathcal{T}$ *is a set of time points with continuous domain, and* $\mathcal{C}$ *is a set of constraints of the form* $X - Y \leq k$ *with* X, Y *time points and* $k \in \mathbb{R} \cup \{-\infty, \infty\}$ *[14].*

A Simple Temporal Constraint Satisfaction problem (STCP) *is the problem of finding a complete assignment of values to the time points in* $\mathcal{T}$ *satisfying all constraints in* $\mathcal{C}$ *[14].*

An STN can also be represented as a directed graph where each node represents a time point of $\mathcal{T}$ and each edge $X \xrightarrow{[x,y]} Y$ (called *requirement link* or *link*, for short) represents the two constraints $Y - X \leq y$ and $X - Y \leq -x$ belonging to $\mathcal{C}$. For each pair of time points in a directed graph representing an STN, there exists only one edge between them, which is labeled exactly by one range. We can also represent it through an equivalent directed weighted graph (called *distance graph* G_d), where the set of nodes is still the set of time points and each constraint $Y - X \leq k$ is mapped to a weighted edge $X \xrightarrow{k} Y$. That is, each edge of the STN $X \xrightarrow{[x,y]} Y$ is mapped to $X \xrightarrow{y} Y$ and $Y \xrightarrow{-x} X$ in the distance graph.

To avoid confusion, hereinafter *edges* will refer to the edges in the distance graph, whereas *(requirement) links* will refer to the edges in the STN graph.

To find the ranges of distance values allowed between time points, one can run the *all pairs shortest paths algorithm* on the distance graph G_d [9]. If G_d contains a negative cycle, the given STP does not admit solutions, i.e., it is *inconsistent.* The upper bound of the range between the ith time point and the origin time point Z corresponds to the shortest path from node Z to that node, whereas the lower bound corresponds to the negation of the shortest path in the opposite direction.

Assuming that the origin time point Z is the starting point, to find a complete solution $\mathtt{S} = \{Z = 0, X_1 = t_{X_1}, \dots\}$ for each time point X, we choose a value among those allowed in its range adding the link $Z \xrightarrow{[x,x]} X$ to the STN (if a link $Z \to X$ already exists in the STN graph, then we replace it with the new one). This translates into adding $X - Z \leq x$ and $Z - X \leq -x$ to $\mathcal{C}$, which fixes the value for X. To get the new updated ranges for the remaining time points, we *propagate* the effect of this assignment recomputing the shortest paths on the distance graph containing now the two new constraints $Z \xrightarrow{x} X$ and $X \xrightarrow{-x} Z$. Managing in such way all time points, we obtain a complete solution.

2.2 STN with Uncertainty

Definition 2. A Simple Temporal Network with Uncertainty (STNU) *extends an STN by adding a set of contingent links [20]. Formally, an STNU is a triple* $\mathcal{S} = \langle \mathcal{T}, \mathcal{C}, \mathcal{L} \rangle$ *where:*

- $\langle \mathcal{T}, \mathcal{C} \rangle$ *is an STN,*
- $\mathcal{L}$ *is a set of* contingent links *of the form* (A, x, y, C) *(or, equivalently,* $A \overset{[x,y]}{\Longrightarrow} C$ *in the STNU graph), where the* activation *point* A *and the* contingent *point* C *are different time points* ($A \not\equiv C$)*,* x *and* y *are such that* $0 < x < y < \infty$*, and*
  - *for each* $(A, x, y, C) \in \mathcal{L}$*,* $\mathcal{C}$ *contains* $C - A \leq y$ *and* $A - C \leq -x$*,*
  - *if* (A_1, x_1, y_1, C_1) *and* (A_2, x_2, y_2, C_2) *are two distinct contingent links, then* $C_1 \not\equiv C_2$*,*
  - *the contingent time point of a contingent link may play the role of an activation point for another one.*

When we are not interested in talking about the range of a link, we simply write $A \Rightarrow C$ *(for contingents) or* $X \to Y$ *(for requirements) omitting* $[x, y]$*. As notation, we write* A *to refer to activation time points,* C *to contingent time points and* X *to generic time points. If* X *is not a contingent time point, then it is also called* control time point.

It is easy to see that each STN $\langle \mathcal{T}, \mathcal{C} \rangle$ is also an STNU $\langle \mathcal{T}, \mathcal{C}, \mathcal{L} \rangle$ where $\mathcal{L} = \emptyset$ (i.e., without contingent links).

When the network is being executed, the system incrementally assigns a fixed time value to each control time point (i.e., to each non-contingent time point) among those allowed in its range. The system can only *observe* the occurrence of any contingent C_i, which is not under the control of the system and is however guaranteed to occur in such a way that that $C_i - A_i \in [x_i, y_i]$.

The meaning of contingency can be thought as representing processes that are not under the control of the workflow systems and whose exact duration is unknown *but* bounded by the range $[x, y]$. For example, the writing of this paper once started (i.e., once A has been executed) will last at least a minimum amount of time x to allow authors to get a polished version to be submitted and at most y ($> x$), which in this context is related to the submission deadline. However, the exact moment when the authors will have it finished (and consequently the paper will have been submitted) is unknown at this stage.

In an STNU, we need to move from the concept of *consistency* to that of *controllability*, because we now have to deal with "uncertainty", which is by definition out of our control. We must make sure that no execution will violate any constraint. Hence, an STNU is *controllable* if we are able to execute all control time points satisfying all constraints in $\mathcal{C}$ no matter what the durations of the contingent links turn out to be. The rest of this section provides everything we need to define the various types of controllability (see [27] for details).

A *situation* $\omega = (d_1, \ldots, d_n)$ is defined by fixing a chosen duration for each contingent link. Fixing a situation is equivalent to transforming an STNU into an STN as each $A_i \overset{[x_i,y_i]}{\Longrightarrow} C_i$ is replaced with $A_i \xrightarrow{[d_i,d_i]} C_i$ ($d_i \in [x_i, y_i]$). A *(situation) projection* is a mapping $sitPrj : \langle \mathcal{T}, \mathcal{C}, \mathcal{L} \rangle \times \Omega \to \langle \mathcal{T}, \mathcal{C}' \rangle$, which considers all contingent links as if they were requirement links with a fixed distance. Therefore, an STNU represents an infinite family of STNs (each one *projecting* a different situation). The *space of all situations* is represented by Ω. A *schedule* is a mapping $\psi : \mathcal{T} \to \mathbb{R}$ that assigns a real value to each time point. The *space of all schedules* (since an STNU can be executed in infinite ways) is represented by Ψ. An *execution strategy* for $\mathcal{S}$ is a mapping $\sigma : \Omega \to \Psi$ such that for each situation $\omega \in \Omega$, $\sigma(\omega)$ is a complete schedule for the time points in $\mathcal{T}$.

Three main kinds of controllability for STNUs have been originally defined in [27]. An STNU is *weakly controllable* if there exists a viable execution strategy, i.e., if every projection is consistent. An STNU is *strongly controllable* if there exists a set of viable execution strategies considering all possible projections, where each control time point is assigned the same value by the schedule in all the strategies. An STNU is *dynamically controllable* if there exists an execution strategy for $\mathcal{S}$ that is both viable and dynamic*, where an execution strategy is dynamic* whenever: if the durations of all contingent time points executed before the next time point X are equal in all different situations ω_1 and ω_2, then the schedule must assign the same value to X in both ω_1 and ω_2.

Checking the dynamic controllability of an STNU is polynomial. The first algorithm was proposed in [20] and further improvements were given in [17, 19]. The main idea behind the controllability check is that of restricting the execution strategies ruling out those that would squeeze the contingent links, where a contingent link is *squeezed* if the other constraints imply a tighter lower and/or upper bound for the link. Hereinafter, we will refer to the basic algorithm introduced in [19] for STNU dynamic controllability, avoiding the discussion related to subtle further optimizations. The algorithm takes as input a labeled distance graph built from the STNU according to the following mapping: each requirement link $X \xrightarrow{[x,y]} Y$ is mapped to $X \xrightarrow{y} Y$ and $Y \xrightarrow{-x} X$ in the labeled distance graph. For each contingent link $A \overset{[x,y]}{\Longrightarrow} C$, we have the same edges $A \xrightarrow{y} C$ and $C \xrightarrow{-x} A$, but we also have $A \xrightarrow{c:x} C$ and $C \xrightarrow{C:-y} A$ which are the *lower-case* and the *upper-case* edge, respectively.

The algorithm proposed in [19] iteratively checks if the *AllMax* projection (i.e., the projection in which all contingent links take their maximal duration) is consistent in the STN-sense, where the *AllMax* projection is the unlabeled distance graph obtained by deleting all lower-case edges and all labels from the upper-case edges (whenever we remove labels from edges or we add new edges, if an edge of the same type already exists in the graph we are operating on, then we usually keep that specifying the tighter constraint with respect to the type of edge). If so, it generates new edges according to suitable edge generation rules given in [19], until either quiescence (i.e., no further constraints are added or the existing ones are tightened) or the cutoff bound used to make the algorithm strongly polynomial, is reached. A detailed analysis of the execution of this algorithm as well as how the proposed rules work can be found in [19].

2.3 Workflow Modeling

A *workflow* consists of a set of tasks to be executed in some order to achieve some (business) goal(s). A *temporal workflow* extends the classical one by taking into account temporal constraints that typically require a lower and an upper bound on the duration of tasks. A temporal workflow also allows one to express relative constraints restricting the allowed time distance between the start or the end of two (not necessarily consecutive) tasks.

In this paper, we only consider *structured* workflows that can be described by a well-defined grammar and, without loss of generality, we do not consider alternative/choice/conditional paths. Thus, we will focus on the workflow specification where all the specified tasks have to be properly executed. An example of the basic constructs of this grammar is given in Table 1 (WORKFLOW BLOCKS), where, for each block, the equivalent STNU is depicted on the right of it (EQUIVALENT STNU).

The table shows the basic workflow block task (first row), which can be thought of as a terminal symbol, and then the sequence (second row) and parallel (third row), which can be thought of as non-terminal symbols. The last component (relative constraint) in the fourth row only imposes further temporal constraints between the start/end of two tasks and it has nothing to do with the control flow that is regulated by the grammar. If the workflow model is structured, we will "structure" the corresponding STNU.

2.4 Temporal RBAC Models

So far, we have not talked about workflow security, but, as we mentioned above, our aim is to put a temporal *Role-Based Access Control (RBAC, [25])* model on top of a workflow model. As the name says, RBAC models rely on the concept of *role*, which is different from that of group, as it is a collection of both users and permissions (thus, it acts as an interface between them), rather than a collection of users only [24]. The main components of an RBAC model are:

- `Users`, `Roles`, `Perm`, `Sess` representing the set of users, roles, permissions and sessions, respectively.
- $UA \subseteq$ `Users` $\times$ `Roles` and $PA \subseteq$ `Roles` $\times$ `Perm` representing many to many user-role and permission-role assignment relations, respectively.
- $user$: `Sess` $\to$ `Users` and $role$: `Sess` $\to 2^{\texttt{Roles}}$ representing functions assigning each session to a single user and to a set of roles, respectively.

Table 1: Workflow to STNU mapping.

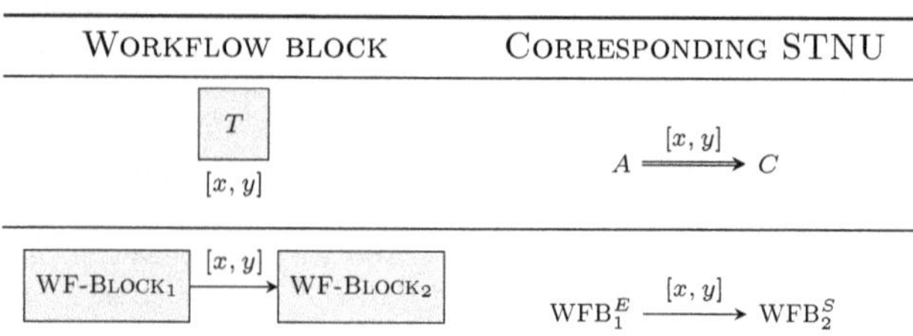

WFB_2^S (resp., WFB_1^E) is a convention to represent the start (resp., the end) time point of the workflow block WF-BLOCK$_2$ (resp., WF-BLOCK$_1$).

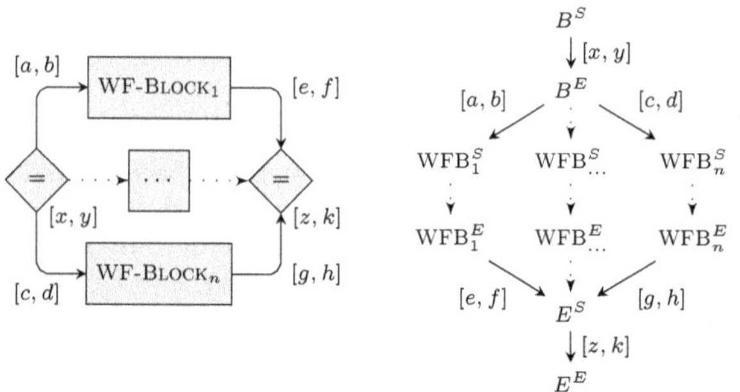

$B^S \to B^E$ (resp., $E^S \to E^E$) is a convention to represent the branch (resp., join) component as an internal task.

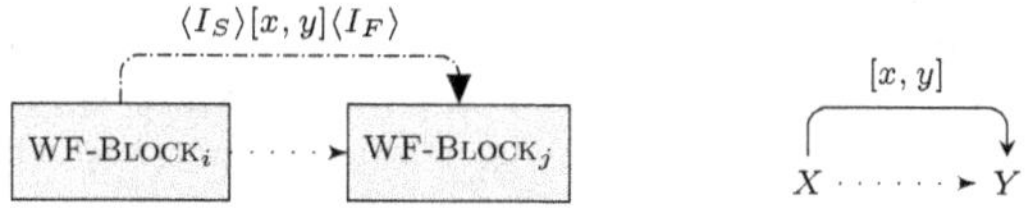

X is either an activation point (if $\langle I_S \rangle \equiv S$) or a contingent point (if $\langle I_S \rangle \equiv E$) of some task inside WF-BLOCK$_i$ and Y is the same but with respect to WF-BLOCK$_j$.

- $RH \subseteq$ `Roles` $\times$ `Roles` representing a partially ordered role hierarchy relation $\geq$.

Moreover, in the classical RBAC model a role R is always `enabled` and can be activated in a session by a user u such that $(u, R) \in UA$. Thus, to deal with the lack of constraints on role enabling and disabling, TRBAC was proposed as a first temporal extension [3]. In this model, a user u can activate a role R provided that both he is authorized to do so and the role is `enabled` at the time of the request, i.e., $R \in ST(t)$, where $ST(t)$ is the set of `enabled` roles at time t. It follows that the concept of *status* {`active`, `inactive`} of a role is implicitly augmented by adding {`enabled`, `disabled`}. Note that, if a role is `active` (i.e., there is an associated user playing it in some session), then it is also `enabled`. In general, the vice versa does not hold.

Roles are `enabled` and `disabled` according to the content of the *role enabling base* (REB) $\mathcal{R}$, which mainly consists of periodic events and triggers. A *periodic event* has the form $(I, P, p{:}E)$, where: I is a time interval, P is a periodic expression using calendars [21], and $p : E$ is a prioritized event expression where p is a priority and E has the form `enable` R or `disable` R for some $R \in$ `Roles`. For example

`([01/01/15,`∞`], WorkingHours, H:enable director)`

tells the system to enable (with high priority) the role `director` from 1 January 2015 onwards, as soon as current time gets to the starting point of each interval spanned by `WorkingHours`, which is a periodic expression representing all time instants from 9AM to 1PM and from 2PM to 6PM of week days (i.e., from Monday to Friday).

A *role trigger* has the form $B \to p : E$ and its meaning is to fire the periodic event on the right of $\to$ whenever all preconditions on the left (the body of the trigger consisting of periodic expressions and role status expressions) become true [3]. A role status expression is either `enabled` R or $\neg$`enabled` R. When firing a role trigger these expressions will be evaluated true or false depending on the status of R at that time. For example, the trigger

`enable director` $\to$ `enable cashier`

tells the system to enable the role `cashier` whenever the role `director` gets `enabled`.

In this paper, we consider the fragment of TRBAC consisting of non-conflicting complementary periodic events. For sake of simplicity, we do not consider *non-complementary periodic events* and *conflicting events*. Thus, we assume that each interval spanned by the periodic expression is not influenced by other periodic events. Moreover, we do not consider *runtime request expressions* (and thus *individual exceptions*) because they allow a security officer to override any execution. We also do not consider *role triggers* because they may lead to the previous problems. Thus, under these assumptions, priorities will not influence the behavior of the system.

3. ACCESS-CONTROLLED WORKFLOWS

We first focus on how a controllable workflow can be executed with respect to a given fragment of TRBAC, where the assumptions made at the end of Section 2.4 hold. Then, in Section 3.3 we derive the set of users authorized to execute a time point. In Section 4, we introduce a running example to discuss a possible real application. In Section 5, we introduce security constraints and related propagation rules to enforce security policies at execution time. In Section 6, we discuss how to execute the access-controlled workflow.

Let us start by supposing that we want to understand whether a controllable workflow can be executed with respect to the considered fragment of TRBAC. In such a model, the set `Perm` $= \{T_1, \ldots, T_n\}$ of permissions consists of the workflow tasks, and the interpretation of the role-permission assignment relation $(R, T) \in PA$ is "all users belonging to R are authorized to execute task T".

As we have already said, roles are `enabled` during certain time intervals and typically `disabled` in the complementary. Consequently, since a workflow task T is represented as a contingent link $A \xRightarrow{[x,y]} C$ where there is no control on the contingent point C, the interval where the associated role is `enabled` is supposed to be at least as large as the maximal duration of the contingent link, i.e., y (otherwise, the workflow would not be consistent with the access control model). Thus, since the workflow and the access control model do not depend on each other, we first need to reduce both models to a common representation to be able to analyze their interplay. To that end, we have chosen to translate the enabling/disabling intervals of roles belonging to the access control model into an equivalent STN to be connected to the STNU representing the workflow model.

We proceed as follows: Section 3.1 introduces a mapping to translate such intervals into an equivalent STN, and then Section 3.2 explains how to connect the resulting STN to the workflow-related STNU.

3.1 From Periodic Expressions to STNs

Let $\mathtt{C}_i$ be a calendar (*Hours*, *Days*, *Weeks*, ...) and $\mathtt{C}_i \sqsubseteq \mathtt{C}_j$ be the sub calendar relation (e.g., *Days* $\sqsubseteq$ *Weeks*). A *periodic expression* has the form $\sum_{i=1}^{n} O_i \cdot \mathtt{C}_i \triangleright r \cdot \mathtt{C}_d$, where $O_1 = all$, $O_i \in 2^{\mathbb{N}} \cup \{all\}$, $\mathtt{C}_i \sqsubseteq \mathtt{C}_{i-1}$ for $i = 2, \ldots, n$, $\mathtt{C}_d \sqsubseteq \mathtt{C}_n$ and $r \in \mathbb{N}$ [21]. The part on the left of $\triangleright$ specifies the set of starting points (O_is) of the spanned intervals with respect to each calendar ($\mathtt{C}_i$) involved, whereas the part on the right specifies the duration of those intervals in terms of time units (r) in the minimum granularity calendar ($\mathtt{C}_d$). For example, assuming that Monday is the first day of every week, **WorkingHours** can be formalized as follows:

$$all \cdot Weeks + \{1,2,3,4,5\} \cdot Days + \{10,15\} \cdot Hours \triangleright \{4\} \cdot Hours\,.$$

Periodic expressions implicitly talk about intervals according to the minimum granularity chosen (in this case *Hours*). The xth hour of the day starts at time instant $x-1$ and ends at x. For instance, the time instant corresponding to 9AM corresponds to the left bound of the 10th hour of the day. Likewise, 1PM corresponds to the right bound of the 4th hour of the first interval spanned by **WorkingHours** starting from the 10th (i.e., the 13th hour since this interval contains the 10th, 11th, 12th, and 13th hour of the day).

Every periodic expression can be translated into an equivalent set of simple periodicity constraints. That is, *linear repeating intervals of integers* along with a *gap constraint* that limits its applicability as described in [2] (which was inspired by [26]). Let P be a periodic expression, *Periodicity*(P) the number of time units in which P repeats, *Granularity*(P) the duration of each spanned interval and *Displacement*(P) the set of integers representing the starting points of the spanned intervals. Then, the *set of equivalent linear repeating intervals of integers* is formally represented by:

$$I^P = \{I^P_{n+1,z} \mid 1 \leq y \leq Granularity(P) \land z \in Displacement(P)\}\,,$$

where each $I^P_{n+1,z} = [t_1, \ldots, t_{Granularity(P)}]$ represents the $(n+1)^{\text{th}}$ interval of integers spanned by the periodic expression P according to the displacement z, and in turn $t_1, \ldots, t_{Granularity(P)}$ are generated according to the following equation representing the class of integers

$$t \equiv_{Periodicity(P)} (y + z - 1)\,,$$

for every $y \in \{1, \ldots, Granularity(P)\}$ once we have fixed $z \in Displacement(P)$ and $n \in \mathbb{N}$, where $t \equiv_k c$ denotes the set of integers of the form $c + kn$, ranging from $-\infty$ to $+\infty$ in $\mathbb{Z}$. For each $z \in Displacement(P)$, the set of all start and end points of all intervals spanned by P is computed with respect to $y = 1$ and $y = Granularity(P)$, respectively.

For example, consider the first complete week of 2015 only (i.e., that starting on 5 January). **WorkingHours** translates to $t \equiv_{168} (y + z - 1)$ for $y = 1,2,3,4$ and $z = 106$, 111, 130, 135, 154, 159, 178, 183, 202, 207, i.e., from the 10th and the 15th hour from Monday to Friday of that week for 4 hours.

To get time intervals of real instants, we modify this translation so that it computes directly such intervals considering only the left and the right bounds. In other words, given P and an interval $I = $ `[begin,end]` where `begin`, `end` are two date expressions identifying a specific granule according to the minimal granularity adopted[1] and $0 \leq$ `begin` $\leq$ `end` $< \infty$, the resulting intervals $I^P_{n+1,z}$ can be computed as $t \equiv_{168} (y + z - 1)$ for $y = 0, 4$ by fixing each time the value of $n \in \mathbb{N}$ and z as before (where 168 is the number of hours in a week). Depending on the chosen $z \in Displacement(P)$, and for $p = Periodicity(P)$ and $g = Granularity(P)$, intervals have thus the form

$$[pn + z - 1, pn + z - 1 + g]$$

that instantiated for our **WorkingHours** becomes

$$[168n + z - 1, 168n + z + 3]\,.$$

For instance, if we restrict the applicability of P to $I = $ `[05/01/15,05/01/15]`[2] (i.e., the first Monday of 2015), then we will obtain:

$$\overbrace{[106,107,108,109]}^{\texttt{05/01/15, (9AM-1PM)}} \cup \overbrace{[111,112,113,114]}^{\texttt{05/01/15, (2PM-6PM)}}$$
$$= 105 \leq t \leq 109 \cup 110 \leq t \leq 114$$

where the first line is the computation of linear repeating intervals of integers, and the second one the conversion in intervals of real time instants.

Once we have translated P in a finite number of intervals of real values representing the intervals spanned by P itself, we can generate an equivalent STN representing them. We will refer to this mapping $\mu_{pt2stn} : P \times I \to \langle \mathcal{T}, \mathcal{C} \rangle$ as *periodic time to STN*. Note that for an STN to be generated it is important that the upper bound of the interval limiting the applicability of the expression P is $\neq \infty$. Thus, the resulting STN is represented in Figure 1.

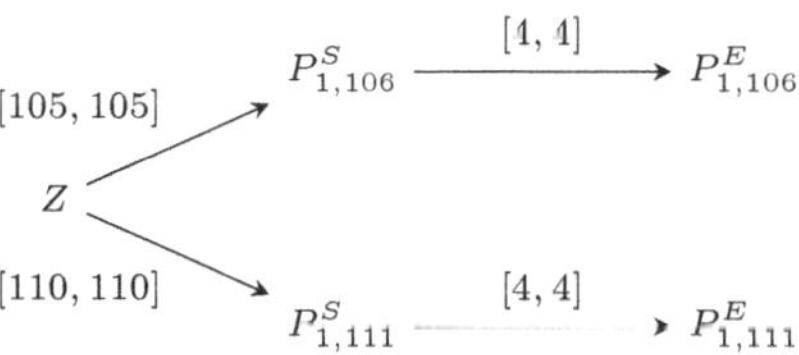

Figure 1: μ_{pt2stn}(**WorkingHours, [05/01/15,05/01/15]**).

THEOREM 1. *Given any periodic expression P whose applicability is limited by an interval I whose upper bound is $\neq \infty$, the mapping μ_{pt2stn} returns an equivalent STN that is (i) consistent and (ii) admits exactly one solution.*

The proof is given in [8]. As a convention, when we write $P^{sup}_{n+1,z}$ we mean the start (if *sup* is S) or the end (if *sup* is E) point of the $(n+1)^{\text{th}}$ ($n \in \mathbb{N}$) interval spanned by P choosing the displacement z according to the mapping μ_{pt2stn}.

Since the TRBAC periodic events we consider are *non-conflicting* and *complementary*, applying the mapping μ_{pt2stn} on the bounded periodic expressions associated to the periodic events involving only an "`enable` R" entails that for each n and z, $P^S_{n+1,z} \to P^E_{n+1,z}$ represents a time interval (of fixed duration) in which the roles associated to this expression in

[1] In this case, a date expression has the form `dd/mm/yy:hh` where `hh` identifies the $(\mathtt{hh})^{\text{th}}$ hour of `dd/mm/yy`.

[2] When we write $[\mathtt{dd}_1/\mathtt{mm}_1/\mathtt{yy}_1, \mathtt{dd}_2/\mathtt{mm}_2/\mathtt{yy}_2]$ we mean that $\mathtt{hh}_1 = \mathtt{01}$ whereas $\mathtt{hh}_2 = \mathtt{24}$.

the TRBAC role enabling base $\mathcal{R}$ are `enabled`. Furthermore, it also turns out that the complementary intervals have the form $[P^E_{n+1,z}, P^S_{n+2,z}]$, where the bounds correspond to the real values given by the scheduler $\psi : \mathcal{T} \to \mathbb{R}$ (which always assigns the same fixed values to these points depending on n and z and P). The next subsection explains how an STN generated by the mapping μ_{pt2stn} restricted to a given upper bound can be connected to the STNU describing the workflow to check if the workflow itself can be executed with respect to the given access control model. We point out that, in general, the mapping μ_{pt2stn} returns different STNs depending on the time window we consider (where a time window is, e.g., the first complete day of the current year, or the 2nd complete week of the 3rd month of the next year). Keeping this flexibility allows us to analyze the access control model in different time windows to leave room for investigating whether or not a workflow is controllable for all possible STNs generated by μ_{pt2stn}.

3.2 Connecting the Access Control Model

We are now ready to explain how we can put an access control model on top of a workflow by connecting the STN describing the access control model to the STNU describing the workflow. When we connect these two networks we say that the resulting network, which is still an STNU, is a *configuration.*

Assume a workflow consists of n tasks $T_1, \ldots, T_n$ corresponding to the n contingent links $A_1 \Rightarrow C_1, \ldots, A_n \Rightarrow C_n$ in the workflow STNU. Also, assume the role R is authorized to execute the task T (i.e., $(R,T) \in PA$) during the time interval $I^P_{n+1,z} = [P^S_{n+1,z}, P^E_{n+1,z}]$ represented by the requirement link $P^S_{n+1,z} \xrightarrow{[k,k]} P^E_{n+1,z}$, for some P, n, z and $k = P^E_{n+1,z} - P^S_{n+1,z}$. Then, to get a configuration we need to impose that the start of T has to occur *after* $P^S_{n+1,z}$, whereas the end *before* $P^E_{n+1,z}$.

In other words, role R cannot start T before getting `enabled`, and cannot end it after getting `disabled`. A *connection mapping* $\mu_{con} : \langle \mathcal{T}, \mathcal{C}, \mathcal{L} \rangle \times \langle \mathcal{T}', \mathcal{C}' \rangle \to \langle \mathcal{T}'', \mathcal{C}'', \mathcal{L}' \rangle$ is formally depicted in Table 2, where on the left the STN representing the access control (above) and the STNU representing the workflow (below) are still not connected, whereas on the right they are. Note that due to lack of space the node Z (zero time point) and the requirement link $Z \xrightarrow{[j,j]} P^S_{n+1,z}$ (for some $j = P^S_{n+1,z} - Z$) have not been shown (but are in [8]). Also, note that we have added a new label ρ on the links connecting the STN to STNU. In general, this new label $\rho = R_1 R_2 \ldots R_n$ consists of a conjunction of roles saying which roles we want to consider during the interval in which they are `enabled` (as more roles can be `enabled` during the same interval).

LEMMA 1. *Given a task represented as a contingent link $A \overset{[x,y]}{\Longrightarrow} C$ connected to a requirement link of access control STN $P^S_{n+1,z} \xrightarrow{[k,k]} P^E_{n+1,z}$ by means of the connection mapping μ_{con} shown in Table 2, then if $k < y$ the resulting STNU is uncontrollable.*

The proof is given in [8].

3.3 Deriving Authorized Users

Once we have connected the two networks, we are able to derive new information on which are the users authorized

Table 2: Connection mapping.

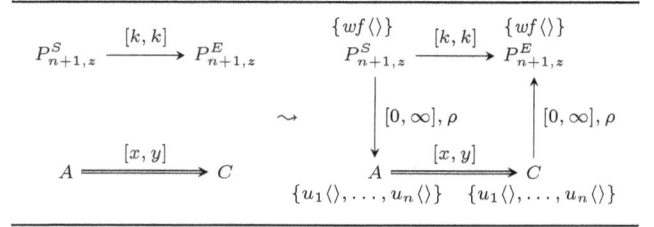

$$P^S_{n+1,z} \xrightarrow{[k,k]} P^E_{n+1,z} \qquad\qquad A \overset{[x,y]}{\Longrightarrow} C$$

$$\leadsto$$

$$\{wf\langle\rangle\}\ P^S_{n+1,z} \xrightarrow{[k,k]} P^E_{n+1,z}\ \{wf\langle\rangle\} \qquad \{u_1\langle\rangle, \ldots, u_n\langle\rangle\}\ A \overset{[x,y]}{\Longrightarrow} C\ \{u_1\langle\rangle, \ldots, u_n\langle\rangle\}$$

with $P^S_{n+1,z} \xrightarrow{[0,\infty],\rho} A$ and $C \xrightarrow{[0,\infty],\rho} P^E_{n+1,z}$

to execute the time points. To represent this piece of information, we associate to each time point $X \in \mathcal{T}$ the set $\mathcal{A}(X) \subseteq$ `Users` of users authorized to execute it as follows.

- For each contingent link $A \Rightarrow C$ representing task T, the set of authorized users is $\mathcal{A}(A) = \mathcal{A}(C) = \{u_1\langle c_1\rangle, \ldots, u_n\langle c_n\rangle\}$, where $c_1, \ldots c_n$ are security constraints we define in Section 5 and $u_1, \ldots, u_n$ are users belonging to all roles R_i such that:
  1. $(R_i, T) \in PA \wedge (u_i, R_i) \in UA$ for $j = 1, \ldots, n$ (in the TRBAC model), and
  2. R_i belongs to ρ specified on the requirement links connecting $P^S_{n+1,z}$ to A and C to $P^E_{n+1,z}$, where P is the associated periodic expression in the periodic event enabling R_i in the REB $\mathcal{R}$.
- For each other time point X different from an activation or a contingent point, $\mathcal{A}(X) = \{wf\langle\rangle\}$ which is a special user we consider to advance the execution of "internal tasks" (e.g., branching points). To be more precise we assume that: (i) $wf \in$ `Users`, (ii) for all $R \in$ `Roles`, $(wf, R) \notin UA$, (iii) for all $X \not\equiv A$ and $\not\equiv C$, $wf\langle\rangle \in \mathcal{A}(X)$, and (iv) for all $X \equiv A$ or $\equiv C$, $wf\langle c\rangle \notin \mathcal{A}(X)$.

To conclude this section we extend the form of the classical solution $\mathtt{S} = \{X = t_X, \ldots\}$ of a network to the new one $\mathtt{S} = \{(u_i : X = t_X), \ldots\}$ for it to take into account who has executed the time point. The contingency is modeled by the fact that once a task has started we do not know when exactly the user will tell the system that he has finished. Of course, we assume the user to finish within the bounds imposed by the contingent link, otherwise the system raises an exception to cope with the situation.

4. CASE STUDY

Before we discuss *how* to enforce security policies at runtime, we introduce a running example.

4.1 Workflow

We consider a workflow modeling a round-trip from London to Edinburgh. It starts with the task `OutwardJourney` in which the train travels from London to Edinburgh. The journey takes from 4 to 5 hours to be completed. After the train has arrived to Edinburgh train station, the `ReturnJourney` to London starts within 5 hours since 1 hour after arrival. Once the train has returned, before the next round trip starts, a `SecurityCheck` and a `SystemCheck` are done in parallel. The first check takes 1 to 2 hours, the second 1 to 3 hours. Figure 2 shows the workflow consisting of 4 tasks, where we have used the graphical components specified in Table 1 (on the left) and decorated each task by a label that specifies the role authorized to carry it out.

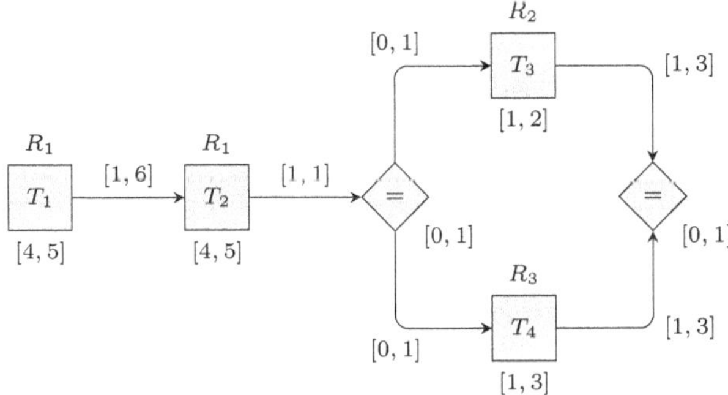

Figure 2: Access-controlled workflow. Tasks T_1, T_2, T_3, T_4 stand for `OutwardJourney`, `ReturnJourney`, `SystemCheck` and `SecurityCheck`, respectively. Roles R_1, R_2, R_3 stand for *TrainDriver*, *SystemEngineer* and *SecurityEngineer*, respectively.

$\mathcal{R}$

PE$_1$: ([01/01/15,∞], P_1, enable *TrainDriver*)
PE$_2$: ([01/01/15,∞], P_2, enable *SystemEngineer*)
PE$_3$: ([01/01/15,∞], P_3, enable *SecurityEngineer*)

Figure 3: The Role Enabling Base of the case study.

4.2 Access Control

The instantiation of the TRBAC is as follows:

- `Users` = {*Alice*, *Bob*, *Charlie*, *Eve*, *Kate*}
- `Roles` = {*TrainDriver*, *SystemEngineer*, *SecurityEngineer*}
- `Perm` = {`OutwardJourney`, `ReturnJourney`, `SystemCheck`, `SecurityCheck`}
- *UA* = {(*Alice*, *TrainDriver*), (*Bob*, *TrainDriver*), (*Charlie*, *SystemEngineer*), (*Charlie*, *SecurityEngineer*), (*Eve*, *SecurityEngineer*), (*Kate*, *SystemEngineer*)}
- *PA* = {(*TrainDriver*, `OutwardJourney`), (*TrainDriver*, `ReturnJourney`), (*SystemEngineer*, `SystemCheck`), (*SecurityEngineer*, `SecurityCheck`)}

The role enabling base $\mathcal{R}$ (Figure 3) consists of periodic events only. Each line represents a periodic event as described in Section 2.4, where the periodic expressions associated to the roles[3] are:

- $P_1 = all \cdot Days + \{9\} \cdot Hours \triangleright \{12\} \cdot Hours$
- $P_2 = all \cdot Days + \{16\} \cdot Hours \triangleright \{9\} \cdot Hours$
- $P_3 = all \cdot Days + \{16\} \cdot Hours \triangleright \{12\} \cdot Hours$

In other words, these periodic expressions say that the role *TrainDriver* is enabled every day from 8AM to 8PM, *SystemEngineer* every day from 3PM to 12AM (midnight) and *SecurityEngineer* from 3PM until 3AM of the day after. Now consider the time window [01/01/15:01,02/01/15:03] limiting P_1, P_2 and P_3. Role *TrainDriver* is enabled during $[8, 20]$, *SystemEngineer* during $[15, 24]$ and *SecurityEngineer* during $[15, 27]$. Figure 4 shows the resulting configuration.

[3]We assume $\mathcal{R}$ also contains the complementary expressions to disable the roles.

4.3 (Temporal) Security Policies

To conclude the case study section we formalize three security policies that are supposed to hold in this context.

Security Policy 1. A user who starts a task ends it too.

Security Policy 2. A user is allowed to execute no more than one task at a time.

Security Policy 3. If the train driver from Edinburgh to London is the same as the one who drove the train from London to Edinburgh, he must rest at least 2 hours before driving again.

We assume that policies 1, 2 and 3 hold for our case study. Without security constraint propagation rules, it is rather easy to note that, if every time we start or end a task we are free to choose any authorized user among those contained in that set, then our example violates all the previous security policies. Therefore, the next section provides a language to define security constraints along with a set of security constraint propagation rules to propagate them when executing.

5. PROPAGATION OF SECURITY CONSTRAINTS

In Section 3.3, we discussed how to compute the set of authorized users for a time point once we have obtained a configuration (Section 3.2). We now proceed by giving its canonical form as further contribution.

Definition 3. For each time point X belonging to a configuration, the set of authorized users has the canonical form *$\mathcal{A}(X) = \{u_1\langle c_1\rangle, u_2\langle c_2\rangle, \ldots, u_n\langle c_n\rangle\}$, where $u_1, \ldots, u_n$ are the authorized users and $c_1, \ldots, c_n$ are (temporal) security constraints defined according to the grammar*

$$c ::= t_k, \square \mid X + k, \square \qquad \square ::= > \mid < \mid \geq \mid \leq \mid = \mid \neq,$$

where $t_k, k \in \mathbb{R}^{\geq 0}$. $c = t_k, \square$ is a Type-1 security constraint, *whereas $c = X + k, \square$ is* Type-2.

Every Type-2 security constraint $c = X + k, \square$ is reducible to a Type-1 by substituting X with a real value taken from its range, plus k (if $k \neq 0$). As an example, let $c = X + 1, \leq$. Once the value of X becomes known, say the scheduler executes it at time 3 ($\psi(X) = 3$), we substitute it for X also adding the constant $k = 1$. After that, the Type-2 security constraint reduces to the Type-1 $c' = 4, \leq$.

$$\underbrace{c = X + 1, \leq}_{t<3} \quad \overset{\psi(X)=3}{\rightsquigarrow} \quad \underbrace{c' = 4, \leq}_{t\geq 3}$$

The main idea behind a security constraint is that of blocking the associated user in order to prevent him from executing some time point if a security policy is violated.

Definition 4. We define interpretation *of security constraints with respect to current time t as follows:*

1. $t \models t_k, >$ *iff* $t > t_k$	*7.* $t \not\models X + k, >$
2. $t \models t_k, <$ *iff* $t < t_k$	*8.* $t \models X + k, <$
3. $t \models t_k, \geq$ *iff* $t \geq t_k$	*9.* $t \not\models X + k, \geq$
4. $t \models t_k, \leq$ *iff* $t \leq t_k$	*10.* $t \models X + k, \leq$
5. $t \models t_k, =$ *iff* $t = t_k$	*11.* $t \not\models X + k, =$
6. $t \models t_k, \neq$ *iff* $t \neq t_k$	*12.* $t \models X + k, \neq$

A user u is blocked *for the time point X if $u\langle c\rangle \in \mathcal{A}(X)$, and current time $t \models c$.*

It is clear from the context that 1–6 regard Type-1 security constraints, whereas 7–12 regard the Type-2. The interpretation of the first group with respect to the chosen $\Box$ operator substantially states that those constraints will be true if current time t is greater than the value specified (1), less than it (2), greater than or equal to it (3), less than or equal to it (4), equal to it (5), or different from it (6). Instead, that of the second group (Type-2) is a little bit subtle since the value of time point specified in it is still unknown.

The interpretation with respect to the chosen $\Box$ operator states that, since X will be executed in the future and is thus yet unknown, the Type-2 constraint is interpreted false (7), true (8), false (9), true (10), false (11) and true (12). When X executes the Type-2 constraint is reduced to a Type-1 and interpreted accordingly.

As an example, consider $c = X + 3, >$. The current time satisfies this constraint iff it is greater than $X + 3$, where the value of X is still unknown. Therefore, at current time t this constraint is false.

Furthermore, when X executes, this constraint remains false for 3 other time units. Now consider the complementary case $c = X + 3, \leq$. The current time satisfies c iff it is less than or equal to $X + 3$, where the value of X is still unknown. Even if X is still unknown, this constraint at time t is trivially true since current time is of course less than (or equal to) some other value in the future plus some *positive* constant. Furthermore, when X executes, this constraint remains true for 3 other time units. Similar explanations apply to the other Type-2 constraints.

Security constraint propagation rules say how security constraints propagate when executing.

Definition 5. A security constraint propagation rule (SC-PR) *is a 4-tuple of the form: $\langle X, \langle c\rangle, \mathcal{Y}, \Diamond\rangle$, where X is a time point, c a security constraint, $\mathcal{Y}$ a set of time points, and $\Diamond$ is either $=$ or $\neq$.*

The semantics of an SCPR says that when X is executed, the security constraint c has to be set to all users in $\mathcal{A}(Y)$ ($Y \in \mathcal{Y}$) equal to (if $\Diamond$ is $=$) or different from (if $\Diamond$ is $\neq$) the user who executed X.

5.1 From Security Policies to SCPRs

We can use SCPRs as a means to embed the (temporal) security policies we want to hold. We exemplify this at hand of the three security policies defined in Section 4.3 by sketching a few constructs of an high-level language to define security policies for the workflow we are currently designing. This language allows Security Officers to specify security policies in an easier way without even mentioning time points. Then, an intermediate step is that of generating a set S of SCPRs starting from the constructs of this language for the system to be able to do a safeness check first and propagate SCs while executing.

We know that by means of the mapping μ_{pt2stn} each task T is represented as a contingent link describing its start and end point. Thus we need constructs such as `start`(T) end `end`(T) to model these aspects.

To express conditions on who did what, we envision to have primitives like `hasExecuted`(u,T), `hasStarted`(u,T), `hasEnded`(u,T) as binary predicates modeling the fact that user u has executed/started/ended task T.

Instead, to model who is not allowed to start or end a task we envision to have primitives `cannotStart`(u,T), `cannotEnd`(u,T) as well as clauses such as $u_1 = u_2$ and $u_1 \neq u_2$ (resp. $T_1 = T_2$ and $T_1 \neq T_2$) to intend the same or a different user (resp. task).

This language also needs to quantify over the sets of authorized users and tasks to formalize properties such as `for all ... [in ...]` other than conditional blocks such as `if ... then ... [else ...]`. Note that since we are considering structured workflows, we are able to formalize statements such as "for all tasks in the first parallel block".

Last but not least, we need "temporal constructs" such as `before` k `after end`(T) to model security properties such as Temporal Separation of Duties (TSoD).

Security Policy 1 requires that an authorized user who starts a task ends it too. In the high-level language we expect to formalize it this way:

```
for all T if hasStarted(u,T) then
    for all u' in A(T)
    if u' ≠ u then cannotEnd(u',T)
```

This rule is translated in n SCPRs having the form:

$$r_i : \langle A_i, \langle C_i, \leq\rangle, C_i, \neq\rangle$$

where n is the number of tasks which the workflow consists of. In our case study is translated to 4 rules (since the workflow of Figure 2 consists of 4 tasks):

$$r_1 : \langle A_1, \langle C_1, \leq\rangle, C_1, \neq\rangle \qquad r_3 : \langle A_3, \langle C_3, \leq\rangle, C_3, \neq\rangle$$
$$r_2 : \langle A_2, \langle C_2, \leq\rangle, C_2, \neq\rangle \qquad r_4 : \langle A_4, \langle C_4, \leq\rangle, C_4, \neq\rangle$$

That is, every time an authorized user u executes an activation point A, the system sets the constraint $C, \leq$ to all users $u' \in \mathcal{A}(C)$ where $u' \neq u$. Those users will be blocked until $t \models C, \leq$ (i.e., until C is executed).

Security Policy 2 requires that an authorized user is allowed to execute one task at a time.

```
for all T in ParallelBlock if hasStarted(u,T) then
    for all T' in ParallelBlock if T' ≠ T then
        cannotStart(u,T') before end(T)
```

This rule is translated in n SCPRs having the form:

$$r_i : \langle A_i, \langle C_i, \leq\rangle, \{A_j\}, =\rangle$$

where $i \neq j$ and n is the number of tasks in the considered parallel block (because we model all possible cases). In our case study is translated to:

$$r_5 : \langle A_3, \langle C_3, \leq\rangle, \{A_4\}, =\rangle \qquad r_6 : \langle A_4, \langle C_4, \leq\rangle, \{A_3\}, =\rangle$$

In the case study introduced in Section 4 there is only one parallel block which consists of tasks T_3, T_4 (Figure 2) or equivalently contingent links $A_3 \Rightarrow C_3, A_4 \Rightarrow C_4$ (Figure 4). Therefore, if a user can execute both tasks (where the execution order of T_3, T_4 is not well defined), we must prevent him from executing the other until the current is not finished. Relying on r_1 it is enough to set the constraint (i.e., to block the user) only on the activation points A_3, A_4 depending on which task executes first.

Security Policy 3 requires that if the same authorized user executes T_1 and T_2, then between the end of T_1 and the start

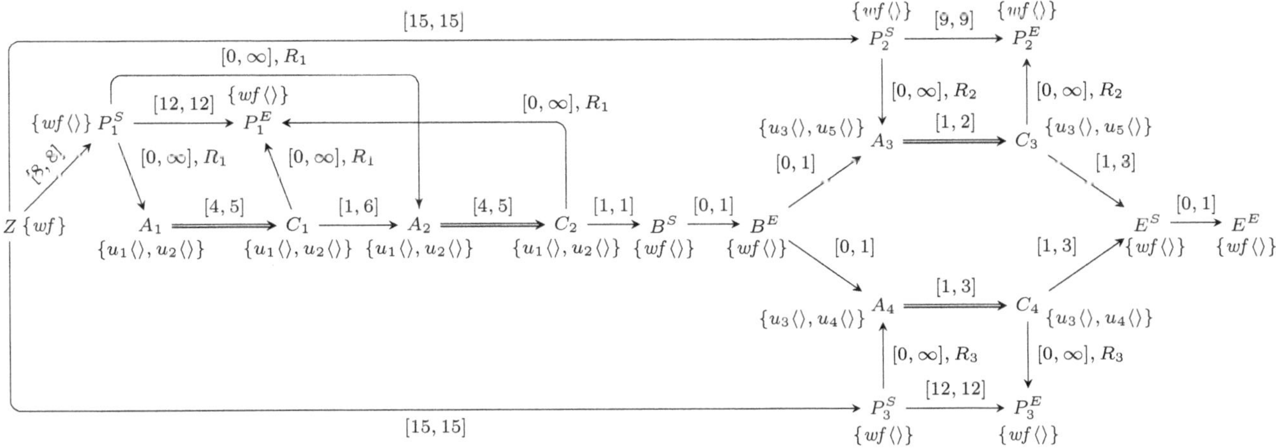

Figure 4: STNU equivalent to the access-controlled workflow depicted in Figure 2. Users u_1, u_2, u_3, u_4, u_5 represent *Alice*, *Bob*, *Charlie*, *Eve*, and *Kate*, respectively.

of T_2 at least 2 hours have to elapse.

for all u **in** $\mathcal{A}(T_1)$ **if** **hasStarted**(u, T_1) **then**
cannotStart(u, T_2) **before** 2 **after** **end**(T_1)

This rule is translated in a single SCPR having the form:

$$r_i : \langle C_i, \langle C_i + 2, \leq\rangle, \{A_j\}, =\rangle$$

where $i \neq j$. In our case study is translated to:

$$r_7 : \langle C_1, \langle C_1 + 2, \leq\rangle, \{A_2\}, =\rangle$$

The same reason of r_5, r_6 (i.e., *relying on* r_1) applies here to avoid writing a redundant C_2 in r_7's $\mathcal{Y}$.

Separation of Duties (SoD) requires that the same user ought not be able to carry out two sensitive tasks in the same execution. *Temporal Separation of Duties (TSoD)* is an extension of SoD that allows the same user to do so, but *only if* a further temporal constraints is satisfied. In our example, the train driver can bring the train back to London as long as he has rested at least 2 hours (the further temporal constraint). Furthermore, imposing this constraint at workflow level (e.g., tightening the STNU by means of a requirement link $C_1 \xrightarrow{[2+\epsilon,\infty]} A_2$, for some $\epsilon > 0$) would be wrong. Indeed, it would prevent *all* train drivers different from the one who drove the train during the outward journey from driving the train in the return journey *as soon as possible* since the arrival at Edinburgh station. That is, exactly after 1 hour considering that we have the constraint $C_1 \xrightarrow{[1,6]} A_2$ (Figure 4).

5.2 Safeness of a set of SCPRs

We are left to specify the notion of *safeness* for a set S of SCPRs. We recall that an STNU is executed incrementally [18]. To do that, we must define (i) *conflicting rules*, and (ii) an *algorithm* to check if a set S of SCPRs does not contain any pair of conflicting rules. We proceed by providing the definition of conflicting rules and then a safeness check algorithm.

Definition 6. Two SCPRs $r_1 = \langle X_1, c_1, \mathcal{Y}_1, \diamond_1\rangle$ and $r_2 = \langle X_2, c_2, \mathcal{Y}_2, \diamond_2\rangle$ are in conflict *iff the following four conditions hold all together: (1) $X_1 = X_2$, (2) $c_1 \neq c_2$, (3) $\mathcal{Y}_1 \cap \mathcal{Y}_2 \neq \emptyset$, and (4) $\diamond_1 = \diamond_2$.*

Algorithm 1 A safeness-checker for a set S of SCPRs

```
procedure SafenessChecker(S)
    for all r1, r2 ∈ S do
        if r1 ≠ r2 and r1 and r2 are conflicting then
            return false
        end if
    end for
    return true
end procedure
```

As an example, the following two SCPRs are conflicting:

$$r_1 : \langle X, \langle Y + 2, \leq\rangle, \{Z, V\}, \neq\rangle \quad r_2 : \langle X, \langle Y, >\rangle, \{W, Z\}, \neq\rangle$$

Rule r_1 says that when X has been executed by $u \in \mathcal{A}(X)$ the security constraint $Y+2, \leq$ has to be set for all users different from u belonging to the sets $\mathcal{A}(Z)$ and $\mathcal{A}(V)$, whereas r_2 says that the complementary constraint $(Y, >)$ has to be set, again, for all users different from u belonging to $\mathcal{A}(W)$ and $\mathcal{A}(Z)$. These two rules are conflicting since the four conditions hold all together: (1) $X = X$, (2) $Y + 2, \leq \neq Y, >$, (3) $\{Z, V\} \cap \{W, Z\} = \{Z\} \neq \emptyset$, and (4) both $\diamond$ are $\neq$. In other words, they are trying to set *at the same time* a different constraint for the same users belonging to $\mathcal{A}(Z)$.

It is quite easy now to see that the set $S = \{r_1, \ldots, r_7\}$ containing the seven SCPRs translating the three security policies of our case study is *safe*, since there does not exist any pair of conflicting rules. A first brute-force procedure to check the safeness of a set $S = \{r_1, \ldots, r_n\}$ of SCPRs is given in Algorithm 1, which takes as input S and tests the four conditions of Definition 6 for all different pairs of rules $r_i, r_j \in S$. The algorithm runs exactly in $\Theta(|S|^2)$.

6. WORKFLOW EXECUTION

In order to propagate security constraints when the workflow is being executed we are left to do one thing: to specify how SCPRs are taken into account at runtime. To do so, we extend the STNU execution algorithm in [18] for it to take as input also a (safe) set of SCPRs that shall be evaluated each time a time point is executed. If the executed time point matches the guard of some rules, then the constraints in them have to be set (thus propagated) before

Algorithm 2 A configuration execution algorithm

```
procedure Executor(S)
    A = set of all control points of the network
    t = 0
    while A ≠ ∅ do
        Wait for some time point live and enabled X ∈ A
        Arbitrary pick a live and enable time point X ∈ A
        Arbitrary pick u⟨c⟩ ∈ 𝒜(X) such that t ⊭ c
        S = S ∪ (u : X = t)
        Propagate all ⟨X_i, c_i, 𝒴_i, ◇_i⟩ ∈ S s.t. X = X_i
        Advance t propagating all temporal constraints
    end while
end procedure
```

the execution continues according to all we have said so far (Algorithm 2).

Now it is time to be more concrete by writing down how the state of the system evolves during the execution. Of course, there are infinite different ways of executing a workflow since time is dense; consequently, each range $[x, y]$ where $x \neq y$ (e.g., those belonging to contingent links) consists of infinite points. For instance, in our case study we have chosen *a possible execution* with the only purpose of showing how security constraints propagate. The execution is given in Table 3 (in the appendix), where cells in bold-face point out the security constraint(s) being applied.

7. RELATED WORK

Related work on defining, validating, and enforcing access control policies in workflow contexts can be grouped in four main areas: (i) access control and workflow models, (ii) authorization constraints, (iii) planning, and (iv) run-time execution.

RBAC models [25] are the default choice for many organizations that need to balance security with flexibility. Classical RBAC models are however unable to deal with security policies at user level, such as separation or binding of duties.

In [5], Bertino et al. give a language for defining authorization constraints on role and user assignment to tasks in a workflow. They also provide algorithms for constraint consistency check and task assignment. This proposal assumes the workflow to verify a total order on tasks (i.e., no parallel tasks are allowed). Furthermore, temporal constraints are not investigated.

The Temporal Authorization Base model described in [4] is able to enforce authorization constraints in heterogeneous distributed systems. It allows users to assign periodic authorizations to other users on sets of objects. This model is quite expressive. In order to use it in a workflow context, we conjecture that it would be required to restrict access modes to `execute` and constrain objects to be `tasks`. However, a thorough investigation is needed, as in our context we also need to deal with the temporal aspects related to workflows.

A number of proposals (Wang and Li in [28] and Crampton et al. in [6, 10, 11, 12, 13], to name a few) have addressed the workflow satisfiability problem (WSP) and the resiliency problem. WSP is the problem of assigning tasks to users so that the execution of the access controlled workflow is guaranteed to reach the end, when dealing with authorization constraints that might prevent some user from doing some action in the future. In general, solving WSP requires exponential time, but some of the cited approaches proved (by using parameterized complexity and kernelization) that for some workflow instances (those where the number of users equals the number of tasks) the WSP can be solved in polynomial time. In our work, we have not dealt with WSP yet, but only with the satisfaction of temporal constraints. As for current and future work, we are trying to extend our approach to deal with WSP, by refining the classical STNU DC-check to take into account authorization constraints as well. If an STNU passes this check, then we can also generate an execution strategy to execute the workflow (planning phase), being guaranteed to always get to the end by satisfying all constraints.

On the other hand, the *resiliency problem* faces the issue of how to deal with the execution of plans if some authorized users become unavailable, when the workflow is being executed. To the best of our knowledge, no solution to the WSP and to the resiliency problems using temporal networks has been proposed so far and the related temporal aspects of such problems deserve further attention.

Finally, in [22], Paci et al. proposed proposed *RBAC-WS-BPEL*, a role-based access control model for the web services business process execution language *WS-BPEL*. The language is based on XML and does not deal with temporal constraints, which makes it unsuitable for our context.

8. CONCLUSIONS AND FUTURE WORK

In this paper we focused on the issue of managing in a seamless way role-based access control mechanisms in temporal workflows, where temporal aspects are both in the access control model and in the workflow model. We based our approach on temporal constraint networks. To the best of our knowledge, all of the existing approaches are unsuitable to deal with a workflow having both temporal constraints related to the execution control model and in the access control model.

We have provided mappings to translate a workflow into an equivalent STNU and a time window of TRBAC into an equivalent STN to be connected to STNU describing the workflow. This allowed us to answer the question about whether or not the resulting configuration is executable. Then, we have derived for each time point the set of authorized users and defined security constraints along with their propagation rules in order to set, update and propagate security constraints also discussing safeness and execution issues.

We view this paper as a first step of a more general research work, where we will consider and face the following research directions: considering *conditional STNUs* [15] in order to augment expressiveness to model different workflow paths; allowing the *combination of temporal security constraints* such as $u\langle c_1 \wedge c_2\rangle$ or $u\langle \neg c\rangle$ to express security policies such as "(not) during"; defining a *high-level security policy language*; and considering the *temporal workflow satisfiability problem* (TWSP) (i.e., *controllability with respect to security*), to do an automated validation of security policies with respect to different possible temporal configurations and user assignments.

9. REFERENCES

[1] A. Armando and S. Ranise. Automated Symbolic Analysis of ARBAC-Policies. In *Proc. of STM*, pages 17–34, 2010.

[2] E. Bertino, C. Bettini, E. Ferrari, and P. Samarati. An access control model supporting periodicity

constraints and temporal reasoning. *ACM Trans. Database Syst.*, 23(3):231–285, 1998.
[3] E. Bertino, P. A. Bonatti, and E. Ferrari. TRBAC: A temporal role-based access control model. *ACM Trans. Inf. Syst. Secur.*, 4(3):191–233, 2001.
[4] E. Bertino, P. A. Bonatti, E. Ferrari, and M. L. Sapino. Temporal authorization bases: From specification to integration. *Journal of Computer Security*, 8(4):309–353, 2000.
[5] E. Bertino, E. Ferrari, and V. Atluri. The specification and enforcement of authorization constraints in workflow management systems. *ACM Trans. Inf. Syst. Secur.*, 2(1):65–104, 1999.
[6] D. Cohen, J. Crampton, A. Gagarin, G. Gutin, and M. Jones. Iterative plan construction for the workflow satisfiability problem. *JAIR*, 51:555–577, 2014.
[7] C. Combi, M. Gambini, S. Migliorini, and R. Posenato. Representing business processes through a temporal data-centric workflow modeling language: An application to the management of clinical pathways. *IEEE T. Systems, Man, and Cybernetics: Systems*, 44(9):1182–1203, 2014.
[8] C. Combi, L. Viganò, and M. Zavatteri. Security Constraints in Temporal Role-Based Access-Controlled Workflows (Extended Version). http://arxiv.org/abs/1512.06404, 2015.
[9] T. H. Cormen, C. E. Leiserson, R. L. Rivest, and C. Stein. *Introduction to Algorithms*. MIT Press, 2009.
[10] J. Crampton. A reference monitor for workflow systems with constrained task execution. In *Proc. of SACMAT*, pages 38–47. ACM Press, 2005.
[11] J. Crampton, A. V. Gagarin, G. Gutin, and M. Jones. On the Workflow Satisfiability Problem with Class-independent Constraints. In *Proc. of IPEC*, pages 66–77, 2015.
[12] J. Crampton, G. Gutin, and A. Yeo. On the parameterized complexity and kernelization of the workflow satisfiability problem. *ACM Trans. Inf. Syst. Secur.*, 16(1):4, 2013.
[13] J. Crampton, M. Huth, and J. H. Kuo. Authorized workflow schemas: deciding realizability through LTL(F) model checking. *STTT*, 16(1):31–48, 2014.
[14] R. Dechter, I. Meiri, and J. Pearl. Temporal Constraint Networks. In *Proc. of KR*, pages 83–93, 1989.
[15] L. Hunsberger, R. Posenato, and C. Combi. The Dynamic Controllability of Conditional STNs with Uncertainty. In *Proc. of PlanEx*, pages 1–8, 2012.
[16] S. Mondal and S. Sural. Security analysis of temporal-rbac using timed automata. In *Proc. of IAS 2008*, pages 37–40, 2008.
[17] P. H. Morris. A structural characterization of temporal dynamic controllability. In *Proc. of CP*, pages 375–389, 2006.
[18] P. H. Morris and N. Muscettola. Execution of temporal plans with uncertainty. In *Proc. of AAAI*, pages 491–496, 2000.
[19] P. H. Morris and N. Muscettola. Temporal Dynamic Controllability Revisited. In *Proc. of AAAI*, pages 1193–1198, 2005.
[20] P. H. Morris, N. Muscettola, and T. Vidal. Dynamic Control Of Plans With Temporal Uncertainty. In *Proc. of IJCAI*, pages 494–502, 2001.
[21] M. Niezette and J. Stevenne. An Efficient Symbolic Representation of Periodic Time. In *Proc. of CIKM*, pages 161–168. ISMM, 1992.
[22] F. Paci, E. Bertino, and J. Crampton. An access-control framework for WS-BPEL. *Int. J. Web Service Res.*, 5(3):20–43, 2008.
[23] S. Ranise, A. Tuan Truong, and L. Viganò. Automated analysis of RBAC policies with temporal constraints and static role hierarchies. In *Proc. of SAC*, pages 2177–2184, 2015.
[24] R. S. Sandhu. Roles versus groups. In *ACM Workshop on Role-Based Access Control*, 1995.
[25] R. S. Sandhu, E. J. Coyne, H. L. Feinstein, and C. E. Youman. Role-based access control models. *IEEE Computer*, 29(2):38–47, 1996.
[26] D. Toman and J. Chomicki. Datalog with integer periodicity constraints. *J. Log. Program.*, 35(3):263–290, 1998.
[27] T. Vidal and H. Fargier. Handling contingency in temporal constraint networks: from consistency to controllabilities. *J. Exp. Theor. Artif. Intell.*, 11(1):23–45, 1999.
[28] Q. Wang and N. Li. Satisfiability and resiliency in workflow authorization systems. *ACM Trans. Inf. Syst. Secur.*, 13(4):40, 2010.

APPENDIX

Train TR2015 from London to Edinburgh departs at 08:00 AM (from platform 1). The system (wf) starts the workflow at 12AM of the 1st of January 2015. That is, it executes the zero time point Z without propagating any security constraint. The system also executes at 8 o'clock P_1^S enabling R_1.

At 8 o'clock Bob (u_2), who is a train driver, starts the outward journey from London to Edinburgh. Rule r_1 (enforcing Security Policy 1) constrains *Bob* to be the only user to end the task (i.e. to execute C_1) between 12PM and 1PM by applying the security constraint $C_1, \leq$ for all users apart from him in $\mathcal{A}(C_1)$ (row 1). Suppose the outward journey takes 4 hours. Thus, *Bob* tells the system the train has arrived at Edinburgh station at midday (row 2). Furthermore, rule r_7 (enforcing Security Policy 3) prevents *Bob* from starting the return journey before current time does not pass 2 o'clock by applying the security constraint $14, \leq^4$ for him in $\mathcal{A}(A_2)$ (again, row 2). Meanwhile at 3 o'clock the system starts both P_2^S and P_3^S enabling R_2 and R_3, respectively without applying any security constraint.

Now let us say that Bob starts the return journey at 3 o'clock. Rule r_1 constrains him to finish the journey between 7PM and 8PM. That is, $C_2, \leq$ is applied for all users apart from him in $\mathcal{A}(C_2)$ (row 3). Assume this time the return journey takes its maximal duration (5 hours). Since there is no security policy which says something upon the arrival of the return journey there is not any rule r whose guard is C_2 either (row 4). The system also disables R_1 by executing P_1^E at the same time.

[4] Instead of applying $C_1 + 2, \leq$ (as formalized in r_1), the system applies directly $14, \leq$ since the value of C_1 (12) is known.

Table 3: Example of execution of the case study. $\mathcal{A}(A_i)$ (resp., $\mathcal{A}(C_i)$ is the set of users authorized to start (resp., end) task T_i. The first column shows when which user has executed which time point.

Executed TP	$\mathcal{A}(A_1)$	$\mathcal{A}(C_1)$	$\mathcal{A}(A_2)$	$\mathcal{A}(C_2)$	$\mathcal{A}(A_3)$	$\mathcal{A}(C_3)$	$\mathcal{A}(A_4)$	$\mathcal{A}(C_4)$
$(wf : Z = 0)$	$\{u_1\langle\rangle, u_2\langle\rangle\}$	$\{u_1\langle\rangle, u_2\langle\rangle\}$	$\{u_1\langle\rangle, u_2\langle\rangle\}$	$\{u_1\langle\rangle, u_2\langle\rangle\}$	$\{u_3\langle\rangle, u_5\langle\rangle\}$	$\{u_3\langle\rangle, u_5\langle\rangle\}$	$\{u_3\langle\rangle, u_4\langle\rangle\}$	$\{u_3\langle\rangle, u_4\langle\rangle\}$
$(wf : P_1^S = 8)$	$\{u_1\langle\rangle, u_2\langle\rangle\}$	$\{u_1\langle\rangle, u_2\langle\rangle\}$	$\{u_1\langle\rangle, u_2\langle\rangle\}$	$\{u_1\langle\rangle, u_2\langle\rangle\}$	$\{u_3\langle\rangle, u_5\langle\rangle\}$	$\{u_3\langle\rangle, u_5\langle\rangle\}$	$\{u_3\langle\rangle, u_4\langle\rangle\}$	$\{u_3\langle\rangle, u_4\langle\rangle\}$
$(u_2 : A_1 = 9)$	$\{u_1\langle\rangle, u_2\langle\rangle\}$	$\{\mathbf{u_1}\langle\mathbf{C_1}, \leq\rangle, \mathbf{u_2}\langle\rangle\}$	$\{u_1\langle\rangle, u_2\langle\rangle\}$	$\{u_1\langle\rangle, u_2\langle\rangle\}$	$\{u_3\langle\rangle, u_5\langle\rangle\}$	$\{u_3\langle\rangle, u_5\langle\rangle\}$	$\{u_3\langle\rangle, u_4\langle\rangle\}$	$\{u_3\langle\rangle, u_4\langle\rangle\}$
$(u_2 : C_1 = 12)$	$\{u_1\langle\rangle, u_2\langle\rangle\}$	$\{\mathbf{u_1}\langle\mathbf{12}, \leq\rangle, \mathbf{u_2}\langle\rangle\}$	$\{\mathbf{u_1}\langle\rangle, \mathbf{u_2}\langle\mathbf{14}, \leq\rangle\}$	$\{u_1\langle\rangle, u_2\langle\rangle\}$	$\{u_3\langle\rangle, u_5\langle\rangle\}$	$\{u_3\langle\rangle, u_5\langle\rangle\}$	$\{u_3\langle\rangle, u_4\langle\rangle\}$	$\{u_3\langle\rangle, u_4\langle\rangle\}$
$(wf : P_2^S = 15)$	$\{u_1\langle\rangle, u_2\langle\rangle\}$	$\{u_1\langle 12, \leq\rangle, u_2\langle\rangle\}$	$\{u_1\langle\rangle, u_2\langle 14, \leq\rangle\}$	$\{u_1\langle\rangle, u_2\langle\rangle\}$	$\{u_3\langle\rangle, u_5\langle\rangle\}$	$\{u_3\langle\rangle, u_5\langle\rangle\}$	$\{u_3\langle\rangle, u_4\langle\rangle\}$	$\{u_3\langle\rangle, u_4\langle\rangle\}$
$(wf : P_3^S = 15)$	$\{u_1\langle\rangle, u_2\langle\rangle\}$	$\{u_1\langle 12, \leq\rangle, u_2\langle\rangle\}$	$\{u_1\langle\rangle, u_2\langle 14, \leq\rangle\}$	$\{u_1\langle\rangle, u_2\langle\rangle\}$	$\{u_3\langle\rangle, u_5\langle\rangle\}$	$\{u_3\langle\rangle, u_5\langle\rangle\}$	$\{u_3\langle\rangle, u_4\langle\rangle\}$	$\{u_3\langle\rangle, u_4\langle\rangle\}$
$(u_2 : A_2 = 15)$	$\{u_1\langle\rangle, u_2\langle\rangle\}$	$\{u_1\langle 12, \leq\rangle, u_2\langle\rangle\}$	$\{u_1\langle\rangle, u_2\langle 14, \leq\rangle\}$	$\{\mathbf{u_1}\langle\mathbf{C_2}, \leq\rangle, \mathbf{u_2}\langle\rangle\}$	$\{u_3\langle\rangle, u_5\langle\rangle\}$	$\{u_3\langle\rangle, u_5\langle\rangle\}$	$\{u_3\langle\rangle, u_4\langle\rangle\}$	$\{u_3\langle\rangle, u_4\langle\rangle\}$
$(u_2 : C_2 = 20)$	$\{u_1\langle\rangle, u_2\langle\rangle\}$	$\{u_1\langle 12, \leq\rangle, u_2\langle\rangle\}$	$\{u_1\langle\rangle, u_2\langle 14, \leq\rangle\}$	$\{\mathbf{u_1}\langle\mathbf{20}, \leq\rangle, \mathbf{u_2}\langle\rangle\}$	$\{u_3\langle\rangle, u_5\langle\rangle\}$	$\{u_3\langle\rangle, u_5\langle\rangle\}$	$\{u_3\langle\rangle, u_4\langle\rangle\}$	$\{u_3\langle\rangle, u_4\langle\rangle\}$
$(wf : P_1^E = 20)$	$\{u_1\langle\rangle, u_2\langle\rangle\}$	$\{u_1\langle 12, \leq\rangle, u_2\langle\rangle\}$	$\{u_1\langle\rangle, u_2\langle 14, \leq\rangle\}$	$\{u_1\langle 20, \leq\rangle, u_2\langle\rangle\}$	$\{u_3\langle\rangle, u_5\langle\rangle\}$	$\{u_3\langle\rangle, u_5\langle\rangle\}$	$\{u_3\langle\rangle, u_4\langle\rangle\}$	$\{u_3\langle\rangle, u_4\langle\rangle\}$
$(wf : B^S = 21)$	$\{u_1\langle\rangle, u_2\langle\rangle\}$	$\{u_1\langle 12, \leq\rangle, u_2\langle\rangle\}$	$\{u_1\langle\rangle, u_2\langle 14, \leq\rangle\}$	$\{u_1\langle 20, \leq\rangle, u_2\langle\rangle\}$	$\{u_3\langle\rangle, u_5\langle\rangle\}$	$\{u_3\langle\rangle, u_5\langle\rangle\}$	$\{u_3\langle\rangle, u_4\langle\rangle\}$	$\{u_3\langle\rangle, u_4\langle\rangle\}$
$(wf : B^E = 21)$	$\{u_1\langle\rangle, u_2\langle\rangle\}$	$\{u_1\langle 12, \leq\rangle, u_2\langle\rangle\}$	$\{u_1\langle\rangle, u_2\langle 14, \leq\rangle\}$	$\{u_1\langle 20, \leq\rangle, u_2\langle\rangle\}$	$\{u_3\langle\rangle, u_5\langle\rangle\}$	$\{u_3\langle\rangle, u_5\langle\rangle\}$	$\{u_3\langle\rangle, u_4\langle\rangle\}$	$\{u_3\langle\rangle, u_4\langle\rangle\}$
$(u_3 : A_3 = 22)$	$\{u_1\langle\rangle, u_2\langle\rangle\}$	$\{u_1\langle 12, \leq\rangle, u_2\langle\rangle\}$	$\{u_1\langle\rangle, u_2\langle 14, \leq\rangle\}$	$\{u_1\langle 20, \leq\rangle, u_2\langle\rangle\}$	$\{u_3\langle\rangle, u_5\langle\rangle\}$	$\{\mathbf{u_3}\langle\rangle, \mathbf{u_5}\langle\mathbf{C_3}, \leq\rangle\}$	$\{\mathbf{u_3}\langle\mathbf{C_3}, \leq\rangle, \mathbf{u_4}\langle\rangle\}$	$\{u_3\langle\rangle, u_4\langle\rangle\}$
$(u_4 : A_4 = 22)$	$\{u_1\langle\rangle, u_2\langle\rangle\}$	$\{u_1\langle 12, \leq\rangle, u_2\langle\rangle\}$	$\{u_1\langle\rangle, u_2\langle 14, \leq\rangle\}$	$\{u_1\langle 20, \leq\rangle, u_2\langle\rangle\}$	$\{u_3\langle\rangle, u_5\langle\rangle\}$	$\{u_3\langle\rangle, u_5\langle C_3, \leq\rangle\}$	$\{u_3\langle C_3, \leq\rangle, u_4\langle\rangle\}$	$\{\mathbf{u_3}\langle\rangle, \mathbf{u_4}\langle\mathbf{C_4}, \leq\rangle\}$
$(u_3 : C_3 = 23)$	$\{u_1\langle\rangle, u_2\langle\rangle\}$	$\{u_1\langle 12, \leq\rangle, u_2\langle\rangle\}$	$\{u_1\langle\rangle, u_2\langle 14, \leq\rangle\}$	$\{u_1\langle 20, \leq\rangle, u_2\langle\rangle\}$	$\{u_3\langle\rangle, u_5\langle\rangle\}$	$\{\mathbf{u_3}\langle\rangle, \mathbf{u_5}\langle\mathbf{23}, \leq\rangle\}$	$\{\mathbf{u_3}\langle\mathbf{23}, \leq\rangle, \mathbf{u_4}\langle\rangle\}$	$\{u_3\langle\rangle, u_4\langle C_4, \leq\rangle\}$
$(wf : P_2^E = 24)$	$\{u_1\langle\rangle, u_2\langle\rangle\}$	$\{u_1\langle 12, \leq\rangle, u_2\langle\rangle\}$	$\{u_1\langle\rangle, u_2\langle 14, \leq\rangle\}$	$\{u_1\langle 20, \leq\rangle, u_2\langle\rangle\}$	$\{u_3\langle\rangle, u_5\langle\rangle\}$	$\{u_3\langle\rangle, u_5\langle 23, \leq\rangle\}$	$\{u_3\langle 23, \leq\rangle, u_4\langle\rangle\}$	$\{u_3\langle\rangle, u_4\langle C_4, \leq\rangle\}$
$(u_4 : C_4 = 25)$	$\{u_1\langle\rangle, u_2\langle\rangle\}$	$\{u_1\langle 12, \leq\rangle, u_2\langle\rangle\}$	$\{u_1\langle\rangle, u_2\langle 14, \leq\rangle\}$	$\{u_1\langle 20, \leq\rangle, u_2\langle\rangle\}$	$\{u_3\langle\rangle, u_5\langle\rangle\}$	$\{u_3\langle\rangle, u_5\langle 23, \leq\rangle\}$	$\{u_3\langle 23, \leq\rangle, u_4\langle\rangle\}$	$\{\mathbf{u_3}\langle\rangle, \mathbf{u_4}\langle\mathbf{25}, \leq\rangle\}$
$(wf : E^S = 26)$	$\{u_1\langle\rangle, u_2\langle\rangle\}$	$\{u_1\langle 12, \leq\rangle, u_2\langle\rangle\}$	$\{u_1\langle\rangle, u_2\langle 14, \leq\rangle\}$	$\{u_1\langle 20, \leq\rangle, u_2\langle\rangle\}$	$\{u_3\langle\rangle, u_5\langle\rangle\}$	$\{u_3\langle\rangle, u_5\langle 23, \leq\rangle\}$	$\{u_3\langle 23, \leq\rangle, u_4\langle\rangle\}$	$\{u_3\langle\rangle, u_4\langle 25, \leq\rangle\}$
$(wf : E^E = 26)$	$\{u_1\langle\rangle, u_2\langle\rangle\}$	$\{u_1\langle 12, \leq\rangle, u_2\langle\rangle\}$	$\{u_1\langle\rangle, u_2\langle 14, \leq\rangle\}$	$\{u_1\langle 20, \leq\rangle, u_2\langle\rangle\}$	$\{u_3\langle\rangle, u_5\langle\rangle\}$	$\{u_3\langle\rangle, u_5\langle 23, \leq\rangle\}$	$\{u_3\langle 23, \leq\rangle, u_4\langle\rangle\}$	$\{u_3\langle\rangle, u_4\langle 25, \leq\rangle\}$
$(wf : P_3^E = 27)$	$\{u_1\langle\rangle, u_2\langle\rangle\}$	$\{u_1\langle 12, \leq\rangle, u_2\langle\rangle\}$	$\{u_1\langle\rangle, u_2\langle 14, \leq\rangle\}$	$\{u_1\langle 20, \leq\rangle, u_2\langle\rangle\}$	$\{u_3\langle\rangle, u_5\langle\rangle\}$	$\{u_3\langle\rangle, u_5\langle 23, \leq\rangle\}$	$\{u_3\langle 23, \leq\rangle, u_4\langle\rangle\}$	$\{u_3\langle\rangle, u_4\langle 25, \leq\rangle\}$

Executed TP (cont.)	$\mathcal{A}(Z)$	$\mathcal{A}(P_1^S)$	$\mathcal{A}(P_1^E)$	$\mathcal{A}(P_2^S)$	$\mathcal{A}(P_2^E)$	$\mathcal{A}(P_3^S)$	$\mathcal{A}(P_3^E)$	$\mathcal{A}(B^S)$	$\mathcal{A}(B^E)$	$\mathcal{A}(E^S)$	$\mathcal{A}(E^E)$
$(wf : Z = 0)$	$\{wf\langle\rangle\}$	$\{wf\langle\rangle\}$	$\{wf\langle\rangle\}$	$\{wf\langle\rangle\}$	$\{wf\langle\rangle\}$	$\{wf\langle\rangle\}$	$\{wf\langle\rangle\}$	$\{wf\langle\rangle\}$	$\{wf\langle\rangle\}$	$\{wf\langle\rangle\}$	$\{wf\langle\rangle\}$
$(wf : P_1^S = 8)$	$\{wf\langle\rangle\}$	$\{wf\langle\rangle\}$	$\{wf\langle\rangle\}$	$\{wf\langle\rangle\}$	$\{wf\langle\rangle\}$	$\{wf\langle\rangle\}$	$\{wf\langle\rangle\}$	$\{wf\langle\rangle\}$	$\{wf\langle\rangle\}$	$\{wf\langle\rangle\}$	$\{wf\langle\rangle\}$
$(u_2 : A_1 = 9)$	$\{wf\langle\rangle\}$	$\{wf\langle\rangle\}$	$\{wf\langle\rangle\}$	$\{wf\langle\rangle\}$	$\{wf\langle\rangle\}$	$\{wf\langle\rangle\}$	$\{wf\langle\rangle\}$	$\{wf\langle\rangle\}$	$\{wf\langle\rangle\}$	$\{wf\langle\rangle\}$	$\{wf\langle\rangle\}$
$(u_2 : C_1 = 12)$	$\{wf\langle\rangle\}$	$\{wf\langle\rangle\}$	$\{wf\langle\rangle\}$	$\{wf\langle\rangle\}$	$\{wf\langle\rangle\}$	$\{wf\langle\rangle\}$	$\{wf\langle\rangle\}$	$\{wf\langle\rangle\}$	$\{wf\langle\rangle\}$	$\{wf\langle\rangle\}$	$\{wf\langle\rangle\}$
$(wf : P_2^S = 15)$	$\{wf\langle\rangle\}$	$\{wf\langle\rangle\}$	$\{wf\langle\rangle\}$	$\{wf\langle\rangle\}$	$\{wf\langle\rangle\}$	$\{wf\langle\rangle\}$	$\{wf\langle\rangle\}$	$\{wf\langle\rangle\}$	$\{wf\langle\rangle\}$	$\{wf\langle\rangle\}$	$\{wf\langle\rangle\}$
$(wf : P_3^S = 15)$	$\{wf\langle\rangle\}$	$\{wf\langle\rangle\}$	$\{wf\langle\rangle\}$	$\{wf\langle\rangle\}$	$\{wf\langle\rangle\}$	$\{wf\langle\rangle\}$	$\{wf\langle\rangle\}$	$\{wf\langle\rangle\}$	$\{wf\langle\rangle\}$	$\{wf\langle\rangle\}$	$\{wf\langle\rangle\}$
$(u_2 : A_2 = 15)$	$\{wf\langle\rangle\}$	$\{wf\langle\rangle\}$	$\{wf\langle\rangle\}$	$\{wf\langle\rangle\}$	$\{wf\langle\rangle\}$	$\{wf\langle\rangle\}$	$\{wf\langle\rangle\}$	$\{wf\langle\rangle\}$	$\{wf\langle\rangle\}$	$\{wf\langle\rangle\}$	$\{wf\langle\rangle\}$
$(u_2 : C_2 = 20)$	$\{wf\langle\rangle\}$	$\{wf\langle\rangle\}$	$\{wf\langle\rangle\}$	$\{wf\langle\rangle\}$	$\{wf\langle\rangle\}$	$\{wf\langle\rangle\}$	$\{wf\langle\rangle\}$	$\{wf\langle\rangle\}$	$\{wf\langle\rangle\}$	$\{wf\langle\rangle\}$	$\{wf\langle\rangle\}$
$(wf : P_1^E = 20)$	$\{wf\langle\rangle\}$	$\{wf\langle\rangle\}$	$\{wf\langle\rangle\}$	$\{wf\langle\rangle\}$	$\{wf\langle\rangle\}$	$\{wf\langle\rangle\}$	$\{wf\langle\rangle\}$	$\{wf\langle\rangle\}$	$\{wf\langle\rangle\}$	$\{wf\langle\rangle\}$	$\{wf\langle\rangle\}$
$(wf : B^S = 21)$	$\{wf\langle\rangle\}$	$\{wf\langle\rangle\}$	$\{wf\langle\rangle\}$	$\{wf\langle\rangle\}$	$\{wf\langle\rangle\}$	$\{wf\langle\rangle\}$	$\{wf\langle\rangle\}$	$\{wf\langle\rangle\}$	$\{wf\langle\rangle\}$	$\{wf\langle\rangle\}$	$\{wf\langle\rangle\}$
$(wf : B^E = 21)$	$\{wf\langle\rangle\}$	$\{wf\langle\rangle\}$	$\{wf\langle\rangle\}$	$\{wf\langle\rangle\}$	$\{wf\langle\rangle\}$	$\{wf\langle\rangle\}$	$\{wf\langle\rangle\}$	$\{wf\langle\rangle\}$	$\{wf\langle\rangle\}$	$\{wf\langle\rangle\}$	$\{wf\langle\rangle\}$
$(u_3 : A_3 = 22)$	$\{wf\langle\rangle\}$	$\{wf\langle\rangle\}$	$\{wf\langle\rangle\}$	$\{wf\langle\rangle\}$	$\{wf\langle\rangle\}$	$\{wf\langle\rangle\}$	$\{wf\langle\rangle\}$	$\{wf\langle\rangle\}$	$\{wf\langle\rangle\}$	$\{wf\langle\rangle\}$	$\{wf\langle\rangle\}$
$(u_4 : A_4 = 22)$	$\{wf\langle\rangle\}$	$\{wf\langle\rangle\}$	$\{wf\langle\rangle\}$	$\{wf\langle\rangle\}$	$\{wf\langle\rangle\}$	$\{wf\langle\rangle\}$	$\{wf\langle\rangle\}$	$\{wf\langle\rangle\}$	$\{wf\langle\rangle\}$	$\{wf\langle\rangle\}$	$\{wf\langle\rangle\}$
$(u_3 : C_3 = 23)$	$\{wf\langle\rangle\}$	$\{wf\langle\rangle\}$	$\{wf\langle\rangle\}$	$\{wf\langle\rangle\}$	$\{wf\langle\rangle\}$	$\{wf\langle\rangle\}$	$\{wf\langle\rangle\}$	$\{wf\langle\rangle\}$	$\{wf\langle\rangle\}$	$\{wf\langle\rangle\}$	$\{wf\langle\rangle\}$
$(wf : P_2^E = 24)$	$\{wf\langle\rangle\}$	$\{wf\langle\rangle\}$	$\{wf\langle\rangle\}$	$\{wf\langle\rangle\}$	$\{wf\langle\rangle\}$	$\{wf\langle\rangle\}$	$\{wf\langle\rangle\}$	$\{wf\langle\rangle\}$	$\{wf\langle\rangle\}$	$\{wf\langle\rangle\}$	$\{wf\langle\rangle\}$
$(u_4 : C_4 = 25)$	$\{wf\langle\rangle\}$	$\{wf\langle\rangle\}$	$\{wf\langle\rangle\}$	$\{wf\langle\rangle\}$	$\{wf\langle\rangle\}$	$\{wf\langle\rangle\}$	$\{wf\langle\rangle\}$	$\{wf\langle\rangle\}$	$\{wf\langle\rangle\}$	$\{wf\langle\rangle\}$	$\{wf\langle\rangle\}$
$(wf : E^S = 26)$	$\{wf\langle\rangle\}$	$\{wf\langle\rangle\}$	$\{wf\langle\rangle\}$	$\{wf\langle\rangle\}$	$\{wf\langle\rangle\}$	$\{wf\langle\rangle\}$	$\{wf\langle\rangle\}$	$\{wf\langle\rangle\}$	$\{wf\langle\rangle\}$	$\{wf\langle\rangle\}$	$\{wf\langle\rangle\}$
$(wf : E^E = 26)$	$\{wf\langle\rangle\}$	$\{wf\langle\rangle\}$	$\{wf\langle\rangle\}$	$\{wf\langle\rangle\}$	$\{wf\langle\rangle\}$	$\{wf\langle\rangle\}$	$\{wf\langle\rangle\}$	$\{wf\langle\rangle\}$	$\{wf\langle\rangle\}$	$\{wf\langle\rangle\}$	$\{wf\langle\rangle\}$
$(wf : P_3^E = 27)$	$\{wf\langle\rangle\}$	$\{wf\langle\rangle\}$	$\{wf\langle\rangle\}$	$\{wf\langle\rangle\}$	$\{wf\langle\rangle\}$	$\{wf\langle\rangle\}$	$\{wf\langle\rangle\}$	$\{wf\langle\rangle\}$	$\{wf\langle\rangle\}$	$\{wf\langle\rangle\}$	$\{wf\langle\rangle\}$

Assume now the system decides the duration of the branch block starting the parallel (which can be viewed as an internal task) is instantaneous and starts exactly after 1 hour since the train has got back to London. That is, the system executes B^S and B^E at 9 o'clock without applying any security constraint.

Suppose now that Charlie (u_3) starts the system check at 9PM. Rule r_5 (enforcing Security Policy 2) prevents him from executing the security check until he has finished the current task by applying $C_3, \leq$ for him in $\mathcal{A}(A_4)$ (row 5). The motivation is that Charlie is both a System and a Security Engineer, thereby he is authorized to execute both tasks. Furthermore, r_3 fires too by constraining Charlie to be the only one authorized to end the task applying $\langle C_3, \leq\rangle$ for all users apart from him in $\mathcal{A}(C_3)$ (again, row 5).

Assume now that while system check is being executed, Eve (u_4) starts the security check at 10PM. Rule r_6 does the same of r_5 but with respect to Eve and task `SystemCheck`. However, since Eve is not a System Engineer (consequently $u_4 \notin \mathcal{A}(A_3)$) this rules has no effect on the state of the system (row 6). Instead, r_4 applies as usual by setting $C_4, \leq$ for all users apart from Eve in $\mathcal{A}(C_4)$ (again, row 6). Now suppose Charlie and Eve terminate the tasks they are executing at 11PM and at 1AM (of the day after), respectively (rows 7 and 8). What happens next is that no security constraint is applied (because there are no rules whose guards contain C_3 or C_4) and the system disables R_3 at midnight (by executing P_2^E) and R_4 at 3AM of the day after (by executing P_3^E).

Finally, as for the branch block, the system decides the duration of the join block is instantaneous and starts after 1 hour since the last task (`SecurityCheck` in this strategy) has terminated, i.e., the system executes E^S and E^E at 1AM of the day after without applying any security constraint.

ARPPM: Administration in the RPPM Model

Jason Crampton
Royal Holloway University of London
Egham, United Kingdom
jason.crampton@rhul.ac.uk

James Sellwood
Royal Holloway University of London
Egham, United Kingdom
james.sellwood.2010@live.rhul.ac.uk

ABSTRACT

The RPPM model of access control uses relationships, paths and principal-matching in order to make access control decisions for general computing systems [8, 9]. Recently Stoller introduced a variant of an early RPPM model supporting administrative actions [20]. Stoller's RPPM^2 model is able to make authorization decisions in respect of actions which affect the system graph and some policy elements.

We also see utility in the RPPM model and believe that providing effective administration of the access control model is key to increasing the model's usefulness to real-world implementations. However, whilst we find inspiration in some aspects of Stoller's work, we believe that an alternative approach making use of the latest RPPM model [10] as its basis will offer a wider range of operational and administrative capabilities.

We motivate this work with specific requirements for an administrative model and then propose a decentralised discretionary access control approach to administration, whereby users are able to manage model components in the system graph through the addition and deletion of edges. The resulting Administrative RPPM (ARPPM) model supports administration of all of the model's components: the system model, the system graph, the authorization policies and all of their elements.

CCS Concepts

•**Security and privacy** → **Access control; Operating systems security;** *Formal security models; Authorization;* Social network security and privacy; •**Theory of computation** → Theory of database privacy and security;

Keywords

access control; path condition; relationship; principal matching; authorization; administration; entity condition

CODASPY'16, March 09 - 11, 2016, New Orleans, LA, USA

ISBN 978-1-4503-3935-3/16/03...$15.00

DOI: http://dx.doi.org/10.1145/2857705.2857711

1. INTRODUCTION

For any access control model to be effective it must keep track of the current state of the system it models. Most systems are not static and, therefore, the associated access control model instance will not be static either. Even for systems which are static, initial configuration will be required. Whatever the reason behind a change to a model instance, there is a need for that change to be controlled. Without this control, unauthorized changes could cause legitimate authorization requests to be denied (type I errors), or allow illegitimate authorization requests to be approved (type II errors). Uncontrolled changes could also cause the model instance to become inconsistent with the model's underlying assumptions or requirements. The administration of an access control model instance is, therefore, a critical aspect of the model's effectiveness.

Consistency is a necessary property which is determined by the definition of the access control model's components. In the case of the RPPM model there is, for example, a requirement for the system graph to be well-formed, with its "shape" constrained by the underlying system model [10]. Any model instance must be well-formed and any interaction must preserve that property. We will not consider other consistency requirements within this paper but reserve their considerations in respect of administration for future work. Instead, the focus of this paper is the authorization of administrative requests in an RPPM-based model.

There are various approaches to the administration of access control models. Models supporting mandatory access control (MAC) employ security labels (such as classifications) assigned to subjects by a security controller. The ability of those subjects to perform particular operations is then determined by a comparison of their label with that of the object they are interacting with [1, 2]. The policy which defines the acceptable combinations of subject and object labels for a particular operation is system-wide. Usually only the security controller can modify labels for subjects, and so the administrative policies are reasonably simple [19]. In contrast, models supporting discretionary access control (DAC) employ names for subjects and objects. Particular operations on an object are then controlled at a per named individual (or named group) level [11]. The definition of policies granting permission to named individuals or groups is carried out by any authorized subject. This allows for a wider variety of administrative architectures and leads to the notions of a hierarchy of administrators, administrative scope and resource ownership [19].

In this paper we introduce the Administrative RPPM (ARPPM) model as a discretionary model for the authorization of operational and administrative requests using relationships, paths and principal-matching. Section 2 identifies the user requirements for our administrative model and the resulting design decisions. Section 3 contains background information on the latest RPPM model (upon which our model is based) whilst Section 4 describes our ARPPM model and Section 5 describes its function in practice. We discuss related work in Section 6 and draw conclusions in Section 7. Appendix A contains the TargetSatisfactionTester algorithm supporting the discussion of Section 5.

2. USER REQUIREMENTS

Given the importance of administration within access control models, we first identify user requirements for any administrative RPPM model. When specifying these requirements we consider commonly applied best practice as well as desirable properties relevant to the practicality, robustness and usability of implementations of relationship-based access control.

UR1: Use the model's concepts to administer itself. It is only natural that authorization of administrative requests in respect of an access control model should be determined using the model itself (see ARBAC [18] for RBAC [12], for example). For the access control model designer such an approach is instinctive and preserves an "economy of concept", thus easing human comprehension[1]. Our first user requirement is, therefore, to *use the model's concepts to administer itself.* The Administrative RPPM (ARPPM) model described here meets this requirement by enhancing the RPPM model described in [10] so as to enable administrative actions to be authorized.

UR2: Support multiple administrators. It is widely accepted that the use of a single "global" administrator account to perform all administrative tasks is undesirable from organisational, auditing and least privilege perspectives [17]. Our second user requirement is, therefore, that the model be able to *support multiple administrators.* In the case of ARPPM, we desire that any user (or other authorized entity) be able to perform administrative actions where the relationships necessary to satisfy the specified administrative policies exist. The ARPPM model described here is capable of supporting any number of administrative entities, administrative hierarchies and scopes of administration.

UR3: Minimise extra-model administration. Many administrative models rely heavily on a benevolent, correct and complete extra-model administrator in order to boot-strap and manage the intra-model administrative capabilities. We require that the model should *minimise extra-model administration* and, as much as possible, be self-contained and ensure "complete mediation" [17]. To this end, in ARPPM we initialize the model instance with a *root* administrator entity and policy elements. This administrator entity may then make controlled changes to the model instance (managed within the model instance) until it reflects the state of the system being modelled or until other users have been assigned the necessary relationships to perform desired administrative actions.

UR4: Control the addition and deletion of model components. Given that an update action may be modelled through the combined use of deletion and addition actions, our fourth user requirement is that the model *control the addition and deletion of model components.* As ARPPM employs a graph-based model of a system, we chose to perform (and control) administration using two actions: addEdge and deleteEdge.

UR5: Support multiple controlling paths. As entities may be connected to numerous other entities through their relationships it is desirable, in some systems, for actions to be controlled through the existence (or otherwise) of multiple paths of relationships. Stoller demonstrates such a need through his healthcare example [20] and we show a similar requirement in our higher-education example (see Section 4). Our fifth user requirement is, therefore, that the model *support multiple controlling paths.* The ARPPM model extends the capabilities of RPPM by allowing multiple positive and negative paths to be used during the evaluation of authorization requests.

UR6: Control changes to all parts of the model. In order to be a complete model of administration it is necessary for administrative requests targeting types, permissible relationships, entities, relationships, and authorization policies and their elements to be managed. The sixth user requirement to *control changes to all parts of the model* increases the utility of the administrative model and is in line with the "complete mediation" design principle [17], drawing parallels with UR3. As the ARPPM model utilises paths in the system graph to evaluate and control actions we initialize the system graph with entities representing the various model components. This enables complete mediation of administrative requests.

UR7: Perform request evaluation efficiently. The RPPM model is designed to be a practical access control model for general computing applications. In order to ensure that it remains practical to implement we require the model *perform request evaluation efficiently.* ARPPM makes use of polynomial time algorithm [10] and follows a design chosen to maximise practicality, such as in its use of a simple typed entity condition in Definition 11.

Whilst the ARPPM model, detailed here meets all of these user requirements, Stoller's $RPPM^2$ model fails to meet several. $RPPM^2$ "is comprehensive in the sense that it allows and controls changes to all aspects of the ReBAC policy" [20]. However, it fails to allow and control changes to other model components (UR6) which are left, presumably, to some extra-model administrator (UR3).

3. THE RPPM MODEL

The RPPM model employs a system graph to represent a system's entities and their (inter-)relationships [8, 9, 10]. Within this graph the entities are nodes whilst the relation-

[1]Some [15, 20] have identified this approach as "economy of mechanism" (as described in [17]); however, that principle requires that a design be "simple and small as possible" which may not always align with the natural desire to protect the protection mechanism with its own capabilities.

ships are edges. Entities may be physical or logical system components. The "shape" of the system graph is governed by a system model, which identifies types of entities and the relationships which may exist between these entities.

DEFINITION 1. *A* system model *comprises a set of* types T, *a set of* relationship labels R, *a set of* symmetric *relationship labels* $S \subseteq R$ *and a* permissible relationship graph $G_{PR} = (V_{PR}, E_{PR})$, *where* $V_{PR} = T$ *and* $E_{PR} \subseteq T \times T \times R$.

DEFINITION 2. *Given a system model* (T, R, S, G_{PR}), *a* system instance *is defined by a* system graph $G = (V, E)$, *where* V *is the set of entities and* $E \subseteq V \times V \times R$, *and a function* $\tau : V \to T$ *which maps an entity to its type. We say* G *is* well-formed *if for each entity* v *in* V, $\tau(v) \in T$, *and for every edge* $(v, v', r) \in E$, $(\tau(v), \tau(v'), r) \in E_{PR}$.

Requests within the RPPM model take the form $q = (s, o, a)$ where a subject $s \in V$ requests to perform a specific action $a \in A$ on object $o \in V$. Such *operational* requests are evaluated using a two step process by first determining a set of matching security principals for the request and then by determining whether this set is authorized to perform the requested action. The use of security principals in this manner abstracts the authorization policy away from subjects, easing the administration burden. It also enables the application of powerful policy models such as a *policy graph*, whereby principals may be activated when specific other principals are matched to a request. We reserve this topic, as applied to operational and administrative requests, for future work.

Principals are matched to requests through the satisfaction of a chain of relationships between the subject and object in the system graph. A path condition π is used to define such a chain of relationships using specific labels from the set of relationship labels R.

DEFINITION 3. *Given a set of relationships* R, *we define a* path condition *recursively:*

- $\diamond$ *is a path condition;*
- r *is a path condition, for all* $r \in R$;
- *if* π *and* π' *are path conditions, then* (π), $\pi ; \pi'$, π^+ *and* $\overline{\pi}$ *are path conditions.*

A path condition of the form r *or* $\overline{r}$, *where* $r \in R$, *is said to be an* edge condition.

DEFINITION 4. *Given a system graph* $G = (V, E)$ *and* $u, v \in V$, *we write* $G, u, v \models \pi$ *to denote that* G, u *and* v satisfy path condition π. *Then, for all* G,u,v,π,π':

- $G, u, v \models \diamond$ *iff* $v = u$;
- $G, u, v \models r$ *iff* $(u, v, r) \in E$;
- $G, u, v \models (\pi)$ *iff* $G, u, v \models \pi$;
- $G, u, v \models \pi ; \pi'$ *iff there exists* $w \in V$ *such that* $G, u, w \models \pi$ *and* $G, w, v \models \pi'$;
- $G, u, v \models \pi^+$ *iff* $G, u, v \models \pi$ *or* $G, u, v \models \pi ; \pi^+$;
- $G, u, v \models \overline{\pi}$ *iff* $G, v, u \models \pi$.

To enable a robust request evaluation process, principals are matched based on two targets, one of which must be satisfied and one of which must not. (A target is a path condition or one of two special targets: all or none, where all is always satisfied and none is never satisfied.) Where such principal-matching rules are deemed applicable to a request their associated principals are added to the set of matched principals.

DEFINITION 5. *Let* P *be a set of authorization principals. A* principal-matching rule *has the form* (ϕ, ψ, p), *where* $p \in P$ *and* ϕ *and* ψ *are targets. A* principal-matching policy *(PMP) is a set of principal-matching rules.*

DEFINITION 6. *We say a principal-matching rule* (ϕ, ψ, p) *is* applicable *to a request* $q = (s, o, a)$ *if and only if* $G, q \models \phi$ *and* $G, q \not\models \psi$. *Given a system graph* $G = (V, E)$, *a PMP* ρ *and a request* $q = (s, o, a)$, *where* $s, o \in V$, *we define the set of* matched principals*:*

$$[\![\rho]\!]_q^G \stackrel{\text{def}}{=} \{p \in P : (\phi, \psi, p) \in \rho \text{ is applicable to } q\}.^2$$

Once the set of matched principals is determined, a set of authorization decisions is produced by evaluating authorization rules defined for those principals.

DEFINITION 7. *An* authorization rule *has the form* (p, x, y, b), *where* $p \in P$, $x \in V \cup T \cup \{\star\}$, $y \in A \cup \{\star\}$ *and* $b \in \{0, 1\}$. *Given a PMP* ρ, *an authorization rule* (p, x, y, b) *is applicable to a request* $q = (s, o, a)$ *if all of the following conditions hold:* (i) $p \in [\![\rho]\!]$ (ii) $x \in \{o, \tau(o), \star\}$ (iii) $y \in \{a, \star\}$.

An authorization policy *is a set of authorization rules. Given an authorization policy* ϱ *and a request* $q = (s, o, a)$, *we define the set of* authorization decisions*:*

$$[\![\rho, \varrho]\!]_q^G \stackrel{\text{def}}{=} \{b \in \{0, 1\} : (p, x, y, b) \in \varrho \text{ is applicable to } q\}.$$

Where necessary a conflict resolution strategy (CRS) (e.g. DenyOverride or AllowOverride) may be employed to ensure a single decision results. If a decision cannot be determined then default decisions are applied. This may occur when no principals are matched to the request ($[\![\rho]\!] = \emptyset$) or no explicit authorizations exist for the set of matched principals ($[\![\rho, \varrho]\!] = \emptyset$). Default decisions are applied in order, where they are defined, of the default-per-subject (only if $[\![\rho]\!] = \emptyset$), default-per-object, default-per-type or system-wide default.

4. THE ARPPM MODEL

We use the RPPM model described in [10], and summarised above, as the basis for our Administrative RPPM (ARPPM) model (in line with UR1). In order to support the evaluation of administrative requests we make several modifications which are detailed here.

4.1 ARPPM Requests

As indicated in response to UR4, we choose to model all administrative requests through the addition and deletion of edges to the system graph. An entity is automatically added to the system graph upon the addition of its first incident edge, and is automatically deleted upon deletion of its last incident edge. We, therefore, extend RPPM's definition of a request to enable actions to target edges as well as entities.

[2]We will abbreviate $[\![\rho]\!]_q^G$ to $[\![\rho]\!]_q$ or $[\![\rho]\!]$ when G, or G and q, are obvious from context.

DEFINITION 8. *An* administrative request *has the form* $(s, (v_1, t_1, v_2, t_2, r), a)$*, where* $s, v_1, v_2 \in V$*,* $t_1, t_2 \in T$*,* $r \in R$ *and* $a \in \{\textsf{addEdge}, \textsf{deleteEdge}\}$*. In order to be* well-formed *any administrative request requires* $\tau(v_1) = t_1$*,* $\tau(v_2) = t_2$ *and* $(t_1, t_2, r) \in E_{PR}$*. Additionally, a well-formed* **addEdge** *request requires* $V \cap \{v_1, v_2\} \neq \emptyset$ *and* $(v_1, v_2, r) \notin E$*, whilst a well-formed* **deleteEdge** *request requires* $(v_1, v_2, r) \in E$*.*

The effect of granting the well-formed request $(s, (v_1, t_1, v_2, t_2, r), \textsf{addEdge})$ is to add (v_1, v_2, r) to E (having added v_1 or v_2 to V, if necessary). The effect of granting the well-formed request $(s, (v_1, t_1, v_2, t_2, r), \textsf{deleteEdge})$ is to remove (v_1, v_2, r) from E; any vertex that is no longer connected to any other vertex as a result of the edge deletion will also be deleted.

RPPM's first step for deciding whether to grant an operational request (s, v, a) attempts to match principals to the request by evaluating principal-matching rules. The targets of each principal-matching rule are evaluated in respect of paths between s and v in the system graph. This is insufficient when deciding whether to grant the administrative request $(s, (v_1, t_1, v_2, t_2, r), a)$ for two reasons.

Firstly, we believe, as Stoller's healthcare example illustrates [20], that multiple paths of relationships may be relevant to the authorization of administrative requests. Secondly, there is no node in the system graph representing the object edge (v_1, t_1, v_2, t_2, r) and, even if such entities were introduced, logically one would not be present at the time a request to first add the edge is made. Evaluating paths between s and (v_1, t_1, v_2, t_2, r) is, therefore, impractical and insufficient.

In order to evaluate administrative requests we must, therefore, refine RPPM's existing policy definition and request evaluation process. We wish to support the evaluation of multiple paths between arbitrary entities when evaluating requests (as per UR5) and so we take inspiration from Stoller's approach of associating path conditions with constraints defining the entities between which the satisfying paths must exist. However, our approach is more rigorously structured and, thereby, enables us to constrain path conditions to entities by their label, their type, their role in the request, or one of two kinds of variable (which can be used to constrain multiple paths to involving the same entity, without specifying beforehand the identity of that entity).

Throughout this paper we shall use a higher-education example to illustrate the ARPPM model. Given the system graph fragment G_1 shown in Figure 1a, we can imagine the need for user ca_1 to submit a request $q_1 = (ca_1, (d_1, dept, c_1, course, runs), \textsf{addEdge})$. The goal of this request is to add an edge labelled *runs* between department d_1 and course c_1. We can, further, imagine the desired policy being that the user who is the course administrator for course c_1 (and no other course administrator) is authorized to perform such an action. In order to match this principal to the request it may be that several paths of relationships must exist within the system graph. We might wish, for example, for the subject of the request to be a member of the department in question and also to be a manager of the course in question.

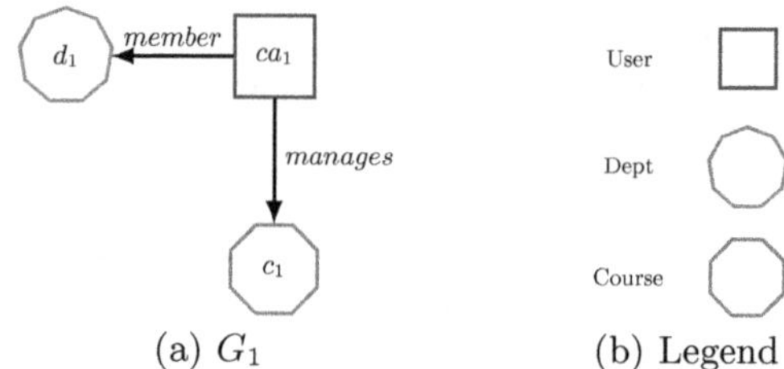

(a) G_1 (b) Legend

Figure 1: Higher-education system graph fragment

4.2 Extended Path Conditions

To support satisfying paths between arbitrary entities we introduce the concept of an *extended path condition* as an RPPM path condition with two typed *entity conditions*, one at each end. One or more extended path conditions may be grouped together within a set called a *path expression.*

DEFINITION 9. *An* untyped entity condition *is either an entity variable* x*, an entity* v *in* V*, or an entity label* ℓ *in* RL*, where* $RL = \{\textsf{subject}, \textsf{object}, \textsf{object-start}, \textsf{object-start}\}$*.*

The set of entities that *satisfies* an untyped entity condition e with respect to a request q, denoted $[\![e, q]\!]$ is defined as follows:

$$\begin{aligned} \text{for any entity variable } x,\ [\![x, q]\!] &= V \\ \text{for any entity } v \text{ in } V,\ [\![v, q]\!] &= \{v\} \\ [\![\textsf{subject}, (s, o, a)]\!] = [\![\textsf{subject}, (s, (v_1, t_1, v_2, t_2, r), a)]\!] &= \{s\} \\ [\![\textsf{object}, (s, o, a)]\!] &= \{o\} \\ [\![\textsf{object-start}, (s, (v_1, t_1, v_2, t_2, r), a)]\!] &= \{v_1\} \\ [\![\textsf{object-end}, (s, (v_1, t_1, v_2, t_2, r), a)]\!] &= \{v_2\} \\ [\![\textsf{object}, (s, (v_1, t_1, v_2, t_2, r), a)]\!] &= \emptyset \\ [\![\textsf{object-start}, (s, o, a)]\!] = [\![\textsf{object-end}, (s, o, a)]\!] &= \emptyset \end{aligned}$$

DEFINITION 10. *A* typed entity condition *has the form* (e, f)*, where* e *is an untyped entity condition and* f *either belongs to* T *or is a type variable.*

Let Var_V denote the set of entity variables and Var_T denote the set of type variables. We assume that $Var_V \cap Var_T = \emptyset$. The set of entities that *satisfies* a typed entity condition (e, f) with respect to a request q, denoted $[\![(e, f), q]\!]$ is defined as follows:

$$[\![(e, f), q]\!] = \begin{cases} V & \text{if } f \in Var_T,\ e \in Var_V \\ \{v : \tau(v) = f\} & \text{if } f \in T,\ e \in Var_V \\ \emptyset & \text{if } f \in T,\ e \notin Var_V,\ \tau(e) \neq f \\ [\![e, q]\!] & \text{otherwise.} \end{cases}$$

A typed entity condition (e, f) in which e is not an entity variable is said to be a *simple* typed entity condition. Note that for any simple typed entity condition (e, f) and any request q, $[\![(e, f), q]\!]$ is either the empty set or $[\![e, q]\!]$ (which is either a singleton set or the empty set). For example, the simple typed entity condition $(u, \tau(u))$, where $u \in V$, is satisfied by $\{u\}$ for any request. Henceforth, we will be working exclusively with typed entity conditions and we will, therefore, refer to entity conditions and simple entity conditions.

DEFINITION 11. *An* extended path condition *has the form* $\eta \cdot \pi \cdot \eta'$*, where* η *is a simple entity condition,* η' *is an entity condition, and* π *is a path condition. A* path expression *is a set of extended path conditions.*

We define satisfaction of path expressions based on the satisfaction of all constituent extended path conditions; we, in turn, define their satisfaction based on the satisfaction of the contained path condition between entities meeting the specified entity conditions. Let $\nu : Var_V \cup Var_T \to V \cup T$ be a function mapping entity variables to entities and type variables to types. We write $\nu(\eta) = (\nu(x), \nu(y))$ to denote the entity condition $\eta = (x, y)$ once variables have been replaced by entities and types.

DEFINITION 12. *An extended path condition* $\eta \cdot \pi \cdot \eta'$ *is satisfied by system graph* G *and request* q*, denoted* $G, q \models \eta \cdot \pi \cdot \eta'$*, iff there exists a function* $\nu : Var_V \cup Var_T \to V \cup T$ *such that:*

- $[\![\nu(\eta), q]\!] \neq \emptyset$*, and*
- *there exists* $v \in [\![\nu(\eta'), q]\!]$ *such that* $G, [\![\nu(\eta), q]\!], v \models \pi$.

A path expression $\{\eta_1 \cdot \pi_1 \cdot \eta'_1, \ldots, \eta_k \cdot \pi_k \cdot \eta'_k\}$ *is satisfied by system graph* G *and request* q*, denoted* $G, q \models \{\eta_1 \cdot \pi_1 \cdot \eta'_1, \ldots, \eta_k \cdot \pi_k \cdot \eta'_k\}$*, iff* $\eta_i \cdot \pi \cdot \eta'_i$ *is satisfied for all* $i \in \{1, \ldots, k\}$.

Returning to Figure 1a and request $q_1 = (ca_1, (d_1, dept, c_1, course, runs), \mathsf{addEdge})$, the extended path condition $(\mathsf{subject}, user) \cdot member \cdot (ev_1, dept)$ identifies the path condition *member* between the subject of the request, if it is a user, and any entity which is a department, referred to using the entity variable ev_1. Only if such a combination of entities and path exist will the extended path condition be satisfied. In the case of this example it is satisfied with $[\![(\mathsf{subject}, user)]\!] = \{ca_1\}$, $[\![(ev_1, dept)]\!] = \{d_1\}$, and $G_1, ca_1, d_1 \models member$.

Note that a path expression may not be satisfied even if it contains no variables. In particular, given the extended path condition $(e, f) \cdot \pi \cdot (e', f')$,

- It may be the case that $e, e' \in V$ but $G, e, e' \not\models \pi$; or
- It may be the case that $e \in RL$ and $f \neq \tau(e)$; or
- It may be the case that $e' \in RL$ and $f' \neq \tau(e')$.

In each of these cases, there can be no mapping ν such that the extended path condition is satisfied. We write $G, q \not\models (e, f) \cdot \pi \cdot (e', f')$ in each of these cases.

Note also that a variable occurring only once in a path expression is essentially a "free" variable and can be assigned to any entity (or type, depending on the nature of the variable). Hence, $\{(\mathsf{subject}, f) \cdot \pi \cdot (\mathsf{object}, f')\}$, where $f, f' \in Var_T$ and $f \neq f'$, is equivalent to the RPPM path condition π. In other words, ARPPM is backwards compatible with RPPM.

It is also important to note the requirement that a simple entity condition is the first part of an extended path condition. This means that an extended path condition may only be satisfied by a path starting from a single specific entity within the system graph, which significantly reduces the complexity of request evaluation (in line with UR7). We do not believe that such a constraint will significantly reduce the applicability of the ARPPM model, especially as $\overline{\pi}$ enables all extended path conditions to be reversed. This approach is in line with, but less restrictive than, that of Stoller's authorization checking algorithm [20]. His recommendation is to entirely reject rules which begin with "unbound variables" whilst we only preclude rules which begin with a constraint which may be satisfied by more than one entity in the system graph.

4.3 ARPPM Principal Matching

Stoller's administrative model replaced RPPM's principal-matching policy with a path-expression naming mechanism [20]. We believe that the two-step request evaluation process used in RPPM, in which principals are analogous to roles in role-based access control, is far more powerful a concept than simply a shorthand naming mechanism. The principal graph and principal activation concepts of [10] offer an insight into how principals may be utilised to a greater effect. We, therefore, maintain RPPM's usage of the security principal in line with the definition given by Saltzer and Schroeder [17]: "The entity in a computer system to which authorizations are granted". That is not to say that Stoller's naming mechanism may not be a helpful shortcut when defining policies (although we do not demonstrate it in this paper). It is simply not an equally powerful substitute for the principal-matching policy.

ARPPM's principal matching rules (ϕ, ψ, p), therefore, take the same basic form as those of RPPM, comprising two targets and a principal. The positive target ϕ must be satisfied and the negative target ψ must not be satisfied for the principal p to apply to the request. Each target may be a path expression or alternatively one of the special targets all or none. Consequently each principal-matching rule may now depend on multiple mandatory (and precluded) paths being found (and not found) within the system graph.

In the case of our higher-education example from Figure 1a we may, for example, employ a principal-matching rule of the form:

$$\begin{aligned}&(\{(\mathsf{subject}, user) \cdot member \cdot (ev_1, dept),\\&(\mathsf{subject}, user) \cdot manages \cdot (\mathsf{object\text{-}end}, course)\},\\&\mathsf{none}, \mathsf{course\text{-}admin}) \in \rho_1\end{aligned}$$

Here the positive target comprises a path expression containing two extended path conditions, whilst the negative target is never satisfied.

We now demonstrate the use of variables within path expressions. Given the system graph fragment G_2 shown in Figure 2a, there may exist a principal-matching rule for a course-admin2 principal:[3]

$$\begin{aligned}&(\{(\mathsf{subject}, user) \cdot member \cdot (ev_1, dept),\\&(\mathsf{subject}, user) \cdot manages \cdot (\mathsf{object\text{-}end}, course),\\&(\mathsf{object\text{-}end}, course) \cdot \overline{runs} \cdot (ev_1, dept)\},\\&\mathsf{none}, \mathsf{course\text{-}admin2}) \in \rho_2\end{aligned}$$

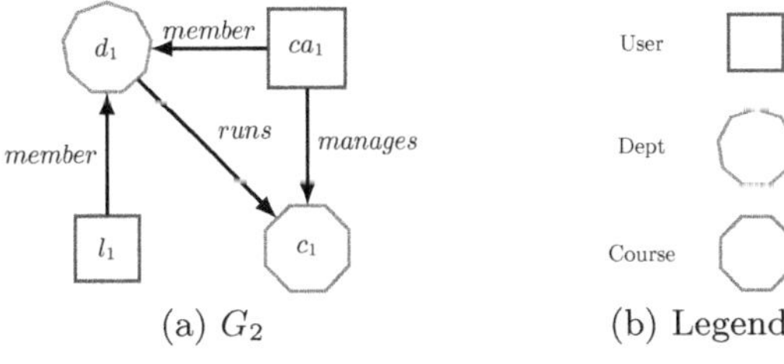

Figure 2: Higher-education system graph fragment

[3]Notice that the third extended path condition utilises the path condition $\overline{runs}$, rather than $runs$, to ensure the extended path condition is constructed as per Definition 11.

Let us consider the evaluation of a request $q_2 = (ca_1, (l_1, user, c_1, course, lectures), \mathsf{addEdge})$ and use the mapping $\nu((ev_1, dept)) = (d_1, dept)$. Consequently, $G_2, q_2 \models (\mathsf{subject}, user) \cdot member \cdot (ev_1, dept)$ between the entities ca_1 and d_1. Similarly, $G_2, q_2 \models (\mathsf{subject}, user) \cdot manages \cdot (\mathsf{object\text{-}end}, course)$ (between the entities ca_1 and c_1) and $G_2, q_2 \models (\mathsf{object\text{-}end}, course) \cdot \overline{runs} \cdot (ev_1, dept)$ (between the entities c_1 and d_1). The positive target is satisfied. The negative target is never satisfied and, therefore, the first stage of request evaluation determines the rule applies and consequently adds the course-admin2 principal to the set of matched principals $[\![\rho_2]\!]_{q_2}^{G_2}$.

The matching of security principals through the satisfaction (or otherwise) of positive and negative targets enables the "layout" of a relevant part of the system graph to be used to inform the request. This matching of principals does not take into consideration the requested action. Therefore, the notion of a principal may be seen as that of a label given to the subject of a request by the request's object, independent of the intended action. Such a notion is comparable to that of Unix where, for example, the "owner" principal may apply independent of whether a read or write request was made. In the case of the example above, the course-admin2 principal would apply whether the request had been to add the *lectures* edge between l_1 and c_1, or to delete it.

4.4 ARPPM Authorizations

Whilst principal matching is independent of action, the second step of request evaluation determines whether the matched security principals have been authorized to perform the requested action. However, when evaluating this second step it is, once again, desirable to consider the relationships amongst participating (and potentially arbitrary) entities. A similar approach was employed by Sandhu *et al.* within ARBAC [18] in their "prerequisite condition" and by Rizvi *et al.* [16] in their "applicability conditions". Therefore, we once again make use of positive and negative targets based on path expressions and the special targets all and none.

DEFINITION 13. *An* authorization rule *has the form* (p, ϕ, ψ, y, d), *where* $p \in P$, ϕ *and* ψ *are positive and negative targets, respectively,* $y \in A \cup \{\star\}$ *and* $d \in \{0,1\}$. *Given a system graph* $G = (V, E)$, *a set of types* T *and a PMP* ρ, *an authorization rule* (p, ϕ, ψ, y, d) *is applicable to a request* $q = (s, o, a)$ *if all of the following conditions hold:* (i) $p \in [\![\rho]\!]$ (ii) $G, q \models \phi$ (iii) $G, q \not\models \psi$ (iv) $y \in \{a, \star\}$.

An authorization policy *is a set of authorization rules. Given an authorization policy* ϱ *and a request* q, *we define the set of* authorization decisions*:*

$$[\![\rho, \varrho]\!]_q^G \stackrel{\text{def}}{=} \{d \in \{0,1\} : (p, \phi, \psi, y, d) \in \varrho \text{ is applicable to } q\}.$$

Returning to system graph fragment G_2 and request $q_2 = (ca_1, (l_1, user, c_1, course, lectures), \mathsf{addEdge})$, we may envisage an authorization rule for the course-admin2 principal requesting the action addEdge:

$$\begin{aligned}&(\mathsf{course\text{-}admin2},\\ &\{(\mathsf{object\text{-}start}, user) \cdot member \cdot (ev_1, dept),\\ &\quad (\mathsf{object\text{-}end}, course) \cdot \overline{runs} \cdot (ev_1, dept)\},\\ &\{(\mathsf{object\text{-}start}, user) \cdot student \cdot (\mathsf{object\text{-}end}, course)\},\\ &\mathsf{addEdge}, 1) \in \varrho_2.\end{aligned}$$

When this rule is considered along with the mapping $\nu((ev_1, dept)) = (d_1, dept)$, the positive target is satisfied because $G_2, q_2 \models (\mathsf{object\text{-}start}, user) \cdot member \cdot (ev_1, dept)$ (between the entities l_1 and d_1) and $G_2, q_2 \models (\mathsf{object\text{-}end}, course) \cdot \overline{runs} \cdot (ev_1, dept)$ (between the entities c_1 and d_1). The negative target is, however, not satisfied because $G_2, q_2 \not\models (\mathsf{object\text{-}start}, user) \cdot student \cdot (\mathsf{object\text{-}end}, course)$. Therefore, as the positive target is satisfied and the negative target is not, the constraints of the authorization rule are met and the rule's approve decision is added to the set of authorization decisions.[4]

Having determined the set of authorization decisions, we determine whether a request is authorized in the same manner as RPPM, employing default decisions and a conflict resolution strategy where appropriate. We believe that default decision-making associated with administrative requests should be distinct from that of operational requests. The default-per-object and default-per-type are certainly redundant as administrative actions are performed on edges rather than single entities. We, therefore, allow for specific administrative default decisions at the default-per-subject and system-wide default levels only.

DEFINITION 14. *Given a system graph* $G = (V, E)$, $V_{so} \subseteq V \times \{\mathsf{sub}, \mathsf{obj}\}$, *a set of types* T, *and an operational request* $q = (s, v, a)$, *a* default decision function

$$\omega : V_{so} \cup T \cup \{\mathsf{sys}\} \rightarrow \{\bot, 0, 1\}$$

is a function which maps entities within the system graph to default decisions for operational requests, where $\bot$ *is undefined,* 0 *is deny and* 1 *is allow. The function maps default decisions on a per subject* (u, sub), *per object* (u, obj), *per object type* $t \in T$ *and* system*-wide basis. When initialized,* $\omega(\mathsf{sys}) = 0$ *and the function maps all other inputs to* $\bot$.

DEFINITION 15. *Given a system graph* $G = (V, E)$, *a set of types* T, *and an administrative request* $q = (s, (v_1, t_1, v_2, t_2, r), a)$, *a* default administrative decision function

$$\omega_a : V \cup \{\mathsf{sys}\} \rightarrow \{\bot, 0, 1\}$$

is a function which maps entities within the system graph to default decisions for administrative requests, where $\bot$ *is undefined,* 0 *is deny and* 1 *is allow. The function maps default decisions on a per subject* $u \in V$ *and* system*-wide basis. When initialized,* $\omega_a(\mathsf{sys}) = 0$ *and the function maps all other inputs to* $\bot$.

Our approach described here enables ARPPM to authorize operational and administrative requests to any subject able to satisfy the specified path conditions through the presence of paths of relationships within the system graph. We are, therefore, not restricted to a single administrative user as demanded by UR2. Further, the separate target pairs for principal-matching and authorization enable complex sets of relationships to independently determine the principals matched to the request and the decision for the requested action.

[4]Note that the positive and negative targets for authorizing the addEdge action to course-admin2 are different from those which determined whether the principal should be matched to a request. We believe this to be likely but not necessary.

It should be noted that if every path expression within the principal-matching policy were to contain a single extended path condition of the form $(\mathsf{subject}, tv_1) \cdot \pi \cdot (\mathsf{object}, tv_2)$, with $tv_1 \neq tv_2$, and only operational requests, of the form $q = (s, v, a)$, were to be submitted then ARPPM would exactly replicate the functionality of RPPM with respect to the first step of request evaluation. In addition, if every authorization rule were to contain the constraints $\phi = \mathsf{all}$ and $\psi = \mathsf{none}$ then, with respect to the second step of request evaluation, ARPPM would exactly replicate the functionality of RPPM when all authorization rules apply to all objects (that is, when x equals $\star$ for all (p, x, y, b) in ϱ).

It is also important to note that in the context of operational requests ARPPM is able to make use of RPPM's typed edges [10] and may, therefore, support caching, auditing, and policy configurations enforcing separation of duty and Chinese Wall with respect to such requests. Typed edges are not so consistently applicable in the context of administrative requests targeting object edges and so we leave their consideration for future work.

4.5 Automated Agents

Whilst we focus the attention of our examples on "users" performing administrative actions, the concepts equally apply to entities of other types. It should be clear that given the appropriate underlying system model and relationships within the system graph, an automated administrative entity of type *auto* may have administrative requests authorized. Such an automated agent could be employed to manage the system graph on behalf of the system and could be responsible for adding the caching and auditing edges described in [10]. With the necessary logic, such automated agents could also be employed to prune caching edges based on an appropriate cache management strategy, or could prune relationship edges which are temporary in nature and associated with some timeout criteria. We leave the details of automated administrative agents to future work.

5. ARPPM IN PRACTICE

5.1 ARPPM Initialization

The ARPPM model described so far is able to meet all but two of our user requirements. In order to control changes to all parts of the model (UR6) and minimise extra-model administration (UR3) we must populate the system graph with entities reflecting model components and define an initial state for the system graph. The minimum requirements for such an initial state involve an interplay of the entities, relationship labels, system graph layout, and the model's policies. Due to limitations of space a non-prescriptive discussion of the minimum requirements is not possible and so we detail a recommended arrangement instead.

In this arrangement we require all system graphs to be *initialized* as per Figure 3a. For ease of exposition, we omit from Figure 3a, and the following discussion, reversed edges (i.e. the existence of an edge $(T, root, \overline{r_a}) \in E$ where the edge $(root, T, r_a) \in E$), caching edges and audit edges. In addition, to allow a comprehensible diagram, we omit from Figure 3a edges from E_{PR_I} (we use the suffix I to indicate initialization) and also edges related to default decision entries mapped to $\perp$.

The initial underlying system model, principals, actions, principal-matching policy and extended authorization policy for this system graph are:

$$T_I = \{t_s, t_f, t_t, t_r, t_a, t_p, t_{pmr}, t_{ar}, t_{dd}, t_{crs}, user\}$$

$$\widetilde{R}_I = \{r_m, r_a, \overline{r_m}, \overline{r_a}\} \qquad S_I = \emptyset$$

$$E_{\mathrm{PR}_I} = \{(t, t_s, r_m) : t \in T_I \setminus \{t_f, t_{dd}, t_{crs}, user\}\} \cup \{(t_{dd}, t_f, r_m)\} \cup \{(user, t', r_a) : t' \in T_I\}$$

$$G_{\mathrm{PR}_I} = (T_I, E_{\mathrm{PR}_I})$$

$$P_I = \{\mathsf{model\text{-}admin}\} \qquad A_I = \{\mathsf{addEdge}, \mathsf{deleteEdge}\}$$

$$\rho_I = \{(\{(\mathsf{subject}, user) \cdot r_a \cdot (\mathsf{object\text{-}end}, tv_1)\}, \mathsf{none}, \mathsf{model\text{-}admin}), (\{(\mathsf{subject}, user) \cdot r_a ; \overline{r_m}^+ \cdot (\mathsf{object\text{-}end}, tv_1)\}, \mathsf{none}, \mathsf{model\text{-}admin})\}$$

$$(\varrho_I, \chi_I) = (\{(\mathsf{model\text{-}admin}, \mathsf{all}, \mathsf{none}, \mathsf{addEdge}, 1), (\mathsf{model\text{-}admin}, \mathsf{all}, \mathsf{none}, \mathsf{deleteEdge}, 1)\}, \mathsf{DenyOverride})$$

At its core, the initial system graph contains an administrative user *root* and entities representing the initial sets of types, relationship labels, principals, actions, principal-matching rules and authorization rules. The initial relationship entities are those necessary to construct this initial system graph: namely entities representing an administrate relationship r_a, a member-of relationship r_m and their reversed counterparts, $\overline{r_a}$ and $\overline{r_m}$ respectively. These have member-of relationships with an entity $\widetilde{R}$ which represents the set of relationship labels.[5] There are no initial symmetric relationship labels, although an entity S representing the set of symmetric relationship labels is present. The initial type entities represent the sets type t_s, the functions type t_f, the types type t_t, the relationships type t_r, the actions type t_a, the principals type t_p, the principal-matching rules type t_{pmr}, the authorization rules type t_{ar}, the default decisions type t_{dd}, the conflict resolution strategy type t_{crs} and the users type $user$. These have member-of relationships with T which represents the set of types.

There is a single initial principal entity representing a model-admin principal which has a member-of relationship with the entity representing the set of principals P. The administrative actions addEdge and deleteEdge are represented by similarly named entities which have member-of relationships with the entity representing the set of actions A. There are two initial principal-matching rules and authorization rules which have member-of relationships with the entities representing the policies, ρ and ϱ respectively. The initial principal-matching rules enable the model-admin principal to be matched to administrative requests made in respect of edges directed towards entities with which the subject has an administrate relationship $((\mathsf{subject}, user) \cdot r_a \cdot (\mathsf{object\text{-}end}, tv_1))$, or edges directed towards entities with which the subject can satisfy the path expression $\{(\mathsf{subject}, user) \cdot r_a ; \overline{r_m}^+ \cdot (\mathsf{object\text{-}end}, tv_1)\}$.[6] The initial authorization rules grant the addEdge and deleteEdge actions to the model-admin principal without constraint.

[5] As per [10], we define the set of relationship labels to be $\widetilde{R} = R \cup \overline{R}$, where $\overline{R}$ is defined to be $\{\overline{r} : r \in R\}$.

[6] Whilst these initial principal-matching rules only apply to requests directed towards one of the initial entities, any object edge directed away may be converted to an object edge directed towards by simply switching the entities and replacing the path condition π with $\overline{\pi}$.

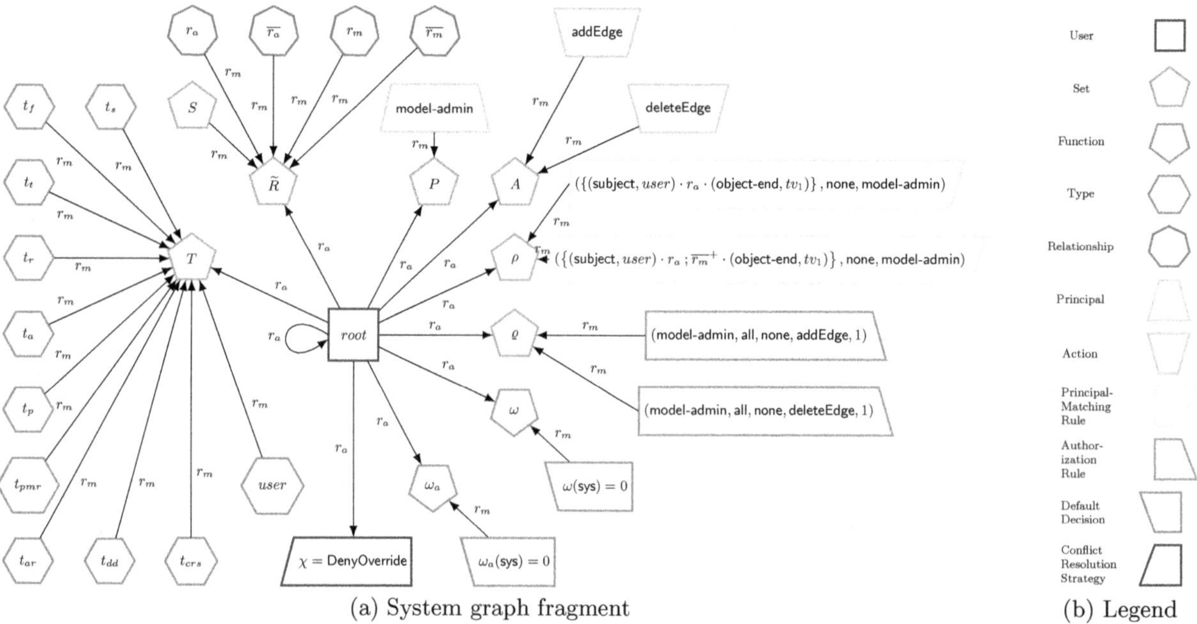

(a) System graph fragment (b) Legend

Figure 3: Initial system graph (simplified)

In addition, the initial system-wide default decisions, $\omega(\mathsf{sys}) = 0$ and $\omega_a(\mathsf{sys}) = 0$, have member-of relationships with the entities representing the default decision function ω and the default administrative decision function ω_a, respectively. Finally, an entity representing the initial conflict resolution strategy, DenyOverride is also present. *root* has an administrate relationship with the conflict resolution strategy entity, the entities representing the default decision functions, all of the set entities previously described and with itself. From this initial system graph, changes are made through the addition and deletion of edges using administrative requests. (Recall that an entity is automatically added to the system graph upon the addition of its first incident edge, and is automatically deleted upon deletion of its last incident edge.)

In order to configure an ARPPM system graph for an actual system the *root* user would add entities, by adding edges, to the newly initialized system graph. In so doing, *root* would be able to modify the underlying system model to support the desired entity types and relationships, and could then introduce concrete and logical system entities into the graph by adding edges such as $(root, u, r_a)$. How the structure of the system graph develops will be up to the *root* user and, subsequently, to any entities granted the ability to administer the system graph through the existence (or otherwise) of relationships satisfying the requisite paths. Such design choices are likely to be instance, if not system, specific and are not constrained by ARPPM.

To prevent an ARPPM model from becoming unusable we do not allow any of the initial system graph's edges to be deleted except those involving entities of the types t_{dd} and t_{crs} (which may need to be deleted in order to change the system-wide default decisions or conflict resolution strategy). All other changes to the system graph are managed by the processes defined in this paper. Whilst changes to the system model $(T, R, S, G_{\mathrm{PR}})$, where $G_{\mathrm{PR}} = (T, E_{\mathrm{PR}})$, are triggered through the system graph, we require that they are enacted by an authorized and correct "system administrator".[7] We introduce the following restrictions to those changes:

- Changes to $t \in T$, $s \in S$ or $r \in \widetilde{R} \setminus S$ are triggered, respectively, by administrative requests of the form $(u, (t, t_t, T, t_s, r_m), a')$, $(u, (s, t_r, S, t_s, r_m), a')$, and $(u, (r, t_r, \widetilde{R}, t_s, r_m), a')$ where $a' \in \{\mathsf{addEdge}, \mathsf{deleteEdge}\}$. Changes to E_{PR} are triggered by administrative requests adding or deleting edges between the entities representing types in G. In each case the authorized administrative request is only considered complete once the system administrator has updated the system model to reflect any desired changes.
- $\{(user, t, r_a) : t \in T\} \subset E_{\mathrm{PR}}$;
- $E_{\mathrm{PR}} \cap \{(t, t'', r) : t \in T, t'' \in \{t_s, t_f\}, r \notin \{r_m, r_a\}\} = \emptyset$;
- Given $T'' = \{t_t, t_r, t_a, t_p, t_{pmr}, t_{ar}, t_{dd}\}$, $E_{\mathrm{PR}} \cap \{(t, t'', r) : t \in T, t'' \in T'', r \neq r_a\} = \emptyset$;
- Given $T' = \{t_s, t_t, t_r, t_a, t_p, t_{pmr}, t_{ar}, t_{dd}\}$, $E_{\mathrm{PR}} \cap \{(t', t'', r) : t' \in T', t'' \neq t_s, r \neq r_m\} = \emptyset$.

The last three restrictions require that edges connecting to entities of the sets type t_s or functions type t_f are either member-of or administrate relationships, that edges connecting to entities of the types found in the set T'' are administrate relationships, and that edges connecting from entities of the types found in the set T' can only connect to the sets type t_s using a member-of relationship.

Finally, in his RPPM[2] model Stoller introduces a complex "strictness order" on authorization rules in order to prevent

[7]This is our one concession to UR3, as some aspect of the system model must be external to the system graph it constrains.

undesirable ramifications of changes to his authorization policy (a combination of our principal-matching policy and authorization policy). Whilst we agree that it should not be possible to circumvent the access control model we believe that a far simpler approach is to explicitly deny undesirable actions by subjects. We assume that the *root* user is trustworthy and correct, and we believe that such restrictions can be implemented by *root* through the use of denial authorizations within the ARPPM authorization policy.

5.2 ARPPM Request Evaluation

We use non-deterministic finite automata (NFA) as the core component of ARPPM's request evaluation process, as used in [10]. We employ the NFA construction and intersection techniques [10, §3.1] only modifying the manner in which intersection NFAs are used to determine target satisfaction.

As ARPPM path expressions may contain multiple extended path conditions, each of which must be satisfied (or not) between entities identified by the entity conditions, we may need to consider multiple intersection NFAs for each target. We achieve this for each extended path condition $(e_i, f_i) \cdot \pi_i \cdot (e'_i, f'_i)$ by:[8]

- Using the simple entity condition (e_i, f_i) to determine the single start state for M_{q_i};
- Using the entity condition (e'_i, f'_i) to determine the set of accepting states for M_{q_i};
- Retrieving the path condition NFA M_{π_i};
- Producing the intersection NFA $M_{\cap_i}$ of M_{q_i} and M_{π_i}.

We then ensure that across all of the intersection NFAs for the path expression, entity conditions using the same entity variable identify the same entity and those using the same type variable identify the same type of entity. Satisfaction of each extended path condition (and, thereby, the path expression) is then determined by the existence of an accepting language for each intersection NFA constrained by the entity conditions.

Pseudo-code for the ARPPM request evaluation process is shown in Algorithm 1; this relies upon a number of other algorithms for specific processing. (For clarity we omit the passing of the core model components $G = (V, E)$, $\widetilde{R}$, $q = (s, o, a)$, ρ, (ϱ, χ), ω, and ω_a between the algorithms.)

We determine the set of matched principals using Algorithm 2 (ComputePrincipals). Having identified the set of matched principals, the set of authorizations is determined using Algorithm 3 (ComputeAuthorizations). These algorithms employ TargetSatisfactionTester (Algorithm 5) shown in Appendix A. The ApplyDefaults functionality is shown in Algorithm 4.

Algorithm 1 RequestEvaluation

```
Require:
Ensure: Returns authorization decision
  ⟦ρ⟧ ← ComputePrincipals()
  if ⟦ρ⟧ = ∅ then
      ⟦ρ, ϱ⟧ ← ApplyDefaults(true)
  else
      ⟦ρ, ϱ⟧ ← ComputeAuthorizations()
      if ⟦ρ, ϱ⟧ = ∅ then
          ⟦ρ, ϱ⟧ ← ApplyDefaults(false)
      end if
  end if
  if ⟦ρ, ϱ⟧ = {0} then
      return false // deny
  else if ⟦ρ, ϱ⟧ = {1} then
      return true // allow
  end if
```

Algorithm 2 ComputePrincipals

```
Require:
Ensure: Returns set of matched principals ⟦ρ⟧
  ⟦ρ⟧ ← ∅
  for all (φ, ψ, p) ∈ ρ do
      if TargetSatisfactionTester(φ, true) then
          if TargetSatisfactionTester(ψ, false) then
              ⟦ρ⟧ ← ⟦ρ⟧ ∪ p
          end if
      end if
  end for
```

Algorithm 3 ComputeAuthorizations

```
Require:
Ensure: Returns set of authorization decisions ⟦ρ, ϱ⟧
  ⟦ρ, ϱ⟧ ← ∅
  for all (p, φ, ψ, y, d) ∈ ϱ do
      if (p ∈ ⟦ρ⟧) and ((y = a) or (y = ⋆)) then
          if TargetSatisfactionTester(φ, true) then
              if TargetSatisfactionTester(ψ, false) then
                  ⟦ρ, ϱ⟧ ← ⟦ρ, ϱ⟧ ∪ d
              end if
          end if
      end if
  end for
  if (χ = DenyOverride) and (0 ∈ ⟦ρ, ϱ⟧) then
      ⟦ρ, ϱ⟧ ← {0}
  else if (χ = AllowOverride) and (1 ∈ ⟦ρ, ϱ⟧) then
      ⟦ρ, ϱ⟧ ← {1}
  end if
```

6. RELATED WORK

Relationship-based access control (ReBAC) continues to receive growing attention as a more context-aware paradigm for request authorization than the commonly deployed role-based access control. Early research on ReBAC focused on social networks [5, 6, 7, 13], while more recent work has considered its use in general computing applications [8, 9, 10, 16]. However, the administration of these access control models has received limited attention so far.

Models applied to social networking have focused on how users specify policies controlling access to existing resources. Who is authorized to define such policies is determined in one of three ways: (i) an "ownership" relation [4], (ii) the existence of more senior users within the system [6, 14], or (iii) by an external system administrator (of some kind) [3]. As these models do not abstract authorization policy in the manner that we do, the policies in question are ap-

[8]We advocate pre-computing, as far as possible, the generic request automaton M_q (which forms the basis for each extended path condition-specific NFA M_{q_i}) and the path condition NFAs for all path expressions in the authorization policies so as to reduce the processing involved during request evaluation.

Algorithm 4 ApplyDefaults

Require: Check default-per-subject indicator *cdpsi*
Ensure: Returns a single element set of authorization decisions, $\{0\}$ or $\{1\}$

if $o = (v_1, t_1, v_2, t_2, r)$ **then**
  if $(cdpsi = \textbf{true})$ **and** $(\omega_a(s) \neq \bot)$ **then**
    return $\emptyset \cup \omega_a(s)$
  else
    return $\emptyset \cup \omega_a(\mathsf{sys})$
  end if
else if $o = v$ **then**
  if $(cdpsi = \textbf{true})$ **and** $(\omega(s) \neq \bot)$ **then**
    return $\emptyset \cup \omega(s)$
  else if $\omega(o) \neq \bot$ **then**
    return $\emptyset \cup \omega(o)$
  else if $\omega(\tau(o)) \neq \bot$ **then**
    return $\emptyset \cup \omega(\tau(o))$
  else
    return $\emptyset \cup \omega(\mathsf{sys})$
  end if
end if

proximately equivalent to a combination of our principal-matching policy and authorization policy.

Cheng *et al.* [6] make use of a "controlling user" to define policies for entities under their control. Whilst they use an ownership relation as an example indicator of this control, alternative relationships are acceptable. However, no indication is given as to how policy specification is authorized to these controlling users. Nor is consideration given as to how the necessary relationships are initially acquired.

Hu *et al.* [14] allow for a variable number of controllers (owner, contributor, stakeholders and disseminator) contributing to the policy. Whilst these controllers are identified with implementation specific constructs (based on a "space" within a social network) it is easy to imagine that they could be determined by the existence of relationships with a shared data item entity. As with the work by Cheng *et al.*, whilst the presence of the necessary relationships is clear, an actual authorization mechanism seems to be unspecified and no consideration is given to the creation and deletion of data items or relationships.

Carminati *et al.* [3] introduced *admin policies* as one of three policy types within their semantic web model for social network access control. The admin policies are determined by the "Security Administrator" of a social network. A policy of the form *antecedent* $\Rightarrow$ *consequent* is based on relationships between a user and a resource such that if the combination of properties and relationships identified in the *antecedent* are true then the *consequent* results. The *consequent* indicates the actions the user can grant or prohibit on that resource. However, they do not manage the creation and deletion of resources, being limited to actions performed on resources that already exist.

It is only recently that the more fundamental question of how the addition and deletion of entities and their relationships are administered has been considered. Stoller's RPPM^2 model [20] provided the ability to add and delete edges, entities, and authorization rules (once again a combination of our principal-matching policy and authorization policy), as well as the ability to set defaults and a conflict resolution strategy. However, RPPM^2 does not support the modification of the underlying system model and actions (unlike ARPPM). Moreover RPPM^2 is unable to support the more advanced features of RPPM that we do, and, we believe, requires more intensive computation to evaluate requests.

In their healthcare implementation of ReBAC, Rizvi *et al.* [16] identify specific administrative actions which are associated with "applicability preconditions" and have "effects" which add or delete edges. The applicability precondition is equivalent to a set of path conditions which must be satisfied between the "participants" of the action (including the subject and object). This construction is not dissimilar to the one described in this paper; however, ours is more generic still as it does not bind graph modifications to implementation specific actions and it also supports path condition satisfaction between arbitrary entities.

7. CONCLUSION

We have identified a set of seven user requirements for any administrative RPPM model. These requirements motivate the work described in this paper, highlighting best practice and desirable properties of the administration of a relationship-based access control model. Our main contribution is to introduce ARPPM – an administrative RPPM model which meets these requirements.

The ARPPM model defines the syntax for administrative policies and requests, and an evaluation mechanism for administrative authorization requests, which together control the addition and deletion of entities and edges in the system graph. In conjunction with the definition of an initial system graph, this allows ARPPM to support the complete administration of an ARPPM instance.

The matching of security principals to requests is performed in a similar manner to that used in the RPPM model. However, in order to provide full administrative control we introduce the notion of entity conditions, extended path conditions and path expressions. Entity conditions are used to specify the region in the system graph, relative to the entities in a request, within which the path condition must be satisfied (or not). When used in path expressions, these extended path conditions allow robust policy rules to be defined enforcing the existence (or otherwise) of multiple paths between pairs of entities within the system graph. Those entities may be directly involved in the request, independent of the request but individually specified, or more arbitrary.

As well as employing path expressions within principal-matching rules we also use them in authorization rules. In this way, certain paths of relationships may define the requirements for which principals are matched to a request, whilst others define the constraints determining which actions those principals are authorized to perform.

The ARPPM model can equally well support administrative requests made by non-user entities as those by users. We believe that such automated administrative agents may be useful for supporting existing, and future, advanced model features. We plan to develop the details of these automated administrative agents in the future. We also plan to consider strategies for partitioning the system graph into sub-graphs. We believe "hub" entities may be used to create "bridges" between these sub-graphs, thus enabling system graph partitioning, which, in turn, may reduce the storage required for the system graph and policies and the time required for request evaluation. The policies for each sub-graph would be managed independently, thus allowing for a more distributed administration model.

8. REFERENCES

[1] Bell, D., and La Padula, L. Secure computer systems: A mathematical model. volume ii. Tech. rep., The MITRE Corporation, Bedford, Massachusetts, Nov 1973. AD0771543.

[2] Bell, D., and La Padula, L. Secure computer systems: Mathematical foundations. Tech. rep., The MITRE Corporation, Bedford, Massachusetts, Nov 1973. AD0770768.

[3] Carminati, B., Ferrari, E., Heatherly, R., Kantarcioglu, M., and Thuraisingham, B. M. A semantic web based framework for social network access control. In *SACMAT 2009, 14th ACM Symposium on Access Control Models and Technologies, Stresa, Italy, June 3-5, 2009, Proceedings* (2009), B. Carminati and J. Joshi, Eds., ACM, pp. 177–186.

[4] Carminati, B., Ferrari, E., and Perego, A. Rule-based access control for social networks. In *On the Move to Meaningful Internet Systems 2006: OTM 2006 Workshops, OTM Confederated International Workshops and Posters, AWeSOMe, CAMS, COMINF, IS, KSinBIT, MIOS-CIAO, MONET, OnToContent, ORM, PerSys, OTM Academy Doctoral Consortium, RDDS, SWWS, and SeBGIS 2006, Montpellier, France, October 29 - November 3, 2006. Proceedings, Part II* (2006), R. Meersman, Z. Tari, and P. Herrero, Eds., vol. 4278 of *Lecture Notes in Computer Science*, Springer, pp. 1734–1744.

[5] Carminati, B., Ferrari, E., and Perego, A. Enforcing access control in web-based social networks. *ACM Trans. Inf. Syst. Secur. 13*, 1 (2009).

[6] Cheng, Y., Park, J., and Sandhu, R. S. Relationship-based access control for online social networks: Beyond user-to-user relationships. In *SocialCom/PASSAT* (2012), IEEE, pp. 646–655.

[7] Cheng, Y., Park, J., and Sandhu, R. S. A user-to-user relationship-based access control model for online social networks. In *DBSec* (2012), N. Cuppens-Boulahia, F. Cuppens, and J. García-Alfaro, Eds., vol. 7371 of *Lecture Notes in Computer Science*, Springer, pp. 8–24.

[8] Crampton, J., and Sellwood, J. Caching and auditing in the RPPM model. In *Security and Trust Management - 10th International Workshop, STM 2014, Wroclaw, Poland, September 10-11, 2014. Proceedings* (2014), S. Mauw and C. D. Jensen, Eds., vol. 8743 of *Lecture Notes in Computer Science*, Springer, pp. 49–64.

[9] Crampton, J., and Sellwood, J. Path conditions and principal matching: a new approach to access control. In *SACMAT* (2014), S. L. Osborn, M. V. Tripunitara, and I. Molloy, Eds., ACM, pp. 187–198.

[10] Crampton, J., and Sellwood, J. Relationships, paths and principal matching: a new approach to access control. *CoRR abs/1505.07945* (2015).

[11] Department of Defense. Trusted computer system evaluation criteria. *Department of Defense Standard* (1985). DoD 5200.28-STD.

[12] Ferraiolo, D. F., and Kuhn, D. R. Role-based access controls. In *Proceedings of the Fifteenth National Computer Security Conference* (1992), NSA/NIST.

[13] Fong, P. W. L. Relationship-based access control: protection model and policy language. In *CODASPY* (2011), R. S. Sandhu and E. Bertino, Eds., ACM, pp. 191–202.

[14] Hu, H., and Ahn, G. Multiparty authorization framework for data sharing in online social networks. In *Data and Applications Security and Privacy XXV - 25th Annual IFIP WG 11.3 Conference, DBSec 2011, Richmond, VA, USA, July 11-13, 2011. Proceedings* (2011), Y. Li, Ed., vol. 6818 of *Lecture Notes in Computer Science*, Springer, pp. 29–43.

[15] Li, N., and Mao, Z. Administration in role-based access control. In *Proceedings of the 2007 ACM Symposium on Information, Computer and Communications Security, ASIACCS 2007, Singapore, March 20-22, 2007* (2007), F. Bao and S. Miller, Eds., ACM, pp. 127–138.

[16] Rizvi, S. Z. R., Fong, P. W. L., Crampton, J., and Sellwood, J. Relationship-based access control for an open-source medical records system. In *Proceedings of the 20th ACM Symposium on Access Control Models and Technologies, Vienna, Austria, June 1-3, 2015* (2015), E. R. Weippl, F. Kerschbaum, and A. J. Lee, Eds., ACM, pp. 113–124.

[17] Saltzer, J. H., and Schroeder, M. D. The protection of information in computer systems. *Proceedings of the IEEE 63*, 9 (1975), 1278–1308.

[18] Sandhu, R. S., Bhamidipati, V., and Munawer, Q. The ARBAC97 model for role-based administration of roles. *ACM Trans. Inf. Syst. Secur. 2*, 1 (1999), 105–135.

[19] Sandhu, R. S., and Samarati, P. Access control: principle and practice. *Communications Magazine, IEEE 32*, 9 (1994), 40–48.

[20] Stoller, S. An administrative model for relationship-based access control. In *Data and Applications Security and Privacy XXIX* (2015), pp. 53–68.

APPENDIX

A. SUPPORTING ALGORITHM

Algorithm 5 (TargetSatisfactionTester) supports the ComputePrincipals and ComputeAuthorizations algorithms by performing the key NFA and path expression-related processing required to determine whether a target is satisfied within the system graph, in the context of the current request. This processing involves iterations over each extended path condition within the target path expression in order to produce the necessary intersection NFAs, to determine whether accepting languages exist for these NFAs, and to ensure that the entity constraints are met in producing those accepting languages.

We have created a Python implementation of the complete ARPPM request evaluation process (Algorithms 1 through 5) and have tested it, successfully, using the examples within this paper and those within the appendix example of [9].

Algorithm 5 TargetSatisfactionTester

Require: Target φ (one of the special targets all or none, or a path expression containing $|\varphi|$ extended path conditions), and positive target indicator *pti*
Ensure: Returns **true** if the target satisfaction matches the positive target indicator and **false** otherwise

if ($\varphi =$ all) **and** ($pti =$ **true**) **then**
  return true
else if ($\varphi =$ none) **and** ($pti =$ **false**) **then**
  return true
else if ($\varphi =$ all) **or** ($\varphi =$ none) **then**
  return false
else
  $f_{EC} : \mathbb{N}_{\leq|\varphi|} \times \{\text{start-node}, \text{end-node}\} \rightarrow 2^V$ // maps extended path conditions' entity conditions to entities
  for all $(e_i, f_i) \cdot \pi_i \cdot (e_i', f_i') \in \varphi$ **do**
    $f_{EC}(i, \text{start-node}) \leftarrow \emptyset$
    $f_{EC}(i, \text{end-node}) \leftarrow \emptyset$
    $s_{M_{q_i}} \leftarrow [\![(e_i, f_i), q]\!]$
    $F_{M_{q_i}} \leftarrow [\![(e_i', f_i'), q]\!]$
    if $(s_{M_{q_i}} = \emptyset)$ **or** $(F_{M_{q_i}} = \emptyset)$ **then**
      continue
    end if
    $M_{\pi_i} \leftarrow \text{PathExpressionNFA}(\pi_i)$ // produce $M_{\pi_i} = (Q_{\pi_i}, \Sigma_{\pi_i}, \delta_{\pi_i}, s_{\pi_i}, F_{\pi_i})$ as per [10]
    $M_{q_i} \leftarrow (V, \widetilde{R}, E, s_{M_{q_i}}, F_{M_{q_i}})$
    $M_{\cap_i} \leftarrow M_{\pi_i} \cap M_{q_i}$ // note $M_{\cap_i} = (V \times Q_{\pi_i}, \widetilde{R} \cap \Sigma_{\pi_i}, \delta_{\cap_i}, (s_{M_{q_i}}, s_{\pi_i}), F_{M_{q_i}} \times F_{\pi_i})$
    if $L(M_{\cap_i}) = \emptyset$ **then**
      continue
    else
      $f_{EC}(i, \text{start-node}) \leftarrow s_{M_{q_i}}$
      $AP = \{h_0, \ldots, h_x : h_0 = (s_{M_{q_i}}, s_{\pi_i}), h_y \in V \times Q_{\pi_i} \text{ for } y > 0, h_x \in F_{M_{q_i}} \times F_{\pi_i}, (h_z, h_{z+1}, \sigma_{z+1}) \in \delta_{\cap_i} \text{ for } 0 \leq z \leq x-1\}$
      $f_{EC}(i, \text{end-node}) \leftarrow \{u_{q_i} \in V : h_0, \ldots, h_x \in AP, h_x = (u_{\pi_i}, u_{q_i})\}$
    end if
  end for
  for all $(e_j, f_j) \cdot \pi_j \cdot (e_j', f_j') \in \varphi$ **do**
    if $f_j \in Var_T$ **then**
      // simple entity condition containing a type variable
      $T_{j_{sn}} \leftarrow \{t \in T : \exists u_{j_{sn}} \in f_{EC}(j, \text{start-node}), \tau(u_{j_{sn}}) = t\}$
      if $f_j' = f_j$ **then**
        $f_{EC}(j, \text{end-node}) \leftarrow \{u_{j_{en}} \in f_{EC}(j, \text{end-node}) : \tau(u_{j_{en}}) \in T_{j_{sn}}\}$
      end if
      for all $(e_k, f_k) \cdot \pi_k \cdot (e_k', f_k') \in \varphi$ **do**
        if $(k \neq j)$ **and** $(f_k = f_j)$ **then**
          $f_{EC}(k, \text{start-node}) \leftarrow \{u_{k_{sn}} \in f_{EC}(k, \text{start-node}) : \tau(u_{k_{sn}}) \in T_{j_{sn}}\}$
        else if $(k \neq j)$ **and** $(f_k' = f_j)$ **then**
          $f_{EC}(k, \text{end-node}) \leftarrow \{u_{k_{en}} \in f_{EC}(k, \text{end-node}) : \tau(u_{k_{en}}) \in T_{j_{sn}}\}$
        end if
      end for
    else if $f_j' \in Var_T$ **then**
      // entity condition containing a type variable
      $T_{j_{en}} \leftarrow \{t \in T : \exists u_{j_{en}} \in f_{EC}(j, \text{end-node}), \tau(u_{j_{en}}) = t\}$
      for all $(e_l, f_l) \cdot \pi_l \cdot (e_l', f_l') \in \varphi$ **do**
        if $(l \neq j)$ **and** $(f_l = f_j')$ **then**
          $f_{EC}(l, \text{start-node}) \leftarrow \{u_{l_{sn}} \in f_{EC}(l, \text{start-node}) : \tau(u_{l_{sn}}) \in T_{j_{en}}\}$
        else if $(l \neq j)$ **and** $(f_l' = f_j')$ **then**
          $f_{EC}(l, \text{end-node}) \leftarrow \{u_{l_{en}} \in f_{EC}(l, \text{end-node}) : \tau(u_{l_{en}}) \in T_{j_{en}}\}$
        end if
      end for
    else if $e_j' \in Var_V$ **then**
      // entity condition containing an entity variable
      for all $(e_m, f_m) \cdot \pi_m \cdot (e_m', f_m') \in \varphi$ **do**
        if $(m \neq j)$ **and** $(e_m' = e_j')$ **then**
          $f_{EC}(m, \text{end-node}) \leftarrow \{u_{m_{en}} \in f_{EC}(m, \text{end-node}) : u_{m_{en}} \in f_{EC}(j, \text{end-node})\}$
        end if
      end for
    end if
  end for
  if $pti =$ **true then**
    if $\forall (e_n, f_n) \cdot \pi_n \cdot (e_n', f_n') \in \varphi$: $(f_{EC}(n, \text{start-node}) \neq \emptyset)$ **and** $(f_{EC}(n, \text{end-node}) \neq \emptyset)$ **then**
      return true
    end if
  else
    if $\forall (e_o, f_o) \cdot \pi_o \cdot (e_o', f_o') \in \varphi$: $(f_{EC}(o, \text{start-node}) = \emptyset)$ **and** $(f_{EC}(o, \text{end-node}) = \emptyset)$ **then**
      return true
    end if
  end if
  return false
end if

Interoperability of Relationship- and Role-Based Access Control

Syed Zain R. Rizvi Philip W. L. Fong
University of Calgary
Alberta, Canada
{szrrizvi, pwlfong}@ucalgary.ca

ABSTRACT

Relationship-Based Access Control (ReBAC) was recently proposed as a general-purpose, application-layer access control paradigm, such that authorization decisions are based on the relationship between the access requestor and the resource owner. A first, large-scale implementation of ReBAC in an open-source medical records system was recently attempted by Rizvi *et al.*

In this work, we extend the ReBAC model of Rizvi *et al.* to support fine-grained interoperability between the ReBAC model and legacy Role-Based Access Control (RBAC) models. This is achieved by the introduction of the notion of demarcations as well as an authorization-time constraint system. Also presented are the design of two authorization algorithms (one of which has an algorithmic structure akin to an SMT solver), their optimization via memoization, and the empirical evaluation of their performances.

CCS Concepts

•**Security and privacy** → **Access control;**

Keywords

Relationship-based access control, role-based access control, interoperability, demarcations, constraints, lazy evaluation, memoization.

1. INTRODUCTION

Access Control is a cornerstone of application security. For several decades, ***Role-Based Access Control (RBAC)*** [26] has been the dominant access control model for the application layer of computer systems. RBAC facilitates administration by having roles as an intermediary abstraction between users and privileges.

Recent authors have advocated the use of ***Relationship-Based Access Control (ReBAC)*** as a general-purpose access control paradigm [14, 16, 7, 10, 9, 15, 13, 24] for organizational applications. This is mainly motivated by the need for fine-grained authorization, such that access is not only determined by job functions (as in RBAC), but also by how the access requestor and the resource owner are related to one another within the organization (e.g., not all doctors can access, but only my family doctor may access). ReBAC policies also facilitate the expression of trust delegation (e.g., consultants referred by my family doctor may access) [14]. Electronic Health Records (EHR) systems are considered an archetypical application domain for deploying ReBAC. Rizvi *et al.* recently reported the first large-scale implementation of ReBAC in an open-source EHR system, OpenMRS [24].

Due to significant investment, RBAC is not going to disappear soon. Any extension of an existing software application to incorporate ReBAC must find a way for the new access control model to interoperate harmoniously with the legacy RBAC model. One path of least resistance is taken by Rizvi *et al.*'s implementation: an access request is granted when both the ReBAC and RBAC authorization mechanisms grant access. Otherwise, ReBAC and RBAC are essentially orthogonal to one another.

In this work, we argue that there are important reasons to allow ReBAC and RBAC to interact with one another in more fine-grained ways than in the work of Rizvi *et al.* In particular, there are important classes of access control policies that applications may need to support:

- **Privilege inheritance between roles and relationships.** For example, a family doctor (a relationship-based principal) is also a general practitioner, or GP (a role-based principal). Privileges granted to a GP shall also be granted to any family doctor. This is an example in which relationship-based principals inherit the privileges of role-based principals. The other direction (role-based principals inheriting from relationship-based principals) shall also be supported.
- **Mutual exclusion between roles and relationships.** When a requestor attempts to justify her access by a certain relationship, the security policy may not allow her to simultaneously justify her access using certain roles. For example, suppose a specialist is a role-based principal, and, as before, a family doctor is a relationship-based principal. If a clinician attempts to justify access by claiming she is both a specialist and a family doctor, then something suspicious maybe going on. One either acts as a specialist or a family doctor, but not both.
- **Qualification and refinement between roles and relationships.** In order to supervise a medical intern (a relationship-based principal), one needs to have the

CODASPY'16, March 9–11, 2016, New Orleans, LA, USA.

DOI: http://dx.doi.org/10.1145/2857705.2857706

qualification of a doctor (a role-based principal). In short, the principal supervisor is a refinement of the principal doctor.

In this work, we extend the ReBAC model of Rizvi *et al.* to support the above fine-grained interactions between roles and relationships. Our specific contributions are the following:

1. We introduce the notion of demarcations [20] into Rizvi *et al.*'s ReBAC model. This minor extension allows privilege inheritance to work across the boundary of ReBAC and RBAC (§2).
2. We propose an *authorization-time* constraint system that supports (a) using roles as qualification requirements of relationships (and vice versa), and (b) preventing the use of an incompatible pair of role and relationship to justify access (§3).
   Note that constraint enforcement is performed at the time of an authorization check. This stands in sharp contrast to static constraints in RBAC systems, in which constraints are enforced at the time when a session is initiated. Authorization time enforcement is necessitated by the fact that membership in relationship-based principals is established at the time of authorization (just like how it is done in UNIX [12]).
   At the time of authorization, the access control subsystem attempts to construct a rationale that justifies the requested access. This access justification consists of a set of role- and relationship-based principals. Our constraints essentially restrict how a legitimate access justification can be formed by the various principals.
3. As one would expect, constraint enforcement is computationally hard (NP-complete). To repeatedly verify constraint satisfaction for each authorization is, at least in theory, a computational challenge. We thus propose two authorization procedures, based respectively on eager and lazy evaluation, for enforcing constraints. The lazy authorization procedure has an algorithmic structure akin to an SMT solver: it uses a SAT solver to opportunistically discover computationally intensive subtasks, and uses learned clauses to constrain its search space (§4).
4. We propose three caching schemes to optimize the two authorization procedures above (§5).
5. We evaluate the performance of our authorization algorithms and caching schemes in a simulated environment (§6). A surprising result is that, even though in theory constraint enforcement is computationally hard, our authorization algorithms and caching strategies deliver competitive performance, thereby demonstrating that our scheme for ReBAC/RBAC interoperability is computationally feasible in practice.

2. ReBAC/DEMARCATIONS

We use the umbrella term ***ReBAC2015*** to refer to the family of access control models presented in this paper as well the one presented in Rizvi *et al.* [24]. We begin this section by reviewing the first member of this family: the ReBAC model of Rizvi *et al.* (§2.1). Then in §2.2 we present a minor extension of Rizvi *et al.*'s model to incorporate the notion of ***demarcations*** [20]. This is followed by a discussion of how the provision of demarcations enables RBAC and ReBAC to interoperate in interesting ways (§2.3). By the end of this section, we will have all the notational devices needed for defining the constraint system of §3.

2.1 A Review of Core ReBAC2015

Recent authors have advocated the application of ReBAC to domains other than social computing [14, 16, 7, 10, 9, 15, 13, 24]. A general-purpose model of ReBAC was proposed in [14], in which the protection state is a social network — an edge-labelled, directed graph in which vertices represent users, edges represent interpersonal relationships, and edge labels represent relationship types.[1] Access control policies have the form "*grant access to o if rp*," where o is the resource protected by the policy, and rp is a ***relationship predicate*** of the form $rp(G, u, v)$, returning a boolean authorization decision based on whether the requestor v is related to the owner u of resource o in a specific way within the social network G. For example, a relationship predicate that returns 1 whenever u and v are within a distance of 2 in G captures the friend-of-friend policy. An innovation of [14] is the use of modal logic as a policy language for specifying predicates of the form $rp(G, u, v)$. The modal policy language was later found to be limited in expressiveness [16]. ***Hybrid logic*** (an extension of modal logic to incorporate first-order features) was subsequently proposed as a policy language for ReBAC, to overcome the aforementioned limitations [7].

Crampton and Sellwood proposed another general-purpose ReBAC model [13]. A first innovation is that the protection state is no longer a social network, but an edge-labelled, directed graph with vertices representing both users and resources. This ***authorization graph*** therefore captures not only user-to-user relationships, but also resource-to-resource relationships as well as user-to-resource relationships (cf. [9]). Consequently, authorization decisions can be based on a much wider class of relationships among system entities. A second innovation is the notion of ***authorization principals***, which is a relationship-based analogue of roles originally inspired by UNIX [12]. In UNIX there are three fixed principals — owner, group and world — permissions are granted to principals, and principal membership is determined by how the requester is related to the requested resource (e.g., owner, same group, etc). In the ReBAC model of Crampton and Sellwood, the administrator may define an arbitrary set of principals. The authorization decision is a function of two sets of rules. Firstly, ***principal matching rules*** associate principals with relationship predicates. At the time of request, if the requestor and the resource satisfy the relationship predicate associated with a principal, then the requestor is considered a member of that principal. This contrasts with the static membership of roles in RBAC. Secondly, ***authorization rules*** assign permissions (either positive or negative) to principals. At request time, users beloning to a principal will be granted the permissions associated with that principal. Because of the presence of both positive and negative permissions, conflict resolution strategies are also considered. A third innovation is the employment of a regular expression-based policy language for specifying relationship predicates (cf. [10, 9]).

Rizvi *et al.* implemented ReBAC in an open source medical records system, OpenMRS [24]. The implemented ReBAC model incorporates the authorization graph and au-

[1]More precisely, the protection state is a number of social networks, one for each ***context***. We overlook this subtlety to simplify discussion.

thorization principals of Crampton and Sellwood, and the hybrid logic of Bruns *et al.* as the specification language for relationship predicates. The methods of OpenMRS are protected by privilege requirements called ***guards***. To accommodate these guards, Rizvi *et al.* invented two different semantics for principal matching: ***liberal-grant*** and ***strict-grant*** semantics. In the rest of this paper, we call this ReBAC model of Rizvi *et al.* ***Core ReBAC2015***.[2]

2.2 Enters Demarcations

The rest of this section presents ***ReBAC2015/Demarcations***, which is a minor extension of Core ReBAC2015 to incorporate the notion of demarcations [20]. The aims of this presentation are (a) to standardize notations for the rest of the paper, (b) to demonstrate how RBAC and ReBAC can interoperate in interesting ways due to the provision of demarcations, and (c) to pave the way to the introduction of a new model ***ReBAC2015/Constraints*** in §3. The description of his model is accompanied by a running example in order to demonstrate the purpose of each component.

A demarcation is an abstract grouping of privileges, just like a role or an authorization principal is an abstract grouping of users. Access control policies are expressed partly by associating authorization principals with demarcations. Such a scheme decouples the management of privilege grouping, user grouping, and user-group/privilege-group association.

DEFINITION 1. *The protection state of ReBAC2015/Demarcations has the following components.*

- *O: The set of objects (resources).*
- *$S \subseteq O$: The set of subjects (users).*
- *I: The set of relation identifiers (i.e., relationship types).*
- *$G \subseteq I \times O \times O$: The authorization graph, in which $(i, u, v) \in G$ refers to an edge from vertex u to vertex v that is labelled with the relation identifier i.*
- *AP: The set of authorization principals.*
- *RP: The set of relationship predicates supported by the system. A relationship predicate is a function with signature $\mathcal{P}(I \times O \times O) \times O \times S \rightarrow \mathbb{B}$. That is, a relationship predicate $rp(G, o, s)$ is a function that takes an authorization graph G, a resource o and a requestor s as inputs, and returns a boolean value as output.*
- *$AR : AP \rightarrow RP$: The assignment of a relationship predicate to each authorization principal (i.e., the principal matching rules).*
- *DM: The set of demarcations.*
- *$\leq \subseteq DM \times DM$: The demarcation hierarchy is a partial ordering over the set of demarcations (i.e., reflexive, transitive, anti-symmetric). Given two demarcations $d_1, d_2 \in DM$ for which $d_1 \leq d_2$, we say that d_1 is* **inferior**, *and d_2 is* **superior**. *Intuitively, superior demarcations "inherit" privileges from inferior demarcations. See Definition 8 for details.*
- *$AD : AP \rightarrow DM$: A principal-demarcation assignment (i.e., the authorization rules).*
- *PR: The set of privileges.*
- *$PD \subseteq PR \times DM$: The privilege-demarcation assignment relation.*
- *MD: A set of methods (actions) that can be applied to objects.*
- *GD: A set of guards (privilege requirements) for methods (to be further defined in Definition 4).*
- *$MG : MD \rightarrow GD$: An assignment of a guard to every method.*

It is assumed that O, I, AP, PR, DM and MD are pairwise disjoint.

DEFINITION 2. *An* **authorization request** *(or simply* **request***) is a triple $(m, o, s) \in MD \times O \times S$, whereby user s requests that method m be applied to resource o.*

EXAMPLE 3. *Alice, a doctor, wishes to read the health record of Bob, her patient. Suppose the health record is composed of identification information, demographic information, clinical visits history, and prescriptions history. Alice wishes to read these all together instead of reading each component individually. To do this, she invokes the method* read_hr(bob_hr) *where* bob_hr *is Bob's health record. This method invocation gets translated to the authorization request (*read_hr*,* bob_hr*, Alice).*

DEFINITION 4. *A* **guard** *g is a specification of privilege requirements that must be satisfied by the requestor in order for the authorization request to be granted. A guard g can have either of the two forms:*

1. `one-of`*(ϕ), where $\phi \subseteq PR$, requires* one *of the privileges in ϕ.*
2. `all-of`*(ϕ), where $\phi \subseteq PR$, demands* all *of the privileges in ϕ.*

Formally, the following rules specify when we say that a privilege set $\varphi \subseteq PR$ **satisfies** *a guard g, written $\varphi \models g$.*

$$\varphi \models \texttt{one-of}(\phi) \text{ iff } \phi \cap \varphi \neq \emptyset$$
$$\varphi \models \texttt{all-of}(\phi) \text{ iff } \phi \subseteq \varphi$$

EXAMPLE 5. *Once the authorization request of Example 3 is issued, the guard $g_{\mathsf{read\_hr}} = MG(\mathsf{read\_hr})$ is looked up. Since a health record is composed of four components (Example 3), a separate privilege is required to read each component, and thus $g_{\mathsf{read\_hr}}$ is an* `all-of` *guard:*

$$g_{\mathsf{read\_hr}} = \texttt{all-of}(\{\, r_{id\_info}, r_{dem\_info}, r_{cv\_history}, r_{pres\_history} \,\}).$$

As an abstract grouping of users, authorization principals are the ReBAC analogue of roles in RBAC. Membership in a principal, however, depends on the resource that is being accessed, and thus principal membership is determined at the time of request. This contrasts sharply with role membership in RBAC, which is statically defined.

DEFINITION 6 (PRINCIPAL MATCHING). *Given a request (m, o, s), we say that an authorization principal $ap \in AP$ is* **enabled by** *s* **for** *o (or simply* **enabled***) whenever $rp(G, o, s) = 1$, where $rp = AR(ap)$. We write $\mathsf{enabled}_o(s)$ for the set of all authorization principals enabled by s for o:*

$$\mathsf{enabled}_o(s) = \{\, ap \in AP \mid AR(ap)(G, o, s) = 1 \,\} \quad (1)$$

EXAMPLE 7. *Continuing Example 5, we illustrate below how $\mathsf{enabled}_{\mathsf{bob\_hr}}(Alice)$ is computed.*

Suppose the system defines a principal FamDoc, for which $AR(FamDoc)$ is a relationship predicate rp such that

[2]Rizvi *et al.* also discuss a basic administrative model for ReBAC, but that is not relevant to this work.

$rp(G, o, s) = 1$ *whenever there is a directed edge with label* Family-Doctor *from the owner of o to the requestor s. Suppose further that Alice is indeed the family doctor of Bob, and thus such an edge exists. It follows that FamDoc* $\in \mathsf{enabled}_{bob\_hr}(Alice))$.

For subsequent examples, let us suppose the following:

$$\mathsf{enabled}_{bob\_hr}(Alice)) = \{\, FamDoc, GP, AuthUser \,\} \quad (2)$$

Intuitively, Alice is a member of the principal GP because she works as a general practitioner in the hospital, and she is a member of the principal AuthUser because she is an authenticated user.

DEFINITION 8 (PRIVILEGE INHERITANCE). *Suppose* $\alpha \subseteq AP$. *We define* $\mathsf{dem}(\alpha)$ *to be the set of demarcations associated with the authorization principals in* α, *and* $\mathsf{priv}(\alpha)$ *to be the set of privileges granted to the principals in* α. *Formally,*

$$\mathsf{dem}(\alpha) = \{\, d \in DM \mid \exists\, ap \in \alpha \,.\, d \leq AD(ap) \,\} \quad (3)$$

$$\mathsf{priv}(\alpha) = \{\, p \in PR \mid \exists\, d \in \mathsf{dem}(\alpha) \,.\, (p, d) \in PD \,\} \quad (4)$$

Note how superior demarcations inherit privileges from inferior ones.

EXAMPLE 9. *By* (2), (3) *and* (4), *we know the following:*

$$\mathsf{priv}(\mathsf{enabled}_{bob\_hr}(Alice)) = \mathsf{priv}(\{FamDoc\}) \cup \mathsf{priv}(\{GP\}) \cup \mathsf{priv}(\{AuthUser\})$$

Let us suppose that $\leq$, *AD and PD are defined such that the three principals are assigned the following privileges:*

$$\mathsf{priv}(\{FamDoc\}) = \{\, r_{id\_info}, r_{dem\_info}, r_{cv\_history}, r_{pres\_history}, \ldots \}$$
$$\mathsf{priv}(\{GP\}) = \{\, r_{id\_info}, r_{dem\_info}, \ldots \}$$
$$\mathsf{priv}(\{AuthUser\}) = \{ \ldots \}$$

We therefore have the following:

$$\mathsf{priv}(\mathsf{enabled}_{bob\_hr}(Alice)) = \{\, r_{id\_info}, r_{dem\_info}, r_{cv\_history}, r_{pres\_history}, \ldots \}$$

Like Core ReBAC2015 (§2.1), ReBAC2015/Demarcations can be configured with one of two authorization semantics — liberal grant or strict grant. Intuitively, a request is authorized in the liberal-grant semantics whenever the set of *all* enabled principals jointly supply the privileges required by the guard. In strict-grant semantics, a request is authorized when there exists *one* enabled principal that can "single-handedly" satisfy the guard.

DEFINITION 10 (LIBERAL GRANT). *A request* (m, o, s) *is authorized according to the* **liberal-grant semantics**, *denoted by the predicate* $\mathsf{auth}_{lib}(m, o, s)$, *iff the following holds:*

$$\mathsf{priv}(\mathsf{enabled}_o(s)) \models MG(m) \quad (5)$$

DEFINITION 11 (STRICT GRANT). *A request* (m, o, s) *is authorized according to the* **strict-grant** *semantics, denoted by the predicate* $\mathsf{auth}_{str}(m, o, s)$, *iff the following holds:*

$$\exists\, ap \in \mathsf{enabled}_o(s) \,.\, \Big(\mathsf{priv}(\{ap\}) \models MG(m) \Big) \quad (6)$$

It can be shown that the two semantics induce identical authorization decisions for `one-of` guards. They differ in behaviour only for `all-of` guards [24, footnote 7]. Moreover, if a request is authorized in the strict-grant semantics, then it is also authorized in the liberal-grant semantics [24, footnote 8].[3]

EXAMPLE 12. *If the system enforces liberal-grant semantics then the authorization decision will be based on* $\mathsf{priv}(\mathsf{enabled}_{bob\_hr}(Alice))$, *and access will be granted since:*

$$\mathsf{priv}(\mathsf{enabled}_{bob\_hr}(Alice)) \models g_{read\_hr}$$

On the other hand, if the system enforces strict-grant semantics, then access must be justifiable by a single principal. In this case, access is granted because FamDoc $\in \mathsf{enabled}_{bob\_hr}(Alice)$ *can "single-handedly" satisfy the guard:*

$$\mathsf{priv}(\{FamDoc\}) \models g_{read\_hr}$$

2.3 Interfacing ReBAC and RBAC

In Rizvi *et al.*'s implementation of ReBAC for OpenMRS, the ReBAC authorization scheme is layered on top of the legacy RBAC authorization scheme in an orthogonal manner: access is granted whenever both RBAC and ReBAC allow access [24]. Otherwise, the two authorization schemes do not interact with one another. Our extension of ReBAC with demarcations, as we shall see below, provides a clean mechanism for ReBAC2015 to interact with RBAC.

Embedding RBAC in ReBAC2015/Demarcations. We first describe how an RBAC protection state can be entirely embedded in a ReBAC2015/Demarcations protection state. Suppose an RBAC protection state is given: (R, RH, PA, UA). Here R is a set of roles. $RH \subseteq R \times R$, the role hierarchy, is a partial ordering such that $(r_1, r_2) \in RH$ means that r_1, a more senior role, dominates r_2, a more junior role, and thus r_1 inherits all privileges granted to r_2. $PA \subseteq PR \times R$ is the privilege assignment relation. $UA \subseteq S \times R$ is the user assignment relation. This RBAC protection state can be embedded in a ReBAC2015/Demarcations protection state using the following two-step construction.

1. *Role Predicates.* We define a principal ap_r for each role $r \in R$. The user assignment relation UA can be simulated by appropriately defined relationship predicates. Specifically, we formulate $AR(ap_r) = rp_r$ such that $rp_r(G, o, s) = 1$ whenever $(s, r) \in UA$. When formulated to capture role membership, a relationship predicate is also called a ***role predicate***. Otherwise, the relationship predicate is said to be ***proper***.
2. *Isometric Demarcations.* We create a demarcation d_r for each role $r \in R$, such that $AD(ap_r) = d_r$. Such an arrangement, in which each principal is paired with a distinct demarcation, is called ***isometric demarcations***. In addition, we define PD in such a way that $(p, d_r) \in PD$ whenever $(p, r) \in PA$. we define $\leq$ in such a way that $d_{r_1} \leq d_{r_2}$ iff $(r_2, r_1) \in RH$.

When ReBAC Interacts with RBAC. The more interesting scenario is when the ReBAC2015 protection state contains both principals defined by role predicates (a.k.a.

[3]There are two main differences between the present treatment of ReBAC2015/Demarcations and that of Core ReBAC2015 in [24]: (1) The treatment here is a mathematical formalization of the implementation-oriented description in [24]; (2) Demarcations are added into the model of [24].

role-based principals) as well as principals defined by proper relationship predicates (a.k.a. ***relationship-based principals***). Suppose FamDoc is a relationship-based principal, such that s belongs to FamDoc iff she is the family doctor of the owner of a patient record o. Say GP is a role-based principal, indicating that the requestor is a general practitioner. If $AD(\mathsf{GP}) \leq AD(\mathsf{FamDoc})$, then family doctors inherit the privileges granted to GPs. This illustrates how the demarcation hierarchy and authorization principals jointly support privilege inheritance across the boundary of ReBAC and RBAC.

3. REBAC2015/CONSTRAINTS

Comparing Definitions 10 and 11, one would notice that in both semantics, authorization is granted when a certain principal set $\alpha \subseteq \mathsf{enabled}_o(s)$ satisfies the condition below:

$$\mathsf{priv}(\alpha) \models MG(m) \quad (7)$$

For liberal-grant, α is $\mathsf{enabled}_o(s)$ itself; for strict-grant, α is constrained to be a singleton subset of $\mathsf{enabled}_o(s)$. To borrow RBAC terminology, the set α of enabled principals are "activated" to satisfy the guard of m. More precisely, the set α constitutes the justification of access.

Liberal- and strict-grant represent the two extreme ends of the design spectrum. Liberal-grant imposes no restriction on the choice of α, and thus α is chosen to be the maximal such set: i.e., $\mathsf{enabled}_o(s)$ itself. In strict-grant, it is required that privileges be contributed only by one principal, and thus α must be a singleton set. The intuition is that perhaps the set of privileges in `all-of` guards are so sensitive that access must be justified by a single principal capable enough to contribute all of them.

In some applications, however, restrictions on the selection of authorization principals for justifying access must be imposed according to the specific security needs of the application domain. For example, it may be the case that one authorization principal shall not be activated along with another authorization principal (mutual exclusion), or it may be the case that an authorization principal can only be activated in conjunction with another principal (prerequisite). Capturing these security restrictions in the form of a one-size-fits-all authorization semantics (e.g., liberal- or strict-grant) makes the access control model more rigid than necessary. In the following, we propose an extension of ReBAC2015 to incorporate the notion of authorization-time constraints, which specify restrictions over the choice of α, the set of principals to be activated to justify access. Note the difference between our authorization-time constraints and the traditional session-based constraints in RBAC. In the latter case, constraints such as static mutually exclusive roles are enforced at the time when a session is initiated. In our case, constraints are enforced every time when an access request is authorized, to ensure that a proper justification can be constructed for each authorized access.

3.1 The Extended Model

ReBAC2015/Constraints builds on ReBAC2015/Demarcations. Specifically, constraints are imposed over the constitution of the set α of principals in (7).

DEFINITION 13. *The protection state of ReBAC2015/Constraints is made up of the same components as ReBAC2015/Demarcations (Definition 1), plus the following two additional components.*

- $\# \subseteq AP \times AP$: *The* **Mutually Exclusive Authorization Principal (MEAP)** *constraints form an irreflexive binary relation $\#$ over AP. (A binary relation R is irreflexive if xRx is never true.) Intuitively, if $ap_1 \# ap_2$, then either ap_1 or ap_2, but not both, can be activated to satisfy a guard.*
- $\sqsubseteq \subseteq AP \times AP$: *The* **Prerequisite Authorization Principal Requirement (PAPR)** *constraints form a partial ordering $\sqsubseteq$ over AP (i.e., reflexive, transitive and anti-symmetric). Intuitively, if $ap_1 \sqsubseteq ap_2$, then ap_2 cannot be activated unless ap_1 is also activated.*

Intuitively, a MEAP constraint $ap_1 \# ap_2$ prevents the two principals ap_1 and ap_2 from being used simultaneously for forming access justification. Therefore, MEAP constraints are therefore used for modelling incompatibilities among access rationales.

On the other hand, a PAPR constraint $ap_1 \sqsubseteq ap_2$ ensures that ap_2 is used for justifying an access only if ap_1 is also used for justifying the same access. In other words, to activate ap_2, the requestor s must satisfy not only the relationship predicate $AR(ap_2)$, but also $AR(ap_1)$. PAPR constraints model the refinement of principal membership.

Constraint semantics is formalized in the definition below.

DEFINITION 14 (CONSTRAINT SATISFACTION). *Given a set $\alpha \subseteq AP$, we write* $\mathsf{consistent}(\alpha)$, *and say that α is* **consistent**, *iff the following conditions hold:*

$$\forall ap_1, ap_2 \in AP \,.\, (ap_1 \# ap_2 \Rightarrow (ap_1 \notin \alpha \vee ap_2 \notin \alpha)) \quad (8)$$

$$\forall ap_1, ap_2 \in AP \,.\, (ap_1 \sqsubseteq ap_2 \Rightarrow (ap_1 \in \alpha \vee ap_2 \notin \alpha)) \quad (9)$$

DEFINITION 15. *A request (m, o, s) is authorized by ReBAC2015/Constraints, denoted by the predicate $\mathsf{auth}_{con}(m, o, s)$, iff the following holds:*

$$\exists \alpha \subseteq \mathsf{enabled}_o(s) \,.\, \mathsf{consistent}(\alpha) \wedge (\mathsf{priv}(\alpha) \models MG(m)) \quad (10)$$

The principals in the set α above are said to be **activated** *(to satisfy $MG(m)$).*

Theorem 17 below formally justifies our previous characterization of liberal- and strict-grant semantics as the two extreme ends of the design spectrum. It turns out that, ReBAC2015/Constraints can be configured to various points between the two ends of the spectrum.

DEFINITION 16. *The protection state is said to be* **prerequisite-free** *iff $ap_1 \sqsubseteq ap_2$ implies $ap_1 = ap_2$. The protection state is* **conflict-free** *iff $\#$ is an empty relation (i.e., $ap_1 \# ap_2$ never holds). The protection state is* **conflict-complete** *iff $\#$ is maximal (i.e., $ap_1 \neq ap_2$ implies $ap_1 \# ap_2$).*

THEOREM 17 (EXPRESSIVENESS). *Suppose the protection state is prerequisite-free. Then:*

$$\mathsf{auth}_{str}(m, o, s) \Rightarrow \mathsf{auth}_{con}(m, o, s) \Rightarrow \mathsf{auth}_{lib}(m, o, s) \quad (11)$$

The first implication above is strengthened to a logical equivalence (i.e., $\mathsf{auth}_{str}(m, o, s) \Leftrightarrow \mathsf{auth}_{con}(m, o, s)$) when the protection state is conflict-complete. The second implication is strengthened to a logical equivalence (i.e., $\mathsf{auth}_{lib}(m, o, s) \Leftrightarrow \mathsf{auth}_{con}(m, o, s)$) when the protection state is conflict-free. In short, liberal- and strict-grant semantics are but two instantiations of ReBAC2015/Constraints.

The theorem follows directly from the definition.

3.2 Interfacing ReBAC and RBAC

The provision of MEAP and PAPR constraints allows one to express interesting interactions between ReBAC and RBAC. The following are some possibilities:

- Consider the role-based principal Specialist and the relationship-based principal FamDoc. Imposing the MEAP constraint Specialist # FamDoc ensures that the requestor acts as either a specialist or a family doctor, but not both. This constraint prevents inconsistent explanation of access rationale.
- Consider the role-based principal Doctor and the relationship-based principal Supervisor. Imposing the PAPR constraint Doctor $\sqsubseteq$ Supervisor ensures that only doctors can supervise medical interns, thus capturing the qualification requirement for a relationship.

4. ENFORCEMENT MECHANISMS

In ReBAC2015/Constraints, authorization involves the testing of condition (10). Two authorization algorithms, based respectively on the eager and lazy evaluation of relationship predicates, are presented in this section for testing (10). Comparison of their performance is deferred to §6.

4.1 Authorization via Eager Evaluation

Given an authorization request (m, o, s), a straightforward procedure for computing authorization decisions operationalizes (10) into the following two steps:

1. Compute the principal set $E = \mathsf{enabled}_o(s)$.
2. Decide if there exists $\alpha \subseteq E$ such that:

$$\mathsf{consistent}(\alpha) \land (\mathsf{priv}(\alpha) \models MG(m)) \qquad (12)$$

Step 1 involves going through each principal $ap \in AP$, and invoking a model checker to evaluate $AR(ap)(G, o, s)$ (assuming that relationship predicates are specified in hybrid logic [7]). Since multiple principals may share the same relationship predicate, the implementation may cache and reuse the result of evaluating $AR(ap)$ to prevent duplicated computations. Specifically, an empty cache is initialized every time Step 1 begins. Whenever a relationship predicate rp is evaluated to a Boolean value b, the pair $\langle rp, b\rangle$ is cached, so that next time the value of rp is needed, a cache lookup is performed. This optimization is called ***RP-caching***. Three different caching schemes will be discussed in §5.

Step 2 is a computationally hard problem:

The ReBAC2015/Constraints Authorization Problem (RE-AUTH)

Instance: A protection state (Def. 13), a set $E \subseteq AP$, and a method $m \in MD$.

Question: Does there exist $\alpha \subseteq E$ such that (12) holds?

THEOREM 18. RE-AUTH *is NP-complete.*

A proof of Thm 18 is given in Appendix A, which also shows that the MEAP constraints (#) are the source of complexity.

Step 2 can be implemented by a reduction of the RE-AUTH instance to a SAT instance, and using a SAT solver to solve the latter. Such a reduction is described in §4.3. Despite the NP-completeness result, performance profiling tells us that modern SAT solvers (such as [2]) can cope with Step 2 gracefully, because (a) the number of principals is only moderate in magnitude, and (b) most of the naturally-occurring RE-AUTH instances are easy.

Algorithm 1 Authorization Checking via Lazy Evaluation

Input: (m, o, s)

1: $F \leftarrow getSATInstance(AP, m)$
2: $satInitSolver(F)$
3: initialize $E[\cdot]$ to an empty map
4: $\sigma \leftarrow satNextModel()$
5: **if** $satNextModel()$ fails **then**
6: **return** "deny access"
7: **end if**
8: $\alpha \leftarrow extractPrincipals(\sigma)$
9: **for all** $ap \in \alpha$ **do**
10: $rp \leftarrow AR(ap)$
11: **if** $E[rp]$ is undefined **then**
12: $E[rp] \leftarrow rp(G, o, s)$
13: **end if**
14: **if** $E[rp] = 0$ **then**
15: $satAddClause((\neg ap))$
16: **goto** 4
17: **end if**
18: **end for**
19: **return** "allow access"

4.2 Authorization via Lazy Evaluation

From the experiences reported in [24, §10], a significant computational challenge lies within Step 1 above, in which the relationship predicate of each authorization principal is evaluated to determine if the principal is enabled. The hybrid logic model checker [22] must be invoked over an authorization graph of potentially formidable size. The process involves both backtracking as well as queries against very large databases. This motivates an alternative enforcement mechanism that employs a lazy strategy in discovering whether principals are enabled. This contrasts sharply with the previous authorization procedure, which eagerly evaluates the relationship predicates of all principals.

Our lazy strategy employs a SAT solver to enumerate all possible principal sets $\alpha \subseteq AP$ for which $\mathsf{priv}(\alpha) \models MG(m)$. For each α, the relationship predicates of principals in α are then model checked. Again, predicate value caching is applied (§4.1). Consequently, model checking is conducted only when it is needed.

Modern SAT solvers (e.g., [2]) offer two features that make this strategy possible. First, users may iterate through the models of a formula. Second, while iterating through the models, the user may add additional clauses to the formula in order to forbid certain models from being generated in subsequent iterations. This second feature is exploited by the lazy strategy, to exclude from future consideration those principals that have been found to be disabled. This effectively cuts down the number of models that need to be examined. Consequently, the algorithmic structure of our authorization procedure is akin to the structure of a modern SMT solver, in which a SAT solver drives the invocation of a theory solver, and learns new clauses to guide backtracking.

Algorithm 1 presents the lazy authorization procedure in the form of pseudocode. A line-by-line explanation of Algorithm 1 is provided in Appendix B. This particular incarnation of lazy authorization incorporates RP-caching (§4.1). Other caching schemes are discussed in §5.

4.3 Reducing RE-AUTH to SAT

We describe here a reduction of RE-AUTH to a CNF-SAT instance, so that a standard SAT solver can be employed to solve the problem. We start by fixing a data representation for the PAPR constraints and the demarcation hierarchy.

DEFINITION 19. *Suppose $ap_1 \sqsubseteq ap_2$ but $ap_1 \neq ap_2$. Then we write $ap_1 \sqsubset ap_2$. Suppose further, for every $ap \in AP$ for which $ap_1 \sqsubseteq ap \sqsubseteq ap_2$, either $ap = ap_1$ or $ap = ap_2$. Then we write $ap_1 \sqsubset' ap_2$.*

Similarly, we can define $<$ and $<'$ for the demarcation hierarchy ($\leq$).

We assume that $\sqsubset'$ and $<'$ are available to the reduction algorithm. The algorithm would run correctly even if $\sqsubset$ and $<$ are used in place of $\sqsubset'$ and $<'$, but the CNF generated by the reduction would not be as compact.

Our reduction produces a CNF formula F with $|E|+|DM|$ variables: one for each principal in E, and one for each demarcation in DM. As $E \subseteq AP$, the number of variables is bounded by $|AP| + |DM|$. To simplify our notation, we write ap_i to denote the variable corresponding to principal ap_i, and d_j to denote the variable representing demarcation d_j. By construction, if the formula F is satisfied by a truth assignment σ, then:

- Let α be the set of principals $ap \in E$ for which $\sigma(ap) = 1$, and let δ be the set of demarcations $d \in DM$ for which $\sigma(d) = 1$.
- We know that $\delta = \mathsf{dem}(\alpha)$ and α satisfies (12).

Thus, both the activated principals and their corresponding demarcations can be recovered from a model of F.

Given a request (m, o, s), the formula F produced by the reduction has the following form:

$$F = F_{guard} \wedge F_{MEAP} \wedge F_{PAPR} \wedge F_{DH} \tag{13}$$

Each of F_{guard}, F_{MEAP}, F_{PAPR} and F_{DH} is a CNF formula (i.e., a set of clauses). F_{guard} encodes the guard of the method involved in the request. The other three encode the protection state. We describe their construction in turn.

Construction of F_{guard}. This formula contains clauses that encode the privilege requirements of method m. Let g be the guard $MG(m)$. Then g can be in either one of two forms: `one-of(`ϕ`)` or `all-of(`ϕ`)`.

Case g = `one-of(`ϕ`)`: Let $\delta(\phi) = \{ d \in DM \mid \exists p \in \phi \,.\, (p, d) \in PD \}$, the set of demarcations that offer at least one privilege in ϕ. The clause $\left(\bigvee_{d \in \delta(\phi)} d\right)$ is added into F_{guard}. This ensures that at least one demarcation that provides at least one of the privileges in ϕ is granted.

Case g = `all-of(`ϕ`)`: Let $\delta(p) = \{ d \in DM \mid (p, d) \in PD \}$, the set of demarcations that offers p. For each $p \in \phi$, the clause $\left(\bigvee_{d \in \delta(p)} d\right)$ is added into F_{guard}. This ensures every privilege in ϕ is provided by a granted demarcation.

Construction of F_{MEAP}. The clauses in F_{MEAP} enforce the MEAP constraints (#). For every (unordered) pair of principals $ap_1, ap_2 \in E$ such that $ap_1 \# ap_2$, the clause $(\neg ap_1 \vee \neg ap_2)$ is added into F_{MEAP}. This ensures that ap_1 and ap_2 are not both activated.

Construction of F_{PAPR}. The clauses in F_{PAPR} enforce PAPR constraints ($\sqsubseteq$). These clauses are of two kinds.

First, for each pair of principals $ap_1, ap_2 \in E$ for which $ap_1 \sqsubset' ap_2$, the clause $(ap_1 \vee \neg ap_2)$ is added into F_{PAPR}. This ensures that ap_2 is not activated unless ap_1 is activated.

Second, for each principal $ap_2 \in E$ for which there is a principal $ap_1 \in AP \setminus E$ such that $ap_1 \sqsubset' ap_2$, the unit clause $(\neg ap_2)$ is added into F_{PAPR}. This ensures that principals with prerequisites outside of E are not activated.

Construction of F_{DH}. This formula models the demarcation hierarchy ($\leq$) and the authorization rules (AD). For each $d \in DM$, a clause C_d is added into F_{DH}. The clause C_d has the form

$$\left(\neg d \vee \left(\bigvee_{ap \in \alpha} ap \right) \vee \left(\bigvee_{d \in \delta} d \right) \right) \tag{14}$$

where $\alpha = \{ ap \in E \mid AD(ap) = d \}$ and $\delta = \{ d' \in DM \mid d <' d' \}$. This clause ensures that the demarcation d is granted only if either one of the principals associated with it is activated, or one of its immediate superior demarcations is granted. Note that, if α and δ are both empty, C_d becomes the unit clause $(\neg d)$, and d will not be activated at all.

Additional implementation strategies for generating and storing these SAT instances are described in Appendix C.

5. CACHING STRATEGIES

Preliminary tests revealed that evaluating relationship predicates by a model checker is computationally more demanding than solving RE-AUTH instances using a SAT solver, and thus reducing the amount of work done by the model checker can potentially optimize the enforcement mechanism. This can be achieved by caching the results of computations previously performed by the model checker and reusing those results when possible. This section presents three caching strategies that can potentially improve the performance of the authorization procedure. Comparison of their performance is deferred to §6.2.

Note that these caching strategies do not cache authorization decions across authorization requests. The purpose of these caching strategies is to facilitate the computation of a single authorization decision.

AP-Caching. The idea behind this caching strategy is to prevent repeating principal membership tests. During the authorization of a request (m, o, s), we ensure that $AR(ap)(G, o, s)$ is computed at most once for each ap, and the result is cached. If membership in ap needs to be checked again during the authorization of the same request, then the cached result is reused. This caching strategy is not useful for the eager evaluation strategy, as membership in each principal is checked only once. AP-caching, however, is effective for the lazy evaluation strategy. Recall that the lazy evaluation strategy repeatedly generates sets $\alpha \subseteq AP$ for which $\mathsf{consistent}(\alpha) \wedge \left(\mathsf{priv}(\alpha) \models MG(m)\right)$. For each such α, it tests if $\alpha \subseteq \mathsf{enabled}_o(s)$ by making an invocation of the model checker for each $ap \in \alpha$. Now, suppose α_1 and α_2 are two candidate principal sets generated by the lazy authorization procedure. Then membership for those principals in $\alpha_1 \cap \alpha_2$ will be tested twice. AP caching is designed to optimize away such repeated membership tests.

RP-Caching. The idea behind this caching strategy is to prevent computing $rp(G, o, s)$ more than once, for any given $rp \in RP$. During the authorization of a request (m, o, s), suppose membership in principal ap is to be tested. Let $rp = AR(ap)$. The model checker is invoked to compute $b = rp(G, o, s)$. The pair $\langle rp, b \rangle$ is then cached. When membership of another principal ap' is to be tested later during the authorization of the same request, if a pair $\langle AR(ap'), b' \rangle$

Parameter	Values
$\|PR\|$	$\{3 \times \|AP\|\}$
$\|PD\|$	$\{7 \times \|AP\|\}$
$\|\phi\|$	$\{3\}$
$\|AP\|$	{50, 100, 150, 200}
$\|\#\|$	{50, 100, 150, ..., 500}
$\|\sqsubset'\|$	{50, 100, 150, ..., 500}
$\|<'\|$	{50, 100, 150, ..., 500}

Table 1: Parameters used for test cases.

is found in the cache, the value b' is reused rather than computed from scratch. This caching strategy utilizes the fact that multiple authorization principals may share a common relationship predicate. This reduces the number of times the model checker is invoked during an authorization check, for both the eager and lazy evaluation strategy. More specifically, the model checker is invoked at most $|RP'|$ times for an authorization check, where RP' is the range of the function AR on input AP. It should be simple to observe that if each authorization principal has a distinct relationship predicate (i.e. $|AP| = |RP'|$), then RP-caching behaves the same as AP-caching. In general, AP-caching is no more effective than RP-caching.

MC-Cross-Caching. This third caching scheme exploits the memoization mechanism of the hybrid logic model checker in a creative way. The model checker in the ReBAC Java Library implements the inductively specified semantics of Bruns *et al.* [7]. As such, the model checker has a recursive structure. To prevent pathological cases and to speed up model checking, the model checking procedure caches the return values of recursive calls — a technique commonly known as ***memoization*** in functional programming literature [28, §19.6]. The cache is local to the model checker instance. In the implementation of AP- and RP-caching, every time model checking is conducted, a new model checker instance is created. Consequently, the model checker cache is discarded after each test of principal membership.

In MC-cross-caching, only one instance of the model checker is created for a given authorization check. The same model checker instance is reused for all principal membership tests during this authorization check. This means that, unlike AP- and RP-caching, in which the values of relationship predicates are cached, MC-cross-caching allows the values of the *subformulas* of the relationship predicates to be reused.

In general, RP-caching is no more effective than MC-cross-caching. They behave identically only when relationship predicates do not share common subformulas.

6. PERFORMANCE EVALUATION

An empirical study has been conducted to evaluate and compare the performance of the eager and lazy authorization procedures (§4) as well as the caching schemes (§5). The study was conducted in a simulated environment with synthetic data. Below we describe our experimental set-up followed by the results of the experiments comparing the authorization procedures (§6.1) and the experiments comparing the caching schemes (§6.2).

Core ReBAC2015 Components. We reused part of the ReBAC protection state in the work of Rizvi *et al.* [24]. First, we reused their authorization graph, which consists of 1.6 million nodes and 32 million edges. It was constructed from the social network dataset, soc-Pokec, from the Stanford Large Network Dataset Collection [3]. 10,000 of the nodes were taken as users (S), and the rest patients ($O \setminus S$). Consult [24, §10 and Appendix B] for details such as edge labelling. Second, we reused their values for $|PR|$, $|PD|$ and $|\phi|$ (Table 1, first 3 lines). Explanations of how these parameter settings are deduced from previously published experimental works on RBAC can be found in [24, §10 and Appendix A]. Third, we reused the hybrid logic formulas in [24, Appendix C] as relationship predicates. These formulas were adapted from the ones used in the Electronic Health Records System case study in [14, §5]. There is a total of 10 distinct formulas, and they are randomly assigned to authorization principals in the experiments (via a randomly generated AR). Consequently, some principals may share the same formulas.

Test Generation Scheme. Table 1 summarizes the parameter combinations used in our experiments. The last 4 lines of the table specify ranges of values for $|AP|$, $|\#|$, $|\sqsubset'|$ and $|<'|$, and account for 4,000 distinct parameter combinations. For each of the four experimental profiles, 20 test cases are randomly generated for each parameter combination. This amounts to 80,000 test cases for each profile.

To generate a test case, the parameter values are first fixed, and then the principals (AP), the principal matching rules (AR), isometric demarcations (DM for which $|DM| = |AP|$), privileges (PR), privilege-demarcation assignment (PD), the demarcation hierarchy ($<'$), and the constraints ($\#$ and $\sqsubset'$) are randomly generated in turn. Lastly, a triple consisting of an object ($o \in O$), a subject ($s \in S$) and a guard ($g \in GD$) is randomly generated to represent the authorization request of the test case.

Experimental Profiles. Four experimental profiles were generated, each is described below.

Profile 1. As discussed above, 80,000 test cases were generated for this profile. The 80,000 corresponding RE-AUTH instances (with $E = AP$) were reduced to SAT instances and solved by a SAT solver. The running time of the SAT solver was recorded for each test case. The 500 test cases with the highest SAT solver running time were then selected. The eager and lazy authorization procedures were then fed these 500 test cases, and their running times were recorded.

This profile is designed to highlight the effect of hard RE-AUTH instances on the two authorization procedures.

Since there were only 10 distinct hybrid logic formulas, and they were randomly assigned to 50–200 principals. This level of duplication is not representative. We therefore adopt RP-caching for this profile, but force the caching mechanism to treat the relationship predicate of each principal to be unique. This effectively turns off the effect of caching.

Profile 2. Again, 80,000 test cases were generated and fed to the lazy authorization procedure. The 500 test cases with the highest running time were selected. The two authorization procedures were then given these 500 test cases, and their running times were recorded. This profile compares the performance of the two authorization procedures on the test cases that are the hardest for lazy evaluation.

As in Profile 1, the hybrid logic formula of each principal was considered unique by the RP-caching mechanism.

Profile 3. This profile is similar to Profile 2, except that the 500 toughest test cases for the eager authorization procedure were selected.

Profile 4. This profile reuses the 500 test cases of Profile 1, but the relationship predicate of each principal is not forced to be unique: i.e., *RP*-caching is in full effect. Recall that the 10 hybrid logic formulas inherited from [24] were randomly distributed among the authorization principals. With *RP*-caching, we expect the overhead of model checking to diminish significantly.

Hardware Configuration. The experiments were conducted on desktop machine with AMD FX-8350 8-core processor (16 MB cache), 16 GB RAM (1866 MHz, DDR3), and 840 EVO solid state drive running Windows 8.1.

Software Configuration. The eager and lazy authorization procedures were implemented in Java 7, with the hybrid logic model checker supplied by the open-source ReBAC Java Library [22]. We did not incorporate the optimization described in Appendix C, and thus all the timings recorded include the overhead of computing the reduction to SAT. We used Sat4j [2] as the SAT solver in the two authorization procedures. This SAT solver offers the two features mentioned in §4.2: model enumeration and learnt clauses. Following [24], the authorization graph was stored in a graph database, Neo4j [1], to obtain a more competitive performance than traditional relational databases.

6.1 Comparing Authorization Procedures

Fig. 1 depicts the average running times of the two authorization procedures in the four experimental profiles.

Finding 1: RE-AUTH ***is not the bottleneck.*** The performance of both authorization procedures are competitive in Profile 1, indicating that the hardest RE-AUTH instances do not slow down performance. Despite the need to solve an NP-complete problem at authorization time, ReBAC2015/Constraints exhibits competitive performance.

Finding 2: Lazy Evaluation is more efficient when model checking is expensive. The performance of lazy evaluation is significantly faster than that of eager evaluation in Profiles 2 and 3. This performance advantage remains whether the test cases are hard for lazy or eager evaluation.

To better understand this phenomenon, we examine the internal behaviour of the two authorization procedures in Table 2 (see the statistics for Profile 3). Eager evaluation makes many more invocations to the model checker (MC) than lazy evaluation. In contrast, eager evaluation makes only (at most) 1 invocation to the SAT solver, while lazy evaluation makes multiple invocations. Since the average time of a model checker invocation is much higher than that of the SAT solver, model checking time dominates the running time. (Note that reduction time is negligible in both authorization procedures.)

Rizvi *et al.* pointed out a major bottleneck of model checking large authorization graphs is database access [24]. We anticipate the performance advantage of lazy evaluation will become even more prominent when, for example, storing the authorization graph in an SSD is not possible due to hardware constraints, or the authorization graph must be stored in a legacy relational database rather than a graph database.

Finding 3: Eager evaluation has a performance advantage when model checking cost is low. In Profile 4, the performances of both lazy and eager evaluation are highly competitive, with eager evaluation exhibiting a performance advantage. In Profile 4, only 10 distinct relationship predicates are involved, and thus the benefit of predicate value caching becomes exceptionally prominent (Table 2, Profile 4). Such a performance advantage can be expected when the diversity of relationship predicates are low among the principals, or when the nesting depth of modal operators in hybrid logic formulas is small.

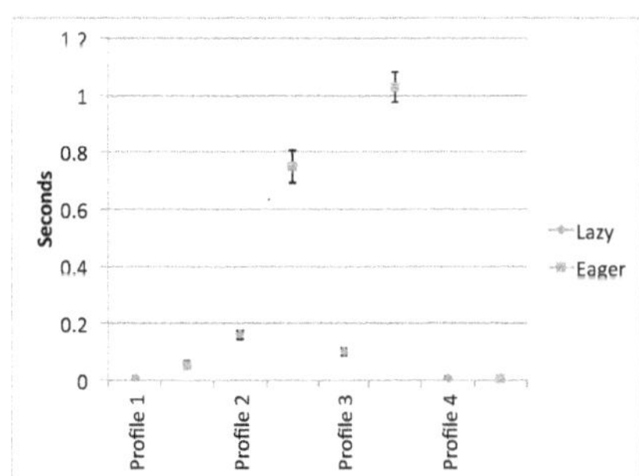

Figure 1: Average time of authorization checks (with 95% confidence interval).

Profile 3		
Avg. Stat.	**Lazy**	**Eager**
# MC calls	13.806	161.206
Time / MC call	0.007 secs	0.007 secs
# SAT calls	13.758	0.994
Time / SAT call	6.6×10^{-7} secs	1.1×10^{-4} secs
Reduction time	4.8×10^{-4} secs	4.9×10^{-4} secs
Profile 4		
Avg. Stat.	**Lazy**	**Eager**
# MC calls	3.838	9.976

Table 2: Statistics of Profiles 3 and 4

6.2 Comparing Caching Schemes

We generated scenarios that potentially challenge the caching strategies (§5). One such scenario would be to generate relationship predicates that do not share common subformulas. A limitation of this scenario is that it does not effect *AP*- and *RP*-caching since these strategies are not concerned with the subformulas of the relationship predicates. The unique subformulas scenario potentially challenges *MC*-cross-caching by preventing cached results from being used across different invocations of the model checker. This scenario is discussed in [23, Chapter 9].

This section presents an extreme scenario where the cost of model checking is extremely high. This scenario is achieved using the test cases of Profile 1 and prepending each relationship predicate with the prefix:

$$\langle \text{agent} \rangle \langle \text{agent} \rangle \langle \text{agent} \rangle$$

This results in an increased workload for the model checker. The test cases of Profile 1 were used to keep the results from being biased towards either of the authorization procedures.

A secondary purpose of this test is to stress-test the *MC*-cross-caching strategy by forcing it to cache a high amount of data such that it results in the cache being full and thus forcing a data dump. The prefix causes the cache to be filled faster and potentially forcing invocations of the cache data dump, thereby countering the benefit of *MC*-cross-caching.

The average running time of the two evaluation schemes using the various caching strategies are summarized in Fig. 2.

Finding 4: As the depth of $\langle \cdot \rangle$ ***increases, the performance advantage of*** ***RP-caching and MC-cross-caching becomes highly pronounced, especially in the case of eager evaluation.*** Recall that the authorization graph consists of 30,622,564 edges between 1,632,803 nodes. For the

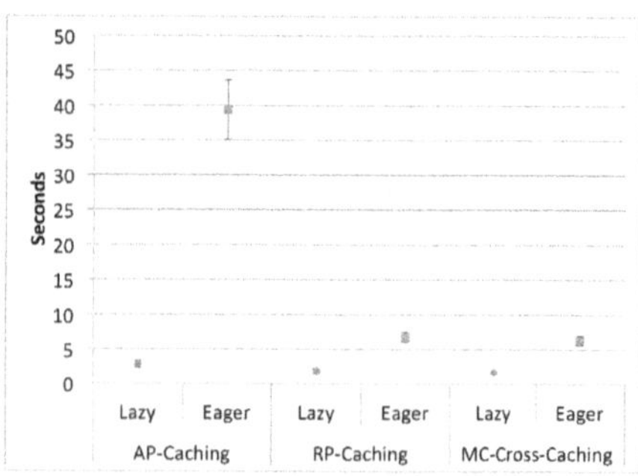

Figure 2: Average time of authorization checks using the caching strategies (w/ 95% CI).

construction of the authorization graph, Rizvi *et al.* separated the top 10,000 nodes with the highest in-degrees and labeled them as users, and the rest were labeled as patients. As a result of their construction, there are 28,538,682 patient-to-patient edges with the agent label, which means that there are approximately 18 (actually 17.586) outgoing agent edges per patient on average. The prefix used for the relationship predicates for this case results in an increase in the workload of the model checker. In the average worst case the workload is increased by a magnitude of 18^3 (= 5,832).

The results show significant performance advantage for using *RP*-caching or *MC*-cross-caching compared to *AP*-caching. The most prominent results are from the eager evaluation scheme. More specifically, the result of *RP*-caching with lazy evaluation or *MC*-cross-caching with lazy evaluation offer the best performance in the worst case scenario.

Finding 5: The MC-Cross-Caching does not invoke a data dump for this case. A surprising result here is that even at this depth, the cache used by the model checker does not invoke a single data dump for either the lazy or eager evaluation schemes. The cache used for the model checker for these experiments is the one provided by the ReBAC Java Library [22], which has a maximum size of 8,000,000 nodes. Since there is no data dump for the cache, all of its nodes are retained and already computed data is not lost. The relationship predicates can be further altered to force even more data to be stored within the model checker cache. For instance, one could use the $\downarrow x$ hybrid logic operator to bind each node to a variable and create the following prefix:

$$\langle \mathsf{agent} \rangle \downarrow x \; \langle \mathsf{agent} \rangle \downarrow y \; \langle \mathsf{agent} \rangle \downarrow z$$

Using the modified prefix would certainly result in a performance slowdown even more so than the original prefix. However, the performance using the original prefix already results in unacceptable running times and thus slowing it down further would not provide any benefits.

7. RELATED WORKS

The evolution of Fong's ReBAC model [14] to the Core ReBAC2015 model [24] has already been discussed in details in §2.1. Compared to [24], this work introduces the demarcation hierarchy (ReBAC2015/Demarcations) and an authorization-time constraint system (ReBAC2015/Constraints). These extensions increase the expressiveness of the model: the liberal- and strict-grant semantics of [24] are but two instantiations of our new model (Thm. 17). Furthermore, the new features support fine-grained interactions between RBAC and ReBAC (§2.3 and §3.2). This compares favourably with [24], in which ReBAC and the legacy RBAC models operate independently. Eager and lazy versions of principal matching algorithms are also presented in [24], but they cannot accommodate an authorization-time constraint system. This gap motivates our design of authorization checking algorithms in §4, which solve an NP-complete problem using a SAT solver, and our lazy authorization algorithm has an algorithmic structure akin to an SMT solver.

Independent of [13], Cheng *et al.* also considered the incorporation of user-to-resource and resource-to-resource relationships into the ReBAC protection state [9]. While relationship predicates are assumed to be specified in hybrid logic formulas [7] in this work, Cheng *et al.* [10, 9] and Crampton and Sellwood [13] advocate the use of regular expressions to specify relationship predicates. The two specification paradigms are incomparable in expressive power. Since backtracking is still involved in the checking of relationship predicates that are specified in regular expressions, our proposal of lazy evaluation would still apply. Lastly, the presence of negative permissions in [9, 13] necessitates conflict resolution schemes. We do not consider negative permissions in this work.

The constraint system presented in this paper stands on the shoulders of prior literature on RBAC constraints [21, 8, 26, 11, 5, 6, 4, 17, 18, 19, 27, 29]. For example, our MEAP constraints are direct descendants of mutual exclusion constraints, which are used to enforce separation of duty policies [25, 21]. Our work is unique in two ways. First, while mutual exclusion constraints (e.g., the SMER constraints in [21]) are imposed statically in a typical RBAC system (i.e., when a session is initiated), our MEAP and PAPR constraints are imposed dynamically (i.e., at the time of a ReBAC authorization check). This dynamism is necessitated by the fact that membership in authorization principals is defined dynamically. But then constraint solving is NP-complete, and there is no *a priori* reason to believe that authorization-time constraint enforcement is feasible. Thus the second uniqueness of this work is the demonstration of the surprising result that modern SAT solving technologies can be employed in a creative way (via our lazy evaluation strategy) to render authorization-time constraint enforcement a feasible task.

8. CONCLUSION AND FUTURE WORK

By introducing demarcations and constraints to the recently proposed ReBAC model of [24], we allow ReBAC and RBAC to interoperate in interesting ways. Constraints are checked at authorization time, via a lazy evaluation strategy akin to SMT solving. The performance of the authorization procedure have been shown empirically to be competitive.

A number of research opportunities arise from this work. First, one could consider negative permissions and study their impact on the constraint system. Second, one could extend ReBAC2015 to incorporate a richer guard language for specifying complex privilege requirements.

Acknowledgments

This work is supported in part by an NSERC Discovery Grant (RGPIN-2014-06611) and a Canada Research Chair (950-229712).

9. REFERENCES

[1] Neo4J. http://neo4j.com/.

[2] Sat4j. http://www.sat4j.org/.

[3] Stanford Large Network Dataset Collection. http://snap.stanford.edu/data.

[4] AHN, G.-J. *The RCL 2000 Language for Specifying Role-based Authorization Constraints.* PhD thesis, Fairfax, VA, USA, 2000. AAI9951117.

[5] AHN, G.-J., AND SANDHU, R. The RSL99 language for role-based separation of duty constraints. In *Proceedings of the Fourth ACM Workshop on Role-based Access Control (RBAC'99)* (New York, NY, USA, 1999), ACM, pp. 43–54.

[6] AHN, G.-J., AND SANDHU, R. Role-based authorization constraints specification. *ACM Trans. Inf. Syst. Secur. 3*, 4 (Nov. 2000), 207–226.

[7] BRUNS, G., FONG, P. W. L., SIAHAAN, I., AND HUTH, M. Relationship-based access control: Its expression and enforcement through hybrid logic. In *Proceedings of the 2nd ACM Conference on Data and Application Security and Privacy (CODASPY'12)* (San Antonio, TX, USA, Feb. 2012).

[8] CHEN, H., AND LI, N. Constraint generation for separation of duty. In *Proceedings of the Eleventh ACM Symposium on Access Control Models and Technologies (SACMAT'06)* (New York, NY, USA, 2006), ACM, pp. 130–138.

[9] CHENG, Y., PARK, J., AND SANDHU, R. Relationship-based access control for online social networks: Beyond user-to-user relationships. In *Proceedings of the 4th IEEE International Conference on Information Privacy, Security, Risk and Trust (PASSAT'12)* (Amsterdam, Netherlands, Sept. 2012).

[10] CHENG, Y., PARK, J., AND SANDHU, R. A user-to-user relationship-based access control model for online social networks. In *Proceedings of the 26th Annual IFIP WG 11.3 Working Conference on Data and Applications Security and Privacy (DBSec'12)* (Paris, France, July 2012), vol. 7371 of *LNCS.*

[11] CRAMPTON, J. Specifying and enforcing constraints in role-based access control. In *Proceedings of the Eighth ACM Symposium on Access Control Models and Technologies (SACMAT'03)* (New York, NY, USA, 2003), ACM, pp. 43–50.

[12] CRAMPTON, J. Why we should take a second look at access control in Unix. In *Proceedings of the 13th Nordic Workshop on Secure IT Systems (NordSec'08)* (Copenhagen, Denmark, Oct. 2008).

[13] CRAMPTON, J., AND SELLWOOD, J. Path conditions and principal matching: A new approach to access control. In *Proceedings of the 19th ACM Symposium on Access Control Models and Technologies (SACMAT'14)* (New York, NY, USA, 2014), ACM, pp. 187–198.

[14] FONG, P. W. Relationship-based access control: Protection model and policy language. In *Proceedings of the First ACM Conference on Data and Application Security and Privacy (CODASPY'11)* (New York, NY, USA, 2011), ACM, pp. 191–202.

[15] FONG, P. W. L., MEHREGAN, P., AND KRISHNAN, R. Relational abstraction in community-based secure collaboration. In *Proceedings of the 20th ACM Conference on Computer and Communications Security (CCS'13)* (Berlin, Germany, Nov. 2013), pp. 585–598.

[16] FONG, P. W. L., AND SIAHAAN, I. Relationship-based access control policies and their policy languages. In *Proceedings of the 16th ACM Symposium on Access Control Models and Technologies (SACMAT'11)* (Innsbruck, Austria, June 2011), pp. 51–60.

[17] GLIGOR, V., GAVRILA, S., AND FERRAIOLO, D. On the formal definition of separation-of-duty policies and their composition. In *Security and Privacy, 1998. Proceedings. 1998 IEEE Symposium on* (May 1998), pp. 172–183.

[18] JAEGER, T. On the increasing importance of constraints. In *Proceedings of the Fourth ACM Workshop on Role-based Access Control (RBAC'99)* (New York, NY, USA, 1999), ACM, pp. 33–42.

[19] JAEGER, T., AND TIDSWELL, J. E. Practical safety in flexible access control models. *ACM Trans. Inf. Syst. Secur. 4*, 2 (May 2001), 158–190.

[20] KUIJPER, W., AND ERMOLAEV, V. Sorting out role based access control. In *Proceedings of the 19th ACM Symposium on Access Control Models and Technologies (SACMAT'14)* (New York, NY, USA, 2014), ACM, pp. 63–74.

[21] LI, N., TRIPUNITARA, M. V., AND BIZRI, Z. On mutually exclusive roles and separation-of-duty. *ACM Trans. Inf. Syst. Secur. 10*, 2 (May 2007).

[22] RIZVI, S. Z., AND HOSSEINKHANI, M. ReBAC Java Library. http://sourceforge.net/p/rebac/.

[23] RIZVI, S. Z. R. ReBAC2015: Interoperability of Relationship- and Role-Based Access Control. Master's thesis, University of Calgary, Calgary, Canada, 2015.

[24] RIZVI, S. Z. R., FONG, P. W. L., CRAMPTON, J., AND SELLWOOD, J. Relationship-based access control for an open-source medical records system. In *Proceedings of the 20th ACM Symposium on Access Control Models and Technologies (SACMAT'15)* (Vienna, Austria, June 2015), pp. 113–124.

[25] SALTZER, J., AND SCHROEDER, M. The protection of information in computer systems. *Proceedings of the IEEE 63*, 9 (Sept 1975), 1278–1308.

[26] SANDHU, R., COYNE, E., FEINSTEIN, H., AND YOUMAN, C. Role-based access control models. *IEEE Computer 29*, 2 (Feb 1996), 38–47.

[27] SIMON, R., AND ZURKO, M. E. Separation of duty in role-based environments. In *Proceedings of the 10th IEEE Workshop on Computer Security Foundations (CSFW'97)* (Washington, DC, USA, 1997), IEEE Computer Society, pp. 183–.

[28] THOMPSON, S. *Haskell: The Craft of Functional Programming*, 3rd edition ed. Addison-Wesley, 2012.

[29] TIDSWELL, J. E., AND JAEGER, T. An access control model for simplifying constraint expression. In *Proceedings of the 7th ACM Conference on Computer and Communications Security (CCS'00)* (New York, NY, USA, 2000), ACM, pp. 154–163.

APPENDIX

A. NP-COMPLETENESS OF RE-AUTH

To prove that RE-AUTH is NP-complete, we show that it is in NP, and that it is NP-hard.

RE-AUTH ***is in NP.*** A nondeterministic algorithm can decide RE-AUTH by first guessing subset $\alpha \subseteq E$, and then verifying that (a) $\mathsf{consistent}(\alpha)$, and (b) $\mathsf{priv}(\alpha) \models MG(m)$, both can be accomplished in time polynomial to the size of the protection state.

RE-AUTH ***is NP-hard.*** We reduce the Independent Set problem to RE-AUTH. The Independent Set problem, which is known to be NP-complete, asks, given an undirected graph $G = \langle V_G, E_G \rangle$ and a positive integer k, does there exist a set of vertices, $U \subseteq V_G$, with $|U| = k$, such that for every pair of vertices, $u, v \in U$, $uv \notin E_G$?

Suppose an instance of Independent Set is given: $G = \langle V_G, E_G \rangle$ and k, where $V_G = \{v_1, ..., v_n\}$. We describe below the construction of a corresponding instance of RE-AUTH consisting of a ReBAC2015/Constraints protection state, a method $m \in MD$, and a set $E \subseteq AP$ (where MD and AP are part of the protection state).

We construct a protection state that is order-free (i.e., no PAPR constraint) and has a flat demarcation hierarchy (i.e., no two distinct demarcations are related by $\leq$). Construct $PR = \{p_1, \ldots, p_k\}$ (i.e., $|PR| = k$). Let $MD = \{m\}$, where $MG(m) = \texttt{all-of}(PR)$. Construct an AP with $k \times n$ principals: ap_{ij}, where $1 \leq i \leq k$ and $1 \leq j \leq n$. The protection state has isometric demarcations: i.e., there is a corresponding demarcation d_{ij} for each ap_{ij} such that $AD(ap_{ij}) = d_{ij}$. We also define $PD = \{(p_i, d_{ij}) \mid p_i \in PR, d_{ij} \in DM\}$. Consequently, $\mathsf{dem}(\{ap_{ij}\}) = \{p_i\}$.

The last component of the protection state is #, the MEAP constraints:

1. *Edge constraints:* For every $1 \leq x < y \leq n$ for which $v_x v_y \in E_G$, impose $ap_{ix} \# ap_{jy}$ for each $1 \leq i \leq k$ and $1 \leq j \leq k$.
2. *Vertex constraints:* For every $1 \leq x < y \leq n$, impose $ap_{ix} \# ap_{iy}$ for each $1 \leq i \leq k$.
3. *Privilege constraints:* For every $1 \leq i < j \leq k$, impose $ap_{ix} \# ap_{jx}$ for each $1 \leq x \leq n$.

Now the rest of the RE-AUTH instance consists of the only method m and the principal set $E = AP$.

It is not hard to see that a solution $\alpha \subseteq E$ exists iff the Independent Set instance has a solution. The constructed protection state consists of k privileges, $k \times n$ principals, $O(k^2 \times n^2)$ edge constraints, $O(n^2 \times k)$ vertex constraints, and $O(k^2 \times n)$ privilege constraints. The reduction can therefore be computed in $O(k^2 n^2)$ time.

Discussion. Note that the constructed RE-AUTH instance is order-free, and its demarcation hierarchy is flat. This means the MEAP constraints (#) form the core of complexity for RE-AUTH. The demarcation hierarchy ($\leq$) and the PAPR constraints ($\sqsubseteq$) are not hard at all. This is easy to see because the reflexive transitive closures for $<'$ and $\sqsubset'$ can be computed in polynomial time.

B. LAZY EVALUATION IN DETAILS

There are three main steps in Algorithm 1.

Step 1: Prepare (lines 1–3). Line 1 reduces the present RE-AUTH instance to a SAT instance F using the reduction in §4.3. The function $getSATInstance(E, m)$ takes two arguments: a principal set E and a requested method m. Note that on line 1, the entire AP is passed as E. Distilling from AP what principals are enabled belongs to Step 3 below. Then on line 2 the SAT solver is initialized to work with F.[4] A map $E[\cdot]$ is used for caching the result of model checking: if $E[rp]$ is defined, then it is the value of $rp(G, o, s)$. $E[\cdot]$ is initialized to an empty map on line 3.

Step 2: Construct Principal Set (lines 4–8). First, the SAT solver is invoked to find the next model of F (line 4). If no such model is found (line 5), then we have exhausted all models of F, and thus access is denied (line 6). Otherwise, a model σ of F is found, and it encodes a principal set α that satisfies (12). The set α is extracted from σ on line 8. More specifically, $extractPrincipals(\sigma)$ returns $\{\, ap \in AP \mid \sigma(ap) = 1 \,\}$. See §4.3 for a justification.

Step 3: Verify That Principals Are Enabled (lines 9–19). The goal of this block of code is to check if all the principals in α are enabled. The for loop on lines 9–18 examines each principal ap in α in turn. Let rp be the relationship predicate that defines membership in ap (line 10). The value of $rp(G, o, s)$ is evaluated by an invocation to the model checker (line 12) if that value has not already been cached in the map $E[\cdot]$ (line 11). If ap is found not to be enabled (line 14), then the clause $(\neg ap)$ is added to F to prevent the SAT solver from attempting to enable ap in subsequently found models (line 15). As soon as α is found to contain a disabled principal, Step 2 is repeated (line 16). However, if all ap in α are confirmed to be enabled, then access will be granted (line 19).

C. EFFICIENT GENERATION AND STORAGE OF SAT INSTANCES

Note that formula F is independent of the resource (o) and requestor (s) from the request. Not only that, in the lazy authorization procedure (§4.2), E is fixed to AP, and thus F_{MEAP}, F_{PAPR} and F_{DH} do not vary across requests. Therefore, to increase efficiency, one can simply generate F once, offline, for each m, and reuse it for all requests involving m. More specifically, F_{MEAP}, F_{PAPR} and F_{DH} are the same for all methods. This means they need only be generated once offline, and stored globally. One can then generate the corresponding F_{guard} for each method m, and store it along with m. When a request is to be authorized, one can retrieve F_{guard} from m, and combine it with the globally stored F_{MEAP}, F_{PAPR} and F_{DH}, to obtain the appropriate F.

[4] Functions that interact with the SAT solvers have the prefix "*sat-*".

A Model-driven Approach to Representing and Checking RBAC Contextual Policies

Ameni Ben Fadhel, Domenico Bianculli, Lionel Briand
SnT Centre - University of Luxembourg, Luxembourg
{ameni.benfadhel,domenico.bianculli,lionel.briand}@uni.lu

Benjamin Hourte
HITEC Luxembourg
benjamin.hourte@hitec.lu

ABSTRACT

Among the various types of Role-based access control (RBAC) policies proposed in the literature, contextual policies take into account the user's location and the time at which she requests an access. The precise characterization of the context in such policies and the definition of an access decision procedure for them are non-trivial tasks, since they have to take into account the various facets of the temporal and spatial expressions occurring in these policies. Existing approaches for modeling contextual policies do not support all the various spatio-temporal concepts and often do not provide an access decision procedure.

In this paper, we propose a model-driven approach to representing and checking RBAC contextual policies. We introduce GemRBAC+CTX, an extension of a generalized conceptual model for RBAC, which contains all the concepts required to model contextual policies. We formalize these policies as constraints, using the Object Constraint Language (OCL), on the GemRBAC+CTX model, as a way to operationalize the access decision for user's requests using model-driven technologies. We show the application of GemRBAC+CTX to model the RBAC contextual policies of an application developed by HITEC Luxembourg, a provider of situational-aware information management systems for emergency scenarios. The use of GemRBAC+CTX has allowed the engineers of HITEC to define several new types of contextual policies, with a fine-grained, precise description of contexts. The preliminary experimental results show the feasibility of applying our model-driven approach for making access decisions in real systems.

1. INTRODUCTION

Several types of Role-based access control (RBAC) policies[1] have been proposed in the literature, together with the corresponding conceptual models that support them (see, for example, the recent taxonomy in [5]). In this paper we focus on *contextual policies.* A contextual policy restricts a user to perform an action depending on her context, e.g., her location and/or the time at which the action should happen. For example, a policy that refers to a temporal context (also called *temporal policy*) can be expressed in English as "assign role *program chair* to user *AP* from March 4, 2015 to March 11, 2016". Similarly, a policy that refers to a spatial context (also called *spatial policy*) can be expressed as "assign role *general chair* to user *RS* if he is located in San Antonio, TX".

Contextual policies play a fundamental role in defining the security level of a system in different types of application domains. Consider, for example, the case of proximity-based payment systems, in which a user can access her credit card details stored on a mobile device only in proximity of a compatible point-of-sale. Another example is represented by enterprise policies that restrict the hours in which an employee can connect to the corporate network when working from home. Finally, we remark that this type of policies is vital in the domain of disaster relief intervention, where HITEC Luxembourg (the partner for the research project in which this work has been carried out) is a provider of situational-aware information management systems for emergency scenarios. In such systems, restricting access to resources (e.g., satellite photos, sensors data) based on the user context is an essential and critical requirement.

Precisely characterizing the context in a contextual policy is non-trivial. For example, temporal policies can refer to individual time instants (e.g., a specific date and/or time) or to time intervals. They can also contain periodic expressions (e.g., "every 3 months") or complex expressions like "in February, from the second Monday to third Friday, from 10:00 to 12:00". In the case of spatial policies, the context can be expressed, for instance, using a distance and a direction with respect to another location (e.g., "6 miles West from coordinates 48.86N, 2.29E") or just with a qualitative attribute (e.g., "100 meters outside the White House"). All these facets have to be considered when defining an RBAC model that supports contextual policies. On a par with the problem of expressing and modeling these policies, there is also the issue of how to make an access decision (i.e., granting/denying access requests) based on such policies.

Several RBAC models have been proposed in the literature to support contextual policies. However, none of them fully support all the facets of these policies. Moreover, only some of them provide algorithms to evaluate contextual policies in order to make an access decision. Furthermore, these

[1] RBAC policies are also referred to as "(authorization) constraints". In this paper we will use the word "policies" to avoid the confusion with "(OCL) constraints".

CODASPY'16, March 9–11, 2016, New Orleans, LA, USA.

DOI: http://dx.doi.org/10.1145/2857705.2857709

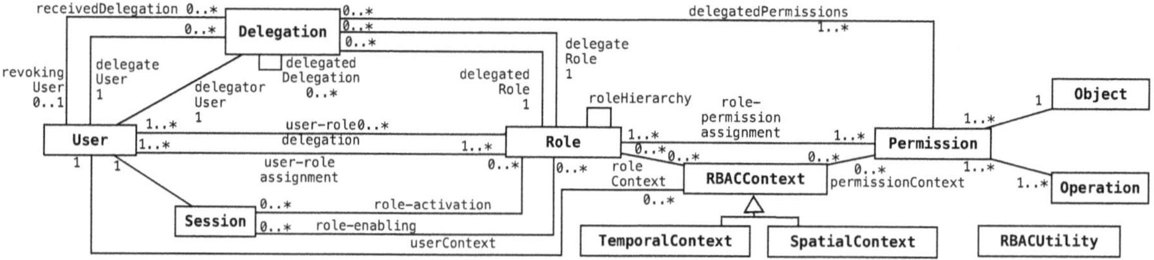

Figure 1: A simplified version of the GemRBAC conceptual model.

models are based on the original RBAC model [23] and do not support advanced non-contextual policies like binding of duty, delegation, revocation.

Our goal is to define a conceptual model significantly more expressive than the state of the art, on top of which we can operationalize the access decision procedure. A more expressive and operational model critically determines its applicability in real scenarios. To achieve this goal, we follow a model-driven approach, based on UML and the Object Constraint Language (OCL) [17].

To represent RBAC contextual policies, we present GEMRBAC+CTX, a conceptual model—expressed in UML—that contains all the conceptual entities required to accurately specify temporal and spatial contexts in RBAC policies. GEMRBAC+CTX is defined as an extension of GEMRBAC [5], our previous proposal for a generalized framework for defining RBAC policies. Since GEMRBAC+CTX is an extension of GEMRBAC, it inherits all its benefits, in particular the support for all types of (non-contextual) RBAC policies surveyed in [5]. In this way, GEMRBAC+CTX supports both complex contextual policies and all types of non-contextual policies (including binding of duty, delegation, revocation).

Regarding the operationalization of the access decision procedure for contextual policies, our model-driven approach is based on the formalization of contextual policies as OCL constraints on the GEMRBAC+CTX model. The problem of making an access decision for contextual policies can be thus reduced to checking the corresponding OCL constraints on an instance of the GEMRBAC+CTX model. We use OCL since it is the common, standardized language for expressing constraints in model-driven engineering and it is well-supported by industry-strength tools. The proposed OCL-based formalization can facilitate the precise understanding of contextual policies by practitioners and paves the way for the practical verification of these policies, based on UML modeling tools and OCL checkers (such as Eclipse OCL [11]).

Furthermore, we report on the application of the proposed approach to modeling the RBAC contextual policies of a real system. The use of GEMRBAC+CTX has allowed the engineers of HITEC to define *19 new types* of contextual policies, with a fine-grained, precise description of contexts. Based on the results of the three policies in the case study section, the time taken by our model-driven approach for making an access decision ranges from few milliseconds to less than three seconds per policy, confirming its suitability for the practical operationalization of access decision procedures.

To summarize, the specific contributions of the paper are: 1) the GEMRBAC+CTX conceptual model, to express contextual RBAC policies; 2) the templates for the formalization of OCL constraints over the GEMRBAC+CTX model, as a way to operationalize the access decision of contextual RBAC policies; 3) the application of the GEMRBAC+CTX model for the specification of real RBAC policies in an industrial setting with high contextual requirements.

The paper is structured as follows. Section 2 briefly illustrates the GEMRBAC model. Section 3 shows how to model contextual policies with GEMRBAC+CTX. Section 4 illustrates the templates for the formalization of contextual policies as OCL constraints on the GEMRBAC+CTX model. Section 5 reports on an industrial application of the proposed approach. Section 6 discusses related work and Section 7 concludes the paper.

2. BACKGROUND: THE GEMRBAC MODEL

The GEMRBAC model, previously introduced in [5], is a richer and more expressive extension of the original RBAC model [23]. GEMRBAC has been designed after surveying the various types of RBAC policies (and the corresponding model extensions) proposed in the literature. We defined GEMRBAC with the goal of filling the gap among these extensions by proposing a generalized model that includes *all* the conceptual entities required to define all the types of constraints classified in the survey. In the rest of this section we describe the main entities of the GEMRBAC model providing some background information on RBAC. A simplified version of the GEMRBAC model is shown in the class diagram of Figure 1; we refer the reader to [5] for a complete description.

At the basis of GEMRBAC there are the concepts of `User`, `Session`, `Role` and `Permission`. A `Permission` is represented as a set of `Operations` on an `Object`. `Permissions` are assigned to `Roles` and `Roles` are assigned to `Users`; these assignments are captured with associations between the respective classes. A `Session` maps a `User` to a subset of the `Roles` that have been assigned to her; this mapping activates the role(s) for a certain user. A role that can be activated is called *enabled*. Role enabling and activation relations are modeled as associations between the `Role` and `Session` classes. A permission is enabled if the user is allowed to perform its associated operations. By analogy to role assignment and enabling, we model the enabled permissions of a given role with the `enabledPermissions` association between the `Role` and `Permission` classes. A user can delegate her role or a subset of its permissions to another user via a `Delegation`.

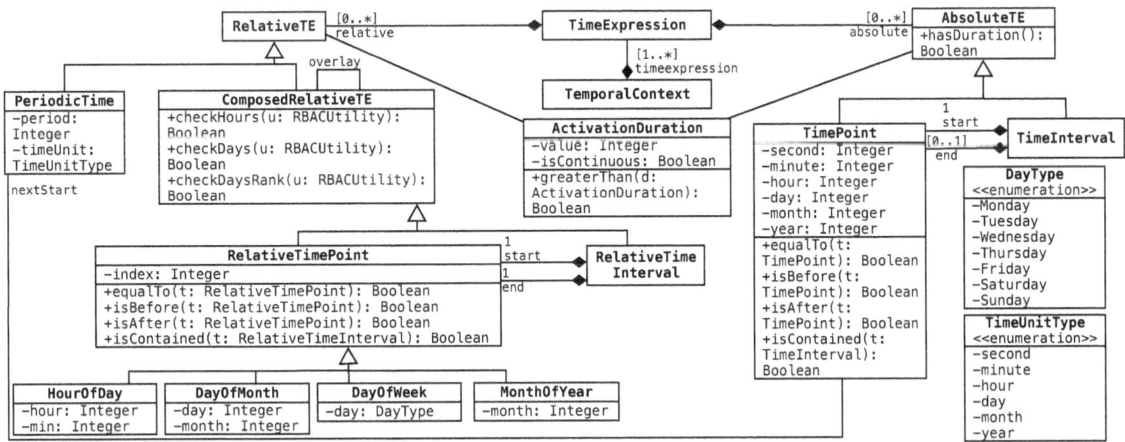

Figure 2: Temporal context in GemRBAC+CTX.

For a `Delegation` we keep track of the delegator, the delegate (the user that receives the delegation), their roles at the time of the delegation, and the delegated role, with associations between classes `Delegation` and `User`, and classes `Delegation` and `Role`. A delegation is put to an end through a revocation action, which can be explicitly performed by a user or automatically triggered depending on the context. Contextual information is modeled with the class `RBACContext` and its subclasses `TemporalContext` and `SpatialContext`. A temporal (respectively, spatial) context models the time (location) on which a given role, or permission, can be enabled/assigned; a role or permission can be enabled/assigned if its contextual information matches the user's one.

3. MODELING CONTEXTUAL POLICIES WITH GEMRBAC+CTX

The GEMRBAC model has limited support for contextual policies. More specifically: (1) the context assigned to a role (or a permission) restricts either its assignment or its enabling but not both; (2) temporal and spatial information are represented in a symbolic way, without an explicit characterization of the actual context. Limitation (1) implies that two policies such as "assign role r to user u in context ctx_1" and "enable role r in context ctx_2", which respectively restricts the assignment and the enabling of the same role r, cannot be defined on the same model instance. As for limitation (2), the GEMRBAC model cannot be used to model explicitly the specific aspects of temporal and spatial context, because GEMRBAC represents contexts in a symbolic way (i.e., with identifiers). For example, from the point of view of temporal context, one cannot explicitly refer to time instants (e.g., "(on) *January 21, 2014 at 8:00*") or periodic expressions (e.g., "*every Monday, from 9.00 to 11.00*"). From the point of view of spatial context, in GEMRBAC, for instance, one cannot define a geo-fence, i.e., a precise geometric characterization of a context (e.g., "*within a radius of 20 miles from the main building*") or a relative location (e.g., "*100 meters outside the White House*").

To overcome these limitations, we introduce the GEMRBAC+CTX model, an extension of the GEMRBAC model that supports the definition of richer contextual policies. To address limitation (1), in the GEMRBAC+CTX model we separate contextual assignment and enabling, both for role and permission. More explicitly, the context in which a role should be assigned (as prescribed by a contextual policy) is modeled with the `roleContextAssignment` association between the `RBACContext` and `Role` classes; similarly, the context in which a role should be enabled (as prescribed by a contextual policy) is modeled with the `roleContextEnabling` association between these two classes. The context for permission enabling and assignment is modeled in a similar way with the `permissionContextAssignment` and `permissionContextEnabling` associations between the `RBACContext` and `Permission` classes. To tackle limitation (2), we enrich the GEMRBAC model with new entities that support the specification of more detailed temporal and spatial context in policies. We illustrate these new entities in the rest of this section.

3.1 Modeling Temporal Context

We support richer temporal context specification in the GEMRBAC+CTX model by introducing a new class hierarchy under class `TemporalContext` of the GEMRBAC model. The new classes and their associations are shown in the class diagram in Figure 2.

We extend class `TemporalContext` by introducing (with a composition relation) the concept of `TimeExpression`. A time expression is composed of absolute and/or relative time expressions; these concepts are modeled as classes `AbsoluteTE` and `RelativeTE`.

An absolute time expression refers to a concrete point or interval in the timeline. An absolute time point, modeled with the class `TimePoint`, corresponds to a given time instant, e.g., "*January 21, 2014 at 8:00:00*". Hereafter, to improve the readability we will omit the hours from a time point when we refer to midnight. A time interval, modeled with class `TimeInterval`, corresponds to a segment in the timeline; a time interval can be either of type bounded or unbounded. A bounded time interval corresponds, for example, to the expression "*from January 21, 2014 to April 25, 2015*". This interval has a start `TimePoint` (*January 21, 2014*) and an end `TimePoint` (*April 25, 2015*). An unbounded interval corresponds to the expression "*starting from October 15, 2013*"; it has only the start `TimePoint` (*October 15, 2013*) and is unbounded to the right.

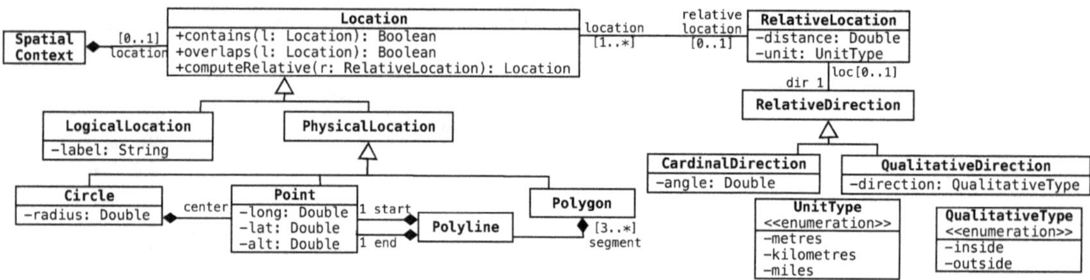

Figure 3: Spatial context in GemRBAC+CTX.

A relative time expression is an expression that cannot be mapped *directly* to a point or an interval in the timeline. For example, the common expression "*(at) 9 a.m.*" by itself cannot be directly mapped to a point in the timeline unless another expression, e.g., "*(on) May 2, 2015*" is specified. Class `RelativeTE` has two subclasses, `RelativeTime` and `PeriodicTime`. By analogy with the class `AbsoluteTE`, the class `RelativeTime` has two subclasses, `RelativeTimePoint` and `RelativeTimeInterval`. Class `RelativeTimePoint` has four subclasses: `HourOfDay` refers to a specific hour of the day, e.g., "*(at) 9 a.m.*"; `DayOfWeek` corresponds to a given day of the week, e.g.,"*(on) Monday*" refers to any Monday; `DayOfMonth` refers to a day in a month such as "*(on) April, 5*"; `MonthOfYear` refers to a given month, e.g., "*(in) April*". Unlike class `TimeInterval`, class `RelativeTimeInterval` always refers to a bounded time interval, whose start and end points have both the same type (a subclass of `RelativeTimePoint`).

Class `ComposedRelativeTE` can be recursively composed with itself through the association `overlay`, to represent composite time expressions. These composite expressions are required to have composite elements of different granularity. We enforce this requirement by defining a structural constraint on the model. Informally, a `MonthOfYear` can overlay either a `DayOfWeek` or an `HourOfDay`; a `DayOfWeek` or a `DayOfMonth` can overlay only an `HourOfDay`. The same constraint applies if any subclass *c* of `RelativeTimePoint` mentioned in it is replaced with a `RelativeTimeInterval` with bounds of type *c*. An example of an expression that can be modeled by composing different instances of `ComposedRelativeTE` by means of the `overlay` association is "*in February, from the second Monday to third Friday, from 10:00:00 to 12:00:00*". This expression is modeled by an instance of `MonthOfYear` (*February*) overlaid with an instance of `RelativeTimeInterval`, with start- and end-point of type `DayOfWeek` (*from Monday to Friday*), overlaid with an instance of `RelativeTimeInterval`, with start- and end-point of type `HourOfDay` (*from 10:00:00 to 12:00:00*). The indexes that refer to a specific occurrence of Monday and Friday are modeled with the `index` attribute, which is defined only for class `DayOfWeek`.

Class `RelativeTE` can also represent periodicity in temporal expressions such as "*every 3 months*". The periodicity is modeled with its subclass `PeriodicTime`. Its attribute `period` is a numeric value associated with a time unit (e.g., day, hour, month) modeled with the attribute `timeUnit`. A `PeriodicTime` is always part of a `TimeExpression` that has exactly one `AbsoluteTE`; the latter defines either the starting time of the period (as in "*every 3 months, starting from April 5, 2015*") or the time interval in which it applies (as in "*every 3 months, from April 5, 2015 to June 8, 2017*"). We assume that each `PeriodicTime` has a `nextStart` association with a `TimePoint` corresponding to the beginning of the next period.

In the context of RBAC, a temporal context can have a time-based policy that represents a bound for the sum of activation durations of a given role (or permission). For instance, a security engineer could enable a certain role from Monday to Friday but allow users to activate it only for two hours over the five days. We keep track of this duration with class `ActivationDuration`, which is associated with classes `RelativeTE` and `AbsoluteTE`. Moreover, this duration can be cumulative (i.e., related to multiple sessions) or non-cumulative (i.e., related to the current session); this concept is represented by the boolean attribute `isContinuous` of the class `ActivationDuration`.

3.2 Modeling Spatial Context

Similarly to what we have done for temporal context, we support richer spatial context specification in the GemRBAC+CTX model by introducing a new class hierarchy under class `SpatialContext` of the GemRBAC model. The new classes and their associations are shown in the class diagram in Figure 3.

We extend class `SpatialContext` by introducing (with a composition relation) the concept of `Location`. At a very high-level, a location represents a specific bounded area or point in space. A location can be either physical or logical; these concepts are modeled as classes `PhysicalLocation` and `LogicalLocation`.

A physical location identifies a precise position in a geometric space. We consider three possible ways to express a physical location and we model them as subclasses of `PhysicalLocation`. Class `Point` represents a geographic coordinate with latitude, longitude and altitude. Class `Circle` represents a circular area, characterized by a radius and a center. Class `Polygon` is an area enclosed by at least three segments, which are modeled with class `Polyline`; each `Polyline` is a segment composed of a start and an end `Point`. Notice that a `Polygon` (as a set of `Polylines`) can model areas with complex shapes, such as the border of a city.

A logical location is an abstraction of one or many physical locations. For instance, the logical location "*offices on the second floor*" refers to the set of physical locations corresponding to the actual office rooms in the second floor of a building. A logical location can also be a convenient shorthand to identify a geographical landmark without providing its coordinates. The concept of logical location is modeled with class `LogicalLocation`. We assume that there is a geocoding function that maps each `LogicalLocation` to the corresponding `PhysicalLocation`(s). A location can be defined *relatively* to another location by providing a direction and optionally a distance. We model these concepts with class `RelativeLocation`, which is associated with class `RelativeDirection`, and has a `distance` attribute. The latter has two subclasses, `CardinalDirection` and `QualitativeDirection`. Class `CardinalDirection` represents the degrees of rotation based on cardinal points on a compass. An example of a location using a relative location denoted with a cardinal direction is "*6 miles West from the Tour Eiffel*". This expression contains a distance (*6 miles*), a cardinal direction (*Southwest, i.e., 225°*) and a logical location (*Tour Eiffel*). Class `QualitativeDirection` represents a relative proximity to a location, such as "*inside*" or "*outside*". An example of a location using a relative location denoted with a qualitative direction is "*100 meters outside the White House*". This expression contains a distance (*100 meters*), a qualitative direction (*outside*) and a logical location (*White House*).

Class `Location` provides some operations that check for topological relations between locations: operation `contains` checks if a location is a part of another one; operation `overlaps` checks if two locations share a common area.

In the GemRBAC+CTX model, we model the user's position with an association between classes `User` and `SpatialContext`. This association provides more precise information than the association between `User` and `RBACContext` that was included in the GemRBAC model (and that is not present in the GemRBAC+CTX model anymore).

4. CHECKING CONTEXTUAL POLICIES WITH OCL

The GemRBAC+CTX model can be used to represent the state of the system from the point of view of RBAC. As explained in Section 3, the context in which a `Role` (or a `Permission`) can be enabled or assigned (as prescribed by a contextual policy), is captured on the UML model. RBAC contextual policies can then be checked by verifying OCL constraints on the GemRBAC+CTX model. In this way, an access decision (e.g., allowing a user to activate a role) can be performed by checking whether an instance of the GemRBAC+CTX satisfies the OCL constraints associated with it. In the rest of this section we provide several templates that can be used to formalize contextual RBAC policies for role enabling or assignment as OCL constraints on the GemRBAC+CTX model. These RBAC policies are based on real policies defined in our industrial case study.

In the definition of the OCL constraints, we make some working assumptions. We assume that each snapshot contains the time at which it was taken (modeled as an association between classes `RBACUtility` and `TimePoint`) and the current day of week (modeled as an association between classes `RBACUtility` and `DayOfWeek`). This assumption can be guaranteed by applying a timestamp to each snapshot. We also assume that the position of the user is always known, by means of a GPS; this is very reasonable nowadays. Lastly, we assume that policies are not conflicting with each other; e.g., we avoid the case of having two policies, one enabling (assigning) and another one disabling (unassigning) the same role/permision in the same context; consistency check of RBAC policies (which guarantees conflict-free policies) is outside the scope of the paper.

All OCL constraints have been made publicly available, together with an Ecore version of the GemRBAC+CTX model, at
https://github.com/AmeniBF/GemRBAC-CTX-model.git.

4.1 Policies with temporal context

A policy on role enabling with an absolute time expression restricts the time interval at which a role can be enabled, as in "role r_1 is enabled from January 21, 2014 to April 25, 2015". This policy can be checked by verifying the following OCL invariant of the class `Session`:

```
1  context Session inv AbsoluteBTIRoleEnab:
2  let u : RBACUtility = RBACUtility.allInstances(),
3      r : Role = Role.allInstances() ->
4         select(r : Role|r.idRole = 'r1'),
5      temporalContext: Set(RBACContext) =
6         r.roleContextEnabling -> select(c |
7         c.oclIsTypeOf(TemporalContext)),
8      timeE: Set(AbsoluteTE) = temporalContext.
9         oclAsType(TemporalContext).timeexpression.
10        absolute ->flatten()->asSet(),
11     timeI: Set(AbsoluteTE) = timeE -> select(e |
12        e.oclIsTypeOf(TimeInterval) and
13        e.oclAsType(TimeInterval).end->notEmpty())
14 in if timeI.oclAsType(TimeInterval) ->
15    exists(i| u.getCurrentTime().isContained(i)) then
16             self.enabledRoles -> includes(r)
17             or self.activeRoles -> includes(r)
18    endif
```

In this OCL expression, we first select the instance corresponding to role r_1 (lines 3–4). Then, we retrieve the list `temporalContext` of temporal contexts in which the role should be enabled (lines 5–7) and compute, over the elements of this list, the list `timeE` of absolute expressions assigned to them (lines 8–10). In this example, since there is only one `TemporalContext` object containing one `AbsoluteTE` object, the `timeE` list will include only one instance of `TimeInterval` whose start and end `TimePoints` corresponds to "January 21, 2014" and "April 25, 2015". Since the enabling temporal context in the policy is expressed as a bounded time interval, we have to select, among the elements of `timeE`, the list `timeI` of expressions in the form of a time interval (lines 11–13) with a bounded end point; this last condition is checked with the expression at line 13. Afterwards, we check if the time when the snapshot was taken—obtained by calling the operation `getCurrentTime` of class `RBACUtiliy`—is contained in one of the time intervals in list `timeI` (lines 14–15). If this is the case, we check whether role r_1 is in the list of enabled or active role of the current session (lines 16–17).

A policy on permission assignment with a relative time expression restricts the time at which a permission can be assigned to a role. As explained in Section 3, we support different forms of relative time expression. For the purpose of illustration, we consider a relative time expression structured as a `DayOfWeek` (or a `RelativeTimeInterval` with bounds of type `DayOfWeek`), which, subsequently, can overlay an `Hour` (or a `RelativeTimeInterval` with bounds of type `Hour`). An example of a policy with a relative time expression of this form is "assign role r_1 to user u_1 *only* from Wednesday to Friday, from 10:00 to 14:00". Such a policy can be checked by verifying the following OCL invariant of the class Permission:

```
1 context Permission inv DayOfWeekHourPermAssign:
2 if self.idPermission = 'p1' then
3  let u: RBACUtility = RBACUtility.allInstances(),
4    day: RelativeTimePoint = u.getDayOfWeek(),
5    r: Role = Role.allInstances() ->
6        select(r : Role | r.idRole = 'r1'),
7    temporalContext: Set(RBACContext) = self.
8        permissionContextAssignment -> select(c |
9        c.oclIsTypeOf(TemporalContext)),
10   timeE: Set (ComposedRelativeTE) = temporalContext.
11       oclAsType(TemporalContext).timeexpression.
12       relative.oclAsType(ComposedRelativeTE)
13       -> flatten() -> asSet(),
14   days: Set (ComposedRelativeTE) = timeE ->select(t|
15      (t.oclIsTypeOf(RelativeTimeInterval) and
16       t.oclAsType(RelativeTimeInterval).start.
17       oclIsTypeOf(DayOfWeek) and day.isContained
18      (t.oclAsType(RelativeTimeInterval)))
19      or (t.oclIsTypeOf(DayOfWeek) and
20      day.equalTo(t.oclAsType(DayOfWeek))))
21  in if days -> exists (t| t.checkHours(u)) then
22             self.roles -> includes (r)
23      else
24            self.roles -> excludes (r)
25      endif
26 endif
```

In this OCL expression if the current permission is p_1, we select the day corresponding to the day of week at which the snapshot was taken, by calling the getDayOfWeek operation of the class RBACUtility (lines 3–4). Then, we select the instance corresponding to role r_1 (lines 5–6). We retrieve the list of temporal contexts temporalContext in which the permission should be assigned to role r_1 (lines 7–9) and compute, over the elements of this list, the list timeE of relative time expressions assigned to them (lines 10–13). Based on the type of policy described above, we have to select, among the elements of timeE, the list days of relative time expressions having a ComposedRelativeTE of type DayOfWeek or of type RelativeTimeInterval with bounds of type DayOfWeek (lines 14–20). While selecting the time expressions in this list, we check whether the day at which the snapshot was taken is contained in the selected TimeExpression. To do so, we check separately for the DayOfWeek, by calling operation equalTo of class RelativeTimePoint (line 20), and for the RelativeTimeInterval by calling operation isContained of class RelativeTimePoint (line 17). In this specific example, list days will include a TimeExpression that contains two ComposedRelativeTE. These objects are: a RelativeTimeInterval (whose start and end RelativeTimePoints correspond to "Wednesday" and "Friday"); and a RelativeTimeInterval (whose start and end RelativeTimePoints correspond to "10:00" and "14:00"). We remark that the first object overlays the second. We check whether the time at which the snapshot was taken is contained in one of the TimeExpressions in days. To do so, we check the hours overlaid by the day(s) of the week by calling operation checkHours of class ComposedRelativeTE (line 21). If the check succeeds, we require role r_1 to belong to the list of roles of permission p_1 (line 22). Otherwise, we require the role not to be in this list (line 24). Because of space limitations, in the remaining of this section we focus only on the specification of policies at the role level.

A policy on role assignment with a relative time expression containing an index of a specific DayOfWeek restricts the day in which a given user can acquire a given role, as in *"assign role r_1 to user u_1 on the 2nd Monday of June"*. This policy can be checked by verifying an OCL invariant of the class Role:

```
1 context Role inv indexRoleAssign:
2 let u: RBACUtility = RBACUtility.allInstances(),
3    month: ecore::EInt = u.getCurrentTime().month,
4    day: RelativeTimePoint =  u.getDayOfWeek(),
5    u1: User = User.allInstances() ->
6        select(m : User | m.idUser = 'u1'),
7    temporalContext: Set(RBACContext) = self.
8        roleContextAssignment -> select(c |
9        c.oclIsTypeOf(TemporalContext)),
10   timeE: Set(ComposedRelativeTE) = temporalContext.
11       oclAsType(TemporalContext).timeexpression.
12       relative.oclAsType(ComposedRelativeTE)
13       -> flatten() -> asSet()
14 in self.idRole = 'r1'
15    and self.users -> includes (u1) implies
16    timeE -> exists(t | t.oclIsTypeOf(MonthOfYear)
17    and t.oclAsType(MonthOfYear).month  = month
18    and t.checkDayIndex(u))
```

In this invariant we first select the month and day of week at which the snapshot was taken by calling the getCurrentTime and getDayOfWeek operations of class RBACUtility (lines 3–4). Then, we select the instance corresponding to user u_1 (line 6). We retrieve the list temporalContext of temporal contexts in which the role should be assigned (lines 7–9) and compute, over the elements of this list, the list timeE of time expressions assigned to them (lines 10–13). The implication at lines 14–18 states that if the current role is r_1 and user u_1 is a member of this role, the temporal context for role assignment should match the current DayOfWeek; this condition is verified by calling operation checkDayIndex of class ComposedRelativeTE.

A policy on role assignment with time expression containing a periodic expression restricts the time at which a role can be assigned to a user as in "user u_1 acquires role r_1 every 5 days starting from July 10, 2014 at 16:00". This policy can be checked in OCL as an invariant of class Role:

```
1 context Role inv periodicUnboundTIRoleAssign:
2 let u: RBACUtility = RBACUtility.allInstances(),
3    u1: User = User.allInstances() ->
4        select(m : User | m.idUser = 'u1'),
5    temporalContext: Set(RBACContext) =
6       self.roleContextAssignment -> select(c |
7       c.oclIsTypeOf(TemporalContext)),
8    timeE: Set (TimeExpression) =
9        temporalContext.oclAsType(TemporalContext).
10       timeexpression.absolute
11       -> flatten() -> asSet(),
12   absoluteE: Set (TimeExpression) = timeE ->
13     select (t | t.absolute.oclAsType(TimeInterval)
14    ->exists(a| a.start.equalTo(u.getCurrentTime())
15     or a.start.isBefore(u.getCurrentTime()))),
16   periodicE: Set(PeriodicTime)= absoluteE.
17      relative.oclAsType(PeriodicTime)
```

```
18         -> flatten() -> asSet()
19 in self.idRole= 'r1' and self.users->includes(u1)
20      implies periodicE.nextStart->select( a |
21      a.equalTo(u.getCurrentTime()))->notEmpty()
```

In this invariant, we first select the instance corresponding to user u_1 (lines 3–4). We retrieve the list temporalContext of temporal contexts in which the role should be assigned to user u_1 (lines 5–7) and compute, over the elements of this list, the list timeE of time expressions assigned to them (lines 8–11). In this example, the list timeE will include a TimeExpression with an unbounded TimeInterval whose start TimePoint corresponds to "July 10, 2014 at 16:00". Then we select among the element of list timeE, the list (absoluteE) of expressions having an absolute TimeInterval that contains the TimePoint at which the snapshot was taken (lines 12–15). We check this containment by comparing the time at which the snapshot was taken with the start TimePoint of the unboundedTimeInterval. Afterwards, we retrieve the list of PeriodicTime objects in each expression in list absoluteE (lines 16–18). The implication at lines 19–21 states that if the current role is r_1, and user u_1 is member of this role, the time at which the snapshot was taken should match the starting time (derived from the nextStart association) of the next period.

A policy on role enabling with a duration associated with an absolute time expression restricts the activation of a role up to a specific duration, as in "enable all roles on April 23, 2015 from 8:00 to 18:00; each role can be active for 3 hours cumulatively". This policy can be checked in OCL as an invariant of class Session:

```
1 context Session inv DurationAbsoluteBTIRoleEnab:
2 let u : RBACUtility = RBACUtility.allInstances(),
3    rolesA: Set(Role) = self.enabledRoles ->
4         select (r:Role| r.getCurrentAbsoluteTE(u)
5         -> notEmpty() and
6         r.getCurrentAbsoluteTE(u).hasDuration())
7 in rolesA -> forAll(r: Role |
8       r.getCurrentAbsoluteTE(u).duration.
9       greaterThan(u.getCumulativeActiveDuration
10      (r,self.user, r.getCurrentAbsoluteT(u).
11      duration.timeUnit)))
```

In this OCL constraint, we select a subset (list rolesA) of the roles enabled in the current session (lines 3–6). This subset includes the roles whose temporal context for enabling contains an absolute time expression that matches the time at which the snapshot was taken (checked by calling the operation getCurrentAbsoluteTE of the class Role). For each role in rolesA, this absolute time expression should be associated with a duration (checked by calling the operation hasDuration of the class AbsoluteTE). Then, we check whether the duration of each role in the list is less than the duration specified in its temporal context for enabling (lines 7–11). We assume that the duration of the activation of each role for each user is recorded in a database and made available through the operation getCumulativeActiveDuration of class RBACUtility.

4.2 Policies with spatial context

A policy on role assignment with a physical location forbids the role assignment when the user is not located in a physical location belonging to the role spatial context for assignment, as in "role r_1 is assigned to user u_1 *only* if the latter is in location loc_1". We assume that loc_1 is of type PhysicalLocation. This policy can be checked in OCL as an invariant of class Role:

```
1 context Role inv physicalLocationRoleAssign:
2 let  u1 : User = User.allInstances() ->
3           select(m: User | m.idUser = 'u1'),
4       spatialContext: Set(RBACContext) = self.
5           roleContextAssignment -> select(c |
6           c.oclIsTypeOf(SpatialContext)),
7       locPh: Set(PhysicalLocation) = spatialContext.
8         oclAsType(SpatialContext).location.
9         oclAsType(PhysicalLocation)->flatten()
10         ->asSet()
11 in if self.idRole = 'r1' and loc -> exists(l|
12        l.contains(u1.userLocation.location.
13        oclAsType(PhysicalLocation))) then
14              self.users -> includes(u1)
15      else
16              self.users -> excludes(u1)
17      endif
```

In this OCL expression, we first select the instance corresponding to user u_1 (lines 2–3). Then, we retrieve the list spatialContext of spatial contexts at which the role should be assigned to user u_1 (lines 4–6) and compute, over the elements of this list, the list locPh of physical locations assigned to them (lines 7–10). We check if the current role is r_1 and if a physical location in list locPh matches the user's location, by calling the operation contains of class Location. If this is the case, the list of roles assigned to user u_1 should contain role r_1 (lines 11–14). If it is not the case, the role should not be included in this list (line 16).

A policy on role assignment with a logical location is checked in a similar way by replacing the instances of PhysicalLocation with instances of LogicalLocation.

A policy on role assignment with a relative location forbids the role assignment when the user is not located in a relative location belonging to the role spatial context for assignment, as in "enable role r_1 *only* within 3 meters outside location loc_1". Location loc_1 can be either of type PhysicalLocation or LogicalLocation. This policy is checked in OCL as an invariant of class Session:

```
1 context Session inv relativeLocationRoleEnabling:
2 let r1 : Role = Role.allInstances() ->
3        select(r : Role| r.idRole = 'r1'),
4     spatialContext: Set(RBACContext) = self.
5         roleContextEnabling -> select(c |
6         c.oclIsTypeOf(SpatialContext)),
7     loc: Set(Location) = spatialContext.
8         oclAsType(SpatialContext).location
9         ->select(l|l.relativelocation->notEmpty())
10        ->flatten()->asSet(),
11      relativeLoc: Set(Location)= loc -> collect(l|
12        l.computeRelative(l.relativelocation))
13        ->flatten()->asSet()
14 in if relativeLoc -> exists(l|self.user.
15        userLocation.location -> exists(pos|
16        l.contains(pos))) then
17            self.enabledRoles -> includes(r1)
18            or self.activeRoles -> includes(r1)
19     else
```

```
20            self.enabledRoles -> excludes(rl)
21            and  self.activeRoles -> excludes(rl)
22    endif
```

In this OCL invariant, we first select the instance corresponding to role r_1 (lines 2–3). We retrieve list `spatialContext` of spatial contexts at which the role should be enabled (lines 4–6) and compute, over the locations assigned to each element in this list, the list `loc` of all locations associated with a relative one (lines 7–10). For each location in list `loc`, we compute in `relativeLoc` the location resulting from the call to operation `computeRelative` of class `Location` (lines 11–13). This operation takes in input `RelativeLocation` and is applied to a `PhysicalLocation` or `LogicalLocation`, hereafter called *base location*. It returns the location resulting from the application to the base location of the parameters (distance and direction) of the relative location. The resulting location is always of type `PhysicalLocation`. We check if any of locations in `relativeLoc` matches the user's position (lines 14–16). If it is the case, the role r_1 should be enabled or active (lines 17–18). Otherwise, the role should be disabled (lines 20–21).

Closing remarks. In this section we have shown how the access decision for spatial and temporal RBAC policies defined according to the GEMRBAC+CTX model can be reduced to the verification of OCL constraints of an instance of the GEMRBAC+CTX model. For space reasons, we have considered temporal and spatial policies in isolation. Nevertheless, we support also *composite context-based policies*, i.e., policies that contain both a temporal and a spatial context. These policies can be checked in OCL by a logical conjunction of the individual OCL constraints corresponding to the composite spatial and temporal policies. The OCL formalization presented here is at the core of a model-driven approach for checking RBAC policies, whose complete description (including technological aspects) is outside the scope of the paper. For example, we have assumed that at any time during the execution of the system for which RBAC policies are defined, we could take a snapshot of the system state and represent it as an instance of the GEMRBAC+CTX model. This assumption is based on previous work of some of the authors on model-driven run-time verification [10], which shows how a run-time system can be represented as a "live" instance of a conceptual model, on which to check OCL constraints.

5. INDUSTRIAL APPLICATION

In this section we report on the application of our approach based on GEMRBAC+CTX for the modeling of a real application and of its RBAC contextual policies. This application has been developed by a provider of situational-aware information management systems for emergency scenarios. The application allows different (humanitarian) organizations to participate to various missions by providing emergency aid to refugees and casualties. An RBAC system controls the access to mission resources. Due to space limitations, we present a small excerpt of the application and consider only a subset of the actual RBAC entities. Moreover, the description has been sanitized for confidentiality reasons. We assume the system to have two `Users`, *Joe* and *Kim*; three `Roles`, *agencyAdmin*, *missionAdmin* and *missionMember*; one `Permission` *noBandwidthLimit*; one `TemporalContext` (hereafter referred to with the id *freeTime*) that ranges from 00.00 to 06.00 and from 20.00 to 23.59 during weekdays and all-day during the weekend; one `SpatialContext` *Zone1*. The following contextual policies are defined for the system:

PL1: *permission* noBandwidthLimit *is assigned to role* missionMember *only during* freeTime. This policy is typically used to ensure a fair use of the available bandwidth.

PL2: *role* agencyAdmin *is enabled only outside Zone1.* This policy is typically used to ensure that administrative tasks are performed, for security reasons, outside the area of the mission.

PL3: *role* missionAdmin *is enabled only inside Zone1.* This policy is typically used for guaranteeing that mission management is done locally.

The object diagram in Figure 4 depicts a small subset of the instance of the GEMRBAC+CTX model that corresponds to a system state during the mission. Roles *agencyAdmin* and *missionMember* are assigned both to *Joe* and to *Kim*. Role `missionAdmin` is assigned to *Joe*. According to policy **PL1**, the temporal context for assignment of permission *noBandwidthLimit* is `freeTime`. It is modeled as a `TimeExpression` composed of four `RelativeTimeIntervals`. Interval `weekend` has a start (`Saturday`) and end (`Sunday`) `RelativeTimePoint` of type `DayOfWeek`. Interval `weekDays` has a start (`Monday`) and end (`Friday`) `RelativeTimePoint` of type `DayOfWeek`. Interval `weekDays` overlays `hours1` and `hours2`: these intervals are of type `HourOfDay`. Let us consider the case in which one wants to check policy **PL1** on this instance. This policy can be checked using the OCL invariant `DayOfWeekHourPermAssign` introduced in Section 4.1. The `if` condition at line 21 is `false` because the time at which the snapshot was taken is not included in the temporal context for enabling permission *noBandwidthLimit*. Hence, we follow the `else` branch, calling operation `excludes` at line 24. Since role *missionMember* is not assigned to permission *noBandwidthLimit*, policy **PL1** is not violated.

According to policy **PL2**, the spatial context for enabling role `AgencyAdmin` is modeled as a `LogicalLocation` (*LLAgencyAdmin*) associated with a `RelativeLocation` (*rloc1*) that contains a `QualitativeDirection` (`inside`). The spatial context for enabling role `MissionAdmin`, indicated in policy **PL3**, is modeled in a similar way (see *LLMissionAdmin*, *rloc2*). The snapshot in Figure 4 includes an instance of `RBACUtility` that captures the `TimePoint` and the `DayWeek` at which it was taken (*Monday, May 4, 2015 at 12:15:23*). In this snapshot, users are connected to the system; we model this with `Sessions`. In session *sesJoe*, role `missionAdmin` is active and role `missionMember` is enabled for user *Joe*. In session `sesKim`, roles `missionMember` and `agencyAdmin` are enabled for user *Kim*. This model instance also captures the location of the two users at the time of their connection. Each of these locations is represented with an association between each `User` and his `SpatialContext`, which contains an object of type `Point`. Objects `pK` and `pJ` refers to the position of users *Kim* and *Joe*. We assume that only *Joe* is located in the defined zone *Zone1*. We now consider the case in which one wants to check policy **PL2** on this model instance. This policy can be checked on both `Sessions`, `sesKim` and `sesJoe`, using the OCL invariant `relativeLocationRoleEnabling` (shown in section 4.2) parametrized with role *agencyAdmin*. For `Session` `sesKim`, the `if` condition at lines 14–16 is true because *Kim*, according to the assumption made above, is outside *Zone1*, meaning that her position (object `pK`) is contained in the lo-

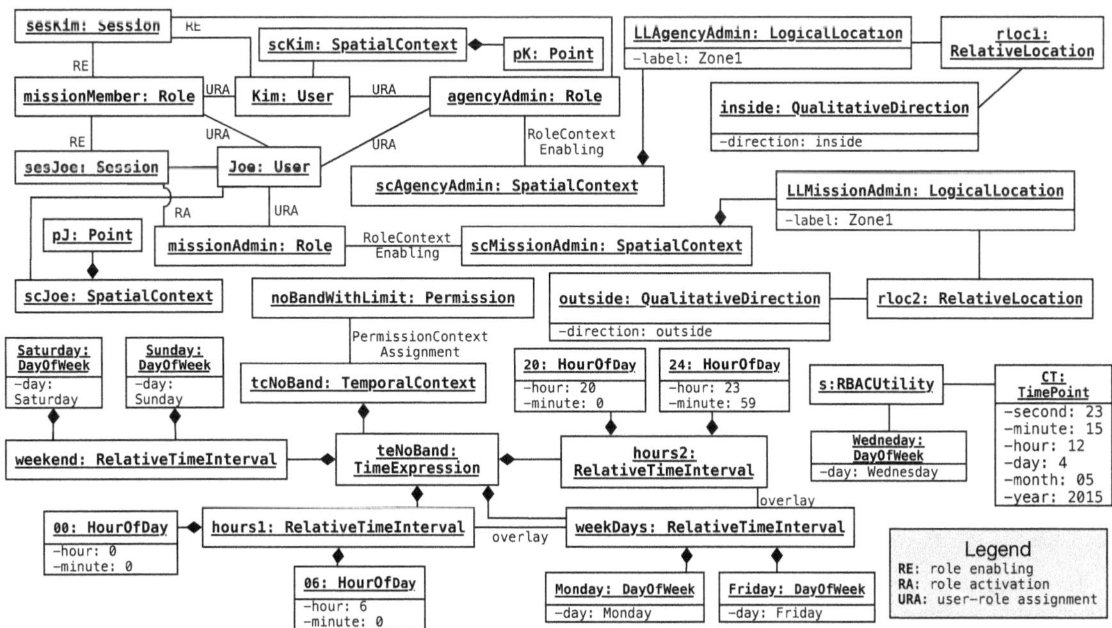

Figure 4: An instance of the GemRBAC+CTX model representing a system state of the example application.

cation `LLAgencyAdmin` associated with the spatial context for enabling role *agencyAdmin* (object `scAgencyAdmin`). Hence, we follow the `then` branch, calling the operation `includes` at lines 17–18. Since role `agencyAdmin` is enabled in the session, this operation returns true, meaning that policy **PL2** is not violated for Kim. Policy **PL3** is checked in a similar way on sessions `sesKim` and `sesJoe`, using the same OCL invariant parametrized with role *missionAdmin*. This policy is not violated since role *missionAdmin* is not enabled for `Kim` (i.e., there is no association between objects `sesKim` and `missionAdmin`) and is active for `Joe` (i.e., there is an association between `sesJoe` and `missionAdmin`).

Evaluation. In the evaluation of the industrial application, we mainly focused on assessing whether all contextual policies required by the application could be expressed with our approach. The new model has allowed the security engineers of our partner to define *19 new types* of RBAC contextual policies. With these new policies, engineers can now tune the definition of fine-grained (from the point of view of context) RBAC policies. This is a major improvement over the previous solution, which granted permissions under any context, for the lack of better specification methods. Moreover, since the GEMRBAC+CTX defines structural constraints among entities, it will prevent end-users to define RBAC policies that are not well-formed.

Overall, the application of the modeling approach supported by GEMRBAC+CTX has been warmly welcome by the security engineers of HITEC. Nevertheless, the engineers also reported some drawbacks of our current approach. In particular, they remarked that defining RBAC policies as OCL constraints on the GEMRBAC+CTX class model was sometimes cumbersome, especially for complex policies (with large corresponding models). To address this limitation, as part of future work, we plan to define a domain-specific language (DSL) on top of the GEMRBAC+CTX model, to allow the definition of policies at a higher-level of abstraction, using a syntax close to natural language.

We also assessed the performance of our model-driven approach in terms of the time required to provide an access decision, i.e., the time needed to evaluate an OCL constraint corresponding to a certain contextual RBAC policy. We used a laptop with a 2.2 GHz Intel Dual-Core i7 CPU and 16GB of memory, running Eclipse Mars Service Release 1, JavaSE-1.8, Eclipse OCL v.4.1.0. The evaluation of policies **PL1–PL3** on the complete model (with 67 roles, 252 permissions, 914 users, 400 temporal contexts and 700 spatial contexts) took 24 ms for **PL1**, 2847 ms for **PL2**, and 2405 ms for **PL3**. We considered the worst-case scenario when all the roles are active and all the roles are assigned to permission p_1. These results confirm the suitability of our approach for operationalizing access decisions for contextual policies in real applications. Although scalability studies on policy checking are out of the scope of this paper, we are confident in the scalability of our approach also for much larger models. For example, community experience [19] shows that Eclipse OCL can check complex OCL constraints on models with millions of elements in few seconds.

6. RELATED WORK

Several extensions of the original RBAC model [23] have been proposed in the literature to express temporal and/or spatial contexts. The first proposed temporal model, TRBAC [6], introduces temporal policies on role enabling. It supports absolute, relative and periodic time. A generalization of this model, called GTRBAC [13], includes temporal policies on role assignment. It also supports the specification of temporal policies restricting the activation duration of a given role. A limitation of these two models is the lack of support for temporal policies at the permission level. As for spatial extensions of RBAC, GeoRBAC [7] introduces spatial policies on role enabling. LRBAC [20] and SRBAC [12] support policies with spatial context not only for role enabling but also for user-role and role-permission

Table 1: Support of policies in RBAC models

	Contextual policies								Scope				Decision	Non-contextual
	ART	PTE	I	AD	PL	LL	RL	CP	PA	PE	RA	RE	algorithm	policies [5]
TRBAC [6]	+	+	+	-	-	-	-	N/A	-	-	-	+	+	2/18
GTRBAC [13]	+	+	+	+	-	-	-	N/A	-	-	+	+	+	9/18
GeoRBAC [7]	-	-	-	-	+	+	-	N/A	-	-	-	+	+	4/18
LRBAC [20]	-	-	-	-	+	+	-	N/A	+	-	+	+	+	2/18
SRBAC [12]	-	-	-	-	+	+	-	N/A	+	-	+	+	-	3/18
STARBAC [2]	+	+	-	-	+	+	-	+	-	+	-	+	-	0/18
ESTRBAC [1]	+	+	+	-	+	+	-	+	+	-	+	+	+	3/18
STRBAC [22]	+	+	-	-	+	+	-	-	+	-	+	+	+	7/18
GSTRBAC [18]	+	+	-	-	+	+	-	+	+	-	+	+	-	8/18
OrBAC [9]	+	+	-	-	+	+	-	+	-	+	-	+	+	5/18
LotRBAC [8]	+	+	+	+	+	+	+	+	+	-	+	+	-	6/18
GemRBAC+CTX	+	+	+	+	+	+	+	+	+	+	+	+	+	18/18

Legend. ART: Absolute and Relative TE; PTE: Periodic TE; I: Index; AD: Activation Duration; PL: Physical Location; LL: Logical Location; RL: Relative Location; CP: Composite context-based policies, RA: User-role Assignment, RE: Role Enabling, PA: Role-permission Assignment, PE: Permission Enabling.

assignment. However, these models do not support spatial policies for permission enabling and have limited support for role disabling. Among RBAC extensions that support both temporal and spatial policies, there is STARBAC [2], with support for contextual policies for role enabling. ESTRBAC [1] extends STARBAC to support contextual policies for role enabling and both user-role and role-permission assignment. STRBAC [22] does not support the definition of composite context-based policies. This limitation is overcome by GSTRBAC [18]. OrBAC [9] defines context as an additional condition restricting the user access in different organizations, and abstracts away from the usual concepts of spatial and temporal context. STRBAC, GSTRBAC, and OrBAC do not support the concepts of index and activation duration for temporal policies, and the concept of relative location for spatial policies. LotRBAC [8] extends GTRBAC by assigning a location to each user, role and permission. It does not support permission enabling and the specification of the perimeter of physical locations.

Regarding checking contextual policies defined over the models surveyed above, the SRBAC [12], STARBAC [2], GSTRBAC [18] and LotRBAC [8] models do not come with any access decision algorithm.

Table 1 summarizes to which extent the RBAC models discussed above support the various concepts related to contextual policies. It also indicates the scope (assignment/enabling of permissions and/or roles) in which such policies can be used, the availability of an access decision algorithm, and the number of types of non-contextual policies (as identified in the taxonomy presented in [5]) they support. As one can see, the GemRBAC+CTX model proposed in this paper is the only one that supports 1) all the various spatio-temporal concepts for contextual policies; 2) the use of such policies for the assignment and enabling of both roles and permissions; 3) a checking procedure for these policies; 4) a complete support for non-contextual properties.

As for the use of UML and OCL for modeling and checking RBAC policies, several approaches have been proposed (such as [4, 16, 24, 15, 21, 25]); we refer the reader to our previous work [5] for a detailed discussion.

7. CONCLUSION AND FUTURE WORK

Several application domains require the definition of RBAC policies that restrict access based on the location of the user or the time at which she requests the access. These policies are called contextual policies and come with many facets, ranging from complex types of temporal expressions to different types of locations and their topological relations. The conceptual RBAC models proposed so far in the literature do not support all the facets of contextual policies and provide limited support to evaluate these policies in order to make an access decision.

In this paper we presented GemRBAC+CTX, a conceptual model that contains all the entities required to accurately specify temporal and spatial contexts in RBAC policies. We formalized these policies as OCL constraints on the GemRBAC+CTX model, as a way to operationalize the access decision for user's requests. We reported on the application of GemRBAC+CTX to model the RBAC policies of a real application in the domain of disaster relief intervention. The use of GemRBAC+CTX has allowed security engineers to define 19 new types of contextual policies, with a fine-grained, precise description of contexts. The preliminary experimental results show the suitability of our model-driven approach for checking RBAC contextual policies.

As part of future work, we plan to extend GemRBAC+CTX based on the recent proposals that support proximity-based policies [14] and geo-social ones [3]. We also plan to define a domain-specific language on top of the GemRBAC+CTX model, to allow the definition of RBAC policies using a syntax close to natural language. The proposed model-driven approach for policy checking could also be integrated into a platform for model-driven run-time enforcement, tailored for checking policies defined using GemRBAC+CTX.

8. ACKNOWLEDGMENTS

This work has been supported by the National Research Fund, Luxembourg (FNR/P10/03) and by a grant by HITEC Luxembourg. Ameni Ben Fadhel is also supported by the Faculty of Science, Technology and Communication of the University of Luxembourg.

9. REFERENCES

[1] S. Aich, S. Mondal, S. Sural, and A. Majumdar. Role Based Access Control with Spatiotemporal Context for Mobile Applications. In *Trans. on Comput. Sci. IV*, volume 5430 of *LNCS*, pages 177–199. Springer, 2009.

[2] S. Aich, S. Sural, and A. Majumdar. STARBAC: Spatiotemporal Role Based Access Control. In *Proc. of the OTM Conferences 2007*, volume 4804 of *LNCS*, pages 1567–1582. Springer, 2007.

[3] N. Baracaldo, B. Palanisamy, and J. Joshi. Geo-Social-RBAC: A location-based socially aware access control framework. In *Proc. of NSS 2014*, volume 8792 of *LNCS*, pages 501–509. Springer, 2014.

[4] D. Basin, J. Doser, and T. Lodderstedt. Model Driven Security: From UML Models to Access Control Infrastructures. *ACM Trans. on Soft. Eng. and Meth.*, 15:39–91, 2006.

[5] A. Ben Fadhel, D. Bianculli, and L. Briand. A comprehensive modeling framework for role-based access control policies. *Journal of Systems and Software*, 107:110–126, September 2015.

[6] E. Bertino, P. A. Bonatti, and E. Ferrari. TRBAC: A Temporal Role-based Access Control Model. *ACM Trans. Inf. Syst. Secur.*, 4(3):191–233, Aug. 2001.

[7] E. Bertino, B. Catania, M. L. Damiani, and P. Perlasca. GEO-RBAC: A Spatially Aware RBAC. In *Proc. of SACMAT 2005*, pages 29–37. ACM, 2005.

[8] S. Chandran and J. Joshi. LoT-RBAC: A Location and Time-Based RBAC Model. In *Proc. of WISE 2005*, volume 3806 of *LNCS*, pages 361–375. Springer, 2005.

[9] F. Cuppens and N. Cuppens-Boulahia. Modeling contextual security policies. *Int. JIS*, 7(4):285–305, 2008.

[10] W. Dou, D. Bianculli, and L. Briand. Revisiting model-driven engineering for run-time verification of business processes. In *Proc. of SAM 2014*, volume 8769 of *LNCS*, pages 190–197. Springer, September 2014.

[11] Eclipse. Eclipse OCL tools. http://www.eclipse.org/modeling/mdt/?project=ocl.

[12] F. Hansen and V. Oleshchuk. SRBAC: A spatial role-based access control model for mobile systems. In *Proc. of NORDSEC2003*, pages 129–141, 2003.

[13] J. B. D. Joshi, E. Bertino, U. Latif, and A. Ghafoor. A Generalized Temporal Role-based Access Control Model. *IEEE Trans. Knowl. Data Eng.*, 17(1):4–23, January 2005.

[14] M. S. Kirkpatrick, M. L. Damiani, and E. Bertino. Prox-RBAC: A proximity-based spatially aware RBAC. In *Proc. of GIS 2011*, pages 339–348. ACM, 2011.

[15] M. Kuhlmann and M. Gogolla. Modeling and validating Mondex scenarios described in UML and OCL with USE. *Formal Aspects of Computing*, 20:79–100, 2008.

[16] M. Kuhlmann, L. Hamann, and M. Gogolla. Extensive validation of OCL models by integrating SAT solving into USE. In *Proc. of TOOLS 2011*, volume 6705 of *LNCS*, pages 290–306, 2011.

[17] OMG. Object Constraint Language. http://www.omg.org/spec/OCL/, 2012.

[18] A. Ramadan, A.-L. Mustafa, R. Indrakshi, and F. Robert B. Specification, Validation, and Enforcement of a Generalized Spatio-Temporal Role-Based Access Control Model. *IEEE Syst. J.*, 7(3):501–515, September 2013.

[19] I. Ràth and E. Willink. Fast, faster and super-fast queries. http://www.eclipse.org/modeling/mdt/ocl/docs/publications/EclipseConEurope2012/FastQueries.pdf, October 2012. EclipseCon Europe.

[20] I. Ray, M. Kumar, and L. Yu. LRBAC: A Location-Aware Role-Based Access Control Model. In *Proc. of ICISS 2006*, volume 4332 of *LNCS*, pages 147–161. Springer, 2006.

[21] I. Ray, N. Li, R. France, and D.-K. Kim. Using UML to visualize role-based access control constraints. In *Proc. of SACMAT 2004*, pages 115–124, 2004.

[22] I. Ray and M. Toahchoodee. A Spatio-temporal Role-Based Access Control Model. In *Proc. of DBSec 2007*, volume 4602 of *LNCS*, pages 211–226. Springer, 2007.

[23] R. S. Sandhu, E. J. Coyne, H. L. Feinstein, and C. E. Youman. Role-based Access Control Models. *Computer*, 29(2):38–47, 1996.

[24] K. Sohr, T. Mustafa, X. Bao, and G.-J. Ahn. Enforcing role-based access control policies in web services with UML and OCL. In *Proc. of ACSAC 2008*, pages 257–266. IEEE, 2008.

[25] M. Strembeck and J. Mendling. Modeling Process-related RBAC Models with Extended UML Activity Models. *Information and Software Technology*, 53:456–483, 2011.

SDN Research Challenges and Opportunities

Anita Nikolich
The National Science Foundation

Abstract

The National Science Foundation has made investments in Software Defined Networking (SDN) and Network Function Virtualization (NFV) for many years, in both the research and infrastructure areas. SDN and NFV enable systems to become more open to transformative research, with implications for revolutionary new applications and services. Additionally, the emerging concept of Software-Defined Exchanges will enable large-scale interconnection of Software Defined infrastructures, owned and operated by many different organizations, to provide logically isolated ³on demand² global scale infrastructure on an end-to-end basis, with enhanced flexibility and security for new applications.

This talk will examine past NSF investments and successes in SDN/NFV, identify new research opportunities available to the community and present challenges that need to be overcome to make SDN/NFV a reality in operational cyberinfrastructure.

CODASPY'16, March 9–11, 2016, New Orleans, LA, USA.
ACM ISBN: 978-1-4503-3935-3/16/03.
DOI: http://dx.doi.org/10.1145/2857705.2857730

Detecting Malicious Exploit Kits using Tree-based Similarity Searches

Teryl Taylor†, Xin Hu‡, Ting Wang*, Jiyong Jang‡, Marc Ph. Stoecklin‡, Fabian Monrose†, and Reiner Sailer‡
† University of North Carolina at Chapel Hill, {tptaylor, fabian}@cs.unc.edu
‡ IBM T.J. Watson Research Center, {huxin, jjang, mpstoeck}@us.ibm.com
* Lehigh University, ting@cse.lehigh.edu

ABSTRACT

Unfortunately, the computers we use for everyday activities can be infiltrated while simply browsing innocuous sites that, unbeknownst to the website owner, may be laden with malicious advertisements. So-called malvertising, redirects browsers to web-based exploit kits that are designed to find vulnerabilities in the browser and subsequently download malicious payloads. We propose a new approach for detecting such malfeasance by leveraging the inherent structural patterns in HTTP traffic to classify exploit kit instances. Our key insight is that an exploit kit leads the browser to download payloads using multiple requests from malicious servers. We capture these interactions in a "tree-like" form, and using a scalable index of malware samples, model the detection process as a subtree similarity search problem. The approach is evaluated on 3800 hours of real-world traffic including over 4 billion flows and reduces false positive rates by four orders of magnitude over current state-of-the-art techniques with comparable true positive rates. We show that our approach can operate in near real-time, and is able to handle peak traffic levels on a large enterprise network — identifying 28 new exploit kit instances during our analysis period.

1. INTRODUCTION

Today, our computers are routinely compromised while performing seemingly innocuous activities like reading articles on trusted websites [43] (e.g., the NY Times). All too often, these compromises are perpetrated via complex interactions involving the advertising networks that monetize these sites. Since crime typically follows the money, it is not too surprising then that miscreants have turned their attention to exploiting advertising networks as a way to reach wider audiences. In 2012 alone, web-based advertising generated revenues of over $36 billion [28], and its wide-spread reach makes it an excellent target for fraudsters and deviants. Furthermore, the many players in the online advertising industry — publishers (who display ads), advertising networks (who deliver ads), and advertisers (who create content) — offer a multitude of vantage points for attackers to leverage, and many of these compromises can go unnoticed for extended periods. A well known example is the widely publicized case involving advertising networks from Google and Microsoft that were tricked into displaying malicious content by miscreants posing as legitimate advertisers [16]. Sadly, such abuses are not isolated incidents and so-called *malvertising* has plagued many popular websites [29], exploited mobile devices [33], and have even been utilized as vessels for botnet activity [3]. For the most part, these exploits are delivered over HTTP, and detecting and defending against such attacks require accurate and efficient analytical techniques to help network operators better understand the attacks being perpetrated on their networks.

Many of these HTTP-based attacks are launched through the use of exploit kits [9, 6], which are web-based services designed to exploit vulnerabilities in web browsers by downloading malicious Java, Silverlight, or Flash files. Exploit kits, such as Fiesta and Blackhole represent an entire software-as-a-service subindustry. The exploitation of a user's system typically follows a four-step process wherein a user navigates to a website (e.g., CNN) that — unbeknownst to the user — contains an external link (e.g., an advertising link) with an injected `iframe` that in turn directs the user's browser to an invisible exploit kit landing page. At that point, information about the victim's system is passed along to the attacker's server, which is then used to select a malicious exploit file that is automatically downloaded. The downloaded file exploits a vulnerability on the system that allows the attacker to install a malicious binary or otherwise control the victim's machine.

Security analysts typically defend enterprise networks from these attacks using network monitoring devices (such as intrusion detection systems) that search HTTP traffic as it passes through the network's edge for signature matches, statistical patterns or known malicious domain names. Unfortunately, the attack landscape constantly changes as the attackers attempt to hide their nefarious web-based services and avoid blacklisting. As a result, current approaches typically incur high false positive and negative rates.

In this paper, we explore a network-centric technique for identifying agile web-based attacks with a focus on reducing false positives over existing approaches while maintaining or improving false negatives. We improve detection rates by leveraging the structural patterns inherent in HTTP traffic to classify specific exploit kit instances. Our key insight is that to infect a client browser, a web-based exploit kit must lead the client browser to visit its landing page (possibly through redirection across multiple compromised/malicious servers), download an exploit file and download a malicious payload, necessitating multiple requests to several malicious servers. Our approach captures the structure of these web requests in a tree-like form, and uses the encoded information for classification purposes. To see how this can help, consider the example where a user visits a website, and that action in turn sets off a chain of web requests that loads various web resources, including the main page, images, and advertisements. The overall

CODASPY'16, March 09-11, 2016, New Orleans, LA, USA
 ISBN 978-1-4503-3935-3/16/03...$15.00
DOI: http://dx.doi.org/10.1145/2857705.2857718

structure of these web requests forms a tree, where the nodes of the tree represent the web resources, and the edges between two nodes represent the causal relationships between these resources. For instance, loading an HTML page which contains a set of images might require one request for the page (the root node) and a separate set of requests (the children) for the images. When a resource on a website loads an exploit kit, the web requests associated with that kit form a subtree of the main tree representing the entire page load. Also, the exploitation is a multi-stage process involving multiple correlated sessions. By providing context through structure, we can capture the correlation among sessions, thereby providing improved detection accuracy.

Intuitively, identifying the malicious subtree within a sea of network traffic can be modeled as a subtree similarity problem. We demonstrate that we can quickly identify the presence of similar subtrees given only a handful of examples generated by an exploit kit. In order to do so, we build an index of malicious tree samples using information retrieval techniques. The malware index is essentially a search engine seeded with a small set of known malicious trees. A device monitoring network traffic can then query the index with subtrees built from the observed client traffic. The traffic is flagged as suspicious if a similar subtree can be found in the index. We note that our decision to use techniques from the field of information retrieval is motivated by the fact that these techniques are known to work well with extremely sparse feature sets (e.g., words and phrases), and the feature space for network analysis can be equally as sparse. Moreover, in information retrieval, the desire is to access a set of documents based on a user's query, and in most cases, the resulting set typically comprises a very small portion of the overall set of documents in the data store. Similarly, in network security, the malicious instances in the dataset tend to comprise only a fraction of the overall network traffic.

In the remainder of this paper, we present several contributions including a network-centric approach based on subtree similarity searching for detecting HTTP traffic related to malicious exploit kits on enterprise networks. We show that using the structural patterns of HTTP traffic can significantly reduce false positives with comparable false negative rates to current approaches. We also provide a novel solution to the subtree similarity problem, by modelling each node in the subtree as a point in a potentially high dimensional feature space. Finally, we utilize this technique to identify agile exploit kits found in a large network deployment.

2. RELATED WORK

Over the past decade, the web has become a dominant communication channel, and its popularity has fueled the rise of malicious websites [39] and malvertising as a vector for infecting vulnerable hosts. Provos et al. [26] examined the ways in which web page components could be used to exploit web browsers and infect clients through drive-by downloads. That study was later extended [27] to include an understanding of large-scale infrastructures of malware delivery networks, and provided overall statistics on the impact of these networks at a macro level. Their analysis found that ad syndication significantly contributed to drive-by downloads. Similarly, Zarras et al. [43] performed a large scale study of the prevalence of malvertising in ad networks. They showed that certain ad networks are more prone to serving malware than others. Grier et al. [9] studied the emergence of the exploit-as-a-service model for drive-by browser compromise and found that many of the most prominent families of malware are propagated through drive-by downloads from a handful of exploit kit flavors.

Since then, detecting malicious landing pages has been a hot topic of research. The most popular approach involves crawling the web for malicious content using known malicious websites as a seed [15, 17, 18, 8]. The crawled websites are verified using statistical analysis techniques [17] or by deploying honeyclients in virtual machines to monitor OS and browser changes [27]. Other approaches include the use of a PageRank algorithm to rank the maliciousness of crawled sites [18] and the use of mutual information to detect similarities among content-based features derived from malicious websites [38]. Eshete and Venkatakrishnan [8] identified content and structural features using samples of 38 exploit kits to build a set of classifiers that can analyze URLs by visiting them through a honey client. These approaches are complimentary to ours, but require significant resources to comb the Internet at scale.

Other approaches involve analyzing the source code of exploit kits to understand their behavior. For example, De Maio et al. [6] studied 50 kits to understand the conditions which triggered redirections to certain exploits. Such information can be leveraged for drive-by download detection. Stock et al. [34] clustered exploit kit samples to build host-based signatures for anti-virus engines and web browsers. Closer to our work are approaches that try to detect malicious websites using HTTP traffic. Cova et al. [5], for example, designed a system to instrument JavaScript run-time environments to detect malicious code execution while Rieck et al. [31] described an online approach that extracts all code snippets from web pages and loads them into a JavaScript sandbox for inspection. Unfortunately, these techniques do not scale well, and require precise client environment conditions to be most effective.

Other approaches focus on using statistical machine learning techniques to detect malicious pages by training a classifier with malicious samples and analyzing traffic in a network environment [31, 2, 1, 20, 21, 22, 24]. More comprehensive techniques focus on extracting javascript elements that are heavily obfuscated or `iframes` that link to known malicious sites [26, 5]. Cova et al. [5] and Mekky et al. [22] note that malicious websites often require a number of redirections, and build a set of features around that fact. Canali et al. [2] describes a static prefilter based on HTML, javascript, URL and host features while Ma et al. [20, 21] use mainly URL characteristics to identify malicious sites. Some of these approaches are used as pre-filter steps to eliminate likely benign websites from further dynamic analysis [27, 26, 2]. Unfortunately, these techniques take broad strokes in terms of specifying suspicious activity, and as such, tend to have high false positive rates. They also require large training sets that are often not available. By contrast, we provide a framework for detecting various flavors of exploit kits, and utilize the interactions between HTTP flows to reduce false positives from a small seed of examples.

Yegneswaran et al. [42] describe a framework for building semantic signatures for client-side vulnerabilities packet traces collected from a honeypot. The work shares the similar observation with ours that correlating flows can help to reduce false positives; however, our work focuses on the specific problem of detecting server-side exploit kits using the structure of HTTP traffic. As such, our approach is different in that we model kits as trees, and take advantage of structural similarity properties to reduce FPs. We also use thresholding to control false positive and negative rates. More recently, Stringhini et al. [35] proposed a learning approach to detect malicious redirection chains using a proprietary dataset. The technique requires traffic from a large crowd of diverse users from different countries, using different browsers and OSes to visit the same malicious websites in order to train a classifier. Unfortunately, as shown in the work, the approach leads to relatively high false positives and negatives with modest data labels and can only detect chains whereby the last node is deemed malicious. By contrast, our work does not model client usage patterns and is not lim-

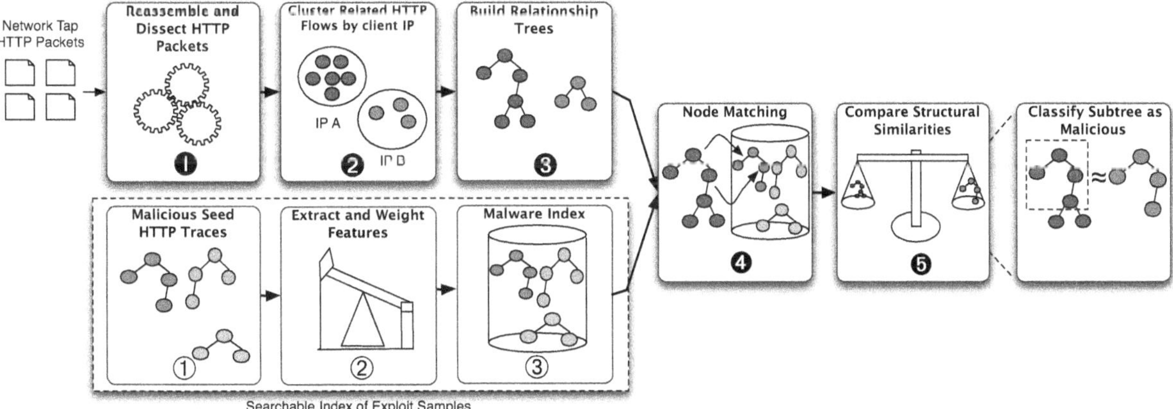

Figure 1: High level overview of the search-based malware system.

ited to the presence of redirection chains to identify exploit kits. Our technique is based on structural similarity; therefore, the last node in the structure does not need to be malicious. Finally, our approach is designed to specifically reduce false positives and negatives in light of a small amount of malicious training data.

Subtree Similarity Search Problem: Lastly, we note that the subtree similarity-search problem on large datasets remains an open research problem. Most proposals require scanning each tree in the dataset and then applying tree edit distance techniques to prune the search space. Recently, Cohen [4] combined the general structural commonalities of trees as well as the uncommon elements to reduce the number of trees checked in a similarity search. The drawback of that work is that the indices are 10x the size of the input data and only works with single-labeled nodes. Our work is based on similar ideas to Cohen [4] but works on trees where the nodes themselves have a large number of features. To make the approach practical, we leverage the sparsity of the feature space in network traffic.

3. APPROACH

For the most part, today's network-centric approaches for detecting HTTP-based malware use HTTP flows individually when performing analytics, but doing so can lead to high false positive rates. By contrast, we focus on the interactions *between* flows to identify malicious cases in network traffic in order to reduce false positives and identify exploit kits — hopefully before they have an opportunity to exploit a vulnerable client. Our key insight is that to infect a client, a web-based exploit kit will lead the client browser to download a malicious payload by making multiple web requests to one or more malicious servers. We use those multiple requests to build a tree-like structure and model the problem as a subtree similarity search problem.

A high-level overview of our approach is shown in Figure 1. There are two main components: an index of known exploit kits (Figure 1 (bottom)) and an online component that monitors HTTP traffic and performs comparisons with the index to identify and label potentially malicious traffic (Figure 1 (top)).

Indexing stage: In step ①, we collect HTTP traffic samples representing client browser interactions with various flavors of exploit kits (e.g., Fiesta) and convert them into tree-like representations. Flow-level and structure information are extracted from these trees (step ②) and then stored in a tree-based invertible index (step ③) called a malware index as described in more detail in Section 3.2.

Classification stage: HTTP traffic is monitored at the edge of an enterprise network, and packets are dissected and reassembled into bidirectional flows (see step ❶). The reassembled flows are grouped by client IP addresses (step ❷) and assembled into tree-like structures (step ❸, § 3.1) called web session trees. The nodes in the web session tree are then mapped to "similar" nodes of the trees in the malware index using content features (step ❹, § 3.3.1), and finally, the mapped nodes are structurally compared to the trees in the index to classify subtrees as malicious (step ❺, § 3.3.2). Given a web session tree and an index of malware trees, the goal is to find all malicious subtrees in the tree that are similar to a tree in the index.

3.1 On Building Trees

In both components of our system (indexing and classification), HTTP traffic is grouped and converted into tree-like structures called web session trees. We use a two-step process to build these session trees for analysis. The first step in the process is to assemble HTTP packets into bidirectional TCP flows and then group them based on their client IP addresses. Flows are ordered by time, and then associated by web session using a technique similar to that used by Ihm and Pai [14] and Provos et al. [27]. A web session tree is defined as all HTTP web requests originating from a single root request over a rolling time window of a tuneable parameter $\triangle t_w$ (empirically set to five seconds in our implementation). A node in the tree is an HTTP flow representing some web resource (e.g., webpage, picture, executable, and so on) with all related flow attributes including URL, IP, port, and HTTP header and payload information. An edge between nodes represents the causal relationship between the nodes (e.g., a webpage *loads* an image). For example, a client surfing to Facebook creates a single root request for the Facebook main page (i.e., the root node of the web session tree), which in turn *loads* images and JavaScript files (i.e., the child nodes). All related files form a client "web session" and the relationships between these resources form a tree-like structure as outlined below.

Each HTTP flow is compared with flow groups that have been active in the last $\triangle t_w$ window for the associated client IP address. Flows are assigned to a particular group based on specific header and content-based attributes that are checked in a priority order. The highest priority attributes are the HTTP `Referer` and the `Location` fields. The `Referer` field identifies the URL of the webpage that linked the resource requested. Valid `Referer` fields are used in approximately 80% of all HTTP requests [14] making them a useful attribute in grouping. The `Location` field is present during a `302` server redirect to indicate where the client browser should query next. After a time window expires, a web session tree is built from the associated flows. Note that our approach can analyze HTTPS traffic in cases where there is a man-in-the-middle proxy that can decrypt SSL sessions.

We chose this tree building technique because our dataset lacked the full packet payloads required to use more complex and exact

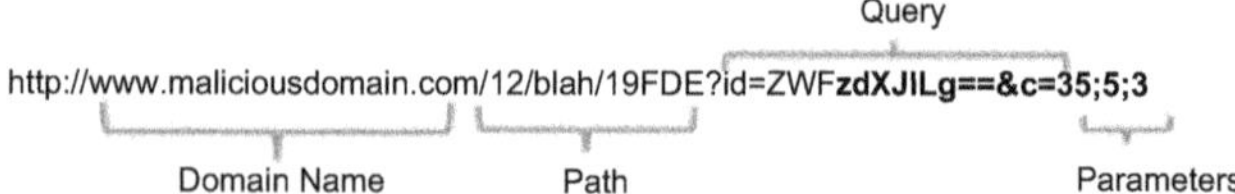

Figure 2: The components of a URL for feature extraction.

approaches [23]. Even so, the tree building approach we used has been effectively applied in other studies [14, 27, 22] and aptly demonstrates the utility of our similarity algorithm. In Section 5.3, we discuss how our algorithm can be utilized to scalably build trees using more complex and time intensive techniques.

3.2 On Building the Malware Index

The malware index is built using HTTP traces from samples of well-known exploit kits (e.g., Fiesta). These samples are gathered by crawling malicious websites [15, 17, 18] using a honeyclient. A honeyclient is a computer with a browser designed to detect changes in the browser or operating system when visiting malicious sites. The first step in building the index is to compile a list of URLs of known malicious exploit kits from websites such as threatglass.com, and urlquery.net. Next, each page must be automatically accessed using the honeyclient and the corresponding HTTP traffic is recorded. Each trace is transformed into a tree using the process in Section 3.1, and then content-based (node-level) and structural features are extracted and indexed.

Content-based (Node-level) Indexing: An exploit kit tree is comprised of N nodes, where each node represents a bidirectional HTTP request/response flow with packet header, HTTP header, and payload information available for extraction and storage in a document style inverted index. Each bidirectional flow (or node in a tree) can be thought of as a document, and its features as the words of the document, which are indexed. Each node is given a unique integer ID and three types of features are extracted: token features, URL structural features, and content-based features.
Token features are mainly packet header and URL features. They are gathered from the URL by breaking it down into its constituent parts: domain names, top level domain, path, query strings, query key/value pairs, parameters, destination IP addresses, and destination subnets. All attributes are stored as bags of tokens. For example, the token features for the URL shown in Figure 2 would be: `www.maliciousdomain.com`, `com`, `12`, `blah`, `19FDE`, `id=ZWFzdXJILg==`, `c=35`, `5`, and `3`.
URL structural features abstract the components of the URL by categorizing them by their data types rather than their actual data values (as in the token features). We use 6 common data types in URLs: numeric, hexadecimal, base64 encoding, alphanumeric, and words. These datatype encodings are used in conjunction with the lengths or ranges of lengths of corresponding tokens to generate structural URL features. For example, the URL structural features for the URL shown in Figure 2 `12/blah/19FDE` would be broken into 3 features: path-num-2, path-word-4, path-hex-5.
Content-based features are extracted from the HTTP headers or payloads where possible. They include binned content lengths, content types, and redirect response codes.

Structural Indexing: Each malware tree in the index is assigned a unique tree identifier, while each node has a unique node identifier. The tree is stored as a string of node identifiers in a canonical form that encodes the tree's structure. The canonical string is built by visiting each node in the tree in a preorder traversal, and appending node identifiers to the end of the string. Note that each indexed node contains the identifier for its corresponding tree to allow for easy mapping from node to tree while each tree structure is labelled by exploit kit type (e.g., Flashpack, Fiesta).

3.3 On Subtree Similarity Searches

With a malware index at hand, we then monitor HTTP traffic at the edge of an enterprise network, and convert the traffic into web session trees. Our task is to determine whether any of the trees contain a subtree that is similar to a sample in the index. If so, the tree is flagged as malicious and labeled by its exploit flavor.

We approach the subtree similarity search problem using a two-step process: node level similarity search and structural similarity search. First, we determine whether any nodes in a web session tree T are "similar" to any nodes in the malware index. If there are multiple nodes in T that are similar to a tree E in the index, then we extract the subtree S containing those nodes, and compare S structurally with E using a tree edit distance technique. Subtrees with sufficient node overlap and structural similarity with E are flagged as malicious. Structural similarity is used because it significantly reduces false positives over grouping HTTP flow sequences (§ 5).

3.3.1 Node Level Similarity Search

To determine whether any nodes in T are sufficiently similar to nodes in the malware index, we extract the set of token, URL structure, and content-based features from each node x in T. These node features are then used to query the index and return any nodes i that have a feature in common with node x. Node similarity is measured by a score based on the overlapping features between nodes.

In this work, we compare two node similarity approaches: the Jaccard Index, and the weighted Jaccard Index to determine how weighting affects the accuracy of the algorithm. The Jaccard Index [10] is a similarity metric that measures the similarity of two sets $X = \{x_1, ..., x_n\}$ and $I = \{i_1, ..., i_n\}$ by calculating $J(X, I) = \frac{|X \cap I|}{|X \cup I|}$. This generates a score between 0 and 1, with higher scores meaning higher similarity. More precisely, we use a variant of the Jaccard Index, called relevance to determine how relevant the set of node features of x in T is to the set of node features of i in the index. To calculate the relevance of X to I, the Jaccard Index becomes: $J(X, I) = \frac{|X \cap I|}{|I|}$.

Two flows x and i are considered similar if $J(X, I) > \epsilon$, where X and I are feature sets of x and i respectively, and ϵ is a user defined threshold. If a node in tree T is similar to a node in the index, the node in T is assigned the ID from the node in the index. The node IDs are used to compare the structural similarities of the subtrees of T with the matching trees in the index (Section 3.3.2).

A weighted Jaccard Index [10] introduces weighting to the features of the set. A higher weight value on a feature emphasizes those features that are most distinctive to a malicious flow; thereby, increasing the similarity score of two nodes that are malicious. The weighted intersection of X and I is defined as

$$W(X, I) = \sum_{x \in X \cap I} w(x),$$

where w is the weight of each feature x.

Then, the weighted Jaccard Index becomes:

$$WJ(X, I) = \frac{|X \cap I|}{|X \cup I|} = \frac{W(X, I)}{C(X) + C(I) - W(X, I)},$$

where $C(X) = |X| = \sum_{x \in X} w(x)$. Again, we use a variant of the weighted Jaccard Index to calculate the relevance of X to I:

$$WJ(X, I) = \frac{|X \cap I|}{|I|} = \frac{W(X, I)}{C(I)},$$

We apply a probabilistic term weighting technique first introduced by Robertson and Jones [32] which gives an ideal weight to term t from query Q. The terms are used in a similarity-based scoring scheme to find a subset of the most relevant documents to query Q. Here, term t is a feature extracted from node x.

To calculate a feature weight $w(f)$, we first consider a dataset of N benign HTTP flows, and R tree instances from a particular

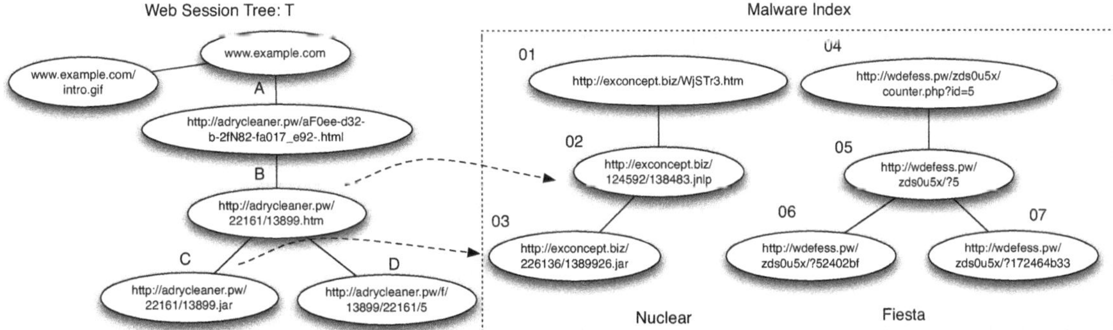

Figure 3: A simplified similarity search on the index. Web session tree T contains nodes that are similar to nodes of one of the Nuclear trees in the index. Those nodes in T are subsequently mapped to their corresponding nodes in the index to form subtrees.

exploit kit flavor (e.g., Nuclear, Fiesta, etc.). Let some feature f index r of the malicious trees in R and n of the benign flows in N. As such, $p = \frac{r}{R}$ is the probability that feature f indexes an exploit kit, while $q = \frac{(n-r)}{(N-R)}$ is the probability that f indexes a benign flow. Therefore, the weight of feature f becomes:

$$w(f) = log(\frac{p(1-q)}{(1-p)q}) = log(\frac{r(N-R-n+r)}{(R-r)(n-r)}).$$

When $r = 0$, i.e. feature f does not index any of malicious trees, the formulation is not stable; therefore, we apply the following modification as suggested by Robertson and Jones [32]:

$$w(f) = log(\frac{(r+1/2)(N-R-n+r+1/2)}{(R-r+1/2)(n-r+1/2)}).$$

Our technique requires a node-level similarity threshold for each exploit kit family stored in the malware index in order to determine that a node in T is similar to nodes in the index. To compute the thresholds, we compare the node similarities scores of each tree in the malware index, against all the other trees in the malware index that are in the same exploit kit family. An average node similarity score is calculated for each node in each tree in an exploit kit family. The node-level threshold for the kit is calculated by finding the node in the tree with the lowest average similarity score.

This process is presented in Algorithm 1. For pedagogical reasons, we use Fiesta tree samples from the malware index to illustrate the approach. For each tree t in the set of Fiesta trees, we first find all trees s that have a tree edit distance similarity score above zero (lines 3-5). For any node in t that has a similarity score above 0.1 with s, its score is recorded (lines 7-9). Finally, we store the minimum average score as the threshold for the kit. During the feature extraction stage, token and content-based features are ignored in order to provide a conservative lower bound on the threshold.

Algorithm 1 Finding the node level similarity threshold for the Fiesta exploit kit using the set of all Fiesta tree samples in the index

```
1: T_f ← set of all Fiesta Trees in Index
2: minval = 1.0
3: for all ( do t ← T_f)
4:     for all ( do s ← T_f)
5:         if TreeSimScore(s, t) > 0.0 then
6:             for all ( do n_s ← Node(s); n_t ← Node(t))
7:                 if score ← NodeSimScore(n_s, n_t) ≥ 0.1 then
8:                     n_t.totalScore+ = score
9:                     n_t.numberScores+ = 1
10:                end if
11:            end for
12:        end if
13:    end for
14:    for all ( do n_t ← Node(t) )
15:        avg = n_t.totalScore/n_t.numberScores
16:        if avg ≤ minval then
17:            minval ← avg
18:        end if
19:    end for
20: end for
21: threshold = minval
```

3.3.2 *Structural Similarity Search*

After a node level similarity search between a tree T (built from the network) and the trees in the malware index, there will be 0 or more nodes in T that are considered "similar" to nodes in the malware index. A node in tree T may be similar to multiple nodes in a single tree in the index or even in multiple trees. The next step is to extract the subtrees S within T that map to the corresponding trees in the index. Figure 3 shows a simplified example of a structural similarity search. Node B in tree T maps to node 02 based on node similarity for a Nuclear tree in the index. Similarly, node C in T maps to node 03. These node mappings are used to build subtrees of T that are compared to the corresponding trees in the index.

Subtrees from tree T are compared to the trees in the index using tree edit distance [11]. Tree edit distance uses the number of deletions, insertions, and label renamings to transform one tree into another. We enforce ancestor-descendant relationships in our setup. For example, if a node was an ancestor of another node in a tree in the index, the relationship must be maintained in the subtree S. As shown later, this restriction helps to reduce false detections. The result of the tree edit distance calculation is a structural similarity score between 0 and 1 that is then used to classify the subtree as either being benign or similar to a specific exploit kit.

4. DATASET AND TRAINING

The efficacy of our approach is evaluated using logs collected from a commercial HTTP proxy server (called BlueCoat) that monitors all web traffic for a large enterprise network. The proxy server records all client-based bidirectional HTTP/HTTPS flows from eight sensors at edge routers around the network and acts as a man-in-the-middle for HTTPS sessions providing a view into encrypted traffic. Each sensor saves flow records into its own set of hourly log files. Flows contain both TCP and HTTP headers.

For our first set of experiments, we analyzed 628 hours worth of labeled log data spanning different days during November 2013 and July 2014. The log files were chosen because they contained known instances of Nuclear, Fiesta, Fake, FlashPack, and Magnitude exploit kits along with several instances of a clickjacking [13] scheme that we refer to as ClickJack. Statistics for the dataset are summarized in Table 1 (labeled Dataset 1). We also utilized a separate three-week long dataset from January 2014 which was *unlabeled* to show the operational impact of our technique. Statistics for the dataset are also described in Table 1 (labeled Dataset 2) and are discussed in Section 6.

Table 1: Summary of datasets.

	Dataset 1	Dataset 2
Network sensors	8	8
Hours analyzed	628	3264
Client IP addresses	345K	> 300K
Bidirectional flows processed	800M	4B
HTTP tree structures processed	116M	572M

4.1 Implementation

The implementation is a multi-threaded application written in approximately 10,000 lines of `Python` and `C++` code. It processes archived bidirectional HTTP flows that are read and converted into web session trees on the fly while node and tree features are stored in the `Xapian` search engine. The prototype uses separate threads to read and parse each flow, to build HTTP web session trees, and to compare the most recently built tree to the malware index.

System Environment: All experiments were conducted on a multi-core Intel Xeon 2.27 GHz CPU with 500 GBs of memory and a 1 TB local disk. Notice that the platform is chosen because it facilitates our large-scale experiments by enabling multiple instances of the prototype to be run in parallel. The actual memory allocated for each prototype instance is 20G.

4.2 Building the Malware Index

As mentioned in Section 3.2, the malware index is essentially the "training data" used to detect malicious subtrees in the dataset. As such, the index is populated with exploit kit samples from a completely disjoint data source. We populated the malware index with exploit kit samples downloaded from a malware analysis website [7]. The operator collected HTTP traces of exploit kits using a honeyclient and stored them in a pcap format. We built a tool that transforms these traces into HTTP trees that are in turn indexed. The 3rd column of Table 2 provides a count of how many instances of each kit were downloaded and indexed. Note that none of the instances installed in the index appear in the proxy data logs. The clickjacking sample was downloaded from another website [25].

Table 2: Testing and training sets. Exploit kits collected from www.malware-traffic-analysis.net used to build the malware index.

Exploit Kit	Instances in Dataset 1	Instances in Malware Index
Fiesta	29	26
Nuclear	7	10
Magnitude	47	12
ClickJack	130	1
FlashPack	2	7
Fake	575	12

The second aspect of building the malware index is to calculate feature weights for all node features in the index when using the weighted Jaccard Index for node similarity. This requires malicious samples from the malware index as well as samples of normal traffic in order to determine how prevalent a feature is in both the malicious and benign dataset. In our experiment, we used 10 days worth of benign data from a single sensor in the BlueCoat logs to calculate feature weights. The benign data included over 4.4 million bidirectional flows.

Finally, we calculate the node similarity thresholds for each exploit using Algorithm 1 (§3.3.1). The thresholds for the weighted and non-weighted node similarity scores ranged between 0.2 to 0.25 depending on the exploit kit as shown in Table 3.

4.3 Establishing Ground Truth

In order to establish a ground truth as a test set for our experiments, we compiled a list of regular expressions from various sources in order to identify exploit kit instances in Dataset 1. First, we ran the Snort Sourcefire exploit kit regular expression rules from the Vulnerability Report Team [37] over the entire dataset. The ruleset included signatures for detecting exploit kits, such as Nuclear, Styx, Redkit, Blackhole, Magnitude, FlashPack, and Fiesta. We augmented these signatures with regular expressions gathered from a malware signatures website (www.malwaresigs.com) that included regular expressions for Fiesta, Angler, FlashPack, Styx, and Redkit. Through manual inspection of flows in Dataset 1 that match these signatures/regexes, we were able to identify several instances of the Fiesta, Nuclear, ClickJack, FlashPack, Fake, and Magnitude exploit kits (see the middle column of Table 2). False positives were painstakingly removed by grouping URLs by domain names, and by comparing them against publicly available blacklists and whitelists, including online searches against various API's engines (e.g., VirusTotal, GoogleSafe Browsing, URLQuery.net, Alexa, malwaredomainlist.com, and Google).

Table 3: Node-level thresholds computed by Algorithm 1.

Exploit Kit	Threshold (Weighted JI)	Threshold (JI)
Fiesta	0.25	0.25
Nuclear	0.23	0.25
Magnitude	0.25	0.25
ClickJack	0.25	0.25
FlashPack	0.23	0.2
Fake	0.23	0.25

Unfortunately, our analysis was conducted shortly after the author of the Blackhole and Cool exploit kits was arrested in Russia [36]. Hence, these exploit kits, which were once credited with over 90% of new infections [36], collapsed leaving attackers scrambling to find an alternative. Although, we were unable to obtain traces of the Blackhole or Cool exploit kits, we procured many instances of the Fiesta and Magnitude kits, which became prevalent after Blackhole's demise [30]. Recent studies [30, 9] show that there are approximately 6-8 exploit kit types dominating the Internet at any one time, accounting for the relatively small number of different but popular kits found on the analyzed network.

5. FINDING THE NEEDLE IN A HAYSTACK

In this section, we evaluate and compare our approach on Dataset 1 against the Snort Intrusion Detection System as well as two recent machine-learning approaches to detect exploit kit instances.

5.1 Comparison with Snort

In all cases, but FlashPack, the weighted and non-weighted node similarity approaches yielded the same results; therefore we leave indepth discussion of these approaches for Section 5.3.

■ *Fiesta*: In evaluating Fiesta, we compared our approach against the Snort rule 29443, which detects Fiesta outbound connections attempts. The rule focuses on the single flow related to the exploit payload and detects Fiesta instance by searching a particular alpha numeric pattern in the URL. As a result, it also flags 597 benign flows that match the regex pattern. On the contrary, our technique focuses on the structural path of flows taken to arrive at the exploit payload. As such, in our technique, not only are we able to eliminate these accidental matches that are unlikely to share similar structures with Fiesta instances, but also identify the exploit before the payload is reached, and even cases where no payload was downloaded at all. The results are summarized in Table 4.

Table 4 shows that using structure eliminated all 597 false positives flagged by the Snort rule and also identified cases that Snort missed. In most cases, our approach detected a Fiesta instance in as little as two or three nodes. Furthermore, it detected three instances that were not originally flagged in the ground truth, because our approach was able to detect the path of requests to the payload. In six cases, the exploit kit never reached a payload, and in another two, the payload string did not match Snort's regex. We missed two instances of Fiesta that accessed the same landing page but at different times. These instances were missed because there were no structures in the index similar enough to the instance to attain a structural score. There was no overlap between the false negatives missed by both techniques.

■ *Nuclear*: To track Nuclear, we used three Snort rules 28594, 28595, and 28596, which search for numeric `jar` and `tpl` file name of malicious payloads as well as specific directory structures in URLs. As noted in Table 4, the Snort signatures performed reasonably well for detecting all five Nuclear instances; because in all these cases, Nuclear was able to proceed to the payload-download stage. However, by looking for specific file types, these regexes missed an instance of Nuclear that was downloading a malicious `pdf` (which we detected). Furthermore, the generality of the signatures (e.g., matching numeric jar or tpl names) leads to 24 false alarms on legitimate websites that download benign jar files with numeric names. Our approach, on the other hand, strikes a better balance between specificity and generality. By leveraging structural properties of multi-stage exploit kits, it eliminates all false positive cases (which do not share similar tree structures with Nuclear exploit kits) and is able to generalize to new variation of exploit kits with previously unseen payloads. Although our approach failed to detect two instances of Nuclear that were structurally the same, that failure arose because our index did not have a similar example in the datastore.

The most interesting instance of Nuclear found in the data was downloaded through an advertisement on a popular foreign news site. That exploit successfully downloaded both a `Java` exploit and a malicious binary to the unsuspecting client machine.

■ *Magnitude*: In order to evaluate Magnitude, we utilized Snort rules 29188 and 28108, which search for hex encoded `eot` and `swf` files, respectively. Results for all techniques are shown in Table 4. The Snort rules generated over 60,000 false positives and missed an instance that did not download a payload while the classifier detected all exploit kit instances but with a high FP rate. By contrast, using the structure of correlated flows, we had zero false positives and zero false negatives.

■ *FlashPack*: Our empirical analysis shows that FlashPack is one of the more difficult exploit kits to detect because of its use of common php file names such as `index.php`, `flash.php`, and `allow.php`. Snort uses rule 29163 to identify a subset of these files (i.e., those which have a specific query string to reduce false positives). However, the query string can be easily manipulated by attackers to evade detection and it often varies across different FlashPack variations. As a result, the Snort rule was unable to detect the two instances of FlashPack variations in the data. We experimented with a much looser regular expression to identify all instances; however, it generated over 43,000 false positives.

Using our approach, we were able to identify both instances in the dataset, with only 68 false positives (weighted node similarity) and 109 false positives (non-weighted) — four orders of magnitude reduction over the loose regular expression. The added false positives in the non-weighted case are due to the increased number of node-level false matches in the non-weighted Jaccard Index calculation. FlashPack was the only exploit kit analyzed where setting a minimum *structural threshold* had a significant impact on the false positive rate (We return to that later in §5.3). The two true instances had similarity scores of 0.75 and 0.85 respectively. With a conservative structural similarity score of 0.5, the number of FPs is reduced to three (weighted) and 19 (non-weighted) (Table 4).

Forensic analysis revealed that both instances of FlashPack were loaded through banner ads when two separate clients visited entertainment websites. In one of these cases, the exploit successfully downloaded both a malicious Flash file as well as a `Java` archive to the vulnerable client.

■ *ClickJack*: Clickjacking is a technique in which an attacker tries to fool a web user into clicking on a malicious link by injecting code or script into a button on a webpage [13]. To detect instances of the ClickJack kit, we loaded a single instance of its structure into the index and then performed searches on the entire dataset. There was no equivalent Snort rule for finding such an exploit and so a comparison to Snort was not possible. Our approach identified 130 instances of the clickjacking scheme with zero false positives and zero false negatives. Interestingly, our analysis found that the ClickJack subtree was the initial entry point into various exploits including an instance of the Magnitude exploit kit, and several trojans. With an online version of our approach, we would have been able to detect the exploit before it was downloaded.

■ *Fake - Installer*: Our final case study focuses on the Fake Installer exploit kit, which is an exploit that attempts to install a fake Adobe update for an unsuspecting client. This kit is identifiable by the `checker.php` file it uses to check the system and attempt a download of a malicious payload. This common file name can trigger an excessive number of false positives, so because of this, there was no corresponding Snort rule. We conducted our own analysis on our dataset specifically looking for the checker.php file and found 1,200 cases of this file in a three month period. Of those 1,200 cases, we were able to confirm 575 to be the Fake Installer. Utilizing our approach, we successfully identify all such cases with zero false positives and zero false negatives.

Summary: Table 4 summarizes the detection results of our approach and Snort. Regarding exploit kits for which Snort rules are available (i.e., Fiesta, Nuclear, Magnitude, and FlashPack), our structure similarity-based approach achieved a 95% detection accuracy while outperforming Snort (at 84%). Considering that false positives place undue burden on analysts to perform a deeper investigation on each reported incident, reducing false positives by over three orders of magnitude is a non-trivial improvement. In addition, our approach identified all instances of two exploit kits for which Snort rules were not available (i.e., Clickjacking and Fake). The approach reduces false positives by utilizing both content and structure, effectively creating a larger feature space.

Table 4: Comparison (weighted) to Snort signatures.

Exploit kits	#	Structural Sim			Snort		
		TPs	FPs	FNs	TPs	FPs	FNs
Fiesta	29	25	0	4	19	597	10
Nuclear	7	5	0	2	5	24	2
Magnitude	47	47	0	0	46	60000+	1
FlashPack	2	2	3	0	0	9	2
Total	85	79 (95%)	3	4	70 (84%)	60630+	13
ClickJack	130	130	0	0	-	-	-
Fake	575	575	0	0	-	-	-
Total	705	705 (100%)	0	0	-	-	-

5.2 Comparison with State of the Art

Next we compare our approach with a statistical classifier proposed by Ma et al. [21]. The classifier is based on Logistic Regression with Stochastic Gradient Descent using features similar to those described in Section 3.2. The classifier labels URLs as either malicious or benign and is trained with all 1,000 URLs used to build the malware index, as well as 10,000 benign URLs collected from BlueCoat logs with a $10x$ class weight applied to the "malicious" class. Parameters for the algorithm are tuned using a grid search and five fold cross validation on the would be training set. Results are shown in Table 5 indicating that the classifier performed well at detecting exploit kit instances. The classifier was able to detect two more instances of Fiesta than our approach because both clients visited a landing page for an exploit kit, but did not reach a payload, exposing no web structure for our technique to detect. In the case of Nuclear, the classifier was unable to identify the instances that only used `.tpl` and `.pdf` file types.

Unfortunately, the technique flagged over 500,000 URLs as malicious in Dataset 1. Through a painstaking analysis of the URLs using malware reports, blacklists, and google searches, we were able to confirm 4,000 of the URLs to be malicious — 2,500 of the URLs were associated with the exploits kits found as ground truth in Dataset 1 (Table 2), which were also detected by our approach. Note that Table 2 represents numbers of trees, with each tree containing multiple URLs. The other 1,500 URLS were comprised of web requests to algorithmically generated domain names used by botnets [41], phishing sites, and malware download sites and were unrelated to exploit kit traffic. False positives were attributed to many different websites including content distribution networks, URL shorteners, and advertising networks. Clearly, due to the high false positive rate, the approach of Ma et al. [21] is infeasible in an operational environment.

Table 5: Comparison (weighted) to binary URL classifier.

Exploit kits	Ins-tances	Structural Sim			Classifier		
		TPs	FPs	FNs	TPs	FPs	FNs
Fiesta	29	25	0	4	27	-	2
Nuclear	7	5	0	2	5	-	2
Magnitude	47	47	0	0	47	-	0
FlashPack	2	2	3	0	2	-	0
ClickJack	130	130	0	0	130	-	0
Fake	575	575	0	0	575	-	0
Total	790	784 (99%)	3	6	786 (99%)	500,000+ (URLs)	4

Recently, Stringhini et al. [35], Mekky et al. [22], Cova et al. [5], Eshete and Venkatakrishnan [8] proposed detecting malicious websites by counting the number of HTTP redirects (i.e., 302, javascript, or HTML) to hop from a compromised website to the malicious exploit. The key insight is that attackers utilize statistically more intermediate HTTP redirects than benign traffic in order to avoid detection. Our intention was to provide a comparative analysis to Stringhini et al. [35], but unfortunately, the approach of Stringhini et al. [35] requires modeling a diverse set of redirect chains of users visiting the same malicious websites with different environments (e.g. OSes and browsers) at geographically dispersed locations. Given that such widely heterogenous environments are not available in most enterprises, we evaluate the utility of using redirects as a main feature to detect exploit kits in traffic by exploring the full packet payload HTTP traces associated with 110 exploit kit instances. The instances included 14 distinct exploit kits: Angler, Blackhole, Dotka Chef, Fake, Fiesta, Flashpack, Goon, Hello, Magnitude, Neutrino, Nuclear, Styx, Sweet Orange, and Zuponic.

Redirection chains were built from each trace by extracting server and HTML (meta tag) redirects. Additionally, we manually analyzed a subset of 50 traces using an instrumented HTML parser, javascript engine(Rhino) and DOM (envjs) in order to build chains that included javascript redirections. We found that the traces had relatively short redirection chains, and the length the chain was dictated by the type of exploit kit. Exploit kits such as Blackhole, Nuclear, Fiesta, Goon DotkaChef, Fake, and Sweet Orange consistently had a single indirection to the exploit kit server. Indeed, server and meta redirections were rare with the main form of redirection being an `iframe` injection into the compromised site, or a `javascript` injection that built an `iframe`. Magnitude, Angler, Flashpack, Zuponic and Neutrino saw anywhere from 1 to 3 redirects with a combination of server, meta and javascript redirects. In fact, Styx was the only instance that had more than 4 redirects. These results are in stark contrast to the results of Mekky et al. [22] that show that over 80% of all malicious chains have 4 or more server redirects or that the average number of exploit kit server redirects are five [8].

Not only are we not seeing large redirect chains for exploit kits, but we are also seeing comparable length redirect chains in benign traffic due primarily to advertising networks. We built server and meta redirection chains on 24 hours worth of data from a large enterprise network consisting of 12 million bidirectional HTTP flows. In that time period, 400,000 redirection chains were generated including 35,000 chains of length 2 to 5, making the redirection feature prone to false positives. By contrast, our approach can utilize redirection chains, but focuses on the process by which an exploit kit attempts to compromise a host and models that into a tree-like structure in order to reduce false positives.

5.3 Findings and Discussion

We now take a closer look at why the use of structural information (especially, the ancestor-descendant relationship) is important in reducing false positives. We begin our analysis by focusing on the node-level similarity scores using the weighted and non-weighted Jaccard Index calculated between the HTTP flows in the archival logs (i.e., Dataset 1 in Table 2) and those in the malware index. The results are shown as a cumulative distribution function in Figure 4. Notice that over 98% of the flows in the dataset had a similarity score below the conservative lower bound thresholds (of 0.23/0.2) derived from Algorithm 1 while all nodes associated with malicious trees had a node similarity score of 0.22 or higher.

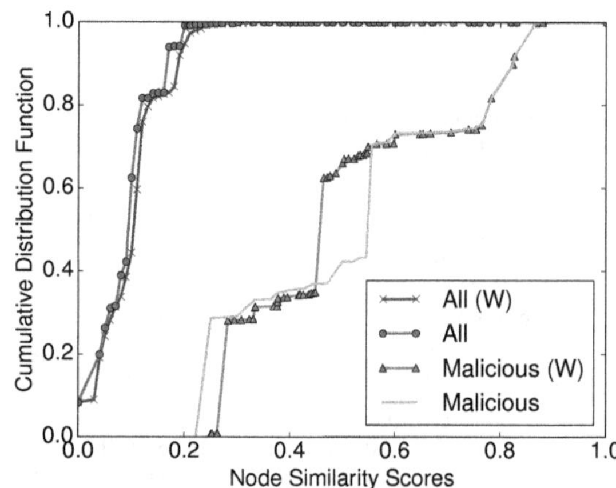

Figure 4: The CDF of node similarity scores between our test dataset and the malware index. "All" represents similarity scores between all nodes in the dataset and the malware index, while "Malicious" represents the node scores for trees in the dataset that were flagged as malicious(W = weighted).

The similarity scores for both node similarity metrics followed the same distribution; however, the non-weighted Jaccard Index generated on average lower similarity scores than the weighted approach (weighted mean = 0.10, non-weighted = 0.09) with similar standard deviations. As can be seen from Figure 4, the similarity gap between the malicious and benign nodes is smaller in the non-weighted case than in the weighted case. This leads to more node-level false positives, and, as a result, structural false positives as seen in the case of FlashPack. Intuitively, because the weighted Jaccard Index is weighted according to the importance of the feature, an unweighted version will be more likely to have false positives due to common features that are prevalent both in benign and malicious nodes. Even though the weighted version provides marginally better accuracy, the non-weighted Jaccard Index may be more desirable from an operational perspective because it does not require any feature training.

As shown in Table 6, there were a large number of false positives if we considered only node-level similarity (like Snort signatures that focus only on individual flows) for both weighted and non-weighted similarities. The false positive rate started to decrease when considering *multiple nodes* in a tree (without considering structure), as the probability of a benign website having two or more nodes in the same tree that match malicious patterns was an order of magnitude smaller. The false positive rate decreased further by another order of magnitude once a *structural score* was established using tree edit distance. After imposing the *ancestor-descendent requirement* on the tree structure, the false positives were reduced to 68 for the total of over 800 million flows. The results show that tree structure is the primary determining factor in reducing false positives.

Table 6: FPs for single node matching, multi-node matching without considering structure, structural similarity, and structural similarity with ancestor-descendant requirement.

	Threshold (Alg 1) non-weighted	Threshold (Alg 1) weighted	Tight Threshold weighted
Single Node	2,141,493	360,150	141,130
Multi-node (no structure)	79,321	32,130	5,878
Structural	5,967	3,800	420
Structural (w/ restriction)	109	68	68

As shown in Table 6 there is a several orders of magnitude reduction in the number of nodes (flows) that are similar to nodes in the index, w.r.t the total number of nodes (flows) in a given dataset (Table 1). We can leverage this result, by only building trees for flow clusters that have multiple similar nodes in common with a tree in the malware index, thus enabling us to scalably apply much more computationally expensive (and correct) tree building techniques to the wire (i.e., [23]) when full payloads are available. Table 6 also shows the detection rates under the optimal tight node-level similarity thresholds using weighted similarity. This bound is the maximum node similarity threshold allowed to still detect all true positives, and was calculated using the ground truth dataset. Even with the optimal bound, structural information was still needed to reduce the false positives.

Our empirical analysis also showed that in the majority of cases, a relatively low minimum structural threshold (less than 0.05) for the tree-similarity score was sufficient because the flagged tree was indeed malicious in almost every case. The structural similarity threshold is specific to the similarity metric chosen and was set conservatively low to maximize true positives with few false positives, creating a clear separation between benign and malicious cases. Figure 5 shows the cumulative distribution of the tree edit distance scores for the malicious subtrees analyzed. The scores ranged anywhere from 0.2 to a perfect 1.0 due to a few factors. First, in some cases there may be multiple nodes added or missing from the subtree as compared to the malware index, causing an imperfect score. The second reason was that, especially in the case of ClickJack, the exploit may lead into other exploits or websites causing the subtree in the dataset to look different from any of the ones in the malware index. Taken together, these findings underscore the power of using structural information and subtree mining, particularly when there may be subtrees that are incomplete or contain previously unseen nodes compared to those encoded in the index. The combination allows us to attain maximum flexibility and reduce both false negatives and false positives over contemporary approaches.

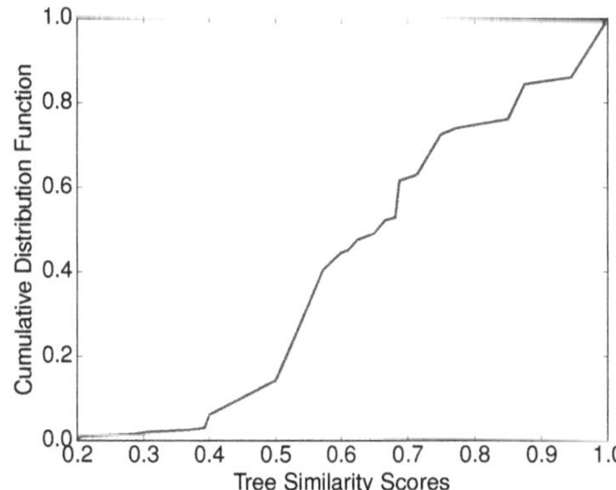

Figure 5: The CDF of tree similarity scores for malicious subtrees.

6. OPERATIONAL DEPLOYMENT

To further demonstrate the utility of our approach in a large enterprise environment, we analyzed three consecutive weeks of BlueCoat logs from January 6-31, 2014 (Dataset 2 in Table 1) using the weighted version of our approach. During the time period, over 4 billion bidirectional flows and 572 million HTTP trees were generated and analyzed using a malware index consisting of the Fiesta, Nuclear, Fake, ClickJack, and Magnitude exploit kits.

During the deployment we were able to identify 28 exploit kit instances with no false positives, compared with Snort signatures that generated over 22K false positives and missed most of the Fiesta instances, as shown in Table 7. Two of the Fiesta instances downloaded malicious `Java` files, while two others downloaded spyware. The Nuclear instance successfully downloaded a malicious `PDF` file followed by a malicious binary. We also discovered that two of the Clickjacking instances downloaded Popup Trojans. By contrast, the URL classifier of Ma et al. [21] generated an average of 143,000 alerts per day for a total of 3.6 million alerts in the month. Unfortunately, the sheer volume of alerts made it infeasible to vet each flagged URL.

Table 7: Live comparison to Snort signatures.

Exploit kits	Structural Similarity		Snort		
	TPs	FPs	TPs	FPs	FNs
Fiesta	20	0	2	340	≥ 18
Nuclear	1	0	1	0	-
Magnitude	1	0	1	22,224	-
Clickjacking	6	0	N/A	N/A	-
Fake	0	0	N/A	N/A	-

The fact that we were able to successfully detect these abuses on a large enterprise network underscores the operational utility of our technique. Indeed, one of the main motivating factors for pursuing this line of research and subsequently building our prototype was the fact that the high false positives induced by existing approaches made them impractical to network operators at our enterprise — who inevitably disabled the corresponding signatures or ignored the flood of false alerts altogether.

From an operational perspective, speed is as equally important as accuracy in order to keep up with the live traffic in a large enterprise network. Therefore, to assess our runtime performance, we evaluated the processing speed for the various components when processing one days worth of traffic across all eight sensors. Note that eight prototype instances were run — one for each sensor. The experiment shows that a single instance of our current prototype is able to process an entire day of traffic in 8 hours. Figure 6 illustrates the performance breakdown of different components of our prototype, indicating that on average, the prototype can parse 3.5K flows per second (302M flows per day), build trees at a rate of approximately 350 per second and conduct the similarity search at a rate of 170 trees per second. Profiling the similarity search module showed that over half the runtime was spent performing feature extraction and memory allocation, while only 5% of the time was spent searching the index. Sensors 5, 6, and 8 were slower than the other sensors because they received a larger portion of the traffic.

Lastly, we note that although our prototype was able to keep up with the average volume of traffic in the target enterprise, the same was not true at peak load. Statistics collected from one day of traffic across all eight sensors showed that at its peak, the network generated 6,250 flows and 550 trees per second. While our prototype falls short of processing at that speed, we note that by design, all the components (e.g., flow parsing, tree building and feature extraction) are parallelizable; as such, with modest hardware provisions we believe our prototype could efficiently handle the peak loads and operate in real-time. We leave this for future work.

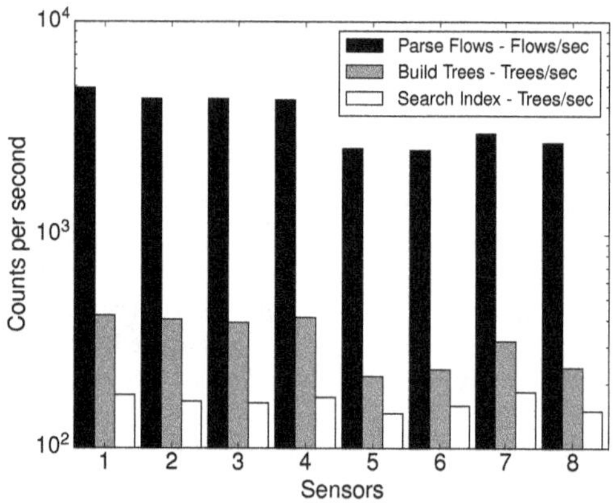

Figure 6: The performance of bidirectional flow parsing, tree building, and malware searching for one day of data across 8 sensors.

7. LIMITATIONS

As with any security solution, attackers will inevitably seek ways to bypass it. An obvious evasive strategy would be to hinder our ability to build subtrees from HTTP flows by using JavaScript and other obfuscation techniques that hide the relationship (e.g., redirection, reference) between HTTP flows. As mentioned previously, we believe our two step similarity algorithm allows us to significantly reduce the overall number of trees that need to built, allowing more computationally expensive and correct techniques to be used such as dynamic analysis [23], JavaScript de-obfuscation [19, 40], and statistical means [12, 24, 44] — all of which could be easily adopted in our setting to thwart evasive techniques. Moreover, in many enterprise environments, there is strict control over the software configuration of client devices in the network, and as such, a mandatory browser plugin could be enforced to make building web session trees easier than our current approach. Nevertheless, we reiterate that the focus of this work is not to build better HTTP trees, but to demonstrate the benefits of a tree structure-based detection approach in reducing false negatives and false positives.

In addition, because our approach relies on *node-level* and *structure-level* similarity to detect exploit kits, a skilled adversary might attempt to circumvent similarity matching by obfuscating flow features and dramatically modifying tree structures. Although the approach suggested herein is no silver bullet, we believe it raises the bar for attackers and makes evasion more difficult. For instance, by using an edit-distance based subtree mining algorithm to compare observed session trees, our approach offers resilience to common obfuscation and variation techniques (e.g., adding redirection nodes or changing malicious payloads). More importantly, a structural similarity based approach provides security analysts with flexibilities in tuning the thresholds such that changes to a few nodes in the web session trees are unlikely to significantly influence the matching results. On the other hand, generating functionally equivalent but structurally distinct exploit paths would be a non-trivial task for attackers. As future work, we plan to quantify our resilience against such obfuscation strategies.

From an operational perspective, the fact that our approach involves some manual effort on the part of the analyst (e.g., to find and install representative examples of exploits kits into the malware index) might appear as a limitation. Indeed, like most tasks in network security, performing this particular step requires some expertise and domain knowledge. That said, the burden on the operator could be lessened with automated techniques for building these indices, for example, from data made available through websites like threatglass.com. Furthermore, techniques applied in automated signature generation [42] may be useful.

Finally, like all network-based detection techniques that require packet inspection, the approach herein cannot operate on encrypted traffic. For many enterprises, however, the ability to inspect encrypted traffic is enforced at the border by using proxy servers specifically designed to decrypt and monitor encrypted traffic. This was precisely the case for the enterprise evaluated in this paper.

8. CONCLUSION

In this paper, we present a network-centric approach that uses structural similarity to accurately and scalably detect web-based exploit kits in enterprise network environments. By exploiting both the content and the structural interactions among HTTP flows, our approach allows us to not only reason about the likelihood of a sequence of HTTP flows being malicious, but to also pinpoint the exact subset of flows relevant to malvertising. By modelling HTTP traffic as trees, we can also determine from which root sites, or advertising networks, an exploit kit was launched. Our prototype implementation, which was evaluated on real world data collected from a large-scale enterprise network, worked remarkably well. In particular, our empirical results show significant improvement over the state-of-the-art methods in terms of false positive and false negative rates across a variety of exploit kits. Lastly, a preliminary analysis in an operational deployment demonstrates that our techniques can easily scale to handle massive HTTP traffic volumes with only modest hardware requirements.

9. ACKNOWLEDGMENTS

We express our gratitude to the Computer Science networking staff (especially, Murray Anderegg and Bil Hayes) for their efforts in deploying some of the infrastructure used in this study. We also thank Douglas L. Schales for help with data procurement as well as Jan Werner, Kevin Snow, Andrew White, and the anonymous reviewers for their insightful comments. This work is supported in part by the National Science Foundation (with a supplement from the Department of Homeland Security) under award numbers 1127361 and 1421703. Any opinions, findings, and conclusions or recommendations expressed in this paper are those of the authors and do not necessarily reflect the views of the National Science Foundation or the Department of Homeland Security.

10. REFERENCES

[1] A. Blum, B. Wardman, T. Solorio, and G. Warner. Lexical feature based phishing url detection using online learning. In *ACM Workshop on Artificial Intelligence and Security*, 2010.

[2] D. Canali, M. Cova, G. Vigna, and C. Kruegel. Prophiler: a fast filter for the large-scale detection of malicious web pages. In *World Wide Web Conference*, 2011.

[3] J. Clark. Malicious javascript flips ad network into rentable botnet, July 2013. URL http://goo.gl/8mFLvQ.

[4] S. Cohen. Indexing for subtree similarity-search using edit distance. In *ACM SIGMOD Conference on Management of Data*, 2013.

[5] M. Cova, C. Kruegel, and G. Vigna. Detection and analysis of drive-by-download attacks and malicious javascript code. In *World Wide Web Conference*, 2010.

[6] G. De Maio, A. Kapravelos, Y. Shoshitaishvili, C. Kruegel, and G. Vigna. PExy: The Other Side of Exploit Kits. In *Conference on Detection of Intrusions and Malware, and Vulnerability Assessment*, 2014.

[7] B. Duncan. Malware-traffic-analysis.net blog, July 2014. URL http://goo.gl/fXdSZz.

[8] B. Eshete and V. N. Venkatakrishnan. Webwinnow: Leveraging exploit kit workflows to detect malicious urls. In *ACM Conference on Data and Application Security and Privacy*, 2014.

[9] C. Grier, L. Ballard, J. Caballero, N. Chachra, C. J. Dietrich, K. Levchenko, P. Mavrommatis, D. McCoy, A. Nappa, A. Pitsillidis, N. Provos, M. Z. Rafique, M. A. Rajab, C. Rossow, K. Thomas, V. Paxson, S. Savage, and G. M. Voelker. Manufacturing compromise: the emergence of exploit-as-a-service. In *ACM Conference on Computer and Communications Security*, 2012.

[10] M. Hadjieleftheriou and D. Srivastava. Weighted set-based string similarity. *IEEE Data Engineering.*, 33(1), 2010.

[11] X. Hu, T.-c. Chiueh, and K. G. Shin. Large-scale malware indexing using function-call graphs. In *ACM Conference on Computer and Communications Security*, 2009.

[12] X. Hu, M. Knysz, and K. G. Shin. Rb-seeker: Auto-detection of redirection botnets. In *Symposium on Network and Distributed System Security*, 2009.

[13] L.-S. Huang, A. Moshchuk, H. J. Wang, S. Schechter, and C. Jackson. Clickjacking: attacks and defenses. In *USENIX Security Symposium*, 2012.

[14] S. Ihm and V. S. Pai. Towards understanding modern web traffic. In *ACM Internet Measurement Conference*, 2011.

[15] L. Invernizzi, S. Benvenuti, P. M. Comparetti, M. Cova, C. Kruegel, and G. Vigna. Evilseed: A guided approach to finding malicious web pages. In *IEEE Symposium on Security and Privacy*, 2012.

[16] R. Lemos. The doubleclick attack and the rise of malvertising, Dec. 2010. URL http://goo.gl/1HzmLF.

[17] Z. Li, K. Zhang, Y. Xie, F. Yu, and X. Wang. Knowing your enemy: understanding and detecting malicious web advertising. In *ACM Conference on Computer and Communications Security*, 2012.

[18] Z. Li, S. Alrwais, Y. Xie, F. Yu, and X. Wang. Finding the linchpins of the dark web: a study on topologically dedicated hosts on malicious web infrastructures. In *IEEE Symposium on Security and Privacy*, 2013.

[19] G. Lu and S. Debray. Automatic simplification of obfuscated javascript code: A semantics-based approach. In *Conference on Software Security and Reliability*, 2012.

[20] J. Ma, L. K. Saul, S. Savage, and G. M. Voelker. Beyond blacklists: learning to detect malicious web sites from suspicious urls. In *Conference on Knowledge Discovery and Data Mining*, 2009.

[21] J. Ma, L. K. Saul, S. Savage, and G. M. Voelker. Learning to detect malicious urls. *ACM Transactions on Intelligent Systems Technology*, 2(3), May 2011.

[22] H. Mekky, R. Torres, Z.-L. Zhang, S. Saha, and A. Nucci. Detecting malicious http redirections using trees of user browsing activity. In *IEEE Conference on Computer Communications*, 2014.

[23] C. Neasbitt, R. Perdisci, K. Li, and T. Nelms. Clickminer: Towards forensic reconstruction of user-browser interactions from network traces. In *ACM Conference on Computer and Communications Security*, 2014.

[24] T. Nelms, R. Perdisci, M. Antonakakis, and M. Ahamad. Webwitness: Investigating, categorizing, and mitigating malware download paths. In *USENIX Security Symposium*, 2015.

[25] J. Nieto. Zeroaccess trojan - network analysis part ii, July 2013. URL http://goo.gl/LYssOV.

[26] N. Provos, D. McNamee, P. Mavrommatis, K. Wang, and N. Modadugu. The ghost in the browser analysis of web-based malware. In *USENIX Workshop on Hot Topics in Understanding Botnet*, 2007.

[27] N. Provos, P. Mavrommatis, M. A. Rajab, and F. Monrose. All your iframes point to us. In *USENIX Security Symposium*, 2008.

[28] PWC. IAB internet advertising revenue report: 2012 full year results. Technical report, PricewaterhouseCoopers, Interactive Advertising Bureau, Apr. 2013.

[29] D. Raywood. Major league baseball website hit by malvertising that may potentially impact 300,000 users, June 2012. URL http://goo.gl/upKVXe.

[30] S. M. G. T. Response. Six months after blackhole: Passing the exploit kit torch, Apr. 2014. URL http://goo.gl/nAsxj0.

[31] K. Rieck, T. Krueger, and A. Dewald. Cujo: efficient detection and prevention of drive-by-download attacks. In *Annual Computer Security Applications Conference*, 2010.

[32] S. E. Robertson and K. S. Jones. Relevance weighting of search terms. *Journal of the American Society for Information Science*, 27(3), 1976.

[33] M. J. Schwartz. Android malware being delivered via ad networks, Aug. 2013. URL http://goo.gl/CrfKzo.

[34] B. Stock, B. Livshits, and B. Zorn. Kizzle: A signature compiler for exploit kits. Technical Report MSR-TR-2015-12, Microsoft Research, February 2015.

[35] G. Stringhini, C. Kruegel, and G. Vigna. Shady paths: leveraging surfing crowds to detect malicious web pages. In *ACM Conference on Computer and Communications Security*, 2013.

[36] Trend Micro. The aftermath of the blackhole exploit kit's demise, Jan. 2014. URL http://goo.gl/DsjYUp.

[37] S. VRT. Snort vrt signatures, July 2014. URL http://www.snort.org/vrt.

[38] G. Wang, J. W. Stokes, C. Herley, and D. Felstead. Detecting malicious landing pages in malware distribution networks. In *IEEE/IFIP International Conference on Dependable Systems and Networks*, 2013.

[39] L. Xu, Z. Zhan, S. Xu, and K. Ye. Cross-layer detection of malicious websites. In *ACM Conference on Data and Application Security and Privacy*, 2013.

[40] W. Xu, F. Zhang, and S. Zhu. Jstill: Mostly static detection of obfuscated malicious javascript code. In *ACM Conference on Data and Application Security and Privacy*, 2013.

[41] S. Yadav, A. K. K. Reddy, A. N. Reddy, and S. Ranjan. Detecting algorithmically generated malicious domain names. In *ACM Internet Measurement Conference*, 2010.

[42] V. Yegneswaran, J. T. Giffin, P. Barford, and S. Jha. An architecture for generating semantics-aware signatures. In *USENIX Security Symposium*, 2005.

[43] A. Zarras, A. Kapravelos, G. Stringhini, T. Holz, C. Kruegel, and G. Vigna. The dark alleys of madison avenue: Understanding malicious advertisements. In *ACM Internet Measurement Conference*, 2014.

[44] H. Zhang, D. D. Yao, and N. Ramakrishnan. Detection of stealthy malware activities with traffic causality and scalable triggering relation discovery. In *ACM Symposium on Information, Computer and Communications Security*, 2014.

PANDDE: Provenance-based ANomaly Detection of Data Exfiltration

Daren Fadolalkarim
Computer Science Department
Purdue University
West Lafayette, IN 47906
dfadolal@purdue.edu

Asmaa Sallam
Computer Science Department
Purdue University
West Lafayette, IN 47906
asallam@purdue.edu

Elisa Bertino
Cyber Center and Computer Science Department
Purdue University
West Lafayette, IN 47906
bertino@purdue.edu

ABSTRACT

Preventing data exfiltration by insiders is a challenging process since insiders are users that have access permissions to the data. Existing mechanisms focus on tracking users' activities while they are connected to the database, and are unable to detect anomalous actions that the users perform on the data once they gain access to it. Being able to detect anomalous actions on the data is critical as these actions are often sign of attempts to misuse data. In this paper, we propose an approach to detect anomalous actions executed on data returned to the users from a database. The approach has been implemented as part of the Provenance-based ANomaly Detection of Data Exfiltration (PANDDE) tool. PANDDE leverages data provenance information captured at the operating system level. Such information is then used to create profiles of users' actions on the data once retrieved from the database. The profiles indicate actions that are consistent with the tasks of the users. Actions recorded in the profiles include data printing, emailing, and storage. Profiles are then used at run-time to detect anomalous actions.

Keywords

Operating System; Security and Reliability; Insider Attacks; Anomaly Detection; Provenance Collection

1. INTRODUCTION

Protecting data from insider threats is a critical requirement as many different organizations are witnessing an increasing amount of insider attacks. Although Database Management Systems (DBMSs) provide access control mechanisms, which allow one to grant users access permissions to the data based on the user tasks and roles within the organizations, this is not sufficient to protect data against misuse by insiders if these insiders have the proper data access permissions.

CODASPY'16, March 09-11, 2016, New Orleans, LA, USA
© 2016 ACM. ISBN 978-1-4503-3935-3/16/03...$15.00
DOI: http://dx.doi.org/10.1145/2857705.2857710

Protection against data exfiltration from insiders thus requires combining different techniques [2]. A relevant category of techniques is represented by Anomaly Detection (AD) tools that create profiles of normal database accesses by users. Then, based on these profiles, accesses to the database are monitored to detect anomalous ones [9]. By using such AD tools, one can detect, for example, that a user, that usually accesses 20% of the data in a table as part of every-day work activity, suddenly downloads the entire table. Such variations in access patterns are important indicators of possible attempts of data theft and misuse [14]. Other mechanisms, recently proposed, extend such approach to create profiles of application programs [8]. Such profiles succinctly represent the normal behaviors of the applications in terms of their interactions with the database. Also, they are used to detect changes in the database accesses performed by the applications. Such changes may be an indication of possible malicious changes to application programs by insiders.

However, the above mechanisms, as well as other proposed techniques, are not enough to secure data from insiders. The reason is that these mechanisms are not able to track and check what the users do with the data once they have gained access to the data. Users can exfiltrate some data by storing the data in a file on their computers, and then printing or emailing such file. It is important to notice that for an insider to be able to steal some data, the insider must not only get access to the data, but he/she must also transfer, in some manner, the data outside of the organization.

To address this problem, we propose PANDDE (Provenance-based ANomaly Detection of Data Exfiltration) tool that tracks the actions executed by users on the data after downloading it from the database to their machines. PANDDE creates a profile of these actions during a training phase, and later uses such profile to detect users' anomalous actions on the data during a detection phase. For example, by using our mechanism, we can detect if a user that usually only inspects some data on a computer screen, now saves this data in a file. Even though there could be legitimate reasons for such change in behavior, it is nevertheless important to flag such a change and perhaps execute additional actions, such as checking with the user.

The *key idea* of PANDDE is to exploit provenance information collected at the file system level. Such provenance information allows us to track and record the sources, direct and indirect, of any piece of data written into a file. As such we can record, for example, that a database record has been stored into a file once it has been retrieved from the database. PANDDE is the first tool that tracks database users' actions on data after the users disconnect from the database to detect data exfiltration attempts unlike existing mechanisms that track users' activities while they are connected to the database. However, PANDDE can be easily integrated with such mechanisms to provide a second level of defense against insider threats by monitoring files at the operating system level as we will show in this paper.

The rest of this paper is structured as follows. Section 2 discusses the design overview. Then, section 3 presents the system architecture and shows how PANDDE can be integrated with other existing mechanisms, whereas section 4 provides details on PANDDE algorithms of operation. Later, section 5 reports experimental results. Section 6 discusses the related work. Lastly, section 7 concludes the paper and outlines the future work. [1]

2. DESIGN OVERVIEW

In this section, we discuss different aspects of PANDDE; those are the system parties, input to PANDDE, design choices, detection workflow, and limitations.

The system parties (actors) are the database owner (DBO) and the exfiltration detection provider (EDP). The DBO is the owner of a database that contains data that he/she wants to defend against exfiltration attempts from the database users. The EDP uses PANDDE to provide the service that performs online inspection to detect anomalies in data usage and report such anomalies to the DBO. Input to PANDDE is the file system operations that the user of the database performs on the data returned by the queries submitted to the database; examples of such operations are printing, emailing, and copying.

2.1 Design choices

PANDDE is designed to detect exfiltration attacks by collecting provenance at the file system level. In general, file systems are categorized into two types: (1) resident native kernel file systems (KFS) which directly work with lower levels of the system architecture, and (2) user level file systems that are based on NFS [21]. Collecting provenance in each type of system has its own advantages and disadvantages. At the kernel level, collecting provenance is fast; however, it is not portable, and makes developing and debugging difficult. On the other hand, collecting provenance at the user level file systems makes developing and debugging easier. However, working at this level affects the performance of the system because of the additional context switches required to serve a user request and record provenance [21]. In PANDDE, we decided to use Wrap file system (WFS), which is a kernel resident stackable file system that is based on virtual file system (VFS). This file system has performance close to the performance of the native KFS since it interacts directly with device drivers [21].

[1]We refer the reader to Table 1 for the list of the acronyms used in this paper.

Table 1: Acronym Table

Acronym	Term
AD	Anomaly Detection
DBMSs	Database Management Systems
DBO	Database Owner
EDP	Exfiltration Detection Provider
KFS	Kernel File System
ML	Monitored List
PL	Provenance Log
PP	Provenance Processor
PS	Provenance Storage
VFS	Virtual File System
WFS	Wrap File System

Since kernel space provenance collection produces large amounts of provenance data, processing this data at the kernel level would impact the performance of the kernel. Hence, we decided to transfer the collected provenance information from kernel space to user space. To do that, we used relayfs, which is a file system designed to provide an efficient mechanism to relay large and continuous data streams from kernel space to user space. Relayfs is a set of per-cpu kernel buffers that can be efficiently written into by the kernel. The buffers are represented as files, and they can be read in user space. These files can only be modified by a user that has root privileges. The FUSE mechanism is similar to relayfs. We refer the reader to [13] and [5] for details about relayfs and FUSE.

2.2 Detection Workflow

The workflow of the detection and response of exfiltration attempts in PANDDE is explained in this subsection. First, the user logs in and submits SQL queries. At that time, normal database security operations, such as user authentication and access control, are executed. According to the access control decision, the user either obtains the data requested in the query or is denied access to it. If the user obtains the data, the data is displayed on a terminal and the user can perform further operations on it on the file system level. PANDDE analyzes such actions and detects exfiltration attempts. Upon the detection of an exfiltration attempt, possible different responses can be taken, for example, blocking the file operation, or logging such action and warning the security administrator.

2.3 Limitations

PANDDE can detect some types of cyber attacks; those are masquerading attacks in which the attacker obtains non-permitted access to the database through legitimate access identification, and general insider threats like when an insider tries to perform operations on the data that are not required by the normal job activities.

It is important to note that PANDDE has to be integrated with other mechanisms to provide full protection against insider attacks. For example, external security has to be adopted to protect against the case when the attacker uses a camera to take a picture of the data. In this case, surveillance cameras can be used to detect the user's action. Also, PANDDE should be integrated with a database level insider attack protection, such as DBSAFE, to detect when a

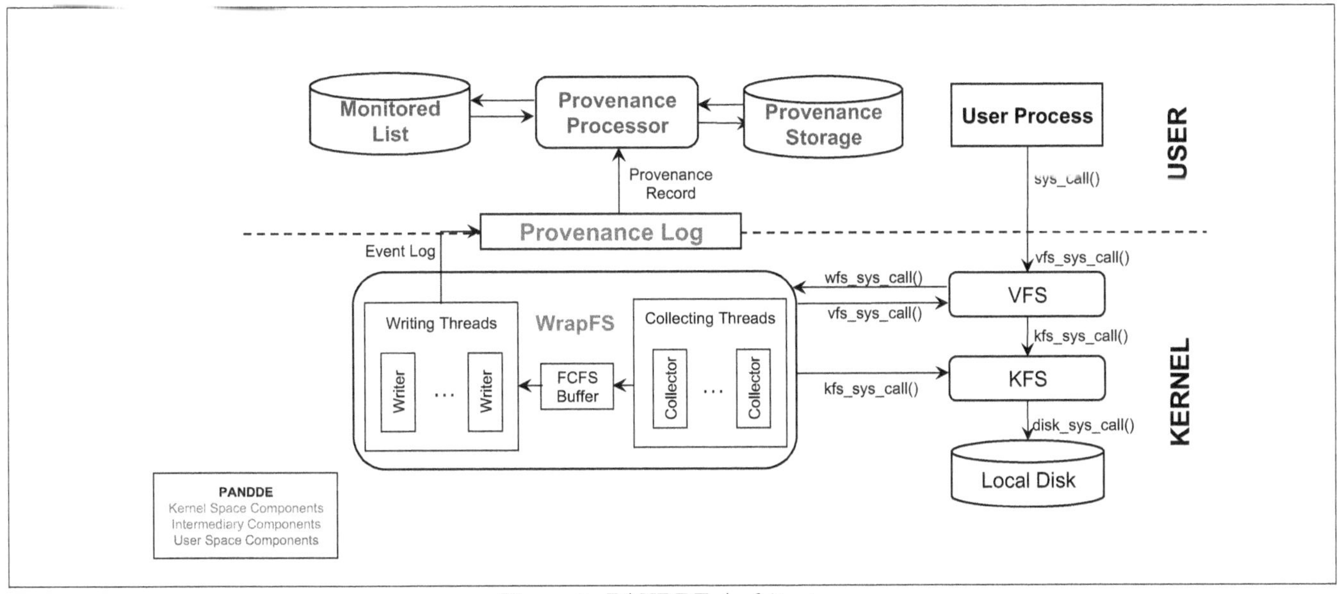

Figure 1: PANDDE Architecture

user's query is anomalous with respect to retrieved data. In PANDDE, we deal with the case in which the user interacts directly with the database; however, in some cases, the user might use a database application program. In such case, systems like DetAnom [8] can be used.

3. SYSTEM ARCHITECTURE

In this section, we describe the main components of PANDDE. Then, we show how PANDDE can be integrated with DBSAFE, which is a database-level AD system [14]. This integration aims at strengthening the protection against malicious insiders.

3.1 PANDDE Architecture

PANDDE consists of the following components: Wrap File System (WFS), Provenance Log (PL), Provenance Processor (PP), Provenance Storage (PS), and Monitored List (ML). As shown in Figure 1, the WFS [21] is located in the kernel space. The WFS is a file system that can be mounted on top of many linux kernel file systems which enhances the portability of our mechanism. The PL, which is located between the kernel and user spaces, is a medium to transmit the metadata of system calls, which are captured in the kernel space, to the user space. Three components of PANDDE are located in the user space: (1) The PP accesses the data in the PL, and then processes it to characterize legitimate access patterns. (2) The PS, which is a PANDDE component, is accessed by the PP to compare the performed action to the existing valid patterns during the detection phase. (3) The ML is a list that includes information about files that contain data from the database. In what follows, we describe in more details the main modules of our mechanism's architecture.

3.1.1 Kernel Space Components

As shown in Figure 1, the WFS is placed in the kernel space, and it is stacked between the virtual file system (VFS) layer and the kernel file system (KFS). In order to access a file, a process invokes a system call (sys_call()). Such system call in-turn invokes the VFS's system call (vfs_sys_call()). Then, the VFS invokes the KFS's function (kfs_sys_call()). When the WFS is mounted on top of the KFS, it intercepts the VFS's calls and copies their arguments and all information that we need from kernel data structures. This provenance information is shown in Table 2.

In our implementation, the WFS consists of several components. The two main components are the Collector, and the Writer (See Figure 1). The task of the WFS's Collector is to capture the metadata of the system calls from the kernel by observing provenance-generating events like writing to a file, reading from a file, opening a file, and reading a directory. In PANDDE, the Collector intercepts the following system calls: open() and write(). Hence, it is able to capture many events, e.g., emailing, printing, and copying. Once the metadata is captured, the Collector writes an entry recording the metadata associated with the specific system call to an in-memory first-come-first-served (FCFS) buffer. Then, the WFS's Writer dequeues a log event as a record from the buffer and writes the record in the PL. In our design, the Collector and the Writer have multiple threads to enhance the performance and speed up the tracking of processes.

3.1.2 Intermediary Components

As shown in Figure 1, the Provenance Log (PL) is located between the kernel space and the user space. It is a medium to communicate provenance events across both spaces. We decided to process the captured data in the user space since provenance collection produces large amount of data [1], and processing such data in the kernel space will be time consuming. Therefore, we used relayfs which is a medium to transfer kernel data to the user space in an efficient way, and to write to an on-disk log file by using expanded printk buffer [13].

After the provenance data is transmitted to the PL using relayfs, the PP accesses the PL to present the event log to the user space in the form of provenance records. The format of each record is shown in Table 2. We use the PName field,

Table 2: Metadata included in a Provenance Record

Field	Explanation
InodeNo	Unique number for each file to describe it
FName	Name of the file on which the user performs an action
UID	The id of the user that performs the activity on the file
GID	The id of the group that the user is currently a member of
PID	Unique number to identify an active process in the kernel
PPID	The identifier of the parent of the process that accesses the file
PName	The name of the process that accesses the file
Args	Arguments that are passed to the captured system call

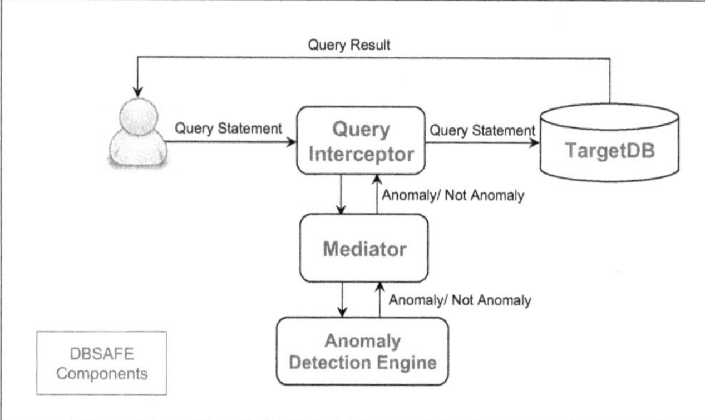

Figure 2: DBSAFE System

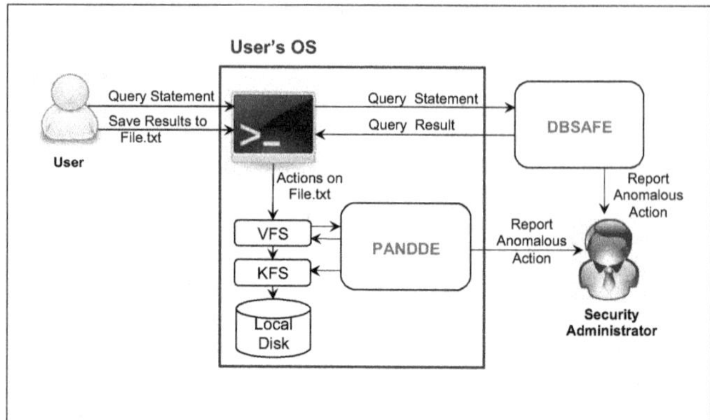

Figure 3: Integration of PANDDE and DBSAFE

which is the name of the running process, to identify the source of the data written to a file. Hence, we can detect if the source of the data is the database. For example, if the PName is "psql", we know that PostgreSQL wrote data to the file.

3.1.3 User Space Components

In the user space, there are three main components: Provenance Processor(PP), Provenance Storage (PS), and Monitored List (ML).

1. The PP plays an important role in both the training and detection phases. During the training phase, the PP processes and stores the information about the collected provenance. The PP is separated from the collection in the kernel space; thus, we can analyze the metadata as we want and use it to support our needs to detect anomalous actions on data. We can concatenate provenance information, or truncate information before saving it to the PS. This separation helps keep the Collector simple without the difficulty of processing data. Besides processing provenance data, the PP works as a detection engine during the detection phase. It compares the current activity of each user to the patterns in the profile. Then, if the PP does not find a match, it decides that the current action is anomalous, and sends a message indicating an anomalous action.

2. The PS stores the profiles of users' legitimate actions. The PP refers to the PS during the detection phase to determine whether the current activity is anomalous. In our implementation, we use two files. The first file is used to store provenance records that consist of the data shown in Table 2. The second one is used to store users' actions (Print, Email, Store, or Copy) to characterize the legitimate access patterns. Each record in such file has the form (<UID>, <Action>), e.g., (1000, Print), which indicates that the user, whose UID is 1000, usually prints files that contain data from the database and therefore such actions are not considered anomalous.

3. The ML is created during the training phase, and PANDDE continues adding files' information to this list during the detection phase. This file contains a list of inode numbers and names of files that contain data from the database. The PP decides that a file should be added to the ML when it captures a system call that is indicating that the database is writing to this file. This list is used to monitor users' actions on files whose source is the database. The PP refers to this list during both the training and detection phases to decide if the current activity should be stored in the PS or not.

3.2 Integration with DBSAFE

In this section, in order to show how PANDDE can be integrated with an AD system for database accesses, we discuss how PANDDE can be integrated with DBSAFE. DBSAFE is an AD system developed for relational databases [14]. It creates profiles of normal SQL user queries and then uses these profiles to detect anomalous queries.

Figure 2 shows the components of DBSAFE. The main components of the system are the mediator, the AD engine and the query interceptor. When the user sends a query to the target database, which is the protected database, the query is intercepted by the query interceptor, also referred to as database activity monitor, which in-turn forwards the query to the AD engine through the mediator component. DBSAFE works in two phases: the training phase and the detection phase. During the training phase, the mediator component receives past logs of the users' SQL queries and use them to train a classifier. In the detection phase, the mediator receives input queries from the query interceptor and sends them to the AD system for classification to detect anomalous SQL queries. This is done by analyzing the syntactic features of the query, e.g., the tables accessed in the query and the columns projected in the answer of the query, as well as some semantic features of the query, that is, the amount of data selected from each table to appear in the query result. Figure 3 shows how PANDDE can be integrated to DBSAFE.

Algorithm 1 Training Phase

Input: Provenance Record R

```
function GetActionType(R)
    if R.PName = "lp"|"lpr" then
        Action= Print
    else if R.PName = "mail"|"mutt" then
        Action= Email
    else if R.PName = "cp" then
        Action= Copy
    else if R.PName = "psql" then
        Action= Store
    else if R.PName = "script" then
        if R.Args = "psql" then
            Action= Store
        end if
    end if
    return Action
end function

function AddToProfileAndML(R)
    Action = GetActionType(R)
    CopyFlag = False        ▷ This flag is used to show that a file from the ML was copied because copying a file invokes two consecutive system calls. The first system call operates on the source file while the second one operates on the destination file.
    if R.InodeNo ∈ ML then
        if Action = Print|Email then
            Add (R.UID, Action) to the Profile
        else if Action = Copy then
            CopyFlag = true
        end if
    else if R.InodeNo ∉ ML then
        if Action = Store then
            Add (R.UID, Store) to the Profile
            Add (R.InodeNo, R.FName) to ML
        else if Action = Copy&CopyFlag = true then
            Add (R.UID, Copy) to the Profile
            Add (R.InodeNo, R.FName) to ML
            CopyFlag = false
        end if
    end if
end function
```

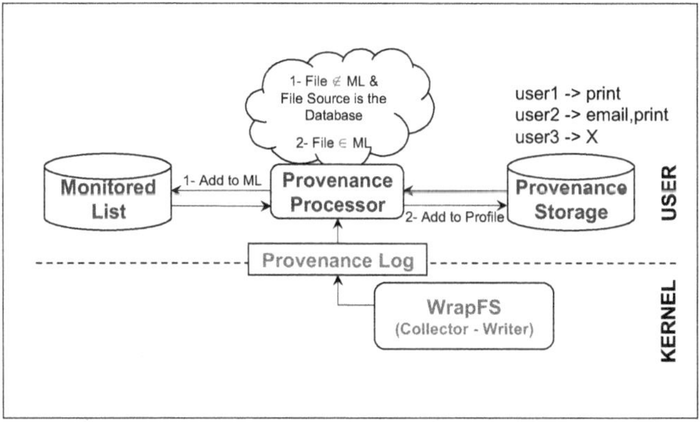

Figure 4: The Training Phase

4. DETECTION OF ANOMALOUS ACTIONS

As mentioned earlier, PANDDE operates in two phases: training phase and detection phase. During the training phase, all files that contain data extracted from the database are monitored, and all actions performed on these files are stored in profiles. During the detection phase, actions issued by users are compared with the actions in the profiles of users to detect anomalous activities. In what follows, a detailed description of both phases is presented.

4.1 Training Phase (Profile Creation)

As shown in Figure 4, the profile of users' actions is created as follows. When the PP captures a provenance record, it processes the data to check if the file does not exist in the ML. If so, it checks whether the action is a creation of a new file and its source is the database. If this is the case, the PP adds this file information to the ML, and adds to the profile that the user usually stores data from the database.

However, if the file is already listed in the ML, the PP checks the type of the action performed by the user. If the action is Print, Email or Copy, the PP will add a record of the action in the PS associated with the user id in the form (<UID>, <Action>), e.g., (1004, Print). If the action is copying to another file, the PP adds the new file to the ML since it also contains data from the database. Algorithm 1 is a pseudo code that shows how the PP works during the training phase. The algorithm assumes a PostgreSQL database. Example 1 below illustrates the discussion.

Example 1: User-A, whose UID is 1000, performed one of these actions:

Action 1: He/She logged in to PostgreSQL and stored the outputs of his/her queries to a file called FILE1.txt by using one of these commands ("\o", "script psql", ... etc).

Actions by the PP: The PP would execute the following steps during the training phase:

1. It adds the name and inode number of FILE1.txt to the ML.
2. It adds a record of the form (1000, Store) to indicate that this user stores data from the database.
3. It adds a record that contains the data in Table 2.

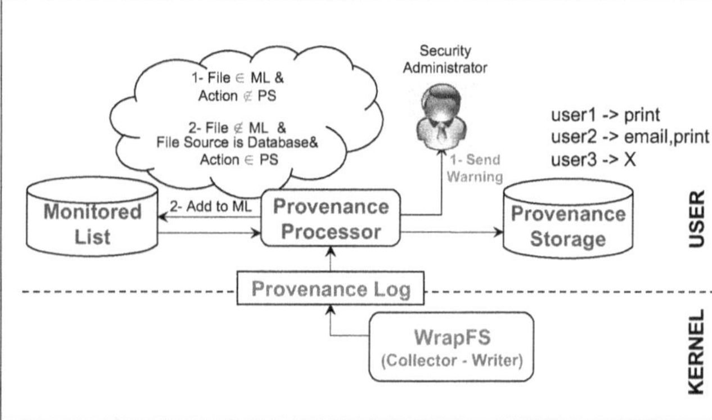

Figure 5: The Detection Phase

Action 2: He/She emailed FILE1.txt by using one of these commands ("mail", "mutt", ...etc).

Actions by the PP: During the training phase, the PP responds as follows :

It checks if FILE1.txt belongs to the ML:

1. If so, it means this file has data from the database.
   (a) The PP stores this action as a record of the form (1000, Email) to indicate that this user emails data from the database.
   (b) It adds a record that contains the data in Table 2 to the PS.
2. Otherwise, the PP does not store this action into the PS.

These profiles can be inspected by a security officer to confirm that the actions recorded in the profiles are consistent with the user normal activities.

4.2 Detection Phase

After the training phase ends, the PP executes the following steps (see Figure 5). Upon intercepting file provenance information, the PP checks whether the file and the action being executed on a file are present in the ML and the PS.

1. First case: the file is not listed in the ML and the file's source is the database. In this case, the PP checks if the PS contains a record which indicates that this user usually stores data from the database. If this is the case, the PP adds this file to the ML; otherwise, it sends a message indicating the detection of an anomaly.
2. Second case: the file is listed in the ML and there is a record in the PS that indicates that it is normal for the user to perform such action. In this case, the PP will allow such action.
3. Third case: the file exists in the ML and the profile does not contain a record of the action. In such case, the PP will send a message indicating the detection of an anomalous action.

Algorithm 2 is a pseudo code that shows how the PP woks during the detection phase. The algorithm assumes a PostgreSQL database. Example 2 below illustrates the detection phase.

Example 2: User-A, whose UID is 1000, performed the following action during the detection phase:

Action: He/She printed a file called FILE2.txt by using one of these commands ("lp", "lpr").

Actions by the PP: During the detection phase, the PP would work as follows:

It checks if FILE2.txt exists in the ML:

1. If so, it means that this file includes data from the database; hence, the PP checks if User-A used to print files by checking the Profile.
   (a) If so, the PP will allow such action.
   (b) Otherwise, the PP will send a warning message to the administrator.
2. If FILE2.txt does not belong to the ML, the PP ignores this action.

Algorithm 2 Detection Phase

Input: Provenance Record R
Output: Detection Engine Response

```
function CheckAnomaly(R)
    Action = GetActionType(R)        ▷ GetActionType works as shown in Algorithm 1
    CopyFlag = False
    if R.InodeNo ∈ ML then
        if (R.UID, Action) ∉ Profile then
            Send a warning message
        else if (R.UID, Action) ∈ Profile then
            if Action = Copy then
                CopyFlag = true
            end if
        end if
    else if R.InodeNo ∉ ML then
        if Action = Store then
            if (R.UID, Store) ∈ Profile then
                Add (R.InodeNo, R.FName) to ML
            else
                Send a warning message
            end if
        else if Action = Copy then
            if (R.UID, Copy) ∈ Profile then
                if CopyFlag = true then
                    Add (R.InodeNo, R.FName) to ML
                    CopyFlag = false
                end if
            else
                if CopyFlag = true then
                    Send a warning message
                end if
            end if
        end if
    end if
end function
```

5. EXPERIMENTAL RESULTS

In this section, we report the results of the experiments assessing the performance of PANDDE. We implemented PANDDE in Ubuntu 12.04 that has 3.8.1 linux kernel, and

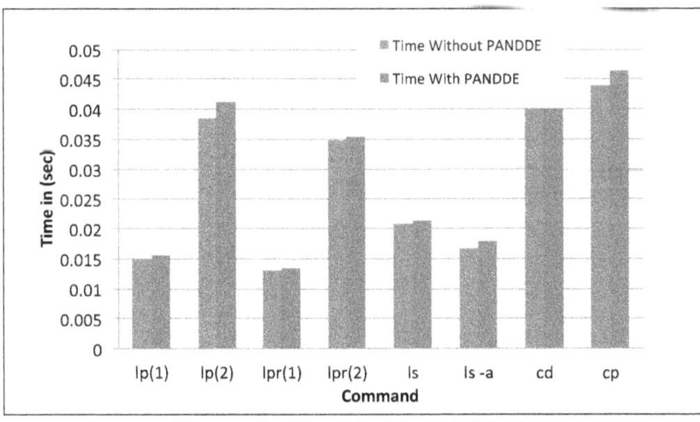

Figure 6: Time in Kernel Mode

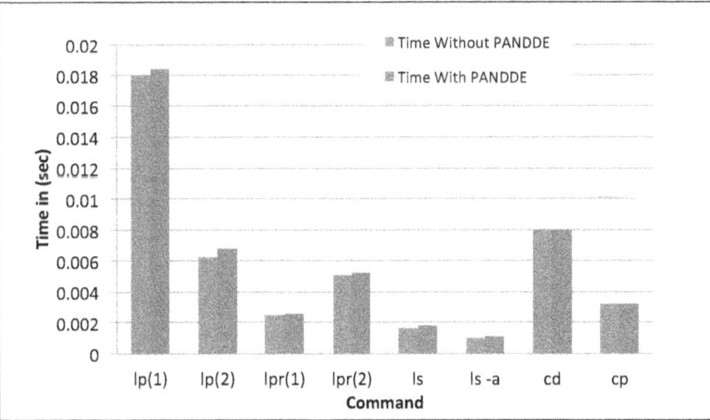

Figure 7: Time in User Mode

used PostgreSQL as DBMS. The database had server and client components. We installed PANDDE at the operating system where the client component is located. The goal of our experiments is to measure the overhead that PANDDE adds to the operating system, and the time that PANDDE takes to detect anomalies.

5.1 Time Overhead

To measure the overhead due to the introduction of our system into the operating system, we measured the required time of executing some widely used commands, namely: "ls", "ls -a", "cd", "lp", "lpr", and "cp". We used the "time" linux command to measure the execution time. This command displays in seconds the total time that the process takes to execute the command, the time that the process spends in kernel mode, and the time spent in user mode. Since the precision of this command is small, we wrote bash scripts to execute each command several times. The ML during the testing time included information of 50 files.

After mounting the WFS and running the PP, we executed each bash script twice. In the first execution run, the script executed through the mounting point which means the executed commands passed through the WFS, and PANDDE processed the collected provenance records. During the second execution run, we ran the bash script outside the mounting point which means that the executed commands sent system calls to the KFS without going through the WFS and the PP was not able to detect such system calls. Therefore, the overhead introduced by PANDDE is obtained as the difference between the execution time obtained from the first execution run and the one obtained from the second execution run.

To measure the overhead that PANDDE adds to the "cd" command, we wrote a bash script that executes this command 500 times. Figures 7 and 6 show that our system did not add overhead to this command. The reason is that PANDDE, as we mentioned earlier, does not capture unnecessary file operations, and this command calls readdir() system call which PANDDE does not capture since such operation is not relevant to AD.

The "lp" and "lpr" commands are used to print files in Linux. To evaluate the time that is added by PANDDE, we wrote two bash scripts to test the "lp" command: (1) The first script calls "lp" to print eight files that were in the ML. (2) The second script calls "lp" 16 times to print files that were not in the ML. In Figures 7, 6 and 8, we refer to the first case as "lp(1)" and to the second case as "lp(2)". The figures show that the execution times increases in kernel mode, in user mode, and in the total execution time. The reason is that such command calls open() system call; hence, it is captured by our system and its provenance record is processed by the PP. The first case, in which files were monitored, the percentage of the increase in the total elapsed time is 8.4. Surprisingly, the increase in the second case, which operated on files that were not monitored, was slightly higher than the first one. The reason is that the PP in the second case had to search the ML file to the end since files did not belong to the ML, and such searching process is linear. It is thus clear that an enhanced organization of the file by the use of, for example, hash techniques is critical for improving the performance. The same method was applied on the "lpr" command, and we obtained similar results.

For the other commands, that is, "ls", "ls -a", and "cp", the results were similar to the results for "lp". They call either open() or write() system calls, and thus they are captured by PANDDE and the collected provenance records are processed by the PP. Thus, they add a slight load to the operating system. It is worth to point out that the results of the "cp" command were noticeable since this command issues two system calls when it is executed. The first system call operates on the source file while the other one operates on the destination file. Hence, we expected higher overhead when using this command. Nonetheless, there was no overhead added to the time in user mode, and the overhead that PANDDE added to the time in kernel mode was lower than the time that was added to other commands like "ls -a", and "lpr".

After testing all these commands, we aggregated the results. Table 3 reports the aggregated results for the average load that PANDDE added on the operating system in real time, in kernel mode and in user mode. This overhead is due to collecting provenance information in the kernel space, transferring such information to the user space, processing the provenance records in the PP, and searching the ML and PS and writing to them.

5.2 Time to Detect Anomalous Actions

For measuring the elapsed time to detect anomalous actions, we wrote bash scripts to execute some actions and

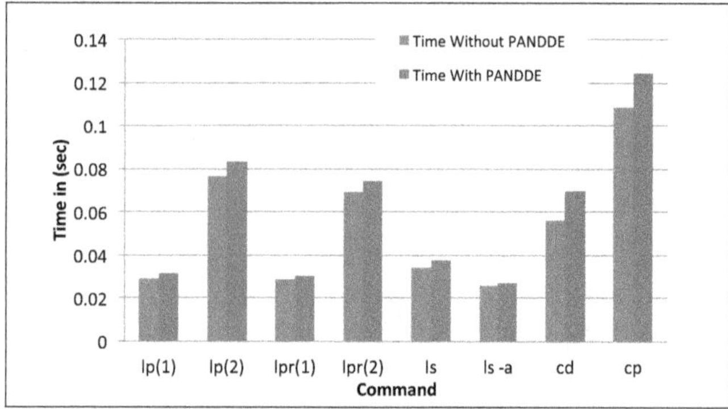

Figure 8: Real Elapsed Time

Table 3: The average overhead imposed by PANDDE

Real Elapsed Time	9.33%
Time in User Mode	3.94%
Time in Kernel Mode	4.35%

called the "date" command to get the current time. Then, we recorded the time at which an AD message was issued by PANDDE in order to obtain the time spent in detecting anomalous actions. Also, in this experiment the number of files in the ML was set to 200. We created 16 scenarios in which the users performed anomalous actions.

- In the first scenario, the user, whose UID is 1000, uses to store data from the database in files, and copy such files; however, he does not email files and thus such action is not in his profile. In this scenario, user 1000 tries to email a file listed in the ML, and PANDDE detected this action in (0.014) seconds.

- In the second scenario, the user, whose UID is 1001, has in the profile records indicating that he only stores, and emails files listed in the ML. In this scenario, user 1001 tries to print a file monitored by PANDDE. The suspiciousness of the action could be detected by PANDDE in (0.009) seconds.

- In the third scenario, for the user, whose UID is 1002, the profile does not have any record which indicates that user 1002 saves data. Hence, when he tries to store data from the database, this action was classified as anomalous. PANDDE took (0.072) seconds to detect the anomaly and send a warning message.

- In the fourth scenario, the user, whose UID is 1003, according to the profile, uses to store, print and email files listed in the ML. She, however, does not copy data from a file that contains data from the database to another file. For this, when she tried to perform such action, PANDDE detected the anomaly and sent a warning message in (0.012) seconds.

We implemented 16 similar scenarios, and calculated the average elapsed time taken by PANDDE to detect each one of the following actions: storing data from the database in a file, printing, emailing or copying such a file. Table 4 shows the results from this experiment.

Table 4: The average elapsed time to detect anomalous actions

Action	Average Detection time in Seconds
Store	0.07825
Print	0.00825
Copy	0.014
Email	0.00675

6. RELATED WORK

Our work is related to work in the area of provenance collection and in the area of AD for database systems. In what follows, we discuss related work in those two areas.

6.1 Provenance Techniques

Provenance information is critical in many different application domains, such as business, archiving, and scientific computing [12]. Hence, many provenance-based systems have been developed to address a large variety of requirements. Notable provenance systems include PASS [12], LinFS [15], and Story Book [17]. All these systems are similar to each other in terms of operating on file systems. Each system has advantages and disadvantages. For example, LinFS and Story Book run in the user space which simplifies their implementation; yet, they incur high overhead in kernel. On the other hand, PASS is implemented in the kernel space which requires more complicated implementation, but has better performance.

Unlike LinFS and Story Book, PANDDE is implemented in the kernel space like PASS. However, PANDDE differs with respect to PASS in the approach used to transmit the event log to the user space. None of those systems was developed with the goal of supporting AD in actions executed upon data retrieved from a database. Trio collects provenance information on databases rather than files [1] [12]. Trio and PANDDE are complementary since Trio focuses on databases and our system focuses on files. In addition, Trio does not support AD.

6.2 Anomaly Detection in Databases

In this section, we discuss other proposed mechanisms that are complementary to PANDDE at different levels. At the database level, there are many approaches that were proposed to detect anomalies in database system access. Chung et al. propose DEMIDS [4] that is a system to detect misuse of relational database systems. This approach derives profiles describing valid access patterns of database users by using the data in audit logs. On the other hand, Spalka et al. [16] propose a system to detect misuse of databases, and to perform AD.

At the database application level, other systems have been proposed. For example, DIDAFIT [10] is a detection system for detecting suspicious database accesses by comparing statements against a known set of valid database transaction fingerprints. DetAnom [8] assures the correct order of SQL commands is preserved in the user transactions by using concolic testing techniques to capture the control flow and data flow of the program. Another approach has been proposed based on the use of data-access correlations to capture anomalies in indirect transactions [3] [7].

Several approaches [11], [19] and [20] have been proposed that are complementary to both PANDDE and DBSAFE. Those approaches use dependency relationships to determine the amount of knowledge that can be inferred about objects of the database. Insiders can use this knowledge to expand their knowledge about the database. Other approaches [18] [22] analyze network traffic in order to detect data exfiltration performed by malware. Combining these approaches with ours can strengthen data protection against insiders' attacks.

7. CONCLUSION AND FUTURE WORK

In this paper, we proposed PANDDE, a system for detecting anomalous actions executed by users on data retrieved from databases. PANDDE focuses on the stage after the data is out of the database and thus works on the operating system level. PANDDE tracks files that are saved from the database query output results. In the training phase, PANDDE records the normal actions executed by the database users on files by collecting provenance information. During the detection phase, PANDDE detects anomalous actions by referring to the recorded profiles. We showed how our mechanism can be integrated with existing systems to provide stronger defense against insider threats.

We plan to extend our work in AD of insider threats against databases in different directions. We plan to enrich the profiles in several ways. First, information about the database tables from which data is returned to users should be added to the profiles to support more detailed access patterns. Second, the temporal aspect of users' actions should be taken into account. We plan to account for the rate of actions that are performed by the user. Adding this will allow us to detect data harvesting attacks where the user gets chuncks of data from the database as a result of performing separate actions, and combines these chuncks to exfiltrate the intended portion of the database.

Another important extension is to take into account queries sent from application programs. This has to be considered at two levels: the database level and the operating system level. Dealing with application programs is different than dealing with the case where the user can send any query to the database engine, since the queries sent from the program are restricted by the control path that the program follows based on the input data. Initial approaches have been proposed based on concolic testing in order to identify queries issued by an application program for different input parameters of the application [8]. We plan on adopting and extending this work to create profiles of actions executed on the data by application programs. This requires capturing the file and print operations performed on the data returned by the database to the application program by using data and control dependency techniques [6].

8. ACKNOWLEDGMENTS

The authors would like to thank Salmin Sultana for assistance with the development of PANDDE.

9. REFERENCES

[1] P. Agrawal, O. Benjelloun, A. D. Sarma, C. Hayworth, S. Nabar, T. Sugihara, and J. Widom. Trio: A system for data, uncertainty, and lineage. In *Proceedings of the 32Nd International Conference on Very Large Data Bases*, VLDB '06, pages 1151–1154. VLDB Endowment, 2006.

[2] E. Bertino. Data protection from insider threats. *Synthesis Lectures on Data Management*, 4(4):1–91, 2012.

[3] M. Chagarlamudi, B. Panda, and Y. Hu. Insider threat in database systems: Preventing malicious users' activities in databases. In *Proceedings of the 2009 Sixth International Conference on Information Technology: New Generations*, ITNG '09, pages 1616–1620, Washington, DC, USA, 2009. IEEE Computer Society.

[4] C. Y. Chung, M. Gertz, and K. Levitt. Integrity and internal control information systems. chapter DEMIDS: A Misuse Detection System for Database Systems, pages 159–178. Kluwer Academic Publishers, Norwell, MA, USA, 2000.

[5] FUSE: Filesystem in userspace. http://fuse.sourceforge.net/.

[6] J. L. Hennessy and D. A. Patterson. *Computer Architecture, Fifth Edition: A Quantitative Approach.* Morgan Kaufmann Publishers Inc., San Francisco, CA, USA, 5th edition, 2011.

[7] Y. Hu and B. Panda. Identification of malicious transactions in database systems. In *Database Engineering and Applications Symposium, 2003. Proceedings. Seventh International*, pages 329–335, July 2003.

[8] S. R. Hussain, A. M. Sallam, and E. Bertino. Detanom: Detecting anomalous database transactions by insiders. In *Proceedings of the 5th ACM Conference on Data and Application Security and Privacy*, CODASPY '15, pages 25–35, New York, NY, USA, 2015. ACM.

[9] A. Kamra, E. Terzi, and E. Bertino. Detecting anomalous access patterns in relational databases. *The VLDB Journal*, 17(5):1063–1077, August 2008.

[10] S. Y. Lee, W. L. Low, and P. Y. Wong. Learning fingerprints for a database intrusion detection system. In *Proceedings of the 7th European Symposium on Research in Computer Security*, ESORICS '02, pages 264–280, London, UK, UK, 2002. Springer-Verlag.

[11] W. Li, B. Panda, and Q. Yaseen. Mitigating insider threat on database integrity. In V. Venkatakrishnan and D. Goswami, editors, *Information Systems Security*, volume 7671 of *Lecture Notes in Computer Science*, pages 223–237. Springer Berlin Heidelberg, 2012.

[12] K.-K. Muniswamy-Reddy, D. A. Holland, U. Braun, and M. Seltzer. Provenance-aware storage systems. In *Proceedings of the Annual Conference on USENIX '06 Annual Technical Conference*, ATEC '06, pages 4–4, Berkeley, CA, USA, 2006. USENIX Association.

[13] D. J. Pohly, S. E. McLaughlin, P. McDaniel, and K. R. B. Butler. Hi-fi: collecting high-fidelity whole-system provenance. In R. H. Zakon, editor, *ACSAC*, pages 259–268. ACM, 2012.

[14] A. M. Sallam, E. Bertino, S. R. Hussain, D. Landers, R. M. Lefler, and D. Steiner. Dbsafe - an anomaly detection system to protect databases from exfiltration attempts. Under Submission, September 2014.

[15] C. Sar and P. Cao. Lineage file system. Online at http://crypto.stanford.edu/ cao/lineage.html, January 2005.

[16] A. Spalka and J. Lehnhardt. A comprehensive approach to anomaly detection in relational databases. In S. Jajodia and D. Wijesekera, editors, *Data and Applications Security XIX*, volume 3654 of *Lecture Notes in Computer Science*, pages 207–221. Springer Berlin Heidelberg, 2005.

[17] R. Spillane, R. Sears, C. Yalamanchili, S. Gaikwad, M. Chinni, and E. Zadok. Story book: An efficient extensible provenance framework. In *First Workshop on on Theory and Practice of Provenance*, TAPP'09, pages 11:1–11:10, Berkeley, CA, USA, 2009. USENIX Association.

[18] H. Xiong, P. Malhotra, D. Stefan, C. Wu, and D. Yao. User-assisted host-based detection of outbound malware traffic. In *Proceedings of the 11th International Conference on Information and Communications Security*, ICICS'09, pages 293–307, Berlin, Heidelberg, 2009. Springer-Verlag.

[19] Q. Yaseen and B. Panda. Knowledge acquisition and insider threat prediction in relational database systems. In *Computational Science and Engineering, 2009. CSE '09. International Conference on*, volume 3, pages 450–455, August 2009.

[20] Q. Yaseen and B. Panda. Predicting and preventing insider threat in relational database systems. In P. Samarati, M. Tunstall, J. Posegga, K. Markantonakis, and D. Sauveron, editors, *Information Security Theory and Practices. Security and Privacy of Pervasive Systems and Smart Devices*, volume 6033 of *Lecture Notes in Computer Science*, pages 368–383. Springer Berlin Heidelberg, 2010.

[21] E. Zadok and I. Bădulescu. A stackable file system interface for Linux. In *LinuxExpo Conference Proceedings*, pages 141–151, Raleigh, NC, May 1999.

[22] H. Zhang, D. D. Yao, and N. Ramakrishnan. Detection of stealthy malware activities with traffic causality and scalable triggering relation discovery. In *Proceedings of the 9th ACM Symposium on Information, Computer and Communications Security*, ASIA CCS '14, pages 39–50, New York, NY, USA, 2014. ACM.

Program-object Level Data Flow Analysis with Applications to Data Leakage and Contamination Forensics

Gaoyao Xiao, Jun Wang, Peng Liu, Jiang Ming, and Dinghao Wu
College of Information Sciences and Technology
The Pennsylvania State University
University Park, PA 16802, USA
{gzx102, jow5222, pliu, jum310, dwu}@ist.psu.edu

ABSTRACT

We introduce a novel Data Flow Analysis (DFA) technique, called PoL-DFA (Program-object Level Data Flow Analysis), to analyze the dynamic data flows of server programs. PoL-DFA symbolically analyzes every instruction in the execution trace of a process to keep track of the data flows among program objects (*e.g.,* integers, structures, arrays), and concatenates these pieces of data flows to obtain the overall data flow graph of the execution. We leverage PoL-DFA to identify malicious data flows in data leakage and contamination forensics. In two mocked digital forensic scenarios, for data leakage and contamination respectively, we tested the ability of PoL-DFA to identify data flows among multiple inputs and outputs of server programs. Our results show that PoL-DFA can accurately determine whether the data (or the processed results) from a source file or socket flow to a certain output channel. Based on this information, security administrators can pinpoint the path of data leakage or data contamination. Different from existing dynamic DFA techniques that require excessive amount of instrumentation, PoL-DFA only requires logging the execution traces of the processes being monitored. The measured performance overhead for server programs is 4.24%, on average. The results indicate PoL-DFA is a lightweight DFA solution for data leakage and contamination forensics.

1. INTRODUCTION

We consider the following scenario: A company has a web server that hosts some web services to users on the Internet. The web page files in the web server can be updated or added through FTP by authorized employees. An employee uses FTP to upload a file that contains sensitive information to the web server (we assume the employee has the needed authority). He also uploads a modified index.html, which contains a link to that file, to overwrite the index.html file on the web server. After he goes home, he starts a web browser and downloads the file, which contains the sensitive information, from the company's web server. Later, the administrator identifies this file on the web server and wants to investigate who uploaded the file and whether the sensitive information has been leaked out. If so, the admin also wants to know which IP addresses the information has been leaked to.

We explored the literature for possible solutions. Causality relationships can be inferred from system events such as file operations, network I/O, and memory read/write, and be used for attack provenance analysis[16, 28, 18, 21]. This type of relationship is unsuitable for data flow analysis – taking the aforementioned data leakage scenario for example, even if the web server opens the file containing sensitive information and later sends a packet to the Internet, it does not necessarily indicate the packet contains the information from that file. Using system events to correlate objects and processes may result in a large number of false positive data dependencies, namely *dependence explosion.* Dynamic Taint Analysis (DTA) can trace data flows at the byte level and is free from dependence explosion. However, the high runtime overhead of DTA restricts itself as an *offline analysis* technique, *e.g.,* automatic generation of malware and exploit signatures [7, 25], and automatic configuration troubleshooting [5]. By "offline analysis", we mean the server programs being protected (*e.g.,* HTTP service), are *not* running at full speed serving a large number of online requests from clients.

In this work, we propose to tackle dependence explosion using a new fine-grained scheme named PoL-DFA (Program-object Level Data Flow Analysis). Different from DTA which is at the byte level, PoL-DFA targets at program object level. Data flows are tracked among network packets, program objects, files, and any devices modeled as file descriptors by the operating system. PoL-DFA only requires the logging of the basic blocks that the program executes. A data flow graph containing program objects, network packets, and files can then be built based on the analysis of the execution trace. While both PoL-DFA and DTA conduct instruction-by-instruction analysis, we have dramatically different design goals. DTA on binary code typically relies on dynamic binary instrumentation to propagate taint tags at the instruction level. By contrast, PoL-DFA tracks the data flow at program-object level. Our system models program objects, call stacks, and heaps of each process, and simulates the process creation operations. Compared to DTA, although PoL-DFA does not log complete runtime values, we show that our approach can still achieve a similar level of precision and better runtime performance.

CODASPY'16, March 9–11, 2016, New Orleans, LA, USA

DOI: http://dx.doi.org/10.1145/2857705.2857747

2. OVERVIEW

This section overviews the intuitions behind our approach and the system work flow.

2.1 Program-object Level Data Flow Analysis (PoL-DFA)

We define PoL-DFA (**P**rogram-**o**bject **L**evel **D**ata **F**low **A**nalysis) as *the procedure of inferring the data flow dependencies among the files and sockets ever accessed by a program through analyzing the execution trace.* We define the *execution trace* as a sequence of program statements or instructions in the order in which they have been executed at runtime. A data flow is essentially the consequence of a program execution. Involved in the execution are a series of program objects and the corresponding operations against them. The below observations show the intuitions of how PoL-DFA works.

Observation 1. The execution trace constructs, such as program statements, instructions, symbols and so forth, inherently imply data flows, even if the corresponding runtime variable values and memory addresses are unknown. The following code in Listing 1 shows a network packet being received, stored in a buffer, and then saved into a file. Knowing neither the runtime memory address of `buf` nor the runtime value of `sockfd/fd`, one can still conclude the data flow purely based on static analysis. In addition, by correlating with the system call log, one can draw an object-level data flow graph as shown in Figure 1.

Listing 1: An example of object level data flow.

```
buf = malloc(1024);
recvfrom(sockfd, buf, len, src_addr, addr_len);
fd = fopen('download.exe', 'w+');
fwrite(buf, 1024, 1, fd);
```

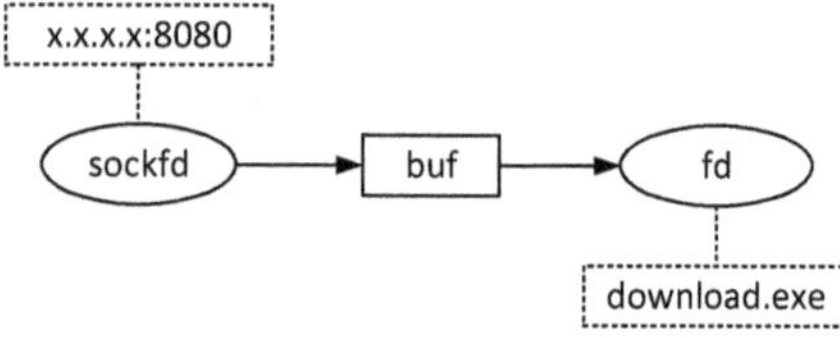

Figure 1: An object-level data flow graph resulted from the static code analysis and runtime system call log.

Observation 2. In many cases, data flow that cannot be statically determined can instead be resolved using the runtime control flow information embedded in the execution trace, including branches and loop iterations. Take the following pseudo code as an example. If the `condition` is true, the data flow will be `file A -> socket C`; otherwise, the data flow will become `file B -> socket C`. If we know which branch has indeed been taken at runtime, we can decide the correct data flow.

```
if (condition)
    read in file A to buffer;
else
    read in file B to buffer;
write buffer to socket C;
```

Observation 3. We realize that there are some cases wherein the data flow cannot be precisely derived solely based on the execution trace. The major portion falls into the situation that a variable (instead of an immediate constant) is used as an index to an array or an offset to a buffer. In such cases, one can choose to log all such concrete index/offset values at runtime. We find that by treating an array/buffer as an atomic unit, we can still correctly identify data flow in most cases (see §3.3 for further discussion).

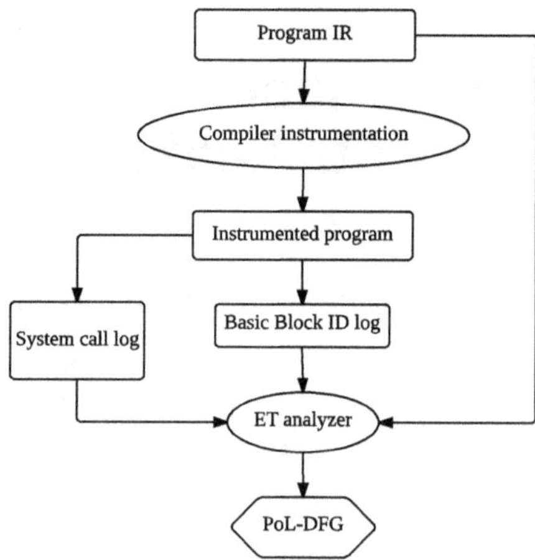

Figure 2: System work flow.

We devise a PoL-DFA mechanism, inspired by the aforementioned three observations. In particular, we sequentially go through every instruction in the execution trace, analyze and translate the instructions into data flow propagation operations between the source operand(s) and the destination operand(s), and in the meantime maintain and populate the data flow states for the corresponding program objects (an operand typically represents an object or part of an object). Finally, a data flow starting from an input file (or socket) to an output file (or socket) can be bridged by a series of intermediate program objects. Currently, the intermediate program objects include data type instances (*e.g.,* integers, floats, pointers), data structure subfields, and arrays. Note that a file descriptor, which refers to a socket or file, is represented as an integer data type as well.

2.2 System Workflow

The workflow of our system is shown in Figure 2. The first step to deploying our system is instrumentation. We implemented a compiler extension to instrument the LLVM IR (Intermediate Representation) of the programs being monitored. The binary executables produced by our instrumentation automatically log the basic block trace of each process into files during runtime. The basic block log contains a sequence of basic block IDs, using which we can recover the execution trace of the program. The second part of the work flow is trace recovering and analysis, which is conducted by ET(Execution Trace)-Analyzer. ET-Analyzer takes basic block log, system call log (used for annotation purpose, *e.g.,* annotating the file name of a file descriptor), and LLVM IR of the program being monitored as inputs. Based on the inputs, ET-Analyzer recovers the execution trace, conducts PoL-DFA against the trace, and outputs a PoL-DFG (Program-object Level Data Flow Graph) which shows the data flows resulted from the program execution.

3. DESIGN

This section introduces the concept of LLVM IR-level execution trace, and how we infer data flows based on the trace.

3.1 LLVM IR-Level Execution Trace

For an execution of a program, the *IR-level execution trace* is a sequence of IR instructions that correspond to the native machine instructions executed. As we know, the IR of a program can be compiled into machine code, which can be executed. When the program runs, a sequence of machine instructions is executed and this sequence of machine instructions has a sequence of IR instructions as a counterpart in the form of IR. This sequence of IR instructions is called the IR-level execution trace of this execution.

The LLVM IR of a program contains a number of basic blocks. An LLVM Basic Block is simply "a container of instructions that execute sequentially" [3]. An example LLVM basic block is as below. In this LLVM Basic Block, a value `%2` is loaded through a pointer `%i`, and used as the parameter of function `%foo`. The return value `%call` is stored through a pointer `%ret`. Then the basic block exits. The execution of a program involves entering and exiting a sequence of basic blocks.

Listing 2: An example of IR basic block.

```
for.body:                              ; preds = %for.cond
  %2 = load i32* %i
  %call = call i32 @foo(i32 %2)
  store i32 %call, i32* %ret
  br label %for.inc
```

We statically assign a unique ID to each basic block and then at the beginning of each basic block, we insert instructions to store the ID to the buffers. We also create a thread to write the logs to hard disk at runtime. The logs show the sequence in which basic blocks are entered. With the logs, we are able to recover the IR level execution trace.

3.2 The PoL-DFA Model

Data Sources. Data sources are the files that a program reads data from and the sockets that a program receives packets from. Data sources are introduced via system calls like `read` and `recv/recvfrom/recvmsg`, as well as library functions like `fread`. Each incoming data source will be assigned a unique *tag*, which represents a unique data source. The tag will then be propagated to other program objects throughout the entire analysis whenever there is a data flow.

Data Sinks. Data sinks are the files that a program writes data to and the sockets that a program sends packets to. Tags can be propagated to data sinks via system calls such as `write`, `send/sendto/sendmsg`, and library functions like `fwrite`. A program-object level data flow graph can be built based on the tags that have arrived at each data sink. In a program-object level data flow graph, a data source could have multiple outgoing edges connecting to different data sinks; and a data sink could have multiple incoming edges starting from different data sources. Note that a file/-socket could be the data sink of one data flow, and the data source of another data flow.

Data Flow. A data flow happens when the contents of a data source are 1) directly copied and written to a data sink, or 2) computationally modified (*e.g.,* compression, encryption/decryption) before being written to a data sink. We aim to extract the data flow by looking at the operations in the execution trace and keeping track of the tag propagation among the program objects. Particularly, we build *data flow paths* between data sources and data sinks. A data flow path is a sequence of nodes through which the data flows. The start node is the data source and end node is data sink. All nodes in between are program objects involved in the operations. The operations against these program objects can be broken down into three categories: data movement, arithmetic, and neither. For a data movement operation, the tags of the source operand(s) will be propagated to the destination operand(s). For an arithmetic operation, all the tags that have arrived at any operand will be propagated to the destination.

To hold the tags, we associate each program object with an abstract metadata structure, called *object state.* For non-pointer variables, the object state contains only tags. For pointers, the object state consists of tags, the symbolic link to the program object being pointed to, and, if it belongs to a subfield of a aggregated data type (*i.e.,* struct, array, and vector), the relative offset of the target object to its "container" object. Here "container" object means the aggregate object that contains the pointer. For aggregated data types, the object state is a list of `<offset, size, tags, polPtr>` tuples, which indicates the tags associated with each subfield starting from `offset` and ending at `offset+size`. The `polPtr` stands for program-object level pointer. In case the subfield happens to be a pointer, the `polPtr` element will then be used to store a pointer object state, which links to the target object being pointed to. Table 1 summarizes the object states and the corresponding program objects.

For the lookup purpose, we build a hash map for the object states, which we call *object state map.* The object state map is a one-to-one mapping from program objects to each of their object states. When tags need to be propagated among program objects, we first look up the corresponding object states in the object state map and then copy and update the tags accordingly. We define two types of object state maps: global object state map and local object state map. There is only one global object state map throughout the entire analysis, keeping track of the object states for global variables. Local object state maps are per-function based. In other words, local object state maps are analogous to function stacks and global object state map is comparable to data segment.

3.3 Policies on Tag Propagation

In this section, we focus on tag propagation. We realize that the tags could be propagated in several possible ways. We denote the possible ways as PoL-DFA policies. We also realize that no single PoL-DFA policy is perfect. Below we present our policy based on the following principles. Principle 1—simplicity: we want everything to be as simple as possible. Principle 2—clear semantics: to avoid ambiguity. Principle 3—utility: it can handle the security officers' needs (*e.g.,* the case studies (§5.1)). We group our policy into three categories: *direct tag propagation, indirect tag propagation,* and *block tag propagation.* It should be noted that since the semantics of LLVM IR is at a higher level, certain types of IR instructions[1] do not have the correspondence in the assembly language. This results in the uniqueness of IR-based

[1]LLVM IR Instruction Set:
http://llvm.org/docs/LangRef.html.

Table 1: Primitive data types of object state and corresponding program objects.

Object State	Elements	Corresponding Program Objects
polVar	tags	variables (*e.g.,* i16 %i)
polPtr	tags, ptr, offset	pointers (*e.g.,* i32* %ptr)
polObj	<offset, size, tags, polPtr>	arrays (*e.g.,* [4 x i8]), structures (*e.g.,* {i32, i32, i32}), and vectors (*e.g.,* <4 x i16*>)

policy over assembly-based policy. Our PoL-DFA policy is presented as follows.

I. Direct tag propagation If there is a direct data flow from source operand(s) to destination operand(s), we do direct tag propagation, that is, we make a union of the tags in the source operands' object states and copy to that of the destination. Immediate constants are considered untagged. The types of instructions involved in this category include arithmetic instructions (*e.g.,* `add`, `sub`), bit instructions (*e.g.,* `and`, `or`, `shl`), and conversion instructions (*e.g.,* `truc`, `bitcast`). Figure 3(a) shows an example of direct propagation.

There is one particular instruction `select` that needs a subtle treatment. The `select` instruction assigns either one of two source operands to the destination operand based on a condition. Due to the lack of the runtime value of the condition, we cannot determine which candidate operand to assign. In many cases one of the two source operands cannot be seen in the earlier trace because the corresponding branch has not been executed. As a result, the object state of that operand will not be found and thus we can do the tag propagation normally. If both object states can be found, we then conservatively propagate both of the two candidates' tags and give them a *Possible flag (P flag)*. Basically, we use P flags to incorporate such conservative tag propagation situations.

II. Indirect tag propagation For many instructions, there is no direct data flow among the operands. Instead, either source or destination operand is a reference (*i.e.,* pointer) to a real program object that is involved in the data flow. This type of instructions comprise a major portion of the execution trace, including `load` (reading data from memory) and `store` (writing data to memory). In such cases, we first look up the real program object (via the symbolic link kept in the object state) and then propagate tags from the real source to the real destination, based on the types of the pointer.

First, if the pointer points to a variable, we simply do the tag propagation using the object state of the variable. For example, Figure 3(b) depicts how the tag is propagated for a `load` instruction in this case. The handling of `store` instruction is similar, just with a reverse direction of tag propagation.

Second, a pointer could point to a subfield of an aggregated data type. In LLVM IR, there are mainly two categories of aggregated data types: 1) `array/vector` type which arranges element sequentially in memory, and 2) `struct` type which is a predefined collection of data members. The `GEP` (*i.e.,* `getelementptr`) instruction is normally used to return the pointer to a subfield of an aggregate data type. For the `struct` type, the `GEP` instruction will always see literal values as the offset to the subfields of a data structure. Therefore, we propagate the tag corresponds to the particular offset. For the `array/vector` type, we conservatively treat the whole array as an atomic unit and do tag propagation for the array as a whole. Figure 3(c) shows how a `GEP` involved in `struct` indexing and how a `load` in such a case is handled.

III. Block tag propagation As direct and indirect tag propagations are both for data flow between individual variables, there is another important data flow existing among buffers, *i.e.,* large pieces of contiguous memory. We also consider file and socket as such kind of buffer. So in general we call them "blocks". Instructions that can lead to data flow between blocks include system calls `read/write`, `send/recv`, and library functions `memcpy` *etc.* Generally, we treat a block as an atomic unit whenever the `size` and/or `offset` arguments are variables whose run-time values are unknown. Therefore, for the source blocks, we copy out all the tags to the destination block, including those with the P flag. For the destination blocks, we use a heuristic to decide whether to clean up existing tags:

- First, if data is stored to a block from the *beginning* (*e.g.,* reading a file `fd` to a buffer `buf`: `read(fd,buf,sz)`), we clean up all the tags in the block's object state and copy the new tag(s) into it. This policy is based on the common practice that a block is always used as an atomic buffer to *relay* data from/to a file or socket. Even if an array could be used for multiple files/sockets in different iterations, an access to it at a certain time is only meant to get its most recent content. Moreover, a `size` parameter is always used in a very careful way by programmers to enforce boundary checks in order to avoid buffer over-read bugs. Nevertheless, buffer over-read bugs do exist in reality such as the notorious Heartbleed bug [2]. Since there are better approaches addressing such vulnerabilities, here we simply assume the program is free from such over-read bugs.
- Second, if data is stored to the *middle* of a block (*e.g.,* `read(fd,buf+offset,sz)`), this indicates that the block is most likely used as a buffer to *accumulate* data from multiple data sources (*e.g.,* files concatenation). Since it is impossible to predict which part of the buffer a later-on access intends to get, we cannot simply remove all the existing tags. Instead our policy is to first set the P flag for all existing tags of the array, if any, and then merge the new tag(s) into it.

3.4 Program-object Level Data Flow Graph Generation

Our system is designed to generate two types of PoL-DFG, with program objects versus without program objects. For the PoL-DFG without program objects, it contains a set of nodes and directed edges. Each node is a system object represented by a file descriptor, *e.g.,* file, socket, standard I/O, *etc.* Each directed edge means the existence of data flow from the start node to the end node. For the PoL-DFG with program objects, a node could also be a program object. For many digital forensic needs, the details about data flow through program objects are not needed. For some

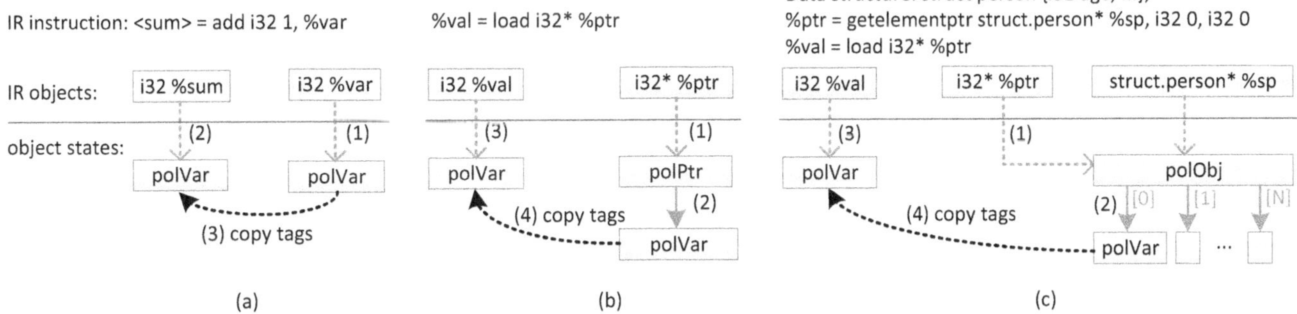

Figure 3: Tag propagation examples. (a) An example of direct tag propagation; (b) An example of indirect tag propagation; (c) An example of indirect tag propagation involving aggregated data types.

other, the officer may also want to see the data flow through program objects, so we also provide this as an option.

Node Annotation. For a node representing a file or a socket, the file name or bound IP of the node is annotated using the system call log. For one execution of a program, I/O related system calls, such as `open`, `socket`, `connect`, *etc.*, are logged in the order they are called. In the IR-level execution trace of this execution, the instructions that call these system calls (or library calls, such as `fopen`, implemented using these system calls) appear in the same order. We simply sequentially match each call instruction, which results in an I/O system call, against the corresponding entry in the system call log. The file names and IP addresses can be extracted from the arguments of system calls. Especially, a socket might be created using `socket` system call and bound with an IP address using `connect` system call. The IP address bound to this socket is extracted from the arguments of `connect`.

Edge Generation. For PoL-DFG without program objects, the edges are created when outputting system calls and library calls, such as `write`, `fwrite`, `sendmsg`, *etc.*, are found in the IR-level execution trace. An outputting system call usually write the contents in a buffer to a file or socket represented by a `fd`. If the tag list of the buffer's object state is not empty, we propagate these tags to the `fd`. For each propagated tag, an edge is created from the data source, corresponding to the tag, to the data sink represented by the `fd`. For PoL-DFG with program objects, each propagation operation of a tag results in the creation of an edge, which starts at the source node of tag propagation and ends at the destination node. The tag propagation operations include data assignment, reading from a file, writing to a file, *etc.*

4. IMPLEMENTATION

Since assembly language does not offer type abstractions (*i.e.*, integers, pointers, structure, *etc.*), we leverage LLVM [20] to base our system. The benefit is twofold: First, LLVM infrastructure enables us to conduct analysis for programs written in various programming languages (*e.g.*, C, C++, Fortran) and running on different platforms (*e.g.*, x86, PowerPC, ARM), making our tool widely applicable. Second, LLVM IR (*i.e.*, intermediate representation) has a well-defined type system and preserves high level program abstractions which can greatly ease our analysis, especially compared with low level assembly language from which the high level semantics has already been removed.

We implemented a prototype PoL-DFA system. The instrumentation component is implemented as an LLVM IR transformation pass, which has 290 LOC. The IR of programs is obtained through compiling source code using clang. The IR is instrumented and then transformed by clang to binary program. The ET-Analyzer is implemented in C++ and it has 5408 LOC. The system calls that create data sources and sinks are logged by Auditd. We use Python scripts to parse the system call logs to extract the file names and IP addresses of data sources and sinks. The PoL-DFG generation is also implemented in Python. We use a Python library named *pydot* to generate PoL-DFG based on the results of PoL-DFA. The Python scripts for parsing system call log and generating PoL-DFG have 340 LOC in total.

5. EVALUATION

We measure the logging overhead, analysis efficiency, and space overhead, on a machine with Intel(R) Xeon(R) CPU X3440 2.53GHz, 12GB DDR3 RAM, and Samsung SSD of 250GB of model 840.

5.1 Solving Dependence Explosion

We conducted two case studies to investigate whether PoL-DFA can solve the dependence explosion problem in data leakage and contamination forensics. We consider two scenarios in which, without PoL-DFA, security administrators would have difficulty to spot malicious data flows, due to the undecidability of data flows.

Case Study 1. Information Leakage: We consider the information leakage scenario mentioned in the introduction. By conducting causality analysis, *i.e.*, inferring data dependencies based on system events, the data flow graph can reach the extent as shown in Figure 4(a). Because there is no publicly available tool for causality analysis, we infer this graph based on algorithms introduced in existing causality analysis works. The graph shows several files were sent to the web server through FTP clients on two different workstations. After the files were uploaded, the web server served requests from 40 different IP addresses. Processing these requests involved six files. Based on this graph, the admin cannot determine who uploaded the file that contains sensitive information and whether it was leaked through the 40 connections (although this file was opened by the web server, this does not mean it was sent to any client). In addition, if the admin assumes the information is leaked through the 40 connections, the graph does not tell which of the 40 is more likely to be the sink.

Figure 4(b) shows the PoL-DFG generated by ET-analyzer.

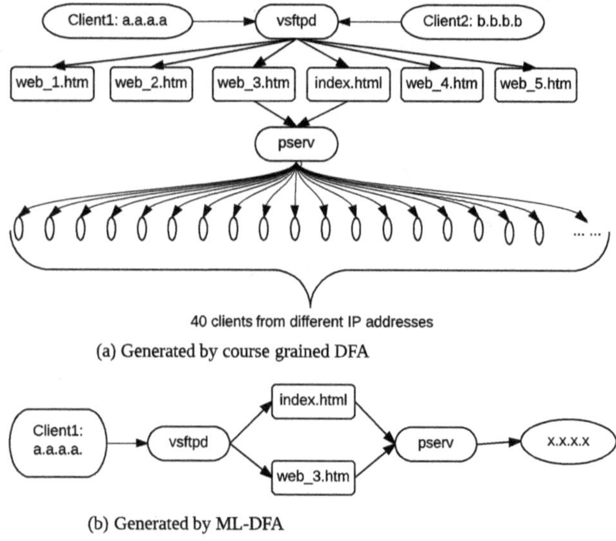

(a) Generated by course grained DFA

(b) Generated by ML-DFA

Figure 4: Information leakage.

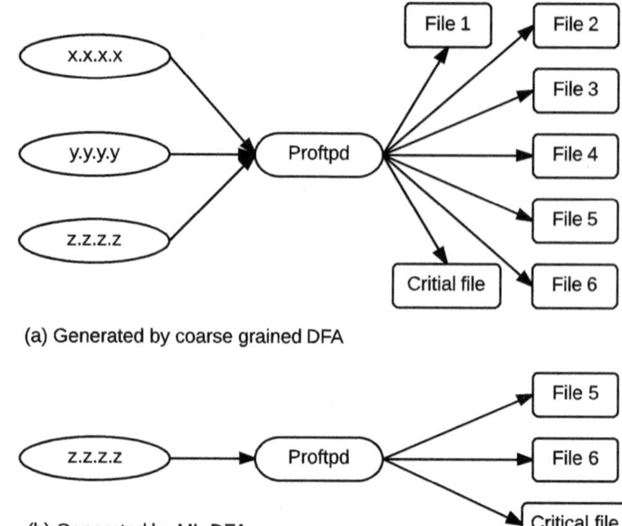

(a) Generated by coarse grained DFA

(b) Generated by ML-DFA

Figure 5: Data contamination.

Table 2: Data flow graph comparison of information leakage case.

Statistics	Causality analysis	PoL-DFA
No. of nodes	50	6
No. of edges	50	6

Table 3: Data flow graph comparison of data contamination case.

Statistics	Causality analysis	PoL-DFA
No. of nodes	12	5
No. of edges	11	4

It precisely identifies that the file, which contains sensitive information, was uploaded to the web server from the FTP client of IP address $a.a.a.a$. The PoL-DFG also pinpoints that the file was indeed leaked out and the destination IP address was $x.x.x.x$. Compared with causality analysis, PoL-DFA slashes off false data flow edges and resolves the dependence explosion problem. Without false data flow edges, the admin can precisely identify who is responsible for the information leakage.

The comparison of the two graphs is shown in Table 2. The graph created by PoL-DFA has 6 nodes and 6 edges, while the other graph has 50 nodes and 50 edges. PoL-DFA narrows the scope to much fewer nodes and edges.

Case Study 2. Data Contamination: We consider a data contamination scenario as follows. A company has a file server which runs FTP service. Employees can use FTP clients on workstations to upload and download files. There are some critical files on the server. Later, the company finds that a critical file on the server was corrupted. The security administrator suspects someone overwrote the original file through FTP and wants to identify who conducted the actions. The admin constructs a data flow graph related to the critical file. Causality analysis based on system events would result in a graph as shown in Figure 5(a). There were three clients connected to the proftpd server, and seven files were uploaded to the server. Because causality analysis treats programs as black boxes, it cannot identify which IP address each file comes from. Hence the graph does not give enough information for the admin to attribute the data contamination actions to the culprit.

Figure 5(b) shows the PoL-DFG generated by ET-Analyzer. It shows that the content of the contaminated file came from packets sent from IP address $z.z.z.z$. With the PoL-DFG, the admin can determine that it was the employee from IP address $z.z.z.z$ that contaminated the critical file.

The comparison of the two graphs is shown in Table 3. The graph created by PoL-DFA has 5 nodes and 4 edges, while the other graph has 12 nodes and 11 edges. The table shows that the PoL-DFG precisely pinpoints the small subset of files and sockets that are involved in the data contamination.

5.2 P-flag Edges and Accuracy

The numbers of nodes and edges for each program produced by ET-Analyzer in our case studies are shown in Table 4. Please note that some files (e.g. log file) opened or created by the server processes are not relevant to any data leakage or contamination and thus we omit these files from the table. Also, even if the data flow between two files involves multiple rounds of `read` and `write`, we use only one edge to denote this data flow.

As it shows, no P-flag edge is found in our case studies. As mentioned in the description of direct tag propagation in §3.3, a P-flag edge indicates that a data flow between two program objects (or between a data source and a data sink) had possibly happened, but the ET-analyzer is not 100% sure. Having no P-flag edge means in the data flow paths from each input file (or socket) to each output file (or socket), there is no conservative propagation of tags. That is, ET-Analyzer is 100% accurate in the two case studies.

5.3 Logging Overhead

The logging overhead on server programs is measured using standard benchmark loaders if available, random inputs

Table 4: Number of P-flag Edges.

Program	# Nodes	# edges	# P-flag edges
vsftpd	4	3	0
pserv	4	3	0
pro-ftpd	5	4	0

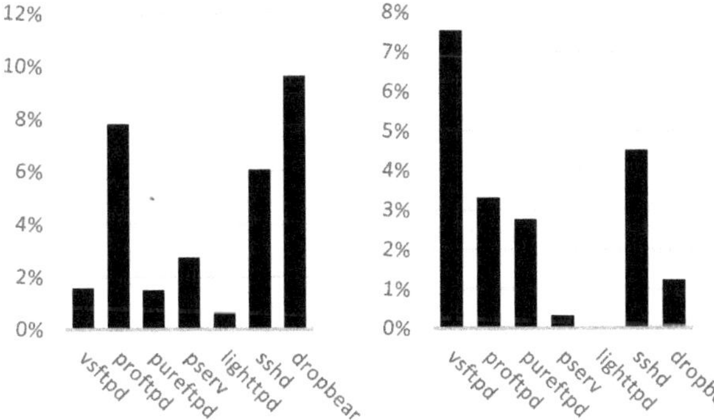

(a) Audit on with logging execution trace to disk. (b) Audit off with logging execution trace to disk.

Figure 6: Logging overhead on server programs.

otherwise. For lighttpd and pserv (*i.e.*, pico server), we use ApacheBench and curl-loader, respectively. For the FTP server programs, including vsftpd, proftpd, and pureftpd, we use concurrent clients to upload files of random sizes, and measure the time it takes until finishing. For sshd and dropbear server, we measure the time it takes to accept a set of randomly sized files from scp, which is a remote file copy program on Linux.

Figure 6 shows the logging overhead of the PoL-DFA system under different conditions. Figure 6a shows the logging overhead with Auditd running. Figure 6b shows the overhead measured with Auditd turned off. Figure 6 shows that in both conditions, the logging overhead is minimal. For simple programs, such as pure-ftpd, pico server, and lighttpd, the overhead is less than 5%. For more complicated programs like sshd and dropbear server, the overhead tends to be higher than 5%, but still lower than 10%. This indicates that PoL-DFA is a lightweighted DFA solution.

6. RELATED WORK

Causality Analysis based on System Events. System call logging has been widely used for building or recovering system object level dependence for the purpose of forensic analysis. It can be used to investigate attack provenance [16, 35], to track attack scope [17], and track information flows [34]. The granularity can be refined through tracking page level memory operations [18], file offsets [28], and process loops [21]. However, causality analysis is unsuitable for data flow analysis, since it cannot decisively identify existence of data flows. For example, even if a program reads from a file, it does not necessarily indicate the outputs will contain information from that file.

Dynamic information flow tracking. Dynamic information flow tracking, *a.k.a.* dynamic taint analysis (DTA) or dynamic data flow tracking (DFT), is being widely used in many domains including attack prevention [25, 31], information flow control [36, 30], data lifetime analysis [9], configuration debugging [6], malware analysis [32], and mobile security [13]. Existing dynamic information flow tracking approaches can be categorized into three categories: binary instrumentation, source code transformation, and hardware-assisted tracking. There are many optimization techniques to improve the efficiency of binary instrumentation based approaches [25, 24, 10, 15, 22, 23], and the best performance overhead reported so far [14] is about 2-3 times slowdown. Second, source code based approaches embed data flow tracking and policy checking operations into source code through source code rewriting [31, 19, 8, 33, 26, 12]. They require source code and depend on particular programming language due to their compiler-based implementation. In comparison, since ET-Analyzer is based on LLVM IR, it is language independent and does not necessarily rely on the availability of source code as there are some existing tools for transforming binary into LLVM byte code [1][4]. Hardware-assisted approaches [29, 11] can achieve very good performance, relying on specially designed hardware.

7. DISCUSSIONS AND LIMITATIONS

PoL-DFA potentially has the following limitations. First, the current implementation of PoL-DFA is vulnerable to kernel level attacks. PoL-DFA relies on Auditd to log some system calls, in order to annotate data sinks and sources, and uses system call `write` to write basic block logs to files. If the kernel is compromised, the attacker can either disable Auditd or tamper with `write` system call. However, this is not a fundamental issue. We can implement system call logging and basic block logging inside a hypervisor and get rid of this concern.

Secondly, our current implementation of logger imposes up to 10% slow down on some server programs. This overhead might be significant in efficiency-critical production systems. This issue can be eased through some optimizations. For example, we can reduce the amount of log data through logging the ID of every other IR basic block instead of logging that of every IR basic block. The IR basic block that has not been logged can be inferred based on the IR basic blocks in the context. Also, for each IR basic block, we can identify, through dynamic profiling, the most frequent successor IR basic block into which it branches. We can treat the most frequent successor as default and only need to instrument the infrequent successor IR basic block. This optimization technique is originally introduced in ShadowReplica [14]. With these techniques the runtime overhead can be further reduced.

Thirdly, it is possible that the PoL-DFG generated by our tool contains many P-flag edges, which means possible existence of data flows. Even with P-flag edges, the PoL-DFG generated by our tool still provides more knowledge to the security officer than causality analysis based on system event logging. Furthermore, while theoretically it is possible for a PoL-DFG to contain many P-flag edges, in our case studies we did not find any P-flag edge.

Finally, in this paper we don't handle control-flow-based data dependencies, *a.k.a.* implicit flows. In the field of dynamic data flow analysis such as DTA, handling implicit flows is still an open problem [27]. Our work does not aim to handle implicit flows. It aims to conduct data flow analysis at a new abstraction level.

8. CONCLUSIONS

In this paper, we present a new type of dynamic data flow analysis, called PoL-DFA, a system prototype that conducts Program-object Level DFA for the purposes of data leakage and contamination forensics. PoL-DFA is based on a new concept, straight-line execution trace enabled data flow analysis, which is a novel combination of "white-box" analysis inside a program and taint logic decoupling. PoL-DFA is designed, implemented and systematically evaluated. Experimental results show that the performance overhead is 4.24% on average for server programs, which means that PoL-DFA is a lightweight DFA solution. Our case studies show that for such security needs as data leakage and contamination forensics, PoL-DFA can solve the undecidability of data flows and help analysts spot malicious data flows.

9. ACKNOWLEDGEMENTS

This work was supported in part by NSF CNS-1223710, NSF CCF-1320605, NSF CNS-1422594, and ARO W911NF-13-1-0421 (MURI).

10. REFERENCES

[1] Dagger: decompilation to llvm ir. http://dagger.repzret.org/.

[2] The heartbleed bug. http://heartbleed.com/.

[3] Llvm basicblock class reference. http://llvm.org/docs/doxygen/html/classllvm_1_1BasicBlock.html.

[4] K. Anand, M. Smithson, K. Elwazeer, A. Kotha, J. Gruen, N. Giles, and R. Barua. A compiler-level intermediate representation based binary analysis and rewriting system. In *ECCS'13*.

[5] M. Attariyan and J. Flinn. Automating configuration troubleshooting with dynamic information flow analysis. In *OSDI*, 2010.

[6] M. Attariyan and J. Flinn. Automating configuration troubleshooting with dynamic information flow analysis. In *OSDI*, 2010.

[7] D. Brumley, J. Newsome, D. Song, H. Wang, and S. Jha. Towards automatic generation of vulnerability-based signatures. In *SP'06*.

[8] W. Chang, B. Streiff, and C. Lin. Efficient and extensible security enforcement using dynamic data flow analysis. In *CCS'08*.

[9] J. Chow, B. Pfaff, T. Garfinkel, K. Christopher, and M. Rosenblum. Understanding data lifetime via whole system simulation. In *USENIX*, 2004.

[10] J. Clause, W. Li, and A. Orso. Dytan: A generic dynamic taint analysis framework. In *ISSTA '07*.

[11] J. R. Crandall and F. T. Chong. Minos: Control data attack prevention orthogonal to memory model. In *MICRO-37*.

[12] K. O. Elish, X. Shu, D. D. Yao, B. G. Ryder, and X. Jiang. Profiling user-trigger dependence for android malware detection. *Computers & Security'15*.

[13] W. Enck, P. Gilbert, B.-G. Chun, L. P. Cox, J. Jung, P. McDaniel, and A. N. Sheth. Taintdroid: An information-flow tracking system for realtime privacy monitoring on smartphones. In *OSDI'10*.

[14] K. Jee, V. P. Kemerlis, A. D. Keromytis, and G. Portokalidis. Shadowreplica: efficient parallelization of dynamic data flow tracking. In *SIGSAC'13*.

[15] V. P. Kemerlis, G. Portokalidis, K. Jee, and A. D. Keromytis. libdft: Practical dynamic data flow tracking for commodity systems. In *VEE*, 2012.

[16] S. T. King and P. M. Chen. Backtracking intrusions. In *SOSP '03*.

[17] S. T. King, Z. M. Mao, D. G. Lucchetti, and P. M. Chen. Enriching intrusion alerts through multi-host causality. In *NDSS*, 2005.

[18] S. Krishnan, K. Z. Snow, and F. Monrose. Trail of bytes: efficient support for forensic analysis. In *CCS'10*.

[19] L. C. Lam and T.-c. Chiueh. A general dynamic information flow tracking framework for security applications. In *ACSAC'06*.

[20] C. Lattner and V. Adve. Llvm: A compilation framework for lifelong program analysis & transformation. In *CGO*, 2004.

[21] K. H. Lee, X. Zhang, and D. Xu. High accuracy attack provenance via binary-based execution partition. In *NDSS*, 2013.

[22] C.-K. Luk, R. Cohn, R. Muth, H. Patil, A. Klauser, G. Lowney, S. Wallace, V. J. Reddi, and K. Hazelwood. Pin: Building customized program analysis tools with dynamic instrumentation. In *PLDI '05*.

[23] J. Ming, D. Wu, G. Xiao, J. Wang, and P. Liu. Taintpipe: pipelined symbolic taint analysis. In *USENIX Security'15*.

[24] N. Nethercote and J. Seward. Valgrind: A framework for heavyweight dynamic binary instrumentation. In *PLDI '07*.

[25] J. Newsome and D. Song. Dynamic taint analysis for automatic detection, analysis,and signature generation of exploits on commodity software. In *NDSS 2005*.

[26] I. Roy, D. E. Porter, M. D. Bond, K. S. McKinley, and E. Witchel. Laminar: practical fine-grained decentralized information flow control. In *PLDI'09*.

[27] E. J. Schwartz, T. Avgerinos, and D. Brumley. All you ever wanted to know about dynamic taint analysis and forward symbolic execution (but might have been afraid to ask). In *SP'10*.

[28] S. Sitaraman and S. Venkatesan. Forensic analysis of file system intrusions using improved backtracking. In *Information Assurance*, 2005.

[29] G. E. Suh, J. W. Lee, D. Zhang, and S. Devadas. Secure program execution via dynamic information flow tracking. In *ASPLOS XI*.

[30] N. Vachharajani, M. J. Bridges, J. Chang, R. Rangan, G. Ottoni, J. A. Blome, G. A. Reis, M. Vachharajani, and D. I. August. Rifle: An architectural framework for user-centric information-flow security. In *MICRO-37*.

[31] W. Xu, S. Bhatkar, and R. Sekar. Taint-enhanced policy enforcement: A practical approach to defeat a wide range of attacks. In *Usenix Security*, 2006.

[32] H. Yin, D. S. amd M. Egele, C. Kruegel, and E. Kirda. Panorama: Capturing system-wide information flow for malware detection and analysis. In *CCS 2007*.

[33] A. Yip, X. Wang, N. Zeldovich, and M. F. Kaashoek. Improving application security with data flow assertions. In *SIGOPS'09*.

[34] N. Zeldovich, S. Boyd-Wickizer, E. Kohler, and D. Mazières. Making information flow explicit in histar. In *OSDI'06*.

[35] H. Zhang, D. D. Yao, and N. Ramakrishnan. Detection of stealthy malware activities with traffic causality and scalable triggering relation discovery. In *ASIACCS'14*.

[36] D. Y. Zhu, J. Jung, D. Song, T. Kohno, and D. Wetherall. Tainteraser: protecting sensitive data leaks using application-level taint tracking. *SIGOPS*.

TPRIVEXEC: Private Execution in Virtual Memory

Judicael B. Djoko
University of Pittsburgh
jbriand@cs.pitt.edu

Brandon Jennings
University of Pittsburgh
bbj5@pitt.edu

Adam J. Lee
University of Pittsburgh
adamlee@cs.pitt.edu

ABSTRACT

Private Browsing Mode has become a popular feature in modern browsers. However, despite its prevalence, a similar privacy enhancing technology has not been replicated in other user applications. PRIVEXEC is an operating system service that provides an application-agnostic, system-wide private execution mode [15]. We present TPRIVEXEC, a novel approach to system-level privacy support that affords faster application execution over PRIVEXEC. TPRIVEXEC uses memory as its principal backing store but falls back to system swap on high memory pressure. Upon swapping, it encrypts and decrypts private application data as it transits into and out of disk. By doing away with much of persistent disk as primary storage, TPRIVEXEC provides stronger privacy guarantees and faster application runtime. As shown by our evaluation, TPRIVEXEC application performance is indistinguishable from a vanilla system and compared to PRIVEXEC, it is up to 30 times faster in writes and 38 times faster in reads for I/O bound tasks.

CCS Concepts

•**Security and privacy** → *Software security engineering;*

Keywords

private browsing, private execution, virtual memory

1. INTRODUCTION

Modern computer applications provide little support for privacy. Although Web Browsers represent a canonical case of potentially severe privacy violations, there are other pressing examples. A number of applications — e.g., email clients, text editors, standalone webapps, and commandline terminals — routinely handle sensitive user information. Unfortunately, these applications are not usually equipped with a "private mode" feature that would allow users to selectively dictate what information is persistent. Even when applications are privacy-conscious (e.g., Spotify [22] has "Private Session"), they remain exposed to data compromises. Adopting "private mode" as a per-application feature would not only lead to much code duplication, it also has a significant limitation: incomplete data sanitization. During the execution of a program, data could propagate out of the application's reach (e.g., kernel buffers) making it impossible for all its copies to be deleted. Therefore, even when deleted, there would be no guarantee that the data could not be recovered using forensic analysis. With an application-based approach being an imperfect stopgap, this calls for privacy support as a system service.

CODASPY'16, March 09 - 11, 2016, New Orleans, LA, USA

ISBN 978-1-4503-3935-3/16/03...$15.00

DOI: http://dx.doi.org/10.1145/2857705.2857724

Onarlioglu et al. [15] provide an Operating System level implementation of private execution called PRIVEXEC. It achieves private execution by binding a Private Execution Key (PEK) to a process. Using the kernel's built-in cryptographic library, the PEK is used to encrypt all data written to disk during file I/O and swapping. In addition, IPC communication by private processes is restricted to avoid leakage of data to public processes. The PEK is kept in kernel memory and is deleted when the process terminates. Figure 1 shows the high-level design of PRIVEXEC. Amongst public processes, IPC communications and disk access are unaffected; their functioning follows on operating system semantics. However, there are IPC restrictions between public and private processes: data only moves from public processes to private ones. Private processes that execute within the same logical context are managed as groups. Within a group, private processes share the same PEK and are allowed to read and write from one another. As for filesystem access, all private process writes are redirected to a secure private container. Data stored in the private container is encrypted with the group's PEK making its contents inaccessible to public processes and "other" private processes. By enforcing these directives, PRIVEXEC prevents the leakage of data generated by private processes.

PRIVEXEC has a few design limitations. First and foremost, as our evaluation shows, it incurs a significant performance overhead during application runtime. By committing every I/O request to persistent storage, when coupled with encryption, the resulting latency makes PRIVEXEC not well suited to disk-intensive tasks. Second, during hibernation, all kernel data are written to disk in plaintext, thereby allowing the PEK of private applications to be retrieved and private container data recovered.

The PRIVEXEC prototype is only one possibility in the design space of system-level privacy support service. We present TPRIVEXEC, a Linux Kernel patch that *provides confidentiality to user's information when running applica-*

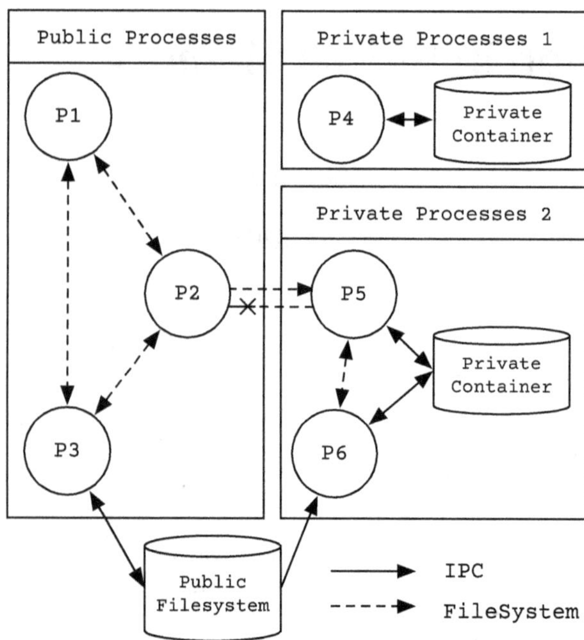

Figure 1: Design of PrivExec.

tions in private execution. The crucial insight in its design is the increasing amount of RAM in computer systems. Hardware trends show a significant drop in the price of RAM, making it possible to pack more memory in commodity systems. In addition, a user study conducted by the Mozilla Foundation reckons that the average private browsing session is only about 10–15 minutes long[1]. Likewise, we expect a similar behavior to occur with other applications run in private mode. By combining increasing system memory with the presumed ephemeral nature of private executions, confidentiality of user information could be achieved without a significant drop in application performance. In the PrivExec model, by encrypting before writing to disk, persistent storage is deemed untrusted. On the other hand, as memory is deemed trusted, we could do away with writes to disk and keep application data in RAM. This is the approach that we employ in TPrivExeC: both I/O and runtime data of private applications are predominantly kept in memory. However, this significantly limits the amount of memory available to other applications. TPrivExeC addresses this shortcoming by allowing encrypted writes to persistent storage in the event of low system memory.

At its core, the TPrivExeC prototype uses an ephemeral *private execution key* (PEK) to trap all the generated application data into a private container. Inter-Process Communication (IPC) restrictions are enforced to avoid private processes from disclosing information to other applications. Application data comprises of both runtime information (stack, heap, shared memory) and I/O data. In addition to native OS process isolation, the PEK is used to enforce permissions on private containers ensuring private application data is inaccessible to the rest of the system. TPrivExeC leverages the system's virtual memory for its private container thereby permitting private application data to be swapped in the event of high memory pressure. Before being written to swap, the pages are encrypted using the PEK. As the swapped pages are read back into memory, they are decrypted before the private application accesses them. The key is generated per private execution environment and is inaccessible to other user processes. Once the private application terminates, in-memory application data is cleared and the PEK is deleted making the recovery of data written to swap infeasible.

TPrivExeC is coercion-resistant (key is ephermeral), requires no explicit application support and does not rely on any specialized hardware. Its implementation is lightweight (involves non-critical modifications to the kernel) and is based on PrivExec [15]. The root motivation for its implementation is performance improvement over PrivExec, while improving on its security guarantees. Contributions include:

(1) Implemented a system-level privacy execution service leveraged on RAM called TPrivExeC. In addition, we implemented a variant of TPrivExeC that permanently locks application data in memory.

(2) An approach against the event of hibernation. The system image written to disk should not contain any sensitive information belonging to Private Processes.

(3) Evaluated the performance of both prototypes. Using the vanilla kernel as the baseline, we show our prototypes incur minimal runtime overhead compared to PrivExec. We show negligible impact on real-life applications with performance akin to (or even better) a vanilla kernel.

The paper is organized as follows: In Section 2, we describe our objectives with TPrivExeC. Sections 3 and 4, we dive into the architecture and implementation of our prototypes. Evaluation is performed in Section 5. We discuss the limitations and possible future work in Section 6. Finally, Section 7 reviews related work on memory encryption and, we conclude in Section 8.

2. BACKGROUND

In this section, we describe our threat model followed by the privacy properties and design goals for our approach.

2.1 Threat Model and Assumptions

To maximize overall system throughput, the OS mediates access to common system resources. However, this pooling of system resources weakens the isolation between processes. For example, consider the case where the browser attempts to access a URL. The request is forwarded to the DNS resolver which, after performing the request, may cache the domain name to serve future requests. Since the DNS resolver's memory is "public", this provides an opportunity (however small and fleeting) for a curious attacker to access private application data. Such a scenario highlights the difficulty of running private applications without leaking any information. Thus, providing absolute confidentiality would require substantial system changes such as making separate copies of system resources. As this heavyweight solution is incompatible with our philosophy, our lightweight approach adopts a best effort in limiting the exposure of private application data.

We assume the user is running a commodity system with an unmodified version of the Linux Kernel. Also, we assume that the user and the private applications he runs are not

[1] https://blog.mozilla.org/metrics/2010/08/23/understanding-private-browsing/

deliberately malicious. The kernel is trusted and maintains customary process isolation primitives: i.e., a running process cannot access another process' memory. In addition, the kernel cannot allocate memory containing the runtime data of another process: i.e., we assume the kernel implicitly zeroes memory reclaimed from another process. Kernel space is inaccessible to user processes and cannot be swapped. At its essence, TPRIVEXEC extends the concept of Private Browsing Mode to generic applications. Therefore, like PRIVEXEC, we chose to adapt the threat and security model of Private Browsing Mode by Aggarwal et al. [1] from browsers to generic applications. We consider two types of adversaries: a local adversary and a remote adversary. We assume their objective is to violate the user's confidentiality by trying to access private application data.

A local adversary is one who has physical access to the machine. He is not allowed to make changes to the system and does not have access to the machine while the private process is running. As this would be too restrictive, we relax this requirement to a non-sophisticated curious local adversary. It excludes adversaries who could install keyloggers or trace applications using side-channel attacks. When the application is terminated, the adversary should be able to use forensic analysis to recover data from private execution sessions. A remote adversary has access to network packets generated by the application. The adversary could add, delete or rearrange network packets or control remote endpoints communicating with an application. Data leaks from network traffic are out of the scope of our threat model, as is data stored in remote servers and device caches.

2.2 Privacy properties

As previously mentioned in the threat model, TPRIVEXEC intends to minimize the exposure of sensitive information. In summary, as in PRIVEXEC, we intend to satisfy the following privacy properties [15]:

PP1: Data explicitly written to storage must never be recoverable without knowledge of a secret bound to an application for the duration of its private execution.

PP2: Application memory that is swapped to disk must never be recoverable without knowledge of the application secret.

PP3: Data produced during a private execution must never be passed to processes outside the private process group via IPC channels.

PP4: Application secrets must never be persisted, and never be exposed outside of protected volatile memory.

PP5: Once a private execution has terminated, application secrets and data must be securely discarded.

2.3 Design goals

In designing TPRIVEXEC, our target audience was users running a commodity operating system. Although being more secure seems intuitively beneficial, it usually comes at the expense of usability and performance. However, there's a limit to which users would sacrifice the latter in achieving the former. To strike an acceptable balance, the following design goals were set:

DG1: TPRIVEXEC should be able to run any unmodified application in "private mode".

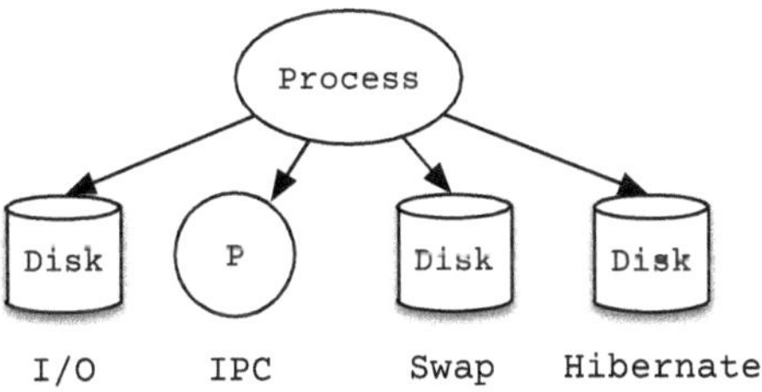

Figure 2: Ways by which data can exit an application's context.

DG2: TPRIVEXEC should allow users to select which application to run "privately". Users should be able to execute "private" and "public" applications concurrently.

DG3: TPRIVEXEC should require no additional input once the application is launched in private mode.

DG4: TPRIVEXEC should not incur any significant overhead in the application's execution; it should not affect the performance of other running applications.

3. ARCHITECTURE

In this section, we present a design overview of TPRIVEXEC. Recall from Section 2.1 that we assume the user is running a Linux Kernel with customary memory isolation: one process cannot access the memory contents of another. To push this requirement further, debugging facilities and access to devices that expose physical memory of private processes are disabled. However, even with this requirement, as shown by Figure 2, there are other means by which process' data could be exposed. Therefore, to provide an adequate private execution environment, the design is split in two phases:

1) **Logical separation**. This foremost requirement involves distinguishing "private" processes from "public" ones. By doing so, it allows design goals (*DG1* to *DG4*) to be satisfied as "private" processes would be isolated from their "public" counterparts.

2) **Privacy enforcement**. Selectively apply restrictions on "private" processes to prevent the leakage of application data. By addressing each venue of data exit, we ensure that TPRIVEXEC satisfies its privacy properties.

3.1 Public vs Private

In TPRIVEXEC, a process is either public or private. A public process is one whose execution occurs on the normal software stack; its execution is per OS primitives. On the other hand, a private process runs in "private mode" and is uniquely identified by a randomly generated *Private Execution Key* (PEK). Using the PEK, access to a private process resources is controlled per private execution semantics. However, private processes that share a common *private execution context* (hence a common PEK) are grouped in *enclaves* allowing them to have unrestricted sharing of resources. Upon termination of all processes in an enclave, their resources are clobbered and the private context is destroyed.

3.2 I/O - Private Containers

A private container refers to the filesystem within which the I/O of an enclave occurs. In TPRIVEXEC, I/O data has a dual nature: primarily memory-resident and alternately disk-persistent on low memory. Thus, to uphold the privacy properties, access to the in-memory data must be restricted and the data written to disk must be irrecoverable. By leveraging the PEK, permissions are enforced on the private container such that only the processes in the enclave can access its contents. Again using the PEK, the I/O data is encrypted before it is written to disk. Once all the processes in the enclave are terminated, the contents of the private container are clobbered and the PEK is destroyed. However, programs often need to access files stored in the public filesystem; config files, shared objects i.e. files whose content are not initially available in the private container. Therefore, for proper functioning, I/O needs to be appropriately coordinated between the public and private filesystems. A straightforward solution would be to make a separate copy of requested files in the private container. Once completed, all I/O requests of the file would be redirected to its private copy. This ensures changes made to the file are not propagated to the public filesystem. To summarize:

- A private process can read and write files in its enclave.
- A private process can read files from the public filesystem.
- All private process writes are done in its private container.
- A process which does not belong to an enclave is not allowed access to the private container.

3.3 Inter-process Communication

In a commodity operating system, processes are allowed to communicate with one another. In TPRIVEXEC, to prevent the inadvertent leakage of sensitive information from private applications, IPC restrictions are enforced. These are performed on top of existing permissions imposed by the OS. Once again, using the PEK for enforcement, the following scenarios are considered:

- A private process is allowed to read and write on an IPC channel with any other private process in the same enclave.
- A private process is allowed to read from any process.

3.4 Swap

Virtual memory allows processes to allocate more memory than there is available in the system. Frequently accessed pages are kept in physical memory, while stale pages are saved to secondary storage called swap. The pages in swapspace are stored in cleartext and persist beyond process execution. If left unaddressed, this presents a potential violation of privacy, as private application data could be recovered from swapspace. Therefore, using the PEK as an encryption key, the pages from private processes are encrypted and decrypted as they transit in and out of swap space. In addition, the following conditions are imposed:

- Only the OS's swap subsystem should be able to decrypt a private process' swapped page using the PEK.
- Once a page is no longer referenced by its process(es), the key must be securely deleted.

3.5 Hibernation

Hibernation saves the contents of RAM to permanent storage. On system restore, the hibernation image is reloaded in memory and system execution is resumed. In case any private application was executing, the hibernation image would contain both the plaintext memory contents and the PEK of the private process. This violates the Privacy Properties as the application secrets written to permanent storage are made recoverable (*PP1*). In TPRIVEXEC, this is exacerbated by the fact that much of private application I/O data resides in memory. Therefore, to withhold the privacy guarantees, before the hibernation image is built, all private applications in-memory data (including I/O) and their private execution keys are cleared. This ensures that the contents of the system state written to disk do not contain any application data and with the PEK deleted, the data already on the disk (which is encrypted) is feasibly irrecoverable.

4. IMPLEMENTATION

We implemented TPRIVEXEC by making changes to Linux Kernel 3.12RC2+. Using the original PRIVEXEC patch as base code, some of its changes were reverted to serve as scaffold for our implementation.

4.1 Private Context

The `struct privexec_context` (Snippet 1) represents a private execution context. The `key` and `token` attributes are randomly generated at instantiation and together, they serve as the PEK of the private context. The `tfm` attribute defaults to the kernel crypto API's AES cipher in CBC mode and uses the `key` for symmetric encryption. On the other hand, the `token` is used to perform comparisons when enforcing permissions. Since this is a common operation, the `token` is conveniently aliased as a `struct privexec_tag`. Lastly, the `ref` variable stores the number of processes pointing to the `privexec_context` and indirectly serves as a count of the number of processes in an enclave. Its value is decremented whenever a process terminates and when it drops to zero, the private context is deleted.

Snippet 1 Private Context descriptor

```
struct privexec_context {
    unsigned char key[PRIVEXEC_KEY_LEN];
    unsigned char token[PRIVEXEC_TOKEN_LEN];
    struct crypto_blkcipher *tfm;
    atomic_t ref;
};
```

Linux represents every process by a `struct task_struct` descriptor. To differentiate a private process from a public one, a `private` attribute of type `privexec_context` was added to the `task_struct`. In Linux, new processes are created by *forking* existing processes. Forking takes a series of flags specifying which resources would be shared by the child and its parent. If the `CLONE_PRIVEXEC` flag is found, a new private context is instantiated and assigned to the process' `private` attribute; otherwise, the cloning is performed per OS semantics (maintaining the creation of public processes). However, if the process being cloned is already a private process, its private attribute is copied to the new process (the `CLONE_PRIVEXEC` flag is ignored) ensuring that a child process does not breakaway from the enclave. In addition, the memory descriptor (`struct mm_struct`) of the private process is set to nondumpable. This prevents the kernel from producing a coredump of the process's memory when it abruptly terminates.

4.2 Filesystems

The Virtual File System (VFS) is a software layer that defines basic abstract interfaces and data structures of filesytems. At its core, the VFS translates generic file operations to the corresponding filesystem implementation. For example, when a program issues a `open()` system call on a file found on an `ext4` filesystem, the VFS calls the `ext4_file_open()` function defined in `fs/ext4/file.c`. Therefore, to implement our private container, a naive approach would be to use one of the native filesystems in the kernel source as a template. Unfortunately, not only would this be cumbersome (`ext4` has about 30k lines of code), but also error prone; modifying native filesystems such as `ext4` not only requires an intimate knowledge of how it organizes data on disk, but also how it interacts with the kernel. An alternative approach is to introduce an additional layer by employing a stackable filesystem. Stackable filesystems do not store data themselves, but use another filesystem as their backend. Their relatively small and simple codebase provides much welcomed reliability and efficiency. With this, Figure 3 is a first implementation of our private container. The private container sits between the VFS layer and the `ext4` filesystem. To the underlying filesystem, the stackable filesystem appears as the VFS. Alas, this design has a severe limitation: the files accessible in the private container are limited to those created in it. In our design of TPRIVEXEC, we wanted private processes to view the *entire* filesystem as it would allow programs to access the existing files for proper functioning.

To address this, we employ a specialized stackable filesystem called a union filesystem. A union filesystem combines two or more filesystems to produce a singular virtual filesystem. The filesystem is made by stacking an 'upper' filesystem over multiple 'lower' filesystems; i.e., the 'upper' filesystem presents a unified namespace of the 'lower' directories. By design, the upper filesystem is writable and the lower filesystems are read-only; all writes are performed in the namespace of the upper directory. Overlayfs [16] is an example of an existing union filesystem. It is limited at combining only two filesystems (one upper and one lower) at a time. However, multiple directories can be unioned by using an Overlayfs filesystem as a lower directory. It works as such:

- When upper and lower objects are directories, a merged directory is formed.
- If an object in the upper directory is deleted, it should not be "shown" again even if it exists in a lower directory.
- If a file is accessed and does not exist in the upper directory, it is read from the lower directory.
- If a file exist in both the lower and upper directory, the copy in the upper directory is presented.

This design is a perfect fit in fulfilling the requirements for our private container. If the appropriate system mount points are added as the lower directory, it provides the private container with a virtual view of the entire filesystem. This is the scheme employed in PRIVEXEC (Figure 4a); the eCryptfs filesystem [7] — a disk-backed filesystem— serves as the upper directory. In a similar fashion, TPRIVEXEC adopts this scheme by using a RAM-based filesystem.

Figure 4b shows the filesystem tree of a private process in TPRIVEXEC. The tmpfs filesystem serves as the private container and it is unioned with the "public" filesystem by Overlayfs. Tmpfs is a volatile filesystem that keeps every-

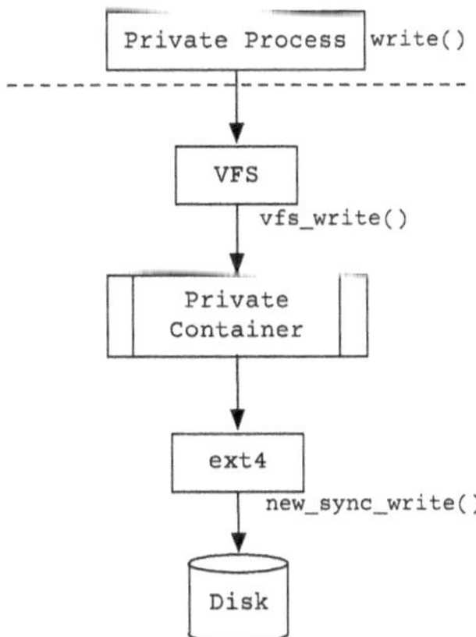

Figure 3: Naive approach to private containers.

thing in virtual memory i.e. it stores its data in both RAM and swap. It primarily resides on the kernel's page cache and swaps to disk on memory pressure. As mentioned in Section 3.2, to satisfy our privacy properties, we need to prevent unauthorized access to I/O data residing in memory and encrypt pages written to disk. To enforce permissions, a `private` attribute of type `struct privexec_context` field was added to the tmpfs superblock. The `private` attribute is set whenever the `tprivexec` flag is detected and the process performing the mount is a private process. Later, when the inode belonging to the private container is been accessed, its corresponding superblock is resolved and a token check is performed against the current process' private context. If there is a mismatch, access to the inode is disallowed.

The linux page cache is the set of all physical pages. With I/O operations performed at page level, the page cache minimizes the amount of disk I/O operations by caching pages in RAM. For example, when a read (or write) operation is requested, the page cache first checks if the requested page resides in memory. If found (*cache hit*), disk access is forgone and the operation is performed on the page cache. Periodically (or through *fsync* system call), the dirty pages are written to permanent storage. For every filesystem, the VFS defines a set of callback functions implement I/O operations. The `readpage` and `writepage` operations read pages in and write pages out of the cache respectively. For TPRIVEXEC, during a `writepage` operation, the page is encrypted before it is copied to swap. As for the `readpage` operation, if the page being read belongs to a private container, the page is decrypted after it is read into the page cache.

4.3 IPC permissions

Linux provides several IPC primitives to allow processes to communicate with one another. Those of concern are: *i*) *message queues*, allow a process to write messages that would be read by one or more processes. *ii*) *pipes*, a unidirectional byte stream from one process to another. *iii*) *shared memory*, allows multiple processes to communicate through memory that appears in their address space. *iv*) *sockets*, provides a facility for processes to communicate using network primitives. (e.g., communicating with the X server).

Other IPC primitives such as *signals* and *semaphores* were not included in the scope of IPC restrictions. Their messages are short and are meant to alert about an event happening, not to explicitly exchange data. Modifications done to

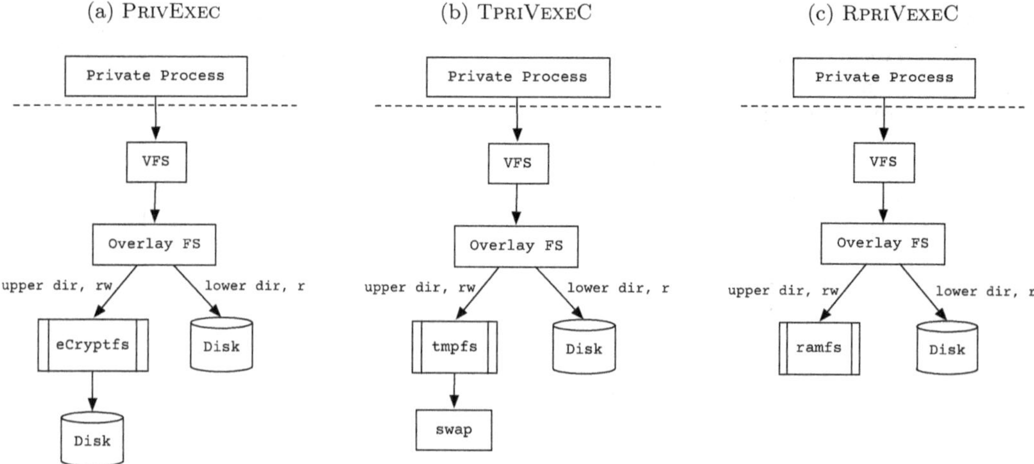

Figure 4: Filesystem configurations of respective systems.

IPC were completely inherited from PrivExec. All IPC primitives listed above share a common model: a parent process creates an IPC descriptor via a system call, passes the descriptor to its children by cloning and the children communicate using file-like operations. To enforce permissions compatible with our privacy properties, the system needs to detect when an IPC descriptor is created or accessed by a private process. The structure describing each of the IPC primitives was augmented with a `privexec_tag` initialized from the private context of the creating process. Then, as in filesystems, using the scenarios described in our architecture, token comparisons are performed to ensure that only authorized processes are allowed to access the descriptor.

4.4 Swap space

In the Linux memory model, a page could be shared amongst multiple processes. To retrieve the list of all page table entries referencing a page, the kernel stores a list of memory regions (which correspond to process page tables) mapping the page. Before copying the page to swap, the page is "unmapped" (removed) from the page tables pointing to it. The PrivExec implementation only encrypts pages that exclusively belong to a process. Therefore, during swapping, shared pages are left unencrypted. However, this approach has a serious limitation when the page is read back into memory. In Linux, from within a page, one cannot link together the list of processes it belongs to. Therefore, when a shared page is swapped-in on behalf of a private process, it would not be aware the page is shared with other processes (including private processes in the same enclave). Subsequently, it would decrypt an unencrypted shared page, thereby resulting to a segmentation fault in userspace. After realizing this significant flaw, we chose a different approach. In Linux, swapping involves copying pages from the page cache to the swap cache. The swap cache is the set of all pages written out to swap and its principal role is buffering pages before committing them to disk. By design, each page in the swap cache correspond to a unique page frame. This implies that shared memory pages (with different PTEs pointing to the same page frame) although mapped in multiple process address spaces, their PTEs eventually correspond to the same page frame in the swap cache. Therefore, for private processes, our solution is to modify the swapping process to take into account when a page is mapped by a private process. It required extending the object representing a swap entry with a pointer to the corresponding private context. Using the process' private context, the kernel swap routine was modified to encrypt and decrypt pages as they move in and out of swap the cache.

4.5 Hibernation

Before writing the system image to disk, it *freezes* the processes to ensure the system is in a valid state. The `try_to_freeze_tasks()` function in `kernel/power/process.c` iterates through every process in the system to perform the freeze. When a private process is found, a `SIGKILL` signal is sent to the process. This should cause the program to exit immediately. However, signals are only executed when the process is scheduled, which in this case would be at system startup. By then, private program data and files would be written to disk. Therefore, to uphold the privacy properties, the files and private data are cleared explicitly. On every memory area of the process' address space, an iteration is performed over each page and if the page is in memory, its content is cleared (filled with zeros). Pages swapped to disk are ignored as they are encrypted and thus, do not require explicit erasure. A similar operation is performed on the pages of private containers; every page of every inode belonging to a private container is iterated and if found in memory, the page is filled with zeros. When completed, the private context of the process is erased to ensure encrypted pages on disk are not recoverable.

4.6 RPRIVEXEC

For comparison, we implemented a variant of TPrivExeC called RPrivExeC. It locks all the application data in memory and employs a RAM-based filesystem for its private container. Consequently, application data is *never* written to disk and with all the I/O performed in RAM, minimal overhead is incurred on the overall process execution. Upon termination, the generated application data is cleared from memory. At a high level, RPrivExeC differs from TPrivExeC in its absence of swap (pages are locked in memory) and the type of private container. In addition, at process instantiation, protection flags of the private process' memory descriptor were set to lock the pages in memory.

Figure 4c shows the filesystem tree for a typical private process in RPRIVEXEC. The ramfs filesystem serves as the private container and is the upper directory of the union filesystem. Ramfs is a simple filesystem that exports the linux caching mechanism as a filesystem. It is resizable (limited by the amount of free RAM), completely resides in the page cache and has no backing store. As done in TPRIVEXEC, private data confidentiality is withheld by disallowing non-enclave access and preventing data persistence.

4.7 Launching Private Applications

To launch private processes, a userspace wrapper application creates and destroys the private environment. As argument, it takes the path of the application to be executed. The wrapper clones itself with the `CLONE_PRIVEXEC` flag and then issues a `wait()` system call. In the newly cloned private process, the private containers are created by mounting the respective filesystems (ramfs and tmpfs for RPRIVEXEC and TPRIVEXEC respectively). Using a config file filled by the user, the necessary number of nested union filesystems are created. It then loads the target application in a chroot environment with the top Overlayfs mountpoint as its root. When the target application terminates, the wrapper unmounts the filesystems and exits. Please note that even if the wrapper application is killed prematurely, the private container remains inaccessible to unauthorized processes (permission enforcement is done in kernel space).

5. EVALUATION

We performed the tests on an Intel Core 2 duo 3.06GHz with 4GB of RAM running Debian 7.8 (wheezy). Different kernel images were compiled for each system: vanilla Linux kernel, TPRIVEXEC, RPRIVEXEC and PRIVEXEC. For GUI applications, each kernel build was configured with relaxed IPC permissions on X as in [15].

Preliminary modifications. Before starting the tests, three changes were made to the PRIVEXEC patch from [15]. First, there was a bug in the swap procedure, which led to kernel panics. A virtual address was incorrectly used as an argument `kunmap` after the page was processed. This was changed to use the page descriptor. Second, when determining the "owner" of a page before paging out, an uninitialized pointer was passed to the `try_to_unmap` function. This sometimes caused a kernel crash when the caller later tries to dereference the dangling pointer. To fix this, the pointer was initialized to null before the function call. Finally, for GUI applications, the path used to detect X was set to `/usr/bin/X` which is not the one used by Debian. The code was changed to also check the `/usr/bin/Xorg` path.

For the remainder of this paper, we use T&R to serve as a shorthand for "TPRIVEXEC and RPRIVEXEC".

5.1 Private Browsing

We compared how the "private execution" in T&R tallies against traditional Private Browsing Mode of modern browsers. Before starting the tests, the Firefox browsing data (history, bookmarks, cache etc.) was cleared. Firefox was launched in private execution and some websites were visited at random (some articles on wikipedia). The browser was terminated and Firefox was restarted in public mode. When checked, the history was found to be still clear. To further the test, we installed Adblock; a popular browser extension which blocks ads on webpages. According to Lerner et al. [12], a known flaw in traditional Private Browsing Mode is browser extensions still able to leave behind data. To verify this behavior, Firefox was launched in Private Browsing Mode with Adblock enabled. Then, from the Adblock icon, `http://cnet.com` was whitelisted; effectively preventing Adblock from blocking ads on the website. After restarting Firefox in normal mode, `http://cnet.com` was visited and was found to be whitelisted by Adblock; the actions performed in Private Browsing Mode persisted into future browsing sessions. The procedure was repeated with Firefox launched as a private application in T&R. Likewise, the `http://cnet.com` website was whitelisted and Firefox was relaunched as a public process. The website was then visited and its ads were found to be blocked by Adblock. This shows that the changes made in private execution did not persist across sessions.

5.2 Browsing Performance

Continuing in the realm of browsers, we tried to estimate the latency imposed by different implementations when loading webpages. Using Selenium Webdriver [19], we automated the Firefox Browser to load two sets of webpages: the top 50 websites from Alexa and 300 random links from Wikipedia. The tests were ran 10 times and the averages (after removing extreme values) are shown in Table 1. Both experiments show little disparity in latency across all implementations which could be accounted with network fluctuations. The varying nature of the Alexa pages and the homogeneity of wikipedia pages made little difference in browser performance.

	Alexa	Wikipedia
Normal	126.78s	205.56s
RPRIVEXEC	124.46s	199.39s
TPRIVEXEC	125.46s	203.28s
PRIVEXEC	124.45s	209.69s

Table 1: Average latency in loading webpages

5.3 Application benchmark

To ensure that TPRIVEXEC satisfies its design goals, we tested multiple Linux applications for proper functioning. However, for our performance evaluation, we focused on tasks a user might employ regularly and for which I/O performance is desirable. The applications were executed in cascade to highlight the merits of the different filesystems.

- *grep* is a command-line utility for searching files that match a pattern. Using grep, "Torvalds" was searched across all the source files in the Linux Source tree.
- *wget* is a console-based network downloader. Raw `TIFF` image files from the Sintel[2] movie score were downloaded (totaling 1.8GB).
- *feh* is a console-based image viewer. Using *feh*, the downloaded `TIFF` files were displayed in a slideshow.
- *ffmpeg* is a command line utility for video and image processing. Using its image conversion utility, all the downloaded `TIFF` files were converted to `PNG` format.

[2] `ftp.nluug.nl/pub/graphics/blender/demo/movies/Sintel_4k/tiff16/`

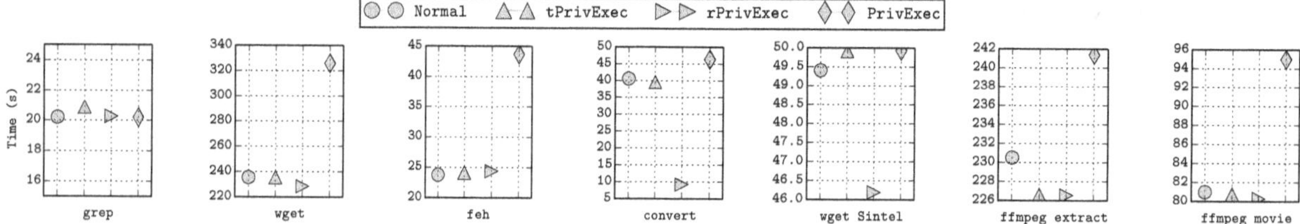

Figure 5: Application benchmarks

- This last test was divided in 3 portions: downloading the movie (*wget Sintel*), extracting images from it (*ffmpeg extract*) and reconstructing a movie from the extracted images (*ffmpeg movie*). Firstly, the previously generated **TIFF** and **GIF** image files were deleted from the current folder (to provide enough space for RPRIVEXEC). Then, using *wget*, the Sintel[3] movie in 1080p was downloaded. The 15min movie is in Matroska (mkv) format and is about 1.2GB in size. Next, using the *ffmpeg* utility, an image was extracted every 3s; generating 297 **PNG** images of about 1MB each. Finally, with the *ffmpeg* utility, the images were used to create a video slideshow.

The tests were done 10 times and the results are plotted in Figure 5. In every test, TPRIVEXEC and RPRIVEXEC performed at least as well as the vanilla kernel. Expectedly, all systems performed almost equally on the *grep* and *wget Sintel* tests; in the former, all prototypes take equal time to copy data from the disk to the page cache and for the latter, network transfer was the bulk portion of the task. However, PRIVEXEC incurs significant overhead in the remaining tasks. As previously mentioned in [15], the eCryptfs filesystem (the PRIVEXEC private container), is very slow in dealing with a large number of files. The overhead comes from allocating multiple inodes and individually performing a number of disk-dependent operations on each of them. This problem is not apparent in either TPRIVEXEC or RPRIVEXEC– with much of the data residing in RAM, filesystem operations can occur at much greater speed.

5.4 I/O benchmark

To evaluate I/O and filesystem performance, we used the Bonnie++ [3] filesystem benchmarking suite. For the test to fit in memory, we used a dataset of 2.5GB. Using 16 files, the test was ran 10 times on each system for comparison. The results displayed in Table 2 show that RPRIVEXEC and TPRIVEXEC have a massive speedup in read, write and rewrites. Compared to PRIVEXEC, both prototypes are about 22x faster in writes and 37x faster in reads. Bonnie++ returned no values for random seeks of RPRIVEXEC and TPRIVEXEC. With all the data in memory, little delay is incurred when finding the blocks of data. RPRIVEXEC and TPRIVEXEC are considerably slower in deleting files when compared to the vanilla system. Since they explicitly clobber their file contents, some overhead is incurred in trying to complete a delete operation.

[3] `https://durian.blender.org/download/`

	Normal	RPRIVEXEC	TPRIVEXEC	PRIVEXEC
W	95.2 MB/s	1.7 GB/s	1.6 GB/s	52.8 MB/s
Rw	99.2 MB/s	1.3 GB/s	1.3 GB/s	22.3 MB/s
R	3.3 GB/s	3.3 GB/s	3.2 GB/s	84.8 MB/s
S	2720 sk/s	–	–	262.2 sk/s
C	18990 μs	507 μs	344 μs	93361 μs
R	761 μs	460 μs	468 μs	4003 μs
D	709 μs	2490 μs	2610 μs	4563 μs

Table 2: I/O benchmarking under memory limits
W:Write Rw:Rewrite R:Read S:Seeks C:Create D:Delete

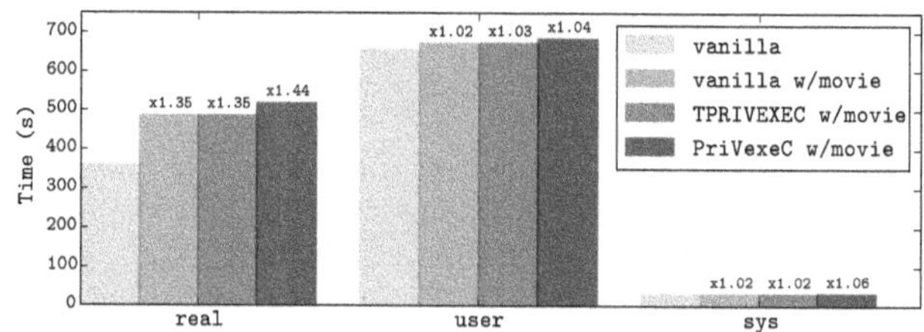

Figure 6: Overhead imposed by player on Node.js compilation.

5.5 System Impact

The typical user workload involves running multiple programs with disparate objectives. For this test, we ran an application in private execution to investigate its impact on the compilation of the Node.js Javascript runtime [13], which internally compiles the V8 JavaScript Engine [8]. In addition to being CPU intensive, the compilation of V8 involves multiprocessing, multithreading, disk access and memory consumption. Although most users would not consider compiling V8 in their workflow, we believe the resources involved emulates the simultaneous execution of multiple processes. First, Node.js was first built on the vanilla kernel to establish a baseline. Then, for each system (vanilla, TPRIVEXEC and PRIVEXEC), Node.js was recompiled (as a public process) while playing the Sintel Movie using mplayer. When under TPRIVEXEC or PRIVEXEC, mplayer was ran as a private process. In all runs, Node.js was compiled with 4 threads and the time required for the compilation was recorded.

Figure 6 shows the runtime of each test. The time slots are divided in 3 categories: *a*) *Real*: the time lapse between launch and termination of the process. This would be the amount of time the user waits for the process to completes the task. *b*) *User*: amount of time spent in user mode. The actual CPU time involved in running the program's code. *c*) *Sys*: time spent in kernel mode. This only includes the time the kernel spent in the process' behalf.

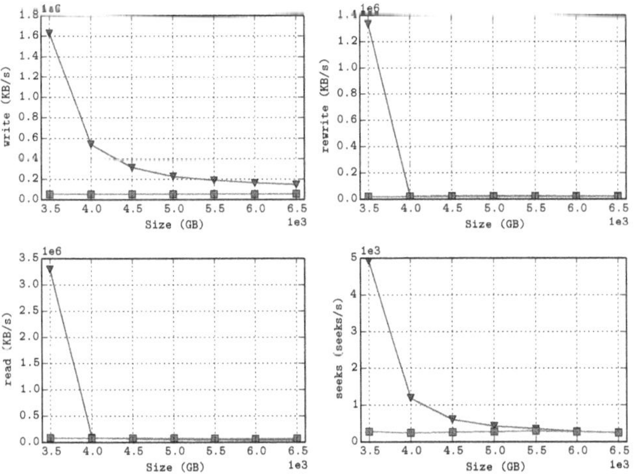

Figure 7: Comparing TPRIVEXEC against PRIVEXEC on I/O benchmarks with sizes bigger than the memory.

From the runtime results, TPRIVEXEC again outperforms PRIVEXEC on every metric. Irrespective of whether a private or public process, mplayer introduces at least a 35% overhead to the *real* time. This is acceptable considering that the task involved rendering a 1080p movie; the context switch required would severely impact compilation time. No noticeable difference could be observed in either the *user* or *sys* time. Therefore, TPRIVEXEC incurs minimal system overhead when executing a private process.

5.6 Stress Test

In this test, TPRIVEXEC and PRIVEXEC were compared on datasets bigger than the size of RAM. The idea was to simulate the I/O performance in applications whose dataset could not fit in memory. Using Bonnie++, I/O tasks were iteratively performed to measure *read*, *write*, *rewrite* and *seek time*. Before each run, kernel filesystem caches were dropped to make sure they did not interfere with the results. The test was repeated 10 times and the results were plotted in Figure 7. On all metrics, TPRIVEXEC performs better than PRIVEXEC but converges to the same value as the dataset increases. With a bigger portion of the data to be written to disk, TPRIVEXEC's advantage with performing I/O in memory is gradually diminished.

6. DISCUSSION

TPRIVEXEC and RPRIVEXEC are geared towards users of commodity systems. They provide a mechanism for selectively running applications in private mode. By holding a non-negligible portion of application data in memory (complete application data in case of RPRIVEXEC), compared to PRIVEXEC, we believe T&R provide better security guarantees for private execution. Regardless of the protection used on permanent storage, there is still a chance the data could be recovered. As we would now discuss, there are some limitations in the guarantees offered by T&R.

Protection of kernel memory is the most principal pillar on which the privacy properties of T&R rests on. Although both prototypes attempt to delete much of the application data, neither of them erases the kernel buffers that might contain traces of private data. An attacker who has privileged access to the system could load a module and would be able read private application data from kernel memory. This vulnerability could be abated by employing a *secure deallocation* [5] implementation such as PaX [14]. T&R does not support applications that bypass the VFS before writing to persistent storage. This method is called DirectIO, commonly used in database suites where data organization on disk is of paramount importance. Also, T&R offers no defense against cold boot [11] or any other hardware-based memory attacks. Although the efficacy of cold boot attacks has been questioned in modern DDR3 memory chips [10], they still remain a potent attack. To protect the PEKs, TPRIVEXEC could make use of the Trusted Platform Module [9] or Exposure-Resilient Functions [4].

With most user applications having a GUI, it is likely the kernel will be compilied with loose IPC permissions on X. Consequently, this introduces a potential privacy violaton, as X would contain contextual information about the application. Furthermore, in the event of hibernation, even though the private application's runtime is cleared, X still bears some application information. A simple workaround is to run X as a private process and then run the application as a child process. A side effect of this arrangement would be all GUI applications being private (and part of the same enclave). A future improvement could be setting up a passphrase used to encrypt the hibernation image saved to disk. Upon system restoration, the user would "unlock" the system by entering the correct passphrase.

7. RELATED WORK

Though there exists multiple systems that assist users in achieving confidentiality, in this section, we focus on work accomplished in the context of private execution.

In 2008, Halderman et al. [11] demonstrated that cryptographic keys and other sensitive information could be extracted from DRAM cells even after they were removed from the motherboard. In response to the "cold boot" attack, Peterson [17] designs the CryptKeeper system, which splits RAM into two portions; a presumably larger encrypted portion and a smaller plaintext portion. The data from the unencrypted section is locked in memory and readily available for use, while the encrypted portion is allowed to write to disk. The intent is to reduce the total amount of sensitive information in RAM at any time. Cryptkeeper offers no fine-grained control on what applications are ran in private mode. By pooling the whole userspace data into the two memory portions, it incurs significant system-wide overhead.

Provos et al. [18] proposed the encryption of of memory pages as they are swapped out. Boneh and Lipton [2] introduced the concept of erasing data by encrypting it and then erasing the key. TPRIVEXEC combines the ideas from the above systems and adds per-application granularity and coercion-resitance. Recently, Xu et al. [21] proposed UCognito, a sandbox-like service that runs the browser under private browsing semantics. It overlays a sandbox filesystem over the main filesystem and intercepts system calls issued by the browser. Although its approach is similar to TPRIVEXEC, there are differences. Not only is this protection limited to browsers but it is implemented in userspace. Consequently, UCognito does not provide the same level of privacy guarantees as TPRIVEXEC.

Lacuna [6] introduces the concept *ephemeral channels* to provide *forensic deniability* for programs as they communicate with devices. Using a modified QEMU hypervisor, it runs the private application in a virtual machine. When the private execution is terminated, the ephemeral channels are clobbered thereby making any state generated by the private process irrecoverable. Though the design goals of lacuna considerably overlaps with ours, the approach employed by Lacuna is deemed heavyweight. By copying OS resources and running the private application in a VM makes Lacuna inappropriate for resource-constrained systems.

By taking advantage of cloud connectivity in mobile devices, CleanOS [20] modifies the Android runtime to encrypt sensitive data. It stores the encryption keys in the cloud and uses tainting to select which data objects to encrypt. In case of mobile theft, the confidentiality of user data is maintained as all sensitive data stored on the device is encrypted. However, CleanOS overhead is prohibitively high and not well suited to already energy-constrained devices such as phones.

8. CONCLUSIONS AND FUTURE WORK

In this paper, we presented the design and implementation of TPRIVEXEC, a system-level private execution service. By trapping all the application data in a private container, it provides confidentiality by preventing unauthorized access during application execution, and securely deleting application data upon exit. To the best of knowledge, TPRIVEXEC is the first system to leverage RAM-backed storage for system-level privacy. As shown by our evaluation, TPRIVEXEC supports a large range of applications, is effective at leaving no usable information on application exit and introduces negligible overhead on application execution. For hibernation, TPRIVEXEC explicitly clears the memory contents and files of private processes before the hibernation image is written to disk. Our justification was that applications ran in private execution are likely short-lived and user does not intend to store the data. However a future improvement is to allow the user set a passphrase to encrypt the PEK. Upon system restore, the user could "unlock" the application by entering the passphrase.

Acknowledgements. This work was supported in part by the National Science Foundation under awards CNS–1228697 and CNS–1253204.

9. REFERENCES

[1] Gaurav Aggarwal, Elie Bursztein, Collin Jackson, and Dan Boneh. An analysis of private browsing modes in modern browsers. In *USENIX Security Symposium*, pages 79–94, 2010.

[2] Dan Boneh and Richard J Lipton. A revocable backup system. In *Usenix Security*, pages 91–96, 1996.

[3] Bonnie++. `http://www.coker.com.au/bonnie++/`.

[4] Ran Canetti, Yevgeniy Dodis, Shai Halevi, Eyal Kushilevitz, and Amit Sahai. Exposure-resilient functions and all-or-nothing transforms. In *Advances in Cryptology—EUROCRYPT 2000*, pages 453–469. Springer, 2000.

[5] Jim Chow, Ben Pfaff, Tal Garfinkel, and Mendel Rosenblum. Shredding your garbage: Reducing data lifetime through secure deallocation. In *USENIX Security*, 2005.

[6] Alan M Dunn, Michael Z Lee, Suman Jana, Sangman Kim, Mark Silberstein, Yuanzhong Xu, Vitaly Shmatikov, and Emmett Witchel. Eternal sunshine of the spotless machine: Protecting privacy with ephemeral channels. In *OSDI*, pages 61–75, 2012.

[7] eCryptfs. `http://ecryptfs.org/`.

[8] V8 Javascript Engine. `https://code.google.com/p/v8/`.

[9] Trusted Computing Group. Tpm main specification. `http://www.trustedcomputinggroup.org/resources/tpm_main_specification`.

[10] Michael Gruhn and T Muller. On the practicability of cold boot attacks. In *Availability, Reliability and Security (ARES), 2013 Eighth International Conference on*, pages 390–397. IEEE, 2013.

[11] J Alex Halderman, Seth D Schoen, Nadia Heninger, William Clarkson, William Paul, Joseph A Calandrino, Ariel J Feldman, Jacob Appelbaum, and Edward W Felten. Lest we remember: cold-boot attacks on encryption keys. *Communications of the ACM*, 52(5):91–98, 2009.

[12] Benjamin S Lerner, Liam Elberty, Neal Poole, and Shriram Krishnamurthi. Verifying web browser extensions' compliance with private-browsing mode. In *Computer Security–ESORICS 2013*, pages 57–74. Springer, 2013.

[13] Node.js. `http://nodejs.org/`.

[14] Homepage of The PaX Team. `http://pax.grsecurity.net/`.

[15] Kaan Onarlioglu, Collin Mulliner, William Robertson, and Engin Kirda. Privexec: Private execution as an operating system service. In *IEEE Symposium on Security and Privacy (S&P)*, May 2013.

[16] Overlayfs. `https://www.kernel.org/doc/Documentation/filesystems/overlayfs.txt`.

[17] Peter AH Peterson. Cryptkeeper: Improving security with encrypted ram. In *Technologies for Homeland Security (HST), 2010 IEEE International Conference on*, pages 120–126. IEEE, 2010.

[18] Niels Provos. Encrypting virtual memory. In *USENIX Security Symposium*, pages 35–44, 2000.

[19] Selenium. `http://www.seleniumhq.org/`.

[20] Yang Tang, Phillip Ames, Sravan Bhamidipati, Ashish Bijlani, Roxana Geambasu, and Nikhil Sarda. Cleanos: Limiting mobile data exposure with idle eviction. In *OSDI*, volume 12, pages 77–91, 2012.

[21] Meng Xu, Yeongjin Jang, Xinyu Xing, Taesoo Kim, and Wenke Lee. Ucognito: Private browsing without tears. In *Proceedings of the 22nd ACM SIGSAC Conference on Computer and Communications Security*, pages 438–449. ACM, 2015.

[22] What you share and how to control it | Spotify Blog. `https://news.spotify.com/us/2011/09/27/what-to-share/`.

Hacking the DBMS to Prevent Injection Attacks

Ibéria Medeiros[1] Miguel Beatriz[2] Nuno Neves[3] Miguel Correia[2]
[1]INESC-ID, Faculdade de Ciências, Universidade de Lisboa, Portugal
[2]INESC-ID, Instituto Superior Técnico, Universidade de Lisboa, Portugal
[3]LaSIGE, Faculdade de Ciências, Universidade de Lisboa, Portugal
ibemed@gmail.com, miguel.beatriz@tecnico.ulisboa.pt, nuno@di.fc.ul.pt, miguel.p.correia@tecnico.ulisboa.pt

ABSTRACT

After more than a decade of research, web application security continues to be a challenge and the backend database the most appetizing target. The paper proposes preventing injection attacks against the database management system (DBMS) behind web applications by embedding protections in the DBMS itself. The motivation is twofold. First, the approach of embedding protections in operating systems and applications running on top of them has been effective to protect these applications. Second, there is a semantic mismatch between how SQL queries are believed to be executed by the DBMS and how they are actually executed, leading to subtle vulnerabilities in protection mechanisms. The approach – SEPTIC – was implemented in MySQL and evaluated experimentally with web applications written in PHP and Java/Spring. In the evaluation SEPTIC has shown neither false negatives nor false positives, on the contrary of alternative approaches, causing also a low performance overhead in the order of 2.2%.

Keywords

web applications; injection attacks; DBMS self-protection; security; software security.

1. INTRODUCTION

Web applications are an important component of today's economy, with major players such as Google, Facebook and Yahoo. However, after more than a decade of research, web application security continues to be a challenge. For example, recently SQL injection (SQLI) attacks have allegedly victimized 12 million Drupal sites [4], SQLI attacks were considered an important threat against critical infrastructures [16], and stored cross-site scripting (XSS) was used to inject malicious code in servers running Wordpress [29].

The mechanisms most commonly used to protect web applications from malicious inputs are web application firewalls (WAFs), sanitization/validation functions, and prepared statements in the application source code. The first two mechanisms, respectively, inspect web application inputs and block and sanitize those that are considered malicious/dangerous, whereas the third bounds inputs to placeholders in the query. Other anti-SQLI mechanisms have been presented in the literature, but barely adopted. Some of these mechanisms monitor SQL queries and block them if they deviate from certain query models, but the queries are inspected without full knowledge about how the server-side scripting language and the DBMS process them [6, 7, 13, 34, 20]. In all these cases, administrators and programmers make assumptions about how the server-side language and the DBMS work and interact, which sometimes are simplistic, others blatantly wrong. For example, programmers often assume that PHP function `mysql_real_escape_string` always effectively sanitizes inputs and prevents SQLI attacks, which is not true, or they may ignore that data may be unsanitized when inserted in the DBMS leading to second-order SQLI vulnerabilities.

We argue that such simplistic or wrong assumptions are caused by a *semantic mismatch* between how an SQL query is expected to run and what actually occurs when it is executed. This mismatch leads to unexpected vulnerabilities in the sense that mechanisms such as those mentioned above can become ineffective, resulting in false negatives (attacks not detected). To avoid this problem, these attacks could be handled after the server-side code processes the inputs and the DBMS validates the queries, reducing the amount of assumptions that are made. The mismatch and this solution are not restricted to web applications.

Today operating systems are much more secure than years ago due to the deployment of automatic protection mechanisms in themselves, in core libraries (e.g., .NET and glibc), and in compilers. For example, address space layout randomization, data execution prevention, or canaries/stack cookies are widely deployed in Windows and Linux [15, 19]. These mechanisms block a large range of attacks irrespectively of the programmer following secure programming practices or not. Clearly, something similar would be desirable for web applications. The DBMS is an interesting location to add these protections as it is a common target for attacks.

We propose modifying – "hacking" – DBMSs to detect and block attacks in runtime without programmer intervention. We call this approach *SElf-Protecting daTabases preventIng attaCks* (SEPTIC). In this paper, we focus on the two main categories of attacks related with databases: *SQL injection* attacks, which continue to be among those with highest risk [37] and for which new variants continue to appear [27], and *stored injection attacks*, which also involve SQL queries. For

CODASPY'16, March 09-11, 2016, New Orleans, LA, USA

DOI: http://dx.doi.org/10.1145/2857705.2857723

SQLI, we propose detecting attacks essentially by comparing queries with query models, taking to its full potential an idea that has been previously used only outside of the DBMS [6, 7, 13, 34] and circumventing the semantic mismatch problem. For stored injection, we propose having plugins to deal with specific attacks before data is inserted in the database.

We demonstrate the concept with a popular deployment scenario: MySQL, probably the most popular open-source DBMS [30], and PHP, the language more used in web applications (more than 77%) [17]. We also explore Java/Spring, the second most employed programming language. We evaluate SEPTIC experimentally to assess its effectiveness to block attacks, including a set of novel SQLI attacks presented recently [27]. SEPTIC is compared with a set of alternative solutions, including the ModSecurity WAF and recent anti-SQLI mechanisms proposed in the literature, with SEPTIC showing neither false negatives nor false positives, on the contrary of the others. We also evaluate the impact of our approach on the performance of web applications using BenchLab [8]. The overhead was very low, around 2.2%.

The main contribution of this paper is a mechanism that comes out of the box with the DBMS to detect and block injection attacks against the DBMS inside the DBMS itself. Moreover, by being placed inside the DBMS, the mechanism is able to mitigate the semantic mismatch problem and handle sophisticated SQL injection and stored injection attacks.

2. DBMS INJECTION ATTACKS

We define *semantic mismatch* as the distance between how programmers assume SQL queries are executed by the DBMS and how queries are effectively executed. This mismatch often leads to mistakes in the implementation of protections in the source code of web applications, letting these applications vulnerable to SQL injection and other attacks involving the DBMS. The semantic mismatch is subjective in the sense that it depends on the programmer, but some mistakes are usual. A common way to try to prevent SQLI consists in sanitizing user inputs before they are used in SQL queries. For instance, in PHP `mysql_real_escape_string` precedes special characters like the prime or the double prime with a backslash, transforming these delimiters into normal characters. However, sanitization functions do not behave as envisioned when the special characters are represented differently from expected. This problem has lead us to use the term semantic mismatch to refer to the gap between how the SQL queries that take these sanitized inputs are believed to be executed by the programmer, and how they are actually processed by the DBMS.

We identified several DBMS injection attacks in the literature, including a variety of cases related to semantic mismatch [9, 11, 12, 22, 27, 31]. Table 1 organizes these attacks in classes. The first three columns identify the classes, whereas the fourth and fifth state what PHP sanitization functions and the DBMS do to the example malicious inputs in the sixth column.

As mentioned in the introduction, we consider two main classes of attacks: *SQL injection* and *stored injection* (first column). These classes are divided in sub-classes for common designations of attacks targeted at DBMSs (A to C). Obfuscation attacks (class A) are the most obvious cases of semantic mismatch. Classes S.1 and S.2 classify attacks in terms of the way they affect the syntactic structure of the SQL query. Class S.1 is composed of attacks that modify this structure. Class S.2 is composed of attacks that modify the query but mimic its original structure.

Class A, obfuscation, contains five subclasses. Consider the code excerpt in Fig. 1 that shows a login script that checks if the credentials the user provides (username, password) exist in the database.[1] The user inputs are sanitized by the `mysql_real_escape_string` function (lines 1-2) before they are inserted in the query (line 3) and submitted to the DBMS (line 4). If an attacker injects the `admin'--` string as username (line 1), the `$user` variable receives this string sanitized, with the prime character preceded by a backslash. The user `admin\'--` does not exist in the database so this SQLI attack is not successful.

```
1 $user = mysql_real_escape_string($_POST['username']);
2 $pass = mysql_real_escape_string($_POST['password']);
3 $query = "SELECT * FROM users WHERE username='$user'
      AND password='$pass'";
4 $result = mysql_query($query);
```

Figure 1: Script vulnerable to SQLI with encoded characters.

On the contrary, this sanitization is ineffective if the input uses URL encoding [5], leading to an attack of class A.1. Suppose the attacker inserts the username URL-encoded: `%61%64%6D%69%6E%27%2D%2D%20`. `mysql_real_escape_string` function does not sanitize the input because it does not recognize `%27` as a prime. However, MySQL receives that string as part of a query and decodes it, so the query executed is `SELECT * FROM users WHERE username='admin'-- ' AND password='foo'`. The attack is therefore effective because this query is equivalent to `SELECT * FROM users WHERE username='admin'` (no password has to be provided). This is also an attack of class S.1 as the structure of the query is modified (the part that checks the password disappears). The other subclasses of class A involve similar techniques. In class A.2 the attacker encodes some characters in Unicode, e.g., the prime as `U+02BC`. In A.3 decoding involves calling dynamically a function (e.g., the prime is encoded as `char(39)`). Class A.4 attacks use spaces and equivalent strings to manipulate queries (e.g., concealing a space with a comment like `/**/`) [9]. A.5 attacks abuse the fact that numeric fields do not require values to be enclosed with primes, so a tautology similar to the example we gave for A.1 can be caused without these characters, fooling sanitization functions like `mysql_real_escape_string`.

Stored procedures that take user inputs may be exploited similarly to queries constructed in the application code (class B). These inputs may modify or mimic the syntactic structure of the query, leading to attacks of classes S.1 or S.2. Blind SQLI attacks (class C) aim to extract information from the database by observing how the application responds to different inputs, so they also fall in classes S.1 or S.2.

Class D attacks – stored injection – are characterized by being executed in two steps: the first involves doing an SQL query that inserts attacker data in the database (`INSERT`, `UPDATE`); the second uses this data to complete the attack. The specific attack depends on the data inserted in the database and how it is used in the second step. In a second order SQLI attack (class D.1) the data inserted is a string specially crafted to be inserted in a second SQL query executed in the second step. This second query is the attack

[1]All examples included in the paper were tested with Apache 2.2.15, PHP 5.5.9 and MySQL 5.7.4

Class		Class name	PHP sanit. func.	DBMS	Example malicious input
SQL injection	**A**	Obfuscation			
	A.1	- Encoded characters	do nothing	decodes and executes	`%27, 0x027`
	A.2	- Unicode characters	do nothing	translates and executes	`U+0027, U+02BC`
	A.3	- Dynamic SQL	do nothing	completes and executes	`char(39)`
	A.4	- Space character evasion	do nothing	removes and executes	`char(39)/**/OR/**/1=1--`
	A.5	- Numeric fields	do nothing	interprets and executes	`0 OR 1=1--`
	B	Stored procedures	sanitize	executes	`admin' OR 1=1`
	C	Blind SQLI	sanitize	executes	`admin' OR 1=1`
sted. inj.	**D**	Stored injection code			
	D.1	- Second order SQLI	–	executes	any of the above
	D.2	- Stored XSS	–	–	`<script>alert('XSS')</script>`
	D.3	- Stored RCI, RFI, LFI	–	–	`malicious.php`
	D.4	- Stored OSCI	–	–	`; cat /etc/passwd`
	S.1	Syntax structure	sanitize	executes	`admin' OR 1=1`
	S.2	Syntax mimicry	sanitize	executes	`admin' AND 1=1--`

RCI: Remote Code Injection; RFI:Remote File Inclusion; LFI: Local File Inclusion; OSCI: OS Command Injection

Table 1: Classes of attacks against DBMSs.

itself, which may fall in classes S.1 or S.2. This is another case of semantic mismatch as the sanitization created by functions like `mysql_real_escape_string` is removed by the DBMS when the string is inserted in the database (first step of the attack). A stored XSS (class D.2) involves inserting a browser script (typically JavaScript) in the database in the first step, then returning it to one or more users in the second step. In class D.3 the data inserted in the database can be a malicious PHP script or an URL of a website containing such a script, resulting on local or remote file inclusion, or on remote code injection. In class D.4 attacks the data that is inserted is an operating system command, which is executed in the second step.

3. THE SEPTIC APPROACH

This section presents the SEPTIC approach. The idea consists in having a module inside the DBMS that processes every query it receives in order to detect attacks against the DBMS. We designate both the approach and this module by SEPTIC. This approach circumvents the semantic mismatch problem as detection is executed near the end of the data flow entering the DBMS, just before it executes the query.

3.1 SEPTIC overview

This section presents an overview of the approach. Fig. 2(a) represents the architecture of a web application, including the DBMS and SEPTIC. This module is placed inside the DBMS, after the parsing and validation of the queries. There may be also hooks inside the server-side language engine (Section 3.3).

In runtime SEPTIC works basically the following way:

1. *Server-side application code:* requests the execution of a query Q;

2. *Server-side language engine:* receives Q and sends it to the DBMS; it may add an identifier (ID) to Q;

3. *DBMS:* receives, parses, validates, and executes Q; between validation and execution, SEPTIC detects and possibly blocks an incoming attack.

Fig. 2(b) provides more details on the operation of SEPTIC. The figure should be read starting from the gray arrow at the top/left. Dashed arrows and dashed processes represent alternative paths.

When a web application is started, SEPTIC has to undergo some training before it enters in normal execution. Training is typically done by putting SEPTIC in *training mode* and running the application for some time without attacks (Section 3.5). Training results in a set of query models (QM) stored in SEPTIC.

In normal execution, for every query SEPTIC receives, it extracts the query ID and the query structure (QS). If no ID is provided, SEPTIC generates one (Section 3.3). SEPTIC detects attacks first by comparing the query structure (QS) with the query model(s) stored for that ID. If there is no match, an SQLI attack was detected. Otherwise, SEPTIC uses a set of *plugins* to discover stored injection attacks. If no attack is detected the query is executed.

The action taken when an attack is detected depends on the mode SEPTIC is running. In *prevention mode*, SEPTIC aborts the attacks, i.e., it drops the queries and the DBMS stops the query processing. In *detection mode*, queries are executed, not dropped. In both modes of operation, SEPTIC logs information about the attacks detected.

In summary, SEPTIC runs in three modes, one for training (*training mode*) and two for normal operation (*prevention mode* and *detection mode*).

The following sections present the approach in detail.

3.2 Query structures and query models

As explained in the previous section, in prevention and detection modes SEPTIC finds out if a query is an attack by comparing the *query structure* with the *query model(s)* associated to the query's ID.

We consider that SEPTIC receives the parse tree of every query represented as a *list of stacks* data structure. Each stack of the list represents a clause of the query (e.g., `SELECT`, `FROM`, `WHERE`), and each of its nodes contains data about the query element, such as category (e.g., field, function, operator), data type (e.g., integer, string), and data.

The *query structure* (QS) of a query is constructed by creating a single stack with the content of all the stacks in the list of stacks of a query. Fig. 3 depicts a generic query structure, showing from bottom to top the clauses and their elements. Each *node* (a row) represents an element of the query. Each node is composed by the element type (category) and the element data: ⟨ELEM_TYPE, ELEM_DATA⟩. The single exception is the alternative format ⟨DATA_TYPE, DATA⟩ that represents an input inserted in the query and its (primitive) data type (DATA_TYPE). A part of the query is considered to be an input if its type is primitive (e.g., a string or an integer) or if it is compared to something in a predicate. For the clauses with conditional expressions (e.g., `WHERE`) the elements are inserted in QS by doing post-order traversal of the parse tree of the query (i.e., the left child is

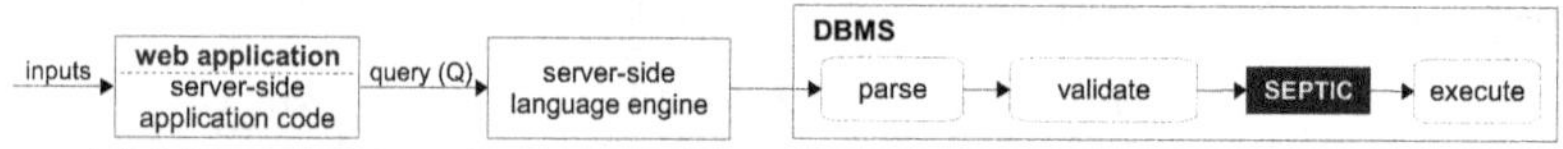

(a) Main modules of a web application backed by a DBMS with SEPTIC.

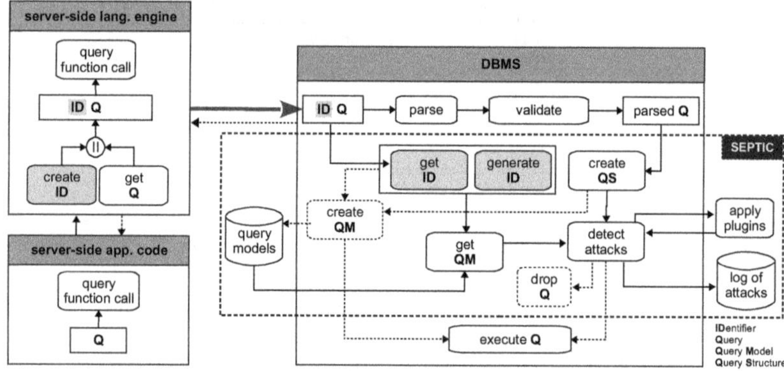

(b) SEPTIC approach data flows.

Figure 2: Architecture and data flows of a web application and SEPTIC (optional components in gray).

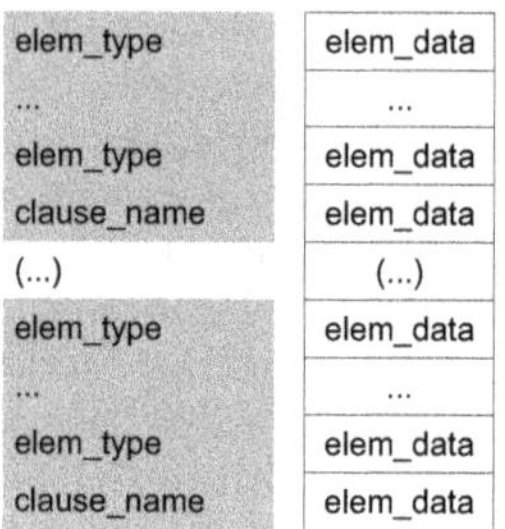

elem_type	elem_data
...	...
elem_type	elem_data
clause_name	elem_data
(...)	(...)
elem_type	elem_data
...	...
elem_type	elem_data
clause_name	elem_data

Figure 3: A generic query structure.

visited and inserted in the stack first, then the right child, and so on until the root).

As mentioned in the previous section, in training mode SEPTIC creates query models. Specifically, it creates a *query model* (QM) whenever the DBMS processes a query, but stores it only if that model is not yet stored for that query ID. The query model is created based on the query structure of the query. The process consists simply in substituting DATA by a special value $\perp$ in all $\langle$DATA_TYPE, DATA$\rangle$ nodes to denote that these fields shall not be compared during attack detection (Section 3.4). All the other nodes are identical in QM and QS.

Take as example the query `SELECT name FROM users WHERE user='alice' AND pass='foo'`. Fig. 4 represents its (a) parse tree, (b) structure (QS), and (c) model (QM). In Fig. 4(b) and (c) the gray items at the bottom have data about the `SELECT` and `FROM` clauses, whereas the rest are about the `WHERE` clause. In Fig. 4(b) the inputs are represented in bold and in Fig. 4(c) they have the special value $\perp$ as explained. In the left-hand column, each item of the query takes a category (field, data type, condition operator, etc.), whereas the right-hand column has the query's keywords, variables and primitive data type. Primitive data types (real, integer, decimal and string) also take a category, such as STRING_ITEM (e.g., in the third row).

3.3 Query identifiers

Each query received by the DBMS has to be verified against one or more query models. *Query identifiers* (IDs) are used to match queries to their models. More specifically, each query is assigned an ID and for each ID the training mode creates a set of one or more models. The SEPTIC module matches a query to a set of models. From the point of view of the module, IDs are opaque, i.e., their structure is not relevant.

SEPTIC can use three kinds of IDs, depending on where they are generated: in the server-side language engine (SSLE), in the DBMS, and outside both the SSLE and the DBMS. We explain them below.

3.3.1 SSLE-generated IDs

The SSLE is arguably the best place to generate the IDs, because this can let the application administrator oblivious to the existence of IDs. Fig. 2(b) shows how this would work generically (SSLE in the left-hand side).

Ideally, every query issued by an application should have a unique ID (Section 3.4) and the SSLE can provide this in many cases. For instance, in the example of Fig. 1 there should be a unique ID for the query constructed in line 3 and issued in line 4. In training mode a model with this ID would be constructed and in prevention/detection modes any query issued there would have the same ID. This would allow comparing the queries against the model without confusion with queries issued elsewhere in the application source code. The SSLE can create this ID when it sees a call to function `mysql_query`. The ID may contain data such as file / line number in which the query is issued. However, this is not enough because many applications have a single function that calls the DBMS with different queries. This function is called from several places in the application, but the file and line number that calls the DBMS is always the same.

We consider the ID format to be a sequence of *file:line* pairs separated by the character |, one pair per each function entered while the query is being composed. Specifically, the first pair corresponds to the line where the DBMS is called and the rest to lines where the query is passed as argument to some function. *file* contains the complete path to allow distinguishing even queries from different applications using the same DBMS.

Assume that the code sample of Fig. 1 is in file `login.php`. The query is created in the same function that calls the func-

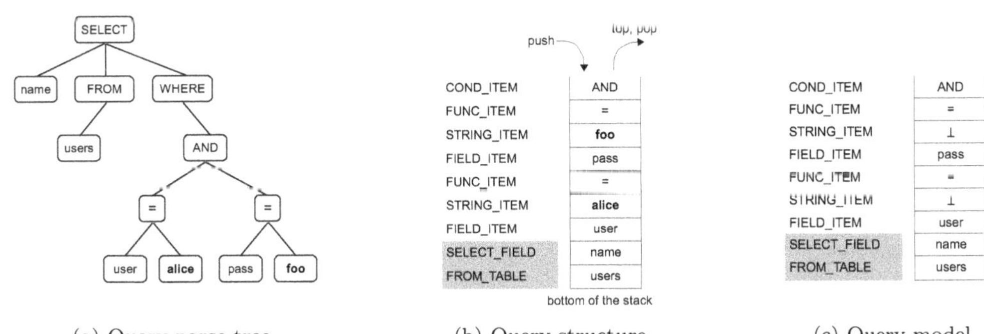

(a) Query parse tree (b) Query structure (c) Query model

Figure 4: Representation of a query as parse tree, structure (QS) and model (QM).

tion `mysql_query`, so the ID is simply *login.php:4*, meaning that the DBMS is called in line 4 of file `login.php`. Consider a second example in which line 4 is substituted by `$result = my_db_query($query)`, that function `my_db_query` is defined in file `my_db.php`, and that that function calls the DBMS using `mysql_query` in line 10 of that file. In this example, the ID is *my_db.php:10 | login.php:4*. This ID format is not guaranteed to generate unique IDs in all situations, but we observed no cases in which it did not. In these examples we show the filename without the full pathname for readability.

3.3.2 DBMS-generated IDs

Whenever the SEPTIC module in the DBMS receives a query without ID (e.g., because the SSLE does not generate IDs), it generates an ID automatically (Fig 2(b), gray boxes inside SEPTIC). The DBMS is unaware of what kind of client calls it (e.g., if it is an SSLE), much less about the web application source code. Therefore this ID has a different format. Similarly to SSLE-generated IDs, the application administrator can be oblivious to DBMS-generated IDs.

The ID format is the SQL command (typically `SELECT`) followed by the number of nodes of the query structure. For the example of Fig. 1 that has the query structure of Fig. 4(b) the ID would be *select_9*.

3.3.3 IDs generated outside the DBMS and the SSLE

In the previous two kinds of IDs the web application administrator is left aside from the process of assigning IDs to queries. If for some reason these kinds of IDs are not desirable, the administrator can define his own IDs. These IDs can have any format, e.g., a sequential number or the same format used in SSLE-generated IDs. They can be added to the queries in a few ways: (1) they may be appended to the query when it is defined or when the DBMS is called; or (2) a wrapper may be inserted between the applications code and the DBMS.

3.4 Attack detection

This section explains how SEPTIC detects attacks by dividing the categories of Table 1 in two groups that are detected differently: SQL injection and stored injection. The former contains the classes A to C and D.1, whereas the latter contains class D (except D.1). Class D.1 is also a form of stored injection, but it more convenient to detect these attacks using the approach to discover SQLI.

3.4.1 SQLI detection

SEPTIC detects SQLI attacks by verifying if queries fall in classes S.1 and S.2. We say that attack classes S.1 and S.2 are *primordial for SQL injection* because any SQLI attack falls in one of these two categories. The rationale is that if an SQLI attack neither modifies the query structure (class S.1) nor modifies the query mimicking the structure (class S.2), then it must leave the query unmodified, but then it is not an SQL injection attack.

SEPTIC detects SQLI attacks by comparing each query with the query models for the query's ID *structurally* (for class S.1) and *syntactically* (for class S.2). An attack is flagged if there are differences between the query and all the models for its ID.

Given a query Q with a certain ID and its query structure QS, detection involves iterating all the models QM_i stored for ID. For every QM_i there are two steps: (1) *Structural verification* – if the number of items in QS is different from the number of items in QM_i, then Q does not match the model QM_i and detection for QM_i ends. (2) *Syntactical verification* – if the data type of any of the items of QS is different from the type of any of the items of QM_i (except primitive types), then Q does not match the model QM_i and detection for QM_i ends. Items are compared starting at the top and going down the QS and QM stacks as represented in Figures 4(b)–(c). Primitive data types (real, integer, decimal and string) are an exception because DBMSs implicitly make type-casting between them (e.g., integer to string), so these types are considered equivalent. This process is iterated for all query models QM_i stored for ID. If Q matches one of the models, there is no attack; otherwise there is an attack. The action taken depends on the mode in which SEPTIC is running: in prevention mode the query processing is aborted; in detection mode the query is executed.

As mentioned in Section 3.3, IDs should be unique, so that a single query model QM would be stored for each ID during training. From that point of view *DBMS-generated IDs* are the worst option as they do not ensure uniqueness, except in applications with a very small number of queries. *SSLE-generated IDs* tend to be unique and *IDs generated outside the DBMS and the SSLE* may be created unique.

3.4.2 Stored injection detection

Stored injection attacks have two steps. In the first, malicious data is inserted in the database; in the second that data is taken from the database and used. For example, for stored XSS (D.2) the data includes a script to be executed at the victims' browsers; in the first step it is stored in the database; in the second step that script is taken from the database and sent to a browser. These attacks cannot be detected as SQLI because they do not work by modifying queries. Therefore, we employ a different solution based on the idea of detecting the presence of malicious data.

SEPTIC detects the presence of malicious data in queries that insert data in the database (first step of the attacks). To do this detection, SEPTIC contains a set of *plugins*, typically one for each type of attack. The plugins analyze the queries searching for code that might be executed by browsers (JavaScript, VB Script), by an operating system (shell script, OS commands, binary files) or by server-side scripts (php). Since running the plugins may introduce some overhead, the mechanism is applied in two steps: (1) *Filtering* – searches for suspicious strings such as: <, >, `href`, and *javacsript* attributes (D.2); protocol keywords (e.g., `http`) and extensions of executable or script files (e.g., *exe, php*) (D.3); special characters (e.g., *;* and |) (D.4). If none is found, detection ends. (2) *Testing* – consists in passing the input to the proper plugin for inspection. For example, if the filtering phase finds the `href` string, the data is provided to a plugin that detects stored XSS attacks. This plugin inserts the input in a simple HTML page with the three main tags (`<html>`, `<head>`, `<body>`), and then calls an HTML parser to determine if other tags appear in the page indicating the presence of a script.

3.5 Training

As explained in Section 3.1, whenever an application is put to run, SEPTIC has to be subjected to training. This is necessary for SEPTIC to create the models of the queries for SQLI detection (Section 3.4.1). There are two methods to do training: *training phase* and *incremental.*

The first method – *training phase* – involves putting SEPTIC in training mode and executing all queries of the web application with correct inputs (i.e., inputs that are not attacks). For every query a model is created and stored, unless the same model is already stored for the same ID. If there is already a model (or more) associated to that ID and the model created is different, then ID becomes associated to two (or more) models. After this is done, SEPTIC can be put in prevention or detection mode and no further intervention from the administrator is needed. The execution of all queries can be achieved in two fashions: (1) using the unit tests of the application; or (2) with the assistance of an external module, called *septic_training.* This module is a web client that works as a crawler. For each web page, it searches for HTML forms and extracts information about the submission method, action, variables and values. Then, it issues HTTP requests for all forms, causing the SQL queries to be sent to the DBMS. These queries can contain user inputs generated by the training module, can be static, or can depend on the results of other queries.

In the second training method – *incremental* – SEPTIC runs in prevention or detection mode all the time, without the need to switch modes and run an explicit training phase. This is very convenient and efficient as long as no attacks happen before the models are created. In both modes, for every query SEPTIC obtains the query structure (QS), gets the set of QMs associated to the query ID, and compares QS with every QM in the set, as explained in Section 3.4.1. From the point of view of training, the relevant case is when there is no QM associated with the ID. In this situation, SEPTIC behaves as if it was in the training phase and creates and stores the query model. The administrator is notified and should confirm that the model was built with a correct query, as it did not appear previously. This verification, however, is not critical for two reasons: (1) it is highly unlikely that the first query with a certain ID in a web application is malicious (attackers take time to find the application and to learn how it works); (2) in the unlikely case of the model being built with a malicious query, this will become conspicuous as correct queries will start being detected as attacks, which will call attention.

In case there are modifications to the application code we envisage two cases. If the changes are not significant, SEPTIC can continue in detection or prevention mode, building new QMs incrementally (incremental method). If the application code suffers many changes, SEPTIC can be put in training mode (training phase method) and all QMs of the application are rebuilt. In this case, the existent QMs are substituted for the new ones. However, in both cases the administrator can opt for either training method. An interesting case is if a query changes from line x to line y in the new version of application with SSLE-generated IDs. This is not problematic if the training phase method is used, as all QMs are rebuilt. In the incremental method two unlikely scenarios may happen: (1) the QM of the query of line y is created and associated to a IDy not in use or to an existent IDy; (2) the IDx (query from line x) receives a new QM, if the line x has now a different query. In both cases the old QMs stored for IDx and IDy are checked for the queries that come with those IDs with the new version of the application. Even if SEPTIC checks that they do not match the old QMs, they match the new QMs, so SEPTIC does not flag an attack (no false positives). False negatives (attacks not detected) are possible as a wrong QM will be associated to an ID, but this is unlikely to happen for two reasons: the two scenarios above are unlikely as a query would have to move to the same line of another; an attack against one of the queries would have to match the QM of the other query.

4. IMPLEMENTATION IN MYSQL AND LANGUAGE RUNTIMES

This section explains how SEPTIC was implemented in MySQL and the creation of identifiers implemented in two contexts: for PHP applications by modifying the PHP runtime (Zend engine); and for web applications implemented in the Spring framework in Java, using aspect oriented programming and a pair of alternatives. The first solution involves a few modifications to the engine's source code, whereas the second does not. Table 2 summarizes the changes made to those software packages.

The implementation of query identifiers has to be compatible with all the components we have been discussing: application source code, SSLE, and DBMS. Specifically, it is important that having SEPTIC in the DBMS or generating IDs in the SSLE does not require modifications to the other components. The solution is to place the identifiers inside DMBS comments. SEPTIC assumes that the first comment in a query is the ID. We place the comment at the beginning of the query, before the query proper.

4.1 Protecting MySQL

We implemented SEPTIC – i.e., the center and right-hand side of Fig. 2(b) – in MySQL 5.7.4. We modified a single file of the package (`sql_parser.cc`) and added a new header file (SEPTIC detector) and a configuration file (SEPTIC setup),

Software	sfm	sfc	loc	sa
MySQL 5.7.4				
- `sql_parser.cc`	1	–	14	–
- SEPTIC detector	–	1	1570	plugins
- SEPTIC setup	–	1	15	–
- *septic_training*	–	1	380	–
Zend engine / PHP 5.5.9				
- mysql extension	1	–	6	–
- mysqli extension	2	–	21	–
- SEPTIC identifier	–	1	249	–
Spring 4.0.5 / Java				
- `JdbcTemplate.java`	1	–	16	–
- SEPTIC identifier	–	1	–	–

sfm: source file modified loc: lines of code
sfc: source file created sa: software added

Table 2: Summary of modifications to software packages.

plus the plugins, which are external to the DBMS (e.g., for stored XSS the plugin is essentially the *jsoup* library [18]). The *septic_training* module is not only external but also runs separately from the DBMS.

The lines added to the `sql_parser.cc` file were inserted in function `mysql_parse`, and just before the call to the function `mysql_execute_command` that executes the query. These lines call the SEPTIC detector with an input corresponding to the query parsed and validated by MySQL. The module performs the previously described operations: builds the query structure (QS); compares QS with its query model (QM); logs que query and the ID if an attack is detected; and optionally drops the query.

SEPTIC is configured using a few switches. The first allows putting SEPTIC in training mode, detection mode (logs attacks), or prevention mode (logs and blocks attacks). The other two allow enabling and disabling respectively the detection of SQLI and stored injection attacks. The values for these switches are defined in a configuration file (SEPTIC setup) that is read by MySQL whenever it is started or restarted. A typical routine consists in setting the first switch to training mode and the other two to *on*, starting the DBMS and the web server, running the *septic_training* module, modifying the first switch to prevention or detection mode, and restarting the DBMS and the application server.

4.2 Inserting identifiers in Zend

In Section 3.3 we discussed three kinds of IDs. We implemented the first kind – *SSLE-generated IDs* – for the PHP language, with the Zend engine as SSLE. As explained in that section, those IDs can be formed of pairs *file:line* separated by |, so the comments we consider in this section have the format `/* file:line | file:line | ... | file:line */`.

Table 2 shows the two Zend engine extensions to which we added a few lines of code to create and insert query IDs. Extensions are used in Zend to group related functions. The table shows also the new header file that we developed for the same purpose (SEPTIC identifier).

The identifiers have to be inserted when the DBMS is called, so we modified in Zend the 11 functions used for this purpose (e.g., `mysql_query`, `mysqli::real_query`). Specifically, the ID is inserted in these functions just before the line that passes the query to the DBMS. This involved modifying three files: `php_mysql.c`, `mysqli_api.c` and `mysqli_nonapi.c`.

When a PHP program is executed, Zend keeps in a stack data about every function call. This stack contains data about the functions called, such as function name, full pathname of the file and line of code where the function was called. This stack allows backtracking the query until a function that does not contain it as argument. This provides the places where the query has been composed and/or passed and allows obtaining query IDs in the format above.

4.3 Inserting identifiers in Spring / Java

We implemented the third kind of IDs explained in Section 3.3 – *IDs generated outside the DBMS and the SSLE* – in Spring / Java. Spring is a framework aimed at simplifying the implementation of enterprise applications in the Java programming language [1]. It allows building Java web applications using the Model-View-Controller (MVC) model. In Spring applications connect to the DBMS via a JDBC driver.

We used three different forms to insert the IDs to show that there are different ways of doing it. The first form consists in inserting the ID directly in the query in the source code of the application. Before the query is issued a comment with the ID is inserted. This is a very simple solution that has the inconvenient of requiring modifications to the source code. The second form uses a *wrapper* to catch the query request before it is sent to JDBC and MySQL, and insert the ID in a comment prefixing the query (e.g., the file and line data). Using a wrapper avoids the need to modify the source code of the application, except for the substitution of the calls to JDBC by calls to the wrapper.

The third form is the most interesting as it does not involve modifications to the application source code. We used *Spring AOP*, an implementation of Aspect-Oriented Programming for Spring, essentially to create a wrapper without modifying the applications' source code [32]. Spring AOP allows the programmer to create *aspects* for the application. These aspects allow intercepting method calls from the application, to insert code that is executed before the methods. These operations are performed without the programmer making changes to the application source code. On the contrary, the programmer develops new files with the *aspects* and their *point cuts*, where the point cuts are the application methods that will be intercepted. We used aspects for intercepting in runtime calls to JDBC, inserting the query ID in the query and proceeding with the query request to MySQL.

5. EXPERIMENTAL EVALUATION

The objective of the experimental evaluation was to answer the following questions: (1) Is SEPTIC able to detect and block attacks against code samples? (2) Is it more efficient than other tools in the literature? (3) Does it solve the semantic mismatch problem better than other tools? (4) How does it perform in terms of false positives and false negatives? (5) Is SEPTIC able to detect and block attacks against real (open source) software? (6) Is the performance overhead acceptable? The evaluation was carried out with the implementation of SEPTIC in MySQL and PHP/Zend.

5.1 Attack detection

This section presents the evaluation of SEPTIC in terms of its ability to detect attacks – questions (1) to (5).

5.1.1 Detection with code samples

To answer questions (1) to (4), we evaluated SEPTIC with: (1) a set of (small) code samples that perform attacks of all classes in Table 1 (17 for the semantic mismatch problem, 7 for other SQLI attacks, 5 for stored injection); (2) 23 code samples from the *sqlmap* project [33], unrelated

Case		Attack/code
1	SELECT balance FROM acct WHERE password='' OR 1=1 -- '	Yes
2	SELECT balance FROM acct WHERE pin= exit()	Yes
3	...WHERE flag=1000>GLOBAL	Yes
4	SELECT * FROM properties WHERE filename='f.e'	No
5	...pin=exit()	Yes
6	...pin=aaaa()	Yes
7	SELECT * FROM t WHERE flag=TRUE	No
8	...pin=aaaa()	Yes
9	SELECT * FROM t WHERE password=password	Yes
10	CREATE TABLE t (name CHAR(40))	No
11	SELECT * FROM t WHERE name='x'	No

Table 3: Code (attacks) and non-code (non-attacks) cases defined by Ray and Ligatti [27]. Although these authors consider case 10 code/attack we disagree because the input is an integer, which is the type expected by the *char* function.

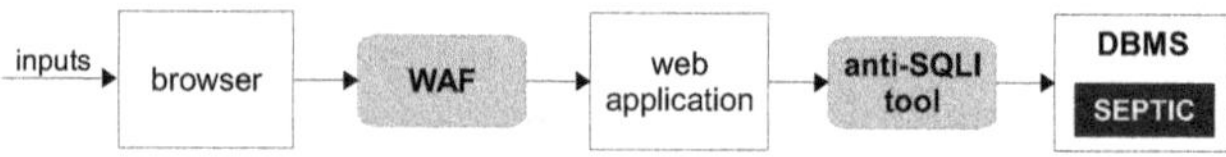

Figure 5: Placement of the protections considered in the experimental evaluation: SEPTIC, anti-SQLI tools, and WAF.

with semantic mismatch; (3) 11 samples with the code and non-code injection cases defined in [27] (Table 3).

We compare SEPTIC with a WAF and four anti-SQLI tools. Fig. 5 shows the place where the WAF and the anti-SQLI tools act and intercept, respectively, the user inputs sent in HTTP requests and the query sent by the web application. SEPTIC acts inside the DBMS. The WAF, ModSecurity 2.7.3.3 [35], was configured with the OWASP Core Rule Set 2.2.9. ModSecurity is the most adopted WAF worldwide, with a stable rule set developed by experienced security administrators. In fact, it has been argued that its ability to detect attacks is hard to exceed [23]. It detects SQLI and other types of attacks by inspecting HTTP requests. The anti-SQLI tools used were: CANDID [3], AMNESIA [13], DIGLOSSIA [31] and SQLrand [6]. The evaluation of these tools was made manually by analyzing the data in [27] and the papers that describe them. More information about them can be found in Section 6.

In the experiments, first with SEPTIC turned *off* we injected malicious user inputs created manually in the code samples to confirm the presence of the vulnerabilities. We also used the *sqlmap* tool to exploit the vulnerabilities from the first two groups of code samples. *sqlmap* is a tool widely used to perform SQLI attacks, both by security professionals and hackers. Second, with SEPTIC turned *on* and in training mode we injected benign inputs in the code samples for the mechanism to learn the queries and to get their models. Then, we run the same attacks from the first phase in detection mode and analyzed the results to determine if they were detected.

Table 4 shows the results of the evaluation. There were 63 tests executed (third column), 4 of which not attacks (the 4 non-attack cases in Table 3). SEPTIC (last column) correctly detected all 59 attacks (row 34) and correctly did not flag as attacks the 4 non-attack cases defined by Ray and Ligatti (row 11). SEPTIC had neither false negatives nor positives (rows 35–36) and correctly handled the semantic mismatch problem by detecting all attacks from classes A (rows 17–21), B (7), C (8–9), and D.2–D.4 (26–30).

The other tools can also detect the syntax structure 1st order (row 3), blind SQLI syntax structure (8), and sqlmap (12) attacks, all from class S.1, but not stored procedure (7) and stored injection attacks (26–30). The anti-SQLI tools, from the semantic mismatch attacks detected only the attack from class A.5 (row 21). ModSecurity detected this attack plus 1st order SQLI attacks with encoding and space evasion (A.1 and A.4, rows 17 and 19). Furthermore, ModSecurity cannot detect 2nd order SQLI attacks, because in the second step of these attacks the malicious input comes from the DBMS, not from outside. All tools other than SEPTIC had a few false positives (except DIGLOSSIA) and many false negatives (around 50% of the attacks). This is essentially justified by the non-detection of semantic mismatch attacks and the Ray and Ligatti code cases (row 10) where the injected code does not contain malicious characters recognized by the tools.

Globally ModSecurity and DIGLOSSIA had a similar performance (35 attacks detected). The latter was the best of the four anti-SQLI tools and the only one that detected the syntax mimicry 1st order attack (row 5). ModSecurity does not detect 2nd order attacks, because it just analyses queries reached by user inputs (rows 18 and 20). On the contrary, SQLrand and AMNESIA detect this type of attack. CANDID does not detect either of them. The false positive reported for ModSecurity was case 11 from [27], as the input contained the prime character that is considered malicious by this WAF.

The answer to the first four questions is positive. We conclude that the proposed approach to detected and block injection attacks inside the DBMS is effective because it uses the information given by the DBMS – that processes the queries – without the need of assumptions about how the queries are executed, which is the root of the semantic mismatch problem.

5.1.2 Detection with real software

We used SEPTIC with real web applications to verify if it detects attacks against them – question (5). We evaluated it with five open source PHP web applications: *ZeroCMS*, a content management system [39]; *WebChess*, an application to play chess online [36]; *measureit*, an energy metering application that stores and visualizes voltage and temperature data [21]; *PHP Address Book*, a web-based address/phone book [25]; and *refbase*, a web reference database [28].

Table 5 shows the detection results. The *ZeroCMS* version used contains three SQLI vulnerabilities that appeared in the Common Vulnerabilities and Exposures (CVE) [10] and the Open Source Vulnerability Database (OSVDB) [24]: CVE-2014-4194, CVE-2014-4034 and OSVDB ID 108025. Using *sqlmap*, we performed SQLI attacks to exploit these vulnerabilities and to verify if SEPTIC detected them. SEPTIC successfully detected the attacks and blocked them, protecting the vulnerable web application. Also, we performed attacks against a patched version of *ZeroCMS* and verified that the attacks were no longer successful or detected by SEPTIC.

With *WebChess* and *measureit*, we performed attacks manually and with *sqlmap*. SEPTIC blocked 13 different attacks against *WebChess* and one stored XSS against *measureit*. To confirm the detection, we repeated the attacks with SEPTIC in detection mode (instead of prevention mode), allowing attack detection but without blocking them, and we verified their impact. Also, we confirmed the vulnerabilities explored by these attacks by inspecting the source code with the assistance of identifiers registered in the log file. We recall that our approach detects in runtime attacks and registers

1	Type of attack	N. Tests	SQLrand	AMNESIA	CANDID	DIGLOSSIA	ModSecurity	SEPTIC
2	**SQLI without sanitization and semantic mismatch (S.1, S.2, B, C, D.1)**							
3	Syntax structure 1st order	1	Yes	Yes	Yes	Yes	Yes	Yes
4	Syntax structure 2nd order	1	Yes	Yes	No	No	No	Yes
5	Syntax mimicry 1st order	1	No	No	No	Yes	Yes	Yes
6	Syntax mimicry 2nd order	1	No	No	No	No	No	Yes
7	Stored procedure	1	No	No	No	No	No	Yes
8	Blind SQLI syntax structure	1	Yes	Yes	Yes	Yes	Yes	Yes
9	Blind SQLI syntax mimicry	1	No	No	No	Yes	Yes	Yes
10	Ray & Ligatti code	7	2	3	3	7	2	7
11	Ray & Ligatti non-code	4 (non-attacks)	2	1	2	0	1	0
12	sqlmap project	23	23	23	23	23	23	23
13	Flagged as attack	–	30	30	30	34	30	37
14	False positives	–	2	1	2	0	1	0
15	False negatives	–	9	8	9	3	8	0
16	**SQLI with sanitization and semantic mismatch (S.1, S.2, A.1–A.5, D.1)**							
17	Syntax structure 1st order	4	0	0	0	0	2	4
18	Syntax structure 2nd order	4	0	0	0	0	0	4
19	Syntax mimicry 1st order	4	0	0	0	0	2	4
20	Syntax mimicry 2nd order	4	0	0	0	0	0	4
21	Numeric fields	1	1	1	1	1	1	1
22	Flagged as attack	–	1	1	1	1	5	17
23	False positives	–	0	0	0	0	0	0
24	False negatives	–	16	16	16	16	12	0
25	**Stored injection (D.2–D.4)**							
26	Stored XSS	1	No	No	No	No	No	Yes
27	RFI	1	No	No	No	No	No	Yes
28	LFI	1	No	No	No	No	No	Yes
29	RCI	1	No	No	No	No	No	Yes
30	OSCI	1	No	No	No	No	No	Yes
31	Flagged as attack	–	0	0	0	0	0	5
32	False positives	–	0	0	0	0	0	0
33	False negatives	–	5	5	5	5	5	0
34	**Flagged as attack**	–	31	31	31	35	35	59
35	**False positives**	–	2	1	2	0	1	0
36	**False negatives**	–	30	29	30	24	25	0

Table 4: Detection of attacks with code samples.

Application	SQLI	Stored inj.	Registered
measureit	–	1	–
PHP Address Book	–	–	–
refbase	–	–	–
WebChess	13	–	–
ZeroCMS	3	–	CVE-2014-4194 CVE-2014-4034 OSVDB ID 108025
Total	16	1	3

Table 5: Detection of attacks in real applications.

the source code location of the vulnerabilities explored by attacks when they are detected. SEPTIC does not registered any attack against the *PHP Address Book* and *refbase* applications, meaning that these applications are secure against attacks injection. So these results allow us to answer affirmatively to question (5).

5.2 Performance overhead

To answer question (6), the performance overhead of SEPTIC was evaluated using BenchLab v2.2 [8] with the *PHP Address Book*, *refbase* and *ZeroCMS* applications. BenchLab is a testbed for web application benchmarking. It generates realistic workloads, then replays their traces using real web browsers, while measuring the application performance.

We have set up a network composed of six identical machines: Intel Pentium 4 CPU 2.8 GHz (1-core and 1-thread) with 2 GB of RAM, running Linux Ubuntu 14.04. Two machines played the role of servers: one run the MySQL DBMS with SEPTIC; the other an Apache web server with Zend to run the web applications, and Apache Tomcat to run the BenchLab server. The other four machines were used as client machines, running BenchLab clients and Firefox web browsers to replay workloads previously stored by the BenchLab server, i.e., to issue a sequence of requests to the web application being benchmarked. The BenchLab server has te role of managing the experiments.

We evaluated SEPTIC with its four combinations of protections turned on and off (SQLI and stored injection on/off) and compared them with the original MySQL without SEPTIC installed (base). For that purpose, we created several scenarios, varying the number of client machines and browsers. The *ZeroCMS* trace was composed of 26 requests to the web application with queries of several types (`SELECT`, `UPDATE`, `INSERT` and `DELETE`). The traces for the other applications were similar but for *PHP Address Book* the trace had 12 requests, while for *refbase* it had 14 requests. All traces involved downloading images, cascading style sheets documents, and other web objects. Each browser executes the traces in a loop many times.

Table 6 summarizes the performance measurements. The main metric assessed was the *latency*, i.e., the time elapsed between the browser starts sending a request and finishes receiving the corresponding reply. For each configuration the table shows the *average latency* and the *average latency overhead* (i.e., the average latency divided by the latency obtained with MySQL without SEPTIC with the same configuration, multiplied by 100 to become percentage). These values are presented as a pair *(latency (ms), overhead (%))* and are shown in the 2nd to 6th columns of the table. The 1st column characterizes the scenario tested, varying the number of client machines (*PCs*) and browsers (*brws*). The latency obtained with MySQL without SEPTIC is shown in the 2nd column and the SEPTIC combinations in the next four. The last two columns show the number of times that each configuration was tested with a trace (*num exps*) and the total number of requests done in these executions (*total reqs*). Each configuration was tested with 5500 trace executions, in a total of 87,200 requests (last row of the table).

The first set of experiments evaluated the overhead of SEPTIC with the *refbase* application (rows 3–6). We run a single Firefox browser in each client machine but varied the number of these machines from 1 to 4. For each additional machine we increase the number of experiments (*num exps*) by 50. Fig. 6 represents graphically these results, showing the latency measurements (a) and the latency overhead of the different SEPTIC configurations (b). The most interesting conclusion taken from the figure is that the overhead of running SEPTIC is very low, always below 2%. Another in-

N. PCs & brws	Base	SEPTIC: SQL injection – stored injection				Num exps	Total reqs
		off–off	on–off	off–on	on–on		
refbase **varying the number of PCs, one browser per PC**							
1 PC	430, –	431, 0.23	432, 0.47	433, 0.70	434, 0.93	70	980
2 PCs	430, –	433, 0.70	433, 0.70	433, 0.70	436, 1.40	120	1680
3 PCs	435, –	437, 0.46	440, 1.15	441, 1.38	442, 1.61	170	2380
4 PCs	435, –	438, 0.69	439, 0.92	442, 1.61	443, 1.84	220	3080
refbase **with four PCs and varying the number of browsers**							
8 brws	504, –	506, 0.40	510, 1.19	513, 1.79	516, 2.38	420	5880
12 brws	530, –	532, 0.38	535, 0.94	539, 1.70	544, 2.64	620	8680
16 brws	540, –	541, 0.19	545, 0.93	550, 1.85	553, 2.41	820	11480
20 brws	570, –	573, 0.53	575, 0.88	581, 1.93	584, 2.46	1020	14280
PHP Address Book **with four PCs**							
20 brws	79, –	79.26, 0.33	79.50, 0.63	80.60, 2.03	81, 2.53	1020	12240
ZeroCMS **with four PCs**							
20 brws	239, –	240, 0.42	241, 0.84	243, 1.67	245, 2.51	1020	26520
Avg. overhead / Total		*0.41%*	*0.82%*	*1.65%*	*2.24%*	5500	87200

Table 6: Performance overhead of SEPTIC measured with Benchlab for three web applications: *PHP Address Book*, *refbase* and *ZeroCMS*. Latencies in ms, overheads in %.

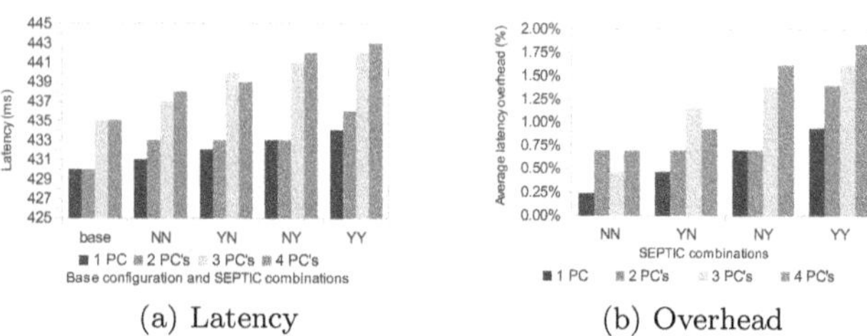

(a) Latency (b) Overhead

Figure 6: Latency and overhead with *refbase* varying the number of PCs, each one with a single browser.

teresting conclusion is that SQLI detection has less overhead than stored injection detection, as the values for configuration NY are just slightly higher than those for YN. Finally, the overhead tends to increase with the number of PCs and browsers generating traffic as the load increases.

The second set of experiments were again with *refbase*, this time with the number of client machines (PCs) set to 4 and varying the number of browsers (Table 6, rows 8–11). Fig. 7 shows how the overhead varies when going from 1 to 4 PCs with one browser each (a) then from 8 browsers (2 per PC) to 20 browsers (5 per PC). The figure allows extracting some of the same conclusions as the first set of experiments. However, they also show that increasing the number of browsers initially increases the overhead (Fig. 7(a)), then stabilizes (b), as neither the CPU at the PCs nor the bandwidth of the network were the performance bottleneck.

The third and fourth sets of experiments used the *PHP Address Book* and *ZeroCMS* web applications and 20 browsers in 4 PCs (Table 6, rows 13 and 15). Fig. 8 shows the overhead of these two applications and *refbase* with the same number of browsers and PCs. The overhead of all applications is similar for each SEPTIC configuration. This is interesting because the applications and their traces have quite different characteristics, which suggests that the over-

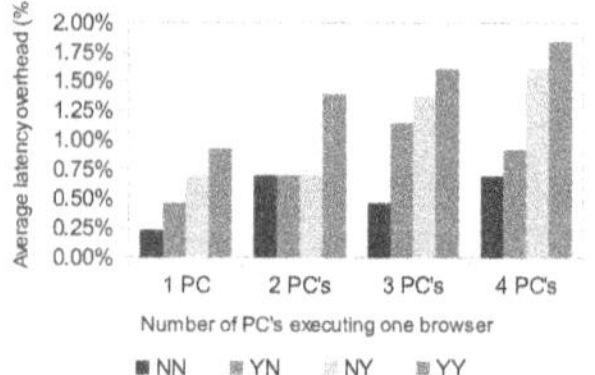

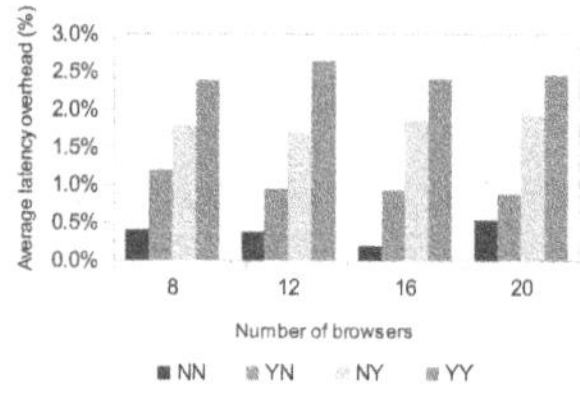

(a) Overhead (1 browser per PC) (b) Overhead (varying browsers)

Figure 7: Overhead with *refbase* with 4 PCs and varying the number browsers.

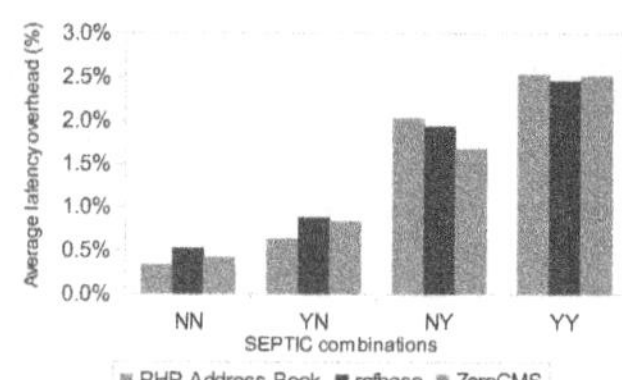

Figure 8: Overhead of SEPTIC with *PHP Address Book*, *refbase* and *ZeroCMS* applications using 20 browsers.

head imposed by SEPTIC is independent of the server-side language and web application.

The average of the overheads varied between 0.82% and 2.24% (last row of the table). This seems to be a reasonable overhead, suggesting that SEPTIC is usable in real settings, answering positively question (6).

6. RELATED WORK

There is a vast corpus of research in web application security, so we survey only related runtime protection mechanisms, which is the category in which SEPTIC fits.

All the works we describe have a point in common that makes them quite different from our work: their focus is on *how to do detection or protection*. On the contrary, our work is more concerned with an architectural problem: *how to do detection/protection inside the DBMS*, so that it runs out of the box when the DBMS is started. None of the related works does detection inside the DBMS.

AMNESIA [13] and CANDID [3] are two of the first works about detecting SQLI by comparing the structure of an SQL query before and after the inclusion of inputs and before the DBMS processes the queries. Both use query models to represent the queries and do detection. AMNESIA creates models by analyzing the source code of the application and extracting the query structure. Then, AMNESIA instruments the source code with calls to a wrapper that compares queries with models and blocks attacks. CANDID also analyses the source code of the application to find database queries, then simulates their execution with benign strings to create the models. On the contrary, SEPTIC does not involve source code analysis or instrumentation. With SEPTIC we aim to make the DBMS protect itself, so both model creation and attack detection are performed inside the DBMS. Moreover, SEPTIC aims to handle the semantic mismatch problem, so it analyses queries just before they are executed, whereas AMNESIA and CANDID do it much earlier. These two tools also cannot detect attacks that do not change the structure of the query (syntax mimicry).

Buehrer et al. [7] present a similar scheme that manages to detect mimicry attacks by enriching the models (parse trees) with comment tokens. However, their scheme cannot deal with most attacks related with the semantic mismatch problem. SqlCheck [34] is another scheme that compares parse trees to detect attacks. SqlCheck detects some of the attacks related with semantic mismatch, but not those involving encoding and evasion. Again, both these mechanisms involve modifying the application code, unlike SEPTIC.

DIGLOSSIA [31] is a technique to detect SQLI attacks that was implemented as an extension of the PHP interpreter. The technique first obtains the query models by mapping all query statements' characters to shadow characters except user inputs, and computes shadow values for all string user inputs. Second, for a query execution it computes the query and verifies if the root nodes from the two parsed trees are equal. Like SEPTIC, DIGLOSSIA detects syntax structure and mimicry attacks but, unlike SEPTIC, it neither detects second-order SQLI once it only computes queries with user inputs, nor encoding and evasion space characters attacks as these attacks do not alter the parse tree root nodes before the malicious user inputs are processed by the DBMS. Although better than AMNESIA and CANDID, it does not deal with all semantic mismatch problems.

Recently, Masri et al. [20] and Ahuja et al. [2] presented two works about prevention of SQLI attacks. The first presents a tool called SQLPIL that simply transforms SQL queries created as strings into prepared statements, preventing SQLI in the source-code. The second, presents three new approaches to detect and prevent SQLI attacks based on rewriting queries, encoding queries and adding assertions to the code. However, these approaches are not even evaluated experimentally. Again, both works involve instrumenting and modifying the application code, unlike SEPTIC that works inside the DBMS.

Dynamic taint analysis tracks the flow of user inputs in the application and verifies it they reach dangerous instructions. Xu et al. [38] show how this technique can be used to detect SQLI and reflected XSS. They annotate the arguments from source functions and sensitive sinks as untrusted and instrument the source code to track the user inputs to verify if they reach the untrusted arguments of sensitive sinks (e.g., functions that send queries to the database). A different but related idea is implemented by CSSE that protects PHP applications from SQLI, XSS and OSCI by modifying the platform to distinguish between what is part of the program and what is external (input), defining checks to be performed to the latter [26] (e.g., if the query structure becomes different due to inputs). WASP does something similar to block SQLI attacks [14]. SEPTIC does not track inputs in the application, but runs in the DBMS.

7. CONCLUSION

The paper explores a new form of protection from attacks against web application databases. It presents the idea of "hacking" the DBMSs to let it protected from SQLI and stored injection attacks. Moreover, by putting protection inside the DBMS, we show that it is possible to detect and block sophisticated attacks, including those related with the semantic mismatch problem. The mechanism was experimented both with synthetic code with vulnerabilities inserted on purpose and with open source PHP web applications. This evaluation suggests that the mechanism can detect and block the attacks it is programmed to handle, performing better that all other tools in the literature and the WAF most used in practice. The performance overhead evaluation shows an impact of around 2.2%, suggesting that our approach can be used in real systems.

Acknowledgments

We thank the anonymous reviewers and our shepherd Anna Squicciarini for their valuable comments. This work was partially supported by the EC through project FP7-607109 (SEGRID), and by national funds through Fundação para a Ciência e a Tecnologia (FCT) with references UID/CEC/50021/2013 (INESC-ID) and UID/CEC/00408/2013 (LaSIGE).

8. REFERENCES

[1] Spring framework, 2014. http://spring.io/.

[2] B. Ahuja, A. Jana, A. Swarnkar, and R. Halder. On preventing SQL injection attacks. *Advanced Computing and Systems for Security*, 395:49–64, 2015.

[3] S. Bandhakavi, P. Bisht, P. Madhusudan, and V. N. Venkatakrishnan. CANDID: preventing SQL injection attacks using dynamic candidate evaluations. In *Proceedings of the 14th ACM Conference on Computer and Communications Security*, pages 12–24, Oct. 2007.

[4] BBC Technology. Millions of websites hit by Drupal hack attack, Oct. 2014. http://www.bbc.com/news/technology-29846539.

[5] T. Berners-Lee, R. Fielding, and L. Masinter. Uniform resource identifier (URI): Generic syntax. IETF Request for Comments: RFC 3986, Jan. 2005.

[6] S. W. Boyd and A. D. Keromytis. SQLrand: Preventing SQL injection attacks. In *Proceedings of the 2nd Applied Cryptography and Network Security Conference*, pages 292–302, 2004.

[7] G. T. Buehrer, B. W. Weide, and P. Sivilotti. Using parse tree validation to prevent SQL injection attacks. In *Proceedings of the 5th International Workshop on Software Engineering and Middleware*, pages 106–113, Sept. 2005.

[8] E. Cecchet, V. Udayabhanu, T. Wood, and P. Shenoy. Benchlab: An open testbed for realistic benchmarking of web applications. In *Proceedings of the 2nd USENIX Conference on Web Application Development*, 2011.

[9] J. Clarke. *SQL Injection Attacks and Defense.* Syngress, 2009.

[10] CVE. http://cve.mitre.org.

[11] A. Douglen. SQL smuggling or, the attack that wasn't there. Technical report, COMSEC Consulting, Information Security, 2007.

[12] M. Dowd, J. Mcdonald, and J. Schuh. *Art of Software Security Assessment.* Pearson Professional Education, 2006.

[13] W. Halfond and A. Orso. AMNESIA: analysis and monitoring for neutralizing SQL-injection attacks. In *Proceedings of the 20th IEEE/ACM International Conference on Automated Software Engineering*, pages 174–183, Nov. 2005.

[14] W. Halfond, A. Orso, and P. Manolios. WASP: protecting web applications using positive tainting and syntax-aware evaluation. *IEEE Transactions on Software Engineering*, 34(1):65–81, 2008.

[15] M. Howard and D. LeBlanc. *Writing Secure Code for Windows Vista.* Microsoft Press, 1st edition, 2007.

[16] ICS-CERT. Incident response/vulnerability coordination in 2014. ICS-CERT Monitor, Set.-Feb. 2015.

[17] Imperva. Hacker intelligence initiative, monthly trend report #8. Apr. 2012.

[18] JSoup. http://jsoup.org.

[19] M. Koschany. Debian hardening, 2013. https://wiki.debian.org/ Hardening.

[20] W. Masri and S. Sleiman. SQLPIL: SQL injection prevention by input labeling. *Security and Communication Networks*, 8(15):2545–2560, 2015.

[21] Measureit. https://code.google.com/p/measureit/.

[22] I. Medeiros, N. F. Neves, and M. Correia. Automatic detection and correction of web application vulnerabilities using data mining to predict false positives. In *Proceedings of the International World Wide Web Conference*, pages 63–74, Apr. 2014.

[23] G. Modelo-Howard, C. Gutierrezand, F. Arshad, S. Bagchi, and Y. Qi. Psigene: Webcrawling to generalize SQL injection signatures. In *Proceedings of the 44th IEEE/IFIP International Conference on Dependable Systems and Networks*, June 2014.

[24] OSVDB. http://osvdb.org.

[25] PHP Address Book. http://php-addressbook.sourceforge.net.

[26] T. Pietraszek and C. V. Berghe. Defending against injection attacks through context-sensitive string evaluation. In *Proceedings of the 8th International Conference on Recent Advances in Intrusion Detection*, pages 124–145, 2005.

[27] D. Ray and J. Ligatti. Defining code-injection attacks. In *Proceedings of the 39th Annual ACM SIGPLAN-SIGACT Symposium on Principles of Programming Languages*, pages 179–190, 2012.

[28] refbase. http://http://www.refbase.net.

[29] Search Security TechTarget. Wordpress vulnerable to stored XSS, Apr. 2015. http://searchsecurity.techtarget.com/news/4500245137/WordPress-vulnerable-to-stored-XSS-researchers-find.

[30] SolidIT. DB-Engines Ranking. http://db-engines.com/en/ranking, accessed Aug. 10th, 2015.

[31] S. Son, K. S. McKinley, and V. Shmatikov. Diglossia: detecting code injection attacks with precision and efficiency. In *Proceedings of the 20th ACM Conference on Computer and Communications Security*, pages 1181–1192, 2013.

[32] Spring. http://docs.spring.io/spring/docs/2.5.4/reference/aop.html.

[33] sqlmap. https://github.com/sqlmapproject/testenv/tree/master/mysql.

[34] Z. Su and G. Wassermann. The essence of command injection attacks in web applications. In *Proceedings of the 33rd ACM SIGPLAN-SIGACT Symposium on Principles of Programming Languages*, pages 372–382, Jan. 2006.

[35] Trustwave SpiderLabs. ModSecurity Open Source Web Application Firewall. http://www.modsecurity.org.

[36] WebChess. http://sourceforge.net/projects/webchess/.

[37] J. Williams and D. Wichers. OWASP Top 10: The ten most critical web application security risks. Technical report, OWASP Foundation, 2013.

[38] W. Xu, S. Bhatkar, and R. Sekar. Practical dynamic taint analysis for countering input validation attacks on web applications. Technical Report SECLAB-05-04, Department of Computer Science, Stony Brook University, 2005.

[39] ZeroCMS. Content management system built using PHP and MySQL. http://www.aas9.in/zerocms/.

JSLINQ: Building Secure Applications across Tiers

Musard Balliu
Chalmers

Benjamin Liebe
Chalmers

Daniel Schoepe
Chalmers

Andrei Sabelfeld
Chalmers

ABSTRACT

Modern web and mobile applications are complex entities amalgamating different languages, components, and platforms. The rich features span the application tiers and components, some from third parties, and require substantial efforts to ensure that the insecurity of a single component does not render the entire system insecure. As of today, the majority of the known approaches fall short of ensuring security across tiers.

This paper proposes a framework for end-to-end security, by tracking information flow through the client, server, and underlying database. The framework utilizes homogeneous meta-programming to provide a uniform language for programming different components. We leverage .NET meta-programming capabilities from the F# language, thus enabling language-integrated queries on databases and interoperable heterogeneous execution on the client and the server. We develop a core of our security enforcement in the form of a security type system for a functional language with mutable store and prove it sound. Based on the core, we develop JSLINQ, an extension of the WebSharper library to track information flow. We demonstrate the capabilities of JSLINQ on the case studies of a password meter, two location-based services, a movie rental database, an online Battleship game, and a friend finder app. Our experiments indicate that JSLINQ is practical for implementing high-assurance web and mobile applications.

1. INTRODUCTION

There is no such thing as a free lunch - building secure and robust web applications is a complex and error prone task. A recurrent fact attested by investigations from security organizations and communities of security experts [8, 4], and very frequently reported by the media [9, 7], is that vulnerabilities in web and mobile applications dominate the classifications of the most dangerous security attacks. The reason can be attributed to different factors, including the myriad of programming languages, technologies and platforms which are used to build modern applications. This process requires substantial efforts and skills on the programmer's side for getting the application logic right, let alone secure and reliable. In this paper, we set out to study the challenge of heterogeneity and provide practical solutions with formal evidence, that help a programmer to build web and mobile applications in a secure manner. In particular, we focus on vulnerabilities that go beyond injection attacks and affect the business logic of the entire web application.

CODASPY'16, March 09 - 11, 2016, New Orleans, LA, USA

ISBN 978-1-4503-3935-3/16/03... $15.00

DOI: http://dx.doi.org/10.1145/2857705.2857717

A closer look at a typical web architecture shows that web applications are often distributed over several tiers: (a) a client tier, where most of the UI logic runs in a web browser as JavaScript and HTML including third-party libraries; (b) a server tier, where the bulk of the application logic is executed in a language like F#, Java or other; (c) and a database tier that serves as persistent store and executes e.g. SQL code. Common security attacks rely on the fact that applications are implemented in different languages that span tiers with different trust relationships. As a result, many security policies are application-specific and tightly connected to the application logic and the trust relationships between the involved parties.

Motivating Scenarios: The following scenarios illustrate the need for cross-tier security analysis and policies.

Password Meter: The first scenario considers a client-side password meter, which is a program used to estimate the strength of passwords provided by users. It is important that the chosen password is not leaked to an application server or other third parties. A reasonable security policy treats the password field as sensitive, and the third-party and the RPC functions used to communicate with the application as public, while enforcing that no sensitive information flows to the public destinations.

Location-based Service: The second scenario is a location-based service, which uses location information to query a web service for the list of nearby points of interest, and a third-party map library to display these points. However, users concerned about privacy may not want to reveal the exact coordinates of their location. A reasonable security policy allows for a declassification function to obfuscate the real location, and only send approximate coordinates to the location server. Moreover, the map library should only be used to display the points of interest and not to, for instance, leak the browser's cookie to the library provider.

Friend Finder App: The third scenario is a mobile app. The user wants to know if a friend is using a certain app, say WhatsApp, without revealing the friend's phone number to the remote server in case they are not using that app. This can be avoided by using a hash function to hide the phone number before sending it to the database server, which in turn compares the hashed value to the list of its users' phone numbers and replies whether or not that user is using the app. A reasonable policy considers the phone address book as sensitive and ensures that only hashed values are sent to the untrusted application server for discovery.

These are all examples of how a security attack can occur across all three tiers of an application. Hence, a satisfactory security analysis needs to express and validate policies for applications that span client, server and database tiers.

Attacker Model: Different attacker models arise in multi-tier web applications. Sensitive or untrusted data may originate from any of the components, for instance it can be a user location from the client, a password from the database or an authentication key from the server. Consequently, any tier can be subject to unintentional or malicious information leaks toward another tier. The policies for the first two scenarios constrain the sensitive data of a trusted client wrt. an untrusted third-party library and a (partially) trusted server. The third scenario illustrates policies for a trusted client wrt. to a completely untrusted server. The client can also be untrusted. For example a trusted server, after authenticating a user, may read his personal data from a trusted database and send back a customized web page, however, no information about other users in the database should flow to the client. Meaningful combinations of tiers and attacker models will be discussed in Section 4. We do not address network attackers who intercept, alter or deny communication between tiers, while techniques like SSL can be used to prevent these types of attacks.

State of the Art: Information-flow control (IFC) tracks sensitive (untrusted) data throughout the computation ensuring that no illegal information flows from sensitive (untrusted) sources toward public (trusted) sinks. This provides end-to-end security guarantees as required in the scenarios above. In general, we mark sources and sinks with labels from a lattice of security levels that expresses the trust relationships between parties. E.g., horizontal privilege-escalation attacks can be prevented by assigning separate security labels for separate users. A large body of work has studied dynamic and static enforcement techniques for all levels of the hardware and software stack [22, 34], including web applications [26] and distributed systems [42]. The majority of these works tackles the problem of information flow for different components in isolation [38, 29, 23]. This is unsatisfactory because tracking information across tiers is necessary for end-to-end security. A few works, as discussed in Section 5, bridge IFC across components allowing for policies that regulate information flows for a web application as a whole. Noteworthy, recent frameworks integrate database queries into programming languages for client and server applications providing a uniform way to program an entire web application, including reasoning about security [18, 16, 15].

Contributions: In this paper we leverage homogeneous meta-programming to obtain a uniform language for reasoning about web and mobile application security across the client-server-database boundaries. The .NET facilities provide support for language-integrated queries on databases and interoperable heterogeneous execution for client and server applications, embedding them seamlessly in the F# language [40]. This allows to implement an entire web or mobile application as a simple F# program and then let the compiler split the code transparently for each tier. In this work we enrich a subset of the language with security types which allow to express security policies. We implement the security types by custom attributes as a separate F# module on top of existing fully-fledged development in F#, providing a complete separation between the program code and the security policy. We then execute the security type check as a separate verification step followed by the F# compilation and thus leaving the F# type system untouched. Finally, we split the program into three parts, producing JavaScript and HTML code to run on the browser, SQL code to run on the database and F# code to run on the server.

On the formal side (Section 2), we develop a model for a functional language with references (a subset of F#), quotations and antiquotations, and establish the soundness of the security type system. Our soundness proof extends and generalizes the proof technique introduced by Pottier and Simonet [30] with support for arbitrary data types and declassification policies. The query language is based on the one introduced by Cheney et al. [14] and uses quotation and normalization of quoted terms to model the semantics of the database language. For simplicity, our results assume a two-point security lattice for confidentiality, however, they apply to arbitrary lattices, including integrity, in a similar fashion.

On the practical side (Section 3), we have implemented JSLINQ, an extension of WebSharper [10] and LINQ [1] libraries with IFC. With JSLINQ, a developer can use a fully-fledged language such as F# for writing secure web and mobile applications. A security analyst is expected to know what sources and sinks are sensitive, which is a reasonable assumption so long as they are partially trusted. If the developer is malicious, one can leverage techniques from [27, 31] to automatically extract sources and sinks used by the application (this is out of scope in this work). The policy module requires to specify security signatures once and only for the APIs that are actually used, thus making it easier and less time-consuming for the programmer. Our experience shows that JSLINQ provides a good trade-off between annotation burden and security assurance for developers with some security background, while user studies with non-expert developers are subject to future work.

We demonstrate the capabilities of JSLINQ on several realistic case studies (Section 4), including the scenarios discussed above, a password meter and an online Battleship game. The case studies leave out user interfaces and other boilerplate code, and only focus on the security-critical parts of the applications to demonstrate the potential of our technique. Moreover, compositionality of the security type checking makes the approach scalable to arbitrary lines of code. The experiments show that JSLINQ is useful for building secure applications and it enjoys several advantages compared to existing tools (Section 5 and Table 2).

A precursor of our approach is SELINQ by Schoepe et al. [36]. SELINQ uses a security type system to enforce policies for server-database applications written in F#, as we do. Rather than enriching F# with security types, SELINQ implements a subset of the language presented in Section 2 and uses a compiler implemented in Haskell to type check and generate F# executable code. By contrast, JSLINQ closes the end-to-end loop by supporting client-side, including third-party code, for fully-fledged F# applications. A distinguishing feature of JSLINQ is that security type checking does not interfere with the normal development process. In practical terms, this translates to a big gain as the programmers can use a production-grade system to develop applications, yet leverage a security type system to verify the critical parts of the code. Moreover, practicality of JSLINQ is supported by several case studies and security policies. Declassification allows us to handle richer policies, e.g. only friends can view a user's profile data, while dynamic policies would require extending the type system with techniques from [43]. While both SELINQ and JSLINQ use the framework by Cheney et al. [14], JSLINQ significantly extends that formalism with mutable references and declassification using a different technique to show noninterference.

While our main focus is on multi-tier application-level attacks, JSLINQ inherits protection against XSS and SQL injection attacks from its components, respectively, from WebSharper and LINQ. Such attacks are impossible due to strong typing [32], similar to frameworks as GWT. For instance, an SQL injections are prevented by the use of LINQ, which leverages the underlying F# type system to strongly type all database queries.

The full details of the framework, including semantics and proofs, and the code for JSLINQ are available online [11].

2. FRAMEWORK

In this section we present the formal underpinnings of the framework. The client and the server components are written in the *host* language, while the database component is written in the *quoted* language. The framework consists of a functional language with mutable storage and support for product types, records, lists, quotations and antiquotations, the security type system, and shows that the type system enforces noninterference and declassification policies with respect to the operational semantics. The host and the quoted language represent a core of the F# language as implemented by JSLINQ.

2.1 Language

The language is presented in Figure 1. It includes the usual constructs of a functional language with references, extended with quotations and antiquotations to account for database queries. The syntax consists of security levels, types, and terms. $\overline{x}$ denotes a sequence of entities x.

$\ell ::= \mathtt{L} \mid \mathtt{H}$ (security types)

$b ::= \mathbf{bool}^\ell \mid \mathbf{int}^\ell \mid \mathbf{float}^\ell \mid \mathbf{string}^\ell$ (base types)

$t ::= b \mid \mathbf{unit} \mid t \xrightarrow{\ell} t \mid t\ \mathbf{ref}^\ell \mid t * t \mid \{\overline{f : t}\} \mid (t\ \mathbf{list})^\ell \mid \mathbf{Expr}\langle t \rangle$ (general types)

$T ::= (\{\overline{f : b}\})\ \mathbf{list}^\ell$ (database tables)

$\Gamma, \Delta, M ::= \cdot \mid \Gamma, x : t \mid \Delta, x : t \mid M, l : t$ (type environment)

$e ::= () \mid c \mid x \mid l \mid op(\overline{e}) \mid \mathbf{lift}\ e \mid \mathbf{fun}(x) \to e$ (terms)
$\mid \mathbf{rec}\ f(x) \to e \mid (e, e) \mid \mathbf{fst}\ e \mid \mathbf{snd}\ e \mid \{\overline{f = e}\} \mid e.f$
$\mid \mathbf{yield}\ e \mid [] \mid e \mathbin{@} e \mid \mathbf{for}\ x\ \mathbf{in}\ e\ \mathbf{do}\ e \mid \mathbf{exists}\ e$
$\mid \mathbf{if}\ e\ \mathbf{then}\ e\ \mathbf{else}\ e \mid \mathbf{if}\ e\ \mathbf{then}\ e \mid \mathbf{run}\ e \mid \texttt{<@}\ e\ \texttt{@>} \mid \texttt{(\%}\ e\ \texttt{)}$
$\mid \mathbf{database}(x) \mid \mathbf{ref}\ e \mid !e \mid e := e$

Figure 1: Syntax of language and types

We remark on some of the interesting constructs: c denotes built-in constants, such as booleans, integers, floats and strings. op denotes built-in operators, such as addition and logical connectives. **if** e_1 **then** e_2 **else** e_3 evaluates to e_2 if e_1 evaluates to **true** and to e_3 otherwise. The language includes mutable state. Terms **ref** e (reference creation), $!e$ (dereference) and $e := e$ (assignment) denote, respectively, allocating, dereferencing and updating memory locations. () denotes a value of type **unit**. Database queries are modelled by quoted expressions `<@` e `@>` of type $\mathbf{Expr}\langle t \rangle$. The language allows only closed quoted terms, since this simplifies the semantics of the language and is still able to express all the desired concepts. Quoted functions can be expressed by abstracting in the quoted term as opposed to abstracting on the level of the host language. `(%` e `)` denotes antiquotation of the expression e, and allows splicing of quoted expressions into quoted expressions in a type-safe way. **lift** e lifts an expression of type t to type $\mathbf{Expr}\langle t \rangle$. **for** x **in** e_1 **do** e_2 is used to express list comprehensions where x is bound successively to elements in e_1 when evaluating e_2. The results of evaluating e_2 for each element are then concatenated. **run** e denotes running a quoted expression e, which involves generating an SQL query based on the quoted term. $e_1 \mathbin{@} e_2$ denotes concatenation of e_1 and e_2. **exists** e evaluates to **true** if and only if the expression e does not evaluate to the empty list. This can be used to check if the result of a query is empty. **if** e_1 **then** e_2 evaluates to e_2 if e_1 evaluates to a non-empty list and to [] otherwise. **yield** e denotes a singleton list consisting of expression e.

Security type language: Security types are defined by annotating a standard type language for a functional fragment with quotations and references with security levels ℓ. The security levels are taken from the two-element lattice $\langle\{\mathtt{L},\mathtt{H}\}, \sqsubseteq\rangle$ consisting of a level L for low-confidentiality (dually high-integrity) information and a level H for high-confidentiality (dually low-integrity) information. The ordering relation requires that $\mathtt{L} \sqsubseteq \mathtt{H}$. The types are split into base types (b), which can occur as types of columns in tables (T), and general types (t) which include unit, functions, references, tuples, records, lists, and quoted expression types. Function types include a level ℓ, which is a lower bound on the level of locations that might be written to when the function is called. To avoid such leakages the function is only allowed to write to memory cells with security levels greater than ℓ. Reference types $t\ \mathbf{ref}^\ell$, besides the security level t of the value stored at the associated location, carry a level ℓ which represents the security level of the reference itself. This is because references are themselves first-class values and can hence be used to leak confidential information.

As is common, a database is a collection of tables. Each table consists of at least one named column, each of which equipped with a fixed security type. The security levels on types for database columns express the confidentiality of the data contained in that column. In particular, each database is given a type signature Σ to express security policies for databases. A type signature describes tables as lists of records. Each record field corresponds to a column in the sense that the field name matches the name of the column in the database. The security level of a column is specified by using a suitable type for the corresponding field in the record. The ordering of elements in a list is irrelevant.

Types are equipped with a subtyping relation $\sqsubseteq$, which is an extension of the lattice ordering relation. The subtyping relation is standard [30, 24], therefore we do not report it here. With a little abuse of notation, we use the subtyping relation to compare security annotations ℓ with types t. In particular, if the type carries a security annotation ℓ', we compare the security levels $\ell \sqsubseteq \ell'$. Otherwise, we need to open the type and look inside the type constructor as described in Figure 5 in the Appendix.

To illustrate the addition of security levels to the type system in the case of multi-tier applications, consider an example involving a database of people locations and friends, `LocationDB`. The locations are confidential, while the names are not, which leads to the following type for `LocationDB`.

```
LocationDB :
  { People :
    { Id : int^L; Name : string^L;
      Lon : float^H; Lat : float^H } list^L
  ; Friends :
    { Id1 : int^L ; Id2 : int^L } list^L
  }
```

Suppose John wants to know whether there are any friends within the range of 1km from his current location. We can query the database for the list of John's friends and later calculate the distance relative to John's location. This can be done by iterating once over all friends in the database to retrieve the list of John's friends and twice over all people in the database to retrieve the result information. After finding John's **Id** in the database, we check that whenever it occurs in the **Friends** table as **Id1**, the corresponding friend as **Id2** occurs in the People table as **Id**. In that case, the name, the latitude and the longitude of that friend is returned as part of the result.

```
let db = <@ database "LocationDB" @>
type ResultType={name:string^L; lon:float^H; lat:float^H}

let friendsLoc : Expr < ResultType list^L > =
  <@ for f in (% db).Friends do
     for p1 in (% db).People do
     for p2 in (% db).People do
     if (p1.Name = "John") &&  (p1.Id = f.Id1) &&
        (f.Id2 = p2.Id) then
     yield ({name = p2.Name; lon = p2.Lon; lat = p2.Lat})
  @>
```

The information flow policy for the program is specified by giving a type annotation to the quoted expression that generates the query, i.e., a type annotation for **friendsLoc**. In particular the **name** component of the result is public, while the location information is confidential as described by **ResultType**. This matches the policy specified for the database contents, i.e., **LocationDB**, in which the name of people are public while their locations are not. Changing the security annotation of the **name** field from public to confidential should result in a type error, since the security level of the **Name** field of the result is public. The example so far illustrates secure information flows from the database to the server for an attacker model where the server is untrusted.

The server uses the result of the database query to calculate the distance between John's location and his friends location, and then send to John the list of nearby friends. The function **dist** : $(float^{\ell} * float^{\ell}) * (float^{\ell} * float^{\ell}) \xrightarrow{\ell'} float^{\ell}$ is side-effect free and it computes the Euclidean distance between two points. The security annotations are parametric on the security levels of inputs and outputs.

```
let friendNames : float^L * float^L -> string^L list^L =
  <@ fun  publicLoc ->
     let res = run friendsLoc in
     for r in res do
     if dist((r.lon, r.lat), publicLoc) <= 1 then
     yield ({ name = r.name}) @>
```

The function **friendNames** takes as input a public location **publicLoc**, executes the query represented by the function **friendsLoc** on the database and returns a list of public names of nearby friends. Since the location information contained in the result of **friendsLoc** is confidential, there is an implicit flow from the location to the list of names. In fact, a public observer learns that the location of everyone in the returned list of names is within 1km from the location **publicLoc**. Therefore, the security type checking should fail. However, one may consider acceptable to leak the distance information as long as the exact location is protected. This can be achieved by *declassifying* the function **dist**, i.e., considering its result as public, although part of the input is confidential. At last, John can call the remote function **friendNames** on the client-side by providing his current location **locJohn**.

```
let locJohn : (float^L, float^L) = GetLocation()

let friends : string^L list^L = friendNames locJohn
```

The function is executed on the server-side and it interacts with the database to retrieve information as described above. Then the list of names of nearby friends is returned back to John on the client-side. The security type checker will ensure that there are no insecure information flows, except the allowed ones, from the database to the client.

2.2 Operational Semantics

The operational semantics of the language evaluates terms in the context of a mutable store μ and a database Ω. A partial mapping $\mu : Loc \rightarrow Val$ from locations to values models the semantics of memory effects. We write $\mu[l \mapsto v]$ for a store μ which maps location l to value v, otherwise agrees with μ. A *configuration* (e, μ) is a pair of a term e and a store μ. We write e when μ is empty. We denote evaluation of a configuration (e, μ) using database data in Ω to another configuration (e', μ') by $(e, \mu) \longrightarrow_{\Omega} (e', \mu')$. Ω is a function that maps database names to the actual content of the database it refers to, and δ is a function that maps operators to their corresponding semantics. Σ maps constants and databases to their respective types. We assume that Ω is consistent with the typing for databases given in Σ: for each database $\Omega(db)$ is assumed to be a value of type $\Sigma(db)$. Let $\longrightarrow_{\Omega}^{*}$ be the reflexive-transitive closure of $\longrightarrow_{\Omega}$. Evaluation and normalization of the quoted language is denoted by $eval_{\Omega}(norm(e))$. This evaluation generates database queries that can be translated to SQL and executed by actual database servers. For instance, higher-order features such as nested records or function applications need to be evaluated to obtain computations that can be expressed in SQL. The syntax of values and evaluation contexts can be defined both for the host language and the quoted language. The quoted language is purely functional and contains no recursion. The evaluation contexts ensure that the semantics is call-by-value with left-to-right evaluation of terms. Quotation contexts $\mathcal{Q}$ are used to ensure that there are no antiquotations left of the hole. The evaluation rules for the host language are standard. For instance, the rule $((\mathbf{fun}(x) \rightarrow e)\ v, \mu) \longrightarrow (e[x \mapsto v], \mu)$ defines function application. We denote the substitution of free occurrences of variable x in term e with another term e' by $e[x \mapsto e']$. The evaluation contexts entail sequentiality and let-binding between terms; we write $e_1; e_2$ for $(\mathbf{fun}(x) \rightarrow e_2)e_1$, where x is not free in e_2 and $\mathbf{let}\ x = e\ \mathbf{in}\ e'$ for $(\mathbf{fun}(x) \rightarrow e')\ e)$. Similarly, the evaluation rules for the query language follow Cheney et al. [14].

2.3 Security Condition

The security condition expresses the notion of noninterference for a functional language with references and databases. Noninterference is an information flow policy that formalizes computational independence between confidential and public information, guaranteeing that no information about the former can be inferred from the latter. More precisely, this is expressed as the preservation of an equivalence relation under pairwise execution; given two inputs that are equal in the components that are visible to an attacker, evaluation should result in two output values that also coincide in the components that can be observed by the attacker. Memory locations are not directly observable by the attacker, however their contents may affect the output returned by the computations and thus leak information. For example, the program **let** $l =$ **ref true**$^{\mathtt{H}}$ **in** $!l$ uses a public location l, which stores a confidential value **true**, to leak that value to an attacker through the dereference $!l$.

To establish the behavior of a secure program from the perspective of an attacker, we introduce the notion of low-equivalence denoted by $\sim$ that demands that parts of values with types that are annotated with L are equal, while placing no demands on the high counterparts. Low-equivalence is formalized as a family of equivalence relations $\sim_t$ on values parametrized by types. We omit the subscript on $\sim$ when the type is clear from the context and write $\sim$ for sequences of values. Built-in values c of base type b are compared using equality if the values are public. In the case of function types and quoted expressions, $\sim_t$ corresponds to noninterference for the bodies of the functions. Moreover, functions are related by $\sim_{t \xrightarrow{\ell} t'}$ if for all input values related by $\sim_t$ they evaluate to values related by $\sim_{t'}$ and the memory effects are upper bounded by the security level of the result $\ell \sqsubseteq t'$. Records are related by $\sim$ if they contain the same fields, and each field's contents are also related by $\sim$. Similarly, tuples are related by $\sim$ if the corresponding components are related by $\sim$. Two lists are required to have the same length if the list type is annotated with L, but their contents may differ based on the element type. Memory locations are compared using equality if the locations are public.

With this we are ready to define the top-level notion of security based on *noninterference* [20]. Since the family of low-equivalence relations is parametrized by types the definition is done with respect to the initial host type, the initial database type and the final result type.

Definition 1 ($NI(e_1, e_2)_{t,\Sigma,t'}$). *Two expressions e_1 and e_2 are noninterfering with respect to the host type t, the database type Σ and the final type t' if for all Ω_i, v_i, v_i' and μ_i such that $v_1 \sim_t v_2$, $\Omega_1 \sim_\Sigma \Omega_2$, and $e_i[x \mapsto v_i] \longrightarrow^*_{\Omega_i} (v_i', \mu_i)$ for $i \in \{1, 2\}$ it holds that $v_1' \sim_{t'} v_2'$.*

Given an open expression e, $NI(e, e)_{t,\Sigma,t'}$ should be read as e is secure with respect to the security policy expressed by t, Σ and t', i.e., no secret parts of host and the database as defined, respectively, by t and Σ is able to influence the public parts of the result value as defined by t'. Note that the definition can represent expressions with multiple inputs by using record values. Moreover, the noninterference policy is *termination-insensitive* [41, 34], namely it ignores leaks via the observation of (non)termination.

Declassification: Noninterference is overly restrictive for programs that leak confidential information in a controlled manner, as shown by the example in Section 2.1. To account for these cases, we extend the framework with support for declassification policies that regulate what information can be released by the program. The policies are expressed in terms of *escape hatches* from a set $\mathcal{D} = \{d_1, \cdots, d_k\}$ and correspond to the *What* dimension in [35]. Escape hatches were introduced to express a similar notion, called *delimited release*, for imperative languages [33]. The security condition is then refined to also take into account the equivalence between declassification expressions. This requires to extend the low-equivalence relations used for noninterference with declassification.

Definition 2 ($DNI(e_1, e_2)_{\mathcal{D},t,\Sigma,t'}$). *Two expressions e_1 and e_2 are noninterfering with respect to the declassification expressions $\mathcal{D}$, the host type t, the database type Σ and the final type t' if for all Ω_i, v_i, v_i' and μ_i such that $v_1 \sim_t v_2$, $\Omega_1 \sim_\Sigma \Omega_2$, $d_j[x \mapsto v_1] \sim_{t,\Sigma} d_j[x \mapsto v_2]$ and $e_i \longrightarrow^*_{\Omega_i} (v_i, \mu_i)$ for $i \in \{1, 2\}$ it holds that $v_1' \sim_{t'} v_2'$.*

2.4 Security Type System

The goal of the security type system is to enforce the notion of noninterference for a functional language with references and databases. Typing judgments are of the form $pc, \Gamma, M \vdash e : t$ where pc is the program counter level, Γ is a typing context mapping variables to types, M is a typing context mapping locations to types, e is an expression and t is a type. They denote that expression e has type t in context pc, Γ, M. We also write H for pc, Γ, M. Intuitively, the program counter level approximates the information that can be learned by observing that the program has reached a particular point during the execution and it is used to control implicit flows due to branching on high values. For uniformity, we write $pc, \Gamma, M \vdash v : t$ for typing judgments dealing with values, although pc is redundant given that values have no computational effects. $\ell \sqcup \ell'$ denotes the join of levels ℓ and ℓ', i.e., $\ell \sqcup \ell' = \mathtt{H}$ iff $\mathtt{H} \in \{\ell, \ell'\}$, and $\ell \sqcup \ell' = \mathtt{L}$ otherwise.

The typing rules for the quoted language are similar to those for the host language as reported in the Appendix. Typing judgments have the form $H, \Delta \vdash c : t$, where H is the typing context for the host language and Δ is the typing context for the quoted language. We present some of the typing rules for the host language and the quoted language in Figure 2 and report the remaining rules in the Appendix.

Most types contain a level ℓ that denotes whether the "structure" of the value is confidential. In the case of base types, this means that their values are confidential or not. In the case of $(t \textbf{ list})^\ell$, the level ℓ indicates whether the length of the list is confidential. If $\ell = \mathtt{H}$, the entire list is considered a secret, otherwise the length of the list may be disclosed to a public observer. However, the elements of the list may or may not be confidential depending on the level of the elements given by the type t. For types for quoted expressions, the security annotation is contained in the type t. Function types contain the usual input and output types together with a security level pc which represents a lower bound on the security level of locations that may be written when calling the function. In order to securely call the function in a context pc' it must be the case that $pc' \sqsubseteq pc$. The intuition is that, in the presence of side-effects, the function can disclose information via its result or via its side-effects. We assume that types for operators, constants, and databases are given by the mapping Σ. Moreover, we also assume that each query only uses a single database.

We now comment on a few typing rules. Rule VAR assigns a type to the variable by looking it up in the environment. FUN uses the program counter level appearing in the function type to check the function body. APPLY is used to check function application. The rule ensures that the side-effects pc' of the caller function are not visible in contexts for which the program counter level is pc, namely $pc \sqsubseteq pc'$. As a re-

$$\frac{x : t \in \Gamma}{pc, \Gamma, M \vdash x : t}\ \textsc{Var} \qquad \frac{pc, \Gamma, x : t, M \vdash e : t'}{pc', \Gamma, M \vdash \mathbf{fun}(x) \rightarrow e : (t \overset{pc}{\rightarrow} t')}\ \textsc{Fun} \qquad \frac{\Sigma(db) = \{\overline{f : t}\}}{H, \Delta \vdash \mathbf{database}(db) : \{\overline{f : t}\}}\ \textsc{DatabaseQ} \qquad \frac{H \vdash e : \mathbf{Expr}\langle t \rangle}{H, \Delta \vdash (\%\ e\ ) : t}\ \textsc{Antiquote}$$

$$\frac{pc, \Gamma, M \vdash e_1 : t \overset{pc'}{\rightarrow} t' \quad pc, \Gamma, M \vdash e_2 : t \quad pc \sqsubseteq pc'}{pc, \Gamma, M \vdash e_1\ e_2 : t'}\ \textsc{Apply} \qquad \frac{pc, \Gamma, M \vdash e : (t\ \mathbf{list})^{\ell} \quad pc, \Gamma, x : t, M \vdash e' : (t'\ \mathbf{list})^{\ell'}}{pc, \Gamma, M \vdash \mathbf{for}\ x\ \mathbf{in}\ e\ \mathbf{do}\ e' : (t'\ \mathbf{list})^{\ell \sqcup \ell'}}\ \textsc{For}$$

$$\frac{pc, \Gamma, M \vdash e : t\ \mathbf{ref}^{\ell} \quad \ell \sqsubseteq t}{pc, \Gamma, M \vdash !e : t}\ \textsc{Deref} \qquad \frac{pc, \Gamma, M, \cdot \vdash e : t}{pc, \Gamma, M \vdash \texttt{<@}\ e\ \texttt{@>} : \mathbf{Expr}\langle t \rangle}\ \textsc{Quote} \qquad \frac{t \sqsubseteq t' \quad pc, \Gamma, M \vdash e : t}{pc, \Gamma, M \vdash e : t'}\ \textsc{Sub}$$

$$\frac{pc, \Gamma, M \vdash e : \mathbf{Expr}\langle t \rangle}{pc, \Gamma, M \vdash \mathbf{run}\ e : t}\ \textsc{Run} \qquad \frac{pc, \Gamma, M \vdash e : t \quad pc \sqsubseteq t}{pc, \Gamma, M \vdash \mathbf{ref}\ e : t\ \mathbf{ref}^{pc}}\ \textsc{Ref} \qquad \frac{pc, \Gamma, M \vdash e_1 : t\ \mathbf{ref}^{\ell} \quad pc, \Gamma, M \vdash e_2 : t \quad pc \sqcup \ell \sqsubseteq t}{pc, \Gamma, M \vdash e_1 := e_2 : \mathbf{unit}}\ \textsc{Assn}$$

Figure 2: Excerpt of type system for host and quoted language

sult, it prevents a function to write to low memory locations in a high context and thus leak information through implicit flows. REF checks memory allocation operations. It ensures that a low reference is not created in a high context and that it does not contain a high value. DEREF checks dereference operations and ensures that the reference level is upper bounded by the level of its contents to avoid information leakage through aliases. ASSN checks memory updates and ensures that no low memory writes occur in a high context or in a high location. The following example captures the intuition behind the typing rules for mutable storage. Let `l, l'` be variables of type $\mathbf{int}^{L}\ \mathbf{ref}^{H}$, `l''` of type $\mathbf{int}^{H}\ \mathbf{ref}^{H}$ and `h` of type $\mathbf{bool}^{H}$. The program is insecure since the returned value at location `l` reveals the initial value of variable `h` through aliasing.

```
l = ref 0; l' = ref 1; let  l'' =
if h then l else l' in l'':= 2; !l
```

The program is correctly rejected by the type system. By rule REF the first two references are typable for pc = H. The conditional is also typable by rule IF, since `l` and `l'` are high references. The successive assignment is typable by rule ASSN provided that 2 has type $\mathbf{int}^{H}$. The type checking fails when considering the dereference $!l$, since the rule DEREF requires $\ell \sqsubseteq t$, which is not true for `l` of type $\mathbf{int}^{L}\ \mathbf{ref}^{H}$.

Rule QUOTE ensures that its arguments are typed in an empty context for quoted expressions. This expresses that only closed quoted terms are allowed in this language. Running a quoted expression e of type $\mathbf{Expr}\langle t\rangle$ using $\mathbf{run}\ e$ results in an expression of type t (rule RUN). Expressions for $\mathbf{database}(db)$ get their type from the mapping Σ. Rule ANTIQUOTE allows to entities defined in the host language from within a quoted expression. The argument of an antiquotation must itself be a quoted expression. Rules SUB allows raising the security level of an expression.

2.5 Soundness

The soundness result is stated as the preservation of a low-equivalence relation under pairwise execution. If we start out in any two low-equivalent environments then the result of running a well-typed program will be low-equivalent with respect to the type of the program. Assuming that the typing of the execution environment corresponds to the capabilities of the attacker, noninterference guarantees that all information observable by the attacker is independent of confidential information. To make the connection between the host policy Γ, the database policy Σ and the type system explicit we write $\Gamma, \Sigma \vdash e : t$ even though Σ was kept implicit in the typing rules.

Theorem 1 (Soundness). *If $x : t, \Sigma \vdash e : t'$, then $NI(e, e)_{t,\Sigma,t'}$.*

Proof sketch. The theorem is proved by adapting the proof technique introduced by by Pottier and Simonet [38] for an ML-like security-typed language. This is done by defining an extension of the language which allows reasoning about pairs of program configurations, and then showing that the type system for the extended language enjoys the subject reduction property. Then noninterference follows as a result of the subject reduction theorem. The proof can be found in the full version of the paper [11]. □

The type system for the host language and the quoted language can be extended with two additional rules which take into account declassification through expressions from the set $\mathcal{D}$. Intuitively, the rules allow to downgrade the security level of an expression if that expression is in the set of declassified expressions $\mathcal{D}$ and the level pc is upper bounded by the level of the declassified expression. The latter is used to enforce that no sensitive information is released implicitly through the declassification mechanism. For the host language the rule is as follows:

$$\frac{pc, \Gamma, M, \mathcal{D} \vdash d : t \qquad pc \sqsubseteq t \qquad (d, t') \in \mathcal{D}}{pc, \Gamma, M \vdash d : t'}\ \textsc{Decl}$$

Theorem 2 (Soundness under Declassification). *If $x : t, \Sigma, \mathcal{D} \vdash e : t'$, then $DNI(e, e)_{\mathcal{D},t,\Sigma,t'}$.*

3. JSLINQ

Figure 3 shows the architecture of JSLINQ. The input is an F# project consisting of the security policy and the application code. The right branch of the figure shows how a project is first compiled to a 3-tier application using the unmodified build process for web applications based on WebSharper. The code of the project is used to create a 3-tier application consisting of JavaScript created using WebSharper, .NET assemblies for server-side logic and SQL queries for the database, created using LINQ. Upon successful compilation, JSLINQ's security type checker can be used on the F# project to determine if the application complies to the

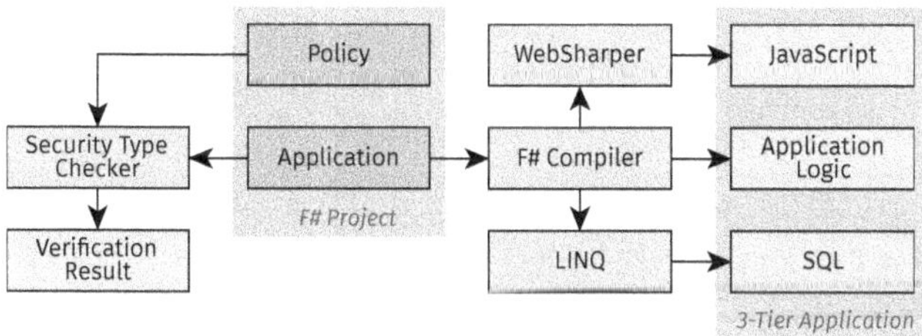

Figure 3: JSLINQ Architecture

specified information-flow policy. How the resulting 3-tier application and the verification result are used depends on the use case of JSLINQ: one possibility is to discard non-compliant application builds and to deploy compliant applications into production. The remainder of the section discusses JSLINQ components in more detail.

WebSharper: WebSharper is a fully-featured and commercially supported framework for web application development in F#, providing powerful functional abstractions such as sitelets for document definition, formlets for data entry forms and flowlets for workflows [21]. Moreover, it offers abstractions for essential web concepts such as the DOM or JavaScript code. Importantly, these abstractions enjoy type safety properties, allowing to leverage the F# type system to build robust applications. One of WebSharper's key features is the translation of F# functions into JavaScript code for execution in the browser. Server-side functions can be designated as remote procedure calls (RPC), and can be transparently called in client-side code, as in the example:

```
// Server-side function called by the client via AJAX.
[<Remote>]
let getText () = "JSLINQ"
// Client-side function translated to JavaScript and HTML.
[<JavaScript>]
let Main () = Text (getText ())
```

WebSharper supports extensions of the client with third-party libraries, for example a map service. Third-party libraries usually consist of JavaScript code that is embedded into the page. Calls from the client-side F# code to the embedded third-party library are handled by wrappers that provide an F# interface to the JavaScript code. This approach requires full trust on the JavaScript code provided by the third party. However, JSLINQ can be used to type-check third-party libraries written in F#. This allows rewriting crucial third-party JavaScript libraries in F# to make them amenable to security analysis using JSLINQ.

F# Project: JSLINQ is designed to perform the verification step after successful compilation of the project. JSLINQ processes MSBuild projects and it is integrated with Microsoft Visual Studio. Code within a project is either part of the policy or part of the program. The policy controls information flows via security type signatures which are added to the definitions of functions and databases. The program implements the application and is subject to the security type check according to the policy. Since the policy is expressed within normal F# syntax, the use of JSLINQ does not interfere with the normal build process of the application and the use of standard tools.

Policy: The policy is specified by adding custom attributes with security type signatures to declarations. Signatures are represented as strings that follow the language in Section 2.1, and use variables for security levels in order to support polymorphism. If no security level is specified within a signature, the corresponding level variable is unconstrained. The following code fragment demonstrates how signatures are added to F# declarations:

```
[<SecT("_^H")>]
let boolH = true

[<SecT("unit ->^L  _^L")>]
let f () = 1
```

We divide a web-application policy into three types: a library policy, an RPC policy and a database policy. Each type deals with different tiers and the meaning of a security type signature depends on the tier in which it is located.

The policy for library functions is defined in a separate module, which is marked with a policy attribute. All library functions used by the program need to be wrapped in the policy, otherwise their use is not allowed. Since HTML and JavaScript abstractions of WebSharper are also library functions, the policy for client-side functionality is specified in this part. Each wrapper function has a mandatory security type signature that governs which security levels are used when the wrapper is called. The following snippet demonstrates a wrapper that uses WebSharper functions to generate a masked input field for passwords, labelled as high:

```
[<Policy>]
module Policy =
  [<JavaScript>][<SecT("unit -> _^H")>]
  let InputPW () = Input [Attr.Type "password"]
```

The policy for RPCs from the client to the server consists of attributes to the declarations of RPC functions within the program. We define the RPC policy and the program in the same file for sake of simplicity. However, JSLINQ allows a complete separation of policy and program into separate files, as we do for the other parts of the policy. Type signatures on RPC functions restrict the information flow from the client to the server (via function arguments) and from the server to the client (via return values). The following fragment demonstrates flows in both directions:

```
[<Remote>][<SecT("unit -> _^L")>]
let untrustedClient () = true

[<Remote>][<SecT("_^L ->^L unit")>]
let untrustedServer (x:bool) = ()
```

The database policy is defined by adding security type signatures to an attribute-based mapping for LINQ [3]. Security type signatures are added to table and column definitions as shown in the following example:

```
[<Table>][<SecT("_^L")>] // Public table length
type Account =
  [<Column>][<SecT("_^L")>] // Public username
  abstract member Username : string
  [<Column>][<SecT("_^H")>] // Confidential password
  abstract member Password : string
```

Security Type Checker: The design of JSLINQ as a verification step after compilation allows us to assume that the code has correct syntax, data types and satisfied dependencies, hence the implementation can only focus on the security type check. Noteworthy, we leave the F# type system untouched and maintain a completely separate security type system during the verification. We perform the security type checking in two steps, which we repeat for each top-level declaration found in the code: first we recursively traverse AST for the declaration to obtain set of constraints and a security type signature by means of the FParsec library [6]. The second step substitutes level variables with actual security levels by solving the constraint set. The resulting types and possibly remaining constraints are added to the environment before proceeding with the next declaration. JSLINQ uses the AST generated by the F# compiler, which is retrieved using the library FSharp Compiler Services [5]. We thus do not duplicate compiler features that are unrelated to the security type check and benefit from F#'s desugaring. This is a clear advantage over prototypes, e.g. SELINQ or SIF, that enhance existing type systems.

4. CASE STUDIES

We have used JSLINQ to implement several case studies as F# projects. In this section we first describe the general design of the policy language and then remark on the policy requirements for the case studies that we have implemented.

4.1 Library Policy

The largest part of the library policy are the signatures for the DOM and JavaScript abstractions. The documents shown in the browser are constructed using these abstractions at runtime. For simplification, we consider the HTML elements as trusted sinks. The rationale behind this is that the user has full access to the data once it has arrived in the browser, independently of that data being displayed or not. However, this assumption does not hold for the full WebSharper API, as it would allow to write and read the elements in the DOM tree in various ways. Therefore, the policy only permits basic operations on the DOM. An important exception from our trusted sink assumption are HTML elements which load external resources, such as images and IFrames. These elements can be used to leak data either directly within the source attribute or indirectly via externally observable HTTP requests. Therefore, we annotate the creation of the source attribute with low security level, both for the URL argument and the side-effects.

4.2 Scenario Discussion

We now comment on different aspects of the policy and provide examples for vulnerabilities captured by JSLINQ.

Password Meter We have included the password meter to demonstrate a policy with full client isolation, where the password is not allowed to leave the browser. The policy declares password fields as sensitive sources. Leaks to third parties and to the application server are prevented by assigning low levels to the source attribute and to the arguments and side-effects of RPC functions, respectively. The scenario assumes that the server is untrusted, as it should not receive the password. A problem with this view is that the JavaScript code executed by the client is usually delivered by an untrusted server. This means that the integrity of the client-side code after the security type check is not guaranteed. Such changes are not subject to the security policy and can thus be abused to leak confidential data. Therefore we have to put trust in the integrity of the code delivered by the application server, which we summarize as *partial trust*. Alternatively, remote attestation methods such as code or certificate signatures can ensure code integrity. The following snippets show a secure password check and two leaks via the source attribute that are handled correctly by JSLINQ. The scenario consists of 53 F# and 6215 generated JS LOCs.

```
let content = // Allowed: Secret only in browser.
  if (containsLetters password)
  then Text "Passed" else Text "Failed"

let content' = // Blocked: Leak via source attribute.
  Image [Src ("http://example.com/img.png?" + password)]
// Blocked: Leak via side-effects.
let content'' = Src (if secret == "jSL!Nq42"
  then "http://example.com/true.jpg"
  else "http://example.com/false.jpg")
```

Location-Based Service This scenario demonstrates declassification of a client-side secret, in this case the user's position. Third parties and the application server can only receive declassified (obfuscated) coordinates. We define declassification as a function that adds a random offset to the position. The function is applied to the confidential latitude and longitude values. The real coordinates are isolated in the browser in the same way as for the password meter. We provide two variants of the location-based service to showcase two different attacker models. The first example embeds a map via an IFrame, where the position is an argument to the source attribute of the IFrame. The following snippet shows how the use of declassified coordinates is permitted, while real coordinates are blocked:

```
let iframeSrc = Src // Allowed: Obfuscated coordinate.
  "https://maps.example.com/?q=" +
  (string (randomize Lat)) + "," + (string (randomize Lon))

let iframeSrc' = Src // Blocked: Exact coordinate.
  "https://maps.example.com/?q=" +
  (string Lat) + "," + (string Lon)
```

The second example includes a third-party library called via F#. We use the Google Maps extension for WebSharper and wrap the initialization and panning of the map within the policy, both having low side-effects and low values. Since the extension wraps the original JavaScript code, we have to fully trust the F#-to-JavaScript extension and JavaScript code implementing the WebSharper APIs. The scenario consists of 76 F# and 6279 generated JS LOCs.

Movie Rental This scenario demonstrates the use of security policies on databases. The database consists of a list of items (e.g. movies) subject to events (e.g. movie rentals) happening at a certain location and time. The location of an event is confidential, while all other information is public. The database policy assigns to the latitude and longitude high-security levels. Leaks to the client are prevented by labelling the return values of RPC functions as public. The following LINQ query joins rentals with movies and returns a list of movie titles. Movie titles are input to an RPC function which is only allowed to return public values. As a result the first `yield` statement is allowed to return the movie titles. If instead we use the second `yield` statement, JSLINQ rejects the program.

```
let events = query {
    for e in db.Event do
    for i in db.Item do
    if e.ItemId = i.Id then
      (* Allowed *) yield i.Name
      (* Blocked *) yield (string e.Lat) }
```

Moreover, we allow the user to retrieve a ranking of popular movies within an area. The implementation contains a pre-defined set of areas which are addressed using indexes. The user can only specify the index for an area of interest. The application server filters the list of movie rentals based on the coordinate values. JSLINQ will infer a high-security level for the length of the resulting list, as it depends on the coordinate values. Our policy allows that geographic information about rentals is disclosed on the granularity of fixed-size areas, therefore we can directly declassify the length of the list. The scenario consists of 87 F# and 6231 generated JS LOCs.

Figure 4: Simplified IFC policy for Battleship

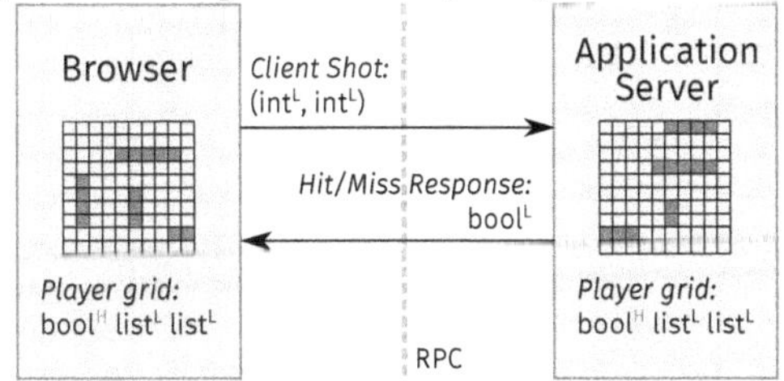

Friend Finder App In this scenario we consider a completely untrusted application server. The client obtains the code from a trusted source. We use the Apache Cordova framework [2] to package the client-side functionality as an app that can be distributed via a trusted channel. Cordova also provides access to the address book of the device. The app can access the address book only via a function defined in the policy, which assigns a high-security level to the contact details. The policy allows declassification by means of a hash function on strings. Leakage of plain contact details to the untrusted server is prevented by assigning a low security level to the arguments and side-effects of RPC functions. The following snippet illustrates a secure and an insecure RPC call:

```
// Allowed: Look-up of hashed phone number
let rpcResult = remoteLookup (Hash phoneNumber)
// Blocked: Look-up of plain phone number
let rpcResult' = remoteLookup phoneNumber
```

The scenario has 62 F# and 9966 generated JS LOCs.

Battleship We implement a simplified version of the classical Battleship game [29, 39]. The client uses the browser to play against the server and the goal of each player is to hide the exact position of their ships on a grid. Both sides trust each other to correctly follow the rules of the game, so we are only concerned about confidentiality. A desirable IFC policy for this game is to mark the values indicating individual ship positions as confidential and all parameters and return values of RPC functions as public, so that confidential information is not allowed to pass the barrier between the browser and the server. This allows us to re-use the same security policy on both sides, as shown in Figure 4. The game rules require declassification, since the response to a shot requires disclosure of one bit of information ("hit" or "miss") to the other player per round. On each side we have to perform declassification twice: firstly for the hit/miss response to a shot, as it directly depends on the presence of a ship at that location, and secondly for indicating to the opponent if a player is defeated, which requires to test all occupied cells. The latter can be done locally, but for implementation reasons players report their own defeat to the opponent. The following example shows this for the client-side:

```
let serverShotResult = {
  shot = response.shot;
  hit = DeclassifyBool !serverTarget.occupied;
  defeated = DeclassifyBool clientDefeated }
```

The scenario has 255 F# and 6348 generated JS LOCs.

4.3 Case Study Results

Table 1 summarizes our case studies. The different combinations of client, third party and server trust illustrate the attacker models handled by JSLINQ. The initial effort of defining the API policy annotations comes with the benefit of minor burden on application programmer side. The policy for JSLINQ requires only very few annotations within the application code. As reported above, the LOCs for F# and JavaScript refer to the application (excluding comments and blank lines) and wrappers in the policy. The difference between the number of lines in F# code and resulting JavaScript shows WebSharper and its libraries at work. This allows the programmer to focus on the application logic and its security-critical parts (subject to security type check in JSLINQ) while standard boilerplate code is automatically generated by the framework. Real-world applications contain considerably more code to offer a better user experience. We omit the verification time, as execution time mostly consists of the compilation required to retrieve the AST. As the security type check is based on a simple constraint solver, we expect it to scale well to larger programs.

Table 1: Overview of implemented scenarios

	Trust			# of Annotations		
Scenario	Client	3rd Party	Server	API	RPC	DB
Password Meter	Yes	No	Partial	10	0	0
POI IFrame	Yes	No	Yes	10	1	5
POI Embedded	Yes	Yes	Yes	11	1	5
Movie Rental	No	No	Yes	9	1	8
Friend Finder	Yes	No	No	9	1	0
Battleship	Yes	No	Yes	12	4	0

5. RELATED WORK

Securing web applications with IFC has been the subject of a large array of research studies. Here we contrast our approach with closely related works on IFC for web security.

Information Flow Security. Much research on formal models for end-to-end security guarantees has followed Goguen and Meseguer's seminal work on noninterference [20]. Heintze and Riecke [24] introduce the SLam calculus to enforce noninterference for a functional language with higher-order features and present a soundness proof for a functional fragment of that language. Pottier and Simonet [30] introduce a security type system for a core of ML with references and higher-order features and implement type checking for the FlowCaml tool [38]. Our framework extends the soundness proof technique from [30] with support for higher-order types, quotations and antiquotations, and declassification. A plethora of static, dynamic and hybrid analysis have been proposed to enforce noninterference-like policies [34]. Our work uses static analysis by means a security type system.

Web Application Security. Common security mechanisms proposed for web applications, including IFC, only secure components in isolation. Database systems such as MySQL provide access controls at the level of tables and columns, which are decoupled from the applications. Similarly, web browsers [23, 13] and application servers [34, 22] leverage dynamic and static techniques to enforce policies in isolation. None of these approaches can express security policies that regulate information flows across component boundaries as we do in this paper. Many existing web application frameworks augment the capabilities of a specific language with homogeneous meta-programming to ease the construction of Internet applications. WebSharper, Rails, GWT and many others are used in industry to develop complex web and mobile applications. For instance, GWT is used by many products at Google, including Flights, Hotel Finder, Offers and Wallet. While there is some framework

Table 2: Comparison of web application frameworks

Tool	Client	Server	DB	3rd Party	Dec	Sound Core	Enforcement	Language	P#C
SIF/SWIFT	✓	✓	✗	✗	✓	✗	TS	Java, HTML	✗
WebSSARI	✗	✓	✓	✗	✓	✗	TS	PHP, SQL	✓
IFDB	✗	✓	✓	✗	✓	✗	Dynamic	PHP, SQL	✗
SELINKS	✓	✓	✓	✗	✓	✓	TS	Links	✗
UR/WEB	✓	✓	✓	✗	✓	✗	ATP	UR	✓
SELINQ	✗	✓	✓	✗	✗	✓	TS	F#	✗
JSFLOW	✓	✗	✗	✓	✗	✓	Dynamic	JavaScript	✗
JSLINQ	✓	✓	✓	✓	✓	✓	TS	F#	✓

support as prepared statements and custom sanitizers, the burden of securing code is largely placed on the developer. JSLINQ provides a smooth integration of security requirements in the development process, which allows F# programmers to check whether their code, or the code developed by external contractors, complies with desired security policies.

A few existing works aim at bridging IFC for multi-tier web applications. Chong et al. implement SIF [17] and SWIFT [16] as extensions of the JIF compiler [29] to enforce information flow policies for web applications written in Java. Web applications are checked against these policies by a combination of static and runtime enforcements. The ability to enforce fine-grained policies in the *decentralized label model* [28] is an attractive feature. At the same time, SIF and SWIFT interweave security annotations with program code and do not provide support for databases. JSLINQ addresses soundness formally and provides integration for third-party libraries. Huang et al. [25] propose WebSSARI, a tool that combines static analysis with runtime checks to detect vulnerabilities in PHP applications that interact with SQL databases. WebSSARI is very effective at discovering security vulnerabilities, although no support for client-side applications is provided and soundness is only addressed informally. Schultz and Liskov [37] propose IFDB, a database management system with decentralized IFC. IFDB is implemented by modifying PostgreSQL as well as the application environments in PHP and Python. Their *Query by Label* model provides abstractions for dealing with expressive information flow policies in relational databases, including decentralization and declassification. IFDB supports policies for server and database tiers and does not provide language integration for database queries. Corcoran et al. [18] present SELINKS which builds on the Links programming language. Links is a strongly-typed functional language for multi-tier web applications and it supports higher-order queries. SELINKS implements an expressive type system which allows to define a variety of policies, including dynamic IFC, provenance, and general access control. JSLINQ only requires the programmer write code in a mainstream language such as F# and express policies in a less sophisticated, but standard type system. Chlipala introduces UrFlow [15], which implements a static information flow analysis as part of the Ur/Web domain-specific language for development of web applications. UrFlow allows to express policies as SQL queries leveraging the users' runtime knowledge. The enforcement is done by symbolic execution over a model of the web application. UrFlow shares similar aspects with SELINKS and scalability depends on capabilities of the underlying theorem prover. While JSLINQ separates security checking from type checking, it can be extended with techniques from [43] to cope with dynamic security policies. Hedin et al. [23] present JSFlow, a security-enhanced JavaScript interpreter for fine-grained tracking of information flow. The interpreter enables deployment as a browser extension providing dynamic IFC on the client-side including third-party scripts. JSFlow only applies to applications written in JavaScript.

Secure Compilation JSLINQ relies on the WebSharper compiler to translate F# code to JavaScript code deployed in the web browser, leaving out a formal investigation of the translation correctness. Fournet et al. [19] show full abstraction for a compiler which translates an ML-like language with higher-order functions and references to JavaScript. Their language is similar to F#, hence the same ideas can be used to show full abstraction for the JSLINQ compiler. Baltopoulos and Gordon [12] study secure compilation by augmenting the Links compiler with encryption and authentication for data stored on the client-side.

Tools Table 2 provides a comparison of existing web application frameworks with support for IFC. We classify each tool depending on whether they allow for IFC on the client, server, databases (DB) or third-party libraries. We also compare against support for declassification policies (Dec), soundness of a core calculus, type of enforcement mechanism (a type system (TS), a dynamic monitor or an automated theorem prover (ATP)), programming languages used and separation between code and policy (P#C). The comparison shows that JSLINQ enjoys many desirable properties.

6. CONCLUSION

We have presented a framework for end-to-end security, by leveraging IFC for a functional language with mutable store and language-integrated queries. The framework puts homogeneous meta-programming to work by developing a security type system that tracks information flows through the client, server, and underlying database. We have implemented JSLINQ and shown through different case studies that it is practical. JSLINQ can be used by organizations to build high-assurance applications. It can automatically verify the information flows within code written by internal developers or external contractors against the security policy. This helps to improve code quality and to demonstrate compliance with information security regulations, for instance when sensitive information like trade secrets or personal data is being processed. As future work, we plan to add to JSLINQ support for dynamic policies and finer-grained third-party libraries from F# and ensure their secure compilation to JavaScript.

Acknowledgments This work was funded by the European Community under the ProSecuToR project and the Swedish research agencies SSF and VR.

7. REFERENCES

[1] LINQ (Language-Integrated Query). http://msdn.microsoft.com/en-us/library/bb397926.aspx, 2014. Accessed: 2015-08-25.

[2] Apache Cordova. http://cordova.apache.org/, 2015. Accessed: 2015-09-11.

[3] Attribute-Based Mapping. https://msdn.microsoft.com/en-us/library/bb386971.aspx, 2015. Accessed: 2015-09-11.

[4] Critical Security Controls. http://www.sans.org/critical-security-controls/, 2015. Accessed: 2015-08-25.

[5] F# Compiler Services. http://fsharp.github.io/FSharp.Compiler.Service/, 2015. Accessed: 2015-09-11.

[6] FParsec. http://www.quanttec.com/fparsec/, 2015. Accessed: 2015-09-11.

[7] 'Mouse over' security flaw causes Twitter trouble. http://edition.cnn.com/2010/TECH/social.media/09/21/twitter.security.flaw/, 2015. Accessed: 2015-08-25.

[8] OWASP Top 10 2013. https://www.owasp.org/index.php/Top_10_2013-Top_10, 2015. Accessed: 2015-08-25.

[9] Sites hit in massive web attack. http://www.bbc.com/news/technology-12933053, 2015. Accessed: 2015-08-25.

[10] WebSharper. http://websharper.com/, 2015. Accessed: 2015-08-25.

[11] M. Balliu, B. Liebe, D. Schoepe, and A. Sabelfeld. JSLINQ: Building Secure Applications across Tiers. https://sites.google.com/site/jslinqcodaspy16/, September 2015. Software and Extended Version.

[12] I. G. Baltopoulos and A. D. Gordon. Secure compilation of a multi-tier web language. In *TLDI*, 2009.

[13] N. Bielova. Survey on JavaScript security policies and their enforcement mechanisms in a web browser. *JLAP*, 2013.

[14] J. Cheney, S. Lindley, and P. Wadler. A practical theory of language-integrated query. In *ICFP*, 2013.

[15] A. Chlipala. Static Checking of Dynamically-Varying Security Policies in Database-Backed Applications. In *OSDI*, 2010.

[16] S. Chong, J. Liu, A. C. Myers, X. Qi, K. Vikram, L. Zheng, and X. Zheng. Secure web applications via automatic partitioning. *Comm. of the ACM*, 2009.

[17] S. Chong, K. Vikram, and A. C. Myers. SIF: Enforcing Confidentiality and Integrity in Web Applications. In *USENIX*, 2007.

[18] B. J. Corcoran, N. Swamy, and M. W. Hicks. Cross-tier, label-based security enforcement for web applications. In *SIGMOD*, 2009.

[19] C. Fournet, N. Swamy, J. Chen, P. Dagand, P. Strub, and B. Livshits. Fully abstract compilation to javascript. In *POPL '13*, 2013.

[20] J. A. Goguen and J. Meseguer. Security Policies and Security Models. In *IEEE SP*, 1982.

[21] A. Granicz. Functional web and mobile development in F#. In *CEFP*, 2013.

[22] G. L. Guernic. *Confidentiality Enforcement Using Dynamic Information Flow Analyses*. PhD thesis, Kansas State University, 2007.

[23] D. Hedin, A. Birgisson, L. Bello, and A. Sabelfeld. JSFlow: tracking information flow in JavaScript and its APIs. In *SAC*, 2014.

[24] N. Heintze and J. G. Riecke. The SLam Calculus: Programming with Secrecy and Integrity. In *POPL*, 1998.

[25] Y.-W. Huang, F. Yu, C. Hang, C.-H. Tsai, D.-T. Lee, and S.-Y. Kuo. Securing web application code by static analysis and runtime protection. In *WWW*, 2004.

[26] X. Li and Y. Xue. A survey on server-side approaches to securing web applications. *ACM Surv.*, 2014.

[27] V. B. Livshits, A. V. Nori, S. K. Rajamani, and A. Banerjee. Merlin: specification inference for explicit information flow problems. In *PLDI*, 2009.

[28] A. C. Myers and B. Liskov. Protecting privacy using the decentralized label model. *ACM Trans. Softw. Eng. Methodol.*, 2000.

[29] A. C. Myers, L. Zheng, S. Zdancewic, S. Chong, and N. Nystrom. Jif: Java Information Flow. Software release. http://www.cs.cornell.edu/jif, July 2001.

[30] F. Pottier and V. Simonet. Information flow inference for ML. In *POPL*, 2002.

[31] S. Rasthofer, S. Arzt, and E. Bodden. A machine-learning approach for classifying and categorizing android sources and sinks. In *NDSS*, 2014.

[32] W. K. Robertson and G. Vigna. Static enforcement of web application integrity through strong typing. In *USENIX*, 2009.

[33] A. Sabelfeld and A. C. Myers. A Model for Delimited Information Release. In *ISSS*, 2003.

[34] A. Sabelfeld and A. C. Myers. Language-based information-flow security. *JSAC*, 2003.

[35] A. Sabelfeld and D. Sands. Declassification: Dimensions and Principles. *JCS*, 2009.

[36] D. Schoepe, D. Hedin, and A. Sabelfeld. SeLINQ: tracking information across application-database boundaries. In *ICFP*, 2014.

[37] D. A. Schultz and B. Liskov. IFDB: decentralized information flow control for databases. In *EuroSys*, 2013.

[38] V. Simonet. The Flow Caml system. Software. http://cristal.inria.fr/~simonet/soft/flowcaml, 2003.

[39] A. Stoughton, A. Johnson, S. Beller, K. Chadha, D. Chen, K. Foner, and M. Zhivich. You sank my battleship!: A case study in secure programming. 2014.

[40] D. Syme. Leveraging .NET Meta-programming Components from F#: Integrated Queries and Interoperable Heterogeneous Execution. In *ML*, 2006.

[41] D. Volpano, G. Smith, and C. Irvine. A Sound Type System for Secure Flow Analysis. *JCS*, 1996.

[42] N. Zeldovich, S. Boyd-Wickizer, and D. Mazières. Securing distributed systems with information flow control. In *5th USENIX Symposium on Networked Systems Design & Implementation, NSDI 2008, April 16-18, 2008, San Francisco, CA, USA, Proceedings*, pages 293–308, 2008.

[43] L. Zheng and A. C. Myers. Dynamic security labels and static information flow control. *Int. J. Inf. Sec.*, 2007.

APPENDIX

$$\frac{\ell \sqsubseteq \ell'}{\ell \sqsubseteq t^{\ell'}} \qquad \frac{}{\ell \sqsubseteq \textbf{unit}} \qquad \frac{\ell \sqsubseteq pc \quad \ell \sqsubseteq t}{\ell \sqsubseteq t' \xrightarrow{pc} t} \qquad \frac{\ell \sqsubseteq t_1 \quad \ell \sqsubseteq t_2}{\ell \sqsubseteq t * t} \qquad \frac{\ell \sqsubseteq t_i}{\ell \sqsubseteq \{\overline{f:t}\}} \qquad \frac{\ell \sqsubseteq t}{\ell \sqsubseteq \textbf{Expr}\langle t\rangle}$$

Figure 5: Security annotation constraints

$$\textsc{Unit}\ \frac{}{pc, \Gamma, M \vdash () : \textbf{unit}} \qquad \textsc{Const}\ \frac{\Sigma(c) = t}{pc, \Gamma, M \vdash c : t^{\ell}} \qquad \textsc{Loc}\ \frac{l : t \in M}{pc, \Gamma, M \vdash l : t} \qquad \textsc{Nil}\ \frac{}{pc, \Gamma, M \vdash [] : (t\ \textbf{list})^{\ell}} \qquad \textsc{Project}\ \frac{pc, \Gamma, M \vdash e : \{\overline{f:t}\}}{pc, \Gamma, M \vdash e.f_i : t_i}$$

$$\textsc{Lift}\ \frac{pc, \Gamma, M \vdash e : t}{pc, \Gamma, M \vdash \textbf{lift}\ e : \textbf{Expr}\langle t\rangle} \qquad \textsc{Snd}\ \frac{pc, \Gamma, M \vdash e : t_1 * t_2}{pc, \Gamma, M \vdash \textbf{snd}\ e : t_2} \qquad \textsc{If}\ \frac{pc, \Gamma, M \vdash e : \textbf{bool}^{\ell} \quad pc \sqcup \ell, \Gamma, M \vdash e_i : t \quad \ell \sqsubseteq t \quad i \in \{1,2\}}{pc, \Gamma, M \vdash \textbf{if}\ e\ \textbf{then}\ e_1\ \textbf{else}\ e_2 : t}$$

$$\textsc{Rec}\ \frac{pc, \Gamma, x : t, f : t \xrightarrow{pc} t', M \vdash e : t'}{pc', \Gamma, M \vdash \textbf{rec}\ f(x) \to e : t \xrightarrow{pc} t'} \qquad \textsc{Pair}\ \frac{pc, \Gamma, M \vdash e_1 : t_1 \quad pc, \Gamma, M \vdash e_2 : t_2}{pc, \Gamma, M \vdash (e_1, e_2) : t_1 * t_2} \qquad \textsc{Record}\ \frac{\overline{pc, \Gamma, M \vdash e : t}}{pc, \Gamma, M \vdash \{\overline{f = e}\} : \{\overline{f:t}\}}$$

$$\textsc{Op}\ \frac{\Sigma(op) = \overline{t} \to t \quad \overline{pc, \Gamma, M \vdash e : t^{\ell}}}{pc, \Gamma, M \vdash op(\overline{e}) : t^{\bigsqcup \ell_i}} \qquad \textsc{Exists}\ \frac{pc, \Gamma, M \vdash e : (t\ \textbf{list})^{\ell}}{pc, \Gamma, M \vdash \textbf{exists}\ e : \textbf{bool}^{\ell}} \qquad \textsc{Yield}\ \frac{pc, \Gamma, M \vdash e : t}{pc, \Gamma, M \vdash \textbf{yield}\ e : (t\ \textbf{list})^{\ell}}$$

$$\textsc{Union}\ \frac{pc, \Gamma, M \vdash e : (t\ \textbf{list})^{\ell} \quad pc, \Gamma, M \vdash e' : (t\ \textbf{list})^{\ell'}}{pc, \Gamma, M \vdash e'\ @\ e : (t\ \textbf{list})^{\ell \sqcup \ell'}} \qquad \textsc{If1}\ \frac{pc, \Gamma, M \vdash e : \textbf{bool}^{\ell} \quad pc, \Gamma, M \vdash e' : (t\ \textbf{list})^{\ell'}}{pc, \Gamma, M \vdash \textbf{if}\ e\ \textbf{then}\ e' : (t\ \textbf{list})^{\ell \sqcup \ell'}}$$

$$\textsc{Fst}\ \frac{pc, \Gamma, M \vdash e : t_1 * t_2}{pc, \Gamma, M \vdash \textbf{fst}\ e : t_1}$$

Figure 6: Type system for host language

$$\textsc{ConstQ}\ \frac{\Sigma(c) = t}{H, \Delta \vdash c : t^{\ell}} \qquad \textsc{FunQ}\ \frac{H, \Delta, x : t \vdash e : t'}{H, \Delta \vdash \textbf{fun}(x) \to e : t \to t'} \qquad \textsc{VarQ}\ \frac{x : t \in \Delta}{H, \Delta \vdash x : t} \qquad \textsc{ApplyQ}\ \frac{H, \Delta \vdash e_1 : t \to t' \quad H, \Delta \vdash e_2 : t}{H, \Delta \vdash e_1\ e_2 : t'}$$

$$\textsc{OpQ}\ \frac{\Sigma(op) = \overline{t} \to t \quad \overline{H, \Delta \vdash M : t^{\ell}}}{H, \Delta \vdash op(\overline{M}) : t^{\bigsqcup \ell_i}} \qquad \textsc{PairQ}\ \frac{H, \Delta \vdash e_1 : t_1 \quad H, \Delta \vdash e_2 : t_2}{H, \Delta \vdash (e_1, e_2) : t_1 * t_2} \qquad \textsc{FstQ}\ \frac{H, \Delta \vdash e : t_1 * t_2}{H, \Delta \vdash \textbf{fst}\ e : t_1} \qquad \textsc{SndQ}\ \frac{H, \Delta \vdash e : t_1 * t_2}{H, \Delta \vdash \textbf{snd}\ e : t_2}$$

$$\textsc{RecordQ}\ \frac{\overline{H, \Delta \vdash M : t}}{H, \Delta \vdash \{\overline{f = M}\} : \{\overline{f:t}\}} \qquad \textsc{ProjectQ}\ \frac{H, \Delta \vdash L : \{\overline{f:t}\}}{H, \Delta \vdash L.f_i : t_i} \qquad \textsc{YieldQ}\ \frac{H, \Delta \vdash M : t}{H, \Delta \vdash \textbf{yield}\ M : (t\ \textbf{list})^{\ell}} \qquad \textsc{NilQ}\ \frac{}{H, \Delta \vdash [] : (t\ \textbf{list})^{\ell}}$$

$$\textsc{ExistsQ}\ \frac{H, \Delta \vdash M : (t\ \textbf{list})^{\ell}}{H, \Delta \vdash \textbf{exists}\ M : \textbf{bool}^{\ell}} \qquad \textsc{IfQ}\ \frac{H, \Delta \vdash L : \textbf{bool}^{\ell} \quad H, \Delta \vdash M : (t\ \textbf{list})^{\ell'}}{H, \Delta \vdash \textbf{if}\ L\ \textbf{then}\ M : (t\ \textbf{list})^{\ell \sqcup \ell'}} \qquad \textsc{UnionQ}\ \frac{H, \Delta \vdash M : (t\ \textbf{list})^{\ell} \quad H, \Delta \vdash N : (t\ \textbf{list})^{\ell'}}{H, \Delta \vdash N\ @\ M : (t\ \textbf{list})^{\ell \sqcup \ell'}}$$

$$\textsc{ForQ}\ \frac{H, \Delta \vdash M : (t\ \textbf{list})^{\ell} \quad H, \Delta, x : t \vdash N : (t'\ \textbf{list})^{\ell'}}{H, \Delta \vdash \textbf{for}\ x\ \textbf{in}\ M\ \textbf{do}\ N : (t'\ \textbf{list})^{\ell \sqcup \ell'}} \qquad \textsc{SubQ}\ \frac{t \sqsubseteq t' \quad H, \Delta \vdash M : t}{H, \Delta \vdash M : t'}$$

Figure 7: Typing rules for quoted language

Efficient Network Path Verification for Policy-routed Queries

Sushama Karumanchi
College of Information Sciences & Technology, Pennsylvania State University
sik5273@ist.psu.edu

Jingwei Li
College of Computer and Control Engineering, Nankai University
lijwl987@gmail.com

Anna Squicciarini
College of Information Sciences & Technology, Pennsylvania State University
acs20@psu.edu

ABSTRACT

Resource discovery in unstructured peer-to-peer networks causes a search query to be flooded throughout the network via random nodes, leading to security and privacy issues. The owner of the search query does not have control over the transmission of its query through the network. Although algorithms have been proposed for policy-compliant query or data routing in a network, these algorithms mainly deal with authentic route computation and do not provide mechanisms to actually verify the network paths taken by the query. In this work, we propose an approach to deal with the problem of verifying network paths taken by a search query during resource discovery, and detection of malicious forwarding of search query. Our approach aims at being secure and yet very scalable, even in the presence of huge number of nodes in the network.

Keywords

resource discovery, security, privacy, network routing, path verification, malicious node detection, query routing, peer-to-peer security, P2P security

1. INTRODUCTION

Resource discovery and data packet routing is a well-known problem in the context of computer networks [9]. Resources in networks such as peer-to-peer networks, are discovered by the requester propagating a search query throughout the network. In case of an unstructured peer-to-peer network, where there is no central directory to keep track of the resources in the network, resources are discovered through search query flooding throughout the network.

Although relatively simple and easy to deploy, search query propagation throughout the network via random nodes raises security and privacy issues, for both the query owner and the search query itself [20]. The query may contain sensitive information related to the query owner, because of which the query owner would want to forward the query only through those nodes that satisfy certain properties. For instance, the search query can be combined with the requested resource and the requester's IP address to produce a comprehensive database about the requester [27]. Also consider an example where a content distribution network (CDN) employs a peer-to-peer network (hybrid-CDN [30]) to host the contents of its client. For example, the CDN provider Akamai could host the contents of Netflix in its network, and to further increase the availability and bandwidth consumption, Akamai could use a P2P network of its users to host the contents of Netflix. Given this context, the users accessing the content and the content providers could have security and privacy issues related to data traversal in the content hosting network. Again, the search query traverses through random nodes in the content hosting network, which might not comply with the business rules and laws associated with the query, or which might not comply with personal privacy preferences.

Approaches for policy-based search for resource discovery and routing have been recently proposed (e.g. [12, 25]). However, policy-enforcement verification, that is, verifying that the network paths or routes taken by the data or the search query during resource discovery are in accordance with the given policy is still a challenging and open problem. Challenges arise due to the following main reasons: (i) the number of nodes whose policy-compliance is to be verified might explode even in small networks, (ii) there is no easy way to check the nodes' behavior during a distributed search and, (iii) even if there exists a way to check nodes' behavior, it is hard to verify node compliance without introducing large computational overhead on the verifier(s).

In this work, we take a step toward addressing the above challenges by proposing an efficient approach to verify policy-compliant routing.

We assume the existence of policy-compliant routing algorithms in decentralized networks such as [12] and [25]. A policy-compliant routing algorithm defines a *policy* which is a machine-readable expression of the query owner's requirements that are imposed on the nodes which are part of the network. Only those nodes that satisfy the requirements specified in the policy are able to receive the search query. It should be noted that our focus is *not on the problem of protection of the content of the search query.* Preventing the nodes in the network from learning the content of search query can be easily achieved using one-to-many encryptions as in [2, 24, 5]. *Our main focus* is two-fold: (i) we aim to develop new mechanisms to verify the policy-compliance of every node in the network that has received the search query, and (ii) we aim to leverage these mechanisms to efficiently

CODASPY'16, March 09-11, 2016, New Orleans, LA, USA
© 2016 ACM. ISBN 978-1-4503-3935-3/16/03...$15.00
DOI: http://dx.doi.org/10.1145/2857705.2857715

detect the malicious behavior of the nodes in the network with respect to query forwarding. In other words, we aim to detect incorrect forwarding of query in the network.

Our contributions are summarized as follows:

- To prevent the problem of explosion of the number of paths or nodes to verify for policy compliance, we design an approach that efficiently filters paths or nodes that are not required to be verified. Our experiments show that our approach saves a large amount of computational overhead compared to an approach that does not use path or node filtering.
- We propose three approaches for verifying the policy-compliance of the paths yielded by successful search queries. Our baseline approach relies on random message challenges. In particular, we challenge the target node (i.e. the node to be verified) with two random messages encrypted using CP-ABE [2]. Policy-compliance is verified by checking which of these two random messages is successfully decrypted. To reduce verification overhead, we propose an optimization approach, which is based on using "honesty-verified" nodes in the paths and offloading verification computations to them. Our approach guarantees that query owner's local computation is minimized while neither affecting the correctness of verification nor imposing heavy computational burden on the nodes. Finally, our third approach is based on the idea of re-using ABE ciphertext, which maintains the same randomness for all the ABE ciphertexts in verification. This approach is extremely efficient: the requester just needs to compute one pair of CP-ABE encryptions, whereas the computation of our previous two approaches is linear with the number of nodes to be verified.

We evaluate our approach extensively, and compare our efficient verification method with baseline cryptographic algorithms. Our results show that our approach is very efficient and effective.

The rest of the paper is organized as follows. Section 2 discusses related work. We provide a cryptographic background that is relevant to this work in Section 3. Section 4 introduces our design goals, and approach overview. Section 5 and Section 6 present our approach in detail. Section 7 presents the results of our performance evaluation. We conclude in Section 8 with pointers to future work.

2. RELATED WORK

Resource discovery in networks has been a popular topic of research in the recent years ([9, 26, 22, 21, 15]). Most existing approaches relate to resource discovery in the context of a large network such as a peer-to-peer network, a content-hosting network or an ad-hoc network. Shojafar et al [26] propose an Improved Adaptive Probabilistic Search algorithm to search for files in unstructured peer-to-peer (P2P) networks. They compare their approach with Random Walk and Adaptive Probabilistic Search algorithms for various P2P network scenarios in terms of response rates, duplicate messages and success rates. Their results show that Shojafar's proposed approach obtains a better trade-off between the performance and cost of search compared to the two classic algorithms. With a similar goal in mind, Qu et al [23] propose multiple algorithms for searching shared files in unstructured P2P networks. The computational overhead of their approach for searching is small, and their approach would be able to accommodate any network topology. Mashayekhi and Habibi [18] propose a framework for search in unstructured P2P networks, which is based on reputation of nodes in the network. They build indexes based on trust and semantic data to search for resources. While all of the above works propose efficient and effective approaches to resource discovery in networks, none of them take into account the security issues that could lead to malicious query forwarding, which is the main focus of this work.

Recent works on policy-compliant routing have also been proposed in the literature ([13, 12, 25]). Common to these approaches are user-specified policies to protect user data as it traverses through a network. Only nodes that satisfy the policy are able to access the data. While we take a similar approach as the above works, we also work towards solving the challenging task of detecting malicious nodes in the network that wrongly forward the search query. Also, there is a significant amount of work on routing security ([4, 7, 19, 29, 8, 14, 31, 16]).These works concentrate on the authenticity of route computation, but do not tackle the problem of detection of malicious forwarding as well as do not build a method to ensure that the computed routes are being correctly followed by the data packets. Naous et al [20] and Jiang et al [10] propose approaches that try to detect inconsistencies in network routes. These approaches would work for pre-computed network routes, where the route the data takes is known to the data owner before hand. Our approach instead focuses on dynamically computed routes. Policy-based routing is dynamic in the sense that the routing decision is made by a node which receives the data on the fly, and there is no pre-defined route that is known to the owner in this case. We enable the data owner to attach a policy to its data, and empower the data owner to actually check the properties of each node that receives its data.

3. CRYPTOGRAPHIC BACKGROUND

In this section, we discuss Attribute-Based Encryption (ABE), which is at the heart of our verification protocol and then introduce bilinear maps which are considered a common tool for designing ABE.

3.1 Attribute-based Encryption

ABE has been widely applied to impose fine-grained access control on encrypted data [24]. Two kinds of ABE have been proposed so far: Key-Policy Attribute-Based Encryption (KP-ABE) [5] and Ciphertext-Policy Attribute-Based Encryption (CP-ABE) [2]. In KP-ABE, each ciphertext is labeled with a set of descriptive attributes, and each private key is associated with an access policy that specifies which type of ciphertexts the key can decrypt. In CP-ABE, the access policy is specified in ciphertext and the private key is associated with a set of attributes. In this paper, we will utilize a variant of CP-ABE for policy-compliance checking, and thus introduce its main primitives below.

- $\mathsf{Setup}(\lambda)$: The setup algorithm takes as input ÂĂÂŞ a security parameter λ, and outputs (pk, msk), where pk denotes the public key and msk denotes the master secret key of ABE system.
- $\mathsf{KeyGen}(\omega, msk)$: The key generation algorithm takes

as input an attribute set ω and the master secret key msk, and outputs the private key sk.

- Encrypt(m, pol) : The encryption algorithm takes as input a message m and the policy pol, and outputs the ciphertext $[m]_{pol}$ with respect to access policy pol.
- Decrypt$([m]_{pol}, sk)$: The decryption algorithm takes as input a ciphertext $[m]_{pol}$ which was assumed to be encrypted under a policy pol and the private key sk for attribute set ω, and outputs the original message m if and only if ω satisfies pol.

3.2 Bilinear Maps

Bilinear map [3] is the common tool for designing the aforementioned KP-ABE primitives. In this subsection, we give the definition of the bilinear map.

Definition 1 (Bilinear Map). *Denote $\mathbb{G}, \mathbb{G}_T$ as cyclic groups of prime order p, writing the group action multiplicatively. g is a generator of $\mathbb{G}$. Let $e : \mathbb{G} \times \mathbb{G} \rightarrow \mathbb{G}_T$ be a map with the following properties:*

- *Bilinearity: $e(g_1^a, g_2^b) = e(g_1, g_2)^{ab}$ for all $g_1, g_2 \in \mathbb{G}$, and $a, b \in_R \mathbb{Z}_p$;*
- *Non-degeneracy: There exists $g_1, g_2 \in \mathbb{G}$ such that $e(g_1, g_2) \neq 1$, in other words, the map does not send all pairs in $\mathbb{G} \times \mathbb{G}$ to the identity in $\mathbb{G}_T$;*
- *Efficiency: There exists an efficient polynomial time algorithm to compute the bilinear map $e(\cdot, \cdot)$.*

As we describe in the next sections, our protocol involves some modification of the basic CP-ABE primitive. By utilizing the bilinear maps we are able to make CP-ABE more efficient and suitable to our problem.

4. APPROACH OVERVIEW

We discuss our design goals, assumptions, and provide an overview of our approach in what follows.

4.1 Design Goals and Threat Model

We aim to solve the problem of detection of malicious behavior in computer networks, specific to malicious behavior detection during distributed search. This problem applies to any large network, such as a content hosting peer-to-peer network [26]. We support both static networks (where there is no constant addition or removal of nodes from the network) and dynamic networks (where constant addition and removal of nodes takes place). We assume that every node is assigned a private key sk according to the CP-ABE algorithm, by a certificate authority. For example, the attributes of a node could be $Domain = 198.62.X.X$ and $ProcessingFee = \$100$. We assume nodes do not share information about their private key with other nodes due to privacy concerns.

Our approach is to verify and enforce network paths taken by a search query in a network, carried out using a "resource discovery" paradigm [26]. Under this paradigm, a query owner (or resource requester) is an entity or a node in the network which creates a search query in order to find a resource within the nodes in the network. The query owner might also wish to obtain certain security and privacy guarantees from the network so as to protect the access of its query by random nodes in the network. Hence, we enable the query owner to attach a *policy* to its query. A *policy* is a machine readable representation of the requirements of the query owner. The requirements are a set of constraints applied on the nodes in the network which carry the query, so as to restrict access of the query by random nodes. Our goal is to verify whether the search query is actually forwarded only to those nodes that satisfy the policy established by the query owner.

We assume that nodes only know their neighbors. In case of peer-to-peer networks which are unstructured (i.e., do not have a central directory of resources), the nodes would not know what resources other nodes have, as these may change over time. Therefore, search queries are forwarded for resolution without following a pre-defined route. A query traverses nodes in the network through various paths. When a resource is found, the resource along with the node IDs (path information) is passed to the query owner, through the same path through which the resource is found. We assume that the path information is reliable, in that, the exact path taken by the query is provided to the query owner without any modification. This can be achieved by cryptographically signing the path information, according to protocols such as [11]. A node maintains the record of its queries and its respective policy, and the path information of past (resolved) queries. We assume that nodes are collaborative, and share policy and path history periodically with the neighboring nodes. Note that the nodes listed in path history are nodes whose selected properties have been verified for compliance with their corresponding query policy. This information is distributed throughout the network nodes to form a consistent history of policies and paths, similar to well-known existing routing algorithms such as [6].

If a node is verified to correctly forward a given search query, we assume the node to be *honest* for the purpose of that specific search. Note that honest nodes may not be fully trusted, and they might be "curious" about the information passing through them. Also, honest nodes are not required to report errors or malicious forward operations of other nodes.

Under the threat assumptions described above, we summarize our objectives as follows.

- **Network Path Compliance**: We aim to guarantee that the network paths followed by the query are in accordance with the policies attached to the query. By meeting this goal, we are able to detect the *malicious* nodes that forward query to the nodes that do not satisfy the requirements specified in the policy.
- **Cost Effectiveness**: Our second goal is to ensure that the network path compliance can be checked in a cost effective way. In other words, we aim to ensure that implementing our approach does not pose a huge computational overhead on the nodes in the network as well as the query owner.

4.2 Approach overview

We now discuss our main approach, and introduce some important notations.

A requester or the query owner (which is a node part of the network) creates a search query to search for his required resource throughout the network. When the requester submits the request for a resource, its query is forwarded across the nodes in the network, in search of a node able to satisfy the request. A search query SQ can be issued by any node, and includes resource requirements in terms of its features and quality.

Example 1. *As a simple example, consider* $SQ = (\{Location\}, \{Fee < \$50, ExecTime < 5s\})$. *The requester is looking for a resource belonging to the Location category, and querying for this resource should charge the requester less than 50 dollars fee and should execute in less than 5 seconds.*

Search queries are associated with and travel along with their policies. Informally, a policy is a set of requirements which are to be satisfied by the nodes that the receive and process the query. A node receiving a query may either solve it, or (if unable) forward the query to neighbor nodes. That is, only the nodes satisfying the requirements are able to obtain the query from the previous node in a path. A policy is formally defined as follows.

Definition 2 (Policy). *A policy pol is a conjunction of atomic conditions,* $pol = cond_1 \wedge .. \wedge cond_{n_i}$. *Condition* $cond_i$ *is defined in the form of* `ATT OP value`, *where* `ATT` *is an attribute;* `OP` *is a matching operator (e.g., $=$, $\geq$, $\leq$); and* `value` *is the requester node preferred value for* `ATT`, *which could be a constant or a variable.*

Example 2. *An example policy is* $pol = \{(OS = Windows) \wedge (Domain = 192.168.250.X) \wedge (SSL = Yes)\}$. *The policy requires a node to have a Windows OS, exist in the network domain 192.168.250.X, and support SSL protocol for communication.*

We use the notation pol_{own} to denote the policy of the query generator or the owner of the query, to which the routing of the query needs to comply with. We denote $SetPol_{hist}$ as the set of policies that have been issued by other nodes in the network prior to pol_{own}. pol_{hist_i} denotes a policy from the history $SetPol_{hist}$.

The search query is to be forwarded according to the policy associated with the query throughout the network.

Definition 3 (Network Path). *A network path* $\mathcal{NP}$ *is a sequence of connected nodes* $\{ID_{N_1}, \ldots, ID_{N_k}\}$ *in a network, where* ID_{N_i} *is the ID of a node* N_i. *We denote a path of nodes compliant with a policy pol as* $\mathcal{NP}_{pol} = \{ID_{N_1}, \ldots, ID_{N_k}\}$, *where pol is the policy to which the nodes in the path adhere to.*

In addition to forwarding according to the search query, the nodes can employ any forwarding strategy such as flooding the query to all the neighbors or selectively forwarding to k-nodes, or so forth. Whenever a query is resolved by finding a resource, the resource traverses along the same path that the query has taken to find the resource. Note that the required resource may be found, that is, there could be multiple nodes that host the resource originally requested by SQ. For any resource, the resource is obtained along with the path information. The path information includes the set of node IDs in the path through which the resource has been discovered[1].

The history of policies $SetPol_{hist}$ is generated as follows. Every node in the network, given its respective query and associated policy, receives information about the network paths through which the query has found the required resource, where a network path is in the form $\{ID_{N1}, \ldots, ID_{Nk}\}$. A node receives as many network paths as the number of places the query is able to find the resource. Every node saves the set of paths as part of history along with the related policies associated with the search queries. The policy and path history is then periodically distributed throughout the entire network.

Our approach includes three different steps to achieve the secure path verification goals specified in Section 4.1.

Firstly, as SQ is resolved and the results of the query are forwarded back to the requester, the first step of our approach is to obtain the network paths taken by the owner's query. Upon launching a search query, the owner of the query, in addition to the query output, is able to obtain the actual set of reliable network paths taken by its query. The paths are assumed to be reliable and verified.

Next, we determine the set of paths taken by the query that are worthy of verification. Depending on the size of the network, the "strictness" of the policy, and the exact routes taken, the number of paths taken by the query might explode. In order to filter out irrelevant paths, our approach relies on checking the "policy and path" history, that is, the known paths taken by previous query routing tasks, which were controlled according to some known policies, as mentioned earlier. The intuition is that *queries associated with similar policies should take similar or same routes.* Our approach for filtering is reported in greater detail in Section 5.

Finally, we *accurately* verify the compliance of the nodes in the set of the paths obtained after filtering, and check whether they correctly forward the query to the nodes based on the requirements specified in the policy for a given search query. Our verification protocols rely on CP-ABE by generating two "complementary" ciphertexts for a challenge. To further improve our verification protocol, we propose an optimization approach by offloading partial CP-ABE encryption to nodes whose honesty has already been verified. We also present a trade-off approach, which is more efficient at the cost of being less resilient than the first optimization method. We describe the baseline approach and two optimizations in Section 6.

5. POLICY SUBSUMPTION FOR PATH FILTERING

A query owner with his policy pol_{own} obtains a set of paths $\mathcal{P}_{pol_{own}}$ traversed by his query SQ. After obtaining $\mathcal{P}_{pol_{own}}$, the query owner tests for malicious paths or nodes among $\mathcal{P}_{pol_{own}}$. An intuitive approach would be to verify policy compliance for every path and every node in the path. This is however a computationally expensive method, that could potentially require an exponential number of nodes to be checked. We overcome this problem by comparing the paths taken by the query in question to the recent network paths traversed by similar queries. Given a search query SQ, each of its returned paths will eventually be classified into one of three categories: *non-malicious* (NM), *possibly malicious* (PM), and *malicious* (M). We leverage the path history of previous policies to classify paths from $\mathcal{P}_{pol_{own}}$. We can obtain reliable path history by employing methods that are used in reliable reputation systems [28].

[1]Depending on the specific network setup and infrastructure, additional meta data and cryptographic guarantees may be added

To check for policy similarity, we adopt the following notion of policy subsumption, building on the well-known subsumption relation between two constraints [1]. The subsumption relation states that a computable subsumption $\Rightarrow$ relation on two constraints $cond_1, cond_2$ is true if all substitutions (i.e. values) that satisfy $cond_1$ also satisfy $cond_2$.

Definition 4 (Policy Subsumption). *Given two policies pol_1 and pol_2, we say that pol_1 is subsumed by pol_2, denoted as $pol_1 \Rightarrow pol_2$ if there exists for every condition $cond_i$ in pol_1 there exists at least one condition $cond_j$ in pol_2 such that either $cond_i = cond_j$ or $cond_i \Rightarrow cond_j$.*

Note that in the definition above, if pol_2 has extra conditions it does not matter, as the policy being subsumed (pol_1) is still fully verified upon verifying pol_2. We provide two examples for better understanding of policy subsumption.

Example 3. *The following two cases to demonstrate policy subsumption. As the first case, consider two simple policies $pol_1 = \{a > 20 \wedge b > 45 \wedge c = 97\}$, and $pol_2 = \{a > 10 \wedge c > 30\}$. pol_1 is a subsumption of pol_2. This is because pol_1 has a condition $\{a > 20\}$ and a condition $\{c = 97\}$, and a node which satisfies these conditions also satisfies the conditions $\{a > 10\}$ and $\{c > 30\}$ in pol_2. As the second case, consider two other simple policies $pol_1 = \{a = 50 \wedge b > 45 \wedge c = 97\}$, and $pol_2 = \{a = 50 \wedge c > 30\}$. pol_1 is a subsumption of pol_2. This is because both pol_1 and pol_2 have an identical condition $\{a = 50\}$, and a node that satisfies the condition $\{c = 97\}$ in pol_1 also satisfies the condition $\{c > 30\}$ in pol_2.*

Path filtering includes two steps. We first compare the policy of the query owner pol_{own}, with all the existing policies in the history policy set $SetPol_{hist}$. All the policies in $SetPol_{hist}$ which have a subsumption relation with policy pol_{own} as per Def. 4 are extracted and stored in $SetPol'_{hist}$. Next, we compare the paths generated under pol_{own} and the paths generated under the set of policies $SetPol'_{hist}$, and filter non-malicious paths, as described next.

5.1 Policy and Path Comparison

We match paths of the history with the set of paths generated by SQ under the constraints imposed by policy pol_{own}. The matching process results in placing nodes from $SetPol'_{hist}$ into one of the three different classes namely, non-malicious, malicious, and maybe-malicious. Two cases are possible, depending on the subsumption relation between the owner's policy and the policy being matched:

1. Let pol_{hist_i} be a policy from $SetPol'_{hist}$ which is a subsumption of the owner's policy pol_{own} per Def. 4, that is $pol_{hist_i} \Rightarrow pol_{own}$. Let $\mathcal{P}_{pol_{own}}$ denote all the paths traversed according to pol_{own} and $\mathcal{P}_{pol_{hist_i}}$ be the paths traversed according to pol_{hist_i}, respectively.

   - *Non-malicious* nodes are nodes belonging to any of the paths in $\mathcal{P}_{pol_{own}}$ that also appear in any path in the path set $\mathcal{P}_{pol_{hist_i}}$
   - *Possibly-malicious* nodes, are nodes belonging to any of the paths in $\mathcal{P}_{pol_{own}}$ that *do not* appear in any path in the path set $\mathcal{P}_{pol_{hist_i}}$

   Note that the union of the two malicious and possibly malicious sets include all nodes in $\mathcal{P}_{pol_{own}}$.

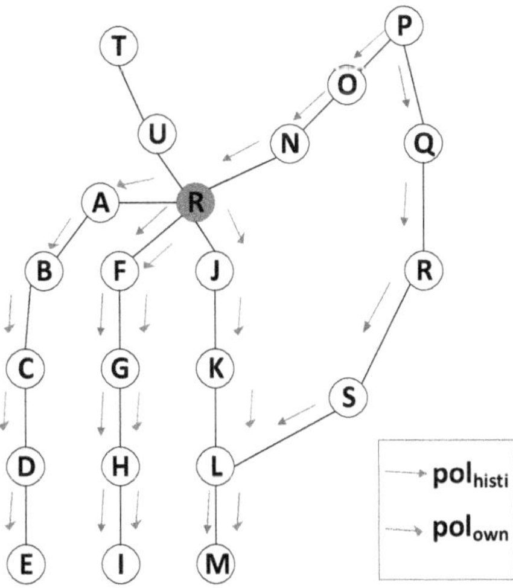

Figure 1: Path Filtering Example

2. Let pol_{hist_i} be a policy from $SetPol'_{hist}$ which subsumes the owner's policy pol_{own} per Def. 4, that is $pol_{own} \Rightarrow pol_{hist_i}$. Let $\mathcal{P}_{pol_{own}}$ denote all the paths traversed according to pol_{own} and $\mathcal{P}_{pol_{hist_i}}$ be the paths traversed according to pol_{hist_i}, respectively.

   - *Malicious nodes* are nodes belonging to any of the paths in $\mathcal{P}_{pol_{own}}$ that *do not* appear in any path in the path set $\mathcal{P}_{pol_{hist_i}}$.
   - *Possibly-malicious nodes* are nodes belonging to any of the paths in $\mathcal{P}_{pol_{own}}$ that appear in any path in the path set $\mathcal{P}_{pol_{hist_i}}$.

   Again, the two sets include all nodes in $\mathcal{P}_{pol_{own}}$.

Note that, policy subsumption checks are carried out for all policies pol_{hist_x} in $SetPol'_{hist}$. If there does not exist even a single subsumption relation between the policies in the history and the owner's policy P_{own} (for example if the node has only recently joined the network or the whole network is in itself new), all the paths taken by SQ of the requester $\mathcal{P}_{pol_{own}}$ need to be verified.

Example 4. *Figure 1 shows an example view of a network. Let R be the requester node which sends out the query. Let the paths represented by red arrows be the paths traversed by the query associated with policy pol_{own}, and the paths represented by blue arrows be the paths traversed by a policy in the history pol_{hist_i}. Let the two policies hold the following subsumption relation $pol_{hist_i} \Rightarrow pol_{own}$. All the nodes in the path taken by pol_{own} $\{R,F,G,H,I\}$ need not be verified as they have been traversed by pol_{hist_i} as can seen by the blue arrows. In the path $\{R,J,K,L,M\}$, nodes L and M need not be verified as they have been traversed by pol_{hist_i}, whereas nodes J and K need to be verified, as they have not been* *traversed by pol_{hist_i}. Since, the path {A,B,C,D,E} has not been traversed by pol_{hist_i}, all the nodes A, B, C, D, and E need to be verified.*

6. PATH COMPLIANCE VERIFICATION

After obtaining the filtered paths or nodes from the *path filtering* step, we verify the compliance of nodes in the filtered paths with regards to policy-compliant query forwarding. Our approaches for path compliance verification rely on verifying the attributes of each node in the paths taken by the query according to the original policy linked to *SQ*. We first present a baseline method, and then propose two optimizations.

6.1 Baseline Method

Without loss of generality, we assume that the requester wants to verify the attributes or properties of a node N_i, called target node. Our baseline method relies on *random message challenges*. The requester creates two random messages m_0 and m_1, and flips a bit coin $b \in_R \{0,1\}$ for encrypting m_0, m_1 respectively under the policy pol_{own} and its complementary policy $\overline{pol}_{own}$ using CP-ABE. That is, the requester encrypts m_b under pol_{own} for obtaining $[m_b]_{pol_{own}}$, while m_{1-b} under $\overline{pol}_{own}$ for obtaining $[m_{1-b}]_{\overline{pol}_{own}}$. Both ciphertexts $[m_b]_{pol_{own}}$ and $[m_{1-b}]_{\overline{pol}_{own}}$ are sent (in random order) to the target node for decryption.

According to our assumption, each node has a private key with respect to its attributes, which it obtains from a certificate authority. Thus, the target node *can only* decrypt either $[m_b]_{pol_{own}}$ or $[m_{1-b}]_{\overline{pol}_{own}}$. This is because the underlying policies in $[m_b]_{pol_{own}}$ and $[m_{1-b}]_{\overline{pol}_{own}}$ are complementary: If the attributes of the target node do not satisfy one underlying policy, they must satisfy the other policy. We employ complementary ciphertexts so that the node that is being verified does not lie by responding that it is unable to decrypt both the ciphertexts. We, hence, prevent the nodes in the network to be lazy. The target node attempts to decrypt both ciphertexts (but it is only able to decrypt one message among the two), and returns back the results m'_0 and m'_1 (in the same order) to requester. Requester verifies if $m_b = m'_b$ and $m_{1-b} \neq m'_{1-b}$. If both the conditions hold, then the target node N_i satisfies the policy pol_{own}. Thus, the node N_{i-1}, which is the neighboring node and has forwarded query to N_i, is considered to be non-malicious and honest as it correctly forwarded the query according to the policy established by the requester, without any disruption. Otherwise, the node N_i does not satisfy the policy and hence N_{i-1} maliciously forwarded the query to a non-satisfying node N_i, hence, N_{i-1} is a malicious node.

We note that our baseline method allows to verify the policy compliance of a certain node with significant probability. The false positive exists only when the non-satisfying target node correctly guesses the random messages, which is negligible provided that the CP-ABE scheme is secure.

One limitation of this baseline method is its overhead. Specifically, our baseline method requires to verify every node (in the path) by encrypting random messages with the original and complementary policies, introducing a massive overhead for the requester. To address this issue, we propose an improved approach, which aims at reducing the computational overhead for the requester node.

6.2 Offloading Partial Computation to Verified Nodes

Our improved approach is based on reusing the verified nodes in the path. Specifically, if we have already verified the honesty of one node, we then trust that it can also honestly perform some (carefully crafted) delegated computations. In other words, the idea underlying this approach is to offload the computation to verified nodes so that the requester's overhead is minimized.

A näive approach is to directly send the random messages m_0 and m_1 to a verified node for encryption (with pol_{own} and $\overline{pol}_{own}$) which *eliminates* the ABE computation at requester side. However, this approach is infeasible, because it requires to *fully trust* the verified node. That is, the näive approach is based on the assumption that the verified node would not leak the challenge messages to target nodes. We argue this assumption is unconvincing. This is because in policy compliant verification, we can only verify the *honesty* of node, which is weaker than *trust*. Even if a verified node is honest, it can still extract or leak secret information to others. Hence the *goal of our optimization is offloading computation to verified nodes, while preserving the confidentiality* of both m_0 and m_1.

By Definition 2, the policy pol_{own} is in a conjunctive form, i.e., $pol_{own} = cond_1 \wedge cond_2 \wedge \ldots \wedge cond_n$, where $cond_i$ is the condition. We use γ_i to denote the satisfying attribute set in which the attributes satisfy $cond_i$. We introduce a few notations in order to elaborate on our approach.

Recall that each node N_i has an attribute private key as sk_i, constructed as $(g^{(\alpha+r_i)/\beta}, \{g^{r_i}\mathsf{H}(j)^{r_j}, g^{r_j}\}_{j \in \omega_i \cup ID_i})$, where ω_i is the attribute set of N_i and ID_i is the ID of node N_i, α, β are the master secrets identical with each node, $r_i \in_R \mathbb{Z}_p$ is the random number per key, $r_j \in_R \mathbb{Z}_p$ $(j \in \omega_i \cup ID_i)$ is the random number per attribute (in a certain secret key). The parameters $g \in \mathbb{G}, g^\beta$ and $e(g,g)^\alpha$ are published after system setup.

Assuming the honesty of a node N_k (called the verified node) is verified, we can offload the ABE computation [17] to N_k as shown in Figure 2. Specifically, after generating the random test messages $m_0, m_1 \in \mathbb{G}_T$, the requester (i.e. the query owner in the first verification step) picks integers s, s_1,
$s_2, s', s'_1, s'_2 \in_R \mathbb{Z}_p$, with $s = s_1 + s_2$ and $s' = s'_1 + s'_2$. Next, the requester sends the target policy pol_{own} as well as the *delegating secrets* s_1 and s'_1 to the verified node for partial ABE encryption on both m_0 and m_1.

Upon receiving (pol_{own}, s_1, s'_1), the verified node respectively uses s_1 and s'_1 to compute partial ABE ciphertexts with respect to pol_{own} and $\overline{pol}_{own}$. We illustrate this offloaded computation to the verified node in Figure 3. Precisely, policy pol_{own} is normalized into a tree-based structure. The root node is an "$\wedge$" gate connecting n sub-trees (corresponding to each condition $cond_i$). To produce a (partial) ciphertext with respect to pol_{own} (using s_1), verified node firstly computes the satisfying attribute set γ_i and generates the ciphertext $(g^{s_{1i}}, \{\mathsf{H}(\theta)^{s_{1i}}\}_{\theta \in \gamma_i})$ of each condition $cond_i$ for $i = 1, 2, \ldots, n$, where $\sum_{i=1}^{n} s_{1i} = s_1$. Finally we can get the partial ciphertext of policy pol_{own} as $\{(g^{s_{1i}}, \{\mathsf{H}(\theta)^{s_{1i}}\}_{\theta \in \gamma_i})\}_{i=1}^{n}$. Similarly, verified node also computes the partial ciphertext with respect to $\overline{pol}_{own}$. It firstly calculates the complementary policy $\overline{pol}_{own}$ of pol_{own}, normalizes $\overline{pol}_{own}$ into a tree-based structure and then uses s'_1

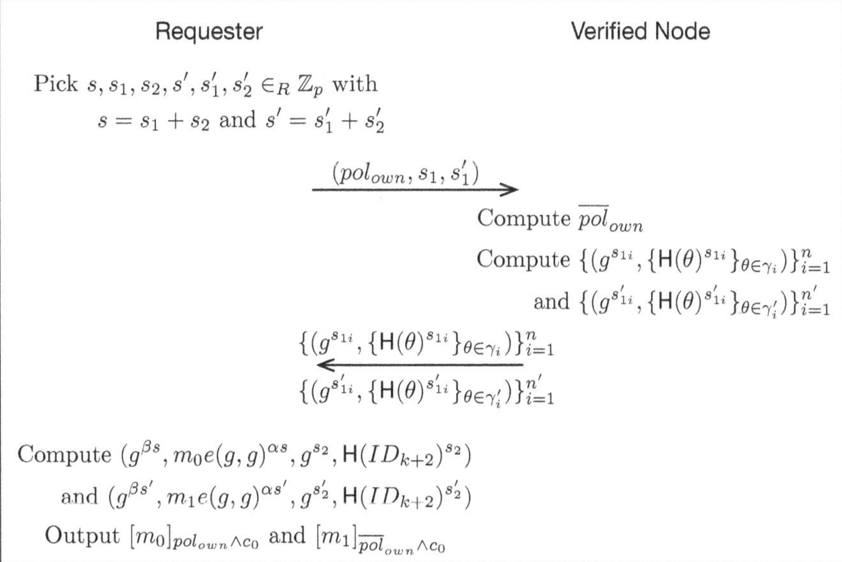

Figure 2: Workflow of Offloading Partial Computations to Verified Nodes

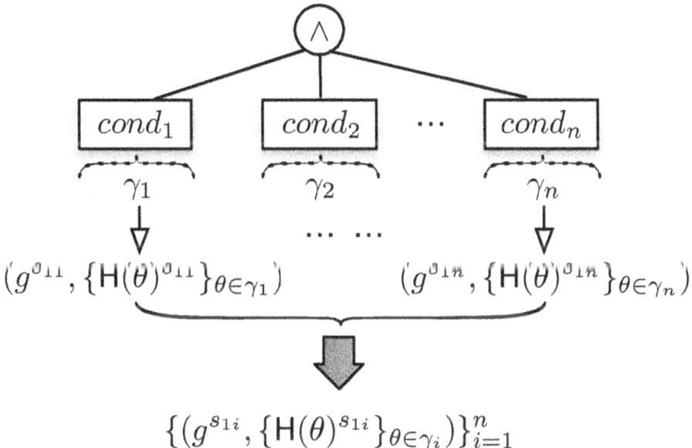

Figure 3: Offloaded Computations to the Verified Nodes

to compute the partial ciphertext $\{(g^{s'_{1i}}, \{\mathsf{H}(\theta)^{s'_{1i}}\}_{\theta \in \gamma'_i})\}_{i=1}^{n}$, where $\sum_{i=1}^{n'} s'_{1i} = s'_1$, γ'_i is the satisfying attribute set in $\overline{pol}_{own}$ and n' is the number of conditions involved in $\overline{pol}_{own}$. Both (partial) ciphertexts are sent back to requester. The requester uses s_2 and s'_2 respectively to compute the partial ciphertexts $(g^{s_2}, \mathsf{H}(ID_{k+2})^{s_2})$ and $(g^{s'_2}, \mathsf{H}(ID_{k+2})^{s'_2})$ where ID_{k+2} is the ID of the node N_{k+2} whose attribute satisfaction is to be checked. After checking the satisfaction of policy by node N_{k+2}, we will be able to detect the forwarding compliance of node N_{k+1}. Requester also computes the encryptions $(g^{\beta s}, m_0 e(g,g)^{\alpha s})$ and $(g^{\beta s'}, m_1 e(g,g)^{\alpha s'})$. Finally the ABE ciphertexts for m_0 and m_1 are output as

$$[m_0]_{pol_{own} \wedge c_0} = (pol_{own} \wedge c_0, g^{s_2}, \mathsf{H}(ID_{k+2})^{s_2}, m_0 e(g,g)^{\alpha s}, g^{\beta s}, \{(g^{s_{1i}}, \{\mathsf{H}(\theta)^{s_{1i}}\}_{\theta \in \gamma_i})\}_{i=1}^{n})$$

and

$$[m_1]_{\overline{pol}_{own} \wedge c_0} = (\overline{pol}_{own} \wedge c_0, g^{s'_2}, \mathsf{H}(ID_{k+2})^{s'_2}, m_1 e(g,g)^{\alpha s'}, g^{\beta s'}, \{(g^{s'_{1i}}, \{\mathsf{H}(\theta)^{s'_{1i}}\}_{\theta \in \gamma'_i})\}_{i=1}^{n'})$$

where c_0 is the introduced clause satisfied by the attribute ID_{k+2}. Both outputs are sent to the target node N_{k+2} for challenge.

Note that $[m_0]_{pol_{own} \wedge c_0}$ and $[m_1]_{\overline{pol}_{own} \wedge c_0}$ follow the same structure of ciphertexts in [2] with respect to policy $pol_{own} \wedge c_0$ and $\overline{pol}_{own} \wedge c_0$. At the same time, the node N_{k+2} has a private key related to $\omega_i \cup \{ID_{k+2}\}$.

Since the verified node cannot access the original test messages m_0, m_1, it can only "aid the encryption process", without compromising the protocol. Therefore, our offloading method would not degrade the security guarantee of the baseline approach. Also, there is no scope of collusion attacks for this approach as the messages are encrypted with the policy which contains the ID of the recipient node. Any recipient node will have a unique private key. A recipient node which did not satisfy the policy cannot collude with another node that satisfies the policy to decrypt the messages for it.

6.3 Reusing ABE Ciphertexts

We now discuss an alternative approach which is more efficient compared to the offloading of partial computation approach. The intuition underlying this alternative approach is reusing the ABE ciphertexts. In particular, we observe that all the test ciphertexts (i.e., encryption of m_0 and m_1) are intended for the same *policy*, and the most part of the ciphertexts could be *re-used* for saving the computations for the following ciphertexts. We describe our approach as follows.

Let us assume that a node N_{i-1} which is a neighbor of the requester, in one of the paths in $\mathcal{P}_{pol}$, has correctly forwarded the query according to the policy and hence, is considered honest. Since N_{i-1} is honest, the requester delegates N_{i-1} the task of verifying the policy compliance of N_i, the neighbor of N_{i-1}. Assume the requester has computed the *initial* CP-ABE ciphertexts $(m_0 e(g,g)^{\alpha s}, g^{\beta s}, \{(g^{s_i}, \mathsf{H}(\theta)^{s_i})\}_{\theta \in \gamma_i, i=1,\dots,n})$ and $(m_1 e(g,g)^{\alpha s'}, g^{\beta s'}, \{(g^{s'_i}, \mathsf{H}(\theta)^{s'_i})\}_{\theta \in \gamma'_i, i=1,\dots,n'})$ with respect to pol_{own} and $\overline{pol}_{own}$, where α, β are the master secrets, s, s' are the randomness satisfying

$\sum_{i=1}^{n} s_i = s$ and $\sum_{i=1}^{n'} s'_i = s'$, and γ_i and γ'_i respectively denote the attribute set satisfying the conditions $cond_i$ and $cond'_i$ in pol_{own} and $\overline{pol}_{own}$.

To generate the ciphertexts for the following nodes, the requester sends the delegatee node N_{i-1} the two ciphertexts as described above. The delegatee node N_{i-1} can leverage the *malleable* property of CP-ABE and modify existing ciphertexts. Specifically, delegatee keeps the other components of ciphertexts, but multiplies $m_0 e(g,g)^{\alpha s}$ with a random message m'_0 and $m_1 e(g,g)^{\alpha s}$ with m'_1. This way generates ciphertexts for a new pair of random messages $m_0 m'_0$ and $m_1 m'_1$, that could be used for the next node's verification. We note that since m'_0 and m'_1 are random, $m_0 m'_0$ and $m_1 m'_1$ are random as well, the target node cannot get knowledge of the challenge messages unless correctly decrypts them. The delegatee node N_{i-1} then sends the new $[m_0 m'_0]_{pol_{own}}$ and $[m_1 m'_1]_{\overline{pol}_{own}}$ to the node N_{i+1} whose attributes are to be verified in order to verify the policy compliance of its neighboring node N_i. This procedure of verifying the attributes of alternate nodes continues until every node in the set of paths from the path information is verified.

In this approach, the requester just needs to compute *one pair of CP-ABE encryption*, each for pol_{own} and $\overline{pol}_{own}$ respectively, and the the ciphertexts resulting from the two CP-ABE encryptions are modified by the delegatee nodes to carry on the verification of rest of the nodes in the path. Nevertheless, we note that this approach essentially trades security for efficiency, and could suffer from a *single-point-of-failure*. In particular, since our approach *re-uses* the same randomness (i.e., s and s') involved in the ABE ciphertexts for verification, it inevitably suffers from failure if nodes collude on s and s'. If some node passes the verification process, but leaks the common randomness in the form of $e(g,g)^{\alpha s}$ or $e(g,g)^{\alpha s'}$, all the following nodes can thus directly recover the message without any decryption.

As mentioned in Section 4, both our schemes would work for both static and dynamic networks. In the context of dynamic networks, when a new node is added to the network, the requester node need not verify the compliance of this node. The reason is intuitive; the newly added node could not have participated in the query forwarding procedure prior to compliance verification. If a node has participated in the query forwarding process but disconnects from the network in order to not participate in the verification process, we flag such a node malicious.

7. PERFORMANCE EVALUATION

We carried out several experiments to test the computational overhead of our approach. Our tests include the computational overhead caused by both the path filtering step and the policy compliance verification step. We conducted the experiments on a 4GB and 1.4 GHz Intel Core i5 processor machine. We conduct our experiments on a peer to peer network topology whose structure is obtained from http://snap.stanford.edu/data/. The network consists of 10,000+ nodes. In the experiments, we do not consider possible network latency.

Our first experiment aims to test the computational overhead of the policy comparison, where we determine the policies in the history that subsume pol_{own} or are a subsumption of pol_{own}. We conducted the experiment for 1000 policies in the history to be compared with pol_{own}, and for up to

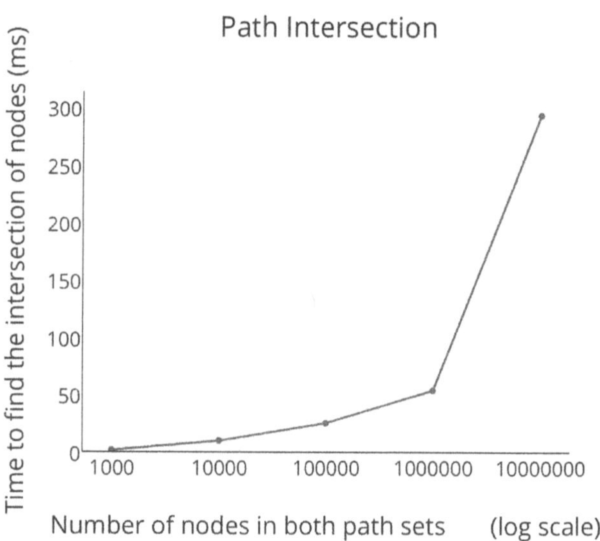

Figure 4: Path Intersection

100 attributes or conditions in each policy of the history and pol_{own}. The time taken to find the policies that have a subsumption relation with pol_{own} grows linearly with the number of attribute conditions to check. With 1000 policies in the history, the overhead ranges from less than 5 milliseconds to around 400 milli seconds for 100 attributes in each policy.

Our second experiment consists of computing the overhead for filtering out the nodes in $\mathcal{P}_{pol_{own}}$ that do not require any further verification (Section 5). We vary the number of nodes in both the sets exponentially, as seen in Figure 4. Our approach scales well, as the time taken to find the intersection of nodes is in the order of milliseconds. Even for a huge number of nodes in the path sets such as 10000000, the computational overhead is in the order of milliseconds.

The third experiment consists of measuring the computational overhead of policy compliance verification protocol using our two approaches. We also compare the overhead introduced by our approaches with that of the basic CP-ABE approach. Results are shown in Figure 5.

Our results for every approach include the time taken to perform the intersection of nodes in the set of paths $\mathcal{P}_{P_{hist_{P_i}}}$ and $\mathcal{P}_{pol_{own}}$.

For the optimization based on "Resuing Ciphertexts", we compute the time taken for a single CP-ABE encryption which is computed by the requester node. The time taken for the modification of the encrypted CP-ABE component (i.e. finite-field multiplication) in order to generate new random messages m_0 and m_1 by the delegatee nodes in the paths, is negligible. The entire verification process does not even consume 1 second as opposed to several hundreds and thousands of seconds depending upon the number of nodes to verify.

For our "Offloading Partial Computation" approach, the computational overhead for the requester just includes three modular exponentiations and one bilinear mapping for a single CP-ABE encryption. If the requester encrypts the messages using CP-ABE for every node that has to be verified (as with baseline approach), the computational time

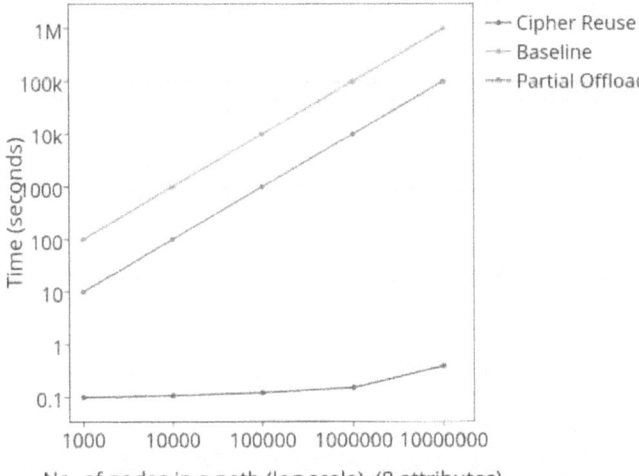

Figure 5: Our Approaches vs. Baseline CP-ABE

explodes as the number of nodes to be verified increases. Since in our approach the requester needs to perform only three modular exponentiations and one bilinear mapping instead of a whole CP-ABE encryption operation as part of the encryption is delegated to "honesty-verified" nodes, there is a huge difference in the computational overhead compared to the baseline CP-ABE approach. For all the three approaches, the number of attributes in the policy is equal to 8, while we increased the number of nodes to verify, as shown in Figure 5. We ran the same experiment multiple times by increasing the number of attributes in the policy and observed the difference of computational overhead between the offloading and the baseline approach. As the number of attributes in the policy increases, the computational overhead of the baseline CP-ABE approach increases, while that of our offloading approach remains the same irrespective of the number of attributes in the policy. This is because our approach requires the requester to compute the partial cipher-text for one attribute only. That is, the ID and the rest of the cipher-text computation for the attributes in the policy is offloaded to the honest nodes. Hence, as the number of attributes in the policy increases, we can observe a huge difference in the computational overhead between our *offloading* approach and the *baseline* approach.

8. CONCLUSION

In this paper, we presented an efficient and yet secure solution for policy compliance verification of distributed search in networks hosting content such as peer-to-peer networks. Our proposed solution includes methods to both reduce the number of nodes to be verified, and make the actual node verification mechanism efficient and yet secure by leveraging a secure cryptographic scheme.

We assumed that the path information about previous queries is available to all nodes and that it is trustworthy. We note that our current scheme would be secure even in case of unreliable path history, although the number of nodes to verify would potentially be very high. As part of our future work, we will explore how to relax this assumption without compromising the main verification approach underlying our solution.

9. REFERENCES

[1] M. Becker and P. Sewell. Cassandra: Distributed access control policies with tunable expressiveness. In *Proceedings of the Fifth IEEE International Workshop on Policies for Distributed Systems and Networks*, Washington, DC, USA, 2004.

[2] J. Bethencourt, A. Sahai, and B. Waters. Ciphertext-policy attribute-based encryption. In *IEEE Symposium on Security and Privacy*, pages 321–334, May 2007.

[3] D. Boneh and M. Franklin. Identity-based encryption from the weil pairing. In *Advances in Cryptology – CRYPTO 2001*, volume 2139 of *Lecture Notes in Computer Science*, pages 213–229, 2001.

[4] K. Butler, T. Farley, P. McDaniel, and J. Rexford. A survey of bgp security issues and solutions. *Proceedings of the IEEE*, 98(1):100–122, Jan 2010.

[5] V. Goyal, O. Pandey, A. Sahai, and B. Waters. Attribute-based encryption for fine-grained access control of encrypted data. In *Proceedings of the 13th ACM Conference on Computer and Communications Security*, pages 89–98. ACM, 2006.

[6] C. Hedrick. Routing information protocol. RFC 1058, June 1988.

[7] Y. Hu, A. Perrig, and D. B. Johnson. Efficient security mechanisms for routing protocolsa. In *Proceedings of the Network and Distributed System Security Symposium*, 2003.

[8] Y.-C. Hu, A. Perrig, and M. Sirbu. Spv: Secure path vector routing for securing bgp. In *Proceedings of the 2004 Conference on Applications, Technologies, Architectures, and Protocols for Computer Communications*, pages 179–192. ACM, 2004.

[9] N. Jafari Navimipour and F. Sharifi Milani. A comprehensive study of the resource discovery techniques in peer-to-peer networks. *Peer-to-Peer Networking and Applications*, 8(3):474–492, 2015.

[10] J. Jiang, W. Li, J. Luo, and J. Tan. A network accountability based verification mechanism for detecting inter-domain routing path inconsistency. *Journal of Network and Computer Applications*, 36:1671 – 1683, 2013.

[11] S. Karumanchi, J. Li, and A. C. Squicciarini. Securing resource discovery in content hosting networks. In *International Conference on Security and Privacy in Communication Networks - 10th International ICST Conference, SecureComm 2014, Beijing, China, September 24-26, 2014, Revised Selected Papers, Part I*, pages 153–173, 2014.

[12] S. Karumanchi, A. C. Squicciarini, and B. Carminati. Policy-compliant search query routing for web service discovery in peer to peer networks. In *IEEE 20th International Conference on Web Services*, pages 387–394, 2013.

[13] S. Karumanchi, A. C. Squicciarini, and D. Lin. Privacy-aware access control for message exchange in vehicular ad hoc networks. *Telecommunication Systems*, 58(4):349–361, 2015.

[14] S. Kent, C. Lynn, J. Mikkelson, and K. Seo. Secure border gateway protocol (s-bgp). *IEEE Journal on Selected Areas in Communications*, 18:103–116, 2000.

[15] T. Kocak and D. Lacks. Design and analysis of a distributed grid resource discovery protocol. *Cluster Computing*, 15(1):37–52, 2012.

[16] M. Lad, D. Massey, D. Pei, Y. Wu, B. Zhang, and L. Zhang. Phas: A prefix hijack alert system. In *Proceedings of the 15th Conference on USENIX Security Symposium*, 2006.

[17] J. Li, C. Jia, J. Li, and X. Chen. Outsourcing encryption of attribute-based encryption with mapreduce. In *Information and Communications Security*, volume 7618 of *Lecture Notes in Computer Science*, pages 191–201, 2012.

[18] H. Mashayekhi and J. Habibi. Combining search and trust models in unstructured peer-to-peer networks. *The Journal of Supercomputing*, 53(1):66–85, 2010.

[19] P. McDaniel, W. Aiello, K. Butler, and J. Ioannidis. Origin authentication in interdomain routing. *Computer Networks*, 50(16):2953–2980, 2006.

[20] J. Naous, M. Walfish, A. Nicolosi, D. Mazières, M. Miller, and A. Seehra. Verifying and enforcing network paths with icing. In *Proceedings of the Seventh Conference on Emerging Networking Experiments and Technologies*, pages 30:1–30:12, 2011.

[21] N. J. Navimipour, A. M. Rahmani, A. H. Navin, and M. Hosseinzadeh. Resource discovery mechanisms in grid systems: A survey. *Journal of Network and Computer Applications*, 41(0):389 – 410, 2014.

[22] C. Pittaras, C. Papagianni, A. Leivadeas, P. Grosso, J. van der Ham, and S. Papavassiliou. Resource discovery and allocation for federated virtualized infrastructures. *Future Generation Computer Systems*, 42(0):55 – 63, 2015.

[23] W. Qu, W. Zhou, and M. Kitsuregawa. Sharable file searching in unstructured peer-to-peer systems. *J. Supercomput.*, 51(2):149–166, feb 2010.

[24] A. Sahai and B. Waters. Fuzzy identity-based encryption. In *Advances in Cryptology – EUROCRYPT 2005*, pages 457–473, 2005.

[25] M. Salmanian and M. Li. Enabling secure and reliable policy-based routing in manets. In *Military Communications Conference*, pages 1–7, Oct 2012.

[26] M. Shojafar, J. Abawajy, Z. Delkhah, A. Ahmadi, Z. Pooranian, and A. Abraham. An efficient and distributed file search in unstructured peer-to-peer networks. *Peer-to-Peer Networking and Applications*, 8(1):120–136, 2015.

[27] M. Suvanto. Privacy in peer-to-peer networks. In *Seminar on Internetworking*, Helsinki University of Technology.

[28] G. Swamynathan, K. Almeroth, and B. Zhao. The design of a reliable reputation system. *Electronic Commerce Research*, 10(3-4):239–270, 2010.

[29] H. Yih-Chun and A. Perrig. A survey of secure wireless ad hoc routing. *IEEE Security Privacy*, 2(3):28–39, May 2004.

[30] G. Zhang, W. Liu, X. Hei, and W. Cheng. Unreeling xunlei kankan: Understanding hybrid cdn-p2p video-on-demand streaming. *Multimedia, IEEE Transactions on*, 17(2):229–242, Feb 2015.

[31] X. Zhang, H.-C. Hsiao, G. Hasker, H. Chan, A. Perrig, and D. G. Andersen. Scion: Scalability, control, and isolation on next-generation networks. In *Proceedings of the 2011 IEEE Symposium on Security and Privacy*, pages 212–227, 2011.

Author Index

www.ingramcontent.com/pod-product-compliance
Lightning Source LLC
Chambersburg PA
CBHW080918220326
41598CB00034B/5614

* 9 7 8 1 4 5 0 3 4 4 7 0 8 *